The 2010 Golf Course Guide

24th edition published 2009
Published by AA Publishing, which is a trading name of
AA Media Limited, whose registered office is:
Fanum House, Basingstoke, Hampshire RG21 4EA
Registered number 06112600

Advertisement Sales: advertisingsales@theAA.com
Editorial: lifestyleguides@theAA.com

The Automobile Association would like to thank the
following photographers, companies and picture libraries
for their assistance in the preparation of this book.

Abbreviations for the picture credits are as follows: (t) top;
(b) bottom; (l) left; (r) right; (c) centre; (AA) AA World Travel
Library.

Front cover (t) Druids Glen; (bl) Getty Images/MedioImages;
(br) Corbis; Back cover (l) Corbis; (c) Getty Images/
MedioImages; (r) Corbis;
1 Getty Images/MedioImages; 3t Corbis; 3bl Getty Images/
MedioImages; 3br Getty Images/MedioImages; 4t Getty
Images/MedioImages; 4b Getty Images/MedioImages; 6
Getty Images/MedioImages; 7 Corbis; 8 Getty Images/
MedioImages; 9t Corbis; 9b AA/S Whitehorne; 10 Getty
Images/MedioImages; 11 Corbis; 12t Getty Images/
MedioImages; 12b Corbis;

Every effort has been made to trace the copyright holders,
and we apologise in advance for any accidental errors. We
would be happy to apply any corrections in the following
edition of this publication.

Typeset/repro by Servis Filmsetting Ltd, Manchester
Printed and bound in Italy by Printer Trento S.r.l

A CIP catalogue record for this book is available from
the British Library

ISBN 978-0-7495-6281-6
A03988

Maps prepared by the
Mapping Services Department
of AA Publishing.
© AA Media Limited 2009.

Contents

Welcome

Welcome to the AA Golf Course Guide 2010. The guide includes revised and updated information for over 2500 courses.

Golf is one of the most democratic of sports. Unlike football or rugby, amateur players always have the opportunity of following in the actual footsteps of the some of the most famous names in the game.

On pages 10-11 you'll find the Championship Course finder which will give you at-a-glance information about the top courses (feature pages and extensive descriptions can be found within the main gazetteer). Throughout the guide, courses of particular merit or interest are highlighted. Whether you're an armchair golf enthusiast or enjoy the thrill of seeing the game live, there's also a selection of dates and events to look forward to in the upcoming golfing calendar (see page 12).

This guide also contains AA-recommended Hotels and Guest Accommodation establishments.

After most entries you'll find details of local hotels or B&Bs, complete with their ratings. See pages 6-9 for more details on how to use this information.

The expanded index section means there are several ways to find a course to play. To browse by place name see page 505, or if you know a specific course you could try the Course Name Index on page 515. Alternatively, if you just want to practice your swing, there's the Driving Range index on page 495.

So, if you are interested in reliving the glories of a well-known golfing moment, looking to organise a golfing trip with friends or just feel like playing a few holes down the back nine of your local municipal course, you'll be able to find a place to play and stay in the AA Golf Course Guide 2010.

To recommend a new course for the guide, please write to: The Editor, AA Golf Course Guide, Fanum House, Basingstoke, Hampshire RG21 4EA

How to Use the Guide

The golf courses in the AA Golf Course Guide are selected by the AA and their entry is free of charge. The guide is updated every year for new courses, changes, closures and new features, and AA recommended accommodation follows most entries. To avoid disappointment we recommend that you phone before visiting a golf course; please mention the guide when you make an enquiry. The country directories are arranged alphabetically by county, then by town or village name. The town or village locations are shown on the atlas and listed in the index. A sample entry is explained below.

① **Town name and map reference**
The atlas at the end of the guide shows the locations of the courses. The map reference includes the atlas page number and the National Grid reference. The grid references for the Republic of Ireland are unique to this atlas.

② **Club name and contact details**
Where the club name appears in *italics* we have been unable to verify current course details with the club. If a club or course has not responded to our invitation to amend their details for two or more years, we show reduced details for them. You should check any details with the club before your visit.

③ **Description** The description highlights the significant features of the course or courses.

④ **Course statistics** The number of holes, distance, par, Standard Scratch Score, Course Record, and the number of club members.

⑤ **Visitor information** Playing days, booking requirements or restrictions are noted. A small number of courses in the guide are not open to visitors and we have included their details for information only.

⑥ **Society information** Booking requirements or restrictions for societies.

⑦ **Green fees** The most up-to-date green fees are given, including any variations or restrictions. Where green fees are not confirmed you should contact the club for current rates.

---

①—**ENFIELD**   **Map 4 TQ39**

②—**Crews Hill** Cattlegate Rd, Crews Hill EN2 8AZ
☎ 020 8363 6674 📠 020 8363 2343
e-mail: info@crewshillgolfclub.com
web: www.crewshillgolfclub.com

③—Parkland course in countryside within the M25 and little changed from its original design by Harry Colt. Considered to have possibly the best back nine in North London.

④—*18 Holes, 6281yds, Par 70, SSS 70, Course record 65. Club membership 600.*   —**⑦**

⑤—**Visitors** Mon-Fri except BHs. Handicap certificate. Dress code.
⑥—**Societies** welcome **Green Fees** phone **Course Designer** Harry Colt
⑧—**Prof** Neil Wichelow **Facilities** ⑫ 🍴 by prior arrangement 🏌 —**⑨**
🍺 🍷 🏌 🏪 ♨ 🛒 ♨ **Conf** facs Corporate Hospitality Days —**⑩**
⑪—**Location** M25 junct 24, A1005 for Enfield, signed
⑫—**Hotel** ★★★★ 77% HL Royal Chace, The Ridgeway, ENFIELD ☎
020 8884 8181 📠 020 8884 8181 92 en suite

---

⑧ **Professional** The name of the club professional(s).

⑨ **Facilities** See the key to symbols on page 7.

⑩ **Conference facilities** The available conference facilities are noted, and corporate hospitality days.

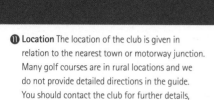

⓫ Location The location of the club is given in relation to the nearest town or motorway junction. Many golf courses are in rural locations and we do not provide detailed directions in the guide. You should contact the club for further details, or use the AA Route Planner at theAA.com.

⓬ Accommodation An AA recognised hotel is provided for most entries. This does not imply that the hotel offers special terms for the golf club, though in some cases the golf course is in the grounds of the hotel. The Star rating, and Merit (%) score appear as applicable. Contact details and the number of rooms are given. Where there is no nearby AA recognised hotel, an AA guest accommodation is recommended. See pages 8-9 for details of AA ratings. Where golf courses offer club accommodation the bed symbol appears under Facilities. Unless the club accommodation has an AA Star classification, the only AA recognised accommodation is the hotel or guest house that follows the entry.

Golf courses and hotels in the guide can illustrate their entry with a photograph or an advertisement.

Championship courses

Major championship courses have a full-page entry in the guide with an extensive description. A list of championship courses can be found on pages 10-11.

Selected courses

Courses considered to be of particular merit or interest are highlighted with a green box. These may include historic clubs, particularly testing or enjoyable courses, or those in holiday areas popular with visiting golfers. The selection is not exhaustive nor totally objective, but it is independent - courses cannot pay to have an entry in the guide, nor can they pay to have a highlighted entry. Highlighted courses do not represent any formal category on quality or other grounds.

Key to symbols

☎	Phone number
🖹	Fax number
€	Euro (Republic of Ireland)
Ⓣ	Lunch
⦿	Dinner
⌷	Bar snacks
⌷	Tea/coffee
⌷	Bar open midday and evenings
◇	Accommodation at club
⌷	Changing rooms
⌷	Well stocked shop
⌷	Clubs for hire
⌷	Motorized cart/trolley for hire
⌷	Buggies for hire
⌷	Trolley for hire
⌷	Driving range
★	AA star rating
Ⓤ	Hotel not yet rated by the AA

Links to other sections of the book

Please note:– Most courses accept credit/debit card payments but some do not. If you intend to pay by credit or debit cards please do check that your chosen course accepts this method of payment.

AA Hotel & Guest Accommodation

The AA inspects and rates establishments under two different accommodation schemes. Guest houses, B&Bs, farmhouses and inns are rated under the Guest Accommodation Scheme and hotels are rated under the Hotel Scheme. Establishments recognised by the AA pay an annual fee according to the rating and the number of bedrooms.

Star Quality

Stars shown in the guide indicate where the accommodation has been rated by the AA under a common standard rating agreed between the AA, VisitBritain, VisitScotland and Visit Wales. Under the common standards, guests can be confident that, for example, a guest house anywhere in the UK and Ireland will offer consistent quality and facilities. The system also uses a brief description or designatorto classify the establishment (abbreviations for these designators are described in the box opposite).

The Inspection Process

Establishments applying for AA recognition are visited by a qualified AA accommodation inspectors as a mystery guest. Inspectors stay overnight to make a thorough test of the accommodation, food, and hospitality. After paying the bill the following morning, they identify themselves and ask to be shown around the premises. The inspector completes a full report, resulting in a recommendation for the appropriate star rating. After this first visit, the establishment will receive an annual visit to check that standards are maintained. If it changes hands, the new owners must re-apply for rating, as standards can change.

AA Hotel Classification

★ In a one-Star hotel you should expect relatively informal yet competent service and an adequate range of facilities, including a television in the lounge or bedroom, and a reasonable choice of hot and cold dishes. The majority of bedrooms are en suite with a bath or shower room always available.

★★ Run by professionally presented staff and offers at least one restaurant or dining room for breakfast and dinner.

★★★ Three-Star hotels have direct-dial phones, a wide selection of drinks in the bar, and last orders for dinner no earlier than 8pm.

★★★★ A four-Star hotel is characterised by uniformed, well-trained staff, additional services, a night porter and a serious approach to cuisine.

★★★★★ Finally, and most luxurious of all, five-Star hotels offer many extra facilities, attentive staff, top-quality rooms and a full concierge service. A wide selection of drinks, including cocktails, are available in the bar, and the impressive menu reflects the hotel's own style of cooking.

% The Merit score appears after the Star rating for hotels in this guide. This is an additional assessment made by AA hotel inspectors, covering everything the hotel has to offer, including hospitality. The score allows a quick comparison between hotels with the same Star rating: the higher the score the better the hotel.

★ Red stars highlight the very best hotels in Britain and Ireland across all ratings. Such hotels offer outstanding levels of quality, comfort, cleanliness and customer care, and serve food of at least one-Rosette standard. No Merit score is shown for hotels with red Stars.

AA Guest Accommodation Classification

Guests can expect to find the following minimum standards at all levels:
- Pleasant and helpful welcome and service, and sound standards of housekeeping and maintenance
- Comfortable accommodation equipped to modern standards

- Bedding and towels changed for each new guest, and at least weekly if the room is taken for a long stay
- Adequate storage, heating, lighting and comfortable seating
- A sufficient hot water supply at reasonable times
- A full cooked breakfast. (If this is not provided, the fact must be advertised and a substantial continental breakfast must be offered.)

There are additional requirements for an establishment to achieve three, four or five Stars:

- Three Stars and above - access to both sides of all beds for double occupancy.
- Three Stars and above – bathrooms/shower rooms cannot be shared by the proprietor.
- Three Stars and above – a washbasin in every guest bedroom (either in the bedroom or the en suite/private facility).
- Four Stars – half of the bedrooms must be en suite or have private facilities.

- Five Stars – all bedrooms must be en suite or have private facilities.
- ★ Yellow stars highlight the top 10% of establishments within the 3, 4 and 5 star ratings.

Designators

B&B	Private house managed by owner
GH	Guest house, a larger B&B
GA	Guest Accommodation
INN	Traditional inn with pub atmosphere
FH	B&B on working farm
HL	Hotel
SHL	Small hotel managed by owner
RR	Restaurant with rooms
THH	Town House Hotel
CHH	Country House Hotel
MH	Metro Hotel
BUD	Budget Hotel

Championship Courses

Name	Location	Course(s)	Map Ref	Page
Sunningdale	Sunningdale, Berkshire	Old Course: 18 holes, 6063yds, Par 70 New Course: 18 holes, 6083yds, Par 70	Map 04 SU96	23
Woburn	Little Brickhill, Buckinghamshire	Duke's Course: 18 holes, 6976yds, Par 72 Duchess Course: 18 holes, 6651yds, Par 72 Marquess Course: 18 holes, 7214yds, Par 72	Map 04 SP93	31
St Mellion	St Mellion, Cornwall	Nicklaus Signature Course: 18 holes, 6592yds, Par 72 Kernow Course: 18 holes, 5500yds, Par 68	Map 04 SX36	51
Old Thorns Golf & Country Estate	Liphook, Hampshire	18 holes, 6461 yds, Par 72	Map 04 SU83	123
Marriot Hanbury Manor	Ware, Hertfordshire	18 holes, 7052yds, Par 72	Map 05 TL31	137
Royal St George's	Sandwich, Kent	18 holes, 7204, Par 70	Map 05 TR35	147
Royal Lytham & St Annes	Lytham St Annes, Lancashire	18 holes, 6882yds, Par 71	Map 07 SD32	157
The National Golf Centre	Woodhall Spa, Lincolnshire	The Hotchkin: 18 holes, 7080yds, Par 73 The Bracken: 18 holes, 6719yds, Par 72	Map 08 TF16	171
Royal Liverpool	Hoylake, Merseyside	18 holes, 6452yds, Par 72	Map 07 SJ28	181
Royal Birkdale	Southport, Merseyside	18 holes, 6726yds, Par 72	Map 07 SD31	183
Wentworth	Virginia Water, Surrey	West Course: 18 holes, 7324yds, Par 73 East Course: 18 holes, 6201yds, Par 68 Edinburgh Course: 18 holes, 7059yds, Par 72	Map 04 TQ06	239
Walton Heath	Walton-on-the-Hill, Surrey	Old Course: 18 holes, 7462yds, Par 72 New Course: 18 holes, 7171yds, Par 72	Map 04 TQ25	243
East Sussex National	Uckfield, East Sussex	East Course: 18 holes, 7138yds, Par 72 West Course: 18 holes, 7154yds, Par 72	Map 05 TQ42	249
The Belfry	Wishaw, Warwickshire	The Brabazon: 18 holes, 7196yds, Par 72 PGA National: 18 holes, 7033yds, Par 72 The Derby: 18 holes, 6057yds, Par 69	Map 07 SP19	263
Marriott Forest of Arden	Meriden, West Midlands	Arden Course: 18 holes, 6707yds, Par 72 Aylesford Course: 18 holes, 5801, Par 69	Map 04 SP28	267
Carnoustie Golf Links	Carnoustie, Angus	Championship: 18 holes, 6941yds, Par 72 Burnside: 18 holes, 6028, Par 68 Buddon Links: 18 holes, 5420yds, Par 66	Map 12 NO53	321

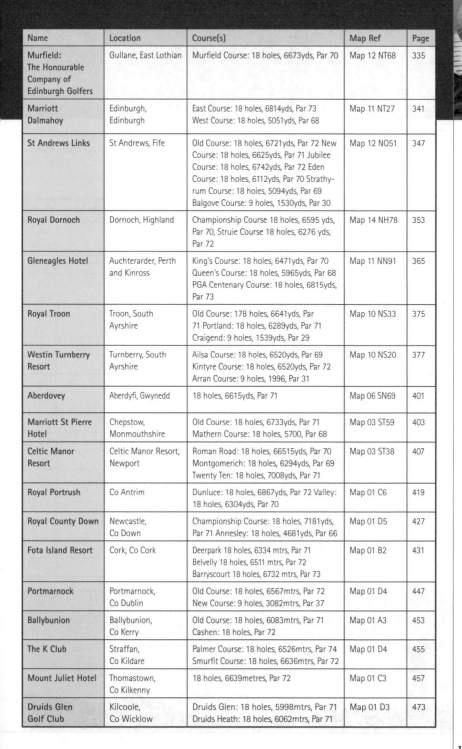

Name	Location	Course(s)	Map Ref	Page
Murfield: The Honourable Company of Edinburgh Golfers	Gullane, East Lothian	Murfield Course: 18 holes, 6673yds, Par 70	Map 12 NT68	335
Marriott Dalmahoy	Edinburgh, Edinburgh	East Course: 18 holes, 6814yds, Par 73 West Course: 18 holes, 5051yds, Par 68	Map 11 NT27	341
St Andrews Links	St Andrews, Fife	Old Course: 18 holes, 6721yds, Par 72 New Course: 18 holes, 6625yds, Par 71 Jubilee Course: 18 holes, 6742yds, Par 72 Eden Course: 18 holes, 6112yds, Par 70 Strathy-rum Course: 18 holes, 5094yds, Par 69 Balgove Course: 9 holes, 1530yds, Par 30	Map 12 NO51	347
Royal Dornoch	Dornoch, Highland	Championship Course 18 holes, 6595 yds, Par 70, Struie Course 18 holes, 6276 yds, Par 72	Map 14 NH78	353
Gleneagles Hotel	Auchterarder, Perth and Kinross	King's Course: 18 holes, 6471yds, Par 70 Queen's Course: 18 holes, 5965yds, Par 68 PGA Centenary Course: 18 holes, 6815yds, Par 73	Map 11 NN91	365
Royal Troon	Troon, South Ayrshire	Old Course: 178 holes, 6641yds, Par 71 Portland: 18 holes, 6289yds, Par 71 Craigend: 9 holes, 1539yds, Par 29	Map 10 NS33	375
Westin Turnberry Resort	Turnberry, South Ayrshire	Ailsa Course: 18 holes, 6520yds, Par 69 Kintyre Course: 18 holes, 6520yds, Par 72 Arran Course: 9 holes, 1996, Par 31	Map 10 NS20	377
Aberdovey	Aberdyfi, Gwynedd	18 holes, 6615yds, Par 71	Map 06 SN69	401
Marriott St Pierre Hotel	Chepstow, Monmouthshire	Old Course: 18 holes, 6733yds, Par 71 Mathern Course: 18 holes, 5700, Par 68	Map 03 ST59	403
Celtic Manor Resort	Celtic Manor Resort, Newport	Roman Road: 18 holes, 66515yds, Par 70 Montgomerich: 18 holes, 6294yds, Par 69 Twenty Ten: 18 holes, 7008yds, Par 71	Map 03 ST38	407
Royal Portrush	Co Antrim	Dunluce: 18 holes, 6867yds, Par 72 Valley: 18 holes, 6304yds, Par 70	Map 01 C6	419
Royal County Down	Newcastle, Co Down	Championship Course: 18 holes, 7181yds, Par 71 Annesley: 18 holes, 4681yds, Par 66	Map 01 D5	427
Fota Island Resort	Cork, Co Cork	Deerpark 18 holes, 6334 mtrs, Par 71 Belvelly 18 holes, 6511 mtrs, Par 72 Barryscourt 18 holes, 6732 mtrs, Par 73	Map 01 B2	431
Portmarnock	Portmarnock, Co Dublin	Old Course: 18 holes, 6567mtrs, Par 72 New Course: 9 holes, 3082mtrs, Par 37	Map 01 D4	447
Ballybunion	Ballybunion, Co Kerry	Old Course: 18 holes, 6083mtrs, Par 71 Cashen: 18 holes, Par 72	Map 01 A3	453
The K Club	Straffan, Co Kildare	Palmer Course: 18 holes, 6526mtrs, Par 74 Smurfit Course: 18 holes, 6636mtrs, Par 72	Map 01 D4	455
Mount Juliet Hotel	Thomastown, Co Kilkenny	18 holes, 6639metres, Par 72	Map 01 C3	457
Druids Glen Golf Club	Kilcoole, Co Wicklow	Druids Glen: 18 holes, 5998mtrs, Par 71 Druids Heath: 18 holes, 6062mtrs, Par 71	Map 01 D3	473

Dates & Events

The tables below provides a list of events to look out for over the next golfing year. The page references link to details about the course in the main gazetteer. All dates were correct at the time of going to press.

Event	Date	Location and course	Page
European Tour, Alfred Dunhill Links Championships	1-4 October 2009	Kingsbarns St Andrews	345 347
Irish Open Championship	May 2010 (dates tbc)	TBC	
English Seniors Championship	2-4 June 2010	Carlisle Crosby on Eden	54 55
British Amateur Championship	14-19 June 2010	Muirfield North Berwick	335
Ladies' British Amateur Championship	22-26 June 2010	Ganton	287
Brabazon Trophy	24-27 June 2010	Royal Liverpool	181
Junior Open	12-14 July 2010	Lundin Links	348
139th British Open Championship	15-18 July 2010	St Andrews	347
Ladies' British Open Championship	29 July – 1 August 2010	TBC	
Boys' International Matches	3-5 August 2010	Southerness	329
Girls' International Matches	3-5 August 2010	TBC	
British Seniors Open Amateur Championship	4-7 August 2010	Walton Heath	243
Ladies' British Seniors Championship	14-16 September 2010	TBC	
Mens' Senior Home Internationals	14-16 September 2010	Scotland – TBC	
Ladies' Senior Home Internationals	28-30 September 2010	TBC	
Ryder Cup	27 Sep-3 Oct 2010	Celtic Manor	407

Running on empty?

Fill up your finances with a loan from the AA

For years motorists have trusted us to come to their rescue.
But you might be surprised to know that as well as rescuing people
at the roadside, the UK's largest motoring organisation has also been
providing financial services for more than a million customers for over
20 years. So if you are looking for a loan, you know who to call.

With an AA Loan you could:

- Borrow from £1,000 to £25,000
- Repay your loan between 1 and 7 years
- Get a decision in minutes
- Receive the money within 24 hours if you use our optional courier service
  at a charge of £55

Call us now on
0800 60 50 30
quoting ref GUIDES or visit **theAA.com/loans**

Loans

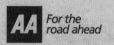

England

BEDFORDSHIRE

ASPLEY GUISE
Map 4 SP93

Aspley Guise & Woburn Sands West Hill MK17 8DX
☎ 01908 583596 🖹 01908 583596 (Secretary)
e-mail: info@aspleyguisegolfclub.co.uk
web: www.aspleyguisegolfclub.co.uk

A fine undulating course in expansive heathland interspersed with many attractive clumps of gorse, broom and bracken. Some well-established silver birch is a feature. The really tough 7th, 8th and 9th holes complete the first half. Accuracy is the premium and a good putting touch will be required to score well. Built on sandy foundations, the course plays well all year.

18 Holes, 6079yds, Par 71, SSS 70, Course record 65. Club membership 590.

Visitors Mon-Sun & BHs. Booking required. Handicap certificate. Dress code. **Societies** booking required. **Green Fees** £34 per round weekdays (£50 weekends) **Course Designer** Sandy Herd **Prof** Colin Clingan **Facilities** 🍴 🍽 🖬 🖵 🏋 🛎 🏠 ⛳ 🏌 🛺 🏌
Conf Corporate Hospitality Days **Location** M1 junct 13, 2m W
Hotel ★★★ 74% HL Best Western Moore Place, The Square, ASPLEY GUISE, Woburn ☎ 01908 282000 🖹 01908 282000 62 en suite

BEDFORD
Map 4 TL04

Bedford & County Green Ln, Clapham MK41 6ET
☎ 01234 352617 🖹 01234 357195
e-mail: enquiries@bedfordandcountygolfclub.co.uk
web: www.bedfordandcountygolfclub.co.uk

A mature, undulating parkland course established in 1912 with views over Bedford and surrounding countryside. Beware of the brook that discreetly meanders through the 7th, 10th, 11th and 15th holes. The testing par 4 15th is one of the most challenging holes in the area.

18 Holes, 6420yds, Par 70, SSS 70, Course record 66. Club membership 600.

Visitors Mon-Fri except BHs. Handicap certificate required. Dress code. **Societies** booking required. **Green Fees** £42 per day, £34 per round **Prof** R Tattersall **Facilities** 🍴 🍽 🖬 🖵 🏋 🛎 🏠 🏌
Conf Corporate Hospitality Days **Location** 2m N of Bedford, off A6 in Clapham village
Hotel ★★★★ 70% HL The Barns Hotel, Cardington Road, BEDFORD ☎ 0870 609 6108 🖹 0870 609 6108 49 en suite

Bedford Great Denham Golf Village, Carnoustie Dr, Biddenham MK40 4FF
☎ 01234 320022 🖹 01234 320023
e-mail: info@thebedfordgc.com
web: www.thebedfordgc.com

American-style course with 89 bunkers, eight large water features and large contoured USPGA specification greens. Built on sand and gravel the course is open all year round and provides a good test of golf for both the beginner and the seasoned player.

The Bedford Golf Club: 18 Holes, 6471yds, Par 72, SSS 72, Course record 63. Club membership 500.

Visitors Mon-Sun & BHs. Booking required. Handicap certificate. Dress code. **Societies** booking required. **Green Fees** £25 per 18 holes (£35 weekends) **Course Designer** David Pottage **Prof** Geoff Swain **Facilities** 🍴 🍽 🖬 🖵 🏋 🛎 🏠 🏌 ⛳ 🛺 🏌 🏌

Conf facs Corporate Hospitality Days **Location** 2.5m W of Bedford off A428
Hotel BUD Innkeeper's Lodge Bedford, 403 Goldington Road, BEDFORD ☎ 0845 112 6056 🖹 0845 112 6056 47 en suite

Bedfordshire Spring Ln, Stagsden MK43 8SR
☎ 01234 822555 🖹 01234 825052
e-mail: ross.ellens@bedfordshiregolf.com
web: www.bedfordshiregolf.com

A challenging 18-hole course on undulating terrain with established trees and woods and water hazards. Magnificent views.

18 Holes, 6565yds, Par 70, SSS 71, Course record 65. Academy Course: 9 Holes, 1354yds, Par 28, SSS 28. Club membership 700.

Visitors Mon-Sun & BHs. Dress code. **Societies** booking required. **Green Fees** £42 per day, £32 per 18 holes. 9 hole course £6.50 (£7.50 weekends) **Course Designer** Cameron Sinclair **Prof** Geraint Dixon **Facilities** 🍴 🍽 by prior arrangement 🖬 🖵 🏋 🛎 🏠 🏌 🛺 🏌 🏌 🏌 **Conf** facs Corporate Hospitality Days **Location** 3m W of Bedford on A422 at Stagsden
Hotel BUD Travelodge Bedford Marston Moretaine, Beancroft Road Junction, MARSTON MORETAINE ☎ 08719 846 011 🖹 08719 846 011 54 en suite

Mowsbury Cleat Hill, Kimbolton Rd, Ravensden MK41 8BJ
☎ 01234 772700 🖹 01234 772700

Parkland municipal course in rural surroundings. Long and testing 14-bay driving range.

18 Holes, 6182yds, Par 72, SSS 69. Club membership 360.

Visitors Mon-Sun & BHs. Dress code. **Societies** welcome. **Green Fees** £15.20 per round (£19.85 weekends) **Course Designer** Hawtree **Prof** Malcolm Summers **Facilities** 🍴 🍽 by prior arrangement 🖬 🖵 🏋 🛎 🏠 🏌 🛺 🏌 **Leisure** squash **Location** 2m N of town centre on B660
Hotel BUD Innkeeper's Lodge Bedford, 403 Goldington Road, BEDFORD ☎ 0845 112 6056 🖹 0845 112 6056 47 en suite

CHALGRAVE
Map 4 TL02

Chalgrave Manor Dunstable Rd LU5 6JN
☎ 01525 876556 & 876554
e-mail: steve@chalgravegolf.co.uk
web: www.chalgravegolf.co.uk

Undulating parkland course set in 150 acres of Bedfordshire countryside. No two consecutive holes play in the same direction. Four holes have water hazards including the signature tenth hole, playing 130yds across water to a sloping green. The par 5 9th, at 621yds, is one of the longest holes in the country.

18 Holes, 6382yds, Par 72, SSS 70, Course record 68. Club membership 550.

Visitors Mon-Sun & BHs. Booking required weekends & BHs. Dress code. **Societies** booking required. **Green Fees** £22 per round (£34 weekends & BHs) **Course Designer** M Palmer **Prof** Martin Heanue **Facilities** 🍴 🍽 by prior arrangement 🖬 🖵 🏋 🛎 🏠 🏌 **Conf** facs Corporate Hospitality Days **Location** M1 junct 12, A5120 through Toddington, signed 1m
Hotel ★★★ 81% HL Old Palace Lodge, Church Street, DUNSTABLE ☎ 01582 662201 🖹 01582 662201 68 en suite

COLMWORTH
Map 4 TL15

Colmworth & North Bedfordshire New Rd MK44 2NN
☎ 01234 378181 🗎 01234 376678
e-mail: colmworth@btopenworld.com
web: www.colmworthgolfclub.co.uk
An easy walking course with well-bunkered greens, opened in 1991. The course is often windy and plays longer than the yardage suggests. Water comes into play on three holes.

Colmworth & North Bedfordshire Golf Course: 18 Holes, 6435yds, Par 72, SSS 71, Course record 69. Club membership 200.
Visitors Mon-Sun & BHs. Booking required weekends & BHs. Dress code. **Societies** welcome. **Green Fees** £15 per 18 holes, £12 per 12 holes, £9 per 9 holes (£25/£17/£14 weekends & BHs) **Course Designer** John Glasgow **Prof** Graham Bithrey **Facilities** ⑪ ⑩ by prior arrangement 🝙 ⬚ ⬚ 🜲 🝙 🝖 ♢ 🝘 ♢ 🝗
Leisure fishing, par 3 course **Conf** facs Corporate Hospitality Days
Location off A1 between Bedford & St Neots
Hotel ★★★★ 70% HL The Barns Hotel, Cardington Road, BEDFORD ☎ 0870 609 6108 🗎 0870 609 6108   49 en suite

DUNSTABLE
Map 4 TL02

Caddington Chaul End Rd, Caddington LU1 4AX
☎ 01582 415573 🗎 01582 415314
e-mail: info@caddingtongolfclub.co.uk
web: www.caddingtongolfclub.co.uk
A challenging 18-hole parkland course with ponds and lakes on top of Blows Downs.

18 Holes, 6226yds, Par 71, SSS 70. Club membership 400.
Visitors Mon-Sun & BHs. Dress code. **Societies** booking required.
Green Fees £19 per round (£30 weekends) **Prof** Daren Turner
Facilities ⑪ ⑩ by prior arrangement 🝙 ⬚ 🝙 🜲 🝙 🝖 ♢ **Conf** Corporate Hospitality Days **Location** M1 junct 11 towards Dunstable, after 0.5m exit left at Tesco rdbt, towards Luton
Hotel ★★★ 81% HL Old Palace Lodge, Church Street, DUNSTABLE ☎ 01582 662201 🗎 01582 662201   68 en suite

Dunstable Downs Whipsnade Rd LU6 2NB
☎ 01582 604472 🗎 01582 478700
e-mail: dunstabledownsgc@btconnect.com
web: www.dunstable-golf.co.uk
A fine downland course set on two levels with far-reaching views and frequent sightings of graceful gliders. The 9th hole is one of the best short holes in the country.

18 Holes, 6320yds, Par 70, SSS 70, Course record 64. Club membership 600.
Visitors Mon-Fri except BHs. Dress code. **Societies** booking required. **Green Fees** £50 per day, £35 per round **Course Designer** James Braid **Prof** Darren Charlton **Facilities** ⑪ ⑩ 🝙 ⬚ 🝙 🜲 🝙 🝖 ♢ **Conf** facs Corporate Hospitality Days
Location 2m S off B4541
Hotel ★★★ 81% HL Old Palace Lodge, Church Street, DUNSTABLE ☎ 01582 662201 🗎 01582 662201   68 en suite

LEIGHTON BUZZARD
Map 4 SP92

Leighton Buzzard Plantation Rd LU7 3JF
☎ 01525 244800 (Office) 🗎 01525 244801
e-mail: lbgc.secretary1@btopenworld.com
web: www.leightonbuzzardgolf.net

Mature parkland and heathland with easy walking. The 17th and 18th holes are challenging tree-lined finishing holes with tight fairways. The par 3 11th is the signature hole.

18 Holes, 6101yds, Par 71, SSS 70, Course record 63. Club membership 700.
Visitors Mon-Fri except BHs. Handicap certificate. Dress code. **Societies** welcome. **Green Fees** phone **Prof** Maurice Campbell **Facilities** ⑪ ⑩ 🝙 ⬚ 🝙 🜲 🝙 🝖 ♢ **Conf** facs Corporate Hospitality Days **Location** 1.5m N of town centre off A4146
Hotel ★★★ 81% HL Old Palace Lodge, Church Street, DUNSTABLE ☎ 01582 662201 🗎 01582 662201   68 en suite

LOWER STONDON
Map 4 TL13

Mount Pleasant Station Rd SG16 6JL
☎ 01462 850999
e-mail: manager@mountpleasantgolfclub.co.uk
web: www.mountpleasantgolfclub.co.uk
Undulating meadowland course with three ponds in play and many tree plantations. A deep ditch, sometimes with water, runs through the middle of the course and is crossed four times per nine holes. The main feature of the course is its presentation and superb greens. The course is seldom closed by bad weather.

Mount Pleasant Golf Course: 9 Holes, 6185yds, Par 70, SSS 70, Course record 68. Club membership 300.
Visitors Mon-Sun & BHs. Booking required. Dress code. **Societies** booking required. **Green Fees** £18 per 18 holes, £10 per 9 holes (£22/£12.50 weekends & BHs) **Course Designer** Derek Young **Prof** Glen Kemble **Facilities** ⑪ ⑩ by prior arrangement 🝙 ⬚ 🝙 🜲 🝙 🝖 ♢ **Leisure** undercover driving nets **Conf** Corporate Hospitality Days **Location** 0.75m W of A600, 4m N of Hitchin
Hotel ★★★ 71% SHL Redcoats Farmhouse Hotel, Redcoats Green, HITCHIN ☎ 01438 729500 🗎 01438 729500   13 en suite

ENGLAND

LUTON
Map 4 TL02

South Beds Warden Hill Rd LU2 7AE
☎ 01582 591500 🖹 01582 495381
e-mail: office@southbedsgolfclub.co.uk
web: www.southbedsgolfclub.co.uk
18-hole and nine-hole chalk downland courses, slightly undulating.
Galley Hill Course: 18 Holes, 6401yds, Par 71, SSS 71,
Course record 64.
Warden Hill Course: 9 Holes, 2364yds, Par 64, SSS 63.
Club membership 1000.
Visitors Mon-Sun & BHs. Handicap certificate required for Galley Hill course. Dress code. **Societies** booking required. **Green Fees** Phone **Prof** Michael Davis **Facilities** ⓣ ⟨◎⟩ ⏚ ⌷ ▜ ⏛ 🖻 🖦 ⌗
Conf Corporate Hospitality Days **Location** 3m N of Luton on A6
Hotel BUD Ibis Luton, Spittlesea Road, LUTON ☎ 01582 424488
🖹 01582 424488 98 en suite

Stockwood Park London Rd LU1 4LX
☎ 01582 413704 (pro shop)
e-mail: spgc@hotmail.co.uk
A well-laid out municipal parkland course with established trees and several challenging holes.
18 Holes, 6049yds, Par 69, SSS 69, Course record 67.
Club membership 600.
Visitors Mon-Sun & BHs. Booking required. Dress code.
Societies booking required. **Green Fees** phone **Course Designer** Charles Lawrie **Prof** Matt Green **Facilities** ⓣ ⟨◎⟩ ⏚ ⌷
▜ ⏛ 🖻 ⌗ 🖦 ⌗ ⌗ **Conf** facs Corporate Hospitality
Days **Location** 1m S
Hotel ★★★★★ 86% HL Luton Hoo Hotel, Golf and Spa,
The Mansion House, LUTON ☎ 01582 734437 🖹 01582 734437
144 en suite

MILLBROOK
Map 4 TL03

Millbrook Millbrook Village MK45 2JB
☎ 01525 840252 & 402269 (booking) 🖹 01525 406249
e-mail: info@themillbrook.com
web: www.themillbrook.com
Long parkland course on rolling countryside high above the Bedfordshire plains. Laid out on well-drained sandy soil with many fairways lined with silver birch, pine and larch. The course provides a continuous test of the tee where length and accuracy pay a huge premium.
The Millbrook Golf Club: 18 Holes, 6966yds, Par 73,
SSS 73, Course record 68. Club membership 560.
Visitors Mon-Fri. Weekends & BHs pm only. Dress code.
Societies booking required. **Green Fees** £25 per 18 holes (£35 weekends & BHs pm only) **Course Designer** William Sutherland **Prof** Robert Brightman **Facilities** ⓣ ⟨◎⟩ ⏚ ⌷ ▜ ⏛ 🖻
⌗ ⌗ 🖦 ⌗ **Conf** facs Corporate Hospitality Days **Location** M1 junct 12/13, A507 Woburn-Ampthill road
Hotel ★★★ 74% HL Best Western Moore Place, The Square, ASPLEY GUISE, Woburn ☎ 01908 282000 🖹 01908 282000
62 en suite

PAVENHAM
Map 4 SP95

Pavenham Park High St MK43 7PE
☎ 01234 822202
e-mail: pavenhampark@o2.co.uk
Mature, undulating parkland with fast contoured greens.
18 Holes, 6400yds, Par 72, SSS 71, Course record 63.
Club membership 790.
Visitors Mon-Sun & BHs. Booking required weekends & BHs. Dress code. **Societies** booking required. **Green Fees** £25 per round (£30 weekends & BHs) **Course Designer** Zac Thompson **Prof** Zac Thompson **Facilities** ⓣ ⟨◎⟩ ⏚ ⌷ ▜ ⏛ 🖻 ⌗ ⌗ 🖦 ⌗
Leisure 100 yd short game zone **Conf** facs Corporate Hospitality Days **Location** 1.5m from A6, N of Bedford
Hotel BUD Travelodge Bedford Marston Moretaine, Beancroft Road Junction, MARSTON MORETAINE ☎ 08719 846 011 🖹 08719 846 011
54 en suite

SANDY
Map 4 TL14

John O'Gaunt Sutton Park SG19 2LY
☎ 01767 260360 🖹 01767 262834
e-mail: admin@johnogauntgolfclub.co.uk
web: www.johnogauntgolfclub.co.uk
Two magnificent parkland courses - John O'Gaunt and Carthagena - covering a gently undulating and tree-lined terrain. The John O'Gaunt course makes the most of numerous natural features, notably a river which crosses the fairways of four holes. The Carthagena course has larger greens, longer tees and from the back tees is a challenging course.
John O'Gaunt Course: 18 Holes, 6513yds, Par 71, SSS 71,
Course record 64.
Carthagena Course: 18 Holes, 5869yds, Par 69, SSS 69.
Club membership 1500.
Visitors Mon-Sun & BHs. Handicap certificate required. Dress code.
Societies booking required. **Green Fees** not confirmed **Course Designer** Hawtree **Prof** Lee Scarbrow **Facilities** ⓣ ⟨◎⟩ ⏚ ⌷ ▜
⏛ 🖻 ⌗ 🖦 ⌗ **Conf** Corporate Hospitality Days **Location** 3m NE of Biggleswade on B1040
Hotel ★★★★ 70% HL The Barns Hotel, Cardington Road, BEDFORD ☎ 0870 609 6108 🖹 0870 609 6108 49 en suite

SHEFFORD
Map 4 TL13

Beadlow Manor Hotel & Golf & Country Club SG17 5PH
☎ 01525 860800 🖹 01525 861345
web: www.beadlowmanor.co.uk
Baroness Course: 18 Holes, 6072yds, Par 71, SSS 69,
Course record 67.
Baron Course: 18 Holes, 6619yds, Par 73, SSS 72,
Course record 67.
Prof Gordon Morrison **Facilities** ⓣ ⟨◎⟩ ⏚ ⌷ ▜ ⏛ 🖻 ⌗
◇ ⌗ 🖦 ⌗ ⌗ **Conf** facs Corporate Hospitality Days **Location** on A507
Telephone for further details
Hotel ★★★★ 73% CHH Menzies Flitwick Manor, Church Road, FLITWICK, BEDFORDSHIRE ☎ 01525 712242 🖹 01525 712242
18 en suite

TILSWORTH
Map 4 SP92

Tilsworth Dunstable Rd LU7 9PU
☎ 01525 210721/2 ▤ 01525 210465
e-mail: nick@tilsworthgolf.co.uk
web: www.tilsworthgolf.co.uk
The course is in first-class condition and, although not a long course, is particularly demanding and challenging where the key is straight driving. The course has its own Amen Corner between the 14th and 16th holes, which will challenge all golfers. Panoramic views of three counties from the 6th tee.

Tilsworth Golf Centre: 18 Holes, 5306yds, Par 69, SSS 66, Course record 61. Club membership 400.

Visitors Mon-Sun & BHs. **Societies** booking required. **Green Fees** £17 for 18 holes (£19.50 weekends/BHs) **Prof** Nick Webb **Facilities** ⑪
⫶◉⫶ 🄱 ▱ 📶 ⟁ 🛋 ⑨⁺ ✔ 🖼 ✔ ꭍ **Conf** facs Corporate Hospitality Days **Location** 0.5m NE off A5, N of Dunstable
Hotel ★★★ 81% HL Old Palace Lodge, Church Street, DUNSTABLE ☎ 01582 662201 ▤ 01582 662201 68 en suite

WYBOSTON
Map 4 TL15

Wyboston Lakes Great North Rd MK44 3AL
☎ 01480 212625 ▤ 01480 223000
e-mail: golf@wybostonlakes.co.uk
web: www.wybostonlakes.co.uk

Parkland with narrow fairways and small greens, set around four lakes and a river, which provide the biggest challenge on this very scenic course.

Wyboston Lakes: 18 Holes, 5955yds, Par 70, SSS 69, Course record 65. Club membership 375.

Visitors Mon-Sun & BHs. Booking required weekends & BHs.
Societies booking required. **Green Fees** phone **Course Designer** N Oakden **Prof** Paul Ashwell **Facilities** ⑪ ⫶◉⫶ 🄱 ▱ 📶 ⟁
🛋 ⑨⁺ ♢ ✔ 🖼 ✔ ꭍ **Leisure** heated indoor swimming pool, fishing, sauna, gymnasium, watersports **Conf** facs Corporate Hospitality Days **Location** 1m S of St Neots off A1/A428
Hotel ★★★★ 70% HL The Barns Hotel, Cardington Road, BEDFORD ☎ 0870 609 6108 ▤ 0870 609 6108 49 en suite

BERKSHIRE

ASCOT
Map 4 SU96

Berkshire Swinley Rd SL5 8AY
☎ 01344 621495 ▤ 01344 623328
e-mail: secretary@theberkshire.co.uk
web: www.theberkshiregolfclub
Two classic heathland courses, with splendid tree-lined fairways, that have remained the same since they were constructed in 1928. The Red Course, on slightly higher ground, is a little longer than the Blue. It has an unusual assortment of holes, six par 3s, six par 4s and six par 5s, the short holes, particularly the 10th and 16th, being the most intimidating. The Blue Course starts with a par 3 and shares with the 16th the reputation of being the finest holes of the 18.

Red Course: 18 Holes, 6452yds, Par 72, SSS 71.
Blue Course: 18 Holes, 6358yds, Par 71, SSS 71.
Club membership 1000.

Visitors Mon-Fri except BHs. Sun pm only. Booking required. Dress code. **Societies** booking required. **Green Fees** £125 per day, £95 per round (£125 Sun pm) **Course Designer** H Fowler **Prof** P Anderson
Facilities ⑪ 🄱 ▱ 📶 ⟁ 🛋 ⑨⁺ ✔ 🖼 ✔ ꭍ **Conf** facs Corporate Hospitality Days **Location** M3 junct 3, 2.5m NW on A332
Hotel ★★★★ 78% HL Macdonald Berystede Hotel & Spa, Bagshot Road, Sunninghill, ASCOT ☎ 0844 879 9104 ▤ 0844 879 9104 126 en suite

Lavender Park Swinley Rd SL5 8BD
☎ 01344 893344
e-mail: lavenderpark@yahoo.com
web: www.lavenderparkgolf.co.uk
Public parkland course, ideal for the short game featuring challenging narrow fairways. Driving range with nine-hole par 3 course, floodlit until 10pm.

Lavender Park Golf Centre: 9 Holes, 1102yds, Par 27, SSS 28.

Visitors Mon-Sun & BHs. **Societies** welcome. **Green Fees** phone **Prof** David Johnson **Facilities** ▱ 📶 🛋 ⑨⁺ ✔ ꭍ
Leisure snooker **Location** 1.5m W of Ascot, off the A329 on the B3017
Hotel ★★★★ 78% HL Macdonald Berystede Hotel & Spa, Bagshot Road, Sunninghill, ASCOT ☎ 0844 879 9104 ▤ 0844 879 9104
126 en suite

Mill Ride Mill Ride SL5 8LT
☎ 01344 886777 ▤ 01344 886820
web: www.mill-ride.com
18 Holes, 6807yds, Par 72, SSS 72, Course record 64.
Course Designer Donald Steel **Location** 2m W of Ascot
Telephone for further details
Hotel ★★★★ 78% HL Macdonald Berystede Hotel & Spa, Bagshot Road, Sunninghill, ASCOT ☎ 0844 879 9104 ▤ 0844 879 9104
126 en suite

ENGLAND

Swinley Forest Coronation Rd SL5 9LE
☎ 01344 295283 (Secretary) & 620197 (clubhouse)
🖷 01344 874733
e-mail: swinleyfgc@tiscali.co.uk
An attractive and immaculate course of heather and pine situated in the heart of Swinley Forest. The 17th is as good a short hole as can be found, with a bunkered plateau green, and the 12th is one of the most challenging par 4s.
18 Holes, 6100yds, Par 69, SSS 70, Course record 62. Club membership 350.
Visitors Mon-Fri except BHs. Booking required. Handicap certificate. Dress code. **Societies** welcome. **Green Fees** not confirmed **Course Designer** Harry Colt **Prof** Stuart Hill **Facilities** ⑪ ⮞ ⚏ 🏌 ⚸
🏡 ⚑ 🏌 🛒 🏌 **Conf** Corporate Hospitality Days **Location** 2m S of Ascot, off A30
Hotel ★★★★ 78% HL Macdonald Berystede Hotel & Spa, Bagshot Road, Sunninghill, ASCOT ☎ 0844 879 9104 🖷 0844 879 9104 126 en suite

---

BINFIELD Map 4 SU87

Blue Mountain Golf Centre Wood Ln RG42 4EX
☎ 01344 300200 🖷 01344 360960
e-mail: bluemountain@crown-golf.uk.com
web: www.bluemountaingolf.co.uk
An 18-hole Pay and Play course with many testing holes with water hazards. Greens are large, undulating and strategically placed bunkers provide a fair challenge.
Blue Mountain Golf Centre: 18 Holes, 6097yds, Par 70, SSS 70, Course record 63. Club membership 250.
Visitors Mon-Sun & BHs. Dress code. **Societies** booking required. **Green Fees** Mon-Thu £20, Fri £21, weekends £26 (9 holes £12/£12.60/£15.60) **Prof** Rob Spurrier **Facilities** ⑪ 🍽 ⮞ ⚏
🏌 ⚸ 🏡 ⚑ 🏌 🛒 🏌 **Conf** facs Corporate Hospitality Days **Location** From M4 junct 10, take A329(M) signed Bracknell. 1st exit signed B3408 Binfield. Straight over roundabout and traffic lights to next roundabout. 2nd exit, first left into Wood Lane.
Hotel ★★★★ 75% HL Coppid Beech, John Nike Way, BRACKNELL ☎ 01344 303333 🖷 01344 303333 205 en suite

---

CAVERSHAM Map 4 SU77

Caversham Heath Chazey Heath RG4 7UT
☎ 0118 947 8600 🖷 0118 947 8700
e-mail: info@cavershamgolf.co.uk
web: www.cavershamgolf.co.uk
A course in a beautiful heathland setting which has matured well and rewards golfers of all levels. The course, built to exacting USGA standards, is unusually dry in winter whilst fully irrigated in summer, and therefore offers dependable year round play.
18 Holes, 7151yds, Par 73, SSS 73, Course record 66. Club membership 600.
Visitors Mon-Sun & BHs. Booking required. Handicap certificate. Dress code. **Societies** booking required. **Green Fees** £40 per 18 holes, £26 per 9 holes (£56/£32 Sat & Sun) **Course Designer** David Williams **Prof** Adam Harrison **Facilities** ⑪ 🍽 ⮞ ⚏ 🏌 ⚸ 🏡 ⚑ ◇
🏌 🛒 🏌 **Conf** facs Corporate Hospitality Days **Location** 2m NE of Caversham on A4074 towards Oxford
Hotel ★★★★ 77% HL Novotel Reading Centre, 25b Friar Street, READING ☎ 0118 952 2600 🖷 0118 952 2600 178 en suite

---

CHADDLEWORTH Map 4 SU47

West Berkshire RG20 7DU
☎ 01488 638574 🖷 01488 638781
e-mail: info@thewbgc.co.uk
web: www.thewbgc.co.uk
Challenging and interesting downland course with views of the Berkshire Downs. The course is bordered by ancient woodland and golfers will find manicured fairways with well-constructed greens and strategically placed hazards. The testing 627yd 5th hole is one of the longest par 5s in southern England. Bunkers are well placed from tees and around the greens to catch any wayward shots.
West Berkshire Golf Course: 18 Holes, 7022yds, Par 73, SSS 74. Club membership 450.
Visitors Mon-Fri. Weekends & BHs pm only. Booking required weekends & BHs. Dress code. **Societies** booking required. **Green Fees** £28 per round (£35 per round weekends & bank holidays - pm only) **Prof** Paul Simpson **Facilities** ⑪ ⮞ ⚏ 🏌 ⚸ 🏡 🛒 🏌
🏌 **Conf** Corporate Hospitality Days **Location** 1m S of village off A338
Hotel ★★★★ 73% HL Ramada Newbury Elcot Park, ELCOT, Newbury ☎ 01488 658100 & 0844 815 9060 🖷 01488 658100 73 en suite

---

COOKHAM Map 4 SU88

Winter Hill Grange Ln SL6 9RP
☎ 01628 527613 🖷 01628 527479
e-mail: winterhill_administration@johnlewis.co.uk
web: www.winterhillgolfclub.net
Peaceful parkland course owned by the John Lewis partnership and set in a curve of the Thames with wonderful views across the river to Cliveden.
18 Holes, 6408yds, Par 72, SSS 71, Course record 63. Club membership 770.
Visitors Mon-Fri except BHs. Handicap certificate. **Societies** booking required. **Green Fees** not confirmed **Course Designer** Charles Lawrie **Prof** Julian Goodman **Facilities** ⑪ 🍽 by prior arrangement ⮞
⚏ 🏌 ⚸ 🏡 🏌 🛒 🏌 **Conf** facs Corporate Hospitality Days **Location** 1m NW off B4447
Hotel ★★★★ HL Macdonald Compleat Angler, Marlow Bridge, MARLOW ☎ 0844 879 9128 🖷 0844 879 9128 64 en suite

---

CROWTHORNE Map 4 SU86

East Berkshire Ravenswood Ave RG45 6BD
☎ 01344 772041 🖷 01344 777378
e-mail: thesecretary@eastberkshiregolfclub.com
web: www.eastberkshiregolfclub.com
An attractive heathland course with an abundance of heather and pine trees. Walking is easy and the greens are exceptionally good. Some fairways become tight where the heather encroaches on the line of play. The course is testing and demands great accuracy.
18 Holes, 6236yds, Par 69, SSS 70, Course record 65. Club membership 766.
Visitors contact club for details. **Societies** welcome. **Green Fees** £60 per day, £40 per round **Course Designer** P Paxton **Prof** Jason Brant **Facilities** ⑪ 🍽 ⮞ ⚏ 🏌 ⚸ 🏡 🏌
Conf Corporate Hospitality Days **Location** W side of town centre off B3348
Hotel ★★★★★ CHH Pennyhill Park Hotel & The Spa, London Road, BAGSHOT ☎ 01276 471774 🖷 01276 471774 123 en suite

DATCHET
Map 4 SU97

Datchet Buccleuch Rd SL3 9BP
☎ 01753 543887 & 541872 🖹 01753 541872
e-mail: secretary@datchetgolfclub.co.uk
web: www.datchetgolfclub.co.uk
Meadowland course, easy walking.

*9 Holes, 6087yds, Par 70, SSS 69, Course record 63.
Club membership 430.*

Visitors Mon-Fri. Weekends & BHs after 2pm. Dress code.
Societies booking required. **Green Fees** £25 per 18 holes (£30 weekends & BHs) **Course Designer** J H Taylor **Prof** Paul Cook
Facilities ⓘ ⦿ 🍴 ☕ 🍽 ⛳ 🛒 ⛵ 🏌 **Location** NW side of Datchet off B470
Hotel ★★★★ 77% HL Mercure Castle, 18 High Street, WINDSOR
☎ 01753 851577 🖹 01753 851577 108 en suite

MAIDENHEAD
Map 4 SU88

Bird Hills Drift Rd, Hawthorn Hill SL6 3ST
☎ 01628 771030 🖹 01628 631023
e-mail: info@birdhills.co.uk
web: www.birdhills.co.uk

A gently undulating course with easy walking and several water hazards. Challenging holes include the par 5 6th dog-leg, par 3 9th surrounded by water and bunkers, and the 16th which is a long uphill par 4 with a two-tier green. Bent grass green and grass teeing areas.
Bird Hills Golf Centre: 18 Holes, 6176yds, Par 72, SSS 69, Course record 65. Club membership 400.

Visitors Mon-Sun & BHs. Booking required Thu-Sun & BHs. Dress code
Societies booking required. **Green Fees** phone **Prof** N Slimming/C Connell/J Dovey **Facilities** ⓘ ⦿ 🍴 ☕ 🍽 ⛳ 🛒 ⛵ 🏌 **Leisure** pool tables. **Conf** facs Corporate Hospitality Days
Location M4 junct 8/9, 4m S on A330
Hotel ★★★ 80% HL Stirrups Country House, Maidens Green, BRACKNELL ☎ 01344 882284 🖹 01344 882284 30 en suite

Maidenhead Shoppenhangers Rd SL6 2PZ
☎ 01628 624693 🖹 01628 780758
e-mail: manager@maidenheadgolf.co.uk
web: www.maidenheadgolf.co.uk
Pleasant parkland with excellent greens and some challenging holes. The long par 4 4th and short par 3 13th are only two of the many outstanding aspects of this course.
*18 Holes, 6338yds, Par 70, SSS 70.
Club membership 650.*

Visitors Mon-Thu except BHs. Handicap certificate required. Dress code. **Societies** booking required. **Green Fees** £47 per day, £37 per

round **Course Designer** Alex Simpson **Prof** Steve Geary **Facilities** ⓘ ⦿ 🍴 ☕ 🍽 ⛳ 🛒 ⛵ **Conf** facs Corporate Hospitality Days **Location** S side of town centre off A308
Hotel ★★★★ HL Fredrick's Hotel Restaurant Spa, Shoppenhangers Road, MAIDENHEAD ☎ 01628 581000 🖹 01628 581000 34 en suite

Temple Henley Rd SL6 5LH
☎ 01628 824795 🖹 01628 828119
web: www.templegolfclub.co.uk
18 Holes, 6266yds, Par 70, SSS 70.
Course Designer Willie Park (Jnr) **Location** M4 junct 8/9, A404M then A4130, signed Henley
Telephone for further details
Hotel ★★★★ HL Macdonald Compleat Angler, Marlow Bridge, MARLOW ☎ 0844 879 9128 🖹 0844 879 9128 64 en suite

MORTIMER
Map 4 SU66

Wokefield Park Wokefield Park RG7 3AE
☎ 0118 933 4072 🖹 0118 933 4031
web: www.deverevenues.co.uk
18 Holes, 6579yds, Par 72, SSS 72, Course record 65.
Course Designer Jonathan Gaunt **Location** M4 junct 11, A33 towards Basingstoke. 1st rdbt, 3rd exit towards Grazeley. After 2.5m right bend, club on right
Telephone for further details
Hotel ★★★ 67% HL Holiday Inn Reading West, Bath Road, PADWORTH ☎ 0118 971 4411 🖹 0118 971 4411 50 en suite

NEWBURY
Map 4 SU46

Donnington Valley Snelsmore House, Snelsmore Common RG14 3BG
☎ 01635 568140 🖹 01635 41889
e-mail: golf@donningtonvalley.co.uk
web: www.donningtonvalleygolfclub.co.uk

Undulating, testing course with mature trees and elevated greens, some protected by water. The closing four holes present a real challenge to all levels of golfer.
*18 Holes, 6353yds, Par 71, SSS 71, Course record 71.
Club membership 370.*

Visitors Mon-Sun & BHs. Dress code. **Societies** welcome. **Green Fees** £27 per 18 holes (£36 weekends) **Course Designer** Mike Smith **Prof** Martin Balfour **Facilities** ⓘ ⦿ by prior arrangement 🍴 ☕ 🍽 ⛳ 🛒 ⛵ ◇ 🏌 **Leisure** heated indoor swimming

continued

pool, sauna, gymnasium **Conf** facs Corporate Hospitality Days **Location** from M4 junct 13 take A34 for Newbury and turn left at sign for Donnington/Services. At next rdbt take 2nd exit signed for Donnington and at following rdbt turn left for 2m, club on right **Hotel** ★★★★ 85% HL Donnington Valley Hotel & Spa, Old Oxford Road, Donnington, NEWBURY ☎ 01635 551199 🖹 01635 551199 111 en suite

Newbury & Crookham Bury's Bank Rd, Greenham RG19 8BZ
☎ 01635 40035
e-mail: steve.myers@newburygolf.co.uk
web: www.newburygolf.co.uk
A traditional English parkland course, whose tree-lined fairways and small fast greens provide a challenge of consistency and accuracy.
18 Holes, 5961yds, Par 69, SSS 69, Course record 63. Club membership 700.
Visitors Mon-Fri except BHs. Handicap certificate. Dress code. **Societies** booking required. **Green Fees** £50 per day, £40 per round. **Course Designer** J H Taylor **Prof** David Harris **Facilities** ⓣ ⓞ︎ ⓛ ⌁ 🍴 ⌁ 🏠 🛺 ⚑ **Conf** Corporate Hospitality Days **Location** 4m S of M4 off A339
Hotel ★★★★ 73% HL Ramada Newbury Elcot Park, ELCOT, Newbury ☎ 01488 658100 & 0844 815 9060 🖹 01488 658100 73 en suite

READING   Map 4 SU77

Calcot Park Bath Rd, Calcot RG31 7RN
☎ 0118 942 7124   🖹 0118 945 3373
e-mail: info@calcotpark.com
web: www.calcotpark.com
A delightfully picturesque, slightly undulating parkland course just outside the town. The subtle borrows on the greens challenge all categories of golfer. Hazards include streams, a lake and many trees. The 6th is a 503yd par 5, with the tee-shot hit downhill over cross-bunkers to a well-guarded green; the 7th (156yds) is played over the lake to an elevated green and the 13th (also 156yds) requires a carry across a valley to a plateau green.
18 Holes, 6216yds, Par 70, SSS 70, Course record 63. Club membership 730.
Visitors Mon-Fri except BHs. Booking required. Handicap certificate. Dress code. **Societies** booking required. **Green Fees** £50 per day/round. Off peak rates **Course Designer** H S Colt **Prof** Mark Grieve **Facilities** ⓣ ⓞ︎ ⓛ ⌁ 🍴 ⌁ 🏠 🛺 ⚑ **Leisure** fishing **Conf** facs Corporate Hospitality Days **Location** 1.5m from M4 junct 12 on A4 towards Reading
Hotel ★★★ 72% HL Best Western Calcot Hotel, 98 Bath Road, Calcot, READING ☎ 0118 941 6423 🖹 0118 941 6423 78 en suite

Hennerton Crazies Hill Rd, Wargrave RG10 8LT
☎ 0118 940 1000 & 0118 940 4778   🖹 0118 940 1042
e-mail: info@hennertongolfclub.co.uk
web: www.hennertongolfclub.co.uk
Overlooking the Thames Valley, this course has many existing natural features and a good number of hazards such as bunkers, mature trees and two small lakes.
18 Holes, 4187yds, Par 65, SSS 62, Course record 62. Club membership 450.
Visitors Mon-Sun & BHs. Dress code. **Societies** booking required. **Green Fees** £18 per 18 holes, £12 per 9 holes (£24/£15 weekends and

BHs) **Course Designer** Col D Beard **Prof** William Farrow **Facilities** ⓣ ⓛ ⌁ 🍴 ⌁ 🏠 🏴 ⚑ 🛺 ⚑ **Conf** Corporate Hospitality Days **Location** signed from A321 Wargrave High St

Mapledurham Chazey Heath, Mapledurham RG4 7UD
☎ 0118 946 3353   🖹 0118 946 3363
e-mail: d.mullen@theclubcompany.com
web: www.theclubcompany.com
An 18-hole parkland and woodland course designed by Bob Sandow. Flanked by hedgerows and mature woods, it is testing for players of all levels.
The Club at Mapledurham: 18 Holes, 5700yds, Par 69, SSS 67, Course record 65. Club membership 750.
Visitors Mon-Sun & BHs. Booking required. Dress code. **Societies** welcome. **Green Fees** £25 per round (£30 weekends) **Course Designer** Robert Sandow **Prof** Tim Gilpin **Facilities** ⓣ ⓞ︎ ⓛ ⌁ 🍴 ⌁ 🏠 ⚑ **Leisure** sauna, gymnasium **Conf** Corporate Hospitality Days **Location** on A4074 to Oxford
Hotel ★★★ 81% HL French Horn, SONNING ON THAMES ☎ 0118 969 2204 🖹 0118 969 2204 22 en suite

Reading 17 Kidmore End Rd, Emmer Green RG4 8SG
☎ 0118 947 2909 (Secretary)   🖹 0118 946 4468
e-mail: secretary@readinggolfclub.com
web: www.readinggolfclub.com
Pleasant parkland, part hilly and part flat with interesting views and several challenging par 3s. After the opening holes the course moves across the valley. The par 4 5th is played from an elevated tee and although relatively short, the well-placed bunkers and trees come into play. The 470yd par 4 12th is a great hole. It has a slight dog-leg and requires an accurate second shot to hit a well-guarded green. The finishing hole requires two great shots to have any chance of reaching par. Club centenary in 2010.
18 Holes, 6212yds, Par 70, SSS 70, Course record 65. Club membership 600.
Visitors Mon-Sun & BHs. Dress code. **Societies** booking required. **Green Fees** £50 per day, £40 per round. **Course Designer** James Braid **Prof** Scott Fotheringham **Facilities** ⓣ ⓞ︎ ⓛ ⌁ 🍴 ⌁ 🏠 🛺 ⚑ **Leisure** indoor nets **Conf** Corporate Hospitality Days **Location** 2m N off B481
Hotel ★★★ 81% HL French Horn, SONNING ON THAMES ☎ 0118 969 2204 🖹 0118 969 2204 22 en suite

SINDLESHAM   Map 4 SU76

Bearwood Mole Rd RG41 5DB
☎ 0118 976 0060
e-mail: barrytustin@btconnect.com
Flat parkland with one water hazard, the 40-acre lake that features on the challenging 6th and 7th holes.
9 Holes, 5610yds, Par 70, SSS 68, Course record 66. Club membership 500.
Visitors Mon-Fri. Weekends & BH pm only. Booking required weekends & BHs. Dress code. **Societies** booking required. **Green Fees** phone **Course Designer** Barry Tustin **Prof** Bayley Tustin **Facilities** ⓣ ⓛ ⌁ 🍴 ⌁ 🏠 ⚑ 🛺 ⚑ **Conf** Corporate Hospitality Days **Location** 1m SW on B3030
Hotel ★★★★ 79% HL Millennium Madejski Hotel Reading, Madejski Stadium, READING ☎ 0118 925 3500 🖹 0118 925 3500 201 en suite

SUNNINGDALE

BERKSHIRE - SUNNINGDALE - MAP 4 SU96

The club has two championship courses, laid out on the most glorious piece of heathland and both courses have their own individual characteristics. The Old Course, founded in 1900, was designed by Willie Park. It is a classic course at just 6627yds long, with gorse and pines, silver birch, heather and immaculate turf. The New Course was created by H S Colt in 1922. At 6729yds, it is a mixture of wood and open heath with long carries and tight fairways.

Ridgemount Rd SL5 9RR ☎ 01344 621681 📄 01344 624154
e-mail: info@sunningdalegolfclub.co.uk **web:** www.sunningdale-golfclub.co.uk
Old Course: 18 Holes, 6063yds, Par 70, SSS 69.
New Course: 18 Holes, 6083yds, Par 70, SSS 70. Club membership 1000.
Visitors may play Mon-Thu except BHs. Booking required. Handicap certificate required. Dress code.
Societies booking required. **Green Fees** Old Course £190 per round, New Course £155 per round. 36 holes £265.
Reduced winter fees. **Course Designer** W Park (Old) H Colt (New) **Prof** Keith Maxwell **Facilities** ⑨ 🍴 ⬜ 🏌️ ⚒
🏠 ✂️ 🏌️ **Conf** Corporate Hospitality Days **Location** 1m S off A30
Hotel ★★★★★ CHH Pennyhill Park Hotel & The Spa, London Road, BAGSHOT ☎ 01276 471774
📄 01276 471774 123 en suite

SONNING
Map 4 SU77

Sonning Duffield Rd RG4 6GJ
☎ 0118 969 3332 📠 0118 944 8409
e-mail: secretary@sonning-golf-club.co.uk
web: www.sonning-golf-club.co.uk

A quality parkland course and the scene of many county championships. Wide fairways, not over-bunkered, and very good greens. Holes of changing character through wooded belts. Four challenging par 4s over 450yds.

18 Holes, 6366yds, Par 70, SSS 70, Course record 65.
Club membership 750.

Visitors contact club for details. **Societies** welcome. **Green Fees** £50 before 10.30am or £40 after 10.30am **Course Designer** J H Taylor **Prof** R McDougall **Facilities** ⓣ ⦿ 🄻 ⬛ ⬛ 🄻 🅲 **Conf** facs Corporate Hospitality Days **Location** 1m S off A4
Hotel ★★★ 81% HL French Horn, SONNING ON THAMES
☎ 0118 969 2204 📠 0118 969 2204 22 en suite

STREATLEY
Map 4 SU58

Goring & Streatley RG8 9QA
☎ 01491 873229 📠 01491 875224
e-mail: secretary@goringgc.org
web: www.goringgc.org

A parkland and moorland course that requires negotiating. Four well-known holes lead up to the heights of the 5th tee, to which there is a 300ft climb. Wide fairways, not over-bunkered, with nice rewards on the way home down the last few holes. A delightful course that commands magnificent views of the Ridgeway & the River Thames.

18 Holes, 6355yds, Par 71, SSS 70, Course record 65.
Club membership 740.

Visitors handicap certificate. Dress code. **Societies** booking required. **Green Fees** phone **Course Designer** Tom Morris **Prof** Jason Hadland **Facilities** ⓣ ⦿ 🄻 ⬛ 🅲 🄻 🄻 🅲 **Location** N of village off A417
Hotel ★★★★ 75% HL The Swan at Streatley, High Street, STREATLEY ☎ 01491 878800 📠 01491 878800 45 en suite

SUNNINGDALE
Map 4 SU96

Sunningdale see page 23
Ridgemount Rd SL5 9RR
☎ 01344 621681 📠 01344 624154
e-mail: info@sunningdalegolfclub.co.uk
web: www.sunningdale-golfclub.co.uk

Sunningdale Ladies Cross Rd SL5 9RX
☎ 01344 620507 📠 01344 620507
e-mail: clbsec.slgc@tiscali.co.uk
web: www.sunningdaleladies.co.uk

A short but challenging 18-hole course with a typical Surrey heathland layout. A very tight course and the heather can be punishing. Excellent test for all levels of golfer.

18 Holes, 3705yds, Par 61, SSS 61. Club membership 400.

Visitors Mon-Sun & BHs. Dress code. **Societies** booking required.
Green Fees £30 per round (£35 weekends & BHs) **Course Designer** H Colt **Facilities** ⓣ 🄻 ⬛ 🅲 🄻 🅲 **Leisure** practice net **Conf** Corporate Hospitality Days **Location** 1m S off A30

Hotel ★★★★ 78% HL Macdonald Berystede Hotel & Spa, Bagshot Road, Sunninghill, ASCOT ☎ 0844 879 9104 📠 0844 879 9104 126 en suite

THEALE
Map 4 SU67

Theale North St RG7 5EX
☎ 0118 930 5331
e-mail: natalielowe125@btinternet.com
web: www.thealegolf.com

Challenging parkland course set in the heart of the Berkshire countryside

18 Holes, 6395yds, Par 72, SSS 71, Course record 68.
Club membership 300.

Visitors Mon-Sun & BHs. Dress code. **Societies** booking required.
Green Fees £35 per day, £20 per 18 holes, £14 per 9 holes.
(£45/£27/£18 weekends & BHs) **Course Designer** Mike Lowe
Facilities ⓣ 🄻 ⬛ 🅲 🄻 🅲 🄻 🄻 🅲 🅲 **Conf** facs
Corporate Hospitality Days **Location** Off M4 junct 12
Hotel ★★★ 72% HL Best Western Calcot Hotel, 98 Bath Road, Calcot, READING ☎ 0118 941 6423 📠 0118 941 6423 78 en suite

WOKINGHAM
Map 4 SU86

Downshire Easthampstead Park RG40 3DH
☎ 01344 302030 📠 01344 301020
e-mail: downshiregc@bracknell-forest.gov.uk
web: www.bracknell-forest.gov.uk

Beautiful municipal parkland course with mature trees. Water hazards come into play on the 14th & 18th holes, & especially on the short 7th, a testing downhill 169yds over the lake. Pleasant easy walking. Challenging holes: 7th (par 4), 15th (par 4), 16th (par 3). Rated as one of the finest municipal courses in the country.

Downshire Golf Complex: 18 Holes, 6416yds, Par 73,
SSS 71. Club membership 1000.

Visitors Mon-Sun & BHs. Booking required. Dress code.
Societies booking required. **Green Fees** £19.65 per 18 holes Mon-Thu, £21.65 Fri, £26.15 weekends & BHs. Reduced winter prices **Prof** W Owers/R Iolo/M Billies **Facilities** ⓣ 🄻 ⬛ 🅲 🄻 🅲 🄻 🄻 🅲 🅲 **Leisure** 9 hole pitch & putt, power tees **Conf** facs Corporate Hospitality Days **Location** 3m SW of Bracknell. M4 junct 10, signs for Crowthorne
Hotel ★★★★ 75% HL Coppid Beech, John Nike Way, BRACKNELL ☎ 01344 303333 📠 01344 303333 205 en suite

Sand Martins Finchampstead Rd RG40 3RQ
☎ 0118 9792711 📠 0118 977 0282
e-mail: info@sandmartins.com
web: www.sandmartins.com

The course has been designed with two distinct and contrasting nine holes. An outward nine set in parkland and a links style inward nine with sandbanks and broom.

18 Holes, 6212yds, Par 70, SSS 70, Course record 64.
Club membership 800.

Visitors Mon-Fri. Weekends & BHs after 12.30 pm. Booking required. Dress code. **Societies** booking required. **Green Fees** phone **Course Designer** Edward Fox **Prof** Andrew Hall/Stephen Cox **Facilities** ⓣ ⦿ 🄻 ⬛ 🅲 🄻 🅲 🅲 🄻 🄻 🅲 🅲 **Conf** facs Corporate Hospitality Days **Location** 1m S of Wokingham

continued

Sand Martins

Hotel ★★★ 74% HL The Waterloo Hotel, Duke's Ride, CROWTHORNE ☎ 0870 609 6111 & 01344 777711 📄 0870 609 6111 79 en suite

BRISTOL

BRISTOL

Map 3 ST57

Bristol and Clifton Beggar Bush Ln, Failand BS8 3TH
☎ 01275 393474 📄 01275 394611
e-mail: mansec@bristolgolf.co.uk
web: www.bristolgolf.co.uk

Utilising the aesthetics and hazards of a former quarry, a valley, stone walls and spinneys of trees, the course is a stern challenge but one always in tip top condition, due in summer to the irrigation and in winter to the natural draining land upon which it is situated. Par 3s from 120 to 220yds, dog-legs which range from the gentle to the brutal and a collection of natural obstacles and hazards add to the charm of the layout.

18 Holes, 6387yds, Par 70, SSS 71, Course record 63. Club membership 850.

Visitors contact club for details. **Societies** welcome. **Green Fees** £40.50 per day (£55.50 weekends) **Prof** Paul Mitchell
Facilities ⊕ ⑩ ⓘ ☐ ⑭ ⚬ 🗄 ☂ ✦ ✦ ✦
Leisure chipping green, practice bunkers **Conf** facs Corporate Hospitality Days **Location** M5 junct 19, A369 for 4m, onto B3129, club 1m on right
Hotel ★★★★ 70% HL Redwood Hotel & Country Club, Beggar Bush Lane, Failand, BRISTOL ☎ 0870 609 6144 📄 0870 609 6144 112 en suite

Filton Golf Course Ln, Filton BS34 7QS
☎ 0117 969 4169 📄 0117 931 4359
e-mail: thesecretary@filtongolfclub.co.uk
web: www.filtongolfclub.co.uk

Interesting and challenging mature parkland course situated on high ground north of the city. Extensive views can be enjoyed from the course to the Concorde and Severn bridges.

18 Holes, 6173yds, Par 70, SSS 70, Course record 61. Club membership 650.

Visitors Mon-Fri. Weekends & BHs pm only. Dress code
Societies booking required. **Green Fees** £34 per round **Prof** D Kelley
Facilities ⊕ ⑩ ⓘ ☐ ⑭ ⚬ 🗄 ✦ ✦ **Conf** Corporate Hospitality Days **Location** M5 junct 15, off A38
Hotel ★★★★ 80% HL Aztec Hotel & Spa, Aztec West Business Park, Almondsbury, BRISTOL ☎ 01454 201090 📄 01454 201090 128 en suite

Henbury Henbury Rd, Westbury-on-Trym BS10 7QB
☎ 0117 950 0044 & 950 2121 (Pro) 📄 0117 959 1928
e-mail: thesecretary@henburygolfclub.co.uk
web: www.henburygolfclub.co.uk

A parkland course in mature woodland bordering the Blaise Castle Estate. The course provides a number of different challenges including the par 3 7th over the River Trym and the par 4 8th which follows the river along the valley.

18 Holes, 6007yds, Par 69, SSS 70, Course record 65. Club membership 740.

Visitors Mon-Sun & BHs. Booking required. Handicap certificate. Dress code. **Societies** booking required. **Green Fees** £36 per day/round **Prof** Nick Riley **Facilities** ⊕ ⑩ by prior arrangement ⓘ ☐ ⑭ ⚬ 🗄 ☂ 🛒 ✦ **Conf** facs Corporate Hospitality Days **Location** M5 junct 17, take A4018 S, right at 1st traffic lights.
Hotel 66% Henbury Lodge, Station Road, Henbury, BRISTOL ☎ 0117 950 2615 📄 0117 950 2615 20 en suite

Knowle Fairway, Brislington BS4 5DF
☎ 0117 977 0660 📄 0117 972 0615
e-mail: admin@knowlegolfclub.co.uk
web: www.knowlegolfclub.co.uk

Undulating course set in 100 acres of parkland with superb views over Bristol and North Somerset. Mature trees line many fairways and the club is involved a rolling development programme to upgrade and improve the layout of bunkers and teeing areas. Includes natural conservation areas attracting an abundance of wild life and several scarce varieties of flora.

18 Holes, 6061yds, Par 69, SSS 69, Course record 61. Club membership 700.

Visitors Mon-Sun & BHs. Handicap certificate. Dress code.
Societies booking required. **Green Fees** £40 per day, £30 per round (£50/£40 weekends) **Course Designer** Hawtree/J H Taylor
Prof Robert Hayward **Facilities** ⊕ ⑩ ⓘ ☐ ⑭ ⚬ 🗄 ☂ ✦ 🛒 ✦ **Location** 3m SE of city centre off A37
Hotel ★★★ 82% CHH Hunstrete House, HUNSTRETE, Pensford, Nr Bath ☎ 01761 490490 📄 01761 490490 25 en suite

Shirehampton Park Park Hill, Shirehampton BS11 0UL
☎ 0117 982 2083
e-mail: info@shirehamptonparkgolfclub.co.uk
web: www.shirehamptonparkgolfclub.co.uk
Lovely parkland course with views across the Avon Gorge.

18 Holes, 5453yds, Par 67, SSS 67, Course record 63. Club membership 530.

Visitors Mon-Sun & BHs. Booking required weekends & BHs.

continued

25

Societies booking required. **Green Fees** £36 per day, £24 per round (£27/18 winter). Twilight rates available **Prof** Jon Palmer **Facilities** ⊕ ⍥ by prior arrangement 🐾 ♿ 🍴 ⛳ 📷 ♨ ✦ **Conf** facs Corporate Hospitality Days **Location** M5 junct 18, 2m E on B4054 **Hotel** ★★★★ 70% HL Redwood Hotel & Country Club, Beggar Bush Lane, Failand, BRISTOL ☎ 0870 609 6144 🖹 0870 609 6144 112 en suite

Shortwood Lodge Carsons Rd, Mangotsfield BS16 9LW
☎ 0117 956 5501 🖹 0117 957 3640
e-mail: info@shortwoodlodge.com
web: www.shortwoodlodge.com

An easy walking parkland course with well-placed bunkers.

18 Holes, 5337yds, Par 68, SSS 66, Course record 61. Club membership 200.

Visitors Mon-Sun & BHs. **Societies** welcome. **Green Fees** £14 (£16 weekends & BHs) **Course Designer** John Day **Facilities** ⊕ ⍥ 🐾 ♿ 🍴 ⛳ 📷 ♨ ✦ 🚲 ✦ **Conf** facs Corporate Hospitality Days **Location** 6m NE of city centre off B4465 **Hotel** ★★★ 74% HL Arno's Manor, 470 Bath Road, Arno's Vale, BRISTOL ☎ 0117 971 1461 🖹 0117 971 1461 73 en suite

Woodlands Trench Ln, Almondsbury BS32 4JZ
☎ 01454 619319 🖹 01454 619397
e-mail: info@woodlands-golf.com
web: www.woodlands-golf.com

Situated on the edge of the Severn Valley, bordered by Hortham Brook and Shepherds Wood, this course has been designed to the highest standards with USGA greens. Both courses have 10 holes where water comes into play, most notably on the 17th hole (Island Green) of the Signature course.

Masters Course: 18 Holes, 6111yds, Par 70, SSS 69. Signature Course: 18 Holes, 5541yds, Par 70, SSS 69. Club membership 100.

Visitors Mon-Sun & BHs. **Societies** welcome. **Green Fees** £14 per round (£16 weekends & BHs) **Prof** L Riddiford **Facilities** ⊕ ⍥ 🐾 ♿ 🍴 ⛳ 📷 ♨ 🚲 ✦ **Leisure** fishing **Conf** facs Corporate Hospitality Days **Location** M5 junct 16, A38 towards Bradley Stoke **Hotel** ★★★★ 71% CHH Grange, Northwoods, Winterbourne, BRISTOL ☎ 01454 777333 🖹 01454 777333 68 en suite

BUCKINGHAMSHIRE

AYLESBURY   Map 4 SP81

Aylesbury Golf Centre Hulcott Ln, Bierton HP22 5GA
☎ 01296 393644

Parkland with magnificent views to the Chiltern Hills. A good test of golf with out of bounds coming into play on nine of the holes, plus a number of water hazards and bunkers.

Aylesbury Golf Centre: 18 Holes, 5965yds, Par 71, SSS 69. Club membership 200.

Visitors Mon-Sun & BHs. Booking required weekends & BHs. Dress code. **Societies** booking required. **Green Fees** phone **Course Designer** T S Benwell **Prof** Richard Wooster **Facilities** ⊕ ⍥ 🐾 ♿ 🍴 ⛳ 📷 ♨ ✦ ✦ **Conf** Corporate Hospitality Days **Location** 1m N of Aylesbury on A418 **Hotel** ★★★★ HL Hartwell House Hotel, Restaurant & Spa, Oxford Road, AYLESBURY ☎ 01296 747444 🖹 01296 747444 46 en suite

Aylesbury Park Andrews Way, Off Coldharbour Way, Oxford Rd HP17 8QQ
☎ 01296 399196
e-mail: info@aylesburyparkgolf.com
web: www.aylesburyparkgolf.com

Parkland with mature trees, located just south-west of Aylesbury.

18 Holes, 6166yds, Par 70, SSS 69, Course record 66. Club membership 360.

Visitors Mon-Sun & BHs. Dress code. **Societies** booking required. **Green Fees** £20 per round (£25 weekends) **Course Designer** M Hawtree **Prof** John Scheu **Facilities** ⊕ 🐾 ♿ 🍴 ⛳ 📷 ♨ ✦ 🚲 ✦ **Leisure** 9 hole par 3 course **Location** 0.5m SW of Aylesbury, on the A418 **Hotel** ★★★★ HL Hartwell House Hotel, Restaurant & Spa, Oxford Road, AYLESBURY ☎ 01296 747444 🖹 01296 747444 46 en suite

Chiltern Forest Aston Hill, Halton HP22 5NQ
☎ 01296 631267 🖹 01296 632709
e-mail: secretary@chilternforest.co.uk
web: www.chilternforest.co.uk

The course nestles in the Chiltern Hills above Aylesbury with stunning views of the surrounding countryside and meanders around challenging wooded terrain. Although not a long course the tightly wooded holes and smallish greens present a challenge to all standards of golfer.

18 Holes, 5765yds, Par 70, SSS 69, Course record 65. Club membership 650.

Visitors Mon-Fri except BHs. Handicap certificate. Dress code. **Societies** welcome. **Green Fees** £36 Mon-Thu, £40 Fri per 18 holes **Prof** Simon Perks **Facilities** ⊕ ⍥ 🐾 ♿ 🍴 ⛳ 📷 ✦ 🚲 ✦ **Conf** Corporate Hospitality Days **Location** off A41 between Tring and Aylesbury **Hotel** BUD Innkeeper's Lodge Aylesbury East, London Road, ASTON CLINTON, Aylesbury ☎ 0845 112 6094 🖹 0845 112 6094 11 en suite

Ellesborough Wendover Rd, Butlers Cross HP17 0TZ
☎ 01296 622114 🖹 01296 622114
e-mail: admin@ellesboroughgolf.co.uk
web: www.ellesboroughgolf.co.uk

Once part of the property of Chequers, and under the shadow of the famous Coombe monument at the Wendover end of the Chilterns. A downland course, it is rather hilly with most holes enhanced by far-ranging views over the Aylesbury countryside.

18 Holes, 6360yds, Par 71, SSS 71, Course record 64. Club membership 700.

Visitors Mon-Fri except BHs. Booking required Tue. Handicap certificate. Dress code. **Societies** Booking required. **Green Fees** not confirmed **Course Designer** James Braid **Prof** Mark Squire **Facilities** ⊕ ⍥ by prior arrangement 🐾 ♿ 🍴 ⛳ 📷 🚲 ✦ **Conf** Corporate Hospitality Days **Location** 1m W of Wendover on B4010 towards Princes Risborough **Hotel** BUD Innkeeper's Lodge Aylesbury South, 40 Main Street, Weston Turville, AYLESBURY ☎ 0845 112 6095 🖹 0845 112 6095 16 en suite

BEACONSFIELD · Map 4 SU99

Beaconsfield Seer Green HP9 2UR
☎ 01494 676545 🖷 01494 681148
e-mail: secretary@beaconsfieldgolfclub.co.uk
web: www.beaconsfieldgolfclub.co.uk
An interesting and, at times, testing tree-lined and parkland course
which frequently plays longer than appears on the card. Each hole
differs to a considerable degree and here lies the charm. Walking is
easy, except perhaps to the 6th and 8th. Well bunkered.
18 Holes, 6506yds, Par 72, SSS 71, Course record 63.
Club membership 900.
Visitors Mon-Fri except BHs. Booking required. Handicap certificate.
Dress code. **Societies** welcome. **Green Fees** not confirmed **Course
Designer** H S Colt **Prof** Michael Brothers **Facilities** ⑪ 🍴 ⊑ ☜ ☷
🏌 📷 ⛳ ⚑ 🏌 **Conf** Corporate Hospitality Days **Location** M40
junct 2, next to Seer Green railway station
Hotel BUD Innkeeper's Lodge Beaconsfield, Aylesbury End,
BEACONSFIELD ☎ 0845 112 6096 🖷 0845 112 6096 31 en suite

BLETCHLEY · Map 4 SP83

Windmill Hill Tattenhoe Ln MK3 7RB
☎ 01908 631113
e-mail: info@golfinmiltonkeynes.co.uk
Long, open-parkland course, the first championship course designed
by Henry Cotton, opened in 1972. Proprietary Pay & Play. No winter
greens.
Windmill Hill Golf Centre: 18 Holes, 6720yds, Par 73,
SSS 72, Course record 68. Club membership 400.
Visitors contact centre for details. **Societies** welcome. **Green
Fees** not confirmed **Course Designer** Henry Cotton **Prof** Colin Clingan
Facilities ⑪ 🍴 ⊑ ☜ ☷ 🏌 📷 ⚑ **Leisure** pool table **Conf** facs Corporate Hospitality Days **Location** W
side of town centre on A421
Hotel BUD Campanile Milton Keynes, 40 Penn Road - off Watling
St, Fenny Stratford, Bletchley, MILTON KEYNES ☎ 01908 649819
🖷 01908 649819 80 en suite

BUCKINGHAM · Map 4 SP63

Buckingham Tingewick Rd MK18 4AE
☎ 01280 815566 🖷 01280 821812
e-mail: admin@buckinghamgolfclub.co.uk
web: www.buckinghamgolfclub.co.uk
Undulating parkland with a stream and river affecting eight holes.
18 Holes, 6162yds, Par 71, SSS 70, Course record 66.
Club membership 740.
Visitors Mon-Fri except BHs. Dress code. **Societies** booking required.
Green Fees £45 per day, £40 per 18 holes **Course Designer** Peter
Jones **Prof** Greg Hannah **Facilities** ⑪ 🍴 ⊑ ☜ ☷ 🏌 📷
⛳ 🏌 **Leisure** snooker room **Conf** Corporate Hospitality Days
Location 1.5m W on A421
Hotel ★★★ 72% HL Best Western Buckingham Hotel, Buckingham
Ring Road, BUCKINGHAM ☎ 01280 822622 🖷 01280 822622
70 en suite

BURNHAM · Map 4 SU98

Burnham Beeches Green Ln SL1 8EG
☎ 01628 661448 🖷 01628 668968
e-mail: enquiries@bbgc.co.uk
web: www.bbgc.co.uk
Wooded parkland on the edge of the historic Burnham Beeches
Forest with a good variety of holes.
18 Holes, 6449yds, Par 70, SSS 71, Course record 66.
Club membership 670.
Visitors Mon-Fri except BHs. Booking required. Handicap certificate.
Dress code. **Societies** booking required. **Green Fees** £45 per round
Course Designer J H Taylor **Prof** Ronnie Bolton **Facilities** ⑪
🍴 ⊑ ☜ ☷ 🏌 📷 ⚑ ⛳ 🏌 **Conf** Corporate
Hospitality Days **Location** 0.5m NE of Burnham
Hotel ★★★★ 74% HL Burnham Beeches Hotel, Grove Road,
BURNHAM ☎ 0844 736 8603 & 01628 603994 🖷 0844 736 8603
82 en suite

Huntswood Taplow Common Rd SL1 8LS
☎ 01628 667144 🖷 01628 663145
e-mail: info@huntswoodgolf.com
web: www.huntswoodgolf.com
Well presented course, which opened in 1996 and has now matured
into one of the most popular courses in the county. Sweeping fairways
set in the heart of a picturesque valley and small greens guarded by
numerous bunkers, making a good second shot a must.
18 Holes, 5286yds, Par 68, SSS 66, Course record 66.
Club membership 365.
Visitors Mon-Sun & BHs. Dress code. **Societies** welcome. **Green
Fees** £16 per 18 holes, £11 per 9 holes (£20.50/£16 weekends)
Prof Graham Benyon **Facilities** ⑪ 🍴 ⊑ ☜ ☷ 🏌 📷 ⚑
🏌 **Conf** facs Corporate Hospitality Days **Location** M4 junct 7, take
first exit at rdbt, at next rdbt take third exit into Lent Rise Road. Under
railway bridge and over mini-rdbt with petrol station on right. Straight
across next min-rdbt into Taplow Common Rd, golf club on left
Hotel ★★★★ 76% HL Grovefield House Hotel, Taplow Common
Road, BURNHAM ☎ 01628 603131 🖷 01628 603131 40 en suite

Lambourne Dropmore Rd SL1 8NF
☎ 01628 666755 🖷 01628 663301
e-mail: info@lambourneclub.co.uk
A championship standard 18-hole parkland course. Undulating terrain
with many trees and several lakes, notably on the tricky 7th hole which
has a tightly guarded green reached via a shot over a lake. Seven
par 4s over 400yds with six picturesque lakes, excellent drainage and
full irrigation.
The Lambourne Club: 18 Holes, 6798yds, Par 72, SSS 73,
Course record 67. Club membership 650.
Visitors contact club for details. **Societies** booking required. **Green
Fees** £60 per round **Course Designer** Donald Steel **Prof** David Hart
Facilities ⑪ 🍴 ⊑ ☜ ☷ 🏌 📷 ⚑ ⛳ 🏌 🏌
Leisure sauna **Conf** facs Corporate Hospitality Days **Location** M4
junct 7 or M40 junct 2, towards Burnham
Hotel ★★★★ 74% HL Burnham Beeches Hotel, Grove Road,
BURNHAM ☎ 0844 736 8603 & 01628 603994 🖷 0844 736 8603
82 en suite

CHALFONT ST GILES
Map 4 SU99

Harewood Downs Cokes Ln HP8 4TA
☎ 01494 762184   📠 01494 766869
e-mail: secretary@hdgc.co.uk
web: www.hdgc.co.uk
A testing undulating parkland course with sloping greens and plenty of trees.

18 Holes, 6028yds, Par 69, SSS 70, Course record 63.
Club membership 600.

Visitors Mon-Fri except BHs. Booking required weekends. Handicap certificate. Dress code. Societies booking required. Green Fees £40 per round Course Designer J H Taylor Prof G C Morris Facilities ⓘ 🍴 by prior arrangement 🛍 ♿ 🏌 ⚲ 🏨 ✦ 🚐 ✦
Conf facs Corporate Hospitality Days Location 2m E of Amersham on A413
Hotel ★★★ 77% HL The Bedford Arms Hotel, CHENIES
☎ 01923 283301 📠 01923 283301 18 en suite

Oakland Park Threehouseholds HP8 4LW
☎ 01494 871277 & 877333 (pro)   📠 01494 874692
e-mail: info@oaklandparkgolf.co.uk
web: www.oaklandparkgolf.co.uk
Parkland with mature trees, hedgerows and water features, designed to respect the natural features of the land and lakes while providing a good challenge for players at all levels.

18 Holes, 5246yds, Par 67, SSS 66, Course record 66.
Club membership 650.

Visitors Mon-Sun & BHs. Booking required. Dress code.
Societies booking required. Green Fees £25 per 18 holes (£30 weekends & BHs) Course Designer Jonathan Gaunt Prof Dale Moore
Facilities ⓘ 🛍 ♿ 🏌 ⚲ 🏨 ✦ 🚐 ✦ 🏆 Conf facs
Corporate Hospitality Days Location M40 junct 2, 3m N
Hotel ★★★ 77% HL The Bedford Arms Hotel, CHENIES
☎ 01923 283301 📠 01923 283301 18 en suite

CHARTRIDGE
Map 4 SP90

Chartridge Park HP5 2TF
☎ 01494 791772   📠 01494 786462
e-mail: info@cpgc.co.uk
web: www.cpgc.co.uk
A family run, easy walking parkland course set high in the beautiful Chiltern Hills, affording breathtaking views.

18 Holes, 5409yds, Par 68, SSS 67, Course record 65.
Club membership 700.

Visitors Mon-Fri. Weekends and BHs by arrangement. Dress code.
Societies booking required. Green Fees not confirmed Course
Designer John Jacobs Prof Jeremy Reilly Facilities ⓘ 🍴 🛍
♿ 🏌 ⚲ 🏨 🚐 ✦ Conf facs Corporate Hospitality Days
Location 3m NW of Chesham
Hotel ★★★ 70% HL The Rose & Crown Hotel, High Street, TRING
☎ 01442 824071 📠 01442 824071 27 en suite

CHESHAM
Map 4 SP90

Chesham & Ley Hill Ley Hill Common HP5 1UZ
☎ 01494 784541   📠 01494 785506
web: www.cheshamgolf.co.uk
9 Holes, 5296yds, Par 67, SSS 65, Course record 62.

Prof James Short Facilities ⓘ 🍴 🛍 ♿ 🚐 ✦ ♿
Leisure practice net Conf facs Location 2m E of Chesham, off A41 on B4504 to Ley Hill
Telephone for further details
Hotel ★★★ 77% HL The Bobsleigh Inn, Hempstead Road, Bovingdon, HEMEL HEMPSTEAD ☎ 0844 879 9033 📠 0844 879 9033 47 en suite

DAGNALL
Map 4 SP91

Whipsnade Park Studham Ln HP4 1RH
☎ 01442 842330   📠 01442 842090
e-mail: whipsnadeparkgolfc@btopenworld.com
web: www.whipsnadeparkgolf.co.uk
Parkland on downs adjoining Whipsnade Zoo. Easy walking, good views and great test of golf.

Whipsnade Park: 18 Holes, 6800yds, Par 73, SSS 72,
Course record 66. Club membership 500.

Visitors Mon-Fri. Weekends & BHs after 1pm. Booking required. Dress code. Societies booking required. Green Fees not confirmed Prof Mark Day Facilities ⓘ 🍴 by prior arrangement 🛍 ♿ 🏌 ⚲ 🏨
⚲ ✦ 🚐 ✦ 🏆 Conf Corporate Hospitality Days Location M1 junct 8, follow signs for Whipsnade Zoo to Dagnall. Golf club off B4506
Hotel ★★★ 81% HL Old Palace Lodge, Church Street, DUNSTABLE
☎ 01582 662201 📠 01582 662201 68 en suite

DENHAM
Map 4 TQ08

Buckinghamshire Denham Court Dr UB9 5PG
☎ 01895 835777   📠 01895 835210
e-mail: enquiries@buckinghamshiregc.co.uk
web: www.buckinghamshiregc.com
The course runs in two loops of nine starting and finishing at the clubhouse. The fairways wander through three distinct areas incorporating woodland, lakes and rivers and undulating links style land, providing a variety of golfing terrain calling for careful thought on every shot. The greens are constructed to USGA specification with excellent drainage and smooth true putting surfaces.

18 Holes, 6880yds, Par 72, SSS 73, Course record 62.
Club membership 550.

Visitors contact club for details. Societies booking required. Green Fees £90 per 18 holes (£100 Fri-Sun & BHs) Course Designer John Jacobs Prof Paul Schunter Facilities ⓘ 🍴 🛍 ♿ 🏌 ⚲
🏨 ⚲ ✦ 🏆 Conf facs Corporate Hospitality Days Location M25 junct 16, signed Uxbridge
Hotel ★★★ 78% HL Barn Hotel, West End Road, RUISLIP
☎ 01895 636057 📠 01895 636057 73 en suite

Denham Tilehouse Ln UB9 5DE
☎ 01895 832022   📠 01895 835340
web: www.denhamgolfclub.co.uk
18 Holes, 6462yds, Par 70, SSS 71, Course record 66.
Course Designer H S Colt Location 0.5m N of North Orbital Road, 2m from Uxbridge
Telephone for further details
Hotel ★★★ 78% HL Barn Hotel, West End Road, RUISLIP
☎ 01895 636057 📠 01895 636057 73 en suite

FLACKWELL HEATH
Map 4 SU89

Flackwell Heath Treadaway Rd, High Wycombe HP10 9PE
☎ 01628 520929 📠 01628 530040
e-mail: secretary@fhgc.co.uk
web: www.fhgc.co.uk
Open sloping heath and tree-lined course on hills overlooking the Chilterns. Some good challenging par 3s and several testing small greens.
18 Holes, 6211yds, Par 71, SSS 70, Course record 63. Club membership 550.
Visitors Mon-Fri. Booking required. Handicap certificate. Dress code. **Societies** booking required **Green Fees** £36 per round **Course Designer** J H Taylor **Prof** Paul Watson **Facilities** 🛈 🍴 🍺 ▱ 🗏 🏖 🖼 🏌 🛒 🏌 **Conf** facs Corporate Hospitality Days **Location** E side of High Wycombe, NE side of town centre
Hotel ★★★ 70% HL Best Western Alexandra, Queen Alexandra Road, HIGH WYCOMBE ☎ 01494 463494 📠 01494 463494 29 en suite

GERRARDS CROSS
Map 4 TQ08

Gerrards Cross Chalfont Park SL9 0QA
☎ 01753 883263 (Sec) & 885300 (Pro)
📠 01753 883593
web: www.gxgolf.co.uk

18 Holes, 6212yds, Par 69, SSS 70, Course record 64.
Course Designer Bill Pedlar **Location** NE side of town centre off A413
Telephone for further details
Hotel ★★ 67% HL Long Island, 2 Victoria Close, RICKMANSWORTH ☎ 01923 779466 📠 01923 779466 50 en suite

HIGH WYCOMBE
Map 4 SU89

Hazlemere Penn Rd, Hazlemere HP15 7LR
☎ 01494 719300 📠 01494 713914
e-mail: enquiries@hazlemeregolfclub.co.uk
web: www.hazlemeregolfclub.co.uk
Undulating parkland course located in the Chiltern Hills in an Area of Outstanding Natural Beauty. Deceiving in its yardage and a challenge to golfers of all standards.
18 Holes, 5833yds, Par 70, SSS 69, Course record 61. Club membership 600.
Visitors Mon-Sun & BHs. Booking required. Handicap certificate. Dress code. **Societies** booking required. **Green Fees** phone **Course Designer** Terry Murray **Prof** G Cousins/C Carsberg **Facilities** 🛈 🍺

▱ 🖼 🏖 🗏 🍴 🛒 🏌 **Conf** facs **Location** on B474, 2m NE of High Wycombe
Hotel ★★★ 70% HL Best Western Alexandra, Queen Alexandra Road, HIGH WYCOMBE ☎ 01494 463494 📠 01494 463494 29 en suite

IVER
Map 4 TQ08

Iver Hollow Hill Ln SL0 0JJ
☎ 01753 655615 📠 01753 654225
9 Holes, 6288yds, Par 72, SSS 72, Course record 66.
Prof Jim Lynch **Facilities** 🛈 🍺 ▱ 🖼 🏖 🗏 🍴 🏌 🏌
Leisure bunker & chipping area, par 3 course **Location** M4 junct 5, 1.5m SW off B470
Telephone for further details
Hotel ★★★★ 75% HL Heathrow/Windsor Marriott, Ditton Road, Langley, SLOUGH ☎ 01753 544244 📠 01753 544244 382 en suite

Richings Park Golf & Country Club North Park SL0 9DL
☎ 01753 655370 & 655352(pro shop) 📠 01753 655409
e-mail: info@richingspark.co.uk
web: www.richingspark.co.uk
Set among mature trees and attractive lakes, this testing par 70 parkland course provides a suitable challenge to golfers of all abilities. Well-irrigated greens and abundant wildlife.
Richings Park Golf Club: 18 Holes, 6144yds, Par 70, SSS 69, Course record 63. Club membership 500.
Visitors Mon-Sun & BHs. Booking required. Dress code.
Societies booking required. **Green Fees** not confirmed **Course Designer** Alan Higgins **Prof** Ryan Kirby **Facilities** 🛈 🍴 🍺 ▱ 🖼 🏖 🗏 🍴 🛒 🏌 🏌 **Conf** facs Corporate Hospitality Days **Location** M4 junct 5, A4 towards Colnbrook, left at lights, Sutton Lane, right at next lights North Park
Hotel ★★★ 73% HL Quality Hotel Heathrow, London Road, Brands Hill, SLOUGH ☎ 01753 684001 📠 01753 684001 128 en suite

Thorney Park Thorney Mill Rd SL0 9AL
☎ 01895 422095 📠 01895 431307
e-mail: sales@thorneypark.com
web: www.thorneypark.com
An 18-hole parkland course which will test both the beginner and established golfer. Fairway irrigation ensures lush green fairways and smooth putting surfaces. Many interesting holes including the testing par 4 9th which needs a long drive to the water's edge and a well-hit iron onto the bunker-guarded green. The back nine finishes with two water holes, the 17th, a near island green and the shot of 150yds makes this a picturesque and testing round. The 18th has more water than grass.
18 Holes, 5765yds, Par 69, SSS 68, Course record 69. Club membership 350.
Visitors Mon-Sun & BHs. Booking required. Dress code.
Societies Booking required. **Green Fees** not confirmed **Course Designer** David Walker **Prof** Andrew Killing **Facilities** 🛈 🍴 🍺
▱ 🖼 🏖 🗏 🍴 🛒 🏌 **Conf** facs Corporate Hospitality Days **Location** M4 junct 5, left onto A4, left onto Sutton Ln, right for Thorney Mill Rd
Hotel ★★★★ 75% HL Heathrow/Windsor Marriott, Ditton Road, Langley, SLOUGH ☎ 01753 544244 📠 01753 544244 382 en suite

LITTLE BRICKHILL — Map 4 SP93

Woburn Golf & Country Club see page 31
MK17 9LJ
☎ 01908 370756 & 626600 (shop) 🖷 01908 378436
e-mail: enquiries@woburngolf.com
web: www.woburn.co.uk/golf

LITTLE CHALFONT — Map 4 SU99

Little Chalfont Lodge Ln HP8 4AJ
☎ 01494 764877
Gently undulating parkland surrounded by mature trees.

9 Holes, 5752yds, Par 70, SSS 68, Course record 66.
Club membership 110.

Visitors Mon-Sun & BHs. Dress code. **Societies** booking required.
Green Fees £14 per 18 holes (£16 weekends) **Course Designer** J M
Dunne **Prof** M Dunne **Facilities** ⑪ ⦿ ⓛ ⊑ ⛳ ⅄ 🕋 ⚑
⚐ **Leisure** one motorised cart for hire by arrangement **Conf** facs
Corporate Hospitality Days **Location** M25 junct 18, on A404
Hotel ★★★ 77% HL The Bedford Arms Hotel, CHENIES
☎ 01923 283301 🖷 01923 283301 18 en suite

LOUDWATER — Map 4 SU89

Wycombe Heights Golf Centre Rayners Ave HP10 9SZ
☎ 01494 816686 🖷 01494 816728
e-mail: sales@wycombeheightsgc.co.uk
web: www.wycombeheightsgc.co.uk
An impressive tree-lined parkland course with panoramic views of the
Chilterns. The final four holes are particularly challenging. A delightful
18 hole par 3 course and floodlit driving range complement the High
Course.

High Course: 18 Holes, 6265yds, Par 70, SSS 71,
Course record 64. Club membership 600.

Visitors Mon-Sun & BHs. Dress code. **Societies** booking required.
Green Fees £20 per round (£26 weekends & BHs) **Course**
Designer John Jacobs **Prof** Chris Reeves **Facilities** ⑪ ⦿ ⓛ ⊑
⛳ ⅄ 🕋 ⚑ ⚐ 🛒 ⚐ 🏌 **Leisure** par 3 course **Conf** facs
Corporate Hospitality Days **Location** M40 junct 3, A40 towards High
Wycombe. 0.5m right onto Rayners Ave at lights
Hotel ★★★ 70% HL Best Western Alexandra, Queen Alexandra
Road, HIGH WYCOMBE ☎ 01494 463494 🖷 01494 463494
29 en suite

MARLOW — Map 4 SU88

Harleyford Harleyford Estate, Henley Rd SL7 2SP
☎ 01628 816161 🖷 01628 816160
e-mail: info@harleyfordgolf.co.uk
web: www.harleyfordgolf.co.uk
Set in 160 acres, this Donald Steel designed course, founded in
1996, makes the most of the natural rolling contours of the beautiful
parkland of the historic Harleyford Estate. A challenging course to
golfers of all handicaps. Stunning views of the Thames Valley.

18 Holes, 6708yds, Par 72, SSS 72, Course record 68.
Club membership 750.

Visitors Mon-Sun except BHs. Booking required. Dress code.
Societies booking required. **Green Fees** £45 per round (£65
weekends) **Course Designer** Donald Steel **Prof** Graham Finch

Facilities ⑪ ⦿ ⓛ ⊑ ⛳ ⅄ 🕋 ⚑ ⚐ 🛒 ⚐ 🏌
Conf facs Corporate Hospitality Days **Location** S side A4156 Marlow-
Henley road

Harleyford

Hotel ★★★★ 85% HL Danesfield House Hotel & Spa, Henley
Road, MARLOW-ON-THAMES ☎ 01628 891010 🖷 01628 891010
84 en suite

MENTMORE — Map 4 SP91

Mentmore Golf & Country Club LU7 0UA
☎ 01296 662020 🖷 01296 662592
web: www.theclubcompany.com
Two 18-hole courses - Rosebery and Rothschild - set within the
wooded estate grounds of Mentmore Towers. Gently rolling parkland
course with mature trees and lakes and two interesting feature holes;
the long par 5 (606 yds) 9th on the Rosebery course with fine views of
the Chilterns and the par 4 (340yd) 14th on the Rothschild course, in
front of the Towers.

Rosebery Course: 18 Holes, 6777yds, Par 72, SSS 72,
Course record 68.
Rothschild Course: 18 Holes, 6700yds, Par 72, SSS 72.
Club membership 1100.

Visitors Mon-Sun except BHs. Dress code. **Societies** welcome. **Green**
Fees not confirmed **Course Designer** Bob Sandow **Prof** Alister Halliday
Facilities ⑪ ⦿ ⓛ ⊑ ⛳ ⅄ 🕋 ⚑ ⚐ 🛒 ⚐ 🏌
Leisure hard tennis courts, heated indoor swimming pool, fishing,
sauna, gymnasium **Conf** facs Corporate Hospitality Days **Location** 4m
S of Leighton Buzzard
Hotel ★★★ 81% HL Old Palace Lodge, Church Street, DUNSTABLE
☎ 01582 662201 🖷 01582 662201 68 en suite

MILTON KEYNES — Map 4 SP83

Abbey Hill Monks Way, Two Mile Ash MK8 8AA
☎ 01908 563845
e-mail: info@abbeyhillgc.co.uk
Undulating parkland course within the city. Tight fairways and well-
placed bunkers. A stream comes into play on five holes and the last
two holes provide a great finish.

18 Holes, 6122yds, Par 71, SSS 69, Course record 66.
Club membership 700.

Visitors Mon-Sun & BHs. Booking required. Dress code.
Societies booking required. **Green Fees** £19.50 per 18 holes (£24.50
weekends & BHs) **Course Designer** Howard Swann **Prof** Ricky Carvell
Facilities ⑪ ⦿ ⓛ ⊑ ⛳ ⅄ 🕋 ⚑ ◇ ⚐ 🛒 ⚐ 🏌
Leisure heated indoor swimming pool, gymnasium, 9 hole par 3

continued

WOBURN

BUCKINGHAMSHIRE - LITTLE BRICKHILL - MAP 4 SP93

Easily accessible from the M1, Woburn is famed not only for its golf courses but also for the magnificent stately home and wildlife park, which are both well worth a visit. Charles Lawrie of Cotton Pennink designed two great courses here among trees and beautiful countryside. From the back tees they are rather long for the weekend amateur golfer. The Duke's Course is a tough challenge for golfers at all levels. The Duchess Course, although relatively easier, still demands a high level of skills to negotiate the fairways guarded by towering pines. A third course, the Marquess, opened in June 2000 and has already staged the British Masters twice. The town of Woburn and the abbey are in Bedfordshire, while the golf club is over the border in Buckinghamshire.

MK17 9LJ ☎ 01908 370756 & 626600 (shop) 📠 01908 378436
e-mail: enquiries@woburngolf.com **web:** www.woburn.co.uk/golf
Duke's Course: 18 Holes, 6976yds, Par 72, SSS 74, Course record 62.
Duchess Course: 18 Holes, 6651yds, Par 72, SSS 72.
Marquess Course: 18 Holes, 7214yards, Par 72, SSS 74.
Visitors Mon-Fri except BHs. Booking required. Handicap certificate required. Dress code. **Societies** booking required. **Green Fees** phone **Course Designer** Charles Lawrie/Peter Alliss & others **Prof** Luther Blacklock
Facilities ⑪ ⌨ 🍴 ♨ 🏠 ⛳ 🏌 🛒 ⚐ **Conf** Corporate Hospitality Days **Location** M1 junct 13, 4m W off A5130
Hotel ★★★ 81% HL The Inn at Woburn, George Street, WOBURN, Milton Keynes ☎ 01525 290441
📠 01525 290441 57 en suite

course **Conf** facs Corporate Hospitality Days **Location** 2m W of town centre off A5
Hotel ★★ **75%** HL Different Drummer, 94 High Street, Stony Stratford, MILTON KEYNES ☎ 01908 564733 🖹 01908 564733 23 en suite

Three Locks Great Brickhill MK17 9BH
☎ 01525 270050   🖹 01525 270470
e-mail: info@threelocksgolfclub.co.uk
web: www.threelocksgolfclub.co.uk
Parkland course offering a challenge to beginners and experienced golfers, with water coming into play on ten holes. Magnificent views. Good winter course with trolleys allowed.

18 Holes, 6036yds, Par 70, SSS 69, Course record 60.
Club membership 300.
Visitors contact club for details. **Societies** welcome. **Green Fees** £30 per day, £19 per round (£37/£26 weekends & BHs) **Course Designer** MRM Sandown **Facilities** ⊕ ⍰ 🍴 📶 🖥 🍴 🎿 🛋 ⊰ 🍴 🏌 **Leisure** fishing **Conf** facs Corporate Hospitality Days **Location** A4146 between Leighton Buzzard & Bletchley **Hotel** BUD Campanile Milton Keynes, 40 Penn Road - off Watling St, Fenny Stratford, Bletchley, MILTON KEYNES ☎ 01908 649819 🖹 01908 649819 80 en suite

PRINCES RISBOROUGH   Map 4 SP80

Whiteleaf Upper Icknield Way, Whiteleaf HP27 0LY
☎ 01844 274058   🖹 01844 275551
e-mail: whiteleafgc@tiscali.co.uk
web: www.whiteleafgolfclub.co.uk
A picturesque nine-hole course on the edge of the Chilterns. Good views over the Vale of Aylesbury. A short challenging course requiring great accuracy.

9 Holes, 5391yds, Par 66, SSS 66, Course record 64.
Club membership 320.
Visitors Mon-Fri except BHs. Dress code. **Societies** booking required. **Green Fees** £35 per day, £25 per 18 holes, £15 per 9 holes **Prof** Ken Ward **Facilities** ⊕ 🍴 🖥 📶 🍴 🎿 🛋 ⊰ **Conf** Corporate Hospitality Days **Location** 1m NE off A4010
Hotel ★★★ **75%** HL Kings Hotel, Oxford Road, HIGH WYCOMBE ☎ 01494 609090 🖹 01494 609090 43 en suite

STOKE POGES   Map 4 SU98

Farnham Park Park Rd SL2 4PJ
☎ 01753 643332   🖹 01753 647065
e-mail: nigel.whitton@southbucks.gov.uk
web: www.farnhamparkgolfcourse.co.uk
Fine, public course set in 130 acres of attractive mature wooded parkland. The Colt/Hawtree design is both challenging and rewarding in equal measure with several good birdie opportunities and a selection of memorable holes in the 6th, 10th, 11th, 13th and 16th.

Farnham Park Golf Course: 18 Holes, 6172yds, Par 70, SSS 69, Course record 68. Club membership 300.
Visitors Mon-Sun & BHs. Booking required. Dress code. **Societies** booking required. **Green Fees** £15.50 per round (£21.50 weekends) **Course Designer** Hawtree **Prof** Nigel Whitton **Facilities** ⊕ 🍴 🖥 📶 🍴 🎿 🛋 ⊰ 🍴 🏌 **Conf** Corporate Hospitality Days **Location** W side of village off B416
Hotel ★★★★ **75%** HL Heathrow/Windsor Marriott, Ditton Road, Langley, SLOUGH ☎ 01753 544244 🖹 01753 544244 382 en suite

Stoke Park Stoke Park, Park Rd SL2 4PG
☎ 01753 717171   🖹 01753 717181
e-mail: info@stokepark.com
web: www.stokepark.com
Judgement of the distance from the tee is all important on this classic parkland course made up of three 9 hole courses, Colt, Alison and Lane Jackson. Fairways are wide and the challenge seemingly innocuous - testing par 4s, superb bunkering and fast putting surfaces. The 7th hole is the model for the well-known 12th hole at Augusta. Recent improvements have seen a complete reconstruction of the 15th hole with new bunkers and a new tee and on the 16th hole a new championship tee has been built.

Old Course: 18 Holes, 6721yds, Par 71, SSS 72,
Course record 65.
Colt/LaneJackson: 18 Holes, 6569yds, Par 72, SSS 70.
Alison/Lane Jackson: 18 Holes, 6318yds, Par 71, SSS 70.
Club membership 2500.
Visitors Hotel residents only. Handicap certificate. Dress code.
Societies welcome. **Green Fees** contact hotel for details. **Course Designer** Harry Shapland Colt **Prof** Stuart Collier **Facilities** ⊕ 🍴 🖥 📶 🍴 🎿 🛋 ⊰ 🍴 ♦ 🏌 🛋 🏌 🏌 **Leisure** hard and grass tennis courts, heated indoor swimming pool, fishing, sauna, gymnasium, indoor tennis courts. treatment room spa **Conf** facs Corporate Hospitality Days **Location** off A4 at Slough onto B416 Stoke Poges Ln, club 1.5m on left

STOWE   Map 4 SP63

Silverstone Silverstone Rd MK18 5LH
☎ 01280 850005   🖹 01280 850156
e-mail: enquiries@silverstonegolfclub.co.uk
web: www.silverstonegolfclub.co.uk
A challenging parkland course situated opposite the Grand Prix circuit. Suitable for both high and low handicap players but care must be taken with the water hazards that are a distinctive feature of the course.

Silverstone Golf Course: 18 Holes, 6472yards, Par 72, SSS 71, Course record 65. Club membership 500.
Visitors Mon-Sun & BHs. Booking required Fri-Sun & BHs. Dress code **Societies** booking required. **Green Fees** phone **Course Designer** David Snell **Prof** Rodney Holt **Facilities** ⊕ 🍴 🖥 📶 🍴 🎿 🛋 ⊰ ♦ 🏌 🏌 **Conf** facs Corporate Hospitality Days **Location** from Silverstone signs to Grand Prix track. Club 1m past entrance on right
Hotel ★★★★ **74%** HL Villiers, 3 Castle Street, BUCKINGHAM ☎ 01280 822444 🖹 01280 822444 49 en suite

WAVENDON   Map 4 SP93

Wavendon Golf Centre Lower End Rd MK17 8DA
☎ 01908 281811   🖹 01908 281257
e-mail: wavendon@jack-barker.co.uk
web: www.jack-barker.co.uk
Pleasant parkland course set within mature oak and lime trees and incorporating several small lakes as water hazards. Easy walking.

Wavendon Golf Centre: 18 Holes, 5570yds, Par 69, SSS 68.
Club membership 300.
Visitors contact centre for details. **Societies** welcome. **Green Fees** phone **Course Designer** J Drake/N Elmer **Prof** Greg Iron

continued

Facilities ⑪ ⑩ 📇 🖵 🍴 ⚖ 🏠 ⛳ 🛒 ✎ ☂
Leisure 9 hole par 3 course Conf facs Location M1 junct 13, off A421

Wavendon Golf Centre

Hotel ★★★ 74% HL Best Western Moore Place, The Square, ASPLEY GUISE, Woburn ☎ 01908 282000 📠 01908 282000 62 en suite

WESTON TURVILLE   Map 4 SP81

Weston Turville Golf New Rd HP22 5QT
☎ 01296 424084   📠 01296 395376
e-mail: westonturvillegc@btconnect.com
web: www.westonturvillegolfclub.co.uk
Flat easy walking parkland at the foot of the Chiltern Hills, with water hazards and many interesting holes, notably the testing dog-leg 15th (418yds). An excellent challenge for the accomplished golfer, yet not too daunting for the higher handicap player.

Weston Turville Golf Club: 18 Holes, 6008yds, Par 69, SSS 69, Course record 68. Club membership 450.
Visitors Mon-Sun & BHs. Booking required. Dress code.
Societies booking required. Green Fees not confirmed Prof Gary George Facilities ⑪ ⑩ by prior arrangement 📇 🖵 🍴 ⚖ 🏠 ⛳ ✎ 🛒 ✎ Conf facs Corporate Hospitality Days Location 2m SE of Aylesbury, off A41
Hotel BUD Innkeeper's Lodge Aylesbury South, 40 Main Street, Weston Turville, AYLESBURY ☎ 0845 112 6095 📠 0845 112 6095 16 en suite

WEXHAM STREET   Map 4 SU98

Wexham Park SL3 6ND
☎ 01753 663271   📠 01753 663318
e-mail: info@wexhamparkgolfcourse.co.uk
web: www.wexhamparkgolfcourse.co.uk
Gently undulating parkland. Three courses, an 18 hole, a challenging nine hole, and another nine hole suitable for beginners.

Blue: 18 Holes, 5346yds, Par 68, SSS 66.
Red: 9 Holes, 2822yds, Par 34.
Green: 9 Holes, 2233yds, Par 32. Club membership 950.
Visitors contact club for details. Societies welcome. Green Fees not confirmed Course Designer E Lawrence/D Morgan Prof John Kennedy Facilities ⑪ 📇 🖵 🍴 ⚖ 🏠 ⛳ 🛒 ✎ ☂ Conf Corporate Hospitality Days Location 0.5m S
Hotel ★★★★ 75% HL Heathrow/Windsor Marriott, Ditton Road, Langley, SLOUGH ☎ 01753 544244 📠 01753 544244 382 en suite

WING   Map 4 SP82

Aylesbury Vale Stewkley Rd LU7 0UJ
☎ 01525 240196   📠 01525 240848
e-mail: info@avgc.co.uk
web: avgc.co.uk
This gently undulating course is set amid tranquil countryside. There are five ponds to pose the golfer problems, notably on the par 4 420yd 13th - unlucky for some - where the second shot is all downhill with an inviting pond spanning the approach to the green.

18 Holes, 6612yds, Par 72, SSS 72, Course record 67. Club membership 515.
Visitors Mon-Sun & BHs. Dress code. Societies Booking required. Green Fees not confirmed Course Designer D Wright Prof Terry Bunyan Facilities ⑪ ⑩ 📇 🖵 🍴 ⚖ 🏠 ⛳ ✎ 🛒 ✎ ☂ Conf facs Corporate Hospitality Days Location 2m NW of Leighton Buzzard on unclassified Stewkley road, between Wing & Stewkley
Hotel ★★★ 81% HL Old Palace Lodge, Church Street, DUNSTABLE ☎ 01582 662201 📠 01582 662201 68 en suite

CAMBRIDGESHIRE

BAR HILL   Map 5 TL36

Menzies Cambridgeshire Bar Hill CB23 8EU
☎ 01954 780098   📠 01954 780010
e-mail: cambridge.golfpro@menzieshotels.co.uk
web: www.menzieshotels.co.uk
Mature undulating parkland course with tree-lined fairways, easy walking. Challenging opening and closing holes with water on the right and out of bounds on the left of both.

18 Holes, 6750yds, Par 72, SSS 73, Course record 68. Club membership 500.
Visitors Mon-Sun & BHs. Booking required. Dress code.
Societies booking required. Green Fees £30 per round (£40 weekends & BHs). Winter £25/£30 Prof Mike Clemons Facilities ⑪ ⑩ 📇 🖵 🍴 ⚖ 🏠 ⛳ ♡ ✎ 🛒 ✎ Leisure hard tennis courts, heated indoor swimming pool, sauna, gymnasium, 2 practice grounds Conf facs Corporate Hospitality Days Location M11/A14, then B1050 (Bar Hill
Hotel ★★★★ 82% HL Hotel Felix, Whitehouse Lane, CAMBRIDGE ☎ 01223 277977 📠 01223 277977 52 en suite

BOURN   Map 5 TL35

Bourn Toft Rd CB3 7TT
☎ 01954 718958   📠 01954 718908
Bourn Golf Course: 18 Holes, 6417yards, Par 72, SSS 71.
Course Designer J Hull
Telephone for further details
Hotel BUD Travelodge Cambridge Lolworth, Huntingdon Road, LOLWORTH ☎ 08719 846 046 📠 08719 846 046 20 en suite

33

BRAMPTON · Map 4 TL27

Brampton Park Buckden Rd PE28 4NF
☎ 01480 434700 & 434705 (pro shop) 🖷 01480 411145
e-mail: admin@bramptonparkgc.co.uk
web: www.bramptonparkgc.co.uk

Set in truly attractive countryside, bounded by the River Great Ouse and bisected by the River Lane. Great variety with mature trees, lakes and water hazards. One of the most difficult holes is the 4th, a par 3 island green, 175yds in length.

18 Holes, 6300yds, Par 71, SSS 72, Course record 62. Club membership 650.

Visitors Mon-Sun except BHs. Booking required Wed and weekends. Dress code. **Societies** welcome. **Green Fees** £37 per day, £27 per round (£46 per round weekends) **Course Designer** Simon Gidman **Prof** Alisdair Currie **Facilities** ⓣ ⍥ ⬛ ☐ ⌨ 🏋 ☐ ◇ ✦ 🛒 ✦ ✦ **Conf** facs Corporate Hospitality Days **Location** signs from A1 or A14 to RAF Brampton
Hotel ★★★★ 75% HL Huntingdon Marriott Hotel, Kingfisher Way, Hinchingbrooke Business Park, HUNTINGDON ☎ 01480 446000 🖷 01480 446000 150 en suite

CAMBRIDGE · Map 5 TL45

Gog Magog Shelford Bottom CB22 4AB
☎ 01223 247626 🖷 01223 414990
e-mail: secretary@gogmagog.co.uk
web: www.gogmagog.co.uk

Gog Magog, established in 1901, is situated just outside the centre of the university town. The chalk downland courses are on high ground, and it is said that if you stand on the highest point and could see far enough to the east the next highest ground would be the Ural Mountains. The courses are open but there are enough trees and other hazards to provide plenty of problems. Views from the high parts are superb. The nature of the ground ensures good winter golf. The area has been designated a Site of Special Scientific Interest.

Old Course: 18 Holes, 6367yds, Par 70, SSS 71, Course record 63.
Wandlebury: 18 Holes, 6735yds, Par 72, SSS 72, Course record 67. Club membership 1400.

Visitors Mon, Tue, Thu & Fri except BHs. Handicap certificate. Dress code. **Societies** booking required. **Green Fees** £60 per day, £45 per round. **Course Designer** Hawtree Ltd **Prof** Ian Bamborough **Facilities** ⓣ ⍥ ⬛ ☐ ⌨ 🏋 ☐ ◇ ✦ 🛒 ✦ ✦ **Conf** Corporate Hospitality Days **Location** 3m SE on A1307
Hotel ★★★ 75% HL Duxford Lodge, Ickleton Road, DUXFORD ☎ 01223 836444 🖷 01223 836444 15 en suite

ELY · Map 5 TL58

Ely City 107 Cambridge Rd CB7 4HX
☎ 01353 662751 (Office) 🖷 01353 668636
e-mail: info@elygolf.co.uk
web: www.elygolf.co.uk.

Slightly undulating parkland with water hazards formed by lakes and natural dykes. Demanding par 4 5th hole (467yds), often into a headwind, and a testing par 3 2nd hole (160yds) played over two ponds. Magnificent views of the cathedral.

18 Holes, 6627yds, Par 72, SSS 72, Course record 65. Club membership 750.

Visitors Mon-Sun & BHs. Handicap certificate. Dress code. **Societies** booking required. **Green Fees** £34 per day (£40 weekends) **Course Designer** Sir Henry Cotton **Prof** Andrew George **Facilities** ⓣ ⍥ ⬛ ☐ ⌨ 🏋 ☐ ◇ ✦ 🛒 ✦ **Conf** Corporate Hospitality Days **Location** S of city on A10
Hotel ★★★ 72% HL Lamb, 2 Lynn Road, ELY ☎ 01353 663574 🖷 01353 663574 31 en suite

GIRTON · Map 5 TL46

Girton Dodford Ln CB3 0QE
☎ 01223 276169 🖷 01223 277150
e-mail: info@girtongolf.co.uk
web: www.girtongolf.co.uk

Flat, open, easy walking parkland with many trees and ditches.

18 Holes, 6012yds, Par 69, SSS 69, Course record 66. Club membership 800.

Visitors Mon-Sun except BHs. Booking required. Dress code. **Societies** booking required. **Green Fees** £25 weekdays **Course Designer** Allan Gow **Prof** Scott Thomson **Facilities** ⓣ ⍥ ⬛ ☐ ⌨ 🏋 ☐ ◇ 🛒 ✦ **Conf** facs Corporate Hospitality Days **Location** 3m from Cambridge, off A14 junct 31
Hotel ★★★★ 82% HL Hotel Felix, Whitehouse Lane, CAMBRIDGE ☎ 01223 277977 🖷 01223 277977 52 en suite

HEMINGFORD ABBOTS · Map 4 TL27

Hemingford Abbots Cambridge Rd PE28 9HQ
☎ 01480 495000 & 493900 🖷 01480 4960000

Hemingford Abbots Golf Course: 9 Holes, 5468yds, Par 68, SSS 68, Course record 69.

Course Designer Ray Paton **Location** A14 Hemingford Abbots **Telephone for further details**
Hotel ★★★ 83% HL The Old Bridge, 1 High Street, HUNTINGDON ☎ 01480 424300 🖷 01480 424300 24 en suite

LONGSTANTON · Map 5 TL36

Cambridge Station Rd CB24 5DS
☎ 01954 789388
e-mail: cambridgegolfclub@tiscali.co.uk
web: www.cambridgegolfclub.net

Undulating parkland with bunkers and ponds.

18 Holes, 6736yds, Par 72, SSS 73, Course record 64. Club membership 350.

Visitors Mon-Sun & BHs. Booking required weekends & BHs. Dress code. **Societies** welcome. **Green Fees** £14 per 18 holes (£18 weekends) **Prof** Phil Rains **Facilities** ⓣ ⍥ ⬛ ☐ ⌨ 🏋 🛒 ✦ 🏌 ✦ **Leisure** fishing, hot air ballons **Conf** facs Corporate Hospitality Days **Location** A14, junct 29 onto B1050 towards Willingham. Straight over 1st rdbt, turn right at 2nd and 3rd rdbt. Club entrance on left
Hotel BUD Travelodge Cambridge Swavesey, Cambridge Road, SWAVESEY ☎ 08719 846 021 🖷 08719 846 021 36 en suite

MARCH
Map 5 TL49

March Frogs Abbey, Grange Rd PE15 0YH
☎ 01354 652364
e-mail: secretary@marchgolfclub.co.uk
web: www.marchgolfclub.co.uk

A nine-hole parkland course with a particularly challenging par 3 9th hole, with out of bounds on the right and high hedges to the left.

9 Holes, 6204yds, Par 70, SSS 70, Course record 65. Club membership 315.

Visitors Mon-Sun & BHs. Dress code. **Societies** booking required. **Green Fees** phone **Prof** Alex Oldham **Facilities** ⊕ ⅃ ⊏ ☜ ⅃ ☒ ⏁ ⚏ ♂ **Conf** facs Corporate Hospitality Days **Location** 0.5m off A141, March bypass
Hotel ★★ 82% HL Crown Lodge, Downham Road, Outwell, WISBECH ☎ 01945 773391 & 772206 ▤ 01945 773391   10 en suite

MELDRETH
Map 5 TL34

Malton Malton Rd, Malton SG8 6PE
☎ 01763 262200   ▤ 01763 262209
e-mail: desk@maltongolf.co.uk
web: www.maltongolf.co.uk

Set among 230 acres of beautiful undulating countryside. The River Cam bisects part of the course which is surrounded by woodlands and wetlands.

Malton Golf Course: 18 Holes, 6708yards, Par 72, SSS 72, Course record 67.

Visitors Mon-Sun & BHs. Booking required Fri-Sun & BHs. Dress code. **Societies** booking required. **Green Fees** not confirmed **Prof** Kevin Evans **Facilities** ⊕ ⎀⎖ ⅃ ⊏ ☜ ⅃ ☒ ⏁ ⚏ **Location** between Orwell
Hotel ★★★ 75% HL Duxford Lodge, Ickleton Road, DUXFORD ☎ 01223 836444 ▤ 01223 836444   15 en suite

PETERBOROUGH
Map 4 TL19

Elton Furze Bullock Rd, Haddon PE7 3TT
☎ 01832 280189 & 280614 (Pro shop)   ▤ 01832 280299
e-mail: helen@efgc.co.uk
web: www.efgc.co.uk

Elton Furze Golf Club is set in the picturesque surroundings of the Cambridgeshire countryside. The course has been designed in and around mature woodland with ponds and slopes, which provides the golfer with an interesting and enjoyable round of golf.

18 Holes, 6279yds, Par 70, SSS 71, Course record 63. Club membership 620.

Visitors Mon-Sun & BHs. Dress code. **Societies** booking required **Green Fees** £48 per day, £35 per round (£55/£39 weekends) **Course Designer** Roger Fitton **Prof** Glyn Krause **Facilities** ⊕ ⎀⎖ by prior arrangement ⅃ ⊏ ☜ ⅃ ☒ ⏁ ⚏ ♂ **Conf** facs Corporate Hospitality Days **Location** 4m SW of Peterborough, off A605/A1
Hotel ★★★★ 75% HL Peterborough Marriott, Peterborough Business Park, Lynchwood, PETERBOROUGH ☎ 01733 371111 ▤ 01733 371111   163 en suite

Orton Meadows Ham Ln, Orton Waterville PE2 5UU
☎ 01733 237478   ▤ 01733 332774
e-mail: enquiries@ortonmeadowsgolfcourse.co.uk
web: www.ortonmeadowsgolfcourse.co.uk

Picturesque course with trees, lakes and an abundance of water fowl, providing some challenges with water featuring on 10 holes.

Orton Meadows Golf Centre: 18 Holes, 5269yds, Par 67, SSS 68, Course record 64. Club membership 650.

Visitors contact club for details. **Societies** welcome. **Green Fees** £14.30 per round (£19.10 weekends & BHs) **Course Designer** D & R Fitton **Prof** Stuart Brown **Facilities** ⊕ ⎀⎖ ⅃ ⊏ ☜ ⅃ ☒ ⏁ ⚏ ♢ ♂ **Leisure** 12 hole pitch & putt **Location** 3m W of town on A605
Hotel ★★★ 79% HL Best Western Orton Hall, Orton Longueville, PETERBOROUGH ☎ 01733 391111 ▤ 01733 391111   72 en suite

Peterborough Milton Milton Ferry PE6 7AG
☎ 01733 380489   ▤ 01733 380489
e-mail: secretary@peterboroughmiltongolfclub.co.uk
web: www.peterboroughmiltongolfclub.co.uk

Designed by James Braid, this well-bunkered parkland course is set in the grounds of the Milton Estate, many of the holes being played in full view of Milton Hall. Challenging holes are the difficult dog-leg 10th and 15th. Easy walking.

18 Holes, 6516yds, Par 71, SSS 72, Course record 69. Club membership 800.

Visitors Mon-Sun & BHs. Handicap certificate. Dress code. **Societies** booking required. **Green Fees** £40 per 36 holes **Course Designer** James Braid **Prof** Jasen Barker/Matt Thorpe **Facilities** ⊕ ⎀⎖ ⅃ ⊏ ☜ ⅃ ☒ ⏁ ♂ ⚏ ♂ **Conf** facs Corporate Hospitality Days **Location** 2m W of Peterborough on A47
Hotel BUD Travelodge Peterborough Eye Green, Crowlands Road, PETERBOROUGH ☎ 08719 846 303 ▤ 08719 846 303   42 en suite

Thorpe Wood Thorpe Wood, Nene Parkway PE3 6SE
☎ 01733 267701   ▤ 01733 332774
e-mail: enquiries@thorpewoodgolfcourse.co.uk
web: www.thorpewoodgolfcourse.co.uk

Gently undulating, parkland course designed by Peter Alliss and Dave Thomas. Challenging holes include the 5th, the longest hole, usually played with prevailing wind, and the 14th, which has a difficult approach shot over water to a two-tier green.

Thorpe Wood Golf Course: 18 Holes, 7086yds, Par 73, SSS 74, Course record 68. Club membership 750.

Visitors Mon-Sun & BHs. Dress code. **Societies** booking required **Green Fees** £14.60 per round (£19.50 weekends & BHs) **Course Designer** Peter Allis/Dave Thomas **Prof** Roger Fitton **Facilities** ⊕ ⎀⎖ ⅃ ⊏ ☜ ⅃ ☒ ⏁ ♂ ⚏ ♂ **Location** 3m W of city centre on A47
Hotel ★★★ 79% HL Best Western Orton Hall, Orton Longueville, PETERBOROUGH ☎ 01733 391111 ▤ 01733 391111   72 en suite

PIDLEY
Map 5 TL37

Lakeside Lodge Fen Rd PE28 3DF
☎ 01487 740540   ▤ 01487 740852
e-mail: info@lakeside-lodge.co.uk
web: www.lakeside-lodge.co.uk

A well-designed, spacious course incorporating eight lakes, 12,000 trees and a modern clubhouse. The 9th and 18th holes both finish

continued

dramatically alongside a lake in front of the clubhouse. Also nine-hole par 3, and 25-bay driving range. The Manor provides an interesting contrast with its undulating fairways and angular greens.

Lodge Course: 18 Holes, 6885yds, Par 72, SSS 73.
The Manor: 9 Holes, 2601yds, Par 34, SSS 33.
The Church: 12 Holes, 3290yds, Par 44.
Club membership 1200.

Visitors Mon-Sun & BHs. Dress code. **Societies** welcome. **Green Fees** £17 per 18 holes (£27 weekends & BHs), £10 per 9/12 holes (£13 weekends & BHs). **Course Designer** A W Headley **Prof** Scott Waterman **Facilities** ⊕ ⏀ ⓑ ⌷ ⏀ ⏁ ⏂ ⏃ ◇ ◈ ⏄ ◈ ⏅ **Leisure** gymnasium, ten pin bowling **Conf** facs Corporate Hospitality Days **Location** A141 from Huntingdon, then B1040 **Hotel 74%** Olivers Lodge, Needingworth Road, ST IVES, Cambridge ☎ 01480 463252 📄 01480 463252 17 en suite

RAMSEY   Map 4 TL28

Old Nene Golf & Country Club Muchwood Ln PE26 2XQ
☎ 01487 815622   📄 01487 813610
Old Nene Golf & Country Club: 9 Holes, 5605yds, Par 68, SSS 68, Course record 64.
Course Designer R Edrich **Location** 0.75m N of Ramsey towards Ramsey Mereside
Telephone for further details
Hotel ★★★ **83%** HL The Old Bridge, 1 High Street, HUNTINGDON ☎ 01480 424300 📄 01480 424300 24 en suite

Ramsey 4 Abbey Ter PE26 1DD
☎ 01487 812600   📄 01487 815746
e-mail: admin@ramseyclub.co.uk
web: www.ramseyclub.co.uk
Flat parkland with water hazards and well-irrigated greens, mature tees and fairways - a good surface whatever the conditions. The impression of wide-open spaces will soon punish the wayward shot.
Ramsey Golf & Bowls Club: 18 Holes, 5998yds, Par 70, SSS 69, Course record 64. Club membership 600.
Visitors Mon-Fri except BHs. Booking required. Handicap certificate. Dress code. **Societies** booking required. **Green Fees** £25 per 18 holes **Course Designer** J Hamilton Stutt **Prof** Stuart Scott **Facilities** ⊕ ⓑ ⌷ ⏀ ⏃ ⏁ ⏂ ◈ ⏆ **Leisure** snooker tables, bowls rinks **Location** 12m SE of Peterborough on B1040
Hotel ★★★ **83%** HL The Old Bridge, 1 High Street, HUNTINGDON ☎ 01480 424300 📄 01480 424300 24 en suite

ST IVES   Map 4 TL37

St Ives Westwood Rd PE27 6DH
☎ 01480 468392   📄 01480 468392
e-mail: manager@stivesgolfclub.co.uk
web: www.stivesgolfclub.co.uk
Picturesque parkland course.
9 Holes, 6180yds, Par 70, SSS 70, Course record 68. Club membership 500.
Visitors Mon-Fri except BHs. Handicap certificate. Dress code. **Societies** booking required. **Green Fees** £26 per day (£13 winter) **Prof** Mark Pond **Facilities** ⊕ ⏀ ⓑ ⌷ ⏀ ⏃ ⏁ ⏂ ⏆ **Location** W side of town centre off A1123
Hotel ★★★ **68%** HL Dolphin, London Road, ST IVES ☎ 01480 466966 📄 01480 466966 67 en suite

ST NEOTS   Map 4 TL16

Abbotsley Golf & Squash Club Eynesbury Hardwicke PE19 6XN
☎ 01480 474000   📄 01480 403280
e-mail: abbotsley@crown-golf.co.uk
Set in 250 acres of idyllic countryside, with two 18-hole courses and a nine-hole par 3. The Cromwell course is the less challenging of the two, offering a contrast to the renowned Abbotsley course with its holes meandering through woods and streams. One of the most memorable holes is the Abbotsley 2nd hole known as the Mousehole, which requires an accurate tee shot to a green that is protected by a stream and shaded by the many trees that surround it.
Abbotsley Course: 18 Holes, 6311yds, Par 73, SSS 72, Course record 69.
Cromwell Course: 18 Holes, 6134yds, Par 70, SSS 69, Course record 66. Club membership 550.
Visitors Mon-Sun & BHs. Booking required. Dress code **Societies** welcome. **Green Fees** Abbotsley £26 per 18 holes (£42.50 weekends & bank holidays) Cromwell £17 per 18 holes (£23 weekends & bank holidays). Reduced winter rates **Course Designer** D Young/V Saunders **Prof** Steve Connolly **Facilities** ⊕ ⏀ ⓑ ⌷ ⏀ ⏃ ⏁ ⏂ ◇ ◈ ⏄ ◈ ⏅ **Leisure** squash, gymnasium **Conf** facs Corporate Hospitality Days **Location** off A1 & A428
Hotel ★★★ **83%** HL The George Hotel & Brasserie, High Street, Buckden, ST NEOTS ☎ 01480 812300 📄 01480 812300 12 en suite

St Neots Crosshall Rd PE19 7GE
☎ 01480 472363   📄 01480 472363
e-mail: office@stneots-golfclub.co.uk
web: www.stneots-golfclub.co.uk
Set in picturesque rolling parkland and divided by the river Kym, the course offers a challenge to all standards of golfer with tree-lined fairways, water hazards and outstanding greens. Fine views of the Ouse on several holes.
18 Holes, 6087yds, Par 70, SSS 70, Course record 64. Club membership 630.
Visitors Mon-Fri except BHs. Booking required. Handicap certificate. Dress code. **Societies** booking required. **Green Fees** £45 per day, £35 per round **Course Designer** H Vardon **Prof** Paul Toyer **Facilities** ⊕ ⏀ ⓑ ⌷ ⏀ ⏃ ⏁ ◈ ⏄ ◈ **Conf** Corporate Hospitality Days **Location** A1 onto B1048 into St Neots
Hotel ★★★ **83%** HL The George Hotel & Brasserie, High Street, Buckden, ST NEOTS ☎ 01480 812300 📄 01480 812300 12 en suite

THORNEY   Map 4 TF20

Thorney English Drove, Thorney PE6 0TJ
☎ 01733 270570   📄 01733 270842
web: www.thorneygolfcentre.com
The 18-hole Fen course is ideal for the beginner, while the Lakes Course has a challenging links-style layout with eight holes around water.
Fen Course: 18 Holes, 6104yds, Par 70, SSS 69, Course record 66.
Lakes Course: 18 Holes, 6441yds, Par 71, SSS 71. Club membership 500.
Visitors Mon-Sun & BHs. Booking required weekends & BHs. Dress code. **Societies** booking required. **Green Fees** phone **Course Designer** A Dow **Prof** Mark Templeman **Facilities** ⊕ ⏀ ⓑ ⌷

continued

🍴 ⛏ 🏠 📠 ☂ ⚙ 🏌 **Leisure** par 3 course **Location** off A47, 7m NE of Peterborough
Hotel BUD Travelodge Peterborough Eye Green, Crowlands Road, PETERBOROUGH ☎ 08719 846 303 🖨 08719 846 303   42 en suite

TOFT
Map 5 TL35

Cambridge Meridian Comberton Rd CB23 2RY
☎ 01223 264700 & 264702   🖨 01223 264701
e-mail: meridian@golfsocieties.com
web: www.cambridgemeridiangolf.co.uk
Set in 207 acres to a Peter Allis and Clive Clark design with sweeping fairways, lakes and well-bunkered greens. The 4th hole has bunker complexes, a sharp dog-leg and a river with the green heavily guarded by bunkers. The 9th and 10th holes challenge the golfer with river crossings.
Cambridge Meridian Golf Course: 18 Holes, 6651yds, Par 73, SSS 72, Course record 72. Club membership 450.
Visitors Mon-Sun & BHs. Dress code. **Societies** welcome. **Green Fees** £28 per 18 holes (£35 weekends) **Course Designer** Peter Alliss/ Clive Clark **Prof** Craig Watson **Facilities** ⑪ ⦿| by prior arrangement 🍴 ⛏ 🏠 📠 ⚙ **Leisure** indoor golf simulator **Conf** facs Corporate Hospitality Days **Location** 3m W of Cambridge, on B1046
Hotel ★★★★ 82% HL The Cambridge Belfry, Back Street, CAMBOURNE ☎ 01954 714600 🖨 01954 714600   120 en suite

TYDD ST GILES
Map 5 TH41

Tydd St Giles Golf & Country Club Kirkgate PE13 5NZ
☎ 01945 871007   🖨 01945 870566
e-mail: enquiries@tyddgolf.co.uk
web: www.tyddgolf.co.uk
This is a comparatively new course. All the greens are around 50 yards long so pin positions in the summer months will add approximately 400 yards to the course making the length around 6,700 yards. Even in its early years, it is a challenge for even the most talented of golfers and with a few more years of maturity, this course should become one of the finest in the area.
Tydd St Giles Golf & Leisure Centre: 18 Holes, 6264yds, Par 70, SSS 70, Course record 66. Club membership 1000.
Visitors Dress code. **Societies** welcome. **Green Fees** £17 per day (£20 weekends & BHs). Twilight £10 everyday from 1pm **Course Designer** Adrian Hurst **Facilities** ⑪ ⦿| 🍴 ⛏ 🏠 📠 ◇ 🚗 ⚙ 🏌 **Leisure** fishing **Conf** facs Corporate Hospitality Days **Location** A1101 N of Wisbech to Long Sutton, turn left into Hannath Rd at Tydd Gate/River
Hotel ★★★ 68% HL Elme Hall, Elm High Road, WISBECH ☎ 01945 475566 🖨 01945 475566   8 en suite

CHESHIRE

ALDERLEY EDGE
Map 7 SJ87

Alderley Edge Brook Ln SK9 7RU
☎ 01625 586200
e-mail: honsecretary@aegc.co.uk
web: www.aegc.co.uk
Well-wooded, undulating pastureland course. A stream crosses seven of the nine holes. A challenging course even for the low handicap player.

9 Holes, 5823yds, Par 68, SSS 68, Course record 62. *Club membership 400.*
Visitors Mon, Wed-Fri, Sun & BHs. Booking required. Handicap certificate. Dress code. **Societies** booking required. **Green Fees** not confirmed **Prof** Peter Bowring **Facilities** ⑪ ⦿| 🍴 ⛏ 📠 🏠 ⚙ **Conf** facs Corporate Hospitality Days **Location** 1m NW on B5085
Hotel ★★★ 85% HL Alderley Edge, Macclesfield Road, ALDERLEY EDGE ☎ 01625 583033 🖨 01625 583033   50 en suite

ALDERSEY GREEN
Map 7 SJ45

Aldersey Green CH3 9EH
☎ 01829 782157
e-mail: bradburygolf@aol.com
web: www.alderseygreengolfclub.co.uk
An exciting, tricky, beautiful parkland course set in 200 acres of countryside. With tree-lined fairways and 14 lakes.
18 Holes, 6145, Par 70, SSS 69, Course record 72. Club membership 350.
Visitors Mon-Sun & BHs. Booking required. Dress code. **Societies** booking required. **Green Fees** £25 per day, £15 per round (£30/£20 weekends) **Prof** Stephen Bradbury **Facilities** ⑪ ⦿| 🍴 📠 🏠 ⛏ 🏠 ⚙ **Conf** Corporate Hospitality Days **Location** On A41 Whitchurch Rd, 6m S of Chester
Hotel ★★★★ 79% HL De Vere Carden Park, Carden Park, BROXTON, Chester ☎ 01829 731000 🖨 01829 731000   196 en suite

ALSAGER
Map 7 SJ75

Alsager Golf & Country Club Audley Rd ST7 2UR
☎ 01270 875700   🖨 01270 882207
web: www.alsagergolfclub.com
Alsager Golf & Country Club: 18 Holes, 6225yds, Par 70, SSS 70, Course record 67.
Prof Richard Brown **Facilities** ⛏ 📠 🍴 ⛏ 🏠 ⚙ **Leisure** bowling green **Conf** facs **Location** M6 junct 16, 2m NE **Telephone for further details**
Hotel ★★★ 83% HL Best Western Manor House, Audley Road, ALSAGER, Stoke-on-Trent ☎ 01270 884000 🖨 01270 884000   57 en suite

ANTROBUS
Map 7 SJ68

Antrobus Foggs Ln CW9 6JQ
☎ 01925 730890
web: www.antrobusgolfclub.co.uk
A challenging parkland course where water is the main feature with streams and ponds in play on most holes. Large undulating greens.
18 Holes, 6220yards, Par 71, SSS 71, Course record 65. Club membership 400.
Visitors Mon-Wed, Fri, Sun & BHs. Booking required. Dress code. **Societies** booking required. **Green Fees** £28 per day (£30 Sun and BHs) **Course Designer** Mike Slater **Prof** Paul Farrance **Facilities** ⑪ ⦿| 🍴 📠 🍴 ⛏ 🏠 ⚙ 🏌 **Leisure** fishing **Conf** facs **Location** M56 junct 10, A559 towards Northwich, 2nd left after Birch pub onto Knutsford Rd, 1st left into Foggs Ln
Hotel ★★★★ 77% HL The Park Royal, Stretton Road, Stretton, WARRINGTON ☎ 01925 730706 🖨 01925 730706   146 en suite

BROXTON
Map 7 SJ45

De Vere Carden Park Hotel Carden Park CH3 9DQ
☎ 01829 731000 📠 01829 731032
e-mail: reservations-carden@devere-hotels.com
web: www.devere-hotels.com

A superb golf resort set in 900 acres of beautiful Cheshire countryside. Facilities include the mature parkland Cheshire Course, the Nicklaus Course, the Golf School and a luxurious clubhouse.

Cheshire: 18 Holes, 6824yds, Par 72, SSS 72, Course record 63.
Nicklaus: 18 Holes, 7045yds, Par 72, SSS 72.
Club membership 250.

Visitors Mon-Sun & BHs. Dress code. **Societies** welcome. **Green Fees** phone **Course Designer** Jack Nicklaus (Nicklaus course) **Prof** Alastair Taylor **Facilities** 🏵 🍽 🏌 🖵 🍴 🏖 🏠 ⛳ ♢ 🍺 🛒 🍴 🏌 **Leisure** hard tennis courts, heated indoor swimming pool, sauna, gymnasium, residential golf school, archery, quad biking **Conf facs** Corporate Hospitality Days **Location** S of City on A41, right at Broxton rdbt onto A534 signed Wrexham. Situated 1.5m on left **Hotel** ★★★★ 79% HL De Vere Carden Park, Carden Park, BROXTON, Chester ☎ 01829 731000 📠 01829 731000 196 en suite

CHESTER
Map 7 SJ46

Chester Curzon Park CH4 8AR
☎ 01244 677760 📠 01244 676667
web: www.chestergolfclub.co.uk

18 Holes, 6508yds, Par 72, SSS 71, Course record 66.
Prof Scott Booth **Facilities** 🏵 🍽 🏌 🖵 🍴 🏖 🏠 ⛳ 🍺 **Location** 1m W of city centre
Telephone for further details
Hotel ★★★★ 74% HL Grosvenor Pulford Hotel & Spa, Wrexham Road, Pulford, CHESTER ☎ 01244 570560 📠 01244 570560 73 en suite

Eaton Guy Ln, Waverton CH3 7PH
☎ 01244 335885 📠 01244 335782
e-mail: office@eatongolfclub.co.uk
web: www.eatongolfclub.co.uk

Parkland with a liberal covering of mature trees and new planting enhanced by natural water hazards.

18 Holes, 6562yds, Par 72, SSS 71, Course record 68.
Club membership 550.

Visitors Mon, Tue, Thu-Sun & BHs. Booking required. Handicap certificate. Dress code. **Societies** booking required. **Green Fees** not confirmed **Course Designer** Donald Steel **Prof** William Tye **Facilities** 🏵 🍽 🏌 🖵 🍴 🏖 🏠 ⛳ 🍺 🛒 🍴 **Conf** Corporate Hospitality Days **Location** 3m SE of Chester off A41 **Hotel** ★★★★★ HL The Chester Grosvenor & Spa, Eastgate, CHESTER ☎ 01244 324024 📠 01244 324024 80 en suite

Upton-by-Chester Upton Ln, Upton-by-Chester CH2 1EE
☎ 01244 381183 📠 01244 376955
web: www.uptonbychestergolfclub.co.uk

Pleasant, tree-lined parkland. Not easy for low-handicap players to score well. Testing holes are 2nd (par 4), 14th (par 4) and 15th (par 3).

18 Holes, 5807yds, Par 69, SSS 68, Course record 63.
Club membership 750.

Visitors Mon-Sun & BHs. Dress code. **Societies** booking required. **Green Fees** not confirmed **Course Designer** Bill Davies **Prof** Stephen

Dewhurst **Facilities** 🏵 🍽 🏌 🖵 🍴 🏖 🏠 ⛳ 🍺 🛒 🍴 **Conf** Corporate Hospitality Days **Location** N side off A5116 **Hotel** ★★★★ 81% HL Hoole Hall Country Club, Hotel & Spa, Warrington Road, Hoole Village, CHESTER ☎ 01244 408800 📠 01244 408800 105 en suite

Vicars Cross Tarvin Rd, Great Barrow CH3 7HN
☎ 01244 335595 📠 01244 335686
e-mail: manager@vicarscrossgolf.co.uk
web: www.vicarscrossgc.co.uk

Tree-lined parkland course, in rural surroundings.

18 Holes, 6446yds, Par 72, SSS 71, Course record 64.
Club membership 750.

Visitors Mon-Sun & BHs except competition days. Dress code. **Societies** welcome. **Green Fees** £35 per day (£40 weekends & BHs). £25 per round after 3pm **Course Designer** J Richardson **Prof** Gavin Beddow **Facilities** 🏵 🍽 🏌 🖵 🍴 🏖 🏠 ⛳ 🍺 🛒 🍴 🏌 **Conf** facs Corporate Hospitality Days **Location** 4m E on A51 **Hotel** ★★★★ 81% HL Rowton Hall Country House Hotel & Spa, Whitchurch Road, Rowton, CHESTER ☎ 01244 335262 📠 01244 335262 37 en suite

CONGLETON
Map 7 SJ86

Astbury Peel Ln, Astbury CW12 4RE
☎ 01260 272772 📠 01260 276420
e-mail: admin@astburygolfclub.com
web: www.astburygolfclub.com

Parkland course in open countryside, bisected by a canal. The testing 12th hole involves a long carry over a tree-filled ravine. Large practice area.

18 Holes, 6296yds, Par 71, SSS 70, Course record 61.
Club membership 720.

Visitors Mon-Fri except BHs. Dress code. **Societies** booking required. **Green Fees** £30 per round (£20 winter) **Prof** Neil Dawson **Facilities** 🏵 🏌 🖵 🍴 🏖 🏠 🍺 🍴 **Location** 1.5m S of Congleton on A34, turn into Peel Lane by Astbury Church for 1m **Guesthouse** ★★★★ INN Egerton Arms, Astbury Village, CONGLETON ☎ 01260 273946 📠 01260 273946 6 en suite

Congleton Biddulph Rd CW12 3LZ
☎ 01260 273540

9 Holes, 5103yds, Par 68, SSS 65.
Prof Andrew Preston **Facilities** 🏵 🍽 🏌 🖵 🍴 🏖 🏠 🍴 **Conf** Corporate Hospitality Days **Location** 1.5m SE on A527
Telephone for further details
Guesthouse ★★★★ INN Egerton Arms, Astbury Village, CONGLETON ☎ 01260 273946 📠 01260 273946 6 en suite

CREWE
Map 7 SJ75

Crewe Fields Rd, Haslington CW1 5TB
☎ 01270 584099 📠 01270 256482
e-mail: secretary@crewegolfclub.co.uk
web: www.crewegolfclub.co.uk

Undulating parkland.

Crewe Golf Club Ltd: 18 Holes, 6414yds, Par 71, SSS 71, Course record 63. Club membership 674.

Visitors dress code. **Societies** booking required. **Green Fees** £30 per

continued

day **Course Designer** James Braid **Prof** David Wheeler **Facilities** ⊕
⊚ ⬚ ⬚ ⬚ ⬚ ⬚ ⬚ **Location** 2.25m NE off A534
Hotel ★★★ 80% HL Hunters Lodge, Sydney Road, Sydney, CREWE
☎ 01270 539100 ⬚ 01270 539100 57 en suite

Queen's Park Queen's Park Dr CW2 7SB
☎ 01270 666724 ⬚ 01270 569902

*Queen's Park Golf Course: 9 Holes, 4920yds, Par 68,
SSS 64, Course record 67.*

Facilities ⊕ ⬚ ⬚ ⬚ ⬚ ⬚ ⬚ **Leisure** hard
tennis courts, Bowling green **Conf** Corporate Hospitality Days
Location Located behind Queen's Park. Well signposted
Telephone for further details
Hotel ★★★ 80% HL Hunters Lodge, Sydney Road, Sydney, CREWE
☎ 01270 539100 ⬚ 01270 539100 57 en suite

Wychwood Park Wychwood Park, Weston CW2 5GP
☎ 01270 829247 (manager) & 829248 (pro)
⬚ 01270 829201
e-mail: jfarmer@deverevenues.co.uk
web: www.deverevenues.co.uk
Parkland style course opened in 2002, built to USGA standards, with
water features on many holes and wildlife protected areas.

18 Holes, 6736yds, Par 72, SSS 73. Club membership 570.

Visitors dress code. **Societies** booking required. **Green Fees** £50 per
18 holes (£60 weekends) **Course Designer** Hawtree & Co **Prof** Frank
Kiddie **Facilities** ⊕ ⊚ ⬚ ⬚ ⬚ ⬚ ⬚ ⬚ ⬚ ⬚ ⬚
⬚ **Leisure** sauna, gymnasium **Conf** facs Corporate Hospitality Days
Location M6 junct 16, A500 for Nantwich, A531 for Keeleo
Hotel ★★★ 72% HL Crewe Arms, Nantwich Road, CREWE
☎ 01270 213204 ⬚ 01270 213204 61 en suite

DELAMERE Map 7 SJ56

Delamere Forest Station Rd CW8 2JE
☎ 01606 883800 ⬚ 01606 889444
e-mail: info@delameregolf.co.uk
web: www.delameregolf.co.uk

Played mostly on undulating open heath there is great charm in
the way this course drops down into the occasional pine sheltered
valley. Six of the first testing nine holes are from 420 to 455yds in
length.

*18 Holes, 6101yds, Par 72, SSS 71, Course record 65.
Club membership 500.*

Visitors dress code. **Societies** booking required. **Green Fees** £70 per
day, £50 per round (£70 per round weekends) **Course Designer** H
Fowler **Prof** Martin Brown **Facilities** ⊕ ⊚ by prior arrangement
⬚ ⬚ ⬚ ⬚ ⬚ ⬚ ⬚ ⬚ **Conf** Corporate Hospitality

Days Location 1.5m NE, off B5152
Hotel ★★★ 78% CHH Willington Hall, Willington, TARPORLEY
☎ 01829 752321 ⬚ 01829 752321 10 en suite

DISLEY Map 7 SJ98

Disley Stanley Hall Ln SK12 2JX
☎ 01663 764001 ⬚ 01663 762678
e-mail: secretary@disleygolfclub.co.uk
web: www.disleygolfclub.co.uk

Straddling a hilltop site above Lyme Park, this undulating parkland
and moorland course affords good views and requires accuracy of
approach to almost all the greens which lie on either a ledge or a
plateau. Testing holes are the 3rd and 4th.

*18 Holes, 6015yds, Par 70, SSS 69, Course record 63.
Club membership 650.*

Visitors Mon-Wed, Fri-Sun & BHs. Booking required Wed & weekends.
Handicap certificate. Dress code. **Societies** booking required. **Green
Fees** £28 per day (£40 weekends) **Course Designer** James Braid
Prof Andrew Esplin **Facilities** ⊕ ⊚ ⬚ ⬚ ⬚ ⬚ ⬚ ⬚
⬚ **Conf** facs Corporate Hospitality Days **Location** NW side of village
off A6
Hotel ★★★ 72% HL Best Western Moorside Grange Hotel &
Spa, Mudhurst Lane, Higher Disley, DISLEY ☎ 01663 764151
⬚ 01663 764151 98 en suite

FRODSHAM Map 7 SJ57

Frodsham Simons Ln WA6 6HE
☎ 01928 732159 ⬚ 01928 734070
e-mail: paulw@frodshamgolf.co.uk
web: www.frodshamgolfclub.co.uk
Undulating parkland with pleasant views from all parts. Emphasis
on accuracy over the whole course, the long and difficult par 5 18th
necessitating a drive across water to the green. Crossed by two
footpaths so extreme care needed.

*18 Holes, 6328yds, Par 70, SSS 70, Course record 63.
Club membership 600.*

Visitors contact club for details. **Societies** welcome. **Green
Fees** £40 per round (weekdays only) **Course Designer** John Day
Prof Graham Tonge **Facilities** ⊕ ⊚ ⬚ ⬚ ⬚ ⬚ ⬚ ⬚
⬚ **Leisure** snooker **Location** M56 junct 12, 1.5m SW, signs for Forest
Hills Hotel, golf club 1st left on Simons Ln
Hotel ★★★ 79% HL Forest Hills Hotel & Leisure Complex, Overton
Hill, FRODSHAM ☎ 01928 735255 ⬚ 01928 735255 58 en suite

HELSBY
Map 7 SJ47

Helsby Towers Ln WA6 0JB
☎ 01928 722021 📠 01928 726816
e-mail: secretary@helsbygolfclub.org
web: www.helsbygolfclub.org

This gentle but challenging parkland course was originally designed by James Braid. With a wide variety of trees and natural water hazards interspersed throughout the course, it is an excellent test of golfing ability. The last six holes are reputed to be perhaps among the most difficult home stretch in Cheshire, with the last being a par 3 of 205yds to a narrow green guarded by bunkers. A wide variety of wildlife lives around the several ponds which are features to be noted (and hopefully avoided).

18 Holes, 6221yds, Par 70, SSS 70, Course record 65. Club membership 640.

Visitors Mon-Fri except BHs. Dress code. **Societies** booking required. **Green Fees** £37 per day, £27.50 per round **Course Designer** James Braid (part) **Prof** Matthew Jones **Facilities** ⓨ ⏀ ⬝ ⬝ ⬝ ⬝ ⬝ ⬝ ⬝ ⬝ ⬝ **Conf** Corporate Hospitality Days **Location** M56 junct 14, 1m. 6m from Chester

Hotel ★★★★★ HL The Chester Grosvenor & Spa, Eastgate, CHESTER ☎ 01244 324024 📠 01244 324024 80 en suite

KNUTSFORD
Map 7 SJ77

Heyrose Budworth Rd, Tabley WA16 0HZ
☎ 01565 733664 📠 01565 734578
e-mail: info@heyrosegolfclub.com
web: www.heyrosegolfclub.com

An 18-hole course in wooded and gently undulating terrain. The par 3 16th (237yds), bounded by a small river in a wooded valley, is an interesting and testing hole - one of the toughest par 3s in Cheshire. Several water hazards. Both the course and the comfortable clubhouse have attractive views.

18 Holes, 6499yds, Par 73, SSS 71, Course record 66. Club membership 600.

Visitors Mon-Sun & BHs. Booking required. Dress code. **Societies** booking required. **Green Fees** £26 per round weekdays and BHs (£31 weekends) **Course Designer** E & C N Bridge **Prof** Philip Bills **Facilities** ⓨ ⏀ ⬝ ⬝ ⬝ ⬝ ⬝ ⬝ ⬝ ⬝ **Leisure** practice bunker, practice nets **Conf** facs Corporate Hospitality Days **Location** M6 junct 19, 1m, follow tourist signs

Hotel ★★★★ 80% HL Cottons Hotel & Spa, Manchester Road, KNUTSFORD ☎ 01565 650333 📠 01565 650333 109 en suite

High Legh Park Country Club Warrington Rd, Mere & High Legh WA16 0WA
☎ 01565 830012 (office) & 830888 (pro shop)
📠 01565 830999
e-mail: enquiries@highleghpark.com
web: www.highleghpark.com

Gentle parkland set in 200 acres of a former medieval deer park with 20 lakes and streams. USGA greens for all-year play.

Championship: 18 Holes, 6715yds, Par 72.
South: 18 Holes, 6281yds, Par 70.
North: 18 Holes, 6472yds, Par 70. Club membership 700.

Visitors Mon-Sun & BHs. Booking required. Handicap certificate. Dress code. **Societies** booking required. **Green Fees** phone **Prof** Anthony Sproston **Facilities** ⓨ by prior arrangement ⏀ by prior arrangement

⬝ ⬝ ⬝ ⬝ ⬝ ⬝ **Leisure** sauna **Conf** facs Corporate Hospitality Days **Location** M6 junct 20, A50 to High Legh

High Legh Country Club

Hotel ★★★★ 80% HL Cottons Hotel & Spa, Manchester Road, KNUTSFORD ☎ 01565 650333 📠 01565 650333 109 en suite

Knutsford Mereheath Ln WA16 6HS
☎ 01565 633355

Parkland course set in a beautiful old deer park. It demands some precise iron play.

9 Holes, 6196yds, Par 70, SSS 70. Club membership 230.

Visitors Mon, Tue, Thu, Fri, Sun & BHs. Handicap certificate required. Dress code. **Societies** booking required. **Green Fees** phone **Prof** Tim Maxwell **Facilities** ⓨ ⏀ ⬝ ⬝ ⬝ ⬝ ⬝ ⬝ **Location** N side of town centre off A50

Hotel ★★★★ 80% HL Cottons Hotel & Spa, Manchester Road, KNUTSFORD ☎ 01565 650333 📠 01565 650333 109 en suite

Mere Golf & Country Club Chester Rd, Mere WA16 6LJ
☎ 01565 830155 📠 01565 830713
e-mail: enquiries@meregolf.co.uk
web: www.meregolf.co.uk

A gracious parkland championship course designed by James Braid in the Cheshire sand belt, with several holes close to a lake. The round has a tight finish with four testing holes.

Mere Golf & Country Club: 18 Holes, 6817yds, Par 71, SSS 73, Course record 64. Club membership 550.

Visitors Mon, Tue & Thu except BHs. Booking required. Handicap certificate. Dress code. **Societies** booking required **Green Fees** not confirmed **Course Designer** James Braid/George Duncan **Prof** Peter Eyre **Facilities** ⓨ ⏀ ⬝ ⬝ ⬝ ⬝ ⬝ ⬝ ⬝ ⬝ ⬝ ⬝ **Leisure** hard tennis courts, heated indoor swimming pool, squash, sauna, gymnasium **Conf** facs Corporate Hospitality Days **Location** M6 junct 19, 1m E. M56 junct 7, 1m W

Hotel ★★★★ 80% HL Cottons Hotel & Spa, Manchester Road, KNUTSFORD ☎ 01565 650333 📠 01565 650333 109 en suite

Peover Plumley Moor Rd, Lower Peover WA16 9SE
☎ 01565 723337 📠 01565 723311
e-mail: mail@peovergolfclub.co.uk
web: www.peovergolfclub.co.uk

Tees and greens have been positioned to maximise the benefits of the natural contours of the land. An excellent mix of holes varying in design and character, with many dog-legs and water hazards, and a river that three of the fairways cross, including the 1st.

18 Holes, 6702yds, Par 72, SSS 72, Course record 69.
Club membership 400.
Visitors Mon-Sun & BHs. Booking required Fri-Sun & BHs.
Societies booking required. **Green Fees** phone **Course Designer** P A Naylor **Prof** Mike Grantham **Facilities** 🎲 🍽️ 🏌 ⌑ 🏌 🏌 🏠
🏌 🏌 🏌 🏌 **Conf** facs Corporate Hospitality Days **Location** M6 junct 19, A556 onto Plumley Moor Rd
Hotel ★★ 81% HL The Longview Hotel & Stuffed Olive Restaurant, 55 Manchester Road, KNUTSFORD ☎ 01565 632119 📠 01565 632119 32 en suite

---

LITTLE SUTTON Map 7 SJ47

Ellesmere Port Chester Rd CH66 1QF
☎ 0151 339 7689
web: www.active8leisure.ltd.uk
Municipal parkland course set in beautiful woodland surroundings with natural hazards of woods, brook and ponds.

Ellesmere Port Golf Centre: 18 Holes, 6296yds, Par 71,
SSS 70. Club membership 120.
Visitors Mon-Sun & BHs. Booking required weekends. Dress code.
Societies booking required. **Green Fees** £10.50 (£11.50 weekends & BHs) **Course Designer** Cotton, Pennick & Lawrie **Prof** Karl Oultram/ Dave Woodland **Facilities** ⌑ 🏌 🏌 🏠 🏌 🏌 🏌 🏌
Leisure squash, gymnasium **Conf** facs Corporate Hospitality Days **Location** NW side of town centre. M53 junct 5, A41 for Chester, club 2m on left
Hotel ★★★ 77% HL Brook Meadow, Health Lane, CHILDER THORNTON ☎ 0151 339 9350 📠 0151 339 9350 25 en suite

---

LYMM Map 7 SJ68

Lymm Whitbarrow Rd WA13 9AN
☎ 01925 755020 📠 01925 755020
e-mail: lymmgolfclub@btconnect.com
web: www.lymm-golf-club.co.uk
First ten holes are gently undulating with the Manchester Ship Canal running alongside the 6th hole. The remaining holes are comparatively flat.

18 Holes, 6341yds, Par 71, SSS 70. Club membership 800.
Visitors Mon-Sun & BHs. Booking weekends & BHs. Dress code.
Societies booking required. **Green Fees** £36 per round weekday **Prof** Steve McCarthy **Facilities** 🎲 🍽️ 🏌 ⌑ 🏌 🏌 🏠 🏌
🏌 **Location** 0.5m N off A6144
Hotel ★★★ 73% HL The Lymm Hotel, Whitbarrow Road, LYMM ☎ 01925 752233 📠 01925 752233 62 en suite

---

MACCLESFIELD Map 7 SJ97

Barcelo Shrigley Hall Hotel & Country Club Shrigley Park, Pott Shrigley SK10 5SB
☎ 01625 575626 📠 01625 575437
e-mail: shrigleyhall.golfretail@barcelo-hotels.co.uk
web: www.barcelo-hotels.co.uk

Parkland course set in a 262-acre estate with breathtaking views of the Peak District and Cheshire plain. Designed by Donald Steel, this championship standard course provides a real sporting challenge.

Barcelo Shrigley Hall Hotel & Country Club:
18 Holes, 6281yds, Par 71, SSS 71, Course record 68.
Club membership 350.
Visitors Mon-Sun & BHs. Booking required. Dress code.
Societies booking required. **Green Fees** phone **Course Designer** Donald Steel **Prof** Anthony Herbert **Facilities** 🎲 🍽️ 🏌
⌑ 🏌 🏠 🏠 🏌 🏌 🏌 🏌 🏌 **Leisure** hard tennis courts, heated indoor swimming pool, squash, fishing, sauna, gymnasium **Conf** facs Corporate Hospitality Days **Location** off A523 Macclesfield-Stockport road
Hotel ★★★★ 74% HL Barceló Shrigley Hall, Golf & Country Club, Shrigley Park, Pott Shrigley, MACCLESFIELD ☎ 01625 575757 📠 01625 575757 148 en suite

Macclesfield The Hollins SK11 7EA
☎ 01625 423227 📠 01625 260061
e-mail: secretary@maccgolfclub.co.uk
web: maccgolfclub.co.uk
Hillside heathland course situated on the edge of the Pennines with excellent views across the Cheshire Plain. The signature hole is the 410yd 3rd, which drops majestically to a plateau green situated above a babbling brook. The temptation is to over-club, thus bringing the out of bounds behind into play. The 7th hole is aptly named Seven Shires as seven counties can be seen on a clear day, as well as the mountains.

18 Holes, 5714yds, Par 70, SSS 68, Course record 63.
Visitors Mon-Wed, Fri, Sun & BHs. Booking required. Dress code.
Societies booking required. **Green Fees** £30 per 18 holes (£40 Sun and BHs) **Course Designer** Hawtree & Son **Prof** Tony Taylor

continued

Facilities ⑪ ⑩ ⓛ ⓓ ⓢ ⓐ ⓦ ♂ **Conf** facs
Corporate Hospitality Days **Location** SE side of town centre off A523
Hotel ★★★ 79% HL Bridge, The Village, PRESTBURY
☎ 01625 829326 📖 01625 829326 23 en suite

Tytherington Dorchester Way, Tytherington SK10 2JP
☎ 01625 506000   📖 01625 506040
e-mail: tytherington.events@theclubcompany.com
web: www.theclubcompany.com/clubs/tytherington
Modern championship course in beautiful, mature parkland setting
with eight water features and over 100 bunkers. Testing holes,
notably the signature 12th hole (par 5), played from an elevated tee
with adjacent snaking ditch and a lake guarding the green.

The Tytherington Club: 18 Holes, 6765yds, Par 72,
SSS 74. Club membership 3000.

Visitors Mon-Sun & BHs. Handicap certificate. Dress code.
Societies booking required. **Green Fees** £39 (£49 weekends).
£15/£20 twilight **Course Designer** Dave Thomas/Patrick Dawson
Prof Gavin Beddon **Facilities** ⑪ ⑩ ⓛ ⓓ ⓢ ⓐ ⓐ
🚗 ♂ ♦ **Leisure** hard tennis courts, sauna, gymnasium,
halfway house at weekends **Conf** facs Corporate Hospitality Days
Location 1m N of Macclesfield off A523
Hotel ★★★★ 74% HL Barceló Shrigley Hall Hotel, Golf
& Country Club, Shrigley Park, Pott Shrigley, MACCLESFIELD
☎ 01625 575757 📖 01625 575757 148 en suite

NANTWICH Map 7 SJ65

Reaseheath Reaseheath College CW5 6DF
☎ 01270 625131   📖 01270 625665
e-mail: chrisb@reaseheath.ac.uk
web: www.reaseheath.ac.uk
The course here is attached to Reaseheath College, which is one of the
major centres of green-keeper training in the UK. It is a short nine-
hole parkland course with challenging narrow fairways, bunkers and a
water hazard, all of which make accuracy essential.

9 Holes, 1882yds, Par 62, SSS 58, Course record 55.
Club membership 520.

Visitors Mon-Sun & BHs. Booking required. Dress code.
Societies booking required. **Green Fees** £10 per day **Course**
Designer D Mortram **Prof** Andrew Pointon **Facilities** ⓓ ⓐ
Conf facs **Location** 1.5m NE of Nantwich, off A51
Hotel ★★★★ 85% HL Rookery Hall Hotel and Spa, Main
Road, Worleston, NANTWICH ☎ 01270 610016 & 0845 072 7533
📖 01270 610016 70 en suite

OSCROFT Map 7 SJ56

Pryors Hayes Willington Rd CH3 8NL
☎ 01829 741250 & 740140   📖 01829 749077
e-mail: info@pryors-hayes.co.uk
web: www.pryorshayes.com
A picturesque 18-hole parkland course set in the heart of Cheshire.
Gently undulating fairways demand accurate drives, and numerous
trees and water hazards make the course a challenging test of golf.

18 Holes, 6054yds, Par 69, SSS 69, Course record 65.
Club membership 530.

Visitors Mon-Sun & BHs. Dress code. **Societies** booking required.
Green Fees £30 per round (£40 weekends). **Course Designer** John Day
Prof Martin Redrup **Facilities** ⑪ ⑩ ⓛ ⓓ ⓢ ⓐ ⓐ ♂ 🚗

♂ **Conf** Corporate Hospitality Days **Location** between A51 & A54, 6m
E of Chester
Hotel ★★★ 78% CHH Willington Hall, Willington, TARPORLEY
☎ 01829 752321 📖 01829 752321 10 en suite

POYNTON Map 7 SJ98

Davenport Worth Hall, Middlewood Rd SK12 1TS
☎ 01625 876951   📖 01625 877489
e-mail: elaine@davenportgolf.co.uk
web: www.davenportgolf.co.uk
Gently undulating parkland. Extensive view over the Cheshire plain
from elevated 18th tee. Testing 1st hole, par 4. Several long par 3s,
water hazards and tree-lined fairways make this a challenging test
of golf.

18 Holes, 6034yds, Par 69, SSS 69, Course record 64.
Club membership 700.

Visitors Mon-Sun & BHs. Booking required. Handicap certificate. Dress
code. **Societies** booking required. **Green Fees** £32 (£43 weekends).
£27/£32 winter **Prof** Tony Stevens **Facilities** ⑪ by prior arrangement
⑩ by prior arrangement ⓛ ⓓ ⓢ ⓐ ⓐ ♂ **Leisure** snooker
Conf facs Corporate Hospitality Days **Location** 1m E off A523
Hotel ★★★ 72% HL Best Western Moorside Grange Hotel &
Spa, Mudhurst Lane, Higher Disley, DISLEY ☎ 01663 764151
📖 01663 764151 98 en suite

PRESTBURY Map 7 SJ97

Prestbury Macclesfield Rd SK10 4BJ
☎ 01625 828241   📖 01625 828241
e-mail: office@prestburygolfclub.com
web: www.prestburygolfclub.com

Undulating parkland with many plateau greens. The 9th hole has
a challenging uphill three-tier green and the 17th is over a valley.
Host to county and inter-county championships, including having
hosted Open qualifying events

18 Holes, 6371yds, Par 71, SSS 71, Course record 64.
Club membership 730.

Visitors Mon-Fri except BHs. Booking required Mon. Thu & Fri. Dress
code. **Societies** booking required **Green Fees** £50 per day **Course**
Designer Harry S Colt **Prof** Nick Summerfield **Facilities** ⑪ ⑩
ⓛ ⓓ ⓢ ⓐ ⓐ ♂ **Conf** Corporate Hospitality Days
Location S side of village off A538
Hotel ★★★★ 79% HL De Vere Mottram Hall, Wilmslow Road,
Mottram St Andrew, Prestbury, WILMSLOW ☎ 01625 828135
📖 01625 828135 131 en suite

RUNCORN
Map 7 SJ58

Runcorn Clifton Rd WA7 4SU
☎ 01928 574214 📠 01928 574214
e-mail: secretary@runcorngolfclub.ltd.uk
Easy walking parkland with tree-lined fairways. Fine views over Mersey and Weaver valleys. Testing holes: 7th par 5; 14th par 5; 17th par 4.
Runcorn Golf Club Ltd: 18 Holes, 6048yds, Par 69, SSS 69, Course record 63. Club membership 570.
Visitors Mon, Wed and Thu except BHs. Dress code. **Societies** booking required. **Green Fees** £30 per round **Prof** Kevin Hartley **Facilities** ⑪ 🍽️ by prior arrangement 🛍️ ⛳ 🚩 ⛏️ 🏆 ✏️ **Location** 1.25m S of Runcorn Station
Hotel ★★★ 79% HL Forest Hills Hotel & Leisure Complex, Overton Hill, FRODSHAM ☎ 01928 735255 📠 01928 735255 58 en suite

SANDBACH
Map 7 SJ76

Malkins Bank Betchton Rd, Malkins Bank CW11 4XN
☎ 01270 765931 📠 01270 764730
e-mail: phil.pleasance@congleton.gov.uk
web: www.congleton.gov.uk
This parkland course has a different challenge around every corner. The four par 3s on the course are all a challenge, especially the signature hole 14th. Trees in all directions make the short par 3 a really exciting hole. In fact, holes 12, 13 and 14 are the Amen Corner of Malkins Bank. Three very tricky holes, yet for straight hitters low scores are possible.
Malkins Bank Golf Course: 18 Holes, 6005yds, Par 70, SSS 69, Course record 65. Club membership 500.
Visitors Mon-Sun & BHs. Booking required. Dress code. **Societies** booking required. **Green Fees** not confirmed **Course Designer** Hawtree **Facilities** ⑪ 🍽️ 🛍️ ⛳ 🚩 ⛏️ 🏆 ✏️ **Location** 1.5m SE off A533
Hotel ★★★ 76% HL The Chimney House Hotel, Congleton Road, SANDBACH ☎ 0870 609 6164 📠 0870 609 6164 50 en suite

SANDIWAY
Map 7 SJ67

Sandiway Chester Rd CW8 2DJ
☎ 01606 883247 (Secretary) 📠 01606 888548
e-mail: info@sandiwaygolf.fsnet.co.uk
web: www.sandiwaygolf.co.uk
Delightful undulating wood and heathland course with long hills up to the 8th, 16th and 17th holes. Many dog-leg and tree-lined holes give opportunities for the deliberate fade or draw. True championship test and one of the finest inland courses in north-west England.
18 Holes, 6404yds, Par 70, SSS 72, Course record 65. Club membership 750.
Visitors handicap certificate. Dress code. **Societies** welcome. **Green Fees** £55 per day, £45 per round (£60 per round weekends) **Course Designer** Ted Ray **Prof** William Laird **Facilities** ⑪ 🍽️ 🛍️ 🚩 🛍️ ⛳ 🏆 ✏️ **Conf** facs Corporate Hospitality Days **Location** 2m W of Northwich on A556
Hotel ★★★★ HL Nunsmere Hall Hotel, Tarporley Road, SANDIWAY ☎ 01606 889100 📠 01606 889100 36 en suite

SUTTON WEAVER
Map 7 SJ57

Sutton Hall Aston Ln WA7 3ED
☎ 01928 790747 📠 01928 759174
Sutton Hall Golf Course: 18 Holes, 6608yards, Par 72, SSS 72, Course record 69.
Course Designer Ace Golf Associates **Location** M56 junct 12, follow signs for A56 to Warrington, on entering Sutton Weaver take 1st turn right
Telephone for further details
Hotel ★★★ 79% HL Forest Hills Hotel & Leisure Complex, Overton Hill, FRODSHAM ☎ 01928 735255 📠 01928 735255 58 en suite

TARPORLEY
Map 7 SJ56

Macdonald Portal Hotel Golf & Spa Cobbler's Cross Ln CW6 0DJ
☎ 01829 734160 📠 01829 733928
e-mail: golf.portal@macdonald-hotels.co.uk
web: www.macdonaldhotels.co.uk
Opened in 1991, there are two 18-hole courses here - Championship and Premier - one 9-hole course - Arderne and the largest indoor golf academy in the UK. They are set in mature, wooded parkland. There are fine views over the Cheshire Plain and numerous water hazards. The Championship 14th is just a short iron through trees, but its green is virtually an island surrounded by water.
Championship Course: 18 Holes, 7058yds, Par 73, SSS 74, Course record 64.
Premier Course: 18 Holes, 6508yds, Par 71, SSS 72, Course record 64.
Arderne Course: 9 Holes, 1724yds, Par 30.
Club membership 300.
Visitors Mon-Sun & BHs. Booking required. Handicap certificate. Dress code. **Societies** welcome. **Green Fees** phone **Course Designer** Donald Steel **Prof** Adrian Hill/Judy Statham **Facilities** ⑪ 🍽️ 🛍️ ⛳ 🚩 🛍️ ⛏️ 🏆 🏅 ✏️ 💎 ✏️ ⛏️ ✏️ 🏆 **Leisure** heated indoor swimming pool, sauna, gymnasium, indoor golf academy **Conf** facs Corporate Hospitality Days **Location** off A49
Hotel ★★★★ 77% HL Macdonald Portal, Cobblers Cross Lane, TARPORLEY ☎ 0844 879 9082 📠 0844 879 9082 83 en suite

WARRINGTON
Map 7 SJ68

Birchwood Kelvin Close WA3 7PB
☎ 01925 818819 (Club) & 816574 (Pro)
📠 01925 822403
web: www.birchwoodgolfclub.co.uk
Pilgrims: 18 Holes, 6727yds, Par 71, SSS 73, Course record 66.
Progress: 18 Holes, 6359yds, Par 71, SSS 72.
Mayflower (ladies course): 18 Holes, 5849yds, Par 74, SSS 74.
Course Designer T J A Macauley **Location** M62 junct 11, signs for Science Park North, course 2m
Telephone for further details
Hotel 75% Rhinewood Country House, Glazebrook Lane, Glazebrook, WARRINGTON ☎ 0161 775 5555 📠 0161 775 5555 32 en suite

Leigh Kenyon Hall, Broseley Ln, Culcheth WA3 4BG
☎ 01925 762943 (Secretary) 🖹 01925 765097
e-mail: golf@leighgolf.fsnet.co.uk
web: www.leighgolf.co.uk
This compact parkland course has benefited in recent years from intensive tree planting and extra drainage and the rebuilding of 12 greens. An interesting course to play with narrow fairways making accuracy from the tees essential.
18 Holes, 5908yds, Par 69, SSS 69, Course record 64.
Club membership 770.
Visitors Mon-Sun & BHs. Booking required. Handicap certificate. Dress code **Societies** booking required. **Green Fees** Summer: £30 per day, £28 per 18 holes. Winter £15 per 18 holes **Course Designer** Harold Hilton **Prof** Andrew Baguley **Facilities** ⑪ 🍴 🛍 🖂 🏌 🛄 🏠 ⑨° ⚡ **Conf** facs Corporate Hospitality Days **Location** 5m NE off A579
Hotel ★★★ 78% HL Best Western Fir Grove, Knutsford Old Road, WARRINGTON ☎ 01925 267471 🖹 01925 267471 52 en suite

Poulton Park Dig Ln, Cinnamon Brow, Padgate WA2 0SH
☎ 01925 822802 & 825220 (pro) 🖹 01925 822802
e-mail: secretary@poultonparkgolfclub.com
web: www.poultonparkgolfclub.co.uk
A short but rather testing course which runs between houses and the motorway embankment. Easy walking with water coming into play on four holes, which together with trees and out of bounds require straight hitting. The 7th/16th hole has a brook in front of the green which demands respect or you may lose your ball. The 4th, 13th and 17th can also wreck a scorecard. If you can play well here, you should be able to play well anywhere.
9 Holes, 5650yds, Par 68, SSS 67, Course record 66.
Club membership 350.
Visitors Mon-Sun & BHs. Booking required Tue, weekends & BHs. Dress code. **Societies** booking required. **Green Fees** not confirmed **Course Designer** Mike Millington **Prof** Ian Orrell **Facilities** ⑪ 🍴 🛍 🖂 🏌 🛄 🏠 ⚡ **Conf** Corporate Hospitality Days **Location** M6 junct 12, follow Woolston Grange Av parallel to motorway across 6 rdbts onto Crab Lane. Cross mini-rdbt and car park on right. M62 junct 11, follow A574 to Warrington. Cross M6 and turn right into Crab Lane.
Hotel ★★★ 78% HL Best Western Fir Grove, Knutsford Old Road, WARRINGTON ☎ 01925 267471 🖹 01925 267471 52 en suite

Walton Hall Warrington Rd WA4 5LU
☎ 01925 263061 (bookings) 🖹 01925 263061
Walton Hall Golf Course: 18 Holes, 6647yds, Par 72, SSS 73, Course record 70.
Course Designer Peter Allisss/Dave Thomas **Location** M56 junct 11, 2m
Telephone for further details
Hotel ★★★★ 75% HL De Vere Daresbury Park, Chester Road, Daresbury, WARRINGTON ☎ 01925 267331 🖹 01925 267331 189 en suite

Warrington Hill Warren, London Rd, Appleton WA4 5HR
☎ 01925 261775 (Secretary) 🖹 01925 265933
e-mail: secretary@warringtongolfclub.co.uk
web: www.warringtongolfclub.co.uk
Meadowland, with varied terrain and natural hazards. Major work has been carried out on both the clubhouse and the course to ensure high standards. The course is a constant challenge with ponds, trees and bunkers threatening the errant shot.
18 Holes, 6211yds, Par 71, SSS 71, Course record 63.
Club membership 840.
Visitors contact club for details. **Societies** welcome. **Green Fees** £45 per day, £35 per round (£40 per round weekends & BHs) **Course Designer** James Braid **Prof** Reay Mackay **Facilities** ⑪ 🍴 🛍 🖂 🏌 🛄 🏠 ⑨° ⚡ **Conf** Corporate Hospitality Days **Location** M56 junct 10, 1.5m N on A49
Hotel ★★★★ 77% HL The Park Royal, Stretton Road, Stretton, WARRINGTON ☎ 01925 730706 🖹 01925 730706 146 en suite

---

WIDNES
Map 7 SJ58

Mersey Valley Golf & Country Club Warrington Rd, Bold Heath WA8 3XL
☎ 0151 4246060 🖹 0151 2579097
e-mail: chrismgerrard@yahoo.co.uk
web: www.merseyvalleygolfclub.co.uk
Parkland with very easy walking.
Mersey Valley Golf & Country Club: 18 Holes, 6374yards, Par 72, SSS 71, Course record 68. Club membership 500.
Visitors contact club for details. **Societies** welcome. **Green Fees** not confirmed **Course Designer** R Bush **Prof** Andy Stevenson **Facilities** ⑪ 🛍 🖂 🍴 🏌 🛄 🏠 ⑨° ⚡ 🚌 ⚡ **Leisure** fishing **Conf** facs Corporate Hospitality Days **Location** M62 junct 7, A57 towards Warrington, club 2m on left
Hotel ★★★ 67% HL The Hillcrest Hotel, 75 Cronton Lane, WIDNES ☎ 0844 736 8610 & 0151 424 1616 🖹 0844 736 8610 50 en suite

St Michael Jubilee Dundalk Rd WA8 8BS
☎ 0151 424 6230 🖹 0151 495 2124
St Michael Jubilee: 18 Holes, 5925yds, Par 69, SSS 67.
Prof Darren Chapman **Facilities** ⑪ 🛍 🖂 🍴 🏌 🏠 ⑨°
Location W side of town centre off A562
Telephone for further details
Hotel BUD Travelodge Widnes, Fiddlers Ferry Road, WIDNES ☎ 0871 984 6183 🖹 0871 984 6183 52 en suite

Widnes Highfield Rd WA8 7DT
☎ 0151 424 2440 & 424 2995 🖹 0151 495 2849
e-mail: office@widnesgolfclub.co.uk
web: www.widnes-golfclub.co.uk
An easy walking parkland course, challenging in parts.
18 Holes, 5719yds, Par 69, SSS 68, Course record 64.
Club membership 700.
Visitors Mon-Sun & BHs. Booking required. Handicap certificate. Dress code. **Societies** booking required. **Green Fees** £26 per 18 holes (£35 weekends) **Prof** J O'Brien **Facilities** ⑪ 🍴 🛍 🖂 🏌 🛄 🏠 **Conf** Corporate Hospitality Days **Location** M62 junct 7, A57 to Warrington, right at lights onto Wilmere Ln, right at T-junct. 1st left at rdbt onto Birchfield Rd, right after 3rd pelican crossing onto Highfield Rd, right before lights
Hotel BUD Travelodge Widnes, Fiddlers Ferry Road, WIDNES ☎ 0871 984 6183 🖹 0871 984 6183 52 en suite

WILMSLOW — Map 7 SJ88

De Vere Mottram Hall Wilmslow Rd, Mottram St Andrew
SK10 4QT
☎ 01625 828135   📠 01625 829312
e-mail: dmhgolf@devere-hotels.com
web: www.deveregolf.co.uk
Championship-standard course - flat meadowland on the front nine
and undulating woodland on the back nine, with well-guarded greens.
The course is unusual as each half opens and closes with par 5s. Good
test for both professional and novice golfers alike. Excellent drainage.
*De Vere Mottram Hall: 18 Holes, 7006yds, Par 72, SSS 74,
Course record 63. Club membership 275.*
Visitors Mon-Sun & BHs. Booking required. Dress code.
Societies booking required. **Green Fees** £60 per round summer,
£30 per round winter **Course Designer** Dave Thomas **Prof** Matthew
Turnock **Facilities** ⑪ ⑩ 🏋 ☕ 🍴 ♨ 🛋 🏌 ◇ ♂
🚌 ♂ 🎯 **Leisure** hard tennis courts, heated indoor swimming
pool, squash, sauna, gymnasium, bag store & drying room, satellite
navigation buggies **Conf** facs Corporate Hospitality Days **Location** on
A538 between Wilmslow and Prestbury
Hotel ★★★★ 79% HL De Vere Mottram Hall, Wilmslow Road,
Mottram St Andrew, Prestbury, WILMSLOW ☎ 01625 828135
📄 01625 828135 131 en suite

Styal Station Rd, Styal SK9 4JN
☎ 01625 531359   📠 01625 416373
e-mail: gtraynor@styalgolf.co.uk
web: www.styalgolf.co.uk
Well-designed flat parkland course with USGA specification greens.
Challenging and enjoyable test for all standards of golfer. The par 3
course is widely regarded as one of the finest short courses in the
country.
*18 Holes, 6238yds, Par 70, SSS 70, Course record 63.
Club membership 800.*
Visitors Mon-Sun & BHs. Dress code. **Societies** booking required.
Green Fees £25 per round (£30 weekends). Par 3 course £8 per
9 holes, £12 per 18 holes **Course Designer** Tony Holmes **Prof** Simon
Forrest **Facilities** ⑪ ⑩ 🏋 ☕ 🍴 ♨ 🛋 🏌 ♂ 🚌 ♂
🎯 **Leisure** par 3 9 hole course. **Conf** facs Corporate Hospitality Days
Location M56 junct 5, 5 mins from Wilmslow/Manchester Airport
Hotel ★★★★ 80% HL Stanneylands, Stanneylands Road,
WILMSLOW ☎ 01625 525225 📄 01625 525225 56 en suite

Wilmslow Great Warford, Mobberley WA16 7AY
☎ 01565 872148   📠 01565 872172
e-mail: info@wilmslowgolfclub.co.uk
web: www.wilmslowgolfclub.co.uk
Peaceful parkland in the heart of the Cheshire countryside offering
golf for all levels.
*18 Holes, 6635yds, Par 72, SSS 72, Course record 62.
Club membership 800.*
Visitors dress code. **Societies** booking required. **Green Fees** £55
per day, £45 per round (£65/£55 weekends & BHs) **Prof** John
Nowicki **Facilities** ⑪ ⑩ 🏋 ☕ 🍴 ♨ 🛋 🏌 🚌 ♂
Conf Corporate Hospitality Days **Location** 2m SW off B5058
Hotel ★★★ 85% HL Alderley Edge, Macclesfield Road, ALDERLEY
EDGE ☎ 01625 583033 📄 01625 583033 50 en suite

WINSFORD — Map 7 SJ66

Knights Grange Grange Ln CW7 2PT
☎ 01606 552780
e-mail: knightsgrangewinsford@valeroyal.gov.uk
web: www.valeroyal.gov.uk/leisure
An 18-hole course set in beautiful Cheshire countryside on the town
outskirts. The front nine is mainly flat but players have to negotiate
water, ditches and other hazards along the way. The back nine takes
the player deep into the countryside, with many of the tees offering
panoramic views. A lake known as the Ocean is a feature of many
holes - a particular hazard for slicers of the ball. There are also many
mature woodland areas to catch the wayward drive.
*Knights Grange Golf Course & Sports Complex: 18 Holes,
5921yds, Par 70, SSS 68.*
Visitors Mon-Sun & BHs. Booking required. **Societies** booking
required **Green Fees** not confirmed **Course Designer** Steve Dawson
Facilities ☕ 🛋 ♨ ♂ **Leisure** hard and grass tennis courts
Location N side of town off A54
Hotel BUD Travelodge Middlewich, MIDDLEWICH ☎ 08719 846 163
📄 08719 846 163 32 en suite

WINWICK — Map 7 SJ69

Alder Root Alder Root Ln WA2 8R2
☎ 01925 291919   📠 01925 291961
e-mail: office@alderrootgolfclub.com
web: www.alderroot.com
A woodland course, flat in nature but with many undulations. Several
holes have water hazards. One of the most testing short courses in
the north-west.
*11 Holes, 6017yds, Par 70, SSS 68, Course record 67.
Club membership 400.*
Visitors Mon-Sun & BHs. Booking required Thu, weekends & BHs.
Dress code. **Societies** booking required. **Green Fees** phone **Course
Designer** Mr Lander/Mr Millington **Prof** C McKevitt **Facilities** ⑪ 🏋
☕ 🍴 🛋 🏌 ♂ 🚌 ♂ 🎯 **Location** M62 junct 9, A49 N
for 800yds, left at lights right into Alder Root Ln
Hotel ★★ 74% HL Paddington House, 514 Old Manchester Road,
WARRINGTON ☎ 01925 816767 📄 01925 816767 37 en suite

CORNWALL & ISLES OF SCILLY

BODMIN — Map 2 SX06

Lanhydrock Hotel Lostwithiel Rd PL30 5AQ
☎ 01208 262570   📠 01208 262579
e-mail: info@lanhydrockhotel.com
web: www.lanhydrockhotel.com
An acclaimed parkland course adjacent to the National Trust property
of Lanhydrock House. Nestling in a picturesque wooded valley of oak
and birch, this undulating course provides an exciting and enjoyable
challenge.
*Lanhydrock Hotel & Golf Club: 18 Holes, 6100yds, Par 70,
SSS 70, Course record 66. Club membership 300.*
Visitors Mon-Sun & BHs. Dress code. **Societies** welcome. **Green
Fees** £40-£50 per day, £25-£35 per round **Course Designer** Hamilton
Stutt **Prof** Richard O'Hanlon **Facilities** ⑪ ⑩ 🏋 ☕ 🍴 🛋 🏌 🚌
♨ ◇ 🚌 ♂ 🎯 **Conf** facs Corporate Hospitality Days **Location** 1m
S of Bodmin off B3268

continued

Lanhydrock Hotel

Hotel ★★★ 73% HL Best Western Restormel Lodge, Castle Hill, LOSTWITHIEL ☎ 01208 872223 📄 01208 872223 36 en suite

---

BUDE
Map 2 SS20

Bude & North Cornwall Burn View EX23 8DA
☎ 01288 352006 📄 01288 356855
e-mail: secretary@budegolf.co.uk
web: www.budegolf.co.uk

A traditional links course established in 1891. Situated in the centre of Bude with magnificent views to the sea. A challenging course with super greens and excellent drainage enables course to be playable throughout the year off regular tees and greens.

18 Holes, 6057yds, Par 71, SSS 70. Club membership 800.
Visitors Mon-Sun & BHs. Dress code. **Societies** welcome. **Green Fees** £30 per day (£30 per round weekends & BHs) **Course Designer** Tom Dunn **Prof** Mark Yeo **Facilities** ⊕ ⓘⓞ] ⓛ ⊑ 🍴 ⚓ 🏠 ⚑ 🛺 ♂ **Leisure** snooker room **Conf** facs Corporate Hospitality Days **Location** N side of town
Hotel ★★★ 75% HL Camelot, Downs View, BUDE
☎ 01288 352361 📄 01288 352361 24 en suite

BUDOCK VEAN
Map 2 SW73

Budock Vean Hotel on the River Mawnan Smith, Helford Passage TR11 5LG
☎ 01326 252102 (shop) 📄 01326 250892
e-mail: relax@budockvean.co.uk
web: www.budockvean.co.uk

Set in 65 acres of mature grounds with a private foreshore to the Helford River, this 18-tee undulating parkland course has a tough par 4 5th hole (456yds) which dog-legs at halfway around an oak tree. The 16th hole measures 572yds, par 5.

Budock Vean Hotel on the River: 9 Holes, 5255yds, Par 68, SSS 66, Course record 58. Club membership 200.
Visitors dress code. **Societies** booking required. **Green Fees** £23 per day (£27 weekends & BHs) **Course Designer** James Braid **Prof** David Short **Facilities** ⊕ ⓘⓞ] by prior arrangement ⓛ ⊑ 🍴 ⚓ 🏠 ⚑ ◇ ♂ 🛺 ♂ **Leisure** hard tennis courts, heated indoor swimming pool, fishing, sauna, boating facilities, health spa, outdoor hot tub **Conf** facs Corporate Hospitality Days **Location** 1.5m SW of Mawnan Smith
Hotel ★★★★ 79% CHH Budock Vean-The Hotel on the River, MAWNAN SMITH, Falmouth ☎ 01326 252100 & 0800 833927 📄 01326 252100 57 en suite

---

CAMBORNE
Map 2 SW64

Tehidy Park TR14 0HH
☎ 01209 842208 📄 01209 842208
e-mail: secretary-manager@tehidyparkgolfclub.co.uk
web: www.tehidyparkgolfclub.co.uk

A well-maintained parkland course providing good holiday golf and a challenge for golfers of all abilities.

18 Holes, 6241yds, Par 71, SSS 71, Course record 62. Club membership 700.
Visitors Mon-Sun & BHs. Handicap certificate. Dress code **Societies** booking required. **Green Fees** £30.50 per day (£40.50 weekends & BHs) **Course Designer** C K Cotton **Prof** Jonathan Lamb **Facilities** ⊕ ⓘⓞ] ⓛ ⊑ 🍴 ⚓ 🏠 ⚑ ♂ 🛺 ♂ **Leisure** snooker **Conf** facs Corporate Hospitality Days **Location** on Portreath-Pool road, 2m S of Camborne
Hotel ★★★ 79% HL Penventon Park, REDRUTH ☎ 01209 203000 📄 01209 203000 64 en suite

---

CAMELFORD
Map 2 SX18

Bowood Park Hotel Lanteglos PL32 9RF
☎ 01840 213017 📄 01840 212622
e-mail: info@bowoodpark.org
web: www.bowoodpark.org

A rolling parkland course set in 230 acres of ancient deer park once owned by the Black Prince; 27 lakes and ponds test the golfer and serve as a haven for wildlife.

Bowood Park Hotel & Golf Course: 18 Holes, 6672yds, Par 72, SSS 72, Course record 68. Club membership 300.
Visitors Mon-Sun & BHs. Dress code. **Societies** welcome. **Green Fees** not confirmed **Course Designer** Sandow **Prof** Matt Stewart **Facilities** ⊕ ⓘⓞ] ⓛ ⊑ 🍴 ⚓ 🏠 ⚑ ◇ ♂ 🛺 ♂ ♂ **Leisure** fishing **Conf** facs Corporate Hospitality Days

continued

Location through Camelford, 0.5m turn right Tintagel/Boscastle B3266, 1st left after garage, 300yds on left
Guesthouse ★★★★ BB The Corn Mill, Port Isaac Road, Trelill, PENDOGGETT ☎ 01208 851079 🖹 01208 851079 2 en suite

CARLYON BAY
See **St Austell**

CONSTANTINE BAY   Map 2 SW87

Trevose PL28 8JB
☎ 01841 520208 🖹 01841 521057
e-mail: info@trevose-gc.co.uk
web: www.trevose-gc.co.uk

Well-known links course with early holes close to the sea on excellent springy turf. A championship course affording varying degrees of difficulty appealing to both the professional and higher handicap player. It is a good test with well-positioned bunkers, and a meandering stream, and the wind playing a decisive role in preventing low scoring. Hosted the English Amateur Stroke Play championship (Brabazon Trophy) in 2008.
Championship Course: 18 Holes, 6863yds, Par 72, SSS 73, Course record 66.
New Course: 9 Holes, 3031yds, Par 35.
Short Course: 9 Holes, 1360yds, Par 29.
Club membership 1650.
Visitors contact course for details. **Societies** welcome. **Green Fees** not confirmed **Course Designer** H S Colt **Prof** Gary Lenaghan **Facilities** ⓣ ⑩ 🏌 ⏛ 🍴 🔨 ⛳ 🛍 ◇ 🚗 🛒 🏌 **Leisure** hard tennis courts, heated outdoor swimming pool **Conf facs Location** 4m W of Padstow on B3276, to St Merryn, 500yds past x-rds turn, signed
Hotel ★★★★ 76% CHH Treglos, Constantine Bay, PADSTOW ☎ 01841 520727 🖹 01841 520727 42 en suite

FALMOUTH   Map 2 SW83

Falmouth Swanpool Rd TR11 5BQ
☎ 01326 314296 🖹 01326 317783
e-mail: steve@falmouthgolfclub.com
web: www.falmouthgolfclub.com
One of the oldest courses in the county situated in a picturesque setting with fine sea and coastal views. Excellent greens.
18 Holes, 6037yds, Par 71, SSS 70. Club membership 600.
Visitors dress code. **Societies** booking required. **Green Fees** £38 per day, £32 per round **Prof** Nick Rogers **Facilities** ⓣ ⑩ 🏌 ⏛

🍴 ⏛ 🍴 🔨 ⛳ 🚗 🛒 🏌 **Conf** Corporate Hospitality Days
Location SW of town centre

Falmouth

Hotel ★★★★ 79% HL Royal Duchy, Cliff Road, FALMOUTH ☎ 01326 313042 🖹 01326 313042 43 en suite

HOLYWELL BAY   Map 2 SW75

Holywell Bay TR8 5PW
☎ 01637 832916 🖹 01637 831000
e-mail: golf@trevornick.co.uk
web: www.holywellbay.co.uk/golf
Situated beside a family fun park with many amenities. The course is an 18-hole short course with excellent sea views. Fresh Atlantic winds make the course hard to play and there are several tricky holes, particularly the 18th over the trout pond. The site also has an excellent 18-hole Pitch and Putt course for the whole family.
Holywell Bay Golf Park: 18 Holes, 2784yds, Par 61, Course record 58. Club membership 200.
Visitors Mon-Sun & BHs. **Societies** booking required. **Green Fees** £12.50 per 18 holes (£16 including half set clubs) **Course Designer** Hartley **Facilities** ⓣ ⑩ 🏌 ⏛ 🍴 ⛳ 🏌 **Leisure** heated outdoor swimming pool, fishing, 18 hole pitch & putt course. Touring & camping facilities **Conf** Corporate Hospitality Days **Location** off A3075 Newquay-Perranporth road
Hotel ★★★ 75% HL Crantock Bay, West Pentire, CRANTOCK ☎ 01637 830229 🖹 01637 830229 31 en suite

LAUNCESTON   Map 2 SX38

Launceston St Stephens PL15 8HF
☎ 01566 773442 & 775359 🖹 01566 777506
e-mail: secretary@launcestongolfclub.co.uk
web: www.launcestongolfclub.co.uk
Highly rated course with magnificent views over the historic town and moors. Noted for superb greens and lush fairways.
18 Holes, 6407yds, Par 70, SSS 70, Course record 65.
Club membership 560.
Visitors Mon-Sun & BHs. Booking required. Handicap certificate. Dress code. **Societies** booking advised. **Green Fees** £40 per day, £30 per round. **Course Designer** Hamilton Stutt **Prof** John Tozer **Facilities** ⓣ 🏌 ⏛ 🍴 ⏛ 🍴 🔨 ⛳ 🚗 🛒 🏌 **Leisure** practice nets **Conf** facs Corporate Hospitality Days **Location** NW of town centre on B3254
Hotel ★★ 74% SHL Eagle House, Castle Street, LAUNCESTON ☎ 01566 772036 & 774488 🖹 01566 772036 14 en suite

ENGLAND

Trethorne Kennards House PL15 8QE
☎ 01566 86903 📠 01566 880925
e-mail: reservations@trethornegolfclub.com
web: www.trethornegolfclub.com
Rolling parkland course with well maintained fairways and computer irrigated greens. Plenty of trees and natural water hazards make this well respected course a good challenge.
18 Holes, 6178yds, Par 71, SSS 71, Course record 67.
Club membership 280.
Visitors Mon-Sun & BHs. Dress code. **Societies** booking required.
Green Fees £24 per round (£28 weekends) **Course Designer** Frank Frayne **Prof** Robert Moore **Facilities** ⑪ ⑩ ⬛ ⬜ 🐛 △ 🏠 🚻 ◇ 🥤 🚗 ✔ **Leisure** leisure farm and tenpin bowling.
Conf facs Corporate Hospitality Days **Location** off junct A30, 3m W of Launceston
Hotel ★★ 74% SHL Eagle House, Castle Street, LAUNCESTON
☎ 01566 772036 & 774488 📠 01566 772036 14 en suite

LELANT   Map 2 SW53

West Cornwall TR26 3DZ
☎ 01736 753401 📠 01736 758468
e-mail: secretary@westcornwallgolfclub.co.uk
web: www.westcornwallgolfclub.co.uk
Established in 1889, a seaside links with sandhills and lovely turf adjacent to the Hayle estuary and St Ives Bay. A real test of the player's skill, especially Calamity Corner starting at the 5th on the lower land by the River Hayle.
18 Holes, 5884yds, Par 69, SSS 69, Course record 63.
Club membership 813.
Visitors Mon-Sun & BHs. Handicap certificate. Dress code.
Societies booking required. **Green Fees** £35 per day (£40 Wed, Sat & BHs) **Course Designer** Reverend Tyacke **Prof** Jason Broadway
Facilities ⑪ ⑩ ⬛ ⬜ 🐛 △ 🏠 🚻 ✔ **Location** N side of village off A3074
Hotel ★★★ 78% HL Carbis Bay, Carbis Bay, ST IVES
☎ 01736 795311 📠 01736 795311 40 en suite

LOOE   Map 2 SX25

Looe Bindown PL13 1PX
☎ 01503 240239 📠 01503 240864
web: www.looegolfclub.co.uk
18 Holes, 5940yds, Par 70, SSS 69, Course record 64.
Course Designer Harry Vardon **Location** 3.5m NE off B3253
Telephone for further details
Hotel ★★★ 70% HL Hannafore Point, Marine Drive, West Looe,
LOOE ☎ 01503 263273 📠 01503 263273 37 en suite

LOSTWITHIEL   Map 2 SX15

Lostwithiel Hotel, Golf & Country Club Lower Polscoe
PL22 0HQ
☎ 01208 873550 📠 01208 873479
e-mail: reception@golf-hotel.co.uk
web: www.golf-hotel.co.uk
This 18-hole course is one of the most varied in the county, designed to take full advantage of the natural features of the landscape, combining two distinct areas of hillside and valley. The challenging front nine has magnificent views of the surrounding countryside, while the picturesque back nine runs through parkland flanked by the River Fowey.
Lostwithiel Hotel, Golf & Country Club: 18 Holes, 5984yds,
Par 72, SSS 71, Course record 67. Club membership 500.
Visitors Mon-Sun & BHs. Booking required. Handicap certificate. Dress code. **Societies** booking required. **Green Fees** £28 per round (£33 weekends). Reductions during winter months **Course Designer** S Wood **Prof** Andrew Hooper **Facilities** ⑪ ⑩ ⬛ ⬜ 🐛 △ 🏠 🚻 ◇ 🚗 ✔ **Leisure** hard tennis courts, heated indoor swimming pool, fishing, gymnasium, indoor golf simulator **Conf** facs Corporate Hospitality Days **Location** 1m from Lostwithiel off A390

Lostwithiel Hotel, Golf & Country Club

Hotel ★★★ 67% HL Lostwithiel Hotel Golf & Country Club,
Lower Polscoe, LOSTWITHIEL ☎ 01208 873550 📠 01208 873550
27 en suite

MAWGAN PORTH   Map 2 SW86

Merlin TR8 4DN
☎ 01841 540222 📠 01841 541031
e-mail: play@merlingolfcourse.co.uk
web: www.merlingolfcourse.co.uk
A heathland course with fine views of the coast and countryside. Fairly easy walking. The most challenging hole is the par 4 18th with out of bounds on the left and ponds on either side of the green.
Merlin Golf Course: 18 Holes, 6210yds, Par 71, SSS 71.
Club membership 350.
Visitors Mon-Sun & BHs. Dress code. **Societies** welcome. **Green Fees** £35 per day, £25 per round **Course Designer** Ross Oliver **Prof** John Rule **Facilities** ⑪ ⑩ ⬛ ⬜ 🐛 △ 🏠 🚻 ◇ 🥤 🚗 ✔ **Conf** facs Corporate Hospitality Days **Location** on Newquay-Padstow coast road. After Mawgan Porth signs for St Eval, course on right
Hotel ★★★★ 76% HL Bedruthan Steps Hotel, MAWGAN PORTH
☎ 01637 860555 & 860860 📠 01637 860555 101 en suite

MULLION   Map 2 SW61

Mullion Cury TR12 7BP
☎ 01326 240685 (sec) & 241176 (pro)
📠 01326 241527
e-mail: secretary@mulliongolfclub.plus.com
Founded in 1895, a clifftop and links course with panoramic views over Mounts Bay. A steep downhill slope on the 6th and the 10th descends to the beach with a deep ravine alongside the green. The most southerly course in England.
18 Holes, 6083yds, Par 70, SSS 70.
Club membership 700.

continued

Visitors Mon-Sun & BHs. Handicap certificate. Dress code. **Societies** booking required. **Green Fees** £30 per day (£30 weekends & BHs) **Course Designer** W Sich **Prof** Ian Harris **Facilities** **Leisure** indoor computerised teaching academy **Location** 1.5m NW of Mullion, off A3083
Hotel ★★★ 77% HL Polurrian, MULLION ☎ 01326 240421 🖹 01326 240421 39 en suite

NEWQUAY — Map 2 SW86

Newquay Tower Rd TR7 1LT
☎ 01637 874354 🖹 01637 874066
e-mail: newquaygolf@btconnect.com
web: www.newquaygolfclub.co.uk

One of Cornwall's finest seaside links with magnificent views over Fistral Beach and the Atlantic Ocean. Open to the unpredictable nature of the elements and possessing some very demanding greenside bunkers, the prerequisite for good scoring at Newquay is accuracy.

18 Holes, 6141yds, Par 69, SSS 69, Course record 63. Club membership 600.

Visitors Mon-Sun & BHs. Booking required. Handicap certificate. Dress code. **Societies** booking required. **Green Fees** £30 per round (£35 per round weekends and BHs). **Course Designer** H Colt **Prof** Joel Cant **Facilities** **Conf** Corporate Hospitality Days **Location** from W side of town take Gannel bypass and follow signs for Fistral Beach. At top of by-pass take 2nd exit off roundabout, club signed
Hotel ★★★ 78% HL Best Western Hotel Bristol, Narrowcliff, NEWQUAY ☎ 01637 875181 🖹 01637 875181 74 en suite

PADSTOW

See **Constantine Bay**

PERRANPORTH — Map 2 SW75

Perranporth Budnic Hill TR6 0AB
☎ 01872 573701
e-mail: office.pgc@tiscali.co.uk
web: www.perranporthgolfclub.com

There are three testing par 5 holes on the links course (2nd, 5th, 11th). This seaside links course has magnificent views of the North Cornwall coastline, and excellent greens. The drainage of the course, being sand-based, is also exceptional.

18 Holes, 6296yds, Par 72, SSS 72, Course record 67. Club membership 650.

Visitors Mon-Sun & BHs. Booking required. Dress code. **Societies** booking required. **Green Fees** £34 per round (£40 weekends & BHs). Additional £5 for extra holes **Course Designer** James Braid **Prof** D Michell **Facilities** **Conf** Corporate Hospitality Days **Location** 0.75m NE on B3285
Hotel ★★★ 70% HL Rosemundy House, Rosemundy Hill, ST AGNES ☎ 01872 552101 🖹 01872 552101 46 en suite

PORTWRINKLE — Map 2 SX45

Whitsand Bay Hotel Golf & Country Club PL11 3BU
☎ 01503 230276 🖹 01503 230329
e-mail: whitsandbayhotel@btconnect.com
web: www.whitsandbayhotel.co.uk

Testing seaside course laid out on cliffs overlooking Whitsand Bay. Easy walking after first hole. The par 3 3rd hole is acknowledged as one of the most attractive holes in Cornwall.

Whitsand Bay Hotel Golf & Country Club: 18 Holes, 6030yds, Par 69, SSS 68, Course record 62. Club membership 400.

Visitors Mon-Sun & BHs. Booking required. Dress code. **Societies** booking required. **Green Fees** not confirmed **Course Designer** Fernie **Prof** Steve Dougan **Facilities** **Leisure** heated indoor swimming pool, sauna, gymnasium, spa centre **Conf** Corporate Hospitality Days **Location** from Tamar Bridge, turn left at Treulefoot roundabout for Polbathic. After 2m turn right to Crafthole then Portwrinkle. Golf course on right.
Hotel ★★★ 74% HL Whitsand Bay Hotel & Golf Club, PORTWRINKLE, Torpoint ☎ 01503 230276 🖹 01503 230276 32 en suite

PRAA SANDS — Map 2 SW50

Praa Sands Golf Club & Country Club Germoe Cross Roads TR20 9TQ
☎ 01736 763445
e-mail: simon.spencer@haulfryn.co.uk
web: www.haulfryn.co.uk/leisure/praa-sands-golf

A beautiful parkland course, overlooking Mount's Bay with outstanding sea views from every tee and green.

Praa Sands Golf Club & Country Club: 9 Holes, 4122yds, Par 62, SSS 62, Course record 58.

Visitors Mon-Sun & BHs. Dress code. **Societies** booking required. **Green Fees** not confirmed **Facilities** **Location** A394 between Penzance & Helston

ROCK
Map 2 SW97

St Enodoc PL27 6LD
☎ 01208 863216   🖹 01208 862976
e-mail: enquiries@st-enodoc.co.uk
web: www.st-enodoc.co.uk
Classic links course with huge sand hills and rolling fairways. James Braid laid out the original 18 holes in 1907 and changes were made in 1922 and 1935. On the Church, the 10th is the toughest par 4 on the course and on the 6th is a truly enormous sand hill known as the Himalayas. The Holywell is not as exacting as the Church; it is less demanding on stamina but still a real test of skill for golfers of any handicap.

Church Course: 18 Holes, 6547yds, Par 69, SSS 71, Course record 64.
Holywell Course: 18 Holes, 4082yds, Par 63, SSS 60.
Club membership 1300.
Visitors Mon-Fri, Sun & BHs. Booking required for Church Course. Handicap certificate. Dress code. **Societies** booking required.
Green Fees Church Course £87 per day, £60 per round (£70 per round Sun). Holywell Course: £30 per day, £20 per round **Course Designer** James Braid **Prof** Nick Williams **Facilities** ⑪ 🍴 ⬜ 🍴 🏖 🛅 ⚑ ✦ 🏌 Location W side of village
Hotel ★★★★ 70% HL The Metropole, Station Road, PADSTOW ☎ 01841 532486 🖹 01841 532486 58 en suite

ST AUSTELL
Map 2 SX05

Carlyon Bay Hotel Beach Rd, Carlyon Bay PL25 3RD
☎ 01726 814250   🖹 01726 814250
e-mail: golf@carlyonbay.com
web: www.carlyonbay.com

A championship-length, clifftop parkland course, running east to west and back again - and also uphill and down a fair bit. The fairways stay in excellent condition all year as they have since the course was laid down in 1925. Magnificent views from the course across St Austell Bay; particularly from the 9th green, where an approach shot remotely to the right will plummet over the cliff edge.
18 Holes, 6597yds, Par 72, SSS 71, Course record 63.
Club membership 500.
Visitors handicap certificate. Dress code. **Societies** booking required. **Green Fees** from £25-£45 per round depending on season. £10 for extra round **Course Designer** Hamilton Stutt **Prof** Mark Rowe **Facilities** ⑪ 🍴 🍴 ⬜ 🍴 🏖 🛅 ⚑ ◇ ✦ 🚲 ✦ **Leisure** hard tennis courts, outdoor and indoor heated swimming pool, sauna, gymnasium, 9 hole par 3 course **Conf** facs Corporate Hospitality Days **Location** 3m SE of St Austell off A390, signposted
Hotel ★★★★ 77% HL Carlyon Bay, Sea Road, Carlyon Bay,

ST AUSTELL ☎ 01726 812304 & 811007 🖹 01726 812304 87 en suite

Porthpean Porthpean PL26 6AY
☎ 01726 64613   🖹 01726 64613
e-mail: porthpeangolfclub@hotmail.co.uk
web: www.porthpeangolfclub.co.uk
A picturesque 18-hole course, the outward holes are in a pleasant parkland setting while the return holes command spectacular views over St Austell Bay.
18 Holes, 5474yds, Par 68, SSS 67. Club membership 550.
Visitors Mon-Sun & BHs. **Societies** booking required. **Green Fees** not confirmed **Facilities** ⑪ 🍴 ⬜ 🍴 🏖 🛅 ⚑ ◇ ✦ 🚲 ✦ **Conf** facs Corporate Hospitality Days **Location** 1.5m from St Austell bypass, A390. Signed
Hotel ★★★ 72% HL Pier House, Harbour Front, Charlestown, ST AUSTELL ☎ 01726 67955 🖹 01726 67955 28 en suite

St Austell Tregongeeves Ln PL26 7DS
☎ 01726 74756   🖹 01726 71978
e-mail: office@staustellgolf.co.uk
web: www.staustellgolf.co.uk
Very interesting inland parkland course designed by James Braid and offering glorious views of the surrounding countryside. Undulating, well-covered with tree plantations and well-bunkered. Notable holes are 8th (par 4) and 16th (par 3).
18 Holes, 6089yds, Par 69, SSS 69, Course record 64.
Club membership 600.
Visitors Mon, Wed, Fri & BHs. Dress code. **Societies** booking required. **Green Fees** £28 per round (£30 weekends) **Course Designer** James Braid **Prof** Tony Pitts **Facilities** ⑪ 🍴 ⬜ 🍴 🏖 🛅 ⚑ ✦ 🏌 **Conf** facs Corporate Hospitality Days **Location** 1m W of St Austell on A390

ST IVES
Map 2 SW54

Tregenna Castle Hotel TR26 2DE
☎ 01736 797381   🖹 01736 796066
web: www.tregenna-castle.co.uk
Tregenna Castle Hotel: 14 Holes, 1846yds, Par 42, SSS 42.
Course Designer Abercrombie **Location** off A30 past Hayle onto A3074
Telephone for further details
Hotel ★★★ 73% HL Tregenna Castle Hotel, ST IVES ☎ 01736 795254 🖹 01736 795254 81 en suite

ST JUST (NEAR LAND'S END)
Map 2 SW33

Cape Cornwall Golf & Leisure Resort Cape Cornwall TR19 7NL
☎ 01736 788611   🖹 01736 788611
e-mail: terryglazebrook@capecornwall.com
web: www.capecornwall.com
Coastal parkland, walled course. The walls are an integral part of its design. Britain's first and last 18-hole course overlooking the only Cape in England, with views of the north Cornwall coast and old fishing coves. Features a flat front nine followed by a challenging back nine. Extremely scenic wild coastal views.
Cape Cornwall Golf & Country Club: 18 Holes, 5529yds, Par 69, SSS 68, Course record 64. Club membership 750.

continued

ST MELLION

CORNWALL - ST MELLION - MAP 2 SX36

Set among 450 acres of glorious Cornish countryside, St Mellion with its two outstanding courses is heralded as the premier golf and country club in the south-west. The Old Course is perfect for golfers of all abilities. Complete with well-sited bunkers, strategically tiered greens and difficult water features, this is definitely not a course to be overlooked. But if you really want to test your game, then head to the renowned Nicklaus Course, designed by the great man himself. On its opening in 1998 Jack declared, 'St Mellion is potentially the finest golf course in Europe'. The spectacularly sculptured fairways and carpet greens of the Nicklaus Course are a challenge and an inspiration to all golfers.

PL12 6SD ☎ 01579 351351 ▤ 01579 350537
e-mail: stmellion@crown-golf.co.uk **web:** www.st-mellion.co.uk
Nicklaus Signature Course: 18 Holes, 6592yds, Par 72, SSS 74, Course record 63.
Kernow Course: 18 Holes, 5500yds, Par 68, SSS 68, Course record 60. Club membership 1000.
Visitors Mon-Sun & BHs. Booking required. Dress code. **Societies** booking required. **Green Fees** Nicklaus Course Mon-Wed £60 per 18 holes, Thu-Fri £65, weekends £75. Kernow Course from £25 **Course Designer** Kernow Course H J Stutt/Jack Nicklaus **Prof** David Moon **Facilities** ⑪ ⑩¦ ⅃ ⬚ ⅌ ⅃ ⬥ ◇ ⬦ ⬥ ⬦ ☀
Leisure hard tennis courts, heated indoor swimming pool, sauna, gymnasium, bowling green **Conf** facs Corporate Hospitality Days **Location** A38 to Saltash, onto A388 to Callington
Hotel ★★★ 85% HL Horn of Plenty, GULWORTHY ☎ 01822 832528 ▤ 01822 832528 10 en suite

Visitors Mon–Sun & BHs. Booking required Fri–Sun & BHs. Dress code. **Societies** welcome. **Green Fees** £25 per round (£30 Fri-Sun) **Course Designer** Bob Hamilton **Prof** Jonathan Lamb **Facilities** ⑪ ⑩ ⓵ ⏛ ⏂ ⏄ ⏆ ⏇ ⏈ ⏉ ⏊ ⏋ **Leisure** heated indoor swimming pool, sauna, gymnasium **Conf** facs Corporate Hospitality Days **Location** 1m W of St Just, follow brown signs for Cape Cornwall **Hotel** ★★★ 64% HL The Land's End Hotel, LANDS END ☎ 01736 871844 ▤ 01736 871844 33 en suite

ST MELLION   Map 2 SX36

St Mellion International Resort see page 51
PL12 6SD
☎ 01579 351351   ▤ 01579 350537
e-mail: stmellion@crown-golf.co.uk
web: www.st-mellion.co.uk

ST MINVER   Map 2 SW97

Roserrow Golf & Country Club Roserrow PL27 6QT
☎ 01208 863000   ▤ 01208 863002
e-mail: info@roserrow.co.uk
web: www.roserrow.co.uk/golf-cornwall.htm

Challenging par 72 course in an undulating wooded valley. Stunning views over the Cornish countryside and out to Hayle Bay. Accommodation and numerous facilities on site.

Roserrow Golf & Country Club: 18 Holes, 6551yds, Par 72, SSS 72, Course record 68. Club membership 450.

Visitors Mon–Sun & BHs. Booking required. Dress code. **Societies** booking required. **Green Fees** £17-£27 according to season **Prof** Matthew Stewart **Facilities** ⑪ ⑩ ⓵ ⏛ ⏂ ⏄ ⏆ ⏇ ⏈ **Leisure** hard tennis courts, heated indoor swimming pool, sauna, gymnasium, outdoor bowling green **Conf** facs Corporate Hospitality Days **Location** off B3314 between Wadebridge **Hotel** ★★★ 77% HL The Bedford Arms Hotel, CHENIES ☎ 01923 283301 ▤ 01923 283301 18 en suite

SALTASH   Map 2 SX45

China Fleet Country Club PL12 6LJ
☎ 01752 848668   ▤ 01752 848456
e-mail: golf@china-fleet.co.uk
web: www.china-fleet.co.uk

Parkland with river views. The 14th tee shot has to carry a lake of some 150yds.

China Fleet Country Club: 18 Holes, 6551yds, Par 72, SSS 72, Course record 69. Club membership 600.

Visitors Mon–Sun & BHs. Booking required. Dress code. **Societies** welcome. **Green Fees** phone **Course Designer** Hawtree **Prof** Damien McEvoy **Facilities** ⑪ ⑩ ⓵ ⏛ ⏂ ⏄ ⏆ ⏇ ⏈ ⏉ ⏊ **Leisure** hard tennis courts, heated indoor swimming pool, squash, sauna, gymnasium **Conf** facs Corporate Hospitality Days **Location** 1m from the Tamar Bridge **Hotel** ★★★ 77% HL China Fleet Country Club, SALTASH ☎ 01752 854664 & 854661 ▤ 01752 854664 40 en suite

TRURO   Map 2 SW84

Killiow Park Kea TR3 6AG
☎ 01872 270246   ▤ 01872 240915
e-mail: sec@killiow.co.uk
web: www.killiowgolf.co.uk

A picturesque and testing parkland course in the grounds of Killiow Estate, with mature trees, water hazards, small greens and tight fairways making this a challenge for golfers of all abilities. Five holes are played across or around water. Floodlit, all-weather driving range and practice facilities.

Killiow Golf Club: 18 Holes, 6141yds, Par 72, SSS 71. Club membership 500.

Visitors Mon–Sun & BHs. Dress code. **Societies** booking required. **Green Fees** £25 per 18 holes. Reduced winter rates **Facilities** ⑪ ⑩ ⓵ ⏛ ⏂ ⏄ ⏆ ⏇ **Leisure** 3 hole academy course **Conf** Corporate Hospitality Days **Location** 3m SW of Truro, off A39 **Hotel** ★★★ 81% HL Alverton Manor, Tregolls Road, TRURO ☎ 01872 276633 ▤ 01872 276633 33 en suite

Truro Treliske TR1 3LG
☎ 01872 278684 (manager)   ▤ 01872 225972
e-mail: trurogolfclub@tiscali.co.uk
web: www.trurogolfclub.co.uk

A picturesque and gently undulating parkland course with lovely views of the cathedral city of Truro and the surrounding countryside. The course offers a great challenge to golfers of all standards and ages. The many trees and shrubs offer open invitations for wayward balls, and with many fairways boasting out of bounds markers, play needs to be safe and sensible. Fairways are tight and the greens small and full of character, making it difficult to play to one's handicap.

18 Holes, 5306yds, Par 66, SSS 66, Course record 59. Club membership 600.

Visitors Mon–Sun & BHs. Handicap certificate. Dress code. **Societies** booking required. **Green Fees** £25 per day (£30 weekends & BHs) **Course Designer** Colt, Alison & Morrison **Prof** Nigel Bicknell **Facilities** ⑪ ⑩ ⓵ ⏛ ⏂ ⏄ ⏆ ⏇ **Conf** Corporate Hospitality Days **Location** 1.5m W on A390 towards Redruth, adjacent to Treliske Hospital **Hotel** ★★★ 81% HL Alverton Manor, Tregolls Road, TRURO ☎ 01872 276633 ▤ 01872 276633 33 en suite

WADEBRIDGE   Map 2 SW97

St Kew St Kew Highway PL30 3EF
☎ 01208 841500   ▤ 01208 841500
e-mail: stkewgolf@btconnect.com
web: www.thisisnorthcornwall.com

An interesting, well-laid out nine-hole parkland course with six holes with water and 15 bunkers. In a picturesque setting there are 10 par 4s and eight par 3s. No handicap certificate required but some

continued

experience of the game is essential. Nine extra tees have now been provided allowing a different teeing area for the back nine.

St Kew Golf Course: 9 Holes, 4550yds, Par 64, SSS 62, Course record 63. Club membership 350.

Visitors Mon-Sun & BHs. Booking required. Dress code. **Societies** welcome. **Green Fees** £15 for 18 holes, £11 for 9 holes **Course Designer** David Derry **Prof** Mike Derry **Facilities** ⛳ ⛴ 🏌 🛒 🍴 ⚐ ♣ ⚙ ♣ **Leisure** fishing, ten pin bowling from end of 2005 **Conf** Corporate Hospitality Days **Location** 2m N of Wadebridge main A39
Hotel ★★★ 74% SHL Trehellas House Hotel & Restaurant, Washaway, BODMIN ☎ 01208 72700 🗎 01208 72700 12 en suite

CUMBRIA

ALSTON   Map 12 NY74

Alston Moor The Hermitage CA9 3DB
☎ 01434 381675 & 382614 (Sec)   🗎 01434 381675

10 Holes, 5518yds, Par 68, SSS 66, Course record 67.
Facilities ⛴ 🍴 🛒 **Location** 1 S of Alston on B6277
Telephone for further details
Hotel ★★★ 78% CHH Lovelady Shield Country House, ALSTON ☎ 01434 381203 & 381305 🗎 01434 381203 10 en suite

APPLEBY-IN-WESTMORLAND   Map 12 NY62

Appleby Brackenber Moor CA16 6LP
☎ 017683 51432   🗎 017683 52773
e-mail: enquiries@applebygolfclub.co.uk
web: www.applebygolfclub.co.uk
This remotely situated heather and moorland course offers interesting golf with the rewarding bonus of several long par 4 holes that will be remembered and challenging par 3s. There are superb views of the Pennines and the Lakeland hills. Renowned for the excellent greens and very good drainage.

18 Holes, 5993yds, Par 68, SSS 69, Course record 61. Club membership 800.
Visitors Mon-Sun & BHs. Dress code. **Societies** welcome. **Green Fees** £31 per day, £24 per round (£37/£30 weekends & BHs) **Course Designer** Willie Fernie **Prof** Andrew Sowerby **Facilities** ⛳ 🍴 🏌 🛒 🍴 ⚙ ♣ **Leisure** buggy for disabled use **Conf** Corporate Hospitality Days **Location** 2m E of Appleby 0.5m off A66
Hotel ★★★★ 76% CHH Appleby Manor Country House, Roman Road, APPLEBY-IN-WESTMORLAND ☎ 017683 51571 🗎 017683 51571 30 en suite

ASKAM-IN-FURNESS   Map 7 SD27

Dunnerholme Duddon Rd LA16 7AW
☎ 01229 462675 & 467421 🗎 01229 462675
e-mail: dunnerholmegolfclub@btinternet.com
Unique 10-hole (18-tee) links course with view of the Cumbrian mountains and Morecambe Bay. Two streams run through and around the course, providing water hazards on the 1st, 2nd, 3rd and 9th holes. The par 3 6th is the feature hole on the course, playing to an elevated green on Dunnerholme Rock, an imposing limestone outcrop jutting out into the estuary.

10 Holes, 6138yds, Par 72, SSS 69. Club membership 450.

Visitors handicap certificate required. Dress code. **Societies** welcome. **Green Fees** not confirmed **Facilities** ⛴ 🍴 🛒 **Location** 1m N on A595
Hotel ★★ 67% HL Lisdoonie, 307/309 Abbey Road, BARROW-IN-FURNESS ☎ 01229 827312 🗎 01229 827312 12 en suite

BARROW-IN-FURNESS   Map 7 SD26

Barrow Rakesmoor Ln, Hawcoat LA14 4QB
☎ 01229 825444
e-mail: barrowgolf@supanet.com
Pleasant course laid out on two levels of meadowland, with extensive views of the nearby Lakeland fells and west to the Irish Sea. Upper level is affected by easterly winds.

18 Holes, 6010yds, Par 71, SSS 70, Course record 65. Club membership 520.
Visitors Mon-Sat except BHs. Booking required Sat. Handicap certificate. Dress code. **Societies** welcome. **Green Fees** not confirmed **Course Designer** A M Duncan **Prof** Mike Newton **Facilities** 🛒 🖺 **Location** M6 junct 35, A590 towards Barrow. 2m to K Papermill, left to top of hill
Hotel ★★★ 80% HL Clarence House Country Hotel & Restaurant, Skelgate, DALTON-IN-FURNESS ☎ 01229 462508 🗎 01229 462508 19 en suite

Furness Central Dr LA14 3LN
☎ 01229 471232 🗎 01229 475100
e-mail: furnessgolfclub@chessbroadband.co.uk
web: www.furnessgolfclub.co.uk
Links golf with a fairly flat first half but a much sterner second nine played across subtle sloping ground. There are good views of the Lakes and the Isle of Man.

18 Holes, 6363yds, Par 71, SSS 71, Course record 65. Club membership 600.
Visitors Mon-Sun & BHs. Booking required. Handicap certificate. Dress code. **Societies** booking required. **Green Fees** not confirmed **Facilities** ⛳ 🍴 🏌 🛒 🍴 🛒 ⚙ **Conf** Corporate Hospitality Days **Location** 1.75 W of town centre off A590 to Walney Island
Hotel ★★ 67% HL Lisdoonie, 307/309 Abbey Road, BARROW-IN-FURNESS ☎ 01229 827312 🗎 01229 827312 12 en suite

BOWNESS-ON-WINDERMERE   Map 7 SD49

Windermere Cleabarrow LA23 3NB
☎ 015394 43123 🗎 015394 46370
e-mail: office@windermeregc.demon.co.uk
web: www.windermeregolfclub.net
Located in the heart of the Lake District, just 2m from Windermere. The course offers some of the finest views in the country. Not a long course but makes up for its lack of distance with heather and tight undulating fairways. The 6th hole has a nerve wracking but exhilarating blind shot - 160yds over a rocky face to a humpy fairway with a lake to avoid on the second shot.

18 Holes, 5151yds, Par 67, SSS 65, Course record 58. Club membership 890.
Visitors Mon-Sun & BHs. Dress code. **Societies** welcome. **Green Fees** £38 per round (£44 weekends & BHs) **Course Designer** G Lowe **Prof** Simon Edwards **Facilities** ⛳ 🍴 🏌 🛒 🍴 🛒 🖺 ⚐ ⚙ 🏌 ♣ **Leisure** snooker **Conf** Corporate Hospitality Days **Location** B5284 1.5m from Bowness

continued

Hotel ★★ 72% HL Queen's Head Hotel, Main Street, HAWKSHEAD
☎ 015394 36271 📄 015394 36722 13 en suite

BRAMPTON   Map 12 NY56

Brampton Tarn Rd CA8 1HN
☎ 016977 2255 📄 016977 41487
e-mail: secretary@bramptongolfclub.com
web: www.bramptongolfclub.com

Undulating heathland course set in rolling fell country. A number
of particularly fine holes, the pick of which may arguably be the
lengthy 3rd and 11th. The challenging nature of the course is
complemented by unspoilt panoramic views of the Lake District,
Pennines and southern Scotland.

*18 Holes, 6407yds, Par 72, SSS 71, Course record 64.
Club membership 750.*

Visitors Mon-Sun & BHs. Booking required weekends & BHs.
Handicap certificate. Dress code. **Societies** welcome. **Green
Fees** £44 per day, £33 per round (£50/£40 weekends & BHs) **Course
Designer** James Braid **Prof** Stewart Wilkinson **Facilities** ⑪ 🍴
📠 ⌨ 🍽 ⚲ 🏠 ⛴ 🏌 ⛳ 🏁 **Leisure** games room
Conf Corporate Hospitality Days **Location** 1.5m SE of Brampton on
B6413
Hotel ★★★ HL Farlam Hall, BRAMPTON ☎ 016977 46234
📄 016977 46234 12 en suite

CARLISLE   Map 11 NY35

Carlisle Aglionby CA4 8AG
☎ 01228 513029 (secretary) 📄 01228 513303
e-mail: secretary@carlislegolfclub.org
web: www.carlislegolfclub.org
Majestic, long-established parkland course with great appeal
providing a secure habitat for red squirrels and deer. A complete

but not too severe test of golf, with fine turf, natural hazards,
streams and many beautiful trees; no two holes are similar.

*18 Holes, 6263yds, Par 71, SSS 70, Course record 63.
Club membership 700.*

Visitors Mon, Wed-Fri, Sun & BHs. **Societies** welcome. **Green
Fees** £60 per day, £40 per round **Course Designer** Mackenzie Ross
Prof Graeme Lisle **Facilities** ⑪ 🍴 📠 ⌨ 🍽 ⚲ 🏠 ⛴ 🏌
🚜 ⛳ 🏁 **Conf** facs Corporate Hospitality Days **Location** M6
junct 43, 0.5m E on A69
Hotel ★★★ 80% HL Crown, Wetheral, CARLISLE
☎ 01228 561888 📄 01228 561888 51 en suite

Stony Holme Municipal CA1 1LS
☎ 01228 625511 📄 01228 625511
web: www.carlisleleisure.com

18 Holes, 5783yds, Par 69, SSS 68, Course record 64.
Prof S Ling **Facilities** ⑪ 🍴 📠 ⌨ 🍽 ⚲ 🏠 ⛴ 🏌 ⛳ 🏁
Conf Corporate Hospitality Days **Location** M6 junct 43, A69, 2m W
Telephone for further details
Hotel ★★★ 66% HL The Crown & Mitre, 4 English Street, CARLISLE
☎ 01228 525491 📄 01228 525491 95 en suite

COCKERMOUTH   Map 11 NY13

Cockermouth, Embleton CA13 9SG
☎ 017687 76223 & 76941 📄 017687 76941
e-mail: secretary@cockermouthgolf.co.uk
web: www.cockermouthgolf.co.uk

Fell course, fenced, with exceptional views of Lakeland hills and
valleys and the Solway Firth. A hard climb on the 3rd and 11th holes.
Testing holes: 10th and 16th (rearranged by James Braid).

*18 Holes, 5410yds, Par 69, SSS 66, Course record 62.
Club membership 400.*

Visitors Mon-Sun & BHs. Booking required weekends. Dress code.
Societies booking required. **Green Fees** £22 per day (£27 weekends
and BHs). Winter £15/£20 **Course Designer** J Braid **Facilities** 📠 ⌨
🍽 ⚲ 🏌 **Leisure** snooker table **Conf** Corporate Hospitality Days
Location 3m E off A66
Hotel ★★★ 83% HL The Trout, Crown Street, COCKERMOUTH
☎ 01900 823591 📄 01900 823591 49 en suite

CROSBY-ON-EDEN
Map 12 NY45

Eden CA6 4RA
☎ 01228 573003 📠 01228 818435
e-mail: info@edengolf.co.uk
web: www.edengolf.co.uk

Open, championship-length parkland course following the River Eden. Tight tree lined fairways and numerous natural water hazards mark this course out as a great test of golf. The nine hole Hadrian's course is set in natural undulating surroundings and has a contrasting style to the main 18.

Eden: 18 Holes, 6432yds, Par 72, SSS 71, Course record 64.
Hadrian's: 9 Holes, 6524yds, Par 72, SSS 71.
Club membership 700.

Visitors Mon-Sun & BHs. Booking required weekends & BHs. Dress code. **Societies** booking required. **Green Fees** Eden Course £28 (£35 weekends & BHs). Hadrian's £12/£15 **Course Designer** A G M Wannop **Prof** Steve Harrison **Facilities** ⊕ 🍴 🖿 ⬜ 🏌 ⚲ 🎯 ♪ 🏌 ⚑ **Leisure** hard tennis courts, marquee & garden site for functions **Conf** facs Corporate Hospitality Days **Location** M6 junct 44, 5m on A689 towards Brampton
Hotel BUD Travelodge Carlisle Todhills, A74 Southbound, Todhills, CARLISLE ☎ 08719 846 127 📠 08719 846 127 40 en suite

GRANGE-OVER-SANDS
Map 7 SD47

Grange Fell Fell Rd LA11 6HB
☎ 015395 32536

A fell course with no excessive climbing and dependant on how straight you hit the ball. Fine views in all directions.

9 Holes, 5292yds, Par 70, SSS 66, Course record 65.
Club membership 300.

Visitors Dress code. **Green Fees** £15 per day (£20 weekends & BHs) **Course Designer** A B Davy **Facilities** ⬜ ⚲ **Location** 1m W on Grange-Over-Sands towards Cartmel
Hotel ★★★ 80% HL Netherwood, Lindale Road, GRANGE-OVER-SANDS ☎ 015395 32552 📠 015395 32552 32 en suite

Grange-over-Sands Meathop Rd LA11 6QX
☎ 015395 33180 📠 015395 33754
e-mail: grangegolfclub@tiscali.co.uk
web: www.grangegolfclub.co.uk

Interesting parkland course with well-sited tree plantations, ditches and water features which has recently been drained and extended. The five par 3s are considered to be some of the best in the area.

18 Holes, 6120yds, Par 70, SSS 69, Course record 64.
Club membership 500.

Visitors Mon-Wed, Fri, Sun except BHs. **Societies** welcome. **Green Fees** £35 per day, £28 per round **Course Designer** Dr A Mackenzie (part) **Prof** Nick Lowe **Facilities** ⊕ 🍴 🖿 ⬜ 🏌 ⚲ 🎯 ♪ 🏌 ⚑ ♪ **Conf** Corporate Hospitality Days **Location** NE of town centre off B5277
Hotel ★★★ 68% HL Graythwaite Manor, Fernhill Road, GRANGE-OVER-SANDS ☎ 015395 32001 & 33755 📠 015395 32001 24 en suite

KENDAL
Map 7 SD59

Carus Green Burneside Rd LA9 6EB
☎ 01539 721097 📠 01539 721097
e-mail: info@carusgreen.co.uk
web: www.carusgreen.co.uk

Flat 18-hole course surrounded by the rivers Kent and Mint with an open view of the Kentmere and Howgill fells. The course is a mixture of relatively easy and difficult holes. These rivers come into play on five holes and there are also a number of ponds and bunkers.

Carus Green Golf Course & Driving Range:
18 Holes, 5691yds, Par 70, SSS 68, Course record 65.
Club membership 600.

Visitors Mon-Sun & BHs. Booking required. Dress code, **Societies** booking required. **Green Fees** £20 per round (£22 weekends & BHs). **Course Designer** W Adamson **Prof** D Turner/A Pickering **Facilities** 🖿 ⬜ 🏌 ⚲ 🎯 ♪ 🏌 ⚑ ♪ **Conf** Corporate Hospitality Days **Location** 1m from Kendal centre
Hotel ★★★ 71% HL Riverside Hotel Kendal, Beezon Road, Stramongate Bridge, KENDAL ☎ 01539 734861 📠 01539 734861 47 en suite

Kendal The Heights LA9 4PQ
☎ 01539 723499 (pro)
e-mail: secretary@kendalgolfclub.co.uk
web: www.kendalgolfclub.co.uk

Elevated parkland and fell course with breathtaking views of Lakeland fells and the surrounding district.

18 Holes, 5737yds, Par 70, SSS 68, Course record 65.
Club membership 450.

Visitors Mon-Fri, Sun & BHs. Booking required. Handicap certificate. Dress code. **Societies** booking required. **Green Fees** £36 per day, £25 per round (£44/£30 Sun) **Prof** Ben Waller **Facilities** ⊕ 🍴 🖿 ⬜ 🏌 ⚲ 🎯 ♪ 🏌 ⚑ **Leisure** Golf clinic with computer analysis. **Location** 1m W of town centre, turn left at town hall and follow signposts
Hotel ★★★ 83% HL Best Western Castle Green Hotel in Kendal, KENDAL ☎ 01539 734000 📠 01539 734000 100 en suite

KESWICK
Map 11 NY22

Keswick Threlkeld Hall, Threlkeld CA12 4SX
☎ 017687 79324 📠 017687 79861
e-mail: secretary@keswickgolfclub.com
web: www.keswickgolf.com

A challenging parkland course. Not very long but a good test of golf.

18 Holes, 6225yds, Par 71, SSS 70, Course record 67.
Club membership 586.

Visitors Mon-Sun & BHs. Booking required. Dress code. **Societies** booking required. **Green Fees** not confirmed **Course Designer** Eric Brown **Prof** Gary Watson **Facilities** ⊕ 🍴 🖿 ⬜

continued

🍴 🏌 🏠 ⛳ ✦ 🛺 ✦ Leisure driving net Conf Corporate Hospitality Days Location 4m E of Keswick, off A66
Hotel ★★★★ 78% HL Wordsworth, GRASMERE ☎ 015394 35592 📠 015394 35592 36 en suite

KIRKBY LONSDALE
Map 7 SD67

Kirkby Lonsdale Scaleber Ln, Barbon LA6 2LJ
☎ 015242 76365   📠 015242 76503
e-mail: klgolf@dial.pipex.com
web: www.klgolf.dial.pipex.com
Parkland on the east bank of the River Lune and crossed by Barbon Beck. Mainly following the lie of the land, the gently undulating course uses the beck to provide water hazards.
18 Holes, 6542yds, Par 72, SSS 71, Course record 64.
Club membership 500.
Visitors handicap certificate. Dress code. **Societies** booking required.
Green Fees £35 per day **Course Designer** Bill Squires **Prof** Paul Brunt
Facilities 🍴 🍽 🏌 ⛳ 🍴 🏌 🏠 ⛳ 🛺 ✦ **Conf** Corporate Hospitality Days **Location** 3m NE of Kirkby Lonsdale on A683
Hotel ★★ 75% HL The Whoop Hall, Burrow with Burrow, KIRKBY LONSDALE ☎ 015242 71284 📠 015242 71284 24 en suite

MARYPORT
Map 11 NY03

Maryport Bankend CA15 6PA
☎ 01900 812605   📠 01900 815626
e-mail: maryportgolfclub@tiscali.co.uk
A tight seaside links course exposed to Solway breezes. Fine views across Solway Firth. Course comprises nine links holes and nine parkland holes, and small streams can be hazardous on several holes. The first three holes have the seashore on their left and an errant tee shot can land in the water. Holes 6-14 are parkland in quality, gently undulating and quite open. Holes 15-18 revert to links.
18 Holes, 5982yds, Par 70, SSS 69, Course record 65.
Club membership 486.
Visitors Mon-Sun except BHs. Booking required Wed, Thu, weekends & BHs. Dress code. **Societies** welcome. **Green Fees** not confirmed
Facilities 🍴 🍽 🏌 ⛳ 🍴 🏌 ⛳ 🛺 ✦ **Location** 1m N on B5300
Hotel ★★★ 82% HL Washington Central, Washington Street, WORKINGTON ☎ 01900 65772 📠 01900 65772 46 en suite

PENRITH
Map 12 NY53

Penrith Salkeld Rd CA11 8SG
☎ 01768 891919   📠 01768 891919
e-mail: secretary@penrithgolfclub.co.uk
A beautiful and well-balanced course, always changing direction, and demanding good length from the tee. It is set on rolling moorland with occasional pine trees and some fine views.
18 Holes, 6047yds, Par 69, SSS 69, Course record 63.
Club membership 850.
Visitors Mon-Sun & BHs. Booking required Mon & Fri-Sun. Handicap certificate. Dress code. **Societies** booking required. **Green Fees** £35 per day, £30 per round (£40/£35 weekends). **Prof** Garry Key **Facilities** 🍴 🍽 🏌 ⛳ 🍴 🏌 🏠 ⛳ 🛺 ✦ ✦ **Conf** facs Corporate Hospitality Days **Location** M6 junct 41, A6 to Penrith, left after 30mph sign
Hotel ★★★ 75% HL George, Devonshire Street, PENRITH ☎ 01768 862696 📠 01768 862696 35 en suite

ST BEES
Map 11 NX91

St Bees Peckmill, Beach Rd CA27 0EJ
☎ 01946 824300
Picturesque 10-hole layout on the cliffs overlooking St Bees beach with views of the Solway Firth and the Isle of Man. Not overly long but testing for golfers of all abilities.
9 Holes, 5306yds, Par 66, SSS 66, Course record 64.
Club membership 400.
Visitors Mon-Sun & BHs. Booking required Wed & weekends. Handicap certificate. **Societies** booking required. **Green Fees** £12 per day **Facilities** ⛳ 🍴 🏌 **Location** 0.5m W of village off B5345
Hotel ★★★ 75% HL Ennerdale Country House, CLEATOR ☎ 01946 813907 📠 01946 813907 30 en suite

SEASCALE
Map 6 NY00

Seascale The Banks CA20 1QL
☎ 019467 28202   📠 019467 28042
e-mail: seascalegolfclub@googlemail.com
web: www.seascalegolfclub.co.uk
A tough links requiring length and control. The natural terrain is used to give a variety of holes and considerable character. Undulating greens add to the challenge. Fine views of the western fells, the Irish Sea and the Isle of Man.
18 Holes, 6416yds, Par 71, SSS 72, Course record 64.
Club membership 700.
Visitors Mon, Tues, Thu-Sun & BHs. Booking required. Handicap certificate. Dress code. **Societies** booking required. **Green Fees** £40 per day, £35 per round (£40/£45 weekends & BHs) **Course Designer** Willie Campbell **Facilities** 🍴 🍽 🏌 ⛳ 🍴 🏌 ⛳ 🛺 ✦ ✦ **Conf** facs Corporate Hospitality Days **Location** NW side of village off B5344
Hotel ★★ 74% HL Bower House Inn, ESKDALE GREEN, Holmrook ☎ 019467 23244 📠 019467 23244 29 en suite

SEDBERGH — Map 7 SD69

Sedbergh Dent Rd LA10 5SS
☎ 015396 21551 📠 015396 21551
e-mail: info@sedberghgolfclub.co.uk
web: www.sedberghgolfclub.co.uk

A tree-lined parkland course with superb scenery in the Yorkshire Dales National Park. Undulating fairways cross or are adjacent to the Dee and Rawthey rivers. Well guarded greens and many water features make the course a test for golfers of all abilities.

9 Holes, 5624yds, Par 70, SSS 68, Course record 66. Club membership 250.

Visitors contact club for details. **Societies** booking required. **Green Fees** £20 per 18 holes, £14 per 9 holes **Course Designer** W G Squires **Facilities** ⑪ ▶ ♀ ⑨ ♪ 🐴 ♪ **Leisure** fishing **Conf** facs Corporate Hospitality Days **Location** 1m S off A683
Hotel ★★★ 83% HL Best Western Castle Green Hotel in Kendal, KENDAL ☎ 01539 734000 📠 01539 734000 100 en suite

SILECROFT — Map 6 SD18

Silecroft Silecroft, Millom LA18 4NX
☎ 01229 774250 & 770467 (Sec)
e-mail: silecroftgcsec@aol.com
web: www.silecroftgolfclub.co.uk

Seaside links course parallel to the coast of the Irish Sea with spectacular views inland of Lakeland hills. Looks deceptively easy but an ever present sea breeze ensures a sporting challenge.

9 Holes, 5896yds, Par 68, SSS 68, Course record 66. Club membership 220.

Visitors Mon-Sun. By arrangement BHs. Handicap certificate. Dress code. **Societies** welcome. **Green Fees** £15 per day (£20 weekends & BHs). **Facilities** ▲ **Location** 3m W of Millom
Hotel ★★★ 77% HL Abbey House, Abbey Road, BARROW-IN-FURNESS ☎ 01229 838282 📠 01229 838282 57 en suite

SILLOTH — Map 11 NY15

Silloth on Solway The Clubhouse CA7 4BL
☎ 016973 31304 📠 016973 31782
e-mail: office@sillothgolfclub.co.uk
web: www.sillothgolfclub.co.uk

Billowing dunes, narrow fairways, heather and gorse and the constant subtle problems of tactics and judgement make these superb links on the Solway an exhilarating and searching test. The 13th is a good long hole. Superb views.

18 Holes, 6108yds, Par 72, SSS 69, Course record 59. Club membership 700.

Visitors handicap certificate. Dress code. **Societies** welcome. **Green Fees** £40 per day (£52 per round weekends) **Course Designer** David Grant/Willie Park Jnr **Prof** J Graham **Facilities** ⑪ ⓞ ▶ ♀ ⑨ ▲ 🐴 ♪ **Conf** facs Corporate Hospitality Days **Location** S side of village off B5300
Hotel ★★ 68% HL Golf Hotel, Criffel Street, SILLOTH ☎ 016973 31438 📠 016973 31438 22 en suite

ULVERSTON — Map 7 SD27

Ulverston Bardsea Park LA12 9QJ
☎ 01229 582824 📠 01229 588910
e-mail: enquiries@ulverstongolf.co.uk
web: www.ulverstongolf.co.uk

Undulating parkland course overlooking Morecambe Bay with extensive views to the Lakeland Fells.

18 Holes, 6191yds, Par 71, SSS 70, Course record 64. Club membership 828.

Visitors contact club for details. **Societies** welcome. **Green Fees** phone **Course Designer** A Herd/H S Colt **Prof** P A Stoller **Facilities** ⑪ ⓞ ▶ ♀ ⑨ ▲ 🐴 ♪ **Leisure** practice ball dispensing machine **Conf** Corporate Hospitality Days **Location** 2m S off A5087
Hotel ★★★ 74% HL Whitewater, The Lakeland Village, NEWBY BRIDGE ☎ 015395 31133 📠 015395 31133 35 en suite

WINDERMERE
See **Bowness-on-Windermere**

WORKINGTON — Map 11 NY02

Workington Branthwaite Rd CA14 4SS
☎ 01900 603460 📠 01900 607123
e-mail: workingtongolf@aol.com

Meadowland course, undulating, with natural hazards created by stream and trees. Good views of Solway Firth and Lakeland Hills. 10th, 13th and 15th holes are particularly testing.

Workington Golf Club Ltd: 18 Holes, 6217yds, Par 72, SSS 70, Course record 65. Club membership 735.

Visitors Mon-Sun & BHs. Handicap certificate. Dress code. **Societies** booking required **Green Fees** not confirmed **Course Designer** James Braid **Prof** Aidrian Drabble **Facilities** ⑪ ⓞ ▶ ♀ ⑨ ▲ 🐴 🐴 ♪ **Leisure** snooker table **Conf** facs **Location** 1.75m E off A596
Hotel ★★★ 82% HL Washington Central, Washington Street, WORKINGTON ☎ 01900 65772 📠 01900 65772 46 en suite

DERBYSHIRE

ALFRETON
Map 8 SK45

Alfreton Wingfield Rd, Oakerthorpe DE55 7LH
☎ 01773 832070
e-mail: bradleyalton@aol.com
web: www.alfretongolfclub.co.uk
A small, well-established parkland course with tight fairways and many natural hazards.

11 Holes, 5393yds, Par 67, SSS 66, Course record 66. Club membership 350.

Visitors Mon-Fri & BHs. Booking required. Handicap certificate. Dress code. **Societies** booking required, **Green Fees** £28 per day, £20 per round **Prof** Neville Hallam **Facilities** ⑪ by prior arrangement ⑪ by prior arrangement ⓑ ⌨ ⑪ ⛬ ⌂ ✐ **Conf** facs Corporate Hospitality Days **Location** 1m W on A615
Hotel ★★★ 77% HL Santo's Higham Farm Hotel, Main Road, HIGHAM ☎ 01773 833812 ⓑ 01773 833812 28 en suite

ASHBOURNE
Map 7 SK14

Ashbourne Wyaston Rd DE6 1NB
☎ 01335 347960 (pro shop)
e-mail: ashbourne.golf.club@gmail.com
web: www.ashbournegolfclub.co.uk
With fine views over surrounding countryside, the course uses natural contours and water features.

18 Holes, 6308yds, Par 71, SSS 71. Club membership 650.
Visitors Mon-Fri except BHs. Booking required. Dress code. **Societies** welcome. **Green Fees** £20 per 18 holes **Course Designer** D Hemstock **Prof** Andrew Smith **Facilities** ⑪ ⑪ ⓑ ⌨ ⑪ ⛬ ⌂ ⛟ ✐ **Leisure** snooker table **Location** off Wyaston Rd, club signed
Hotel ★★★ 82% CHH Callow Hall, Mappleton Road, ASHBOURNE ☎ 01335 300900 ⓑ 01335 300900 16 en suite

BAKEWELL
Map 8 SK26

Bakewell Station Rd DE45 1GB
☎ 01629 812307
e-mail: administrator@bakewellgolfclub.co.uk
web: www.bakewellgolfclub.org.uk
Hilly parkland course with plenty of natural hazards to test the golfer. Magnificent views across the Wye Valley.

9 Holes, 5240yds, Par 68, SSS 66, Course record 68. Club membership 340.
Visitors contact club for details. **Societies** booking required. **Green Fees** £20 per day (£25 Sun & BHs) **Facilities** ⑪ ⑪ ⓑ ⌨ ⑪ ⛬ **Conf** Corporate Hospitality Days **Location** from A619 (bridge over River Wye) right up hill (Station Rd) past the industrial estate, club 200 yds on left
Hotel ★★★ 70% HL Rutland Arms, The Square, BAKEWELL ☎ 01629 812812 ⓑ 01629 812812 35 en suite

BAMFORD
Map 8 SK28

Sickleholme Saltergate Ln S33 0BN
☎ 01433 651306 ⓑ 01433 659498
e-mail: sickleholme.gc@btconnect.com
web: www.sickleholme.co.uk
Undulating downland course in the lovely Peak District, with rivers and ravines and spectacular scenery.

18 Holes, 6064yds, Par 69, SSS 69, Course record 62. Club membership 700.
Visitors Mon-Sun & BHs. Booking required. Handicap certificate. Dress code. **Societies** booking required. **Green Fees** £29 per round/day (£34 weekends) **Prof** P H Taylor **Facilities** ⑪ ⑪ ⓑ ⌨ ⑪ ⛬ ⌂ ✐ **Conf** Corporate Hospitality Days **Location** 0.75m S on A6013
Hotel ★★★ 81% HL George Hotel, Main Road, HATHERSAGE ☎ 01433 650436 & 0845 456 0581 ⓑ 01433 650436 22 en suite

BREADSALL
Map 8 SK33

Marriot Breadsall Priory Hotel & Country Club Moor Rd, Morley DE7 6DL
☎ 01332 836016 ⓑ 01332 836089
e-mail: ian.knox@marriotthotels.com
web: www.breadsallpriorygolf.com
Set in 200 acres of mature undulating parkland, the Priory Course is built on the site of a 13th-century priory. Full use has been made of natural features and fine old trees. A degree of accuracy is required to play small protected greens along tree lined fairways. Signature hole is the 16th. In contrast the Moorland Course is a sand based course allowing all year round play to full greens. Slighter wider fairways allow for more attacking tee shots but beware of well-placed bunkers, trees and rough. At the 13th the tee shot is narrow with trees and bushes lining the fairway.

Priory Course: 18 Holes, 6054yds, Par 70, SSS 69, Course record 63.
Moorland Course: 18 Holes, 6028yds, Par 70, SSS 69. Club membership 800.
Visitors Mon-Sun & BHs. Dress code. **Societies** booking required. **Green Fees** from £45 **Course Designer** D Steel **Prof** Darren Steels **Facilities** ⑪ ⑪ ⓑ ⌨ ⑪ ⛬ ⌂ ⛟ ◇ ⛾ ✐ ⚑ **Leisure** hard tennis courts, heated indoor swimming pool, sauna, gymnasium **Conf** facs Corporate Hospitality Days **Location** From S, M1 junct 28, filter left towards Derby at 1st rdbt, left at 2nd rdbt into Breadsall Village, left into Rectory Lane. follow road right and turn left into Moor Rd, hotel on left.
Hotel ★★★★ 74% HL Marriott Breadsall Priory Hotel & Country Club, Moor Road, MORLEY ☎ 01332 832235 ⓑ 01332 832235 112 en suite

BUXTON
Map 7 SK07

Buxton & High Peak, Waterswallows Rd SK17 7EN
☎ 01298 26263 ⓑ 01298 26333
e-mail: admin@bhpgc.co.uk
web: www.bhpgc.co.uk
Bracing, well-drained meadowland course, the highest in Derbyshire. Challenging course where wind direction is a major factor on some holes; others require blind shots to sloping greens.

18 Holes, 5966yds, Par 69, SSS 69. Club membership 650.
Visitors handicap certificate. Dress code. **Societies** booking required.

continued

Green Fees £30 per day, £24 per round (£36/£30 weekends & BHs)
Course Designer J Morris Prof John Lines Facilities ⊕ ⦿ by prior
arrangement 🏌 ♿ 🍴 🚶 🗄 🚲 💈 Conf facs
Corporate Hospitality Days Location 1m NE off A6
Hotel ★★★★ 72% HL Barceló Buxton Palace Hotel, Palace Road,
BUXTON ☎ 01298 22001 📠 01298 22001 122 en suite

Cavendish Gadley Ln SK17 6XD
☎ 01298 79708   📠 01298 79708
e-mail: admin@cavendishgolfcourse.com
web: www.@cavendishgolfcourse.com

This parkland and moorland course with its comfortable clubhouse
nestles below the rising hills. Generally open to the prevailing west
wind, it is noted for its excellent surfaced greens which contain
many deceptive subtleties. Designed by Dr Alastair McKenzie,
the course has skilfully managed to preserve the character of his
original design.

18 Holes, 5721yds, Par 68, SSS 68, Course record 61.
Club membership 500.

Visitors Mon-Fri, Sun & BHs. Booking required. Dress code.
Societies booking required. Green Fees phone Course Designer Dr
Mackenzie Prof Simon Townend Facilities ⊕ by prior arrangement
⦿ by prior arrangement 🏌 ♿ 🍴 🚶 🗄 🚲 💈 💈
Conf facs Corporate Hospitality Days Location 0.75m W of town
centre off A53
Hotel ★★★ 79% HL Best Western Lee Wood, The Park, BUXTON
☎ 01298 23002 📠 01298 23002 40 en suite

CHAPEL-EN-LE-FRITH   Map 7 SK08

Chapel-en-le-Frith The Cockyard, Manchester Rd
SK23 9UH
☎ 01298 812118 & 813943   📠 01298 814990
e-mail: info@chapelgolf.co.uk
web: www.chapelgolf.co.uk

Scenic parkland course surrounded by hills and bordering the
picturesque Combs Reservoir. A tough but fair test for golfers at all
levels.

18 Holes, 6434yds, Par 72, SSS 71, Course record 68.
Club membership 570.

Visitors contact club for details. Societies welcome. Green
Fees phone Course Designer David Williams Prof David J Cullen
Facilities ⊕ ⦿ 🏌 ♿ 🍴 🚶 🗄 🚲 💈 Leisure snooker
room Conf Corporate Hospitality Days Location on B5470
Hotel ★★★ 79% HL Best Western Lee Wood, The Park, BUXTON
☎ 01298 23002 📠 01298 23002 40 en suite

CHESTERFIELD   Map 8 SK37

Chesterfield Walton S42 7LA
☎ 01246 279256   📠 01246 276622
e-mail: secretary@chesterfieldgolfclub.co.uk
web: www.chesterfieldgolfclub.co.uk

A varied and interesting, undulating parkland course with trees
picturesquely adding to the holes and the outlook alike. Stream hazard
on the back nine.

18 Holes, 6281yds, Par 71, SSS 70, Course record 64.
Club membership 600.

Visitors handicap certificate. Dress code. Societies booking required.
Green Fees £40 per round (£45 per round weekends) Prof Mike

McLean Facilities ⊕ ⦿ 🏌 ♿ 🍴 🚶 🗄 🚲 💈 Leisure snooker
Location 2m SW off A632
Hotel ★★★ 67% HL Sandpiper, Sheffield Road, Sheepbridge,
CHESTERFIELD ☎ 01246 450550 📠 01246 450550 46 en suite

Grassmoor Golf Centre North Wingfield Rd, Grassmoor
S42 5EA
☎ 01246 856044   📠 01246 853486
e-mail: enquiries@grassmoorgolf.co.uk
web: www.grassmoorgolf.co.uk

An 18-hole heathland course with interesting and challenging water
features, testing greens and testing par 3s.

Grassmoor Golf Centre: 18 Holes, 5723yds, Par 69, SSS 69,
Course record 67. Club membership 450.

Visitors contact club for details. Societies booking required.
Green Fees £12 per 18 holes (£15 weekends & BHs) Course
Designer Hawtree Prof Gary Hagues Facilities ⊕ 🏌 ♿ 🍴 🚶
♿ 🗄 🚲 💈 💈 Conf facs Corporate Hospitality
Days Location M1 junct 29, 4m off B6038 between Chesterfield &
Grassmoor
Hotel ★★★ 67% HL Sandpiper, Sheffield Road, Sheepbridge,
CHESTERFIELD ☎ 01246 450550 📠 01246 450550 46 en suite

Stanedge Walton Hay Farm, Stonedge, Ashover S45 0LW
☎ 01246 566156
e-mail: chrisshaw56@tiscali.co.uk
web: www.stanedgegolfclub.co.uk

Moorland course in hilly situation open to strong winds. Some
tricky short holes with narrow fairways, so accuracy is paramount.
Magnificent views over four counties.

10 Holes, 5786yds, Par 69, SSS 68, Course record 68.
Club membership 250.

Visitors Mon-Sun & BHs. Dress code. Societies booking required.
Green Fees £15 per round Facilities 🏌 ♿ 🍴 🚶 Conf Corporate
Hospitality Days Location 5m SW off B5057 near Famous Red Lion pub
Hotel ★★ 85% HL The Red House Country Hotel, Old Road, Darley
Dale, MATLOCK ☎ 01629 734854 📠 01629 734854 10 en suite

Tapton Park Tapton Park, Tapton S41 0EQ
☎ 01246 239500 & 273887
web: www.taptonparkgolfcourse.co.uk

Municipal parkland course with some fairly hard walking. The 625yd
(par 5) 5th is a testing hole.

Tapton Main: 18 Holes, 6104yds, Par 72, SSS 69.
Dobbin Clough: 9 Holes, 2613yds, Par 34.
Club membership 322.

Visitors Mon-Sun & BHs. Booking required. Dress code.
Societies booking required. Green Fees £13 per 18 holes, £7.50 per
9 holes (£16/£8.50 Fri-Sun & BHs) Prof Andrew Carnall Facilities ⊕
⦿ 🏌 ♿ 🍴 🚶 🗄 🚲 💈 Leisure 9 hole par 3 course
Conf facs Corporate Hospitality Days Location 0.5m E of Chesterfield
station
Hotel ★★★ 67% HL Sandpiper, Sheffield Road, Sheepbridge,
CHESTERFIELD ☎ 01246 450550 📠 01246 450550 46 en suite

CODNOR
Map 8 SK44

Ormonde Fields Golf & Country Club, Nottingham Rd DE5 9RG

☎ 01773 570043 (Secretary)   📠 01773 742987

Parkland course with undulating fairways and natural hazards. There is a practice area.

Ormonde Fields Golf & Country Club: 18 Holes, 6502yds, Par 71, SSS 72, Course record 68. Club membership 500.

Visitors dress code. **Societies** booking required. **Green Fees** £25 per 18 holes (£30 weekend & BHs) **Course Designer** John Fearn **Prof** Richard White **Facilities** ⑪ 🍴 🏌 ⌨ 🍽 ⚲ 🏠 🏐 🚜 ⛳ **Conf** facs Corporate Hospitality Days **Location** 1m SE on A610 **Hotel** ★★★★ 73% HL Makeney Hall Hotel, Makeney, Milford, BELPer ☎ 01332 842999 📄 01332 842999 46 en suite

DERBY
Map 8 SK33

Allestree Park Allestree Hall DE22 2EU

☎ 01332 550616   📠 01332 541195

Allestree Park Golf Course: 18 Holes, 5806yds, Par 68, SSS 68, Course record 61.

Prof Leigh Woodward **Facilities** ⑪ 🏌 ⌨ 🍽 ⚲ 🏠 🏐 ⛳ **Leisure** fishing, pool table **Conf** Corporate Hospitality Days **Location** N of Derby, A38 onto A6 N, course 1.5m on left **Telephone for further details** **Hotel** ★★★★ 74% HL Marriott Breadsall Priory Hotel & Country Club, Moor Road, MORLEY ☎ 01332 832235 📄 01332 832235 112 en suite

Mickleover Uttoxeter Rd, Mickleover DE3 9AD

☎ 01332 518662 (pro)   📠 01332 516011

Undulating parkland course of two loops of nine holes, in a pleasant setting and affording splendid country views. There is a premium in hitting tee shots in the right place for approaches to greens, some of which are on elevated plateaus. Some attractive par 3s which are considered to be very exacting.

18 Holes, 5727yds, Par 68, SSS 67, Course record 64. Club membership 800.

Visitors dress code. **Societies** booking required. **Green Fees** not confirmed **Course Designer** J Pennink **Prof** Tim Coxon **Facilities** ⑪ 🍴 🏌 ⌨ 🍽 ⚲ 🏠 🏐 ⛳ 🏐 **Conf** Corporate Hospitality Days **Location** 3m W of Derby on A516/B5020 **Hotel** ★★★★ 74% HL Menzies Mickleover Court, Etwall Road, Mickleover, DERBY ☎ 01332 521234 📄 01332 521234 99 en suite

Sinfin Wilmore Rd, Sinfin DE24 9HD

☎ 01332 766462   📠 01332 769004

e-mail: phil.dews@derby.gov.uk
web: www.sinfingolfcourse.co.uk

Municipal parkland course with tree-lined fairways established in 1923. An excellent test of golf and famous for its demanding par 4s. Generally a flat course, it is suitable for golfers of all ages.

Sinfin Golf Course: 18 Holes, 6163yds, Par 70, SSS 70, Course record 65. Club membership 244.

Visitors Mon-Sun & BHs. Dress code. **Societies** welcome. **Green Fees** not confirmed **Prof** Daniel Delaney **Facilities** ⑪ 🍴 🏌 ⌨ 🍽 ⚲ 🏠 🏐 ⛳ **Location** 2.5m S of city centre **Hotel** ★★★ 66% HL International, 288 Burton Road, DERBY ☎ 01332 369321 📄 01332 369321 62 en suite

DRONFIELD
Map 8 SK37

Hallowes Hallowes Ln S18 1UR

☎ 01246 411196   📠 01246 413753

e-mail: john.oates@hallowesgolfclub.org
web: www.hallowesgolfclub.org

Attractive moorland and parkland course in the Derbyshire hills. Several testing par 4s and splendid views.

18 Holes, 6319yds, Par 71, SSS 71, Course record 61. Club membership 630.

Visitors Mon-Fri except BHs. Handicap certificate. Dress code. **Societies** welcome. **Green Fees** not confirmed **Prof** Philip Dunn **Facilities** ⑪ 🍴 🏌 ⌨ 🍽 ⚲ 🏠 🏐 ⛳ **Leisure** short game facility, snooker **Conf** Corporate Hospitality Days **Location** S side of town, off B6057 onto Cemetery Rd and Hallowes Rise/Drive **Hotel** ★★★ 67% HL Sandpiper, Sheffield Road, Sheepbridge, CHESTERFIELD ☎ 01246 450550 📄 01246 450550 46 en suite

DUFFIELD
Map 8 SK34

Chevin Golf Ln DE56 4EE

☎ 01332 841864   📠 01332 844028

e-mail: secretary@chevingolf.fsnet.co.uk
web: www.chevingolf.co.uk

A mixture of parkland and moorland, this course is rather hilly which makes for some hard walking, but with most rewarding views of the surrounding countryside. The 8th hole, aptly named Tribulation, requires an accurate tee shot, and is one of the most difficult holes in the county.

18 Holes, 6057yds, Par 69, SSS 69, Course record 64. Club membership 750.

Visitors Mon-Fri & Sun except BHs. Booking required Tue, Thu, Fri & Sun. Handicap certificate. Dress code. **Societies** booking required. **Green Fees** £35 per day, £30 per round (£35 per round Sun) **Course Designer** J Braid **Prof** Willie Bird **Facilities** ⑪ 🍴 🏌 ⌨ 🍽 ⚲ 🏠 🏐 ⛳ **Conf** facs Corporate Hospitality Days **Location** N side of town off A6 **Hotel** ★★★★ 73% HL Makeney Hall Hotel, Makeney, Milford, BELPer ☎ 01332 842999 📄 01332 842999 46 en suite

GLOSSOP
Map 7 SK09

Glossop and District Hurst Ln, off Sheffield Rd SK13 7PU

☎ 01457 865247(club house)

Moorland course in good position, excellent natural hazards. Difficult closing hole (9th & 18th).

11 Holes, 5800yds, Par 68, SSS 68, Course record 64. Club membership 350.

Visitors dress code. **Societies** booking required. **Green Fees** phone **Prof** Mike Williams **Facilities** ⑪ 🍴 🏌 ⌨ 🍽 ⚲ 🏠 🏐 ⛳ **Location** 1m E off A57 from town centre **Hotel** ★★ 83% HL Wind in the Willows, Derbyshire Level, GLOSSOP ☎ 01457 868001 📄 01457 868001 12 en suite

HORSLEY
Map 8 SK34

Horsley Lodge Smalley Mill Rd DE21 5BL
☎ 01332 780838 🖩 01332 781118
e-mail: enquiries@horsleylodge.co.uk.
web: www.horsleylodge.co.uk.

Parkland course set in 180 acres of Derbyshire countryside, has some very challenging holes. Also floodlit driving range. Big undulating greens designed by former World Champion Peter McEvoy providing the golfer with a great test of ability.

18 Holes, 6400yds, Par 71, SSS 71, Course record 65. Club membership 650.

Visitors Mon-Sun & BHs. Booking required weekends. Dress code **Societies** booking required. **Green Fees** £30 per 18 holes (£35 weekends) **Course Designer** Bill White/Peter McEvoy **Prof** Mark Whithorn **Facilities** ⑪ ⑩ ㅗ ㄷ ㄲ ㅗ 츠 ⌂ 얘 ◇ ✔ 🛒 ✔ ♜ **Leisure** fishing **Conf** facs Corporate Hospitality Days **Location** 4m NE of Derby, off A38 at Belper then follow tourist signs **Hotel** ★★★★ 74% HL Marriott Breadsall Priory Hotel & Country Club, Moor Road, MORLEY ☎ 01332 832235 🖩 01332 832235 112 en suite

KEDLESTON
Map 8 SK34

Kedleston Park DE22 5JD
☎ 01332 840035 🖩 01332 840035
e-mail: secretary@kedleston-park-golf-club.co.uk
web: www.kedlestonparkgolf.co.uk
The course is laid out in flat mature parkland with fine trees and background views of historic Kedleston Hall (National Trust). Many testing holes are included in each nine and there is an excellent modern clubhouse.

18 Holes, 6713yds, Par 72, SSS 72, Course record 65. Club membership 681.

Visitors Mon, Tue, Thu, Fri, Sun & BHs. Booking required except Mon. Handicap certificate. Dress code. **Societies** booking required. **Green Fees** £50 per day, £40 per round (£45 per round Sun & BHs) **Course Designer** James Braid **Prof** Paul Wesselingh **Facilities** ⑪ ⑩ ㅗ ㄷ ㄲ ㅗ 츠 ⌂ 얘 ✔ 🛒 ✔ ♜ **Leisure** sauna **Conf** Corporate Hospitality Days **Location** signposted Kedleston Hall from A38 **Hotel** ★★★ 66% HL International, 288 Burton Road, DERBY ☎ 01332 369321 🖩 01332 369321 62 en suite

LONG EATON
Map 8 SK43

Trent Lock Golf Centre Lock Ln, Sawley NG10 2FY
☎ 0115 946 4398 🖩 0115 946 1183
e-mail: trentlockgolf@aol.com
Main course has two par 5, five par 3 and eleven par 4 holes, plus water features and three holes adjacent to the river. A challenging test of golf. A 22-bay floodlit golf range is available.

Main Course: 18 Holes, 5883yds, Par 69, SSS 68, Course record 67.
9 hole: 9 Holes, 2911yds, Par 36. Club membership 500.

Visitors Mon-Sun & BHs. Booking required. Dress code for Main course. **Societies** booking required. **Green Fees** 18 hole course: £17.50 per round (£22.50 weekends). 9 hole course: £6 per round (£7.50 per round weekends) **Course Designer** E McCausland **Prof** M Taylor **Facilities** ⑪ ⑩ ㅗ ㄷ ㄲ ㅗ 츠 ⌂ ✔ 🛒 ✔ ♜ **Leisure** club fitting centre **Conf** facs Corporate Hospitality Days **Hotel** ★★★ 67% HL Novotel Nottingham East Midlands, Bostock Lane, LONG EATON ☎ 0115 946 5111 🖩 0115 946 5111 108 en suite

MATLOCK
Map 8 SK36

Matlock Chesterfield Rd, Matlock Moor DE4 5LZ
☎ 01629 582191 🖩 01629 582135
e-mail: matlockcs@hotmail.co.uk
web: www.matlockgolfclub.co.uk
Moorland course with fine views of the beautiful Peak District.

18 Holes, 5996yds, Par 70, SSS 69, Course record 63. Club membership 700.

Visitors Mon-Fri except BHs. Booking required. Handicap certificate. Dress code. **Societies** booking required. **Green Fees** £35 per day, £28 per round **Course Designer** Tom Williamson **Prof** Christian Goodman **Facilities** ⑪ ⑩ ㅗ ㄷ ㄲ ㅗ 츠 ✔ **Conf** facs Corporate Hospitality Days **Location** 1.5m NE of Matlock on A632 **Hotel** ★★★ 79% HL Riber Hall, MATLOCK ☎ 01629 582795 🖩 01629 582795 14 en suite

MORLEY
Map 8 SK34

Morley Hayes Main Rd DE7 6DG
☎ 01332 780480 & 782000 (shop) 🖩 01332 781094
e-mail: golf@morleyhayes.com
web: www.morleyhayes.com

Peaceful pay and play course set in a splendid valley and incorporating charming water features and woodland. Floodlit driving range. Challenging nine-hole short course (Tower Course).

continued

*Manor Course: 18 Holes, 6477yds, Par 72, SSS 72,
Course record 63.*
Tower Course: 9 Holes, 1614yds, Par 30.
Visitors Mon-Sun & BHs. Booking required. Dress code.
Societies booking required. **Green Fees** Manor course: £38 per day,
£20 per round (£28 per round weekends & BHs). Tower: £9 per 9 holes
(£11 weekends & BHs) **Prof** James Whatley **Facilities** ⊕ ⑩ ⓑ ⌴
⬚ ⌸ ⌸ ☆ ◇ ⚐ ⚑ ✿ **Conf** facs Corporate Hospitality
Days **Location** on A608 4m N of Derby
Hotel ★★★★ 76% HL The Morley Hayes Hotel, Main Road,
MORLEY ☎ 01332 780480 🖹 01332 780480 32 en suite

NEW MILLS   Map 7 SK08

New Mills Shaw Marsh SK22 4QE
☎ 01663 743485 🖹 01663 743485
web: www.newmillsgolfclub.com
18 Holes, 5604yds, Par 69, SSS 67, Course record 62.
Course Designer Williams **Location** 0.5m N off B6101
Telephone for further details
Hotel ★★★ 72% HL Best Western Moorside Grange Hotel &
Spa, Mudhurst Lane, Higher Disley, DISLEY ☎ 01663 764151
🖹 01663 764151 98 en suite

RENISHAW   Map 8 SK47

Renishaw Park Club House, Mill Ln S21 3UZ
☎ 01246 432044 & 435484 🖹 01246 432116
web: www.renishawparkgolf.co.uk
Part parkland and part meadowland with easy walking.
*18 Holes, 6107yds, Par 71, SSS 70, Course record 64.
Club membership 750.*
Visitors contact club for details. **Societies** booking required. **Green
Fees** phone **Course Designer** Sir George Sitwell **Prof** Nigel Parkinson
Facilities ⊕ ⓑ ⌴ ⌸ ☆ ☆ ⚑ **Conf** Corporate Hospitality
Days **Location** M1 junct 30, 1.5m W
Hotel ★★★ 70% HL Sitwell Arms, Station Road, RENISHAW
☎ 01246 830004 & 435226 🖹 01246 830004 31 en suite

RISLEY   Map 8 SK43

Maywood Rushy Ln DE72 3SW
☎ 0115 939 2306 & 949 0043 (pro)
e-mail: torymoon@btinternet.com
web: www.maywoodgolfclub.com
Wooded parkland with numerous water hazards. Recent improvements
have enhanced this charming and challenging course.
*Maywood Golf Course: 18 Holes, 6424yds, Par 72, SSS 71,
Course record 70. Club membership 400.*
Visitors Mon-Sun & BHs. Dress code. **Societies** booking required.
Green Fees £23 per day, £18 per round (£27/£22 weekends & BHs)
Course Designer P Moon **Prof** Simon Purcell-Jackson **Facilities** ⊕
⑩ ⓑ ⌴ ⌸ ☆ ☆ ⚑ **Location** M1 junct 25
Hotel BUD Days Inn Donnington, Welcome Break Services, A50
Westbound, SHARDLOW ☎ 01332 799666 🖹 01332 799666
47 en suite

SHIRLAND   Map 8 SK45

Shirland Lower Delves DE55 6AU
☎ 01773 834935
e-mail: office@shirlandgolfclub.co.uk
web: www.shirlandgolfclub.co.uk
Rolling parkland and tree-lined course with extensive views of
Derbyshire countryside.
*18 Holes, 6072yds, Par 71, SSS 70, Course record 65.
Club membership 500.*
Visitors Mon-Sun & BHs. Booking required weekends & BHs. Dress
code. **Societies** welcome. **Green Fees** £15 (£18 weekends) **Prof** Ian
Walley **Facilities** ⊕ ⑩ ⓑ ⌴ ⌸ ☆ ☆ ⚑ **Conf** facs
Corporate Hospitality Days **Location** S side of village off A61
Hotel ★★★ 77% HL Santo's Higham Farm Hotel, Main Road,
HIGHAM ☎ 01773 833812 🖹 01773 833812 28 en suite

STANTON BY DALE   Map 8 SK43

Erewash Valley DE7 4QR
☎ 0115 932 3258 🖹 0115 944 0061
e-mail: secretary@erewashvalley.co.uk
web: www.erewashvalley.co.uk
Challenging parkland course with many specimen trees. Greens meet
USGA specification and there is the unique feature of two holes played
into and within an old Victorian sandstone quarry.
*Erewash Valley: 18 Holes, 6557yds, Par 72, SSS 71,
Course record 67. Club membership 750.*
Visitors Mon-Sat except BHs. Handicap certificate. Dress code.
Societies booking required. **Green Fees** not confirmed **Course
Designer** Hawtree **Prof** Darren Bartlett **Facilities** ⊕ ⑩ ⓑ ⌴
⌸ ☆ ☆ ⚑ ☆ ⚑ ✿ **Conf** facs Corporate Hospitality
Days **Location** 1m W. M1 junct 25, 2m
Hotel BUD Days Hotel Derby, Derbyshire C C Ground, Pentagon
Roundabout, Nottingham Road, DERBY ☎ 01332 363600
🖹 01332 363600 100 en suite

UNSTONE   Map 8 SK37

Birch Hall Sheffield Rd S18 4DB
☎ 01246 291979 🖹 01246 412912
Very testing woodland/moorland course demanding respect and a
good straight game if one is to walk away with a respectable card.
Sloping fairways gather wayward drives into thick gorse and deep
ditches. Signature holes are the tough 6th and scenic 13th, the latter
begs a big-hitter to go for a shot to the green.
*Birch Hall Golf Course: 18 Holes, 6379yds, Par 73, SSS 71,
Course record 72. Club membership 320.*
Visitors dress code. **Societies** booking required. **Green Fees** not
confirmed **Course Designer** D Tucker **Prof** Pete Ball **Facilities** ☆
🚗 **Location** off A61 between Sheffield & Chesterfield, outskirts of
Unstone
Hotel ★★★ 67% HL Sandpiper, Sheffield Road, Sheepbridge,
CHESTERFIELD ☎ 01246 450550 🖹 01246 450550 46 en suite

DEVON

AXMOUTH
Map 3 SY29

Axe Cliff Squires Ln EX12 4AB
☎ 01297 21754 📠 01297 24371
web: www.axecliff.co.uk
Axe Cliff Golf Club Ltd: 18 Holes, 6000yds, Par 70, SSS 70, Course record 64.
Course Designer James Braid **Location** 0.75m S on B3172
Telephone for further details
Hotel ★★ 80% HL Swallows Eaves, Swan Hill Road, COLYFORD
☎ 01297 553184 📠 01297 553184 8 en suite

BIGBURY-ON-SEA
Map 3 SX64

Bigbury TQ7 4BB
☎ 01548 810557 📠 01548 810207
e-mail: secretary@bigburygolfclub.co.uk
web: www.bigburygolfclub.com
Clifftop downland and parkland with easy walking. Exposed to winds, but with fine views over the sea and River Avon. The 7th hole is particularly tricky.
18 Holes, 6052yds, Par 70, SSS 69, Course record 65. Club membership 850.
Visitors Mon-Sun & BHs. Booking required. Handicap certificate required. Dress code. **Societies** booking required. **Green Fees** not confirmed **Course Designer** J H Taylor **Prof** Simon Lloyd **Facilities** ⊕ ⦿ by prior arrangement ⛳ ☐ 🍴 ⚐ 🏠 ⛳ ♦ 🛒 ♦
Conf Corporate Hospitality Days **Location** 1m S on B3392 between Bigbury village and Bigbury -on-Sea
Hotel ★★★★ 81% HL Thurlestone, THURLESTONE
☎ 01548 560382 📠 01548 560382 64 en suite

BLACKAWTON
Map 3 SX85

Dartmouth Golf & Country Club TQ9 7DE
☎ 01803 712686 📠 01803 712628
e-mail: info@dgcc.co.uk
web: www.dgcc.co.uk
Both courses are worth a visit and not just for the beautiful views. The Championship is one of the most challenging courses in the West Country with 12 water hazards and a daunting par 5 4th hole that visitors will always remember. The spectacular final hole, looking downhill and over a water hazard to the green, can be difficult to judge and has been described as one of the most picturesque finishing holes in the country.
Championship Course: 18 Holes, 6663yds, Par 72, SSS 72, Course record 64.
Dartmouth Course: 9 Holes, 2539yds, Par 33, SSS 33. Club membership 600.
Visitors Mon-Sun & BHs. Dress code. **Societies** welcome. **Green Fees** Championship: £38 (£48 weekends). Dartmouth: £15 (£16 weekends) **Course Designer** Jeremy Pern **Prof** Rob Glazier/Stuart Barnett **Facilities** ⊕ ⦿ ⛳ ☐ 🍴 ⚐ 🏠 🍴 ♦ 🛒 ♦ 🏇 **Leisure** heated indoor swimming pool, sauna, gymnasium, massage & beauty treatments **Conf** facs Corporate Hospitality Days **Location** A38 from Buckfastleigh. Follow brown leisure signs for Woodlands Leisure Park. 800yds beyond park turn left into club.
Hotel ★★★ 72% HL Stoke Lodge, Stoke Fleming, DARTMOUTH
☎ 01803 770523 📠 01803 770523 25 en suite

BUDLEIGH SALTERTON
Map 3 SY08

East Devon Links Rd EX9 6DG
☎ 01395 443370 📠 01395 445547
e-mail: secretary@edgc.co.uk
web: www.edgc.co.uk
An interesting course with downland turf, much heather and gorse, and superb views over the bay. Laid out on cliffs 250 to 400 feet above sea level, the early holes climb to the cliff edge. The downhill 17th has a heather section in the fairway, leaving a good second to the green. In addition to rare orchids, the course enjoys an abundance of wildlife including deer and peregrine falcons.
18 Holes, 6231yds, Par 70, SSS 70, Course record 61. Club membership 850.
Visitors handicap certificate. Dress code. **Societies** booking required. **Green Fees** £52 per 27/36 holes, £40 per 18 holes
Prof Trevor Underwood **Facilities** ⊕ ⦿ ⛳ ☐ 🍴 ⚐ 🏠 🍴 ♦ **Conf** Corporate Hospitality Days **Location** W side of town centre
Hotel ★★ 64% HL Bulstone, High Bulstone, BRANSCOMBE
☎ 01297 680446 📠 01297 680446 7 en suite

CHITTLEHAMHOLT
Map 3 SS62

Highbullen Hotel EX37 9HD
☎ 01769 540561 📠 01769 540492
web: www.highbullen.co.uk
Highbullen Hotel Golf & Country Club: 18 Holes, 5755yds, Par 68, SSS 67.
Course Designer M Neil/ J Hamilton **Location** 0.5m S of village
Telephone for further details
Hotel ★★★ CHH Northcote Manor, BURRINGTON, Umberleigh
☎ 01769 560501 📠 01769 560501 11 en suite

CHRISTOW
Map 3 SX88

Teign Valley Golf & Hotel EX6 7PA
☎ 01647 253026 📠 01647 253026
e-mail: andy@teignvalleygolf.co.uk
web: www.teignvalleygolf.co.uk

A scenically spectacular 18-hole course set beside the River Teign in Dartmoor National Park. Offering a good challenge to both low and high handicap golfers, it features two lakeside holes, rolling fairways and fine views.
Teign Valley Golf & Hotel: 18 Holes, 5913yds, Par 70, SSS 69. Club membership 500.
Visitors Mon-Sun & BHs. Booking required. Dress code.

continued

Societies booking required. Green Fees not confirmed Course Designer P Nicholson Prof Scott Amiet Facilities ⓘ ⑩ ⛳ 🛒 🏌 ⛾ 🏠 ⛳ ◇ ⛾ 🛺 ⛳ Leisure gymnasium Conf facs Corporate Hospitality Days Location A38 Teign Valley exit, Exeter/ Plymouth Expressway signs on B3193
Hotel ★★★ 73% HL Best Western Lord Haldon Country House, Dunchideock, EXETER ☎ 01392 832483 📄 01392 832483 23 en suite

CHULMLEIGH　　　　　　　　　　　Map 3 SS61

Chulmleigh Leigh Rd EX18 7BL
☎ 01769 580519　📄 01769 580519
e-mail: chulmleighgolf@aol.com
web: www.chulmleighgolf.co.uk
Situated in a scenic area with views to distant Dartmoor, this undulating meadowland course offers a good test for the most experienced golfer and is enjoyable for newcomers to the game. Short 18-hole summer course with a tricky 1st hole; in winter the course is changed to nine holes and made longer for players to extend their game.
Summer Course: 18 Holes, 1407yds, Par 54, SSS 54, Course record 48. Club membership 110.
Visitors contact club for details. **Societies** booking required. **Green Fees** £8.50 per 18 holes, £7.50 before 10am **Course Designer** John Goodban **Facilities** ⛳ 🗗 🛒 🏌 🏠 ⛳ ◇ ⛾ **Location** SW side of village just off A377
Hotel ★★★ CHH Northcote Manor, BURRINGTON, Umberleigh ☎ 01769 560501 📄 01769 560501　11 en suite

CHURSTON FERRERS　　　　　　　Map 3 SX95

Churston Dartmouth Rd TQ5 0LA
☎ 01803 842751 & 842218　📄 01803 845738
web: www.churstongolf.com
Churston Golf Club Ltd: 18 Holes, 6219yds, Par 70, SSS 70, Course record 64.
Prof Neil Holman **Facilities** ⓘ ⑩ ⛳ 🗗 🛒 🏌 🏠 ⛳ ⛾
Location NW side of village on A379
Telephone for further details
Hotel ★★★ 72% HL Berry Head, Berry Head Road, BRIXHAM ☎ 01803 853225 📄 01803 853225　32 en suite

CREDITON　　　　　　　　　　　　Map 3 SS80

Downes Crediton Hookway EX17 3PT
☎ 01363 773025 & 774464　📄 01363 775060
e-mail: secretary@downescreditongc.co.uk
web: www.downescreditongc.co.uk
Parkland with water features. Flat front nine. Hilly and wooded back nine.
18 Holes, 5954yds, Par 70, SSS 69. Club membership 700.
Visitors contact club for details. **Societies** welcome. **Green Fees** £28 per day (£32 weekends) **Prof** Barry Austin **Facilities** ⓘ ⑩ ⛳ 🗗 🛒 🏌 🏠 ⛳ ⛾ **Conf** Corporate Hospitality Days **Location** 1.5m SE off A377
Hotel ★★★ 71% HL Barton Cross Hotel & Restaurant, Huxham, Stoke Canon, EXETER ☎ 01392 841245 📄 01392 841245　9 en suite

CULLOMPTON　　　　　　　　　　Map 3 ST00

Padbrook Park EX15 1RU
☎ 01884 836100　📄 01884 836101
e-mail: padbrookpark@fsmail.net
web: www.padbrookpark.co.uk
Course extended to 18 holes from March 2009 with all tees and greens to USPGA standards. Feature holes are the 3rd (par 4) and the 14th (par 5).
18 Holes, 6450yds, Par 72, SSS 72. Club membership 250.
Visitors Mon-Sun & BHs. Booking required. Dress code.
Societies booking required. **Green Fees** £25 per 18 holes **Course Designer** Bob Sandow/Trevor Spurway **Facilities** ⓘ ⑩ ⛳ 🗗 🛒 🏌 🏠 ⛳ ◇ ⛾ 🛺 ⛾ 🏌 Leisure fishing, gymnasium, indoor bowling centre **Conf** facs Corporate Hospitality Days **Location** M5 junct 28, 1m on S edge of town
Hotel ★★★ 77% HL Padbrook Park, CULLOMPTON ☎ 01884 836100 📄 01884 836100　40 en suite

DAWLISH WARREN　　　　　　　Map 3 SX97

Warren EX7 0NF
☎ 01626 862255
e-mail: golf@dwgc.co.uk
web: www.dwgc.co.uk
Typical flat, genuine links course lying on spit between sea and Exe estuary. Picturesque scenery, a few trees but much gorse. Testing in windy conditions. The 7th hole provides the opportunity to go for the green across a bay on the estuary.
18 Holes, 5954yds, Par 69, SSS 69, Course record 65. Club membership 600.
Visitors Mon-Sun & BHs. Handicap certificate. Dress code.
Societies booking required. **Green Fees** £35 per day (£40 weekends & BHs). **Course Designer** James Braid **Prof** Darren Prowse **Facilities** ⓘ ⑩ ⛳ 🗗 🛒 🏌 🏠 ⛳ ⛾ **Conf** Corporate Hospitality Days **Location** E side of village
Hotel ★★★ 78% HL Langstone Cliff, Dawlish Warren, DAWLISH ☎ 01626 868000 📄 01626 868000　66 en suite

DOWN ST MARY　　　　　　　　Map 3 SS70

Waterbridge EX17 5LG
☎ 01363 85111
web: www.waterbridgegc.co.uk
A testing course of nine holes set in a gently sloping valley. The par of 32 will not be easily gained, with one par 5, three par 4s and five par 3s, although the course record holder has par 29. The 3rd hole which is a raised green is surrounded by water and the 4th (439yds) is demanding for beginners.
Waterbridge Golf Course: 9 Holes, 3910yds, Par 64, SSS 64. Club membership 120.
Visitors contact course for details. **Societies** welcome. **Green Fees** not confirmed **Course Designer** D Taylor **Prof** David Ridyard **Facilities** ⓘ ⛳ 🗗 🛒 🏌 🏠 ⛳ ⛾ **Conf** Corporate Hospitality Days **Location** A377 from Exeter towards Barnstaple, 1m past Copplestone
Hotel ★★★ CHH Northcote Manor, BURRINGTON, Umberleigh ☎ 01769 560501 📄 01769 560501　11 en suite

EXETER
Map 3 SX99

Exeter Golf & Country Club Topsham Rd, Countess Wear
EX2 7AE
☎ 01392 874639 🖷 01392 874914
e-mail: golf@exetergcc.co.uk
web: www.exetergcc.co.uk

Sheltered parkland with very mature tree lined fairways. An easy
walking course set in the grounds of a fine mansion, which is now the
clubhouse. The 15th-18th finishing stretch is one of the toughest in
South West England. Small well guarded greens in excellent condition
all year round.

*Exeter Golf & Country Club: 18 Holes, 6023yds, Par 69,
SSS 69, Course record 62. Club membership 800.*

Visitors Mon-Fri, Sun & BHs. Booking required. Handicap certificate.
Dress code. **Societies** booking required. **Green Fees** £50 per day (£60
Sun & BHs) **Course Designer** J Braid **Prof** Gary Milne **Facilities** ⓣ
🍴 🍸 🖭 🍽 ⚖ 🖾 🏌 **Leisure** hard tennis courts, outdoor
and indoor heated swimming pool, squash, sauna, gymnasium, short
game area **Conf** facs Corporate Hospitality Days **Location** M5 junct 30
towards Topsham, SE side of city centre off A379
Hotel ★★★★ 71% HL Buckerell Lodge Hotel, Topsham Road,
EXETER ☎ 01392 221111 🖷 01392 221111 54 en suite

Woodbury Park Hotel and Golf Club Woodbury Castle
EX5 1JJ
☎ 01395 233500 🖷 01395 233384
web: www.woodburypark.co.uk

*Oaks: 18 Holes, 6578yds, Par 72, SSS 72, Course record 66.
Acorn: 9 Holes, 2297yds, Par 32, SSS 32.*

Course Designer J Hamilton-Stutt **Location** M5 junct 30, A3052
Telephone for further details
Hotel ★★★★ 73% HL Woodbury Park Hotel and Golf
Club, Woodbury Castle, WOODBURY, Exeter ☎ 01395 233382
🖷 01395 233382 60 en suite

See advert on opposite page

HIGH BICKINGTON
Map 2 SS52

Libbaton EX37 9BS
☎ 01769 560269 & 560167 🖷 01769 560342
e-mail: post.libbaton@hotmail.co.uk
web: www.libbatongc.com

Parkland on undulating land. Water comes into play on 11 of the
18 holes, as well as a quarry, ditches, trees and eight raised greens.
Not a heavily bunkered course, but those present are well positioned
and the sharp sand they contain makes them tricky. Five par 5s could

easily get you thinking this course is only for big hitters but as with
many good courses, sound course management is the key to success.

*18 Holes, 6481yds, Par 73, SSS 71, Course record 72.
Club membership 500.*

Visitors Mon-Sun & BHs. Booking required. Handicap certificate.
Dress code. **Societies** booking required. **Green Fees** £26 per 18 holes
(£30 weekends) **Course Designer** Col Badham **Prof** David Jeffs
Facilities ⓣ 🍴 🍸 🖭 🍽 ⚖ 🖾 🖤 🏌 🛆 🛒 🏌
Conf facs Corporate Hospitality Days **Location** B3217 1m fromf High
Bickington, off A377
Hotel ★★★ CHH Northcote Manor, BURRINGTON, Umberleigh
☎ 01769 560501 🖷 01769 560501 11 en suite

HOLSWORTHY
Map 2 SS30

Holsworthy Killatree EX22 6LP
☎ 01409 255390 (pro shop) & 253177 🖷 01409 253177
e-mail: info@holsworthygolfclub.co.uk
web: www.holsworthygolfclub.co.uk

Pleasant parkland with gentle slopes, numerous trees and a few
strategic bunkers. Small greens offer a good test for players of all
abilities.

*18 Holes, 6059yds, Par 70, SSS 69, Course record 64.
Club membership 500.*

Visitors Mon-Sun & BHs. Booking required. Dress code.
Societies booking required. **Green Fees** phone **Prof** Alan Johnston
Facilities ⓣ 🍴 🍸 🖭 🍽 ⚖ 🖾 🖤 🛆 🖾 🛒 🏌
Conf facs Corporate Hospitality Days **Location** 1.5m W on A3072
towards Bude
Hotel ★★★ 79% HL Falcon, Breakwater Road, BUDE
☎ 01288 352005 🖷 01288 352005 29 en suite

HONITON
Map 3 ST10

Honiton Middlehills EX14 9TR
☎ 01404 44422 & 42943 🖷 01404 46383
e-mail: secretary@honitongolfclub.fsnet.co.uk
web: honitongolfclub.fsnet.co.uk

Founded in 1896, this level parkland course is situated on a plateau
850ft above sea level. Easy walking and good views. The 4th hole is
a testing par 3. The 17th and 18th provide a challenging finish. A
premium is placed on accuracy especially from the tee.

*18 Holes, 5910yds, Par 69, SSS 68, Course record 63.
Club membership 800.*

Visitors Mon-Sun & BHs. Booking advised. Handicap certificate
required. Dress code. **Societies** welcome. **Green Fees** not confirmed
Prof Adrian Cave **Facilities** ⓣ 🍴 🍸 🖭 🍽 ⚖ 🖾 🖤
🏌 **Leisure** hardstanding for touring caravans with services
Conf Corporate Hospitality Days **Location** 1.25m SE of Honiton, turn
towards Farway at Tower Cross on A35
Hotel ★★ 76% SHL Home Farm Hotel & Restaurant, Wilmington,
HONITON ☎ 01404 831278 🖷 01404 831278 12 en suite

ILFRACOMBE — Map 2 SS54

Ilfracombe Hele Bay EX34 9RT
☎ 01271 862176   📠 01271 867731
e-mail: ilfracombegolfclub@btinternet.com
web: www.ilfracombegolfclub.com

A challenging coastal heathland course with views over the Bristol Channel and South Wales from every hole.

18 Holes, 5596yds, Par 69, SSS 67, Course record 66. Club membership 520.

Visitors Mon-Sun & BHs. Booking required. **Societies** welcome. **Green Fees** £27.50 per round (£33 weekends & BHs) **Course Designer** T K Weir **Prof** Mark Davies **Facilities** ⓣ 🅘 🖭 ⏦ 🎪 🚶 🏠 ⛽ 🛒 🐾 🚩 **Location** 1.5m E of Ilfracombe, off A399
Hotel ★★★ 88% HL Watersmeet, Mortehoe, WOOLACOMBE ☎ 01271 870333 📠 01271 870333   25 en suite

IPPLEPEN — Map 3 SX86

Dainton Park Totnes Rd TQ12 5TN
☎ 01803 815000
e-mail: info@daintonparkgolf.co.uk
web: www.daintonparkgolf.co.uk

A challenging parkland course in typical Devon countryside, with gentle contours, tree-lined fairways and raised tees. Water hazards make the two opening holes particularly testing.

18 Holes, 6400yds, Par 71, SSS 71, Course record 69. Club membership 550.

Visitors Mon-Sun & BHs. Booking required. Dress code. **Societies** booking required. **Green Fees** £25 per round **Course Designer** Adrian Stiff **Prof** Michael Cayless **Facilities** ⓣ 🅘 🖭 ⏦ 🎪 🚶 🏠 ⛽ 🐾 🚩 **Leisure** gymnasium, fitness gym **Conf** Corporate Hospitality Days **Location** 2m S of Newton Abbot on A381
Hotel ★★ 75% MET Best Western Queens Hotel, Queen Street, NEWTON ABBOT ☎ 01626 363133 📠 01626 363133   26 en suite

IVYBRIDGE — Map 2 SX65

Dinnaton Blachford Rd PL21 9HU
☎ 01752 690020 & 892512   📠 01752 698334
web: www.mccaulays.com

McCauleys Health Clubs - Dinnaton Golf Club: 9 Holes, 4089yds, Par 64, SSS 60.

Course Designer Cotton & Pink **Location** off A38 at Ivybridge junct towards town centre, 1st rdbt brown signs for club 1m
Telephone for further details
Hotel ★★ 76% HL Glazebrook House Hotel, SOUTH BRENT ☎ 01364 73322 📠 01364 73322   10 en suite

MORETONHAMPSTEAD — Map 3 SX78

Bovey Castle TQ13 8RE
☎ 01647 445009   📠 01647 440961
e-mail: richard.lewis@boveycastle.com
web: www.boveycastle.com

This enjoyable parkland course has enough hazards to make any golfer think. Most hazards are natural such as the Rivers Bowden and Bovey which meander through the first eight holes.

Bovey Castle: 18 Holes, 6303yds, Par 70, SSS 70, Course record 63. Club membership 320.

Woodbury Castle, Woodbury
Exeter, Devon EX5 1JJ
Tel: 01395 233382
Fax: 01395 233384

The Oaks: 18 holes par 72, 6578 • Handicap required
The Acorns: 9 hole par 32, 2297 yards
Golf Bookings call 01395 233500

Situated in 550 acres of Devon's most idyllic countryside near Exeter.

Hotel & Lodge
Accommodation available
56 en suite
4 annexe en suite
Hotel: 01395 233382

Website: www.woodburypark.co.uk
Email: golfbookings@woodburypark.co.uk

Visitors contact course for details. **Societies** welcome. **Green Fees** £70 per round **Course Designer** J Abercrombie **Prof** Richard Lewis **Facilities** ⓣ 🅘 🖭 ⏦ 🎪 🚶 🏠 ⛽ ◇ 🛒 🐾 🚩 **Leisure** hard and grass tennis courts, outdoor and indoor heated swimming pool, fishing, sauna, gymnasium **Conf** facs Corporate Hospitality Days **Location** 2m W of Moretonhampstead, off B3212
Hotel ★★★ 78% HL The White Hart Hotel, The Square, MORETONHAMPSTEAD ☎ 01647 441340 📠 01647 441340   28 en suite

MORTEHOE — Map 2 SS44

Mortehoe & Woolacombe Easewell EX34 7EH
☎ 01271 870566 & 870745
e-mail: malcolm_wilkinson@northdevon.gov.uk
web: www.woolacombegolf.co.uk

Attached to a camping and caravan site, this 9-hole course has 2 par 3s and 7 par 4s. The gently sloping clifftop course has spectacular views across Morte Bay.

Easewell: 9 Holes, 4729yds, Par 66, SSS 63, Course record 66. Club membership 200.

Visitors Mon-Sun & BHs. Dress code. **Societies** booking required. **Green Fees** not confirmed **Course Designer** D Hoare **Prof** Paul Adams **Facilities** ⓣ 🅘 🖭 ⏦ 🎪 🚶 🏠 ⛽ ◇ 🐾 **Leisure** heated indoor swimming pool, indoor bowls. **Location** 0.25m before Mortehoe on station road
Hotel ★★★ 88% HL Watersmeet, Mortehoe, WOOLACOMBE ☎ 01271 870333 📠 01271 870333   25 en suite

NEWTON ABBOT   Map 3 SX87

Hele Park Golf Centre Ashburton Rd TQ12 6JN
☎ 01626 336060
e-mail: info@heleparkgolf.co.uk
web: www.heleparkgolf.co.uk

Gently undulating parkland course with views stretching to Dartmoor.
A fair test of golf with water in play on 3 holes.

*Hele Park Golf Centre: 9 Holes, 5228yds, Par 68, SSS 65,
Course record 63. Club membership 400.*

Visitors Mon-Sun & BHs. Dress code. **Societies** welcome. **Green
Fees** £20 per 18 holes, £11.50 per 9 holes. (£22/£12.50 weekends &
BHs) **Course Designer** M Craig **Prof** Duncan Arnold **Facilities** ⑪ ⓛ
🖵 🍴 ⚐ 🛍 ⚑ ⚡ 🛒 ♂ ⛴ **Conf** Corporate Hospitality
Days **Location** W of town off A383 Newton Abbot to Ashburton road.
Hotel ★★★ 71% HL Passage House, Hackney Lane, Kingsteignton,
NEWTON ABBOT ☎ 01626 355515 📄 01626 355515 90 en suite

Stover Bovey Rd TQ12 6QQ
☎ 01626 352460 (Secretary)   📄 01626 330210
e-mail: info@stovergolfclub.co.uk
web: www.stovergolfclub.co.uk

Mature wooded parkland with water coming into play on eight holes.

*18 Holes, 5764yds, Par 69, SSS 69, Course record 63.
Club membership 800.*

Visitors handicap certificate. Dress code. **Societies** booking required.
Green Fees £32 per round **Course Designer** James Braid **Prof** James
Lansmead **Facilities** ⑪ ⓛ ⓛ 🖵 🍴 ⚐ 🛍 ♂ **Conf** facs
Corporate Hospitality Days **Location** 3m N of Newton Abbot on A382.
Bovey Tracey exit on A38
Hotel ★★ 75% MET Best Western Queens Hotel, Queen Street,
NEWTON ABBOT ☎ 01626 363133 📄 01626 363133 26 en suite

OKEHAMPTON   Map 2 SX59

Ashbury Golf Hotel Higher Maddaford EX20 4NL
☎ 01837 55453   📄 01837 55468
web: www.ashburygolfhotel.co.uk

A combination of courses occupying a lightly wooded parkland setting
in rolling Devon countryside on the foothills of Dartmoor National Park.
Extra hazards have been added to the natural ones already present,
with over 100 bunkers and 18 lakes. The courses are open throughout
the year with either larger main greens or purpose built alternate ones.

*Oakwood: 18 Holes, 5400yds, Par 67, SSS 66,
Course record 65.
Pines: 18 Holes, 5901yds, Par 70.
Beeches: 18 Holes, 5765yds, Par 69, SSS 66.*

*Kigbeare: 18 Holes, 6464yds, Par 72.
Alder: 9 Holes, 2770yds, Par 34. Club membership 170.*
Visitors Mon-Sun & BHs. Booking required. Dress code.
Societies booking required. **Green Fees** £25 per round (£30
weekends) **Course Designer** David Fensom **Facilities** ⑪ ⓛ 🖵
🍴 ⚐ 🛍 ⚐ ◇ 🛒 ♂ ⛴ **Leisure** hard tennis courts, fishing,
sauna, par 3 course, indoor bowls, snooker. **Conf** facs Corporate
Hospitality Days **Location** off A3079 Okehampton-Holsworthy
Hotel ★★ 72% HL Ashbury, Higher Maddaford, Southcott,
OKEHAMPTON ☎ 01837 55453 📄 01837 55453 184 en suite

See advert on page 64

Okehampton Tors Rd EX20 1EF
☎ 01837 52113   📄 01837 53541
e-mail: okehamptongc@btconnect.com
web: www.okehamptongc.co.uk

A good combination of moorland, woodland and river makes this one
of the prettiest, yet testing courses in Devon.

*18 Holes, 5294yds, Par 68, SSS 66, Course record 66.
Club membership 600.*

Visitors Mon-Sun & BHs. Booking required. Handicap certificate.
Dress code. **Societies** booking required. **Green Fees** £30 per day;
£25 per round (£30 per round weekends) **Course Designer** J H Taylor
Prof Ashley Moon **Facilities** ⑪ ⓛ ⓛ 🖵 🍴 ⚐ 🛍 ♂
Location 1m S off A30, signed from town centre
Hotel ★★ 71% HL White Hart, Fore Street, OKEHAMPTON
☎ 01837 52730 & 54514 📄 01837 52730 19 en suite

PLYMOUTH   Map 2 SX45

Elfordleigh Hotel, Golf & Leisure Colebrook PL7 5EB
☎ 01752 336428 (hotel) & 348425 (golf shop)
📄 01752 344581
web: www.elfordleigh.co.uk

*Elfordleigh Hotel Golf & Country Club: 18 Holes, 5664yds,
Par 69, SSS 67, Course record 66.*

Course Designer J H Taylor **Location** 2m NE off A374, follow signs
from Plympton town centre
Telephone for further details
Hotel ★★★ 74% HL Elfordleigh Hotel Golf Leisure, Colebrook,
Plympton, PLYMOUTH ☎ 01752 336428 📄 01752 336428
34 en suite

Staddon Heights Plymstock PL9 9SP
☎ 01752 402475   📄 01752 401998
e-mail: golf@shgc.uk.net
web: www.staddon-heights.co.uk

Cliff top course affording spectacular views across Plymouth Sound,
Dartmoor and Bodmin Moor.

*18 Holes, 6164yds, Par 70, SSS 70, Course record 66.
Club membership 900.*

Visitors contact club for details. **Societies** booking required.
Green Fees £28 (£32 weekends & BHs) **Course Designer** Hamilton
Stutt **Facilities** ⑪ ⓛ ⓛ 🖵 🍴 ⚐ 🛍 ♂ **Conf** facs
Location from city centre follow signs for Kingsbridge, Turnchapel and
Staddon Heights
Hotel ★★★ 77% HL Langdon Court Hotel & Restaurant,
Langdon, Wendbury, PLYMOUTH ☎ 01752 862358 & 07944 483162
📄 01752 862358 18 en suite

SAUNTON   Map 2 SS43

Saunton EX33 1LG
☎ 01271 812436   📠 01271 814241
web: www.sauntongolf.co.uk

Two traditional championship links courses. The opening 4 holes
of the East course total over one mile in length. The par 3 5th and
13th holes are short but testing with undulating features and the
16th is notable. On the West course club selection is paramount as
positioning the ball is the key to success. The loop on the back nine,
comprising the 12th, 13th and 14th is as testing as it is pleasing
to the eye.

East Course: 18 Holes, 6427yds, Par 71, SSS 71,
Course record 64.
West Course: 18 Holes, 6138yds, Par 71, SSS 70,
Course record 63. Club membership 1450.

Visitors Mon-Sun & BHs. Booking required. Handicap certificate.
Dress code. **Societies** booking required. **Green Fees** £85 per
36 holes, £65 per 18 holes (£100/£70 weekends) **Course Designer** F
Pennick/W H Fowler **Prof** A T MacKenzie **Facilities** ⓣ 🍴 🖥 🎱 ⚌
⚑ 🏌 **Conf** Corporate Hospitality Days
Location S side of village off B3231
Hotel ★★★★ 78% HL Saunton Sands, SAUNTON
☎ 01271 890212 & 892001 📠 01271 890212 92 en suite

SIDMOUTH   Map 3 SY18

Sidmouth Cotmaton Rd EX10 8SX
☎ 01395 513451   📠 01395 514661
e-mail: secretary@sidmouthgolfclub.co.uk
web: www.sidmouthgolfclub.co.uk

Situated on the side of Peak Hill, offering beautiful coastal views OF
Lyme Bay and Sidmouth. Sheltered, undulating fairways and superb
greens.

18 Holes, 5100yds, Par 66, SSS 65, Course record 59.
Club membership 700.

Visitors Mon-Sun & BHs. Dress code. **Societies** booking required
Green Fees not confirmed **Course Designer** J H Taylor **Prof** Chris
Haigh **Facilities** ⓣ 🍴 🖥 🎱 ⚌ ⚑ 🏌
Location W side of town centre
Hotel ★★★★ 83% HL Victoria, The Esplanade, SIDMOUTH
☎ 01395 512651 📠 01395 512651 61 en suite

SOUTH BRENT   Map 3 SX66

Wrangaton (S Devon) Golf Links Rd, Wrangaton TQ10 9HJ
☎ 01364 73229   📠 01364 73229
e-mail: wrangatongolf@btconnect.com
web: www.wrangatongolfclub.co.uk

Unique 18-hole course with nine holes on moorland and nine holes on
parkland. The course lies within Dartmoor National Park. Spectacular
views towards sea and rugged terrain. Natural fairways and hazards
include bracken, sheep and ponies.

18 Holes, 6065yds, Par 70, SSS 69, Course record 66.
Club membership 600.

Visitors Mon-Sun & BHs. Dress code. **Societies** booking required.
Green Fees phone **Course Designer** D M A Steel **Prof** Glenn Richards
Facilities ⓣ 🍴 by prior arrangement 🖥 🎱 ⚌ ⚑ 🏌
⚑ 🏌 **Location** 2.25m SW off A38, between South Brent and
Ivybridge

Wrangaton (S Devon)

Hotel ★★ 76% HL Glazebrook House Hotel, SOUTH BRENT
☎ 01364 73322 📠 01364 73322 10 en suite

SPARKWELL   Map 2 SX55

Welbeck Manor & Sparkwell Golf Course Blacklands
PL7 5DF
☎ 01752 837219   📠 01752 837219

Welbeck Manor & Sparkwell Golf Course: 9 Holes,
2886yds, Par 68, SSS 68, Course record 68.

Course Designer John Gabb **Location** 1m N of A38 Plymouth-Ivybridge
road
Telephone for further details
Hotel ★★★ 74% HL Elfordleigh Hotel Golf Leisure, Colebrook,
Plympton, PLYMOUTH ☎ 01752 336428 📠 01752 336428
34 en suite

TAVISTOCK   Map 2 SX47

Hurdwick Tavistock Hamlets PL19 0LL
☎ 01822 612746   📠 01822 612746
e-mail: hurdwick@aol.com

An executive parkland course with many bunkers and fine views.
Executive golf originated in America and the concept is that a round
should take no longer than 3 hours while offering a solid challenge.

18 Holes, 5302yds, Par 68, SSS 67, Course record 67.
Club membership 110.

Visitors contact club for details. Dress code. **Societies** welcome.
Green Fees not confirmed **Course Designer** Hawtree **Facilities** 🖥
🎱 ⚌ ⚑ 🏌 **Location** 1m N of Tavistock on the Brentor
Road
Hotel ★★★ 75% HL Bedford, 1 Plymouth Road, TAVISTOCK
☎ 01822 613221 📠 01822 613221 31 en suite

Tavistock Down Rd PL19 9AQ
☎ 01822 612344   📠 01822 612344
e-mail: info@tavistockgolfclub.org.uk
web: www.tavistockgolfclub.org.uk

Set on Whitchurch Down in south-west Dartmoor with easy walking
and magnificent views over rolling countryside into Cornwall.
Downland turf with some heather, and interesting holes on
undulating ground.

18 Holes, 6495yds, Par 71, SSS 71, Course record 60.
Club membership 700.

Visitors handicap certificate. Dress code **Societies** booking
required. **Green Fees** £30 per day/round (£36 weekends & BHs)

continued

Course Designer H Fowler **Prof** S Steel **Facilities** ⊕ ⓘ◎ ⓛ ⎕ ⓡ ⌳ 🏠 ⌣ **Conf** Corporate Hospitality Days **Location** 1m SE of town centre, on Whitchurch Down
Hotel ★★★ 75% HL Bedford, 1 Plymouth Road, TAVISTOCK
☎ 01822 613221 📄 01822 613221 31 en suite

TEDBURN ST MARY   Map 3 SX89

Fingle Glen Golf Hotel EX6 6AF
☎ 01647 61817   📄 01647 61135
web: www.fingleglen.com

Fingle Glen Golf Hotel: 18 Holes, 5878yds, Par 70, SSS 68, Course record 63.

Course Designer Bill Pile **Location** 5m W of Exeter, off A30
Telephone for further details
Hotel ★★★ 75% HL St Olaves, Mary Arches Street, EXETER
☎ 01392 217736 📄 01392 217736 14 en suite

TEIGNMOUTH   Map 3 SX97

Teignmouth Haldon Moor TQ14 9NY
☎ 01626 777070   📄 01626 777304
e-mail: tgc@btconnect.com
web: www.teignmouthgolfclub.co.uk

This fairly flat heathland course is high up with fine panoramic views of sea, moors and river valley. Good springy turf with some heather and an interesting layout makes for very enjoyable holiday golf. Designed by Dr A MacKenzie, the world famous architect who also designed Augusta GC USA.

18 Holes, 6110yds, Par 69, SSS 69, Course record 63. Club membership 900.

Visitors Mon–Sun & BHs. Booking required weekends & BHs. Handicap certificate. Dress code. **Societies** welcome. **Green Fees** £40 per day **Course Designer** Dr Alister Mackenzie **Prof** Rob Selley **Facilities** ⊕ ⓘ◎ ⓛ ⎕ ⓡ ⌳ 🏠 ⌣ **Conf** facs Corporate Hospitality Days **Location** 2m NW off B3192
Hotel ★★ 69% HL Cockhaven Manor Hotel, Cockhaven Road, BISHOPSTEIGNTON ☎ 01626 775252 📄 01626 775252 12 en suite

THURLESTONE   Map 3 SX64

Thurlestone TQ7 3NZ
☎ 01548 560405   📄 01548 562149
e-mail: secretary@thurlestonegolfclub.co.uk
web: www.thurlestonegolfclub.co.uk

Situated on the edge of the cliffs with downland turf and good greens. The course, after an interesting opening hole, rises to higher land with fine sea views, and finishes with an excellent 502yd downhill hole to the clubhouse.

18 Holes, 6340yds, Par 71, SSS 70, Course record 65. Club membership 820.

Visitors handicap certificate. Dress code. **Green Fees** £40 per day/round **Course Designer** Harry S Colt **Prof** Peter Laugher **Facilities** ⊕ ⓘ◎ by prior arrangement ⓛ ⎕ ⓡ ⌳ 🏠 ⌣ **Leisure** hard and grass tennis courts **Location** S side of village
Hotel ★★★★ 81% HL Thurlestone, THURLESTONE
☎ 01548 560382 📄 01548 560382 64 en suite

TIVERTON   Map 3 SS91

Tiverton Post Hill EX16 4NE
☎ 01884 252187
e-mail: tivertongolfclub@lineone.net
web: www.tivertongolfclub.co.uk

Parkland with many different species of tree, and lush pastures that ensure some of the finest fairways in the south-west. The undulating ground provides plenty of variety and there are a number of interesting holes which visitors will find a real challenge.

18 Holes, 6236yds, Par 71, SSS 71, Course record 65. Club membership 750.

Visitors Mon–Sun & BHs. Booking required. Dress code.
Societies booking required. **Green Fees** £36 per 18 holes **Course Designer** Braid **Prof** Michael Hawton **Facilities** ⊕ ⓘ◎ ⓛ ⎕ ⓡ ⌳ 🏠 ⌣ **Conf** Corporate Hospitality Days **Location** 3m E of Tiverton. M5 junct 27, through Sampford Peverell & Halberton
Hotel ★★★ 74% HL Best Western Tiverton, Blundells Road, TIVERTON ☎ 01884 256120 📄 01884 256120 69 en suite

TORQUAY   Map 3 SX96

Torquay 30 Petitor Rd, St Marychurch TQ1 4QF
☎ 01803 314591   📄 01803 316116
e-mail: info@torquaygolfclub.co.uk
web: www.torquaygolfclub.org.uk

Unusual combination of cliff and parkland golf, with wonderful views over the sea and Dartmoor.

18 Holes, 6164yds, Par 69, SSS 69, Course record 63. Club membership 725.

Visitors Mon–Fri, Sun & BHs. Booking required Sun & BHs. Handicap certificate. Dress code. **Societies** booking required. **Green Fees** £40 per day (£45 Sun) **Prof** Martin Ruth **Facilities** ⊕ ⓘ◎ ⓛ ⎕ ⓡ ⌳ 🏠 ⌣ **Location** 1.25m N
Hotel ★★★ 86% HL Orestone Manor Hotel & Restaurant, Rockhouse Lane, Maidencombe, TORQUAY ☎ 01803 328098 📄 01803 328098 12 en suite

TORRINGTON (GREAT)   Map 2 SS41

Torrington Weare Trees EX38 7EZ
☎ 01805 622229 & 623878   📄 01805 623878
e-mail: theoffice@torringtongolf.fsnet.co.uk
web: www.torringtongolfclub.co.uk

Attractive and challenging nine-hole course. Free draining to allow play all year round. Excellent greens and outstanding views.

Great Torrington Golf Club: 9 Holes, 4423yds, Par 64, SSS 62, Course record 58. Club membership 420.

Visitors Mon, Thu & Fri. Other days pm only. Booking required. Dress code. **Societies** booking required. **Green Fees** not confirmed **Facilities** ⊕ ⓛ ⎕ ⓡ ⌳ 🏠 ⌣ **Location** 1m W of Torringdon
Hotel ★★★ 74% HL Royal, Barnstaple Street, BIDEFORD
☎ 01237 472005 📄 01237 472005 32 en suite

WESTWARD HO!   Map 2 SS42

Royal North Devon Golf Links Rd EX39 1HD
☎ 01237 473817 📄 01237 423456
e-mail: info@royalnorthdevongolfclub.co.uk
web: www.royalnorthdevongolfclub.co.uk
Oldest links course in England with traditional links features and a museum in the clubhouse.

18 Holes, 6665yds, Par 72, SSS 72, Course record 64. Club membership 1150.

Visitors Mon-Fri, Sun & BHs. Booking required. Handicap certificate. Dress code. **Societies** booking required. **Green Fees** £60 per day, £45 per 18 holes (£50 per 18 holes Sun & BHs) **Course Designer** Old Tom Morris **Prof** Iain Parker **Facilities** ⑪ ⑩ ⑱ ⑰ ⑲ ⑳ ⑪ ⑥ **Leisure** Museum of Golf Memorabilia, snooker **Conf** facs Corporate Hospitality Days **Location** N side of village off B3236
Guesthouse ★★★ GH Culloden House, Fosketh Hill, WESTWARD HO! ☎ 01237 479421 📄 01237 479421 5 en suite

WOOLFARDISWORTHY   Map 2 SS32

Hartland Forest EX39 5RA
☎ 01237 431777
e-mail: hfgolf@googlemail.com
web: www.hartlandforestgolf.co.uk
Exceptionally varied course with water hazards on 12 holes and gentle slopes.

18 Holes, 6004yds, Par 71, SSS 69. Club membership 100.
Visitors Mon-Sun & BHs. Dress code. **Societies** booking required. **Green Fees** £15 per 9/18 holes **Course Designer** A Cartwright **Facilities** ⑱ ⑰ ⑲ ⑳ ⑪ ⑥ ⑦ ⑥ **Leisure** hard tennis courts, fishing **Conf** facs Corporate Hospitality Days **Location** 4m S of Clovelly Cross, 1.7m E of A39
Hotel ★★★ 71% HL The Hoops Inn & Country Hotel, The Hoops, HORNS CROSS, Nr Clovelly, Bideford ☎ 01237 451222 📄 01237 451222 13 en suite

YELVERTON   Map 2 SX56

Yelverton Golf Links Rd PL20 6BN
☎ 01822 852824 📄 01822 854869
e-mail: secretary@yelvertongc.co.uk
web: www.yelvertongc.co.uk
An excellent course on Dartmoor with plenty of gorse and heather. Tight lies in the fairways, fast greens and challenging hazards with outstanding views.

18 Holes, 6353yds, Par 71, SSS 71, Course record 64. Club membership 650.
Visitors handicap certificate. Dress code. **Societies** booking required. **Green Fees** £40 per day **Course Designer** Herbert Fowler **Prof** Tim McSherry **Facilities** ⑪ ⑩ ⑱ ⑰ ⑲ ⑳ ⑪ **Leisure** indoor golf academy. **Conf** facs Corporate Hospitality Days **Location** 1m S of Yelverton, off A386
Hotel ★★★ 75% HL Moorland Links, YELVERTON ☎ 01822 852245 📄 01822 852245 44 en suite

DORSET

ASHLEY HEATH   Map 4 SU10

Moors Valley Horton Rd BH24 2ET
☎ 01425 479776
e-mail: golf@moorsvalleygolf.co.uk
web: www.moors-valley.co.uk/golf
Skilfully designed by Hawtree, this mature heathland and woodland course is scenically set within a wildlife conservation area, exuding peace and tranquillity. Each hole has its own character, the back seven being in particular very special. The course is renowned for its greens.

Moors Valley Golf Course: 18 Holes, 6337yds, Par 72, SSS 70, Course record 67.
Visitors Mon-Sun & BHs. Booking required. Dress code. **Societies** booking required. **Green Fees** £23 per round **Course Designer** Hawtree & Son **Facilities** ⑪ ⑩ by prior arrangement ⑱ ⑰ ⑲ ⑳ ⑪ ⑥ ⑦ ⑥ **Leisure** fishing, 4 hole game improvement course, bike hire, aerial assault course **Conf** facs Corporate Hospitality Days **Location** 1.5m from A331/A338 rdbt, signed
Hotel BUD Travelodge Ringwood, St Leonards, RINGWOOD ☎ 08719 846 237 📄 08719 846 237 31 en suite

BEAMINSTER   Map 3 ST40

Chedington Court South Perrott DT8 3HU
☎ 01935 891413 📄 01935 891217
e-mail: info@chedingtoncourtgolfclub.com
web: www.chedingtongolfclub.co.uk
This beautiful 18-hole parkland course is set on the Dorset-Somerset borders with mature trees and interesting water hazards. A challenge from the first hole, par 5, blind drive to the elevated tee on the 15th, and the closing holes can be tricky.

18 Holes, 5924yds, Par 70, SSS 70, Course record 68. Club membership 449.
Visitors Mon-Sun & BHs. Booking advised. Dress code. **Societies** booking required. **Green Fees** £25 per round (£30 weekends). **Course Designer** David Hemstock/Donald Steel **Prof** Steve Ritchie **Facilities** ⑪ ⑩ ⑱ ⑰ ⑲ ⑳ ⑪ ⑥ **Conf** facs Corporate Hospitality Days **Location** 5m NE of Beaminster on A356 Dorchester-Crewkerne
Hotel ★★★ 80% HL BridgeHouse, 3 Prout Bridge, BEAMINSTER ☎ 01308 862200 📄 01308 862200 14 en suite

BERE REGIS   Map 3 SY89

Dorset Golf & Country Club BH20 7NT
☎ 01929 472244 📄 01929 471294
e-mail: admin@dorsetgolfresort.com
web: www.dorsetgolfresort.com
Lakeland/Parkland is the longest course in Dorset. Designed by Martin Hawtree with numerous interconnected water features, carefully planned bunkers and sculptured greens. A player who completes a round without hitting into every hazard has every reason to celebrate. The Woodland course, although shorter, is equally outstanding with rhododendron and tree-lined fairways. All holes built to USGA specification.

continued

Lakeland/Parkland Course: 18 Holes, 6580yds, Par 72, SSS 73, Course record 69.
Woodland Course: 9 Holes, 5032yards, Par 66, SSS 64. Club membership 600.

Visitors Mon-Sun & BHs. Dress code. **Societies** booking required. **Green Fees** £39 (£43 weekend & BHs) **Course Designer** Martin Hawtree **Prof** Scott Porter **Facilities** ⓣ ⓘⓞⓛ ⓑ ⓓ ⓦ ⓛ ⓐ ⓥ ⓟ ⓞ ⓓ ⓛ **Leisure** fishing, sauna, gymnasium, 3 rink indoor longmat bowling centre **Conf** facs Corporate Hospitality Days **Location** 5m from Bere Regis on Wool Road
Hotel ★★★ 73% HL Worgret Manor, Worgret Road, WAREHAM ☎ 01929 552957 ᨑ 01929 552957 12 en suite

BLANDFORD FORUM   Map 3 ST80

Ashley Wood Wimborne Rd DT11 9HN
☎ 01258 452253   ᨑ 01258 450590
e-mail: generalmanager@ashleywoodgolfclub.com
web: www.ashleywoodgolfclub.com

The course is one of the oldest in the county. The first record of play on Keyneston Down was in 1896, and part of the course is played over Buzbury Rings, a prehistoric hill fort with magnificent views over the Stour and Tarrant valleys. Constructed on downland, the fairways are undulating and, apart from the 3rd hole with a short sharp hill, all holes are easy walking. Four holes are played within the ancient woodland of Ashley Woods. The natural chalk provides excellent drainage.

The Ashley Wood Golf Club: 18 Holes, 6308yds, Par 70, SSS 70, Course record 66. Club membership 670.

Visitors Mon-Fri. Weekends & BHs pm only. Booking required weekends & BHs. Handicap certificate. Dress code. **Societies** booking required. **Green Fees** £43 per day, £28 per 18 holes after 10am (£33 per 18 holes weekends) **Course Designer** P Tallack **Prof** Jon Shimmons **Facilities** ⓣ ⓘⓞⓛ by prior arrangement ⓑ ⓓ ⓦ ⓐ ⓥ ⓓ ⓦ ⓛ **Conf** Corporate Hospitality Days **Location** 2m E on B3082
Hotel ★★★ 73% HL Best Western Crown Hotel, West Street, BLANDFORD FORUM ☎ 01258 456626 ᨑ 01258 456626 32 en suite

BOURNEMOUTH   Map 4 SZ09

The Club at Meyrick Park Central Dr, Meyrick Park BH2 6LH
☎ 01202 786000   ᨑ 01202 786020
e-mail: meyrickpark.lodge@theclubcompany.com
web: www.theclubcompany.com
Picturesque municipal parkland course founded in 1890.
The Club at Meyrick Park: 18 Holes, 5600yds, Par 69, SSS 69, Course record 63.
Visitors Mon-Sun & BHs. Booking required. Dress code. **Societies** booking required. **Green Fees** not confirmed **Prof** Darren Strathan **Facilities** ⓣ ⓘⓞⓛ ⓑ ⓓ ⓦ ⓐ ⓥ ⓟ ⓞ ⓓ
Leisure sauna, gymnasium, spa and steam room
Hotel ★★★ 66% HL Burley Court, Bath Road, BOURNEMOUTH ☎ 01202 552824 & 556704 ᨑ 01202 552824 38 en suite

Iford Golf Centre Riverside Av, off Castle Lane East BH7 7ES
☎ 01202 436436   ᨑ 01202 436444
e-mail: info@ifordgolfcentre.co.uk
web: www.ifordgolfcentre.co.uk
A well drained meadowland course beside the river Stour with many mature trees and lakes on five holes. Enjoyable for intermediates and beginners off yellow or white tees and a test for any golfer off the back blue tees. Greens are superb and need careful reading.
Bridge Course: 18 Holes, 6277yards, Par 72, SSS 69. Club membership 300.
Visitors Mon-Sun & BHs. Booking required. Dress code. **Societies** booking required. **Green Fees** £16.50 per 18 holes (£21 per 18 holes weekends). Par 3 course from £3 **Course Designer** John Jacobs Golf Associates **Prof** Lawrence Moxon **Facilities** ⓣ ⓘⓞⓛ ⓑ ⓓ ⓦ ⓐ ⓥ ⓟ ⓓ ⓦ ⓓ ⓛ **Leisure** 9 hole par 3 course **Conf** facs Corporate Hospitality Days **Location** off A338 onto A3060 for Christchurch, past Tesco, left onto Riverside Av
Hotel BUD Innkeeper's Lodge Bournemouth, Cooper Dean Roundabout, Castle Lane East, BOURNEMOUTH ☎ 0845 112 6085 ᨑ 0845 112 6085 28 en suite

Knighton Heath Francis Av BH11 8NX
☎ 01202 572633   ᨑ 01202 590774
e-mail: khgc@btinternet.com
web: www.khgc.co.uk
Undulating heathland course on high ground inland from Poole.
18 Holes, 6084yds, Par 70, SSS 69. Club membership 550.
Visitors Mon-Fri except BHs. Handicap certificate. Dress code. **Societies** booking required. **Green Fees** £30 per day, £23 per round **Prof** David Miles **Facilities** ⓣ ⓘⓞⓛ ⓑ ⓓ ⓦ ⓐ ⓥ ⓓ
Conf Corporate Hospitality Days **Location** N side of Poole, junct A348 signed at rdbt
Guesthouse ★★★★ GA Ashton Lodge, 10 Oakley Hill, WIMBORNE ☎ 01202 883423 ᨑ 01202 883423 5 rms (2 en suite)

Queen's Park Queens Park Drive West BH8 9BY
☎ 01202 437807   ᨑ 01202 396817
e-mail: queenspark@bournemouth.gov.uk
web: www.littledowncentre.co.uk/qpgolf
Mature parkland with undulating tree-lined fairways. A demanding test of golf, with each hole having a unique character.

continued

Queen's Park Golf Course: 18 Holes, 6132yds, Par 71, SSS 69, Course record 69. Club membership 190.
Visitors Mon-Sun & BHs. Booking required. Dress code. **Societies** booking required. **Green Fees** £17 per round (£23 weekends & BHs). Reduced winter rates. **Facilities** ⓣ ⦿ ⓛ ⊡ ⓕ ⼈ 🖻 ⼑ 🛒 🏌 **Conf** facs Corporate Hospitality Days **Location** 2m NE of Bournemouth town centre off A338
Hotel ★★★ 77% HL Queens, Meyrick Rd, East Cliff, BOURNEMOUTH ☎ 01202 554415 📄 01202 554415 109 en suite

Solent Meads Rolls Dr, Hengistbury Head BH6 4NA
☎ 01202 420795
e-mail: solentmeads@yahoo.co.uk
web: www.solentmeads.com
An 18-hole par 3 links course overlooking Hengistbury Head with fine views of Christchurch Harbour and the Isle of Wight. Expect a sea breeze. One of the driest courses in the county with no temporary greens.
Solent Meads Golf Centre: 18 Holes, 2182yards, Par 54, Course record 52.
Visitors Mon-Sun & BHs. **Societies** welcome. **Green Fees** £8 per 18 holes **Prof** Warren Butcher **Facilities** ⓣ ⓛ ⊡ 🖻 ⼑ 🏌 🏌 **Leisure** 9 hole fun golf **Conf** Corporate Hospitality Days **Location** from A35 take B3509 (signposted Tuckton/Southbourne). At 2nd roundabout go straight ahead and take 1st left (Broadway). After 0.75m turn left into Rolls Drive.
Hotel ★★★ 77% HL Christchurch Harbour Hotel, 95 Mudeford, CHRISTCHURCH ☎ 01202 483434 📄 01202 483434 64 en suite

---

BRIDPORT
Map 3 SY49

Bridport & West Dorset The Clubhouse, Burton Rd DT6 4PS
☎ 01308 421491 & 421095 📄 01308 421095
e-mail: secretary@bridportgolfclub.org.uk
web: www.bridportgolfclub.org.uk
Seaside links course on the top of the east cliff, with fine views over Lyme Bay and surrounding countryside. The signature 6th hole, known as Port Coombe, is only 133yds but dropping from the top of the cliff to a green almost at sea level far below. Fine sea views along the Chesil Bank to Portland Bill and across Lyme Bay.
18 Holes, 6213yds, Par 70, SSS 68. Club membership 700.
Visitors Mon-Sun & BHs. Booking required weekends & BHs. Handicap certificate. Dress code. **Societies** booking required. **Green Fees** not confirmed **Course Designer** Hawtree **Prof** David Parsons **Facilities** ⓣ ⦿ ⓛ ⊡ ⓕ ⼈ 🖻 🏌 🛒 🏌 **Leisure** pitch & putt (holiday season) **Conf** Corporate Hospitality Days **Location** 1m E of Bridport on B3157
Hotel ★★★ 64% HL Haddon House, West Bay, BRIDPORT ☎ 01308 423626 & 425323 📄 01308 423626 12 en suite

---

BROADSTONE
Map 3 SZ09

Broadstone (Dorset) Wentworth Dr BH18 8DQ
☎ 01202 692595 📄 01202 642520
e-mail: admin@broadstonegolfclub.com
web: www.broadstonegolfclub.com
Undulating and demanding heathland course with the 2nd, 7th, 13th and 16th being particularly challenging holes.
18 Holes, 6349yds, Par 70, SSS 70, Course record 63. Club membership 620.

Visitors Mon-Wed, Fri & Sun except BHs. Thu pm only. Booking required. Handicap certificate. Dress code. **Societies** booking required. **Green Fees** not confirmed **Course Designer** Colt/Dunn **Prof** Mathew Wilson **Facilities** ⓣ ⦿ ⓛ ⊡ ⓕ ⼈ 🖻 ⼑ 🏌 🏌 **Conf** Corporate Hospitality Days **Location** N side of village off B3074

Broadstone (Dorset)

Guesthouse ★★★★ GA Ashton Lodge, 10 Oakley Hill, WIMBORNE ☎ 01202 883423 📄 01202 883423 5 rms (2 en suite)

CHRISTCHURCH
Map 4 SZ19

Dudmoor Farm Dudmoor Farm Rd, Off Fairmile Rd BH23 6AQ
☎ 01202 473826 📄 01202 480207
A testing par 3 and 4 wooded heathland course.
Dudmoor Farm Golf Course: 9 Holes, 1562yds, Par 31.
Visitors contact course for details. **Societies** booking required. **Green Fees** £8.50 per 9/18 holes (£9.50 weekends & BHs) **Facilities** ⊡ ⼈ ⼑ 🏌 🛒 🏌 **Leisure** adjoining riding stables **Location** private road off B3073 Christchurch-Hurn road
Hotel ★★★ 77% HL Best Western Waterford Lodge, 87 Bure Lane, Friars Cliff, CHRISTCHURCH ☎ 01425 282100 & 282101 📄 01425 282100 18 en suite

---

DORCHESTER
Map 3 SY69

Came Down Higher Came DT2 8NR
☎ 01305 813494 (manager) 📄 01305 815122
e-mail: manager@camedowngolfclub.co.uk
web: www.camedowngolfclub.co.uk
Scene of the West of England championships on several occasions, this fine course lies on a high plateau commanding glorious views over Portland. Three par 5 holes add interest to a round. The turf is of the springy, downland type. Connected with Samuel Ryder and the beginnings of the Ryder Cup.
18 Holes, 6255yds, Par 70, SSS 70.
Club membership 750.
Visitors handicap certificate. Dress code. **Societies** booking required. **Green Fees** £36 per day weekdays (£40 weekends) **Course Designer** J H Taylor/H S Colt **Prof** Nick Rodgers **Facilities** ⓣ ⦿ ⓛ ⊡ ⼈ 🏌 🏌 **Location** 2m off A354 between Dorchester & Weymouth)
Guesthouse ★★★★ RR Yalbury Cottage & Restaurant, Lower Bockhampton, DORCHESTER ☎ 01305 262382 📄 01305 262382 8 en suite

FERNDOWN
Map 4 SU00

Dudsbury 64 Christchurch Rd BH22 8ST
☎ 01202 593499 🖷 01202 594555
e-mail: info@dudsburygolfclub.co.uk
web: www.dudsburygolfclub.co.uk
Set in 160 acres of beautiful Dorset countryside rolling down to the
River Stour. Wide variety of interesting and challenging hazards,
notably water which comes into play on 14 holes. The well-drained
greens are protected by large bunkers and water hazards. A feature
hole is the 16th where the green is over two lakes; the more aggressive
the drive, the greater the reward.

*Championship Course: 18 Holes, 6904yds, Par 71, SSS 73,
Course record 64. Club membership 715.*

Visitors Mon-Sun & BHs. Dress code. **Societies** booking required.
Green Fees £50 per 36 holes, £40 per 18 holes (£60/£45 weekend and
BHs) **Course Designer** Donald Steel **Prof** Steve Pockneall **Facilities** ⓣ
ⁱ◎ ⬛ 🖵 🖫 ⚖ ⛫ ◈ ⚐ ⚑ ⚑ Leisure fishing,
6 hole par 3 short game academy course **Conf** facs Corporate
Hospitality Days **Location** 3m N of Bournemouth on B3073
Hotel ★★★★ 70% HL Norfolk Royale, Richmond Hill,
BOURNEMOUTH ☎ 01202 551521 🖷 01202 551521 95 en suite

> *Ferndown* 119 Golf Links Rd BH22 8BU
> ☎ 01202 874602 🖷 01202 873926
> **web:** www.ferndown-golf-club.co.uk
> *Championship Course: 18 Holes, 6505yds, Par 71,
> SSS 71, Course record 63.*
> *Presidents Course: 9 Holes, 5604yds, Par 70, SSS 68.*
> **Course Designer** Harold Hilton **Location** S side of town centre off
> A347
> **Telephone for further details**
> **Hotel** ★★★ 71% SHL Tyrrells Ford Country House, Avon,
> RINGWOOD ☎ 01425 672646 🖷 01425 672646 14 en suite

Ferndown Forest Forest Links Rd BH22 9PH
☎ 01202 876096 🖷 01202 894095
e-mail: golf@ferndownforestgolf.co.uk
web: www.ferndownforestgolf.co.uk
Flat parkland dotted with mature oaks, several interesting water
features, and some tight fairways.

*18 Holes, 5068yds, Par 68, SSS 67, Course record 69.
Club membership 400.*

Visitors Mon-Sun & BHs. **Societies** booking required. **Green Fees** £16
per round (£18 weekends & BHs) **Course Designer** Guy Hunt/Richard
Graham **Prof** Graham Howell **Facilities** ⓣ ⁱ◎ ⬛ 🖵 🖫 ⚖
⛫ ⚐ 🛒 ◈ ⚑ **Conf** Corporate Hospitality Days **Location** off
A31 N of Ferndown, follow signs to Dorset Police Headquarters
Hotel ★★★ 71% SHL Tyrrells Ford Country House, Avon,
RINGWOOD ☎ 01425 672646 🖷 01425 672646 14 en suite

HALSTOCK
Map 3 ST50

Halstock Common Ln BA22 9SF
☎ 01935 891689 & 891968 (pro shop) 🖷 01935 891839
*Halstock Golf Enterprises: 18 Holes, 4481yds, Par 66,
SSS 63, Course record 63.*
Prof Robert Harris **Facilities** ⓣ ⁱ◎ ⬛ 🖵 🖫 ⚖ ⛫ ⚐ ◈
⚑ **Location** 6m S of Yeovil
Telephone for further details
Hotel ★★★★ CHH Summer Lodge Country House Hotel,

Restaurant & Spa, EVERSHOT ☎ 01935 482000 🖷 01935 482000
24 en suite

HIGHCLIFFE
Map 4 SZ29

Highcliffe Castle 107 Lymington Rd BH23 4LA
☎ 01425 272210 🖷 01425 272953
Picturesque parkland with easy walking.

*18 Holes, 4798yds, Par 64, SSS 63, Course record 58.
Club membership 450.*

Visitors Mon-Sun & BHs. Handicap certificate. Dress code.
Societies booking required. **Green Fees** £27.50 per round (£36
weekends) **Facilities** ⓣ ⁱ◎ by prior arrangement ⬛ 🖵 🖫 ⚖
Conf Corporate Hospitality Days **Location** SW side of town on A337
Hotel ★★★ 77% HL Best Western Waterford Lodge, 87 Bure
Lane, Friars Cliff, CHRISTCHURCH ☎ 01425 282100 & 282101
🖷 01425 282100 18 en suite

HURN
Map 4 SZ19

Parley Parley Green lane BH23 6BB
☎ 01202 591600 🖷 01202 579043
e-mail: info@parleygolf.co.uk
web: www.parleygolf.co.uk
Flat testing parkland course with few hazards including par 5s.
Renowned 5th hole, bordering the River Stour.

*Parley Golf Course: 9 Holes, 4938yds, Par 68, SSS 64,
Course record 69. Club membership 100.*

Visitors Mon-Sun & BHs. **Societies** welcome. **Green Fees** £14
for 18 holes, £10 for 9 holes (£15/£11.50 weekends & BHs) **Course
Designer** P Goodfellow **Prof** Richard Hill **Facilities** ⓣ ⬛ 🖵 🖫
⚖ ⚐ ◈ ⚑ **Conf** Corporate Hospitality Days **Location** on
B3073 opp Bournemouth airport
Hotel ★★★ 80% HL Elstead, Knyveton Road, BOURNEMOUTH
☎ 01202 293071 🖷 01202 293071 50 en suite

LYME REGIS
Map 3 SY39

Lyme Regis Timber Hill DT7 3HQ
☎ 01297 442963 🖷 01297 444368
e-mail: secretary@lrgc.eclipse.co.uk
web: www.lymeregisgolfclub.co.uk

Undulating cliff-top course with magnificent views of Golden Cap and
Lyme Bay.

*18 Holes, 6283yds, Par 71, SSS 70, Course record 65.
Club membership 575.*

continued

Visitors Mon-Wed, Fri-Sun & BHs. Handicap certificate. Dress code. **Societies** booking required. **Green Fees** not confirmed **Course Designer** Donald Steel **Prof** Duncan Driver **Facilities** ⊕ ⊘ ▣ ▢ ⊙ ♨ ⊞ ✔ ♣ ✎ ✦ **Conf** Corporate Hospitality Days **Location** W end of Charmouth bypass (A35), take A3052 to Lyme Regis. 1.5m from A3052/A35 rdbt
Hotel ★★★ 77% HL Hotel Alexandra and Restaurant, Pound Street, LYME REGIS ☎ 01297 442010 📄 01297 442010 25 en suite

LYTCHETT MATRAVERS   Map 3 SY99

Bulbury Woods Bulbury Ln BH16 6HR
☎ 01929 459574   📄 01929 459000
web: www.bulbury-woods.co.uk
18 Holes, 6002yds, Par 71, SSS 69.
Facilities ⊕ ⊘ ▣ ▢ ⊙ ♨ ⊞ ✔ ♣ ✎ **Conf** facs Corporate Hospitality Days **Location** A35 Poole-Dorchester, 3m from Poole centre
Telephone for further details
Hotel ★★★ 73% HL Worgret Manor, Worgret Road, WAREHAM ☎ 01929 552957 📄 01929 552957 12 en suite

POOLE   Map 4 SZ09

Parkstone Links Rd, Parkstone BH14 9QS
☎ 01202 707138   📄 01202 706027
e-mail: admin@parkstonegolfclub.co.uk
web: www.parkstonegolfclub.co.uk
Very scenic heathland course with views of Poole Bay. Designed in 1909 by Willie Park Jnr and enlarged in 1932 by James Braid. The result of this highly imaginative reconstruction was an intriguing and varied test of golf set among pines and heather fringed fairways where every hole presents a different challenge.
18 Holes, 6241yds, Par 72, SSS 71, Course record 63. Club membership 700.
Visitors Mon, Thu, Fri & BHs. Booking required. Handicap certificate. Dress code. **Societies** booking required. **Green Fees** £80 per day; £55 per round (£90/£65 BHs). **Course Designer** Willie Park Jnr **Prof** Martyn Thompson **Facilities** ⊕ ⊘ ▣ ▢ ⊙ ♨ ⊞ ✎ ✦ **Conf** Corporate Hospitality Days **Location** E side of town centre off A35
Hotel ★★★ 68% HL Arndale Court, 62/66 Wimborne Road, POOLE ☎ 01202 683746 📄 01202 683746 39 en suite

SHERBORNE   Map 3 ST61

Sherborne Higher Clatcombe DT9 4RN
☎ 01935 814431   📄 01935 814218
e-mail: secretary@sherbornegolfclub.co.uk
web: www.sherbornegolfclub.co.uk
Beautiful mature parkland to the north of Sherborne on the Dorset-Somerset border, with extensive views.
18 Holes, 6414yds, Par 72, SSS 71, Course record 62. Club membership 700.
Visitors Mon-Sun & BHs. Booking required. Dress code. **Societies** booking required. **Green Fees** £30 per day, £25 per round (£36 per round weekends) **Course Designer** James Braid (part) **Prof** Alistair Tresidder **Facilities** ⊕ ⊘ ▣ ▢ ⊙ ♨ ⊞ ⊞ ♨ ✎ **Conf** Corporate Hospitality Days **Location** 2m N off B3145
Hotel ★★★ 75% HL Eastbury, Long Street, SHERBORNE ☎ 01935 813131 📄 01935 813131 23 en suite

STURMINSTER MARSHALL   Map 3 ST90

Sturminster Marshall Moor Ln BH21 4AH
☎ 01258 858444
e-mail: mike@sturminstermarshallgolfclub.co.uk
web: www.sturminstermarshallgolfclub.co.uk
Privately owned club with pay & play facilities set in beautiful Dorset countryside. Played off 18 different tees the course is ideal for golfers of all standards.
Sturminster Marshall Golf Course: 9 Holes, 3850yds, Par 64, SSS 59, Course record 64. Club membership 200.
Visitors dress code. **Societies** booking required. **Green Fees** £15 per 18 holes; £10 per 9 holes **Course Designer** John Sharkey/David Holdsworth **Prof** Mike Dodd/Colin Murray **Facilities** ⊕ ⊘ ▣ ▢ ⊙ ♨ ⊞ ⊞ ✔ ♣ ✎ ✦ **Leisure** children's golf school, ladies academy **Conf** facs Corporate Hospitality Days **Location** on A350, signed from village
Hotel ★★★ 73% HL Best Western Crown Hotel, West Street, BLANDFORD FORUM ☎ 01258 456626 📄 01258 456626 32 en suite

SWANAGE   Map 4 SZ07

Isle of Purbeck BH19 3AB
☎ 01929 450361 & 450354   📄 01929 450501
web: www.purbeckgolf.co.uk
Purbeck Course: 18 Holes, 6295yds, Par 70, SSS 70, Course record 66.
Dene Course: 9 Holes, 4014yds, Par 60.
Course Designer H Colt **Location** 2.5m N on B3351
Telephone for further details
Hotel ★★★ 70% HL Grand, Burlington Road, SWANAGE ☎ 01929 423353 📄 01929 423353 30 en suite

VERWOOD   Map 4 SU00

Crane Valley The Club House BH31 7LE
☎ 01202 814088   📄 01202 813407
e-mail: general@crane-valley.co.uk
web: www.crane-valley.co.uk
Two secluded parkland courses set amid rolling Dorset countryside and mature woodland. The 6th nestles in the bend of the River Crane and there are four long par 5s ranging from 499 to 545yds.
Valley: 18 Holes, 6445yds, Par 72, SSS 71, Course record 65.
Woodland: 9 Holes, 2060yds, Par 33, SSS 30.
Club membership 560.
Visitors Mon-Sun & BHs. Booking required. Dress code. **Societies** booking required. **Green Fees** Valley £25 per round (£30 weekends and BHs). Woodland £10 for 18 holes, £7 for 9 holes (£12/£8 weekends) **Course Designer** Donald Steel **Prof** Darrel Ranson **Facilities** ⊕ ⊘ ▣ ▢ ⊙ ♨ ⊞ ⊞ ✔ ♣ ✎ ✦ **Conf** facs Corporate Hospitality Days **Location** 6m W of Ringwood on B3081
Hotel ★★★ 71% SHL Tyrrells Ford Country House, Avon, RINGWOOD ☎ 01425 672646 📄 01425 672646 14 en suite

WAREHAM
Map 3 SY98

Wareham Sandford Rd BH20 4DH
☎ 01929 554147 📠 01929 557993
e-mail: warehamgolf@tiscali.co.uk
web: www.warehamgolfclub.com

At the entrance to the Purbeck Hills with splendid views over Poole Harbour and Wareham Forest. A mixture of undulating parkland and heathland fairways. A challenge for all abilities.

18 Holes, 5766yds, Par 69, SSS 68, Course record 66. Club membership 400.

Visitors Mon-Sun & BHs. Handicap certificate. Dress code.
Societies booking required. **Green Fees** £36 per day, £25 per round
Facilities ⑪ ⓛ ⌷ ⑪ ⚲ ✧ ⚙ ✧ **Location** 0.5m N of Wareham on A351
Hotel ★★★ 73% HL Worgret Manor, Worgret Road, WAREHAM
☎ 01929 552957 📠 01929 552957 12 en suite

WEYMOUTH
Map 3 SY67

Weymouth Links Rd DT4 0PF
☎ 0844 9809909 (Manager) & 01305 773997(Pro)
📠 01305 788029
e-mail: weymouthgolfclub@aol.com
web: www.weymouthgolfclub.co.uk

A seaside parkland course situated in the heart of the town with views over the Dorset coast and countryside. Recent developments have seen the building and completion of 18 new tees and the club celebrated its centenary in 2009.

18 Holes, 5996yds, Par 70, SSS 69, Course record 60. Club membership 1300.

Visitors Mon-Thu, weekends & BHs. Booking required. Handicap certificate. Dress code. **Societies** booking required. **Green Fees** £40 per day, £32 per round (£38 weekends) **Course Designer** James Braid **Prof** Des Lochrie **Facilities** ⑪ ⑫ ⓛ ⌷ ⑪ ⚲ ⚙ ✧ ⚙ ✧ **Conf** Corporate Hospitality Days **Location** N side of town centre off B3157
Hotel ★★★ 68% HL Hotel Rex, 29 The Esplanade, WEYMOUTH
☎ 01305 760400 📠 01305 760400 31 en suite

WIMBORNE
Map 3 SZ09

Canford Magna Knighton Ln BH21 3AS
☎ 01202 592552 📠 01202 592550
e-mail: admin@canfordmagnagc.co.uk
web: www.canfordmagnagc.co.uk

Lying in 350 acres of Dorset countryside, the Canford Magna Golf Club provides 45 holes of challenging golf for the discerning player. The 18-hole Parkland and Riverside courses are quite different and the new nine-hole Knighton course demands the same level of playing skill. For those wishing to improve their handicap, the Golf Academy offers a covered driving range, pitching greens, a chipping green and bunkers, together with a 6-hole par 3 academy course.

Parkland: 18 Holes, 6519yds, Par 71, SSS 71, Course record 65.
Riverside: 18 Holes, 6173yds, Par 70, SSS 69, Course record 63.
Knighton: 9 Holes, 1377yds, Par 27, Course record 26. Club membership 1000.

Visitors Mon-Sun & BHs. Booking required. Dress code.
Societies booking required **Green Fees** Parkland £23.50 per round

(£27.50 weekends). Riverside £18.50/£21.50. Knighton £7/£8 **Course Designer** Howard Swan **Prof** david Cooper **Facilities** ⑪ ⑫ ⓛ ⌷ ⑪ ⚲ ✧ ⚙ ✧ ✧ **Conf** facs Corporate Hospitality Days
Location on A341
Guesthouse ★★★★ GA Ashton Lodge, 10 Oakley Hill, WIMBORNE
☎ 01202 883423 📠 01202 883423 5 rms (2 en suite)

CO DURHAM

BARNARD CASTLE
Map 12 NZ01

Barnard Castle Harmire Rd DL12 8QN
☎ 01833 638355 📠 01833 695551
e-mail: sec@barnardcastlegolfclub.org.uk
web: www.barnardcastlegolfclub.org.uk

Flat parkland in open countryside. Plantations and natural water add colour and interest to this classic course.

18 Holes, 6406yds, Par 73, SSS 71, Course record 63. Club membership 650.

Visitors Mon-Sun & BHs. Booking required weekends & BHs. Dress code. **Societies** welcome. **Green Fees** £27 per round (£30 weekends & BHs) **Course Designer** A Watson **Prof** Darren Pearce **Facilities** ⑪ ⑫ ⓛ ⌷ ⑪ ⚲ ✧ ⚙ ✧ **Conf** Corporate Hospitality Days **Location** 1m N of town centre on B6278
Hotel ★★ HL Rose & Crown, ROMALDKIRK ☎ 01833 650213
📠 01833 650213 12 en suite

BEAMISH
Map 12 NZ25

Beamish Park DH9 0RH
☎ 0191 370 1382 📠 0191 370 2937
e-mail: info@beamishgolfclub.co.uk
web: www.beamishgolfclub.co.uk

Parkland course designed by Henry Cotton and W Woodend.

Beamish Park Golf Club Ltd: 18 Holes, 6183yds, Par 71, SSS 70, Course record 64. Club membership 630.

Visitors Mon-Fri except BHs. Dress code. **Societies** welcome. **Green Fees** £28 per day, £25 per round **Course Designer** H Cotton **Prof** Chris Cole **Facilities** ⚲ ⌷ ✧ ⚙ ✧ **Conf** Corporate Hospitality Days **Location** 1m NW off A693
Hotel ★★★ 80% HL Beamish Park, Beamish Burn Road, Marley Hill, BEAMISH, Newcastle upon Tyne ☎ 01207 230666
📠 01207 230666 42 en suite

BILLINGHAM
Map 8 NZ42

Billingham Sandy Ln TS22 5NA
☎ 01642 533816 & 557060 (Pro) 🖨 01642 533816
e-mail: billinghamgc@btconnect.com
web: www.billinghamgolfclub.com
Undulating parkland with water hazards.

*Billingham Golf Club Ltd: 18 Holes, 6346yds, Par 71,
SSS 70, Course record 62. Club membership 1050.*

Visitors Mon-Sun & BHs. Booking required weekends & BHs. Dress
code. **Societies** booking required. **Green Fees** not confirmed **Course
Designer** F Pennick **Prof** Michael Ure **Facilities** ⊕ 🍴 ⓘ ┗ ⏢ 🖫
♿ 🏠 ⛳ ⛴ ∅ **Conf** facs **Location** 1m W of town centre
Hotel ★★★ 79% HL Best Western Parkmore Hotel & Leisure Club,
636 Yarm Road, Eaglescliffe, STOCKTON-ON-TEES ☎ 01642 786815
🖨 01642 786815 55 en suite

Wynyard Wellington Dr TS22 5QJ
☎ 01740 644399 🖨 01740 644599
*Wellington: 18 Holes, 7063yds, Par 72, SSS 73,
Course record 63.*

Course Designer Hawtree **Location** off A689 between A19 & A1
Telephone for further details
Hotel ★★★★ 73% HL Thistle Middlesbrough, Fry Street,
MIDDLESBROUGH ☎ 0871 376 9028 🖨 0871 376 9028 132 en suite

BISHOP AUCKLAND
Map 8 NZ22

Bishop Auckland High Plains, Durham Rd DL14 8DL
☎ 01388 661618 🖨 01388 607005
e-mail: enquiries@bagc.co.uk
web: www.bagc.co.uk
A parkland course with many well-established trees offering a
challenging round. A small ravine adds interest to several holes
including the short 7th, from a raised tee to a green surrounded by
a stream, gorse and bushes. Pleasant views over the Wear Valley
and over the residence of the Bishop of Durham. Has the distinction
of having five par 5 holes and five par 3s.

*18 Holes, 6504yds, Par 72, SSS 71, Course record 63.
Club membership 950.*

Visitors Mon-Sun & BHs. Booking required weekends & BHs.
Handicap certificate. Dress code. **Societies** welcome. **Green
Fees** £35 per day, £30 per round (£40/£35 per round weekends)
Course Designer James Kay **Prof** David Skiffington **Facilities** ⊕
🍴 ⓘ ┗ ⏢ 🖫 ♿ 🏠 🛥 ∅ **Leisure** snooker **Conf** facs
Corporate Hospitality Days **Location** 1m NE on A689
Hotel ★★★ 79% CHH Best Western Whitworth Hall Hotel,
Whitworth Hall Country Park, SPENNYMOOR ☎ 01388 811772
🖨 01388 811772 29 en suite

BURNOPFIELD
Map 12 NZ15

Hobson Hobson NE16 6BZ
☎ 01207 270941 🖨 01207 271069
18 Holes, 6403yds, Par 69, SSS 68, Course record 65.
Prof Jack Ord **Facilities** ⊕ 🍴 ⓘ ┗ ⏢ 🖫 ♿ 🏠 ⛳ ∅ 🛥
∅ **Location** 0.75m S on A692
Telephone for further details
Hotel ★★★ 80% HL Beamish Park, Beamish Burn Road,
Marley Hill, BEAMISH, Newcastle upon Tyne ☎ 01207 230666
🖨 01207 230666 42 en suite

CHESTER-LE-STREET
Map 12 NZ25

Chester-le-Street Lumley Park DH3 4NS
☎ 0191 388 3218 (Secretary)
e-mail: clsgcoffice@tiscali.co.uk
web: www.clsgolfclub.co.uk
Parkland course in castle grounds, good views, easy walking.

*18 Holes, 6479yds, Par 71, SSS 71, Course record 67.
Club membership 650.*

Visitors Mon-Fri except BHs. Booking required. Dress code.
Societies booking required. **Green Fees** £30 per day, £25 per round
(£35/£30 weekends) **Course Designer** J H Taylor **Prof** David Fletcher
Facilities ⊕ 🍴 ⓘ ┗ ⏢ 🖫 ♿ 🏠 ⛳ ∅ 🛥 ∅ **Conf** Corporate
Hospitality Days **Location** 0.5m E off B1284
Hotel ★★★★ 71% HL Ramside Hall, Carrville, DURHAM
☎ 0191 386 5282 🖨 0191 386 5282 80 en suite

Roseberry Grange Grange Villa DH2 3NF
☎ 0191 370 0670 🖨 0191 370 0224
e-mail: grahamstephenson@chester-le-street.gov.uk
web: www.chester-le-street.gov.uk
Parkland course providing a good test of golf for all abilities. Fine
panoramic views of County Durham.

*Roseberry Grange Golf Course: 18 Holes, 6152yds, Par 71,
SSS 69. Club membership 620.*

Visitors contact course for details. **Societies** booking required. **Green
Fees** £15 per round (£20 weekends) **Course Designer** Durham County
Council **Prof** Chris Jones **Facilities** ⊕ 🍴 ⓘ ┗ ⏢ 🖫 ♿ 🏠
∅ ⛳ **Location** 5m W of Chester-le-Street. Off A694 into West Pelton,
signed
Hotel ★★★ 75% HL George Washington Golf & Country Club,
Stone Cellar Road, High Usworth, WASHINGTON ☎ 0191 402 9988
🖨 0191 402 9988 103 en suite

CONSETT
Map 12 NZ15

Consett & District Elmfield Rd DH8 5NN
☎ 01207 505060 (secretary) 🖨 01207 505060
e-mail: consettgolfclub@btconnect.com
web: www.consettgolfclub.com
Undulating parkland and moorland course with views across the
Derwent Valley to the Cheviot Hills.

*18 Holes, 6041yds, Par 71, SSS 69, Course record 63.
Club membership 600.*

Visitors Mon-Sun except BHs. Booking required. Dress code.
Societies booking required. **Green Fees** £20 per day (£25 weekends)
Course Designer Harry Vardon **Facilities** ⊕ 🍴 ⓘ ┗ ⏢ 🖫
♿ 🏠 🛥 **Leisure** snooker room **Conf** Corporate Hospitality Days
Location N side of town on A691
Hotel ★★★ 73% HL Best Western Derwent Manor, Allensford,
CONSETT ☎ 01207 592000 🖨 01207 592000 48 en suite

CROOK
Map 12 NZ13

Crook Low Jobs Hill DL15 9AA
☎ 01388 762429   🖶 01388 762137
e-mail: secretary@crookgolfclub.co.uk
web: www.crookgolfclub.co.uk

Meadowland and parkland on an elevated position with natural hazards and varied holes. Panoramic views over Durham and the Cleveland Hills.

18 Holes, 6102yds, Par 70, SSS 69, Course record 64. Club membership 550.

Visitors contact club for details. **Societies** welcome. **Green Fees** phone **Facilities** ⓘ ⑩ ㊐ ㊐ ㊐ ㊐ ㊐ ㊐
🛈 **Conf** facs Corporate Hospitality Days **Location** 0.5m E off A690
Hotel ★★★ 79% CHH Best Western Whitworth Hall Hotel, Whitworth Hall Country Park, SPENNYMOOR ☎ 01388 811772 🖶 01388 811772 29 en suite

DARLINGTON
Map 8 NZ21

Blackwell Grange Briar Close, Blackwell DL3 8QX
☎ 01325 464458   🖶 01325 464458
e-mail: secretary@blackwellgrangegolf.com
web: www.blackwellgrangegolf.com

One of the most attractive courses in north-east England. Clever use of the trees on this easy walking course gives a feeling of having the course to oneself. Three ponds add to the variety of holes on offer.

18 Holes, 5621yds, Par 68, SSS 67, Course record 63. Club membership 600.

Visitors Mon, Tue, Wed-Sun & BHs. Booking required Fri-Sun & BHs. Dress code. **Societies** booking required. **Green Fees** £35 per day; £25 per round (£35 per round weekends & BHs) **Course Designer** F Pennink **Prof** Joanne Furby **Facilities** ⓘ ⑩ ㊐ ㊐ ㊐ ㊐ ㊐ ㊐ 🛈 **Conf** Corporate Hospitality Days **Location** 1.5m SW off A66 into Blackwell, signed
Hotel ★★★ 78% HL The Blackwell Grange Hotel, Blackwell Grange, DARLINGTON ☎ 0870 609 6121 & 01325 509955 🖶 0870 609 6121 108 en suite

Darlington Haughton Grange DL1 3JD
☎ 01325 355324   🖶 01325 366086
e-mail: office@darlington-gc.co.uk
web: www.darlington-gc.co.uk

Fairly flat parkland course with tree-lined fairways, and large first-class greens.

18 Holes, 6181yds, Par 70, SSS 69, Course record 65. Club membership 850.

Visitors dress code. **Societies** welcome. **Green Fees** £30 per 36 holes; £25 per 18 holes **Course Designer** Dr Alistair McKenzie **Prof** Craig Dilley **Facilities** ⓘ ⑩ ㊐ ㊐ ㊐ ㊐ ㊐ ㊐ 🛈 **Conf** Corporate Hospitality Days **Location** N side of town centre off A1150
Hotel ★★★ 85% HL Headlam Hall, Headlam, Gainford, DARLINGTON ☎ 01325 730238 🖶 01325 730238 40 en suite

Hall Garth Hotel, Golf & Country Club Coatham Mundeville DL1 3LU
☎ 01325 379710   🖶 01325 310083
web: www.foliohotels.com/hallgarth

Hall Garth Golf & Country Club Hotel: 9 Holes, 6621yds, Par 72, SSS 72.

Course Designer Brian Moore **Location** 0.5m from A1(M), junct 59 off A167
Telephone for further details
Hotel ★★★ 74% HL Hall Garth Hotel, Golf and Country Club, Coatham Mundeville, DARLINGTON ☎ 0870 609 6131 🖶 0870 609 6131 52 en suite

Headlam Hall Headlam DL2 3HA
☎ 01325 730238   🖶 01325 730790
web: www.headlamhall.co.uk

Headlam Hall Hotel: 9 Holes, 2075yards, Par 31, SSS 56.

Course Designer Ralph Givens **Location** 8m W of Darlington, off A67
Telephone for further details
Hotel ★★★ 85% HL Headlam Hall, Headlam, Gainford, DARLINGTON ☎ 01325 730238 🖶 01325 730238 40 en suite

Stressholme Snipe Ln DL2 2SA
☎ 01325 461002   🖶 01325 461002
web: www.darlington.gov.uk

Picturesque municipal parkland course, long but wide, with 98 bunkers and a par 3 hole played over a river.

18 Holes, 6431yds, Par 71, SSS 70, Course record 69. Club membership 450.

Visitors Mon-Sun & BHs. Booking required. Dress code.
Societies booking required. **Green Fees** £22 per day, £14 per round (£27.25/£16 weekends) **Prof** Ralph Givens **Facilities** ⓘ ⑩ ㊐ ㊐ ㊐ ㊐ ㊐ ㊐ 🛈 **Conf** facs Corporate Hospitality Days **Location** SW of town centre on A67
Hotel ★★★ 78% HL The Blackwell Grange Hotel, Blackwell Grange, DARLINGTON ☎ 0870 609 6121 & 01325 509955 🖶 0870 609 6121 108 en suite

DURHAM
Map 12 NZ24

Brancepeth Castle Brancepeth Village DH7 8EA
☎ 0191 378 0075   🖶 0191 378 3835
e-mail: enquiries@brancepeth-castle-golf.co.uk
web: www.brancepeth-castle-golf.co.uk

Parkland course overlooked at the 9th hole by beautiful Brancepeth Castle.

18 Holes, 6400yds, Par 70, SSS 70, Course record 64. Club membership 780.

Visitors Mon-Sun & BHs. Booking required weekends & BHs. Dress code. **Societies** booking required. **Green Fees** £40 per day, £35 per round (£40 per round weekends & BHs) **Course Designer** H S Colt **Prof** David Howdon **Facilities** ⓘ ⑩ ㊐ ㊐ ㊐ ㊐ ㊐ 🛈 **Conf** Corporate Hospitality Days **Location** 4m from Durham A690 towards Crook, left at x-rds in Brancepeth, left at Castle Gates, 400yds
Hotel ★★★★ 76% HL Durham Marriott Hotel, Royal County, Old Elvet, DURHAM ☎ 0191 386 6821 🖶 0191 386 6821 150 en suite

Durham City Littleburn, Langley Moor DH7 8HL
☎ 0191 378 0069   🖶 0191 378 4265
e-mail: durhamcitygolf@lineone.net
web: www.durhamcitygolf.co.uk

Parkland course bordered on several holes by the River Browney.

18 Holes, 6349yds, Par 71, SSS 70, Course record 66. Club membership 750.

Visitors Mon-Sun & BHs. Booking required. Dress code.

continued

Societies booking required. **Green Fees** £30 (£40 weekends & BHs) **Course Designer** C Stanton **Prof** Steve Corbally **Facilities** ⓣ ⍾◎⍾ ┗ ♉ 🍴 ╻ ⚑ **Conf** Corporate Hospitality Days **Location** 2m W of Durham City, turn left off A690 into Littleburn Ind Est

Hotel ★★★★ 76% HL Durham Marriott Hotel, Royal County, Old Elvet, DURHAM ☎ 0191 386 6821 📋 0191 386 6821 150 en suite

Mount Oswald South Rd DH1 3TQ
☎ 0191 386 7527 📋 0191 386 0975
e-mail: information@mountoswald.co.uk
web: www.mountoswald.co.uk

Picturesque parkland that gently undulates through the Durham countryside. The easy walking course attracts golfers of all levels and abilities.

Mount Oswald Manor & Golf Course: 18 Holes, 5991yds, Par 71, SSS 69. Club membership 124.

Visitors Mon-Sun & BHs. Booking required weekends & BHs. **Societies** welcome. **Green Fees** £16 per round (£18.50 weekends & BHs). Reduced winter rates **Prof** Chris Calder **Facilities** ⓣ ⍾◎⍾ ┗ ♉ 🍴 ╻ ⚑ ╱ ⚑ **Conf** facs Corporate Hospitality Days **Location** on A177, 1m SW of city centre
Hotel ★★★★ 71% HL Ramside Hall, Carrville, DURHAM ☎ 0191 386 5282 📋 0191 386 5282 80 en suite

Ramside Hall Carrville DH1 1TD
☎ 0191 386 9514 📋 0191 386 9519
e-mail: golf@ramsidegolfclub.fsnet.co.uk
web: www.ramsidehallhotel.co.uk

Parkland course consisting of three loops of nine holes, Princes, Bishops, and Cathedral - with 14 lakes and panoramic views surrounding an impressive hotel. Excellent golf academy and driving range on site.

Princes: 9 Holes, 3235yds, Par 36, SSS 36.
Bishops: 9 Holes, 3285yds, Par 36.
Cathedral: 9 Holes, 2874yds, Par 34. Club membership 450.

Visitors Mon-Sun & BHs. Booking required. Dress code. **Societies** booking required. **Green Fees** £35 per 18 holes (£40 weekends) **Course Designer** Jonathan Gaunt **Prof** Kevin Jackson **Facilities** ⓣ ⍾◎⍾ ┗ ♉ 🍴 ╻ ⚑ ◇ ╻ ╱ **Leisure** sauna, steam room **Conf** facs Corporate Hospitality Days **Location** 500yds from junct A1
Hotel ★★★★ 71% HL Ramside Hall, Carrville, DURHAM ☎ 0191 386 5282 📋 0191 386 5282 80 en suite

EAGLESCLIFFE
Map 8 NZ41

Eaglescliffe and District Yarm Rd TS16 0DQ
☎ 01642 780238 (office) 📋 01642 781128
e-mail: secretary@eaglescliffegolfclub.co.uk
web: www.eaglescliffegolfclub.co.uk

Undulating wooded parkland with views over the River Tees to the Cleveland Hills. A tee on the riverbank makes for a daunting tee shot at the 14th signature hole.

18 Holes, 6275yds, Par 72, SSS 70, Course record 64. Club membership 965.

Visitors Mon-Sun & BHs. Booking required. Dress code. **Societies** booking required. **Green Fees** £40 per day, £32 per round (£55/£40 Sun) **Course Designer** J Braid/H Cotton **Prof** Graeme Bell **Facilities** ⓣ ⍾◎⍾ ┗ ♉ 🍴 ╻ ⚑ ╱ ╻ ╱ **Conf** Corporate Hospitality Days **Location** on E side of A135

Hotel ★★★ 79% HL Best Western Parkmore Hotel & Leisure Club, 636 Yarm Road, Eaglescliffe, STOCKTON-ON-TEES ☎ 01642 786815 📋 01642 786815 55 en suite

HARTLEPOOL
Map 8 NZ53

Castle Eden Castle Eden TS27 4SS
☎ 01429 836510 📋 01429 836510

Beautiful parkland course alongside a nature reserve. Hard walking but trees provide wind shelter.

18 Holes, 6262yds, Par 70, SSS 70, Course record 64. Club membership 750.

Visitors Mon, Wed-Sun & BHs. Dress code. **Societies** welcome. **Green Fees** £30 (£38 weekends & BHs) **Course Designer** Henry Cotton **Prof** Peter Jackson **Facilities** ⓣ ⍾◎⍾ ┗ ♉ 🍴 ╻ ⚑ 🛒 ╱ **Leisure** snooker **Location** 2m S of Peterlee on B1281 off A19
Hotel ★★★ 75% HL Best Western Grand, Swainson Street, HARTLEPOOL ☎ 01429 266345 📋 01429 266345 47 en suite

Hartlepool Hart Warren TS24 9QF
☎ 01429 274398 📋 01429 274129
e-mail: hartlepoolgolf@btconnect.com
web: www.hartlepoolgolfclub.co.uk

A seaside course, half links, overlooking the North Sea. A good test and equally enjoyable to all handicap players. The 10th, par 4, demands a precise second shot over a ridge and between sand dunes to a green down near the edge of the beach, alongside which several holes are played.

18 Holes, 6200yds, Par 70, SSS 70, Course record 62. Club membership 700.

Visitors Mon-Sat except BHs. Booking required. Dress code. **Societies** booking required. **Green Fees** £34 per day (£44 Sat) **Course Designer** Partly Braid **Prof** Graham Laidlaw **Facilities** ⓣ ⍾◎⍾ ┗ ♉ 🍴 ╻ ⚑ ╱ **Conf** Corporate Hospitality Days **Location** N of Hartlepool, off A1086
Hotel ★★★ 75% HL Best Western Grand, Swainson Street, HARTLEPOOL ☎ 01429 266345 📋 01429 266345 47 en suite

MIDDLETON ST GEORGE
Map 8 NZ31

Dinsdale Spa Neasham Rd DL2 1DW
☎ 01325 332297 📋 01325 332297
e-mail: dinsdalespagolf@btconnect.com
web: www.dinsdalespagolfclub.co.uk

Mainly flat parkland on high land above the River Tees with views of the Cleveland Hills. Water hazards in front of the 15th tee and green; the prevailing west wind affects the later holes. There is a practice area by the clubhouse.

18 Holes, 6107yds, Par 71, SSS 69, Course record 65. Club membership 700.

Visitors Mon-Sat & BHs. Booking required Sat & BHs. Dress code. **Societies** booking required. **Green Fees** £28 per day **Prof** Martyn Stubbings **Facilities** ⓣ ⍾◎⍾ ┗ ♉ 🍴 ╻ ⚑ 🛒 ╱ ╱ **Conf** Corporate Hospitality Days **Location** 1.5m SW
Hotel ★★★ 74% HL Best Western Croft, Croft-on-Tees, DARLINGTON ☎ 01325 720319 📋 01325 720319 20 en suite

NEWTON AYCLIFFE

Map 8 NZ22

Oakleaf Golf Complex School Aycliffe Ln DL5 6QZ
☎ 01325 310820   📄 01325 318918
Oakleaf Golf Complex: 18 Holes, 5568yds, Par 70, SSS 67, Course record 67.
Prof Ernie Wilson **Facilities** ⊕ ⏶ ⏸ ⏢ ⏷ ⏛ ⏞ ⛯ ⛳
🏌 🏳 **Leisure** squash, fishing **Location** 6m N of Darlington, off A6072
Telephone for further details
Hotel ★★★★ 77% CHH Barceló Redworth Hall Hotel, REDWORTH
☎ 01388 770600 📄 01388 770600   143 en suite

Woodham Golf & Country Club Burnhill Way DL5 4PN
☎ 01325 320574 (Office) & 315257 (Pro Shop)
📄 01325 315254
Woodham Golf & Country Club: 18 Holes, 6688yds, Par 73, SSS 72, Course record 66.
Course Designer James Hamilton Stutt **Location** A1 onto A689 towards Bishop Auckland, 0.5m from Rushford
Telephone for further details
Hotel ★★★★ 77% CHH Barceló Redworth Hall Hotel, REDWORTH
☎ 01388 770600 📄 01388 770600   143 en suite

SEAHAM

Map 12 NZ44

Seaham Dawdon SR7 7RD
☎ 0191 513 0837 & 581 2354
e-mail: seahamgolfclub@btconnect.com
web: www.seahamgolfclub.co.uk
Heathland links course with several holes affected by strong winds.
18 Holes, 6017yds, Par 70, SSS 69, Course record 64. Club membership 600.
Visitors Mon-Fri & BHs. Dress code. **Societies** booking required. **Green Fees** £27 per day (£22 winter) **Prof** Andrew Blunt **Facilities** ⊕ ⏶ ⏸ ⏢ ⏷ ⏛ ⏞ ⛳ **Conf** Corporate Hospitality Days
Location 3m E of A19, exit for Seaham and Murton
Hotel ★★★★ 75% HL Sunderland Marriott, Queen's Parade, Seaburn, SUNDERLAND ☎ 0191 529 2041 📄 0191 529 2041 82 en suite

SEATON CAREW

Map 8 NZ52

Seaton Carew Tees Rd TS25 1DE
☎ 01429 266249   📄 01429 267952
e-mail: seatoncarewgolfclub@btconnect.com
web: www.seatoncarewgolfclub.co.uk
A championship links course taking full advantage of its dunes, bents, whins and gorse. Renowned for its par 4 17th; just enough fairway for an accurate drive followed by another precise shot to a pear-shape sloping green that is severely trapped.
The Old Course: 18 Holes, 6633yds, Par 72, SSS 72. Brabazon Course: 18 Holes, 6857yds, Par 73, SSS 72. Club membership 700.
Visitors Mon-Sun & BHs. Booking required. Handicap certificate. Dress code. **Societies** booking required. **Green Fees** phone **Course Designer** McKenzie **Prof** Clifford Jackson **Facilities** ⊕ ⏶ ⏢ ⏷ ⏛ ⏞ ⛳ ⛳ **Location** SE side of village off A178
Hotel ★★★ 75% HL Best Western Grand, Swainson Street, HARTLEPOOL ☎ 01429 266345 📄 01429 266345   47 en suite

SEDGEFIELD

Map 8 NZ32

Knotty Hill Golf Centre TS21 2BB
☎ 01740 620320   📄 01740 622227
e-mail: knottyhill@btconnect.com
The 18-hole Princes Course is set in rolling parkland with many holes routed through shallow valleys. Several holes are set wholly or partially within woodland and water hazards abound. Bishops Course is a developing 18-hole course with varied water features on attractive terrain. Several holes are routed through mature woodland. Academy course suited for beginners.
Princes Course: 18 Holes, 6433yds, Par 72, SSS 71. Bishops Course: 18 Holes, 5976yds, Par 70. Academy Course: 9 Holes, 2494yds, Par 32.
Visitors Tue-Sun & BHs. Booking required. Dress code.
Societies booking required. **Green Fees** not confirmed **Course Designer** C Stanton **Facilities** ⊕ ⏶ ⏸ ⏢ ⏷ ⏞ ⛯ ⛳ 🏌 **Leisure** gymnasium, tuition range. **Conf** facs Corporate Hospitality Days **Location** A1(M) junct 60, 1m N of Sedgefield on A177
Hotel ★★★★ 77% HL Best Western Hardwick Hall, SEDGEFIELD ☎ 01740 620253 📄 01740 620253   51 en suite

STANLEY

Map 12 NZ15

South Moor The Middles, Craghead DH9 6AG
☎ 01207 232848   📄 01207 284616
e-mail: secretary@southmoorgc.co.uk
web: www.southmoorgc.co.uk
Moorland course with natural hazards, designed by Dr A MacKenzie in 1926 and still one of the most challenging of its type in north east England. Out of bounds features on 11 holes from the tee, and the testing par 5 12th hole is uphill and usually against a strong headwind.
18 Holes, 6293yds, Par 72, SSS 71, Course record 66. Club membership 500.
Visitors Mon-Sun except BHs. Booking required weekends. Dress code. **Societies** booking required. **Green Fees** £23 per day (£30 weekends & BHs) **Course Designer** Dr Alistair Mackenzie **Prof** Shaun Cowell **Facilities** ⊕ ⏶ ⏸ ⏢ ⏷ ⏛ ⏞ ⛯ 🏌 ⛳ 🏌 **Leisure** snooker table **Conf** Corporate Hospitality Days **Location** 1.5m SE on B6313
Hotel ★★★ 80% HL Beamish Park, Beamish Burn Road, Marley Hill, BEAMISH, Newcastle upon Tyne ☎ 01207 230666 📄 01207 230666   42 en suite

STOCKTON-ON-TEES

Map 8 NZ41

Norton Blakeston Ln, Norton TS20 3LQ
☎ 01642 676385   📄 01642 607854
An interesting parkland course with long drives from the 7th and 17th tees. Several water hazards.
Norton Golf Course: 18 Holes, 5855yds, Par 70.
Visitors Dress code. **Societies** booking required. **Green Fees** £13 per 18 holes (£15 weekends and BHs) **Course Designer** T Harper **Facilities** ⏢ 🏌 **Conf** Corporate Hospitality Days **Location** in Norton 2m N off A19
Hotel ★★★ 79% HL Best Western Parkmore Hotel & Leisure Club, 636 Yarm Road, Eaglescliffe, STOCKTON-ON-TEES ☎ 01642 786815 📄 01642 786815   55 en suite

Teesside Acklam Rd, Thornaby TS17 7JS
☎ 01642 616516 & 673822 (pro) 🖳 01642 676252
e-mail: teessidegolfclub@btconnect.com
web: www.teessidegolfclub.co.uk

Flat, easy walking parkland.
18 Holes, 6535yds, Par 72, SSS 71, Course record 64.
Club membership 700.

Visitors handicap certificate. Dress code. **Societies** booking required. **Green Fees** £28 per day (£32 per round weekends & Bhs) **Prof** Stewart Pilgrim **Facilities** 🍴 🍽 🏌 🖿 ⛳ 🏊 🏠 🏌 🛵 🏌
Conf facs Corporate Hospitality Days **Location** 1.5m SE on A1130, off A19 at Mandale interchange
Hotel ★★★ 79% HL Best Western Parkmore Hotel & Leisure Club, 636 Yarm Road, Eaglescliffe, STOCKTON-ON-TEES ☎ 01642 786815 🖳 01642 786815 55 en suite

ESSEX

ABRIDGE
Map 5 TQ49

Abridge Golf and Country Club Epping Ln, Stapleford Tawney RM4 1ST
☎ 01708 688396 🖳 01708 688550
e-mail: info@abridgegolf.com
web: www.abridgegolf.com
Easy walking parkland. The quick drying course is a challenge for all levels. This has been the venue of several professional tournaments. Abridge is a golf and country club and has all the attendant facilities.
Abridge Golf and Country Club: 18 Holes, 6704yds, Par 72, SSS 72, Course record 67. Club membership 600.
Visitors contact club for details. **Societies** welcome. **Green Fees** not confirmed **Course Designer** Henry Cotton **Prof** Stuart Layton **Facilities** 🍴 🏌 🖿 ⛳ 🏊 🏠 🏌 🛵 🏌 🏌
Leisure 3 snooker tables **Conf** facs Corporate Hospitality Days **Location** 1.75m NE

BASILDON
Map 5 TQ78

Basildon Clay Hill Ln SS16 5JP
☎ 01268 533297 🖳 01268 284163
web: www.basildongolfclub.org.uk
18 Holes, 6236yds, Par 72, SSS 70.
Course Designer A Cotton **Location** 1m S off A176
Telephone for further details
Hotel BUD Innkeeper's Lodge Basildon/Wickford, Runwell Road, WICKFORD ☎ 0845 112 6055 🖳 0845 112 6055 24 en suite

BENFLEET
Map 5 TQ78

Boyce Hill Vicarage Hill, South Benfleet SS7 1PD
☎ 01268 793625 & 752565 🖳 01268 750497
e-mail: secretary@boycehillgolfclub.co.uk
web: www.boycehillgolfclub.co.uk
Hilly parkland with good views.
18 Holes, 6003yds, Par 68, SSS 69, Course record 64.
Club membership 700.
Visitors contact club for details. **Societies** booking required. **Green Fees** not confirmed **Course Designer** James Braid **Prof** Graham Burroughs **Facilities** 🍴 🍽 🏌 🖿 ⛳ 🏊 🏠 🏌 🛵 🏌
Conf Corporate Hospitality Days **Location** 0.75m NE of Benfleet Station
Hotel ★★★ 78% HL Balmoral, 34 Valkyrie Road, Westcliff-on-Sea, SOUTHEND-ON-SEA ☎ 01702 342947 🖳 01702 342947 34 en suite

BILLERICAY
Map 5 TQ69

The Burstead Tye Common Rd, Little Burstead CM12 9SS
☎ 01277 631171 🖳 01277 632766
e-mail: info@thebursteadgolfclub.com
web: www.thebursteadgolfclub.com
The Burstead is an attractive parkland course set amidst some of the most attractive countryside in south Essex. It is an excellent test of golf to players of all standards with the greens showing maturity beyond their years. Good management of shots is necessary throughout play and the narrow fairways, ditches and water hazards prove a good test of golf.
18 Holes, 6275yds, Par 71, SSS 70, Course record 69.
Club membership 850.
Visitors Mon-Fri. Weekends & BHs after 11am. Dress code. **Societies** booking required. **Green Fees** phone **Course Designer** Patrick Tallack **Prof** Keith Bridges/Dean Bullock **Facilities** 🍴 🍽 🏌 🖿 ⛳ 🏊 🏠 🏌 🛵 🏌 **Conf** facs Corporate Hospitality Days **Location** M25 onto A127, off A176
Hotel ★★★ 78% HL Chichester, Old London Road, Wickford, BASILDON ☎ 01268 560555 🖳 01268 560555 35 en suite

Stock Brook Golf & Country Club Queens Park Av CM12 0SP
☎ 01277 653616 & 650400 🖳 01277 633063
web: www.stockbrook.com
Stock & Brook Courses: 18 Holes, 6728yds, Par 72, SSS 72, Course record 66.
Manor Course: 9 Holes, 2997yds, Par 35.
Course Designer Martin Gillet **Location** off B1007
Telephone for further details
Hotel ★★★★ 75% HL Marygreen Manor, London Road, BRENTWOOD ☎ 01277 225252 🖳 01277 225252 44 en suite

BRAINTREE
Map 5 TL72

Braintree Kings Ln, Stisted CM77 8DD
☎ 01376 346079 🖳 01376 348677
e-mail: manager@braintreegolfclub.co.uk
web: www.braintreegolfclub.co.uk
Parkland with many rare mature trees. Good par 3s with the 14th - Devils Lair - regarded as one of the best in the county.
18 Holes, 6228yds, Par 70, SSS 69, Course record 64.
Club membership 750.

continued

Visitors Mon-Sun & BHs. Dress code. **Societies** booking required.
Green Fees £47 per day, £36.50 per round (£67/£52 weekends & BHs)
Course Designer Hawtree **Prof** Duncan Woolger **Facilities** ⑪ ⑩Ⓧ
⒧ ⌴ ⬛ ⼌ ⛏ ⚐ 🛒 ⚐ **Conf** Corporate Hospitality Days
Location 1m E, off A120
Hotel ★★★ 77% HL White Hart, Market End, COGGESHALL,
Colchester ☎ 01376 561654 ▤ 01376 561654 18 en suite

Towerlands Park Panfield Rd CM7 5BJ
☎ 01376 326802   ▤ 01376 552487
e-mail: info@towerlands.com
web: www.unextowerlands.com

Undulating, grassland course, nine holes with 18 tees.

9 Holes, 5559yds, Par 68. Club membership 135.

Visitors Mon-Sat & BHs. Sun pm only. Dress code. **Societies** booking
required. **Green Fees** Phone **Course Designer** G Shiels **Facilities** ⼌
Conf facs **Location** on B1053
Hotel ★★★ 77% HL White Hart, Market End, COGGESHALL,
Colchester ☎ 01376 561654 ▤ 01376 561654 18 en suite

BRENTWOOD   Map 5 TQ59

Bentley Ongar Rd CM15 9SS
☎ 01277 373179   ▤ 01277 375097
e-mail: info@bentleygolfclub.com
web: www.bentleygolfclub.com

Mature parkland course with water hazards.

18 Holes, 6703yds, Par 72, SSS 72. Club membership 580.

Visitors Mon, Tue, Thu-Sun except BHs. Handicap certificate.
Dress code. **Societies** welcome. **Green Fees** not confirmed **Course
Designer** Howard Swann **Prof** Nick Garrett **Facilities** ⑪ ⑩Ⓧ ⒧ ⌴
⼌ ⬛ 🛒 ⚐ **Conf** Corporate Hospitality Days **Location** 3m
NW on A128
Hotel ★★★ 71% HL Weald Park Hotel, Golf & Country Club,
Coxtie Green Road, South Weald, BRENTWOOD ☎ 01277 375101
▤ 01277 375101 32 en suite

Hartswood King George's Playing Fields CM14 5AE
☎ 01277 218850   ▤ 01277 218850

18 Holes, 6192yds, Par 70, SSS 69, Course record 68.

Course Designer H Cotton **Location** 0.75m SE of Brentwood town
centre on A128 from A127
Telephone for further details
Hotel ★★★ 71% HL Weald Park Hotel, Golf & Country Club,
Coxtie Green Road, South Weald, BRENTWOOD ☎ 01277 375101
▤ 01277 375101 32 en suite

Warley Park Magpie Ln, Little Warley CM13 3DX
☎ 01277 224891   ▤ 01277 200679
e-mail: enquiries@warleyparkgc.co.uk
web: www.warleyparkgc.co.uk

Parkland with numerous water hazards, reasonable walking. There is
also a golf practice ground.

1st & 2nd: 18 Holes, 5985yds, Par 69, SSS 67,
Course record 66.
1st & 3rd: 18 Holes, 5925yds, Par 71, SSS 69,
Course record 65.
2nd & 3rd: 18 Holes, 5917yds, Par 70, SSS 69,
Course record 65. Club membership 800.

Visitors Mon-Sun & BHs .Dress code. **Societies** welcome. **Green
Fees** £50 per day, £40 per round **Course Designer** Reg Plumbridge

Prof Kevin Smith **Facilities** ⑪ ⑩Ⓧ by prior arrangement ⒧ ⌴
⼌ ⬛ ⚐ 🛒 ⚐ 🏌 **Conf** facs Corporate Hospitality Days
Location M25 junct 29, A127 E onto B186, 0.5m N
Hotel ★★★ 71% HL Weald Park Hotel, Golf & Country Club,
Coxtie Green Road, South Weald, BRENTWOOD ☎ 01277 375101
▤ 01277 375101 32 en suite

Weald Park Hotel, Golf & Country Club Coxtie Green Rd CM14 5RJ
☎ 01277 375101   ▤ 01277 374888
web: www.bw-wealdparkhotel.co.uk

Weald Park Hotel, Golf & Country Club: 18 Holes,
6285yds, Par 71, SSS 70, Course record 65.

Course Designer Reg Plumbridge **Location** 3m from M25
Telephone for further details
Hotel ★★★ 71% HL Weald Park Hotel, Golf & Country Club,
Coxtie Green Road, South Weald, BRENTWOOD ☎ 01277 375101
▤ 01277 375101 32 en suite

BULPHAN   Map 5 TQ68

Langdon Hills Lower Dunton Rd RM14 3TY
☎ 01268 548444   ▤ 01268 490084
web: www.golflangdon.co.uk

Langdon & Bulphan Course: 18 Holes, 6760yds, Par 72,
SSS 72, Course record 67.
Bulphan & Horndon Course: 18 Holes, 6537yds, Par 73,
SSS 72.
Horndon & Langdon Course: 18 Holes, 6279yds, Par 71,
SSS 71.

Course Designer Howard Swan **Location** off A13 onto B1007
Telephone for further details
Hotel ★★★★ 75% HL Marygreen Manor, London Road,
BRENTWOOD ☎ 01277 225252 ▤ 01277 225252 44 en suite

BURNHAM-ON-CROUCH   Map 5 TQ99

Burnham-on-Crouch Ferry Rd, Creeksea CM0 8PQ
☎ 01621 782282   ▤ 01621 784489
e-mail: burnhamgolf@hotmail.com
web: www.burnhamgolfclub.co.uk

Undulating meadowland riverside course, easy walking and stunning
views. Challenging for all standards of player.

18 Holes, 6056yds, Par 70, SSS 69, Course record 66.
Club membership 520.

Visitors Mon-Wed, Fri except BHs. Weekends pm only. Booking
required. Dress code. **Societies** booking required. **Green Fees** £36
per 18 holes (£42 weekends) **Course Designer** Swan **Prof** Steve
Parkin/Ken Light **Facilities** ⑪ ⑩Ⓧ ⒧ ⌴ ⬛ ⼌ ⚐ 🛒 ⚐
Conf Corporate Hospitality Days **Location** 1.25m W off B1010
Hotel ★★ 68% HL The Oakland Hotel, 2-6 Reeves Way, SOUTH
WOODHAM FERRERS ☎ 01245 322811 ▤ 01245 322811 34 en suite

CANEWDON
Map 5 TQ99

Ballards Gore Gore Rd SS4 2DA
☎ 01702 258917   📠 01702 258571
e-mail: secretary@ballardsgore.com
web: www.ballardsgore.com

Parkland course with scenic views, officially the longest course in Essex. Water comes into play on 8 holes demanding good course management and the use of every club in the bag.

18 Holes, 6874yds, Par 73, SSS 73, Course record 69.
Club membership 500.

Visitors Mon-Fri. Weekends & BHs after noon. Handicap certificate. Dress code. **Societies** booking required. **Green Fees** not confirmed **Course Designer** Arthur Elvin **Prof** Gary McCarthy **Facilities** ⑪ ℡ ♨ ⬚ ♨ ⚑ 🛒 🏌 **Leisure** snooker room **Conf** facs Corporate Hospitality Days **Location** 2m NE of Rochford
Guesthouse ★★★★ GA Ilfracombe House, 9-13 Wilson Road, SOUTHEND-ON-SEA ☎ 01702 351000 📠 01702 351000   20 en suite

CANVEY ISLAND
Map 5 TQ78

Castle Point Somnes Av SS8 9FG
☎ 01268 510830 & 511149   📠 01268 511758
e-mail: canveyisland@glendale-services.co.uk
web: www.glendale-golf.co.uk

A flat seaside links and part parkland course with water hazards on 13 holes and views of the estuary and Hadleigh Castle. Always a test for any golfer when the wind starts to blow.

18 Holes, 6176yds, Par 71, SSS 69, Course record 66.
Club membership 275.

Visitors Mon-Sun & BHs. Booking required. Dress code.
Societies booking required. **Green Fees** £15 (£20 weekends)
Prof Nigel Birch **Facilities** ⑪ ℡ ⬚ ♨ ⚑ 🛒 🏌 **Conf** Corporate Hospitality Days **Location** SE of Basildon, A130 to Canvey Island
Hotel ★★★ 78% HL Chichester, Old London Road, Wickford, BASILDON ☎ 01268 560555 📠 01268 560555   35 en suite

CHELMSFORD
Map 5 TL70

Channels Belstead Farm Ln, Little Waltham CM3 3PT
☎ 01245 440005   📠 01245 442032
e-mail: info@channelsgolf.co.uk
web: www.channelsgolf.co.uk

The Channels course is built on land from reclaimed gravel pits, 18 very exciting holes with plenty of lakes providing an excellent test of golf. Belsteads, a nine-hole course, is mainly flat but has three holes where water has to be negotiated.

Channels Course: 18 Holes, 6413yds, Par 71, SSS 71, Course record 65.
Belsteads: 9 Holes, 2467yds, Par 34, SSS 32.
Club membership 800.

Visitors Mon-Fri except BHs. Dress code. **Societies** booking required. **Green Fees** Phone **Course Designer** Cotton & Swan **Prof** Ian Sinclair **Facilities** ⑪ 🍴 ℡ ⬚ ♨ ⚑ 🛒 ◇ 🏌 🛒 🏌 **Leisure** fishing, 9 hole pitch & putt course. **Conf** facs Corporate Hospitality Days **Location** 2m NE on A130
Hotel ★★★★ 74% HL County Hotel, 29 Rainsford Road, CHELMSFORD ☎ 01245 455700 📠 01245 455700   51 en suite

Chelmsford Widford Rd CM2 9AP
☎ 01245 256483   📠 01245 256483
e-mail: office@chelmsfordgc.co.uk
web: www.chelmsfordgc.co.uk

An undulating parkland course, hilly in parts, with three holes in woods and four difficult par 4s. From the reconstructed clubhouse there are fine views over the course and the wooded hills beyond.

18 Holes, 5981yds, Par 68, SSS 69, Course record 61.
Club membership 650.

Visitors Mon-Fri except BHs. Handicap certificate. Dress code.
Societies booking required. **Green Fees** £40 per round **Course Designer** Tom Dunn **Prof** Mark Welch **Facilities** ⑪ ℡ ⬚ ♨ ⚑ 🏌 🛒 🏌 **Conf** Corporate Hospitality Days **Location** 1.5m S of town centre off A12
Hotel ★★★★ 74% HL County Hotel, 29 Rainsford Road, CHELMSFORD ☎ 01245 455700 📠 01245 455700   51 en suite

Regiment Way Back Ln, Little Waltham CM3 3PR
☎ 01245 362210 & 361100   📠 01245 442032
e-mail: info@channelsgolf.co.uk
web: www.regimentway.co.uk

A nine-hole course with alternate tee positions, offering a par 64 18-hole course. Fully automatic tee and green irrigation plus excellent drainage ensure play at most times of the year. The course is challenging but at the same time can be forgiving.

Regiment Way Golf Centre: 9 Holes, 4887yds, Par 65, SSS 64. Club membership 265.

Visitors Mon-Sun & BHs. Booking required weekends
Societies welcome. **Green Fees** £15 per 18 holes, £11 per 9 holes **Course Designer** R Stubbings/R Clark **Prof** David March/Mark Sharman **Facilities** ⑪ 🍴 ℡ ⬚ ♨ ⚑ 🛒 ◇ 🛒 🏌 **Conf** facs Corporate Hospitality Days **Location** off A130 N of Chelmsford
Hotel ★★★ 77% HL Best Western Atlantic, New Street, CHELMSFORD ☎ 01245 268168 📠 01245 268168   59 en suite

CHIGWELL | Map 5 TQ49

Chigwell High Rd IG7 5BH
☎ 020 8500 2059 📠 020 8501 3410
web: www.chigwellgolfclub.co.uk
18 Holes, 6296yds, Par 71, SSS 70, Course record 66.
Course Designer Hawtree/Taylor **Location** 0.5m S on A113
Telephone for further details
Hotel ★★★★ 72% HL Menzies Prince Regent, Manor Road,
WOODFORD BRIDGE, Essex ☎ 020 8505 9966 📠 020 8505 9966
61 en suite

Woolston Manor Abridge Rd IG7 6BX
☎ 0208 500 2549 📠 0208 501 5452
web: www.woolstonmanor.co.uk
*Manor Course: 18 Holes, 6510yards, Par 72, SSS 72,
Course record 67.*
Course Designer Neil Coles **Location** M11 junct 5, 1m
Telephone for further details
Hotel ★★★★ 72% HL Menzies Prince Regent, Manor Road,
WOODFORD BRIDGE, Essex ☎ 020 8505 9966 📠 020 8505 9966
61 en suite

CHIGWELL ROW | Map 5 TQ49

Hainault Forest Golf Complex Romford Rd IG7 4QW
☎ 020 8500 2131 📠 020 8501 5196
e-mail: info@hainaultforestgolf.co.uk
web: www.hainaultforestgolf.co.uk
Two championship courses with spectacular views of Essex
countryside. Parkland courses with modern driving range.
*No 1 Course: 18 Holes, 5687yds, Par 70, SSS 67,
Course record 65.*
*No 2 Course: 18 Holes, 6238yds, Par 71, SSS 71.
Club membership 250.*
Visitors Mon-Sun & BHs. Booking required. Dress code.
Societies booking required. **Green Fees** not confirmed **Course
Designer** Taylor & Hawtree **Prof** C Hope/A Shearn/B Smith
Facilities ⊕ 🎯 ⅃ ⌷ 🍴 ⚐ ⌂ ⚑ ⛳
Leisure sports injury therapy clinic **Conf** Corporate Hospitality Days
Location 0.5m S on A1112
Hotel ★★ 57% SHL Ridgeway, 115/117 The Ridgeway, North
Chingford, LONDON ☎ 020 8529 1964 📠 020 8529 1964 20 en suite

CLACTON-ON-SEA | Map 5 TM11

Clacton West Rd CO15 1AJ
☎ 01255 421919 📠 01255 424602
e-mail: secretary@clactongolfclub.com
web: www.clactongolfclub.com
The course covers 110 acres and runs alongside the sea wall and
then inland. Easy walking layout, part open and part woodland. The
course is well bunkered and a unique feature is the fleets, ditches
and streams that cross and border many of the fairways, demanding
accuracy and good striking.
*Clacton Golf Club Ltd: 18 Holes, 6448yds, Par 71, SSS 71,
Course record 67. Club membership 650.*
Visitors contact club for details. **Societies** welcome. **Green
Fees** not confirmed **Course Designer** Jack White **Prof** S J Levermore

Facilities ⊕ 🎯 ⅃ ⌷ 🍴 ⚐ ⌂ ⚑ ⛳ **Leisure** practice
nets available **Location** 1.25m SW of town centre
Hotel ★★ 68% HL Esplanade Hotel, 27-29 Marine Parade East,
CLACTON-ON-SEA ☎ 01255 220450 📠 01255 220450 29 en suite

COLCHESTER | Map 5 TL92

Birch Grove Layer Rd, Kingsford CO2 0HS
☎ 01206 734276
e-mail: maureen@birchgrove.fsbusiness.co.uk
web: www.birchgrovegolfclub.co.uk
A pretty, undulating course surrounded by woodland - small but
challenging with excellent greens. Challenging 6th hole cut through
woodland with water hazards and out of bounds.
*9 Holes, 4532yds, Par 66, SSS 63, Course record 62.
Club membership 250.*
Visitors dress code. **Societies** booking required. **Green Fees** £16
for 18 holes, £11 for 9 holes **Course Designer** L A Marston
Facilities ⊕ 🎯 ⅃ ⌷ 🍴 ⚐ ⌂ ⛳ **Conf** facs Corporate
Hospitality Days **Location** 2.5m S on B1026
Hotel ★★★ 81% HL Best Western The Rose & Crown, East Street,
COLCHESTER ☎ 01206 866677 📠 01206 866677 38 en suite

Colchester Braiswick CO4 5AU
☎ 01206 853396 📠 01206 852698
e-mail: secretary@colchestergolfclub.com
web: www.colchestergolfclub.com
Fairly flat yet scenic parkland, with tree-lined fairways and small
copses. Mainly level walking.
*18 Holes, 6357yds, Par 70, SSS 70, Course record 63.
Club membership 700.*
Visitors Mon-Sun except BHs. Booking required. Handicap certificate.
Dress code. **Societies** booking required. **Green Fees** £40 per 18 holes
(£45 weekends) **Course Designer** James Braid **Prof** Mark Angel
Facilities ⊕ 🎯 ⅃ ⌷ 🍴 ⚐ ⌂ ⚑ ⛳ ⛳ **Conf** facs
Corporate Hospitality Days **Location** 1.5m NW of town centre on B1508
(West Bergholt Rd)
Hotel ★★★ 81% HL Best Western The Rose & Crown, East Street,
COLCHESTER ☎ 01206 866677 📠 01206 866677 38 en suite

Lexden Wood Bakers Ln CO3 4AU
☎ 01206 843333 📠 01206 854775
e-mail: info@lexdenwood.com
web: www.lexdenwood.com
Challenging 18-hole, parkland course with many water features. A
mix of undulating and flat land with testing greens. Also a nine-hole
pitch and putt course, and a floodlit driving range. The course has
undergone a major redevelopment in recent years and has 60 new
bunkers and many new tees.
*18 Holes, 6000yds, Par 70, SSS 69, Course record 63.
Club membership 500.*
Visitors Mon-Sun & BHs. Booking required. Dress code.
Societies booking required. **Green Fees** not confirmed **Course
Designer** Jonathan Gaunt **Prof** Phil Grice **Facilities** ⊕ 🎯 ⅃ ⌷
🍴 ⌂ ⌂ ⚐ ⛳ ⚑ ⛳ **Leisure** 9 hole par 3 **Conf** facs
Corporate Hospitality Days **Location** A12 towards Colchester Central,
follow tourist signs
Hotel ★★★ 81% HL Best Western The Rose & Crown, East Street,
COLCHESTER ☎ 01206 866677 📠 01206 866677 38 en suite

Stoke-by-Nayland Keepers Ln CO6 4PZ
☎ 01206 262836   📠 01206 263356
web: www.stokebynaylandclub.co.uk
Gainsborough Course: 18 Holes, 6498yds, Par 72, SSS 71, Course record 66.
Constable Course: 18 Holes, 6544yds, Par 72, SSS 71, Course record 67.
Course Designer Howard Swan **Location** 1.5m NW of Stoke-by-Nayland on B1068
Telephone for further details
Hotel ★★★ CHH Maison Talbooth, Stratford Road, DEDHAM ☎ 01206 322367 📠 01206 322367 12 en suite

EARLS COLNE   Map 5 TL82

Colne Valley Station Rd CO6 2LT
☎ 01787 224343   📠 01787 224126
e-mail: info@colnevalleygolfclub.co.uk
web: www.colnevalleygolfclub.co.uk
Opened in 1991, this surprisingly mature parkland course belies its tender years. Natural water hazards, and well-defined bunkers, along with USGA standard greens offer year round playability, and a stimulating test for all abilities.
18 Holes, 6301yds, Par 70, SSS 71, Course record 68.
Club membership 500.
Visitors booking required. Dress code. **Societies** welcome. **Green Fees** £40 per day, £30 per 18 holes (£35 per 18 holes weekends). **Course Designer** Howard Swan **Facilities** ⑪ ⑩ 🍴 🛒 🍺 ⚒ 🏺 🍺 ⚒ **Leisure** fishing **Conf** facs Corporate Hospitality Days **Location** off A1124
Hotel ★★★ 77% HL White Hart, Market End, COGGESHALL, Colchester ☎ 01376 561654 📠 01376 561654 18 en suite

Essex Golf & Country Club CO6 2NS
☎ 01787 224466   📠 01787 224410
web: www.the clubcompany.com
County Course: 18 Holes, 7019yds, Par 73, SSS 73, Course record 67.
Garden Course: 9 Holes, 2190yds, Par 34, SSS 34.
Course Designer Reg Plumbridge **Location** signed off A120 onto B1024
Telephone for further details
Hotel ★★★ 77% HL White Hart, Market End, COGGESHALL, Colchester ☎ 01376 561654 📠 01376 561654 18 en suite

EPPING   Map 5 TL40

Epping Fluxs Ln CM16 7PE
☎ 01992 572282   📠 01992 575512
e-mail: info@eppinggolfcourse.org.uk
web: www.eppinggolfcourse.org.uk
Undulating parkland with extensive views over Essex countryside and excellent fairways. Incorporates many water features designed to use every club in the bag. Some driveable par 4s, and the spectacular 18th, Happy Valley, is rarely birdied. Open all year.
The Epping Golf Course: 18 Holes, 5405yds, Par 68, SSS 65, Course record 62. Club membership 350.
Visitors Mon-Sun & BHs. Booking required weekends & BHs. Dress code. **Societies** welcome. **Green Fees** £15 per day, £11.50 per round (£30/£18.50 weekends & BHs) **Course Designer** Sjoberg **Facilities** ⑪

🛒 🍺 🍴 🏺 ⚒ 🍺 🏺 🍺 ⚒ 🍺 **Conf** facs Corporate Hospitality Days **Location** M11 junct 7, 2.5m on B1393, left in Epping High Rd towards station
Hotel BUD Travelodge Harlow North Weald, A414 Eastbound, Tylers Green, North Weald, HARLOW ☎ 08719 846 033 📠 08719 846 033 61 en suite

Nazeing Middle St, Nazeing EN9 2LW
☎ 01992 893798   📠 01992 893882
web: www.nazeinggolfclub.co.uk
Parkland course built with American sand-based greens and tees and five strategically placed lakes. One of the most notable holes is the difficult par 3 13th with out of bounds and a large lake coming into play.
18 Holes, 6617yds, Par 72, SSS 72, Course record 68.
Club membership 400.
Visitors Mon-Sun & BHs. Booking required. Dress code. **Societies** booking required. **Green Fees** Mon £18 per round, Tue-Thu £22, Fri £25 (£30 weekends & BHs) **Course Designer** M Gillete **Prof** Robert Green **Facilities** ⑪ ⑩ 🛒 🍺 🍴 🏺 🍺 ⚒ 🍺 **Conf** facs Corporate Hospitality Days **Location** M25 junct 26, near Waltham Abbey
Hotel ★★★★ 78% HL Waltham Abbey Marriott, Old Shire Lane, WALTHAM ABBEY ☎ 01992 717170 📠 01992 717170 162 en suite

FRINTON-ON-SEA   Map 5 TM22

Frinton 1 The Esplanade CO13 9EP
☎ 01255 674618   📠 01255 682450
e-mail: frintongolf@lineone.net
web: www.frintongolfclub.com
Deceptive, flat seaside links course providing fast, firm and undulating greens that will test the best putters, and tidal ditches that cross many of the fairways, requiring careful placement of shots. Its open character means that every shot has to be evaluated with both wind strength and direction in mind. Easy walking.
Havers: 18 Holes, 6265yds, Par 71, SSS 70, Course record 63.
Kirkby: 9 Holes, 3062yds, Par 60, SSS 60.
Club membership 850.
Visitors Mon-Sun & BHs. Booking required weekends & BHs. Handicap certificate. Dress code. **Societies** booking required. **Green Fees** Main course £30 (£35 weekends). Short course £11 **Course Designer** Willy Park Jnr/Harry Colt **Prof** Peter Taggart **Facilities** ⑪ by prior arrangement 🛒 🍺 🍴 🏺 🍺 ⚒ 🍺 ⚒ **Leisure** indoor practice nets **Conf** facs Corporate Hospitality Days **Location** SW of town centre
Hotel ★★ 68% HL Esplanade Hotel, 27-29 Marine Parade East, CLACTON-ON-SEA ☎ 01255 220450 📠 01255 220450 29 en suite

GOSFIELD   Map 5 TL72

Gosfield Lake The Manor House, Hall Dr CO9 1RZ
☎ 01787 474747   📠 01787 476044
e-mail: gosfieldlakegc@btconnect.com
web: www.gosfield-lake-golf-club.co.uk
Parkland with bunkers, lakes and water hazards. Designed by Sir Henry Cotton and Howard Swan. Also a nine-hole course; ideal for beginners and improvers.
Lakes Course: 18 Holes, 6615yds, Par 72, SSS 72, Course record 68.

continued

Meadows Course: 9 Holes, 4180yds, Par 64, SSS 61.
Club membership 650.

Visitors dress code. **Societies** welcome. **Green Fees** Lakes £35 per round, Meadows £17 per round. Twilight £20/£10 **Course Designer** Henry Cotton/Howard Swan **Prof** Richard Wheeler **Facilities** ⑪ ⑩ 🏌 ⌨ 🍴 ✔ 🏌 **Conf** Corporate Hospitality Days **Location** 1m W of Gosfield off B1017
Hotel ★★★ 77% HL White Hart, Market End, COGGESHALL, Colchester ☎ 01376 561654 ▤ 01376 561654 18 en suite

HARLOW   Map 5 TL41

Canons Brook Elizabeth Way CM19 5BE
☎ 01279 421482   ▤ 01279 626393
e-mail: manager@canonsbrook.com
web: www.canonsbrook.com

Challenging parkland course designed by Henry Cotton. Accuracy is the key requiring straight driving from the tees, especially on the par 5 11th to fly a gap with out of bounds left and right before setting up the shot to the green.

18 Holes, 6800yds, Par 73, SSS 72, Course record 65.
Club membership 650.

Visitors contact club for details. **Societies** welcome. **Green Fees** phone **Course Designer** Henry Cotton **Prof** Alan McGinn **Facilities** ⑪ ⑩ 🏌 ⌨ 🍴 🏌 🏌 ✔ 🏌 ✔ **Conf** facs **Location** M11 junct 7, 3m NW
Hotel ★★★ 62% HL The Green Man, Mulberry Green, Old Harlow, HARLOW ☎ 01279 442521 ▤ 01279 442521 55 en suite

North Weald Rayley Ln, North Weald CM16 6AR
☎ 01992 522118   ▤ 01992 522881
e-mail: info@northwealdgolfclub.co.uk
web: www.northwealdgolfclub.co.uk

Although only opened in November 1995, the blend of lakes and meadowland give this testing course an air of maturity. Further major improvements include a golf range.

18 Holes, 6377yds, Par 71, SSS 71, Course record 64.
Club membership 500.

Visitors Mon-Sun & BHs. Booking required. **Societies** welcome. **Green Fees** not confirmed **Course Designer** David Williams **Prof** David Rawlings **Facilities** ⑪ ⑩ 🏌 ⌨ 🍴 🏌 🏌 ✔ 🏌 **Leisure** fishing, sauna, gymnasium **Conf** facs Corporate Hospitality Days **Location** M11 exit 7, A414 2m towards Chipping Ongar
Hotel BUD Travelodge Harlow North Weald, A414 Eastbound, Tylers Green, North Weald, HARLOW ☎ 08719 846 033 ▤ 08719 846 033 61 en suite

HARWICH   Map 5 TM23

Harwich & Dovercourt Station Rd, Parkeston CO12 4NZ
☎ 01255 503616   ▤ 01255 503323
e-mail: secretary@harwichanddovercourtgolfclub.com

Flat parkland with easy walking. The 234yd par 3 9th hole to an invisible green is a real experience.

9 Holes, 5900yds, Par 70, SSS 69, Course record 59.
Club membership 420.

Visitors contact club for details. **Societies** booking required. **Green Fees** £24 per 18 holes; £16 per 9 holes **Facilities** ⑪ ⑩ by prior arrangement 🏌 ⌨ 🍴 🏌 🏌 ✔ **Conf** Corporate Hospitality Days **Location** off A120 near Ferry Terminal

Hotel ★★★ 82% HL The Pier at Harwich, The Quay, HARWICH ☎ 01255 241212 ▤ 01255 241212 14 en suite

INGRAVE   Map 5 TQ69

Thorndon Park CM13 3RH
☎ 01277 810345   ▤ 01277 810645
e-mail: office@thorndonpark.com
web: www.thorndonpchulfclub.com

Course is playable even at the wettest time of the year. Holes stand on their own surrounded by mature oaks, some of which are more than 500 years old. The lake in the centre of the course provides both a challenge and a sense of peace and tranquillity. The Palladian Thorndon Hall, site of the old clubhouse, is the magnificent backdrop to the closing hole.

18 Holes, 6511yds, Par 71, SSS 71, Course record 69.
Club membership 630.

Visitors Mon-Fri except BHs. Booking required. Handicap certificate. Dress code. **Societies** booking required. **Green Fees** £65 per day, £50 per 18 holes **Course Designer** Colt **Prof** Brian White **Facilities** ⑪ ⑩ by prior arrangement 🏌 ⌨ 🍴 🏌 🏌 🏌 ✔ **Conf** Corporate Hospitality Days **Location** W side of village off A128
Hotel ★★★ 71% HL Weald Park Hotel, Golf & Country Club, Coxtie Green Road, South Weald, BRENTWOOD ☎ 01277 375101 ▤ 01277 375101 32 en suite

LOUGHTON   Map 5 TQ49

High Beech Wellington Hill IG10 4AH
☎ 020 8508 7323

High Beech Golf Course: 9 Holes, 1477, Par 27,
Course record 25.

Prof Clark Baker **Facilities** ⌨ 🏌 🏌 ✔ **Location** M25 junct 26 **Telephone for further details**
Hotel ★★★★ 78% HL Waltham Abbey Marriott, Old Shire Lane, WALTHAM ABBEY ☎ 01992 717170 ▤ 01992 717170 162 en suite

Loughton Clays Ln, Debden Green IG10 2RZ
☎ 020 8502 2923

Nine-hole parkland course on the edge of Epping Forest. A good test of golf.

9 Holes, 4652yds, Par 66, SSS 63, Course record 69.
Club membership 100.

Visitors contact club for details. **Societies** welcome. **Green Fees** not confirmed **Facilities** 🏌 ⌨ 🍴 🏌 🏌 🏌 ✔ **Location** 1.5m SE of Theydon Bois
Hotel ★★★★ 78% HL Waltham Abbey Marriott, Old Shire Lane, WALTHAM ABBEY ☎ 01992 717170 ▤ 01992 717170 162 en suite

MALDON   Map 5 TL80

Forrester Park Beckingham Rd, Great Totham CM9 8EA
☎ 01621 891406   ▤ 01621 891406
e-mail: info@forresterparkltd.com
web: www.forresterparkltd.com

Set in undulating parkland in the Essex countryside and commanding some beautiful views across the River Blackwater. Accuracy is more important than distance and judgement more important than strength

continued

on this traditional club course. There is a separate 10-acre practice ground.

18 Holes, 6073yds, Par 71, SSS 69, Course record 69.
Club membership 1000.

Visitors contact club for details. **Societies** booking required. **Green Fees** £12-£22 depending on time/day **Course Designer** T R Forrester-Muir **Prof** Gary Pike **Facilities** Ⓟ ⓑ ⓒ ⓓ ⓐ ⓕ ✦ ✦ **Leisure** hard tennis courts, heated indoor swimming pool **Conf** facs Corporate Hospitality Days **Location** 3m NE of Maldon off B1022
Hotel ★★ 69% HL Benbridge Hotel, Holloway Road, The Square, Heybridge, MALDON ☎ 01621 857666 & 853667 🖨 01621 857666 13 en suite

Maldon Beeleigh, Langford CM9 6LL
☎ 01621 853212   🖨 01621 855232
e-mail: maldon.golf@virgin.net
web: www.maldon-golf..co.uk
Flat parkland in a triangle of land bounded by the River Chelmer and the Blackwater Canal. Small greens provide a test for iron shots and the short game. Testing par 3 14th (166yds) demanding particular accuracy to narrow green guarded by bunkers and large trees.

9 Holes, 6253yds, Par 71, SSS 70, Course record 66.
Club membership 380.

Visitors Mon, Thu & Fri. Tue & Wed pm only. Booking Tue & Wed. Dress code. **Societies** booking required. **Green Fees** not confirmed **Course Designer** Thompson of Felixstowe **Facilities** ⓑ ⓒ ⓓ ⓐ ⓕ **Location** 1m NW off B1019
Hotel ★★★ 77% HL Pontlands Park Country Hotel, West Hanningfield Road, Great Baddow, CHELMSFORD ☎ 01245 476444 🖨 01245 476444 35 en suite

ORSETT   Map 5 TQ68

Orsett Brentwood Rd RM16 3DS
☎ 01375 891352   🖨 01375 892471
e-mail: enquiries@orsettgolfclub.co.uk
web: www.orsettgolfclub.co.uk
A very good test of golf - this heathland course with its sandy soil is quick drying and provides easy walking. Close to the Thames estuary it is seldom calm and the main hazards are the prevailing wind and thick gorse. Any slight deviation can be exaggerated by the wind and result in a ball lost in the gorse. Host for regional qualifying for the Open Championship on eleven occasions.

18 Holes, 6682yds, Par 72, SSS 73, Course record 63.
Club membership 650.

Visitors Mon-Wed & Fri except BHs. Thu pm only. Booking required. Handicap certificate. Dress code. **Societies** booking required. **Green Fees** £45 per day, £35 per 18 holes **Course Designer** James Braid **Prof** Richard Herring **Facilities** Ⓟ ⓘ ⓑ ⓒ ⓓ ⓐ ⓔ ✦ ⓖ ✦ **Leisure** coaching **Conf** Corporate Hospitality Days **Location** junct of A13/A128, then S on A128 towards Chadwell St Mary for 0.5m. Entrance on left.

PURLEIGH   Map 5 TL80

Three Rivers Stow Rd CM3 6RR
☎ 01621 828631   🖨 01621 828060
web: www.threeriversclub.com
Kings Course: 18 Holes, 6403yds, Par 72, SSS 71, Course record 66.
Jubilee Course: 18 Holes, 4501yds, Par 64, SSS 62.

Course Designer Hawtree **Location** 2.5m from South Woodham Ferrers
Telephone for further details
Hotel ★★ 68% HL The Oakland Hotel, 2-6 Reeves Way, SOUTH WOODHAM FERRERS ☎ 01245 322811 🖨 01245 322811 34 en suite

ROCHFORD   Map 5 TQ89

Rochford Hundred Hall Rd SS4 1NW
☎ 01702 544302   🖨 01702 541343
e-mail: admin@rochfordhundredgolfclub.co.uk
web: www.rochfordhundredgolfclub.co.uk
Parkland with ponds and ditches as natural hazards.

18 Holes, 6292yds, Par 72, SSS 71, Course record 64.
Club membership 800.

Visitors Mon-Fri except BHs. Booking required. Handicap certificate required. Dress code. **Societies** booking required. **Green Fees** £40 per day/round **Course Designer** James Braid **Prof** Graham Hill **Facilities** Ⓟ ⓘ ⓑ ⓒ ⓓ ⓐ ⓔ ⓕ **Location** W on B1013
Guesthouse ★★★★ GA Ilfracombe House, 9-13 Wilson Road, SOUTHEND-ON-SEA ☎ 01702 351000 🖨 01702 351000 20 en suite

SAFFRON WALDEN   Map 5 TL53

Saffron Walden Windmill Hill CB10 1BX
☎ 01799 522786   🖨 01799 520313
e-mail: office@swgc.com
web: www.swgc.com
Undulating parkland in the former deer park of Audley End House. Fine views over rolling countryside. Two par 3 signature holes, the 5th and 18th.

18 Holes, 6632yds, Par 72, SSS 72, Course record 63.
Club membership 800.

Visitors Mon-Fri, Sun & BHs. Handicap certificate. Dress code. **Societies** booking required. **Green Fees** £55 per day, £44 per 18 holes **Course Designer** Howard Swan **Prof** Philip Davis **Facilities** Ⓟ ⓘ ⓑ ⓒ ⓓ ⓐ ⓔ ✦ ⓖ ✦ ✦ **Conf** facs Corporate Hospitality Days **Location** N side of town centre off B184
Hotel ★★★ 74% HL The Crown House, GREAT CHESTERFORD ☎ 01799 530515 🖨 01799 530515 22 en suite

SOUTHEND-ON-SEA   Map 5 TQ88

Belfairs Eastwood Road North SS9 4LR
☎ 01702 525345 & 520202
web: www.southend.gov.uk
Belfairs Golf Course: 18 Holes, 5840yds, Par 70, SSS 68, Course record 68.

Course Designer H S Colt **Location** off A127/A13
Telephone for further details
Hotel ★★★ 78% HL Balmoral, 34 Valkyrie Road, Westcliff-on-Sea, SOUTHEND-ON-SEA ☎ 01702 342947 🖨 01702 342947 34 en suite

Thorpe Hall Thorpe Hall Av SS1 3AT
☎ 01702 582205 🖥 01702 584498
web: www.thorpehallgc.co.uk
18 Holes, 6290yds, Par 71, SSS 70, Course record 62.
Course Designer Various **Location** 2m E off A13
Telephone for further details
Hotel ★★★ **78%** HL Balmoral, 34 Valkyrie Road, Westcliff-on-Sea,
SOUTHEND-ON-SEA ☎ 01702 342947 🖥 01702 342947 34 en suite

SOUTH OCKENDON   Map 5 TQ58

Belhus Park Belhus Park RM15 4QR
☎ 01708 854260 🖥 01708 854260
Belhus Park Golf Course: 18 Holes, 5589yds, Par 69,
SSS 68, Course record 67.
Course Designer Capability Brown **Location** off B1335, brown tourist
signs to course
Telephone for further details
Hotel BUD Ibis London Thurrock, Weston Avenue, WEST THURROCK,
Grays ☎ 01708 686000 🖥 01708 686000 102 en suite

Top Meadow Fen Ln RM14 3PR
☎ 01708 852239
web: www.topmeadow.co.uk
Top Meadow Golf Course: 18 Holes, 6348yds, Par 72,
SSS 71, Course record 68.
Course Designer Burns/Stock **Location** M25 junct 29, A127 towards
Southend, B186 towards Ockendon
Telephone for further details
Hotel BUD Travelodge Brentwood East Horndon, EAST HORNDON
☎ 08719 846016 🖥 08719 846016 45 en suite

STANFORD LE HOPE   Map 5 TQ68

St Clere's Hall London Rd SS17 0LX
☎ 01375 361565 🖥 01375 361565
18 Holes, 6474yds, Par 72, SSS 71, Course record 71.
Course Designer A Stiff **Location** 5m from M25 on A13, Stanford turn
towards Linford, St Clere on left
Telephone for further details
Hotel ★★★ **77%** HL Best Western Manor Hotel, Hever Court Road,
GRAVESEND ☎ 01474 353100 🖥 01474 353100 59 en suite

STAPLEFORD ABBOTTS   Map 5 TQ59

Stapleford Abbotts Horsemanside, Tysea Hill RM4 1JU
☎ 01708 381108 🖥 01708 386345
e-mail: staplefordabbotts-sales@crown-golf.co.uk
web: www.staplefordabbottsgolf.co.uk
Abbotts course provides a challenging test for players of all abilities
as mature trees, large greenside bunkers and many lakes are all
brought into play. The Priors course with its links-type layout gives a
fresh challenge on each hole.
Abbotts Course: 18 Holes, 6501yds, Par 72, SSS 71.
Priors Course: 18 Holes, 5735yds, Par 70, SSS 69.
Club membership 650.
Visitors Mon-Fri & BHs. After noon weekends. Dress code.
Societies welcome. **Green Fees** phone **Course Designer** Henry
Cotton/Howard Swan **Prof** James Walpole **Facilities** 🍴 🍽 🏌 ⬇

🥤 🏌 🏠 🚩 ✦ 🚜 ✦ **Leisure** sauna **Conf** facs Corporate
Hospitality Days **Location** 1m E of Stapleford Abbotts, off B175
Hotel ★★★★ **75%** HL Marygreen Manor, London Road,
BRENTWOOD ☎ 01277 225252 🖥 01277 225252 44 en suite

STOCK   Map 5 TQ69

Crondon Park Stock Rd CM4 9DP
☎ 01277 843027 🖥 01277 841356
e-mail: paul@crondon.com
web: www.crondon.com
Undulating parkland with many water hazards, set in the Crondon
valley.
18 Holes, 6627yards, Par 72, SSS 72, Course record 67.
Club membership 700.
Visitors Dress code. **Societies** booking required. **Green Fees** not
confirmed **Course Designer** Mr M Gillet **Prof** Chris Wood/Freddie
Sunderland **Facilities** 🍴 🍽 🏌 ⬇ 🥤 🏌 🏠 🚜 ✦ 🚩
Conf facs Corporate Hospitality Days **Location** on B1007, between
Stock and A12 junct16
Hotel ★★★★ **76%** HL Greenwoods Hotel Spa & Retreat, Stock
Road, STOCK ☎ 01277 829990 & 829205 🖥 01277 829990
39 en suite

THEYDON BOIS   Map 5 TQ49

Theydon Bois Theydon Rd CM16 4EH
☎ 01992 812460 (pro) & 813054 (office)
🖥 01992 815602
web: www.theydongolf.co.uk

18 Holes, 5490yds, Par 68, SSS 67, Course record 64.
Course Designer James Braid **Location** M25 junct 26, 2m
Telephone for further details
Hotel BUD Travelodge Harlow North Weald, A414 Eastbound, Tylers
Green, North Weald, HARLOW ☎ 08719 846 033 🖥 08719 846 033
61 en suite

TOLLESHUNT KNIGHTS   Map 5 TL91

Five Lakes Hotel, Golf, Country Club & Spa Colchester
Rd CM9 8HX
☎ 01621 868888 & 862426 🖥 869696
e-mail: golfoffice@fivelakes.co.uk
web: www.fivelakes.co.uk
Set in 320 acres, the two 18-hole courses both offer their own
particular challenges. Water is the predominant feature of the

continued

Lakes Course, coming into play on nine holes. Generous fairways, large greens and water hazards provide a great test for golfers and ensure every club in the bag is used. The Links course presents a very different challenge, testing precision with narrow fairways and strategically placed water hazards, sand-bunkers and well guarded greens. Accuracy is the key to success on this course.

Links Course: 18 Holes, 6181yds, Par 71, SSS 70, Course record 67.
Lakes Course: 18 Holes, 6751yds, Par 72, SSS 72, Course record 63. Club membership 430.

Visitors Mon-Sun & BHs. Booking advisable. Dress code. **Societies** booking required. **Green Fees** not confirmed **Course Designer** Neil Coles **Prof** Gary Carter **Facilities** ⊕ ⦶ ⓘ ⓛ ⓓ ⦶ ⦶ ⦶ ⦶ ⦶ **Leisure** hard tennis courts, heated indoor swimming pool, squash, sauna, gymnasium, snooker, badminton, fitness studio **Conf** facs Corporate Hospitality Days **Location** 1.75m NE on B1026, 15 mins from A12 Kelvedon exit. Brown tourist signs
Hotel ★★★★ 77% HL Five Lakes Hotel, Golf, Country Club & Spa, Colchester Road, TOLLESHUNT KNIGHTS, Maldon ☎ 01621 868888 ▤ 01621 868888 194 en suite

TOOT HILL   Map 5 TL50

Toot Hill School Rd CM5 9PU
☎ 01277 365523   ▤ 01277 364509
Pleasant course with several water hazards and sand greens.
18 Holes, 6053yds, Par 70, SSS 69, Course record 65. Club membership 400.
Visitors contact club for details. **Societies** welcome. **Green Fees** not confirmed **Course Designer** Martin Gillett **Prof** Mark Bishop **Facilities** ⊕ ⦶ ⓘ ⓛ ⓓ ⦶ ⦶ ⦶ ⦶ ⦶ ⦶
Conf facs **Location** 7m SE of Harlow off A414
Hotel ★★★ 62% HL The Green Man, Mulberry Green, Old Harlow, HARLOW ☎ 01279 442521 ▤ 01279 442521 55 en suite

WITHAM   Map 5 TL81

Benton Hall Golf & Country Club Wickham Hill CM8 3LH
☎ 01376 502454   ▤ 01376 521050
e-mail: bentonhall.retail@theclubcompany.com
web: www.theclubcompany.com

Set in rolling countryside surrounded by dense woodland, this challenging course provides a severe test even to the best golfers. The River Blackwater dominates the front nine and natural lakes come into play on five other holes. A multi-million pound refurbishment of the existing clubhouse completed in June 2006 incorporates health and fitness facilities.

Benton Hall Golf & Country Club: 18 Holes, 6413yds, Par 71, SSS 72, Course record 64. Club membership 600.
Visitors contact club for details. **Societies** welcome. **Green Fees** phone **Course Designer** Alan Walker/Charles Cox **Prof** Colin Fairweather **Facilities** ⊕ ⦶ ⓘ ⓛ ⓓ ⦶ ⦶ ⦶ ⦶ ⦶ ⦶ **Leisure** sauna, gymnasium, 9 hole par 3 course **Conf** facs Corporate Hospitality Days **Location** off A12 at Witham, signed
Hotel ★★★ 77% HL Rivenhall, Rivenhall End, WITHAM ☎ 01376 516969 ▤ 01376 516969 55 en suite

WOODHAM WALTER   Map 5 TL80

Bunsay Downs Little Baddow Rd CM9 6RU
☎ 01245 222648   ▤ 01245 223989
9 Holes, 2932yds, Par 70, SSS 68.
Badgers: 9 Holes, 1319yds, Par 54.
Course Designer John Durham **Location** 2m from Danbury on A414, signed
Telephone for further details
Hotel ★★★★ 74% HL County Hotel, 29 Rainsford Road, CHELMSFORD ☎ 01245 455700 ▤ 01245 455700 51 en suite

Warren CM9 6RW
☎ 01245 223258   ▤ 01245 223989
e-mail: enquiries@warrengolfclub.co.uk
web: www.warrengolfclub.co.uk
Attractive parkland with natural hazards and good views.
18 Holes, 6263yds, Par 70, SSS 70, Course record 62. Club membership 765.
Visitors Mon, Tue, Thu-Sun exept BHs. Dress code. **Societies** welcome. **Green Fees** not confirmed **Prof** David Brooks **Facilities** ⊕ ⦶ ⓓ ⦶ ⦶ ⦶ ⦶ ⦶ ⦶ **Location** 0.5m SW
Hotel ★★★★ 74% HL County Hotel, 29 Rainsford Road, CHELMSFORD ☎ 01245 455700 ▤ 01245 455700 51 en suite

GLOUCESTERSHIRE

ALMONDSBURY   Map 3 ST68

Bristol St Swithins Park, Blackhorse Hill BS10 7TP
☎ 01454 620000   ▤ 01454 202700
e-mail: bristol@crown-golf.co.uk
web: www.crown-golf.co.uk
An undulating course set in 200 acres of parkland with magnificent views of the Severn estuary and surrounding countryside.
18 Holes, 6111yds, Par 70, SSS 69, Course record 63. Club membership 700.
Visitors contact club for details. **Societies** booking required. **Green Fees** not confirmed **Course Designer** Pierson **Prof** David Griffin **Facilities** ⊕ ⦶ ⓘ ⓛ ⓓ ⦶ ⦶ ⦶ ⦶ ⦶ ⦶ ⦶
Leisure par 3 academy course **Conf** facs Corporate Hospitality Days **Location** M5 junct 17, 100yds
Hotel 66% Henbury Lodge, Station Road, Henbury, BRISTOL ☎ 0117 950 2615 ▤ 0117 950 2615 20 en suite

Bells Hotel
Forest of Dean Golf Club

Lords Hill, Coleford, Gloucestershire GL16 8BE
Tel: 01594 832583   **Fax:** 01594 832584
Website: www.bells-hotel.co.uk   **Email:** enquiries@bells-hotel.co.uk

AA
★★
Hotel

Situated on its own golf course, featuring lakes, streams and woodland, Bells Hotel is the ideal place for your golf break. With 52 en-suite rooms, including two with wheelchair access, the hotel can cater for the individual as well as groups of varying sizes. The Clubhouse offers a warm welcome and friendly atmosphere, where drinks and homemade food are served throughout the day.

Golf Breaks at Bells include games on our golf course which is easily playable yet offers a challenge to the more experienced golfer. There is a practice chipping and putting green and a well stocked golf shop on site.

The tennis court and bowling green are available free of charge to Hotel guests. A four mat short mat bowling venue is a new addition to *The Forest of Dean Golf Club.*

In addition to the amenities on site, Bells Hotel is in an ideal location from which to explore the Forest of Dean and The Wye Valley. This area of outstanding natural beauty offers the chance to take part in many activities as well as being a place to relax and enjoy the scenery.

CHELTENHAM — Map 3 SO92

Cotswold Hills Ullenwood GL53 9QT
☎ 01242 515264 📠 01242 515317
e-mail: contact.us@cotswoldhills-golfclub.com
web: www.cotswoldhills-golfclub.com
A gently undulating course with open aspects and views of the Cotswolds.

18 Holes, 6557yds, Par 72, SSS 71, Course record 67. Club membership 750.

Visitors Mon-Sun & BHs. Handicap certificate. Dress code.
Societies booking required. **Green Fees** £36 per 18 holes (£42 weekends & BHs) **Course Designer** M D Little **Prof** James Latham **Facilities** ⓣ ⓘⓞⓛ ⓛ ⓓ ⓢⓣ ⓐ ⓑ ⓕ ⓖ ⓗ **Conf** Corporate Hospitality Days **Location** 3m SE on A435
Hotel ★★★★ 72% HL Barceló Cheltenham Park, Cirencester Road, Charlton Kings, CHELTENHAM ☎ 01242 222021 📠 01242 222021 152 en suite

Lilley Brook Cirencester Rd, Charlton Kings GL53 8EG
☎ 01242 526785 📠 01242 256880
e-mail: karl@lilleybrook.co.uk
web: www.lilleybrook.co.uk
Challenging parkland/downland course on the lower slopes of Leckhampton Hill with outstanding views of Cheltenham, the Malverns and the Black Mountains.

18 Holes, 6212yds, Par 69, SSS 70, Course record 61. Club membership 900.

Visitors Mon-Sun & BHs. Booking required weekends & BHs. Handicap certificate. Dress code. **Societies** booking required. **Green Fees** £35 per 18 holes (£40 weekends & BHs) **Course Designer** Dr Alister Mackenzie **Prof** Simon Harrison **Facilities** ⓣ ⓘⓞⓛ ⓛ ⓓ ⓢⓣ ⓐ ⓑ ⓕ ⓖ ⓗ **Conf** facs Corporate Hospitality Days **Location** 2m S of Cheltenham on A435
Hotel ★★★★ 72% HL Barceló Cheltenham Park, Cirencester Road, Charlton Kings, CHELTENHAM ☎ 01242 222021 📠 01242 222021 152 en suite

Shipton Shipton Oliffe, Andoverford GL54 4HT
☎ 01242 890237
e-mail: shiptongolf@tiscali.co.uk
web: www.shiptongolf.co.uk
Deceptive, easy walking course situated in the heart of the Cotswolds giving a fair challenge and panoramic views.

Shipton Golf Course: 9 Holes, 2516yds, Par 35, SSS 63, Course record 33.

Visitors contact course for details. **Societies** welcome. **Green Fees** £12 per 18 holes, £8 per 9 holes (£14/£10 weekends & BHs) **Prof** Noel Boland **Facilities** ⓓ ⓐ ⓑ ⓕ ⓖ ⓗ **Location** on A436, S of A40 junct
Hotel ★★★ 74% SHL Charlton Kings, London Road, Charlton Kings, CHELTENHAM ☎ 01242 231061 📠 01242 231061 13 en suite

CHIPPING SODBURY — Map 3 ST78

Chipping Sodbury Trinity Ln BS37 6PU
☎ 01454 319042 📠 01454 320052
e-mail: info@chippingsodburygolfclub.co.uk
web: www.chippingsodburygolfclub.co.uk
Founded in 1905, a parkland course of championship proportions on the edge of the Cotswolds. The easy walking terrain, delicately

interrupted by a medley of waterways and lakes, is complimented by a stylish clubhouse.

Beaufort Course: 18 Holes, 6912yds, Par 73, SSS 73, Course record 65. Club membership 800.

Visitors Mon-Fri & BHs. Dress code. **Societies** booking required.
Green Fees £35 per round **Course Designer** Hawtree **Prof** Mike Watts **Facilities** ⓣ ⓘⓞⓛ ⓛ ⓓ ⓢⓣ ⓐ ⓑ ⓕ ⓖ ⓗ
Leisure 6 hole academy course **Conf** facs Corporate Hospitality Days **Location** 0.5m N
Hotel ★★ 76% HL Best Western Compass Inn, TORMARTON ☎ 01454 218242 & 218577 📠 01454 218242 26 en suite

CIRENCESTER — Map 4 SP00

Cirencester Cheltenham Rd, Bagendon GL7 7BH
☎ 01285 652465 📠 01285 650665
e-mail: info@cirencestergolfclub.co.uk
web: www.cirencestergolfclub.co.uk

Undulating open Cotswold course with excellent views.
18 Holes, 6030yds, Par 70, SSS 69, Course record 65. Club membership 800.

Visitors Mon-Sun & BHs. Handicap certificate. Dress code.
Societies booking required. **Green Fees** £35 per round/day (£40 weekends) **Course Designer** J Braid **Prof** Ed Goodwin **Facilities** ⓣ ⓘⓞⓛ ⓛ ⓓ ⓢⓣ ⓐ ⓑ ⓕ ⓖ ⓗ **Leisure** 6 hole par 3 academy course. **Conf** facs Corporate Hospitality Days **Location** 2m N of Cirencester on A435
Hotel ★★★ 79% HL Best Western Stratton House, Gloucester Road, CIRENCESTER ☎ 01285 651761 📠 01285 651761 39 en suite

CLEEVE HILL — Map 3 SO92

Cleeve Hill GL52 3PW
☎ 01242 672025 📠 01242 67444
web: www.cleevehillgolfcourse.com
18 Holes, 6448yds, Par 72, SSS 71, Course record 66.
Prof Dave Finch **Facilities** ⓣ ⓘⓞⓛ ⓛ ⓓ ⓐ ⓑ ⓕ ⓖ
Conf facs Corporate Hospitality Days **Location** 1m NE on B4632
Telephone for further details
Hotel ★★★ 80% HL George Hotel, St Georges Road, CHELTENHAM ☎ 01242 235751 📠 01242 235751 31 en suite

COALPIT HEATH
Map 3 ST68

The Kendleshire Henfield Rd BS36 2TG
☎ 0117 956 7007   ▤ 0117 957 3433
e-mail: info@kendleshire.com
web: www.kendleshire.com

Opened in 1997, the course has 27 holes with water coming into play on 18 holes. Notable holes are the 11th, the 16th and the 27th. The 11th is a short hole with an island green set in a 3-acre lake and the 16th has a second shot played over water. The course is never short of interest and the greens have been built to USGA specification.

The Kendleshire Golf Course: 18 Holes, 6567, Par 71, SSS 72, Course record 63.
The Kendleshire Golf Course: 18 Holes, 6249, Par 71, SSS 70, Course record 68.
The Kendleshire Golf Course: 18 Holes, 6353, Par 70, SSS 70, Course record 68. Club membership 900.

Visitors Mon-Sun & BHs. Booking required Fri-Sun & BHs. Dress code. **Societies** booking required. **Green Fees** Mon £25 per round, Tue-Thu £36, Fri-Sun £40 **Course Designer** A Stiff/P McEvoy **Prof** Tony Mealing **Facilities** ⓟ ⑩ ⓛ ☐ 🏐 ⚤ 🏠 ⛳ ✦ 🛒 ✦ ♣ **Conf** facs Corporate Hospitality Days **Location** M32 junct 1, on Avon Ring Road

Hotel ★★★★ 74% HL Jurys Bristol Hotel, Prince Street, BRISTOL ☎ 0117 923 0333 ▤ 0117 923 0333 192 en suite

CODRINGTON
Map 3 ST78

Players Club BS37 6RZ
☎ 01454 313029   ▤ 01454 323446
e-mail: enquiries@theplayersgolfclub.com
web: www.theplayersgolfclub.com

This Adrian Stiff designed layout can measure up to 7617yds. Often described as an inland links, the rolling sand based fairways encounter an unusual mix of gorse and water.

Championship: 18 Holes, 6547yards, Par 72, SSS 72, Course record 63. Club membership 2000.

Visitors Mon-Sun & BHs. Booking required. Dress code. **Societies** booking required. **Green Fees** not confirmed **Course Designer** Adrian Stiff **Prof** Mark Brookes **Facilities** ⓟ ⑩ ⓛ ☐ 🏐 ⚤ 🏠 ⛳ ✦ 🛒 ✦ ♣ **Leisure** fishing, 9 hole par 3 course **Conf** facs Corporate Hospitality Days **Location** M4 junct 18, 1m on B4465

Hotel ★★ 76% HL Best Western Compass Inn, TORMARTON ☎ 01454 218242 & 218577 ▤ 01454 218242 26 en suite

COLEFORD
Map 3 SO51

Forest Hills Mile End Rd GL16 7QD
☎ 01594 810620   ▤ 01594 810823
e-mail: foresthills@btconnect.com
web: foresthillsgolfclub.co.uk

Parkland on a plateau with panoramic views of Coleford and Forest of Dean. Some testing holes with the par 5 13th hole sitting tight on a water hazard, and the challenging 18th with second shot over large pond to a green protected by another pond and bunker - all in front of the clubhouse.

18 Holes, 6385yds, Par 72, SSS 70, Course record 64. Club membership 470.

Visitors contact club for details. **Societies** welcome. **Green Fees** £22 per 18 holes (£33 weekends) **Course Designer** A Stiff **Prof** Richard Ballard **Facilities** ⓟ ⑩ ⓛ ☐ 🏐 ⚤ 🏠 ⛳ ✦ 🛒 ✦ ♣ **Leisure** fishing **Conf** facs Corporate Hospitality Days
Hotel ★★★ 66% HL Speech House, COLEFORD ☎ 01594 822607 ▤ 01594 822607 37 en suite

Forest of Dean Golf Club & Bells Hotel Lords Hill GL16 8BE
☎ 01594 832583   ▤ 01594 832584
web: www.bells-hotel.co.uk

Forest of Dean Golf Club & Bells Hotel: 18 Holes, 6033yds, Par 70, SSS 69, Course record 63.

Course Designer John Day **Location** 0.25m from Coleford town centre on B4431 Coleford-Parkend road
Telephone for further details
Hotel ★★ 71% HL Bells Hotel & The Forest of Dean Golf Club, Lords Hill, COLEFORD ☎ 01594 832583 ▤ 01594 832583 52 en suite

See advert on page 90

DURSLEY
Map 3 ST79

Stinchcombe Hill Stinchcombe Hill GL11 6AQ
☎ 01453 542015   ▤ 01453 549545
e-mail: secretary@stinchcombehill.plus.com
web: www.stinchcombehillgolfclub.com

High on the hill with splendid views of the Cotswolds, the River Severn and the Welsh hills. A downland course with good turf, some trees and an interesting variety of greens. Protected greens make this a challenging course in windy conditions.

18 Holes, 5734yds, Par 68, SSS 68, Course record 61. Club membership 550.

Visitors handicap certificate. Dress code. **Societies** welcome. **Green Fees** not confirmed **Course Designer** Arthur Hoare **Prof** Paul Bushell **Facilities** ⓟ ⑩ by prior arrangement ⓛ ☐ 🏐 ⚤ 🏠 ✦ **Conf** Corporate Hospitality Days **Location** 1m W off A4135
Hotel ★★★★ 74% HL Tortworth Court Four Pillars, Tortworth, WOTTON-UNDER-EDGE ☎ 0800 374 692 & 01454 263000 ▤ 0800 374 692 189 en suite

DYMOCK
Map 3 SO73

Dymock Grange The Old Grange GL18 2AN
☎ 01531 890840   ▤ 01531 890860
Old Course: 9 Holes, 5786yards, Par 72, SSS 70, Course record 71.
New Course: 9 Holes, 3390yards, Par 60, SSS 60.

continued

BURLEIGH COURT HOTEL

Burleigh Court Hotel, Burleigh, Minchampton,
Stroud, Gloucestershire GL5 2PF

Tel: +44 (0) 1453 883804   Fax: +44 (0) 1453 886870
Website: burleighcourthotel.co.uk
Email: burleighcourt@aol.com

Nestling on the edge of a steep hillside, overlooking the Golden Valley, Burleigh Court is an 18th century Cotswold stone gentlemen's manor house, a hidden gem in the heart of Royal Gloucestershire.

Renowned for its warmth and quality of service, you are beguiled into enjoying the relaxed and tranquil atmosphere that Burleigh Court exudes.

Course Designer Cufingham **Location** on B4215 Leominster road
Telephone for further details
Hotel ★★★ 80% HL Feathers, High Street, LEDBURY
☎ 01531 635266 📠 01531 635266 22 en suite

GLOUCESTER   Map 3 SO81

Brickhampton Court Golf Complex Cheltenham Rd,
Churchdown GL2 9QF
☎ 01452 859444 📠 01452 859333
e-mail: info@brickhampton.co.uk
web: www.brickhampton.co.uk
Rolling parkland featuring lakes, streams, strategic white-sand
bunkers, plantations - but no steep hills.

Spa: 18 Holes, 6449yds, Par 71, SSS 71, Course record 65.
Glevum: 9 Holes, 1859yds, Par 31, SSS 31.
Club membership 860.

Visitors Mon-Sun & BHs. Dress code. **Societies** booking required.
Green Fees Spa £23 per round (£26 Fri, £30 weekends & BHs).
Glevum £8.50 per 9 holes (£10.50 weekends & BHs) **Course**
Designer Simon Gidman **Prof** Bruce Wilson **Facilities** ⊕ ⊚⏐
🏐 ⛳ 🐾 🏌 📷 ⛳ 🏐 🚶 ⛳ 🏁 **Conf** facs Corporate
Hospitality Days **Location** M5 junct 11, A40 towards Gloucester, at
Elmbridge Court rdbt B4063 signed Churchdown, 2m
Hotel ★★★ 80% HL Hatherley Manor, Down Hatherley Lane,
GLOUCESTER ☎ 01452 730217 📠 01452 730217 50 en suite

Ramada Gloucester Matson Ln, Robinswood Hill
GL4 6EA
☎ 01452 525653 📠 01452 307212
web: www.gloucestergolf.com
Undulating, wooded course, built around a hill with superb views
over Gloucester and the Cotswolds. The 12th is a drive straight up a
hill, nicknamed 'Coronary Hill'.

18 Holes, 6170yds, Par 70, SSS 69, Course record 65.
Club membership 600.

Visitors Mon-Sun & BHs. Booking required. Dress code.
Societies booking required. **Green Fees** phone **Prof** Keith Wood
Facilities ⊕ ⊚⏐ 🏐 ⛳ 🏌 🚶 📷 ⛳ ⛳ 🏁 ⛳ 🏌
Leisure hard tennis courts, heated indoor swimming pool, squash,
sauna, gymnasium, 9 hole par 3 course **Conf** facs Corporate
Hospitality Days **Location** 2.5m SE of Gloucester, off B4073
Hotel ★★★ 70% HL Ramada Gloucester Hotel and Country Club,
Matson Lane, Robinswood Hill, GLOUCESTER ☎ 0844 815 9044
📠 0844 815 9044 97 en suite

Rodway Hill Newent Rd, Highnam GL2 8DN
☎ 01452 384222 📠 01452 313814
e-mail: info@rodway-hill-golf-course.co.uk
web: www.rodway-hill-golf-course.co.uk
A challenging 18-hole course with superb panoramic views. Testing
front five holes and the par 3 13th and par 5 16th affected by strong
crosswinds off the River Severn.

Rodway Hill Golf Course: 18 Holes, 6040yds, Par 70,
SSS 69, Course record 66. Club membership 400.
Visitors Mon-Sun & BHs. Booking required. Dress code.

continued

Societies welcome. **Green Fees** £15 per 18 holes, £9 per 9 holes (£17-£18/£9-£10 weekends) **Course Designer** John Gabb **Prof** Chris Murphy **Facilities** **Conf** facs Corporate Hospitality Days **Location** 2m outside Gloucester on B4215

Hotel ★★★ **80%** HL Hatherley Manor, Down Hatherley Lane, GLOUCESTER ☎ 01452 730217 01452 730217 50 en suite

LYDNEY Map 3 SO60

Lydney Lakeside Av GL15 5QA
☎ 01594 841186
web: www.lydneygolfclub.org.uk

Flat parkland and meadowland course with prevailing wind along fairways.

9 Holes, 5298yds, Par 66, SSS 66, Course record 63. Club membership 240.

Visitors Mon-Fri & BHs. Dress code. **Societies** welcome. **Green Fees** £11 per day/round **Facilities** **Location** SE side of town centre

Hotel ★★★ **66%** HL Speech House, COLEFORD ☎ 01594 822607 01594 822607 37 en suite

MINCHINHAMPTON Map 3 SO80

Minchinhampton (New Course) New Course GL6 9BE
☎ 01453 833866 01453 837360
e-mail: alan@mgcnew.co.uk
web: www.mgcnew.co.uk

Set high on the Cotswolds, both courses offer scenic countryside and outstanding tests of golf.The Cherington is a testing inland links course and was an Open Qualifying venue from 2002-2007. The Avening is a parkland course offering a different but no less challenging experience.

Avening: 18 Holes, 6263yds, Par 70, SSS 70, Course record 61.
Cherington: 18 Holes, 6430yds, Par 71, SSS 71, Course record 61. Club membership 1200.

Visitors Mon-Sun & BHs. Booking required. Handicap certificate. Dress code. **Societies** welcome. **Green Fees** not confirmed **Course Designer** Hawtree & Son **Prof** Chris Steele **Facilities** **Conf** Corporate Hospitality Days **Location** B4014 from Nailsworth into Avening, left at Cross pub towards Minchinhampton, club 0.25m on right

Hotel ★★★ **79%** HL Burleigh Court, Burleigh, Minchinhampton, STROUD ☎ 01453 883804 01453 883804 18 en suite

See advert on page 93

Minchinhampton (Old Course) Old Course GL6 9AQ
☎ 01453 832642 & 836382 01453 832642
e-mail: alan@mgcold.co.uk
web: www.mgcold.co.uk

An open grassland course 600 feet above sea level, best described as an inland links course with no water or sand bunkers. The numerous humps and hollows around the greens test the golfer's ability to play a variety of shots - often in difficult windy conditions. Panoramic Cotswold views. Two of the par 3s, the 8th and the 16th, often require an accurate long iron or wood depending on the strength and direction of the wind.

Minchinhampton Old Course: 18 Holes, 6088yds, Par 71, SSS 69, Course record 61. Club membership 550.

Visitors Mon-Sun & BHs. Booking required Tue, Thu-Sun & BHs. Dress code. **Societies** booking preferable. **Green Fees** £18 per day (£22 weekends and BHs) **Prof** Peter Dangerfield **Facilities** **Location** 1m NW

Hotel ★★ **76%** HL Egypt Mill, NAILSWORTH ☎ 01453 833449 01453 833449 28 en suite

NAUNTON Map 4 SP12

Naunton Downs GL54 3AE
☎ 01451 850090 01451 850091
e-mail: admin@nauntondowns.co.uk
web: www.nauntondowns.co.uk

Naunton Downs course plays over beautiful Cotswold countryside. A valley running through the course is one of the main features, creating one par 3 hole that crosses over it. The prevailing wind adds extra challenge to the par 5s (which play into the wind), combined with small undulating greens.

18 Holes, 6191yds, Par 71, SSS 70, Course record 67. Club membership 750.

Visitors Mon-Sun & BHs. Booking required. Dress code. **Societies** booking required. **Green Fees** Mon £20 per round, Tue-Fri £25 (£29 weekends and BHs) **Course Designer** J Pott **Prof** Nick Ellis **Facilities** **Leisure** hard tennis courts **Conf** facs Corporate Hospitality Days **Location** off B4068

Hotel ★★★★ CHH Lords of the Manor, UPPer SLAUGHTER ☎ 01451 820243 01451 820243 26 en suite

PAINSWICK Map 3 SO80

Painswick GL6 6TL
☎ 01452 812180
e-mail: hello@painswickgolf.com
web: www.painswickgolf.com

Downland course set on the Cotswolds at Painswick Beacon, with fine views. Short course more than compensated by natural hazards and tight fairways.

18 Holes, 4895yds, Par 67, SSS 63, Course record 61. Club membership 250.

Visitors Mon-Sat & BHs. Booking required Sat & BHs. Dress code **Societies** booking required. **Green Fees** £19 per 18 holes (£22 Sat). Winter £11.50/£19 **Facilities** **Conf** Corporate Hospitality Days **Location** 1m N of Painswick, off A46 to Cheltenham

Hotel ★★★ **71%** HL Hatton Court, Upton Hill, Upton St Leonards, GLOUCESTER ☎ 01452 617412 01452 617412 45 en suite

TEWKESBURY

Map 3 SO83

Hilton Puckrup Hall Puckrup GL20 6EL
☎ 01684 271550   📠 01684 271550
web: www.hilton.co.uk/tewkesbury

Set in 140 acres of undulating parkland with lakes, existing trees and marvellous views of the Malvern hills. There are water hazards at the 5th, and a cluster of bunkers on the long 14th, before the challenging tee shot across the water to the par 3 18th.

Hilton Puckrup Hall: 18 Holes, 6219yds, Par 70, SSS 68, Course record 63. Club membership 380.

Visitors Mon-Fri. Weekends & BHs pm only. Booking required. Dress code. **Societies** welcome. **Green Fees** not confirmed **Course Designer** Simon Gidman **Prof** Mark Fenning **Facilities** ⓣ †◎† 🍴 �🛒 🏌 🧍 🏠 ◇ 🛵 🛺 🐎 **Leisure** heated indoor swimming pool, sauna, gymnasium **Conf** facs Corporate Hospitality Days **Location** 4m N of Tewkesbury on A38
Hotel ★★★★ 72% HL Tewkesbury Park Hotel Golf & Country Club, Lincoln Green Lane, TEWKESBURY ☎ 0870 609 6101 📠 0870 609 6101   82 en suite

---

Tewkesbury Park Hotel Golf & Country Club Lincoln Green Ln GL20 7DN
☎ 01684 295405   📠 01684 292386
e-mail: tewkesburypark@foliohotels.com
web: www.bespokehotels.com/tewkesburypark

Scenic course overlooking the Malvern Hills and surrounding countryside. It offers many interesting and testing holes, with wooded areas and water hazards early in the round, opening up onto spacious fairways on the back nine of the undulating course.

Tewkesbury Park Hotel Golf & Country Club: 18 Holes, 6533yds, Par 73, SSS 71, Course record 66. Club membership 500.

Visitors Mon-Sun & BHs. Booking required. Handicap certificate. Dress code. **Societies** booking required. **Green Fees** phone **Course Designer** Frank Pennick **Prof** Richard Harber **Facilities** ⓣ †◎† 🍴 �🛒 🏌 🧍 🏠 ◇ 🛵 🛺 🐎 **Leisure** hard tennis courts, heated indoor swimming pool, squash, sauna, gymnasium **Conf** facs Corporate Hospitality Days **Location** M5 junct 9, take A438 into town centre, 1st exit at rdbt passing abbey on left, 3rd right into Lincoln Green Lane
Hotel ★★★★ 72% HL Tewkesbury Park Hotel Golf & Country Club, Lincoln Green Lane, TEWKESBURY ☎ 0870 609 6101 📠 0870 609 6101   82 en suite

See advert on this page

THORNBURY

Map 3 ST69

Thornbury Golf Centre Bristol Rd BS35 3XL
☎ 01454 281144   📠 01454 281177
e-mail: info@thornburygc.co.uk
web: www.thornburygc.co.uk

Two 18-hole pay and play courses designed by Hawtree and set in undulating terrain with views towards the Severn estuary. The Low 18 is a par 3 with holes ranging from 80 to 207yds and is ideal for beginners. The High course puts to test the more experienced golfer. Excellent 25 bay floodlit driving range.

High Course: 18 Holes, 6308yds, Par 71, SSS 69.
Low Course: 18 Holes, 2195yds, Par 54.
Club membership 510.

Visitors Mon-Sun & BHs. Dress code. **Societies** booking required. **Green Fees** High Course £22 (£26 weekends & BHs). Low Course £6 **Course Designer** Hawtree **Prof** Mike Smedley **Facilities** ⓣ †◎†

continued

ENGLAND

🛒 ☕ 🍽 🎿 🛍 ❡ ◇ 🚜 ✂ 🏐 **Conf** facs Corporate Hospitality Days **Location** M5 junct 16, off A38 towards Gloucester **Hotel** ★★ 71% HL Thornbury Golf Lodge, Bristol Road, THORNBURY ☎ 01454 281144 🖹 01454 281144 11 en suite

WESTONBIRT
Map 3 ST88

Westonbirt Westonbirt School GL8 8QG
☎ 01666 880242 & 881338   🖹 01666 880385

Westonbirt Golf Course: 9 Holes, 4504yds, Par 64, SSS 64.
Facilities 🍸 ☕ 🎿 🏐 **Conf** facs **Location** E side of village off A433
Telephone for further details
Hotel ★★★ 77% HL Hare & Hounds, Westonbirt, TETBURY
☎ 01666 880233 & 881000 🖹 01666 880233 45 en suite

WICK
Map 3 ST77

Park Resort Tracy Park Estate BS30 5RN
☎ 0117 937 1800   🖹 0117 937 1813
web: www.theparkresort.com

Crown Course: 18 Holes, 6201yds, Par 69, SSS 70.
Cromwell Course: 18 Holes, 6157yds, Par 71, SSS 70.

Prof Richard Berry **Facilities** 🍴 🛒 ☕ 🍽 🎿 🛍 ❡ ◇ ✂ 🚜 ✂ 🏐 **Conf** facs Corporate Hospitality Days **Location** M4 junct 18, then follow A46 towards Bath followed by A420. Course off A420 E of village of Wick
Telephone for further details
Hotel ★★★ HL Queensberry, Russel Street, BATH
☎ 01225 447928 🖹 01225 447928 29 en suite

WOTTON-UNDER-EDGE
Map 3 ST79

Cotswold Edge Upper Rushmire GL12 7PT
☎ 01453 844167   🖹 01453 845120
e-mail: nnewman@cotswoldedgegolfclub.org.uk
web: www.cotswoldedgegolfclub.org.uk
Meadowland course situated in a quiet Cotswold valley with magnificent views. First half flat and open, second half more varied.
18 Holes, 6170yds, Par 71, SSS 71. Club membership 800.
Visitors booking required. Dress code. **Societies** booking required. **Green Fees** not confirmed **Prof** Rod Hibbitt **Facilities** 🍸 🛒 ☕ 🍽 🎿 🛍 ❡ ✂ 🚜 ✂ **Location** N of town on B4058 Wotton-Tetbury road
Hotel ★★ 76% HL Egypt Mill, NAILSWORTH ☎ 01453 833449 🖹 01453 833449 28 en suite

GREATER LONDON

ADDINGTON
Map 5 TQ36

The Addington 205 Shirley Church Rd CR0 5AB
☎ 020 8777 1055   🖹 020 8777 6661
e-mail: info@addingtongolf.com
web: www.addingtongolf.com
This heather and woodland course is considered to be one of the best laid out courses in Southern England with the world famous 13th, par 3 at 230yds. A good test of golfing ability with no two holes the same.

18 Holes, 6284yds, Par 69, SSS 71, Course record 66.
Visitors Mon-Sun & BHs. Booking required. Dress code **Societies** welcome. **Green Fees** phone **Course Designer** J F Abercromby **Prof** M Churchill **Facilities** 🍸 🍴 🛒 ☕ 🍽 🎿 🛍 ❡ ✂ 🚜 ✂ **Conf** Corporate Hospitality Days **Location** M25 junct 7, 3m from Croydon

The Addington

Hotel BUD Innkeeper's Lodge London Beckenham, 422 Upper Elmers End Road, BECKENHAM ☎ 0845 112 6126 🖹 0845 112 6126 24 en suite

Addington Court Featherbed Ln CR0 9AA
☎ 020 8657 0281 (booking) & 8651 5270 (admin)
🖹 020 8651 0282

Championship Course: 18 Holes, 5577yds, Par 68, SSS 67, Course record 60.
Falconwood: 18 Holes, 5472yds, Par 68, SSS 67.
9 Hole: 9 Holes, 1804yds, Par 31.

Course Designer Hawtree Snr **Location** 1m S off A2022
Telephone for further details
Hotel ★★★ 74% HL South Park Hotel, 3-5 South Park Hill Road, South Croydon, CROYDON ☎ 020 8688 5644 🖹 020 8688 5644 30 en suite

Addington Palace Addington Park, Gravel Hill CR0 5BB
☎ 020 8654 3061   🖹 020 8655 3632
e-mail: info@addingtonpalacegolf.co.uk
web: www.addingtonpalacegolf.co.uk
Set in the grounds of Addington Palace, which was the home of the Archbishops of Canterbury for a number of years. There are a number of tree-lined fairways and the 17th hole follows one of the original roads into the Palace and has a fine array of horse chestnut trees. The course winds its way through tree-lined fairways for the first nine holes. The second nine holes opens out and needs full concentration to achieve a good score. The 12th hole is one to remember, over a fountain and onto a green bunkered on all sides.

18 Holes, 6404yds, Par 71, SSS 70, Course record 63. Club membership 700.
Visitors Mon-Wed & Fri except BHs. Thu pm only. Booking required. Handicap certificate. Dress code. **Societies** booking required. **Green Fees** £45 per day, £40 per round **Course Designer** J H Taylor **Prof** Roger Williams **Facilities** 🍸 🍴 by prior arrangement 🛒 ☕ 🍽 🎿 🛍 ✂ 🚜 ✂ **Leisure** snooker **Conf** facs Corporate Hospitality Days **Location** 2m SE of Croydon station on A212
Hotel ★★★ 74% HL South Park Hotel, 3-5 South Park Hill Road, South Croydon, CROYDON ☎ 020 8688 5644 🖹 020 8688 5644 30 en suite

BARNEHURST

Map 5 TQ57

Barnehurst Mayplace Road East DA7 6JU
☎ 01322 523746 📠 01322 523860
e-mail: barnehurstgolfcourse@bexley.gov.uk
Public parkland course with well matured greens. Easy walking.

Barnehurst Public Pay & Play Golf Course: 9 Holes, 4796yds, Par 70, SSS 67. Club membership 180.

Visitors Mon-Sun & BHs. Dress code. **Societies** booking required. **Green Fees** not confirmed **Course Designer** James Braid **Prof** Bob Cameron **Facilities** ⑪ ⑩ ⓛ ☐ ⒏ ⚘ ☂ ⚐ ⦿ ✓ **Conf** facs Corporate Hospitality Days **Location** 0.75m NW of Crayford off A2000 **Hotel** ★★★★ 75% HL Bexleyheath Marriott Hotel, 1 Broadway, BEXLEYHEATH ☎ 020 8298 1000 📄 020 8298 1000 142 en suite

BARNET

Map 4 TQ29

Arkley Rowley Green Rd EN5 3HL
☎ 020 8449 0394 📠 020 8440 5214
e-mail: secretary@arkleygolfclub.co.uk
web: arkleygolfclub.co.uk
Wooded parkland on high ground with fine views.

9 Holes, 6046yds, Par 69, SSS 69. Club membership 400.
Visitors Mon-Sun & BHs. Booking required Tue, weekends & BHs. Dress code. **Societies** booking required. **Green Fees** £32 per day, £25 per round. £15 twilight after 4pm except Thu. **Course Designer** Braid **Prof** Andrew Hurley **Facilities** ⑪ ⑩ ⓛ ☐ ⚘ ☂ ⚐ ✓ **Conf** Corporate Hospitality Days **Location** off A1 at Arkley sign **Hotel** ★★★ 74% HL Corus hotel Elstree, Barnet Lane, ELSTREE ☎ 020 8953 8227 & 0844 736 8602 📄 020 8953 8227 49 en suite

Old Fold Manor Old Fold Ln, Hadley Green EN5 4QN
☎ 020 8440 9185 📠 020 8441 4863
e-mail: manager@oldfoldmanor.co.uk
web: www.oldfoldmanor.co.uk
Superb heathland course with some fine greens, breathtaking views and a challenge for all levels of golfer. Slightly undulating in parts but an enjoyable golfing experience.

18 Holes, 6447yds, Par 71, SSS 71, Course record 66. Club membership 560.
Visitors Mon-Fri. Weekends & BHs after 2.30pm. Booking required. Dress code. **Societies** booking required. **Green Fees** £48 per 36 holes, £45 per 27 holes, £35 per 18 holes **Course Designer** H S Colt **Prof** Peter McEvoy **Facilities** ⑪ ⑩ ⓛ ☐ ⚘ ☂ ⚐ ✓ ☂ ✓ **Conf** Corporate Hospitality Days **Location** off A1000 between Barnet & Potters Bar
Hotel ★★★★ 80% HL West Lodge Park, Cockfosters Road, HADLEY WOOD ☎ 020 8216 3900 & 8216 3903 📄 020 8216 3900 59 en suite

The Shire London St Albans Rd EN5 4RE
☎ 020 8441 7649 📠 020 8440 2757
e-mail: golf@theshirelondon.com
web: www.theshirelondon.com
A 27-hole golf complex, opened in May 2007 and designed by Seve Ballesteros, his first full golf course in the UK. The 18-hole Seve Masters course is a championship style layout with six par threes, six par fours and six par fives. The 9-hole Seve Challenge course is a mix of par fours and threes on a smaller scale, ideal for juniors, beginners and as a warm-up nine. The complex is also home to the Seve School

Of Natural Golf, a large driving range and practice area, where Seve's golfing philosophy is unveiled in a world-first teaching package.

Seve Masters: 18 Holes, 7100yds, Par 72, SSS 75. Seve Challenge: 9 Holes, 1501yds, Par 30, SSS 30. Club membership 400.

Visitors Mon-Sun & BHs. Booking required. Dress code. **Societies** booking required. **Green Fees** £50 per 18 holes (£65 weekends) **Course Designer** Severiano Ballesteros **Prof** Cox/Whitelegg/Menai-Davis **Facilities** ⑪ ⑩ ⓛ ☐ ⚘ ☂ ⚐ ✓ ☂ ✓ ☂ **Leisure** sauna, gymnasium, Severiano Ballesteros School of Natural Golf **Conf** facs Corporate Hospitality Days **Location** M25 junct 23 (A1/M25 interchange), take A1081 towards Barnet, Course on right
Hotel ★★★ 74% HL Corus hotel Elstree, Barnet Lane, ELSTREE ☎ 020 8953 8227 & 0844 736 8602 📄 020 8953 8227 49 en suite

BECKENHAM

Map 5 TQ36

Beckenham Place Park The Mansion BR3 2BP
☎ 020 8650 2292 📠 020 8663 1201

Beckenham Place Park Golf Course: 18 Holes, 5722yds, Par 68, SSS 69.

Prof John Denham/Carl Denham **Facilities** ⑪ ⓛ ☐ ⚘ ☂ ⚐ ⦿ ✓ ☂ ✓ **Leisure** hard tennis courts **Conf** facs **Location** off A2015
Telephone for further details
Hotel ★★★ 77% HL Best Western Bromley Court, Bromley Hill, BROMLEY ☎ 020 8461 8600 📄 020 8461 8600 114 en suite

Langley Park Barnfield Wood Rd BR3 6SZ
☎ 020 8658 6849 📠 020 8658 6310
e-mail: manager@langleyparkgolf.co.uk
web: www.langleyparkgolf.co.uk
A pleasant but difficult, well-wooded parkland course. Natural hazards include a lake at the par 3 18th hole. Although most fairways are bordered by woodland, they are wide with forgiving rough and friendly bunkers.

18 Holes, 6453yds, Par 69, SSS 71, Course record 65. Club membership 700.

Visitors Mon-Fri except BHs. Handicap certificate. Dress code. **Societies** booking required. **Green Fees** not confirmed **Course Designer** J H Taylor **Prof** Colin Staff **Facilities** ⑪ ⑩ ⓛ ☐ ⚘ ☂ ⚐ ⦿ ✓ **Conf** Corporate Hospitality Days **Location** 0.5 N of Beckenham on B2015
Hotel ★★★ 77% HL Best Western Bromley Court, Bromley Hill, BROMLEY ☎ 020 8461 8600 📄 020 8461 8600 114 en suite

BEXLEYHEATH

Map 5 TQ47

Bexleyheath Mount Rd DA6 8JS
☎ 020 8303 6951

9 Holes, 5162yds, Par 66, SSS 66, Course record 65.
Facilities ☂ **Location** 1m SW
Telephone for further details
Hotel ★★★★ 75% HL Bexleyheath Marriott Hotel, 1 Broadway, BEXLEYHEATH ☎ 020 8298 1000 📄 020 8298 1000 142 en suite

BIGGIN HILL
Map 5 TQ45

Cherry Lodge Jail Ln TN16 3AX
☎ 01959 572250   🖻 01959 540672
e-mail: info@cherrylodgegc.co.uk
web: www.cherrylodgegc.co.uk
Undulating parkland 600ft above sea level with panoramic views of the surrounding countryside. An enjoyable test of golf for all standards. The 14th is 434yds across a valley and uphill, requiring two good shots to reach the green.

18 Holes, 6593yds, Par 72, SSS 72, Course record 66.
Club membership 1500.

Visitors dress code. **Societies** booking required. **Green Fees** £55 per day **Course Designer** John Day **Prof** Craig Sutherland **Facilities** ⑪ ⑩ ⓱ ⌑ ⑪ ⏃ 🖻 🛒 ✆ 🏌 **Conf** Corporate Hospitality Days **Location** 1m E of Biggin Hill Airport
Hotel ★★★ 79% HL Best Western Donnington Manor, London Road, Dunton Green, SEVENOAKS ☎ 01732 462681 🖻 01732 462681 60 en suite

BROMLEY
Map 5 TQ46

Bromley Magpie Hall Ln BR2 8JF
☎ 020 8462 7014   🖻 020 8462 6916
Bromley Golf Course: 9 Holes, 2745yds, Par 70, SSS 67.
Prof Alan Hodgson **Facilities** ⌑ 🖻 ⏉ ✆ **Location** 2m SE off A21
Telephone for further details
Hotel ★★★ 77% HL Best Western Bromley Court, Bromley Hill, BROMLEY ☎ 020 8461 8600 🖻 020 8461 8600 114 en suite

Sundridge Park Garden Rd BR1 3NE
☎ 020 8460 0278   🖻 020 8289 3050
e-mail: gm@spgc.co.uk
web: www.spgc.co.uk
The East Course is longer than the West but many think the shorter of the two courses is the more difficult. The East is surrounded by trees while the West is more hilly, with good views. Both are certainly a good test of golf. An Open qualifying course with year round irrigation of fairways.

East Course: 18 Holes, 6538yds, Par 71, SSS 71,
Course record 63.
West Course: 18 Holes, 6019yds, Par 69, SSS 69,
Course record 65. Club membership 1200.

Visitors Mon-Fri except BHs. Handicap certificate. Dress code. **Societies** welcome. **Green Fees** £60 per day, £45 per round **Course Designer** Willie Park **Prof** Stuart Dowsett **Facilities** ⑪ ⑩ ⓱ ⌑ ⑪ ⏃ 🖻 ✆ 🛒 ✆ **Conf** facs Corporate Hospitality Days **Location** N side of town centre off A2212
Hotel ★★★ 77% HL Best Western Bromley Court, Bromley Hill, BROMLEY ☎ 020 8461 8600 🖻 020 8461 8600 114 en suite

CARSHALTON
Map 4 TQ26

Oaks Sports Centre Woodmansterne Rd SM5 4AN
☎ 020 8643 8363   🖻 020 8661 7880
e-mail: info@theoaksgolf.co.uk
web: www.theoaksgolf.co.uk
Public parkland course with floodlit, covered driving range.

Oaks Sports Centre Ltd: 18 Holes, 6026yds, Par 70, SSS 69,
Course record 65.
Oaks Sports Centre Ltd: 9 Holes, 1497yds, Par 28, SSS 28.
Club membership 230.

Visitors Mon-Sun & BHs. Booking required weekends & BHs. Dress code. **Societies** booking required. **Green Fees** £19 for 18 holes, £10 for 9 holes (£25/£12 weekends) **Prof** Horley/Pilkington/Mulcahy **Facilities** ⑪ ⑩ ⓱ ⌑ ⑪ ⏃ 🖻 ⏉ 🛒 ✆ 🏌 **Conf** facs Corporate Hospitality Days **Location** 0.5m S on B278
Hotel ★★★ 80% HL Aerodrome, Purley Way, CROYDON ☎ 020 8710 9000 & 8680 1999 🖻 020 8710 9000 110 en suite

CHESSINGTON
Map 4 TQ16

Chessington Garrison Ln KT9 2LW
☎ 020 8391 0948   🖻 020 8397 2068
e-mail: info@chessingtongolf.co.uk
web: www.chessingtongolf.co.uk
Tree-lined parkland course designed by Patrick Tallack, with panoramic views over the Surrey countryside.

Chessington Golf Centre: 9 Holes, 1679yds, Par 30, SSS 28.
Club membership 90.

Visitors contact centre for details. **Societies** welcome. **Green Fees** £9 per round (£11 weekends and BHs) **Course Designer** Patrick Tallack **Prof** Mark Janes **Facilities** ⑪ ⓱ ⌑ ⑪ 🖻 ⏉ 🛒 ✆ 🏌 **Leisure** automated ball teeing facility on driving range **Conf** facs Corporate Hospitality Days **Location** M25 junct 9, 3m N on A243, 0.5m from Chessington World of Adventure
Hotel ★★★★ 71% HL Holiday Inn London-Chessington, Leatherhead Road, CHESSINGTON ☎ 01372 734600 🖻 01372 734600 150 en suite

CHISLEHURST
Map 5 TQ47

Chislehurst Camden Park Rd BR7 5HJ
☎ 020 8467 2782   🖻 020 8295 0874
e-mail: thesecretary@chislehurstgolfclub.co.uk
web: www.chislehurstgolfclub.co.uk
The course was established in 1894 and is dominated by an imposing 17th century building of great historical interest. The challenging parkland course has an overall area of less than 70 acres and accuracy is always more important than distance off the tee. There are trees, hills and dales and the excellent greens are neither too large or too flat. Only the 7th hole remains from the original nine-hole course.

18 Holes, 5120yds, Par 66, SSS 66, Course record 61.
Club membership 760.

Visitors Booking required. Handicap certificate. Dress code. **Societies** booking required. **Green Fees** £40 per round **Course Designer** Park **Prof** David Bicknell **Facilities** ⑪ ⓱ ⌑ ⑪ ⏃ 🖻 ✆ 🛒 ✆ **Leisure** snooker room **Conf** facs Corporate Hospitality Days
Hotel ★★★ 77% HL Best Western Bromley Court, Bromley Hill, BROMLEY ☎ 020 8461 8600 🖻 020 8461 8600 114 en suite

COULSDON
Map 4 TQ25

Coulsdon Manor Hotel Coulsdon Court Rd CR5 2LL
☎ 020 8668 0414   📄 020 8668 3118
e-mail: reservations.coulsdon@ohiml.com
web: www.oxfordhotelsandinns.com
Designed by Harry S Colt and set in its own 140 acres of landscaped parkland.

Coulsdon Manor Hotel Golf Course: 18 Holes, 6037yds, Par 70, SSS 68. Club membership 150.

Visitors Mon-Sun & BHs. Booking required weekends & BHs. Dress code. **Societies** booking required. **Green Fees** £23 per round (£29.50 weekends and BHs) **Course Designer** Harry Colt **Prof** Matt Asbury **Facilities** ⓦ 🍴 🏌 ☕ 🍽 🏃 🏠 ⛺ ◇ 🛒 ✦ **Leisure** hard tennis courts, squash, sauna, gymnasium **Conf** facs Corporate Hospitality Days **Location** 0.75m E off A23 on B2030
Hotel ★★★ 73% HL Coulsdon Manor, Coulsdon Court Road, Coulsdon, CROYDON ☎ 020 8668 0414 📄 020 8668 0414 35 en suite

Woodcote Park Meadow Hill, Bridle Way CR5 2QQ
☎ 020 8668 2788   📄 020 8660 0918
e-mail: info@woodcotepgc.com
web: www.woodcotepgc.com
Slightly undulating parkland.

18 Holes, 6720yds, Par 71, SSS 72, Course record 66. Club membership 700.

Visitors Mon-Fri except BHs. Booking required. Dress code.
Societies booking required. **Green Fees** £50 per day/round **Course Designer** H S Colt **Prof** Wraith Grant **Facilities** ⓦ 🍴 🏌 ☕ 🍽 🏃 🏠 ✦ 🛒 ✦ ✦ **Conf** facs Corporate Hospitality Days **Location** 1m N of town centre off A237
Hotel ★★★ 80% HL Aerodrome, Purley Way, CROYDON ☎ 020 8710 9000 & 8680 1999 📄 020 8710 9000   110 en suite

CROYDON
Map 4 TQ36

Croham Hurst Croham Rd CR2 7HJ
☎ 020 8657 5581   📄 020 8657 3229
e-mail: secretary@chgc.co.uk
web: www.chgc.co.uk
Easy walking parkland with tree-lined fairways and bounded by wooded hills.

18 Holes, 6290yds, Par 70, SSS 70. Club membership 800.
Visitors booking required. Handicap certificate. Dress code.
Societies booking required. **Green Fees** not confirmed **Course Designer** Hawtree/Braid **Prof** David Green **Facilities** ⓦ 🍴 🏌 ☕ 🍽 🏃 🏠 ✦ 🛒 ✦ **Conf** facs Corporate Hospitality Days **Location** 1.5m SE of Croydon on B269
Hotel ★★★ 74% HL South Park Hotel, 3-5 South Park Hill Road, South Croydon, CROYDON ☎ 020 8688 5644 📄 020 8688 5644 30 en suite

Selsdon Park Hotel, Addington Rd, Sanderstead CR2 8YA
☎ 020 8768 3116   📄 020 8651 6171
e-mail: chris.baron@principal-hayley.com
web: www.principal-hayley.com
Parkland course in 250 acres of rolling woodland only 12 miles from the centre of London.

Selsdon Park Hotel & Golf Club: 18 Holes, 6473yds, Par 73, SSS 71, Course record 63.
Visitors Mon-Sun & BHs. Dress code. **Societies** booking required. **Green Fees** not confirmed **Course Designer** J H Taylor **Prof** Chris Baron **Facilities** ⓦ 🍴 🏌 ☕ 🍽 🏃 🏠 ⛺ ◇ 🛒 ✦ ✦ **Leisure** hard and grass tennis courts, outdoor and indoor heated swimming pool, squash, sauna, gymnasium **Conf** facs Corporate Hospitality Days **Location** 3m S on A2022
Hotel ★★★ 74% HL South Park Hotel, 3-5 South Park Hill Road, South Croydon, CROYDON ☎ 020 8688 5644 📄 020 8688 5644 30 en suite

Shirley Park 194 Addiscombe Rd CR0 7LB
☎ 020 8654 1143   📄 020 8654 6733
web: www.shirleyparkgolfclub.co.uk
18 Holes, 6210yds, Par 71, SSS 69, Course record 64.
Course Designer Tom Simpson/Herbert Fowler **Location** E of town centre on A232
Telephone for further details
Hotel ★★★ 74% HL South Park Hotel, 3-5 South Park Hill Road, South Croydon, CROYDON ☎ 020 8688 5644 📄 020 8688 5644 30 en suite

DOWNE
Map 5 TQ46

High Elms High Elms Rd BR6 7JL
☎ 01689 853232 & 858175 (bookings)
📄 01689 856326
High Elms Golf Course: 18 Holes, 6210yds, Par 71, SSS 70, Course record 68.
Course Designer Hawthorn **Location** 2m E of A21
Telephone for further details
Hotel ★★★ 77% HL Best Western Bromley Court, Bromley Hill, BROMLEY ☎ 020 8461 8600 📄 020 8461 8600   114 en suite

West Kent Milking Ln BR6 7LD
☎ 01689 851323   📄 01689 858693
e-mail: golf@wkgc.co.uk
web: www.wkgc.co.uk
Undulating woodland course close to south London but providing a quiet rural setting in three valleys.

18 Holes, 6426yds, Par 71, SSS 71, Course record 68. Club membership 700.
Visitors Mon-Fri except BHs. Booking required. Handicap certificate. Dress code. **Societies** booking required. **Green Fees** £50 per day, £40 per round **Course Designer** H S Colt **Prof** Chris Forsyth **Facilities** ⓦ 🍴 🏌 ☕ 🍽 🏃 🏠 ✦ 🛒 ✦ **Conf** Corporate Hospitality Days **Location** M25 junct 4, A21 towards Bromley, left signed Downe, through village on Luxted road 0.5m, West Hill on right
Hotel ★★★ 77% HL Best Western Bromley Court, Bromley Hill, BROMLEY ☎ 020 8461 8600 📄 020 8461 8600   114 en suite

ENFIELD
Map 4 TQ39

Crews Hill Cattlegate Rd, Crews Hill EN2 8AZ
☎ 020 8363 6674 📄 020 8363 2343
e-mail: info@crewshillgolfclub.com
web: www.crewshillgolfclub.com

Parkland course in countryside within the M25 and little changed from its original design by Harry Colt. Considered to have possibly the best back nine in North London.

18 Holes, 6281yds, Par 70, SSS 70, Course record 65.
Club membership 600.

Visitors Mon-Fri except BHs. Handicap certificate. Dress code. **Societies** welcome **Green Fees** phone **Course Designer** Harry Colt **Prof** Neil Wichelow **Facilities** ⓟ ⓘⓞⓘ by prior arrangement 🏌 ⌷ 🍴 ⚲ 🏠 ✆ 🚮 ✆ **Conf** facs Corporate Hospitality Days **Location** M25 junct 24, A1005 for Enfield, signed
Hotel ★★★★ 77% HL Royal Chace, The Ridgeway, ENFIELD
☎ 020 8884 8181 📄 020 8884 8181 92 en suite

Enfield Old Park Road South EN2 7DA
☎ 020 8363 3970 📄 020 8342 0381
e-mail: secretary@enfieldgolfclub.co.uk
web: www.enfieldgolfclub.co.uk
Parkland with tree-lined fairways and a meandering brook that comes into play on nine holes. There are no hidden or unfair hazards and, although not easy, the course is highly playable and always attractive.

18 Holes, 6154yds, Par 72, SSS 70, Course record 61.
Club membership 600.

Visitors Mon-Sun & BHs. Booking required weekends & BHs.. Handicap certificate. Dress code. **Societies** booking required. **Green Fees** not confirmed **Course Designer** James Braid **Prof** Martin Porter **Facilities** ⓟ ⓘⓞⓘ 🏌 ⌷ 🍴 ⚲ 🏠 ⚲ ✆ **Conf** facs Corporate Hospitality Days **Location** M25 jnct 24, A1005 to Enfield to rdbt with church on left, right down Slades Hill, 1st left to end
Hotel ★★★★ 77% HL Royal Chace, The Ridgeway, ENFIELD
☎ 020 8884 8181 📄 020 8884 8181 92 en suite

Whitewebbs Park Whitewebbs Ln EN2 9HH
☎ 020 8363 4454 📄 020 8366 2257
e-mail: gary.sherriff1@btinternet.com
web: www.enfield.gov.uk
This challenging parkland course was first opened for play in 1932 and is set in over 140 acres of attractive rolling countryside with mature woodland and the meandering Cuffley brook that comes into play on four holes.

Whitewebbs Park Golf Course: 18 Holes, 5782yds, Par 68, SSS 68, Course record 64. Club membership 350.

Visitors Mon-Sun & BHs. Dress code. **Societies** booking required.

Green Fees not confirmed **Facilities** ⓟ ⓘⓞⓘ 🏌 ⌷ 🍴 ⚲ 🏠
🏌 ⚲ ✆ **Location** N of town centre
Hotel ★★★★ 77% HL Royal Chace, The Ridgeway, ENFIELD
☎ 020 8884 8181 📄 020 8884 8181 92 en suite

GREENFORD
Map 4 TQ18

C & L Golf & Country Club Westend Rd, Northolt UB5 6RD
☎ 020 8845 5662 📄 020 8841 5515
Demanding parkland course with long par 3s and ideal for all golfers.

C & L Golf & Country Club: 18 Holes, 4458yds, Par 67, SSS 62, Course record 58. Club membership 150.

Visitors contact club for details. **Societies** welcome. **Green Fees** not confirmed **Course Designer** Patrick Tallack **Prof** Richard Kelly **Facilities** ⓟ ⓘⓞⓘ 🏌 ⌷ 🍴 **Leisure** gymnasium **Conf** facs **Location** junct Westend Rd
Hotel ★★★ 78% HL Barn Hotel, West End Road, RUISLIP
☎ 01895 636057 📄 01895 636057 73 en suite

Ealing Perivale Ln UB6 8SS
☎ 020 8997 0937 📄 020 8998 0756
e-mail: info@ealinggolfclub.co.uk
web: www.ealinggolfclub.com
A classic parkland layout with the river Brent providing a natural hazard and some of the finest greens around.

18 Holes, 6191yds, Par 70, SSS 70, Course record 62.
Club membership 650.

Visitors Mon-Fri except BHs. Booking required. Handicap certificate. Dress code. **Societies** welcome. **Green Fees** £40 per 18 holes (£50 weekends) **Course Designer** H S Colt **Prof** Ricky Willison **Facilities** ⓟ ⓘⓞⓘ by prior arrangement 🏌 ⌷ 🍴 ⚲ 🏠 🏌 ✆ ⚲ ✆ **Conf** facs Corporate Hospitality Days **Location** exit at the Perivale turn-off on the A40
Hotel ★★★ 79% HL Ramada London Ealing, Ealing Common, LONDON ☎ 0844 815 9035 📄 0844 815 9035 189 en suite

Horsenden Hill Woodland Rise, Whitton Av UB6 0RD
☎ 020 8902 4555 📄 020 8902 4555
A distinctive picturesque course designed over hilly landscape. Very challenging comprising eight par 3s (3 over 200yds) and a par 4 of 292yds. Overlooks the London skyline to Canary Wharf and the London Eye.

9 Holes, 1632yds, Par 28, SSS 28. Club membership 135.

Visitors contact club for details. **Societies** welcome. **Green Fees** not confirmed **Prof** Jeff Quarshie **Facilities** ⓟ ⓘⓞⓘ 🏌 ⌷ 🍴 🏠 🏌 ✆ **Conf** Corporate Hospitality Days **Location** 3m NE on A4090
Hotel ★★★ 71% HL Quality Hotel, Wembley, Empire Way, WEMBLEY ☎ 020 8733 9000 📄 020 8733 9000 165 en suite

Perivale Park Stockdove Way UB6 8TJ
☎ 020 8575 7116
Parkland beside the River Brent.

Perivale Park Golf Course: 9 Holes, 2667yds, Par 68, SSS 67. Club membership 250.

Visitors Mon-Sun & BHs. Booking required weekends. **Green Fees** £8 per 9 holes (£9 weekends & BHs) **Prof** Peter Bryant **Facilities** 🏌 ⌷ ⚲ 🏠 🏌 ✆ **Location** E side of town centre, off A40
Hotel ★★★ 72% MET Best Western Cumberland, 1 St Johns Road, HARROW ☎ 020 8863 4111 📄 020 8863 4111 84 en suite

ENGLAND

HADLEY WOOD
Map 4 TQ29

Hadley Wood Beech Hill EN4 0JJ
☎ 020 8449 4328 & 4486 📄 020 8364 8633
web: www.hadleywoodgc.com

18 Holes, 6514yds, Par 72, SSS 71, Course record 67.
Course Designer Alister Mackenzie **Location** M25 junct 24, take
A111 to Cockforsters, 2m to 3rd turning right
Telephone for further details
Hotel ★★★★ **80%** HL West Lodge Park, Cockfosters Road,
HADLEY WOOD ☎ 020 8216 3900 & 8216 3903 📄 020 8216 3900
59 en suite

HAMPTON
Map 4 TQ17

Fulwell Wellington Rd, Hampton Hill TW12 1JY
☎ 020 8977 3844 📄 020 8977 7732
e-mail: secretary@fulwellgolfclub.co.uk
web: www.fulwellgolfclub.co.uk

Championship-length parkland course with easy walking. The 575-
yd 17th and the water feature 9th are notable.
18 Holes, 6544yds, Par 71, SSS 71.
Club membership 750.
Visitors Mon-Sun & BHs. Booking required weekends & BHs. Dress
code. **Societies** welcome. **Green Fees** £40 per round (£55 per
round weekends) **Course Designer** John Morrison **Prof** Nigel Turner
Facilities ⊕ ⬛ ⬜ 🍴 ⬙ 👝 🎯 🏆 ♂ **Conf** Corporate
Hospitality Days **Location** off M3/M25 junct, 1.5m N on A311
Hotel ★★★★ **73%** HL Richmond Hill, Richmond Hill,
RICHMOND UPON THAMES ☎ 020 8940 2247 📄 020 8940 2247
149 en suite

HAMPTON WICK
Map 4 TQ16

Hampton Court Palace Home Park KT1 4AD
☎ 020 8977 2423 📄 020 8614 4747
e-mail: hamptoncourtpalace@crown-golf.co.uk
web: www.hamptoncourtgolf.co.uk

Flat course with easy walking situated in the grounds of Hampton
Court Palace. Unique blend of parkland and inland links built on a
base of sand and gravel, making it one of the finest winter courses in
the country.
18 Holes, 6513yds, Par 71, SSS 71, Course record 64.
Club membership 750.
Visitors contact club for details. **Societies** booking required. **Green
Fees** Mon-Thu £40 per 18 holes, £45 Fri, £45 weekends after noon.
£29 twilight Mon-Thu, £31.50 Fri-Sun **Course Designer** Willie Park

Prof Karl Nesson **Facilities** ⊕ 🍴 ⬛ ⬜ 🍴 ⬙ 👝 🎯 ♂
🏳 **Conf** facs Corporate Hospitality Days **Location** Off A308 on W side
of Kingston Bridge
Hotel ★★★★ **73%** HL Richmond Hill, Richmond Hill, RICHMOND
UPON THAMES ☎ 020 8940 2247 📄 020 8940 2247 149 en suite

HARROW
Map 4 TQ18

Playgolf Northwick Park Watford Rd HA1 3TZ
☎ 020 8864 2020 📄 020 8864 4040
e-mail: info@northwickpark.com
web: www.northwickpark.com

The 'Majors' course consists of 7 par 3 holes and 2 par 4's
incorporating links and parkland styles. It is unique with nine
full-scale tributes to some of the world's most famous golf holes -
including 12th and 16th at Augusta National and the 8th 'Postage
Stamp' hole from Royal Troon.
Majors Course: 9 Holes, 1804yds, Par 29, SSS 29.
Club membership 300.
Visitors Mon-Sun & BHs. Dress code. **Societies** booking required.
Green Fees £25 per two rounds, £15 per round. Fees include
facilities on short game practice area **Course Designer** Peter
McEvoy **Facilities** ⊕ 🍴 ⬛ ⬜ 🍴 ⬙ 👝 🎯 ♂
Leisure gymnasium, short game practice area, adventure golf course,
baseball & softball cages **Conf** facs Corporate Hospitality Days
Location SE of Harrow on A404 Watford road. Follow directions to
Northwick Park Hospital, course adjacent
Hotel ★★★ **72%** MET Best Western Cumberland, 1 St Johns Road,
HARROW ☎ 020 8863 4111 📄 020 8863 4111 84 en suite

HOUNSLOW
Map 4 TQ17

Airlinks Southall Ln TW5 9PE
☎ 020 8561 1418 📄 020 8813 6284

18 Holes, 6000yds, Par 71, SSS 69, Course record 63.
Course Designer P Alliss/D Thomas **Location** M4 junct 3, W of
Hounslow
Telephone for further details
Hotel ★★ **69%** HL Best Western Master Robert, 366 Great West
Road, HOUNSLOW ☎ 020 8570 6261 📄 020 8570 6261 96 en suite

Hounslow Heath Municipal Staines Rd TW4 5DS
☎ 020 8570 5271 📄 020 8570 5205

*Hounslow Heath Golf Course: 18 Holes, 5901yds, Par 69,
SSS 68, Course record 62.*
Course Designer Fraser M Middleton **Location** On A315 towards
Bedfont
Telephone for further details
Hotel ★★ **69%** HL Best Western Master Robert, 366 Great West
Road, HOUNSLOW ☎ 020 8570 6261 📄 020 8570 6261 96 en suite

ILFORD
Map 5 TQ48

Ilford Wanstead Park Rd IG1 3TR
☎ 020 8554 2930 🖷 020 8554 0822
e-mail: info@ilfordgolfclub.com
web: www.ilfordgolfclub.com

Fairly flat parkland on the River Roding. The river borders four holes, and is crossed by three holes. While not a particularly long course, the small greens, and many holes requiring brains rather than brawn, provide a challenging test to all.

18 Holes, 5299yds, Par 67, SSS 66, Course record 61.
Club membership 500.

Visitors Mon-Sun & BHs. Dress code. **Societies** booking required.
Green Fees phone **Course Designer** Whitehead **Prof** G Cant
Facilities ⑪ 🍴 🛍 🖵 🍴 ⚒ 📤 🏌 **Conf** facs Corporate
Hospitality Days **Location** NW of town centre off A12
Hotel BUD Travelodge London Ilford, Clements Road, ILFORD
☎ 08719 846 194 🖷 08719 846 194 91 en suite

ISLEWORTH
Map 4 TQ17

Wyke Green Syon Ln TW7 5PT
☎ 020 8847 0685 (Pro) & 8560 8777 (Sec)
🖷 020 8569 8392
e-mail: office@wykegreengolfclub.co.uk
web: www.wykegreengolfclub.co.uk

Fairly flat parkland. Seven par 4 holes over 420yds.

18 Holes, 6182yds, Par 69, SSS 70, Course record 64.
Club membership 500.

Visitors Mon-Fri except BHs. Dress code. **Societies** booking required.
Green Fees £25 per round (£30 weekends) **Course Designer** Hawtree
Prof Neil Smith **Facilities** ⑪ 🛍 🖵 🍴 ⚒ 📤 🏌 🏌 🏌
Conf Corporate Hospitality Days **Location** 0.5m N on B454, off A4 at
Gillette Corner
Hotel ★★ 69% HL Best Western Master Robert, 366 Great West
Road, HOUNSLOW ☎ 020 8570 6261 🖷 020 8570 6261 96 en suite

KINGSTON UPON THAMES
Map 4 TQ16

Coombe Hill Golf Club Dr, Coombe Lane West KT2 7DF
☎ 020 8336 7600 🖷 020 8336 7601
e-mail: thesecretary@chgc.net
web: www.coombehillgolfclub.com

Charming heathland course featuring a fine display of rhododendrons during May and June. The course presents a challenge to golfers of all standards offering superb greens, quality short holes and a number of testing long holes requiring approach shots to elevated greens.

18 Holes, 6028yds, Par 71, SSS 71, Course record 67.
Club membership 520.

Visitors Mon, Tue, Thu & Fri. Other days pm only. Booking required.
Handicap certificate. Dress code. **Societies** booking required.
Green Fees not confirmed **Course Designer** J F Abercromby
Prof Andy Dunn **Facilities** ⑪ 🛍 🖵 🍴 📤 📤 🏌 🏌
Leisure sauna, halfway house **Conf** Corporate Hospitality Days
Location 1.75m E on A238
Hotel BUD Travelodge London Kingston upon Thames, 21-23
London Road, KINGSTON-UPON-THAMES ☎ 08719 846 241
🖷 08719 846 241 72 en suite

Coombe Wood George Rd, Kingston Hill KT2 7NS
☎ 020 8942 0388 🖷 020 8942 5665
e-mail: geoff.seed@coombewoodgolf.com
web: www.coombewoodgolf.com

Mature parkland with seven varied and challenging par 3s.

18 Holes, 5299yds, Par 66, SSS 66, Course record 59.
Club membership 700.

Visitors Mon, Wed & Thu. Tue pm only. Other times by arrangement..
Dress code. **Societies** welcome. **Green Fees** not confirmed **Course
Designer** Tom Williamson **Prof** Phil Wright **Facilities** ⑪ 🍴 🛍
🖵 🍴 📤 📤 🏌 🏌 **Conf** facs Corporate Hospitality Days
Location 1.25m NE on A308
Hotel BUD Travelodge London Kingston upon Thames, 21-23 London
Road, KINGSTON-UPON-THAMES ☎ 08719 846 241 🖷 08719 846 241
72 en suite

MITCHAM
Map 4 TQ26

Mitcham Carshalton Rd, Mitcham Junction CR4 4HN
☎ 020 8640 4280 🖷 020 8647 4197
e-mail: mitchamgc@hotmail.co.uk
web: www.mitchamgolfclub.co.uk

A wooded heathland course on a gravel base, playing as an inland links course.

18 Holes, 6022yds, Par 69, SSS 69, Course record 65.
Club membership 500.

Visitors Mon-Sun & BHs. Booking required. Dress code.
Societies booking required. **Green Fees** £19 per 18 holes (£27
weekends, £29 BHs) **Course Designer** T Scott/T Morris **Prof** Paul
Burton **Facilities** ⑪ 🍴 🛍 🖵 🍴 📤 📤 🍴 🏌
Conf Corporate Hospitality Days **Location** adjacent Mitcham Junction
railway station
Hotel ★★★ 80% HL Aerodrome, Purley Way, CROYDON
☎ 020 8710 9000 & 8680 1999 🖷 020 8710 9000 110 en suite

NEW MALDEN
Map 4 TQ26

Malden Traps Ln KT3 4RS
☎ 020 8942 0654 🖷 020 8336 2219
web: www.maldengolfclub.com

18 Holes, 6252yds, Par 71, SSS 70.

Prof Robert Hunter **Facilities** ⑪ 🍴 🛍 🖵 🍴 📤 📤 🏌
📤 🏌 **Conf** Corporate Hospitality Days **Location** N of town centre
off B283
Telephone for further details
Hotel BUD Travelodge London Kingston upon Thames, 21-23 London
Road, KINGSTON-UPON-THAMES ☎ 08719 846 241 🖷 08719 846 241
72 en suite

NORTHWOOD   Map 4 TQ09

Haste Hill The Drive HA6 1HN
☎ 01923 825224
Parkland with stream running through. Excellent views.

Haste Hill: 18 Holes, 5787yds, Par 68, SSS 68,
Course record 63. Club membership 250.

Visitors Mon-Sun & BHs. Booking required. Handicap certificate. Dress code **Societies** welcome. **Green Fees** not confirmed **Prof** Cameron Smilie **Facilities** ⑪ ⑩ by prior arrangement ⓑ ⌹ ⑨ ⚐ ⊞ ⛳ ✐ ⛟ ✐ **Location** 0.5m S off A404
Hotel ★★★ 74% HL The Harrow Hotel, 12-22 Pinner Road, HARROW ☎ 020 8427 3435 ⎙ 020 8427 3435 79 en suite

Northwood Rickmansworth Rd HA6 2QW
☎ 01923 821384 ⎙ 01923 840150
e-mail: secretary@northwoodgolf.co.uk
web: www.northwoodgolf.co.uk

A high quality parkland course. The course provides a good test of golf to the experienced golfer and can hold many surprises for the unsuspecting. The par 4 10th hole, Death or Glory, has wrecked many good cards in the past, while the long par 4 5th hole requires two very good shots to make par.

18 Holes, 6514yds, Par 71, SSS 71, Course record 67.
Club membership 650.

Visitors handicap required. Dress code. **Societies** booking required. **Green Fees** £43 per round **Course Designer** James Braid **Prof** C J Holdsworth **Facilities** ⑪ ⑩ ⓑ ⌹ ⑨ ⊞ ⛳ ⛟ ✐ **Conf** Corporate Hospitality Days **Location** on A404
Hotel ★★★ 74% HL The Harrow Hotel, 12-22 Pinner Road, HARROW ☎ 020 8427 3435 ⎙ 020 8427 3435 79 en suite

Sandy Lodge Sandy Lodge Ln HA6 2JD
☎ 01923 825429 ⎙ 01923 824319
e-mail: info@sandylodge.co.uk
web: www.sandylodge.co.uk

A links-type, very sandy, heathland course. Excellent drainage giving good all year playing conditions.

18 Holes, 6347yds, Par 71, SSS 71, Course record 64.
Club membership 780.

Visitors Mon-Fri except BHs. Booking required Mon & Thu. Handicap certificate. Dress code. **Societies** booking required. **Green Fees** £45 per round. **Course Designer** H Vardon **Prof** Jeff Pinsent **Facilities** ⑪ ⑩ ⓑ ⌹ ⑨ ⊞ ⛳ ✐ ⛟ ✐ ✐ **Conf** facs Corporate Hospitality Days **Location** N of town centre off A4125
Hotel ★★★ 73% HL Best Western White House, Upton Road, WATFORD ☎ 01923 237316 ⎙ 01923 237316 57 en suite

ORPINGTON   Map 5 TQ46

Chelsfield Lakes Golf Centre Court Rd BR6 9BX
☎ 01689 896266 ⎙ 01689 824577
e-mail: chelsfieldlakes@crown-golf.co.uk
web: www.chelsfieldlakesgolf.co.uk

A downland course but some holes are played through the orchards which used to occupy the site. The 9th and 18th holes are separated by a hazardous lake. The newly constructed nine hole course is due to reopen during 2009

Chelsfield Lakes Golf Centre: 18 Holes, 6077yds, Par 71, SSS 69, Course record 64. Club membership 220.

Visitors Mon-Sun & BHs. Booking required. Dress code. **Societies** welcome. **Green Fees** £20 Mon-Thu, £25 Fri, £29 weekends **Course Designer** M Sandow **Prof** N Lee **Facilities** ⑪ ⑩ ⓑ ⌹ ⑨ ⊞ ⛳ ⚐ ⛟ ✐ ✐ **Conf** facs Corporate Hospitality Days **Location** M25 junct 4, on A224
Hotel ★★★ 77% HL Best Western Bromley Court, Bromley Hill, BROMLEY ☎ 020 8461 8600 ⎙ 020 8461 8600 114 en suite

Orpington Golf Centre Sandy Ln, St Paul's Cray BR5 3HY
☎ 01689 839677 ⎙ 01689 891428
e-mail: orpington@crown-golf.co.uk
web: www.orpingtongolf.co.uk

Easy walking open parkland courses comprising two with 18 holes and a nine hole. Challenging for all standards of golfers.

Cray Valley 18: 18 Holes, 5669yds, Par 70, SSS 67.
Ruxley Park: 18 Holes, 5703yds, Par 70, SSS 68, Course record 63.
Cray Valley 9: 9 Holes, 2140yds, Par 32.
Club membership 400.

Visitors Mon-Sun & BHs. **Societies** booking required. **Green Fees** £10-£26 **Prof** Brad McLean **Facilities** ⑪ ⓑ ⌹ ⑨ ⊞ ⛳ ⚐ ✐ ⛟ ✐ ✐ **Conf** Corporate Hospitality Days **Location** 1m off A20, Crittals Corner junction
Hotel ★★★ 77% HL Best Western Bromley Court, Bromley Hill, BROMLEY ☎ 020 8461 8600 ⎙ 020 8461 8600 114 en suite

PINNER   Map 4 TQ18

Grims Dyke Oxhey Ln, Hatch End HA5 4AL
☎ 020 8428 4539 ⎙ 020 8421 5494
e-mail: info@grimsdyke.co.uk
web: www.club-noticeboard.co.uk/grimsdyke
Pleasant, undulating parkland.

18 Holes, 5596yds, Par 69, SSS 67, Course record 61.
Club membership 460.

Visitors contact club for details. **Societies** booking required. **Green Fees** £36 per round (£40 weekends) **Course Designer** James Baird **Prof** Lee Curling **Facilities** ⑪ ⓑ ⌹ ⑨ ⊞ ⛳ ✐ ⛟ ✐ **Conf** facs Corporate Hospitality Days **Location** 3m N of Harrow on A4008
Hotel ★★★ 72% MET Best Western Cumberland, 1 St Johns Road, HARROW ☎ 020 8863 4111 ⎙ 020 8863 4111 84 en suite

Pinner Hill Southview Rd, Pinner Hill HA5 3YA
☎ 020 8866 0963 ⎙ 020 8868 4817
e-mail: phgc@pinnerhillgc.com
web: www.pinnerhillgc.com

On the top of Pinner Hill surrounded by rolling parkland and mature woods, this peaceful atmosphere will make you feel a million miles from North West London's suburbia. Two nine-hole loops of mature fairways and undulating greens will lift and challenge your game.

18 Holes, 6392yds, Par 71, SSS 71, Course record 69.
Club membership 620.

Visitors Mon-Sun except BHs.Booking required. Handicap certificate. Dress code. **Societies** booking required. **Green Fees** phone. **Course Designer** J H Taylor **Prof** Chris Duck **Facilities** ⑪ ⑩ ⓑ ⌹ ⑨ ⊞ ⛳ ⚐ ✐ ✐ **Leisure** snooker room **Conf** facs **Location** 2m NW off A404
Hotel ★★★ 74% HL The Harrow Hotel, 12-22 Pinner Road, HARROW ☎ 020 8427 3435 ⎙ 020 8427 3435 79 en suite

PURLEY
Map 5 TQ36

Purley Downs 106 Purley Downs Rd CR2 0RB
☎ 020 8657 8347 📠 020 8651 5044
e-mail: info@purleydowns.co.uk
web: www.purleydownsgolfclub.co.uk

Hilly downland course which is a good test for golfers and is in play all year round.

18 Holes, 6262yds, Par 70, SSS 70, Course record 64.
Club membership 750.

Visitors Mon-Fri & BHs. Booking required. Handicap certificate. Dress code. **Societies** welcome. **Green Fees** not confirmed **Course Designer** J Taylor/H S Colt **Prof** Simon Iliffe **Facilities** ⓣ ⒱ 🍴 ⌕ ⌷ 🍷 🛋 🏠 🚲 ♿ **Conf** facs **Location** E of town centre off A235

Hotel ★★★ 80% HL Aerodrome, Purley Way, CROYDON
☎ 020 8710 9000 & 8680 1999 📠 020 8710 9000 110 en suite

RICHMOND (UPON THAMES)
Map 4 TQ17

Richmond Sudbrook Park TW10 7AS
☎ 020 8940 4351 (office) & 8940 7792 (shop)
📠 020 8940 8332/7914
web: www.the richmondgolfclub.com

The Richmond Golf Club: 18 Holes, 6100yds, Par 70, SSS 70, Course record 65.

Course Designer Tom Dunn **Location** 1.5m S off A307 between Kingston & Richmond
Telephone for further details
Hotel ★★★★ 73% HL Richmond Hill, Richmond Hill, RICHMOND UPON THAMES ☎ 020 8940 2247 📠 020 8940 2247 149 en suite

Royal Mid-Surrey Old Deer Park, Twickenham Rd TW9 2SB
☎ 020 8940 1894 📠 020 8939 0150
e-mail: secretary@rmsgc.co.uk
web: www.rmsgc.co.uk

A long playing historic parkland course. The flat fairways are cleverly bunkered. The 1st hole at 245yds from the medal tees is a tough par 3 opening hole. The 18th provides an exceptionally good par 4 finish with a huge bunker before the green to catch the not quite perfect long second. The Inner Course, while shorter than the Outer, offers a fair challenge to all golfers. Again the 18th offers a strong par 4 finish with bunkers threatening from the tee. A long second to a sloping, well-bunkered green will reward the accurate player.

Outer Course: 18 Holes, 6343yds, Par 69, SSS 71, Course record 62.
Inner Course: 18 Holes, 5544yds, Par 68, SSS 67.
Club membership 1400.

Visitors Mon-Fri except BHs. Handicap certificate. Dress code. **Societies** booking required. **Green Fees** Outer Course £75, Inner Course £60 **Course Designer** J H Taylor **Prof** Matthew Paget **Facilities** ⓣ 🛋 ⌷ 🍷 🛋 🏠 ⌕ ♿ ⚹ **Leisure** snooker **Conf** facs Corporate Hospitality Days **Location** 0.5m N of Richmond off A316

Hotel ★★★★ 73% HL Richmond Hill, Richmond Hill, RICHMOND UPON THAMES ☎ 020 8940 2247 📠 020 8940 2247 149 en suite

ROMFORD
Map 5 TQ58

Maylands Colchester Rd, Harold Park RM3 0AZ
☎ 01708 341777 📠 01708 343777
e-mail: maylands@maylandsgolf.com
web: www.maylandsgolf.com

Picturesque undulating parkland course.

18 Holes, 6361yds, Par 71, SSS 70, Course record 62.
Club membership 550.

Visitors Mon-Sun & BHs. Booking required. Dress code. **Societies** booking required. **Green Fees** from £25 per round **Course Designer** H S Colt **Prof** Darren Parker **Facilities** ⓣ ⒱ 🍴 ⌕ ⌷ 🍷 ⌀ 🏠 ♿ 🚲 ♿ ⚹ **Conf** Corporate Hospitality Days **Location** M25 junct 28, A12, 0.5m towards London, club on right
Hotel ★★★★ 75% HL Marygreen Manor, London Road, BRENTWOOD ☎ 01277 225252 📠 01277 225252 44 en suite

Risebridge Golf Centre Risebridge Chase RM1 4DG
☎ 01708 741429 📠 01708 741429
web: www.jackbarker.com

Risebridge Golf Centre: 18 Holes, 6000yds, Par 71, SSS 70, Course record 66.

Course Designer Hawtree **Location** between Collier Row and Harold Hill
Telephone for further details
Hotel ★★★ 77% HL Harefield Manor Hotel, 33 Main Road, ROMFORD ☎ 01708 751901 📠 01708 751901 36 en suite

Romford Heath Dr RM2 5QB
☎ 01708 740986 📠 01708 752157

18 Holes, 6410yds, Par 72, SSS 70, Course record 64.

Course Designer H Colt **Location** 1m NE on A118
Telephone for further details
Hotel ★★★ 77% HL Harefield Manor Hotel, 33 Main Road, ROMFORD ☎ 01708 751901 📠 01708 751901 36 en suite

RUISLIP
Map 4 TQ08

Ruislip Ickenham Rd HA4 7DQ
☎ 01895 638081 & 638835 📠 01895 635780
e-mail: ruislipgolf@btconnect.com

Municipal parkland course. Flat with easy walking. Greens are fairly small placing a premium on accuracy.

18 Holes, 5700yds, Par 69, SSS 68, Course record 65.
Club membership 300.

Visitors contact club for details. **Societies** welcome. **Green Fees** £16.50 (£24 weekends & BHs). Winter £12/£18 **Course Designer** Sand Herd **Prof** Paul Glozier **Facilities** ⓣ ⒱ 🍴 🛋 ⌷ 🍷 🏠 🚲 ⌕ ♿ ⚹ **Conf** facs **Location** from A40, 0.5m SW on B466 opposite West Ruislip underground station
Hotel ★★★ 74% HL The Harrow Hotel, 12-22 Pinner Road, HARROW ☎ 020 8427 3435 📠 020 8427 3435 79 en suite

SIDCUP
Map 5 TQ47

Sidcup Rear of Hurstmere School, Hurst Rd DA15 9AW
☎ 020 8300 2150   ▤ 020 8300 2150
e-mail: sidcupgolfclub@tiscali.co.uk
web: www.sidcupgolfclub.co.uk
Easy walking parkland with two lakes and the River Shuttle running through. Water hazards on six holes.
Sidcup Golf Club 1926 Ltd: 9 Holes, 5722yds, Par 68, SSS 68, Course record 62. Club membership 330.
Visitors Mon-Fri except BHs. Booking required. Handicap certificate. Dress code. **Green Fees** £25 per 18 holes **Course Designer** James Braid **Facilities** ⑪ ▙ ⤶ ⚑ ⚐ Location N of town centre off A222
Hotel ★★★★ 75% HL Bexleyheath Marriott Hotel, 1 Broadway, BEXLEYHEATH ☎ 020 8298 1000 ▤ 020 8298 1000   142 en suite

SOUTHALL
Map 4 TQ17

West Middlesex Greenford Rd UB1 3EE
☎ 020 8574 3450   ▤ 020 8574 2383
e-mail: westmid.gc@virgin.net
web: www.westmiddxgolfclub.co.uk
Gently undulating parkland course founded in 1891, the oldest private course in Middlesex designed by James Braid.
18 Holes, 6119yds, Par 69, SSS 69, Course record 64. Club membership 396.
Visitors Mon-Sun & BHs. Booking required. Handicap certificate. Dress code. **Societies** booking required. **Green Fees** Mon £18 per round; Tue-Fri £22, weekends & BHs £30 **Course Designer** James Braid **Prof** T Talbot **Facilities** ⑪ ⑩ ▙ ⤶ ⚑ ⚐ ⚐ ✐
Leisure fishing, snooker **Conf** facs Corporate Hospitality Days **Location** W of town centre on A4127
Hotel ★★ 69% HL Best Western Master Robert, 366 Great West Road, HOUNSLOW ☎ 020 8570 6261 ▤ 020 8570 6261   96 en suite

STANMORE
Map 4 TQ19

Stanmore 29 Gordon Av HA7 2RL
☎ 020 8954 2599   ▤ 020 8954 2599
e-mail: secretary@stanmoregolfclub.co.uk
web: www.stanmoregolfclub.co.uk
A quiet and peaceful parkland course in the suburbs of north-west London, with incredible views over the Thames basin from the 3th and 5th tees. The course is short but very challenging as all the fairways are lined with trees. Accuracy plays a major role and notable holes are the 2nd, 8th, 11th and 13th. The signature hole is the par 4 7th, played over a fir tree from an elevated tee onto the fairway.
18 Holes, 5885yds, Par 68, SSS 68, Course record 61. Club membership 500.
Visitors Mon-Sun & BHs. Booking required Mon, Fri-Sun & BHs. Dress code. **Societies** booking required. **Green Fees** not confirmed **Course Designer** Dr A Mackenzie **Prof** J Reynolds **Facilities** ⑪ ⑩ ▙ ⤶ ⚑ ⚐ ⚐ ⚑ ⚑ ✐ **Conf** facs Corporate Hospitality Days **Location** S of town centre between Stanmore & Belmont
Hotel ★★★ 74% HL The Harrow Hotel, 12-22 Pinner Road, HARROW ☎ 020 8427 3435 ▤ 020 8427 3435   79 en suite

SURBITON
Map 4 TQ16

Surbiton Woodstock Ln KT9 1UG
☎ 020 8398 3101 (Sec)   ▤ 020 8339 0992
web: www.surbitongolfclub.com
18 Holes, 6055yds, Par 70, SSS 69, Course record 63.
Course Designer Tom Dunn **Location** A3 Hook junct, A309 S 2m, left onto Woodstock Ln
Telephone for further details
Hotel ★★★★ 72% HL The Carlton Mitre, Hampton Court Road, HAMPTON COURT ☎ 020 8979 9988 & 8783 3505 ▤ 020 8979 9988   36 en suite

TWICKENHAM
Map 4 TQ17

Amida Staines Rd TW2 5JD
☎ 020 8783 1698   ▤ 020 8783 9475
web: www.amidaclubs.com
Amida Golf: 9 Holes, 2788yds, Par 35, SSS 69.
Prof Jamie Skinner **Facilities** ⑪ ⑩ ▙ ⤶ ⚑ ⚐ ⚐ ✐
Leisure hard tennis courts, heated indoor swimming pool, squash, sauna, gymnasium, indoor virtual golf **Conf** facs Corporate Hospitality Days **Location** 2m W on A305
Telephone for further details
Hotel ★★★★ 73% HL Richmond Hill, Richmond Hill, RICHMOND UPON THAMES ☎ 020 8940 2247 ▤ 020 8940 2247   149 en suite

Strawberry Hill Wellesley Rd, Strawberry Hill TW2 5SD
☎ 020 8894 0165 & 8898 2082
e-mail: secretary@shgc.net
web: www.shgc.net
Parkland with easy walking.
9 Holes, 4762yds, Par 64, SSS 63, Course record 59. Club membership 300.
Visitors Mon-Fri except BHs. Dress code. **Societies** booking required **Green Fees** £30/£20 per day, £20/£13 per 18 holes, £15/£10 per 9 holes **Course Designer** J H Taylor **Prof** Peter Buchan **Facilities** ⑪ ⑩ by prior arrangement ▙ ⤶ ⚑ ⚐ ⚐ ✐ **Location** S of town centre off A316, next to Strawberry Hill railway station
Hotel ★★★★ 73% HL Richmond Hill, Richmond Hill, RICHMOND UPON THAMES ☎ 020 8940 2247 ▤ 020 8940 2247   149 en suite

UPMINSTER
Map 5 TQ58

Upminster 114 Hall Ln RM14 1AU
☎ 01708 222788 (Secretary)   ▤ 01708 222484
e-mail: secretary@upminstergolfclub.co.uk
web: www.upminstergolfclub.co.uk
The meandering River Ingrebourne features on several holes of this partly undulating parkland course, situated on one side of the river valley. It provides a challenge for golfers of all abilities. The clubhouse is a beautiful Grade II listed building.
18 Holes, 6076yds, Par 69, SSS 69, Course record 62. Club membership 1000.
Visitors contact club for details. **Societies** welcome. **Green Fees** phone **Course Designer** W G Key **Prof** Jodie Dartford **Facilities** ⑪ ⑩ ▙ ⤶ ⚑ ⚐ ⚐ ✐
Leisure bowling, snooker **Location** M25 junct 29, take A127 W towards Romford for 1m to Hall Lane slip road signed Upminster/Cranham. Proceed S on Hall Lane for 0.5m, entrance past park on left

continued

Hotel ★★★★ 77% HL De Rougemont Manor, Great Warley Street, BRENTWOOD ☎ 01277 226418 & 220483 📄 01277 226418 79 en suite

UXBRIDGE
Map 4 TQ08

Stockley Park Stockley Park UB11 1AQ
☎ 020 8813 5700   📄 020 8813 5655
web: www.stockleyparkgolf.com
18 Holes, 6754yds, Par 72, SSS 71.
Course Designer Robert Trent Jones Snr **Location** M4 junct 4, 1m N off A408
Telephone for further details
Hotel ★★★★ 72% HL Novotel London Heathrow, Cherry Lane, WEST DRAYTON ☎ 01895 431431 📄 01895 431431 178 en suite

Uxbridge The Drive, Harefield Place UB10 8AQ
☎ 01895 272457   📄 01895 813539
e-mail: uxbridgegolfclub@btconnect.com
web: www.uxbridgegolfclub.co.uk
Municipal parkland course, undulating and tricky.
Uxbridge Golf Course: 18 Holes, 5677yds, Par 68, SSS 68, Course record 64. Club membership 200.
Visitors Mon-Sun & BHs. Booking required. Dress code.
Societies booking required **Green Fees** not confirmed **Prof** Phil Howard **Facilities** ⊕ ⊧◯▐ ▐▄ ⌑ ⋺▐ ⌃ 🖼 ⋎ 🛒 ♂
Conf facs Corporate Hospitality Days **Location** 2m N off B467
Hotel ★★★ 78% HL Barn Hotel, West End Road, RUISLIP ☎ 01895 636057 📄 01895 636057 73 en suite

WEMBLEY
Map 4 TQ18

Sudbury Bridgewater Rd HA0 1AL
☎ 020 8902 3713   📄 020 8902 3713
e-mail: enquiries@sudburygolfclubltd.co.uk
web: www.sudburygolfclubltd.co.uk

Undulating parkland near the centre of London.
18 Holes, 6282yds, Par 69, SSS 70, Course record 63. Club membership 650.
Visitors Mon-Fri except BHs. Handicap certificate. Dress code.
Societies welcome. **Green Fees** £35 per 18 holes. £25 Mon. **Course Designer** Harry Colt **Prof** Neil Jordan **Facilities** ⊕ ⊧◯▐ ▐▄ ⌑ ⋺▐ ⌃ 🖼 ♂ 🛒 ♂ **Conf** facs **Location** SW of town centre on A4090
Hotel ★★★ 71% HL Quality Hotel, Wembley, Empire Way, WEMBLEY ☎ 020 8733 9000 📄 020 8733 9000 165 en suite

WOODFORD GREEN
Map 5 TQ49

Woodford Sunset Av IG8 0ST
☎ 020 8504 3330 & 8504 0553   📄 020 8559 0504
e-mail: office@woodfordgolf.co.uk
web: www.woodfordgolf.co.uk
Forest land course on the edge of Epping Forest. Views over the Lea valley to the London skyline. When played as 18 holes from dual tees, the course is comprised of four par 3s, two par 5s and twelve par 4s. Although fairly short, the tree-lined fairways and subtle undulations provide and excellent test of golfing skill. Noted for its fine greens.
9 Holes, 5852yds, Par 70, SSS 69, Course record 66. Club membership 310.
Visitors Mon-Sun & BHs. Booking required weekends & BHs. Dress code. **Societies** booking required. **Green Fees** £18 per 18 holes, £12 per 9 holes (£20£14 weekends) **Course Designer** Tom Dunn **Prof** Adam Baker **Facilities** ⊕ ⊧◯▐ by prior arrangement ⌑ ⋺▐ ⌃ 🖼 ♂ **Conf** Corporate Hospitality Days **Location** NW of town centre off A104
Hotel ★★ 57% SHL Ridgeway, 115/117 The Ridgeway, North Chingford, LONDON ☎ 020 8529 1964 📄 020 8529 1964 20 en suite

GREATER MANCHESTER

ALTRINCHAM
Map 7 SJ78

Altrincham Stockport Rd WA15 7LP
☎ 0161 928 0761   📄 0161 928 8542
web: www.altrinchamgolfclub.org.uk
18 Holes, 6385yds, Par 71, SSS 69.
Prof Scott Partington **Facilities** ⊕ ▐▄ ⋺▐ ⌃ 🖼 ⋎ ♂ 🏌
Conf Corporate Hospitality Days **Location** 0.75m E of town ventre on A560
Telephone for further details
Hotel ★★★ 77% HL Best Western Cresta Court, Church Street, ALTRINCHAM ☎ 0161 927 7272 & 927 2601 📄 0161 927 7272 140 en suite

Dunham Forest Oldfield Ln WA14 4TY
☎ 0161 928 2605   📄 0161 929 8975
e-mail: enquiries@dunhamforest.com
web: www.dunhamforest.com
An attractive parkland course cut through magnificent beech woods.
Dunham Forest Golf & Country Club: 18 Holes, 6636yds, Par 72, SSS 72, Course record 63. Club membership 680.
Visitors Mon-Fri. Restricted play weekends & BHs. Handicap certificate. Dress code. **Societies** booking required. **Green Fees** £58 per 18 holes (£68 weekends) **Course Designer** Dave Thomas **Prof** Ian Wrigley **Facilities** ⊕ ⊧◯▐ by prior arrangement ▐▄ ⌑ ⋺▐ ⌃ 🖼 ⋎ ♂ 🛒 ♂ 🏌 **Leisure** hard tennis courts **Conf** facs Corporate Hospitality Days **Location** 1.5m W off A56
Hotel ★★★ 77% HL Best Western Cresta Court, Church Street, ALTRINCHAM ☎ 0161 927 7272 & 927 2601 📄 0161 927 7272 140 en suite

Ringway Hale Mount, Hale Barns WA15 8SW
☎ 0161 980 2630   📄 0161 980 4414
e-mail: fiona@ringwaygolfclub.co.uk
web: www.ringwaygolfclub.co.uk
Parkland with interesting natural hazards. Easy walking and good views of the Pennines and the Peak District.   *continued*

18 Holes, 6482yds, Par 71, SSS 71, Course record 65. Club membership 800.

Visitors Mon-Thu, weekends & BHs. Booking required. Dress code. **Societies** booking required. **Green Fees** £40 (£50 weekends & BHs) **Course Designer** Colt **Prof** Nick Ryan **Facilities** ⊕ ⑩ ⓛ ⌒ ⏚ ⑯ ⚑ ✦ ✦ **Conf** Corporate Hospitality Days **Location** M56 junct 6, A538 for 1m signed Hale, right onto Shay Ln
Hotel ★★★ 77% HL Best Western Cresta Court, Church Street, ALTRINCHAM ☎ 0161 927 7272 & 927 2601 📄 0161 927 7272 140 en suite

---

ASHTON-IN-MAKERFIELD　　　Map 7 SJ59

Ashton-in-Makerfield Garswood Park, Liverpool Rd WN4 0YT
☎ 01942 719330 📄 01942 719330
e-mail: secretary@ashton-in-makerfieldgolfclub.co.uk
web: www.ashton-in-makerfieldgolfclub.co.uk
Well-wooded parkland course. Easy walking.

Ashton-In-Makerfield Golf Club: 18 Holes, 6205yds, Par 70, SSS 70, Course record 63. Club membership 800.

Visitors Mon, Tue, Thu, Fri & Sun except BHs. Booking required. Dress code. **Societies** booking required **Green Fees** phone **Prof** Peter Allan **Facilities** ⊕ ⑩ ⓛ ⌒ ⑯ ⏚ ⏁ ⚑ ✦ **Conf** Corporate Hospitality Days **Location** M6 junct 24, 5m W on A580
Hotel ★★★★ 76% HL Thistle Haydock, Penny Lane, HAYDOCK ☎ 0871 376 9044 📄 0871 376 9044 137 en suite

---

ASHTON-UNDER-LYNE　　　Map 7 SJ99

Ashton-under-Lyne Gorsey Way OL6 9HT
☎ 0161 330 1537 📄 0161 330 6673
web: www.ashtongolfclub.co.uk

18 Holes, 5754yds, Par 69, SSS 68.
Prof Colin Boyle **Facilities** ⊕ ⑩ ⓛ ⌒ ⑯ ⏚ ⏁ ✦
Conf facs Corporate Hospitality Days **Location** N off B6194
Telephone for further details
Hotel ★★★ 80% HL Best Western Hotel Smokies Park, Ashton Road, Bardsley, OLDHAM ☎ 0161 785 5000 📄 0161 785 5000 73 en suite

Dukinfield Lyne Edge, Yew Tree Ln SK16 5DB
☎ 0161 338 2340 📄 0161 303 0205
e-mail: dgclub@tiscali.co.uk
web: www.dukinfieldgolfclub.co.uk
Extended, tricky hillside course with several challenging par 3s and a very long par 5.
18 Holes, 5338yds, Par 67, SSS 66. Club membership 500.

Visitors Mon-Fri. Booking required. Dress code. **Societies** booking required. **Green Fees** not confirmed **Prof** David Green **Facilities** ⊕ ⑩ ⓛ ⌒ ⑯ ⏚ ⏁ ✦ **Conf** Corporate Hospitality Days **Location** S off B6175
Hotel ★★★ 74% HL Holiday Inn Manchester Airport, Altrincham Road, WILMSLOW ☎ 0870 443 6961 📄 0870 443 6961 126 en suite

---

BOLTON　　　Map 7 SD70

Bolton Lostock Park, Chorley New Rd BL6 4AJ
☎ 01204 843067 & 843278 📄 01204 843067
e-mail: secretary@boltongolfclub.co.uk
This well-maintained heathland course is always a pleasure to visit. The 12th hole should be treated with respect and so too should the final four holes which have ruined many a card.
18 Holes, 6237yds, Par 70, SSS 70, Course record 64. Club membership 525.
Visitors Mon, Wed-Fri & BHs. Booking required Wed & BHs. Dress code. **Societies** welcome. **Green Fees** £46 per day, £36 per round **Prof** R Longworth **Facilities** ⊕ ⑩ ⓛ ⌒ ⑯ ⏚ ⏁ ✦ **Conf** Corporate Hospitality Days **Location** 3m W of Bolton on A673
Hotel ★★★ 74% HL Ramada Bolton, Manchester Road, Blackrod, BOLTON ☎ 01942 814598 📄 01942 814598 91 en suite

Breightmet Red Bridge BL2 5PA
☎ 01204 527381 & 399275 📄 01204 399275
Breightmet Golf Club Ltd: 18 Holes, 6405yds, Par 72, SSS 71, Course record 67.
Course Designer D Griffiths **Location** E of town centre off A58
Telephone for further details
Hotel ★★★★ 71% HL Holiday Inn Bolton Centre, 1 Higher Bridge Street, BOLTON ☎ 0870 4420 901 & 01204 879988 📄 0870 4420 901 132 en suite

Deane Broadford Rd, Deane BL3 4NS
☎ 01204 61944 (pro) & 651808(sec) 📄 01204 652047
e-mail: secretary@deanegolfclub.com
Undulating parkland with small ravines on the approach to some holes.
18 Holes, 5677yds, Par 68, SSS 68, Course record 64. Club membership 470.
Visitors handicap certificate. Dress code. **Societies** booking required. **Green Fees** £25 per round (£30 weekends and BHs) **Prof** David Martindale **Facilities** ⊕ ⑩ ⓛ ⌒ ⑯ ⏚ ⏁ ✦ **Conf** facs **Location** M61 junct 5, 1m towards Bolton
Hotel ★★★★ 71% HL Holiday Inn Bolton Centre, 1 Higher Bridge Street, BOLTON ☎ 0870 4420 901 & 01204 879988 📄 0870 4420 901 132 en suite

Dunscar Longworth Ln, Bromley Cross BL7 9QY
☎ 01204 303321 📄 01204 303321
e-mail: dunscargolfclub@uk2.net
web: www.dunscargolfclub.co.uk
A scenic moorland course with panoramic views.
18 Holes, 5982yds, Par 71, SSS 69, Course record 63. Club membership 550.
Visitors Wed-Fri, Sun & BHs. Booking required. Handicap certificate. Dress code. **Societies** booking required. **Green Fees** £30 per round (£36 Sun & BHs) **Course Designer** Mr G Lowe **Prof** Gary Treadgold **Facilities** ⊕ ⑩ ⓛ ⌒ ⑯ ⏚ ⏁ ✦ **Conf** facs Corporate Hospitality Days **Location** 2m N off A666

continued

Hotel BUD Travelodge Bolton West (M61 Southbound), Bolton West Service Area, Horwich, BOLTON ☎ 08719 846 334 🖹 08719 846 334 32 en suite

Great Lever & Farnworth Plodder Ln, Farnworth BL4 0LQ
☎ 01204 656137   🖹 01204 656137
e-mail: greatlever@btconnect.com
Downland course with easy walking.
18 Holes, 5745yds, Par 69, SSS 68, Course record 63.
Club membership 470.
Visitors Mon-Sun & BHs. Booking required. Handicap certificate. Dress code. **Societies** booking required. **Green Fees** £25 per day (£30 weekends & BHs) **Prof** Tony Howarth **Facilities** ⑪ ⑩ ☕ ⌷ 🛆 ☻ 🖍 **Leisure** snooker **Conf** facs **Location** M61 junct 4, 1m **Hotel** ★★★★ 71% HL Holiday Inn Bolton Centre, 1 Higher Bridge Street, BOLTON ☎ 0870 4420 901 & 01204 879988 🖹 0870 4420 901 132 en suite

Harwood Roading Brook Rd, Harwood BL2 4JD
☎ 01204 522878   🖹 01204 524233
e-mail: secretary@harwoodgolfclub.co.uk
web: www.harwoodgolfclub.co.uk
Mainly flat parkland with several water hazards.
Harwood Golf Club (Bolton): 18 Holes, 5915yds, Par 70, SSS 69, Course record 65. Club membership 691.
Visitors Mon-Fri except BHs. Dress code. **Societies** booking required. **Green Fees** £25 per round **Course Designer** G Shuttleworth **Prof** Clive Loydall **Facilities** ⑪ ⑩ ☕ ⌷ 🛆 ☻ 🖍 **Location** 2.5m NE off B6196

Old Links Chorley Old Rd, Montserrat BL1 5SU
☎ 01204 842307   🖹 01204 497549
e-mail: mail@boltonoldlinksgolfclub.co.uk
web: www.boltonoldlinksgolfclub.co.uk
Championship moorland course.
Bolton Old Links Golf Club: 18 Holes, 6469yds, Par 71, SSS 72. Club membership 600.
Visitors handicap certificate. Dress code. **Societies** booking required. **Green Fees** £35 per day (£45 weekends & BHs) **Course Designer** Dr Alistair MacKenzie **Prof** Paul Horridge **Facilities** ⑪ ⑩ ☕ ⌷ 🛆 ☻ 🖍 **Conf** facs **Location** NW of town centre on B6226 **Hotel** BUD Travelodge Bolton West (M61 Southbound), Bolton West Service Area, Horwich, BOLTON ☎ 08719 846 334 🖹 08719 846 334 32 en suite

Regent Park Links Rd, Chorley New Rd BL6 4AF
☎ 01204 495421   🖹 01204 844620
Parkland course with exceptional moorland views.
Regent Park Golf Course: 18 Holes, 6130yds, Par 71, SSS 70, Course record 63. Club membership 200.
Visitors Mon-Sun & BHs. Booking required. Dress code. **Societies** booking required. **Green Fees** £12 per round (£15 weekends) **Course Designer** James Braid **Prof** Neil Brazell **Facilities** ⑪ ⑩ ☕ ⌷ 🛆 ☻ 🖍 **Conf** facs Corporate Hospitality Days **Location** M61 junct 6, 1m E off A673 **Hotel** BUD Travelodge Bolton West (M61 Southbound), Bolton West Service Area, Horwich, BOLTON ☎ 08719 846 334 🖹 08719 846 334 32 en suite

Turton Wood End Farm, Hospital Rd, Bromley Cross BL7 9QD
☎ 01204 852235   🖹 01204 856921
e-mail: info@turtongolfclub.com
web: www.turtongolfclub.com
Moorland course with panoramic views. A wide variety of holes which challenge any golfer's technique.
18 Holes, 6124yds, Par 70, SSS 69, Course record 68.
Club membership 550.
Visitors Mon- Fri, Sun & BHs. Dress code. **Societies** booking required. **Green Fees** £32 per round (£40 Sun & BHs) **Course Designer** Alex Herd **Prof** Andrew Green **Facilities** ⑪ ⑩ ☕ ⌷ 🛆 ☻ 🖍 **Leisure** indoor computer system **Location** 3m N off A666, follow signs for 'Last Drop Village'
Hotel ★★★ 78% HL Egerton House, Blackburn Road, Egerton, BOLTON ☎ 01204 307171 🖹 01204 307171 29 en suite

BRAMHALL   Map 7 SJ88

Bramall Park 20 Manor Rd SK7 3LY
☎ 0161 485 7101   🖹 0161 485 7101
e-mail: secretary@bramallparkgolfclub.co.uk
web: www.bramallparkgolfclub.co.uk
Attractive parkland with some testing, lengthy par 4s
18 Holes, 6247yds, Par 70, SSS 70, Course record 63.
Club membership 829.
Visitors Mon-Sun & BHs. Booking required. Handicap certificate. Dress code. **Societies** booking required. **Green Fees** not confirmed **Course Designer** James Braid **Prof** M Proffitt **Facilities** ⑪ ⑩ ☕ ⌷ 🛆 ☻ 🖍 **Conf** facs Corporate Hospitality Days **Location** NW of town centre off B5149
Hotel ★★★ 75% HL Alma Lodge Hotel, 149 Buxton Road, STOCKPORT ☎ 0161 483 4431 🖹 0161 483 4431 52 en suite

Bramhall Ladythorn Rd SK7 2EY
☎ 0161 439 6092   🖹 0161 439 6092
e-mail: office@bramhallgolfclub.com
web: www.bramhallgolfclub.com
Undulating parkland with easy walking and new USGA greens.
18 Holes, 6347yds, Par 70, SSS 70. Club membership 840.
Visitors Mon, Tue & Fri except BHs. Booking required. Handicap certificate. Dress code. **Societies** booking required. **Green Fees** £44 per 18 holes. Reduced winter rrates. **Course Designer** Alex Herd **Prof** Richard Green **Facilities** ⑪ ⑩ by prior arrangement ☕ ⌷ 🛆 ☻ 🖍 **Conf** Corporate Hospitality Days **Location** E of town centre off A5102
Hotel ★★★ 75% HL Alma Lodge Hotel, 149 Buxton Road, STOCKPORT ☎ 0161 483 4431 🖹 0161 483 4431 52 en suite

BURY   Map 7 SD81

Bury Unsworth Hall, Blackford Bridge, Manchester Rd BL9 9TJ
☎ 0161 766 4897   🖹 0161 796 3480
e-mail: secretary@burygolfclub.com
web: www.burygolfclub.com
Moorland course, difficult in part. Tight and good test of golf.
18 Holes, 5961yds, Par 69, SSS 69, Course record 61.
Club membership 650.

continued

Visitors contact club for details. **Societies** welcome. **Green Fees** not confirmed **Course Designer** Mackenzie **Prof** G Coope **Facilities** ⓉⒾ 🍴 ⓛ ⌨ ⓣ ⌁ 🛍 ✓ **Conf** facs Corporate Hospitality Days **Location** 2m N of M60 junct 17 on A56
Hotel ★★★ 75% HL Fairways Lodge & Leisure Club, George Street, (Off Bury New Road), PRESTWICH, Manchester ☎ 0161 798 8905 📄 0161 798 8905 40 en suite

Lowes Park Hilltop, Lowes Rd BL9 6SU
☎ 0161 764 1231 📄 0161 763 9503
e-mail: lowesparkgc@btconnect.com
web: www.lowesparkgc.co.uk
Moorland with easy walking. Exposed outlook with good views.
9 Holes, 6006yds, Par 70, SSS 69, Course record 65. Club membership 300.
Visitors Mon, Tue, Thu, Fri & Sun except BHs. Booking required. Handicap certificate. Dress code. **Societies** booking required. **Green Fees** £15 per 18 holes **Facilities** ⓉⒾ 🍴 ⓛ ⌨ ⓣ ⌁ **Conf** facs Corporate Hospitality Days **Location** N side of town centre off A56
Hotel ★★★★ 77% HL Mercure Norton Grange Hotel & Spa, Manchester Road, Castleton, ROCHDALE ☎ 0870 1942119 📄 0870 1942119 81 en suite

Pike Fold Pike Fold, Hills Ln, Unsworth BL9 8QP
☎ 0161 766 3561
e-mail: secretary@pikefold.co.uk
web: www.pikefold.co.uk
Inland course that plays like a links with a number of water hazards that come into play. USGA standard greens.
18 Holes, 6252yds, Par 71, SSS 70, Course record 68. Club membership 478.
Visitors Mon-Sat & BHs. Booking required. Handicap certificate. Dress code. **Societies** booking required. **Green Fees** £30 per 18 holes **Prof** Grant Hamerton **Facilities** ⓉⒾ 🍴 ⓛ ⌨ ⓣ ⌁ 🛍 ⌐ ✓ **Leisure** indoor swing room **Conf** facs Corporate Hospitality Days **Location** 4m N of city centre off Rochdale Rd
Hotel ★★★ 75% HL Fairways Lodge & Leisure Club, George Street, (Off Bury New Road), PRESTWICH, Manchester ☎ 0161 798 8905 📄 0161 798 8905 40 en suite

Walmersley Garretts Close, Walmersley BL9 6TE
☎ 0161 764 1429 & 0161 764 7770 📄 0161 764 7770
e-mail: wgcsecretary@btconnect.com
Moorland hillside course, with wide fairways, large greens and extensive views. Testing holes: 2nd (484 yds) par 5 and the 5th par 4 with severe dog leg and various hazards.
18 Holes, 6094yds, Par 71, SSS 70, Course record 65. Club membership 475.
Visitors Mon-Fri & Sun except BHs. Booking required Sun. Dress code. **Societies** booking required. **Green Fees** £30 per day **Course Designer** S Marnoch **Prof** S L Halsall **Facilities** Ⓣ by prior arrangement 🍴 by prior arrangement ⓛ ⌨ ⓣ ⌁ ✓ **Conf** Corporate Hospitality Days **Location** 2m N off A56
Hotel ★★★★ 77% HL Mercure Norton Grange Hotel & Spa, Manchester Road, Castleton, ROCHDALE ☎ 0870 1942119 📄 0870 1942119 81 en suite

CHEADLE
Map 7 SJ88

Cheadle Cheadle Rd SK8 1HW
☎ 0161 491 4452
e-mail: cheadlegolfclub@msn.com
web: www.cheadlegolfclub.com
Parkland with hazards on every hole, from sand bunkers and copses to a stream across six of the fairways.
9 Holes, 5006yds, Par 64, SSS 65. Club membership 350.
Visitors Mon, Wed-Fri & BHs. Handicap certificate . Dress code. **Societies** booking required. **Green Fees** £25 **Course Designer** T Renouf **Prof** D Cain **Facilities** ⓉⒾ 🍴 ⓛ ⌨ ⓣ ⌁ 🛍 ✓ **Conf** facs Corporate Hospitality Days **Location** S of village off A5149
Hotel ★★★ 73% HL Wycliffe, 74 Edgeley Road, Edgeley, STOCKPORT ☎ 0161 477 5395 📄 0161 477 5395 20 en suite

DENTON
Map 7 SJ99

Denton Manchester Rd M34 2GG
☎ 0161 336 3218 📄 0161 336 4751
web: www.dentongolfclub.com
Easy walking parkland course with brook running through. One notable hole is called Death and Glory.
18 Holes, 6443yds, Par 71, SSS 71, Course record 66. Club membership 865.
Visitors Mon-Fri & BHs. Dress code. **Societies** booking required. **Green Fees** phone **Course Designer** R McCauley **Prof** M Hollingworth **Facilities** ⓉⒾ 🍴 by prior arrangement ⓛ ⌨ ⓣ ⌁ 🛍 ✓ **Leisure** indoor teaching facility **Location** M60 junct 24, 1.5m W on A57
Hotel ★★★ 70% HL Old Rectory Hotel, Meadow Lane, Haughton Green, Denton, MANCHESTER ☎ 0161 336 7516 📄 0161 336 7516 36 en suite

FAILSWORTH
Map 7 SD80

Brookdale Medlock Rd M35 9WQ
☎ 0161 681 4534 📄 0161 688 6872
web: www.brookdalegolf.co.uk
Brookdale Golf Club Ltd: 18 Holes, 5864yds, Par 68, SSS 68, Course record 64.
Prof Tony Cuppello **Facilities** ⓉⒾ 🍴 ⓛ ⌨ ⓣ ⌁ 🛍 ⌐ ✓ 🛺 ✓ **Location** M60/A62 Oldham exit, towards Manchester, left at Nat West bank, left at road end. Right at minirdbt, 0.5m on left
Telephone for further details

FLIXTON
Map 7 SJ79

William Wroe Municipal Pennybridge Ln, Flixton Rd M41 5DX
☎ 0161 748 8680 📄 0161 748 8680
web: www.traffordleisure.co.uk/golf.htm
Municipal parkland course with easy walking, rolling contours and many trees.
William Wroe Municipal Golf Course: 18 Holes, 4368yds, Par 64.
Visitors Mon-Sun & BHs. Booking required Tue, Fri-Sun & BHs. Dress code. **Societies** booking required. **Green Fees** £10 per round (£13.50

continued

weekends & BHs) **Prof** Scott Partington **Facilities** ⬚ ♨ 🏠 ⛳
⚐ **Location** E of village off B5158, 3m from Manchester centre
Hotel ★★★ 68% HL Amblehurst Hotel, 44 Washway Road, SALE
☎ 0161 973 8800 📋 0161 973 8800 66 en suite

GATLEY   Map 7 SJ88

Gatley Waterfall Farm SK8 3TW
☎ 0161 437 2091
web: www.gatleygolfclub.com
9 Holes, 5934yds, Par 68, SSS 68, Course record 67.
Prof James Matterson **Facilities** ⓣ 🍴 ⬚ ♨ ♨ 🏠 ⚐
Conf Corporate Hospitality Days **Location** S of village off B5166
Telephone for further details
Hotel ★★★★ 74% HL Crowne Plaza Manchester Airport,
Ringway Road, MANCHESTER ☎ 0870 400 9055 📋 0870 400 9055
294 en suite

HAZEL GROVE   Map 7 SJ98

Hazel Grove Buxton Rd SK7 6LU
☎ 0161 483 3978   📋 0161 483 3978
e-mail: secretary@hazelgrovegolfclub.com
web: www.hazelgrovegolfclub.com
Testing parkland course with tricky greens and water hazards coming
into play on several holes. Year round play on the greens.
18 Holes, 6310yds, Par 71, SSS 70, Course record 62.
Club membership 630.
Visitors Mon-Sun & BHs. Booking required. Dress code.
Societies booking required. **Green Fees** £40.50 per day, £35.50
per 18 holes (£45.50 per 18 holes weekends & BHs) **Course**
Designer McKenzie **Prof** J Hopley **Facilities** ⓣ 🍴 🍴 ⬚ ♨ ♨
🏠 ♨ ⚐ **Leisure** golf electronic teaching system (GASP) **Conf** facs
Corporate Hospitality Days **Location** 1m E off A6
Hotel ★★★ 75% HL Alma Lodge Hotel, 149 Buxton Road,
STOCKPORT ☎ 0161 483 4431 📋 0161 483 4431 52 en suite

HINDLEY   Map 7 SD60

Hindley Hall Hall Ln WN2 2SQ
☎ 01942 255131   📋 01942 253871
18 Holes, 5913yds, Par 69, SSS 68, Course record 64.
Prof David Clarke **Facilities** ⓣ 🍴 🍴 ⬚ ♨ ♨ 🏠 ⚐
Conf Corporate Hospitality Days **Location** M61 junct 6, 3m, 1m N off
A58
Telephone for further details
Hotel ★★★ 74% HL Ramada Bolton, Manchester Road, Blackrod,
BOLTON ☎ 01942 814598 📋 01942 814598 91 en suite

HYDE   Map 7 SJ99

Werneth Low Werneth Low Rd SK14 3AF
☎ 0161 368 2503 & 336 9496(sec)   📋 0161 320 0053
11 Holes, 6113yds, Par 70, SSS 70, Course record 64.
Prof Tony Bacchus **Facilities** ⓣ 🍴 🍴 ⬚ ♨ ♨ 🏠 🍴 ⚐
Conf Corporate Hospitality Days **Location** 2m S of town centre
Telephone for further details
Hotel ★★ 83% HL Wind in the Willows, Derbyshire Level, GLOSSOP
☎ 01457 868001 📋 01457 868001 12 en suite

KEARSLEY   Map 7 SD70

Manor Moss Ln BL4 8SF
☎ 01204 701027   📋 01204 796914
18 Holes, 5010yds, Par 66, SSS 64, Course record 65.
Course Designer Jeff Yates **Location** off A666 Manchester Rd
Telephone for further details
Hotel ★★★ 72% HL Novotel Manchester West, Worsley Brow,
WORSLEY, Manchester ☎ 0161 799 3535 📋 0161 799 3535
119 en suite

LITTLEBOROUGH   Map 7 SD91

Whittaker Whittaker Ln OL15 0LH
☎ 01706 378310
e-mail: whittaker_golf@yahoo.co.uk
web: www.whittakergolfclub.co.uk
Moorland course with outstanding views of Hollingworth Lake
Countryside Park and the Pennine Hills.
9 Holes, 5632yds, Par 68, SSS 67, Course record 61.
Club membership 240.
Visitors Mon-Sat & BHs. Dress code. **Societies** booking required.
Green Fees £15 per 18 holes (£20 Sat). Reduced winter rates
Facilities 🍴 ♨ **Location** 1.5m from Littleborough off A58
Hotel ★★★★ 77% HL Mercure Norton Grange Hotel & Spa,
Manchester Road, Castleton, ROCHDALE ☎ 0870 1942119
📋 0870 1942119 81 en suite

MANCHESTER   Map 7 SJ89

Blackley Victoria Ave East, Blackley M9 7HW
☎ 0161 643 2980 & 654 7770   📋 0161 653 8300
e-mail: office@blackleygolfclub.com
web: www.blackleygolfclub.com
Parkland course crossed by a footpath. The course has recently been
redesigned giving greater challenge and interest including water
features.
18 Holes, 6168yds, Par 70, SSS 71. Club membership 800.
Visitors Mon-Wed, Fri & Sat except BHs. Booking required Sat.
Dress code. **Societies** booking required. **Green Fees** phone **Course**
Designer Gaunt & Marnoch **Prof** Craig Gould **Facilities** ⓣ 🍴 by
prior arrangement 🍴 ⬚ ♨ ♨ 🏠 ⚐ 🍴 ⚐ **Conf** facs
Corporate Hospitality Days **Location** 4m N of city centre
Hotel ★★★ 88% HL Malmaison Manchester, Piccadilly,
MANCHESTER ☎ 0161 278 1000 📋 0161 278 1000 167 en suite

Chorlton-cum-Hardy Barlow Hall, Barlow Hall Rd,
Chorlton-cum-Hardy M21 7JJ
☎ 0161 881 5830   📋 0161 881 4532
e-mail: chorltongolf@hotmail.com
web: www.chorltoncumhardygolfclub.co.uk
Set in the grounds of Barlow Hall, this challenging parkland course
winds its way around the banks of the Mersey. The testing opening
holes lead up to the stroke 1 7th, an impressive 474yd par 4, with
its elevated green. The course then meanders through parkland
culminating at the par 4 18th.
18 Holes, 5994yds, Par 70, SSS 69, Course record 61.
Club membership 650.
Visitors Mon-Sun & BHs. Booking required except Mon. Dress code.
Societies booking required. **Green Fees** £30 (£35 weekends & BHs)

continued

Prof David Valentine **Facilities** ⓧ ⦿ ⧄ ⬜ ⧉ ⛱ ⬚ ✓ **Leisure** snooker **Conf** facs Corporate Hospitality Days **Location** 4m S of Manchester, A5103/A5145
Hotel ★★★ 78% HL Best Western Willow Bank, 340-342 Wilmslow Road, Fallowfield, MANCHESTER ☎ 0161 224 0461 📠 0161 224 0461 116 en suite

Davyhulme Park Gleneagles Rd M41 8SA
☎ 0161 748 2260 📠 0161 747 4067
web: www.davyhulmeparkgolfclub.co.uk
18 Holes, 6237yds, Par 72, SSS 70, Course record 64.
Prof Dean Butler **Facilities** ⓧ ⦿ ⧄ ⬜ ⧉ ⛱ ⬚ ✓
Leisure snooker **Conf** Corporate Hospitality Days **Location** next to Trafford General Hospital
Telephone for further details
Hotel ★★ 67% HL Monton House, 116-118 Monton Road, Eccles, MANCHESTER ☎ 0161 789 7811 📠 0161 789 7811 60 en suite

Didsbury Ford Ln, Northenden M22 4NQ
☎ 0161 998 9278 📠 0161 902 3060
e-mail: golf@didsburygolfclub.com
web: www.didsburygolfclub.com
Parkland course.
18 Holes, 6273yds, Par 70, SSS 70, Course record 60. Club membership 750.
Visitors contact club for details. **Societies** welcome. **Green Fees** not confirmed **Prof** Peter Barber **Facilities** ⓧ ⦿ ⧄ ⬜ ⧉ ⛱ ⬚
✓ ⛟ ✓ **Conf** facs Corporate Hospitality Days **Location** 6m S of city centre off A5145
Hotel BUD Travelodge Manchester Didsbury, Kingsway, DIDSBURY, Manchester ☎ 08719 846 244 📠 08719 846 244 62 en suite

Fairfield 'Boothdale', Booth Rd, Audenshaw M34 5QA
☎ 0161 301 4528 📠 0161 301 4254
e-mail: fairfield.golf@btconnect.com
web: www.fairfieldgolfclub.co.uk
Parkland course set around a reservoir. Course demands particularly accurate placing of shots.
Fairfield Golf and Sailing Club: 18 Holes, 5276yds, Par 68, SSS 66, Course record 63. Club membership 450.
Visitors Mon, Tue, Fri & BHs. Booking required. **Societies** welcome. **Green Fees** phone **Prof** Stephen Pownell **Facilities** ⓧ ⦿ ⧄ ⬜
⧉ ⛱ ⬚ ⚐ ✓ **Location** 5m E of Manchester off A635
Hotel ★★★ 70% HL Old Rectory Hotel, Meadow Lane, Haughton Green, Denton, MANCHESTER ☎ 0161 336 7516 📠 0161 336 7516 36 en suite

Marriott Worsley Park Hotel & Country Club Worsley Park M28 2QT
☎ 0161 975 2043 📠 0161 975 2058
web: www.marriott.co.uk/golf
Marriott Worsley Park Hotel & Country Club: 18 Holes, 6611yds, Par 71, SSS 72, Course record 61.
Course Designer Ross McMurray **Location** M60 junct 13, A585, course 0.5m on left
Telephone for further details
Hotel ★★★★ 80% HL Marriott Worsley Park Hotel & Country Club, Worsley Park, Worsley, MANCHESTER ☎ 0161 975 2000 📠 0161 975 2000 158 en suite

Northenden Palatine Rd, Northenden M22 4FR
☎ 0161 998 4738 📠 0161 945 5592
e-mail: manager@northendengolfclub.com
web: www.northendengolfclub.com

Parkland course surrounded by the River Mersey with 18 USGA specification greens.
18 Holes, 6432yds, Par 72, SSS 71, Course record 64. Club membership 800.
Visitors contact club for details. **Societies** welcome. **Green Fees** £32 per day (£35 weekends & BHs) **Course Designer** Renouf/S Gidman **Prof** J Curtis **Facilities** ⓧ ⦿ ⧄ ⬜ ⧉ ⛱ ⬚ ✓
Leisure indoor teaching facility. **Conf** facs Corporate Hospitality Days **Location** 6.5m S of city centre on B1567
Hotel BUD Travelodge Manchester Didsbury, Kingsway, DIDSBURY, Manchester ☎ 08719 846 244 📠 08719 846 244 62 en suite

Withington 243 Palatine Rd, West Didsbury M20 2UE
☎ 0161 445 9544 📠 0161 445 5210
e-mail: secretary@withingtongolfclub.co.uk
web: www.withingtongolfclub.co.uk
Flat parkland course bordering the River Mersey and only four miles from the city centre. Famed for its tree lined fairways and manicured greens.
18 Holes, 6410yds, Par 71, SSS 70. Club membership 600.
Visitors Mon-Wed, Fri, Sun & BHs. Booking required. Handicap certificate. Dress code. **Societies** booking required. **Green Fees** not confirmed **Prof** S Marr **Facilities** ⓧ ⦿ ⧄ ⬜ ⧉ ⛱ ⬚ ⛟
✓ **Location** 4m SW of city centre off B5167
Hotel BUD Travelodge Manchester Didsbury, Kingsway, DIDSBURY, Manchester ☎ 08719 846 244 📠 08719 846 244 62 en suite

Worsley Stableford Av, Worsley M30 8AP
☎ 0161 789 4202 📠 0161 789 3200
e-mail: secretary@worsleygolfclub.co.uk
web: www.worsleygolfclub.co.uk
Well-wooded parkland course.
18 Holes, 6252yds, Par 71, SSS 70, Course record 65. Club membership 600.
Visitors contact club for details. **Societies** welcome. **Green Fees** not confirmed **Course Designer** James Braid **Prof** Andrew Cory **Facilities** ⓧ ⦿ ⧄ ⬜ ⧉ ⛱ ⬚ ⚐ ✓ **Location** 6.5m NW of city centre off A572
Hotel ★★★ 72% HL Novotel Manchester West, Worsley Brow, WORSLEY, Manchester ☎ 0161 799 3535 📠 0161 799 3535 119 en suite

MELLOR
Map 7 SJ98

Mellor & Townscliffe Gibb Ln, Tarden SK6 5NA
☎ 0161 427 2208 (secretary)
web: www.mellorgolf.co.uk

Scenic parkland and moorland course, undulating with some hard walking. Good views. Testing 200yd 9th hole, par 3.

18 Holes, 5925yds, Par 70, SSS 69. Club membership 550.
Visitors Mon, Tue, Thu, Fri & Sun except BHs. Booking required Mon, Thu, Fri & Sun. Handicap certificate. Dress code. **Societies** booking required. **Green Fees** not confirmed **Prof** Gary R Broadley **Facilities** ⑪ ⑩ ⓑ ⌷ ⑨ ⌳ ⌂ 🏌 ✓ **Location** 7m SE of Stockport off A626
Hotel ★★★ 77% HL Bredbury Hall Hotel & Country Club, Goyt Valley, BREDBURY ☎ 0161 430 7421 📄 0161 430 7421 150 en suite

MIDDLETON
Map 7 SD80

Manchester Hopwood Cottage, Rochdale Rd M24 6QP
☎ 0161 643 3202 📄 0161 643 9174
e-mail: secretary@mangc.co.uk
web: www.mangc.co.uk

Moorland golf of unique character over a spaciously laid out course with generous fairways sweeping along to large greens. A wide variety of holes will challenge the golfer's technique, particularly the testing last four holes.

The Manchester Golf Club: 18 Holes, 6491yds, Par 72, SSS 72, Course record 63. Club membership 650.
Visitors Mon, Tue, Thu, Fri, Sun & BHs. Booking required. Handicap certificate. Dress code. **Societies** booking required. **Green Fees** £50 per day, £40 per round (£65/£55 per round Sun & BHs) **Course Designer** Shapland Colt **Prof** Brian Connor **Facilities** ⑪ ⑩ ⓑ ⌷ ⑨ ⌳ ⌂ ✓ 🏌 ✓ 🏌 **Leisure** snooker **Conf** facs Corporate Hospitality Days **Location** 1m S of M62 junct 20 on A664
Hotel ★★★★ 77% HL Mercure Norton Grange Hotel & Spa, Manchester Road, Castleton, ROCHDALE ☎ 0870 1942119 📄 0870 1942119 81 en suite

New North Manchester Rhodes House, Manchester Old Rd M24 4PE
☎ 0161 643 9033 📄 0161 643 7775
e-mail: tee@nmgc.co.uk
web: www.northmanchestergolfclub.co.uk

Delightful moorland and parkland with several water features. Challenging but fair for the accomplished golfer.

18 Holes, 6436yds, Par 71, SSS 71, Course record 69. Club membership 560.
Visitors Mon-Wed, Fri, Sun & BHs. Booking required. Dress code. **Societies** booking required. **Green Fees** £38 (£40 Sun). Reduced winter rates **Course Designer** J Braid **Prof** Jason Peel **Facilities** ⑪ ⑩ ⓑ ⌷ ⑨ ⌳ ⌂ ✓ **Leisure** 2 full size snooker tables **Conf** facs Corporate Hospitality Days **Location** M60 junct 19, W of town centre off A576

MILNROW
Map 7 SD91

Tunshill Kiln Ln OL16 3TS
☎ 01706 342095

Testing moorland course with two demanding par 5s and out of bounds features on eight of the nine holes.

9 Holes, 5743yds, Par 70, SSS 68, Course record 64. Club membership 300.
Visitors Mon-Fri except BHs. Booking required. Dress code. **Societies** booking required. **Green Fees** £16 per day **Facilities** ⑪ by prior arrangement ⑩ by prior arrangement ⓑ ⌷ ⑨ ⌳ **Location** 1m NE M62 exit junct 21 off B6225
Hotel ★★★★ 77% HL Mercure Norton Grange Hotel & Spa, Manchester Road, Castleton, ROCHDALE ☎ 0870 1942119 📄 0870 1942119 81 en suite

OLDHAM
Map 7 SD90

Crompton & Royton Highbarn, Royton OL2 6RW
☎ 0161 624 0986 📄 0161 652 4711
e-mail: secretary@cromptonandroytongolfclub.co.uk
web: www.cromptonandroytongolfclub.co.uk

Undulating moorland course.

18 Holes, 6214yds, Par 70, SSS 70, Course record 62. Club membership 700.
Visitors Mon, Tue, Wed-Fri, Sun & BHs. Booking required. Handicap certificate. Dress code. **Societies** booking required, **Green Fees** £25 per round (£35 Sun) **Prof** David Melling **Facilities** ⑪ ⑩ ⓑ ⌷ ⑨ ⌳ ⌂ ✓ **Leisure** practice nets **Conf** facs Corporate Hospitality Days **Location** 0.5m NE of Royton

Oldham Lees New Rd OL4 5PN
☎ 0161 624 4986

18 Holes, 5122yds, Par 66, SSS 65, Course record 62.
Prof R Heginbotham **Facilities** ⑪ ⑩ ⓑ ⌷ ⑨ ⌳ ⌂ ✓ ✓ **Location** 2.5m E off A669
Telephone for further details

Werneth Green Ln, Garden Suburb OL8 3AZ
☎ 0161 624 1190
e-mail: secretary@wernethgolfclub.co.uk
web: www.wernethgolfclub.co.uk

Semi-moorland course, with a deep gully and stream crossing eight fairways. Testing hole: 3rd (par 3).

18 Holes, 5363yds, Par 68, SSS 66, Course record 61. Club membership 430.
Visitors Mon, Wed-Fri & BHs. Booking required Thu & BHs. Dress code. **Societies** booking required. **Green Fees** £18 per day **Course Designer** Sandy Herd **Prof** James Matterson **Facilities** ⑪ ⑩ ⓑ ⌷ ⑨ ⌳ ⌂ ⑨ ✓ **Conf** Corporate Hospitality Days **Location** S of town centre off A627

PRESTWICH
Map 7 SD80

Heaton Park Golf Centre Heaton Park, Middleton Rd M25 2SW
☎ 0161 654 9899 📄 0161 653 2003
e-mail: heatonpark@btconnect.com

An award winning municipal parkland-style course in historic Heaton Park, with rolling hills and lakes, designed by five times Open Champion, J H Taylor. It has some spectacular holes and is a good test of skill for golfers of all abilities.

Championship: 18 Holes, 5755yds, Par 70, SSS 68, Course record 67. Club membership 140.
Visitors Mon-Sun & BHs. Booking required weekends & BHs. Dress code. **Societies** booking required. **Green Fees** £15 (£18 weekends)

continued

Course Designer J H Taylor **Prof** Gary Dermott **Facilities** ⑪ ⁺◎⁺ ⓑ
⚑ ⁊⦚ ⚒ ⛽ ◇ ♣ **Leisure** fishing, 18 hole par 3 course.
Conf facs Corporate Hospitality Days **Location** N of Manchester near
M60 junct 19

Heaton Park Golf Centre

Hotel ★★★ 75% HL Fairways Lodge & Leisure Club, George Street,
(Off Bury New Road), PRESTWICH, Manchester ☎ 0161 798 8905
🖹 0161 798 8905 40 en suite

See advert on this page

Prestwich Hilton Ln M25 9XB
☎ 0161 773 1404 🖹 0161 772 0700

18 Holes, 4846yds, Par 65, SSS 65, Course record 60.
Prof Simon Wakefield **Facilities** ⑪ ⁺◎⁺ ⓑ ⚑ ⁊⦚ ⚒ ⛽ ⁊
♣ **Location** N of town centre on A6044
Telephone for further details
Hotel ★★★ 72% HL Novotel Manchester West, Worsley Brow,
WORSLEY, Manchester ☎ 0161 799 3535 🖹 0161 799 3535
119 en suite

ROCHDALE   Map 7 SD81

Castle Hawk Chadwick Ln, Castleton OL11 3BY
☎ 01706 640841 🖹 01706 860587
e-mail: teeoff@castlehawk.co.uk
web: www.castlehawk.co.uk
Two parkland courses that are an ideal place to start for beginners
whilst still offering a stern test for the better golfer. The 18 hole
course consists of 17 par 3s and one par 4. The 9 hole course is a
more traditional test of golf with seven par 4s and two par 3s, each
offering a test of skill be it length, accuracy or both.
New Course: 9 Holes, 2699yds, Par 34, SSS 33,
Course record 30.
Old Course: 18 Holes, 3189yds, Par 55, SSS 55.
Club membership 200.
Visitors Mon-Fri, Sun & BHs. 18 holes only Sat. **Societies** welcome.
Green Fees not confirmed **Course Designer** T Wilson **Prof** David
Royale/Ryan Crumbridge **Facilities** ⑪ ⁺◎⁺ ⓑ ⚑ ⁊⦚ ⚒ ⛽
⁊ ♣ ♟ **Conf** Corporate Hospitality Days **Location** M62 junct 20,
S of Rochdale
Hotel ★★★★ 77% HL Mercure Norton Grange Hotel & Spa,
Manchester Road, Castleton, ROCHDALE ☎ 0870 1942119
🖹 0870 1942119 81 en suite

Marland Park Springfield Park OL11 4RE
☎ 01706 656401 (weekends)

18 Holes, 5237yds, Par 67, SSS 66, Course record 64.
Prof David Wills **Facilities** ⚒ ⁊ ♣ **Location** 1.5m SW off A58
Telephone for further details
Hotel ★★★★ 77% HL Mercure Norton Grange Hotel & Spa,
Manchester Road, Castleton, ROCHDALE ☎ 0870 1942119
🖹 0870 1942119 81 en suite

Rochdale Edenfield Rd OL11 5YR
☎ 01706 643818 🖹 01706 861113
e-mail: rochdale.golfclub@zen.co.uk
Easy walking parkland for enjoyable golf.
18 Holes, 6050yds, Par 71, SSS 69, Course record 65.
Club membership 750.
Visitors Mon, Wed, Fri, Sun & BHs. Booking required. Dress code.
Societies booking required. **Green Fees** £22 per round, £27 Fri,
£30 Sun & BHs **Course Designer** George Lowe **Prof** Andrew Laverty
Facilities ⑪ ⁺◎⁺ ⓑ ⚑ ⁊⦚ ⚒ ⛽ ♣ **Conf** facs Corporate
Hospitality Days **Location** 1.75m W on A680
Hotel ★★★★ 77% HL Mercure Norton Grange Hotel & Spa,
Manchester Road, Castleton, ROCHDALE ☎ 0870 1942119
🖹 0870 1942119 81 en suite

ROMILEY
Map 7 SJ99

Romiley Goose House Green SK6 4LJ
☎ 0161 430 2392   ▤ 0161 430 7258
e-mail: office@romileygolfclub.org
web: www.romileygolfclub.org

Semi-parkland course on the edge of the Derbyshire Hills, providing a good test of golf with a number of outstanding holes, notably the 6th, 9th, 14th and 16th. The latter enjoys magnificent views from the tee.

18 Holes, 6454yds, Par 70, SSS 71, Course record 66.
Club membership 700.

Visitors Mon-Fri, Sun & BHs. Booking required. Handicap certificate. Dress code. **Societies** booking required. **Green Fees** phone **Prof** Matthew Ellis **Facilities** ⓐ ▯ ⓣ ⓘ ⓣ ◻ ◻ ◻ **Location** E of town centre off B6104
Hotel ★★★ 73% HL Wycliffe, 74 Edgeley Road, Edgeley, STOCKPORT ☎ 0161 477 5395 ▤ 0161 477 5395   20 en suite

SALE
Map 7 SJ79

Ashton on Mersey Church Ln M33 5QQ
☎ 0161 976 4390 & 962 3727   ▤ 0161 976 4390
web: www.aomgc.co.uk

9 Holes, 6146yds, Par 71, SSS 69, Course record 66.

Prof Mike Williams **Facilities** ⓐ ⓣ by prior arrangement ◻ ◻ ◻ ◻ ◻ ◻ **Leisure** sauna **Conf** facs **Location** M60 junct 7, 1m W off Glebelands Rd
Telephone for further details
Hotel ★★★ 77% HL Best Western Cresta Court, Church Street, ALTRINCHAM ☎ 0161 927 7272 & 927 2601 ▤ 0161 927 7272   140 en suite

Sale Golf Rd M33 2XU
☎ 0161 973 1638 (Office) & 973 1730 (Pro)
▤ 0161 962 4217
e-mail: mail@salegolfclub.com
web: www.salegolfclub.com

Tree-lined parkland course. Feature holes are the 13th - Watery Gap - and the par 3 3rd hole of 210yds over water.

18 Holes, 6301yds, Par 70, SSS 70, Course record 63.
Club membership 700.

Visitors Mon-Sun & BHs. Dress code. **Societies** welcome. **Green Fees** £40 per day **Prof** Mike Stewart **Facilities** ⓐ ⓣ ◻ ◻ ◻ ◻ ◻ ◻ **Conf** Corporate Hospitality Days **Location** M60 junct 6, 0.5m NW of town centre off A6144
Hotel ★★★ 77% HL Best Western Cresta Court, Church Street, ALTRINCHAM ☎ 0161 927 7272 & 927 2601 ▤ 0161 927 7272   140 en suite

SHEVINGTON
Map 7 SD50

Gathurst 62 Miles Ln WN6 8EW
☎ 01257 255235 (Secretary)   ▤ 01257 255953
e-mail: mail@gathurstgolfclub.ltd.uk
web: www.gathurstgolfclub.co.uk

A testing parkland course. Slightly hilly.

18 Holes, 6016yds, Par 70, SSS 69, Course record 64.
Club membership 630.

Visitors Mon, Tue, Thu & Fri except BHs. Handicap certificate. Dress code. **Societies** booking required. **Green Fees** £30 per round **Course Designer** N Pearson **Prof** David Clarke **Facilities** ⓐ ⓣ ◻ ◻ ◻ ◻ ◻ ◻ **Conf** Corporate Hospitality Days **Location** M6 junct 27, 1m SW of village on B5375
Hotel ★★★★ 73% HL Macdonald Kilhey Court, Chorley Road, Standish, WIGAN ☎ 0870 1942122 ▤ 0870 1942122   62 en suite

STALYBRIDGE
Map 7 SJ99

Stamford Oakfield House, Huddersfield Rd SK15 3PY
☎ 01457 832126
e-mail: admin@stamfordgolfclub.co.uk
web: www.stamfordgolfclub.co.uk

Part parkland, part moorland course with gentle sloping hills. Tree lined fairways with some heather lined rough.

18 Holes, 5701yds, Par 70, SSS 68, Course record 62.
Club membership 600.

Visitors Mon-Fri except BHs. Dress code. **Societies** booking required. **Green Fees** £25 per day **Prof** Brian Badger **Facilities** ⓐ ⓣ ◻ ◻ ◻ ◻ ◻ ◻ **Conf** facs Corporate Hospitality Days **Location** 2m NE off A635
Hotel ★★★ 80% HL Best Western Hotel Smokies Park, Ashton Road, Bardsley, OLDHAM ☎ 0161 785 5000 ▤ 0161 785 5000   73 en suite

STANDISH
Map 7 SD51

Standish Court Rectory Ln WN6 0XD
☎ 01257 425777   ▤ 01257 425777
web: www.standishgolf.co.uk

18 Holes, 4860yds, Par 68, SSS 64, Course record 63.
Course Designer P Dawson **Location** E of town centre on B5239
Telephone for further details
Hotel ★★★★ 73% HL Macdonald Kilhey Court, Chorley Road, Standish, WIGAN ☎ 0870 1942122 ▤ 0870 1942122   62 en suite

STOCKPORT

Map 7 SJ89

Heaton Moor Mauldeth Rd, Heaton Mersey SK4 3NX
☎ 0161 432 2134 📠 0161 432 2134
e-mail: heatonmoorgolfclub@yahoo.co.uk
web: www.heatonmoorgolfclub.co.uk

Gently undulating parkland with two separate nine holes starting from the clubhouse. The narrow fairways are challenging.

18 Holes, 5970yds, Par 70, SSS 69, Course record 66. Club membership 700.

Visitors Mon-Sun & BHs. Booking required.. Dress code.
Societies booking required. **Green Fees** phone **Prof** Simon Marsh
Facilities ⊕ ⊚ ⊫ ⊡ ⊓ ⊼ ⊟ ⊓ ✔ **Location** M60, junct 1, N of town centre off B5169
Hotel ★★★ 77% HL Bredbury Hall Hotel & Country Club, Goyt Valley, BREDBURY ☎ 0161 430 7421 📠 0161 430 7421 150 en suite

Houldsworth Houldsworth Park, Reddish SK5 6BN
☎ 0161 442 1712 📠 0161 947 9678
e-mail: houldsworthsecretary@hotmail.co.uk
web: www.houldsworthgolfclub.co.uk

Flat, tree-lined parkland course with water hazards. Testing holes 11th (par 4) and 13th (par 5).

18 Holes, 6209yds, Par 71, SSS 70, Course record 65. Club membership 680.

Visitors Mon-Sun & BHs. Booking required. Dress code.
Societies booking required. **Green Fees** phone **Course Designer** Dave Thomas **Prof** Daniel Marsh **Facilities** ⊕ ⊚ ⊫ ⊡ ⊓ ⊼ ⊟
⊓ ✔ **Conf** facs **Location** 4m SE of city centre off A6
Hotel ★★★ 78% HL Best Western Willow Bank, 340-342 Wilmslow Road, Fallowfield, MANCHESTER ☎ 0161 224 0461 📠 0161 224 0461 116 en suite

Marple Barnsfold Rd, Hawk Green, Marple SK6 7EL
☎ 0161 427 2311 & 427 1195 (pro) 📠 0161 427 2311
e-mail: secretary@marple-golf-club.co.uk
web: www.marplegolfclub.co.uk

Parkland with several ponds or other water hazards. Gentle slopes overlook the Cheshire plains.

18 Holes, 5552yds, Par 68, SSS 67, Course record 66. Club membership 600.

Visitors Mon-Sun & BHs. Booking advisable. Dress code.
Societies welcome. **Green Fees** not confirmed **Prof** David Myers
Facilities ⊕ ⊚ ⊫ ⊡ ⊓ ⊼ ⊟ ✔ **Leisure** snooker
Conf Corporate Hospitality Days **Location** S of Marple town centre
Hotel ★★★ 77% HL Bredbury Hall Hotel & Country Club, Goyt Valley, BREDBURY ☎ 0161 430 7421 📠 0161 430 7421 150 en suite

Reddish Vale Southcliffe Rd, Reddish SK5 7EE
☎ 0161 480 2359 📠 0161 480 2359
e-mail: admin@rvgc.co.uk
web: www.rvgc.co.uk

Undulating heathland course designed by Dr A MacKenzie and situated in the Tame valley.

18 Holes, 6086yds, Par 69, SSS 69, Course record 64. Club membership 550.

Visitors Mon-Fri, Sun & BHs. Booking required Sun & BHs.
Societies welcome. **Green Fees** not confirmed **Course Designer** Dr A Mackenzie **Prof** Bob Freeman **Facilities** ⊕ ⊚ ⊫ ⊡ ⊓ ⊼
⊟ ⊓ 🛒 ✔ **Conf** facs Corporate Hospitality Days **Location** Off Reddish Road, M6 junct 27

Hotel ★★★ 73% HL Wycliffe, 74 Edgeley Road, Edgeley, STOCKPORT ☎ 0161 477 5395 📠 0161 477 5395 20 en suite

Stockport Offerton Rd, Offerton SK2 5HL
☎ 0161 427 8369 📠 0161 427 8369
e-mail: info@stockportgolf.co.uk
web: www.stockportgolf.co.uk

A beautifully situated course in wide open countryside with views of the Cheshire and Derbyshire hills. It is not too long but requires that the player plays all the shots to excellent greens. Demanding holes include the dog-leg 3rd, 12th and 18th and the 460yd opening hole is among the toughest in Cheshire. Regional qualifying course for Open Championship.

18 Holes, 6326yds, Par 71, SSS 71, Course record 64. Club membership 500.

Visitors Mon, Wed-Fri, Sun & BHs. Booking advised. Dress code.
Societies booking required. **Green Fees** £55 per day, £45 per 18 holes (£60/£50 Sun & BHs) **Course Designer** P Barrie/A Herd
Prof Gary Norcott **Facilities** ⊕ ⊚ ⊫ ⊡ ⊓ ⊼ ⊟ ⊓ ✔
Conf Corporate Hospitality Days **Location** 4m SE on A627
Hotel ★★★ 77% HL Bredbury Hall Hotel & Country Club, Goyt Valley, BREDBURY ☎ 0161 430 7421 📠 0161 430 7421 150 en suite

SWINTON

Map 7 SD70

Swinton Park East Lancashire Rd M27 5LX
☎ 0161 794 0861 📠 0161 281 0698
web: www.spgolf.co.uk

18 Holes, 6472yds, Par 73, SSS 71.

Course Designer James Braid **Location** Entrance off A580
Telephone for further details
Hotel ★★★ 72% HL Novotel Manchester West, Worsley Brow, WORSLEY, Manchester ☎ 0161 799 3535 📠 0161 799 3535 119 en suite

UPPERMILL

Map 7 SD90

Saddleworth Mountain Ash OL3 6LT
☎ 01457 873653 📠 01457 820647
web: www.saddleworthgolfclub.org.uk

18 Holes, 6118yds, Par 71, SSS 69, Course record 61.

Course Designer George Lowe/Dr McKenzie **Location** E of town centre off A670
Telephone for further details
Hotel ★★★ 80% HL Best Western Hotel Smokies Park, Ashton Road, Bardsley, OLDHAM ☎ 0161 785 5000 📠 0161 785 5000 73 en suite

URMSTON

Map 7 SJ79

Flixton Church Rd, Flixton M41 6EP
☎ 0161 748 2116 📠 0161 748 2116
e-mail: flixtongolfclub@mail.com
web: www.flixtongolfclub.co.uk

Meadowland course bounded by the River Mersey.

9 Holes, 6492yds, Par 71, SSS 71. Club membership 430.

Visitors Mon-Fri, Sun & BHs. Dress code. **Societies** booking required.
Green Fees £15 (£25 Sun) **Prof** Gary Coope **Facilities** ⊕ ⊚
⊫ ⊡ ⊓ ⊼ ⊟ ✔ **Conf** facs Corporate Hospitality Days
Location S of town centre on B5213

continued

Hotel ★★★★ 76% HL Copthorne Hotel Manchester, Clippers Quay, Salford Quays, MANCHESTER ☎ 0161 873 7321 📄 0161 873 7321 166 en suite

WALKDEN
Map 7 SD70

Brackley Municipal M38 9TR
☎ 0161 790 6076

9 Holes, 3003yds, Par 35, SSS 69, Course record 68.
Facilities ⬜ ⛳ Location 2m NW on A6
Telephone for further details
Hotel ★★★ 72% HL Novotel Manchester West, Worsley Brow, WORSLEY, Manchester ☎ 0161 799 3535 📄 0161 799 3535 119 en suite

WESTHOUGHTON
Map 7 SD60

Hart Common Wigan Rd BL5 2BX
☎ 01942 813195

A parkland course on green belt land with many water features, including the signature hole, the 7th, which has water all down the left hand side.

18 Holes, 5719yards, Par 71, SSS 68.
Club membership 400.
Visitors contact club for details. Societies welcome. Green Fees £12 per 18 holes (£16 weekends & BHs) Course Designer Mike Shattock Prof Simon Reeves Facilities ⓣ ⛹ ⬜ 🍴 ⛳ ✦ 🚜 ✦
🌱 Leisure par 3 academy course Conf Corporate Hospitality Days Location on A58 between Bolton and Wigan
Hotel ★★★ 74% HL Ramada Bolton, Manchester Road, Blackrod, BOLTON ☎ 01942 814598 📄 01942 814598 91 en suite

Westhoughton Long Island, School St BL5 2BR
☎ 01942 811085 & 608958 📄 01942 811085
e-mail: honsec.wgc@btconnect.com
web: www.westhoughtongolfclub.co.uk
Compact downland course.

18 Holes, 5918yds, Par 70, SSS 71. Club membership 370.
Visitors Mon, Wed-Sat & BHs. Booking required Sat & BHs. Dress code. Societies booking required. Green Fees £20 weekdays Course Designer Jeff Shuttleworth Facilities ⓣ ⛹ ⬜ 🍴 ⛳
Leisure snooker Conf Corporate Hospitality Days Location 0.5m NW off A58
Hotel ★★★★ 76% HL De Vere Whites, De Havilland Way, HORWICH, Bolton ☎ 01204 667788 📄 01204 667788 125 en suite

WHITEFIELD
Map 7 SD80

Stand The Dales, Ashbourne Grove M45 7NL
☎ 0161 766 3197 📄 0161 796 3234
e-mail: secretary@standgolfclub.co.uk
web: www.standgolfclub.co.uk

A semi-parkland course with five moorland holes. Undulating fairways with views of five counties. A fine test of golf with a very demanding finish.

18 Holes, 6411yds, Par 72, SSS 71, Course record 65.
Club membership 500.
Visitors Mon-Fri & BHs. Booking required. Handicap certificate. Dress code. Societies booking required. Green Fees £35 Course Designer G Lowe/A Herd Prof Mark Dance Facilities ⓣ ⛹ ⬜ 🍴 ⛳

📠 🍴 ✦ Conf Corporate Hospitality Days Location M60 junct 17, follow A56/A667
Hotel ★★★★ 77% HL Mercure Norton Grange Hotel & Spa, Manchester Road, Castleton, ROCHDALE ☎ 0870 1942119 📄 0870 1942119 81 en suite

Whitefield Higher Ln M45 7EZ
☎ 0161 351 2700 📄 0161 351 2712
e-mail: enquiries@whitefieldgolfclub.com
web: www.whitefieldgolfclub.co.uk

Picturesque parkland course with stunning views and well-watered greens. Considered to have some of the best par 3 holes in the North West.

18 Holes, 6063yds, Par 69, SSS 69, Course record 64.
Club membership 540.
Visitors dress code. Societies booking required. Green Fees not confirmed Prof Roy Penney Facilities ⓣ 🍴 ⛹ ⬜ 🍴 ⛳ 🏠
📠 ✦ 🚜 ✦ Leisure indoor swing analysis centre, snooker room Conf facs Corporate Hospitality Days Location M60 junct 17, N of town centre on A665
Hotel ★★★ 88% HL Malmaison Manchester, Piccadilly, MANCHESTER ☎ 0161 278 1000 📄 0161 278 1000 167 en suite

WIGAN
Map 7 SD50

Haigh Hall Golf Complex Copperas Ln WN2 1PE
☎ 01942 831107 📄 01942 831417
web: www.haighhall.net

Balcarres Course: 18 Holes, 6300yards, Par 70, SSS 71.
Crawford Course: 9 Holes, 1446yards, Par 28.
Course Designer Steve Marnoch Location M6 junct 27/M61 junct 5 or 6, signed Haigh Hall
Telephone for further details
Hotel ★★★ 74% HL Ramada Bolton, Manchester Road, Blackrod, BOLTON ☎ 01942 814598 📄 01942 814598 91 en suite

Wigan Arley Hall, Haigh WN1 2UH
☎ 01257 421360 📄 01257 426500
e-mail: info@wigangolfclub.co.uk
web: www.wigangolfclub.co.uk

Fairly level parkland with outstanding views and magnificent trees. The fine old clubhouse is the original Arley Hall, and is surrounded by a medieval moat.

18 Holes, 6009yds, Par 70, SSS 69. Club membership 300.
Visitors Mon. Wed-Fri, Sun & BHs. Booking required Sun & BHs. Handicap certificate. Dress code. Societies booking required. Green Fees not confirmed Course Designer Gaunt & Marnoch Facilities ⓣ 🍴 ⛹ ⬜ 🍴 ⛳ Conf facs Corporate Hospitality Days Location M6 junct 27, 3m NE off B5238
Hotel ★★★★ 73% HL Macdonald Kilhey Court, Chorley Road, Standish, WIGAN ☎ 0870 1942122 📄 0870 1942122 62 en suite

WORSLEY
Map 7 SD70

Ellesmere Old Clough Ln M28 7HZ
☎ 0161 799 0554 (office) 📄 0161 790 2122
e-mail: honsec@ellesmeregolfclub.co.uk
web: www.ellesmeregolfclub.co.uk
Parkland with natural hazards and hard walking. Trees and two streams running through the course make shot strategy an important
continued

aspect of the round. Testing holes: 3rd (par 5), 9th (par 3), 15th (par 5).

18 Holes, 6248yds, Par 70, SSS 70, Course record 67. Club membership 700.

Visitors booking required. Dress code. **Societies** welcome. **Green Fees** £40 per day, £30 per round (£35 per round weekends) **Prof** Simon Wakefield **Facilities** ⑪ ⑩ ⓛ ☐ ⌷ ⌷ △ 🖿 ♪ **Conf** Corporate Hospitality Days **Location** N of village off A580 **Hotel** ★★★ 72% HL Novotel Manchester West, Worsley Brow, WORSLEY, Manchester ☎ 0161 799 3535 📄 0161 799 3535 119 en suite

HAMPSHIRE

ALDERSHOT
Map 4 SU85

Army Laffans Rd GU11 2HF
☎ 01252 337272   📄 01252 337562
e-mail: secretary@armygolfclub.com
web: www.armygolfclub.co.uk

One of the oldest clubs in Hampshire situated on 165 acres of low, undulating heathland and woodland. A challenging course with three tricky par threes and the final four holes provide a demanding finish.

18 Holes, 6550yds, Par 71, SSS 71, Course record 66. Club membership 750.

Visitors Mon-Fri except BHs. Handicap certificate. Dress code. **Societies** booking required. **Green Fees** £50 for 36 holes, £37 for 18 holes **Course Designer** Frank Pennine/Mackenzie Ebert **Prof** Graham Cowley **Facilities** ⑪ ⑩ ⓛ ☐ ⌷ △ 🖿 ♪ 🛺 ♪ **Conf** facs Corporate Hospitality Days **Location** 1.5m N of town centre off A323/A325

Hotel ★★★ 64% HL Potters International, 1 Fleet Road, ALDERSHOT ☎ 01252 344000 📄 01252 344000 103 en suite

ALTON
Map 4 SU73

Alton Old Odiham Rd GU34 4BU
☎ 01420 82042
web: www.altongolfclub.org.uk

9 Holes, 5744yds, Par 68, SSS 68, Course record 62.
Course Designer James Braid **Location** 2m N of Alton off B3349 at Golden Pot
Telephone for further details
Hotel ★★★ 77% HL Alton Grange, London Road, ALTON ☎ 01420 86565 📄 01420 86565 30 en suite

Worldham Park Cakers Ln, East Worldham GU34 3BF
☎ 01420 543151   📄 01420 544606
e-mail: manager@worldhamgolfclub.co.uk
web: www.worldhamgolfclub.co.uk

The course is in a picturesque parkland setting with an abundance of challenging holes (dog-legs, water and sand). Suitable for all golfing standards.

Worldham Golf Course: 18 Holes, 6257yds, Par 72, SSS 70. Club membership 400.

Visitors Mon-Sun & BHs. Dress code. **Societies** welcome. **Green Fees** £18 per 18 holes Mon-Thu, £20 Fri (£22 weekends and BHs) **Course Designer** F J Whidborne **Prof** Anthony Cook **Facilities** ⑪ ⑩ by prior arrangement ⓛ ☐ ⌷ △ 🖿 ⌷ 🛺 ♪ ♪ **Conf** Corporate Hospitality Days **Location** A31, on B3004 **Hotel** ★★★ 77% HL Alton Grange, London Road, ALTON ☎ 01420 86565 📄 01420 86565 30 en suite

AMPFIELD
Map 4 SU42

Ampfield Winchester Rd SO51 9BQ
☎ 01794 368480
e-mail: clubhouse@ampfieldgolf.com
web: www.ampfieldgolf.com

Pretty parkland course designed by Henry Cotton in 1963. Well-bunkered greens.

Ampfield Par Three Golf Club: 18 Holes, 2478yds, Par 54, SSS 53, Course record 49. Club membership 230.

Visitors Mon-Sun & BHs. Dress code. **Societies** booking required. **Green Fees** not confirmed **Course Designer** Henry Cotton **Facilities** ⑪ ⑩ ⓛ ☐ ⌷ △ 🖿 ⌷ ◇ ♪ **Conf** facs Corporate Hospitality Days **Location** 4m NE of Romsey on A31 **Hotel** ★★★ 77% HL Chilworth Manor, CHILWORTH, Southampton ☎ 023 8076 7333 📄 023 8076 7333 95 en suite

ANDOVER
Map 4 SU34

Andover 51 Winchester Rd SP10 2EF
☎ 01264 358040   📄 01264 358040
e-mail: secretary@andovergolfclub.co.uk
web: www.andovergolfclub.co.uk

Undulating downland course combining a good test of golf for all abilities with breathtaking views across Hampshire countryside. Well-guarded greens and a notable par 3 9th (225yds) with the tee perched on top of a hill, 100ft above the green. Excellent drainage on the chalk base.

9 Holes, 6096yds, Par 70, SSS 69, Course record 64. Club membership 450.

Visitors Mon-Sun & BHs. Dress code. **Societies** booking required. **Green Fees** £20 per 18 holes (£25 weekends) **Course Designer** J H Taylor **Facilities** ⑪ ⑩ ⓛ ☐ ⌷ △ 🖿 ⌷ ♪ **Conf** facs Corporate Hospitality Days **Location** 0.5m S on A3057 **Hotel** ★★★ 63% HL Quality Hotel Andover, Micheldever Road, ANDOVER ☎ 01264 369111 📄 01264 369111 49 en suite

Hampshire Winchester Rd SP11 7TB
☎ 01264 357555 (pro shop) & 356462 (office)
📄 01264 356606
e-mail: enquiry@thehampshiregolfclub.co.uk
web: www.thehampshiregolfclub.co.uk

Pleasant undulating parkland with fine views and a backdrop of 35,000 young trees and shrubs. The challenging Manor course has two lakes to catch the unwary. Based on chalk which provides very good drainage, with a superb finishing hole.

Manor: 18 Holes, 6145yds, Par 71, SSS 69, Course record 67. Club membership 500.

Visitors Mon-Sun & BHs. Booking required. Dress code. **Societies** booking required. **Green Fees** £22 per 18 holes (£29 weekends & BHs) **Prof** Tim Baker **Facilities** ⑪ ⓛ ☐ ⌷ △ 🖿 ⌷ ♪ 🛺 ♪ 🏌 **Leisure** 9 hole par 3 course **Conf** facs Corporate Hospitality Days **Location** 1.5m S of Andover on A3057 **Hotel** ★★★ 63% HL Quality Hotel Andover, Micheldever Road, ANDOVER ☎ 01264 369111 📄 01264 369111 49 en suite

BARTON-ON-SEA

Map 4 SZ29

Barton-on-Sea Milford Rd BH25 5PP
☎ 01425 615308   📠 01425 621457
e-mail: admin@barton-on-sea-golf.co.uk
web: www.barton-on-sea-golf.co.uk

A cliff top course with 3 loops of nine giving a great variety and challenge to golfers of all handicaps. Fine views over the Solent and to the Isle of Wight and the Needles.

Becton: 9 Holes, 3182yds, Par 36.
Needles: 9 Holes, 3339yds, Par 36.
Stroller: 9 Holes, 3125yds, Par 36. Club membership 750.

Visitors Mon-Sun & BHs. Booking required.. Handicap certificate. Dress code. **Societies** booking required **Green Fees** £44 per day (£55 weekends & BHs) **Course Designer** Vardon/Colt/Stutt **Prof** Peter Rodgers **Facilities** ⑪ 🍴 by prior arrangement 🛒 🖥 🍴 🏌 📷 🎯 🚲 🎣 **Leisure** snooker tables **Conf** Corporate Hospitality Days **Location** B3058 SE of town **Hotel** ★★★★★ HL Chewton Glen Hotel & Spa, Christchurch Road, NEW MILTON ☎ 01425 275341 📠 01425 275341 58 en suite

BASINGSTOKE

Map 4 SU65

See also **Rotherwick**

Basingstoke Kempshott Park RG23 7LL
☎ 01256 465990   📠 01256 331793
e-mail: office@basingstokegolfclub.co.uk
web: www.basingstokegolfclub.co.uk

A well-maintained parkland course. Excellent bunkering requires good course management from the tee and all clubs will be required with many long testing par 4's. A true test of golf, yet fair and playable for the less experienced golfer.

18 Holes, 6350yds, Par 70, SSS 70, Course record 63. Club membership 700.

Visitors Mon-Fri except BHs. Handicap certificate. Dress code. **Societies** booking required. **Green Fees** £52 per day, £42 per round. Reduced winter fees **Course Designer** James Braid **Prof** Richard Woolley **Facilities** ⑪ 🍴 🛒 🖥 🍴 🏌 📷 🎯 🚲 🎣 **Conf** facs Corporate Hospitality Days **Location** M3 junct 7, 1m SW on A30 **Hotel** ★★★★ 73% HL Apollo, Aldermaston Roundabout, BASINGSTOKE ☎ 01256 796700 📠 01256 796700   125 en suite

Dummer Dummer RG25 2AD
☎ 01256 397888 (office) & 397950 (pro)
📠 01256 397889
e-mail: enquiries@dummergolfclub.com
web: www.dummergolfclub.com

Designed by Peter Alliss, this course is set in 165 acres of fine Hampshire countryside with panoramic views. The course meanders around lakes, mature trees and hedgerows. The course combines large, level teeing areas, undulating fairways, fast true greens and cleverly positioned bunkers to provide a challenging golf experience.

18 Holes, 6533yds, Par 72, SSS 71, Course record 62. Club membership 500.

Visitors Mon-Sun & BHs. Booking required. Dress code. **Societies** welcome. **Green Fees** not confirmed **Course Designer** Pete Alliss **Prof** Andrew Fannon **Facilities** ⑪ 🍴 🛒 🖥 🍴 🏌 📷

🍴 🚲 🎣 🎯 **Conf** facs Corporate Hospitality Days **Location** M3 junct 7, towards Dummer, club 0.25m on left **Hotel** ★★★★ 76% CHH Audleys Wood, Alton Road, BASINGSTOKE ☎ 01256 817555 📠 01256 817555   72 en suite

Weybrook Park Rooksdown Ln RG24 9NT
☎ 01256 320347   📠 01256 812973
e-mail: paul.shearman@weybrookpark.co.uk
web: www.weybrookpark.co.uk

An all year course designed to be enjoyable for all standards of player. Easy walking with fabulous views. Extensive new practice facility opened in 2008 and a further 9 holes due to open 2010.

18 Holes, 6468yds, Par 71, SSS 71. Club membership 600.

Visitors Mon-Sun & BHs. Booking required. Handicap certificate. Dress code. **Societies** welcome. **Green Fees** phone **Prof** Anthony Dillon **Facilities** ⑪ 🍴 🛒 🖥 🍴 🏌 📷 🎯 🚲 🎣 **Conf** facs Corporate Hospitality Days **Location** 2m W of town centre via A339 **Hotel** ★★★★ 73% HL Apollo, Aldermaston Roundabout, BASINGSTOKE ☎ 01256 796700 📠 01256 796700   125 en suite

BORDON

Map 4 SU73

Blackmoor Firgrove Rd, Whitehill GU35 9EH
☎ 01420 472775   📠 01420 487666
e-mail: admin@blackmoorgolf.co.uk
web: www.blackmoorgolf.co.uk

A first-class moorland course with a great variety of holes. Fine greens and wide pine tree-lined fairways are a distinguishing feature. The ground is mainly flat and walking easy.

18 Holes, 6164yds, Par 69, SSS 70, Course record 63. Club membership 650.

Visitors Mon-Fri except BHs. Handicap certificate. Dress code. **Societies** booking required. **Green Fees** not confirmed **Course Designer** H S Colt **Prof** Stephen Clay **Facilities** ⑪ 🍴 by prior arrangement 🛒 🖥 🍴 🏌 📷 🎯 **Conf** Corporate Hospitality Days **Location** 6m S from Farnham on A325, through Whitehill, right at rdbt **Hotel** ★★★ 82% HL Old Thorns Hotel Golf & Country Estate, Griggs Green, LIPHOOK ☎ 01428 724555 📠 01428 724555 33 en suite

BOTLEY

Map 4 SU51

Macdonald Botley Park Hotel, Golf & Country Club
Winchester Rd, Boorley Green SO32 2UA
☎ 01489 780888   📠 01489 789242
e-mail: golfbotley@macdonald-hotels.co.uk
web: www.macdonaldhotels.co.uk

Pleasantly undulating course with water hazards. Driving range and country club facilities.

Macdonald Botley Park Hotel, Golf & CC: 18 Holes, 6341yds, Par 70, SSS 70, Course record 67. Club membership 1500.

Visitors Mon-Sun & BHs. Booking required. Dress code. **Societies** booking required. **Green Fees** not confirmed **Course Designer** Ewan Murray **Prof** Tim Barter **Facilities** ⑪ 🍴 🛒 🖥 🍴 🏌 📷 🎯 🍴 🚲 🎣 **Leisure** hard tennis courts, heated indoor swimming pool, squash, sauna, gymnasium, health and beauty spa **Conf** facs Corporate Hospitality Days **Location** 1m NW of Botley on B3354

continued

Hotel ★★★★ 76% CHH Macdonald Botley Park, Golf & Country Club, Winchester Road, Boorley Green, BOTLEY ☎ 01489 780 888 & 0870 194 2132 🗎 01489 780 888   130 en suite

BROCKENHURST   Map 4 SU20

Brokenhurst Manor Sway Rd SO42 7SG
☎ 01590 623332 (Secretary) 🗎 01590 624691
e-mail: secretary@brokenhurst-manor.org.uk
web: www.brokenhurst-manor.org.uk
An attractive forest course set in the New Forest, with the unusual feature of three loops of six holes each to complete the round. Fascinating holes include the short 5th and 12th, and the 4th and 17th, both dog-legs. A stream also features on seven of the holes.
18 Holes, 6222yds, Par 70, SSS 70, Course record 63. Club membership 700.
Visitors contact club for details. **Societies** booking required. **Green Fees** not confirmed **Course Designer** H S Colt **Prof** Bruce Parker **Facilities** ⓗ ⍦ 🌭 ☐ ⍦ 🏌 🏠 🛒 ⚷ **Conf** Corporate Hospitality Days **Location** 1m S on B3055
Hotel ★★ 63% HL Watersplash, The Rise, BROCKENHURST ☎ 01590 622344 🗎 01590 622344   23 en suite

BURLEY   Map 4 SU20

Burley Cott Ln BH24 4BB
☎ 01425 402431 & 403737 🗎 01425 404168
e-mail: secretary@burleygolfclub.co.uk
web: www.burleygolfclub.co.uk
Undulating heather and gorseland. The 7th requires an accurately placed tee shot to obtain par 4. Played off different tees on second nine.
9 Holes, 6151yds, Par 71, SSS 70, Course record 62. Club membership 520.
Visitors Mon-Fri, Sun & BHs. Sat after 4pm. Handicap certificate. Dress code. **Green Fees** £20 per 18 holes (£25 weekends) **Facilities** ⓗ ⍦ 🌭 ☐ ⍦ 🏌 ⚷ **Location** E of village
Hotel ★★★ 71% CHH Moorhill House, BURLEY ☎ 01425 403285 🗎 01425 403285   31 en suite

CORHAMPTON   Map 4 SU62

Corhampton Shepherds Farm Ln SO32 3GZ
☎ 01489 877279 🗎 01489 877680
e-mail: secretary@corhamptongc.co.uk
web: www.corhamptongc.co.uk
Free draining downland course situated in the heart of the picturesque Meon Valley.
18 Holes, 6398yds, Par 71, SSS 71. Club membership 800.
Visitors Mon-Fri except BHs. Handicap certificate. Dress code. **Societies** booking required. **Green Fees** not confirmed **Prof** Ian Roper **Facilities** ⓗ ⍦ 🌭 ☐ ⍦ 🏌 🏠 🛒 ⚷ **Location** 1m W of Corhampton off B3035
Hotel ★★★ 77% HL Old House Hotel & Restaurant, The Square, WICKHAM ☎ 01329 833049 🗎 01329 833049   12 en suite

CRONDALL   Map 4 SU74

Oak Park Heath Ln GU10 5PB
☎ 01252 850850 🗎 01252 850851
e-mail: oakpark@crown-golf.co.uk
web: www.oakparkgolf.co.uk
Oak Park is a gently undulating parkland course overlooking a pretty village. Woodland is undulating on holes 10 to 13. Panoramic views, mature trees and very challenging where every aspect of the game is tested
Woodland: 18 Holes, 6352yds, Par 70, SSS 70, Course record 69.
Village: 9 Holes, 3279yds, Par 36. Club membership 900.
Visitors Mon-Sun & BHs. Booking required Fri-Sun & BHs. Dress code. **Societies** booking required. **Green Fees** not confirmed **Course Designer** Patrick Dawson **Prof** Gary Murton **Facilities** ⓗ ⍦ 🌭 ☐ ⍦ 🏌 🏠 🛒 ⚷ 🏷 **Conf** facs Corporate Hospitality Days **Location** 0.5m E of village off A287 Farnham-Odiham
Hotel ★★★ 75% HL Mercure Bush, The Borough, FARNHAM ☎ 0870 400 8225 & 01252 715237 🗎 0870 400 8225   83 en suite

DENMEAD   Map 4 SU61

Furzeley Furzeley Rd PO7 6TX
☎ 023 9223 1180 🗎 023 9223 0921
A well-laid parkland course with many features including several strategically placed lakes which provide a good test set in beautiful scenery. Straight hitting and club selection on the short holes is the key to manufacturing a low score.
Furzeley Golf Course: 18 Holes, 4488yds, Par 62, SSS 61, Course record 56. Club membership 250.
Visitors Mon-Sun & BHs. **Societies** booking required. **Green Fees** £15 per 18 holes, £9 per 9 holes (£16/£9.50 weekends & BHs) **Course Designer** Mark Sale/Robert Brown **Prof** Derek Brown **Facilities** ⓗ 🏌 ☐ ⍦ 🏠 🛒 ⚷ **Location** from Waterlooville NW onto Hambledon road, signed
Hotel ★★★★ 74% HL Portsmouth Marriott Hotel, Southampton Road, PORTSMOUTH ☎ 0870 400 7285 🗎 0870 400 7285   174 en suite

DIBDEN   Map 4 SU40

Dibden Main Rd SO45 5TB
☎ 023 8020 7508 & 8084 5596
web: www.nfdc.gov.uk/golf
Course 1: 18 Holes, 5931yds, Par 70, SSS 69, Course record 64.
Course 2: 9 Holes, 1520yds, Par 29.
Course Designer Hamilton Stutt **Location** 2m NW of Dibden Purlieu, off A326 to Hythe
Telephone for further details
Hotel ★★★ 74% HL Novotel Southampton, 1 West Quay Road, SOUTHAMPTON ☎ 023 8033 0550 🗎 023 8033 0550   121 en suite

ENGLAND

EASTLEIGH   Map 4 SU41

East Horton Golf Centre Mortimers Ln, Fair Oak SO50 7EA
☎ 023 8060 2111   📠 023 8069 6280
e-mail: info@easthortongolf.co.uk
web: www.easthortongolf.co.uk

Courses set out over 260 acres of Hampshire countryside with parkland fairways and mature trees in abundance. The Greenwood course sets out across a stream and around a large woodland, returning to the stream for the 18th. Fine views from the top holes and from the 16th tee, even the best golfers need to concentrate with a 160yd carry over an imposing lake. The Parkland course has relatively wide fairways and the stream has to be negotiated a few times. The five par 3s may not be as easy as they appear.

Greenwood: 18 Holes, 5960yds, Par 70, SSS 69.
Parkland: 18 Holes, 5907yds, Par 70, SSS 70.
Club membership 700.

Visitors Mon-Sun & BHs. Booking required. Dress code.
Societies booking required. **Green Fees** £18 per 18 holes, Fri £20, weekends £22) **Course Designer** Guy Hunt **Prof** Miles Harding/Conrad Claxton **Facilities** 🅟 🍴 🍺 ⬜ 🍴 ⚒ 🏠 🏴 ◇ ⚘ 🚍
⚘ 🏳 **Leisure** sauna, gymnasium, 9 hole par 3 course **Conf** facs Corporate Hospitality Days **Location** off B3037
Hotel ★★★ 73% HL Marwell, Thompsons Lane, Colden Common, Marwell, WINCHESTER ☎ 01962 777681 📠 01962 777681 66 en suite

Fleming Park Passfield Av SO50 9NL
☎ 023 8061 2797   📠 023 8065 1686

18 Holes, 4524yds, Par 65, SSS 62, Course record 62.

Course Designer David Miller **Location** E of town centre
Telephone for further details
Hotel BUD Travelodge Southampton Eastleigh, Twyford Road, EASTLEIGH ☎ 08719 846 213 📠 08719 846 213 44 en suite

FAREHAM   Map 4 SU50

Cams Hall Cams Hall Estate PO16 8UP
☎ 01329 827222   📠 01329 827111

Two Peter Alliss/Clive Clark designed golf courses. The Creek Course is coastal and has salt and fresh water lakes and the fairways are lined with undulating hills. The Park Course is designed in the grounds of Cams Hall.

Creek Course: 18 Holes, 6244yds, Par 71, SSS 70,
Course record 69.
Park Course: 9 Holes, 3202yds, Par 36, SSS 36.
Club membership 1100.

Visitors Mon-Fri. Weekends & BHs pm only. Booking required.
Dress code. **Societies** booking required. **Green Fees** phone **Course Designer** Peter Alliss **Prof** Jason Neve **Facilities** 🅟 🍴 🍺 ⬜
🍴 ⬚ 🏠 🏴 ⚘ 🚍 ⚘ **Leisure** sauna **Conf** facs **Location** M27 junct 11, A27
Hotel ★★★ 72% HL Lysses House, 51 High Street, FAREHAM
☎ 01329 822622 📠 01329 822622 21 en suite

FARNBOROUGH   Map 4 SU85

Southwood Ively Rd, Cove GU14 0LJ
☎ 01252 548700   📠 01252 549091
e-mail: enquiries@southwoodgolfcourse.co.uk
web: www.southwoodgolfcourse.co.uk

Municipal parkland golf course.

Southwood Golf Course: 18 Holes, 5738yds, Par 69, SSS 68,
Course record 61. Club membership 400.

Visitors Mon-Sun & BHs. Booking advisable. **Societies** booking required. **Green Fees** not confirmed **Course Designer** Hawtree & Son **Prof** Chris Hudson **Facilities** 🅟 🍴 🍺 ⬜ 🍴 ⚒ 🏠 🏴 ⚘
🚍 ⚘ **Conf** facs Corporate Hospitality Days **Location** 0.5m W
Hotel ★★★ 79% HL Holiday Inn Farnborough, Lynchford Road, FARNBOROUGH ☎ 0870 400 9029 & 01252 894300
📠 0870 400 9029 142 en suite

FLEET   Map 4 SU85

North Hants Minley Rd GU51 1RF
☎ 01252 616443   📠 01252 811627
web: www.northhantsgolf.co.uk

18 Holes, 6472yds, Par 70, SSS 72, Course record 65.

Course Designer James Braid **Location** 0.25m N of Fleet station on B3013
Telephone for further details
Hotel ★★★ 72% HL Lismoyne, Church Road, FLEET
☎ 01252 628555 📠 01252 628555 62 en suite

GOSPORT   Map 4 SZ69

Gosport & Stokes Bay Off Fort Rd, Haslar PO12 2AT
☎ 023 9252 7941
e-mail: secretary@gosportandstokesbaygolfclub.co.uk
web: www.gosportandstokesbaygolfclub.co.uk

A testing links course overlooking the Solent, with plenty of gorse and short rough. Changing winds.

9 Holes, 5995yds, Par 70, SSS 69, Course record 65.
Club membership 400.

Visitors contact club for details. **Societies** welcome. **Green Fees** £20 Mon-Fri (£25 Sat). Twilight £10 **Facilities** 🅟 ⬜ 🍴 🏠 🏴 ⚘
Location A32 S from Fareham, E onto Fort Rd to Haslar
Hotel ★★★ 72% HL Lysses House, 51 High Street, FAREHAM
☎ 01329 822622 📠 01329 822622 21 en suite

HARTLEY WINTNEY — Map 4 SU75

Hartley Wintney London Rd RG27 8PT
☎ 01252 844211 (Sec/Gen Mgr) 📠 01252 844211
e-mail: office@hartleywintneygolfclub.com
web: www.hartleywintneygolfclub.com

Easy walking parkland and partly wooded course in pleasant countryside. Provides a challenging test for golfers of all abilities with many mature trees and water hazards.

18 Holes, 6240yds, Par 71, SSS 71, Course record 63.
Club membership 750.

Visitors Mon-Sun & BHs. Booking required weekends. Dress code. **Societies** booking required. **Green Fees** £48 per day, £36 per 18 holes (£42 per 18 holes weekends) **Prof** Martin Smith **Facilities** ⒯ 🍴 ⤴ 🏠 🛎 ✆ **Leisure** indoor teaching studio **Conf** facs Corporate Hospitality Days **Location** NE of village on A30
Hotel ★★★ 79% HL The Elvetham Hotel, HARTLEY WINTNEY ☎ 01252 844871 📠 01252 844871 70 en suite

HAYLING ISLAND — Map 4 SU70

Hayling Links Ln PO11 0BX
☎ 023 9246 4446 📠 023 9246 1119
e-mail: members@haylinggolf.co.uk
web: www.haylinggolf.co.uk

A delightful links course among the dunes offering fine seascapes and views of the Isle of Wight. Varying sea breezes and sometimes strong winds ensure that the course seldom plays the same two days running. Testing holes at the 12th and 13th, both par 4. Club selection is important.

18 Holes, 6531yds, Par 71, SSS 71, Course record 65.
0 Holes, 0. Club membership 1000.

Visitors Mon-Sun except BHs. Booking required Tue & Wed. Handicap certificate. Dress code. **Societies** booking required. **Green Fees** £62 per day, £50 per round **Course Designer** Taylor 1905, Simpson 1933 **Prof** Mark Treleaven **Facilities** ⒯ 🍴 ⤴ 🛒 🏠 ✆ **Conf** facs Corporate Hospitality Days **Location** SW side of island at West Town
Hotel ★★★ 79% HL Brookfield, Havant Road, EMSWORTH ☎ 01243 373363 📠 01243 373363 39 en suite

KINGSCLERE — Map 4 SU55

Sandford Springs RG26 5RT
☎ 01635 296800 & 296808 (Pro Shop)
📠 01635 296801
e-mail: info@sandfordspringsgolf.co.uk
web: www.sandfordsprings.co.uk

The course has unique variety in beautiful surroundings and offers three distinctive loops of nine holes. There are water hazards, woodlands and gradients to negotiate, providing a challenge for all playing categories.

The Park: 9 Holes, 2974yds, Par 34.
The Lakes: 9 Holes, 3127yds, Par 35.
The Wood: 9 Holes, 3148yds, Par 36.
Club membership 700.

Visitors Mon-Fri. Weekends & BHs after 1pm. Booking required. Dress code. **Societies** booking required. **Green Fees** Mon-Thu £35 per 18 holes, Fri-Sun £40 **Course Designer** Hawtree & Son **Prof** Andrew Wild **Facilities** ⒯ 🍴 ⤴ 🛒 🏠 ✆

🛎 ✆ **Conf** facs Corporate Hospitality Days **Location** on A339 between Basingstoke & Newbury

Sandford Springs

Hotel ★★★★ 73% HL Apollo, Aldermaston Roundabout, BASINGSTOKE ☎ 01256 796700 📠 01256 796700 125 en suite

KINGSLEY — Map 4 SU73

Dean Farm GU35 9NG
☎ 01420 489478
web: www.deanfarmgolf.co.uk

Undulating parkland course.

9 Holes, 1600yds, Par 31.

Visitors contact club for details. **Societies** welcome. **Green Fees** weekdays £12 per day, £6 per 9 holes. **Prof** Matthew Howard **Facilities** ⒯ ⤴ 🛒 🏠 🔧 ✆ **Location** W of village off B3004
Hotel ★★★ 77% HL Alton Grange, London Road, ALTON ☎ 01420 86565 📠 01420 86565 30 en suite

LECKFORD — Map 4 SU33

Leckford SO20 6JF
☎ 01264 810320 📠 01264 811122

Old Course: 9 Holes, 6394yds, Par 72, SSS 71.
New Course: 9 Holes, 4562yds, Par 66, SSS 62.

Prof Tony Ashton **Facilities** ⤴ ⤴ ✆ **Location** 1m SW off A3057
Telephone for further details
Hotel ★★★ 63% HL Quality Hotel Andover, Micheldever Road, ANDOVER ☎ 01264 369111 📠 01264 369111 49 en suite

LEE-ON-THE-SOLENT — Map 4 SU50

Lee-on-the-Solent Brune Ln PO13 9PB
☎ 023 9255 1170 📠 023 9255 4233
e-mail: enquiries@leeonthesolentgolfclub.co.uk
web: www.leegolf.co.uk

Predominately heath and oak woodland. While not long in length, still a good test of golf requiring accuracy off the tee to score well. Excellent greens and five very challenging par 3's.

18 Holes, 5962yds, Par 69, SSS 69, Course record 63.
Club membership 725.

Visitors contact club for details. **Societies** welcome. **Green Fees** not confirmed **Prof** Rob Edwards **Facilities** ⒯ 🍴 ⤴ 🛒 🏠 ⤴ 🏠 ✆ 🔧 **Conf** facs Corporate Hospitality Days **Location** 3m S of Fareham
Hotel ★★★ 72% HL Lysses House, 51 High Street, FAREHAM ☎ 01329 822622 📠 01329 822622 21 en suite

LIPHOOK
Map 4 SU83

Liphook Wheatsheaf Enclosure GU30 7EH
☎ 01428 723271 & 723785 🖹 01428 724853
e-mail: secretary@liphookgolfclub.com
web: www.liphookgolfclub.com
Heathland course with easy walking and fine views.

18 Holes, 6167yds, Par 70, SSS 69, Course record 67.
Club membership 800.

Visitors handicap certificate. Dress code. **Societies** booking
required. **Green Fees** £67 per day, £53 per round (£70/£60 Sat,
£70 Sun & BHs pm only) **Course Designer** A C Croome **Prof** Ian
Mowbray **Facilities** ⓣ ⓛ ⊑ ⊡ ⊐ ⊑ ⊟ ⊕ ♛ ◈ ♙ ♘
Conf Corporate Hospitality Days **Location** 1m S on B2070
Hotel ★★★★ 76% HL Lythe Hill Hotel and Spa, Petworth Road,
HASLEMERE ☎ 01428 651251 🖹 01428 651251 41 en suite

Old Thorns Golf & Country Estate see page 123
Griggs Green GU30 7PE
☎ 01428 724555 🖹 01428 725036
e-mail: sales@oldthorns.com
web: www.oldthorns.com

LYNDHURST
Map 4 SU20

Bramshaw Brook SO43 7HE
☎ 023 8081 3433 🖹 023 8081 3460
web: www.bramshaw.co.uk
Manor Course: 18 Holes, 6527yds, Par 71, SSS 71,
Course record 65.
Forest Course: 18 Holes, 5774yds, Par 69, SSS 68,
Course record 65.

Prof Clive Bonner **Facilities** ⓣ ⓛ ⊑ ⊡ ⊐ ⊑ ⊟ ⊕
◇ ♛ 🛒 ◈ **Leisure** practice bunker **Conf** facs Corporate
Hospitality Days **Location** M27 junct 1, 1m W on B3079
Telephone for further details
Hotel ★★★ 83% HL Bell Inn, BROOK ☎ 023 8081 2214
🖹 023 8081 2214 27 en suite

New Forest Southampton Rd SO43 7BU
☎ 023 8028 2484 & 8028 3094 🖹 023 8028 4030
e-mail: secretarynfgc@aol.com
web: www.newforestgolfclub.co.uk
This picturesque heathland course is situated in an area of
outstanding natural beauty above the village of Lyndhurst. The
first two holes are somewhat teasing, as is the 485yd (par 5) 9th.
Walking is easy.

18 Holes, 5536yds, Par 69, SSS 67, Course record 64.
Club membership 500.

Visitors Mon-Sat & BHs. Sun pm. Booking required. Handicap
certificate. Dress code. **Societies** booking required. **Green
Fees** phone **Prof** Kevin Caplehorn **Facilities** ⓣ ⓛ ⊑ ⊡
⊐ ⊑ ⊟ ⊕ ◈ **Conf** facs Corporate Hospitality Days
Location 0.5m NE off A35
Hotel ★★★ 75% HL Best Western Crown, High Street,
LYNDHURST ☎ 023 8028 2922 🖹 023 8028 2922 38 en suite

NEW ALRESFORD
Map 4 SU53

Alresford Cheriton Rd, Tichborne Down SO24 0PN
☎ 01962 733746 & 733998 (pro shop) 🖹 01962 736040
e-mail: secretary@alresfordgolf.co.uk
web: www.alresfordgolf.co.uk

A rolling downland course on well-drained chalk. The five difficult
par 3s, tree-lined fairways and well-guarded fast greens ensure that
the course offers a true test of skill, even for the most experienced
golfer. Regular venue for county tournaments.

18 Holes, 5914yds, Par 69, SSS 69, Course record 63.
Club membership 600.

Visitors Mon-Sun except BHs. Dress code. **Societies** booking required.
Green Fees summer £32 per 18 holes (£40 weekends). Winter
£24/£30 **Course Designer** Scott Webb Young **Prof** Malcolm Scott
Facilities ⓣ ⓛ by prior arrangement ⊑ ⊡ ⊐ ⊑ ⊟
◈ ◈ **Conf** Corporate Hospitality Days **Location** situated 1m S of
Alresford on the B3046 with easy access from the A31 and M3
Hotel ★★ 67% HL Swan, 11 West Street, ALRESFORD
☎ 01962 732302 & 734427 🖹 01962 732302 23 en suite

NEW MILTON
Map 4 SZ29

Chewton Glen Hotel Christchurch Rd BH25 5QS
☎ 01425 275341 🖹 01425 272310
web: www.chewtonglen.com
Chewton Glen Hotel: 9 Holes, 854yds, Par 27.

Facilities ⓣ ⓛ ⊑ ⊡ ⊟ ◇ **Leisure** hard tennis courts,
outdoor and indoor heated swimming pool, sauna, gymnasium, Spa
& health club **Conf** facs Corporate Hospitality Days **Location** off A337
W of town centre
Telephone for further details
Hotel ★★★★★ HL Chewton Glen Hotel & Spa, Christchurch
Road, NEW MILTON ☎ 01425 275341 🖹 01425 275341 58 en suite

OVERTON
Map 4 SU54

Test Valley Micheldever Rd RG25 3DS
☎ 01256 771737 🖹 01256 771285
e-mail: pro@testvalleygolf.com
web: www.testvalleygolf.com
A downland course with excellent drainage, fine year-round greens
and prominent water and bunker features. On undulating terrain with
lovely views over the Hampshire countryside.

18 Holes, 6663yds, Par 72, SSS 69, Course record 62.
Club membership 500.

Visitors Mon-Sun & BHs. Booking required. Dress code.

continued

OLD THORNS

HAMPSHIRE - LIPHOOK - MAP 4 SU83

The wonderful location of this demanding 18 hole championship course makes it a delight for golfers of all standards. Set in a country estate of 400 acres, the course winds its way through rolling hills past natural springs and lakes and offers spectacular views across the beautiful Hampshire countryside. Designed in 1976 by Commander John Harris, the construction was overseen by former golfer and broadcaster Peter Allis, and opened in 1982. The 10th is a particularly tricky hole, while the 16th has a sign reading 'if your tee shot does not come to rest on the green could you please put a pound in the charity box on the bar'. It is a challenging course and one with many rewards.

Griggs Green GU30 7PE ☎ 01428 724555 🖺 01428 725036
e-mail: sales@oldthorns.com **web:** www.oldthorns.com
Old Thorns Golf & Country Estate: 18 Holes, 6461yds, Par 72, SSS 72. Club membership 200.
Visitors Mon-Sun & BHs. Booking required BHs. Dress code. **Societies** booking required. **Green Fees** £40 per round (£50 weekends and BHs) **Course Designer** Peter Alliss **Prof** Peter Chapman **Facilities** ⑨ ⑩ 🖺 🖵 ⑨🗍 ⚊🗐🏌🛇🛋🖋🏌**Leisure** hard tennis courts, heated indoor swimming pool, fishing, sauna, gymnasium
Conf facs Corporate Hospitality Days **Location** off A3 at Griggs Green, S of Liphook, signed Old Thorns
Hotel ★★★ 82% HL Old Thorns Hotel Golf & Country Estate, Griggs Green, LIPHOOK ☎ 01428 724555
🖺 01428 724555 33 en suite

Societies booking required. **Green Fees** not confirmed **Course Designer** Don Wright **Prof** Alastair Briggs/Claire Duffy **Facilities** ⓘ ⌐ 🍴 🛒 💳 ⬆ 🏌 🧳 🏌 🚵 🏌 🏌 **Conf** facs Corporate Hospitality Days **Location** M3 junct 8 southbound, from A303 take junct signed Overton and follow brown signs. M3 junct 9 northbound, take A34 to A303 signed Basingstoke, leave at junct signed Overton and follow brown signs .
Hotel ★★★★ 79% HL The Hampshire Court Hotel, Centre Drive, Chineham, BASINGSTOKE ☎ 01256 319700 🖥 01256 319700 90 en suite

OWER   Map 4 SU31

Paultons Golf Centre Old Salisbury Rd SO51 6AN
☎ 023 8081 3992   🖥 023 8081 3993
e-mail: paultons@crown.golf.co.uk
web: www.paultonsgolf.co.uk

A pay and play parkland and woodland 18-hole course built within the original Paultons parkland which was laid out by Capability Brown. The water features on four of the holes and the tree-lined fairways challenge the ability of all golfers. There is also a nine-hole academy course, ideal for beginners or players wishing to improve their short games as well as a 24-bay floodlit driving range.

Paultons Golf Centre: 18 Holes, 6238yds, Par 71, SSS 70, Course record 67. Club membership 500.

Visitors Mon-Sun & BHs. Booking required. Dress code.
Societies booking required. **Green Fees** not confirmed **Course Designer** J R Smith **Prof** M Williamson/C Farr/C Tyrrell **Facilities** ⓘ ⌐ 🍴 🛒 💳 ⬆ 🏌 🧳 🏌 🚵 🏌 🏌 **Leisure** 9 hole academy course **Conf** facs Corporate Hospitality Days **Location** M27 junct 2, A36 towards Salisbury, 1st rdbt 1st exit, 1st right at Vine pub
Hotel ★★★ 75% HL Bartley Lodge, Lyndhurst Road, CADNAM ☎ 023 8081 2248 🖥 023 8081 2248   31 en suite

PETERSFIELD   Map 4 SU72

Petersfield Tankerdale Ln, Liss GU33 7QY
☎ 01730 895165 (office)   🖥 01730 894713
e-mail: manager@pgc1892.net
web: www.petersfieldgolfclub.co.uk

Gently undulating course of downland and parkland with mature trees and hedgerows. Very free drainage in an Area of Outstanding Natural Beauty.

18 Holes, 6450yds, Par 72, SSS 71, Course record 68. Club membership 725.

Visitors Mon-Sun & BHs. Booking required Tue, Thu, weekends & BHs. Handicap certrificate. Dress code. **Societies** booking required. **Green Fees** £40 per day, £30 per round (£40 per round weekends & BHs) **Course Designer** M Hawtree **Prof** Greg Hughes **Facilities** ⓘ ⌐ 🍴 🛒 💳 ⬆ 🏌 🏌 **Location** off the A3(M), between the Liss/Petersfield exits southbound
Hotel ★★★ 75% HL Langrish House, Langrish, PETERSFIELD ☎ 01730 266941 🖥 01730 266941   13 en suite

PORTSMOUTH   Map 4 SU60

Great Salterns Public Course Burrfields Rd PO3 5HH
☎ 023 9266 4549   🖥 023 9265 0525
e-mail: enquiries@portsmouthgolfcentre.co.uk
web: www.portsmouthgolfcentre.co.uk

Easy walking, seaside course with open fairways and testing shots onto well-guarded, small greens. Testing 13th hole, par 4, requiring 130yd shot across a lake.

Great Salterns Public Course: 18 Holes, 5575yds, Par 69, SSS 67, Course record 64. Club membership 700.

Visitors Mon-Sun & BHs. Booking required. **Societies** booking required. **Green Fees** phone **Prof** Terry Healy **Facilities** ⓘ ⓘ ⌐ 🛒 💳 🏌 ◇ 🏌 **Conf** facs **Location** NE of town centre on A2030
Hotel ★★★★ 74% HL Portsmouth Marriott Hotel, Southampton Road, PORTSMOUTH ☎ 0870 400 7285 🖥 0870 400 7285 174 en suite

ROMSEY   Map 4 SU32

Dunwood Manor Danes Rd, Awbridge SO51 0GF
☎ 01794 340549   🖥 01794 341215
e-mail: admin@dunwood-golf.co.uk
web: www.dunwood-golf.co.uk

Undulating parkland with fine views. Fine holes running through mature woodland.

18 Holes, 5655yds, Par 69, SSS 68, Course record 65. Club membership 587.

Visitors Mon-Sun & BHs. Booking required. Handicap certificate. Dress code. **Societies** booking required. **Green Fees** not confirmed **Prof** Heath Teschner **Facilities** ⓘ ⓘ ⌐ 🍴 🛒 💳 ⬆ 🏌 ◇ 🏌 🏌 **Conf** Corporate Hospitality Days **Location** 4m NW of Romsey off A27
Hotel ★★★ 83% HL Bell Inn, BROOK ☎ 023 8081 2214 🖥 023 8081 2214   27 en suite

Romsey Romsey Rd, Nursling SO16 0XW
☎ 023 8073 4637   🖥 023 8074 1036
e-mail: secretary@romseygolfclub.co.uk
web: www.romseygolfclub.com

Parkland and woodland course with narrow tree-lined fairways. Six holes are undulating, the rest are sloping. There are superb views over the Test valley. Excellent test of golf for all standards.

18 Holes, 5718yds, Par 69, SSS 68, Course record 64. Club membership 800.

Visitors Mon-Fri except BHs. Dress code. **Societies** booking required. **Green Fees** £38 per day, £32 per round **Prof** James Pitcher **Facilities** ⓘ ⓘ ⌐ 🍴 🛒 💳 ⬆ 🏌 🏌 🏌 **Leisure** refreshments at 11th tee **Conf** facs Corporate Hospitality Days **Location** 1m N M27 junct 3 on A3057
Hotel ★★★ 77% HL Chilworth Manor, CHILWORTH, Southampton ☎ 023 8076 7333 🖥 023 8076 7333   95 en suite

Wellow Ryedown Ln, East Wellow SO51 6BD
☎ 01794 323833 & 322872   🖥 01794 323832
web: www.wellowgolfclub.co.uk

Three nine-hole courses set in 217 acres of parkland surrounding Embley Park, former home of Florence Nightingale.

Ryedown & Embley: 18 Holes, 5953yds, Par 70, SSS 69, Course record 65.

continued

Embley & Blackwater: 18 Holes, 6301yds, Par 72, SSS 70.
Blackwater & Ryedown: 18 Holes, 5784yds, Par 70, SSS 68.
Club membership 600.

Visitors Mon-Fri. Weekends & BHs pm. Booking required. Dress code. **Societies** booking required. **Green Fees** £21 per 18 holes (£26 weekends & BHs) **Course Designer** W Wiltshire **Prof** Neil Bratley **Facilities** ⊕ ⏣ 🏌 ♨ ☕ ⛳ ✓ ➤ ✓ **Leisure** gymnasium **Conf** facs Corporate Hospitality Days **Location** M27 junct 2, A36 towards Salisbury, 1m right to Whinwhistle Rd

Hotel ★★★ 77% HL Chilworth Manor, CHILWORTH, Southampton ☎ 023 8076 7333 ⏣ 023 8076 7333 95 en suite

ROTHERWICK   Map 4 SU75

Tylney Park RG27 9AY
☎ 01256 762079   ⏣ 01256 763079
e-mail: contact@tylneypark.co.uk
web: www.tylneypark.co.uk

Set in English Heritage-registered parkland with specimen mature trees. Championship course with U.S.G.A. free-draining sand-based tees and greens allowing year-round quality golf. Undulating with highly profiled greens.

18 Holes, 7017yds, Par 72, SSS 74, Course record 68.
Club membership 580.

Visitors Mon-Sun & BHs. Handicap certificate. Dress code. **Societies** booking required. **Green Fees** £45 per round (including lunch) **Course Designer** D Steel/T Mackenzie **Prof** Alasdair Hay **Facilities** ⊕ ⏣ by prior arrangement 🏌 ♨ ☕ 🏌 ⛳ **Conf** Corporate Hospitality Days **Location** M3 junct 5, 2m NW of Hook. 9m S of M4 junct 11 via A33.

Hotel ★★★★ HL Tylney Hall, ROTHERWICK, Hook ☎ 01256 764881 ⏣ 01256 764881 112 en suite

ROWLAND'S CASTLE   Map 4 SU71

Rowlands Castle 31 Links Ln PO9 6AE
☎ 023 9241 2784   ⏣ 023 9241 3649
e-mail: manager@rowlandscastlegolfclub.co.uk
web: www.rowlandscastlegolfclub.co.uk

Reasonably dry in winter, the flat parkland course is a testing one with a number of tricky dog-legs and bunkers much in evidence. The par 4 13th is a signature hole necessitating a drive to a narrow fairway and a second shot to a two-tiered green. The 7th, at 522yds, is the longest hole on the course and leads to a well-guarded armchair green.

18 Holes, 6630yds, Par 72, SSS 72, Course record 68.
Club membership 800.

Visitors Mon-Fri, Sun & BHs. Handicap certificate. Dress code. **Societies** booking required. **Green Fees** £40 per day (£45 Sun) **Course Designer** Colt **Prof** Peter Klepacz **Facilities** ⊕ ⏣ 🏌 ♨ ☕ ⛳ ✓ ➤ ✓ **Conf** Corporate Hospitality Days **Location** W of village off B2149

Hotel ★★★ 79% HL Brookfield, Havant Road, EMSWORTH ☎ 01243 373363 ⏣ 01243 373363 39 en suite

SHEDFIELD   Map 4 SU51

Marriott Meon Valley Hotel & Country Club Sandy Ln SO32 2HQ
☎ 01329 833455   ⏣ 01329 834411

It has been said that a golf-course architect is as good as the ground on which he has to work. Here Hamilton Stutt had magnificent terrain at his disposal and a very good and lovely parkland course is the result. There are three holes over water.

Meon Course: 18 Holes, 6520yds, Par 71, SSS 71, Course record 66.
Valley Course: 9 Holes, 5758yds, Par 70, SSS 68.
Club membership 560.

Visitors Mon-Sun & BHs. Dress code. **Societies** booking required. **Green Fees** £44 per 18 holes (£54 weekends & BHs) **Course Designer** Hamilton Stutt **Prof** Neal Grist **Facilities** ⊕ ⏣ 🏌 ♨ ☕ ⛳ ♔ ◇ ✓ ➤ ✓ ⚑ **Leisure** hard tennis courts, heated indoor swimming pool, sauna, gymnasium **Conf** facs Corporate Hospitality Days **Location** M27 junct 7, off A334 between Botley & Wickham

Hotel ★★★★ 76% HL Marriott Meon Valley Hotel & Country Club, Sandy Lane, SHEDFIELD ☎ 01329 833455 ⏣ 01329 833455 113 en suite

SOUTHAMPTON   Map 4 SU41

Chilworth Main Rd, Chilworth SO16 7JP
☎ 023 8074 0544   ⏣ 023 8073 3166

A course with two loops of nine holes, with a booking system to allow undisturbed play. The front nine is fairly long and undulating and include water hazards. The back nine is tighter and quite a challenge.

Manor Golf Course: 18 Holes, 5915yds, Par 69, SSS 69, Course record 68. Club membership 600.

Visitors Mon-Sun & BHs. Dress code. **Societies** welcome. **Green Fees** £12 per 18 holes, £6 per 9 holes (£15/£10 weekends & BHs) **Course Designer** J Garner **Prof** Darren Newing **Facilities** ⊕ ⏣ 🏌 ♨ ☕ ⛳ ✓ ⚑ **Location** A27 between Chilworth & Romsey

Hotel ★★★ 77% HL Chilworth Manor, CHILWORTH, Southampton ☎ 023 8076 7333 ⏣ 023 8076 7333 95 en suite

Southampton Golf Course Rd SO16 7LE
☎ 023 8076 0478 & 8076 0546(booking)
⏣ 023 8076 0472

Southampton Municipal Golf Course: 18 Holes, 6103yds, Par 69, SSS 70.
Southampton Municipal Golf Course: 9 Holes, 2395yds, Par 33.

Course Designer Halmree/A P Taylor **Location** 4m N of city centre off A33

Telephone for further details

Hotel ★★ 76% HL Elizabeth House, 42-44 The Avenue, SOUTHAMPTON ☎ 023 8022 4327 ⏣ 023 8022 4327 27 en suite

Stoneham Monks Wood Close, Bassett SO16 3TT
☎ 023 8076 9272   📠 023 8076 6320
e-mail: richard@stonehamgolfclub.org.uk
web: www.stonehamgolfclub.org.uk

Undulating through an attractive parkland and heathland setting with views over the Itchen valley towards Winchester, this course rewards brains over brawn. It is unusual in having 5 par 5's and 5 par 3's and no two holes alike. The quality of the course means that temporary greens are never used and the course is rarely closed.

18 Holes, 6392yds, Par 72, SSS 71, Course record 63. Club membership 800.

Visitors Mon-Sun & BHs. Booking required. Handicap certificate. Dress code. **Societies** booking required. **Green Fees** £58 per day, £48 per round (£62/£52 weekends & BHs) **Course Designer** Willie Park Jnr **Prof** Ian Young **Facilities** ⊕ ⏀⏃ ⬛ ⏄ ⏍ ⏄ ⏮ 🏌 **Conf** facs Corporate Hospitality Days **Location** 4m N of city centre off A27
Hotel ★★★ 77% HL Chilworth Manor, CHILWORTH, Southampton ☎ 023 8076 7333 📠 023 8076 7333 95 en suite

SOUTHWICK   Map 4 SU60

Southwick Park Naval Recreation Centre Pinsley Dr
PO17 6EL
☎ 023 923 80131   📠 0871 8559809
e-mail: southwickpark@btconnect.com
web: www.southwickparkgolfclub.co.uk

Set in 100 acres of parkland played around Southwick Park lake. Tight course with good greens and tough finish. Holes of note are the 4th, 7th, 9th, 11th and 16th. The 15th offers the historic backdrop of a 12th century priory remains.

Southwick Park Golf Club: 18 Holes, 5884yds, Par 69, SSS 69, Course record 64. Club membership 750.

Visitors Mon-Sun & BHs. Booking required Fri-Sun & BHs. Handicap certificate. Dress code. **Societies** booking required. **Green Fees** £32 per 36 holes, £26 per 18 holes (£29 per 18 holes weekends) **Course Designer** C Lawrie **Prof** Eddy Rawlings **Facilities** ⊕ ⏀⏃ ⬛ ⏄ ⏍ ⏄ ⏮ 🏌 **Conf** Corporate Hospitality Days **Location** 0.5m SE off B2177
Hotel ★★★ 77% HL Old House Hotel & Restaurant, The Square, WICKHAM ☎ 01329 833049 📠 01329 833049 12 en suite

TADLEY   Map 4 SU66

Bishopswood Bishopswood Ln RG26 4AT
☎ 0118 981 2200   📠 0118 940 8606
Bishopswood Golf Course: 9 Holes, 6474yds, Par 72, SSS 71, Course record 66.
Course Designer M W Phillips/G Blake **Location** 6m N of Basingstoke off A340
Telephone for further details
Hotel ★★★ 67% HL Holiday Inn Reading West, Bath Road, PADWORTH ☎ 0118 971 4411 📠 0118 971 4411 50 en suite

WATERLOOVILLE   Map 4 SU60

Portsmouth Crookhorn Ln, Purbrook PO7 5QL
☎ 023 9237 2210   📠 023 9220 0766
e-mail: info@portsmouthgc.com
web: www.portsmouthgc.com
Hilly, challenging course with good views of Portsmouth Harbour. Rarely free from the wind and the picturesque 6th, 17th and 18th holes can test the best.

Portsmouth Golf Course: 18 Holes, 6139yds, Par 69, SSS 70, Course record 64. Club membership 600.
Visitors Mon-Sun & BHs. Booking required. Dress code. **Societies** welcome. **Green Fees** not confirmed **Course Designer** Hawtree **Prof** James Green **Facilities** ⊕ ⏀⏃ ⬛ ⏄ ⏍ ⏄ ⏮ 🏌 **Location** 2m S off A3
Hotel ★★★★ 74% HL Portsmouth Marriott Hotel, Southampton Road, PORTSMOUTH ☎ 0870 400 7285 📠 0870 400 7285 174 en suite

Waterlooville Cherry Tree Av, Cowplain PO8 8AP
☎ 023 9226 3388   📠 023 9224 2980
e-mail: secretary@waterloovillegolfclub.co.uk
web: waterloovillegolfclub.co.uk
Easy walking but challenging parkland course, with five par 5s over 500yds and featuring four ponds and a stream running through. The 13th hole, at 556yds, has a carry over a pond for a drive and a stream crossing the fairway and ending in a very small green.

18 Holes, 6602yds, Par 72, SSS 72, Course record 64. Club membership 800.
Visitors Mon-Sun except BHs. Booking required weekends. Handicap certificate. Dress code. **Societies** booking required. **Green Fees** £40 per day/round **Course Designer** Henry Cotton **Prof** John Hay **Facilities** ⊕ ⬛ ⏄ ⏍ ⏄ ⏮ 🚲 🏌 **Conf** Corporate Hospitality Days **Location** NE of town centre off A3
Hotel ★★★ 79% HL Brookfield, Havant Road, EMSWORTH ☎ 01243 373363 📠 01243 373363 39 en suite

WICKHAM   Map 4 SU51

Wickham Park Titchfield Ln PO17 5PJ
☎ 01329 833342 & 836356   📠 01329 834798
e-mail: wickhampark-membership@crown-golf.co.uk
web: www.crown-golf.co.uk
An attractive 18-hole parkland course set in the Meon Valley. Ideal for beginners and established golfers alike. The course is not overly demanding but is challenging enough to provide an enjoyable round of golf.

18 Holes, 5898yards, Par 69, SSS 68, Course record 69. Club membership 600.   *continued*

Visitors Mon-Sun & BHs. Booking required. Dress code.
Societies booking required. Green Fees not confirmed Prof Scott
Edwards Facilities ⓘ †⊙¹ ⓑ ☐ ⟋ ♨ ⌂ ♐ ⌖ ⌀
♐ Leisure chipping area Conf facs Corporate Hospitality Days
Location M27 junct 9/10
Hotel ★★★ 77% HL Old House Hotel & Restaurant, The Square,
WICKHAM ☎ 01329 833049 📄 01329 833049 12 en suite

WINCHESTER   Map 4 SU42

Hockley Twyford SO21 1PL
☎ 01962 713165 📄 01962 713612
e-mail: secretary@hockleygolfclub.com
web: www.hockleygolfclub.com
Downland course with good views.
18 Holes, 6500yds, Par 71, SSS 70, Course record 64.
Club membership 750.
Visitors handicap certiificate for weekend play. Dress code.
Societies booking required. Green Fees not confirmed Course
Designer James Braid Prof Gary Stubbington Facilities ⓘ †⊙¹ ⓑ
☐ ♨ ⟋ ⌂ ⌀ ♨ ⌀ ♐ Conf Corporate Hospitality Days
Location M3 junct 11, signed to Twyford
Hotel ★★★★ 70% HL Mercure Wessex, Paternoster Row,
WINCHESTER ☎ 01962 861611 📄 01962 861611 94 en suite

Royal Winchester Sarum Rd SO22 5QE
☎ 01962 852462 📄 01962 865048
e-mail: manager@royalwinchestergolfclub.com
web: royalwinchestergolfclub.com
The Royal Winchester course is a sporting downland course centred
on a rolling valley, so the course is hilly in places with fine views
over the surrounding countryside. Built on chalk downs, the course
drains extremely well and offers an excellent playing surface.
18 Holes, 6387yds, Par 72, SSS 72, Course record 68.
Club membership 800.
Visitors Mon-Sun except BHs. Handicap certificate. Dress code.
Societies booking required. Green Fees phone Course Designer J H
Taylor Prof Steven Hunter Facilities ⓘ †⊙¹ by prior arrangement
ⓑ ☐ ♨ ⟋ ⌂ ⌀ ♨ ⌀ Conf Corporate Hospitality Days
Location 1.5m W off A3090
Hotel ★★★★ HL Lainston House, Sparsholt, WINCHESTER
☎ 01962 776088 📄 01962 776088 50 en suite

South Winchester Romsey Rd SO22 5QX
☎ 01962 877800 📄 01962 877900
web: www.crown-golf.co.uk/southwinchester
18 Holes, 7086yds, Par 72, SSS 74, Course record 68.
Course Designer Dave Thomas Location M3 junct 11, on A3090
Romsey road
Telephone for further details
Hotel ★★★ 77% HL The Winchester Royal, Saint Peter Street,
WINCHESTER ☎ 01962 840840 📄 01962 840840 75 en suite

HEREFORDSHIRE

BODENHAM   Map 3 SO55

Brockington Hall Golf Club & Country House HR1 3HX
☎ 01568 797877 📄 01568 797877
e-mail: info@brockingtonhall.co.uk
web: www.brockingtonhall.co.uk
A well-maintained course set in attractive countryside with fine greens
and defined fairways separated by mixed plantations. A meandering
brook runs through the course making it a testing but enjoyable game
of golf.
Brockington Hall Golf Club & Country House:
9 Holes, 2344yds, Par 66, SSS 63, Course record 32.
Club membership 178.
Visitors Mon-Sun & BHs. Dress code. Societies welcome. Green
Fees £11 per 18 holes, £7 per 9 holes (£12/£8 weekends) Course
Designer Derek Powell Prof Kevin Davis Facilities ⓘ †⊙¹ ⓑ
☐ ♨ ⟋ ⌂ ♨ ⌀ Conf facs Corporate Hospitality
Days Location on A417 on outskirts of Bodenham village between
Leominster and Hereford.
Hotel ★★★ 75% HL Best Western Talbot, West Street, LEOMINSTER
☎ 01568 616347 📄 01568 616347 28 en suite

CLIFFORD   Map 3 SO24

Summerhill HR3 5EW
☎ 01497 820451 📄 01497 820451
web: www.summerhillgolfcourse.co.uk
Summerhill Golf Course: 9 Holes, 2872yds, Par 70, SSS 67,
Course record 71.
Course Designer Bob Sandow Location 0.5m N from Hay on B4350,
on right
Telephone for further details
Guesthouse ★★★★★ RR The Talkhouse, Pontdolgoch, CAERSWS
☎ 01686 688919 📄 01686 688919 3 en suite

HEREFORD   Map 3 SO53

Belmont Lodge Belmont HR2 9SA
☎ 01432 352666 📄 01432 358090
e-mail: info@belmont-hereford.co.uk
web: www.belmont-hereford.co.uk

Parkland course designed in two loops of nine. The first nine take the
higher ground, offering magnificent views over Herefordshire. The
second nine run alongside the River Wye with five holes in play against
the river. Many golfers find the second nine the harder as the river
comes into play on at least five of the holes. *continued*

Belmont Lodge & Golf: 18 Holes, 6369yds, Par 72, SSS 71, Course record 66. Club membership 500.

Visitors contact for details. **Societies** booking required. **Green Fees** £25 per 18 holes (£30 weekends & BHs). Reduced winter rates **Course Designer** Bob Sandow **Prof** Richard Hemming/Kevin Davis **Facilities** ⓣ ⓘ ⓛ ⌑ 🍴 ⌖ 🏠 🍴 ◇ ♂ 🚗 ♂ **Leisure** hard tennis courts, fishing **Conf** facs Corporate Hospitality Days **Location** 2m S off A465

Hotel ★★★ 74% HL Belmont Lodge & Golf, Belmont, HEREFORD ☎ 01432 352666 📄 01432 352666 30 en suite

Burghill Valley Tillington Rd, Burghill HR4 7RW
☎ 01432 760456   📄 01432 761654
e-mail: info@bvgc.co.uk
web: www.bvgc.co.uk

The course is situated in typically beautiful Herefordshire countryside. The walking is easy on gently rolling fairways with a background of hills and woods and in the distance, the Welsh mountains. Some holes are played through mature cider orchards and there are two lakes to negotiate. A fair but interesting test for players of all abilities.

Burghill Valley Golf Course: 18 Holes, 6204yds, Par 70, SSS 70, Course record 66. Club membership 700.

Visitors contact course for details. **Societies** welcome. **Green Fees** phone **Course Designer** M Barnett **Prof** Keith Preece/Andy Cameron **Facilities** ⓣ ⓘ ⓛ ⌑ 🍴 ⌖ 🏠 ♂ 🚗 ♂ **Leisure** chipping practice area. **Location** 4m NW of Hereford **Hotel** ★★★ 87% HL Castle House, Castle Street, HEREFORD ☎ 01432 356321 📄 01432 356321 15 en suite

Hereford Municipal Hereford Leisure Centre, Holmer Rd HR4 9UD
☎ 01432 344376   📄 01432 266281

This municipal parkland course is more challenging than first appearance. The well-drained greens are open all year round with good drainage for excellent winter golf.

Hereford Municipal Golf Course: 9 Holes, 3060yds, Par 35, SSS 68. Club membership 148.

Visitors Mon-Sun & BHs. **Societies** welcome. **Green Fees** not confirmed **Course Designer** J Leek **Prof** Gary Morgan **Facilities** ⓣ ⓘ ⓛ ⌑ 🍴 ⌖ 🏠 🍴 ♂ **Leisure** squash, gymnasium, Leisure centre **Location** within racecourse on A49 Hereford-Leominster **Hotel** ★★★ 87% HL Castle House, Castle Street, HEREFORD ☎ 01432 356321 📄 01432 356321 15 en suite

KINGTON   Map 3 SO25

Kington Bradnor Hill HR5 3RE
☎ 01544 230340 (club) & 231320 (pro shop)
📄 01544 230340 /231320 (pro)
e-mail: kingtongolf@ukonline.co.uk

The highest 18-hole course in England, with magnificent views over seven counties. A natural heathland course with easy walking on mountain turf cropped by sheep. There is bracken to catch any really bad shots but no sand traps. The greens play true and fast and are generally acknowledged as some of the best in the west Midlands.

18 Holes, 5980yds, Par 70, SSS 69, Course record 63. Club membership 510.

Visitors contact club for details. **Societies** welcome. **Green Fees** £28 per day, £22 per round (£32/£26 weekends & BHs) **Course Designer** Major C K Hutchison **Prof** Andy Gealy **Facilities** ⓣ ⓘ

ⓛ ⌑ 🍴 ⌖ 🏠 🍴 ♂ 🚗 ♂ 🏴 **Location** 0.5m N of Kington off B4355
Hotel ★★★ 74% HL Burton, Mill Street, KINGTON ☎ 01544 230323 📄 01544 230323 16 en suite

LEOMINSTER   Map 3 SO45

Leominster Ford Bridge HR6 0LE
☎ 01568 610055   📄 01568 610055
e-mail: contact@leominstergolfclub.co.uk
web: www.leominstergolfclub.co.uk

On undulating parkland with the lower holes running alongside the River Lugg and others on the higher part of the course affording fine panoramic views over the surrounding countryside.

18 Holes, 6026yds, Par 70, SSS 69. Club membership 500.

Visitors Mon-Sun & BHs. Booking required. Dress code. **Societies** booking required. **Green Fees** £25 per day, £20 per 18 holes (£30 per day, £25 per round weekends & BHs) **Course Designer** Bob Sandow **Prof** Nigel Clarke **Facilities** ⓣ ⓘ ⓛ ⌑ 🍴 ⌖ 🏠 🚗 ♂ **Leisure** fishing **Conf** facs Corporate Hospitality Days **Location** 3m S of Leominster on A49, signed **Hotel** ★★★ 75% HL Best Western Talbot, West Street, LEOMINSTER ☎ 01568 616347 📄 01568 616347 28 en suite

ROSS-ON-WYE   Map 3 SO62

Ross-on-Wye Two Park, Gorsley HR9 7UT
☎ 01989 720267   📄 01989 720212
e-mail: admin@therossonwyegolfclub.co.uk
web: www.therossonwyegolfclub.co.uk

This undulating, parkland course has been cut out of a silver birch forest. The fairways are well-screened from each other and tight, the greens good and the bunkers have been restructured.

18 Holes, 6451yds, Par 72, SSS 71, Course record 68. Club membership 730.

Visitors Mon-Sun & BHs. Booking required. Handicap certificate. Dress code. **Societies** booking required. **Green Fees** £50 per 36 holes, £46 per 27 holes, £40 per round. **Course Designer** Mr C K Cotton **Prof** Paul MIddleton **Facilities** ⓣ ⓘ ⓛ ⌑ 🍴 ⌖ 🏠 🍴 ♂ 🚗 ♂ 🏴 **Leisure** snooker **Conf** Corporate Hospitality Days **Location** M50 junct 3, on B4221 N
Hotel ★★★ 77% HL Best Western Pengethley Manor, Pengethley Park, ROSS-ON-WYE ☎ 01989 730211 📄 01989 730211 25 en suite

continued

Hotel ★★ 72% HL King's Head Hotel, 8 High Street, ROSS-ON-WYE ☎ 01989 763174 📠 01989 769578 15 en suite

South Herefordshire Twin Lakes HR9 7UA
☎ 01989 780535 📠 01989 780535
e-mail: info@herefordshiregolf.co.uk
web: www.herefordshiregolf.co.uk

Impressive 6672yd parkland course fast maturing into one of Herefordshire's finest. Magnificent panoramic views of the Welsh mountains and countryside. Drains well and is playable in any weather. The landscape has enabled the architect to design 18 individual and varied holes.

Twin Lakes: 18 Holes, 6672yds, Par 71, SSS 72,
Course record 71. Club membership 400.

Visitors Mon-Sun & BHs. Booking required. Dress code.
Societies welcome. **Green Fees** £20 per 18 holes (£25 weekends).
Course Designer John Day **Prof** Lewis Hanney **Facilities** ⑪ ⑩ 🍴 ⬛ ⛳ 📶 🧍 🏠 🍴 🏌 🏌 **Leisure** par 3 academy course
Conf Corporate Hospitality Days **Location** M50 junct 4, to Upton Bishop, right onto B4224, 1m left
Hotel ★★★ 70% CHH Pencraig Court Country House Hotel, Pencraig, ROSS-ON-WYE ☎ 01989 770306 📠 01989 770306 11 en suite

UPPER SAPEY   Map 3 SO66

Sapey WR6 6XT
☎ 01886 853288 & 853567 📠 01886 853485
e-mail: anybody@sapeygolf.co.uk
web: www.sapeygolf.co.uk

Easy walking parkland with views of the Malvern Hills. The mixture of long or short holes, including trees, lakes and water hazards, is a demanding challenge for all golfers.

The Rowan: 18 Holes, 5935yds, Par 69, SSS 68,
Course record 63.
The Oaks: 9 Holes, 1203, Par 27, SSS 27.
Club membership 350.

Visitors Mon-Sat & BHs. Dress code. **Societies** booking required.
Green Fees Rowan £27 per round (£32 weekends). Oaks £7 (£9 weekends) **Course Designer** R McMurray **Prof** Chris Knowles
Facilities ⑪ ⑩ by prior arrangement 🍴 ⬛ ⛳ 🧍 🏠 📶 🏌 🏌 🏌 **Leisure** 9 hole par 3 Oaks Course **Conf** Corporate Hospitality Days **Location** B4203 Bromyard-Stourport road
Hotel ★★★ 75% HL Best Western Talbot, West Street, LEOMINSTER ☎ 01568 616347 📠 01568 616347 28 en suite

WORMSLEY   Map 3 SO44

Herefordshire Ravens Causeway HR4 8LY
☎ 01432 830219 & 830465 (pro) 📠 01432 830095
e-mail: herefordshire.golf@breathe.com
web: www.herefordshiregolfclub.co.uk

Undulating parkland with expansive views of the Clee Hills to the east and the Black Mountains to the west. Peaceful and relaxing situation.

18 Holes, 6055yds, Par 70, SSS 70, Course record 61.
Club membership 750.

Visitors Mon-Sun & BHs. Booking required. Handicap certificate. Dress code **Societies** booking required. **Green Fees** £35 per day £30per 18 holes. (£40/£45 weekends & BHs) **Course Designer** James Braid
Prof Julian Parry **Facilities** ⑪ ⑩ 🍴 ⬛ ⛳ 🧍 🏠 📶 🏌 🏌 🏌 **Conf** Corporate Hospitality Days **Location** 7m NW of Hereford on B road to Weobley
Hotel ★★★ 74% HL Belmont Lodge & Golf, Belmont, HEREFORD ☎ 01432 352666 📠 01432 352666 30 en suite

HERTFORDSHIRE

ALDENHAM   Map 4 TQ19

Aldenham Golf and Country Club Church Ln WD25 8NN
☎ 01923 853929 📠 01923 858472
e-mail: info@aldenhamgolfclub.co.uk
web: www.aldenhamgolfclub.co.uk

Gently undulating parkland with woods, water hazards and ditches. Many specimen trees and beautiful views across the countryside.

Church Course: 18 Holes, 6456yds, Par 70, SSS 71.
Berry Grove Course: 9 Holes, 2350yds, Par 33, SSS 32.
Club membership 450.

Visitors Mon-Sun & BHs. Booking required. Dress code.
Societies booking required.. **Green Fees** Church £35 per round (£45 weekends & BHs). Berry Grove £12 (£15 weekends & BHs) **Prof** Tim Dunstan **Facilities** ⑪ ⑩ 🍴 ⬛ ⛳ 🧍 🏠 📶 🏌 🏌 **Conf** facs Corporate Hospitality Days **Location** M1 junct 5, 0.5m to W of village
Hotel ★★★ 73% HL Best Western White House, Upton Road, WATFORD ☎ 01923 237316 📠 01923 237316 57 en suite

BERKHAMSTED   Map 4 SP90

Berkhamsted The Common HP4 2QB
☎ 01442 865832 📠 01442 863730
e-mail: barryh@berkhamstedgc.co.uk
web: www.berkhamstedgolfclub.co.uk

There are no sand bunkers on this championship heathland course but this does not make it any easier to play. The natural hazards will test the skill of the most able players, with a particularly testing hole at the 11th, 568yds, par 5. Fine greens, long carries and heather and gorse

18 Holes, 6605yds, Par 71, SSS 72, Course record 65.
Club membership 700.

Visitors handicap certificate. Dress code. **Societies** booking required.
Green Fees phone **Course Designer** Colt/Braid **Prof** John Clarke
Facilities ⑪ 🍴 ⬛ ⛳ 🧍 🏠 📶 🏌 **Location** 1.5m E
Hotel ★★★★ 76% HL Pendley Manor, Cow Lane, TRING ☎ 01442 891891 📠 01442 891891 73 en suite

BISHOP'S STORTFORD Map 5 TL42

Bishop's Stortford Dunmow Rd CM23 5HP
☎ 01279 654715   📠 01279 655215
e-mail: office@bsgc.co.uk
web: www.bsgc.co.uk

Well-established parkland course, fairly flat, but undulating, with easy walking.

18 Holes, 6404yds, Par 71, SSS 71, Course record 64. Club membership 900.

Visitors Mon-Fri except BHs. Handicap certificate. Dress code. **Societies** booking required. **Green Fees** not confirmed **Course Designer** James Braid **Prof** Simon Sheppard **Facilities** ⓣ 🍴 🕍 ☕ 🍷 👤 📷 🚩 ♂ 🛢 ♂ **Leisure** snooker tables **Conf** facs Corporate Hospitality Days **Location** M11 junct 8, 0.5m W on A1250
Hotel BUD Days Inn London Stansted, BIRCHANGER GREEN ☎ 01279 656477 📠 01279 656477   60 en suite

Great Hadham Golf & Country Club Great Hadham Rd, Much Hadham SG10 6JE
☎ 01279 843558   📠 01279 842122
e-mail: info@ghgcc.co.uk

An undulating meadowland and links course offering excellent country views and a challenge with its ever present breeze.

Great Hadham Golf & Country Club: 18 Holes, 6854yds, Par 72, SSS 73, Course record 67. Club membership 800.

Visitors Mon-Fri except BHs. Weekends after noon. Booking required. Dress code. **Societies** booking required. **Green Fees** £21 per 18 holes, £13 per 9 holes (£28/£16 weekends pm only) **Course Designer** Iain Roberts **Prof** Kevin Lunt **Facilities** ⓣ 🍴 by prior arrangement 🕍 ☕ 🍷 👤 📷 🛢 ♂ **Leisure** sauna, gymnasium **Conf** facs Corporate Hospitality Days **Location** on the B1004, 3m SW of Bishop's Stortford
Hotel ★★★★ 76% HL Down Hall Country House, Hatfield Heath, BISHOPS STORTFORD ☎ 01279 731441 📠 01279 731441   99 en suite

BRICKENDON Map 5 TL30

Brickendon Grange Pembridge Ln SG13 8PD
☎ 01992 511258   📠 01992 511411
e-mail: play@brickendongrangegc.co.uk
web: www.brickendongrangegc.co.uk

Undulating parkland with some fine par 4s. The 17th hole reputed to be best in the county.

18 Holes, 6458yds, Par 71, SSS 71, Course record 67. Club membership 680.

Visitors contact club for details. **Societies** booking required. **Green Fees** not confirmed **Course Designer** C K Cotton **Prof** Graham Tippett **Facilities** ⓣ 🍴 🕍 ☕ 🍷 👤 📷 🛢 ♂ **Conf** facs Corporate Hospitality Days **Location** W of village
Hotel ★★★★ 76% HL Ponsbourne Park Hotel, Newgate Street Village, POTTERS BAR, Nr Hertford ☎ 01707 876191 & 879277 📠 01707 876191   51 en suite

BROOKMANS PARK Map 4 TL20

Brookmans Park Golf Club Rd AL9 7AT
☎ 01707 652487   📠 01707 661851
e-mail: info@bpgc.co.uk
web: www.bpgc.co.uk

Undulating parkland with several cleverly constructed holes. But it is a fair course, although it can play long. The 11th, par 3, is a testing hole which plays across a lake.

18 Holes, 6249yds, Par 71, SSS 71, Course record 65. Club membership 750.

Visitors Mon-Fri except BHs. Handicap certificate. Dress code. **Societies** booking required. **Green Fees** not confirmed **Course Designer** Hawtree/Taylor **Prof** Ian Jelley **Facilities** ⓣ 🍴 🕍 ☕ 🍷 👤 📷 ♂ 🛢 ♂ **Location** N of village off A1000
Hotel ★★★ 77% HL Bush Hall, Mill Green, HATFIELD ☎ 01707 271251 📠 01707 271251   25 en suite

BROXBOURNE Map 5 TL30

Hertfordshire Broxbournebury Mansion, White Stubbs Ln EN10 7PY
☎ 01992 466666 & 441268 (pro shop)
📠 01992 470326
e-mail: hertfordshire@crowngolf.co.uk
web: www.crowngolf.co.uk

An 18 hole course of a 'Nicklaus' design set around a Grade II listed clubhouse to full USGA specifications. Considered to be one of the best private courses to appear in recent years.

Hertfordshire Golf & Country Club: 18 Holes, 6388yds, Par 70, SSS 70, Course record 62. Club membership 600.

Visitors contact club for details. **Societies** welcome. **Green Fees** not confirmed **Course Designer** Jack Nicklaus II **Prof** James Jones **Facilities** ⓣ 🍴 🕍 ☕ 🍷 👤 📷 🚩 🛢 ♂ **Leisure** hard tennis courts, heated indoor swimming pool, fishing, sauna, gymnasium, jacuzzis **Conf** facs Corporate Hospitality Days **Location** off A10 for Broxbourne, signs for Paradise Wildlife Park, left at Bell Ln over A10, on right
Hotel ★★★★ 76% HL Cheshunt Marriott, Halfhide Lane, Turnford, BROXBOURNE ☎ 01992 451245 📠 01992 451245   143 en suite

BUNTINGFORD
Map 5 TL32

East Herts Hamels Park SG9 9NA
☎ 01920 821978 (office) & 821922 (pro)
🖶 01920 823700
e-mail: secretary@easthertsgolfclub.co.uk
web: www.easthertsgolfclub.co.uk
Mature, attractive, undulating parkland course with magnificent specimen trees.
18 Holes, 6451yds, Par 71, SSS 71, Course record 62. Club membership 800.
Visitors Mon, Tue, Thu & Fri except BHs. Handicap certificate. Dress code. **Societies** welcome. **Green Fees** £50 per day, £36 per round **Prof** D Field **Facilities** ⑪ ⑩⑪ ⓛ ⌑ ⓖ⑪ ⌦ 🛢 ⑪ 🛢
🛢 **Conf** Corporate Hospitality Days **Location** 1m N of Puckeridge off A10, opposite Pearce's Farm Shop
Hotel ★★★ 77% HL Novotel Stevenage, Knebworth Park, STEVENAGE ☎ 01438 346100 🖶 01438 346100   101 en suite

BUSHEY
Map 4 TQ19

Bushey Golf & Country Club High St WD23 1TT
☎ 020 8950 2215(pro shop) & 8950 2283 (club)
🖶 020 8386 1181
e-mail: info@busheycountryclub.com
web: www.busheycountryclub.com
Undulating parkland with challenging 2nd and 9th holes. The latter has a sweeping dog-leg left, playing to a green in front of the clubhouse. For the rather too enthusiastic golfer, Bushey offers its own physiotherapist.
Bushey Golf & Country Club: 9 Holes, 6120yds, Par 70, SSS 69, Course record 67. Club membership 475.
Visitors Mon, Tue & Fri except BHs. Wed & Thu after 1pm. Weekends after 2.30pm. Booking required. Dress code. **Societies** welcome. **Green Fees** £22 per 18 holes, £14 per 9 holes (£27/£16 weekends) **Course Designer** Donald Steele **Prof** Martin Siggins **Facilities** ⑪ ⑩⑪ ⓛ ⌑ ⓖ⑪ 🛢 🛢 ⑪ 🎯 **Leisure** sauna, gymnasium, health & fitness club **Conf** facs Corporate Hospitality Days **Location** M1 junct 5
Hotel ★★★ 74% HL Corus hotel Elstree, Barnet Lane, ELSTREE ☎ 020 8953 8227 & 0844 736 8602 🖶 020 8953 8227   49 en suite

Bushey Hall Bushey Hall Dr WD23 2EP
☎ 01923 222253   🖶 01923 229759
e-mail: info@golfclubuk.co.uk
web: www.busheyhallgolfclub.co.uk
A tree-lined parkland course, the oldest established club in Hertfordshire.
18 Holes, 6099yds, Par 69, SSS 69, Course record 62. Club membership 500.
Visitors contact club for details. **Societies** booking required. **Green Fees** not confirmed **Course Designer** J Braid **Prof** Ken Wickham **Facilities** ⑪ by prior arrangement ⓛ ⌑ ⓖ⑪ ⌦ ⑪ 🛢 ⑪ **Leisure** practice nets **Conf** facs Corporate Hospitality Days **Location** M1 junct 5, A41Harrow to Bushey, 4th exit at rdbt, club 150yds on left
Hotel ★★★ 74% HL Corus hotel Elstree, Barnet Lane, ELSTREE ☎ 020 8953 8227 & 0844 736 8602 🖶 020 8953 8227   49 en suite

CHESHUNT
Map 5 TL30

Cheshunt Park Golf Centre Cheshunt Park, Park Ln EN7 6QD
☎ 01992 624009   🖶 01992 637551
e-mail: golf.leisure@broxbourne.gov.uk
web: www.broxbourne.gov.uk
Municipal parkland course, well bunkered with ponds, easy walking.
Cheshunt Park Golf Course: 18 Holes, 6692yds, Par 72, SSS 71. Club membership 480.
Visitors Mon-Sun & BHs. Booking required Fri-Sun & BHs. Dress code.. **Societies** booking required. **Green Fees** £15.50 per 18 holes (£21.50 weekends & BHs) **Course Designer** P Wawtry **Facilities** ⑪ ⑩⑪ ⓛ ⌑ ⓖ⑪ ⌦ 🛢 ⑪ 🎯 **Leisure** Club repair service **Conf** facs Corporate Hospitality Days **Location** 1.5m NW off B156. M25 junct 25, 3m N
Hotel ★★★★ 76% HL Cheshunt Marriott, Halfhide Lane, Turnford, BROXBOURNE ☎ 01992 451245 🖶 01992 451245   143 en suite

CHORLEYWOOD
Map 4 TQ09

Chorleywood Common Rd WD3 5LN
☎ 01923 282009   🖶 01923 286739
e-mail: secretary@chorleywoodgolfclub.co.uk
Very attractive mix of woodland and heathland with natural hazards and good views.
9 Holes, 5686yds, Par 68, SSS 67, Course record 64. Club membership 300.
Visitors Mon-Sat except BHs. Booking required. Handicap certificate. Dress code. **Societies** booking required. **Green Fees** £20 per round, £15 for 9 holes (£25/15 weekends) **Prof** R Mandeville **Facilities** ⑪ ⓛ ⌑ ⓖ⑪ ⌦ ⑪ **Location** M25 junct 18, E of village off A404
Hotel ★★★ 77% HL The Bedford Arms Hotel, CHENIES ☎ 01923 283301 🖶 01923 283301   18 en suite

ELSTREE
Map 4 TQ19

Elstree Watling St WD6 3AA
☎ 020 8953 6115 & 8238 6941   🖶 020 8207 6390
e-mail: admin@elstree-golf.co.uk
web: www.elstree-golfclub.co.uk
Parkland course incorporating ponds and streams and challenging doglegs.
Elstree Golf and Country Club: 18 Holes, 6556yds, Par 73, SSS 72. Club membership 400.
Visitors Mon-Sun & BHs. Dress code. **Societies** booking required. **Green Fees** £20 weekdays (£24 weekends & BHs). **Course Designer** Donald Steel **Prof** Marc Warwick **Facilities** ⑪ ⑩⑪ ⓛ ⌑ ⓖ⑪ ⌦ ⑪ 🛢 ⑪ 🎯 **Leisure** snooker, golf academy **Conf** facs Corporate Hospitality Days **Location** A5183 between Radlett and Elstree, next to Wagon pub
Hotel ★★★ 74% HL Corus hotel Elstree, Barnet Lane, ELSTREE ☎ 020 8953 8227 & 0844 736 8602 🖶 020 8953 8227   49 en suite

ESSENDON

Map 4 TL20

Hatfield London Country Club Bedwell Park AL9 6HN
☎ 01707 260360   📠 01707 278475
e-mail: info@hatfieldlondon.co.uk
web: www.hatfieldlondon.co.uk
Parkland course with many varied hazards, including ponds, a stream and a ditch.

Old Course: 18 Holes, 6808yds, Par 72, SSS 72.
New Course: 18 Holes, 6938yds, Par 72, SSS 73.
Club membership 350.

Visitors Mon-Sun & BHs. Booking required weekends. Dress code. **Societies** booking required. **Green Fees** Old Course £25 (£35 weekends & BHs). New Course £33 (£50 weekends & BHs) **Course Designer** Fred Hawtree **Facilities** ⑪ ⑩ 🛍 ⬛ 🍴 🍺 👟 🐎 **Leisure** sauna, 9 hole pitch and putt, Japanese bath **Conf** facs Corporate Hospitality Days **Location** 1m S on B158
Hotel ★★★★ 76% HL Ponsbourne Park Hotel, Newgate Street Village, POTTERS BAR, Nr Hertford ☎ 01707 876191 & 879277 📠 01707 876191   51 en suite

GRAVELEY

Map 4 TL22

Chesfield Downs Golf & Country Club Jack's Hill SG4 7EQ
☎ 01462 482929   📠 01462 482930
e-mail: chesfielddowns-manager@crown-golf.co.uk
web: www.crown-golf.co.uk
Tree lined parkland golf course with undulating fairways and USGA greens. Playable all year due to its design and its chalk based construction. In addition to the main course is the par 3 Lannock Links, ideal for the novice golfer.

Chesfield Downs Golf & Country Club: 18 Holes, 6648yds, Par 71, SSS 72, Course record 65. Club membership 500.

Visitors Mon-Sun & BHs. Booking advisable. Dress code. **Societies** welcome. **Green Fees** Mon-Thu £23 per round, Fri £26, weekends & BHs £32 **Course Designer** J Gaunt **Prof** Keith Bond **Facilities** ⑪ ⑩ by prior arrangement 🛍 ⬛ 🍴 👟 🍺 🐎 🐎 **Leisure** sauna, gymnasium, par 3 9 hole course, studio relaxation suite **Conf** facs Corporate Hospitality Days **Location** A1 junct 8, B197 to Graveley
Hotel BUD Ibis Stevenage Centre, Danestrete, STEVENAGE ☎ 01438 779955 📠 01438 779955   98 en suite

HARPENDEN

Map 4 TL11

Aldwickbury Park Piggottshill Ln AL5 1AB
☎ 01582 760112   📠 01582 760113
e-mail: info@aldwickburyparkgc.co.uk
web: www.aldwickburyparkgolfclub.com
The combination of mature woodland, undulating parkland and lakes provides an array of challenges enhanced by stunning views over the Lea Valley. Its signature hole, the 18th, requires a good drive, leaving a short iron over a lake to a bunker protected green.

Park Course: 18 Holes, 6368yds, Par 71, SSS 71, Course record 66. Club membership 700.

Visitors Mon-Sun & BHs. Booking required. Dress code. **Societies** booking required. **Green Fees** £40 per 18 holes. Par 3 course £6/£7 **Course Designer** Ken Brown/Martin Gillett **Prof** Robin Turley **Facilities** ⑪ ⑩ 🛍 ⬛ 🍴 👟 🍺 🐎 **Leisure** gymnasium, academy facility including par 3 course

Conf facs Corporate Hospitality Days **Location** M1 junct 9, off Wheathampstead Rd between Harpenden & Wheathampstead
Hotel ★★★★ 72% HL Harpenden House Hotel, 18 Southdown Road, HARPENDEN ☎ 0870 609 6170 📠 0870 609 6170   76 en suite

Harpenden Hammonds End, Redbourn Ln AL5 2AX
☎ 01582 712580   📠 01582 712725
e-mail: office@harpendengolfclub.co.uk
web: www.harpendengolfclub.co.uk
Gently undulating parkland, easy walking.

18 Holes, 6377yds, Par 70, SSS 70, Course record 64.
Club membership 800.

Visitors Mon-Wed, Fri-Sun & BHs. Booking required weekends & BHs. Dress code. **Societies** booking required. **Green Fees** £50 per day, £40 per round (£45 per round weekends & BHs) **Course Designer** Hawtree & Taylor **Prof** Peter Lane **Facilities** ⑪ ⑩ by prior arrangement 🛍 ⬛ 🍴 👟 🍺 🐎 🐎 **Conf** Corporate Hospitality Days **Location** 1m S on B487
Hotel ★★★★ 72% HL Harpenden House Hotel, 18 Southdown Road, HARPENDEN ☎ 0870 609 6170 📠 0870 609 6170   76 en suite

Harpenden Common Cravells Rd, East Common AL5 1BL
☎ 01582 711328 (pro shop)   📠 01582 711321
e-mail: manager@hcgc.co.uk
web: www.hcgc.co.uk
Flat, easy walking, parkland with good greens. Golf has been played on the common for well over 100 years.

18 Holes, 6214yds, Par 70, SSS 70, Course record 64.
Club membership 710.

Visitors contact club for details **Societies** welcome. **Green Fees** £40 per day, £36 per round . £25 per round winter **Course Designer** K Brown **Prof** Danny Fitzsimmons **Facilities** ⑪ ⑩ 🛍 ⬛ 🍴 👟 🐎 🐎 🐎 **Location** on A1081 0.5m S of Harpenden
Hotel ★★★★ 72% HL Harpenden House Hotel, 18 Southdown Road, HARPENDEN ☎ 0870 609 6170 📠 0870 609 6170   76 en suite

HEMEL HEMPSTEAD

Map 4 TL00

Boxmoor 18 Box Ln, Boxmoor HP3 0DJ
☎ 01442 242434
web: www.boxmoorgolfclub.co.uk
The second-oldest course in Hertfordshire. Challenging, hilly, moorland course with sloping fairways divided by trees. Fine views. Testing holes: 3rd (par 3), 4th (par 4). The 3rd has not been holed in one since the course was founded in 1890 and the par for the course (64) has only been broken once.

9 Holes, 4812yds, Par 64, SSS 63, Course record 62.
Club membership 280.

Visitors Mon-Sat & BHs. Sun after 11.30am only. Dress code. **Societies** welcome. **Green Fees** not confirmed **Facilities** 🛍 ⬛ 🍴 👟 **Location** 2m SW on B4505
Hotel ★★★ 74% HL Best Western The Watermill, London Road, Bourne End, HEMEL HEMPSTEAD ☎ 01442 349955 📠 01442 349955   71 en suite

Little Hay Box Ln HP3 0DQ
☎ 01442 833798   📠 01442 831399
Little Hay Golf Complex: 18 Holes, 6300yds, Par 72, SSS 72.

Course Designer Hawtree **Location** 1.5m SW off A41 onto B4505
Telephone for further details

continued

Hotel ★★★ 77% HL The Bobsleigh Inn, Hempstead Road, Bovingdon, HEMEL HEMPSTEAD ☎ 0844 879 9033 📄 0844 879 9033 47 en suite

Shendish Manor Hotel & Golf Course London Rd, Apsley HP3 0AA

☎ 01442 251806 📄 01442 230683
e-mail: golfmanager@shendish.manor.com
web: www.shendish-manor.com

A hilly course with plenty of trees and good greens. A tough course for any golfer.

Shendish Manor Hotel & Golf Course: 18 Holes, 5660yds, Par 70, SSS 67. Club membership 200.

Visitors Mon-Sun & BHs. Booking required. Dress code.
Societies booking required. **Green Fees** phone **Course Designer** D Steel **Facilities** ⑪ ⑩ by prior arrangement 🔜 ⌨ ⑪ ♨ 🏠 ♨ ◇ 🛋 ✆ **Conf** facs Corporate Hospitality Days **Location** off A4251
Hotel ★★★★ 76% HL Pendley Manor, Cow Lane, TRING ☎ 01442 891891 📄 01442 891891 73 en suite

---

KNEBWORTH   Map 4 TL22

Knebworth Deards End Ln SG3 6NL
☎ 01438 812752 📄 01438 815216
e-mail: knebworth1@btconnect.com
web: www.knebworthgolfclub.com

Easy walking parkland.

18 Holes, 6518yds, Par 71, SSS 71, Course record 66. Club membership 900.

Visitors Mon, Tue & Thu except BHs. Booking required.
Societies booking required. **Green Fees** £40 per day/round. **Course Designer** W Park (Jun) **Prof** Garry Parker **Facilities** ⑪ ⑩ 🔜 ⌨ ⑪ 🏠 🛋 🛌 ✆ **Conf** Corporate Hospitality Days **Location** N of village off B197
Hotel ★★★ 71% HL Best Western Roebuck Inn, London Road, Broadwater, STEVENAGE ☎ 01438 365445 📄 01438 365445 26 en suite

---

LETCHWORTH   Map 4 TL23

Letchworth Letchworth Ln SG6 3NQ
☎ 01462 683203 📄 01462 484567
e-mail: secretary@letchworthgolfclub.com
web: www.letchworthgolfclub.com

Planned more than 100 years ago by Harry Vardon, this is an adventurous parkland course. To its variety of natural and artificial hazards is added an unpredictable wind.

18 Holes, 6459yds, Par 71, SSS 71, Course record 66. Club membership 950.

Visitors Mon-Fri except BHs. Handicap certificate. Dress code.
Societies welcome. **Green Fees** phone **Course Designer** Harry Vardon **Prof** Karl Teschner **Facilities** ⑪ ⑩ 🔜 ⌨ ⑪ 🏠 🛋 ♨ ✆ 🛌 ✆ 🍴 **Leisure** 9 hole par 3 course. **Conf** facs Corporate Hospitality Days **Location** S side of town centre off A505
Hotel ★★★ 71% SHL Redcoats Farmhouse Hotel, Redcoats Green, HITCHIN ☎ 01438 729500 📄 01438 729500 13 en suite

---

LITTLE GADDESDEN   Map 4 SP91

Ashridge HP4 1LY
☎ 01442 842244 📄 01442 843770
e-mail: info@ashridgegolfclub.ltd.uk
web: www.ashridgegolfclub.ltd.uk

Classic wooded parkland in Area of Outstanding Natural Beauty.

18 Holes, 6625yds, Par 72, SSS 71, Course record 63. Club membership 720.

Visitors Mon-Fri except BHs. Booking required. Dress code.
Societies booking required. **Green Fees** phone **Course Designer** Sir G Campbell/C Hutchinson/N V Hotchkin **Prof** Peter Cherry **Facilities** ⑪ ⑩ 🔜 ⌨ ⑪ 🏠 🛋 ♨ ✆ ✆ ✆
Conf Corporate Hospitality Days **Location** 5m N of Berkhamsted on B4506
Hotel ★★★★ 72% HL Harpenden House Hotel, 18 Southdown Road, HARPENDEN ☎ 0870 609 6170 📄 0870 609 6170 76 en suite

---

MUCH HADHAM   Map 5 TL41

Ash Valley Little Hadham Rd SG10 6HD
☎ 01279 843253 📄 01279 842389

18 Holes, 6586yds, Par 72, SSS 71, Course record 64.
Course Designer Martin Gillett **Location** 1.5m S of A120 Little Hadham lights
Telephone for further details
Hotel ★★★ 74% HL Roebuck, Baldock Street, WARE ☎ 01920 409955 📄 01920 409955 47 en suite

---

POTTERS BAR   Map 4 TL20

Potters Bar Darkes Ln EN6 1DE
☎ 01707 652020 📄 01707 655051
e-mail: john@pottersbargolfclub.com
web: www.pottersbargolfclub.com

Undulating parkland.

18 Holes, 6279yds, Par 71, SSS 70. Club membership 560.

Visitors Mon, Tue, Thu & Fri except BHs. Dress code **Societies** booking required. **Green Fees** £26 for 18 holes **Course Designer** James Braid **Prof** Gary A'Ris **Facilities** ⑪ 🔜 ⌨ ⑪ 🏠 🛋 ♨ ✆ 🛌 ✆
Location M25 junct 24, 1m N
Hotel BUD Days Inn South Mimms, Bignells Corner, POTTERS BAR ☎ 01707 665440 📄 01707 665440 74 en suite

---

RADLETT   Map 4 TL10

Porters Park Shenley Hill WD7 7AZ
☎ 01923 854127 📄 01923 855475
e-mail: enquiries@porterspark.com
web: www.porterspark.com

A splendid, undulating parkland course with fine trees and lush grass. The holes are all different and interesting - on many, accuracy of shot to the green is of paramount importance.

18 Holes, 6313yds, Par 70, SSS 70, Course record 64. Club membership 700.

Visitors Mon-Fri except BHs. Booking required. Handicap certificate.
Societies booking required. **Green Fees** not confirmed **Course Designer** Braid **Prof** David Gleeson **Facilities** ⑪ ⑩ 🔜 ⌨ ⑪

continued

⚓ 🏠 ⛳ ✏ **Conf** Corporate Hospitality Days **Location** NE of village off A5183
Hotel BUD Innkeeper's Lodge London Borehamwood, Studio Way, BOREHAM WOOD ☎ 0845 112 6120 📠 0845 112 6120 55 en suite

REDBOURN   Map 4 TL11

Redbourn Kinsbourne Green Ln AL3 7QA
☎ 01582 793493 📠 01582 794362
e-mail: info@redbourngc.co.uk
web: www.redbourngolfclub.com

A mature parkland course offering a fair test of golf to all standards. Water comes into play on a number of holes.

Ver Course: 18 Holes, 6506yds, Par 70, SSS 71, Course record 67.
Kingsbourne Course: 9 Holes, 1361yds, Par 27.
Club membership 800.

Visitors Mon-Sun & BHs. Booking required. Dress code.
Societies booking required. **Green Fees** £30 per 18 holes Mon-Thu, £35 Fri-Sun **Prof** Stephen Hunter **Facilities** 🎖 🏌 ⛳ 🏳️ ⚓ 🏠 🚰 ✏ 🌳 **Leisure** 9 hole par 3 course **Conf** Corporate Hospitality Days **Location** M1 junct 9, 1m N off A5183
Hotel ★★★★ 72% HL Harpenden House Hotel, 18 Southdown Road, HARPENDEN ☎ 0870 609 6170 📠 0870 609 6170 76 en suite

RICKMANSWORTH   Map 4 TQ09

The Grove Chandler's Cross WD3 4TG
☎ 01923 294266 📠 01923 294268
e-mail: golf@thegrove.co.uk
web: www.thegrove.co.uk

A course built to USGA specifications but following the slopes, ridges and mounds that occur naturally within the landscape. The fairway grass encourages crisp ball striking and the greens have firm, fast putting surfaces. Continuous cart path around all holes.

The Grove: 18 Holes, 7152yds, Par 72, SSS 74.

Visitors Mon-Sun & BHs. Booking required. **Societies** booking required. **Green Fees** not confirmed **Course Designer** Kyle Phillips **Prof** Spencer Schaub **Facilities** 🎖 🏌 🏳️ ⛳ 🏳️ 🌳 ⚓ 🏠 ◇ ✏ 🚰 🌳 **Leisure** hard tennis courts, outdoor and indoor heated swimming pool, sauna, gymnasium **Conf** facs Corporate Hospitality Days **Location** M25 junct 19/20, follow signs to Watford, At first large rdbt take exit for A411. Proceed for 0.5m and entrance on right.
Hotel ★★★★★ 89% HL The Grove, Chandler's Cross, RICKMANSWORTH ☎ 01923 807807 📠 01923 807807 227 en suite

Moor Park WD3 1QN
☎ 01923 773146 📠 01923 777109
e-mail: enquiries@moorparkgc.co.uk
web: www.moorparkgc.co.uk

Two parkland courses with rolling fairways - High Course is challenging and will test the best golfer and West Course demands a high degree of accuracy. The clubhouse is a Grade 1 Listed Mansion.

High Golf Course: 18 Holes, 6722yds, Par 72, SSS 72, Course record 63.
West Golf Course: 18 Holes, 5815yds, Par 69, SSS 68, Course record 60. Club membership 1500.

Visitors Mon-Sun except BHs. Booking required. Handicap

certificate. Dress code. **Societies** booking required. **Green Fees** High £85 per round, West £55 per round (£125/£85 weekends) **Course Designer** H S Colt **Prof** Lawrence Farmer **Facilities** 🎖 🏌 🏳️ ⛳ 🏳️ ⚓ 🏠 ⛳ ✏ 🚰 🌳 **Leisure** hard and grass tennis courts, chipping green snooker room **Conf** facs Corporate Hospitality Days **Location** M25 junct 17/18, off A404 to Northwood

Moor Park

Hotel ★★★ 77% HL The Bedford Arms Hotel, CHENIES ☎ 01923 283301 📠 01923 283301 18 en suite

Rickmansworth Public Course Moor Ln WD3 1QL
☎ 01923 775278
web: www.rickmansworthgolfcourse.co.uk

Undulating, municipal parkland course, short but tests skills to the full.

Rickmansworth Public Golf Course: 18 Holes, 4656yds, Par 65, SSS 63. Club membership 240.

Visitors Mon-Sun & BHs. Booking required. **Societies** booking required. **Green Fees** £15 per round (£20 weekends). **Course Designer** Colt **Prof** Darren Hodgson **Facilities** 🎖 🏌 🏳️ ⛳ 🏳️ 🌳 ⚓ 🏠 ✏ **Conf** facs Corporate Hospitality Days **Location** 2m S of town off A4145
Hotel ★★★ 77% HL The Bedford Arms Hotel, CHENIES ☎ 01923 283301 📠 01923 283301 18 en suite

ROYSTON   Map 5 TL34

Barkway Park Nuthampstead Rd, Barkway SG8 8EN
☎ 01763 849070
e-mail: gc@barkwaypark.fsnet.co.uk

An undulating course criss-crossed by ditches which come into play on several holes. The challenging par 3 7th features a long, narrow green with out of bounds close to the right edge of the green.

18 Holes, 6997yds, Par 74, SSS 74. Club membership 380.

Visitors Mon-Sun & BHs. Dress code. **Societies** welcome **Green Fees** phone **Course Designer** Vivien Saunders **Prof** Jamie Bates **Facilities** 🎖 🏌 ⛳ 🏳️ ⛳ 🌳 ⚓ 🏠 🚰 ✏ **Location** A10 onto B1368
Hotel ★★★ 75% HL Duxford Lodge, Ickleton Road, DUXFORD ☎ 01223 836444 📠 01223 836444 15 en suite

Heydon Grange Golf & Country Club, Heydon SG8 7NS
☎ 01763 208988 📠 01763 208926
e-mail: enquiries@heydon-grange.co.uk
web: www.heydongrange.co.uk

Three nine-hole parkland courses - the Essex, Cambridgeshire and Hertfordshire - situated in gently rolling countryside. Courses are playable all year round.

continued

*Essex: 9 Holes, 2891yds, Par 36, SSS 35, Course record 64.
Cambridgeshire: 9 Holes, 3057yds, Par 36, SSS 36.
Hertfordshire: 9 Holes, 2937yds, Par 36, SSS 36.
Club membership 250.*

Visitors Mon-Sun & BHs. Booking required weekends & BHs. Dress code. **Societies** welcome. **Green Fees** £20 per 18 holes, £14.50 per 9 holes (£25/£16.50 weekends & BHs) **Course Designer** Cameron Sinclair **Prof** Stuart Smith **Facilities** ⑪ ⑭⑪ ⓑ ▱ ⑪ ⏄ ⌂ ⑪ ✐ ⌂ ⑪ 𝆑 **Conf** Corporate Hospitality Days **Location** M11 junct 10, A505 between Royston and Newmarket
Hotel ★★★ 75% HL Duxford Lodge, Ickleton Road, DUXFORD
☎ 01223 836444 ▤ 01223 836444 15 en suite

Kingsway Cambridge Rd, Melbourn SG8 6EY
☎ 01763 262943   ▤ 01763 263038
e-mail: kingswaygolf@btconnect.com
The Melbourn course is short and deceptively tricky. This nine-hole course provides a good test for both beginners and experienced golfers. Out of bounds and strategically placed bunkers come into play on several holes, in particular the tough par 3 7th. The Orchard course is a cleverly designed par 3 course set among trees. Ideal for sharpening the short game or as a family introduction to golf.
*Melbourn Course: 9 Holes, 2455yds, Par 33, SSS 32.
Orchard Course: 9 Holes, 727yds, Par 27, SSS 27.
Club membership 150.*
Visitors Mon-Sun & BHs. Dress code. **Societies** welcome. **Green Fees** phone **Prof** D Hastings/M Sturgess **Facilities** ⑪ ⓑ ▱ ⑪ ⏄ ⌂ ⑪ ✐ 𝆑 **Leisure** 9 hole par 3 Orchard Course **Location** off A10
Hotel ★★★ 75% HL Duxford Lodge, Ickleton Road, DUXFORD
☎ 01223 836444 ▤ 01223 836444 15 en suite

Royston Baldock Rd SG8 5BG
☎ 01763 242696 & 243476   ▤ 01763 246910
e-mail: roystongolf@btconnect.com
web: www.roystongolfclub.co.uk
Heathland course on undulating terrain and fine fairways. The 8th, 10th and 15th are the most notable holes on this all weather course.
*18 Holes, 6052yds, Par 70, SSS 70, Course record 63.
Club membership 750.*
Visitors Mon-Sun & BHs. Dress code. **Societies** booking required. **Green Fees** from £15 **Course Designer** Harry Vardon **Prof** Sean Clark **Facilities** ⑪ ⑭⑪ ⓑ ▱ ⑪ ⏄ ⌂ ⑪ ✐ ⌂ 𝆑 **Conf** facs Corporate Hospitality Days **Location** 0.5m W of town centre
Hotel ★★★ 75% HL Duxford Lodge, Ickleton Road, DUXFORD
☎ 01223 836444 ▤ 01223 836444 15 en suite

ST ALBANS   Map 4 TL10

Abbey View Westminster Lodge Leisure Ctr AL1 2DL
☎ 01727 868227   ▤ 01727 848468
web: www.leisureconnection.co.uk
Abbey View Golf Course: 9 Holes, 1411yds, Par 29, Course record 27.
Prof Mark Flitton **Facilities** ⏄ ⌂ ⑪ ✐ **Leisure** hard and grass tennis courts, heated indoor swimming pool, sauna, gymnasium, crazy golf **Conf** Corporate Hospitality Days **Location** city centre, off Holywell Hill in Verulamium Park
Telephone for further details
Hotel ★★★★ 77% HL St Michael's Manor, Fishpool Street, ST ALBANS ☎ 01727 864444 ▤ 01727 864444 30 en suite

Batchwood Hall Batchwood Dr AL3 5XA
☎ 01727 844250   ▤ 01727 858506
web: www.stalbans.gov.uk
Batchwood Hall Golf & Tennis Centre: 18 Holes, 6487yds, Par 71, SSS 71.
Course Designer J H Taylor **Location** 1m NW off A5183
Telephone for further details
Hotel ★★★★ 77% HL St Michael's Manor, Fishpool Street, ST ALBANS ☎ 01727 864444 ▤ 01727 864444 30 en suite

Verulam London Rd AL1 1JG
☎ 01727 853327   ▤ 01727 812201
e-mail: gm@verulamgolf.co.uk
web: www.verulamgolf.co.uk
Easy walking parkland with fourteen holes having out of bounds. Water affects the 12th, 13th and 14th holes. Samuel Ryder was captain here in 1927 when he began the now celebrated Ryder Cup competition.
*18 Holes, 6448yds, Par 72, SSS 72, Course record 67.
Club membership 720.*
Visitors Mon-Fri except BHs. Handicap certificate. Dress code. **Societies** welcome. **Green Fees** Mon £25 per round, Tue-Fri £35 **Course Designer** Braid **Prof** Nick Burch **Facilities** ⑪ ⑭⑪ by prior arrangement ⓑ ▱ ⑪ ⏄ ⌂ ⑪ 𝆑 **Conf** facs Corporate Hospitality Days **Location** 0.5m from St Albans centre on A1081 London Rd, signed by railway bridge
Hotel ★★★★ 78% HL Sopwell House, Cottonmill Lane, Sopwell, ST ALBANS ☎ 01727 864477 ▤ 01727 864477 129 en suite

SAWBRIDGEWORTH   Map 5 TL41

Manor of Groves Golf & Country Club High Wych CM21 0JU
☎ 01279 603539 & 0870 410 8833   ▤ 01279 726972
e-mail: golf@manorofgroves.co.uk
web: www.manorofgroves.com
The course is set out over 150 acres of established parkland and rolling countryside and is a challenge to golfers at all levels.
Manor of Groves Golf & Country Club: 18 Holes, 6228yds, Par 71, SSS 70, Course record 63. Club membership 550.
Visitors Mon-Fri. Weekends & BHs after 11am only. Booking required. Dress code. **Societies** booking required. **Green Fees** not confirmed **Course Designer** S Sharer **Prof** Ben Goodey **Facilities** ⑪ ⑭⑪ ⓑ ▱ ⑪ ⏄ ⌂ ⑪ ◇ ✐ ⌂ 𝆑 **Leisure** heated indoor swimming pool, sauna, gymnasium **Conf** facs Corporate Hospitality Days **Location** 1.5m west of town centre
Hotel ★★★ 77% HL Manor of Groves Hotel, Golf & Country Club, High Wych, SAWBRIDGEWORTH ☎ 01279 600777 & 0870 410 8833 ▤ 01279 600777 80 en suite

STANSTEAD ABBOTTS   Map 5 TL31

Briggens Park Briggens Park, Stanstead Rd SG12 8LD
☎ 01279 793867   ▤ 01279 793867
e-mail: briggensparkgolf@aol.co.uk
An attractive nine-hole course set in the grounds of a hotel which was once a stately house in 80 acres of countryside.
*9 Holes, 2793yds, Par 72, SSS 69, Course record 67.
Club membership 200.*

continued

Visitors Mon-Sun & BHs. Booking required weekends & BHs. Dress code. Societies booking required. Green Fees £15 per 18 holes, £10 per 9 holes (£18/£12 weekends & BHs) Facilities 🍴 🖵 🎯 📠 🏌 🏖 🏌 Location off A414 Stanstead road
Hotel ★★★ 74% HL Roebuck, Baldock Street, WARE
☎ 01920 409955 📠 01920 409955 47 en suite

STEVENAGE   Map 4 TL22

Stevenage Golf Centre 6 Aston Ln SG2 7EL
☎ 01438 880223 & 880424 (pro shop)   📠 01438 880040
Bragbury Course: 18 Holes, 6451yds, Par 72, SSS 71, Course record 63.
Aston Course: 9 Holes, 880yds, Par 27, SSS 27.
Course Designer John Jacobs Location 4m SE off B5169
Telephone for further details
Hotel ★★★ 71% HL Best Western Roebuck Inn, London Road, Broadwater, STEVENAGE ☎ 01438 365445 📠 01438 365445 26 en suite

WARE   Map 5 TL31

Chadwell Springs Hertford Rd SG12 9LE
☎ 01920 461447   📠 01920 466596
9 Holes, 6418yds, Par 72, SSS 71, Course record 68.
Prof Mark Wall Facilities 🍴 🍴 🖵 🎯 🏖 🏌
Conf facs Corporate Hospitality Days Location 0.75m W on A119
Telephone for further details
Hotel ★★★ 74% HL Roebuck, Baldock Street, WARE
☎ 01920 409955 📠 01920 409955 47 en suite

Marriott Hanbury Manor Golf & Country Club see page 136
SG12 0SD
☎ 01920 487722   📠 01920 487692
web: www.marriotthanburymanor.co.uk

Whitehill Dane End SG12 0JS
☎ 01920 438495   📠 01920 438891
web: www.whitehillgolf.co.uk
Whitehill Golf: 18 Holes, 6618yds, Par 72, SSS 72.
Prof Matt Belsham Facilities 🍴 🍴 🖵 🎯 🏖 📠 🏌
🏌 🏌 🏌 Leisure snooker room Conf facs Corporate Hospitality Days Location M25 junct 25 towards Cambridge (A10). Take turn for Ware A1170 and turn right at rdbt. After 2m turn left, proceed for 2m, course on left
Telephone for further details
Hotel ★★★ 74% HL Roebuck, Baldock Street, WARE
☎ 01920 409955 📠 01920 409955 47 en suite

WATFORD   Map 4 TQ19

West Herts Cassiobury Park WD3 3GG
☎ 01923 236484   📠 01923 222300
e-mail: gm@westhertsgolf.demon.co.uk
web: www.westhertsgolfclub
Set in parkland, the course is close to Watford but its tree-lined setting is beautiful and tranquil. Set out on a plateau the course is exceedingly dry. It also has a very severe finish with the 17th, a hole of 378yds, the toughest on the course. The last hole measures over 480yds.

18 Holes, 6620yds, Par 72, SSS 72, Course record 65.
Club membership 900.
Visitors Mon-Sun & BHs. Booking required. Dress code. Societies booking required. Green Fees £40 per 18 holes (£50 weekends) Course Designer Tom Morris Prof Charles Gough
Facilities 🍴 🍴 🖵 🎯 🏖 📠 🏌 🏌 🏌 🏌
Leisure indoor teaching facility Conf Corporate Hospitality Days Location W of town centre off A412
Hotel ★★★ 73% HL Best Western White House, Upton Road, WATFORD ☎ 01923 237316 📠 01923 237316 57 en suite

WELWYN GARDEN CITY   Map 4 TL21

Mill Green Gypsy Ln AL7 4TY
☎ 01707 276900 & 270542 (Pro shop)   📠 01707 276898
e-mail: millgreen@crown-golf.co.uk
web: www.millgreengolf.com
A course of two contrasting 9 hole loops. The front 9 plays over a gently undulating landscape. The back 9 plays over fairways winding through ancient woodland and around large lakes. The par 3 course has small greens guarded by testing bunkers.
18 Holes, 6615yds, Par 72, SSS 72, Course record 64.
Club membership 850.
Visitors Mon-Fri. Weekends & BHs pm only. Booking required. Dress code. Societies booking required. Green Fees phone Course Designer Alliss & Clark Prof Ian Parker Facilities 🍴 🍴 🖵
🎯 🏖 📠 🏌 🏌 🏌 Leisure 9 hole par 3 course. Conf facs Corporate Hospitality Days Location exit 4 of A1(M), A414 to Mill Green
Hotel ★★★ 77% HL Bush Hall, Mill Green, HATFIELD
☎ 01707 271251 📠 01707 271251 25 en suite

Panshanger Golf & Squash Complex Old Herns Ln AL7 2ED
☎ 01707 333350   📠 01707 390010
web: www.finesseleisure.com
Panshanger Golf & Squash Complex: 18 Holes, 6347yds, Par 72, SSS 70, Course record 65.
Course Designer Peter Kirkham Location 1m N of town centre signed off B1000
Telephone for further details
Hotel ★★★★ 74% HL Tewin Bury Farm Hotel, Hertford Road (B1000), WELWYN GARDEN CITY, Herts ☎ 01438 717793 📠 01438 717793 39 en suite

Welwyn Garden City Mannicotts, High Oaks Rd AL8 7BP
☎ 01707 325243   📠 01707 393213
e-mail: secretary@welwyngardencitygolfclub.co.uk
web: www.welwyngardencitygolfclub.co.uk
Undulating parkland with a ravine. A former course record holder is Nick Faldo.
18 Holes, 6114yds, Par 70, SSS 69, Course record 63.
Club membership 930.
Visitors dress code. Societies welcome. Green Fees phone Course Designer Hawtree Prof Richard May Facilities 🍴 🍴 by prior arrangement 🖵 🎯 🏖 📠 🏌 🏌 🏌 Conf facs Corporate Hospitality Days Location A1 junct 6, W of city
Hotel ★★★ 74% HL Best Western Homestead Court Hotel, Homestead Lane, WELWYN GARDEN CITY ☎ 01707 324336 📠 01707 324336 67 en suite

MARRIOTT HANBURY MANOR

HERTFORDSHIRE - WARE - MAP 5 TL31

There can be few golf venues that combine so successfully the old and the new. The old is the site itself, dominated since the 19th century by Hanbury Manor, a Jacobean-style mansion; the wonderful grounds included a nine-hole parkland course designed by the legendary Harry Vardon. The new is the conversion of the estate into the golf and country club; the manor now offers a five-star country house hotel, while Jack Nicklaus II redesigned the grounds for an 18-hole course. The American-style design took the best of Vardon's original and added meadowland to produce a course that looks beautiful and plays superbly. Hanbury Manor has hosted a number of professional events, including the Women's European Open in 1996 and the Men's European Tour's English Open from 1997 to 1999, won respectively by Per Ulrik Johannson, Lee Westwood and Darren Clarke.

SG12 0SD ☎ 01920 487722 🖹 01920 487692
web: www.marriotthanburymanor.co.uk
Marriott Hanbury Manor Golf & Country Club: 18 Holes, 7052yds, Par 72, SSS 74, Course record 61. Club membership 674.
Visitors Handicap certificate. Dress code. Must be hotel resident or minimum of 12 golfers. **Societies** booking required. **Green Fees** phone **Course Designer** Jack Nicklaus II **Prof** Tim Good **Facilities** **Leisure** hard tennis courts, heated indoor swimming pool, sauna, gymnasium, Health spa
Conf facs Corporate Hospitality Days **Location** M25 junct 25, 12m N on A10
Hotel ★★★★★ **79%** CHH Marriott Hanbury Manor Hotel & Country Club, WARE ☎ 01920 487722 & 0870 400 7222 🖹 01920 487722 161 en suite

WHEATHAMPSTEAD   Map 4 TL11

Mid Herts Lamer Ln, Gustard Wood AL4 8RS
☎ 01582 832242   📄 01582 834834
e-mail: secretary@mid-hertsgolfclub.co.uk
web: www.mid-hertsgolfclub.co.uk
Commonland, wooded with heather and gorse-lined fairways.

18 Holes, 6060yds, Par 69, SSS 69, Course record 61.
Club membership 760.

Visitors Mon-Sun except BHs. Booking required weekends. Dress code.
Societies welcome. **Green Fees** Phone. **Course Designer** James Braid
Prof Barney Puttick **Facilities** ⑪ ㅏ ☐ ¶ ㅅ 🖨 🛆 ✔
Conf facs **Location** 1m N on B651

Hotel ★★★★ 72% HL Harpenden House Hotel, 18 Southdown
Road, HARPENDEN ☎ 0870 609 6170 📄 0870 609 6170 76 en suite

KENT

ADDINGTON   Map 5 TQ65

West Malling London Rd ME19 5AR
☎ 01732 844785   📄 01732 844795
e-mail: mike@westmallinggolf.com
web: www.westmallinggolf.com
Two 18-hole parkland courses. Year round play on main greens and
tees.

Spitfire Course: 18 Holes, 6142yds, Par 70, SSS 70,
Course record 67.
Hurricane Course: 18 Holes, 6281yds, Par 70, SSS 70,
Course record 69.

Visitors Mon-Sun & BHs. Dress code. **Societies** booking required.
Green Fees phone **Course Designer** Max Falkner **Prof** Duncan
Lambert **Facilities** ⑪ ⑩ ㅏ ☐ ¶ ㅅ 🖨 ✔ 🛆 ✔
✔ **Leisure** sauna, gymnasium, jaccuzi & steam room. **Conf** facs
Corporate Hospitality Days **Location** 1m S off A20
Hotel ★★★ 72% HL Grange Moor, St Michael's Road, MAIDSTONE
☎ 01622 677623 📄 01622 677623 50 en suite

ASH   Map 5 TQ66

The London Stansted Ln TN15 7EH
☎ 01474 879899   📄 01474 879912
e-mail: info@londongolf.co.uk
web: www.londongolf.co.uk
The two championship courses were designed by Jack Nicklaus. The
signature Heritage course is a par 72 parkland course which hosts
The European Open and presents a true golfing challenge with risky
carries over water and sand. It is strictly reserved for members and
their guests. Players of all standards can enjoy the inland links feel
of the International course which is available to visitors. Both courses
feature true fairways and pristine greens and the practice facilities
are among the very best.

Heritage Course: 18 Holes, 7257yds, Par 72, SSS 72,
Course record 63.
International Course: 18 Holes, 7005yds, Par 72, SSS 72,
Course record 64. Club membership 1800.

Visitors International course only. Mon-Sun & BHs. Booking
required. Handicap certificate. Dress code. **Societies** welcome **Green
Fees** International Course £95 per round (£110 Fri-Sun & BHs). Apr
£65/£75, Nov-Mar £55/£65 **Course Designer** Jack Nicklaus/Ron Kirby

Prof Paul Stuart **Facilities** ⑪ ⑩ ㅏ ☐ ¶ ㅅ 🖨 ¶ ✔
🖨 ✔ ✔ **Leisure** on site heli-pad **Conf** facs Corporate Hospitality
Days **Location** off A20, 2m from Brands Hatch
Hotel ★★★★ 75% HL Brandshatch Place Hotel & Spa,
Brands Hatch Road, Fawkham, BRANDS HATCH ☎ 01474 875000
📄 01474 875000 38 en suite

ASHFORD   Map 5 TR04

Ashford (Kent) Sandyhurst Ln TN25 4NT
☎ 01233 622655   📄 01233 627494
e-mail: secretary@ashfordgolfclub.co.uk
web: www.ashfordgolfclub.co.uk
Parkland with good views and easy walking. Considered to be one of
the best inland courses in the county. Narrow fairways and tightly
bunkered greens ensure a challenging game for all levels of golfer.

18 Holes, 6263yds, Par 71, SSS 70, Course record 65.
Club membership 672.

Visitors Mon-Sun & BHs. Booking required weekends & BHs. Dress
code. **Societies** booking required. **Green Fees** £30. Reduced winter
rates. **Course Designer** Cotton **Prof** Hugh Sherman **Facilities** ⑪ ⑩
ㅏ ☐ ¶ ㅅ 🖨 ✔ 🖨 ✔ **Conf** facs Corporate Hospitality
Days **Location** 1m NW M20 junct 9
Hotel ★★★★ 81% HL Ashford International Hotel, Simone Weil
Avenue, ASHFORD ☎ 01233 219988 📄 01233 219988 179 en suite

Homelands Golf Centre Ashford Rd, Kingsnorth TN26 1NJ
☎ 01233 661620
e-mail: info@ashfordgolf.co.uk
web: www.ashfordgolf.co.uk
Challenging nine-hole course designed by Donald Steel to provide
a stern test for experienced golfers and for others to develop their
game. With four par 3s and five par 4s it demands accuracy rather
than length.

Homelands Golf Centre: 9 Holes, 2230yds, Par 32, SSS 31,
Course record 32. Club membership 400.

Visitors Mon-Sun & BHs. Dress code. **Societies** booking required.
Green Fees not confirmed **Course Designer** Donald Steel
Prof Howard Bonaccorsi **Facilities** ⑪ ㅏ ☐ ¶ 🖨 ¶ 🖨
✔ ✔ **Leisure** teaching facilities **Conf** Corporate Hospitality Days
Location M20 junct 10, A2070, signed from 2nd rdbt to Kingsnorth
Hotel ★★★★ 81% HL Ashford International Hotel, Simone Weil
Avenue, ASHFORD ☎ 01233 219988 📄 01233 219988 179 en suite

BARHAM   Map 5 TR25

Broome Park The Broome Park Estate CT4 6QX
☎ 01227 830728   📄 01227 832591
e-mail: golf@broomepark.co.uk
web: www.broomepark.co.uk
Championship-standard parkland course in a valley, with a 350-year-
old mansion clubhouse.

18 Holes, 6580yds, Par 72, SSS 71, Course record 66.
Club membership 700.

Visitors contact club for details. **Societies** welcome. **Green Fees** £40
per round (£50 weekends) **Course Designer** Donald Steel **Prof** Tienne
Britz **Facilities** ⑪ ⑩ ㅏ ☐ ¶ ㅅ 🖨 ¶ ✔ 🖨 ✔ 🏌
Leisure hard tennis courts **Conf** facs Corporate Hospitality Days
Location 1.5m SE on A260
Hotel ★★★ 87% HL Best Western Abbots Barton, New Dover Road
CANTERBURY ☎ 01227 760341 📄 01227 760341 50 en suite

BEARSTED
Map 5 TQ85

Bearsted Ware St ME14 4PQ
☎ 01622 738198 ▤ 01622 735608
e-mail: bearstedgolfclub@tiscali..com
web: www.bearstedgolfclub.co.uk
Parkland with fine views of the North Downs.
18 Holes, 6437yds, Par 72, SSS 71. Club membership 780.
Visitors Mon-Sat except BHs. Booking required. Handicap certificate.
Dress code. **Societies** booking required. **Green Fees** £45 per 36 holes,
£34 per 18 holes **Prof** Tim Simpson **Facilities** ⊕ ⫶⊙⫶ ⊫ ⊡ ⊕⫶
⚐ 🖨 ✐ **Location** M20 junct 7, right at rdbt, left at minirdbt, left
at 2nd minirdbt. Pass Bell pub on right, under bridge, on left
Hotel ★★★★ 79% HL Tudor Park, a Marriott Hotel & Country
Club, Ashford Road, Bearsted, MAIDSTONE ☎ 01622 734334
& 632004 ▤ 01622 734334 120 en suite

BIDDENDEN
Map 5 TQ83

Chart Hills Weeks Ln TN27 8JX
☎ 01580 292222 ▤ 01580 292233
e-mail: info@charthills.co.uk
web: www.charthills.co.uk
Created by Nick Faldo, he has truly left his mark on this course.
Signature features include the 200-yard long snake-like Anaconda
Bunker (one of 138) on the 5th and the island green at the short 17th.
18 Holes, 7119yds, Par 72, SSS 74, Course record 61.
Club membership 500.
Visitors Mon-Sun & BHs. Booking required. Dress code.
Societies booking required. **Green Fees** £65 per 18 holes (£80
weekends), Winter £45/£55 **Course Designer** Nick Faldo **Prof** James
Cornish **Facilities** ⊕ ⫶⊙⫶ ⊫ ⊡ ⊕⫶ ⚐ 🖨 ⫶✐ ✐ 🛺 ✐
✐ **Leisure** fishing **Conf** facs Corporate Hospitality Days **Location** 1m
N of Biddenden off A274
Hotel ★★★ 75% HL London Beach Country Hotel, Spa & Golf
Club, Ashford Road, TENTERDEN, Ashford ☎ 01580 766279
▤ 01580 766279 26 en suite

BOROUGH GREEN
Map 5 TQ65

Wrotham Heath Seven Mile Ln TN15 8QZ
☎ 01732 884800 ▤ 01732 887370
18 Holes, 5954yds, Par 70, SSS 69, Course record 66.
Course Designer Donald Steel (part) **Location** 2.25m E on B2016
Telephone for further details
Hotel ★★★ 77% HL Hadlow Manor, Goose Green, HADLOW
☎ 01732 851442 ▤ 01732 851442 29 en suite

BRENCHLEY
Map 5 TQ64

Kent National Golf & Country Club Watermans Ln
TN12 6ND
☎ 01892 724400 ▤ 01892 723300
web: www.kentnational.com
Kent National Golf & Country Club: 18 Holes, 6693yds,
Par 72, SSS 72, Course record 63.
Course Designer T Saito **Location** 3m N of Brenchley off B2160
Telephone for further details
Hotel ★★ 64% MET Russell Hotel, 80 London Road, TUNBRIDGE
WELLS ☎ 01892 544833 ▤ 01892 544833 25 en suite

BROADSTAIRS
Map 5 TR36

North Foreland Convent Rd CT10 3PU
☎ 01843 862140 ▤ 01843 862663
e-mail: office@northforeland.co.uk
web: www.northforeland.co.uk
A picturesque cliff top course situated where the Thames Estuary
widens towards the sea. One of the few courses where the sea can
be seen from every hole. Walking is easy and the wind is deceptive.
The 8th and 17th, both par 4, are testing holes. There is also an
18-hole approach and putting course.
18 Holes, 6430yds, Par 71, SSS 71, Course record 63.
Club membership 1100.
Visitors Mon-Sun & BHs. Handicap certificate. Dress code.
Societies booking required. **Green Fees** £51 per day, £39 per
round (£51 per round weekends). Par 3 course £8 (£9.50 weekends)
Course Designer Fowler & Simpson **Prof** Darren Parris **Facilities** ⊕
⫶⊙⫶ ⊫ ⊡ ⊕⫶ ⚐ 🖨 ⫶✐ ✐ 🛺 ✐ **Leisure** hard tennis
courts, 18 hole par 3 course **Conf** facs Corporate Hospitality Days
Location 1.5m N off B2052
Hotel ★★★ 79% HL The Fayreness, Marine Drive, KINGSGATE,
Broadstairs ☎ 01843 868641 & 861103 ▤ 01843 868641
29 en suite

CANTERBURY
Map 5 TR15

Canterbury Scotland Hills, Littlebourne Rd CT1 1TW
☎ 01227 453532 ▤ 01227 784277
e-mail: generalmanager@canterburygolfclub.co.uk

Undulating parkland, densely wooded in places, with elevated tees
and challenging drives on several holes.
18 Holes, 6272yds, Par 71, SSS 70, Course record 64.
Club membership 700.
Visitors contact club for details. **Societies** booking required. **Green
Fees** £45 per day, £33 per 18 holes (£34 per 18 holes weekends)
Course Designer Harry Colt **Prof** Paul Everard **Facilities** ⊕ ⫶⊙⫶ ⊫
⊡ ⊕⫶ ⚐ 🖨 ⫶✐ 🛺 ✐ ✐ **Conf** facs Corporate Hospitality
Days **Location** 1.5m E on A257
Hotel ★★★ 87% HL Best Western Abbots Barton, New Dover Road,
CANTERBURY ☎ 01227 760341 ▤ 01227 760341 50 en suite

CRANBROOK — Map 5 TQ73

Hemsted Forest Golford Rd TN17 4AL
☎ 01580 712833 📄 01580 714274
e-mail: golf@hemstedforest.co.uk
web: www.hemstedforest.co.uk

Scenic parkland with easy terrain, backed by Hemsted Forest. The course lies in a beautiful natural setting and offers a tranquil haven. The clubhouse, a converted oast, is the only one of its kind.

18 Holes, 6305yds, Par 70, SSS 71, Course record 64. Club membership 1500.

Visitors Tue-Sun & BHs. Booking required. Dress code. **Societies** booking required. **Green Fees** £25 per round (£40 weekends) **Course Designer** Commander J Harris **Prof** Henry Low **Facilities** ⚑ 🍴 🛉 ⬜ 🍺 🛆 📷 ⚘ **Leisure** practice nets **Conf** facs Corporate Hospitality Days **Location** 2m E
Hotel ★★★ 75% HL London Beach Country Hotel, Spa & Golf Club, Ashford Road, TENTERDEN, Ashford ☎ 01580 766279 📄 01580 766279 26 en suite

DARTFORD — Map 5 TQ57

Birchwood Park Birchwood Rd DA2 7HJ
☎ 01322 662038 & 660554 📄 01322 667283
web: www.birchwoodparkgc.co.uk
Parkland: 18 Holes, 6364yds, Par 71, SSS 70, Course record 64.
Orchard: 9 Holes, 1349yds, Par 29.

Course Designer Howard Swann **Location** B258 between Dartford & Swanley
Telephone for further details
Hotel ★★★★ 75% HL Bexleyheath Marriott Hotel, 1 Broadway, BEXLEYHEATH ☎ 020 8298 1000 📄 020 8298 1000 142 en suite

Dartford Heath Lane (Upper), Dartford Heath DA1 2TN
☎ 01322 226455 📄 01322 226455
e-mail: dartfordgolf@hotmail.com
web: www.dartfordgolfclub.co.uk

Challenging parkland course with tight fairways and easy walking.
18 Holes, 5909yds, Par 69, SSS 69, Course record 61. Club membership 700.

Visitors Mon-Fri except BHs. Handicap certificate. Dress code. **Societies** booking required. **Green Fees** £37 per 36 holes, £26 per 18 holes **Course Designer** James Braid **Prof** John Gregory **Facilities** ⚑ 🍴 🛉 ⬜ 🍺 🛆 📷 ⚘ **Conf** facs Corporate Hospitality Days **Location** 2m from town centre off A2
Hotel ★★★★ 82% HL Rowhill Grange Hotel & Utopia Spa, WILMINGTON, Dartford ☎ 01322 615136 📄 01322 615136 38 en suite

DEAL — Map 5 TR35

Royal Cinque Ports Golf Rd CT14 6RF
☎ 01304 374007 📄 01304 379530
web: www.royalcinqueports.com
18 Holes, 6899yds, Par 72, SSS 73.
Course Designer James Braid **Location** on seafront at N end of Deal
Telephone for further details
Hotel ★★★★ 74% HL Wallett's Court Country House Hotel & Spa, West Cliffe, St Margarets-at-Cliffe, DOVER ☎ 01304 852424 & 0800 035 1628 📄 01304 852424 16 en suite

EDENBRIDGE — Map 5 TQ44

Sweetwoods Park Cowden TN8 7JN
☎ 01342 850729 (Pro shop) 📄 01342 850866
e-mail: golf@sweetwoodspark.com
web: www.sweetwoodspark.com

An undulating and mature parkland course with very high quality greens, testing water hazards and fine views across the Weald from four holes. A good challenge off the back tees. Signature holes include the 7th, 14th and 17th.

Sweetwoods Park: 18 Holes, 6607yds, Par 72, SSS 72, Course record 63. Club membership 700.

Visitors Mon-Sun & BHs. Booking required. Dress code. **Societies** booking required. **Green Fees** £30 per round (£36 weekends and BHs) **Prof** Julian Reason **Facilities** ⚑ 🍴 🛉 ⬜ 🍺 🛆 📷 🏌 ⚘ 🚗 ⚘ 🏳 **Conf** facs Corporate Hospitality Days **Location** 4m E of East Grinstead on A264
Hotel ★★★ HL Gravetye Manor, EAST GRINSTEAD ☎ 01342 810567 📄 01342 810567 18 en suite

EYNSFORD — Map 5 TQ56

Austin Lodge Upper Austin Lodge Rd DA4 0HU
☎ 01322 863000 📄 01322 862406
e-mail: info@pentlandgolf.co.uk
web: www.pentlandgolf.co.uk

A well-drained course designed to lie naturally in three secluded valleys in rolling countryside. Over 7000yds from the medal tees.

18 Holes, 7026yds, Par 73, SSS 71, Course record 68. Club membership 500.

Visitors dress code. **Societies** welcome. **Green Fees** £22 per 18 holes (£29.50 weekends and BHs) **Course Designer** P Bevan **Facilities** ⚑ 🍴 🛉 ⬜ 🍺 🛆 📷 🏌 ⚘ 🚗 ⚘ 🏳 **Leisure** practice nets **Conf** facs Corporate Hospitality Days **Location** 6m S of Dartford
Hotel ★★★★ 75% HL Brandshatch Place Hotel & Spa, Brands Hatch Road, Fawkham, BRANDS HATCH ☎ 01474 875000 📄 01474 875000 38 en suite

FAVERSHAM — Map 5 TR06

Boughton Brickfield Ln ME13 9AJ
☎ 01227 752277 📄 01227 752361
web: www.pentlandgolf.co.uk
Boughton Golf: 18 Holes, 6469yds, Par 72, SSS 71, Course record 68.
Course Designer P Sparks **Location** M2 junct 7, Brenley Corner
Telephone for further details
Hotel ★★★★ HL Eastwell Manor, Eastwell Park, Boughton Lees, ASHFORD ☎ 01233 213000 📄 01233 213000 62 en suite

Faversham Belmont Park ME13 0HB
☎ 01795 890561 📄 01795 890760
e-mail: themanager@favershamgolf.co.uk
web: www.favershamgolf.co.uk

A beautiful inland course laid out over part of a large estate with pheasants walking the fairways quite tamely. Play follows two heavily wooded valleys but the trees affect only the loose shots going out of bounds. Fine views.

18 Holes, 5978yds, Par 70, SSS 69, Course record 62. Club membership 800.

continue▶

Visitors Mon-Fri except BHs. Dress code. **Societies** welcome. **Green Fees** £35 per round **Course Designer** J H Taylor/D Steel **Prof** Stuart Rokes **Facilities** ⑪ ⑩ ⓛ ⓛ ☐ ⓛ ⚑ ⚑ ⚑ ⚑ ⚑ **Conf** Corporate Hospitality Days **Location** 3.5m S on Belmont road

Faversham

Hotel ★★★★ HL Eastwell Manor, Eastwell Park, Boughton Lees, ASHFORD ☎ 01233 213000 📄 01233 213000 62 en suite

FOLKESTONE
Map 5 TR23

Etchinghill Canterbury Rd CT18 8FA
☎ 01303 863863 📄 01303 863210
web: www.pentlandgolf.co.uk
Etchinghill Golf Course: 27 Holes, 6101yds, Par 70, SSS 69, Course record 67.
Course Designer John Sturdy **Location** M20 junct 11/12
Telephone for further details
Hotel ★★★ 75% HL Best Western Clifton, The Leas, FOLKESTONE
☎ 01303 851231 📄 01303 851231 80 en suite

GILLINGHAM
Map 5 TQ76

Gillingham Woodlands Rd ME7 2AP
☎ 01634 853017 (office) 📄 01634 574749
e-mail: golf@gillinghamgolf.idps.co.uk
web: www.gillinghamgolfclub.co.uk
Mature parkland course with views of the estuary.
18 Holes, 5540yds, Par 68, SSS 67, Course record 64. Club membership 900.
Visitors Mon-Wed & Fri except BHs. Handicap certificate. Dress code. **Societies** booking required. **Green Fees** £45 per day, £25 per round **Course Designer** James Braid/Steel **Prof** Martin Daniels **Facilities** ⑪ ⑩ ⓛ ☐ ⓛ ⚑ ⚑ ⚑ **Conf** facs Corporate Hospitality Days **Location** 1.5m SE on A2
Hotel ★★★★ 72% HL Bridgewood Manor Hotel, Bridgewood Roundabout, Walderslade Woods, CHATHAM ☎ 01634 201333 📄 01634 201333 100 en suite

GRAVESEND
Map 5 TQ67

Mid Kent Singlewell Rd DA11 7RB
☎ 01474 568035 📄 01474 564218
e-mail: secretary@mkgc.co.uk
web: www.mkgc.co.uk
A well-maintained downland course with some easy walking and some excellent greens. The first hole is short, but nonetheless a real challenge. The slightest hook and the ball is out of bounds or lost.

18 Holes, 6106yds, Par 70, SSS 69, Course record 60. Club membership 900.
Visitors Mon-Fri except BHs. Handicap certificate. Dress code. **Societies** booking required. **Green Fees** £50 per day, £30 per round **Course Designer** Frank Pennick **Prof** Mark Foreman **Facilities** ⑪ ⑩ by prior arrangement ⓛ ☐ ⓛ ⚑ ⚑ ⚑ ⚑ ⚑ **Leisure** snooker **Location** S of town centre off A227
Hotel ★★★ 77% HL Best Western Manor Hotel, Hever Court Road, GRAVESEND ☎ 01474 353100 📄 01474 353100 59 en suite

Southern Valley Thong Ln, Shorne DA12 4LF
☎ 01474 568568 📄 01474 360366
e-mail: larry@southernvalley.co.uk
web: www.southernvalley.co.uk
All year playing conditions on a course landscaped with gorse, bracken and thorn and designed to enhance the views across the Thames Estuary. The course features undulating greens, large trees and rolling fairways with the 9th and 18th holes located close to the clubhouse.
Southern Valley Golf Course: 18 Holes, 6200yds, Par 69, SSS 69. Club membership 300.
Visitors contact course for details. **Societies** welcome. **Green Fees** £16.50 per 18 holes, £10.50 per 9 holes (£19.50/£12.50 weekends and BHs) **Course Designer** Weller/Richardson **Prof** Larry Batchelor **Facilities** ⑪ ⓛ ☐ ⓛ ⚑ ⚑ ⚑ ⚑ **Conf** facs Corporate Hospitality Days **Location** A2 junct 4, off slip-road left onto Thong Ln, continue 1m, follow signs for Inn on the Lake Hotel
Hotel ★★★ 77% HL Best Western Manor Hotel, Hever Court Road, GRAVESEND ☎ 01474 353100 📄 01474 353100 59 en suite

HALSTEAD
Map 5 TQ46

Broke Hill Sevenoaks Rd TN14 7HR
☎ 01959 533225 📄 01959 532680
web: www.crown-golf.co.uk/brokehill

18 Holes, 6469yds, Par 72, SSS 71, Course record 65.
Course Designer David Williams **Location** M25 junct 4, opp Knockholt station
Telephone for further details
Hotel ★★★ 79% HL Best Western Donnington Manor, London Road, Dunton Green, SEVENOAKS ☎ 01732 462681 📄 01732 462681 60 en suite

HAWKHURST — Map 5 TQ73

Hawkhurst High St TN18 4JS
☎ 01580 752396 🖷 01580 754074
e-mail: hawkhurstgolfclub@tiscali.co.uk
web: hawkhurstgolfclub.org.uk
Undulating parkland.

9 Holes, 5751yds, Par 70, SSS 68, Course record 69.
Club membership 220.

Visitors Mon-Sun except BHs. Handicap certificate. Dress code **Societies** booking required. **Green Fees** £29 per day, £22 per round **Course Designer** W A Baldock **Prof** Peter Chandler **Facilities** ⑪ ⑩ ⓛ ⌖ 🖵 🍴 ⚑ ⚐ 🛄 🏧 ♨ **Leisure** squash, squash **Conf** facs **Location** W of village off A268
Hotel ★★★ 75% HL London Beach Country Hotel, Spa & Golf Club, Ashford Road, TENTERDEN, Ashford ☎ 01580 766279 🖷 01580 766279 26 en suite

HEADCORN — Map 5 TQ84

Weald of Kent Maidstone Rd TN27 9PT
☎ 01622 890866 🖷 01622 890070
e-mail: proshop@weald-of-kent.co.uk
Enjoying delightful views over the Weald, this pay and play course features a range of natural hazards, including lakes, trees, ditches and undulating fairways. A good test for golfers of every standard.

Weald of Kent Golf Course: 18 Holes, 6310yds, Par 70,
SSS 70, Course record 67. Club membership 350.

Visitors dress code. **Societies** booking required. **Green Fees** not confirmed **Course Designer** John Millen **Facilities** ⑪ ⑩ ⓛ ⌖ 🖵 🍴 ⚑ ⚐ ♨ 🛄 **Leisure** training academy **Conf** facs Corporate Hospitality Days **Location** M20 junct 8, through Leeds village, A274 towards Headcorn, course on left
Hotel ★★★★ 79% HL Tudor Park, a Marriott Hotel & Country Club, Ashford Road, Bearsted, MAIDSTONE ☎ 01622 734334 & 632004 🖷 01622 734334 120 en suite

HERNE BAY — Map 5 TR16

Herne Bay Eddington CT6 7PG
☎ 01227 374727

18 Holes, 5567yds, Par 68, SSS 68.

Course Designer James Braid **Location** on junct A291
Telephone for further details
Hotel ★★★ 87% HL Best Western Abbots Barton, New Dover Road, CANTERBURY ☎ 01227 760341 🖷 01227 760341 50 en suite

HEVER — Map 5 TQ44

Hever Castle, Hever Rd, Edenbridge TN8 7NP
☎ 01732 700771 🖷 01732 700775
e-mail: mail@hevercastlegolfclub.co.uk
web: www.hever.co.uk
Originally part of the Hever Castle estate, set in 250 acres of Kentish countryside, the Championship course has matured well and, with the addition of the Princes' nine holes, offers stunning holes to challenge all golfers. Water plays a prominent part in the design of the course, particularly around Amen Corner, holes 11 through 13. The golfer is then met with the lengthy stretch home, especially up the 17th, a daunting 644yd par 5, one of Europe's longest.

Championship: 18 Holes, 6761yds, Par 72, SSS 73,
Course record 69.
Princes 9 Course: 9 Holes, 2784yds, Par 35.
Club membership 450.

Visitors contact club for details. **Societies** booking required. **Green Fees** Championship Course £39.50 summer, £27 winter. Princes 9 Course £10.50 **Course Designer** Dr Nicholas **Prof** Peter Parks **Facilities** ⑪ ⑩ ⓛ ⌖ 🖵 🍴 ⚑ ⚐ 🛄 🏧 ♨ **Conf** facs Corporate Hospitality Days **Location** off B269 between Oxted and Tonbridge, 0.5m from Hever Castle
Hotel ★★★★ 77% HL The Spa, Mount Ephraim, TUNBRIDGE WELLS ☎ 01892 520331 🖷 01892 520331 72 en suite

HILDENBOROUGH — Map 5 TQ54

Nizels Nizels Ln TN11 9LU
☎ 01732 838926 (Bookings) 🖷 01732 833764

Nizels Golf Course: 18 Holes, 6408yds, Par 72, SSS 71,
Course record 65.

Course Designer Donaldson/Edwards Partnership **Location** off B245
Telephone for further details
Hotel ★★★ 72% HL Best Western Rose & Crown, 125 High Street, TONBRIDGE ☎ 01732 357966 🖷 01732 357966 56 en suite

HOO — Map 5 TQ77

Deangate Ridge Dux Court Rd ME3 8RZ
☎ 01634 251180 🖷 01634 250537
Parkland, municipal course designed by Fred Hawtree. 18-hole pitch and putt.

18 Holes, 6300yds, Par 71, SSS 70, Course record 65.
Club membership 500.

Visitors Mon-Sun & BHs. Booking required. Dress code. **Societies** booking required. **Green Fees** not confirmed **Course Designer** Hawtree **Prof** Richard Fox **Facilities** ⑪ ⑩ ⓛ ⌖ 🖵 🍴 ⚑ ⚐ 🛄 ♨ 🏧 ♨ **Leisure** hard tennis courts, gymnasium **Location** 4m NE of Rochester off A228
Hotel ★★★★ 72% HL Bridgewood Manor Hotel, Bridgewood Roundabout, Walderslade Woods, CHATHAM ☎ 01634 201333 🖷 01634 201333 100 en suite

HYTHE — Map 5 TR13

Mercure Hythe Imperial Princes Pde CT21 6AE
☎ 01303 267441 🖷 01303 264610
e-mail: h6862@accor.com
web: www.mercure.com
A nine-hole 18-tee links course bounded by the Royal Military Canal and the English Channel. Although the course is relatively flat, its aspect offers an interesting and challenging round to a wide range of golfers.

Hythe Imperial: 9 Holes, 5560yds, Par 68, SSS 66,
Course record 62. Club membership 300.

Visitors contact hotel for details. **Societies** welcome. **Green Fees** phone. **Facilities** ⑪ ⑩ ⓛ ⌖ 🖵 🍴 ⚑ ⚐ 🛄 🏧 ♨ **Leisure** hard and grass tennis courts, heated indoor swimming pool, squash, sauna, gymnasium, snooker **Conf** facs Corporate Hospitality Days **Location** Exit M20 junct 11. Follow into Hythe towards the town centre. Turn right into Twiss Road. Golf course is in grounds of the Hythe Imperial
Hotel ★★★★ 74% HL Mercure Hythe Imperial, Princes Parade, HYTHE ☎ 01303 267441 🖷 01303 267441 100 en suite

Sene Valley Sene CT18 8BL

☎ 01303 268513 (Manager) 📠 01303 237513
e-mail: senevalleygolf@btconnect.com
web: www.senevalleygolfclub.co.uk

A two-level downland course in excellent condition, standing 350 feet above the town and providing interesting golf over an undulating landscape with sea views. A typical hole that challenges most players, is the par 3, 11th which combines a stunning sea view with a testing tee shot to a green surrounded by bunkers and gorse.

18 Holes, 6271yds, Par 71, SSS 70, Course record 65. Club membership 700.

Visitors Mon-Sun & BHs. Booking required weekends & BHs. Handicap certificate. Dress code. **Societies** booking required. **Green Fees** £32 weekdays. (£45 weekends) **Course Designer** Henry Cotton **Prof** Nick Watson **Facilities** ⓣ ⍰ ⛳ ☕ 🏌 🏠 🛒 ✦ **Conf** facs Corporate Hospitality Days **Location** M20 junct 12, A20 towards Ashford for 3m, left at rdbt, Hythe Rd for 1m
Hotel 74% Best Western Stade Court, West Parade, HYTHE ☎ 01303 268263 📠 01303 268263 42 en suite

KINGSDOWN   Map 5 TR34

Walmer & Kingsdown The Leas CT14 8EP

☎ 01304 373256 📠 01304 382336
e-mail: info@kingsdowngolf.co.uk
web: www.kingsdowngolf.co.uk

This beautiful downland site is situated near Deal and, being situated on top of the famous White Cliffs, offers breathtaking views of the Channel from every hole.

18 Holes, 6471yds, Par 72, SSS 71, Course record 66. Club membership 600.

Visitors Mon-Fri. Summer weekends & BHs pm only. Booking required Mon-Wed & weekends. Handicap certificate. Dress code. **Societies** booking required. **Green Fees** £40 per day, £32 per round (£40 per round weekends & BHs) **Course Designer** Prof Jude Read **Facilities** ⓣ ⍰ ⛳ ☕ 🏌 🏠 🛒 🏓 ✦ **Conf** Corporate Hospitality Days **Location** 1.5m E of Ringwould off A258 Dover-Deal road
Hotel ★★★ 80% HL Dunkerleys Hotel & Restaurant, 19 Beach Street, DEAL ☎ 01304 375016 📠 01304 375016 16 en suite

LAMBERHURST   Map 5 TQ63

Lamberhurst Church Rd TN3 8DT

☎ 01892 890591 📠 01892 891140
e-mail: secretary@lamberhurstgolfclub.com
web: www.lamberhurstgolfclub.com

Parkland course crossing the river twice. Fine views.

18 Holes, 6423yds, Par 72, SSS 71, Course record 65. Club membership 650.

Visitors dress code. **Societies** booking required. **Green Fees** £43 per day, £33 per round **Prof** Brian Impett **Facilities** ⓣ ⍰ ⛳ ☕ 🏌 🏠 ✦ **Conf** Corporate Hospitality Days **Location** N of village on B2162
Hotel ★★★★ 77% HL The Spa, Mount Ephraim, TUNBRIDGE WELLS ☎ 01892 520331 📠 01892 520331 72 en suite

LITTLESTONE   Map 5 TR02

Littlestone St Andrew's Rd TN28 8RB

☎ 01797 363355 📠 01797 362740
e-mail: secretary@littlestonegolfclub.org.uk
web: www.littlestonegolfclub.org.uk

Located in the Romney Marshes, this fairly flat seaside links course calls for every variety of shot. The 8th, 15th, 16th and 17th are regarded as classics by international golfers. Fast running fairways and faster greens.

18 Holes, 6486yds, Par 71, SSS 72, Course record 66. Club membership 350.

Visitors contact club for details. **Societies** welcome. **Green Fees** £70 per day, £50 per round (£90/£65 weekends & BHs). **Course Designer** Laidlaw Purves **Prof** Andrew Jones **Facilities** ⓣ ⛳ ☕ 🏌 🏠 🛒 ✦ **Leisure** hard tennis courts **Conf** Corporate Hospitality Days **Location** from A259 at New Romney take B2071 (Littlestone road)
Hotel ★★★★ 74% HL Mercure Hythe Imperial, Princes Parade, HYTHE ☎ 01303 267441 📠 01303 267441 100 en suite

Littlestone Warren St Andrews Rd TN28 8RB

☎ 01797 362231 📠 01797 363511
web: www.littlestonegolfclub.org.uk

A links-style course, normally very dry. Flat providing easy walking and play challenged by sea breezes. Although not overly long, narrow fairways and small greens place a premium on shot selection and placement.

Littlestone Warren: 18 Holes, 5126yds, Par 67, SSS 65, Course record 63. Club membership 550.

Visitors contact course for details. **Societies** booking required. **Green Fees** £35 per day, £22 per round (£37/£27 weekends) **Course Designer** Evans/Lewis **Prof** Andrew Jones **Facilities** ⓣ ⍰ ⛳ 🏌 🏠 ✦ **Conf** Corporate Hospitality Days **Location** from A259 at New Romney take B2071 (Littlestone road)
Hotel ★★★★ 74% HL Mercure Hythe Imperial, Princes Parade, HYTHE ☎ 01303 267441 📠 01303 267441 100 en suite

LYDD
Map 5 TR02

Lydd Romney Rd TN29 9LS
☎ 01797 320808 🖷 01797 321482
web: www.lyddgolfclub.co.uk

18 Holes, 6529yds, Par 71, SSS 71, Course record 65.
Course Designer Mike Smith **Location** A259 onto B2075 by Lydd Airport
Telephone for further details
Hotel ★★★★ 77% HL George in Rye, 98 High Street, RYE
☎ 01797 222114 🖷 01797 222114 24 en suite

MAIDSTONE
Map 5 TQ75

Cobtree Manor Park Chatham Rd, Sandling ME14 3AZ
☎ 01622 753276 🖶 01622 620387
e-mail: golf.manager@cobtreemanorgolfcourse.co.uk
web: www.cobtreemanorgolfcourse.co.uk
Undulating parkland with some water hazards.

Cobtree Manor Park Golf Course: 18 Holes, 5648yds,
Par 69, SSS 69, Course record 62. Club membership 400.
Visitors contact club for details. **Societies** booking required.
Green Fees phone **Course Designer** Lawtree **Prof** James Eldridge
Facilities 🍸 🍽 🏌 🏞 🛒 🏊 🏠 ⛳ 🚗 ⚡ **Conf** facs
Corporate Hospitality Days **Location** M20 junct 6, 0.25m N on A229
Hotel ★★★ 75% HL Best Western Russell, 136 Boxley Road,
MAIDSTONE ☎ 01622 692221 🖷 01622 692221 42 en suite

Leeds Castle Ashford Rd ME17 1PL
☎ 01622 767828 & 880467 🖷 01622 735616
web: www.leeds-castle.co.uk

Leeds Castle Golf Course: 9 Holes, 2681yds, Par 33,
SSS 33, Course record 29.
Course Designer Neil Coles **Location** M20 junct 8, 4m E of Maidstone
on A20 towards Lenham
Telephone for further details

Hotel ★★★★ 79% HL Tudor Park, a Marriott Hotel & Country
Club, Ashford Road, Bearsted, MAIDSTONE ☎ 01622 734334
& 632004 🖷 01622 734334 120 en suite

See advert on opposite page

Tudor Park, a Marriott Hotel & Country Club Ashford Rd
ME14 4NQ
☎ 01622 734334 🖷 01622 735360
web: www.marriotthotels.com/tdmgs

Milgate Course: 18 Holes, 6085yds, Par 70, SSS 69,
Course record 64.
Course Designer Donald Steel **Location** M20 junct 8, 1.25m W on A20
Telephone for further details
Hotel ★★★★ 79% HL Tudor Park, a Marriott Hotel & Country
Club, Ashford Road, Bearsted, MAIDSTONE ☎ 01622 734334
& 632004 🖷 01622 734334 120 en suite

NEW ASH GREEN
Map 5 TQ66

Redlibbets Manor Ln, West Yoke TN15 7HT
☎ 01474 879190 🖷 01474 879290
e-mail: redlibbets@golfandsport.co.uk
web: www.redlibbetsmembers.co.uk
Delightful rolling Kentish course cut through an attractive wooded
valley.

18 Holes, 6639yds, Par 72, SSS 72, Course record 67.
Club membership 500.
Visitors Mon-Fri except BHs. Dress code. **Societies** booking required.
Green Fees £50 per round **Course Designer** Jonathan Gaunt
Prof Ross Taylor **Facilities** 🍸 🍽 🏌 🏞 🛒 🏊 🏠 ⛳ ⚡
🚗 ⚡ 🏳 **Conf** facs Corporate Hospitality Days **Location** off A20,
close to Brand's Hatch
Hotel ★★★★ 75% HL Brandshatch Place Hotel & Spa,
Brands Hatch Road, Fawkham, BRANDS HATCH ☎ 01474 875000
🖷 01474 875000 38 en suite

RAMSGATE
Map 5 TR36

St Augustine's Cottington Rd, Cliffsend CT12 5JN
☎ 01843 590333 🖷 01843 590444
e-mail: sagc@ic24.net
web: www.staugustinesgolfclub.co.uk
A comfortably flat course in this famous championship area of Kent.
St Augustine's will provide a fair challenge for most golfers. Dykes
run across the course.

18 Holes, 5254yds, Par 69, SSS 66, Course record 61.
Club membership 670.

Visitors Mon-Sun & BHs. Booking required. Dress code. **Societies** booking required. **Green Fees** £24 per 18 holes (£30 weekends) **Course Designer** Tom Vardon **Prof** Derek Scott **Facilities** ⑪ ⏍ ⓑ ⌷ ⌁ ⏃ ⊟ ◈ ⛟ ♂ **Location** off A256 Ramsgate-Sandwich
Hotel ★★★ *77%* HL Pegwell Bay, 81 Pegwell Road, Pegwell Village, RAMSGATE ☎ 01843 599590 ▤ 01843 599590 42 en suite

Stonelees Golf Centre Ebbsfleet Ln CT12 5DJ
☎ 01843 823133 ▤ 01843 850569
e-mail: stoneless@stonelees.com
web: www.stonelees.co.uk
Opened in 1994 Stonelees Golf Centre offers three 9 hole courses, each demanding a different ability level, from the par 3 through the demanding Execeutive course to the challenging full length Heights course.
Executive: 9 Holes, 1510yds, Par 29.
Heights: 9 Holes, 2865yds, Par 35.
Societies booking required. **Green Fees** £9 per round (£12 weekends). Par 3 £5/£6 **Prof** David Bonthron/Mark Belsham **Facilities** ⑪ ⏍ ⓑ ⌷ ⌁ ⏃ ⊟ ⏏ ⛟ ♂ ♂ **Leisure** par 3 course
Conf Corporate Hospitality Days **Location** off A256 between Ramsgate and Sandwich
Hotel ★★★ *77%* HL Pegwell Bay, 81 Pegwell Road, Pegwell Village, RAMSGATE ☎ 01843 599590 ▤ 01843 599590 42 en suite

ROCHESTER
Map 5 TQ76

Rochester & Cobham Park Park Pale ME2 3UL
☎ 01474 823411 ▤ 01474 824446
e-mail: rcpgc@talk21.com
web: www.rochesterandcobhamgc.co.uk
A first-rate course of challenging dimensions in undulating parkland. All holes differ and each requires accurate drive placing to derive the best advantage. Open Championship regional qualifying course.
18 Holes, 6597yds, Par 71, SSS 72, Course record 64. Club membership 730.
Visitors Mon-Fri except BHs. Booking required. Handicap certificate. Dress code. **Societies** booking required. **Green Fees** £40 per round **Course Designer** Donald Steel **Prof** Warren Wood **Facilities** ⑪ ⏍ ⓑ ⌷ ⌁ ⏃ ⊟ ♂ ⛟ ♂ ♂ **Conf** Corporate Hospitality Days **Location** 2.5m W on A2
Hotel ★★★★ *72%* HL Bridgewood Manor Hotel, Bridgewood Roundabout, Waldersdale Woods, CHATHAM ☎ 01634 201333 ▤ 01634 201333 100 en suite

SANDWICH
Map 5 TR35

Prince's Prince's Dr CT13 9QB
☎ 01304 611118 ▤ 01304 612000
web: www.princesgolfclub.co.uk
Dunes: 9 Holes, 3432yds, Par 36, SSS 36.
Himalayas: 9 Holes, 3201yds, Par 35, SSS 35.
Shore: 9 Holes, 3348yds, Par 36, SSS 36.
Course Designer Sir Guy Campbell & J S F Morrison **Location** 2m E via toll road, signs from Sandwich
Telephone for further details
Hotel ★★★ *80%* HL Dunkerleys Hotel & Restaurant, 19 Beach Street, DEAL ☎ 01304 375016 ▤ 01304 375016 16 en suite

Royal St George's see page 147
CT13 9PB
☎ 01304 613090 ▤ 01304 611245
e-mail: secretary@royalstgeorges.com
web: www.royalstgeorges.com

SEAL
Map 5 TR36

Wildernesse, Park Ln TN15 0JE
☎ 01732 761199 ▤ 01732 763809
e-mail: golf@wildernesse.co.uk
web: www.wildernesse.co.uk
A tight inland course, heavily wooded with tree-lined fairways. Straight driving and attention to the well-placed bunkers is essential. With few slopes and easy walking, it is difficult to beat par.
18 Holes, 6532yds, Par 72, SSS 71, Course record 63. Club membership 720.
Visitors Mon, Thu & Fri except BHs. Booking required. Handicap certificate. Dress code. **Societies** welcome. **Green Fees** £90 per day, £60 per round **Course Designer** Braid (part) **Prof** Craig Walker **Facilities** ⑪ ⏍ ⓑ ⌷ ⌁ ⏃ ⊟ ♂ ⛟ ♂ ♂ **Conf** Corporate Hospitality Days **Location** take A25 from Sevenoaks to Seal, turn right into Park Lane, club entrance on left.
Hotel ★★★ *79%* HL Best Western Donnington Manor, London Road, Dunton Green, SEVENOAKS ☎ 01732 462681 ▤ 01732 462681 60 en suite

SEVENOAKS   Map 5 TQ55

Knole Park Seal Hollow Rd TN15 0HJ
☎ 01732 452150   📄 01732 463159
e-mail: secretary@knoleparkgolfclub.co.uk
web: www.knoleparkgolfclub.co.uk

The course is laid out within the grounds of the Knole Estate and can rightfully be described as a natural layout. The course designer has used the contours of the land to produce a challenging course in all weather conditions and throughout all seasons. While, for most of the year, it may appear benign, in summer, when the bracken is high, Knole Park represents a considerable challenge but always remains a fair test of golf.

18 Holes, 6246yds, Par 70, SSS 70, Course record 62.
Club membership 750.

Visitors Mon-Sun & BHs. Booking required weekends & BHs.. Handicap certificate. Dress code. **Societies** booking required. **Green Fees** £50 per day, £40 per round **Course Designer** J A Abercromby **Prof** Marissa Newman **Facilities** ⊕ ⋈ 🏌 🖵 🗭 🎒 🛄
🏌 **Leisure** squash **Conf** Corporate Hospitality Days **Location** NE of town centre off B2019

Hotel ★★★ 79% HL Best Western Donnington Manor, London Road, Dunton Green, SEVENOAKS ☎ 01732 462681 📄 01732 462681   60 en suite

SHEERNESS   Map 5 TQ97

Sheerness Power Station Rd ME12 3AE
☎ 01795 662585   📄 01795 668100
e-mail: secretary@sheernessgolfclub.co.uk
web: www.sheernessgolfclub.co.uk

Semi-links, marshland course, few bunkers, but many ditches and water hazards.

18 Holes, 6390yds, Par 71, SSS 71, Course record 66.
Club membership 650.

Visitors Mon-Fri & Sun except BHs. Booking required. Dress code. **Societies** booking required. **Green Fees** £35 per day, £26 per 18 holes **Prof** L Stanford **Facilities** ⊕ 🏌 🖵 🗭 🎒 🛄 🏌 🚜 🏌
Location 1.5m E off A249

Hotel ★★★★ 72% HL Bridgewood Manor Hotel, Bridgewood Roundabout, Walderslade Woods, CHATHAM ☎ 01634 201333 📄 01634 201333   100 en suite

SHOREHAM   Map 5 TQ56

Darenth Valley Station Rd TN14 7SA
☎ 01959 522922   📄 01959 525089
e-mail: enquiries@dvgc.co.uk
web: www.dvgc.co.uk

Gently undulating parkland in a beautiful Kent valley, with excellent well-drained greens. The course has matured and developed to become a challenge to both high and low handicap golfers.

Darenth Valley Golf Course: 18 Holes, 6193yds, Par 72, SSS 71, Course record 64.

Visitors Mon-Sun & BHs. Dress code. **Societies** booking required. **Green Fees** £32 per 36 holes, £20 per 18 holes (£25 per 18 holes weekends & BHs) **Course Designer** Michael Cross **Prof** Pete Stopford **Facilities** ⊕ ⋈ 🏌 🖵 🗭 🎒 🛄 🏌 🚜 🏌 **Conf** facs Corporate Hospitality Days **Location** 3m N of Sevenoaks off A225 between Otford & Eynsford

Hotel ★★★ 79% HL Best Western Donnington Manor, London Road, Dunton Green, SEVENOAKS ☎ 01732 462681 📄 01732 462681 60 en suite

SITTINGBOURNE   Map 5 TQ96

The Oast Golf Centre Church Rd, Tonge ME9 9AR
☎ 01795 473527
e-mail: info@oastgolf.co.uk
web: www.oastgolf.co.uk

A par 3 approach course of nine holes with 18 tees augmented by a 17-bay floodlit driving range and a putting green.

The Oast Golf Centre: 9 Holes, 1664yds, Par 54, SSS 54.

Visitors Mon-Sun & BHs. **Societies** welcome. **Green Fees** £8 for 18 holes, £6 for 9 holes. Weekdays £6 per am, £8 per pm unlimited. **Course Designer** D Chambers **Prof** D Chambers **Facilities** 🏌 🖵 🗭 🛄 🏌 🏌 **Location** 2m NE, A2 from Sittingbourne, turn left after Bapchild

Hotel ★★★★ 72% HL Bridgewood Manor Hotel, Bridgewood Roundabout, Walderslade Woods, CHATHAM ☎ 01634 201333 📄 01634 201333   100 en suite

Sittingbourne & Milton Regis Wormdale, Newington ME9 7PX
☎ 01795 842261
e-mail: sittingbournegc@btconnect.com
web: www.sittingbournegolfclub.com

A downland course with pleasant vistas and renowned for its greens. There are a few uphill climbs, but the course is far from difficult. The back nine holes are challenging whilst the front nine require accuracy and precision.
continued

ROYAL ST GEORGE'S

KENT - SANDWICH - MAP 5 TR35

Consistently ranked among the leading golf courses in the world, Royal St George's occupies a unique place in the history of golf, playing host in 1894 to the first Open Championship outside Scotland. Set among the dunes of Sandwich Bay, the links provide a severe test for the greatest of golfers. Only three Open winners (Bill Rogers in 1981, Greg Norman in 1993 and Ben Curtis in 2003) have managed to under par after 72 holes. The undulating fairways, the borrows on the greens, the strategically placed bunkers, and the prevailing winds that blow on all but the rarest of occasions; these all soon reveal any weakness in the player. There are few over the years who have mastered all the vagaries in one round. It hosted its thirteenth Open Championship in 2003, won dramatically by outsider Ben Curtis and will be the venue in 2011.

CT13 9PB ☎ 01304 613090 📄 01304 611245
e-mail: secretary@royalstgeorges.com **web:** www. royalstgeorges.com
18 Holes, 7204yds, Par 70, SSS 74, Course record 67. Club membership 750.
Visitors Mon-Fri except BHs. Booking required. Handicap certificate. Dress code. **Societies** booking required.
Green Fees £180 per 36 holes, £140 per 18 holes. Reduced winter rates **Course Designer** Dr Laidlaw Purves
Prof A Brooks **Facilities** ⑪ 🍴 by prior arrangement 🖥 🍺 ⚒ 🏠 ⛳ ◇ ✦ ✦ **Conf** Corporate Hospitality
Days **Location** 1.5m E of Sandwich. Enter town for golf courses
Hotel ★★★ 77% HL Pegwell Bay, 81 Pegwell Road, Pegwell Village, RAMSGATE ☎ 01843 599590
📄 01843 599590 42 en suite

18 Holes, 6291yds, Par 71, SSS 70, Course record 63. Club membership 715.

Visitors Mon, Tue, Thu & Fri except BHs. Dress code. **Societies** booking required. **Green Fees** £32 per day **Course Designer** Donald Steel **Prof** John Hearn **Facilities** ⛳ 🍴 by prior arrangement 🏌 ☕ 🍺 ♨ 🏪 ✦ 🛒 ♂ **Conf** Corporate Hospitality Days **Location** 0.5m from M2 junct 5, off Chestnut St at Danaway

Hotel ★★★★ 72% HL Bridgewood Manor Hotel, Bridgewood Roundabout, Walderslade Woods, CHATHAM ☎ 01634 201333 🖺 01634 201333 100 en suite

Upchurch River Valley Golf Centre Oak lane, Upchurch ME9 7AY

☎ 01634 379592 🖺 01634 387784

Undulating parkland in picturesque countryside. Testing water hazards on several holes. Excellent winter course. The nine-hole course is ideal for beginners and for those keen to sharpen up their short game.

Upchurch River Valley Golf Centre: 18 Holes, 6237yds, Par 70, SSS 70. Club membership 752.

Visitors contact centre for details. **Societies** welcome. **Green Fees** not confirmed **Course Designer** David Smart **Prof** Roger Cornwell **Facilities** ⛳ 🍴 🏌 ☕ ☕ 🍺 ♨ 🏪 ✦ 🛒 ♂ ♂ **Leisure** heated outdoor swimming pool **Conf** facs Corporate Hospitality Days **Location** A2 between Rainham & Newington

Hotel ★★★ 75% HL Best Western Russell, 136 Boxley Road, MAIDSTONE ☎ 01622 692221 🖺 01622 692221 42 en suite

---

SNODLAND   Map 5 TQ76

Oastpark Malling Rd ME6 5LG
☎ 01634 242661 🖺 01634 240744
e-mail: oastparkgolfclub@btconnect.com

A challenging parkland course for golfers of all abilities. The course has water hazards and orchards.

Oastpark Golf Course: 9 Holes, 3150yds, Par 35, SSS 35, Course record 71. Club membership 60.

Visitors contact course for details. **Societies** welcome. **Green Fees** £9 per day (weekends £15 per 18 holes, £10 per 9 holes) **Course Designer** J D Banks **Prof** David Porthouse **Facilities** 🏌 ☕ 🍺 ♨ 🏪 ♂ ♂ **Location** M20 junct 4

Hotel ★★★★ 72% HL Bridgewood Manor Hotel, Bridgewood Roundabout, Walderslade Woods, CHATHAM ☎ 01634 201333 🖺 01634 201333 100 en suite

---

TENTERDEN   Map 5 TQ83

London Beach Country Hotel & Golf Club Ashford Rd TN30 6HX

☎ 01580 766279 🖺 01580 763884
e-mail: enquiries@londonbeach.com
web: www.londonbeach.com

Located in a mature parkland setting in the Weald. A test of golf for all abilities of golfer with its rolling fairways and undulating greens.

London Beach Country Hotel & Golf Club: 9 Holes, 5860yds, Par 70, SSS 69, Course record 66. Club membership 250.

Visitors Mon-Sun & BHs. Booking required. Handicap certificate. Dress code. **Societies** booking required. **Green Fees** £20 per 18 holes, £18 per 9 holes (£25/£20 weekends and BHs) **Course Designer** Golf Landscapes **Prof** Mark Chilcott **Facilities** ⛳ 🍴 🏌 ☕ 🍺 ♨

⛳ 🍴 ♦ 🛒 🖼 ♂ ♂ **Leisure** fishing, sauna, gymnasium, pitch & putt, clay pigeon shooting, spa **Conf** facs Corporate Hospitality Days **Location** M20 Junct 9, A28 towards Tenterden, hotel on right 1m before Tenterden

London Beach Country Hotel & Golf Club

Hotel ★★★ 75% HL London Beach Country Hotel, Spa & Golf Club, Ashford Road, TENTERDEN, Ashford ☎ 01580 766279 🖺 01580 766279 26 en suite

Tenterden Woodchurch Rd TN30 7DR

☎ 01580 763987 🖺 01580 763430
e-mail: enquiries@tenterdengolfclub.co.uk
web: tenterdengolfclub.co.uk

Set in tranquil undulating parkland with beautiful views, the course is challenging with several difficult holes. Open fairways with short rough allows for speedy play. Tree positioning demands accuracy without spoiling enjoyment.

18 Holes, 6071yds, Par 70, SSS 69, Course record 61. Club membership 400.

Visitors Mon-Sun & BHs. Dress code. **Societies** booking required. **Green Fees** £40 per day, £25 per round (£50/£30 weekends & BHs). Winter £20/£25 **Prof** Kyle Kelsall **Facilities** ⛳ 🍴 🏌 ☕ 🍺 ♨ 🏪 🖼 🛒 ♂ **Conf** facs Corporate Hospitality Days **Location** M20 junct 10, take A28 signed Tenterden. Before Tenterden turn left at B2080 signed Appledore/Woodchurch and left at B2067 Woodchurch Rd

Hotel ★★★ 75% HL London Beach Country Hotel, Spa & Golf Club, Ashford Road, TENTERDEN, Ashford ☎ 01580 766279 🖺 01580 766279 26 en suite

---

TONBRIDGE   Map 5 TQ54

Poultwood Higham Ln TN11 9QR

☎ 01732 364039 & 366180 🖺 01732 354640
e-mail: leisure.services@tmbc.gov.uk
web: www.poultwoodgolf.co.uk

There are two public pay and play parkland courses in an idyllic woodland setting. The courses are ecologically designed over predominantly flat land offering challenging hazards and interesting playing conditions for all standards of golfer.

Poult Wood Golf Centre: 18 Holes, 5524yds, Par 68, SSS 66.

Poult Wood Golf Centre: 9 Holes, 1281yds, Par 28.

Visitors Mon-Sun & BHs. Dress code. **Societies** booking required. **Green Fees** 18 hole course £15.50 (£22 weekends & BHs). 9 hole course £6/£7.60 **Course Designer** Hawtree **Prof** David Copsey **Facilities** ⛳ 🍴 🏌 ☕ 🍺 ♨ 🏪 🖼 🛒 ♂ **Leisure** squash

continued

Conf facs Corporate Hospitality Days **Location** off A227 3m N of Tonbridge
Hotel ★★★ **72%** HL Best Western Rose & Crown, 125 High Street, TONBRIDGE ☎ 01732 357966 📄 01732 357966 56 en suite

TUNBRIDGE WELLS (ROYAL)   Map 5 TQ53

Nevill Benhall Mill Rd TN2 5JW
☎ 01892 525818   📄 01892 517861
e-mail: manager@nevillgolfclub.co.uk
web: www.nevillgolfclub.co.uk

The Kent-Sussex border forms the northern perimeter of the course. Open undulating ground, well-wooded with some heather and gorse for the first half. The second nine holes slope away from the clubhouse to a valley where a narrow stream hazards two holes.

18 Holes, 6349yds, Par 71, SSS 70, Course record 64.
Club membership 800.

Visitors Mon, Wed-Fri except BHs. Booking required. Handicap certificate. Dress code. **Societies** booking required. **Green Fees** £50 per day; £40 per round **Course Designer** Henry Cotton **Prof** Nick Duc **Facilities** ⊕ ⏀ ⮢ ⬑ ⬗ 🏌 ⬠ ⬟ ✿ **Conf** facs Corporate Hospitality Days **Location** S of Tunbridge Wells
Hotel ★★★★ **77%** HL The Spa, Mount Ephraim, TUNBRIDGE WELLS ☎ 01892 520331 📄 01892 520331 72 en suite

Tunbridge Wells Langton Rd TN4 8XH
☎ 01892 523034   📄 01892 536918
web: www.tunbridgewellsgolfclub.co.uk

9 Holes, 4725yds, Par 65, SSS 62, Course record 59.
Facilities ⊕ ⏀ ⮢ ⬑ ⬗ ⬠ ⬟ ✿ **Location** 1m W on A264
Telephone for further details
Hotel ★★★★ **77%** HL The Spa, Mount Ephraim, TUNBRIDGE WELLS ☎ 01892 520331 📄 01892 520331 72 en suite

WEST KINGSDOWN   Map 5 TQ56

Woodlands Manor Tinkerpot Ln, Otford TN15 6AB
☎ 01959 523806   📄 01959 524398
e-mail: info@woodlandsmanorgolf.co.uk
web: www.woodlandsmanorgolf.co.uk

Two distinct nine-hole layouts with views over an Area of Outstanding Natural beauty. The course is challenging but fair with varied and memorable holes of which the 7th, 10th and 18th stand out. Good playing conditions all year round.

18 Holes, 6015yds, Par 69, SSS 69, Course record 64.
Club membership 600.

Visitors Mon, Wed-Fri & BHs. Tue & weekends pm. Dress code. **Societies** booking required. **Green Fees** £24 per 18 holes (£30 weekends) **Course Designer** Lyons/Coles **Prof** Philip Womack **Facilities** ⊕ ⏀ by prior arrangement ⮢ ⬗ 🏌 ⬠ ⬟ 🚌 ✿ 🏌 **Conf** facs Corporate Hospitality Days **Location** A20 through West Kingsdown, right opp Portbello Inn onto School Ln, clubhouse left after 2m
Hotel ★★★★ **80%** HL Thistle Brands Hatch, BRANDS HATCH, Dartford ☎ 0871 376 9008 📄 0871 376 9008 121 en suite

WEST MALLING   Map 5 TQ65

Kings Hill Fortune Way, Discovery Dr, Kings Hill ME19 4GF
☎ 01732 875040   📄 01732 875019
e-mail: khatkhgolf@aol.com
web: www.kingshillgolf.co.uk

Set in over 200 acres of undulating terrain and features large areas of protected heath and mature woodland. USGA standard greens and tees.

18 Holes, 6622yards, Par 72, SSS 72.
Club membership 530.

Visitors Mon-Sun & BHs. Booking required. Dress code.
Societies booking required. **Green Fees** £35 (£45 weekends & BHs) **Course Designer** David Williams Partnership **Prof** David Hudspith **Facilities** ⊕ ⏀ ⮢ ⬑ ⬗ 🏌 ⬠ ⬟ **Conf** facs **Location** M20 junct 4, A228 towards Tonbridge
Hotel ★★★ **77%** HL Hadlow Manor, Goose Green, HADLOW ☎ 01732 851442 📄 01732 851442 29 en suite

WESTERHAM   Map 5 TQ45

Park Wood Chestnut Av, Tatsfield TN16 2EG
☎ 01959 577744 & 577177 (pro-shop)
📄 01959 572702
e-mail: mail@parkwoodgolf.co.uk
web: www.parkwoodgolf.co.uk

Situated in an Area of Outstanding Natural Beauty, flanked by an ancient woodland with superb views across Kent and Surrey countryside. An undulating course, tree lined and with some interesting water features. Playable in all weather conditions.

18 Holes, 6835yds, Par 72, SSS 72, Course record 66.
Club membership 500.

Visitors contact club for details. **Societies** welcome. **Green Fees** phone **Prof** Nick Terry **Facilities** ⊕ ⮢ ⬑ ⬗ 🏌 ⬠ ⬟ ✿ 🚌 ✿ **Conf** facs Corporate Hospitality Days **Location** A25 onto B2024 Croydon Rd Ln, at Church Hill junct onto Chestnut Av
Hotel ★★★ **79%** HL Best Western Donnington Manor, London Road, Dunton Green, SEVENOAKS ☎ 01732 462681 📄 01732 462681 60 en suite

Westerham Valence Park, Brasted Rd TN16 1LJ
☎ 01959 567100   📄 01959 567101
e-mail: ben.hammond@westerhamgc.co.uk
web: www.westerhamgc.co.uk

Originally forestry land with thousands of mature pines. The storms of 1987 created natural fairways and the mature landscape makes the course both demanding and spectacular. A clubhouse with first-class facilities and magnificent views.

18 Holes, 6329yds, Par 72, SSS 72. Club membership 600.
Visitors Mon-Fri & BHs. Weekends pm. Booking required. Dress code. **Societies** welcome. **Green Fees** £35 per round Mon-Thu, £40 Fri, £45 weekends and BHs **Course Designer** D Williams **Prof** J Marshall **Facilities** Ⓣ ⓀⒹ ⓀⒹ ⓀⒹ ⓀⒹ ⓀⒹ ⓀⒹ ⓀⒹ ⓀⒹ **Leisure** short game practice area **Conf** facs Corporate Hospitality Days **Location** A25 between Westerham & Brasted
Hotel ★★★ 79% HL Best Western Donnington Manor, London Road, Dunton Green, SEVENOAKS ☎ 01732 462681 📄 01732 462681 60 en suite

WESTGATE ON SEA   Map 5 TR37

Westgate and Birchington 176 Canterbury Rd CT8 8LT
☎ 01843 831115
e-mail: wandbgc@tiscali.co.uk
A fine blend of inland and seaside holes which provide a good test of the golfer despite the apparently simple appearance of the course.

18 Holes, 4926yds, Par 64, SSS 64, Course record 58. Club membership 350.
Visitors Mon-Sun & BHs. Dress code. **Societies** welcome. **Green Fees** £18 per day (£21 weekends & BHs) **Prof** Mark Young **Facilities** Ⓣ ⓀⒹ ⓀⒹ ⓀⒹ ⓀⒹ ⓀⒹ **Conf** Corporate Hospitality Days **Location** E of town centre off A28
Hotel ★★★ 77% HL Pegwell Bay, 81 Pegwell Road, Pegwell Village, RAMSGATE ☎ 01843 599590 📄 01843 599590 42 en suite

WHITSTABLE   Map 5 TR16

Chestfield (Whitstable) 103 Chestfield Rd, Chestfield CT5 3LU
☎ 01227 794411 & 792243   📄 01227 794454
e-mail: secretary@chestfield-golfclub.co.uk
web: www.chestfield-golfclub.co.uk
Changes have been made to this parkland course with undulating fairways and fine views of the sea and countryside. These consist of six new greens and five new tees. The ancient clubhouse, dating back to the 15th century, is reputed to be the oldest building in the world used for this purpose.

18 Holes, 6200yds, Par 70, SSS 70, Course record 66. Club membership 725.
Visitors Mon-Sun & BHs. Dress code. **Societies** welcome. **Green Fees** £44 per day, £36 per round **Course Designer** D Steel/James Braid **Prof** John Brotherton **Facilities** Ⓣ ⓀⒹ ⓀⒹ ⓀⒹ ⓀⒹ ⓀⒹ ⓀⒹ ⓀⒹ **Leisure** half-way house providing snacks/refreshments **Conf** Corporate Hospitality Days **Location** 0.5m S by Chestfield Railway Station, off A2990
Hotel BUD Travelodge Canterbury Whitstable, Thanet Way, FAVERSHAM ☎ 08719 846 022 📄 08719 846 022 40 en suite

Whitstable & Seasalter Collingwood Rd CT5 1EB
☎ 01227 272020   📄 01227 280822
e-mail: wandsgolfclub@talktalkbusiness.net
Links course.

9 Holes, 5357yds, Par 66, SSS 65, Course record 64. Club membership 350.
Visitors contact club for details. **Societies** booking required. **Green Fees** £20 per 18 holes, £13 per 9 holes **Facilities** Ⓣ by prior arrangement ⓀⒹ ⓀⒹ ⓀⒹ ⓀⒹ **Location** W of town centre off B2205
Hotel ★★★ 70% HL Victoria, 59 London Road, CANTERBURY ☎ 01227 459333 📄 01227 459333 33 en suite

LANCASHIRE

ACCRINGTON   Map 7 SD72

Accrington & District Devon Av, Oswaldtwistle BB5 4LS
☎ 01254 231091 & 350112   📄 01254 350111
e-mail: info@accringtongolfclub.com
web: www.accringtongolfclub.com
Moorland course with pleasant views of the Pennines and surrounding areas. The course is a real test for even the best amateur golfers and has hosted many county matches and championships over its 100 plus years of history.

18 Holes, 6031yds, Par 70, SSS 69, Course record 63. Club membership 600.
Visitors Mon-Sun & BHs. Booking required weekends & BHs. Handicap certificate. Dress code. **Societies** booking required. **Green Fees** £25 per round (£35 weekends & BHs) **Course Designer** J Braid **Prof** Mark Harling **Facilities** Ⓣ by prior arrangement Ⓚ by prior arrangement ⓀⒹ ⓀⒹ ⓀⒹ ⓀⒹ ⓀⒹ ⓀⒹ **Conf** Corporate Hospitality Days **Location** between Accrington & Blackburn
Hotel ★★★★ 72% HL Mercure Dunkenhalgh Hotel & Spa, Blackburn Road, Clayton-le-Moors, ACCRINGTON ☎ 01254 398021 📄 01254 398021 175 en suite

Baxenden & District Top o' th' Meadow, Baxenden BB5 2EA
☎ 01254 234555
e-mail: baxgolf@hotmail.com
web: www.baxendengolf.co.uk
Moorland course with panoramic views and a long par 3 to start.

9 Holes, 5740yds, Par 70, SSS 68, Course record 65. Club membership 340.
Visitors contact club for details. **Societies** welcome. **Green Fees** £15 per 18 holes (£25 weekends & BHs) **Facilities** Ⓣ ⓀⒹ ⓀⒹ ⓀⒹ ⓀⒹ **Conf** facs Corporate Hospitality Days **Location** 1.5m SE off A680
Hotel ★★★★ 72% HL Mercure Dunkenhalgh Hotel & Spa, Blackburn Road, Clayton-le-Moors, ACCRINGTON ☎ 01254 398021 📄 01254 398021 175 en suite

Green Haworth Green Haworth BB5 3SL
☎ 01254 237580 & 382510 🖨 01254 396176
e-mail: golf@greenhaworth.co.uk
web: www.greenhaworthgolfclub.co.uk
Moorland course dominated by quarries and difficult in windy conditions.

9 Holes, 5522yds, Par 68, SSS 67, Course record 66.
Club membership 250.

Visitors Mon-Fri & BHs. Dress code. **Societies** welcome. **Green Fees** not confirmed **Facilities** ⊕ ⑩ 🝆 ⊑ 🝆 ⚲ **Conf** Corporate Hospitality Days **Location** 2m S off A680
Hotel ★★★★ 72% HL Mercure Dunkenhalgh Hotel & Spa, Blackburn Road, Clayton-le-Moors, ACCRINGTON ☎ 01254 398021 🖨 01254 398021 175 en suite

BACUP
Map 7 SD82

Bacup Maden Rd OL13 8HY
☎ 01706 873170 🖨 01706 877726
9 Holes, 6018yds, Par 70, SSS 69, Course record 60.
Facilities ⊕ by prior arrangement ⑩ by prior arrangement 🝆 ⊑ 🝆 ⚲ **Conf** Corporate Hospitality Days **Location** W of town off A671
Telephone for further details
Hotel ★★★ 78% HL Rosehill House, Rosehill Avenue, BURNLEY ☎ 01282 453931 🖨 01282 453931 34 en suite

BARNOLDSWICK
Map 7 SD84

Ghyll Skipton Rd BB18 6JH
☎ 01282 842466 & 865582
e-mail: kennethjwilkinson@btinternet.com
web: www.ghyllgc.co.uk
Excellent parkland course with outstanding views, especially from the Ingleborough tee where you can see the Three Peaks. Testing Mast hole is an uphill par 3. Eleven holes in total, nine in Yorkshire and two in Lancashire.

Tudor: 9 Holes, 6233yds, Par 70, SSS 70, Course record 62.
York: 9 Holes, 5744yds, Par 68, SSS 68.
Club membership 345.

Visitors Mon-Sat except BHs. Dress code. **Societies** booking required. **Green Fees** £15 per day **Facilities** ⑩ ⊑ 🝆 ⚲ **Conf** Corporate Hospitality Days **Location** NE of town on B6252
Hotel ★★★ 75% HL Herriots Hotel, Broughton Road, SKIPTON ☎ 01756 792781 🖨 01756 792781 23 en suite

BICKERSTAFFE
Map 7 SD40

Mossock Hall Liverpool Rd L39 0EE
☎ 01695 421717 🖨 01695 424961
e-mail: jackie@mossockhallgolfclub.co.uk
web: www.mossockhallgolfclub.co.uk
Relatively flat parkland with scenic views. USGA greens and water features on four holes.

18 Holes, 6272yards, Par 71, SSS 70, Course record 68.
Club membership 580.

Visitors contact club for details. **Societies** welcome. **Green Fees** £27 per 18 holes (£34 weekends & BHs) **Course Designer** Steve Marnoch **Prof** Brad Millar **Facilities** ⊕ ⑩ 🝆 ⊑ 🝆 ⚲ 🝆 🛒 ⚲ **Conf** facs Corporate Hospitality Days **Location** M58 junct 3
Hotel ★★★ 82% HL West Tower Country House, Mill Lane, Aughton, ORMSKIRK ☎ 01695 423328 🖨 01695 423328 12 en suite

BLACKBURN
Map 7 SD62

Blackburn Beardwood Brow BB2 7AX
☎ 01254 51122 🖨 01254 665578
e-mail: sec@blackburngolfclub.com
web: www.blackburngolfclub.com
Parkland on a high plateau with stream and hills. Superb views of Lancashire coast and the Pennines.

18 Holes, 6144yds, Par 71, SSS 70, Course record 62.
Club membership 550.

Visitors Mon-Sun & BHs. Booking required weekends & BHs.. Handicap certificate. Dress code. **Societies** booking required. **Green Fees** £32 per day (£38 weekends) **Prof** Alan Rodwell **Facilities** ⊕ ⑩ 🝆 ⊑ 🝆 ⚲ 🝆 ⚲ 🛒 ⚲ **Conf** Corporate Hospitality Days **Location** 1.25m NW of town centre off A677
Hotel ★★ 85% HL Millstone at Mellor, Church Lane, Mellor, BLACKBURN ☎ 01254 813333 🖨 01254 813333 23 en suite

BLACKPOOL
Map 7 SD33

Blackpool North Shore Devonshire Rd FY2 0RD
☎ 01253 352054 🖨 01253 591240
e-mail: office@bnsgc.com
web: www.bnsgc.com

Links type course with rolling fairways and good sized greens. Excellent views of the Lake District and Pennine Hills.

18 Holes, 6432yds, Par 71, SSS 71, Course record 62.
Club membership 900.

Visitors Mon-Wed, Fri & Sun except BHs. Booking required Sun. Handicap certificate. Dress code. **Societies** booking required. **Green Fees** £37 per day, £29 per round (£44/£35 Sun) **Course Designer** H S Colt **Prof** Andrew Richardson **Facilities** ⊕ ⑩ 🝆 ⊑ 🝆 ⚲ 🝆 🛒 ⚲ **Conf** Corporate Hospitality Days **Location** on A587 N of town centre
Hotel ★★ 71% HL Hotel Sheraton, 54-62 Queens Promenade, BLACKPOOL ☎ 01253 352723 🖨 01253 352723 104 en suite

Blackpool Park North Park Dr FY3 8LS
☎ 01253 397916 & 478176 (tee times)
🖨 01253 397916
e-mail: secretary@blackpoolparkgc.co.uk
web: www.blackpoolparkgc.co.uk
The course, situated in Stanley Park, is municipal. The golf club (Blackpool Park) is private but golfers may use the clubhouse facilities if playing the course. An abundance of grassy pits, ponds and open dykes.

18 Holes, 6087yds, Par 70, SSS 70, Course record 64.
Club membership 650. *continued*

Visitors Mon-Sun & BHs. **Societies** booking required. **Green Fees** phone **Course Designer** A.McKenzie **Prof** Brian Purdie **Facilities** ⓦ ⦿ 🏌 ⛳ 🍴 👤 🏠 ⛳ ✓ **Conf** Corporate Hospitality Days **Location** 1m E of Blackpool Tower
Hotel ★★★ 75% HL Carousel, 663-671 New South Prom, BLACKPOOL ☎ 01253 402642 🖹 01253 402642 92 en suite

Herons' Reach De Vere Hotel, East Park Dr FY3 8LL
☎ 01253 766156 & 838866   🖹 01253 798800
web: www.deveregolf.co.uk

The course was designed by Peter Alliss and Clive Clarke. There are 10 man-made lakes and several existing ponds. Built to a links design, well mounded but fairly easy walking. Water comes into play on nine holes, better players can go for the carry or shorter hitters can take the safe route. Extensive plantation and landscaping have been carried out as the course matures. The course provides an excellent and interesting challenge for golfers of all standards.

18 Holes, 5848yds, Par 72, SSS 68, Course record 64.
Club membership 450.

Visitors Mon-Fri & BHs. Weekends after 10am. Booking required Fri-Sun & BHs. Handicap certificate. Dress code. **Societies** booking required. **Green Fees** £35 per round (£40 weekends). Winter £22.50/£25 **Course Designer** Peter Alliss/Clive Clark **Prof** Richard Bowman **Facilities** ⓦ ⦿ 🏌 ⛳ 🍴 👤 🏠 ⛳ ◇ ✓ 🛒 ✓ ✔ **Leisure** hard tennis courts, heated indoor swimming pool, squash, sauna, gymnasium, health and beauty facilities. **Conf** facs Corporate Hospitality Days **Location** M55 junct 4, follow signs for zoo, hotel situated just before
Hotel ★★★★ 75% HL De Vere Herons' Reach, East Park Drive, BLACKPOOL ☎ 01253 838866 🖹 01253 838866 172 en suite

BURNLEY   Map 7 SD83

Burnley Glen View BB11 3RW
☎ 0870 3306655   🖹 01282 451281
e-mail: burnleygolfclub@onthegreen.co.uk
web: www.burnleygolf.sitenet.pl

Challenging moorland course with exceptional views.

18 Holes, 5939yds, Par 69, SSS 69, Course record 62.
Club membership 650.

Visitors Mon-Sun & BHs. Handicap certificate. Dress code. **Societies** booking required. **Green Fees** £25 per day (£30 weekends & BHs) **Course Designer** James Braid **Prof** Matthew Baker **Facilities** ⓦ ⦿ 🏌 ⛳ 🍴 👤 🏠 ⛳ ✓ **Leisure** snooker table **Conf** facs Corporate Hospitality Days **Location** S of town off A646
Hotel ★★★ 78% HL Rosehill House, Rosehill Avenue, BURNLEY ☎ 01282 453931 🖹 01282 453931 34 en suite

Towneley Towneley Park BB11 3ED
☎ 01282 438473

18 Holes, 5811yds, Par 70, SSS 68, Course record 67.
Facilities ⓦ ⦿ ⛳ 🍴 👤 🏠 ✓ **Location** 1m SE of town centre on A671
Telephone for further details
Hotel ★★★ 80% HL Oaks, Colne Road, Reedley, BURNLEY ☎ 01282 414141 🖹 01282 414141 52 en suite

CHORLEY   Map 7 SD51

Charnock Richard Preston Rd PR7 5LE
☎ 01257 470707   🖹 01257 791196
web: www.charnockrichardgolfclub.co.uk

18 Holes, 6239yds, Par 71, SSS 70, Course record 68.

Course Designer Martin Turner **Location** on A49, 0.25m from Camelot Theme Park
Telephone for further details
Hotel ★★★ 74% HL Best Western Park Hall, Park Hall Road, Charnock Richard, CHORLEY ☎ 01257 455000 🖹 01257 455000 140 en suite

Chorley Hall o' th' Hill, Heath Charnock PR6 9HX
☎ 01257 480263   🖹 01257 480722
e-mail: secretary@chorleygolfclub.freeserve.co.uk
web: www.chorleygolfclub.co.uk

A splendid moorland course with plenty of fresh air. The well-sited clubhouse affords some good views of the Lancashire coast and of Angelzarke, a local beauty spot. Beware of the short 3rd hole with its menacing out of bounds.

18 Holes, 6269yds, Par 71, SSS 70, Course record 62.
Club membership 550.

Visitors Handicap certificate. Dress code. **Societies** booking required. **Green Fees** not confirmed **Course Designer** J A Steer **Prof** Mark Bradley **Facilities** ⓦ ⦿ 🏌 ⛳ 🍴 👤 🏠 🛒 ✓ **Location** 2.5m SE on A673
Hotel ★★★ 80% HL Pines, 570 Preston Rd, Clayton-Le-Woods, CHORLEY ☎ 01772 338551 🖹 01772 338551 35 en suite

Duxbury Jubilee Park Duxbury Hall Rd PR7 4AT
☎ 01257 265380   🖹 01257 274500

18 Holes, 6390yds, Par 71, SSS 70.

Course Designer Hawtree & Sons **Location** 2.5m S off A6
Telephone for further details
Hotel BUD Welcome Lodge Charnock Richard, Welcome Break Service Area, CHORLEY ☎ 01257 791746 🖹 01257 791746 100 en suite

Shaw Hill Hotel Golf & Country Club Preston Rd, Whittle-Le-Woods PR6 7PP
☎ 01257 269221 & 279222 (pro shop)
🖹 01257 261223
e-mail: golf@shaw-hill.co.uk
web: www.shaw-hill.co.uk

A fine heavily wooded parkland course designed by one of Europe's most prominent golf architects and offering a considerable challenge as well as tranquillity and scenic charm. Six holes are protected by water and signature holes are the 8th and the closing 18th played slightly up hill to the imposing club house.

18 Holes, 6283yds, Par 72, SSS 71, Course record 65.
Club membership 500.

Visitors Mon-Fri except BHs. Handicap certificate. **Societies** booking required. **Green Fees** Mon-Thu £35 per 18 holes, Fri £45 **Course Designer** Harry Vardon **Prof** David Clark **Facilities** ⓦ ⦿ 🏌 ⛳ 🍴 👤 🏠 ⛳ ◇ 🛒 ✓ **Leisure** heated indoor swimming pool, sauna, gymnasium, snooker **Conf** facs Corporate Hospitality Days **Location** 1.5m N on A6
Hotel ★★★ 74% HL Best Western Park Hall, Park Hall Road, Charnock Richard, CHORLEY ☎ 01257 455000 🖹 01257 455000 140 en suite

CLITHEROE
Map 7 SD74

Clitheroe Whalley Rd, Pendleton BB7 1PP
☎ 01200 422292 📠 01200 422292
e-mail: secretary@clitheroegolfclub.com
web: www.clitheroegolfclub.com
One of the best inland courses in the country. Clitheroe is a parkland-type course with water hazards and good scenic views, particularly towards Longridge and Pendle Hill. An Open Championship regional qualifying course from 2010.

18 Holes, 6530yds, Par 71, SSS 71, Course record 63.
Club membership 700.

Visitors Sun-Fri & BHs. Booking required. Handicap certificate. Dress code. **Societies** booking required. **Green Fees** Mon-Thu £48 per day, £38 per 18 holes, Fri & Sun £50/£43 **Course Designer** James Braid **Prof** Paul McEvoy **Facilities** 🄫 🍴 🛈 🖢 🍺 🏌 🏡 ⚑ ✂ ⛳ **Conf** facs Corporate Hospitality Days **Location** 2m S of Clitheroe
Hotel ★★★ 74% HL Shireburn Arms, Whalley Road, Hurst Green, CLITHEROE ☎ 01254 826518 📠 01254 826518 22 en suite

COLNE
Map 7 SD84

Colne Law Farm, Skipton Old Rd BB8 7EB
☎ 01282 863391 📠 01282 870547
e-mail: colnegolfclub@hotmail.co.uk
Moorland course with scenic surroundings.

9 Holes, 6053yds, Par 70, SSS 69, Course record 63.
Club membership 440.

Visitors Mon-Sun & BHs. Booking required weekends & BHs. Dress code. **Societies** booking required. **Green Fees** £20 per day (£25 weekends & BHs) **Facilities** 🄫 🍴 🛈 🖢 🍺 🏌 **Leisure** snooker **Conf** Corporate Hospitality Days **Location** 1m E off A56
Hotel ★★★ 80% HL Oaks, Colne Road, Reedley, BURNLEY ☎ 01282 414141 📠 01282 414141 52 en suite

DARWEN
Map 7 SD62

Darwen Winter Hill BB3 0LB
☎ 01254 701287 (club) & 704367 (office)
📠 01254 773833
e-mail: admin@darwengolfclub.com
web: www.darwengolfclub.com
Built on undulating moorland with the front 9 having more of a parkland setting. The front nine holes have many water features and are pleasurable but challenging to play. The back nine are more undulating with fine views and challenging holes for all levels of golfer.

18 Holes, 6046yds, Par 71, SSS 71. Club membership 600.

Visitors Mon, Wed-Fri, Sun & BHs. Booking required Fri, Sun & BHs. Handicap certificate. Dress code. **Societies** welcome. **Green Fees** £25 per 18 holes (£30 Sun) **Prof** Wayne Lennon **Facilities** 🄫 🍴 🛈 🖢 🍺 🏡 ⛳ **Conf** facs Corporate Hospitality Days **Location** M65 junct 4, 1m NW of Darwen
Hotel BUD Travelodge Blackburn M65, Darwen Motorway Services, DARWEN, Nr Blackburn ☎ 08719 846 122 📠 08719 846 122 48 en suite

FLEETWOOD
Map 7 SD34

Fleetwood Golf House, Princes Way FY7 8AF
☎ 01253 773573
e-mail: secretary@fleetwoodgolf.co.uk
web: www.fleetwoodgolf.co.uk
Championship length, flat seaside links where the player must always be alert to changes of direction or strength of the wind.

18 Holes, 6723yds, Par 72, SSS 72.
Club membership 600.

Visitors Mon-Fri, Sun & BHs. Booking required. Dress code. **Societies** booking required. **Green Fees** £35 per round (£40 Sun). Winter £25/£30 **Course Designer** J A Steer **Prof** Ian Taylor **Facilities** 🄫 🍴 🛈 🖢 🍺 🏡 🏡 ⛳ **Conf** facs Corporate Hospitality Days **Location** W of town centre
Hotel ★★★ 78% HL Briar Dene, 56 Kelso Avenue, Thornton, Cleveleys, BLACKPOOL ☎ 01253 852312 & 338300 📠 01253 852312 16 en suite

GARSTANG
Map 7 SD44

BW Garstang Country Hotel & Golf Centre Garstang Rd, Bowgreave PR3 1YE
☎ 01995 600100 📠 01995 600950
e-mail: reception@ghgc.co.uk
web: www.garstanghotelandgolf.com
Fairly flat parkland course following the contours of the Rivers Wyre and Calder, some greens being close to the hazards. The good

continued

drainage all year and the fine views of the Pennines add to the enjoyment of a challenging game of golf.

BW Garstang Country Hotel & Golf Centre: 18 Holes, 6050yds, Par 68, SSS 68.

Visitors Mon-Sun & BHs. **Societies** booking required. **Green Fees** not confirmed **Course Designer** Richard Bradbeer **Prof** Robert Head **Facilities** ⑪ ⑩| 🍴 ⌸ 🍸 ⚞ 🏠 ⚟ ◇ 🛺 ✆ 🏌
Conf facs Corporate Hospitality Days **Location** 1m S of Garstang on B6430

BW Garstang Country Hotel & Golf Centre

Hotel ★★★ 77% HL Best Western Garstang Country Hotel & Golf Centre, Garstang Road, Bowgreave, GARSTANG ☎ 01995 600100 🖹 01995 600100 32 en suite

See advert on page 153

GREAT HARWOOD   Map 7 SD73

Great Harwood Harwood Bar, Whalley Rd BB6 7TE
☎ 01254 884391
web: www.greatharwoodgolfclub.co.uk
Flat parkland with fine views of the Pendle region.

9 Holes, 6404yds, Par 73, SSS 71, Course record 68. Club membership 400.

Visitors Mon-Fri & BHs. Dress code. **Societies** booking required **Green Fees** £22 per day (£28 BHs) **Facilities** 🍴 ⌸ 🍸 ⚞ **Location** E of town centre on A680
Hotel ★★★★ 72% HL Mercure Dunkenhalgh Hotel & Spa, Blackburn Road, Clayton-le-Moors, ACCRINGTON ☎ 01254 398021 🖹 01254 398021 175 en suite

HASLINGDEN   Map 7 SD72

Rossendale Ewood Lane Head BB4 6LH
☎ 01706 831339 (Secretary) & 213616 (Pro)
🖹 01706 228669
e-mail: admin@rossendalegolfclub.net
web: www.rossendalegolfclub.co.uk
A surprisingly flat parkland course, situated on a plateau with panoramic views and renowned for excellent greens.

18 Holes, 6293yds, Par 72, SSS 71, Course record 64. Club membership 700.

Visitors Mon-Fri, Sun & BHs. Booking required. Handicap certificate. Dress code. **Societies** booking required. **Green Fees** £40 per day, £30 per round (£45/£35 Sun) **Prof** Stephen Nicholls **Facilities** ⑪ ⑩| 🍴 ⌸ 🍸 ⚞ 🏠 ✆ **Location** 0.5m S off A56
Hotel ★★ 85% HL Millstone at Mellor, Church Lane, Mellor, BLACKBURN ☎ 01254 813333 🖹 01254 813333 23 en suite

HEYSHAM   Map 7 SD46

Heysham Trumacar Park, Middleton Rd LA3 3JH
☎ 01524 851011 (Sec) & 852000 (Pro)
🖹 01524 853030
e-mail: secretary@heyshamgolfclub.co.uk
web: www.heyshamgolfclub.co.uk
A seaside parkland course, partly wooded.

18 Holes, 5999yds, Par 68, SSS 69. Club membership 850.

Visitors Mon-Sat & BHs. Handicap certificate. Dress code. **Societies** booking required. **Green Fees** £35 per day, £30 per round (£40 Sat & BHs) **Course Designer** Alex Herd **Prof** Ryan Done **Facilities** ⑪ ⑩| 🍴 ⌸ 🍸 ⚞ ✆ 🛺 ✆ 🏌
Leisure snooker **Conf** Corporate Hospitality Days **Location** 0.75m S off A589
Hotel ★★★ 68% HL Clarendon, 76 Marine Road West, West End Promenade, MORECAMBE ☎ 01524 410180 🖹 01524 410180 29 en suite

KNOTT END-ON-SEA   Map 7 SD34

Knott End Wyreside FY6 0AA
☎ 01253 810576   🖹 01253 813446
e-mail: louise@knottendgolfclub.com
web: www.knottendgolfclub.com

Scenic links and parkland course next to the Wyre estuary. The opening five holes run along the river and have spectacular views of the Fylde Coast. Although the course is quite short, the prevailing winds can add to one's score. Over-clubbing can be disastrous with trouble behind most of the smallish and well-guarded greens.

18 Holes, 5825yds, Par 69, SSS 68, Course record 63. Club membership 650.

Visitors Mon-Fri, Sun & BHs. Booking required. Handicap certificate. Dress code. **Societies** booking required. **Green Fees** £35 per day, £33 per round (£45/£41Sun) **Course Designer** Braid **Prof** Paul Walker **Facilities** ⑪ ⑩| 🍴 ⌸ 🍸 ⚞ 🏠 ✆ 🛺 ✆
Leisure practice net **Conf** Corporate Hospitality Days **Location** W of village off B5377
Hotel BUD Travelodge Lancaster (M6), White Carr Lane, Bay Horse, FORTON, Lancaster ☎ 08719 846 152 🖹 08719 846 152 53 en suite

LANCASTER
Map 7 SD46

Lancaster Golf Club Ashton Hall, Ashton-with-Stodday
LA2 0AJ
☎ 01524 751247 📠 01524 752742
e-mail: office@lancastergc.co.uk
web: www.lancastergc.co.uk

This parkland course is unusual as it is exposed to winds from the Irish Sea. It is situated on the Lune estuary and has some natural hazards and easy walking. There are several fine holes among woods near the old clubhouse. Fine views towards the Lake District.

Lancaster Golf Club: 18 Holes, 6282yds, Par 71, SSS 71, Course record 66. Club membership 900.

Visitors Mon-Fri except BHs. Booking required. Handicap certificate. Dress code. **Societies** booking required. **Green Fees** £52 per day, £43 per round **Course Designer** James Braid **Prof** David Sutcliffe
Facilities ⊕ ❥ ⓛ ⌴ 🍴 ⅄ 🏠 ⅋ ◇ ✔ 🛒 ✔
Conf Corporate Hospitality Days **Location** 3m S on A588
Hotel ★★★★ 76% HL Lancaster House, Green Lane, Ellel, LANCASTER ☎ 01524 844822 📠 01524 844822 99 en suite

Lansil Caton Rd LA1 3PE
☎ 01524 61233

9 Holes, 5540yds, Par 70, SSS 67, Course record 68.

Facilities ⊕ by prior arrangement ❥ by prior arrangement ⓛ ⌴
🍴 **Location** N of town centre on A683
Telephone for further details
Hotel ★★★★ 76% HL Lancaster House, Green Lane, Ellel, LANCASTER ☎ 01524 844822 📠 01524 844822 99 en suite

LANGHO
Map 7 SD73

Mytton Fold Hotel & Golf Complex Whalley Rd BB6 8AB
☎ 01254 245392 📠 01254 248119
web: www.myttonfold.co.uk

The course has panoramic views across the Ribble Valley and Pendle Hill. Tight fairways and water hazards are designed to make this a challenging course for any golfer.

Mytton Fold Hotel & Golf Complex: 18 Holes, 6155yds, Par 72, SSS 70, Course record 69. Club membership 450.

Visitors Mon-Sun & BHs. Booking required Fri-Sun & BHs. Dress code. **Societies** booking required. **Green Fees** £22.50 (£25 weekends) **Course Designer** Frank Hargreaves **Facilities** ⊕ ❥ ⓛ ⌴
🍴 ⅄ 🏠 ◇ 🛒 ✔ **Conf** facs Corporate Hospitality Days
Location on A59 between Langho and Billington
Hotel ★★ 79% HL The Avenue Hotel & Restaurant, Brockhall Village, LANGHO ☎ 01254 244811 📠 01254 244811 21 en suite

LEYLAND
Map 7 SD52

Leyland Wigan Rd PR25 5UD
☎ 01772 436457 📠 01772 435605
e-mail: manager@leylandgolfclub.co.uk
web: www.leylandgolfclub.co.uk

Fairly flat parkland course.

18 Holes, 6298yds, Par 70, SSS 70, Course record 67. Club membership 750.

Visitors Mon-Fri except BHs. Booking required. Handicap certificate. Dress code. **Societies** booking required. **Green Fees** £34 per round. Winter £28 **Prof** Colin Burgess **Facilities** ⊕ ❥ ⓛ ⌴ 🍴 ⅄

📠 ✔ 🛒 ✔ 🍴 **Conf** facs Corporate Hospitality Days **Location** M6 junct 28, turn right to traffic lights at A49, turn right again, course 0.5m on left
Hotel ★★★ 80% HL Pines, 570 Preston Rd, Clayton-Le-Woods, CHORLEY ☎ 01772 338551 📠 01772 338551 35 en suite

LONGRIDGE
Map 7 SD63

Longridge Fell Barn, Jeffrey Hill PR3 2TU
☎ 01772 783291 📠 01772 783022
e-mail: secretary@longridgegolfclub.com
web: www.longridgegolfclub.com

One of the oldest clubs in England, which celebrated its 125th anniversary in 2002. A moorland course with panoramic views of the Trough of Bowland, the Fylde coast and Welsh mountains. Small, sloping greens, difficult to read.

18 Holes, 5975yds, Par 70, SSS 69, Course record 63. Club membership 600.

Visitors Mon-Sun & BHs. Booking required. Dress code. **Societies** booking required. **Green Fees** from £17 per round **Prof** Stephen Taylor **Facilities** ⊕ ❥ ⓛ ⌴ 🍴 ⅄ 🏠 ⅋
✔ 🛒 ✔ **Conf** Corporate Hospitality Days **Location** 8m NE of Preston off B6243
Hotel ★★★ 74% HL Shireburn Arms, Whalley Road, Hurst Green, CLITHEROE ☎ 01254 826518 📠 01254 826518 22 en suite

LYTHAM ST ANNES
Map 7 SD32

Fairhaven Oakwood Av FY8 4JU
☎ 01253 736741 (Secretary) 📠 01253 731461
web: www.fairhavengolfclub.co.uk

18 Holes, 6883yds, Par 74, SSS 73, Course record 64.

Course Designer J A Steer **Location** E of town centre off B5261
Telephone for further details
Hotel ★★★ 79% HL Bedford, 307-313 Clifton Drive South, LYTHAM ST ANNES ☎ 01253 724636 📠 01253 724636 45 en suite

Lytham Green Drive Ballam Rd FY8 4LE
☎ 01253 737390 📠 01253 731350
e-mail: secretary@lythamgreendrive.co.uk
web: www.lythamgreendrive.co.uk

Green Drive provides a stern but fair challenge for even the most accomplished golfer. Tight fairways, strategically placed hazards and small tricky greens are the trademark of this testing course which meanders through pleasant countryside and is flanked by woods, pastures and meadows. The course demands accuracy in spite of the relatively flat terrain.

18 Holes, 6363yds, Par 70, SSS 70, Course record 64. Club membership 700.

Visitors Mon-Fri, Sun & BHs. Handicap certificate. Dress code. **Societies** booking required. **Green Fees** £50 per day, £40 per round **Course Designer** Steer **Prof** Andrew Lancaster **Facilities** ⊕ ❥ ⓛ
⌴ 🍴 ⅄ 🏠 ⅋ ✔ **Conf** Corporate Hospitality Days **Location** E of town centre off B5259
Hotel ★★★ 79% HL Bedford, 307-313 Clifton Drive South, LYTHAM ST ANNES ☎ 01253 724636 📠 01253 724636 45 en suite

Royal Lytham & St Annes see page 157
FY8 3LQ
☎ 01253 724206   🖷 01253 780946
e-mail: bookings@royallytham.org
web: www.royallytham.org

St Annes Old Links Highbury Rd East FY8 2LD
☎ 01253 723597   🖷 01253 781506
e-mail: secretary@stannesoldlinks.com
web: www.stannesoldlinks.com

Seaside links, qualifying course for Open Championship; compact and of very high standard, particularly greens. Windy, very long 5th, 17th and 18th holes. Famous hole: 9th (171yds), par 3.

St Annes Old Links Golf Ltd: 18 Holes, 6684yds, Par 72, SSS 73, Course record 63. Club membership 700.

Visitors Mon-Fri & Sun except BHs. Booking required Sun. Handicap certificate. Dress code. **Societies** welcome. **Green Fees** Mon-Thu £60 per day, £50am only, £45 pm only, Fri & Sun £65/£55/£50 **Course Designer** George Lowe **Prof** D J Webster **Facilities** ⑪ ⚑ 🍽 🛒 🔌 🏐 ⚐ 🚜 ♂ **Leisure** snooker room **Conf** facs Corporate Hospitality Days **Location** N of town centre
Hotel ★★★ 77% HL Chadwick, South Promenade, LYTHAM ST ANNES ☎ 01253 720061 🖷 01253 720061 75 en suite

---

MORECAMBE   Map 7 SD46

Morecambe Marine Road East, Bare LA4 6AJ
☎ 01524 412841   🖷 01524 400088
e-mail: secretary@morecambegolfclub.com
web: www.morecambegolfclub.com

Holiday golf at its most enjoyable. The well-maintained, wind-affected seaside parkland course is not long but full of character. Even so the panoramic views of Morecambe Bay, the Lake District and the Pennines make concentration difficult. The 4th is a testing hole.

Morecambe Golf Club Ltd: 18 Holes, 5791yds, Par 67, SSS 69, Course record 69. Club membership 850.

Visitors Mon-Sun & BHs. Booking required. Handicap certificate. Dress code. **Societies** booking required. **Green Fees** phone **Course Designer** Dr Alister Mackenzie **Prof** Simon Fletcher **Facilities** ⑪ ⚑ 🍽 🛒 🔌 🏐 ⚐ ♂ **Leisure** snooker room **Conf** Corporate Hospitality Days **Location** N of town centre on A5105
Hotel ★★★ 68% HL Elms, Bare Village, MORECAMBE ☎ 01524 411501 🖷 01524 411501 39 en suite

---

NELSON   Map 7 SD83

Marsden Park Townhouse Rd BB9 8DG
☎ 01282 661912 & 661384
e-mail: martin.robinson@pendleleisuretrust.co.uk
web: www.pendleleisuretrust.co.uk

A semi-parkland course offering panoramic views of surrounding countryside, set in the foothills of Pendle Marsden Park, a testing 18 holes for golfers of all abilities.

Marsden Park Golf Course: 18 Holes, 5989yds, Par 70, SSS 69, Course record 65. Club membership 750.

Visitors Mon-Sun & BHs. Booking required weekends & BHs. **Societies** welcome. **Green Fees** £14.50 per 18 holes; £12 per 9 holes (£14 per 9 holes weekends & BHs) **Facilities** ⑪ ⚑ 🍽 ⚐ 🔌 🏐 🚜 🍴 ♂ ♂ **Conf** facs Corporate Hospitality Days

Location take M65 from Blackburn to end, turn right at rdbt, 2nd exit at next roundabout. left at Hour Glass Pub, signed on left
Hotel ★★★ 80% HL Oaks, Colne Road, Reedley, BURNLEY ☎ 01282 414141 🖷 01282 414141 52 en suite

Nelson King's Causeway, Brierfield BB9 0EU
☎ 01282 611834   🖷 01282 611834
e-mail: secretary@nelsongolfclub.com
web: www.nelsongolfclub.com

Moorland course. Dr MacKenzie, who laid out the course, managed a design that does not include any wearisome climbing and created many interesting holes with wonderful panoramic views of the surrounding Pendle area.

18 Holes, 6006yds, Par 70, SSS 69, Course record 64. Club membership 590.

Visitors Mon-Fri, Sun & BHs. Booking required. Handicap certificate. Dress code. **Societies** booking required. **Green Fees** £30 per day (£35 Sun & BHs). **Course Designer** Dr A Mackenzie **Prof** Simon Eaton **Facilities** ⑪ ⚑ 🍽 🛒 🔌 🏐 ⚐ 🍴 ♂ **Conf** Corporate Hospitality Days **Location** M65 junct 12, A682 to Brierfield, left at lights onto Halifax Rd & King's Causeway
Hotel ★★★ 80% HL Oaks, Colne Road, Reedley, BURNLEY ☎ 01282 414141 🖷 01282 414141 52 en suite

---

ORMSKIRK   Map 7 SD40

Hurlston Hall Golf & Country Club Hurlston Ln, Southport Rd, Scarisbrick L40 8HB
☎ 01704 840400 & 842829 (pro shop) 🖷 01704 841404
e-mail: info@hurlstonhall.co.uk
web: www.hurlstonhall.co.uk

Designed by Donald Steel, this gently undulating course offers fine views of the Pennines and Bowland Fells. With generous fairways, large tees and greens, two streams and seven lakes, it provides a good test of golf for players of all standards.

Hurlston Hall Golf & Country Club: 18 Holes, 6757yds, Par 72, SSS 72, Course record 66. Club membership 650.

Visitors contact club for details. **Societies** welcome. **Green Fees** £40 per 18 holes (£45 weekends). **Course Designer** Donald Steel **Prof** Tim Hastings **Facilities** ⑪ ⚑ 🍽 🛒 🔌 🏐 ⚐ 🚜 ♂ ♂ **Leisure** heated indoor swimming pool, fishing, gymnasium **Conf** facs Corporate Hospitality Days **Location** 2m from Ormskirk on A570
Hotel ★★★ 82% HL West Tower Country House, Mill Lane, Aughton, ORMSKIRK ☎ 01695 423328 🖷 01695 423328 12 en suite

Ormskirk Cranes Ln, Lathom L40 5UJ
☎ 01695 572227   🖷 01695 572227
e-mail: mail@ormskirkgollfclub.com
web: www.ormskirkgolfclub.com

Pleasantly secluded, fairly flat parkland with much heath and silver birch. Accuracy from the tees will provide an interesting variety of second shots.

18 Holes, 6358yds, Par 70, SSS 71, Course record 63. Club membership 300.

Visitors Mon-Sun & BHs. Booking required. Dress code. **Societies** booking required. **Green Fees** £55 per day, £45 per round (£60/£50 Sun, £60 per round Sat) **Course Designer** Harold Hilton **Prof** Jack Hammond **Facilities** ⑪ ⚑ 🍽 🛒 🔌 🏐 ⚐ ♂ **Conf** Corporate Hospitality Days **Location** 1.5m NE
Hotel ★★★ 82% HL West Tower Country House, Mill Lane, Aughton, ORMSKIRK ☎ 01695 423328 🖷 01695 423328 12 en suite

ROYAL LYTHAM & ST ANNES

LANCASHIRE - LYTHAM ST ANNES - MAP 7 SD32

Founded in 1886, this huge links course can be difficult, especially in windy conditions. Unusually for a championship course, it starts with a par 3, the nearby railway line and red-brick houses creating distractions that add to the challenge. The course has hosted 10 Open Championships with some memorable victories: amateur Bobby Jones famously won the first here in 1926; Bobby Charles of New Zealand became the only left-hander to win the title; in 1969 Tony Jacklin helped to revive British golf with his win; and the most recent in 2001 was won by David Duval.

Links Gate FY8 3LQ ☎ 01253 724206 📄 01253 780946
e-mail: bookings@royallytham.org
web: www.royallytham.org
18 Holes, 6882yds, Par 71, SSS 74, Course record 64. Club membership 850.
Visitors Mon-Fri & BHs. Weekends only with accommodation in Dormy House. Booking required. Handicap certificate. Dress code. **Societies** booking required. **Green Fees** £208 per 36 holes, £137 per 18 holes (Sun £208 per 18 holes). All prices including lunch **Course Designer** George Lowe **Prof** Eddie Birchenough **Facilities** ⑪ ⑩ 🍴 🖳 💻 🍷 🏊 🏠 ◇ ✐ ✔ **Conf** Corporate Hospitality Days **Location** 0.5m E of St Annes
Hotel ★★★ 77% HL Chadwick, South Promenade, LYTHAM ST ANNES ☎ 01253 720061 📄 01253 720061 75 en suite

PLEASINGTON　　　　　　　　　Map 7 SD62

Pleasington BB2 5JF
☎ 01254 202177　📄 01254 201028
e-mail: secretary-manager@pleasington-golf.co.uk
web: www.pleasington-golf.co.uk

Plunging and rising across lovely parkland and heathland turf, this course tests judgement of distance through the air to greens of widely differing levels. The 11th and 4th are testing holes. A regular regional qualifying course for the Open Championship.

18 Holes, 6402yds, Par 71, SSS 71, Course record 65. Club membership 700.

Visitors Mon-Fri, Sun & BHs. Booking required. Dress code. **Societies** booking required. **Green Fees** £45 per round (£50 Sun & BHs). **Course Designer** George Lowe **Prof** Ged Furey **Facilities** Ⓣ ⏐Ⓞ⏐ ⓑ ▭ ⏐ ⏐ ⏞ 🗄 🖋 🏌 **Conf** facs Corporate Hospitality Days **Location** M65 junct 3, signed for Blackburn
Hotel ★★ 85% HL Millstone at Mellor, Church Lane, Mellor, BLACKBURN ☎ 01254 813333 📄 01254 813333　23 en suite

POULTON-LE-FYLDE　　　　　　Map 7 SD33

Poulton-le-Fylde Breck Rd FY6 7HJ
☎ 01253 892444
e-mail: greenwood-golf@hotmail.co.uk
web: www.poultonlefyldegolfclub.co.uk

A pleasant, municipal parkland course suitable for all standards of golfers although emphasis on accuracy is required. Good mix of holes

Poulton Le Fylde Golf Club: 9 Holes, 2858yds, Par 35, SSS 34, Course record 66. Club membership 300.

Visitors Mon-Sun & BHs. Booking required. Dress code. **Societies** booking required. **Green Fees** £15 per 18 holes, £8.75 per 9 holes (£18/£10 weekends). **Course Designer** H Taylor **Prof** John Greenwood **Facilities** Ⓣ ⏐Ⓞ⏐ ⓑ ▭ ⏐ ⏐ ⏞ 🗄 ⏐ 🖋 🛺 🖋 **Leisure** indoor custom fitting centre **Conf** Corporate Hospitality Days **Location** M55 junct 3, A585 signed Fleetwood, 1st exit at River Wyre rdbt, club 500 yds on right signed
Hotel ★★ 71% HL Hotel Sheraton, 54-62 Queens Promenade, BLACKPOOL ☎ 01253 352723 📄 01253 352723　104 en suite

PRESTON　　　　　　　　　　　Map 7 SD52

Ashton & Lea Tudor Av, Lea PR4 0XA
☎ 01772 735282　📄 01772 735762
e-mail: simonp@ashtonleagolfclub.co.uk
web: www.ashtonleagolfclub.co.uk

Fairly flat, well-maintained parkland course with natural water hazards, offering pleasant walks and some testing holes for golfers of all standards. Water comes into play on seven of the last nine holes. The course has three challenging par 3s.

18 Holes, 6334yds, Par 71, SSS 70, Course record 65. Club membership 650.

Visitors Mon-Sun except BHs. Dress code. **Societies** booking required. **Green Fees** £30 per 18 holes (£35 weekends) **Course Designer** J Steer **Prof** M Greenough **Facilities** Ⓣ ⏐Ⓞ⏐ ⓑ ▭ ⏐ ⏐ ⏞ 🗄 🖋 🛺 🖋 **Leisure** snooker table **Conf** facs Corporate Hospitality Days **Location** 3m W of Preston on A5085
Hotel ★★★★ 76% HL Preston Marriott Hotel, Garstang Road, Broughton, PRESTON ☎ 01772 864087 📄 01772 864087 149 en suite

Fishwick Hall Glenluce Dr, Farringdon Park PR1 5TD
☎ 01772 798300　📄 01772 704600
e-mail: fishwickhallgolfclub@supanet.com
web: www.fishwickhallgolfclub.co.uk

Meadowland course overlooking River Ribble. Natural hazards.

18 Holes, 6045yds, Par 70, SSS 69, Course record 66. Club membership 650.

Visitors Mon-Sun & BHs. Dress code. **Societies** booking required. **Green Fees** not confirmed **Prof** Martin Watson **Facilities** Ⓣ ⏐Ⓞ⏐ ⓑ ▭ ⏐ ⏐ 🗄 🖋 **Conf** Corporate Hospitality Days **Location** M6 junct 31
Hotel ★★★ 75% HL Macdonald Tickled Trout, Preston New Road, Samlesbury, PRESTON ☎ 0870 1942120 📄 0870 1942120 102 en suite

Ingol Tanterton Hall Rd PR2 7BY
☎ 01772 734556　📄 01772 729815
web: www.ingolgolfclub.co.uk

18 Holes, 6294yds, Par 72, SSS 70, Course record 68.
Course Designer Henry Cotton **Location** A5085 onto B5411, signs to Ingol
Telephone for further details
Hotel ★★★ 75% HL Macdonald Tickled Trout, Preston New Road, Samlesbury, PRESTON ☎ 0870 1942120 📄 0870 1942120 102 en suite

Penwortham Blundell Ln, Penwortham PR1 0AX
☎ 01772 744630　📄 01772 740172
e-mail: admin@penworthamgc.co.uk
web: www.penworthamgc.co.uk

A progressive golf club set close to the banks of the River Ribble. The course has tree-lined fairways, excellent greens, and provides easy walking. Testing holes include the 177 yd, par 3 3rd, the 480 yd, par 5 6th, and the 386 yd par 4 16th.

18 Holes, 5865yds, Par 69, SSS 69, Course record 65. Club membership 1100.

Visitors Mon, Wed-Fri except BHs. Booking required. Handicap certificate. Dress code. **Societies** booking required. **Green Fees** not confirmed **Course Designer** Ken Moodie **Prof** Darren Hopwood **Facilities** Ⓣ ⏐Ⓞ⏐ ⓑ ▭ ⏐ ⏐ ⏞ 🗄 🖋 **Conf** Corporate Hospitality Days **Location** 1.5m W of town centre off A59
Hotel ★★★ 75% HL Macdonald Tickled Trout, Preston New Road, Samlesbury, PRESTON ☎ 0870 1942120 📄 0870 1942120 102 en suite

Preston Fulwood Hall Ln, Fulwood PR2 8DD
☎ 01772 700011 📠 01772 794234
e-mail: secretary@prestongolfclub.com
web: www.prestongolfclub.com
Pleasant inland golf at this course set in very agreeable parkland.
There is a well-balanced selection of holes, undulating among groups
of trees, and not requiring great length.
18 Holes, 6312yds, Par 71, SSS 71, Course record 68.
Club membership 800.
Visitors contact club for details. **Societies** welcome. **Green Fees** £45
per day, £40 per round. **Course Designer** James Braid **Prof** Andrew
Greenbank **Facilities** ⑪ ⑩ ⓛ ☐ ☌ ⌂ 🏊 ⚑ ⚐ ✆
Conf facs Corporate Hospitality Days **Location** 1m N of city centre
on A6, right at lights onto Watling St, left onto Fulwood Hall Ln,
course 300yds on left
Hotel ★★★★ 76% HL Preston Marriott Hotel, Garstang
Road, Broughton, PRESTON ☎ 01772 864087 📠 01772 864087
149 en suite

RISHTON   Map 7 SD73

Rishton Eachill Links, Hawthorn Dr BB1 4HG
☎ 01254 884442 📠 01254 887701
e-mail: rishtongc@onetel.net
web: www.rishtongolfclub.co.uk
Undulating moorland course with some interesting holes and fine
views of East Lancashire.
Eachill Links: 10 Holes, 6097yds, Par 70, SSS 69,
Course record 68. Club membership 270.
Visitors dress code. **Green Fees** £20 **Course Designer** Peter Alliss/
Dave Thomas **Facilities** ⑪ ⑩ ⓛ ☐ ☌ ⌂ **Conf** Corporate
Hospitality Days **Location** M65 junct 6/7, 1m. Signed from Station Rd
in Rishton
Hotel ★★★★ 72% HL Mercure Dunkenhalgh Hotel & Spa,
Blackburn Road, Clayton-le-Moors, ACCRINGTON ☎ 01254 398021
📠 01254 398021 175 en suite

SILVERDALE   Map 7 SD47

Silverdale Redbridge Ln LA5 0SP
☎ 01524 701300 📠 01524 702074
e-mail: info@silverdalegolfclub.co.uk
web: silverdalegolfclub.co.uk
Challenging heathland course with rock outcrops, set in an Area
of Outstanding Natural Beauty with spectacular views of the Lake
District hills and Morecambe Bay. It is a course of two halves, being
either open fairways or tight hilly limestone valleys. The 13th hole has
been described as one of Britain's 100 extraordinary golf holes.
18 Holes, 5526yds, Par 70, SSS 67, Course record 67.
Club membership 450.
Visitors Mon-Sun & BHs, Booking required weekends & BHs. Dress
code. **Societies** booking required. **Green Fees** not confirmed **Prof** Ceri
& Chris Cousins **Facilities** ⑪ ⑩ ⓛ ☐ ☌ ⌂ 🏊 ⚑ ✆
Location opp Silverdale station & Leighton Moss RSPB nature reserve
Hotel ★★★ 70% HL Cumbria Grand, GRANGE-OVER-SANDS
☎ 015395 32331 📠 015395 32331 122 en suite

UPHOLLAND   Map 7 SD50

Beacon Park Golf & Country Club Beacon Ln, Dalton
WN8 7RU
☎ 01695 622700 📠 01695 628362
e-mail: info@beaconparkgolf.com
web: www.beaconparkgolf.com

Undulating/hilly parkland course, designed by Donald Steel, with
magnificent view of the Welsh hills. Twenty-four-bay floodlit driving
range.
Beacon Park Golf & Country Club: 18 Holes, 6151yds,
Par 72, SSS 70, Course record 68. Club membership 250.
Visitors Mon-Sun & BHs. Booking required. Dress code.
Societies booking required. **Green Fees** not confirmed **Course**
Designer Donald Steel **Prof** Colin Parkinson **Facilities** ⑪ ⑩ by
prior arrangement ⓛ ☐ ☌ ⌂ ⚑ ✆ ⚐ ✆ **Conf** facs
Corporate Hospitality Days **Location** M6 junct 26, follow signs for
Upholland & Orrell, then brown Beacon Country Park signs
Hotel ★★★ 80% HL Best Western Wrightington Hotel &
Country Club, Moss Lane, Wrightington, WIGAN ☎ 01257 425803
📠 01257 425803 74 en suite

Dean Wood Lafford Ln WN8 0QZ
☎ 01695 622219 📠 01695 622245
e-mail: secretary@deanwoodgolfclub.co.uk
web: www.deanwoodgolfclub.co.uk
This well maintained parkland course has a varied terrain - flat
front nine, undulating back nine. Beware the par 4 11th and 17th
holes, which have ruined many a card.
18 Holes, 6148yds, Par 71, SSS 70, Course record 65.
Club membership 630.
Visitors Mon, Thu & Fri except BHs. Dress code. **Societies** welcome.
Green Fees £30 per day **Course Designer** James Braid
Prof David Clarke **Facilities** ⑪ ⑩ ⓛ ☐ ☌ ⌂ 🏊 ⚑ ✆
Conf Corporate Hospitality Days **Location** M6 junct 26, 1m on A577
Hotel ★★★ 80% HL Best Western Wrightington Hotel &
Country Club, Moss Lane, Wrightington, WIGAN ☎ 01257 425803
📠 01257 425803 74 en suite

WHALLEY   Map 7 SD73

Whalley Long Leese Barn, Clerk Hill Rd BB7 9DR
☎ 01254 822236
e-mail: peterb@whalleygolfclub.com
web: www.whalleygolfclub.com
A parkland course near Pendle Hill, overlooking the Ribble Valley.
Superb views. Ninth hole over pond.

continued

9 Holes, 6258yds, Par 72, SSS 71, Course record 66. Club membership 450.

Visitors Dress code. **Societies** booking required. **Green Fees** not confirmed **Prof** Jamie Hunt **Facilities** ⊕ ⏐⚈⏐ ▟ ◻ ⏗ ⚑ ⏛ 🛜 ⛳ ⚐ ⚑ **Conf** Corporate Hospitality Days **Location** 1m SE off A671 **Hotel** ★★★★ 80% SHL Northcote, Northcote Road, LANGHO, Blackburn ☎ 01254 240555 📄 01254 240555 14 en suite

WHITWORTH   Map 7 SD81

Lobden Lobden Moor OL12 8XJ
☎ 01706 343228 & 345598   📄 01706 343228

Moorland course, with hard walking. Windy with superb views of surrounding hills. Excellent greens.

9 Holes, 5697yds, Par 70, SSS 68, Course record 63. Club membership 250.

Visitors contact club for details. **Societies** welcome. **Green Fees** phone **Facilities** ⚖ **Location** E of town centre off A671 **Hotel** ★★★★ 77% HL Mercure Norton Grange Hotel & Spa, Manchester Road, Castleton, ROCHDALE ☎ 0870 1942119 📄 0870 1942119   81 en suite

WILPSHIRE   Map 7 SD63

Wilpshire 72 Whalley Rd BB1 9LF
☎ 01254 248260   📄 01254 246745
e-mail: admin@wilpshiregolfclub.co.uk
web: www.wilpshiregolfclub.co.uk

Parkland/moorland course with varied and interesting holes. Magnificent views of Ribble Valley, the coast and the Yorkshire Dales. The course is not long by modern standards but it has two excellent par 5's and five par 3's, none of which are easy.

18 Holes, 5843yds, Par 69, SSS 69, Course record 63. Club membership 650.

Visitors Mon-Sun & BHs. Booking required Tue, Fri-Sun & BHs. Handicap certificate. Dress code. **Green Fees** Mon, Wed & Thu £20, Tue & Fri £25, weekends & BHs £30 **Course Designer** James Braid **Prof** Walter Slaven **Facilities** ⊕ ⏐⚈⏐ ▟ ◻ ⏗ ⚖ 🛜 🚌 ⛳ **Conf** facs Corporate Hospitality Days **Location** M6, junct 31, take A59 towards Blackburn, remain on this road at Swallow Hotel towards Clitheroe/Skipton. At next traffic lights turn right onto B6245 towards Blackburn, at next traffic lights turn right onto A666 towards Clitheroe, club 400yds on right **Hotel** ★★★ 77% SHL Sparth House Hotel, Whalley Road, Clayton Le Moors, ACCRINGTON ☎ 01254 872263 📄 01254 872263   16 en suite

LEICESTERSHIRE

ASHBY-DE-LA-ZOUCH   Map 8 SK31

Willesley Park Measham Rd LE65 2PF
☎ 01530 414596   📄 01530 564169
e-mail: info@willesleypark.com
web: www.willesleypark.com

Undulating heathland and parkland with quick-draining sandy subsoil.

18 Holes, 6304yds, Par 70, SSS 70, Course record 63. Club membership 600.

Visitors Mon, Wed-Sun & BHs. Booking required. Handicap certificate.

Dress. code. **Societies** booking required. **Green Fees** £35 per day/round (£40 weekends and BHs) **Course Designer** Cotton/Mackenzie **Prof** Ben Hill **Facilities** ⊕ ⏐⚈⏐ ▟ ◻ ⏗ ⚖ 🛜 🚌 ⛳ **Location** SW of town centre on B5006 **Hotel** ★★★ 68% HL Royal, Station Raod, ASHBY-DE-LA-ZOUCH ☎ 01530 412833 📄 01530 412833   34 en suite

BIRSTALL   Map 4 SK50

Birstall Station Rd LE4 3BB
☎ 0116 267 4322   📄 0116 267 4322
e-mail: sue@birstallgolfclub.co.uk
web: www.birstallgolfclub.co.uk

Parkland with trees, shrubs, ponds and ditches, next to the Great Central Railway Steam Train line.

18 Holes, 6239yds, Par 70, SSS 71. Club membership 650.

Visitors contact club for details. **Societies** welcome. **Green Fees** £35 per day; £30 per round (£40 per round weekends) **Prof** David Clark **Facilities** ⊕ ⏐⚈⏐ ▟ ◻ ⏗ ⚖ 🛜 ⛳ **Leisure** billiard room **Conf** facs Corporate Hospitality Days **Location** 3m N of Leicester on A6 **Hotel** ★★★★ 78% SHL Hotel Maiyango, 13-21 St Nicholas Place, LEICESTER ☎ 0116 251 8898 📄 0116 251 8898   14 en suite

BOTCHESTON   Map 4 SK40

Forest Hill Markfield Ln LE9 9FJ
☎ 01455 824800   📄 01455 828522

18 Holes, 6600yds, Par 72, SSS 71, Course record 63.

Course Designer Gaunt & Marnoch **Location** M1 junct 22, take A50 towards Leicester, turn right at 1st rdbt and follow road for 4m, club on left. **Telephone for further details**

COSBY   Map 4 SP59

Cosby Chapel Ln, Broughton Rd LE9 1RG
☎ 0116 286 4759   📄 0116 286 4484
e-mail: secretary@cosbygolfclub.co.uk
web: www.cosbygolfclub.co.uk

Undulating parkland with a number of tricky, tight driving holes. Challenging holes include the par 4 1st with an unseen meandering brook, the deceptively long par 4 3rd, the 12th from an elevated tee and the hogs-back shape par 3 14th, both affected by the prevailing wind.

18 Holes, 6438yds, Par 71, SSS 71, Course record 65. Club membership 750.

Visitors Mon-Fri except BHs. Booking required. Handicap certificate. Dress code. **Societies** booking required. **Green Fees** £40 per day, £28 per round **Course Designer** Hawtree **Prof** Gary Coysh **Facilities** ⊕ ⏐⚈⏐ ▟ ◻ ⏗ ⚖ 🛜 ⚐ 🚌 ⛳ **Leisure** snooker table **Conf** facs Corporate Hospitality Days **Location** M1 junct 21, B4114 to L-turn at BP service station, signed Cosby **Hotel** ★★★★ 80% HL Sketchley Grange, Sketchley Lane, Burbage, HINCKLEY ☎ 01455 251133 📄 01455 251133   52 en suite

EAST GOSCOTE
Map 8 SK61

Beedles Lake 170 Broome Ln LE7 3WQ
☎ 0116 260 6759 🖷 0116 269 4127
e-mail: jon.coleman@jelson.co.uk
web: www.beedleslake.co.uk

Fairly flat parkland with easy walking situated in the heart of the Wreake Valley with the river meandering through a number of holes. Older trees and thousands of newly planted ones give the course a mature feel. The course is maintained to a high standard and proper tees and greens are used at all times.

Beedles Lake Golf Centre: 18 Holes, 6641yds, Par 72, SSS 72, Course record 68. Club membership 498.

Visitors Mon-Sun & BHs. Booking required weekends & BHs. Dress code. **Societies** booking required. **Green Fees** £15 per 18 holes (£22 weekends & BHs) **Course Designer** D Tucker **Prof** Sean Byrne **Facilities** ⑪ ⑩ ㏒ ☕ 🍴 ㅿ 🏠 🎯 🛒 🏌 🏌 **Leisure** fishing **Conf** facs Corporate Hospitality Days **Location** off A607
Hotel ★★★★ 76% HL Quorn Country Hotel, Charnwood House, 66 Leicester Road, QUORN ☎ 01509 415050 & 415061 🖷 01509 415050 36 en suite

ENDERBY
Map 4 SP59

Enderby Mill Ln LE19 4LX
☎ 0116 284 9388 🖷 0116 284 9388

An attractive gently undulating nine-hole course with various water features. The longest hole is the 2nd at 471yds.

Enderby Golf Course: 9 Holes, 2900yds, Par 72, SSS 71, Course record 71. Club membership 150.

Visitors Mon-Sun & BHs. **Societies** welcome. **Green Fees** £9.50 per 18 holes, £7.85 per 9 holes **Course Designer** David Lowe **Prof** Chris D'Araujo **Facilities** ⑪ ⑩ ㏒ ☕ 🍴 ㅿ 🏠 🎯 🏌 🏌 **Leisure** heated indoor swimming pool, squash, sauna, gymnasium, indoor bowls snooker badminton **Conf** Corporate Hospitality Days **Location** M1 junct 21, 2m S on Narborough road, right at Toby Carvery rdbt, 0.5m on left, signed
Hotel ★★★ 73% HL Westfield House Hotel, Enderby Rd, Blaby, LEICESTER ☎ 0870 609 6106 🖷 0870 609 6106 48 en suite

HINCKLEY
Map 4 SP49

Hinckley Leicester Rd LE10 3DR
☎ 01455 615124 & 615014 🖷 01455 890841
web: www.hinckleygolfclub.com

18 Holes, 6467yds, Par 71, SSS 71, Course record 65.
Course Designer Southern Golf Ltd **Location** 1.5m NE on B4668
Telephone for further details
Hotel ★★★ 68% HL Best Western Weston Hall, Weston Lane, Bulkington, NUNEATON ☎ 024 7631 2989 🖷 024 7631 2989 40 en suite

KIBWORTH
Map 4 SP69

Kibworth Weir Rd, Beauchamp LE8 0LP
☎ 0116 279 2301
e-mail: secretary@kibworthgolfclub.freeserve.co.uk
web: www.kibworthgolfclub.co.uk

Attractive parkland course with two loops of nine holes and easy walking. The fairways are lined with mature trees and a meandering stream crosses eight holes.

18 Holes, 6354yds, Par 71, SSS 71, Course record 63. Club membership 700.

Visitors Mon, Wed-Fri except BHs. Booking required. Handicap certificate. Dress code **Societies** booking required. **Green Fees** £40 per day, £32 per round. **Prof** Bryn Morris **Facilities** ⑪ ⑩ ㏒ ☕ 🍴 ㅿ 🏠 🎯 🛒 🏌 **Conf** Corporate Hospitality Days **Location** S of village off A6
Hotel ★★★ 78% HL Best Western Three Swans, 21 High Street, MARKET HARBOROUGH ☎ 01858 466644 🖷 01858 466644 61 en suite

KIRBY MUXLOE
Map 4 SK50

Kirby Muxloe Station Rd LE9 2EP
☎ 0116 239 3457 🖷 0116 238 8891
e-mail: kirbymuxloegolf@btconnect.com
web: www.kirbymuxloe-golf.co.uk

Pleasant parkland with a lake in front of the 17th green and a short 18th. Easy walking course.

18 Holes, 6485yds, Par 71, SSS 71, Course record 62. Club membership 870.

Visitors Mon, Wed-Fri except BHs. Limited play Tue. Booking required. Handicap certificate. Dress code. **Societies** booking required. **Green Fees** £45 per day, £35 per round **Prof** Bruce Whipham **Facilities** ⑪ ⑩ ㏒ ☕ 🍴 ㅿ 🏠 🎯 🛒 🏌 🏌 **Leisure** two snooker rooms **Conf** Corporate Hospitality Days **Location** S of village off B5380
Hotel ★★★★ 79% HL Leicester Marriott, Smith Way, Grove Park, Enderby, LEICESTER ☎ 0116 282 0100 🖷 0116 282 0100 227 en suite

LEICESTER
Map 4 SK50

Humberstone Heights Gypsy Ln LE5 0TB
☎ 0116 276 3680 & 299 5570 (pro) 🖷 0116 299 5569
e-mail: admin@hhmgolfclub.freeserve.co.uk
web: www.humberstoneheightsgc.co.uk

Municipal parkland course with varied layout.

18 Holes, 6216yds, Par 70, SSS 70, Course record 66. Club membership 400.

Visitors Mon-Sun & BHs. Booking required weekends. Dress code. **Societies** welcome. **Green Fees** £17.50 per 18 holes **Course Designer** Hawtry & Sons **Prof** Jon Alcock **Facilities** ⑪ ⑩ ㏒ ☕ 🍴 ㅿ 🏠 🎯 🛒 🏌 🏌 **Leisure** 9 hole pitch and putt course. **Location** 2.5m NE of city centre
Hotel ★★★ 80% HL Best Western Belmont Hotel, De Montfort Street, LEICESTER ☎ 0116 254 4773 🖷 0116 254 4773 77 en suite

Leicestershire Evington Ln LE5 6DJ
☎ 0116 273 8825 🖷 0116 249 8799
e-mail: colin@leicestershiregolfclub.co.uk
web: www.leicestershiregolfclub.co.uk

Mature parkland course providing a challenging test of golf.

The Leicestershire Golf Club: 18 Holes, 6134yds, Par 68, SSS 70. Club membership 800.

Visitors Mon, Wed-Fri, Sun & BHs. Booking required. Handicap certificate. Dress code. **Societies** booking required. **Green Fees** not confirmed **Course Designer** Hawtree **Prof** Darren Jones **Facilities** ⑪ ⑩ ㏒ ☕ 🍴 ㅿ 🏠 🏌 🛒 🏌 **Location** 2m E of city off A6030
Hotel ★★★ 71% HL Regency, 360 London Road, LEICESTER ☎ 0116 270 9634 🖷 0116 270 9634 32 en suite

Western Scudamore Rd, Braunstone Frith LE3 1UQ
☎ 0116 299 5566   📠 0116 299 5568
web: www.westernparkgc.co.uk

Pleasant, undulating parkland course with open aspect fairways in two loops of nine holes. Not too difficult but a good test of golf off the back tees.

Western Golf Course: 18 Holes, 6486yds, Par 72, SSS 71, Course record 66. Club membership 200.

Visitors Mon-Sun & BHs. Booking required. Dress code.
Societies booking required. **Green Fees** £14.50 per 18 holes, £12 per 9 holes (£17.50/£13 weekends) **Course Designer** Hawtree **Prof** Dave Butler **Facilities** ⊕ 🏐 🖫 ⌑ 🍴 🏖 🍔 ⛳ ✆ **Leisure** inddor practice nets **Conf** Corporate Hospitality Days **Location** 1.5m W of city centre off A47
Hotel ★★★★ 79% HL Leicester Marriott, Smith Way, Grove Park, Enderby, LEICESTER ☎ 0116 282 0100 📠 0116 282 0100 227 en suite

LOUGHBOROUGH   Map 8 SK51

Longcliffe Snell's Nook Ln, Nanpantan LE11 3YA
☎ 01509 239129   📠 01509 231286
e-mail: longcliffegolf@btconnect.com
web: www.longcliffegolf.co.uk

Course of natural heathland, tree-lined fairways with water in play on the 14th and 15th holes. This course is recognised by the English Golf Championship.

18 Holes, 6625yds, Par 72, SSS 73, Course record 65. Club membership 700.

Visitors Mon, Wed-Fri except BHs. Booking required. Handicap certificate. Dress code. **Societies** booking required. **Green Fees** phone **Course Designer** Williamson **Prof** David Mee **Facilities** ⊕ 🏐 🖫 ⌑ 🍴 🏖 🏖 ✆ 🍔 ✆ **Location** 1.5m from M1 junct 23 off A512
Hotel ★★★★ 76% HL Quorn Country Hotel, Charnwood House, 66 Leicester Road, QUORN ☎ 01509 415050 & 415061 📠 01509 415050 36 en suite

LUTTERWORTH   Map 4 SP58

Kilworth Springs South Kilworth Rd, North Kilworth LE17 6HJ
☎ 01858 575082   📠 01858 575078
e-mail: admin@kilworthsprings.co.uk
web: www.kilworthsprings.co.uk

An 18-hole course of two loops of nine: the front nine is links style while the back nine is in parkland. Attractive views over the Avon

valley. Greens to USGA specifications and the construction of the course allows play on main greens and tees all year.

18 Holes, 6718yds, Par 72, SSS 71, Course record 65. Club membership 850.

Visitors Mon-Sun & BHs. Dress code. **Societies** welcome. **Green Fees** £24 (£27 weekends) **Course Designer** Ray Baldwin **Prof** Anders Mankert **Facilities** ⊕ 🏐 🖫 ⌑ 🍴 🏖 🏖 🍔 🍔 ✆ ✆ **Leisure** half way house on course **Conf** facs Corporate Hospitality Days **Location** M1 junct 20, 5m E on A4304 towards Market Harborough between villages of North & South Kilworth
Hotel ★★★★ 76% HL Best Western Ullesthorpe Court Hotel & Golf Club, Frolesworth Road, ULLESTHORPE, Near Lutterworth ☎ 01455 209023 📠 01455 209023 72 en suite

Lutterworth Rugby Rd LE17 4HN
☎ 01455 552532   📠 01455 553586
e-mail: sec@lutterworthgc.co.uk
web: www.lutterworthgc.co.uk

Hilly course with the River Swift running through.

18 Holes, 6226yds, Par 70, SSS 70. Club membership 650.

Visitors Mon-Fri except BHs. Weekends pm. Booking required weekends. Dress code. **Societies** booking required. **Green Fees** £30 per day/round **Prof** Lee Challinor **Facilities** ⊕ 🏐 🖫 ⌑ 🍴 🏖 🏖 🍔 🍔 ✆ **Location** M1 junct 20, 0.25m
Hotel ★★★ 78% HL Brownsover Hall Hotel, Brownsover Lane, Old Brownsover, RUGBY ☎ 0870 609 6104 📠 0870 609 6104 47 en suite

MARKET HARBOROUGH   Map 4 SP78

Market Harborough Oxendon Rd LE16 8NF
☎ 01858 463684   📠 01858 432906
e-mail: proshop@mhgolf.co.uk
web: www.mhgolf.co.uk

A parkland course close to the town. Undulating and in parts hilly. There are wide-ranging views over the surrounding countryside. Lakes feature on four holes; challenging last three holes.

18 Holes, 6086yds, Par 70, SSS 69, Course record 61. Club membership 650.

Visitors Mon-Fri except BHs. Handicap certificate. Dress code. **Societies** booking required. **Green Fees** £30 per round. **Course Designer** H Swan **Prof** Frazer Baxter **Facilities** ⊕ 🏐 🖫 ⌑ 🍴 🏖 🏖 ✆ ✆ **Conf** Corporate Hospitality Days **Location** 1m S on A508
Hotel ★★★ 78% HL Best Western Three Swans, 21 High Street, MARKET HARBOROUGH ☎ 01858 466644 📠 01858 466644 61 en suite

Stoke Albany Ashley Rd, Stoke Albany LE16 8PL
☎ 01858 535208   📠 01858 535505
e-mail: info@stokealbanygolfclub.co.uk
web: www.stokealbanygolfclub.co.uk

A parkland course in the picturesque Welland valley. Affording good views, the course should appeal to the mid-handicap golfer, and provide an interesting test to the more experienced player. There are several water features and the greens are individually contoured, adding to the golfing challenge.

Stoke Albany Golf Course: 18 Holes, 6175yds, Par 71, SSS 70, Course record 65. Club membership 500.

Visitors contact course for details. **Societies** welcome.
Green Fees £21 per 18 holes (£23 weekends & BHs) **Course Designer** Hawtree **Prof** Adrian Clifford **Facilities** 🖫 ⌑ 🍴 🏖

🛏 🍴 🛒 🥂 **Conf** facs Corporate Hospitality Days **Location** N off A427 Market Harborough-Corby road, follow Stoke Albany 500yds towards Ashley
Hotel ★★★ 78% HL Best Western Three Swans, 21 High Street, MARKET HARBOROUGH ☎ 01858 466644 🖥 01858 466644 61 en suite

MELTON MOWBRAY   Map 8 SK71

Melton Mowbray Waltham Rd, Thorpe Arnold LE14 4SD
☎ 01664 562118   🖥 01664 562118
e-mail: meltonmowbraygc@btconnect.com
web: www.mmgc.org

Easy walking heathland course with undulating fairways. Deceptively challenging.
18 Holes, 6222yds, Par 70, SSS 70, Course record 65.
Club membership 650.
Visitors Mon-Sun & BHs. Dress code. **Societies** welcome. **Green Fees** not confirmed **Prof** Neil Curtis **Facilities** ⑪ �🍴 🛒 🖥 🗒 🛒 🛏 🥂 🛒 🔥 **Location** 2m NE of Melton Mowbray on A607
Hotel ★★★ 77% HL Sysonby Knoll, Asfordby Road, MELTON MOWBRAY ☎ 01664 563563 🖥 01664 563563 30 en suite

Stapleford Park Stapleford LE14 2EF
☎ 01572 787000 & 787044   🖥 01572 787001
e-mail: clubs@stapleford.co.uk
web: www.staplefordpark.com
Set in 500 acres of parkland, lake and woods. Reminiscent of some Scottish links, the course wraps around the heart of the estate in two extended loops. Never more than two holes wide, the whole course is spacious and tranquil. The beauty of the surrounding countryside is the perfect backdrop.
Stapleford Park: 18 Holes, 6944yds, Par 73, SSS 73.
Club membership 310.
Visitors Mon-Sun & BHs. Booking required. Handicap certificate. Dress code. **Societies** booking required. **Green Fees** £75 per day, £50 per 18 holes, £25 per 9 holes **Course Designer** Donald Steel **Prof** Richard Alderson **Facilities** ⑪ 🍴 🛒 🖥 🗒 🛏 🖥 🥂 🔥 🛒 🛒 🔥 **Leisure** hard tennis courts, heated indoor swimming pool, fishing, sauna, gymnasium, shooting, falconry, offroading, horseriding, archery **Conf** facs Corporate Hospitality Days **Location** 4m E of Melton Mowbray off B676, follow brown signs
Hotel ★★★★ CHH Stapleford Park, Stapleford, MELTON MOWBRAY ☎ 01572 787000 🖥 01572 787000 55 en suite

OADBY   Map 4 SK60

Glen Gorse Glen Rd LE2 4RF
☎ 0116 271 4159   🖥 0116 271 4159
e-mail: secretary@gggc.org
web: www.gggc.org
Attractive mature parkland course with strategically placed trees encountered on every hole, rewarding the straight hitter. The long approaches and narrow greens require the very best short game. However, a premium is placed on accuracy and length, and no more so than over the closing three holes, considered to be one of the finest finishes in the county.
18 Holes, 6648yds, Par 72, SSS 72, Course record 64.
Club membership 818.
Visitors Mon-Fri & BHs. Booking required. Handicap certificate. Dress code. **Societies** booking required. **Green Fees** phone **Prof** Dominic Fitzpatrick **Facilities** ⑪ 🍴 🛒 🖥 🗒 🛏 🛒 🔥 🛒 **Leisure** snooker room **Conf** facs Corporate Hospitality Days **Location** on A6 between Oadby Glen, 5m S of Leicester
Hotel ★★★ 71% HL Regency, 360 London Road, LEICESTER ☎ 0116 270 9634 🖥 0116 270 9634 32 en suite

Oadby Leicester Rd LE2 4AJ
☎ 0116 270 9052
e-mail: oadbygolf@supanet.com
web: www.oadbygolfclub.co.uk
Flat municipal parkland course with water crossing the course.
18 Holes, 6376yds, Par 72, SSS 71, Course record 69.
Club membership 300.
Visitors Mon-Sun & BHs. Booking required weekends. Dress code. **Societies** booking required. **Green Fees** £14 (£17 weekends) **Prof** Andrew Wells **Facilities** ⑪ 🍴 🛒 🖥 🗒 🛏 🛒 🥂 ◇ 🔥 **Leisure** snooker **Conf** facs **Location** W of Oadby off A6
Hotel ★★★ 71% HL Regency, 360 London Road, LEICESTER ☎ 0116 270 9634 🖥 0116 270 9634 32 en suite

ROTHLEY   Map 8 SK51

Rothley Park Westfield Ln LE7 7LH
☎ 0116 230 2809   🖥 0116 237 4467
e-mail: kaye@rothleypark.co.uk
web: www.rothleypark.co.uk
A picturesque parkland course.
18 Holes, 6501yds, Par 71, SSS 71, Course record 65.
Club membership 600.
Visitors contact club for details. **Societies** welcome. **Green Fees** phone **Facilities** ⑪ 🍴 🛒 🖥 🗒 🛏 🛒 🔥 **Location** N of Leicester, W off A6
Hotel ★★★★ 76% HL Quorn Country Hotel, Charnwood House, 66 Leicester Road, QUORN ☎ 01509 415050 & 415061 🖥 01509 415050 36 en suite

SCRAPTOFT
Map 4 SK60

Scraptoft Beeby Rd LE7 9SJ
☎ 0116 241 9000 📄 0116 241 9000
web: www.scraptoft-golf.co.uk
18 Holes, 6166yds, Par 70, SSS 70.
Prof Simon Wood **Facilities** ⓣ 🍴 🛍 ⬜ 🍺 🔺 🏠 ⛳ 🛒
⛳ **Location** 1m NE
Telephone for further details
Hotel ★★★ 80% HL Best Western Belmont Hotel, De Montfort
Street, LEICESTER ☎ 0116 254 4773 📄 0116 254 4773 77 en suite

SEAGRAVE
Map 8 SK61

Park Hill Park Hill LE12 7NG
☎ 01509 815454 📄 01509 816062
e-mail: mail@parkhillgolf.co.uk
web: www.parkhillgolf.co.uk

Nestled in the heart of Leicestershire, overlooking the Charnwood
Forest and beyond, Park Hill Golf Club has an 18-hole championship
length course that uses the land's natural features to ensure that
no two holes are the same. The combination of water features and
precisely positioned bunkers provide for a challenging, yet enjoyable
course, with excellent playing conditions all year round.

18 Holes, 7219yds, Par 73, SSS 75, Course record 71.
Club membership 500.

Visitors Non-Sun & BHs. Dress code. **Societies** welcome. **Green
Fees** £27 (£33 weekends & BHs). **Prof** Matthew Ulyett **Facilities** ⓣ
🍴 🛍 ⬜ 🍺 🔺 🏠 ⛳ ⛳ 🛒 **Conf** facs Corporate
Hospitality Days **Location** 3m N of Leicester off A46, signs to Seagrave
Hotel ★★★★ 76% HL Quorn Country Hotel, Charnwood House, 66
Leicester Road, QUORN ☎ 01509 415050 & 415061 📄 01509 415050
36 en suite

SIX HILLS
Map 8 SK62

Six Hills Six Hills Rd LE14 3PR
☎ 01509 881225 📄 01509 881846
Flat parkland.
18 Holes, 5826yds, Par 71, SSS 68.
Visitors Mon-Sun & BHs. Booking required weekends & BHs.
Societies booking required. **Green Fees** not confirmed **Prof** James
Hawley **Facilities** ⓣ 🍴 🛍 ⬜ 🍺 🏠 ⛳ 🛒 **Location** on
B676 between Melton Mowbray & Loughborough
Hotel BUD Travelodge Leicester Thrussington, THRUSSINGTON
☎ 08719 846 083 📄 08719 846 083 32 en suite

ULLESTHORPE
Map 4 SP58

BW Ullesthorpe Court Hotel & Golf Club Frolesworth Rd
LE17 5BZ
☎ 01455 209023 📄 01455 202537
e-mail: membership@ullesthorpecourt.co.uk
web: www.bw-ullesthorpecourt.co.uk

Set in 120 acres of parkland surrounding a 17th-century manor house,
this championship length course can be very demanding and offers
a challenge to both beginners and professionals. Excellent leisure
facilities. Water plays a part on four holes.

*BW Ullesthorpe Court Hotel & Golf Club: 18 Holes, 6662yds,
Par 72, SSS 72, Course record 67. Club membership 650.*

Visitors Mon-Fri except BHs. Booking required. Dress code.
Societies booking required. **Green Fees** £35 per day, £25 per round
Prof Jon Salter **Facilities** ⓣ 🍴 🛍 ⬜ 🍺 🔺 🏠 ⛳ ◇
⛳ 🛒 ⛳ **Leisure** hard tennis courts, heated indoor swimming pool,
sauna, gymnasium, snooker room, steam room, beauty treatment
rooms **Conf** facs Corporate Hospitality Days **Location** M1 junct 20,
proceed towards Lutterworth and follow brown signs leading to B577
(Bitteswell and Ullesthorpe), follow road for 3m to Ullesthorpe. Drive
through village and just before exiting turn right at sign posted
Frolesworth and Golf Course

BW Ullesthorpe Court Hotel & Golf Club

Hotel ★★★★ 76% HL Best Western Ullesthorpe Court Hotel
& Golf Club, Frolesworth Road, ULLESTHORPE, Near Lutterworth
☎ 01455 209023 📄 01455 209023 72 en suite

WHETSTONE
Map 4 SP59

Whetstone Cambridge Rd, Cosby LE9 1SJ
☎ 0116 286 1424 📄 0116 286 1424
Easy to walk, parkland course where accuracy rather than length is
required.
18 Holes, 5795yds, Par 68, SSS 68, Course record 63.
Club membership 500.
Visitors contact club for details. **Societies** welcome. **Green Fees** £16
Course Designer E Calloway **Prof** David Raitt **Facilities** ⓣ 🍴 🛍
⬜ 🍺 🔺 🏠 ⛳ 🛒 ⛳ **Location** 1m S of village
Hotel ★★★ 73% HL Westfield House Hotel, Enderby Rd, Blaby,
LEICESTER ☎ 0870 609 6106 📄 0870 609 6106 48 en suite

WOODHOUSE EAVES
Map 8 SK51

Charnwood Forest Breakback Rd LE12 8TA
☎ 01509 890259
e-mail: secretary@charnwoodforestgolfclub.com
web: www.charnwoodforestgolfclub.com

Oldest course in the county, founded in 1890. Hilly heathland course
with hard walking, but no bunkers. Play is round volcanic rock giving
panoramic views over the Charnwood Forest area.

9 Holes, 5972yds, Par 69, SSS 69, Course record 65.
Club membership 360.

Visitors Mon, Wed-Fri except BHs. Handicap certificate. Dress code.
Societies booking required. **Green Fees** not confirmed **Course
Designer** James Braid **Facilities** ⓣ 🍴 🛍 ⬜ 🍺 🔺
Location M1 junct 23, take A512 towards Loughborough. After 0.5m
turn right into Snells Nook Lane. Club 3m on left.
Hotel ★★★★ 76% HL Quorn Country Hotel, Charnwood House, 66
Leicester Road, QUORN ☎ 01509 415050 & 415061 📄 01509 415050
36 en suite

Lingdale Joe Moore's Ln LE12 8TF
☎ 01509 890703
web: www.lingdale-golf-club.com
Parkland in Charnwood Forest with some hard walking at some holes. The par 3 3rd and par 5 8th are testing holes. Several holes have water hazards and the blend of strategic holes requires good club selection.
18 Holes, 6545yds, Par 71, SSS 71, Course record 68. Club membership 659.
Visitors Mon, Wed-Fri & BHs. Booking required BHs. Handicap certificate. Dress code. **Societies** booking required. **Green Fees** phone **Course Designer** David Tucker **Prof** Peter Sellears **Facilities** ⏱ ⵊⵔ ⵐ ⵏ ⵕ ⵌ ⵓ ⵔ **Location** 1.5m S off B5330
Hotel ★★★★ 76% HL Quorn Country Hotel, Charnwood House, 66 Leicester Road, QUORN ☎ 01509 415050 & 415061 📄 01509 415050 36 en suite

LINCOLNSHIRE

BELTON
Map 8 SK93

De Vere Belton Woods Hotel NG32 2LN
☎ 01476 593200   📄 01476 574547
e-mail: belton.woods@devere-hotels.com
web: www.devere.co.uk
Two challenging 18-hole courses, a nine-hole par 3 and a driving range. The Lakes Course has 13 lakes, while The Woodside has the one of the longest holes in Europe at 613yds. Many leisure facilities.
The Lakes Course: 18 Holes, 6831yds, Par 72, SSS 73, Course record 66.
The Woodside Course: 18 Holes, 6623yds, Par 73, SSS 72, Course record 68.
Visitors Mon-Sun & BHs. Dress code. **Societies** booking required. **Green Fees** Lakes £39 per round (£49 weekends). Woodside £39/£49. Winter (both courses) £25/£29. Academy £6 **Prof** Matt Buckley **Facilities** ⏱ ⵊⵔ ⵊ ⵐ ⵏ ⵕ ⵌ ⵓ ⵔ ⵗ ⵖ **Leisure** hard tennis courts, heated indoor swimming pool, squash, fishing, sauna, gymnasium, 9 hole par 3 Red Arrows course **Conf** facs Corporate Hospitality Days **Location** on A607 2m N of Grantham
Hotel ★★★★ 75% HL De Vere Belton Woods, BELTON, Grantham ☎ 01476 593200 📄 01476 593200 136 en suite

BLANKNEY
Map 8 TF06

Blankney LN4 3AZ
☎ 01526 320202   📄 01526 322521
e-mail: grahambradley5@btconnect.com
web: www.blankneygolf.co.uk
Parkland in pleasant surroundings, with mature trees and testing greens offering a challenging test of golf. Set in the Blankney estate and 2004 was the centenary year.
18 Holes, 6634yds, Par 72, SSS 73, Course record 69. Club membership 700.
Visitors Mon-Sun & BHs. Booking required. Dress code. **Societies** booking required. **Green Fees** phone **Course Designer** C Sinclair **Prof** Graham Bradley **Facilities** ⏱ ⵊⵔ ⵊ ⵐ ⵏ ⵕ ⵌ ⵓ ⵔ ⵗ **Leisure** snooker **Conf** facs Corporate Hospitality Days **Location** 10m SW on B1188
Hotel ★★★ 75% CHH Branston Hall, Branston Park, Branston, LINCOLN ☎ 01522 793305 📄 01522 793305 50 en suite

BOSTON
Map 8 TF34

Boston Cowbridge, Horncastle Rd PE22 7EL
☎ 01205 350589   📄 01205 367526
e-mail: steveshaw@bostongc.co.uk
web: www.bostongc.co.uk
Parkland with water coming into play on a number of holes. Renowned for the quality of the greens.
18 Holes, 6415yds, Par 72, SSS 71, Course record 65. Club membership 650.
Visitors Mon, Wed-Sun & BHs. Booking required weekends & BHs. Dress code. **Societies** booking required. **Green Fees** £32 per day, £24 per round before 2.30pm, £16 after 2.30pm (£30 per round weekends & BHs) **Prof** Nick Hiom **Facilities** ⏱ ⵊⵔ ⵊ ⵐ ⵏ ⵕ ⵌ ⵓ ⵔ ⵗ ⵖ **Conf** Corporate Hospitality Days **Location** 2m N of Boston on B1183
Hotel ★★ 72% HL Poacher's Country Hotel, Swineshead Road, Kirton Holme, BOSTON ☎ 01205 290310 📄 01205 290310 16 en suite

Boston West Golf Centre Hubbert's Bridge PE20 3QX
☎ 01205 290670   📄 01205 290725
e-mail: info@bostonwestgolfclub.co.uk
web: www.bostonwestgolfclub.co.uk
A well maintained maturing golf course, nestled in the Lincolnshire countryside featuring excellent greens, well positioned lakes and bunkers. Good test of golf for all levels of golfer.
Boston West Golf Centre: 18 Holes, 6411yards, Par 72, SSS 71, Course record 67. Club membership 500.
Visitors Mon-Sun & BHs. Booking required. Dress code. **Societies** booking required. **Green Fees** £20 per 18 holes (£25 weekends & BHs) **Course Designer** Michael Zara **Prof** Sophie Hunter **Facilities** ⏱ ⵊⵔ ⵊ ⵐ ⵏ ⵕ ⵌ ⵓ ⵔ ⵗ ⵖ **Leisure** 6 hole academy course **Conf** facs Corporate Hospitality Days **Location** 2m W of Boston on A1121/B1192 x-rds
Hotel ★★★ 63% HL Golf Hotel, The Broadway, WOODHALL SPA ☎ 01526 353535 📄 01526 353535 50 en suite

Kirton Holme Holme Rd, Kirton Holme PE20 1SY
☎ 01205 290669
web: www.kirtonholmegolfclub.co.uk
A young parkland course designed for mid to high handicappers. It is flat but has 2500 young trees, two natural water courses plus water hazards. The 2nd is a challenging, 386yd, par 4 dog-leg.
Kirton Holme Golf Course: 9 Holes, 5778yds, Par 70, SSS 68, Course record 66. Club membership 320.
Visitors contact course for details. **Societies** welcome. **Green Fees** £12 per 18 holes, £8 per 9 holes (£13/£9 weekends & BHs) **Course Designer** D W Welberry **Prof** Alison Johns **Facilities** ⏱ ⵊⵔ ⵐ ⵏ ⵕ ⵌ ⵓ ⵔ ⵗ **Conf** Corporate Hospitality Days **Location** 4m W of Boston off A52
Hotel ★★ 72% HL Poacher's Country Hotel, Swineshead Road, Kirton Holme, BOSTON ☎ 01205 290310 📄 01205 290310 16 en suite

ENGLAND

BOURNE   Map 8 TF02

Toft Hotel Toft PE10 0JT
☎ 01778 590616   📄 01778 590264

18 Holes, 6486yds, Par 72, SSS 71, Course record 63.
Course Designer Roger Fitton **Location** on A6121 Bourne-Stamford road
Telephone for further details
Hotel ★★★ 86% HL The George of Stamford, 71 St Martins, STAMFORD ☎ 01780 750750 & 750700 (res) 📄 01780 750750 47 en suite

CLEETHORPES   Map 8 TA30

Tetney Station Rd, Tetney DN36 5HY
☎ 01472 211644   📄 01472 211644
An 18-hole parkland course at the foot of the Lincolnshire Wolds, noted for its challenging water features.

18 Holes, 6245yds, Par 71, SSS 69, Course record 65.
Club membership 300.
Visitors Mon-Sun & BHs. Dress code. **Societies** booking required.
Green Fees £12 per 18 holes (£14 weekends & BHs) **Course Designer** J S Grant **Prof** Jason Abrams **Facilities** ⊕ 🍽 🛒 ⬛ 🍴 ⌃ 🖼 🔪 🛺 🔪 🏌 **Conf** facs **Location** 1m off A16 Louth-Grimsby road
Hotel ★★★ 77% HL Kingsway, Kingsway, CLEETHORPES ☎ 01472 601122 📄 01472 601122 49 en suite

CROWLE   Map 8 SE71

The Lincolnshire DN17 4BU
☎ 01724 711619   📄 01724 711619
The Lincolnshire Golf Course: 18 Holes, 6283yds, Par 71, SSS 70.
Course Designer Stubley/Byrne **Location** M180 junct 2, 0.5m on Crowle road
Telephone for further details
Hotel ★★★ 74% HL Wortley House, Rowland Road, SCUNTHORPE ☎ 01724 842223 📄 01724 842223 45 en suite

ELSHAM   Map 8 TA01

Elsham Barton Rd DN20 0LS
☎ 01652 680291(Sec)   📄 01652 680308
e-mail: office@elshamgolfclub.co.uk
web: www.elshamgolfclub.co.uk
Gently undulating, part parkland and part heathland course in a rural setting with a variety of wildlife, including many pheasants. Each

hole is different and has its own challenge. Very secluded with easy walking, three ponds plus a reservoir to maintain irrigation.

18 Holes, 6426yds, Par 71, SSS 71, Course record 65.
Club membership 650.
Visitors Mon-Fri except BHs. Booking required. Handicap certificate. Dress code. **Societies** booking required. **Green Fees** £40 per 36 holes, £30 per 18 holes **Course Designer** Various **Prof** Stuart Brewer
Facilities ⊕ 🍽 🛒 ⬛ 🍴 ⌃ 🖼 🔪 🛺 🔪 **Conf** facs
Corporate Hospitality Days **Location** 2m NE of Brigg on B1206

Elsham

Hotel ★★★ 74% HL Wortley House, Rowland Road, SCUNTHORPE ☎ 01724 842223 📄 01724 842223 45 en suite

GAINSBOROUGH   Map 8 SK88

Gainsborough Thonock DN21 1PZ
☎ 01427 613088   📄 01427 810172
e-mail: kate@gainsboroughgc.co.uk
web: www.gainsboroughgc..co.uk
Thonock Park course, founded in 1894 is an attractive parkland course with many deciduous trees. Karsten Lakes course is a championship course designed by Neil Coles. Set in rolling countryside the lakes and well bunkered greens provide a true test of golf. Floodlit driving range.

Thonock Park: 18 Holes, 6266yds, Par 70, SSS 70, Course record 63.
Karsten Lakes: 18 Holes, 6721yds, Par 72, SSS 72, Course record 65. Club membership 700.
Visitors Mon-Sun & BHs. Booking required. Dress code.
Societies booking required. **Green Fees** Thonock Park £40 per day, £30 per round. Karsten Lakes £40 per day, £30 per round **Course Designer** Neil Coles **Prof** Stephen Cooper **Facilities** ⊕ 🍽 🛒 ⬛ 🍴 ⌃ 🖼 🔪 ◇ 🔪 🛺 🔪 🏌 **Leisure** fishing **Conf** facs
Corporate Hospitality Days **Location** 1m N off A159. Signed off A631
Hotel ★★ 63% HL Hickman Hill, Cox's Hill, GAINSBOROUGH ☎ 01427 613639 📄 01427 613639 9 en suite

GEDNEY HILL   Map 8 TF31

Gedney Hill West Drove PE12 0NT
☎ 01406 330922   📄 01406 330323
e-mail: gedneyhillgolf@aol.com
web: www.gedneyhillgolfclub.co.uk
Flat parkland course similar to a links course. Made testing by Fen winds and small undulating greens.

Gedney Hill Golf Course: 18 Holes, 5493yds, Par 70, SSS 66, Course record 65. Club membership 200.
Visitors Mon-Sun & BHs. **Societies** welcome. **Green Fees** £10

continued

(£15 weekends & BHs) **Course Designer** Monkwise Ltd **Prof** Kerr Page **Facilities** ⑪ ⑩ ⓛ ⯐ ⯐ ⯐ ⯐ ⯐ ⯐ ⯐ ⯐
Location 10m SE of Spalding
Hotel ★★★ 68% HL Elme Hall, Elm High Road, WISBECH
☎ 01945 475566 📄 01945 475566 8 en suite

GRANTHAM   Map 8 SK93

Belton Park Belton Ln, Londonthorpe Rd NG31 9SH
☎ 01476 542900   📄 01476 592078
e-mail: greatgolf@beltonpark
web: www.beltonpark.co.uk

Three nine-hole courses set in classic mature parkland of Lord Brownlow's country seat, Belton House. Gently undulating with streams, ponds, plenty of trees and beautiful scenery, including a deer park. Famous holes: 5th, 12th, 16th and 18th. Combine any of the three courses for a testing 18-hole round.

Brownlow: 18 Holes, 6472yds, Par 71, SSS 71,
Course record 64.
Ancaster: 18 Holes, 6325yds, Par 70, SSS 70.
Belmont: 18 Holes, 6075yds, Par 69, SSS 69.
Club membership 850.

Visitors Dress code. **Societies** booking required. **Green Fees** £40 per day, £35 per round (£50/£40 Sun & BHs) **Course Designer** Williamson/Allis **Prof** Simon Williams **Facilities** ⑪ ⑩ ⓛ ⯐ ⯐ ⯐ ⯐ ⯐ ⯐ **Conf** facs Corporate Hospitality Days **Location** 1.5m NE of Grantham
Hotel ★★★ 73% HL Best Western Kings, North Parade, GRANTHAM
☎ 01476 590800 📄 01476 590800 21 en suite

Sudbrook Moor Charity St, Carlton Scroop NG32 3AT
☎ 01400 250796
web: www.sudbrookmoor.co.uk

A testing nine-hole parkland and meadowland course in a picturesque valley setting with easy walking.

9 Holes, 4811yds, Par 66, SSS 64, Course record 64.
Club membership 600.

Visitors contact club for details. **Green Fees** £9 per day (£12 weekends and BHs) **Course Designer** Tim Hutton **Prof** Tim Hutton **Facilities** ⑪ ⓛ ⯐ ⯐ ⯐ ⯐ ⯐ **Location** 6m NE of Grantham on A607 in village of Carlton Scroop
Hotel ★★★ 73% HL Best Western Kings, North Parade, GRANTHAM
☎ 01476 590800 📄 01476 590800 21 en suite

GRIMSBY   Map 8 TA21

Grimsby Littlecoates Rd DN34 4LU
☎ 01472 342630   📄 01472 342630
18 Holes, 6057yds, Par 70, SSS 69, Course record 65.
Course Designer Colt **Location** 1m from A180. 1m from A46
Telephone for further details
Hotel ★★★ 71% HL Legacy Oaklands, Barton St, LACEBY
☎ 0870 832 9909 📄 0870 832 9909 45 en suite

Waltham Windmill Cheapside, Waltham DN37 0HT
☎ 01472 824109   📄 01472 828391
e-mail: secretary@walthamwindmillgolfclub.co.uk
web: www.walthamwindmillgolfclub.co.uk

Nestling in 125 acres of Lincolnshire countryside, the natural springs have been used to great effect giving individuality and challenge to every shot. The course has a mixture of long par 5s and water comes into play on nine holes.

18 Holes, 6442yds, Par 71, SSS 71, Course record 64.
Club membership 680.

Visitors Mon-Sun & BHs. Dress code. **Societies** booking required. **Green Fees** £27 per round (£33 weekends). Reduced winter rates **Course Designer** J Payne **Prof** M Stephenson **Facilities** ⑪ ⑩ ⓛ ⯐ ⯐ ⯐ ⯐ ⯐ ⯐ ⯐ **Conf** facs Corporate Hospitality Days **Location** 1m off A16
Hotel ★★★ 77% HL Kingsway, Kingsway, CLEETHORPES
☎ 01472 601122 📄 01472 601122 49 en suite

HORNCASTLE   Map 8 TF26

Horncastle West Ashby LN9 5PP
☎ 01507 526800
e-mail: info@horncastlegolfclub.com
web: www.horncastlegolfclub.com

Parkland course with many water hazards and bunkers; very challenging. There is a 10-bay short game floodlit driving range.

18 Holes, 5717yds, Par 70, SSS 68, Course record 71.
Club membership 145.

Visitors Mon-Sun & BHs. Booking required BHs. **Societies** booking required. **Green Fees** £10 (£15 weekends & BHs) **Course Designer** E C Wright **Facilities** ⑪ ⑩ ⓛ ⯐ ⯐ ⯐ ⯐ ⯐ **Leisure** fishing **Conf** facs Corporate Hospitality Days **Location** off A153/A158 at West Ashby
Hotel ★★★ 71% HL Best Western Admiral Rodney, North Street, HORNCASTLE ☎ 01507 523131 📄 01507 523131 31 en suite

IMMINGHAM Map 8 TA11

Immingham St Andrews Ln, off Church Ln DN40 2EU
☎ 01469 575298 📄 01469 577636
e-mail: immgc@btconnect.com
web: www.immgc.com

An excellent, flat parkland course. The natural exaggerated undulations on the fairways form one of the best local examples of medieval strip farming methods. They are natural to the course, particularly on the front nine and require concentration on fairway play. The Lincolnshire drainage channel, which meanders through the course and comes into play on over half of the holes, can catch the unwary golfer.

18 Holes, 6215yds, Par 71, SSS 70, Course record 69. Club membership 700.

Visitors Mon-Sun & BHs. Booking required weekends & BHs. Dress code. **Societies** welcome. **Green Fees** £24 per round **Course Designer** Hawtree & Son **Prof** Nick Harding **Facilities** ⊕ ⏍ ⌑ ⌷ ⌨ ⌹ 🏠 ⌺ 🚚 ✂ **Conf** facs Corporate Hospitality Days **Location** 7m NW of Grimsby
Hotel ★★★ 72% HL Stallingborough Grange Hotel, Riby Road, STALLINGBOROUGH ☎ 01469 561302 📄 01469 561302 41 en suite

LACEBY Map 8 TA20

Manor Barton St, Laceby Manor DN37 7LD
☎ 01472 873468
e-mail: mackayj@grimsby.ac.uk
web: www.lmgc.co.uk

The first seven holes played as a parkland course lined with mature trees. The second nine are more open fairways with water courses running alongside and through the holes. The 16th hole green is surrounded by water. Holes 17 and 18 are tree-lined like the first seven holes.

18 Holes, 6354yds, Par 71, SSS 70. Club membership 550.

Visitors Mon-Sun & BHs. Booking required. Dress code. **Societies** booking required. **Green Fees** £22 per round (£24 weekends and BHs) **Facilities** ⊕ ⏍ ⌑ ⌷ ⌨ ⌹ 🏠 🚚 ✂ **Leisure** fishing **Conf** facs Corporate Hospitality Days **Location** A18 Laceby-Louth
Hotel ★★★ 71% HL Legacy Oaklands, Barton St, LACEBY ☎ 0870 832 9909 📄 0870 832 9909 45 en suite

LINCOLN Map 8 SK97

See also **Torksey**

Canwick Park Canwick Park, Washingborough Rd LN4 1EF
☎ 01522 542912
e-mail: manager@canwickpark.org
web: www.canwickpark.org

Attractive parkland course with fine views of Lincoln Cathedral. The 5th and 13th holes are particularly testing par 3s.

18 Holes, 6160yds, Par 70, SSS 69, Course record 65. Club membership 650.

Visitors Mon-Fri. Weekends & BHs after 1pm. Dress code. **Societies** booking required. **Green Fees** £19 per round (£25 weekends) **Course Designer** Hawtree & Sons **Prof** S Williamson **Facilities** ⊕ ⏍ ⌑ ⌷ ⌨ ⌹ 🏠 ✂ 🚚 ✂ **Conf** Corporate Hospitality Days **Location** 2m E of city centre on B1190
Hotel ★★★ 74% HL The Lincoln, Eastgate, LINCOLN ☎ 01522 520348 📄 01522 520348 72 en suite

Carholme Carholme Rd LN1 1SE
☎ 01522 523725 📄 01522 533733
e-mail: info@carholme-golf-club.co.uk
web: www.carholme-golf-club.co.uk

Parkland where prevailing west winds can add interest. Good views. First hole out of bounds left and right of fairway, pond in front of bunkered green at 5th, lateral water hazards across several fairways.

18 Holes, 6215yds, Par 71, SSS 70, Course record 67. Club membership 500.

Visitors contact club for details. **Societies** welcome. **Green Fees** £24 per day, £20 per round **Course Designer** Willie Park Jnr **Facilities** ⊕ ⏍ ⌑ ⌷ ⌨ 🏠 ✂ **Conf** Corporate Hospitality Days **Location** 1m W of city centre on A57
Hotel ★★★ 68% HL The White Hart, Bailgate, LINCOLN ☎ 01522 526222 & 563293 📄 01522 526222 50 en suite

LOUTH Map 8 TF38

Kenwick Park Kenwick Park LN11 8NY
☎ 01507 605134 📄 01507 606556
e-mail: secretary@kenwickparkgolf.co.uk
web: www.kenwickparkgolf.co.uk

Situated on the edge of the Lincolnshire Wolds with panoramic views. Course features a mixture of parkland and woodland holes, complemented by a network of lakes.

18 Holes, 6782yds, Par 72, SSS 73, Course record 71. Club membership 520.

Visitors Mon-Fri, Sun & BHs. Booking required Mon-Fri & Sun. Handicap certificate. Dress code. **Societies** booking required. **Green Fees** £40 per 18 holes (£50 weekends & BHs) **Course Designer** Patrick Tallack **Prof** P Spence/M Langford **Facilities** ⊕ ⏍ by prior arrangement ⌑ ⌷ ⌨ ⌹ 🏠 ◇ 🚚 ✂ **Leisure** squash, sauna, gymnasium **Conf** Corporate Hospitality Days **Location** 2m S of Louth on A157 (Louth bypass)
Hotel ★★★ 79% HL Best Western Kenwick Park, Kenwick Park Estate, LOUTH ☎ 01507 608806 📄 01507 608806 34 en suite

Louth Crowtree Ln LN11 9LJ
☎ 01507 603681 📄 01507 608501
e-mail: louthgolfclub@btconnect.com
web: www.louthgolfclub.com

Undulating parkland, fine views in an Area of Outstanding Natural Beauty. No winter greens, offering quality golf throughout the year.

18 Holes, 6430yds, Par 72, SSS 71, Course record 66. Club membership 700.

Visitors Mon-Fri, Sun & BHs. Booking required Sun & BHs. Handicap certificate. Dress code. **Societies** booking required. **Green Fees** £35 per day, £27 per round (£38/£32 Sun & BHs) **Prof** A Blundell **Facilities** ⊕ ⏍ ⌑ ⌷ ⌨ ⌹ 🏠 ✂ 🚚 ✂ **Conf** facs Corporate Hospitality Days **Location** from A157/A16 rdbt take B1521 to Louth, 1st right up Love Lane to top.
Hotel ★★★ 86% HL Brackenborough Hotel, Cordeaux Corner, Brackenborough, LOUTH ☎ 01507 609169 📄 01507 609169 24 en suite

MARKET RASEN
Map 8 TF18

Market Rasen & District Legsby Rd LN8 3DZ
☎ 01673 842319 📠 01673 849245
e-mail: marketrasengolf@onetel.net
web: www.marketrasengolfclub.co.uk

Picturesque, well-wooded heathland course, easy walking, with many natural hazards.

18 Holes, 6239yds, Par 71, SSS 70, Course record 65.
Club membership 600.

Visitors Mon-Fri except BHs. Booking required. Dress code.
Societies booking required **Green Fees** £39 per day, £28 per round
Course Designer Hawtree Ltd **Prof** A M Chester **Facilities** ⓦ ⦿
🛏 ⛴ 🍴 🛎 🏌️ **Conf** Corporate Hospitality Days
Location 1m E, A46 onto A631
Guesthouse ★★★★★ BB Blaven, Walesby Hill, Walesby, MARKET RASEN ☎ 01673 838352 📠 01673 838352 3 rms 2 en suite

Market Rasen Race Course (Golf Course) Legsby Rd LN8 3EA
☎ 01673 843434 📠 01673 844532
web: www.marketrasenraces.co.uk

Market Rasen Race Course (Golf Course): 9 Holes,
2532yds, Par 32.

Course Designer Edward Stenton **Location** 1m E of Market Rasen
Telephone for further details
Guesthouse ★★★★ BB Chuck Hatch, Kingerby Road, West Rasen, MARKET RASEN ☎ 01673 842947 & 07745 288463 📠 01673 842947
4 en suite

NORMANBY
Map 8 SE81

Normanby Hall Normanby Park DN15 9HU
☎ 01724 720226 (Pro shop)
Well-maintained course set in secluded mature parkland. A challenge to golfers of all abilities.

18 Holes, 6547yds, Par 72, SSS 71, Course record 66.
Club membership 320.

Visitors Mon-Sun & BHs. Dress code. **Societies** booking required.
Green Fees phone **Course Designer** Hawtree & Son **Prof** Dean
Worrall **Facilities** ⓦ ⦿ 🛏 ⛴ 🍴 🛎 🏌️ 🛎 🏌️
Location 3m N of Scunthorpe on B1130 next to Normanby Hall
Hotel ★★★ 74% HL Wortley House, Rowland Road, SCUNTHORPE
☎ 01724 842223 📠 01724 842223 45 en suite

SCUNTHORPE
Map 8 SE81

Ashby Decoy Burringham Rd DN17 2AB
☎ 01724 866561 📠 01724 271708
e-mail: info@ashbydecoygolfclub.co.uk
web: www.ashbydecoy.co.uk

Pleasant, flat parkland course to satisfy all tastes, yet test the experienced golfer.

18 Holes, 6281yds, Par 71, SSS 71, Course record 66.
Club membership 650.

Visitors Mon-Fri except BHs. Booking required. Handicap certificate.
Dress code. **Societies** booking required. **Green Fees** £30 per day, £25
per round. **Prof** A Miller **Facilities** ⓦ ⦿ 🛏 ⛴ 🍴 🛎 🏌️
🛎 🏌️ **Conf** facs Corporate Hospitality Days **Location** 2.5m SW on
B1450 near Asda store
Hotel ★★★ 74% HL Wortley House, Rowland Road, SCUNTHORPE
☎ 01724 842223 📠 01724 842223 45 en suite

Forest Pines Hotel & Golf Resort Ermine St, Broughton DN20 0AQ
☎ 01652 650756 📠 01652 650495
e-mail: forestpinesproshop@qhotels.co.uk
web: www.qhotels.co.uk

A 27 hole course set in 185 acres, meandering through majestic pines into open heathland. Forest Pines offers three challenging nine-hole courses - Forest, Pines and Beeches. Any combination can be played.

Forest/Pines: 18 Holes, 6842yds, Par 73, SSS 73,
Course record 64.
Pines/Beeches: 18 Holes, 6653yds, Par 72, SSS 72.
Beeches/Forest: 18 Holes, 6393yds, Par 71, SSS 71.
Club membership 300.

Visitors Mon-Sun & BHs. Booking required. Dress code.
Societies booking required. **Green Fees** £75 per day, £50 per round
(£90/£60 weekends) **Course Designer** John Morgan **Prof** Matthew
Peacock/Dan Greenwood **Facilities** ⓦ ⦿ 🛏 ⛴ 🍴 🛎 🛎
🏌️ ⬦ 🏌️ 🛎 🏌️ 🏌️ **Leisure** heated indoor swimming pool, sauna,
gymnasium **Conf** facs Corporate Hospitality Days **Location** M180
junct 4, 1st exit for Scunthorpe. At next rdbt take 2nd exit, hotel on left
Hotel ★★★★ 79% HL Forest Pines Hotel & Golf Resort, Ermine
Street, Broughton, SCUNTHORPE ☎ 01652 650770 📠 01652 650770
188 en suite

Grange Park Butterwick Rd, Messingham DN17 3PP
☎ 01724 762945 📠 01724 762945
e-mail: info@grangepark.com
web: www.grangepark.com

Challenging parkland course with wide tree lined lush fairways and well manicured greens. There are many testing water hazards to

continued

negotiate, especially the 4th par 3, known as the 'pond hole' requiring a tee shot of over 136 yards to clear the pond and stop the ball dead on the green to have a chance of reaching par.

18 Holes, 6146yds, Par 70, SSS 69, Course record 64. Club membership 320.

Visitors Mon-Sun & BHs. Dress code. **Societies** booking required. **Green Fees** £16 per 18 holes (£18 weekends & BHs) **Course Designer** R Price **Prof** Jonathan Drury **Facilities** ⓉⒾ 🝖 ⌴ 🍴 ⚲ 🏠 ◇ ✦ 🛒 ✦ **Leisure** hard tennis courts, fishing, 9 hole par 3 course **Conf** facs Corporate Hospitality Days **Location** 1.5m W of Messingham towards East Butterwick
Hotel ★★★ 74% HL Wortley House, Rowland Road, SCUNTHORPE ☎ 01724 842223 📄 01724 842223 45 en suite

Holme Hall Holme Ln, Bottesford DN16 3RF
☎ 01724 862078   📄 01724 862081
e-mail: secretary@holmehallgolf.co.uk
web: www.holmehallgolf.co.uk

Natural heathland course with gorse and heather and sandy subsoil. Easy walking. Tight driving holes and good greens.

18 Holes, 6413yds, Par 71, SSS 71, Course record 64. Club membership 650.

Visitors Mon-Sun except BHs. Booking required weekends. Handicap certificate. Dress code. **Societies** welcome. **Green Fees** £40 per day, £35 per 27 holes, £30 per round **Prof** Richard McKiernan **Facilities** Ⓣ ⓉⒾ 🝖 ⌴ 🍴 ⚲ 🏠 ⛳ ✦ 🛒 ✦ **Conf** Corporate Hospitality Days **Location** M180 junct 4, 4m SE of Scunthorpe
Hotel ★★★ 74% HL Wortley House, Rowland Road, SCUNTHORPE ☎ 01724 842223 📄 01724 842223 45 en suite

SKEGNESS   Map 9 TF56

North Shore Hotel & Golf Course North Shore Rd PE25 1DN
☎ 01754 763298   📄 01754 761902
e-mail: info@northshorehotel.co.uk
web: www.northshorehotel.co.uk

Part links, part parkland, with two of the nine holes situated next to the sea. New drainage ditches create additional challenges even for the most accomplished golfer.

North Shore Hotel & Golf Course: 18 Holes, 6200yds, Par 71, SSS 71, Course record 66. Club membership 400.
Visitors Mon-Sun & BHs. Booking required. Dress code. **Societies** booking required. **Green Fees** £41 per day; £31 per round (£51/£39 weekends). **Course Designer** James Braid **Prof** J Cornelius **Facilities** Ⓣ ⓉⒾ 🝖 ⌴ 🍴 ⚲ 🏠 ◇ 🛒 ✦ **Leisure** snooker **Conf** facs Corporate Hospitality Days **Location** 1m N of town centre off A52, opp North Shore Holiday Centre

Hotel ★★ 72% HL North Shore Hotel & Golf Course, North Shore Road, SKEGNESS ☎ 01754 763298 📄 01754 763298 36 en suite

Seacroft Drummond Rd, Seacroft PE25 3AU
☎ 01754 763020   📄 01754 763020
e-mail: enquiries@seacroft-golfclub.co.uk
web: www.seacroft-golfclub.co.uk

A championship seaside links traditionally laid out with tight undulations and hogsback fairways. Adjacent to Gibraltar Point Nature Reserve, overlooking the Wash.

18 Holes, 6492yds, Par 71, SSS 71, Course record 65. Club membership 590.

Visitors Mon-Sun & BHs. Booking required. Handicap certificate. Dress code. **Societies** booking required. **Green Fees** phone **Course Designer** Tom Dunn/Willie Fernie **Prof** Robin Lawie **Facilities** Ⓣ ⓉⒾ 🝖 ⌴ 🍴 ⚲ 🏠 ⛳ ✦ 🛒 ✦ **Conf** Corporate Hospitality Days **Location** S of town centre towards Gibralter Point Nature Reserve
Hotel ★★★ 66% HL Crown, Drummond Road, SKEGNESS ☎ 01754 610760 📄 01754 610760 29 en suite

SLEAFORD   Map 8 TF04

Sleaford Willoughby Rd, Greylees NG34 8PL
☎ 01529 488273   📄 01529 488644
e-mail: sleafordgolfclub@btinternet.com
web: www.sleafordgolfclub.co.uk

Inland links-type course, moderately wooded and fairly flat with sandy well-draining soil, which supports a variety of trees and shrubs. While the lowest index hole is the awkward dog-leg 4th, the 2nd hole requires two mighty hits to be reached. The feature hole is the 12th, where the green is totally protected by a copse of pine trees. A stream running through the course provides water hazards on several holes.

18 Holes, 6503yds, Par 72, SSS 71, Course record 64. Club membership 630.

Visitors Mon-Sun & BHs. Handicap certificate. Dress code. **Societies** booking required. **Green Fees** £35 per day, £28 per round (£36 weekends) **Course Designer** T Williamson **Prof** Nigel Pearce **Facilities** Ⓣ ⓉⒾ 🝖 ⌴ 🍴 ⚲ 🏠 🛒 ✦ **Conf** Corporate Hospitality Days **Location** 2m W of Sleaford off A153
Hotel ★★★ 73% HL Best Western Kings, North Parade, GRANTHAM ☎ 01476 590800 📄 01476 590800 21 en suite

THE NATIONAL GOLF CENTRE

LINCOLNSHIRE - WOODHALL SPA - MAP 8 TF16

The Championship Course at Woodhall Spa, now known as the Hotchkin, is considered to be the best inland course in the UK . This classic course has cavernous bunkers and heather-lined fairways. Golf has been played here for over a century and the Hotchkin has hosted most of the top national and international amateur events. The English Golf Union acquired Woodhall Spa in 1995 to create a centre of excellence. A second course, the Bracken, has been built, along with extensive practice facilities including one of Europe's finest short-game practice areas. The English Golf Union actively encourages visitors to the National Golf Centre throughout the year, to experience the facilities and to enjoy the unique ambience.

The Broadway LN10 6PU ☎ 01526 352511 🖷 01526 351817
e-mail: booking@englishgolfunion.org
web: www.woodhallspagolf.com
The Hotchkin: 18 Holes, 7080yds, Par 73, SSS 75, Course record 64.
The Bracken: 18 Holes, 6719yds, Par 72, SSS 74, Course record 67. *Club membership 520.*
Visitors Mon-Sun & BHs. Booking required. Handicap certificate. Dress code. **Societies** booking required. **Green Fees** Hotchkin £120 per day, £80 per round. Bracken £80 per day, £55 round. £110 per day playing both courses
Course Designer Col S V Hotchkin/Donald Steel (Bracken) **Facilities** ⑪ ⑩ ⬚ ⬚ ⬚ ⬚ ⬚ ⬚ ⬚ ⬚ ⬚
Leisure pitch & putt 9 hole course **Conf** facs Corporate Hospitality Days **Location** Exit A1 just after Colsterworth rdbt onto B6403 to Ancaster. Turn right onto A153 to Coningsby/Tattershall and then left onto B1192.
Hotel ★★★ 74% HL Petwood, Stixwould Road, WOODHALL SPA ☎ 01526 352411 🖷 01526 352411
53 en suite

SOUTH KYME   Map 8 TF14

South Kyme Skinners Ln LN4 4AT
☎ 01526 861113   📠 01526 861113
e-mail: southkymegc@hotmail.com
web: www.skgc.co.uk
A challenging fenland course in a tranquil location, described as an inland links with water hazards, trees and fairway hazards.

18 Holes, 6556yds, Par 72, SSS 72, Course record 67.
Club membership 400.

Visitors Mon-Sun & BHs. Dress code. **Societies** welcome. **Green Fees** £22 per round, £12 per 9 holes (£25/£14 weekends & BHs) **Prof** Peter Chamberlain **Facilities** ⊕ ⦿ 🏌 ⌨ 🏌 ⚐ 🏌
🛺 ⚐ **Leisure** 6 hole short course. **Conf** Corporate Hospitality Days
Location off B1395 into South Kyme
Hotel BUD Travelodge Sleaford, Holdingham, SLEAFORD
☎ 08719 846 104 📠 08719 846 104   40 en suite

SPALDING   Map 8 TF22

Spalding Surfleet PE11 4EA
☎ 01775 680386 (office) & 680474 (pro)
📠 01775 680988
e-mail: secretary@spaldinggolfclub.co.uk
web: www.spaldinggolfclub.co.uk

A pretty, well-laid out course in a fenland area. The River Glen runs beside the 1st, 2nd and 4th holes, and ponds and lakes are very much in play on the 9th, 10th and 11th holes. Challenging holes include the river dominated 2nd and the 17th where a good drive is needed for the right hand side of the fairway to leave a challenging second shot to a well protected green, bunkered in front and right with out of bounds on the left.

18 Holes, 6478yds, Par 72, SSS 71, Course record 62.
Club membership 750.

Visitors Mon-Sun & BHs. Booking required. Handicap certificate. Dress code. **Societies** booking required. **Green Fees** £35 per day, £30 per round (£40 per round weekends & BHs) **Course Designer** Price/Spencer/Ward **Prof** John Spencer/Chris Huggins **Facilities** ⊕ ⦿
🏌 ⌨ 🏌 ⚐ 🏌 🛺 ⚐ **Conf** Corporate Hospitality Days
Location 4m N of Spalding next to A16
Hotel ★★ 74% SHL Cley Hall, 22 High Street, SPALDING
☎ 01775 725157 📠 01775 725157   15 en suite

STAMFORD   Map 4 TF00

Burghley Park St Martins PE9 3JX
☎ 01780 753789   📠 01780 753789
web: www.burghleygolf.org.uk
18 Holes, 6236yds, Par 70, SSS 70, Course record 65.
Prof Glenn Davies **Facilities** ⊕ 🏌 ⌨ 🏌 ⚐ 🏌 🛺 ⚐
Conf Corporate Hospitality Days **Location** 1m S of town on B1081, take roundabout from A1 S of Stamford
Telephone for further details
Hotel ★★★ 86% HL The George of Stamford, 71 St Martins, STAMFORD ☎ 01780 750750 & 750700 (res) 📠 01780 750750 47 en suite

STOKE ROCHFORD   Map 8 SK92

Stoke Rochford NG33 5EW
☎ 01476 530275   📠 01476 530237
e-mail: srg.mail@btinternet.com
web: stokerochfordgolfclub.co.uk
Parkland course designed by C Turnor in 1924 and extended in 1936 to 18 holes by Major Hotchkin.

18 Holes, 6252yds, Par 70, SSS 70, Course record 65.
Club membership 525.

Visitors Mon, Tue, Thu & Fri except BHs. Booking required. Handicap certificate. Dress code. **Societies** booking required. **Green Fees** £28 per round **Course Designer** Major Hotchkin **Prof** Angus Dow **Facilities** ⊕ ⦿ 🏌 ⌨ 🏌 ⚐ 🏌 ⚐ 🛺 ⚐ **Location** 5m S of Grantham off A1 southbound signed Stoke Rochford, onto A1 northbound, enter club via BP service station
Hotel ★★★ 73% HL Best Western Kings, North Parade, GRANTHAM ☎ 01476 590800 📠 01476 590800   21 en suite

SUTTON BRIDGE   Map 9 TF42

Sutton Bridge New Rd PE12 9RQ
☎ 01406 350323
web: www.club-noticeboard.co.uk/suttonbridge
Established in 1914, the nine holes are played along, over and in a Victorian dock basin which was abandoned as a dock in 1881. The original walls of the dock are still intact and help to make the course one of the most interesting courses in the region. The greens are recognised as among the best in Lincolnshire.

9 Holes, 5724yds, Par 70, SSS 68, Course record 64.
Club membership 350.

Visitors Mon-Sun & BHs. Booking required Wed, Thu, weekends & BHs. Dress code. **Societies** welcome. **Green Fees** Apr-Sep £30 per day, Oct-Mar £15 **Prof** Antony Lowther **Facilities** ⊕ ⦿ 🏌 ⌨ 🏌 ⚐
🛺 ⚐ **Conf** Corporate Hospitality Days **Location** E of village off A17
Hotel BUD Travelodge King's Lynn Long Sutton, Wisbech Road, LONG SUTTON ☎ 08719 846 082 📠 08719 846 082   40 en suite

SUTTON ON SEA   Map 9 TF58

Sandilands Roman Bank LN12 2RJ
☎ 01507 441432   📠 01507 441617
e-mail: helen_sherratt@yahoo.co.uk
Well-manicured links course next to the sea, renowned for the standard of its greens. Playable all year and easy walking due to the

continued

subtle undulations. The variety of holes and bunker placement will require the use of every club in the bag

18 Holes, 6021yds, Par 70, SSS 69, Course record 64. Club membership 300.

Visitors Mon-Sun & BHs. **Societies** booking required. **Green Fees** £30.50 per day, £22.50 per round (£38.50/£25.50 weekends & BHs). Reduced winter rates **Prof** Simon Sherratt **Facilities** ⓘ ⓑ ♥ 🐾 👤 🏠 ⛳ ♦ ⛳ ♣ ✦ **Leisure** hard and grass tennis courts, gymnasium **Conf** facs Corporate Hospitality Days **Location** 1.5m S off A52
Hotel ★★★ 73% HL The Grange & Links, Sea Lane, Sandilands, SUTTON-ON-SEA ☎ 01507 441334 📄 01507 441334 23 en suite

---

TORKSEY   Map 8 SK87

Lincoln LN1 2EG
☎ 01427 718721 📄 01427 718721
e-mail: info@lincolngc.co.uk
web: www.lincolngc.co.uk

A mature championship standard course offering a variety of holes, links style to parkland.

18 Holes, 6438yds, Par 71, SSS 71, Course record 65. Club membership 750.

Visitors handicap certificate. Dress code. **Societies** booking required **Green Fees** £45 per day, £35 per round (£50/£40 weekends & BHs) **Course Designer** J H Taylor **Prof** Ashley Carter **Facilities** ⓘ ⓘ ⓑ ♥ 🐾 👤 🏠 ⛳ ✦ **Leisure** 3 hole practice course **Conf** facs Corporate Hospitality Days **Location** NE of village off A156
Hotel ★★★ 68% HL The White Hart, Bailgate, LINCOLN ☎ 01522 526222 & 563293 📄 01522 526222 50 en suite

Millfield Laughterton LN1 2LB
☎ 01427 718255 📄 01427 718473
The Millfield: 18 Holes, 6004yds, Par 72, SSS 69, Course record 68.
The Grenville Green: 18 Holes, 4485yds, Par 65.
Course Designer C W Watson **Location** on A1133 1m N of A57
Telephone for further details
Hotel ★★★ 68% HL The White Hart, Bailgate, LINCOLN ☎ 01522 526222 & 563293 📄 01522 526222 50 en suite

---

WOODHALL SPA   Map 8 TF16

The National Golf Centre see page 171
The Broadway LN10 6PU
☎ 01526 352511 📄 01526 351817
e-mail: booking@englishgolfunion.org
web: www.woodhallspagolf.com

WOODTHORPE   Map 9 TF48

Woodthorpe Hall LN13 0DD
☎ 01507 450000 📄 01507 450000
web: www.woodthorpehallleisure.co.uk
18 Holes, 5140yds, Par 67, SSS 65, Course record 68.
Facilities ⓘ ⓘ ⓑ ♥ 🐾 👤 ♦ 🏠 ✦ **Leisure** fishing **Conf** facs **Location** 3m N of Alford on B1373
Telephone for further details
Hotel ★★★ 73% HL The Grange & Links, Sea Lane, Sandilands, SUTTON-ON-SEA ☎ 01507 441334 📄 01507 441334 23 en suite

---

LONDON

E4 CHINGFORD

Royal Epping Forest Forest Approach, Chingford E4 7AZ
☎ 020 8529 2195 📄 020 8559 4664
e-mail: office@refgc.co.uk
web: www.refgc.co.uk
Woodland course. Red garments must be worn.

18 Holes, 6281yds, Par 71, SSS 70, Course record 64. Club membership 400.

Visitors contact club for details. **Societies** welcome. **Green Fees** £20 (£25 weekends)) **Course Designer** J G Gibson **Prof** A Traynor **Facilities** ⓘ by prior arrangement ⓘ by prior arrangement ⓑ ♥ 🐾 👤 🏠 ⛳ ✦ **Conf** facs **Location** 300yds E of Chingford station on Chingford Plain
Hotel ★★ 57% SHL Ridgeway, 115/117 The Ridgeway, North Chingford, LONDON ☎ 020 8529 1964 📄 020 8529 1964 20 en suite

West Essex Bury Rd, Sewardstonebury, Chingford E4 7QL
☎ 020 8529 7558 📄 020 8524 7870
e-mail: sec@westessexgolfclub.co.uk
web: www.westessexgolfclub.co.uk

Testing parkland course within Epping Forest with spectacular views over Essex and Middlesex. Created by James Braid in 1900 and designed to make full use of the landscape's natural attributes. The front nine is the shorter of the two and provides a test of accuracy with tree-lined fairways that meander through the undulating countryside. The back nine is equally challenging although slightly longer and requiring more long iron play.

18 Holes, 6289yds, Par 71, SSS 70, Course record 63. Club membership 710.

Visitors handicap certificate. Dress code. **Societies** booking required. **Green Fees** not confirmed **Course Designer** James Braid **Prof** Robert Joyce **Facilities** ⓘ ⓘ ⓑ ♥ 🐾 👤 🏠 ⛳ ✦ 🚜 ✦ ✦ **Leisure** halfway house, snooker **Conf** facs Corporate Hospitality Days **Location** M25 junct 26, 1.5m N of Chingford station
Hotel ★★★★ 72% HL Menzies Prince Regent, Manor Road, WOODFORD BRIDGE, Essex ☎ 020 8505 9966 📄 020 8505 9966 61 en suite

---

E11 LEYTONSTONE & WANSTEAD

Wanstead Overton Dr, Wanstead E11 2LW
☎ 020 8989 3938 📄 020 8532 9138
e-mail: wgclub@aol.com
web: www.wansteadgolf.org.uk

Flat, picturesque parkland with many trees and shrubs and easy walking. The par 3 16th involves driving across a lake.

18 Holes, 6015yds, Par 69, SSS 69, Course record 62. Club membership 600.

Visitors Mon-Fri except BHs. Dress code. **Societies** booking required. **Green Fees** £40 per day **Course Designer** James Braid **Prof** David Hawkins **Facilities** ⓘ ⓘ ⓑ ♥ 🐾 👤 🏠 ✦ ✦ **Leisure** fishing **Conf** facs Corporate Hospitality Days **Location** off A12 in Wanstead
Hotel BUD Innkeeper's Lodge London Snaresbrook, 73 Hollybush Hill, Snaresbrook, LONDON ☎ 0845 112 6122 📄 0845 112 6122 24 en suite

N2 EAST FINCHLEY

Hampstead Winnington Rd N2 0TU
☎ 020 8455 0203   📠 020 8731 6194
e-mail: hampsteadgolf@btconnect.com
web: www.hampsteadgolfclub.co.uk
Undulating parkland with many mature trees.

9 Holes, 5822yds, Par 68, SSS 68, Course record 64.
Club membership 526.

Visitors Mon-Fri & Sun except BHs. Dress code. **Green Fees** £30 per 18 holes (£35 Sun) **Course Designer** Tom Dunn **Prof** Peter Brown **Facilities** ⊕ 🍴 🖪 ⬜ 🍴 👤 🖼 🔑 **Location** off Hampstead Ln
Guesthouse ★★★★ GA The Langorf, 20 Frognal, Hampstead, LONDON ☎ 020 7794 4483 📠 020 7794 4483   31 en suite

N6 HIGHGATE

Highgate Denewood Rd N6 4AH
☎ 020 8340 3745   📠 020 8348 9152
e-mail: nick@highgategc.co.uk
web: www.highgategc.co.uk
Parkland with fine views over London. The nearest 18-hole course north of the river from Marble Arch. Many interesting holes with a premium on accuracy. The 15th and 16th holes are very demanding par 4s.

18 Holes, 5985yds, Par 69, SSS 69, Course record 66.
Club membership 700.

Visitors Mon-Fri except BHs. Booking required. Dress code.
Societies booking required. **Green Fees** £50 per day, £35 per round **Course Designer** Cuthbert Butchart **Prof** Robin Turner **Facilities** ⊕ 🍴 🖪 ⬜ 👤 🖼 🔑 🔑 **Conf** facs Corporate Hospitality Days **Location** off B519 Hampstead Ln
Hotel ★★★★ 75% HL London Marriott Hotel Regents Park, 128 King Henry's Road, LONDON ☎ 0870 400 7240 📠 0870 400 7240   304 en suite

N9 LOWER EDMONTON

Lee Valley Leisure Lee Valley Leisure Complex, Meridian Way, Edmonton N9 0AR
☎ 020 8803 3611   📠 020 8884 4975
e-mail: rgarvey@leevalleypark.org.uk
web: www.leevalleypark.org.uk
Testing parkland course with a large lake and the river Lee providing natural hazards. Good quality greens all year round.

Lee Valley Leisure Golf Course: 18 Holes, 5204yds, Par 67, SSS 65, Course record 66. Club membership 200.

Visitors Mon-Sun & BHs. Booking required weekends.
Societies booking required. **Green Fees** not confirmed **Course Designer** John Jacobs **Prof** R Gerken **Facilities** ⊕ 🍴 🖪 ⬜ 🍴 👤 🖼 🔑 🔑
Hotel ★★★★ 77% HL Royal Chace, The Ridgeway, ENFIELD ☎ 020 8884 8181 📠 020 8884 8181   92 en suite

N14 SOUTHGATE

Trent Park Bramley Rd, Oakwood N14 4UW
☎ 020 8367 4653   📠 0208 366 4581
web: crown-golf.co.uk
Parkland course set in 150 acres of green belt area. Seven holes

played across Merryhills brook. Testing holes are 2nd (423 yds) over brook, 190 yds from the tee, and up to a plateau green; 7th (463 yds) dog-leg, over brook, par 4.

18 Holes, 6381yds, Par 70, SSS 69, Course record 64.
Club membership 700.

Visitors Mon-Sun & BHs. Booking required. **Societies** booking required. **Green Fees** £18 per round (£21 weekends) **Course Designer** D McGibbon **Prof** Mark Banning **Facilities** ⊕ 🍴 🖪 ⬜ 🍴 👤 🖼 🔑 🔑 **Conf** facs Corporate Hospitality Days **Location** opp Oakwood tube station
Hotel ★★★★ 80% HL West Lodge Park, Cockfosters Road, HADLEY WOOD ☎ 020 8216 3900 & 8216 3903 📠 020 8216 3900   59 en suite

N20 WHETSTONE

North Middlesex The Manor House, Friern Barnet Ln, Whetstone N20 0NL
☎ 020 8445 1604 & 020 8445 3060   📠 020 8445 5023
e-mail: manager@northmiddlesexgc.co.uk
web: www.northmiddlesexgc.co.uk
Short parkland course with many attractive water features and many mature trees. Renowned for its tricky greens and a spectacular final hole which is a demanding par 3.

18 Holes, 5594yds, Par 69, SSS 67, Course record 64.
Club membership 520.

Visitors Mon-Sun & BHs. Booking advisable weekends & BHs. Handicap certificate. Dress code. **Societies** booking required. **Green Fees** £25 (£30 weekends & BHs). Winter £20/£27 **Course Designer** Willie Park Jnr **Prof** Freddy George **Facilities** ⊕ 🍴 🖪 ⬜ 🍴 👤 🖼 🔑 🛒 🔑 **Conf** facs Corporate Hospitality Days **Location** M25 junct 23, 5m S
Hotel ★★★ 74% HL Corus hotel Elstree, Barnet Lane, ELSTREE ☎ 020 8953 8227 & 0844 736 8602 📠 020 8953 8227   49 en suite

> **South Herts** Links Dr N20 8QU
> ☎ 020 8445 2035   📠 020 8445 7569
> **web:** www.southhertsgolfclub.co.uk
> *18 Holes, 6432yds, Par 72, SSS 71, Course record 63.*
> **Course Designer** Harry Vardon **Location** 2m E of A1 at Apex Corner **Telephone for further details**
> **Hotel** BUD Innkeeper's Lodge Southgate, 22 The Green, Southgate, LONDON ☎ 0845 112 6123 📠 0845 112 6123   19 en suite

N21 WINCHMORE HILL

Bush Hill Park Bush Hill, Winchmore Hill N21 2BU
☎ 020 8360 4103   📠 020 8360 5583
e-mail: info@bushhillparkgolfclub.co.uk
web: www.bushhillparkgolfclub.co.uk
Pleasant parkland course in a tranquil setting. The holes set a challenge due to the vast array of mature trees, which make it an enjoyable course to play. The premium is on accuracy rather than length off the tee. The six par threes are all visually stunning and along with the remodelled 17th contribute to an enjoyable round of golf for all levels of golfer.

18 Holes, 5809yds, Par 70, SSS 68, Course record 59.
Club membership 700.

Visitors Mon-Fri, Sun & BHs. Booking required. Dress code.
Societies booking required. **Green Fees** £29.50 per round (£35 Sun

continued

& BHs). Twilight £19 **Course Designer** Harry Vardon **Prof** Lee Fickling
Facilities ⓣ ⓞ ⓛ ⓓ 🐴 ⚑ ⛳ ♪ 🚗 ♪ ♪
Conf facs Corporate Hospitality Days **Location** 1m S of Enfield off
A105
Hotel ★★★★ 77% HL Royal Chace, The Ridgeway, ENFIELD
☎ 020 8884 8181 ▤ 020 8884 8181   92 en suite

N22 WOOD GREEN

Muswell Hill Rhodes Av, Wood Green N22 7UT
☎ 020 8888 1764   ▤ 020 8889 9380
e-mail: mhgcclubsecretary@btconnect.com
web: www.muswellhillgolf.co.uk
Undulating parkland course with a brook running through the centre,
set in 87 acres.
18 Holes, 6438yds, Par 71, SSS 71, Course record 65.
Club membership 560.
Visitors Mon-Sun & BHs. Booking required weekends & BHs. Handicap
certificate. Dress code. **Societies** welcome. **Green Fees** £35 per round
(£40 weekends). Fees include a drink. **Course Designer** Braid/Wilson
Prof David Wilton **Facilities** ⓣ ⓞ ⓛ ⓓ 🐴 ⚑ ⛳ ♪
Conf facs Corporate Hospitality Days **Location** off N Circular Rd near
Bounds Green
Hotel ★★★ 67% HL Days Hotel London North, Welcome Break
Service Area, LONDON ☎ 020 8906 7000 ▤ 020 8906 7000
200 en suite

NW4 HENDON   Map 4 TQ28

The Metro Golf Centre Barnet Copthall Sports Centre
NW4 1PS
☎ 020 8202 1202   ▤ 020 8203 1203
web: www.metro-golf.co.uk
The Metro Golf Centre: 9 Holes, 898yds, Par 27, SSS 27,
Course record 24.
Course Designer Cousells **Location** M1 junct 2, off A41/A1, in Barnet
Copthall sports complex
Telephone for further details
Hotel ★★★★ 75% HL London Marriott Hotel Regents Park, 128
King Henry's Road, LONDON ☎ 0870 400 7240 ▤ 0870 400 7240
304 en suite

NW7 MILL HILL

Finchley Nether Court, Frith Ln NW7 1PU
☎ 020 8346 2436   ▤ 020 8343 4205
e-mail: secretary@finchleygolfclub.co.uk
web: www.finchleygolfclub.com
Compact and well presented course with rolling parkland. Tree-lined
fairways and heavily contoured greens.
18 Holes, 6356yds, Par 72, SSS 71. Club membership 500.
Visitors Mon, Wed, & Fri. Weekends & BHs pm. Booking required.
Handicap certificate. Dress code. **Societies** booking required. **Green
Fees** £45 per day, £35 per 18 holes (£55/£45 weekends & BHs)
Course Designer James Braid **Prof** Caroline Bradley **Facilities** ⓣ
ⓞ by prior arrangement 🐴 ⓓ 🐴 ⚑ ⛳ ♪ 🚗 ♪
Conf facs Corporate Hospitality Days **Location** near Mill Hill East Tube
Station
Hotel ★★★ 74% HL Corus hotel Elstree, Barnet Lane, ELSTREE
☎ 020 8953 8227 & 0844 736 8602 ▤ 020 8953 8227   49 en suite

Hendon Ashley Walk, Devonshire Rd, Mill Hill NW7 1DG
☎ 020 8346 6023   ▤ 020 8343 1974
e-mail: admin@hendongolfclub.co.uk
web: www.hendongolfclub.co.uk
Easy walking parkland course with a good variety of trees, and
providing testing golf.
18 Holes, 6289yds, Par 70, SSS 70, Course record 63.
Club membership 560.
Visitors Mon-Sun & BHs. Booking required weekends & BHs. Handicap
certificate. Dress code. **Societies** welcome. **Green Fees** £35 (£40 per
round weekends). Winter £25/£33 **Course Designer** H S Colt **Prof** Matt
Deal **Facilities** ⓣ ⓞ ⓛ ⓓ 🐴 ⚑ ⛳ ♪ 🚗 ♪
Conf facs Corporate Hospitality Days **Location** M1 junct 2 southbound
Hotel ★★★ 74% HL Corus hotel Elstree, Barnet Lane, ELSTREE
☎ 020 8953 8227 & 0844 736 8602 ▤ 020 8953 8227   49 en suite

Mill Hill 100 Barnet Way, Mill Hill NW7 3AL
☎ 020 8959 2339   ▤ 020 8906 0731
e-mail: cluboffice@millhillgc.co.uk
web: www.millhillgc.co.uk
A mature course set in 145 acres of parkland. The 18 holes are all
individually designed with many bordered by ancient oaks. Lake
features on the 2nd, 9th, 10th and 17th holes.
18 Holes, 6247yds, Par 70, SSS 70, Course record 68.
Club membership 550.
Visitors Mon-Sun except BHs. Dress code. **Societies** booking required.
Green Fees £30 per round (£37 weekends) **Course Designer** J F
Abercrombie/H S Colt **Prof** David Beal **Facilities** ⓣ ⓞ ⓛ ⓓ 🐴
🐴 ⚑ ⛳ ♪ 🚗 ♪ 🏊 **Leisure** snooker **Conf** facs Corporate
Hospitality Days **Location** M1 junct 4, take A41 towards central
London. At Apex rdbt turn left and immediately right onto A5109, 3rd
turn left into Hankins Lane. From M25 exit junct 23 onto A1, 2nd exit
at Stirling rdbt, A1 on left..
Hotel ★★★ 74% HL Corus hotel Elstree, Barnet Lane, ELSTREE
☎ 020 8953 8227 & 0844 736 8602 ▤ 020 8953 8227   49 en suite

SE9 ELTHAM

Eltham Warren Bexley Rd, Eltham SE9 2PE
☎ 020 8850 4477   ▤ 020 8850 0522
e-mail: secretary@elthamwarren.idps.co.uk
web: www.elthamwarrengolfclub.co.uk
Parkland course founded in 1890 with narrow tree-lined fairways and
small greens.
9 Holes, 5874yds, Par 69, SSS 68, Course record 62.
Club membership 440.
Visitors Mon-Fri & BHs. Booking required. Dress code.
Societies booking required. **Green Fees** £30 per day **Course
Designer** James Braid **Prof** Gary Brett **Facilities** ⓣ ⓛ ⓓ 🐴 🐴
⚑ ♪ 🚗 ♪ **Leisure** snooker **Location** 0.5m from Eltham station
on A210 (Bexley Rd)
Hotel ★★★ 77% HL Best Western Bromley Court, Bromley Hill,
BROMLEY ☎ 020 8461 8600 ▤ 020 8461 8600   114 en suite

Royal Blackheath Court Rd SE9 5AF
☎ 020 8850 1795 📠 020 8859 0150
e-mail: info@rbgc.com
web: www.royalblackheath.com

A pleasant, parkland course of great character, with many great trees and two ponds. The 18th requires a pitch to the green over a thick clipped hedge, which also crosses the front of the 1st tee. The clubhouse dates from the 17th century, and you may wish to visit the club's fine museum of golf.

18 Holes, 6147yds, Par 70, SSS 70, Course record 65. Club membership 720.

Visitors contact club for details. **Societies** welcome. **Green Fees** £70 per day, £50 per round **Course Designer** James Braid **Prof** Matt Johns **Facilities** ⑪ ⑯ ⓵ ⓶ ⓷ ⓸ ⓹ ⓺ ⓻ ⓼ **Leisure** golf museum **Conf** facs Corporate Hospitality Days **Location** M25 junct 3, A20 towards London, 2nd lights right, club 500yds on right

Hotel ★★★ 77% HL Best Western Bromley Court, Bromley Hill, BROMLEY ☎ 020 8461 8600 📠 020 8461 8600 114 en suite

SE18 WOOLWICH

Shooters Hill Eaglesfield Rd, Shooters Hill SE18 3DA
☎ 020 8854 6368 📠 020 8854 0469
e-mail: admin@shgc.uk.com
web: www.shgc.uk.com

Hilly and wooded parkland with good views and natural hazards.

18 Holes, 5721yds, Par 69, SSS 68, Course record 63. Club membership 900.

Visitors Mon-Sun & BHs. Handicap certificate. Dress code. **Societies** booking required. **Green Fees** £35 per day, £28 per round **Course Designer** Willie Park **Prof** David Brotherton **Facilities** ⑪ ⓵ ⓶ ⓷ ⓸ ⓹ ⓺ ⓻ **Conf** Corporate Hospitality Days **Location** Shooters Hill road from Blackheath

Hotel ★★★★ 72% HL Novotel London ExCel, 7 Western Gateway, Royal Victoria Docks, LONDON ☎ 020 7540 9700 & 0870 850 4560 📠 020 7540 9700 257 en suite

SE21 DULWICH

Dulwich & Sydenham Hill Grange Ln, College Rd SE21 7LH
☎ 020 8693 3961 📠 020 8693 2481
e-mail: secretary@dulwichgolf.co.uk
web: www.dulwichgolf.co.uk

Parkland course set among mature oaks on the slopes of Sydenham Hill, overlooking Dulwich College. Demanding par 4's and challenging par 3's are interspersed with reachable but testing par 5's. Tree-lined fairways off the tees, hazards and cannily placed bunkers await the approach shot. Having made the green, the golfer is then faced with tricky but true greens.

18 Holes, 6079yds, Par 69, SSS 69, Course record 63. Club membership 850.

Visitors Mon-Fri except BHs. Dress code. **Societies** booking required. **Green Fees** £55 per day, £40 per round. Winter £30 per round **Course Designer** H Colt **Prof** David Baillie **Facilities** ⑪ ⑯ ⓵ ⓶ ⓷ ⓸ ⓹ ⓺ ⓻ ⓼ **Leisure** short game area **Conf** facs Corporate Hospitality Days **Location** 0.5m from Dulwich College off A205 (South Circular)

Hotel ★★★ 77% HL Best Western Bromley Court, Bromley Hill, BROMLEY ☎ 020 8461 8600 📠 020 8461 8600 114 en suite

SE28 WOOLWICH

Thamesview Fairway Dr, Summerton Way, Thamesmead SE28 8PP
☎ 020 8310 7975
e-mail: golf@tvgc.co.uk
web: www.tvgc.co.uk

A delightful but tricky course with a mix of mature trees, new trees and water hazards. The 6th hole, while only 357 yds, is one of the toughest par 4's a golfer can play.

Thamesview Golf Centre: 9 Holes, 5462yds, Par 70, SSS 66. Club membership 50.

Visitors Mon-Sun & BHs. **Societies** booking required. **Green Fees** Mon-Thu £10 per 18 holes, £7 per 9 holes, Fri £12/£8.50, weekends £14/£10 **Course Designer** Heffernan **Prof** Gary Stewart **Facilities** ⑪ ⑯ ⓵ ⓶ ⓷ ⓸ ⓹ ⓺ **Conf** facs Corporate Hospitality Days **Location** off A2 near Woolwich ferry

Hotel BUD Ibis London Barking, Highbridge Road, BARKING ☎ 020 8477 4100 📠 020 8477 4100 86 en suite

SW15 PUTNEY

Richmond Park Roehampton Gate, Priory Ln SW15 5JR
☎ 020 8876 1795 📠 020 8878 1354
e-mail: richmondpark@glendale-services.co.uk
web: www.glendale-golf.com

Two public parkland courses.

Princes Course: 18 Holes, 5868yds, Par 69, SSS 67. Dukes Course: 18 Holes, 6036yds, Par 69, SSS 68.

Visitors Mon-Sun & BHs. Booking required weekends & BHs. Dress code. **Societies** booking required. **Green Fees** not confirmed **Course Designer** Fred Hawtree **Prof** Stuart Hill & David Bown **Facilities** ⑪ ⓵ ⓶ ⓷ ⓸ ⓹ ⓺ ⓻ ⓼ **Location** inside Richmond Park, entrance via Roehampton Gate

Hotel ★★★★ 73% HL Richmond Hill, Richmond Hill, RICHMOND UPON THAMES ☎ 020 8940 2247 📠 020 8940 2247 149 en suite

SW17 WANDSWORTH

Central London Golf Centre Burntwood Ln, Wandsworth SW17 0AT
☎ 020 8871 2468 📠 020 8874 7447
e-mail: golf@clgc.co.uk
web: www.clgc.co.uk

Attractive flat parkland course in the middle of London. The longest drive is the 430 yard 3rd to one of the course's superb greens. Well placed bunkers trap the careless shot and the course rewards the accurate player.

Central London Golf Centre: 9 Holes, 2277yds, Par 62, SSS 62, Course record 59. Club membership 200.

Visitors Mon-Sun & BHs. Booking required weekends & BHs. **Societies** welcome. **Green Fees** £11.50 (£13.50 weekends) **Course Designer** Patrick Tallack/Michael Anscomb **Prof** G Clements **Facilities** ⑪ ⑯ ⓵ ⓶ ⓷ ⓸ ⓹ ⓺ ⓻ ⓼ ⓽ **Leisure** short game area **Conf** facs Corporate Hospitality Days **Location** between Garatt Ln and Trinity Rd

Hotel ★★★★ 77% CHH Cannizaro House, West Side, Wimbledon Common, LONDON ☎ 020 8879 1464 📠 020 8879 1464 46 en suite

SW19 WIMBLEDON

London Scottish Windmill Enclosure, Wimbledon Common SW19 5NQ
☎ 020 8788 0135 & 8789 1207 📠 020 8789 7517
e-mail: secretary.lsgc@btconnect.com
web: www.londonscottishgolfclub.co.uk

Heathland course. The original course was seven holes around the windmill, laid out by 'Old' Willie Dunn of Musselburgh. His son, Tom Dunn, was the first professional to the club and laid out the 18-hole course.

18 Holes, 5458yds, Par 68, SSS 66, Course record 61.
Club membership 300.

Visitors Mon-Fri except BHs. Handicap certificate. Dress code.
Societies booking required. **Green Fees** Mon £30 per day, £20 per round. Tue-Fri £35/£25 **Course Designer** Tom Dunn **Prof** Steve Barr
Facilities ⊕ †○! ⓑ ☲ ☶! ⌁ 🖻 ☖ 🗲
Hotel ★★★★ 77% CHH Cannizaro House, West Side, Wimbledon Common, LONDON ☎ 020 8879 1464 📠 020 8879 1464 46 en suite

Royal Wimbledon 29 Camp Rd SW19 4UW
☎ 020 8946 2125 📠 020 8944 8652
e-mail: secretary@rwgc.co.uk
web: www.rwgc.co.uk

The third-oldest club in England, established in 1865 and steeped in the history of the game. Mainly heathland with trees and heather, a good test of golf with many fine holes, the 12th being rated as the best.

18 Holes, 6350yds, Par 70, SSS 71, Course record 66.
Club membership 1050.

Visitors Wed & Thu except BHs. Booking required. Handicap certificate. Dress code. **Societies** welcome. **Green Fees** £95 per day, £70 per round **Course Designer** H Colt **Prof** David Jones
Facilities ⊕ ⓑ ☲ ☶! ⌁ 🖻 ☖ 🗲
Conf Corporate Hospitality Days **Location** 1m from Tibbatt's Corner roundabout on A3 off Wimbledon Park before war memorial in village
Hotel ★★★★ 77% CHH Cannizaro House, West Side, Wimbledon Common, LONDON ☎ 020 8879 1464 📠 020 8879 1464 46 en suite

Wimbledon Common 19 Camp Rd SW19 4UW
☎ 020 8946 0294 (Pro shop) 📠 020 8947 8697
e-mail: secretary@wcgc.co.uk
web: www.wcgc.co.uk

Quick-drying course on Wimbledon Common with no temporary greens. Well wooded, with tight fairways, challenging short holes but no bunkers.

18 Holes, 5438yds, Par 68, SSS 66, Course record 63.
Club membership 320.

Visitors Mon-Fri except BHs. Dress code. **Societies** booking required.
Green Fees £35 per day, £25 per round **Course Designer** Tom & Willie Dunn **Prof** J S Jukes **Facilities** ⊕ †○! ⓑ ☲ ☶! ⌁ 🖻
☖ 🗲 **Leisure** snooker room. **Conf** facs Corporate Hospitality Days **Location** 0.5m N of Wimbledon Village
Hotel ★★★★ 77% CHH Cannizaro House, West Side, Wimbledon Common, LONDON ☎ 020 8879 1464 📠 020 8879 1464 46 en suite

Wimbledon Park Home Park Rd SW19 7HR
☎ 020 8946 1250 📠 020 8944 8688
web: www.wpgc.co.uk

18 Holes, 5483yds, Par 66, SSS 66, Course record 59.
Course Designer Willie Park Jnr **Location** 400yds from Wimbledon Park station
Telephone for further details
Hotel ★★★★ 73% HL Richmond Hill, Richmond Hill, RICHMOND UPON THAMES ☎ 020 8940 2247 📠 020 8940 2247 149 en suite

W7 HANWELL

Brent Valley 138 Church Rd W7 3BE
☎ 020 8567 1287
18 Holes, 5426yds, Par 67, SSS 66.
Prof Peter Bryant **Facilities** ⊕ ⓑ ☲ ☶! ⌁ 🖻 ☖ 🗲
Telephone for further details
Hotel ★★ 69% HL Best Western Master Robert, 366 Great West Road, HOUNSLOW ☎ 020 8570 6261 📠 020 8570 6261 96 en suite

MERSEYSIDE

BEBINGTON
Map 7 SJ38

Brackenwood Brackenwood Golf Course, Bracken Ln CH63 2LY
☎ 0151 608 5394
web: www.brackenwoodgolf.co.uk

Municipal parkland course with easy walking, a very testing but fair course in a fine rural setting.

18 Holes, 6285yds, Par 70, SSS 70, Course record 66.
Club membership 250.

Visitors Mon-Sun & BHs. Booking required weekends & BHs. Dress code. **Societies** booking required. **Green Fees** £11 per round **Prof** Ken Lamb **Facilities** ☲ 🖻 ☖ 🗲 **Location** M53 junct 4, 0.75m N on B5151
Hotel ★★★★ 77% HL Thornton Hall Hotel and Spa, Neston Road, THORNTON HOUGH, Wirral ☎ 0151 336 3938 📠 0151 336 3938 63 en suite

BIRKENHEAD　　　　　　　　Map 7 SJ38

Arrowe Park Woodchurch CH49 5LW
☎ 0151 677 1527
Arrowe Park Golf Course: 18 Holes, 6435yds, Par 72, SSS 71, Course record 66.
Prof Colin Disbury **Facilities** ⑪ ⑩ ⓛ ▭ ⓢ 🏠 ⓣ 🛒 ✆
Leisure pitch & putt **Location** M53 junct 3, 1m on A551
Telephone for further details
Hotel ★★★ 80% HL RiverHill, Talbot Road, Prenton, BIRKENHEAD
☎ 0151 653 3773 📄 0151 653 3773　15 en suite

Prenton Golf Links Rd, Prenton CH42 8LW
☎ 0151 609 3426
e-mail: nigel.brown@prentongolfclub.co.uk
web: www.prentongolfclub.co.uk
Parkland with easy walking and views of Welsh hills.
18 Holes, 6429yds, Par 71, SSS 71, Course record 65. Club membership 610.
Visitors dress code. **Societies** booking required. **Green Fees** phone
Course Designer James Braid **Prof** Robin Thompson **Facilities** ⑪
⑩ ⓛ ▭ ⓢ 🏠 ⓣ ✆ **Conf** facs Corporate Hospitality
Days **Location** M53 junct 3, off A552 towards Birkenhead
Hotel ★★★ 80% HL RiverHill, Talbot Road, Prenton, BIRKENHEAD
☎ 0151 653 3773 📄 0151 653 3773　15 en suite

Wirral Ladies 93 Bidston Rd CH43 6TS
☎ 0151 652 1255 📄 0151 651 3775
e-mail: wirral.ladies@btconnect.com
web: www.wirral-ladies-golf-club.co.uk
Compact heathland course with heather and birch, requiring accurate shots.
18 Holes, 5185yds, Par 68, SSS 65. Club membership 620.
Visitors Mon-Sun except BHs. Handicap certificate. Dress code.
Societies booking required. **Green Fees** £30 per round **Prof** Angus
Law **Facilities** ⑪ ⓛ ▭ ⓢ 🏠 ✆ **Leisure** indoor training
suite. **Conf** Corporate Hospitality Days **Location** W of town centre on
B5151
Hotel ★★★ 80% HL RiverHill, Talbot Road, Prenton, BIRKENHEAD
☎ 0151 653 3773 📄 0151 653 3773　15 en suite

BLUNDELLSANDS　　　　　　Map 7 SJ39

West Lancashire Hall Road West L23 8SZ
☎ 0151 924 1076 📄 0151 931 4448
e-mail: golf@westlancashiregolf.co.uk
web: www.westlancashiregolf.co.uk
Challenging, traditional links with sandy subsoil overlooking the
Mersey estuary. The course provides excellent golf throughout the
year. The four short holes are very fine.
18 Holes, 6763yds, Par 72, SSS 73, Course record 66. Club membership 650.
Visitors Mon, Wed-Fri, Sun & BHs. Booking required. Dress code.
Societies booking required. **Green Fees** £85 per day, £70 per
round (£100/£85 Sun) **Course Designer** C K Cotton **Prof** Gary
Edge **Facilities** ⑪ ⑩ ⓛ ▭ ⓢ 🏠 ⓣ ✆ ✆ 🏌
Conf Corporate Hospitality Days **Location** N of village, next to Hall
Road station
Hotel ★★★ 80% HL The Royal, Marine Terrace, Waterloo,
LIVERPOOL ☎ 0151 928 2332 📄 0151 928 2332　25 en suite

BOOTLE　　　　　　　　　　Map 7 SJ39

Bootle 2 Dunnings Bridge Rd L30 2PP
☎ 0151 928 1371 📄 0151 949 1815
18 Holes, 6362yds, Par 70, SSS 70, Course record 64.
Prof Alan Bradshaw **Facilities** ⑪ ⓛ ▭ ⓢ 🏠 ⓣ ✆
Leisure fishing **Location** 2m NE on A5036
Telephone for further details
Hotel ★★★ 80% HL The Royal, Marine Terrace, Waterloo,
LIVERPOOL ☎ 0151 928 2332 📄 0151 928 2332　25 en suite

BROMBOROUGH　　　　　　Map 7 SJ38

Bromborough Raby Hall Rd CH63 0NW
☎ 0151 334 2155 📄 0151 334 7300
e-mail: enquiries@bromboroughgolfclub.org.uk
web: www.bromboroughgolfclub.org.uk
Parkland course.
18 Holes, 6650yds, Par 72, SSS 72, Course record 65. Club membership 800.
Visitors Mon, Wed-Fri, Sun & BHs. Booking required. Dress code.
Societies booking required. **Green Fees** phone **Course Designer** J
Hassall/Hawtree & Son **Prof** Geoff Berry **Facilities** ⑪ ⑩ ⓛ
▭ ⓢ 🏠 ✆ ✆ **Conf** Corporate Hospitality Days
Location 0.5m W of Station
Hotel ★★★★ 77% HL Thornton Hall Hotel and Spa, Neston Road,
THORNTON HOUGH, Wirral ☎ 0151 336 3938 📄 0151 336 3938
63 en suite

CALDY　　　　　　　　　　Map 7 SJ28

Caldy Links Hey Rd CH48 1NB
☎ 0151 625 5660 📄 0151 625 7394
e-mail: golfcaldygc@btconnect.com
web: www.caldygolfclub.co.uk

A heathland and clifftop links course situated on the estuary of the
River Dee with many of the fairways running parallel to the river.
Of championship length, the course offers excellent golf all year,
but is subject to variable winds that noticeably alter the day-to-day
playing of each hole. There are excellent views of the Welsh Hills.
18 Holes, 6133metres, Par 72, SSS 73, Course record 65. Club membership 900.
Visitors Mon,Thu, Fri except BHs.. Booking required. Handicap
certificate. Dress code. **Societies** booking required. **Green Fees** £70
per day, £60 per round **Course Designer** J Braid **Prof** A Gibbons
Facilities ⑪ ⑩ ⓛ ▭ ⓢ 🏠 🛒 ✆ **Leisure** ball

continued

hire & collection **Conf** Corporate Hospitality Days **Location** A540
(Thurstaston to West Kirby), take exit for Caldy at rdbt, club signed
Hotel ★★★★ 77% HL Thornton Hall Hotel and Spa,
Neston Road, THORNTON HOUGH, Wirral ☎ 0151 336 3938
📄 0151 336 3938 63 en suite

EASTHAM
Map 7 SJ38

Eastham Lodge 117 Ferry Rd CH62 0AP
☎ 0151 327 3003   📄 0151 327 7574
e-mail: easthamlodge.g.c@btinternet.com
web: www.easthamlodgegolfclub.co.uk

A parkland course with many mature trees. Most holes have a subtle
dog-leg to left or right. The 1st hole requires an accurate drive to open
up the green which is guarded on the right by a stand of pine trees.

*18 Holes, 5436yds, Par 68, SSS 68, Course record 63.
Club membership 800.*

Visitors Mon-Sun except BHs. Booking required. Dress code.
Societies booking required. **Green Fees** £25.50 per day, £20.50
per round **Course Designer** Hawtree/D Hemstock **Prof** N Sargent
Facilities ⊕ ⦿ 🍴 ♨ 🛒 🏌 👥 ⛳ **Leisure** snooker
Conf Corporate Hospitality Days **Location** 1.5m N, off A41 to Wirral
Metropolitan College Country Park
Hotel ★★★ 77% HL Brook Meadow, Health Lane, CHILDER
THORNTON ☎ 0151 339 9350 📄 0151 339 9350 25 en suite

FORMBY
Map 7 SD30

Formby Golf Rd L37 1LQ
☎ 01704 872164   📄 01704 833028
e-mail: info@formbygolfclub.co.uk
web: www.formbygolfclub.co.uk

Championship seaside links through sandhills and pine trees. Partly
sheltered from the wind by high dunes it features firm, springy turf,
fast seaside greens and natural sandy bunkers. Well drained it
plays well throughout the year.

*18 Holes, 7028yds, Par 72, SSS 72, Course record 65.
Club membership 700.*

Visitors Mon-Fri & BHs. Weekends after 3.30pm. Handicap
certificate. Dress code **Societies** welcome. **Green Fees** not
confirmed **Course Designer** Park/Colt **Facilities** ⊕ ⦿ 🍴 ♨
🛒 🏌 👥 ⛳ **Conf** facs Corporate Hospitality Days
Location N of town next to Freshfield railway station
Hotel 79% Formby Hall Golf Resort & Spa, Southport Old Road,
FORMBY ☎ 01704 875699 📄 01704 875699 62 en suite

Formby Hall Resort & Spa Southport Old Rd L37 0AB
☎ 01704 875699   📄 01704 832134
e-mail: golf@formbyhallresort.co.uk
web: www.formbyhallresort.co.uk

A spectacular parkland course with links style bunkers. American style
design with water on 16 holes. Generous sized fairways with large
undulating greens, many of which are protected by water.

*Formby Hall Golf Resort & Spa: 18 Holes, 7100yds, Par 72,
SSS 74, Course record 69. Club membership 750.*

Visitors Mon-Sun & BHs. Booking required. Handicap certificate. Dress
code. **Societies** booking required. **Green Fees** not confirmed **Course
Designer** Alan Higgens **Prof** Matthew Allen-Chillan **Facilities** ⊕
⦿ 🍴 ♨ 🛒 🏌 👥 ⛳ **Leisure** sauna,
gymnasium, 9 hole par 3 course, clay pigeon shooting, paintball,
archery **Conf** facs Corporate Hospitality Days **Location** 0.5m off A565
Formby bypass, opp RAF Woodvale
Hotel 79% Formby Hall Golf Resort & Spa, Southport Old Road,
FORMBY ☎ 01704 875699 📄 01704 875699 62 en suite

Formby Ladies Golf Rd L37 1YH
☎ 01704 873493   📄 01704 874127
e-mail: secretary@formbyladiesgolfclub.co.uk
web: www.formbyladiesgolfclub.co.uk

Seaside links - one of the few independent ladies' clubs in the country.
The course has contrasting hard-hitting holes in flat country and tricky
holes in sandhills and woods.

*18 Holes, 5374yds, Par 71, SSS 72, Course record 60.
Club membership 500.*

Visitors Mon-Wed, Fri-Sun except BHs. Handicap certificate. Dress
code. **Societies** welcome. **Green Fees** £48 per day (£55 weekends)
Prof Andrew Witherup **Facilities** ⊕ 🛒 ♨ 🍴 🏌 👥 ⛳
Conf Corporate Hospitality Days **Location** N of town centre
Hotel 79% Formby Hall Golf Resort & Spa, Southport Old Road,
FORMBY ☎ 01704 875699 📄 01704 875699 62 en suite

HESWALL
Map 7 SJ28

Heswall Cottage Ln CH60 8PB
☎ 0151 342 1237   📄 0151 342 6140
web: www.heswallgolfclub.com

18 Holes, 6556yds, Par 72, SSS 72, Course record 62.
Course Designer McKenzie/Ebert **Location** 1m S off A540
Telephone for further details
Hotel ★★★★ 77% HL Thornton Hall Hotel and Spa,
Neston Road, THORNTON HOUGH, Wirral ☎ 0151 336 3938
📄 0151 336 3938 63 en suite

MERSEYSIDE

HOYLAKE — Map 7 SJ28

Hoylake Carr Ln, Municipal Links CH47 4BG
☎ 0151 632 2956
web: www.hoylakegolfclub.com
Flat, generally windy semi-links course. Tricky fairways, with some very deep bunkers.
18 Holes, 6313yds, Par 70, SSS 70, Course record 63.
Club membership 303.
Visitors Mon-Sun & BHs. Booking required weekends & BHs. Dress code. **Societies** booking required. **Green Fees** £11.50 per round **Course Designer** James Braid **Prof** Simon Hooton **Facilities** ⬜ 🍴 ♿ 🏌 🚗 ⛳ **Location** SW of town off A540
Hotel ★★★ 77% HL Leasowe Castle, Leasowe Road, MORETON ☎ 0151 606 9191 📠 0151 606 9191 47 en suite

Royal Liverpool see page 181
Meols Dr CH47 4AL
☎ 0151 632 3101 & 632 3102 📠 0151 632 6737
e-mail: secretary@royal-liverpool-golf.com
web: www.royal-liverpool-golf.com

HUYTON — Map 7 SJ49

Bowring L36 4HD
☎ 0151 443 0424 & 489 1901
Bowring Park Golf Club: 18 Holes, 6082yds, Par 70.
Facilities ⬜ ⛳ **Location** M62 junct 5, on A5080
Telephone for further details
Hotel ★★★★ 73% HL Suites Hotel Knowsley, Ribblers Lane, KNOWSLEY, Prescot ☎ 0151 549 2222 📠 0151 549 2222 101 en suite

Huyton & Prescot Hurst Park L36 1UA
☎ 0151 489 3948 📠 0151 489 0797

18 Holes, 5779yds, Par 68, SSS 68, Course record 65.
Prof John Fisher **Facilities** 🍴 🍴 ♿ ⬜ 🍴 🏌 🏠 ⛳
Conf facs **Location** 1.5m NE off B5199
Telephone for further details
Hotel ★★★★ 73% HL Suites Hotel Knowsley, Ribblers Lane, KNOWSLEY, Prescot ☎ 0151 549 2222 📠 0151 549 2222 101 en suite

LIVERPOOL — Map 7 SJ39
See also **Blundellsands**

Allerton Park Allerton Manor Golf Estate, Allerton Rd L18 3JT
☎ 0151 428 7490 📠 0151 428 7490
Parkland course.
18 Holes, 5494yds, Par 67, SSS 66.
Visitors Mon-Sun & BHs. Booking required. **Societies** welcome. **Green Fees** £9 (£10 weekends and BHs) **Prof** Barry Large **Facilities** ♿ ⬜ 🍴 🏠 ⛳ **Leisure** 9 hole par 3 course. **Location** 5.5m SE of city centre off A562
Hotel ★★★ 80% HL The Royal, Marine Terrace, Waterloo, LIVERPOOL ☎ 0151 928 2332 📠 0151 928 2332 25 en suite

The Childwall Naylors Rd L27 2YB
☎ 0151 487 0654 📠 0151 487 0654
web: www.childwallgolfclub.co.uk
18 Holes, 6425yds, Par 72, SSS 71, Course record 66.
Course Designer James Braid **Location** 7m E of city centre off B5178
Telephone for further details
Hotel ★★★★ 79% HL Crowne Plaza Liverpool - John Lennon Airport, Speke Aerodrome, LIVERPOOL ☎ 0151 494 5000 📠 0151 494 5000 164 en suite

Kirkby-Liverpool Municipal Ingoe Ln L32 4SS
☎ 0151 546 5435
Liverpool Municipal Golf Club (Kirby): 18 Holes, 6704yds, Par 72, SSS 72, Course record 68.
Prof Dave Weston **Facilities** 🍴 🍴 ♿ ⬜ 🍴 🏠 ⛳ **Location** 7.5m NE of city centre on A506
Telephone for further details
Hotel ★★★ 80% HL The Royal, Marine Terrace, Waterloo, LIVERPOOL ☎ 0151 928 2332 📠 0151 928 2332 25 en suite

Lee Park Childwall Valley Rd L27 3YA
☎ 0151 487 3882 📠 0151 498 4666
e-mail: lee.park@virgin.net
web: www.leepark.co.uk

Well presented parkland course with easy walking. A test for the short game; being in the right position to attack the pins is a premium.
18 Holes, 5959yds, Par 70, SSS 69, Course record 66.
Club membership 600.
Visitors Dress code. **Societies** booking required. **Green Fees** £32 per day (£42 weekends & BHs) **Course Designer** Frank Pennick **Prof** Chris Crowder **Facilities** 🍴 🍴 ♿ ⬜ 🍴 🏠 ⛳ **Leisure** snooker
continued

ROYAL LIVERPOOL

MERSEYSIDE - HOYLAKE - MAP 7 SJ28

Built in 1869 on the site of a former racecourse, this world-famous championship course was one of the first seaside courses to be established in England. In 1921 Hoylake was the scene of the first international match between the US and Britain, now known as the Walker Cup. Over the years, golfing enthusiasts have come to Hoylake to witness 18 amateur championships and 11 Open Championships, the latest being in 2006. Visitors playing on this historic course can expect a challenging match, with crosswinds, deep bunkers and hollows, all set against the backdrop of stunning Welsh hills. Watch out for the 8th hole, which saw the great Bobby Jones take an 8 on this par 5 on the way to his famous Grand Slam in 1930.

Meols Dr CH47 4AL ☎ 0151 632 3101 & 632 3102 📠 0151 632 6737
e-mail: secretary@royal-liverpool-golf.com
web: www.royal-liverpool-golf.com
18 Holes, 6452yds, Par 72, SSS 71. Club membership 950.
Visitors Wed & Fri. Restricted play on other days. Booking required. Handicap certificate. Dress code.
Societies booking required. **Green Fees** Wed & Fri, May-Sep £150, Oct-Apr £120. Mon, Tue & Thu £175/£145.
Weekends & BHs £200/£170 **Course Designer** R Chambers/G Morris/D Steel **Prof** John Heggarty **Facilities** ⑪ 🏌
🛒 🍴 ⚒ 🏠 ⛳ ✦ 🏴 **Conf** Corporate Hospitality Days **Location** SW side of town on A540

room **Conf** facs Corporate Hospitality Days **Location** M62 junct 6/ M57 junct 1, take A5080 towards Huyton. Turn left at 2nd set of lights into Wheathill Rd. After 1m turn left at 1st set of lights into Childwall Valley Rd, club on right
Hotel ★★★★ 79% HL Crowne Plaza Liverpool - John Lennon Airport, Speke Aerodrome, LIVERPOOL ☎ 0151 494 5000 📄 0151 494 5000 164 en suite

West Derby Yew Tree Ln, West Derby L12 9HQ
☎ 0151 254 1034   📄 0151 259 0505
e-mail: pmilne@westderbygc.freeserve.co.uk
web: www.westderbygc.co.uk

A parkland course always in first-class condition, and flat, giving easy walking. The fairways are well-wooded. Care must be taken on the first nine holes to avoid the brook which guards many of the greens.

18 Holes, 6275yds, Par 72, SSS 70, Course record 65.
Club membership 550.

Visitors Mon, Wed-Fri except BHs. Booking required. Dress code. **Societies** booking required. **Green Fees** £38 per day **Prof** Stuart Danchin **Facilities** ⊕ ⊖ ⓘ ⌂ ⌨ ✆ ⏚ ⌗ **Conf** facs Corporate Hospitality Days **Location** 4.5m E of city centre off A57
Hotel ★★★ 80% HL The Royal, Marine Terrace, Waterloo, LIVERPOOL ☎ 0151 928 2332 📄 0151 928 2332 25 en suite

Woolton Doe Park, Speke Rd, Woolton L25 7TZ
☎ 0151 486 2298   📄 0151 486 1664
e-mail: golf@wooltongolf.co.uk
web: www.wooltongolf.co.uk

Parkland course providing a good round of golf for all standards. A members-owned course that includes two par 5s and five par 3s.

18 Holes, 5717yds, Par 69, SSS 68, Course record 63.
Club membership 600.

Visitors Mon-Fri. Limited play weekends & BHs. Booking required. Handicap certificate. Dress code. **Societies** booking required. **Green Fees** £30 per 18 holes (£40 weekends) **Prof** Dave Thompson **Facilities** ⊕ ⊖ ⓘ ⌂ ⌨ ✆ ⏚ ⌗ ⏏ **Leisure** Indoor teaching unit. **Conf** facs Corporate Hospitality Days **Location** 7m SE of city centre off A562, near Liverpool Airport
Hotel ★★★ 80% HL The Royal, Marine Terrace, Waterloo, LIVERPOOL ☎ 0151 928 2332 📄 0151 928 2332 25 en suite

NEWTON-LE-WILLOWS   Map 7 SJ59

Haydock Park Newton Ln WA12 0HX
☎ 01925 228525   📄 01925 224984
e-mail: secretary@haydockparkgc.co.uk
web: www.haydockparkgc.co.uk

A well-wooded parkland course, close to the well-known racecourse, and always in excellent condition. The pleasant undulating fairways offer some very interesting golf and the 6th, 9th, 11th and 13th holes are particularly testing.

Haydock Park Golf Club Ltd: 18 Holes, 6073yds, Par 70, SSS 69, Course record 65. Club membership 630.

Visitors Mon-Sun except BHs. Booking required. Dress code. **Societies** welcome. **Green Fees** £35 per day, £32 per round **Course Designer** James Braid **Prof** Peter Kenwright **Facilities** ⊕ ⓘ ⌂ ⌨ ✆ ⏚ ⌗ **Conf** Corporate Hospitality Days **Location** 0.75m NE off A49
Hotel ★★ 63% HL Kirkfield Hotel, 2/4 Church Street, NEWTON LE WILLOWS ☎ 01925 228196 📄 01925 228196 15 en suite

RAINHILL   Map 7 SJ49

Blundells Hill Blundells Ln L35 6NA
☎ 0151 430 9551 (secretary) & 430 0100 (pro)
📄 0151 426 5256
web: www.blundellshill.co.uk

18 Holes, 6256yds, Par 71, SSS 70, Course record 69.

Course Designer Steve Marnoch **Location** M62 junct 7, A57 towards Prescot, left after garage, 2nd left onto Blundells Ln
Telephone for further details
Hotel ★★★ 67% HL The Hillcrest Hotel, 75 Cronton Lane, WIDNES ☎ 0844 736 8610 & 0151 424 1616 📄 0844 736 8610 50 en suite

Eccleston Park Rainhill Rd L35 4PG
☎ 0151 493 0033   📄 0151 493 0044
e-mail: epgc@crown-golf.co.uk
web: www.ecclestonparkgolf.co.uk

A tough parkland course designed to test all golfing abilities. Strategically placed water features, bunkers and mounding enhance the beauty and difficulty of this manicured course.

18 Holes, 6477yds, Par 71, SSS 70. Club membership 800.

Visitors Mon-Sun & BHs. Booking required. Dress code. **Societies** booking required. **Green Fees** not confirmed **Prof** Bryan Joelson-Mulhall **Facilities** ⊕ ⊖ ⓘ ⌂ ⌨ ✆ ⏚ ⌗ ⏏ **Conf** facs Corporate Hospitality Days **Location** M62 junct 7, A57 to Prescot, at hump bridge right at lights, course 1m on left
Hotel ★★★ 67% HL The Hillcrest Hotel, 75 Cronton Lane, WIDNES ☎ 0844 736 8610 & 0151 424 1616 📄 0844 736 8610 50 en suite

ST HELENS   Map 7 SJ59

Grange Park Prescot Rd WA10 3AD
☎ 01744 26318   📄 01744 26318
e-mail: secretary@grangeparkgolfclub.co.uk
web: www.grangeparkgolfclub.co.uk

Possibly one of the finest tests of inland golf in the northwest, set in 150 acres only a short distance from the centre of town. While not too long, the contours of the fairways, small greens and penal rough demand the best from players. A wide shot making repertoire is required to gain the best score possible.

18 Holes, 6446yds, Par 72, SSS 71, Course record 65.
Club membership 730.

Visitors Dress code. **Societies** welcome. **Green Fees** not confirmed **Course Designer** James Braid **Prof** Paul Roberts **Facilities** ⊕ ⓘ ⌂ ⌨ ✆ ⏚ ⌗ **Conf** facs Corporate Hospitality Days **Location** 1.5m SW on A58
Hotel ★★ 63% HL Kirkfield Hotel, 2/4 Church Street, NEWTON LE WILLOWS ☎ 01925 228196 📄 01925 228196 15 en suite

ROYAL BIRKDALE

MERSEYSIDE - SOUTHPORT - MAP 7 SD31

Founded in 1889, the Royal Birkdale is considered by many to be the ultimate championship venue, having hosted every major event in the game including eight Open Championships, two Ryder Cup matches, the Walker Cup, the Curtis Cup and many amateur events. The 1st hole provides an immediate taste of what is to come, requiring a well-placed drive to avoid a bunker, water hazard and out-of-bounds and leave a reasonably clear view of the green. The 10th, the first of the inward nine is unique in that it is the only hole to display the significant fairway undulations one would expect from a classic links course. The 12th is the most spectacular of the short holes on the course, and is considered by Tom Watson to be one of the best par 3s in the world; tucked away in the sand hills it continues to claim its fair share of disasters. The approach on the final hole is arguably the most recognisable in golf with the distinctive clubhouse designed to appear like an ocean cruise liner rising out of the sand hills. It's a par 5 for mere mortals, and played as a par 4 in the Open, but it will provide a memorable finish to any round of golf.

Waterloo Rd, Birkdale PR8 2LX ☎ 01704 552020 📠 01704 552021
e-mail: secretary@royalbirkdale.com
web: www.royalbirkdale.com
The Royal Birkdale Golf Club: 18 Holes, 6726yds, Par 72, SSS 73. Club membership 800.
Visitors Mon, Wed, Thu, Sun & BHs. Tue pm only & Fri am only. Booking required. Handicap certificate. Dress code.
Societies booking required. **Green Fees** Apr-Sep £165 per round (£195 weekends). Winter £120/£150. Prices include soup and sandwiches **Course Designer** Hawtree **Prof** Brian Hodgkinson **Facilities** ⑪ 🍴 by prior arrangement 🔔 ⌨
🍴 ⚲ 🏠 ⛳ ⚡ 🏌 **Conf** Corporate Hospitality Days **Location** 1.75m S of town centre on A565
Hotel ★★★ 77% HL Scarisbrick, Lord Street, SOUTHPORT ☎ 01704 543000 📠 01704 543000 88 en suite

Houghwood Golf Billinge Hill, Crank Rd, Crank WA11 8RL
☎ 01744 894444 & 894754 🖷 01744 894754
e-mail: houghwoodgolf@btinternet.com
web: www.houghwoodgolfclub.co.uk

From the course's highest point, the 12th tee, there are panoramic views over the Lancashire plain to the Welsh hills. All greens built to USGA specification with a permanent track around the entire course for buggies and trolleys.

Houghwood Golf: 18 Holes, 6283yds, Par 70, SSS 70, Course record 67. Club membership 580.

Visitors Mon-Sun & BHs. Booking required. Dress code.
Societies booking required. **Green Fees** £30 per round (£40 weekends & BHs) **Course Designer** Neville Pearson **Prof** Paul Dickenson **Facilities** ⊕ ⑩ ⓛ ⬚ ⑨ ⊿ ⌂ ☕ ✧ **Leisure** snooker table **Conf** facs Corporate Hospitality Days **Location** M6, 3.5m N of St Helens off B5205
Hotel BUD Travelodge Haydock St Helens, Piele Road, HAYDOCK, St Helens ☎ 08719 846 145 🖷 08719 846 145 62 en suite

Sherdley Park Sherdley Rd WA9 5DE
☎ 01744 813149 🖷 01744 817967
e-mail: sherdleyparkgolfcourse@sthelens.gov.uk
web: www.sthelens.gov.uk
Fairly hilly, challenging, pay and play parkland course with ponds in places. Excellent greens.

Sherdley Park Golf Course: 18 Holes, 5790yds, Par 71, SSS 67.

Visitors Mon-Sun & BHs. Booking advisable. **Societies** welcome.
Green Fees not confirmed **Prof** Danny Jones **Facilities** ⊕ ⓛ ⬚ ⑨ ⊿ ⌂ ☕ ✧ ✦ **Location** 2m S of St Helens off A570
Hotel ★★ 63% HL Kirkfield Hotel, 2/4 Church Street, NEWTON LE WILLOWS ☎ 01925 228196 🖷 01925 228196 15 en suite

SOUTHPORT

Map 7 SD31

The Hesketh Cockle Dick's Ln, off Cambridge Rd PR9 9QQ
☎ 01704 536897 🖷 01704 539250
e-mail: secretary@heskethgolfclub.co.uk
web: www.heskethgolfclub.co.uk
The Hesketh is the oldest of the six clubs in Southport, founded in 1885. Set at the northern end of south-west Lancashire's dune system, the course sets a unique challenge with half of the holes threaded through tall dunes while the other holes border the Ribble estuary. The course is next to a renowned bird reserve and across the estuary are fine views of the mountains of Lancashire, Cumbria and Yorkshire. Used as a final qualifying course for the Open Championship.

18 Holes, 6685yds, Par 72, SSS 73, Course record 67. Club membership 600.

Visitors Mon, Wed-Fri, Sun & BHs. Tue & Sat am only. Booking required. Dress code. **Societies** booking required. **Green Fees** £70 per day, £55 per round (£75 per round weekends & BHs) **Course Designer** J F Morris/M Hawtree **Prof** Scott Astin **Facilities** ⊕ ⑩ ⓛ ⬚ ⑨ ⊿ ☕ ✧ ✦ **Leisure** snooker **Conf** Corporate Hospitality Days **Location** 1m NE of town centre off A565
Hotel ★★ 81% HL Cambridge House, 4 Cambridge Road, SOUTHPORT ☎ 01704 538372 🖷 01704 538372 16 en suite

Hillside Hastings Rd, Hillside PR8 2LU
☎ 01704 567169 🖷 01704 563192
e-mail: secretary@hillside-golfclub.co.uk
web: www.hillside-golfclub.co.uk
Championship links course with natural hazards open to strong wind. The back nine holes are particularly memorable.

18 Holes, 6850yds, Par 72, SSS 74, Course record 65. Club membership 700.

Visitors Mon, Thu, Fri & Sun except BHs. Tue pm only. Booking required. Handicap certificate. Dress code. **Societies** booking required. **Green Fees** not confirmed **Course Designer** Hawtree/Steel **Prof** Brian Seddon **Facilities** ⊕ ⑩ ⓛ ⬚ ⑨ ⊿ ⌂ ☕ ✧ ☕ ✧ **Conf** Corporate Hospitality Days **Location** 3m S of town centre on A565
Hotel ★★★ 77% HL Scarisbrick, Lord Street, SOUTHPORT ☎ 01704 543000 🖷 01704 543000 88 en suite

Royal Birkdale see page 183
Waterloo Rd, Birkdale PR8 2LX
☎ 01704 552020 🖷 01704 552021
e-mail: secretary@royalbirkdale.com
web: www.royalbirkdale.com

Southport & Ainsdale Bradshaws Ln, Ainsdale PR8 3LG
☎ 01704 578000 🖷 01704 570896
e-mail: secretary@sandagolfclub.co.uk
web: www.sandagolfclub.co.uk
S and A, as it is known in the north, is another of the fine championship courses for which this part of the country is famed. The club has staged many important events and offers golf of the highest order.

18 Holes, 6705yds, Par 72, SSS 74, Course record 64. Club membership 815.

Visitors contact club for details. **Societies** welcome. **Green Fees** £75 per 18 holes; £100 per 36 holes (£100 per 18 holes weekends) **Course Designer** James Braid **Prof** Jim Payne **Facilities** ⊕ ⑩ ⓛ ⬚ ⑨ ⊿ ⌂ ☕ ☕ ✧ **Conf** facs Corporate Hospitality Days **Location** 3m S off A565
Hotel ★★★ 74% HL Best Western Royal Clifton Hotel & Spa, Promenade, SOUTHPORT ☎ 01704 533771 🖷 01704 533771 120 en suite

Southport Municipal Park Road West PR9 0JR
☎ 01704 535286

18 Holes, 6400yds, Par 70, SSS 69, Course record 67.
Prof Bill Fletcher **Facilities** ⑪ 🍴 🖪 ☐ ◐ 🍴 ⚘ 🏡 ⛳ 🚜 ✓
Location N of town centre off A565
Telephone for further details
Hotel ★★★ 74% HL Best Western Royal Clifton Hotel & Spa, Promenade, SOUTHPORT ☎ 01704 533771 📄 01704 533771 120 en suite

Southport Old Links Moss Ln, Churchtown PR9 7QS
☎ 01704 228207 📄 01704 505353
e-mail: secretary@solgc.freeserve.co.uk
web: www.solgc.freeserve.co.uk

Seaside course with tree-lined fairways and easy walking. One of the oldest courses in Southport.

9 Holes, 6461yds, Par 72, SSS 71, Course record 70.
Club membership 450.

Visitors Mon, Tue, Thu-Sat except BHs. Handicap certificate. Dress code. **Societies** booking required. **Green Fees** £25 per 18 holes, £15 per 9 holes (£30/£18 Sat) **Course Designer** James Braid **Prof** Gary Copeman **Facilities** ⑪ 🍴 🖪 ☐ ◐ ⚘ 🏡 ✓
Conf Corporate Hospitality Days **Location** NW of town centre off A5267
Hotel ★★ 81% HL Cambridge House, 4 Cambridge Road, SOUTHPORT ☎ 01704 538372 📄 01704 538372 16 en suite

---

WALLASEY   Map 7 SJ29

Bidston Bidston Link Rd CH44 2HR
☎ 0151 638 3412
e-mail: linda@bidstongolf.co.uk
web: www.bidstongolf.co.uk

Flat, easy walking parkland with westerly winds.

18 Holes, 6233yds, Par 70, SSS 70. Club membership 600.
Visitors dress code. **Societies** welcome. **Green Fees** £20 per 18 holes (£30 weekends). Reduced winter rates **Prof** Alan Norwood **Facilities** ⑪ 🍴 🖪 ☐ ◐ ⚘ 🏡 🍴 ✓ **Location** M53 junct 1, 0.5m W off A551
Hotel ★★★ 77% HL Leasowe Castle, Leasowe Road, MORETON ☎ 0151 606 9191 📄 0151 606 9191 47 en suite

Leasowe Moreton CH46 3RD
☎ 0151 677 5852 📄 0151 641 8519
e-mail: secretary@leasowegolfclub.co.uk
web: www.leasowegolfclub.co.uk

Course built on well draining sand stretching along the north coast of the Wirral peninsula. Tight fairways with intimidating out of bounds are a feature of the course. This, coupled with the fine greens, gives a good test of golf for players of all levels.

18 Holes, 6276yds, Par 71, SSS 70. Club membership 637.
Visitors Sun-Fri & BHs. Booking required. Dress code.
Societies booking required. **Green Fees** £32.50 (£37.50 Sun) **Course Designer** John Ball Jnr **Prof** Andrew Ayre **Facilities** ⑪ 🍴 🖪 ☐ ◐ ⚘ 🏡 🍴 ✓ **Conf** Corporate Hospitality Days **Location** M53 junct 1, 2m W on A551
Hotel ★★★ 77% HL Leasowe Castle, Leasowe Road, MORETON ☎ 0151 606 9191 📄 0151 606 9191 47 en suite

Wallasey Bayswater Rd CH45 8LA
☎ 0151 691 1024 📄 0151 638 8988
e-mail: wallaseygc@aol.com
web: wallaseygolf.com

A well-established links course, adjacent to the Irish Sea. A true test of golf due in part to the prevailing westerly winds and the natural undulating terrain. Spectacular views across Liverpool Bay and the Welsh hills.

18 Holes, 6572yds, Par 72, SSS 72, Course record 65.
Club membership 650.

Visitors Sun-Fri & BHs. Booking required. Handicap certificate. Dress code. **Societies** welcome. **Green Fees** £85 per day, £75 per round (£100/£95 Sun & BHs) **Course Designer** Tom Morris **Prof** Mike Adams **Facilities** ⑪ 🍴 by prior arrangement 🖪 ☐ ◐ ⚘ 🏡 ✓ **Location** N of town centre, M53 junct 1, take A554 to New Brighton
Hotel ★★★ 79% HL Grove House, Grove Road, WALLASEY ☎ 0151 639 3947 & 0151 630 4558 📄 0151 639 3947 14 en suite

Warren Grove Rd CH45 0JA
☎ 0151 639 8323
e-mail: golfer@warrengc.freeserve.co.uk
web: www.warrengc.freeserve.co.uk

Short, undulating links course with first-class greens and prevailing winds off the sea.

9 Holes, 5854yds, Par 72, SSS 68, Course record 68.
Club membership 140.

Visitors Mon-Sat & BHs. Booking required. Dress code.
Societies welcome. **Green Fees** not confirmed **Prof** Mark Eagles **Facilities** 🖪 ☐ ◐ ✓ **Location** N of town centre off A554
Hotel ★★★ 77% HL Leasowe Castle, Leasowe Road, MORETON ☎ 0151 606 9191 📄 0151 606 9191 47 en suite

---

NORFOLK

BARNHAM BROOM   Map 5 TG00

Barnham Broom Hotel, Golf & Restaurant Honingham Rd NR9 4DD
☎ 01603 759552 & 759393 📄 01603 758224
e-mail: golfmanager@barnham-broom.co.uk
web: www.barnham-broom.co.uk

Course meanders through the Yare valley, parkland and mature trees. Hill course has wide fairways, heavily guarded greens and spectacular views.

Valley Course: 18 Holes, 6483yds, Par 72, SSS 71.
Hill Course: 18 Holes, 6495yds, Par 71, SSS 71.
Club membership 500.

Visitors Mon-Sun & BHs. Booking required. Dress code.
Societies welcome. **Green Fees** not confirmed **Course Designer** Frank Pennink **Prof** Ian Rollett **Facilities** ⑪ 🍴 🖪 ☐ ◐ ⚘ 🏡 🍴 ⚘ ✓ 🏸 **Leisure** hard tennis courts, heated indoor swimming pool, squash, sauna, gymnasium, 3 academy holes. Golf school. Squash tuition **Conf** facs Corporate Hospitality Days **Location** off A47 at Honingham
Hotel ★★★ 83% HL Barnham Broom Hotel, Golf & Restaurant, BARNHAM BROOM, Norwich ☎ 01603 759393 📄 01603 759393 52 en suite

ENGLAND

BAWBURGH
Map 5 TG10

Bawburgh Glen Lodge, Marlingford Rd NR9 3LU
☎ 01603 740404 📄 01603 740403
e-mail: info@bawburgh.com
web: www.bawburgh.com

Undulating course, mixture of parkland and heathland. The main feature is a large hollow that meanders down to the River Yare creating many interesting tee and green locations. Excellent 18th hole to finish requiring a long accurate second shot to clear the lake in front of the elevated green.

18 Holes, 6209yds, Par 70, SSS 70, Course record 64. Club membership 650.

Visitors Mon-Sun & BHs. Booking required. Dress code.
Societies booking required. **Green Fees** not confirmed **Course Designer** John Barnard **Prof** Chris Potter **Facilities** ⊗ ⅃ ⊇ ⅋ ⅃ ⅃ ⅃ ⅃ ⅃ ⅃ **Conf** facs Corporate Hospitality Days **Location** S of Royal Norfolk Showground, off A47 to Bawburgh
Hotel ★★★ 82% HL Park Farm, HETHERSETT ☎ 01603 810264 📄 01603 810264 53 en suite

BRANCASTER
Map 9 TF74

Royal West Norfolk PE31 8AX
☎ 01485 210087 📄 01485 210087
e-mail: secretary@rwngc.org
web: www.rwngc.org

A fine links laid out in grand manner characterised by sleepered greens, superb cross bunkers and salt marshes. The tranquil surroundings include a harbour, the sea, farmland and marshland, inhabited by many rare birds. A great part of the year the club is cut off by tidal flooding that restricts the amount of play.

18 Holes, 6428yds, Par 71, SSS 71, Course record 65. Club membership 910.

Visitors Mon-Fri except BHs. Booking required. Handicap certificate. Dress code **Societies** booking required. **Green Fees** £75 per day/round, £50 after 3pm **Course Designer** Holcombe-Ingleby **Prof** S Rayner **Facilities** ⊗ ⅃ ⊇ ⅃ ⅃ ⅃ ⅃ ⅃ ⅃ ⅃ ⅃
Location off A149 in Brancaster 1m to seafront
Hotel ★★★ 79% HL White Horse, BRANCASTER STAITHE, Norfolk ☎ 01485 210262 📄 01485 210262 15 en suite

CROMER
Map 9 TG24

Royal Cromer 145 Overstrand Rd NR27 0JH
☎ 01263 512884 📄 01263 512430
e-mail: general.manager@royal-cromer.com
web: www.royalcromergolfclub.com

Challenging course with spectacular views out to sea and overlooking the town. Strong sea breezes affect the clifftop holes, the most famous being the 14th (the Lighthouse) which has a green in the shadow of a lighthouse.

18 Holes, 6508yds, Par 72, SSS 72, Course record 67. Club membership 700.

Visitors Mon-Sun & BHs. Booking required. Handicap certificate. Dress code. **Societies** booking required. **Green Fees** not confirmed **Course Designer** J H Taylor **Prof** Lee Patterson **Facilities** ⊗ ⅃ ⅃ ⊇ ⅃ ⅃ ⅃ ⅃ ⅃ ⅃ **Location** 1m E on B1159

Hotel ★★★ 74% HL The Cliftonville, CROMER ☎ 01263 512543 📄 01263 512543 30 en suite

DENVER
Map 5 TF60

Ryston Park Ely Rd PE38 0HH
☎ 01366 382133 📄 01366 383834
e-mail: rystonparkgc@talktalkbusiness.net
web: www.club-noticeboard.co.uk

Parkland course with two challenging par 4s to open. Water comes into play on holes 5, 6 and 7. The course is well wooded with an abundance of wildlife.

Ryston Park: 9 Holes, 6138yds, Par 70, SSS 70, Course record 66. Club membership 330.

Visitors Mon-Fri except BHs. Booking required. Handicap certificate. Dress code. **Societies** booking required. **Green Fees** £35 per day, £25 per 18 holes, £15 per 9 holes **Course Designer** James Braid **Facilities** ⊗ ⅃ by prior arrangement ⅃ ⊇ ⅃ ⅃ ⅃ **Conf** facs Corporate Hospitality Days **Location** 0.5m S of Downham Market southern bypass on A10
Hotel ★★ 78% HL Castle, High Street, DOWNHAM MARKET ☎ 01366 384311 📄 01366 384311 12 en suite

DEREHAM
Map 9 TF91

Dereham Quebec Rd NR19 2DS
☎ 01362 695900 📄 01362 695904
e-mail: derehamgolfclub@dgolfclub.freeserve.co.uk
web: derehamgolfclub.com

9 hole parkland course with 17 tees.

9 Holes, 6232yds, Par 71, SSS 70, Course record 66. Club membership 480.

Visitors contact club for details. **Societies** booking required. **Green Fees** not confirmed **Prof** Neil Allsebrook **Facilities** ⊗ ⅃ ⅃ ⊇ ⅃ ⅃ ⅃ ⅃ **Conf** Corporate Hospitality Days **Location** N of town centre off B1110
Hotel ★★★ 83% HL Barnham Broom Hotel, Golf & Restaurant, BARNHAM BROOM, Norwich ☎ 01603 759393 📄 01603 759393 52 en suite

The Norfolk Golf & Country Club Hingham Rd, Reymerston NR9 4QQ
☎ 01362 850297 🖷 01362 850614
e-mail: norfolkgolfsec@ukonline.co.uk
web: www.the norfolkgolfclub.co.uk

The course meanders through more than 200 acres of rolling Norfolk countryside, including ancient ditches, hedges and woodland. Large greens built to USGA specification.

The Norfolk Golf & Country Club: 18 Holes, 6609yds, Par 72, SSS 72, Course record 66. Club membership 400.

Visitors Mon-Sun & BHs. Dress code. **Societies** booking required. **Green Fees** £25. Twilight rates available **Prof** Tony Varney **Facilities** ⓣ ⑩ 🍴 ⛳ ⚐ ≋ 👟 🏠 🚗 🚿 ⛳ **Leisure** sauna, gymnasium, pitch & putt **Conf** facs Corporate Hospitality Days **Location** off B1135

Hotel ★★★ 83% HL Barnham Broom Hotel, Golf & Restaurant, BARNHAM BROOM, Norwich ☎ 01603 759393 🖷 01603 759393 52 en suite

---

FRITTON   Map 5 TG40

Caldecott Hall Golf & Leisure Caldecott Hall, Beccles Rd NR31 9EY
☎ 01493 488488   🖷 01493 488561
web: www.caldecotthall.co.uk

Parkland/links style course with testing dog-leg fairways.
Main Course: 18 Holes, 6685yards, Par 73, SSS 72, Course record 67. Club membership 500.

Visitors Mon-Sun & BHs. Dress code. **Societies** booking required. **Green Fees** £35 per day, £25 per round (£40/£30 weekends) **Prof** Mark Tungate **Facilities** ⓣ ⑩ 🍴 ⛳ ⚐ ≋ 👟 🏠 ◇ ⛳ ⛳ **Leisure** heated indoor swimming pool, gymnasium, 18 hole par 3 course, spa **Conf** facs Corporate Hospitality Days **Location** on A143

Hotel ★★★ 78% HL Caldecott Hall Golf & Leisure, Caldecott Hall, Beccles Road, FRITTON, Great Yarmouth ☎ 01493 488488 🖷 01493 488488 8 en suite

---

GORLESTON ON SEA   Map 5 TG50

Gorleston Warren Rd NR31 6JT
☎ 01493 661911   🖷 01493 661911
e-mail: manager@gorlestongolfclub.co.uk
web: www.gorlestongolfclub.co.uk

Clifftop course, the most easterly in the British Isles. One of the outstanding features of the course is the 7th hole, which was rescued from cliff erosion about 20 years ago. The green, only 8yds from the cliff edge, is at the mercy of the prevailing winds so club selection is critical.

18 Holes, 6391yds, Par 71, SSS 71, Course record 68. Club membership 800.

Visitors Mon, Tue & Thu except BHs. Wed pm & Fri am. Handicap certificate. Dress code. **Societies** welcome. **Green Fees** £40 per day, £30 per 18 holes **Course Designer** J H Taylor **Prof** Nick Brown **Facilities** ⓣ ⑩ by prior arrangement 🍴 ⛳ ⚐ ≋ 👟 🏠 🚗 ⛳ **Conf** Corporate Hospitality Days **Location** between Gt Yarmouth and Lowestoft, signed from A12

Hotel ★★★ 67% HL Burlington Palm Hotel, 11 North Drive, GREAT YARMOUTH ☎ 01493 844568 & 842095 🖷 01493 844568 70 en suite

GREAT YARMOUTH   Map 5 TG50

Great Yarmouth & Caister Beach House, Caister-on-Sea NR30 5TD
☎ 01493 728699   🖷 01493 728831
e-mail: office@caistergolf.co.uk
web: www.caistergolf.co.uk

A traditional links-style course played over tight and undulating fairways and partly set amongst sand dunes with gorse and marram grass. Well drained with excellent greens. A challenge for golfers of all abilities.

18 Holes, 6330yds, Par 70, SSS 71, Course record 65. Club membership 700.

Visitors Mon-Sun & BHs. Booking required Tue, weekends & BHs. Handicap certificate. Dress code. **Societies** booking required. **Green Fees** £35 per day; £25 after noon (£45/£35 weekends & BHs) **Course Designer** H Colt **Prof** Martyn Clarke **Facilities** ⓣ ⑩ 🍴 ⛳ ⚐ ≋ 👟 🏠 🚿 ⛳ **Leisure** snooker **Location** 0.5m N off A149, at S end of Caister

Hotel ★★★★ ⊛ 71% HL Imperial Hotel, North Drive, GREAT YARMOUTH ☎ 01493 842000 🖷 01493 852229 39 en suite

ENGLAND

HEACHAM   Map 9 TF63

Heacham Manor Golf Club & Hotel Hunstanton Rd
PE31 7JX
☎ 01485 536030   📠 01485 533815
e-mail: golf@heacham-manor.co.uk
web: www.heacham-manor.co.uk

This Championship length course has been designed to incorporate the natural features of the of the surrounding landscape. With two rivers and four lakes to negotiate, the course varies between links and parkland styles with views of the Wash. A long course, but with a number of teeing areas on each hole the course is playable for all handicaps. The two rivers are an integral part of several holes and the lakes feature on the 7th hole which demands a long carry of 180 yards straight to the green with water all the way.

Heacham Manor Golf Club & Hotel: 18 Holes, 7075yds, Par 72. Club membership 160.

Visitors Mon-Sun & BHs. Booking required. Handicap certificate. Dress code. **Societies** booking required. **Green Fees** £50 per day, £30 per round (£35 per round weekends). Twilight after 4pm weekday £20. Winter £40/£25/£30 **Course Designer** Paul Searle **Prof** Ray Stocker **Facilities** 🏌 🍴 🍔 🖥 🥤 🏌 🏡 🍴 🛍 🛒 🏌 🏸
Leisure hard tennis courts, fishing, bowls green **Conf** facs Corporate Hospitality Days **Location** A149 from King's Lynn by-pass, straight ahead at traffic lights in Heacham, immediately before approach of hill to Hunstanton take left turning signposted Heacham, hotel on right.
Hotel 🛏 Heacham Manor Hotel, Hunstanton Rd, HEACHAM
☎ 01485 536030 & 579800 📠 01485 536030 45 en suite

See advert on opposite page

HUNSTANTON   Map 9 TF64

Hunstanton Golf Course Rd PE36 6JQ
☎ 01485 532811   📠 01485 532319
e-mail: secretary@hunstantongolfclub.com
web: www.hunstantongolfclub.com
A championship links course set among some of the natural golfing country in East Anglia. Keep out of the numerous bunkers and master the fast greens to play to your handicap - then you only have the wind to contend with. Good playing conditions all year round.

18 Holes, 6759yds, Par 72, SSS 73.
Club membership 675.

Visitors Mon-Sun except BHs. Booking required. Handicap certificate. Dress code. **Societies** booking required. **Green Fees** £80 per day, £65 after noon, £48 after 3pm (£90/£70/£55 weekends)

Course Designer James Braid **Prof** James Dodds **Facilities** 🍴 🍔 🖥 🥤 🏌 🏡 🍴 🛍 🏌 🚗 🏌 **Location** off A149 in Old Hunstanton, signed
Hotel ★★★ 82% HL Best Western Le Strange Arms, Golf Course Road, Old Hunstanton, HUNSTANTON ☎ 01485 534411 📠 01485 534411 36 en suite

Hotel ★★ 78% HL Lifeboat Inn, Ship Lane, THORNHAM
☎ 01485 512236 📠 01485 512323 13 en suite

Searles Leisure Resort South Beach Rd PE36 5BB
☎ 01485 536010   📠 01485 533815
e-mail: golf@searles.co.uk
web: www.searles.co.uk

This nine-hole par 34 course is designed in a links style and provides generous fairways with good greens. A river runs through the 3rd and 4th holes and the par 5 8th follows the ancient reed bed to finish with the lake-sided par 3 9th in front of the clubhouse. Good views of Hunstanton and the surrounding countryside and a challenge for all standards of golfer.

Searles Leisure Resort: 9 Holes, 2773yds, Par 34, SSS 33.
Club membership 200.

continued

Visitors Mon-Sun & BHs. Bbooking required. Handicap certificate. Dress code. **Societies** welcome. **Green Fees** 18 holes £16, 9 holes £10 (£17.50/£11 weekends & BHs) **Course Designer** Prof Ray Stocker/Mitch Kierstenson **Facilities** ⑪ 🏌 ♿ ➗ 🎱 ⚐ 🏖 🍴 ♦ 🏌 ♦ 🏃 **Leisure** hard tennis courts, outdoor and indoor heated swimming pool, fishing, sauna, gymnasium, bowls green **Conf** facs Corporate Hospitality Days **Location** A149 N to Hunstanton, 2nd left at rdbt, over minirdbt, 1st left signed Sports and Country Club

Hotel ★★★ 82% HL Best Western Le Strange Arms, Golf Course Road, Old Hunstanton, HUNSTANTON ☎ 01485 534411 🖹 01485 534411 36 en suite

KING'S LYNN   Map 9 TF62

Eagles 39 School Rd, Tilney All Saints PE34 4RS
☎ 01553 827147   🖹 01553 829777
e-mail: shop@eagles-golf-tennis.co.uk
web: www.eagles-golf-tennis.co.uk
Parkland with a variety of trees and shrubs lining the fairways. A large area of water comes into play on several holes.

Eagles Golf Centre: 9 Holes, 4284yds, Par 64, SSS 61, Course record 64. Club membership 200.

Visitors Dress code. **Societies** welcome. **Green Fees** 18 holes £16.50, 9 holes £12 (£18.50/£13 weekends & BHs). Par 3 18 holes £8.50, 9 holes £5.80 **Course Designer** D W Horn **Prof** Nigel Pickerell **Facilities** ⑪ by prior arrangement 🍴 🏌 ♿ 🍴 ♿ 🏖 ⚐ ♦ 🏃 **Leisure** par 3 course **Conf** Corporate Hospitality Days **Location** off A47 at rdbt to Tilney All Saints, between Kings Lynn & Wisbech

Hotel ★★★ 70% HL Stuart House, 35 Goodwins Road, KINGS LYNN ☎ 01553 772169 🖹 01553 772169 18 en suite

King's Lynn Castle Rising PE31 6BD
☎ 01553 631654   🖹 01553 631036
e-mail: secretary@kingslynngc.co.uk
web: www.club-noticeboard.co.uk

The course is set among silver birch and fir woodland and benefits, especially in the winter, from well-drained sandy soil.

18 Holes, 6609yds, Par 72, SSS 73, Course record 64. Club membership 850.

Visitors contact club for details. **Societies** welcome. **Green Fees** not confirmed **Course Designer** Thomas & Alliss **Prof** John Reynolds **Facilities** ⑪ 🍴 🏌 ♿ 🍴 ♿ 🏖 ♦ 🏖 ♦ 🏃 **Leisure** Snooker **Conf** facs Corporate Hospitality Days **Location** 4m NE off A149

Hotel ★★★ 78% HL Best Western Knights Hill, Knights Hill Village, South Wootton, KING'S LYNN ☎ 01553 675566 🖹 01553 675566 79 en suite

MATTISHALL   Map 9 TG01

Mattishall South Green NR20 3JZ
☎ 01362 850111
Mattishall has the distinction of having the longest hole in Norfolk at a very demanding 638 yd par 5.

Mattishall Golf Course: 9 Holes, 3099yds, Par 36, SSS 35. Club membership 120.

Visitors Mon-Fri except BHs. Dress code. **Societies** booking required. **Green Fees** £20 per day, £14 per 18 holes, £10 per 9 holes **Course Designer** B Todd **Facilities** ♿ 🍴 🏖 ⚐ 🏖 ♦ **Location** 0.75m S of Mattishall Church

Hotel ★★★ 83% HL Barnham Broom Hotel, Golf & Restaurant, BARNHAM BROOM, Norwich ☎ 01603 759393 🖹 01603 759393 52 en suite

MIDDLETON   Map 9 TF61

Middleton Hall Hall Orchards PE32 1RY
☎ 01553 841800 & 841801   🖹 01553 841800
e-mail: enquiries@middletonhallgolfclub.com
web: www.middletonhallgolfclub.com
Natural undulations and mature specimen trees offer a most attractive environment for golf. The architecturally designed course provides a challenge for the competent golfer; there is also a covered floodlit driving range.

18 Holes, 5392yds, Par 71, SSS 67. Club membership 500.

continued

Visitors Mon-Sun & BHs. Dress code. **Societies** booking required. **Green Fees** £40 per day, £25 per round (£40/£30 weekends & BHs) **Course Designer** D Scott **Prof** Steve White **Facilities** ⓘ ⓘ ⓛ ⓓ 🏌 ⚄ 🏠 ⚑ ⚐ 🚗 ⚑ **Conf** Corporate Hospitality Days **Location** 4m from King's Lynn on A47 towards Norwich **Hotel** ★★★ CHH Congham Hall Country House Hotel, Lynn Road, GRIMSTON, King's Lynn ☎ 01485 600250 🖩 01485 600250 14 en suite

MUNDESLEY   Map 9 TG33

Mundesley Links Rd NR11 8ES
☎ 01263 720095   🖩 01263 722849
web: www.mundesleygolfclub.co.uk

Mundesley Golf Club Ltd: 9 Holes, 5377yds, Par 68, SSS 66, Course record 64.

Course Designer Harry Vardon **Location** W of village off B1159 **Telephone for further details** **Hotel** ★★ 78% HL Red Lion, Brook Street, CROMER ☎ 01263 514964 🖩 01263 514964   12 en suite

NORWICH   Map 5 TG20

Costessey Park Old Costessey NR8 5AL
☎ 01603 746333 & 747085   🖩 01603 746185
e-mail: cpgc@ljgroup.com
web: www.costesseypark.com

The course lies in the gently contoured Tud valley, providing players with a number of holes that bring the river and man-made lakes into play. The 1st hole starts a round with a par 3 that requires an accurate drive across the river, to land the ball on a sculptured green beside a reed fringed lake. To end the round at the 18th hole, you need to make a straight drive past the ruined belfry to allow a second shot back over the river to land the ball on a recessed green.

Costessey Park Golf Course: 18 Holes, 5881yds, Par 71, SSS 69, Course record 63. Club membership 200.

Visitors contact course for details. **Societies** welcome. **Green Fees** not confirmed **Prof** Andrew Young **Facilities** ⓘ ⓘ ⓛ ⓓ 🏌 ⚄ ⚑ 🚗 ⚑ **Conf** Corporate Hospitality Days **Location** 4.5m NW of Norwich. A1074 onto Longwater Ln, left onto West End, club on left **Hotel** ★★ 85% HL Stower Grange, School Road, Drayton, NORWICH ☎ 01603 860210 🖩 01603 860210   11 en suite

De Vere Dunston Hall Hotel Ipswich Rd NR14 8PQ
☎ 01508 470444   🖩 01508 471499
web: www.devereonline.co.uk

De Vere Dunston Hall Hotel: 18 Holes, 6300yds, Par 71, SSS 70, Course record 68.

Course Designer M Shaw **Location** on A140 **Telephone for further details** **Hotel** ★★★★ 78% HL De Vere Dunston Hall, Ipswich Road, NORWICH ☎ 01508 470444 🖩 01508 470444   169 en suite

Eaton Newmarket Rd NR4 6SF
☎ 01603 451686   🖩 01603 457539
e-mail: admin@eatongc.co.uk
web: www.eatongc.co.uk

An undulating, tree-lined parkland course. Easy opening par 5 followed by an intimidating par 3 that is well bunkered with deep rough on both sides. Many rate the par 4 3rd as one of the best holes in the county with its elevated tee and undulating fairways. The challenging 17th hole is uphill to a small hidden green and always needs more club than expected.

18 Holes, 6118yds, Par 70, SSS 70, Course record 64. Club membership 800.

Visitors Mon-Sun & BHs. Booking required. Handicap certificate. Dress code. **Societies** booking required. **Green Fees** not confirmed **Course Designer** J H Taylor **Prof** Mark Allen **Facilities** ⓘ ⓘ ⓛ ⓓ 🏌 ⚄ 🏠 ⚑ **Location** 1.5m SW of city centre off A11 **Hotel** ★★★ 82% HL Park Farm, HETHERSETT ☎ 01603 810264 🖩 01603 810264   53 en suite

Marriott Sprowston Manor Hotel & Country Club
Wroxham Rd NR7 8RP
☎ 01603 410871   🖩 01603 423911
web: www.marriottsprowstonmanor.co.uk

Set in 100 acres of parkland, including an impressive collection of oak trees that provide a backdrop to many holes. The signature hole is the 7th, a dog leg par 4 with tricky weirs and a difficult approach. The course benefits from USGA specification tees and greens.

Marriott Sprowston Manor Hotel & Country Club: 18 Holes, 6464yds, Par 71, SSS 71, Course record 64. Club membership 500.

Visitors Mon-Sun & BHs. Booking required. Dress code. **Societies** booking required. **Green Fees** £35 per 18 holes (£40 weekends & BHs) **Course Designer** Ross McMurray **Prof** Guy Ireson **Facilities** ⓘ ⓘ ⓛ ⓓ 🏌 ⚄ ⚑ 🏠 ⚑ ⚐ 🚗 ⚑ 🏌

continued

Leisure heated indoor swimming pool, sauna, gymnasium **Conf** facs
Corporate Hospitality Days **Location** 4m NE from city centre on A1151,
signed
Hotel ★★ SHL The Old Rectory, 103 Yarmouth Road, Thorpe St
Andrew, NORWICH ☎ 01603 700772 📠 01603 700772 8 en suite

Royal Norwich Drayton High Rd, Hellesdon NR6 5AH
☎ 01603 429928 & 408459 📠 01603 417945
e-mail: mail@royalnorwichgolf.co.uk
web: www.royalnorwichgolf.co.uk

Undulating mature parkland course complimented with gorse. Largely
unchanged since the alterations carried out by James Braid in 1924. A
challenging test of golf.

18 Holes, 6506yds, Par 72, SSS 72, Course record 65.
Club membership 630.

Visitors Mon-Sun & BHs. Handicap certificate. Dress code.
Societies booking required. **Green Fees** £48 per day, £30 per round
Course Designer James Braid **Prof** Simon Youd **Facilities** ⓣ ⓞ
by prior arrangement 🏌 🏳 🍴 🎿 🏠 🚌 🏌 **Conf** Corporate
Hospitality Days **Location** 2.5m NW of city centre on A1067
Hotel ★★★ 78% HL Ramada Norwich, 121-131 Boundary Road,
NORWICH ☎ 01603 787260 📠 01603 787260 107 en suite

Wensum Valley Hotel, Golf & Country Club Beech Av, Taverham NR8 6HP
☎ 01603 261012 📠 01603 261664
e-mail: enqs@wensumvalleyhotel.co.uk
web: www.wensumvalleyhotel.co.uk

Two picturesque and contrasting courses set in 350 acres of the
attractive Wensum Valley and designed and built to compliment the
natural landscape. The shorter Valley course has narrow fairways
with strategic bunkers to catch any loose drive. The greens, although
generous in size, have some interesting undulations, putting a
premium on iron play. The Wensum course has smaller well protected
greens making approach play tricky. The 7th hole is a short par 3 that
plays onto an island green over the river, which also comes into play
throughout the 8th and 16th holes.

Valley Course: 18 Holes, 6223yds, Par 72, SSS 70,
Course record 68.
Wensum Course: 18 Holes, 6922yds, Par 72, SSS 73.
Club membership 500.

Visitors Mon-Sun & BHs. Dress code. **Societies** welcome. **Green
Fees** £30 per day/ £25 per round inc bar meal. Twilight £15 **Course
Designer** B Todd **Facilities** ⓣ ⓞ 🏌 🏳 🍴 🎿 🏠 🌂 ◇
🚌 🏌 ☘ **Leisure** heated indoor swimming pool, fishing, sauna,
gymnasium **Conf** facs Corporate Hospitality Days **Location** 5m N of
Norwich off A1067
Hotel ★★ 85% HL Stower Grange, School Road, Drayton, NORWICH
☎ 01603 860210 📠 01603 860210 11 en suite

SHERINGHAM   Map 9 TG14

Sheringham Weybourne Rd NR26 8HG
☎ 01263 823488 📠 01263 826129
e-mail: info@sheringhamgolfclub.co.uk
web: www.sheringhamgolfclub.co.uk

The course is laid out along a rolling, gorse-clad cliff top from where
the sea is visible on every hole. The par 4 holes are outstanding with
a fine view along the cliffs from the 5th tee.

18 Holes, 6456yds, Par 70, SSS 71, Course record 64.
Club membership 760.

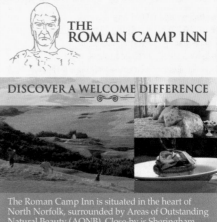
Visitors Mon-Sun & BHs. Booking required. Handicap certificate.
Dress code. **Societies** booking required. **Green Fees** phone **Course
Designer** Tom Dunn **Prof** M W Jubb **Facilities** ⓣ ⓞ 🏌 🏳
🍴 🎿 🏠 🌂 🏌 🚌 🏌 **Conf** Corporate Hospitality Days
Location W of town centre on A149
Hotel ★★★ 78% SHL Roman Camp Inn, Holt Road, Aylmerton,
SHERINGHAM ☎ 01263 838291 📠 01263 838291 15 en suite

See advert on this page

SWAFFHAM
Map 5 TF80

Swaffham Cley Rd PE37 8AE
☎ 01760 721621 📠 01760 721621
e-mail: manager@swaffhamgc.co.uk
web: www.club-noticeboard.co.uk
Heathland course and designated wildlife site in the heart of breckland country. Excellent drainage.

18 Holes, 6525yds, Par 71, SSS 71. Club membership 600.
Visitors Mon-Fri. Limited play weekends & BHs. Booking required. Dress code. **Societies** booking required. **Green Fees** £50 for 36 holes, £30 for 18 holes **Course Designer** Jonathan Gaunt **Prof** Peter Field
Facilities ⊕ ⦿ ⓑ ☐ ☜ ⚒ ♨ 🏊 ⚑ 🛒 ✓ **Location** 1.5m SW of town centre
Hotel ★★★ 74% HL Best Western George Hotel, Station Road, SWAFFHAM ☎ 01760 721238 📠 01760 721238 29 en suite

THETFORD
Map 5 TL88

Feltwell Thor Ave (off Wilton Rd), Feltwell IP26 4AY
☎ 01842 827644 📠 01842 829065
e-mail: sec.feltwellgc@virgin.net
web: www.club-noticeboard.co.uk/feltwell
Inland links course with quality fairways and greens. Well drained for winter play.

9 Holes, 6488yds, Par 72, SSS 71, Course record 71. Club membership 320.
Visitors contact club for details. **Societies** booking required. **Green Fees** £20 per day (£30 weekends & BHs) **Prof** Jonathan Moore
Facilities ⊕ ⦿ ⓑ ☐ ☜ ⚒ ♨ ⚑ ✓ 🍴 **Conf** Corporate Hospitality Days **Location** on B1112 next to RAF Feltwell
Hotel ★★ 68% HL The Thomas Paine Hotel, White Hart Street, THETFORD ☎ 01842 755631 📠 01842 755631 13 en suite

Thetford Brandon Rd IP24 3NE
☎ 01842 752169 📠 01842 766212
e-mail: thetfordgolfclub@btconnect.com
web: www.club-noticeboard.com/thetford
The course has a good pedigree. It was laid out by the fine golfer CH Mayo, later altered by James Braid and then again altered by another famous course designer, Mackenzie Ross. It is a testing heathland course with a particularly stiff finish.

18 Holes, 6849yds, Par 72, SSS 73, Course record 66. Club membership 750.
Visitors contact club for details. **Societies** welcome. **Green Fees** not confirmed **Course Designer** James Braid **Prof** Gary Kitley
Facilities ⊕ ⦿ ⓑ ☐ ☜ ⚒ ♨ ⚑ ✓ **Leisure** short game area **Location** 2m W of Thetford on B1107
Hotel ★★ 68% HL The Thomas Paine Hotel, White Hart Street, THETFORD ☎ 01842 755631 📠 01842 755631 13 en suite

WATTON
Map 5 TF90

Richmond Park Saham Rd IP25 6EA
☎ 01953 881803 📠 01953 881817
e-mail: info@richmondpark.co.uk
web: www.richmondpark.co.uk
Compact parkland course with mature and young trees set around the Little Wissey river and spread over 100 acres of Norfolk countryside. The river and other water hazards create an interesting but not daunting challenge.

18 Holes, 6300yds, Par 71, SSS 70, Course record 69. Club membership 600.
Visitors Mon-Sun & BHs. Handicap certificate. Dress code.
Societies booking required. **Green Fees** £45 per day, £30 per round (£45 per day/round weekends & BHs) **Course Designer** D Jessup/D Scott **Facilities** ⊕ ⦿ ⓑ ☐ ☜ ⚒ ♨ 🏊 ◇ 🛒 ✓ ⚑
Conf facs Corporate Hospitality Days **Location** 500yds NW of town centre
Hotel ★★★ 74% HL Best Western George Hotel, Station Road, SWAFFHAM ☎ 01760 721238 📠 01760 721238 29 en suite

WEST RUNTON
Map 9 TG14

Links Country Park Hotel & Golf Club NR27 9QH
☎ 01263 838675 📠 01263 838264
e-mail: garypottergolf@hotmail.co.uk
web: www.links-hotel.co.uk
Parkland course 500yds from the sea, with superb views overlooking West Runton.

Links Country Park Hotel & Golf Club: 9 Holes, 4842yds, Par 66, SSS 64, Course record 64. Club membership 250.
Visitors Mon-Sun & BHs. Booking required weekends & BHs. Dress code. **Societies** booking required. **Green Fees** £35 per day/round, Twilight £20 summer after 4pm, winter £15 after 1pm **Course Designer** J.H Taylor **Prof** Gary Potter **Facilities** ⊕ ⦿ ⓑ ☐ ☜ ⚒ ♨ ⓑ ⚑ ◇ ✓ 🛒 ✓ **Leisure** hard tennis courts, heated indoor swimming pool, sauna, gymnasium **Conf** facs Corporate Hospitality Days **Location** S of village off A149
Hotel ★★ 79% HL Beaumaris, South Street, SHERINGHAM ☎ 01263 822370 📠 01263 822370 21 en suite

WESTON LONGVILLE
Map 9 TG11

Weston Park NR9 5JW
☎ 01603 872363 📠 01603 873040
e-mail: golf@weston-park.co.uk
web: www.weston-park.co.uk
Superb, challenging course, set in 200 acres of magnificent, mature woodland and parkland.

Weston Park Golf Club Ltd: 18 Holes, 6648yds, Par 72, SSS 72, Course record 67. Club membership 580.
Visitors Mon-Sun & BHs. Booking required. Handicap certificate. Dress code. **Societies** booking required. **Green Fees** £50 per day, £40 per 18 holes (£42 weekends) **Course Designer** Golf Technology **Prof** Michael Few **Facilities** ⊕ ⓑ ☐ ☜ ⚒ ♨ 🏊 ✓ 🛒
✓ **Leisure** hard tennis courts, croquet lawn **Conf** facs Corporate Hospitality Days **Location** brown tourist signs off A1067 or A47
Hotel ★★ 72% HL Old Brewery House, Market Place, REEPHAM ☎ 01603 870881 📠 01603 870881 23 en suite

NORTHAMPTONSHIRE

CHACOMBE
Map 4 SP44

Cherwell Edge OX17 2EN
☎ 01295 711591 📠 01295 713674
e-mail: enquiries@cherwelledgegolfclub.co.uk
web: www.cherwelledgegolfclub.co.uk

Parkland course over chalk giving good drainage. The back nine is short and tight with mature trees. The front nine is longer and more open. The course is well bunkered with three holes where water can catch the wayward golfer.

18 Holes, 6092yds, Par 70, SSS 69, Course record 64. Club membership 500.

Visitors Mon–Sun & BHs. Booking required. Dress code.
Societies booking required. **Green Fees** £20 per 18 holes (£25 weekends) **Course Designer** R Davies **Prof** Jason Newman
Facilities ⑪ 🍴 🏌 ⏰ 🍺 ⚐ 🏠 ➔ 🏆 🏌 ⚐ 🏆
Conf facs Corporate Hospitality Days **Location** M40 junct 11, 0.5m S off B4525, 2m from Banbury
Hotel ★★★ 77% HL Mercure Whately Hall, Banbury Cross, BANBURY ☎ 01295 253261 📠 01295 253261 69 en suite

COLD ASHBY
Map 4 SP67

Cold Ashby Stanford Rd NN6 6EP
☎ 01604 740548
e-mail: info@coldashbygolfclub.com
web: www.coldashbygolfclub.com

Undulating parkland course, nicely matured, with superb views. The 27 holes consist of three loops of nine, which can be interlinked with each other. All three loops have their own challenge and any combination of two loops will give an excellent course. The start of the Elkington loop offers five holes of scenic beauty and testing golf and the 3rd on the Winwick loop is a 200yd par 3 from a magnificent plateau tee.

Ashby-Elkington: 18 Holes, 6308yds, Par 72, SSS 71, Course record 67.
Elkington-Winwick: 18 Holes, 6293yds, Par 70, SSS 71, Course record 67.
Winwick-Ashby: 18 Holes, 6047yds, Par 70, SSS 70, Course record 64. Club membership 500.

Visitors Mon–Sun & BHs. Booking required weekends & BHs. Dress code. **Societies** booking required **Green Fees** £19 per round (£24 weekends & BHs) **Course Designer** David Croxton **Prof** Shane Rose
Facilities ⑪ 🍴 🏌 ⏰ 🍺 ⚐ 🏠 ➔ 🏆 🏌 ⚐ 🏆
Conf facs Corporate Hospitality Days **Location** M1 junct 18 or A14 junct 1
Hotel BUD Ibis Rugby East, Parklands, CRICK ☎ 01788 824331 📠 01788 824331 111 en suite

COLLINGTREE
Map 4 SP75

Collingtree Park Windingbrook Ln NN4 0XN
☎ 01604 700000 & 701202 📠 01604 702600
e-mail: info@collingtreeparkgolf.com
web: www.collingtreeparkgolf.com

An 18-hole resort course designed by former US and British Open champion Johnny Miller. The American-style course has water hazards on 10 holes with a spectacular par 5 18th Island Green.

Collingtree Park Golf Course: 18 Holes, 6776yds, Par 72, SSS 72, Course record 66. Club membership 660.
Visitors Mon–Sun & BHs. Booking required. Handicap certificate. Dress code. **Societies** booking required. **Green Fees** phone **Course Designer** Johnny Miller **Prof** G Pook/B Mudge **Facilities** ⑪ 🍴 🏌 ⏰ 🍺 🏠 ➔ 🚌 🏆 🏆 **Leisure** fishing **Conf** facs Corporate Hospitality Days **Location** M1 junct 15, on A508 to Northampton

Collingtree Park

Hotel ★★★★ 73% HL Northampton Marriott Hotel, Eagle Drive, NORTHAMPTON ☎ 01604 768700 📠 01604 768700 120 en suite

See advert on this page

CORBY
Map 4 SP88

Corby Public Stamford Rd, Weldon NN17 3JH
☎ 01536 260756 🗎 01536 260756
web: www.phgc.org
Parkland course with generous fairways, mature trees and 58 bunkers.

Corby Public Golf Course: 18 Holes, 6677yds, Par 72, SSS 72, Course record 68. Club membership 600.

Visitors contact course for details. **Societies** booking required. **Green Fees** £15 for 18 holes (£19.50 weekends) **Course Designer** F Hawtree **Prof** Jeff Bradbrook **Facilities** ⑦ ⑪ 🗟 ♆ 🍴 🎿 🛋 ⛳ ✐ 🚗 ✐ **Conf** Corporate Hospitality Days **Location** 4m NE on A43
Hotel ★★★ 72% HL Holiday Inn Corby-Kettering A43, Geddington Road, CORBY ☎ 01536 401020 🗎 01536 401020 105 en suite

DAVENTRY
Map 4 SP56

Daventry & District Norton Rd NN11 2LS
☎ 01327 702829
e-mail: ddgc@hotmail.co.uk
web: www.ddgc.co.uk
An undulatory course providing panoramic views and whose tight fairways and small fast greens with large borrows provide a good test of golf.

9 Holes, 5812yds, Par 69, SSS 68, Course record 62. Club membership 285.

Visitors Mon-Sat & BHs. Sun after 10.30pm. Dress code.
Societies booking required. **Green Fees** £15 per day (£20 weekends) **Facilities** ♆ 🍴 🎿 **Conf** facs **Location** 0.5m E of Daventry
Hotel ★★★★ 72% HL Barceló Daventry Hotel, Sedgemoor Way, DAVENTRY ☎ 01327 307000 🗎 01327 307000 155 en suite

FARTHINGSTONE
Map 4 SP65

Farthingstone Hotel & Golf Course Everdon Rd NN12 8HA
☎ 01327 361291 🗎 01327 361645
web: www.farthingstone.co.uk

A mature and challenging course set in picturesque countryside. Woodland, water, naturally sweeping fairways and carefully crafted greens make for a memorable golfing experience.

Farthingstone Hotel & Golf Course: 18 Holes, 6299yds, Par 70, SSS 70, Course record 68. Club membership 350.

Visitors Mon-Sun & BHs. Dress code. **Societies** welcome. **Green Fees** Mon-Thu £32 per day, £20 per 18 holes, £12.50 per 9 holes, Fri £35/£22/£15. Weekends before 10am £50 per day, £35 per 18 holes, after 10am £40 per day, £28 per 18 holes, £17 per 9 holes **Course Designer** Don Donaldson **Prof** Mike Gallagher **Facilities** ⑦ ⑪ 🗟

♆ 🍴 🎿 🛋 ⛳ ♢ ✐ 🚗 ✐ 🏌 **Leisure** squash, Snooker room **Conf** facs Corporate Hospitality Days **Location** M1 junct 16, W near Farthingstone
Hotel ★★★★ HL Fawsley Hall, Fawsley, DAVENTRY ☎ 01327 892000 🗎 01327 892000 58 en suite

HELLIDON
Map 4 SP55

Hellidon Lakes Golf & Spa Hotel NN11 6GG
☎ 01327 262550 🗎 01327 262559
e-mail: hellidonlakesreservations@qhotels.co.uk
web: www.qhotels.co.uk

Nestling in its own peaceful valley, a course of 27 holes running through 220 acres and designed to test golfers of all levels. From the elevated position of the first tee, the eye can wander over the shimmering lakes below, which are a highlight of the course. Many of the holes feature water hazards offering the choice of challenging carries for the bold and daring or safer routes for the less adventurous.

Red & Blue: 18 Holes, 6082yds, Par 72, SSS 71. Club membership 209.

Visitors Mon-Sun & BHs. Booking required. Handicap certificate. Dress code. **Societies** booking required. **Green Fees** £35 per 18 holes (£40 weekends). Nov-Mar £17.50/£25 **Course Designer** D Snell **Prof** Joe Kingston **Facilities** ⑦ ⑪ 🗟 ♆ 🍴 🎿 🛋 ⛳ ♢ 🚗 ✐ 🏌 **Leisure** hard tennis courts, heated indoor swimming pool, fishing, sauna, gymnasium **Conf** facs Corporate Hospitality Days **Location** off A361 into Hellidon, 2nd right
Hotel ★★★★ 70% HL Hellidon Lakes Golf & Spa Hotel, HELLIDON ☎ 01327 262550 🗎 01327 262550 110 en suite

KETTERING
Map 4 SP87

Kettering Headlands NN15 6XA
☎ 01536 511104 🗎 01536 523788
e-mail: secretary@kettering-golf.co.uk
web: www.kettering-golf.co.uk
A mature woodland course with gentle slopes established in 1891. Easy walking.

18 Holes, 6057yds, Par 69, SSS 69, Course record 63. Club membership 600.

Visitors Mon-Fri except BHs. Dress code. **Societies** booking required. **Green Fees** £36 per round. **Course Designer** Tom Morris **Prof** Kevin Theobald **Facilities** ⑦ ⑪ 🗟 ♆ 🍴 🎿 ✐ 🚗 ✐ **Conf** facs Corporate Hospitality Days **Location** A14 junct 8, take A43 towards Kettering and follow golf club signs
Hotel ★★★★ 80% HL Kettering Park Hotel & Spa, Kettering Parkway, KETTERING ☎ 01536 416666 🗎 01536 416666 119 en suite

Pytchley Golf Lodge Kettering Rd, Pytchley NN14 1EY
☎ 01536 511527 📠 01536 790266
e-mail: info@pytchleygolflodgekettering.co.uk
web: www.pytchleygolflodgekettering.co.uk
Academy nine-hole pay and play course, offering a challenge to both experienced and novice players.

Pytchley Golf Lodge: 9 Holes, 2574yards, Par 34, SSS 65, Course record 70. Club membership 200.

Visitors contact course for details. **Societies** welcome. **Green Fees** not confirmed **Course Designer** Roger Griffiths Associates **Prof** Peter Machin **Facilities** 🍴 🛒 🖥 🏌 🏪 ⛳ ✦ **Location** A14 junct 9, A509 towards Kettering signed
Hotel ★★★ 80% HL Kettering Park Hotel & Spa, Kettering Parkway, KETTERING ☎ 01536 416666 📠 01536 416666
119 en suite

NORTHAMPTON   Map 4 SP76

Brampton Heath Sandy Ln, Church Brampton NN6 8AX
☎ 01604 843939 📠 01604 843885
e-mail: crose@bhgc.co.uk
web: www.bhgc.co.uk
Appealing to both the novice and experienced golfer, this beautiful, well drained heathland course affords panoramic views over Northampton. It plays like an inland links in the summer - fast running fairways, true rolling greens with the wind always providing a challenge. Excellent play all year round.

Brampton Heath Golf Centre: 18 Holes, 6533yds, Par 72, SSS 71, Course record 66. Club membership 500.

Visitors Mon-Sun & BHs. Dress code. **Societies** welcome. **Green Fees** £20 per round, £13 for 9 holes (£25/£16 weekends & BHs) **Course Designer** D Snell **Facilities** 🍴 🛒 🖥 🏌 🏪 ⛳ ✦ 🏪 ✦ **Leisure** 9 hole short course (814 yds) **Conf** facs Corporate Hospitality Days **Location** signed off A5199 2m N of Kingsthorpe
Hotel ★★★ 71% HL Best Western Lime Trees, 8 Langham Place, Barrack Road, NORTHAMPTON ☎ 01604 632188 📠 01604 632188
28 en suite

Delapre Golf Complex Eagle Dr, Nene Valley Way NN4 7DU
☎ 01604 764036 📠 01604 706378
e-mail: delapre@jbgolf.co.uk
web: www.jackbarker.com
Rolling parkland course, part of a pay and play golf complex, which includes two nine-hole par 3 courses, pitch and putt, and a 40-bay floodlit driving range.

The Oaks: 18 Holes, 6269yds, Par 70, SSS 70, Course record 66.
Hardingstone Course: 9 Holes, 2109yds, Par 32. Club membership 500.

Visitors contact centre for details. **Societies** welcome. **Green Fees** phone **Course Designer** John Jacobs/John Corby **Prof** J Cuddihy/M Chapman/P Machin **Facilities** 🍴 🛒 🖥 🏌 🏪 ⛳ 🏪 ✦ 🏪 **Leisure** two 9 hole par 3 courses **Conf** facs Corporate Hospitality Days **Location** M1 junct 15, 3m on A508/A45
Hotel ★★★★ 73% HL Northampton Marriott Hotel, Eagle Drive, NORTHAMPTON ☎ 01604 768700 📠 01604 768700 120 en suite

Kingsthorpe Kingsley Rd NN2 7BU
☎ 01604 710610 📠 01604 710610
e-mail: secretary@kingsthorpe-golf.co.uk
web: www.kingsthorpe-golf.co.uk
A compact, undulating parkland course set within the town boundary. Not a long course but the undulating terrain provides a suitable challenge for golfers of all standards. The 18th hole is claimed to be the longest 400yds in the county when played into the wind and is among the finest finishing holes in the area.

18 Holes, 5903yds, Par 69, SSS 69, Course record 63. Club membership 550.

Visitors Mon-Fri, Sun & BHs. Booking required. Handicap certificate. Dress code. **Societies** booking required. **Green Fees** £40 per day, £30 per round. £25 per round winter **Course Designer** Mr Alison/ H Colt **Prof** Paul Armstrong **Facilities** 🍴 🛒 🖥 🏌 🏪 ✦ **Conf** Corporate Hospitality Days **Location** N of town centre on A5095 between Kingsthorpe and racecourse
Hotel ★★★ 71% HL Best Western Lime Trees, 8 Langham Place, Barrack Road, NORTHAMPTON ☎ 01604 632188 📠 01604 632188
28 en suite

Northampton Harlestone NN7 4EF
☎ 01604 845155 📠 01604 820262
e-mail: golf@northamptongolfclub.co.uk
web: www.northamptongolfclub.co.uk
Parkland with water in play on four holes.

18 Holes, 6615yds, Par 72, SSS 72, Course record 63. Club membership 750.

Visitors Mon, Tue, Thu & Fri except BHs. Wed after 3pm. Handicap certificate. Dress code. **Societies** booking required. **Green Fees** phone **Course Designer** Sinclair Steel **Prof** Barry Randall **Facilities** 🍴 🍴 by prior arrangement 🛒 🖥 🏌 🏪 ✦ 🏪 ✦ **Conf** facs Corporate Hospitality Days **Location** NW of town centre on A428
Hotel ★★★ 71% HL Best Western Lime Trees, 8 Langham Place, Barrack Road, NORTHAMPTON ☎ 01604 632188 📠 01604 632188
28 en suite

Northamptonshire County Golf Ln, Church Brampton NN6 8AZ
☎ 01604 843025 📠 01604 843463
e-mail: secretary@countygolfclub.org.uk
web: www.countygolfclub.org
A fine, traditional championship course situated on undulating heathland with areas of gorse, heather and extensive coniferous and deciduous woodland. A river and a railway line pass through the course and there is a great variety of holes. There are three additional holes providing a 9 hole loop returning to the clubhouse, for those wishing to play 9 or 27 holes. The club celebrated its centenary in 2009.

18 Holes, 6721yds, Par 70, SSS 73, Course record 65. Club membership 750.

Visitors Mon, Wed-Sun & BHs. Limited play Tue. Handicap certificate. Dress code. Handicap certificate. **Societies** welcome. **Green Fees** £55 per 27/36 holes, £45 per 18 holes. Winter £40/£35 **Course Designer** H S Colt **Prof** Tim Rouse **Facilities** 🍴 🍴 🛒 🖥 🏌 🏪 ✦ 🏪 ✦ **Leisure** 6 hole par 3 course with artificial tees/greens **Conf** Corporate Hospitality Days **Location** 5m NW of Northampton off A5199
Hotel ★★★ 71% HL Best Western Lime Trees, 8 Langham Place, Barrack Road, NORTHAMPTON ☎ 01604 632188 📠 01604 632188
28 en suite

Overstone Park Billing Ln NN6 0AS
☎ 01604 643555 📠 01604 642635
e-mail: enquiries@overstonepark.com
web: www.overstonepark.com

A testing parkland course, gently undulating within panoramic views of local stately home. Excellent drainage and fine greens make the course great all year round. Water comes into play on three holes.

Overstone Park: 18 Holes, 6472yds, Par 72, SSS 72, Course record 69. Club membership 500.

Visitors contact for details **Societies** booking required. **Green Fees** from £26 per round **Course Designer** Donald Steel **Prof** Stuart Keir **Facilities** ⊕ 🍴 🛏 ⊑ 🏌 ᗱ 🏡 ⛳ ◇ ✦ 🛒 ✦ **Leisure** hard tennis courts, heated indoor swimming pool, fishing, sauna, gymnasium **Conf** facs Corporate Hospitality Days **Location** M1 junct 15, A45 to Billing Aquadrome turn off, course 2m off A5076 Gt Billing Way

Hotel ★★★ 71% HL Best Western Lime Trees, 8 Langham Place, Barrack Road, NORTHAMPTON ☎ 01604 632188 📠 01604 632188 28 en suite

---

OUNDLE   Map 4 TL08

Oundle Benefield Rd PE8 4EZ
☎ 01832 273267 📠 01832 273267
web: www.oundlegolfclub.com

18 Holes, 6265yds, Par 72, SSS 70, Course record 63.
Prof Richard Keys **Facilities** ⊕ 🍴 🛏 ⊑ 🏌 ᗱ 🏡 ⛳ **Leisure** Short game practice area **Conf** facs Corporate Hospitality Days **Location** 1m W on A427
Telephone for further details
Hotel ★★★ 72% HL Holiday Inn Corby-Kettering A43, Geddington Road, CORBY ☎ 01536 401020 📠 01536 401020 105 en suite

---

STAVERTON   Map 4 SP56

Staverton Park Staverton Park NN11 6JT
☎ 01327 705506 📠 01327 311428
e-mail: spgclub@deverevenues.co.uk

Open course, fairly testing with good views. Water hazards and large American style bunkers mean accurate shots are rewarded.

18 Holes, 6593yds, Par 71, SSS 72, Course record 65. Club membership 450.

Visitors Mon-Sun except BHs. Booking required. Handicap certificate. Dress code. **Societies** booking required. **Green Fees** phone **Course Designer** Cmdr John Harris **Prof** Richard Mudge **Facilities** ⊕ 🍴 🛏 ⊑ 🏌 ᗱ 🏡 ⛳ ◇ ✦ 🛒 ✦ 🏈 **Leisure** heated indoor swimming pool, sauna, gymnasium **Conf** facs Corporate Hospitality Days **Location** 0.75m NE on A425

Hotel ★★★★ 72% HL Barceló Daventry Hotel, Sedgemoor Way, DAVENTRY ☎ 01327 307000 📠 01327 307000 155 en suite

---

WELLINGBOROUGH   Map 4 SP86

Rushden Kimbolton Rd, Chelveston NN9 6AN
☎ 01933 418511 📠 01933 418511
e-mail: secretary@rushdengolfclub.org
web: www.rushdengolfclub.org

Undulating parkland with a brook bisecting the course.

10 Holes, 6249yds, Par 71, SSS 70, Course record 68. Club membership 400.

Visitors Mon, Tue, Thu, Fri, Sun & BHs. Wed am. Booking required. Dress code. **Societies** booking required. **Green Fees** £25 per 18 holes, £13 per 9 holes **Prof** Adrian Clifford **Facilities** ⊕ 🍴 🛏 ⊑ 🏌 ᗱ **Conf** Corporate Hospitality Days **Location** 6m E of Wellingborough off B645
Hotel BUD Travelodge Wellingborough Rushden, Saunders Lodge, RUSHDEN ☎ 0871 984 6115 📠 0871 984 6115 40 en suite

Wellingborough Great Harrowden Hall NN9 5AD
☎ 01933 677234 📠 01933 679379
e-mail: info@wellingboroughgolfclub.com
web: www.wellingboroughgolfclub.com

Undulating parkland with many trees set in the grounds of Harrowden Hall with an 18th century clubhouse.

18 Holes, 6721yds, Par 72, SSS 72, Course record 68. Club membership 820.

Visitors contact club for details. **Societies** welcome. **Green Fees** £48 per day **Course Designer** Hawtree **Prof** David Clifford **Facilities** ⊕ 🍴 🛏 ⊑ 🏌 ᗱ 🏡 ⛳ ✦ **Leisure** outdoor swimming pool **Conf** facs Corporate Hospitality Days **Location** 2m N of Wellingborough on A509
Hotel BUD Travelodge Wellingborough Rushden, Saunders Lodge, RUSHDEN ☎ 0871 984 6115 📠 0871 984 6115 40 en suite

---

WHITTLEBURY   Map 4 SP64

Whittlebury Park Golf & Country Club NN12 8WP
☎ 01327 850000 📠 01327 850001
e-mail: enquiries@whittlebury.com
web: www.whittlebury.com

The 36 holes incorporate three loops of tournament-standard nines plus a short course. The 1905 course is a reconstruction of the original parkland course built at the turn of the century, the Royal Whittlewood is a lakeland course playing around copses and the Grand Prix, next to Silverstone Circuit, has a strong links feel playing over gently undulating grassland with many challenging features.

Grand Prix: 9 Holes, 3339yds, Par 36, SSS 36.
Royal Whittlewood: 9 Holes, 3323yds, Par 36, SSS 36.
1905: 9 Holes, 3256yds, Par 36, SSS 36.
Club membership 350.

Visitors Mon-Sun & BHs. Booking required. Dress code. **Societies** booking required. **Green Fees** not confirmed **Course Designer** Cameron Sinclair **Prof** Chris Guy **Facilities** ⊕ 🍴 🛏 ⊑ 🏌 ᗱ 🏡 ⛳ ◇ ✦ 🛒 ✦ 🏈 **Leisure** heated indoor swimming pool, sauna, halfway house for refreshments **Conf** facs Corporate Hospitality Days **Location** M1 junct 15a, on A413 Buckingham Road
Hotel ★★★★ 81% HL Whittlebury Hall, WHITTLEBURY ☎ 01327 857857 📠 01327 857857 211 en suite

NORTHUMBERLAND

ALLENDALE
Map 12 NY85

Allendale High Studdon, Allenheads Rd NE47 9DH
☎ 07005 808246
web: www.allendale-golf.co.uk

Challenging and hilly parkland course set 1000ft above sea level with superb views of East Allen valley.

9 Holes, 4541yds, Par 66, SSS 64, Course record 62.
Club membership 130.

Visitors contact club for details. **Societies** welcome. **Green Fees** £15 per day (£18 weekends) **Facilities** 🏳 ⚘ **Conf** Corporate Hospitality Days **Location** 1m S of Allendale on B6295
Hotel ★★★ 75% HL Best Western Beaumont, Beaumont Street, HEXHAM ☎ 01434 602331 📠 01434 602331 35 en suite

ALNMOUTH
Map 12 NU21

Alnmouth Foxton Hall NE66 3BE
☎ 01665 830231 📠 01665 830922
e-mail: secretary@alnmouthgolfclub.com
web: www.alnmouthgolfclub.com

The original course, situated on the Northumberland coast, was established in 1869, being the fourth oldest in England. The existing course, created in 1930, provides a testing and enjoyable challenge.

18 Holes, 6429yds, Par 71, SSS 71, Course record 64.
Club membership 800.

Visitors Mon-Thu, Sun & BHs. Dress code. **Societies** booking required. **Green Fees** £40 per day, £30 per round (£35 per round weekends) **Course Designer** H S Colt **Prof** Linzi Hardy **Facilities** 🏳 🍴 ⚘ 🏳 🍴 ⚘ 🏠 ◇ 🛒 ✦ **Leisure** snooker room **Conf** Corporate Hospitality Days **Location** 5m E of Alnwick and A1
Hotel ★★★ 80% HL White Swan, Bondgate Within, ALNWICK ☎ 01665 602109 📠 01665 602109 56 en suite

Alnmouth Village Marine Rd NE66 2RZ
☎ 01665 830370
e-mail: bobhill53@live.co.uk
web: www.ukgolfer.com

Seaside course with coastal view. The oldest 9 hole golf club in England.

9 Holes, 6090yds, Par 70, SSS 70, Course record 63.
Club membership 480.

Visitors Mon-Sun & BHs. Booking required Wed, weekends & BHs. Handicap certificate. Dress code. **Societies** booking required. **Green Fees** £20 per 18 holes. Weekly ticket £60 **Course Designer** Mungo

Park Facilities 🍴 ⚘ 🏳 🍴 ⚘ ✦ **Conf** Corporate Hospitality Days **Location** E of village
Hotel ★★★ 80% HL White Swan, Bondgate Within, ALNWICK ☎ 01665 602109 📠 01665 602109 56 en suite

ALNWICK
Map 12 NU11

Alnwick Swansfield Park NE66 2AB
☎ 01665 602632
web: www.alnwickgolfclub.co.uk

A mixture of mature parkland, open grassland and gorse bushes with panoramic views out to sea 5 miles away. Offers a fair test of golf.

18 Holes, 6284yds, Par 70, SSS 70, Course record 66.
Club membership 400.

Visitors Mon-Sun & BHs. Dress code. **Societies** booking required.
Green Fees £35 per day, £25 per round (£27.50 per round weekends & BHs) **Course Designer** Rochester/Rae **Facilities** 🍴 🍴 ⚘ 🏳 🍴 ⚘ ✦ 🛒 ✦ **Location** S of town centre off B6341
Hotel ★★★ 80% HL White Swan, Bondgate Within, ALNWICK ☎ 01665 602109 📠 01665 602109 56 en suite

BAMBURGH
Map 12 NU13

Bamburgh Castle The Club House NE69 7DE
☎ 01668 214378 (club) & 214321 (sec)
📠 01668 214607
web: www.bamburghcastlegolfclub.co.uk

18 Holes, 5621yds, Par 68, SSS 67, Course record 64.

Course Designer George Rochester **Location** 6m E of A1 via B1341 or B1342
Telephone for further details
Hotel ★★ 78% HL The Lord Crewe, Front Street, BAMBURGH ☎ 01668 214243 & 214613 📠 01668 214243 17 en suite

BEDLINGTON
Map 12 NZ28

Bedlingtonshire Acorn Bank, Hartford Rd NE22 6AA
☎ 01670 822457 📠 01670 823048
e-mail: secretary@bedlingtongolfclub.com
web: www.bedlingtongolfclub.com

Meadowland and parkland with easy walking. Under certain conditions the wind can be a distinct hazard.

18 Holes, 6813yards, Par 73, SSS 73, Course record 64.
Club membership 800.

Visitors dress code. **Societies** booking required. **Green Fees** £35 per day; £25 per round (£40/£32 weekends & BHs) **Course Designer** Frank

continued

Pennink **Prof** Marcus Webb **Facilities** ⑪ ⑩ by prior arrangement
⛾ ☕ 🍴 ⛴ 📷 ⛳ 🚗 🏌 **Conf** Corporate Hospitality Days
Location 1m SW on A1068
Hotel ★★★ 78% HL Holiday Inn Newcastle upon Tyne, Great North
Road, Seaton Burn, NEWCASTLE UPON TYNE ☎ 0870 787 3291
& 0191 201 9988 📠 0870 787 3291 154 en suite

BELFORD   Map 12 NU13

Belford South Rd NE70 7DP
☎ 01668 213232 📠 01668 213282
web: www.thebelford.co.uk
The Belford Golf Club: 9 Holes, 3227yds, Par 71, SSS 71.
Course Designer Nigel Williams **Location** off A1 between Alnwick and
Berwick on Tweed
Telephone for further details
Hotel ★★ 74% HL Purdy Lodge, Adderstone Services, BELFORD
☎ 01668 213000 📠 01668 213000 20 en suite

BELLINGHAM   Map 12 NY88

Bellingham Boggle Hole NE48 2DT
☎ 01434 220530 (Secretary)
e-mail: admin@bellinghamgolfclub.com
web: www.bellinghamgolfclub.com

Rolling parkland with many natural hazards. This highly regarded 18-
hole course lies between Hadrian's Wall and the Scottish border. There
is a mixture of testing par 3s, long par 5s and tricky par 4s.
18 Holes, 6093yds, Par 70, SSS 70, Course record 64.
Club membership 500.
Visitors contact club for details. **Societies** booking required. **Green
Fees** £24 per day/round (£30 per round weekends) **Course Designer** E
Johnson/I Wilson **Facilities** ⑪ ⑩ ⛾ ☕ 🍴 ⛴ 📷 🏌
Conf Corporate Hospitality Days **Location** N of village on B6320
Hotel ★★★ 75% HL The Otterburn Tower Hotel, OTTERBURN
☎ 01830 520620 📠 01830 520620 18 en suite

BERWICK-UPON-TWEED   Map 12 NT95

Berwick-upon-Tweed (Goswick) Goswick TD15 2RW
☎ 01289 387256 📠 01289 387334
web: www.goswicklinksgc.co.uk
18 Holes, 6686yds, Par 72, SSS 72, Course record 69.
Course Designer James Braid **Location** 6m S of Berwick off A1
Telephone for further details
Hotel ★★★ 70% CHH Marshall Meadows Country House,
BERWICK-UPON-TWEED ☎ 01289 331133 📠 01289 331133
19 en suite

Magdalene Fields Magdalene Fields TD15 1NE
☎ 01289 306130 📠 01289 306384
e-mail: mail@magdalene-fields.co.uk
web: www.magdalene-fields.co.uk

Seaside course on a clifftop with natural hazards formed by bays. All
holes open to winds. Testing 8th hole over bay (par 3). Scenic views to
Holy Island and north to Scotland.
18 Holes, 6407yds, Par 72, SSS 71, Course record 65.
Club membership 350.
Visitors Mon-Sun & BHs. Booking required weekends. Dress code.
Societies booking required. **Green Fees** £25 per round (£30
weekends) **Course Designer** Willie Park **Facilities** ⑪ ⑩ ⛾ ☕
🍴 ⛴ 📷 🏌 ⛳ 🚗 🏌 **Conf** Corporate Hospitality Days
Location 0.5m E of town centre
Hotel ★★★ 86% CHH Tillmouth Park Country House, CORNHILL-
ON-TWEED, Berwick-upon-Tweed ☎ 01890 882255 📠 01890 882255
14 en suite

BLYTH   Map 12 NZ38

Blyth New Delaval, Newsham NE24 4DB
☎ 01670 540110 (sec) & 356514 (pro)
📠 01670 540134
e-mail: clubmanager@blythgolf.co.uk
web: www.blythgolf.co.uk
Course built over old colliery. Parkland with water hazards. Superb
greens.
18 Holes, 6424yds, Par 72, SSS 71, Course record 63.
Club membership 860.
Visitors Mon-Sun & BHs. Booking required. Dress code.
Societies welcome. **Green Fees** £30 per day, £23.50 per round
(£35/£26 weekends) **Course Designer** Hamilton Stutt **Prof** Andrew
Brown **Facilities** ⑪ ⛾ ☕ 🍴 ⛴ 📷 🏌 🚗 🏌 **Location** 1m
S of town centre
Hotel ★★★ 78% HL Holiday Inn Newcastle upon Tyne, Great North
Road, Seaton Burn, NEWCASTLE UPON TYNE ☎ 0870 787 3291
& 0191 201 9988 📠 0870 787 3291 154 en suite

CRAMLINGTON   Map 12 NZ27

Arcot Hall NE23 7QP
☎ 0191 236 2794 📠 0191 217 0370
web: www.arcothallgolfclub.com
18 Holes, 6329yds, Par 70, SSS 70, Course record 60.
Course Designer James Braid **Location** 2m SW off A1
Telephone for further details
Hotel BUD Innkeeper's Lodge Cramlington, Blagdon Lane,
CRAMLINGTON ☎ 0845 112 6013 📠 0845 112 6013 18 en suite

EMBLETON   Map 12 NU22

Dunstanburgh Castle NE66 3XQ
☎ 01665 576562 📠 01665 576562
e-mail: enquiries@dunstanburgh.com
web: www.dunstanburgh.com

Rolling links designed by James Braid, adjacent to the beautiful
Embleton Bay. Historic Dunstansburgh Castle is at one end of the
course and a National Trust lake and bird sanctuary at the other.
Superb views.

continued

18 Holes, 6298yds, Par 70, SSS 69, Course record 69. Club membership 357.

Visitors Mon-Sun & BHs. **Societies** welcome. **Green Fees** £25 per day (£35 per day; £30 per round weekends & BHs) **Course Designer** James Braid **Facilities** ⓣ ⦿ 🏋 ⬜ 🏌 ⚐ 🏌 🏠 🏌 🚗 ♣
Conf facs Corporate Hospitality Days **Location** 7m NE of Alnwick off A1
Hotel ★★ 78% HL Dunstanburgh Castle Hotel, EMBLETON, Alnwick
☎ 01665 576111 📠 01665 576111 20 en suite

FELTON   Map 12 NU10

Burgham Park NE65 9QP
☎ 01670 787898 (office) & 787978 (pro shop)
📠 01670 787164
e-mail: info@burghampark.co.uk
web: www.burghampark.co.uk

PGA associates designed course, making the most of the gentle rolling landscape with views to the sea and the Northumbrian hills.

Aidan Course: 18 Holes, 6403yards, Par 72, SSS 72, Course record 67. Club membership 560.

Visitors Mon-Sun & BHs. Booking required. Dress code.
Societies booking required. **Green Fees** not confirmed **Course Designer** Andrew Mair **Prof** David Mather **Facilities** ⓣ ⦿ 🏋 ⬜ 🏌 ⚐ 🏠 🏌 🚗 ♣ 🏌 **Leisure** par 3 course
Conf Corporate Hospitality Days **Location** 5m N of Morpeth, 0.5m off A1
Hotel ★★★★ 82% HL Macdonald Linden Hall, Golf & Country Club, LONGHORSLEY, Morpeth ☎ 01670 500000 📠 01670 500000 50 en suite

GREENHEAD   Map 12 NY66

Haltwhistle Wallend Farm CA6 7HN
☎ 016977 47367   📠 01434 344311

Haltwhistle Golf Course: 18 Holes, 5522yds, Par 69, SSS 67, Course record 70.

Facilities ⓣ ⦿ 🏋 ⬜ 🏌 🏠 **Location** N on A69 past Haltwhistle on Gilsland Road
Telephone for further details
Hotel ★★★ HL Farlam Hall, BRAMPTON ☎ 016977 46234
📠 016977 46234 12 en suite

HEDDON-ON-THE-WALL   Map 12 NZ16

Close House NE15 0HT
☎ 01661 852255   📠 01661 856017
e-mail: events@closehouse.co.uk
web: www.closehouse.co.uk

Situated in the grounds of the Close House Estate with stunning views of the River Tyne and surrounding area. The original course dates back to 1964 but a substantial recent development has produced one of the finest courses in the county. The new course offers a great challenge to golfers of all abilities with its USGA specification sloping greens and longer length.

Close House Hotel: 18 Holes, 6000yds, Par 70, SSS 70, Course record 67.

Visitors Mon-Sun & BHs. Booking required. Dress code.
Societies booking required. **Green Fees** £25 per 18 holes (£35 weekends & BHs) **Course Designer** Hawtrees **Prof** Jonathan Lupton **Facilities** ⓣ ⦿ 🏋 ⬜ 🏌 🏠 🏌 ♢ 🚗 ♣ 🏌 **Conf** facs Corporate Hospitality Days **Location** From A1/A69 roundabout, follow

A69 W for 4m to junct signed Close House (B6528). At the junction, turn left. Close House Hotel is signposted on left

Close House

Hotel ★★★★ 75% HL Close House, HEDDON-ON-THE-WALL
☎ 01661 852255 📠 01661 852255 19 en suite

HEXHAM   Map 12 NY96

De Vere Slaley Hall, Golf Resort & Spa Slaley NE47 0BY
☎ 01434 673154   📠 01434 673152
web: www.deveregolf.co.uk

Hunting Course: 18 Holes, 7088yds, Par 72, SSS 74, Course record 63.
Priestman Course: 18 Holes, 6951yds, Par 72, SSS 72, Course record 63.

Course Designer Dave Thomas/Neil Coles **Location** 8m S of Hexham off A68
Telephone for further details
Hotel ★★★★ 80% HL De Vere Slaley Hall, Slaley, HEXHAM
☎ 01434 673350 📠 01434 673350 142 en suite

Hexham Spital Park NE46 3RZ
☎ 01434 603072   📠 01434 601865
e-mail: info@hexhamgolf.co.uk
web: www.hexhamgolf.co.uk

A very pretty, well-drained course with interesting natural contours. Exquisite views from parts of the course of the Tyne valley below. As good a parkland course as any in the north of England.

18 Holes, 6294yds, Par 70, SSS 71, Course record 61. Club membership 700.

Visitors Mon-Sun & BHs. Booking required. Dress code.
Societies booking required. **Green Fees** £35 per round (£45 weekends & BHs) **Course Designer** Vardon/Caird **Prof** Andrew Paisley **Facilities** ⓣ ⦿ 🏋 ⬜ 🏌 🏠 🏌 🚗 ♣ 🏌 **Leisure** squash, squash courts **Conf** facs Corporate Hospitality Days **Location** 1m NW on B6531
Hotel ★★★ 75% HL Best Western Beaumont, Beaumont Street, HEXHAM ☎ 01434 602331 📠 01434 602331 35 en suite

LONGHORSLEY   Map 12 NZ19

Macdonald Linden Hall NE65 8XF
☎ 01670 500011   📠 01670 500001
e-mail: golf.lindenhall@macdonald-hotels.co.uk
web: www.macdonaldhotels.co.uk/lindenhall

Set within the picturesque Linden Hall Estate on a mixture of mature woodland and parkland, established lakes and burns provide

continued

interesting water features to match the peaceful surroundings. This award-winning course is a pleasure to play for all standards of golfer.

Macdonald Linden Hall: 18 Holes, 6846yds, Par 72, SSS 73. Club membership 250.

Visitors Mon-Sun & BHs. Booking required. Dress code. **Societies** booking required. **Green Fees** £36 (£44 weekends) **Course Designer** Jonathan Gaunt **Prof** Gordon Morrison **Facilities** ⓦ ⑩ 🍽 🖥 🏷 🛒 ⛳ ◇ 🛒 ⛳ **Leisure** hard tennis courts, sauna, gymnasium, chipping green **Conf** facs Corporate Hospitality Days **Location** from A1 take A697, 0.5m from village of Longhorsley

Hotel ★★★★ 82% HL Macdonald Linden Hall, Golf & Country Club, LONGHORSLEY, Morpeth ☎ 01670 500000 🗎 01670 500000 50 en suite

MATFEN
Map 12 NZ07

Matfen Hall NE20 0RH
☎ 01661 886400   🗎 01661 886055
e-mail: golf@matfenhall.com
web: www.matfenhall.com

A 27-hole parkland course set in beautiful countryside with many natural and man-made hazards. The course is an enjoyable test for players of all abilities but it does incorporate challenging water features in the shape of a large lake and a fast flowing river. The dry stone wall presents a unique obstacle on several holes. The 4th, 9th, 12th and 14th holes are particularly testing par 4s, the dog-leg 16th is the pick of the par 5s but Matfen's signature hole is the long par 3 17th with its narrow green teasingly sited just over the river.

Matfen Hall Country House Hotel & Golf Club: 27 Holes, 6700yds, Par 72, SSS 72, Course record 63.

Visitors Mon-Sun & BHs. Dress code. **Societies** booking required. **Green Fees** £35 per 18 holes **Course Designer** Mair/James/Gaunt/Harrison/Parkinson **Prof** John Harrison **Facilities** ⓦ ⑩ 🖥 🍽 🏷 🛒 ⛳ ◇ ⛳ 🛒 ⛳ **Leisure** heated indoor swimming pool, sauna, gymnasium, 9 hole par 3 course. 10 bay covered driving range. Leisure complex & health spa **Conf** facs Corporate Hospitality Days **Location** off B6318

Hotel ★★★★ 81% HL Matfen Hall, MATFEN, Newcastle upon Tyne ☎ 01661 886500 & 855708 🗎 01661 886500 53 en suite

MORPETH
Map 12 NZ28

Morpeth The Clubhouse NE61 2BT
☎ 01670 504942   🗎 01670 504918
e-mail: admin@morpethgolf.co.uk
web: www.morpethgolf.co.uk
Parkland course with views of the Cheviots.

18 Holes, 6206yds, Par 71, SSS 69, Course record 65. Club membership 700.

Visitors contact club for details. **Societies** welcome. **Green Fees** not confirmed **Course Designer** Harry Vardon **Prof** Martin Jackson **Facilities** ⓦ ⑩ 🖥 🖥 🍽 🏷 🛒 ⛳ ◇ ⛳ **Location** S of town centre on A197

Hotel ★★★★ 82% HL Macdonald Linden Hall, Golf & Country Club, LONGHORSLEY, Morpeth ☎ 01670 500000 🗎 01670 500000 50 en suite

NEWBIGGIN-BY-THE-SEA
Map 12 NZ38

Newbiggin-by-the-Sea Prospect Place NE64 6DW
☎ 01670 817344
e-mail: info@newbiggingolfclub.co.uk
web: www.newbiggingolfclub.co.uk
Seaside-links course.

Newbiggin Golf Club Ltd: 18 Holes, 6452yds, Par 72, SSS 71, Course record 65. Club membership 694.

Visitors Mon-Fri & Sun except BHs. Dress code. **Societies** booking required. **Green Fees** £27 per day, £20 per round (£27/£25 weekends & BHs) **Course Designer** Willie Park **Prof** James Kerr **Facilities** ⓦ ⑩ 🖥 🖥 🍽 🏷 🛒 ◇ ⛳ 🛒 ⛳ **Leisure** snooker **Conf** facs Corporate Hospitality Days **Location** N of town centre

Hotel ★★★★ 82% HL Macdonald Linden Hall, Golf & Country Club, LONGHORSLEY, Morpeth ☎ 01670 500000 🗎 01670 500000 50 en suite

PONTELAND
Map 12 NZ17

Ponteland 53 Bell Villas NE20 9BD
☎ 01661 822689   🗎 01661 860077
e-mail: secretary@thepontelandgolfclub.co.uk
web: www.thepontelandgolfclub.co.uk
Open parkland course offering testing golf and good views.

18 Holes, 6587yds, Par 72, SSS 72, Course record 65. Club membership 1200.

Visitors Tue, Thu & Sun. Booking required. Handicap certificate. Dress code. **Societies** booking required. **Green Fees** from £15 per round **Course Designer** Harry Fernie **Prof** Alan Robson-Crosby **Facilities** ⓦ ⑩ 🖥 🖥 🍽 🏷 🛒 ⛳ ◇ 🛒 ⛳ **Conf** facs Corporate Hospitality Days **Location** 0.5m E on A696

Hotel ★★★ 78% HL Novotel Newcastle Airport, Ponteland Road, Kenton, NEWCASTLE UPON TYNE ☎ 0191 214 0303 🗎 0191 214 0303 126 en suite

ROTHBURY
Map 12 NU00

Rothbury Whitton Rd NE65 7RX
☎ 01669 621271
web: www.rothburygolfclub.com
18 Holes, 6102yds, Par 70.

Course Designer J Radcliffe **Location** SW of town off B6342
Telephone for further details

Hotel ★★★★ 82% HL Macdonald Linden Hall, Golf & Country Club, LONGHORSLEY, Morpeth ☎ 01670 500000 🗎 01670 500000 50 en suite

SEAHOUSES

Map 12 NU23

Seahouses Beadnell Rd NE68 7XT
☎ 01665 720794
e-mail: secretary@seahousesgolf.co.uk
web: www.seahousesgolf.co.uk
Traditional links course with many hazards. Signature holes are the famous par 3 10th hole, Logans Loch, water hole and the par 3 15th, nominated as one of the most difficult holes in the world. Spectacular views of the coastline to the Farne Islands and Lindisfarne.

18 Holes, 5542yds, Par 67, SSS 67, Course record 63. Club membership 550.

Visitors Mon-Sun & BHs. Booking required weeekends & BHs. Booking required. Dress code. **Societies** booking required **Green Fees** not confirmed **Facilities** ⑪ ⑩ ▤ ⌨ 🍴 ⚖ ✎ 🛒 ✦ **Location** S of village on B1340, 5m E of A1

STOCKSFIELD

Map 12 NZ06

Stocksfield New Ridley Rd NE43 7RE
☎ 01661 843041 ▤ 01661 843046
e-mail: info@sgcgolf.co.uk
web: www.sgcgolf.co.uk
Challenging course: parkland (nine holes), woodland (nine holes). Some elevated greens, giving fine views, and water hazards.

18 Holes, 5991yds, Par 70, SSS 69, Course record 61. Club membership 550.

Visitors Mon-Sun & BHs. Booking required. Handicap certificate. Dress code. **Societies** welcome. **Green Fees** £25 per day, £20 per round (£28 weekends & BHs) **Course Designer** Pennick **Prof** Steven Harrison **Facilities** ⑪ ⑩ ▤ ⌨ 🍴 ⚖ 🛒 ✦ 🛒 ✦ **Leisure** snooker **Conf** Corporate Hospitality Days **Location** 1.5m S off A695

Hotel ★★★ 75% HL Best Western Beaumont, Beaumont Street, HEXHAM ☎ 01434 602331 ▤ 01434 602331 35 en suite

SWARLAND

Map 12 NU10

Percy Wood Golf & Country Retreat Coast View NE65 9JG
☎ 01670 787010
e-mail: enquiries@percywood.co.uk
web: www.percywood.co.uk
A parkland course set in mature woodland with scenic views. There are seven par 4 holes in excess of 400yds. A good challenge for golfers of all levels.

Percy Wood Golf & Country Retreat: 18 Holes, 6335yds, Par 72, SSS 72. Club membership 400.

Visitors Mon-Sun & BHs. Booking required. Dress code. **Societies** booking required. **Green Fees** £20 (£25 weekends) **Prof** Peter Ritchie **Facilities** ⑪ ⑩ ▤ ⌨ 🍴 ⚖ 🏠 🛒 ◇ ✎ 🛒 ✦ 🍴 **Conf** Corporate Hospitality Days **Location** 1m W of A1

Hotel ★★★★ 82% HL Macdonald Linden Hall, Golf & Country Club, LONGHORSLEY, Morpeth ☎ 01670 500000 ▤ 01670 500000 50 en suite

WOOLER

Map 12 NT92

Wooler Dod Law, Doddington NE71 6AN
☎ 01668 282135
web: www.woolergolf.co.uk
Hilltop, moorland course with spectacular views over the Glendale valley. Nine greens played from 18 tees. A very challenging course when windy with one par 5 of 580yds. The course is much under used during the week so is always available.

9 Holes, 6411yds, Par 72, SSS 71, Course record 69. Club membership 300.

Visitors dress code. **Societies** booking required. **Green Fees** £20 per 18 holes, £15 per 9 holes **Facilities** ⑪ by prior arrangement ⑩ by prior arrangement ▤ ⌨ 🍴 ⚖ ✎ 🛒 ✦ **Location** at Doddington on B6525

Hotel ★★ 74% HL Purdy Lodge, Adderstone Services, BELFORD ☎ 01668 213000 ▤ 01668 213000 20 en suite

NOTTINGHAMSHIRE

CALVERTON

Map 8 SK64

Ramsdale Park Golf Centre Oxton Rd NG14 6NU
☎ 0115 965 5600 ▤ 0115 965 4105
e-mail: info@ramsdaleparkgc.co.uk
web: www.ramsdaleparkgc.co.uk
The Seely Course is a challenging and comprehensive test for any standard of golf. A relatively flat front nine is followed by an undulating back nine that is renowned as one of the best in the county. The Lee Course is an 18-hole par 3 course with holes of varying lengths, suitable for beginners and those wishing to improve their short game.

Seely Course: 18 Holes, 6546yds, Par 71, SSS 71, Course record 70.

Visitors Mon-Sun & BHs. Booking required weekends. Dress code. **Societies** booking required. **Green Fees** £22 per 18 holes (£28 weekends) **Course Designer** Hawtree **Prof** Robert Macey **Facilities** ⑪ ⑩ ▤ ⌨ 🍴 ⚖ 🏠 🛒 ✎ 🛒 ✦ 🍴 **Leisure** fishing, 18 hole par 3 Lee Course **Conf** facs Corporate Hospitality Days **Location** 8m NE of Nottingham off B6386

Hotel ★★★ 71% HL Best Western Bestwood Lodge, Bestwood Country Park, Arnold, NOTTINGHAM ☎ 0115 920 3011 ▤ 0115 920 3011 39 en suite

Springwater Moor Ln NG14 6FZ
☎ 0115 965 2129 (pro shop) & 965 4946
🖷 0115 965 2344
e-mail: dave.pullan@springwatergolfclub.com
web: www.springwatergolfclub.com

This attractive course set in rolling countryside overlooking the Trent valley, offers an interesting and challenging game of golf to players of all handicaps. The 18th hole is particularly noteworthy, a 183yd par 3 over two ponds

18 Holes, 6262yds, Par 71, SSS 71, Course record 68.
Club membership 440.

Visitors Mon-Sun & BHs. Booking required. Dress code.
Societies booking required. **Green Fees** £22 per round (£27 weekends & BHs) **Course Designer** Neil Footitt/Paul Wharmsby **Prof** Paul Drew **Facilities** ⑪ ⛳ ⮝ ⌨ ⛴ ⚓ 🏠 🍴 ⛽ 🏌 🏇
Leisure short game academy **Conf** facs Corporate Hospitality Days
Location off A6097 to Calverton, 600yds on left
Hotel ★★★ 74% HL Best Western Westminster, 312 Mansfield Road, Carrington, NOTTINGHAM ☎ 0115 955 5000 🖷 0115 955 5000 73 en suite

EAST LEAKE
Map 8 SK52

Rushcliffe Stocking Ln LE12 5RL
☎ 01509 852959 🖷 01509 852688
e-mail: secretary.rushcliffegc@btopenworld.com
Hilly, tree-lined and picturesque parkland.

The Rushcliffe Golf Club: 18 Holes, 6013yds, Par 70,
SSS 71, Course record 63. Club membership 750.

Visitors dress code. **Societies** booking required. **Green Fees** phone
Course Designer Tom Williamson **Prof** Chris Hall **Facilities** ⑪ ⛳ ⮝ ⌨ ⛴ ⚓ 🏠 🍴 🏌 **Location** M1 junct 24
Hotel ★★★★ 80% HL Best Western Premier Yew Lodge Hotel, Packington Hill, KEGWORTH ☎ 01509 672518 🖷 01509 672518 100 en suite

HUCKNALL
Map 8 SK54

Hucknall Golf Centre Wigwam Ln NG15 7TA
☎ 0115 964 2037 🖷 0115 964 2724
e-mail: leen@jbgolf.co.uk
web: www.jackbarker.com

A course on two different levels. Upper level has a links feel while the lower level with its ponds, streams and ditches has a parkland feel. A relatively short course but still a challenge for all abilities.

Hucknall Golf Centre: 18 Holes, 6026yds, Par 70, SSS 70.
Club membership 250.

Visitors Mon-Sun & BHs. Booking required weekends & BHs.
Dress code. **Societies** welcome. **Green Fees** not confirmed **Course Designer** Tom Hodgetts **Prof** Cyril Jepson **Facilities** ⑪ ⛳ ⮝ ⌨ ⛴ ⚓ 🏠 🍴 ⛽ 🏌 **Conf** facs Corporate Hospitality Days
Location 0.5m from town centre, signs for railway station, right onto Wigwam Ln
Hotel ★★★ 71% HL Best Western Bestwood Lodge, Bestwood Country Park, Arnold, NOTTINGHAM ☎ 0115 920 3011 🖷 0115 920 3011 39 en suite

KEYWORTH
Map 8 SK63

Stanton on the Wolds Golf Course Rd NG12 5BH
☎ 0115 937 4885 🖷 0115 937 1652

18 Holes, 6369yds, Par 73, SSS 71, Course record 67.
Course Designer Tom Williamson **Location** E side of village off A606
Telephone for further details
Hotel ★★★ 81% HL Langar Hall, LANGAR ☎ 01949 860559 🖷 01949 860559 12 en suite

KIRKBY IN ASHFIELD
Map 8 SK55

Notts Derby Rd NG17 7QR
☎ 01623 753225 🖷 01623 753655
e-mail: office@nottsgolfclub.co.uk
web: www.nottsgolfclub.co.uk
Undulating heathland championship course.

18 Holes, 7250yds, Par 72, SSS 76, Course record 66.
Club membership 450.

Visitors Mon-Fri & Sun except BHs. Booking required. Handicap certificate. Dress code. **Societies** booking required. **Green Fees** £100 per day, £70 per round. **Course Designer** Willie Park **Prof** Mike Bradley **Facilities** ⑪ ⛳ ⮝ ⌨ ⛴ ⚓ 🏠 🍴 🏌 🏇 **Conf** Corporate Hospitality Days **Location** 2m SE of Mansfield off A611
Hotel ★★ 70% SHL Pine Lodge, 281-283 Nottingham Road, MANSFIELD ☎ 01623 622308 🖷 01623 622308 20 en suite

MANSFIELD
Map 8 SK56

Sherwood Forest Eakring Rd NG18 3EW
☎ 01623 627403 🖷 01623 420412

18 Holes, 6289yds, Par 71, SSS 71.

Course Designer H S Colt/James Braid **Location** E of Mansfield
Telephone for further details
Hotel ★★ 70% SHL Pine Lodge, 281-283 Nottingham Road, MANSFIELD ☎ 01623 622308 🖷 01623 622308 20 en suite

NEWARK-ON-TRENT
Map 8 SK75

Newark Coddington NG24 2QX
☎ 01636 626282 🖷 01636 626497
e-mail: manager@newarkgolfclub.co.uk
web: www.newarkgolfclub.co.uk
Wooded parkland in a secluded position with easy walking.

18 Holes, 6458yds, Par 71, SSS 71, Course record 66.
Club membership 650.

Visitors Mon, Wed-Sun except BHs. Dress code. **Societies** booking required. **Green Fees** £42 per day, £36 per round (£42 per round

continued

weekends) **Course Designer** T Williamson **Prof** P A Lockley
Facilities ⓣ ⍾ ⍾ ⍾ ⍾ ⍾ ⍾ ⍾ ⍾ ⍾ ⍾
Leisure snooker **Conf** facs Corporate Hospitality Days **Location** 4m E
of Newark on Sleaford road
Hotel ★★★ 82% HL The Grange Hotel, 73 London Road, NEWARK
☎ 01636 703399 🖨 01636 703399 19 en suite

NOTTINGHAM Map 8 SK53

Beeston Fields Old Dr, Wollaton Rd, Beeston NG9 3DD
☎ 0115 925 7062 🖨 0115 925 4280
e-mail: beestonfields@btconnect.com
web: www.beestonfields.co.uk

Parkland course with sandy subsoil and wide, tree-lined fairways. The
par 3 14th has an elevated tee and a small bunker-guarded green.
18 Holes, 6430yds, Par 71, SSS 71, Course record 64.
Club membership 600.
Visitors handicap certificate. Dress code. **Societies** booking required.
Green Fees £43 per day, £34 per round (£39 per round Sun) **Course
Designer** Tom Williamson **Prof** Alun Wardle **Facilities** ⓣ ⍾ by prior
arrangement ⍾ ⍾ ⍾ ⍾ ⍾ ⍾ ⍾ **Conf** facs Corporate
Hospitality Days **Location** 400yds SW off A52 Nottingham-Derby road
Hotel BUD Travelodge Nottingham Trowell (M1), TROWELL
☎ 08719 846 093 🖨 08719 846 093 35 en suite

Bulwell Forest Hucknall Rd, Bulwell NG6 9LQ
☎ 0115 976 3172 (pro shop) 🖨 0115 977 0576
e-mail: secretarybfgc@hotmail.co.uk
web: www.bulwellforestgolfclub.com
Municipal heathland course with many natural hazards. Very tight
fairways and subject to wind. Five challenging par 3s. Excellent
drainage with no winter greens or tees.
18 Holes, 5667yds, Par 68, SSS 68, Course record 62.
Club membership 350.
Visitors Mon-Sun & BHs. Booking required weekends & BHs. Dress
code. **Societies** booking required. **Green Fees** £13 per round (£17
weekends & BHs) **Course Designer** John Doleman **Facilities** ⓣ ⍾
⍾ ⍾ ⍾ ⍾ ⍾ **Leisure** hard tennis courts, children's
playground **Conf** Corporate Hospitality Days **Location** 4m NW of city
on A611
Hotel ★★★ 71% HL Best Western Bestwood Lodge,
Bestwood Country Park, Arnold, NOTTINGHAM ☎ 0115 920 3011
🖨 0115 920 3011 39 en suite

Chilwell Manor Meadow Ln, Chilwell NG9 5AE
☎ 0115 925 8958 🖨 0115 922 0575
e-mail: info@chilwellmanorgolfclub.co.uk
web: www.chilwellmanorgolfclub.co.uk
Flat parkland. Some water, plenty of trees and narrow fairways.
18 Holes, 6255yds, Par 70, SSS 71, Course record 66.
Club membership 750.
Visitors handicap certificate. Dress code. **Societies** booking required
Green Fees £30 per day, £25 per round (weekends £30 per round)
Course Designer Tom Williamson **Prof** Paul Wilson **Facilities** ⓣ
⍾ ⍾ ⍾ ⍾ ⍾ **Conf** facs Corporate Hospitality Days
Location 4m SW on A6005
Hotel BUD Innkeeper's Lodge Nottingham, Derby Road, Wollaton Vale,
NOTTINGHAM ☎ 0845 112 6051 🖨 0845 112 6051 34 en suite

Edwalton Municipal Wellin Ln, Edwalton NG12 4AS
☎ 0115 923 4775 🖨 0115 923 1647
e-mail: edwalton@glendale-services.co.uk
web: www.glendale-golf.com
Gently sloping, challenging nine-hole parkland course. Also a nine-
hole par 3.
Edwalton Municipal Golf Course: 9 Holes, 3336yds, Par 72,
SSS 72, Course record 71. Club membership 650.
Visitors dress code. **Societies** welcome. **Green Fees** not confirmed
Prof Lee Rawlings **Facilities** ⓣ ⍾ by prior arrangement ⍾ ⍾
⍾ ⍾ ⍾ ⍾ ⍾ **Leisure** par 3 course **Conf** facs
Corporate Hospitality Days **Location** S of Nottingham off A606
Hotel ★★★ 67% HL Swans Hotel & Restaurant, 84-90
Radcliffe Road, West Bridgford, NOTTINGHAM ☎ 0115 981 4042
🖨 0115 981 4042 30 en suite

Mapperley Central Av, Plains Rd, Mapperley NG3 6RH
☎ 0115 955 6673 (pro) & 955 6672 (sec)
🖨 0115 955 6670
e-mail: secretary@mapperleygolfclub.org
web: www.mapperleygolfclub.org
Hilly meadowland course but with easy walking.
18 Holes, 6307yds, Par 71, SSS 70, Course record 65.
Club membership 700.
Visitors Mon-Fri. Sun & BHs. Handicap certificate. Dress code.
Societies booking required. **Green Fees** £25 per day/round (£27.50
Sun & BHs) **Course Designer** John Mason **Prof** John Newham
Facilities ⓣ ⍾ ⍾ ⍾ ⍾ ⍾ ⍾ ⍾ ⍾ **Leisure** pool room
Conf facs Corporate Hospitality Days **Location** 3m NE of city centre
off B684
Hotel BUD Travelodge Nottingham Trowell (M1), TROWELL
☎ 08719 846 093 🖨 08719 846 093 35 en suite

Nottingham City Sandhurst Rd NG6 8LF
☎ 0115 927 2767 (pro) & 07740 688694
web: www.nottinghamcitygolfclub.co.uk
18 Holes, 6218yds, Par 69, SSS 70, Course record 63.
Course Designer H Braid **Location** 4m NW of city centre off A6002
Telephone for further details
Hotel ★★★ 71% HL Best Western Bestwood Lodge,
Bestwood Country Park, Arnold, NOTTINGHAM ☎ 0115 920 3011
🖨 0115 920 3011 39 en suite

Wollaton Park Limetree Av, Wollaton Park NG8 1BT
☎ 0115 978 7574 📠 0115 970 0736
e-mail: secretary@wollatonparkgolfclub.com
web: www.wollatonparkgolfclub.com

A traditional parkland course on slightly undulating land, winding through historic woodland and set in a historic deer park. Fine views of 16th-century Wollaton Hall.

18 Holes, 6445yds, Par 71, SSS 71, Course record 64.
Club membership 700.

Visitors Mon-Sun & BHs. Dress code. **Societies** booking required.
Green Fees £51 per day, £37 per round (£55/£42 weekends &
BHs) **Course Designer** T Williamson **Prof** John Lower **Facilities** ⊕
🍴 📶 🍺 🏪 🖥 ⛳ 🛍 ♿ 🏌 **Conf** Corporate Hospitality Days
Location 2.5m W of city centre off ring road at junct A52
Hotel ★★★ 67% HL Swans Hotel & Restaurant, 84-90
Radcliffe Road, West Bridgford, NOTTINGHAM ☎ 0115 981 4042
📠 0115 981 4042 30 en suite

OLLERTON
Map 8 SK66

Rufford Park Golf & Country Club Rufford Ln, Rufford
NG22 9DG
☎ 01623 825253 📠 01623 825254
e-mail: enquiries@ruffordpark.co.uk
web: www.ruffordpark.co.uk

Set in the heart of Sherwood Forest, Rufford Park is noted for its picturesque 18 holes with its especially challenging par 3s. From the unique 175yd par 3 17th over water to the riverside 641yd 13th, the course offers everything the golfer needs from beginner to professional.

Rufford Park Golf & Country Club: 18 Holes, 6368yds,
Par 70, SSS 70, Course record 66. Club membership 600.

Visitors contact club for details. **Societies** welcome. **Green Fees** £22 per 18 holes (£28 weekends) **Course Designer** David Hemstock/Ken
Brown **Prof** John Vaughan/James Thompson **Facilities** ⊕ 🍴 🍺
📶 🏪 🖥 ⛳ 🍺 🛍 ♿ 🏌 **Conf** facs Corporate Hospitality
Days **Location** S of Ollerton, off A614 for Rufford Mill
Hotel ★★★ 79% HL Clumber Park, Clumber Park, WORKSOP
☎ 01623 835333 📠 01623 835333 73 en suite

OXTON
Map 8 SK65

Oakmere Park Oaks Ln NG25 0RH
☎ 0115 965 3545 📠 0115 965 5628
e-mail: enquiries@oakmerepark.co.uk
web: www.oakmerepark.co.uk

Twenty-seven holes set in rolling heathland in the heart of picturesque Robin Hood country. Renowned for its all weather playing qualities.

Admirals: 18 Holes, 6617yds, Par 73, SSS 72,
Course record 64.
Commanders: 9 Holes, 6407yds, Par 72, SSS 71.
Club membership 900.

Visitors Mon-Sun & BHs. Booking required. Dress code.
Societies booking required. **Green Fees** Admirals £22 per 18 holes
(£32 weekends). Commanders £14/£18 **Course Designer** Frank
Pennick **Prof** Daryl St-John Jones **Facilities** ⊕ 🍴 🍺 🖥 📶
♿ 🏪 🖥 ⛳ 🛍 🏌 🍺 🏌 **Conf** facs Corporate Hospitality Days
Location 1m NW of Oxton off A6097 or A614
Hotel ★★★ 74% HL Best Western Westminster, 312 Mansfield
Road, Carrington, NOTTINGHAM ☎ 0115 955 5000 📠 0115 955 5000
73 en suite

RADCLIFFE ON TRENT
Map 8 SK63

Cotgrave Place Golf Club, Stragglethorpe, Nr Cotgrave
Village NG12 3HB
☎ 0115 933 3344 📠 0115 933 4567
e-mail: cotgrave@crown-golf.co.uk
web: www.cotgraveplacegolf.co.uk

The course offers 36 holes of championship golf. The front nine of the Open course is placed around a beautiful lake, man-made ponds and the Grantham Canal. The back nine is set in magnificent parkland with mature trees and wide fairways. Masters has an opening nine set among hedgerows and coppices. The huge greens with their interesting shapes are a particularly challenging test of nerve. The par 5 17th hole is one of the toughest in the country.

Masters: 18 Holes, 5933yds, Par 70, SSS 69,
Course record 66.
Open: 18 Holes, 6302yds, Par 71, SSS 70, Course record 67.
Club membership 850.

Visitors Mon-Sun & BHs. Booking required. Dress code.
Societies booking required. **Green Fees** phone **Course Designer** Peter
Aliss/John Small **Prof** Robert Smith **Facilities** ⊕ 🍴 🍺 🖥
📶 ♿ 🏪 🖥 ⛳ 🛍 🏌 **Conf** facs Corporate Hospitality Days
Location 2m SW of Radcliffe off A52
Hotel ★★★ 81% HL Langar Hall, LANGAR ☎ 01949 860559
📠 01949 860559 12 en suite

Radcliffe-on-Trent Dewberry Ln, Cropwell Rd NG12 2JH
☎ 0115 933 3000 📠 0115 911 6991
e-mail: les.wake@radcliffeontrentgc.co.uk
web: www.radcliffeontrentgc.co.uk

Fairly flat, parkland course with three good finishing holes: 16th (423 yds) par 4; 17th (174 yds) through spinney, par 3; 18th (336 yds) dog-leg par 4. Excellent views.

18 Holes, 6374yds, Par 70, SSS 71, Course record 64.
Club membership 700.

Visitors contact club for details. **Societies** booking required. **Green
Fees** £37 per day, £27 per 18 holes **Course Designer** Tom Williamson
Prof Craig George **Facilities** ⊕ 🍴 🍺 🖥 📶 ♿ 🏪 🖥 ⛳
🍺 🏌 **Conf** Corporate Hospitality Days **Location** 0.5m SE of town
centre off A52
Hotel ★★★ 67% HL Swans Hotel & Restaurant, 84-90
Radcliffe Road, West Bridgford, NOTTINGHAM ☎ 0115 981 4042
📠 0115 981 4042 30 en suite

RETFORD
Map 8 SK78

Retford Brecks Rd, Ordsall DN22 7UA
☎ 01777 711188 (Secretary) 📠 01777 710412
Wooded parkland.

18 Holes, 6507yds, Par 72, SSS 72, Course record 67.
Club membership 700.

Visitors Mon, Wed-Fri & BHs. Tue & weekends pm. Booking required.
Dress code. **Societies** welcome. **Green Fees** £35 per day; £28 per
round (£28 per round weekends) **Course Designer** Tom Williamson
Prof Craig Morris **Facilities** ⑪ 🍴 🖫 ▽ 🍸 🏌 🏡 🏌
🏌 🛺 🏌 **Conf** Corporate Hospitality Days **Location** 1.5m S A620,
between Worksop & Gainsborough
Hotel ★★★ 74% HL Best Western West Retford, 24 North Road,
RETFORD ☎ 01777 706333 📠 01777 706333 63 en suite

RUDDINGTON
Map 8 SK53

Ruddington Grange Wilford Rd NG11 6NB
☎ 0115 921 1951 (pro shop) & 984 6141
📠 0115 940 5165
e-mail: info@ruddingtongrange.com
web: www.ruddingtongrange.com

Undulating parkland with many mature trees and water hazards on
eight holes. Challenging but fair layout.

18 Holes, 6515yds, Par 72, SSS 72, Course record 69.
Club membership 750.

Visitors Mon-Fri except BHs. Booking required. Dress code.
Societies booking required. **Green Fees** £35 per day, £25 per
18 holes. **Course Designer** E MacAusland/J Small **Prof** Robert
Simpson **Facilities** ⑪ 🍴 🖫 ▽ 🍸 🏌 🏡 🏌 🏌
Conf facs Corporate Hospitality Days **Location** 1m N of town centre
on B680
Hotel ★★★ 67% HL Swans Hotel & Restaurant, 84-90
Radcliffe Road, West Bridgford, NOTTINGHAM ☎ 0115 981 4042
📠 0115 981 4042 30 en suite

SERLBY
Map 8 SK68

Serlby Park DN10 6BA
☎ 01777 818268
e-mail: serlbysec@talktalkbusiness.net

Peaceful, picturesque setting on well-drained areas of woodland,
parkland and farmland on the Serlby Hall Estate. Easy walking.

Serlby Park: 11 Holes, 5396yds, Par 66, SSS 66,
Course record 63. Club membership 260.

Visitors Mon-Sun & BHs. Booking required. Handicap certificate. Dress
code. **Societies** booking required. **Green Fees** £15 per round (£20
weekends & BHs) **Course Designer** Tom Williamson **Facilities** ⑪
🍴 🖫 ▽ 🍸 🏌 **Conf** Corporate Hospitality Days **Location** from
A1(M) Blyth take A614 E towards Bawtry for 1m. Turn right signposted
Serlby, clubhouse 0.75 on right.
Hotel ★★★ 82% HL Best Western Charnwood, Sheffield Road,
BLYTH, Worksop ☎ 01909 591610 📠 01909 591610 45 en suite

SOUTHWELL
Map 8 SK65

Norwood Park Norwood Park NG25 0PF
☎ 01636 816626
e-mail: golf@norwoodpark.co.uk
web: www.norwoodpark.co.uk

A parkland course that blends perfectly with the historic setting
of Norwood Park and highlights its natural features. Built to USGA
standards, the course will appeal to all golfers, who will appreciate
the well-shaped fairways, large undulating greens, natural and man-
made water hazards, and fine views over the surrounding countryside.

Norwood Park Golf Course: 18 Holes, 6805yds, Par 72,
SSS 72, Course record 68. Club membership 600.

Visitors Mon-Sun & BHs. Booking required. Dress code.
Societies booking required **Green Fees** £20 per 18 holes (£28
weekends & BHs). Westwood par 3 course £7 per 9 holes (£8
weekends) **Course Designer** Clyde B Johnston **Prof** Paul Thornton
Facilities ⑪ 🍴 🖫 ▽ 🍸 🏌 🏡 🏌 🏌 🛺 🏌 🏌
Leisure 9 holes par 3 Westwood course **Conf** facs Corporate
Hospitality Days **Location** Off A617 Newark to Mansfield road. Take
turning to Southwell in Kirklington, golf course 5m on right.
Hotel ★★★ 73% HL Saracens Head, Market Place, SOUTHWELL
☎ 01636 812701 📠 01636 812701 27 en suite

SUTTON IN ASHFIELD
Map 8 SK45

Coxmoor Coxmoor Rd NG17 5LF
☎ 01623 557359 📠 01623 557435
e-mail: secretary@coxmoorgolfclub.co.uk
web: www.coxmoorgolfclub.co.uk

Undulating moorland and heathland course with easy walking and
excellent views. The clubhouse is traditional with a well-equipped
games room. The course lies adjacent to Forestry Commission land
over which there are several footpaths and extensive views.

18 Holes, 6577yds, Par 73, SSS 72, Course record 65.
Club membership 700.

Visitors Mon-Fri except BHs. Booking required. Handicap certificate.
Dress code. **Societies** booking required. **Green Fees** £58 per day,
£45 per round **Prof** Craig Wright **Facilities** ⑪ 🍴 🖫 ▽ 🍸
🏌 🏡 🏌 **Leisure** snooker **Conf** Corporate Hospitality Days
Location M1 junct 27/28, exit for Mansfield, entrance to club on
B6139
Hotel ★★ 70% SHL Pine Lodge, 281-283 Nottingham Road,
MANSFIELD ☎ 01623 622308 📠 01623 622308 20 en suite

WORKSOP
Map 8 SK57

Bondhay Bondhay Ln, Whitwell S80 3EH
☎ 01909 723608 📠 01909 720226
e-mail: enquiries@bondhay.com
web: www.bondhay.com

The wind usually plays quite an active role in making this flat
championship course testing. Signature holes are the 10th which
requires a second shot over water into a basin of trees; the 11th
comes back over the same expanse of water and requires a mid to
short iron to a long, narrow green; the 18th is a par 5 with a lake - the
dilemma is whether to lay up short or go for the carry. The par 3s are
generally island-like in design, requiring accuracy to avoid the many
protective bunker features.

Devonshire Course: 18 Holes, 6871yds, Par 72, SSS 72,
Course record 67. Club membership 450. *continued*

Visitors Mon–Sun & BHs. Dress code. **Societies** booking required.
Green Fees 18 holes Mon–Tues £16, Wed–Fri £19, weekends £26.
Par 3 course £6 **Course Designer** Donald Steel **Prof** Michael Ramsden
Facilities ⏀ ⦿ ⧉ ☷ ⬚ ⌖ ⚲ ❦ ⚑
Leisure fishing, 9 hole par 3 academy course **Conf** facs Corporate
Hospitality Days **Location** M1 junct 30, 5m W of Worksop off A619
Hotel ★★★ 70% HL Sitwell Arms, Station Road, RENISHAW
☎ 01246 830004 & 435226 📠 01246 830004 31 en suite

College Pines Worksop College Dr S80 3AL
☎ 01909 501431 📠 01909 481227
e-mail: snelljunior@btinternet.com
web: www.collegepinesgolfclub.co.uk

A fine heathland course set in majestic surroundings. Its free draining
characteristics make it suitable for all year round play and full tees
and greens remain open throughout.

*College Pines Golf Course: 18 Holes, 6801yards, Par 73,
SSS 73, Course record 67. Club membership 500.*

Visitors Mon–Sun & BHs. Dress code. **Societies** booking required.
Green Fees £24 per day, £16 per round (£33/£22 weekends & BHs)
Course Designer David Snell **Prof** Charles Snell **Facilities** ⏀ ⦿ ⧉
⬚ ⌖ ☷ ⚲ ⚑ ❦ ⚑ **Conf** Corporate Hospitality Days
Location M1 junct 30/31, S of Worksop on B6034 Edwinstowe road
Hotel ★★★ 79% HL Clumber Park, Clumber Park, WORKSOP
☎ 01623 835333 📠 01623 835333 73 en suite

Kilton Forest Blyth Rd S81 0TL
☎ 01909 486563

*Kilton Forest Golf Course: 18 Holes, 6424yds, Par 72,
SSS 71, Course record 66.*

Prof Stuart Betteridge **Facilities** ⏀ ⧉ ⬚ ⌖ ☷ ⚲ ❦ ⚑
Leisure bowling **Location** 1m NE of town centre on B6045
Telephone for further details
Hotel ★★★ 78% HL Best Western Lion, 112 Bridge Street,
WORKSOP ☎ 01909 477925 📠 01909 477925 46 en suite

Lindrick Lindrick Common S81 8BH
☎ 01909 475282 📠 01909 488685
web: www.lindrickgolfclub.co.uk

18 Holes, 6486yds, Par 71, SSS 71, Course record 63.
Prof John R King **Facilities** ⏀ ⦿ ⧉ ⬚ ⌖ ☷ ⚲ ❦
Leisure buggies for disabled only **Conf** Corporate Hospitality Days
Location M1 junct 31, 4m NW of Worksop on A57
Telephone for further details
Hotel ★★★ 78% HL Best Western Lion, 112 Bridge Street,
WORKSOP ☎ 01909 477925 📠 01909 477925 46 en suite

Worksop Windmill Ln S80 2SQ
☎ 01909 477731 📠 01909 530917
e-mail: thesecretary@worksopgolfclub.co.uk
web: www.worksopgolfclub.com

Adjacent to Clumber Park, this course has heathland terrain, with
gorse, broom, oak and birch trees. Fast, true greens, dry all year round.

18 Holes, 6660yds, Par 72, SSS 72. Club membership 600.
Visitors Mon, Wed & Fri except BHs. Booking required. Dress code.
Societies welcome. **Green Fees** £55 per day, £40 per 18 holes **Course
Designer** Tom Williamson **Prof** K Crossland **Facilities** ⏀ ⦿ ⧉
⬚ ⌖ ☷ ⚲ ❦ ⚑ ❦ **Leisure** snooker **Conf** facs Corporate
Hospitality Days **Location** A57 ring road onto B6034 to Edwinstowe
Hotel ★★★ 79% HL Clumber Park, Clumber Park, WORKSOP
☎ 01623 835333 📠 01623 835333 73 en suite

OXFORDSHIRE

ABINGDON
Map 4 SU49

Drayton Park Steventon Rd, Drayton OX14 4LA
☎ 01235 550607 (Pro Shop) 📠 01235 525731

Set in the heart of Oxfordshire, an 18-hole parkland course designed
by Hawtree. Five lakes and sand-based greens.

*Drayton Park Golf Course: 18 Holes, 6214yds, Par 70,
SSS 70, Course record 63. Club membership 400.*

Visitors Mon–Sun & BHs. Booking required. Dress code.
Societies booking required. **Green Fees** £19.50 (£25.50 weekends)
Course Designer Hawtree **Prof** Jonathan Draycott **Facilities** ⏀
⦿ ⧉ ⬚ ⌖ ☷ ⚲ ❦ ⚑ **Leisure** 9 hole par 3 course
Conf facs Corporate Hospitality Days **Location** off A34 at Didcot
Hotel ★★★ 78% HL Abingdon Four Pillars Hotel, Marcham Road,
ABINGDON ☎ 0800 374 692 & 01235 553456 📠 0800 374 692
63 en suite

BANBURY
Map 4 SP44
See also **Chacombe (Northamptonshire)**

Banbury Aynho Rd, Adderbury OX17 3NT
☎ 01295 810419 & 812880 📠 01295 810056
web: www.banburygolfclub.co.uk

Undulating wooded course with water features and USGA specification
greens.

*Red & Yellow: 18 Holes, 6557yds, Par 71, SSS 71.
Yellow & Blue: 18 Holes, 6603yds, Par 71, SSS 71.
Red & Blue: 18 Holes, 6746yds, Par 72, SSS 72.
Club membership 300.*

Visitors Mon–Sun & BHs. Booking required. Dress code.
Societies booking required. **Green Fees** £23 per 18 holes (£29
weekends) **Course Designer** Reed/Payn **Prof** Mark McGeehan
Facilities ⏀ ⦿ ⧉ ⬚ ⌖ ☷ ⚲ ❦ **Conf** Corporate
Hospitality Days **Location** M40 junct 10, off B4100 between Adderbury
& Aynho
Hotel ★★★ 82% HL Cartwright Hotel, 1-5 Croughton Road,
AYNHO, Banbury ☎ 01869 811885 📠 01869 811885 21 en suite

Rye Hill Milcombe OX15 4RU
☎ 01295 721818 📠 01295 720089
e-mail: info@ryehill.co.uk
web: www.ryehill.co.uk

Well-drained course, set in 200 acres of rolling countryside, with
both parkland and heathland features, including wide fairways, large
undulating greens, dramatic lakes, and fine views of the surrounding
countryside.

continued

18 Holes, 6919yds, Par 72, SSS 73, Course record 62.
Club membership 400.

Visitors Mon-Sun & BHs. Booking required. **Societies** booking required. **Green Fees** not confirmed **Prof** Tony Pennock **Facilities** ⓐ ⓞⓛ by prior arrangement ⓑ ⓒ ⓓ ⓔ ⓕ ⓖ ⓗ ⓘ **Leisure** fishing, tri-golf 9 hole family course, 3 hole academy course **Conf** facs Corporate Hospitality Days **Location** M40 junct 11, A361 towards Chipping Norton, signed 1m out of Bloxham
Hotel ★★★ 80% HL Best Western Wroxton House, Wroxton St Mary, BANBURY ☎ 01295 730777 ▤ 01295 730777 32 en suite

BURFORD
Map 4 SP21

Burford Swindon Rd OX18 4JG
☎ 01993 822583 ▤ 01993 822801
e-mail: secretary@burfordgolfclub.co.uk
web: www.burfordgolfclub.co.uk

Parkland with mature, tree-lined fairways and high quality greens.

18 Holes, 6401yds, Par 71, SSS 71, Course record 64.
Club membership 770.

Visitors Mon, Wed & Fri except BHs. Other days limited play. Booking required. Dress code. **Societies** welcome. **Green Fees** not confirmed **Course Designer** John H Turner **Prof** Michael Ridge **Facilities** ⓐ ⓞⓛ ⓑ ⓒ ⓓ ⓔ ⓕ ⓖ **Location** 0.5m S off A361
Hotel ★★★ 81% SHL The Lamb Inn, Sheep Street, BURFORD ☎ 01993 823155 ▤ 01993 823155 17 en suite

CHESTERTON
Map 4 SP52

Bicester Golf & Country Club OX26 1TE
☎ 01869 242023 ▤ 01869 240754
web: www.bicestergolf.co.uk

Bicester Golf & Country Club: 18 Holes, 6600yds, Par 71, SSS 70, Course record 68.

Course Designer R Stagg **Location** 0.5m W off A4095
Telephone for further details
Hotel ★★ 74% HL Best Western Jersey Arms, BICESTER ☎ 01869 343234 ▤ 01869 343234 20 en suite

CHIPPING NORTON
Map 4 SP32

Chipping Norton Southcombe OX7 5QH
☎ 01608 642383 ▤ 01608 645422
e-mail: golfadmin@chippingnortongolfclub.com
web: www.chippingnortongolfclub.com

Downland course situated at 800ft above sea level, its undulations providing a good walk. On a limestone base, the course dries quickly in wet conditions. The opening few holes provide a good test of golf made more difficult when the prevailing wind makes the player use the extremes of the course.

18 Holes, 6241yds, Par 71, SSS 70, Course record 62.
Club membership 900.

Visitors dress code. **Societies** welcome. **Green Fees** not confirmed **Prof** Neil Rowlands **Facilities** ⓐ ⓞⓛ ⓑ ⓒ ⓓ ⓔ ⓕ ⓖ ⓗ ⓘ **Location** 1.5m E on A44
Hotel ★★★ 81% HL Mill House Hotel & Restaurant, KINGHAM ☎ 01608 658188 ▤ 01608 658188 23 en suite

Wychwood Lyneham OX7 6QQ
☎ 01993 831841 ▤ 01993 831775
e-mail: info@thewychwood.com
web: www.thewychwood.com

Wychwood was designed to use the natural features of its location. It is set in 170 acres on the fringe of the Cotswolds and blends superbly with its surroundings. Lakes and streams enhance the challenge of the course with water coming into play on eight of the 18 holes. All greens are sand based, built to USGA specification.

18 Holes, 6844yds, Par 72, SSS 72, Course record 67.
Club membership 750.

Visitors Mon, Thu-Sun except BHs. Limited play Tue. 3 days booking required. Handicap certificate. Dress code. **Societies** booking required. **Green Fees** £39 per day, £27 per 18 holes (£39/£32 weekends) **Prof** Adam Souter **Facilities** ⓐ ⓞⓛ ⓑ ⓒ ⓓ ⓔ ⓕ ⓖ ⓗ **Leisure** fishing **Conf** facs Corporate Hospitality Days **Location** off A361 between Burford & Chipping Norton
Hotel ★★★ 81% HL Mill House Hotel & Restaurant, KINGHAM ☎ 01608 658188 ▤ 01608 658188 23 en suite

DIDCOT
Map 4 SU59

Hadden Hill Wallingford Rd OX11 9BJ
☎ 01235 510410 ▤ 01235 511260
e-mail: info@haddenhillgolf.co.uk
web: www.haddenhillgolf.co.uk

A challenging course on undulating terrain with excellent drainage. Superb greens and fairways.

18 Holes, 6563yds, Par 71, SSS 71, Course record 65.
Club membership 400.

Visitors Mon-Sun & BHs. Booking required. Dress code. **Societies** booking required. **Green Fees** £20 per 18 holes, £12 per 9 holes (£25/£15 weekends) **Course Designer** Michael V Morley **Prof** Ian Mitchell **Facilities** ⓐ ⓞⓛ by prior arrangement ⓑ ⓒ ⓓ ⓔ ⓕ ⓖ ⓗ ⓘ **Leisure** 6 hole par 3 academy course, teaching academy **Conf** Corporate Hospitality Days **Location** A34 Milton interchange, follow A4130, course located 1m E of Didcot on Wallingford Road
Hotel ★★★ 78% HL Abingdon Four Pillars Hotel, Marcham Road, ABINGDON ☎ 0800 374 692 & 01235 553456 ▤ 0800 374 692 63 en suite

FARINGDON
Map 4 SU29

Carswell Carswell SN7 8PU
☎ 01367 870422
e-mail: info@carswellgolfandcountryclub.co.uk
web: www.carswellgolfandcountryclub.co.uk

An attractive course set in undulating wooded countryside close to Faringdon. Mature trees, five lakes and well-placed bunkers add interest to the course. Floodlit driving range.

Carswell Golf & Country Club: 18 Holes, 6183yds, Par 72, SSS 70. Club membership 520.

Visitors Mon-Sun & BHs. Booking required Fri-Sun & BHs. Handicap certificate. Dress code. **Societies** welcome. **Green Fees** £20 per 18 holes (£28 weekends & BHs) **Course Designer** J & E Ely **Prof** John Strode **Facilities** ⓐ ⓞⓛ ⓑ ⓒ ⓓ ⓔ ⓕ ⓖ ⓗ ⓘ **Leisure** sauna, gymnasium **Conf** facs Corporate Hospitality Days **Location** off A420
Hotel ★★★ 75% HL Best Western Sudbury House Hotel & Conference Centre, London Street, FARINGDON ☎ 01367 241272 ▤ 01367 241272 49 en suite

FRILFORD
Map 4 SU49

Frilford Heath OX13 5NW
☎ 01865 390864 📄 01865 390823
e-mail: secretary@frilfordheath.co.uk
web: www.frilfordheath.co.uk

Fifty-four holes in three layouts of differing character. The Green course is a fully mature heathland course of some 6006yds. The Red Course is of championship length at 6884yds with a parkland flavour and a marked degree of challenge. The Blue Course is of modern design, and at 6728yds, it incorporates water hazards and large shallow sand traps.

Red Course: 18 Holes, 6884yds, Par 73, SSS 73,
Course record 66.
Green Course: 18 Holes, 6006yds, Par 69, SSS 69,
Course record 67.
Blue Course: 18 Holes, 6728yds, Par 72, SSS 72,
Course record 63. Club membership 1300.

Visitors Mon-Fri except BHs. **Societies** booking required. **Green Fees** £69 per day **Course Designer** J Taylor/D Cotton/S Gidman **Prof** Derek Craik Jnr **Facilities** ⓉⒾⓁ 🍴 🖥 ⛳ ⚐ ⛳ **Conf** facs Corporate Hospitality Days **Location** 0.5m N of Frilford off A338
Hotel ★★★ 78% HL Westwood Country Hotel, Hinksey Hill, Boars Hill, OXFORD ☎ 01865 735408 📄 01865 735408 20 en suite

HENLEY-ON-THAMES
Map 4 SU78

Badgemore Park Badgemore RG9 4NR
☎ 01491 637300 📄 01491 576899
e-mail: info@badgemorepark.com
web: www.badgemorepark.com

Formerly a country estate, Badgemore Park was transformed in 1971 into a beautiful 18 hole parkland golf course, cleverly designed to challenge golfers of all standards.

18 Holes, 6129yds, Par 69, SSS 69, Course record 64.
Club membership 600.

Visitors Mon-Sun except BHs. Booking required. Dress code. **Societies** booking required. **Green Fees** £30 per day/round (£39 weekends) **Course Designer** Robert Sandow **Prof** Jonathan Dunn **Facilities** Ⓣ 🖥 ⛳ 🍴 ⚐ 🖥 ⛳ ◇ ⛳ 🏌 ⛳ **Conf** facs Corporate Hospitality Days **Location** N from Henley towards Rotherfield Greys, 1.5m on right
Hotel ★★★★ Hotel du Vin Henley-on-Thames, New Street, HENLEY-ON-THAMES ☎ 01491 848400 📄 01491 848400 43 en suite

Henley Harpsden RG9 4HG
☎ 01491 575742 📄 01491 412179
e-mail: admin@henleygc.com
web: www.henleygc.com

Designed by James Braid in 1907, the course retains many of his classic features, while being a challenge for all golfers even with modern technology. The first four holes are considered the hardest opening holes of any course in Oxfordshire and possibly the UK. The club celebrated its centenary in 2007.

18 Holes, 6329yds, Par 70, SSS 70, Course record 62.
Club membership 700.

Visitors Mon-Fri except BHs. Handicap certificate. Dress code. **Societies** welcome. **Green Fees** £55 per day, £45 per round, £35 after 4pm **Course Designer** James Braid **Prof** Mark Howell **Facilities** Ⓣ 🍴 🖥 🖥 ⚐ 🍴 ⛳ 🖥 ⛳ ⛳ **Conf** Corporate Hospitality Days **Location** 1.25m S off A4155
Hotel ★★★★ Hotel du Vin Henley-on-Thames, New Street, HENLEY-ON-THAMES ☎ 01491 848400 📄 01491 848400 43 en suite

HORTON-CUM-STUDLEY
Map 4 SP51

Studley Wood The Straight Mile OX33 1BF
☎ 01865 351122 & 351144 📄 01865 351166
e-mail: admin@swgc.co.uk.
web: www.studleywoodgolf.co.uk.

Gently undulating woodland course set in a former deer park. Tranquil setting with an abundance of wildlife. USGA specification tees and greens, with lakes coming into play on nine holes. Fine test of golf for golfers of all levels.

18 Holes, 6811yds, Par 72, SSS 72, Course record 65.
Club membership 700.

Visitors Mon-Fri. Weekends & BHs pm only. Booking required. Dress code. **Societies** booking required. **Green Fees** £37.50 per round **Course Designer** Simon Gidman **Prof** Avann/Charlton/Gavrilovic **Facilities** Ⓣ 🍴 🖥 🖥 ⚐ 🍴 ⛳ 🖥 ⛳ ⛳ **Leisure** teaching academy with indoor facilities **Conf** facs Corporate Hospitality Days **Location** M40 junct 8/9, from N take A34 then B4027, from S take A40 then B4027
Hotel ★★★★ 76% HL Barceló Oxford Hotel, Godstow Road, Wolvercote Roundabout, OXFORD ☎ 01865 489988 📄 01865 489988 168 en suite

KIRTLINGTON
Map 4 SP41

Kirtlington OX5 3JY
☎ 01869 351133 📄 01869 351143
e-mail: info@kirtlingtongolfclub.com
web: www.kirtlingtongolfclub.com

An inland links-type course with challenging greens. The course incorporates many natural features and has 102 bunkers and a 110yd par 3 19th when an extra hole is required to determine a winner. The 9 hole course has three par 4's and six par 3's with all year round buggy track.

18 Holes, 6107yds, Par 70, SSS 69, Course record 68.
Academy Course: 9 Holes, 1535yds, Par 30.
Club membership 400.

Visitors Mon-Sun & BHs. Booking required weekends & BHs. Dress code. **Societies** booking required. **Green Fees** £25 per 18 holes. Academy £10 per 9 holes (£30/£12 weekends & BHs) **Course Designer** Graham Webster **Prof** Andy Taylor **Facilities** Ⓣ 🖥 🖥

continued

🍴 ⚲ 📷 ⛳ ✦ 🛺 ✦ 🏌 **Conf** facs Corporate Hospitality Days **Location** M40 junct 9, on A4095 outside Kirtlington **Hotel** ★★★ 78% HL Weston Manor, WESTON-ON-THE-GREEN, Bicester ☎ 01869 350621 📄 01869 350621 35 en suite

Course Designer Willie Park jnr **Location** off A4130 at Nuffield **Telephone for further details Hotel** ★★★ 74% HL Shillingford Bridge, Shillingford, WALLINGFORD ☎ 01865 858567 📄 01865 858567 40 en suite

MILTON COMMON
Map 4 SP60

The Oxfordshire Rycote Ln OX9 2PU
☎ 01844 278300 📄 01844 278003
e-mail: info@theoxfordshiregolfclub.com
web: www.theoxfordshiregolfclub.com

Designed by Rees Jones, The Oxfordshire is considered to be one of the most exciting courses in the country. The strategically contoured holes blend naturally into the surrounding countryside to provide a challenging game of golf. With four lakes and 135 bunkers, the course makes full use of the terrain and the natural elements to provide characteristics similar to those of a links course.

18 Holes, 7192yds, Par 72, SSS 75, Course record 63.
Club membership 510.

Visitors Mon & Wed-Fri. Weekends & BHs pm. Booking required. Handicap certificate. Dress code. **Societies** booking required. **Green Fees** Summer £90 per 18 holes (£110 weekends & BHs). Winter £65/£75 **Course Designer** Rees Jones **Prof** Justin Barns **Facilities** 🍴 🍽 by prior arrangement 🏪 🖵 🍴 ⚲ 📷 ⛳ ✦ 🛺 ✦ 🏌 **Leisure** Japanese ofuro baths, halfway house **Conf** facs Corporate Hospitality Days **Location** M40 junct 7, 1.5m on A329 **Hotel** ★★★★ 76% HL The Oxford Belfry, MILTON COMMON, Thame ☎ 01844 279381 📄 01844 279381 154 en suite

NUFFIELD
Map 4 SU68

Huntercombe RG9 5SL
☎ 01491 641207 📄 01491 642060
web: www.huntercombegolfclub.co.uk

18 Holes, 6271yds, Par 70, SSS 70, Course record 63.

OXFORD
Map 4 SP50

Hinksey Heights South Hinksey OX1 5AB
☎ 01865 327775 📄 01865 736930
e-mail: sec@oxford-golf.co.uk
web: www.oxford-golf.co.uk

Set in an Area of Outstanding Natural Beauty, overlooking the incomparable Dreaming Spires of Oxford and the Thames Valley. The course has a heathland or links feel with several fairways running along the bottom of valleys created by the use of natural and man-made features.

Hinksey Heights Golf Course: 18 Holes, 6936yds, Par 72, SSS 73, Course record 65.
Spires Course: 9 Holes, 2617yds, Par 35, SSS 65.
Club membership 600.

Visitors Mon-Sun & BHs. Booking required. Dress code. **Societies** welcome. **Green Fees** £18 Mon-Fri (£23 weekends) **Course Designer** David Heads **Prof** Dean Davis **Facilities** 🍴 🍽 🏪 🖵 🍴 ⚲ 📷 ⛳ 🛺 ✦ 🏌 **Leisure** 9 hole par 3 course **Conf** facs Corporate Hospitality Days **Location** on A34 Oxford bypass between Hinksey Hill and Botley Junct, signed **Hotel** ★★★ 74% HL Hawkwell House, Church Way, Iffley Village, OXFORD ☎ 01865 749988 📄 01865 749988 66 en suite

North Oxford Banbury Rd OX2 8EZ
☎ 01865 554924 📄 01865 515921
web: www.nogc.co.uk
18 Holes, 5736yds, Par 67, SSS 67, Course record 62.
Prof Robert Harris **Facilities** 🍴 🍽 🏪 🖵 🍴 ⚲ 📷 ⛳ ✦ **Conf** Corporate Hospitality Days **Location** 3m N of city centre on A4165 **Telephone for further details Hotel** ★★★★ 76% HL Barceló Oxford Hotel, Godstow Road, Wolvercote Roundabout, OXFORD ☎ 01865 489988 📄 01865 489988 168 en suite

Southfield Hill Top Rd OX4 1PF
☎ 01865 242158 📄 01865 250023
web: www.southfieldgolf.com

18 Holes, 6325yds, Par 70, SSS 70, Course record 61.
Course Designer H S Colt **Location** 1.5m SE of city centre off B480 **Telephone for further details Hotel** ★★★ 78% HL Westwood Country Hotel, Hinksey Hill, Boars Hill, OXFORD ☎ 01865 735408 📄 01865 735408 20 en suite

SHRIVENHAM
Map 4 SU28

Shrivenham Park Penny Hooks Ln SN6 8EX
☎ 01793 783853
e-mail: info@shrivenhampark.com
web: www.shrivenhampark.com

A flat, mature parkland course with excellent drainage. A good challenge for all standards of golfer.

18 Holes, 5769yds, Par 69, SSS 69, Course record 64. Club membership 250.

Visitors Mon-Sun & BHs. Booking required Fri-Sun & BHs. Dress code. **Societies** booking required. **Green Fees** £15 per 18 holes £12 per 9 holes (£25/£16 weekends & BHs) **Course Designer** Gordon Cox **Prof** Richard Jefferies **Facilities** ⊕ ⏌☺⏌ ⓑ ⌷ 🕏 ⏌ ⌲ 🎒 ⛳ 🛺 🎿 **Conf** Corporate Hospitality Days **Location** 0.5m NE of town centre on A420 towards Oxford
Hotel ★★★ 75% HL Best Western Sudbury House Hotel & Conference Centre, London Street, FARINGDON ☎ 01367 241272 📄 01367 241272   49 en suite

TADMARTON
Map 4 SP33

Tadmarton Heath OX15 5HL
☎ 01608 737278   📄 01608 730548
e-mail: secretary@tadmartongolf.com
web: www.tadmartongolf.com

A mixture of heath and sandy land on a plateau in the Cotswolds. The course opens gently before reaching the scenic 7th hole across a trout stream close to the clubhouse. The course then progressively tightens through the gorse before a challenging 430yd dog-leg completes the round.

18 Holes, 5936yds, Par 69, SSS 69, Course record 62. Club membership 650.

Visitors Mon-Wed, Fri-Sun except BHs. Thu pm. Booking required. Handicap certificate. Dress code. **Societies** booking required. **Green Fees** £45 per day, £40 after 10am (£50 weekends, £40 after 12pm). Reduced winter rates **Course Designer** Col C K Hutchison **Prof** John Stubbs **Facilities** ⊕ ⏌☺⏌ by prior arrangement ⓑ ⌷ 🕏 ⏌ ⌲ 🎒 ⛳ 🛺 🎿 **Leisure** fishing **Conf** facs Corporate Hospitality Days **Location** 1m SW of Lower Tadmarton off B4035, 6m from Banbury
Hotel ★★★ 78% HL Best Western Banbury House, Oxford Road, BANBURY ☎ 01295 259361 📄 01295 259361   64 en suite

WALLINGFORD
Map 4 SU68

The Springs Hotel & Golf Club Wallingford Rd OX10 6BE
☎ 01491 827310   📄 01491 827312
web: www.thespringshotel.com

The Springs Hotel & Golf Club: 18 Holes, 6470yds, Par 72, SSS 71, Course record 67.

Course Designer Brian Hugget **Location** 2m SE of town centre over River Thames
Telephone for further details
Hotel ★★★ 80% HL The Springs Hotel & Golf Club, Wallingford Road, North Stoke, WALLINGFORD ☎ 01491 836687 📄 01491 836687 32 en suite

WATERSTOCK
Map 4 SP60

Waterstock Thame Rd OX33 1HT
☎ 01844 338093   📄 01844 338036
e-mail: wgc_oxfordgolf@btinternet.com
web: www.waterstockgolf.co.uk

Course designed by Donald Steel with USGA greens and tees fully computer irrigated. Four par 3s facing north, south, east and west. A brook and hidden lake affect six holes, with dog-legs being 4th and 10th holes. Five par 5s on the course, making it a challenge for players of all standards.

Waterstock Golf Course: 18 Holes, 6535yds, Par 72, SSS 72, Course record 69. Club membership 500.

Visitors contact course for details. **Societies** welcome. **Green Fees** £40.50 per day, £23 per round, £16.50 twilight, £12.50 for 9 holes (£48/£28/£19/£15 weekends & BHs) **Course Designer** Donald Steel **Prof** Paul Bryant **Facilities** ⊕ ⏌☺⏌ ⓑ ⌷ 🕏 ⏌ ⌲ 🎒 ⛳ 🎿 🛺 🎿 🎿 **Leisure** fishing **Conf** facs Corporate Hospitality Days **Location** M40 junct 8/8A, E of Oxford near Wheatley
Hotel BUD Days Inn Oxford, M40 junction 8A, Waterstock, OXFORD ☎ 01865 877000 📄 01865 877000   59 en suite

WITNEY
Map 4 SP31

Witney Lakes Downs Rd OX29 0SY
☎ 01993 893011   📄 01993 778866
e-mail: golf@witney-lakes.co.uk
web: www.witney-lakes.co.uk

Five large lakes come into play on eight holes. An excellent test of golf that will use every club in the bag.

Witney Lakes Golf Course: 18 Holes, 6700yds, Par 71, Course record 67. Club membership 400.

Visitors Mon-Sun & BHs. Booking required Tue, Thu & weekends. Dress code.. **Societies** welcome. **Green Fees** £23 per 18 holes (£32 weekends). Winter £18/£27 **Course Designer** Simon Gidman **Prof** John Cook **Facilities** ⊕ ⏌☺⏌ ⓑ ⌷ 🕏 ⏌ ⌲ 🎒 ⬦ 🛺 🎿 🎿 **Leisure** heated indoor swimming pool, sauna, gymnasium, trim trail **Conf** facs Corporate Hospitality Days **Location** 2m W of Witney town centre, off B4047 Witney/Burford road
Hotel ★★★★ 73% HL Witney Four Pillars Hotel, Ducklington Lane, WITNEY ☎ 0800 374692 & 01993 779777 📄 0800 374692 87 en suite

RUTLAND

GREAT CASTERTON
Map 4 TF00

Rutland County PE9 4AQ
☎ 01780 460330   📄 01780 460437
e-mail: info@rutlandcountygolf.co.uk
web: www.rutlandcountygolf.co.uk

Inland links-style course with gently rolling fairways, large tees and greens. Playable all year round due to good drainage.

18 Holes, 6425yds, Par 71, SSS 71, Course record 64. Club membership 740.

Visitors Mon-Sun & BHs. Booking required. Dress code. **Societies** booking required. **Green Fees** not confirmed **Course Designer** Cameron Sinclair **Prof** Ian Melville **Facilities** ⊕ ⏌☺⏌ ⓑ ⌷ 🕏 ⏌ ⌲ 🎒 ⛳ 🎿 🛺 🎿 🎿 **Leisure** par 3 course **Conf** facs Corporate Hospitality Days **Location** A1 exit for Pickworth Woolfox Depot

continued

Hotel ★★★ 74% HL Greetham Valley, Wood Lane, GREETHAM
☎ 01780 460444 🖹 01780 460444 35 en suite

GREETHAM
Map 8 SK91

Greetham Valley Hotel, Golf & Conference Centre Wood
Ln LE15 7NP
☎ 01780 460444 🖹 01780 460623
web: www.greethamvalley.co.uk

*Lakes: 18 Holes, 6764yds, Par 72, SSS 72,
Course record 65.
Valley: 18 Holes, 5595yds, Par 68, SSS 67,
Course record 64.*
Course Designer F E Hinch/B Stephens **Location** A1 onto B668
Oakham road, course signed
Telephone for further details
Hotel ★★★★ ◎◎◎◎ 90% CHH Hambleton Hall, Hambleton,
OAKHAM ☎ 01572 756991 🖹 01572 724721 17 en suite

KETTON
Map 4 SK90

Luffenham Heath PE9 3UU
☎ 01780 720205 🖹 01780 722146
e-mail: jringleby@theluffenhamheathgc.co.uk
web: www.luffenham.co.uk
A James Braid course with firm driving fairways framed by swaying
fescue, cross bunkers, grassy wastes and subtly undulating greens,
hemmed in by sculpted traps. Many outstanding and challenging
holes, placing a premium on accuracy. The 17th par 3 signature
hole is downhill over a tangle of mounds and studded with tricky
bunkers.
*18 Holes, 6563yds, Par 70, SSS 72, Course record 64.
Club membership 550.*
Visitors Mon, Wed-Sun & BHs. Booking required BHs. Handicap
certificate. Dress code. **Societies** booking required. **Green Fees** £65

per day, £50 per round **Course Designer** James Braid **Prof** Ian
Burnett **Facilities** ⑪ ⑩ 🏋 ☐ 🍴 🏌 🏖 🛈 ⚌
Conf Corporate Hospitality Days **Location** 1.5m SW of Ketton on
A6121 by Foster's Bridge

Luffenham Heath

Hotel ★★★ 86% HL The George of Stamford, 71 St Martins,
STAMFORD ☎ 01780 750750 & 750700 (res) 🖹 01780 750750
47 en suite

SHROPSHIRE

BRIDGNORTH
Map 7 SO79

Bridgnorth Stanley Ln WV16 4SF
☎ 01746 763315 🖹 01746 763315
e-mail: secretary.bgc@tiscali.co.uk
web: www.bridgnorthgolfclub.co.uk
Pleasant parkland by the River Severn.
*18 Holes, 6582yds, Par 73, SSS 72, Course record 68.
Club membership 725.*
Visitors Sun-Fri & BHs. Booking required Wed. Dress code.
Societies welcome. **Green Fees** £35 per day, £25 per round (£30 per
round Sun & BHs) **Prof** Steve Russell **Facilities** ⑪ ⑩ 🏋 ☐ 🍴
🏖 🛈 ⚌ 🏌 ⚌ **Leisure** fishing **Conf** Corporate Hospitality Days
Location 1m N off B4373
Guesthouse ★★★★ GH The Laurels, Broadoak, Six Ashes,
BRIDGNORTH ☎ 01384 221546 🖹 01384 221546 7 en suite

CHURCH STRETTON
Map 7 SO49

Church Stretton Trevor Hill SY6 6JH
☎ 01694 722281
e-mail: secretary@churchstrettongolfclub.co.uk
web: www.churchstrettongolfclub.co.uk
Hillside course designed by James Braid on the lower slopes of the
Long Mynd, with magnificent views and well-drained turf. One of the
highest courses in Britain.
*18 Holes, 5020yds, Par 66, SSS 65, Course record 57.
Club membership 450.*
Visitors contact club for details. **Societies** booking required. **Green
Fees** £20 (£25 weekends & BHs) **Course Designer** James Braid
Prof J Townsend **Facilities** ⑪ ⑩ 🏋 ☐ 🍴 🏖 🛈 ⚌
Location W of town. From Cardington Valley up steep Trevor Hill
Hotel ★★★ 73% HL Longmynd Hotel, Cunnery Road, CHURCH
STRETTON, Shropshire ☎ 01694 722244 🖹 01694 722244
50 en suite

CLEOBURY MORTIMER

Map 7 SO67

Cleobury Mortimer Wyre Common DY14 8HQ
☎ 01299 271112   📠 01299 271468
web: www.cleoburygolfclub.com

Foxes Run: 9 Holes, 2980yds, Par 34, SSS 34.
Badgers Sett: 9 Holes, 3271yds, Par 36, SSS 36.
Deer Park: 9 Holes, 3167yds, Par 35, SSS 35.

Course Designer E.G.U **Location** on A4117 1m N of Cleobury Mortimer
Telephone for further details
Guesthouse ★★★★ INN The Crown Inn, Hopton Wafers,
CLEOBURY MORTIMER ☎ 01299 270372 📠 01299 270372
18 en suite

LILLESHALL

Map 7 SJ71

Lilleshall Hall TF10 9AS
☎ 01952 604776   📠 01952 604272
e-mail: honsec@lhgc.entadsl.com
web: www. lilleshallhallgolfclub.co.uk
Heavily-wooded parkland course. Easy walking.

18 Holes, 5906yds, Par 68, SSS 68, Course record 65.
Club membership 650.

Visitors Mon-Fri except BHs. Dress code. **Societies** booking required.
Green Fees not confirmed **Course Designer** H S Colt **Prof** Robert
Bluck **Facilities** ⊕ ⊗ ≜ ⊑ ⌶ ⅂ ⌁ ⅄ **Conf** Corporate
Hospitality Days **Location** 3m SE
Hotel ★★★ 78% HL Hadley Park House, Hadley Park, TELFORD
☎ 01952 677269 📠 01952 677269   12 en suite

LUDLOW

Map 7 SO57

Ludlow Bromfield SY8 2BT
☎ 01584 856366   📠 01584 856366
e-mail: secretary@ludlowgolfclub.com
web: www.ludlowgolfclub.com

A long-established heathland course in the middle of the racecourse.
Very flat, quick drying, with broom and gorse-lined fairways, excellent
playing surfaces all year round.

18 Holes, 6277yds, Par 70, SSS 70, Course record 65.
Club membership 700.

Visitors Mon-Sun & BHs. Dress code. **Societies** booking required.
Green Fees £28 per round/£35 per day (£35 per round weekends &
BHs) **Prof** Russell Price **Facilities** ⊕ ⊗ ≜ ⊑ ⌶ ⅂ ⅄
⌁ ⅊ ⌁ **Conf** Corporate Hospitality Days **Location** 1m N of Ludlow
off A49
Hotel ★★★ 80% HL Feathers, The Bull Ring, LUDLOW
☎ 01584 875261 📠 01584 875261   40 en suite

MARKET DRAYTON

Map 7 SJ63

Market Drayton Sutton Ln TF9 2HX
☎ 01630 652266   📠 01630 656564
e-mail: market.draytongc@btconnect.com
web: www.marketdraytongolfclub.co.uk

Undulating parkland course with two steep banks in quiet,
picturesque surroundings, providing a good test of golf.

18 Holes, 6290yds, Par 71, SSS 71, Course record 67.
Club membership 600.

Visitors booking required weekends & BHs. Handicap certificate. Dress

code. **Societies** booking required. **Green Fees** Summer £30 per round,
Winter £25 **Prof** Russell Clewes **Facilities** ⊕ ⊗ ≜ ⊑ ⌶ ⅂
🖭 ⋄ 🛺 ⌁ **Conf** Corporate Hospitality Days **Location** 1m S off
A41/A529
Hotel ★★★ 83% HL Goldstone Hall, Goldstone, MARKET DRAYTON
☎ 01630 661202 📠 01630 661202   12 en suite

NEWPORT

Map 7 SJ72

Aqualate Golf Centre Stafford Rd TF10 9DB
☎ 01952 811699
A parkland course with gentle gradients and hazards.

Aqualate Golf Centre: 9 Holes, 5659yds, Par 69, SSS 67,
Course record 67. Club membership 175.

Visitors Mon-Sun & BHs. **Societies** booking required. **Green
Fees** not confirmed **Prof** Kevin Short **Facilities** ⊑ ⅄ ⌶ ⌁ ⅄
Location 2m E of town centre on A518, 400yds from junct A41
Hotel ★★★ 78% HL Hadley Park House, Hadley Park, TELFORD
☎ 01952 677269 📠 01952 677269   12 en suite

OSWESTRY

Map 7 SJ22

Mile End Mile End, Old Shrewsbury Rd SY11 4JF
☎ 01691 671246   📠 01691 670580
e-mail: info@mileendgolfclub.co.uk
web: www.mileendgolfclub.co.uk

A gently undulating parkland-type course covering over 135 acres and
including a number of water features, notably the 3rd, 8th and 17th
holes, which have greens protected by large pools. The longest hole is
the par 5, 542yd 14th, complete with its two tiered green.

Mile End Golf Course: 18 Holes, 6233yds, Par 71, SSS 70,
Course record 66. Club membership 700.

Visitors contact course for details. **Societies** welcome. **Green Fees** not
confirmed **Course Designer** Price/Gough **Prof** Scott Carpenter
Facilities ⊕ ⊗ ≜ ⊑ ⅄ ⌁ 🛺 ⌁ **Conf** Corporate
Hospitality Days **Location** 1m SE of Oswestry, signposted off A5/A483
Hotel ★★★★ 80% HL Wynnstay, Church Street, OSWESTRY
☎ 01691 655261 📠 01691 655261   34 en suite

Oswestry Aston Park, Queens Head SY11 4JJ
☎ 01691 610535   📠 01691 610535
e-mail: secretary@oswestrygolfclub.co.uk
web: www.oswestrygolfclub.co.uk

Gently undulating mature parkland course set in splendid Shropshire
countryside. Free draining soils make Oswestry an ideal year round
test of golf. New clubhouse opened 2009.

18 Holes, 6050yds, Par 70, SSS 69, Course record 61.
Club membership 910.

Visitors Mon-Sun & BHs. Booking required. Handicap certificate. Dress
code. **Societies** booking required. **Green Fees** £43 per day, £32 per
round (£48/£38 weekends) **Course Designer** James Braid **Prof** Jason
Davies **Facilities** ⊕ ⊗ ≜ ⊑ ⌶ ⅄ 🖭 ⌁ 🛺 ⌁
Conf facs Corporate Hospitality Days **Location** 2m SE on A5
Hotel ★★★★ 80% HL Wynnstay, Church Street, OSWESTRY
☎ 01691 655261 📠 01691 655261   34 en suite

SHIFNAL
Map 7 SJ70

Shifnal Decker Hill TF11 8QL
☎ 01952 460330   📇 01952 460330
web: www.shifnalgolfclub.com
Well-wooded parkland. Walking is easy and an attractive country
mansion serves as the clubhouse.

18 Holes, 6468yds, Par 71, SSS 71, Course record 65.
Club membership 700.

Visitors Mon-Fri & BHs. Booking required. Handicap certificate. Dress
code. **Societies** booking required. **Green Fees** £45 per day, £35 per
18 holes **Course Designer** Pennick **Prof** David Ashton **Facilities** ⑪
🍽 🍸 🖵 🍴 ⚖ 🏌 ✐ **Conf** Corporate Hospitality Days
Location 1m N off B4379
Hotel ★★★★ 76% HL Park House, Park Street, SHIFNAL
☎ 01952 460128 📇 01952 460128 54 en suite

SHREWSBURY
Map 7 SJ41

Arscott Arscott, Pontesbury SY5 0XP
☎ 01743 860114   📇 01743 860881
e-mail: golf@arscott.dydirect.net
web: www.arscottgolfclub.co.uk
At 365ft above sea level, the views from Arscott Golf Club of the hills
of south Shropshire and Wales are superb. Arscott is set in mature
parkland with water features and holes demanding all sorts of club
choice. A challenge to all golfers both high and low handicap.

18 Holes, 6178yds, Par 70, SSS 69, Course record 66.
Club membership 500.

Visitors dress code. **Societies** booking required. **Green Fees** £24 per
round (£29 weekends & BHs) **Course Designer** M Hamer **Prof** Glyn
Sadd **Facilities** ⑪ 🍽 🍸 🖵 🍴 ⚖ 🏌 🍴 ✐
Leisure fishing **Conf** facs Corporate Hospitality Days **Location** off
A488 S of town
Hotel ★★★ 70% HL The Lion, Wyle Cop, SHREWSBURY
☎ 01743 353107 📇 01743 353107 59 en suite

Shrewsbury Condover SY5 7BL
☎ 01743 872977   📇 01743 872977
e-mail: info@shrewsbury-golf-club.co.uk
web: www.shrewsburygolfclub.co.uk
Parkland course. First nine flat, second undulating with good views
of the Long Mynd. Several holes with water features. Fast putting
surfaces.

18 Holes, 6207yds, Par 70, SSS 70. Club membership 872.

Visitors Mon-Sun & BHs. Dress code. **Societies** welcome **Green
Fees** £28 (£32 weekends) **Prof** John Richards **Facilities** ⑪ 🍽
🍸 🖵 🍴 ⚖ 🏌 ✐ 🍴 ✐ **Conf** facs Corporate
Hospitality Days **Location** 4m S off A49
Hotel ★★★ 82% HL Prince Rupert, Butcher Row, SHREWSBURY
☎ 01743 499955 📇 01743 499955 70 en suite

TELFORD
Map 7 SJ60

Shropshire Golf Centre Granville Park, Muxton TF2 8PQ
☎ 01952 677800   📇 01952 677622
e-mail: sales@theshropshire.co.uk
web: www.theshropshire.co.uk
This 27-hole course is set in rolling countryside. The three loops
of nine make the most of the natural undulations and provide a
challenge for golfer of all abilities. Ample stretches of water and
bullrush lined ditches, wide countered fairways and rolling greens
guarded by mature trees, hummocks and vast bunkers. Several
elevated tees with spectacular views.

Blue: 9 Holes, 3286yds, Par 35, SSS 35.
Silver: 9 Holes, 3303yds, Par 36, SSS 36.
Gold: 9 Holes, 3334yds, Par 36, SSS 36.
Club membership 495.

Visitors contact centre for details. **Societies** welcome. **Green
Fees** not confirmed **Course Designer** Martin Hawtree **Prof** Rob Grier
Facilities ⑪ 🍽 🍸 🖵 🍴 ⚖ 🏌 🍴 ✐ 🍴 ✐ 🏌
Leisure par 3 14 hole academy course **Conf** facs Corporate Hospitality
Days **Location** M54/A5 onto B5060 towards Donnington, 3rd exit at
Granville rdbt
Hotel ★★★ 78% HL Hadley Park House, Hadley Park, TELFORD
☎ 01952 677269 📇 01952 677269 12 en suite

Telford Hotel & Golf Resort Great Hay Dr, Sutton Heights
TF7 4DT
☎ 01952 429977   📇 01952 586602
e-mail: telfordgolf@qhotels.co.uk
web: www.qhotels.co.uk

Picturesque course with tree-lined fairways, open greens and
strategically placed water hazards. Challenging for all levels of golfer.

Telford Hotel & Golf Resort: 18 Holes, 6809yds, Par 72,
SSS 72, Course record 66. Club membership 300.

Visitors Mon-Sun & BHs. Booking required. Dress code.
Societies booking required. **Green Fees** £35 per round (£40
weekends) **Course Designer** Bryan Griffiths/John Harris **Prof** George
Boden **Facilities** ⑪ 🍽 🍸 🖵 🍴 ⚖ 🏌 🍴 ◇ 🍴 ✐
🏌 **Leisure** heated indoor swimming pool, sauna, gymnasium, spa
treatments **Conf** facs Corporate Hospitality Days **Location** M54
junct 4, follow signs for A442 towards Bridgnorth, exit at sign for
Madeley/ Ironbridge Gorge. Turn right at first rdbt, left at next rdbt,
take third road on left (Great Hay Drive).
Hotel ★★★★ 75% HL Telford Hotel & Golf Resort, Great Hay
Drive, Sutton Heights, TELFORD ☎ 01952 429977 📇 01952 429977
114 en suite

WELLINGTON

Map 7 SJ61

Wrekin Ercall Woods, Golf Links Ln TF6 5BX
☎ 01952 244032   📄 01952 252906
e-mail: wrekingolfclub@btconnect.com
web: www.wrekingolfclub.co.uk

Downland course with some hard walking but superb views.

18 Holes, 5570yds, Par 66, SSS 67, Course record 62.
Club membership 650.

Visitors Mon, Wed-Sun & BHs. Booking required. Dress code.
Societies booking required. **Green Fees** £35 per day, £27 per round
(£35 per round weekends & BHs) **Prof** O Evans **Facilities** ⊕ ⏺
🍺 ⛳ 🍴 ⛳ 🏠 ✎ 🚗 ✎ **Location** M54 junct 7, 1.25m S
off B5061
Hotel ★★★ 78% HL Hadley Park House, Hadley Park, TELFORD
☎ 01952 677269 📄 01952 677269   12 en suite

WESTON-UNDER-REDCASTLE

Map 7 SJ52

Hawkstone Park Hotel SY4 5UY
☎ 01948 841700   📄 01939 200335
e-mail: info.hawkstonepark@principal-hayley.com
web: www.hawkstone.co.uk

The Hawkstone Course plays through the English Heritage
designated Grade I landscape of the historic park and follies,
providing a beautiful, tranquil yet dramatic back drop to a round
of golf. The Championship Course utilises many American style
features and extensive water hazards and is a challenging
alternative.

Hawkstone Course: 18 Holes, 6497yds, Par 72, SSS 71,
Course record 65.
Championship Course: 18 Holes, 6763yds, Par 72,
SSS 72, Course record 64. Club membership 650.

Visitors Mon-Sun & BHs. Booking required. Dress code.
Societies booking required. **Green Fees** Hawkstone £45 per

round. Championship £35 (£45 weekends) **Course Designer** J
Braid **Facilities** ⊕ ⏺ 🍺 ⛳ 🍴 ⛳ 🏠 🚗 ◇ ✎ 🚗
✎ 🏌 **Leisure** 6 hole par 3 course, snooker. **Conf** facs Corporate
Hospitality Days **Location** off A49/A442
Hotel ★★★ 72% SHL Dodington Lodge, Dodington, WHITCHURCH
☎ 01948 662539 📄 01948 662539   10 en suite

WHITCHURCH

Map 7 SJ54

Hill Valley Terrick Rd SY13 4JZ
☎ 01948 663584 & 667788   📄 01948 665927
web: www.hill-valley.co.uk
Emerald: 18 Holes, 6628yds, Par 73, SSS 72,
Course record 64.
Sapphire: 18 Holes, 4800yds, Par 66, SSS 64.

Course Designer Peter Alliss/Dave Thomas **Location** 1m N. Follow
signs from bypass
Telephone for further details
Hotel ★★★★ 76% HL Macdonald Hill Valley, Tarporley Road,
WHITCHURCH ☎ 0870 194 2133 📄 0870 194 2133   81 en suite

WORFIELD

Map 7 SO79

Chesterton Valley Chesterton WV15 5NX
☎ 01746 783682
Dry course built on sandy soil giving excellent drainage. No temporary
greens and no trolley ban.

18 Holes, 5938yards, SSS 69. Club membership 450.

Visitors Mon-Sun & BHs. Dress code. **Societies** welcome. **Green
Fees** phone **Course Designer** Mike Davis **Facilities** ⛳ 🍴 ⛳ 🏠
✎ 🚗 ✎ **Location** on B4176
Hotel ★★★ SHL Old Vicarage Hotel, Worfield, BRIDGNORTH
☎ 01746 716497 📄 01746 716497   14 en suite

Worfield Roughton WV15 5HE
☎ 01746 716372   📄 01746 716302
e-mail: enquiries@worfieldgolf.co.uk
web: www.worfieldgolf.co.uk

A parkland links mix with three large lakes, many bunkers and large
trees giving a challenge to golfers. Superb views and drainage which
allows play on full greens and tees all year. Water comes into play
on four holes, including the short par 4 18th where it lies in front of
the green.

Worfield Golf Course: 18 Holes, 6545yds, Par 73, SSS 72,
Course record 68. Club membership 520.

Visitors dress code. **Societies** booking required. **Green Fees** £22 per

continued

round **Course Designer** T Williams **Prof** Nick Doody **Facilities** ⓘ ⑩ 🛒 🖥 🍴 🏌 🏡 🖊 🛍 🖊 **Conf** facs Corporate Hospitality Days **Location** 3m W of Bridgnorth, off A454
Hotel ★★★ SHL Old Vicarage Hotel, Worfield, BRIDGNORTH
☎ 01746 716497 🖹 01746 716497 14 en suite

SOMERSET

BACKWELL   Map 3 ST46

Tall Pines Cooks Bridle Path, Downside BS48 3DJ
☎ 01275 472076 🖹 01275 474869
e-mail: terry.murray3@btinternet.com
web: www.tallpinesgolfclub.co.uk
Free draining parkland with views over the Bristol Channel.

18 Holes, 6049yds, Par 70, SSS 70, Course record 65.
Club membership 500.

Visitors Mon-Sun & BHs. Booking required weekends & BHs. Dress code. **Societies** welcome. **Green Fees** £20 per 18 holes **Course Designer** T Murray **Prof** Alex Murray **Facilities** ⓘ ⑩ 🛒 🖥 🍴 🏌 🏡 🖊 🛍 🖊 **Conf** Corporate Hospitality Days
Location next to Bristol Airport, 1m off A38/A370
Hotel ★★★ 71% HL Beachlands, 17 Uphill Road North, WESTON-SUPER-MARE ☎ 01934 621401 🖹 01934 621401 21 en suite

BATH   Map 3 ST76

Bath Sham Castle BA2 6JG
☎ 01225 463834 🖹 01225 331027
web: www.bathgolfclub.org.uk
18 Holes, 6442yds, Par 71, SSS 71, Course record 66.
Course Designer Colt & others **Location** 1.5m SE city centre off A36
Telephone for further details
Hotel ★★★ 73% HL Mercure Francis, Queen Square, BATH
☎ 01225 424105 & 338970 🖹 01225 424105 95 en suite

Entry Hill BA2 5NA
☎ 01225 834248
Entry Hill Golf Course: 9 Holes, 2065yds, Par 33, SSS 30.
Prof Tim Tapley **Facilities** ⓘ 🛒 🖥 🍴 🏡 🏤 🖊 **Location** off A367
Telephone for further details
Hotel ★★★ 79% SHL Haringtons, 8-10 Queen Street, BATH
☎ 01225 461728 & 445883 🖹 01225 461728 13 en suite

Lansdown Lansdown BA1 9BT
☎ 01225 422138 🖹 01225 339252
e-mail: admin@lansdowngolfclub.co.uk
web: www.lansdowngolfclub.co.uk
A level parkland course situated 800ft above sea level, providing a challenge to both low and high handicap golfers. Stunning views from the 5th and 14th holes.

18 Holes, 6428yds, Par 71, SSS 70, Course record 67.
Club membership 600.

Visitors Mon-Sun & BHs. Booking required. Handicap certificate. Dress code. **Societies** welcome. **Green Fees** £35 per day, £30 per round, 9 holes £15 **Course Designer** C A Whitcombe **Prof** Scott Readman **Facilities** ⓘ ⑩ 🛒 🖥 🍴 🏌 🏡 🖊 🛍 🖊 **Leisure** 6 hole

academy course **Conf** facs Corporate Hospitality Days **Location** M4 junct 18, 6m SW by Bath racecourse
Hotel ★★★ 72% HL Pratt's, South Parade, BATH
☎ 01225 460441 🖹 01225 460441 46 en suite

BRIDGWATER   Map 3 ST23

Cannington Cannington Centre for TA5 2LS
☎ 01278 655050 🖹 01278 655055
Cannington Golf Course: 9 Holes, 6072yds, Par 68, SSS 70, Course record 64.
Course Designer Martin Hawtree **Location** 4m NW off A39
Telephone for further details
Hotel ★★★ 75% HL Combe House, HOLFORD ☎ 01278 741382 & 741213 🖹 01278 741382 18 en suite

BURNHAM-ON-SEA   Map 3 ST34

Brean Coast Rd, Brean Sands TA8 2QY
☎ 01278 752111(pro shop) 🖹 01278 752111
e-mail: proshop@brean.com
web: www.breangolfclub.co.uk

Level moorland course with water hazards. Facilities of Brean Leisure Park adjoining.
Brean Golf Club At Brean Leisure Park: 18 Holes, 5715yds, Par 69, SSS 68, Course record 66. Club membership 350.
Visitors Mon-Sun & BHs. Booking required. Dress code.
Societies booking required. **Green Fees** not confirmed **Course Designer** In house **Prof** David Haines **Facilities** ⓘ ⑩ 🛒 🖥 🍴 🏌 🏡 🏤 🖊 🛍 🖊 **Leisure** heated swimming pool and outdoor swimming pool, fishing **Conf** facs Corporate Hospitality Days **Location** M5 junct 22, 4m on coast road
Hotel ★★★ 71% HL Beachlands, 17 Uphill Road North, WESTON-SUPER-MARE ☎ 01934 621401 🖹 01934 621401 21 en suite

Burnham & Berrow St Christopher's Way TA8 2PE
☎ 01278 785760 📠 01278 795440
e-mail: secretary.bbgc@btconnect.com
web: www.burnhamandberrowgolfclub.co.uk

Natural championship links course with panoramic views of the Somerset hills and the Bristol Channel. A true test of golf suitable only for players with a handicap of 22 or better.

Championship Course: 18 Holes, 6383yds, Par 71, SSS 72, Course record 64.
Channel Course: 9 Holes, 5819yds, Par 70, SSS 68. Club membership 900.

Visitors Mon-Sun & BHs. Booking required. Dress code.
Societies booking required. **Green Fees** Championship Course £85 per day, £65 per round (£75 per round Sat) **Course Designer** H S Colt **Prof** Mark Crowther-Smith **Facilities** ⊕ 🍴 🍺 ☐ 🍽 ♨ 🏠 ⛳ ♢ 🏌 🏁 **Location** 1m N of town on B3140
Hotel ★★ 78% HL Woodlands Country House, Hill Lane, BRENT KNOLL ☎ 01278 760232 📠 01278 760232 9 en suite

CHARD
Map 3 ST30

Windwhistle Cricket St Thomas TA20 4DG
☎ 01460 30231 📠 01460 30055
e-mail: info@windwhistlegolfclub.co.uk
web: www.windwhistlegolfclub.co.uk

Parkland course at 735ft above sea level with outstanding views over the Somerset Levels to the Bristol Channel and south Wales.

East/West Course: 18 Holes, 6176yds, Par 72, SSS 70, Course record 69. Club membership 500.

Visitors Mon-Sun & BHs. Dress code. **Societies** booking required.
Green Fees £25 per 18 holes (£30 weekends) **Course Designer** Braid & Taylor/Fisher **Prof** Paul Deeprose **Facilities** ⊕ 🍺 ☐ 🍽 ♨ 🏠 🏁 🏠 ⛳ 🏌 **Leisure** squash **Conf** facs Corporate Hospitality Days **Location** 3m E on A30

Hotel ★★★ 78% HL Best Western Shrubbery, ILMINSTER
☎ 01460 52108 📠 01460 52108 21 en suite

CLEVEDON
Map 3 ST47

Clevedon Castle Rd, Walton St Mary BS21 7AA
☎ 01275 874057 📠 01275 341228
e-mail: secretary@clevedongolfclub.co.uk
web: clevedongolfclub.co.uk

Situated on the cliff overlooking the Severn estuary with distant views of the Welsh coast. Excellent parkland course in first-class condition. Magnificent scenery and some tremendous drop holes.

18 Holes, 6557yds, Par 72, SSS 72, Course record 65. Club membership 750.

Visitors Sun-Fri & BHs. Handicap certificate. Dress code.
Societies booking required. **Green Fees** £35 per day (£45 weekends)
Course Designer J H Taylor **Prof** Robert Scanlan **Facilities** ⊕ 🍴 🍺 ☐ 🍽 ♨ 🏠 ⛳ 🏌 **Conf** Corporate Hospitality Days
Location M5 junct 20, 1m NE of town centre
Hotel ★★★★ 78% HL Cadbury House Hotel, Health Club & Spa, Frost Hill, Congresbury, BRISTOL ☎ 01934 834343 📠 01934 834343 72 en suite

CONGRESBURY
Map 3 ST46

Mendip Spring Honeyhall Ln BS49 5JT
☎ 01934 852322 📠 01934 853021
e-mail: info@mendipspringgolfclub.com
web: www.mendipspringgolfclub.com

Set in peaceful countryside with the Mendip Hills as a backdrop, this 18-hole course includes lakes and numerous water hazards covering some 12 acres of the course. The 11th hole has a stroke index of 1 and there are long drives on the 7th and 13th. The nine-hole Lakeside course is easy walking, mainly par 4. Floodlit driving range.

Brinsea Course: 18 Holes, 6412yds, Par 71, SSS 70, Course record 64.
Lakeside: 9 Holes, 2329yds, Par 34, SSS 66. Club membership 500.

Visitors Mon-Sun & BHs. Booking required for Brinsea course. Handicap certificate for Brinsea course. Dress code. **Societies** booking required. **Green Fees** Brinsea £30 (£40 weekends). Lakeside £9.50/£10 **Prof** John Blackburn & Robert Moss **Facilities** ⊕ 🍴 🍺 ☐ 🍽 ♨ 🏠 🏁 ⛳ ♢ 🏌 🏠 ⛳ 🏌 **Conf** facs Corporate Hospitality Days **Location** 2m S between A370 & A368
Hotel ★★★★ 78% HL Cadbury House Hotel, Health Club & Spa, Frost Hill, Congresbury, BRISTOL ☎ 01934 834343 📠 01934 834343 72 en suite

ENMORE
Map 3 ST23

Enmore Park TA5 2AN
☎ 01278 672100 📠 01278 672101
e-mail: manager@enmorepark.co.uk
web: www.enmorepark.co.uk

A parkland course on the foothills of the Quantocks, with water features. Wooded countryside and views of the Mendips; 1st and 10th are testing holes.

18 Holes, 6411yds, Par 71, SSS 71, Course record 64. Club membership 700.

Visitors Mon-Sun & BHs. Booking required. Handicap certificate Dress

continued

code. **Societies** booking required. **Green Fees** £50 per day £36 per round (£47 per round weekends & BHs) **Course Designer** Hawtree **Prof** Nigel Wixon **Facilities** ⊕ ⦿ ⛳ ⬜ ⛳ ⚲ 🏠 ⚲ ✎ 🏌 ⚲ **Conf** facs Corporate Hospitality Days **Location** 0.5m E of village, 3.5m SW of Bridgwater
Hotel ★★★ 75% HL Combe House, HOLFORD ☎ 01278 741382 & 741213 📠 01278 741382 18 en suite

FARRINGTON GURNEY   Map 3 ST65

Farrington Golf & Country Club Marsh Ln BS39 6TS
☎ 01761 451596   📠 01761 451021
web: www.farringtongolfclub.net
Main Course: 18 Holes, 6335yds, Par 72, SSS 71, Course record 66.
Course Designer Peter Thompson **Location** SE of village off A37
Telephone for further details
Hotel ★★★ 78% HL Best Western Centurion, Charlton Lane, MIDSOMER NORTON ☎ 01761 417711 & 412214 📠 01761 417711 44 en suite

FROME   Map 3 ST74

Frome Golf Centre Critchill Manor BA11 4LJ
☎ 01373 453410
web: www.fromegolfclub.fsnet.co.uk
Frome Golf Club: 18 Holes, 5527yds, Par 69, SSS 67, Course record 64.
Prof Lawrence Wilkin **Facilities** ⊕ ⛳ ⬜ ⚲ 🏠 🏌 **Location** 1m SW of town centre
Telephone for further details
Hotel 67% The George at Nunney, 11 Church Street, NUNNEY ☎ 01373 836458 📠 01373 836458 9 en suite

Orchardleigh BA11 2PH
☎ 01373 454200   📠 01373 454202
web: www.orchardleighgolf.co.uk
18 Holes, 6824yds, Par 72, SSS 73, Course record 67.
Course Designer Brian Huggett **Location** on A362 Frome to Radstock road near village of Buckland Dinham
Telephone for further details
Hotel 67% The George at Nunney, 11 Church Street, NUNNEY ☎ 01373 836458 📠 01373 836458 9 en suite

GURNEY SLADE   Map 3 ST64

Mendip BA3 4UT
☎ 01749 840570   📠 01749 841439
e-mail: secretary@mendipgolfclub.com
web: www.mendipgolfclub.com
Undulating downland course offering an interesting test of golf on superb fairways and extensive views over the surrounding countryside.
18 Holes, 6383yds, Par 71, SSS 71, Course record 65. Club membership 900.
Visitors contact club for details. **Societies** welcome. **Green Fees** £28 per round (£36 weekends) **Course Designer** C K Cotton **Prof** Adrian Marsh **Facilities** ⊕ ⦿ ⛳ ⬜ ⚲ 🏠 ⚲ ✎ 🏌 **Location** 1.5m S off A37
Hotel ★★★ 78% HL Best Western Centurion, Charlton Lane, MIDSOMER NORTON ☎ 01761 417711 & 412214 📠 01761 417711 44 en suite

KEYNSHAM   Map 3 ST66

Stockwood Vale Stockwood Ln BS31 2ER
☎ 0117 986 6505   📠 0117 986 8974
e-mail: stockwoodvale@aol.com
web: www.stockwoodvale.com
Undulating and challenging public course in a beautiful setting with interesting well bunkered holes, in particular the beautiful and challenging 5th and 13th holes.
18 Holes, 6031yds, Par 71, SSS 69. Club membership 600.
Visitors Mon-Sun & BHs. Booking required. Dress code.
Societies booking required. **Green Fees** £16.50 per round (£19.50 weekends). **Facilities** ⊕ ⦿ ⛳ ⬜ ⚲ 🏠 ✎ 🏌 **Conf** facs Corporate Hospitality Days **Location** A4 W from Bath to the Bristol Ring Road (A4174) at the Hicks Gate roundabout. Turn left at rdbt for Keynsham. After 1m turn right at mini rdbt, club signed
Guesthouse ★★★★ GH Grasmere Court, 22-24 Bath Road, KEYNSHAM ☎ 0117 986 2662 📠 0117 986 2662 16 en suite

LONG ASHTON   Map 3 ST57

Long Ashton The Clubhouse BS41 9DW
☎ 01275 392229   📠 01275 394395
web: www.longashtongolfclub.co.uk

18 Holes, 6400yds, Par 71, SSS 71.
Course Designer J H Taylor **Location** 0.5m N on B3128
Telephone for further details
Hotel ★★★★ 70% HL Redwood Hotel & Country Club, Beggar Bush Lane, Failand, BRISTOL ☎ 0870 609 6144 📠 0870 609 6144 112 en suite

Woodspring Golf & Country Club Yanley Ln BS41 9LR
☎ 01275 394378   📠 01275 394473
e-mail: info@woodspring-golf.com
web: www.woodspring-golf.com
Set in 245 acres of undulating Somerset countryside, featuring superb natural water hazards, protected greens and a rising landscape. The course has three individual nine-hole courses, the Avon, Severn and Brunel. The 9th hole on the Brunel Course is a feature hole, with an elevated tee shot over a natural gorge. Long carries to tight fairways, elevated island tees and challenging approaches to greens make the most of the 27 holes.
Avon Course: 9 Holes, 2960yds, Par 35, SSS 34.
Brunel Course: 9 Holes, 3320yds, Par 37, SSS 35.
Severn Course: 9 Holes, 3267yds, Par 36, SSS 35.
Club membership 300.
Visitors Mon-Sun & BHs. Booking required weekends. **Societies** booking

continued

required. **Green Fees** £30 per 18 holes (£34 weekends & BHs) **Course Designer** Clarke/Alliss/Steel **Prof** Kevin Pitts **Facilities** ⑪ ⚑ ⚐ 🖥 🕿 🍴 🛎 ♂ 🏌 ♂ 🏌 **Conf** facs Corporate Hospitality Days **Location** off A38 Bridgwater Road
Hotel ★★★★ 70% HL Redwood Hotel & Country Club, Beggar Bush Lane, Failand, BRISTOL 🕿 0870 609 6144 📠 0870 609 6144 112 en suite

MIDSOMER NORTON   Map 3 ST65

Fosseway Golf Course Charlton Ln BA3 4BD
🕿 01761 412214   📠 01761 418357
web: www.centurionhotel.co.uk
Fosseway Golf Course: 9 Holes, 4565yds, Par 67, SSS 61.
Course Designer C K Cotton/F Pennink **Location** SE of town centre off A367
Telephone for further details
Hotel ★★★ 78% HL Best Western Centurion, Charlton Lane, MIDSOMER NORTON 🕿 01761 417711 & 412214 📠 01761 417711 44 en suite

MINEHEAD   Map 3 SS94

Minehead & West Somerset The Warren TA24 5SJ
🕿 01643 702057   📠 01643 705095
e-mail: secretary@mineheadgolf.co.uk
web: www.minehead-golf-club.co.uk
Flat seaside links, established in 1882, very exposed to wind, with good turf set on a shingle bank. The last five holes adjacent to the beach are testing. The 215yd 18th is wedged between the beach and the club buildings and provides a good finish. Considered to be the oldest links course in Somerset.
18 Holes, 6153yds, Par 71, SSS 69, Course record 65.
Club membership 620.
Visitors Mon-Sun & BHs. Dress code. **Societies** booking required.
Green Fees £40 per day (£47 weekends & BHs) **Prof** Ian Read
Facilities ⑪ 🍴 ⚐ 🖥 ⚑ 🛎 🕿 ♂ **Conf** Corporate Hospitality Days **Location** E end of esplanade
Hotel ★★ 84% SHL Channel House, Church Path, MINEHEAD 🕿 01643 703229 📠 01643 703229 8 en suite

SALTFORD   Map 3 ST66

Saltford Golf Club Ln BS31 3AA
🕿 01225 873513   📠 01225 873525
e-mail: mike@saltfordgolfclub.co.uk
web: www.saltfordgolfclub.co.uk
Set in 150 acres of attractive countryside, the course nestles in a natural wooded setting with extensive views over Bath and the Avon valley. Notable holes are the long par 4 6th hole and the two delightful finishing holes.
18 Holes, 6183yds, Par 71, SSS 71. Club membership 600.
Visitors Mon-Sun & BHs. Booking required. Handicap certificate. Dress code. **Societies** booking required. **Green Fees** £30 per round (£35 weekends). Winter £22/£28 **Course Designer** Harry Vardon
Prof Darren Read **Facilities** ⑪ ⚐ 🖥 ⚑ 🛎 🕿 ♂ 🏌
♂ **Leisure** snooker **Conf** facs Corporate Hospitality Days **Location** S of village, off A4
Hotel ★★★ 82% CHH Hunstrete House, HUNSTRETE 🕿 01761 490490 📠 01761 490490 25 en suite

SOMERTON   Map 3 ST42

Long Sutton Long Sutton TA10 9JU
🕿 01458 241017   📠 01458 241022
web: www.longsuttongolf.com
18 Holes, 6369yds, Par 71, SSS 70, Course record 64.
Course Designer Patrick Dawson **Location** 3.5m E of Langport, 0.5m S of Long Sutton on B3165
Telephone for further details
Hotel ★★★ 79% HL The Hollies, Bower Hinton, MARTOCK 🕿 01935 822232 📠 01935 822232 44 en suite

Wheathill Wheathill TA11 7HG
🕿 01963 240667   📠 01963 240230
e-mail: wheathill@wheathill.fsnet.co.uk
web: www.wheathillgc.co.uk
A parkland course set in quiet countryside. Gently sloping land with the river Cary flowing next to the 13th and 14th holes. There is an 18 hole academy course and an expansive driving range.
18 Holes, 5831yds, Par 68, SSS 65, Course record 67.
Club membership 550.
Visitors Mon-Sun & BHs. Booking required Fri-Sun & BHs. Dress code. **Societies** welcome. **Green Fees** £20 per round **Course Designer** J Pain **Prof** A England **Facilities** ⑪ 🍴 ⚐ 🖥 ⚑ 🛎 🕿
🏌 ♂ 🏌 **Leisure** 8 hole academy course. **Conf** facs Corporate Hospitality Days **Location** 2m off A37, on B3153 between Somerton and Castle Cary
Hotel ★★ 81% HL Walnut Tree, Fore Street, WEST CAMEL 🕿 01935 851292 📠 01935 851292 13 en suite

TAUNTON   Map 3 ST22

Oake Manor Oake TA4 1BA
🕿 01823 461993   📠 01823 461992
e-mail: russell@oakemanor.com
web: www.oakemanor.com
A parkland and lakeland course situated in breathtaking Somerset countryside with views of the Quantock, Blackdown and Brendon hills. Ten holes feature water hazards such as lakes, cascades and a trout stream. The 15th hole (par 5, 476yds) is bounded by water all down the left with a carry over another lake on to an island green. The course is challenging yet great fun for all standards of golfer.
18 Holes, 6109yds, Par 70, SSS 70, Course record 65.
Club membership 600.
Visitors contact club for details. **Societies** welcome. **Green Fees** £26 per 18 holes, £29 Fri, £32 weekends **Course Designer** Adrian Stiff **Prof** R Gardner/J Smallacombe **Facilities** ⑪
🍴 ⚐ 🖥 ⚑ 🛎 🕿 ♂ 🏌 **Leisure** 2 hole academy course, short game area **Conf** facs Corporate Hospitality Days **Location** M5 junct 26, A38 N towards Taunton. Signed at World's End pub
Hotel ★★★ 75% HL Best Western Rumwell Manor, Rumwell, TAUNTON 🕿 01823 461902 📠 01823 461902 20 en suite

Taunton & Pickeridge Corfe TA3 7BY
🕿 01823 421537   📠 01823 421742
e-mail: admin@tauntongolf.co.uk
web: www.taunton-golf.co.uk
Downland course established in 1892 with extensive views of the Quantock and Mendip hills. Renowned for its excellent greens.

continued

18 Holes, 6056yds, Par 69, SSS 69, Course record 66. *Club membership 800.*
Visitors Mon-Fri except BHs. Dress code. **Societies** booking required. **Green Fees** not confirmed **Prof** Simon Stevenson **Facilities** ⚙ ⫙ 🍴 ⛳ 🏌 🏊 ⛿ ✏ **Conf** facs Corporate Hospitality Days **Location** 4m S off B3170
Hotel ★★★ 77% HL The Mount Somerset, Lower Henlade, TAUNTON
☎ 01823 442500 📠 01823 442500 11 en suite

Taunton Vale Creech Heathfield TA3 5EY
☎ 01823 412220   📠 01823 413583
e-mail: admin@tauntonvalegolf.co.uk
web: www.tauntonvalegolf.co.uk
An 18-hole and a nine-hole course in a parkland complex occupying 156 acres in the Vale of Taunton. Views of the Blackdown and Quantock Hills. Floodlit driving range.
Charlton Course: 18 Holes, 6237yds, Par 70, SSS 70.
Durston Course: 9 Holes, 2004yds, Par 32.
Club membership 700.
Visitors Mon-Sun & BHs. Booking required. Dress code.
Societies booking required **Green Fees** 18 hole course £25 per round (£30 weekends & BHs). 9 hole course £12 per round (£14 weekends) **Course Designer** John Payne **Prof** Martin Keitch **Facilities** ⚙ 🍴 by prior arrangement ⫙ ⛳ 🏌 🏊 ⛿ 🏁 **Conf** facs Corporate Hospitality Days **Location** M5 junct 24 or 25, off A38/A361
Hotel ★★★ 77% HL The Mount Somerset, Lower Henlade, TAUNTON
☎ 01823 442500 📠 01823 442500 11 en suite

Vivary Park Municipal Fons George TA1 3JU
☎ 01823 333875   📠 01823 352713
e-mail: n.hobbs@toneleisure.com
web: www.toneleisure.com
A parkland course, tight and narrow with ponds.
Vivary Park Municipal Golf Course: 18 Holes, 4574yds, Par 65, SSS 63, Course record 59. Club membership 800.
Visitors Mon-Sun & BHs. Booking required. **Societies** booking required. **Green Fees** £15 per round (£16 weekends) **Course Designer** W H Fowler **Facilities** ⚙ 🍴 ⫙ ⛳ 🏌 🏊 ⛿ ✏ **Leisure** hard tennis courts **Conf** facs **Location** S of town centre off A38
Hotel ★★★ 68% HL Corner House Hotel, Park Street, TAUNTON
☎ 01823 284683 📠 01823 284683 44 en suite

WEDMORE
Map 3 ST44

Isle of Wedmore Lineage BS28 4QT
☎ 01934 712452 (pro-shop)   📠 01934 713554
e-mail: info@wedmoregolfclub.com
web: www.wedmoregolfclub.com
Gently undulating course designed to maintain natural environment. Existing woodland and hedgerow enhanced by new planting. Magnificent panoramic views of Cheddar valley and Glastonbury Tor from the back nine. The course design provides two loops of nine holes both starting and finishing at the clubhouse.
18 Holes, 6057yds, Par 70, SSS 69, Course record 67.
Club membership 680.
Visitors Mon-Sun & BHs. Booking required Mon, Thu, weekends & BHs. Dress code. **Societies** booking required. **Green Fees** £32 per day, £24 per round. Reduced winter rates **Course Designer** Terry Murray **Prof** Nick Pope **Facilities** ⚙ 🍴 ⫙ ⛳ 🏌 🏊 ⛿ ✏ 🏁

Leisure indoor teaching studio & custom fitting centre **Conf** facs Corporate Hospitality Days **Location** 0.5m N of Wedmore
Hotel ★★★ 85% HL Best Western Swan, Sadler Street, WELLS
☎ 01749 836300 📠 01749 836300 50 en suite

WELLS
Map 3 ST54

Wells (Somerset) Blackheath Lne, East Horrington BA5 3DS
☎ 01749 675005   📠 01749 683170
e-mail: secretary@wellsgolfclub.co.uk
web: www.wellsgolfclub.co.uk
Beautiful wooded course with wonderful views. The prevailing SW wind complicates the 448yd 3rd. Good drainage and paths for trolleys constructed all round the course.
18 Holes, 6053yds, Par 70, SSS 69, Course record 66.
Club membership 670.
Visitors Mon-Sun & BHs. Booking required. Handicap certificate. **Societies** booking required. **Green Fees** £30 per 18 holes (£35 weekends & BHs) **Prof** Adrian Bishop **Facilities** ⚙ 🍴 ⫙ ⛳ 🏌 🏊 ⛿ 🏁 ✏ 🏁 **Conf** facs Corporate Hospitality Days **Location** 1.5m E off B3139
Hotel ★★ 67% HL Ancient Gate House, 20 Sadler Street, WELLS
☎ 01749 672029 📠 01749 672029 8 en suite

WESTON-SUPER-MARE
Map 3 ST36

Weston-Super-Mare Uphill Road North BS23 4NQ
☎ 01934 626968 & 633360 (pro)   📠 01934 621360
e-mail: wsmgolfclub@eurotelbroadband.com
web: www.westonsupermaregolfclub.com
A compact and interesting layout with the opening hole adjacent to the beach. The sandy, links-type course is slightly undulating and has beautifully maintained turf and greens. The 15th is a testing 455yd par 4. Superb views across the Bristol Channel to Cardiff.
18 Holes, 6245yds, Par 70, SSS 70, Course record 65.
Club membership 750.
Visitors contact club for details. **Societies** welcome **Green Fees** £48 per day, £36 per round **Course Designer** T Dunne/Dr Mackenzie **Prof** Mike Laband **Facilities** ⚙ ⫙ ⛳ 🏌 🏊 ⛿ ✏ 🏁 **Location** S of town centre off A370
Hotel ★★★ 71% HL Beachlands, 17 Uphill Road North, WESTON-SUPER-MARE ☎ 01934 621401 📠 01934 621401 21 en suite

Worlebury Monks Hill BS22 9SX
☎ 01934 625789   ▤ 01934 621935
e-mail: secretary@worleburygc.co.uk
web: www.worleburygc.co.uk
Parkland course on the ridge of Worlebury Hill, with fairly easy walking
and extensive views of the Severn estuary and Wales.
18 Holes, 5963yds, Par 70, SSS 68, Course record 66.
Club membership 650.
Visitors contact club for details. **Societies** welcome. **Green Fees** not
confirmed **Course Designer** H Vardon **Prof** Gary Marks **Facilities** ⓣ
🍴 ⓑ 🖵 🕙 🛆 🖿 ✓ **Location** 2m NE off A370
Hotel ★★★ 71% HL Beachlands, 17 Uphill Road North, WESTON-
SUPER-MARE ☎ 01934 621401 ▤ 01934 621401   21 en suite

YEOVIL
Map 3 ST51

Yeovil Sherborne Rd BA21 5BW
☎ 01935 422965   ▤ 01935 411283
e-mail: office@yeovilgolfclub.com
web: www.yeovilgolfclub.com
On the Old Course the opener lies by the River Yeo before the gentle
climb to high downs with good views. The outstanding 14th and 15th
holes present a challenge, being below the player with a deep railway
cutting on the left of the green. The 1st on the Newton Course is played
over the river which then leads to a challenging but scenic course.
Old Course: 18 Holes, 6087yds, Par 71, SSS 70,
Course record 64.
Newton Course: 9 Holes, 4856yds, Par 68, SSS 65,
Course record 63. Club membership 1000.
Visitors Mon-Sun & BHs. Booking required. Handicap certificate.
Dress code. **Societies** booking required. **Green Fees** Old Course £40
per day. Newton Course £25 per day **Course Designer** Hugh Allison
Prof Geoff Kite **Facilities** ⓣ 🍴 ⓑ 🖵 🕙 🛆 🖿 🕙 ✓
🔧 ✓ ✦ **Conf** Corporate Hospitality Days **Location** 1m E on A30
Hotel ★★★ 78% HL The Yeovil Court Hotel & Restaurant, West
Coker Road, YEOVIL ☎ 01935 863746 ▤ 01935 863746   30 en suite

STAFFORDSHIRE

BROCTON
Map 7 SJ91

Brocton Hall ST17 0TH
☎ 01785 661901   ▤ 01785 661591
web: www.broctonhall.com
18 Holes, 6064yds, Par 69, SSS 69, Course record 66.
Course Designer Harry Vardon **Location** NW of village off A34
Telephone for further details
Hotel ★★★★ 85% HL The Moat House, Lower Penkridge Road,
Acton Trussell, STAFFORD ☎ 01785 712217 ▤ 01785 712217
41 en suite

BURTON UPON TRENT
Map 8 SK22

Belmont Belmont Rd, Needwood DE13 9PH
☎ 01283 814381   ▤ 01283 814381
e-mail: belmontpro@belmontgolf.co.uk
web: www.belmontgolf.co.uk
A nine-hole course with five par 4s, the longest being 430 yards. Also
a par 5 of 510 yards. The course comprises trees, bunkers, some water
and great views.

Belmont Driving Range & Golf Course: 9 Holes, 2413yds,
Par 33, Course record 31. Club membership 55.
Visitors Mon-Sun & BHs. Booking required weekends & BHs. Dress
code. **Societies** booking required. **Green Fees** £12.50 per 18 holes,
£8 per 9 holes (£14.50/£9.50 weekends) **Course Designer** R Coy
Prof R Coy/C Roberts **Facilities** 🖵 🖿 🕙 ✓ ✦ **Leisure** fishing
Conf Corporate Hospitality Days **Location** 3m NW of Tutbury, off B5017
towards Tutbury
Hotel ★★★ 74% HL The Boars Head, Lichfield Road, SUDBURY
☎ 01283 820344 ▤ 01283 820344   23 en suite

Branston Burton Rd DE14 3DP
☎ 01283 512211   ▤ 01283 566984
web: www.branston-golf-club.co.uk

Branston Golf & Country Club: 18 Holes, 6697yds, Par 72,
SSS 72, Course record 65.
Course Designer G Ramshall **Location** 1.5m SW on A5121
Telephone for further details
Hotel ★★★ 81% HL Three Queens, One Bridge Street, BURTON
UPON TRENT ☎ 01283 523800 & 0845 230 1332 ▤ 01283 523800
38 en suite

Burton-upon-Trent 43 Ashby Road East DE15 0PS
☎ 01283 544551(sec) & 562240 (pro)
e-mail: the secretary@burtonontrentgolfclub.co.uk
web: www.burtonontrentgolfclub.co.uk
Undulating parkland course with notable trees and water features on
two holes. Testing par 3s at 10th and 12th.
Burton upon Trent Golf Club: 18 Holes, 6579yds, Par 71,
SSS 72, Course record 63. Club membership 700.
Visitors Mon, Tue & Fri except BHs. Handicap certificate. Dress
code. **Societies** booking required. **Green Fees** £50 per day, £38
per round (£57/£44 weekends & BHs) **Course Designer** H S Colt
Prof Gary Stafford **Facilities** ⓣ 🍴 ⓑ 🖵 🕙 🛆 🖿 🕙 ✓
Conf Corporate Hospitality Days **Location** 3m E of Burton on A511
Guesthouse ★★★★ GH The Edgecote, 179 Ashby Road, BURTON
UPON TRENT ☎ 01283 568966 ▤ 01283 568966   11 rms (5 en suite)

Craythorne Craythorne Rd, Rolleston on Dove DE13 0AZ
☎ 01283 564329   ▤ 01283 511908
e-mail: admin@craythorne.co.uk
web: www.craythorne.co.uk
A relatively short and challenging parkland course with tight fairways
and views of the Trent valley. Excellent greens giving all year play.
Suits all standards but particularly good for society players. The
course has matured following development over many years and
recent improvements to tees, paths and greens make the course a
good test of golf.

continued

The Craythorne: 18 Holes, 5642yds, Par 68, SSS 68,
Course record 67. Club membership 450.

Visitors Mon-Sun & BHs. Booking required. Dress code.
Societies booking required. **Green Fees** £34 per day, £22 per round
Course Designer A A Wright **Prof** Steve Hadfield **Facilities** ⊕ ⑩
🏌 ⬜ 🍴 ⚲ 🏠 ⚑ ⚔ 🏌 ⚔ 🏌 **Conf** facs Corporate
Hospitality Days **Location** off A38 through Stretton, tourist signs
Guesthouse ★★★★ GH The Edgecote, 179 Ashby Road, BURTON
UPON TRENT ☎ 01283 568966 🖨 01283 568966 11 rms (5 en suite)

CANNOCK   Map 7 SJ91

Beau Desert Rugeley Rd, Hazel Glade WS12 0PJ
☎ 01543 422626 🖨 01543 451137
e-mail: enquiries@bdgc.co.uk
web: www.bdgc.co.uk
A moorland course with firm and fast fairways and greens, used on
many occasions as an Open qualifier course. The course has many
varied and testing holes ranging from the 1st over a pit, the 10th over
a ravine, to the 18th with a second shot across gorse traversing the
fairway.

18 Holes, 6310yds, Par 70, SSS 71, Course record 64.
Club membership 650.

Visitors Mon-Sun except BHs. Booking required. Handicap certificate.
Dress code. **Societies** booking required. **Green Fees** £60 per day, £50
per round (£70 weekends & BHs) **Course Designer** Herbert Fowler
Prof Barrie Stevens **Facilities** ⊕ ⑩ 🏌 ⬜ 🍴 ⚲ ⚑
⚔ 🏌 **Conf** facs Corporate Hospitality Days **Location** off A460
NE of Hednesford
Hotel 70% Roman Way, Watling Street, CANNOCK ☎ 01543 572121
🖨 01543 572121 56 en suite

Cannock Park Stafford Rd WS11 2AL
☎ 01543 578850
e-mail: seccpgc@yahoo.co.uk
Part of a large leisure centre, this parkland-type course plays
alongside Cannock Chase. Severe slopes on some greens. Good
drainage, open all year.

Cannock Park Golf Course: 18 Holes, 5200yds, Par 67,
SSS 65, Course record 62. Club membership 120.

Visitors Mon-Sat & BHs. Booking required Sat & BHs. Dress code.
Societies welcome. **Green Fees** £11.80 per round (£14.90 Sat) **Course**
Designer John Mainland **Facilities** ⊕ ⑩ 🏌 ⬜ 🍴 ⚲ 🏠
⚑ ⚔ **Leisure** hard tennis courts, heated indoor swimming pool,
sauna, gymnasium **Conf** Corporate Hospitality Days **Location** 0.5m N
of town centre on A34
Hotel 70% Roman Way, Watling Street, CANNOCK ☎ 01543 572121
🖨 01543 572121 56 en suite

ENVILLE   Map 7 SO88

Enville Highgate Common DY7 5BN
☎ 01384 872074 (office) & 873396 (pro shop)
🖨 01384 873396
e-mail: secretary@envillegolfclub.com
web: www.envillegolfclub.com
Easy walking on two fairly flat woodland and heathland courses.
Qualifying course for the Open Championship.

Highgate Course: 18 Holes, 6592yds, Par 72, SSS 73,
Course record 65.

Lodge Course: 18 Holes, 6417yds, Par 71, SSS 71,
Course record 65. Club membership 900.

Visitors Mon-Fri except BHs. Dress code. **Societies** booking
required. **Green Fees** £60 per 36 holes, £50 per 18 holes **Prof** Sean
Power **Facilities** ⊕ ⑩ 🏌 ⬜ 🍴 ⚲ 🏠 ⚔ 🏌 ⚔ 🏌
Conf Corporate Hospitality Days **Location** 2m NE of Enville off A458
Hotel ★★★★ 78% HL Mill Hotel & Restaurant, ALVELEY,
Bridgnorth ☎ 01746 780437 🖨 01746 780437 41 en suite

GOLDENHILL   Map 7 SJ85

Goldenhill Mobberley Rd ST6 5SS
☎ 01782 787678 🖨 01782 787678
web: www.jackbarker.com
Golden Hill Golf Course: 18 Holes, 5957yds, Par 71,
SSS 69.

Facilities ⊕ ⑩ 🏌 ⬜ 🍴 ⚲ 🏠 ⚑ ⚔ 🏌 ⚔ 🏌
Location on A50 4m N of Stoke
Telephone for further details
Hotel ★★★ 83% HL Best Western Manor House, Audley Road,
ALSAGER ☎ 01270 884000 🖨 01270 884000 57 en suite

HIMLEY   Map 7 SO89

Himley Hall Golf Centre Log Cabin, Himley Hall Park
DY3 4DF
☎ 01902 895207 & 0715284196
e-mail: bernie@bsparrow.wanadoo.co.uk
web: www.himleygolf.com
Parkland course set in the grounds of Himley Hall Park, with lovely
views. Large practice area including a pitch and putt.

Himley Hall Golf Centre: 9 Holes, 6215yds, Par 72, SSS 70,
Course record 65. Club membership 120.

Visitors Mon-Sun & BHs. Booking required weekends. Dress code.
Societies welcome. **Green Fees** Summer 18 holes £13, 9 holes £8.80
(Winter £12.50/£8.50) **Course Designer** A Baker **Prof** Mark Sparrow
Facilities 🏌 ⬜ 🏠 ⚔ **Location** 0.5m E on B4176
Hotel BUD Innkeeper's Lodge Dudley Kingswinford, Swindon Road,
KINGSWINFORD ☎ 0845 112 6069 🖨 0845 112 6069 22 en suite

LEEK   Map 7 SJ95

Leek Birchall, Cheddleton Rd ST13 5RE
☎ 01538 384779 & 384767 (pro) 🖨 01538 384779
e-mail: enquiries@leekgolfclub.co.uk
web: www.leekgolfclub.co.uk
Undulating, challenging, mainly parkland course, reputedly one of the
best in the area. In its early years the course was typical moorland
with sparse tree growth but its development since the 1960s has
produced tree-lined fairways which are much appeciated by golfers for
their lush playing qualities.

18 Holes, 6218yds, Par 70, SSS 70, Course record 63.
Club membership 825.

Visitors contact club for details. **Societies** welcome. **Green Fees** not
confirmed **Prof** Paul Toyer **Facilities** ⊕ ⑩ 🏌 ⬜ 🍴 ⚲ 🏠
⚑ ⚔ **Leisure** snooker **Conf** facs **Location** 0.75m S on A520
Hotel ★★★ 75% HL Three Horseshoes Inn & Country Hotel, Buxton
Road, Blackshaw Moor, LEEK ☎ 01538 300296 🖨 01538 300296
26 en suite

Westwood (Leek) Newcastle Rd ST13 7AA
☎ 01538 398385 (office) & 398897 (pro)
🖹 01538 382485
e-mail: westwoodgolfclub-leek@zen.co.uk
web: www.westwoodgolfclubleek.co.uk

A challenging moorland and parkland course set in beautiful open countryside with an undulating front nine. The back nine is more open and longer with the River Churnet coming into play on several holes.

Westwood (Leek) Golf Course: 18 Holes, 6105yds, Par 70, SSS 69, Course record 66. Club membership 700.

Visitors Mon-Sun & BHs. Booking required. Dress code.
Societies booking required. **Green Fees** phone **Prof** Greg Rogula
Facilities ⑪ 🏌 🍴 🍽 👤 🏠 🚿 ⚒ **Conf** facs Corporate
Hospitality Days **Location** on A53 S of Leek
Hotel ★★★ 75% HL Three Horseshoes Inn & Country Hotel, Buxton
Road, Blackshaw Moor, LEEK ☎ 01538 300296 🖹 01538 300296
26 en suite

LICHFIELD   Map 7 SK10

Lichfield Golf & Country Club Elmhurst WS13 8HE
☎ 01543 417333   🖹 01543 418098
e-mail: s.joyce@theclubcompany.com
web: www.theclubcompany.com

A 27-hole course in picturesque parkland scenery. Numerous holes crossed by meandering mill streams. Undulating greens defended by hazards lie in wait for the practised approach.

Mill Course: 18 Holes, 6042yds, Par 72, SSS 70, Course record 67. Club membership 1200.

Visitors contact course for details. **Societies** booking required. **Green Fees** Mill course £35 per 18 holes (£40 weekends), 9 holes £10.50
Course Designer Hawtree & Son **Prof** Simon Joyce **Facilities** ⑪
🍴 🏌 🍽 🍴 👤 🏠 🚿 ⚒ 🏴 **Leisure** heated indoor
swimming pool, sauna, gymnasium, 9 hole par 3 course **Location** 3m
N of Lichfield off B5014
Hotel ★★★ 77% HL Best Western The George, 12-14 Bird Street,
LICHFIELD ☎ 01543 414822 🖹 01543 414822   45 en suite

Whittington Heath Tamworth Rd WS14 9PW
☎ 01543 432317   🖹 01543 433962
e-mail: info@whittingtonheathgc.co.uk
web: www.whittingtonheathgc.co.uk

The 18 magnificent holes wind through heathland and trees, presenting a good test for the serious golfer. Leaving the fairway can be severely punished. The dog-legs are most tempting, inviting the golfer to chance his arm. Local knowledge is a definite advantage. Clear views of the famous three spires of Lichfield Cathedral.

Whittington Heath Golf Club Ltd: 18 Holes, 6490yds, Par 70, SSS 71, Course record 64. Club membership 660.

Visitors Mon & Wed-Fri except BHs. Tue pm. Booking required.
Handicap certificate. Dress code. **Societies** booking required. **Green Fees** £55 per 36 holes; £48 per 27 holes; £40 per 18 holes. **Course Designer** Colt **Prof** Adrian Sadler **Facilities** ⑪ 🍴 🏌 🍽 🍴
👤 🏠 **Leisure** buggy for hire on medical grounds **Conf** Corporate
Hospitality Days **Location** 2.5m SE on A51
Hotel ★★★ 77% HL Best Western The George, 12-14 Bird Street,
LICHFIELD ☎ 01543 414822 🖹 01543 414822   45 en suite

NEWCASTLE-UNDER-LYME   Map 7 SJ84

Jack Barkers Keele Golf Centre Newcastle Rd, Keele ST5 5AB
☎ 01782 627596   🖹 01782 714555
e-mail: keele@jackbarker.com
web: www.jackbarker.com

Parkland with mature trees and great views of Stoke-on-Trent and the surrounding area.

Jack Barkers Keele Golf Centre: 18 Holes, 6396yds, Par 71, SSS 70, Course record 64. Club membership 400.

Visitors Mon-Sun & BHs. **Societies** booking required. **Green Fees** £11 per round, £14 Fri, £16 weekends **Course Designer** Hawtree
Facilities ⑪ 🍴 🏌 🍽 🍴 👤 🏠 🚿 ⚒ 🏴 🏌
Leisure 9 hole par 3 academy course **Conf** Corporate Hospitality Days
Location 2m W on A525 opp Keele University
Hotel ★★★ 67% HL Haydon House, Haydon Street, Basford, STOKE-
ON-TRENT ☎ 01782 711311 & 753690 🖹 01782 711311   17 en suite

Newcastle-Under-Lyme Whitmore Rd ST5 2QB
☎ 01782 617006   🖹 01782 617531
e-mail: info@newcastlegolfclub.co.uk
web: www.newcastlegolfclub.co.uk

Parkland course.

18 Holes, 6395yds, Par 72, SSS 71, Course record 66. Club membership 600.

Visitors Mon-Fri except BHs. Handicap certificate. Dress code.
Societies booking required. **Green Fees** not confirmed **Prof** Ashley
Salt **Facilities** ⑪ 🍴 🏌 🍽 🍴 👤 🏠 🚿 ⚒ **Conf** Corporate
Hospitality Days **Location** 1m SW on A53
Hotel ★★★ 74% HL Holiday Inn Stoke-on-Trent, Clayton Road,
Clayton, NEWCASTLE-UNDER-LYME ☎ 01782 557000 & 557018
🖹 01782 557000   118 en suite

Wolstanton Dimsdale Old Hall, Hassam Pde, Wolstanton ST5 9DR
☎ 01782 622413 (Sec)

A challenging undulating suburban course incorporating six difficult par 3 holes. The 6th hole (par 3) is 233yds from the Medal Tee.

18 Holes, 5533yds, Par 68, SSS 68, Course record 63. Club membership 700.

Visitors Mon-Fri except BHs. Booking required. Dress code.
Societies booking required. **Green Fees** £27.50 per 18 holes
Prof Simon Arnold **Facilities** ⑪ 🍴 🏌 🍽 🍴 👤 🏠 ⚒
Conf facs Corporate Hospitality Days **Location** 1.5m from town centre.
Turn off A34 at MacDonalds
Hotel ★★★★ 74% HL Best Western Stoke-on-Trent Moat
House, Etruria Hall, Festival Way, Etruria, STOKE-ON-TRENT
☎ 0870 225 4601 & 01782 206101 🖹 0870 225 4601   147 en suite

ONNELEY
Map 7 SJ74

Onneley CW3 5QF
☎ 01782 750577 & 846759
web: www.onneleygolf.co.uk
18 Holes, 5728yds, Par 70, SSS 68.
Course Designer A Benson/G Marks **Location** 2m from Woore on A525
Telephone for further details

PATTINGHAM
Map 7 SO89

Patshull Park Hotel Golf & Country Club Patshull Rd
WV6 7HR
☎ 01902 700100 🖷 01902 700874
e-mail: sales@patshull-park.co.uk
web: www.patshull-park.co.uk

Picturesque course set in 280 acres of glorious 'Capability' Brown
landscaped parkland. Designed by John Jacobs, the course meanders
alongside trout fishing lakes. Water comes into play alongside the
3rd hole and there is a challenging drive over water on the 13th.
Wellingtonia and cedar trees prove an obstacle to wayward drives off
several holes. The 12th is the toughest hole on the course and the tee
shot is vital, anything wayward and the trees block out the second to
the green.
Patshull Park Hotel Golf & Country Club: 18 Holes,
6400yds, Par 72, SSS 71, Course record 64.
Club membership 300.
Visitors Mon-Sun & BHs, Booking required. Dress code.
Societies booking required. **Green Fees** £40 per round **Course**
Designer John Jacobs **Prof** Richard Bissell **Facilities** ⑪ 🍴 🖳
🖳 🍴 👤 🏠 🏆 ◇ 🚜 ✦ **Leisure** heated indoor swimming
pool, fishing, sauna, gymnasium **Conf** facs Corporate Hospitality
Days **Location** 1.5m W of Pattingham, at Pattingham Church take the
Patshull Rd, club on right
Hotel ★★★ 77% HL Patshull Park Hotel Golf & Country Club, Patshull
Park, PATTINGHAM ☎ 01902 700100 🖷 01902 700100 49 en suite

PENKRIDGE
Map 7 SJ91

The Chase Pottal Pool Rd ST19 5RN
☎ 01785 712888 🖷 01785 712692
e-mail: chase@crown-golf.co.uk
web: www.crown-golf.co.uk
Parkland course with links characteristics.
18 Holes, 6707yds, Par 72, SSS 74. Club membership 850.
Visitors Mon-Sun & BHs. Booking required. Dress code.
Societies booking required. **Green Fees** phone **Prof** Craig Thomas
Facilities ⑪ 🍴 🖳 🖳 🍴 👤 🏠 🚜 ✦ 🏆 **Leisure** indoor

teaching academy **Conf** facs Corporate Hospitality Days **Location** 2m
E off B5012
Hotel ★★★★ 85% HL The Moat House, Lower Penkridge Road,
Acton Trussell, STAFFORD ☎ 01785 712217 🖷 01785 712217
41 en suite

PERTON
Map 7 SO89

Perton Park Wrottesley Park Rd WV6 7HL
☎ 01902 380073 🖷 01902 326219
e-mail: admin@pertongolfclub.co.uk
web: www.pertongolfclub.co.uk
Challenging inland links style course set in picturesque Staffordshire
countryside.
18 Holes, 6520yds, Par 72, SSS 72, Course record 61.
Club membership 600.
Visitors Mon-Sun & BHs. Booking advisable. Dress code.
Societies booking required **Green Fees** not confirmed **Prof** Jeremy
Harrold **Facilities** ⑪ 🍴 🖳 🖳 🍴 👤 🏠 🏆 🚜 ✦ 🏆
Leisure hard tennis courts, 2 bowling greens. **Conf** facs Corporate
Hospitality Days **Location** SE of Perton off A454
Hotel ★★★ 88% HL The Elms Hotel & Restaurant, Stockton Road,
ABBERLEY ☎ 01299 896666 🖷 01299 896666 23 en suite

RUGELEY
Map 7 SK01

St Thomas's Priory Armitage Ln WS15 1ED
☎ 01543 492096 🖷 01543 492096
18 Holes, 5969yds, Par 70, SSS 70, Course record 64.
Course Designer P I Mulholland **Location** A51 onto A513
Telephone for further details
Hotel BUD Travelodge Rugeley, Western Springs Road, RUGELEY
☎ 08719 846 102 🖷 08719 846 102 32 en suite

STAFFORD
Map 7 SJ92

Stafford Castle Newport Rd ST16 1BP
☎ 01785 223821 🖷 01785 223821
Undulating parkland-type course built around Stafford Castle.
9 Holes, 6383yds, Par 71, SSS 70, Course record 68.
Club membership 400.
Visitors Mon-Sat except BHs. Booking required. Dress code.
Societies booking required. **Green Fees** £18 per day (£22 Sat)
Facilities ⑪ 🖳 🖳 🍴 👤 **Conf** Corporate Hospitality Days
Location SW of town centre off A518
Hotel ★★★ 78% HL The Swan, 46 Greengate Street, STAFFORD
☎ 01785 258142 🖷 01785 258142 31 en suite

STOKE-ON-TRENT
Map 7 SJ84

Burslem Wood Farm, High Ln, Tunstall ST6 7JT
☎ 01782 837006
e-mail: alanporterburslemgc@yahoo.co.uk
On the outskirts of Tunstall, a moorland course with hard walking.
9 Holes, 5354yds, Par 66, SSS 66, Course record 66.
Club membership 250.
Visitors dress code. **Societies** booking required. **Green Fees** £16 per
day, £10 per round **Facilities** ⑪ by prior arrangement 🍴 by prior
arrangement 🖳 🖳 👤 **Location** 4m N of city centre on B5049
Hotel ★★★ 70% HL Quality Hotel Stoke, 66 Trinity Street, Hanley,
STOKE-ON-TRENT ☎ 01782 202361 🖷 01782 202361 136 en suite

Greenway Hall Stanley Rd, Stockton Brook ST9 9LJ
☎ 01782 503158 📄 01782 504691
e-mail: greenway@jackbarker.com
web: www.jackbarker.com

Moorland course with fine views of the Pennines.

18 Holes, 5678yds, Par 68, SSS 67, Course record 65.
Club membership 300.

Visitors Mon-Sun & BHs. Booking required. Dress code.
Societies welcome. **Green Fees** £12, Fri £14, weekends £16
Facilities ⑪ ⑩↾ ⅃ ☕ ⑨ॵ ⚫ 🛒 ⚫
Conf Corporate Hospitality Days **Location** 5m NE off A53
Hotel ★★★ 70% HL Quality Hotel Stoke, 66 Trinity Street, Hanley,
STOKE-ON-TRENT ☎ 01782 202361 📄 01782 202361 136 en suite

Trentham 14 Barlaston Old Rd, Trentham ST4 8HB
☎ 01782 658109 📄 01782 644024
e-mail: generalmanager@trenthamgolf.org
web: www.trenthamgolf.org

Traditional parkland course with mature trees lining most fairways.
A well placed approach shot is required to help navigate the many
undulating greens. An Open Championship regional qualifying course
for five years.

18 Holes, 6644yds, Par 72, SSS 72, Course record 67.
Club membership 600.

Visitors Mon-Fri, Sun & BHs. Booking required. Handicap certificate.
Dress code. **Societies** booking required. **Green Fees** phone **Course
Designer** Colt & Alison **Prof** Shane Owen **Facilities** ⑪ ⑩↾ ⅃ ☕
⑨ॵ ⅄ ☕ ⊔ ⚫ 🛒 ⚫ **Leisure** squash **Conf** Corporate
Hospitality Days **Location** off A5035 in Trentham
Hotel ★★★ 67% HL Haydon House, Haydon Street, Basford,
STOKE-ON-TRENT ☎ 01782 711311 & 753690 📄 01782 711311
17 en suite

Trentham Park Trentham Park ST4 8AE
☎ 01782 658800 📄 01782 658800
e-mail: admin@trenthamparkgolfclub.com
web: www.trenthamparkgolfclub.com

Fine woodland course. Set in established parkland with many
challenging and interesting holes making excellent use of water
features.

18 Holes, 6425yds, Par 71, SSS 71, Course record 67.
Club membership 850.

Visitors handicap certificate. Dress code. **Societies** booking required.
Green Fees not confirmed **Prof** Simon Lynn **Facilities** ⑪ ⑩↾ ⅃
☕ ⑨ॵ ⅄ ☕ ⚫ 🛒 ⚫ **Conf** Corporate Hospitality Days
Location M6 junct 15, 1m E. 3m SW of Stoke off A34

Hotel ★★★ 67% HL Haydon House, Haydon Street, Basford,
STOKE-ON-TRENT ☎ 01782 711311 & 753690 📄 01782 711311
17 en suite

STONE   Map 7 SJ93

Barlaston Meaford Rd ST15 8UX
☎ 01782 372795 & 372867 📄 01782 373648
e-mail: barlaston.gc@virgin.net
web: www.barlastongolfclub.co.uk

Picturesque parkland course designed by Peter Alliss. A number of
water features come into play on several holes.

18 Holes, 5800yds, Par 69, SSS 68, Course record 65.
Club membership 600.

Visitors Mon-Sun & BHs. Dress code. **Societies** booking required.
Green Fees phone **Course Designer** Peter Alliss **Prof** Ian Rogers
Facilities ⑪ ⑩↾ ⅃ ☕ ⑨ॵ ⅄ ☕ 🛒 ⚫ ⚫ **Conf** Corporate
Hospitality Days **Location** M6 junct 15, 5m S
Hotel ★★★ 74% HL Crown, 38 High Street, STONE
☎ 01785 813535 📄 01785 813535 32 en suite

Izaak Walton Eccleshall Rd, Cold Norton ST15 0NS
☎ 01785 760900
e-mail: secretary@izaakwaltongolfclub.co.uk
web: www.izaakwaltongolfclub.co.uk

A gently undulating meadowland course with streams and ponds as
features.

18 Holes, 6370yds, Par 72, SSS 72, Course record 66.
Club membership 450.

Visitors Mon-Sun & BHs. Booking required. Dress code.
Societies booking required. **Green Fees** £35 per day, £25 per round
(£40/£30weekends & BHs) **Prof** Paul Brunt **Facilities** ⑪ ⑩↾ ⅃
☕ ⑨ॵ ⅄ ☕ 🛒 ⚫ ⚫ **Location** on B5026 between Stone &
Eccleshall
Hotel ★★★ 74% HL Crown, 38 High Street, STONE
☎ 01785 813535 📄 01785 813535 32 en suite

Stone Filleybrooks ST15 0NB
☎ 01785 813103
e-mail: enquiries@stonegolfclub.co.uk
web: www.stonegolfclub.co.uk

Nine-hole parkland course with easy walking and 18 different tees.

9 Holes, 6307yds, Par 71, SSS 70, Course record 67.
Club membership 310.

Visitors Mon-Fri except BHs. Dress code. **Societies** welcome. **Green
Fees** £20 per day/round **Facilities** ⑪ ⑩↾ ⅃ ☕ ⑨ॵ ⅄ ⚫
Conf Corporate Hospitality Days **Location** 0.5m W on A34
Hotel ★★★ 74% HL Crown, 38 High Street, STONE
☎ 01785 813535 📄 01785 813535 32 en suite

TAMWORTH
Map 7 SK20

Drayton Park Drayton Park, Fazeley B78 3TN
☎ 01827 251139 📠 01827 284035
e-mail: draytonparkgc.co.uk
web: www.draytonparkgc.co.uk
Parkland course designed by James Braid. Club established since 1897.
18 Holes, 6439yds, Par 71, SSS 71, Course record 62.
Club membership 550.
Visitors dress code. **Societies** welcome. **Green Fees** £40 per day
Course Designer James Braid **Prof** M W Passmore **Facilities** ⓣ
🍴 🔼 🖥 🍽️ ♨ 🏌 🛒 ✆ **Conf** Corporate Hospitality Days
Location 2m S on A4091, next to Drayton Manor Leisure Park
Hotel ★★ 81% HL Drayton Court Hotel, 65 Coleshill Street, Fazeley, TAMWORTH ☎ 01827 285805 📠 01827 285805 19 en suite

Tamworth Municipal Eagle Dr B77 4EG
☎ 01827 709303 📠 01827 709305
web: www.tamworth.gov.uk
Tamworth Municipal Golf Course: 18 Holes, 6488yds,
Par 73, SSS 72, Course record 63.
Course Designer Hawtree & Son **Location** 2.5m E off B5000
Telephone for further details
Hotel ★★ 81% HL Drayton Court Hotel, 65 Coleshill Street, Fazeley, TAMWORTH ☎ 01827 285805 📠 01827 285805 19 en suite

UTTOXETER
Map 7 SK03

Manor Leese Hill, Kingstone ST14 8QT
☎ 01889 563234 📠 01889 563234
e-mail: manorgc@btinternet.com
web: www.manorgolfclub.org.uk
A short but tough course set in the heart of the Staffordshire countryside with fine views of the surrounding area.
18 Holes, 6206yds, Par 71, SSS 69, Course record 67.
Club membership 400.
Visitors Mon-Sun & BHs. Booking required Thu & weekends. Dress code. **Societies** welcome. **Green Fees** £20 per day (£30 weekends)
Course Designer Various **Prof** Chris Miller **Facilities** ⓣ 🍴 🔼
🖥 🍽️ 🏌 🍔 ♨ ✆ 🏌 **Leisure** fishing **Conf** Corporate Hospitality Days **Location** 2m from Uttoxeter on A518 towards Stafford
Hotel ★★★ 74% HL The Boars Head, Lichfield Road, SUDBURY ☎ 01283 820344 📠 01283 820344 23 en suite

Uttoxeter Wood Ln ST14 8JR
☎ 01889 564884 (Pro) & 566552 (Office)
📠 01889 566552
e-mail: admin@uttoxeter.com
web: uttoxetergolfclub.com
Undulating, challenging course with excellent putting surfaces, manicured fairways, uniform rough and extensive views across the Dove valley to the rolling hills of Staffordshire and Derbyshire.
18 Holes, 5801yds, Par 70, SSS 69, Course record 64.
Club membership 700.
Visitors Mon-Sun & BHs. Booking required. Dress code.
Societies booking required. **Green Fees** £28 per day (£30 weekends)
Course Designer G Rothera **Prof** Adam McCandless **Facilities** ⓣ 🍴
🔼 🖥 🍽️ 🏌 🍔 ✆ **Location** near A50, 0.5m beyond main entrance to racecourse

Hotel ★★★ 74% HL The Boars Head, Lichfield Road, SUDBURY ☎ 01283 820344 📠 01283 820344 23 en suite

WESTON
Map 7 SJ92

Ingestre Park ST18 0RE
☎ 01889 270845 📠 01889 271434
e-mail: office@ingestregolf.co.uk
web: www.ingestregolf.co.uk
Parkland course set in the grounds of Ingestre Hall, former home of the Earl of Shrewsbury, with mature trees and pleasant views.
18 Holes, 6352yds, Par 70, SSS 70, Course record 67.
Club membership 750.
Visitors Mon-Fri except BHs. Handicap certificate. Dress code.
Societies welcome. **Green Fees** £50 per day, £40 per round **Course Designer** Hawtree **Prof** Danny Scullion **Facilities** ⓣ 🍴 🔼 🖥
🍽️ 🏌 🍔 ✆ 🛒 ✆ **Conf** facs Corporate Hospitality Days
Location 2m SE off A51
Hotel ★★★ 78% HL The Swan, 46 Greengate Street, STAFFORD ☎ 01785 258142 📠 01785 258142 31 en suite

WHISTON
Map 7 SK04

Whiston Hall Mansion Court Hotel ST10 2HZ
☎ 01538 266260 📠 01538 266820
e-mail: enquiries@whistonhall.com
web: www.whistonhall.com
A challenging 18-hole course in scenic countryside incorporating many natural obstacles and providing a test for all golfing abilities.
18 Holes, 5742yds, Par 71, SSS 69, Course record 70.
Club membership 400.
Visitors Mon-Sun & BHs. **Societies** welcome. **Green Fees** not confirmed **Course Designer** T Cooper **Facilities** ⓣ 🍴 🔼 🖥
🍽️ 🏌 ♨ 🍔 ✆ **Leisure** fishing, snooker **Conf** facs Corporate Hospitality Days **Location** E of village centre off A52
Hotel ★★★ 79% HL Izaak Walton, Dovedale, ASHBOURNE ☎ 01335 350555 📠 01335 350555 35 en suite

SUFFOLK

ALDEBURGH
Map 5 TM45

Aldeburgh Saxmundham Rd IP15 5PE
☎ 01728 452890 📠 01728 452937
e-mail: info@aldeburghgolfclub.co.uk
web: www.aldeburghgolfclub.co.uk
Good natural drainage provides year round golf in links-type conditions. Accuracy is the first challenge on well-bunkered, gorse-lined holes. Fine views over an Area of Outstanding Natural Beauty.
18 Holes, 6349yds, Par 68, SSS 71, Course record 65.
River Course: 9 Holes, 4228yds, Par 64, SSS 61,
Course record 62. Club membership 900.
Visitors Mon-Sun & BHs. Booking required weekends & BHs. Handicap certificate. Dress code. **Societies** booking required.
Green Fees £70 per day, £50 after 12 noon (weekends £75/£55)
Course Designer Thompson, Fernie, Taylor, Park. **Prof** Keith Preston
Facilities ⓣ 🔼 🖥 🍽️ 🏌 🍔 ✆ 🛒 ✆ **Conf** Corporate Hospitality Days **Location** 1m W on A1094

continued

ENGLAND

Hotel ★★★ 88% HL Wentworth, Wentworth Road, ALDEBURGH
☎ 01728 452312 📄 01728 452312   35 en suite

See advert on opposite page

BECCLES
Map 5 TM48

Beccles The Common NR34 9BX
☎ 01502 712244
e-mail: brianlever@hotmail.com
Commons course with gorse bushes, no water hazards or bunkers.
9 Holes, 5566yds, Par 68, SSS 67, Course record 66. Club membership 76.
Visitors dress code. **Societies** booking required. **Green Fees** £5 per day (£10 weekends) **Facilities** 🏠 🖵 🍴 🥢 **Location** NE of town centre

BUNGAY
Map 5 TM38

Bungay & Waveney Valley Outney Common NR35 1DS
☎ 01986 892337 📄 01986 892222
e-mail: bungaygolfclub@uwclub.net
web: www.club-noticeboard.co.uk
Heathland course, lined with fir trees and gorse. Excellent greens all-year-round, easy walking.
18 Holes, 6044yds, Par 69, SSS 69, Course record 64. Club membership 730.
Visitors Mon-Sun & BHs. Booking required. Dress code. **Societies** booking required. **Green Fees** £38 per day, £32 per round (£35 per round weekends) **Course Designer** James Braid **Prof** Andrew Collison **Facilities** 🛈 🍴 🏠 🖵 🍴 🥢 🍷 ✎ 🚽 ✎ **Conf** Corporate Hospitality Days **Location** 0.5m NW on A143 at junct with A144

BURY ST EDMUNDS
Map 5 TL86

Bury St Edmunds Tut Hill IP28 6LG
☎ 01284 755979 📄 01284 763288
e-mail: info@burygolf.co.uk
web: www.clubnoticeboard.co.uk/burystedmunds
A mature, undulating course, full of character with some challenging holes. The nine-hole pay and play course consists of five par 3s and four par 4s with modern construction greens.
18 Holes, 6675yds, Par 72, SSS 72, Course record 65.
9 Holes, 2184yds, Par 62, SSS 62. Club membership 850.
Visitors Mon-Fri except BHs. 9 hole course Mon-Sun & BHs. Handicap certificate. Dress code. **Societies** booking required. **Green Fees** 18 hole course £45 per day, £37 per round, 9 hole course £16 per

round (£18 weekends) **Course Designer** Ted Ray **Prof** Mark Jillings **Facilities** 🛈 🍴 by prior arrangement 🏠 🖵 🍴 🥢 🚽 🍷 🍴 ✎ 🚽 ✎ **Conf** Corporate Hospitality Days **Location** A14 junct 42, 0.5m NW on B1106
Hotel ★★★★ Angel, Angel Hill, BURY ST EDMUNDS
☎ 01284 714000 📄 01284 714000 75 en suite

Suffolk Hotel Golf & Leisure Club Fornham St Genevieve IP28 6JQ
☎ 01284 706801 📄 01284 706721
web: www.oxfordhotelsandinns.com
A classic parkland course with the River Lark running through it. Criss-crossed by ponds and streams with rich fairways. Considerable upgrading of the course in recent years and the three finishing holes are particularly challenging.
The Genevieve Course: 18 Holes, 6392yds, Par 72, SSS 71, Course record 69. Club membership 600.
Visitors Mon-Sun & BHs. Booking required. Dress code. **Societies** welcome. **Green Fees** £32 per round (£37 weekends & BHs). £25 Nov-Mar anytime. **Facilities** 🛈 🍴 🏠 🖵 🍴 🥢 🚽 🍷 🍴 ✎ **Leisure** heated indoor swimming pool, sauna, gymnasium **Conf** facs Corporate Hospitality Days **Location** off A14 at Bury St Edmunds, W onto B1106 towards Brandon, club 2.5m on right
Hotel ★★★★ Angel, Angel Hill, BURY ST EDMUNDS
☎ 01284 714000 📄 01284 714000 75 en suite

CRETINGHAM
Map 5 TM26

Cretingham IP13 7BA
☎ 01728 685275 📄 01728 685488
e-mail: cretinghamgolfclub@hotmail.co.uk
web: www.club-noticeboard.co.uk/cretingham
Parkland course, tree-lined with numerous water features, including the River Deben which runs through part of the course.
18 Holes, 5278yds, Par 68, SSS 66. Club membership 350.
Visitors contact club for details. **Societies** welcome. **Green Fees** £20 per 18 holes, £11 per 9 holes (£22/£12 weekends) **Course Designer** J Austin **Prof** Neil Jackson/Tim Johnson **Facilities** 🛈 🍴 🏠 🖵 🍴 🥢 🚽 🍷 🍷 ✎ ✎ **Leisure** hard tennis courts, fishing **Conf** facs Corporate Hospitality Days **Location** NE of village off A1120
Hotel ★★★ 72% HL Cedars, Needham Road, STOWMARKET
☎ 01449 612668 📄 01449 612668 25 en suite

FELIXSTOWE
Map 5 TM33

Felixstowe Ferry, Ferry Rd IP11 9RY
☎ 01394 286834 📄 01394 273679
e-mail: secretary@felixstowegolf.co.uk
web: www.felixstowegolf.co.uk
An 18-hole seaside links with pleasant views, easy walking. Nine-hole pay and play course. Both courses a good test of golf.
Martello Course: 18 Holes, 6178yds, Par 72, SSS 70, Course record 66.
Kingsfleet: 9 Holes, 2941yds, Par 35, SSS 68. Club membership 900.
Visitors Martello course Mon-Fri. Weekends & BHs pm only. Booking required. Handicap certificate. Dress code. **Societies** booking required. **Green Fees** Martello £45 per day (£35 after 1pm), £50 weekends & BHs. Kingsfleet £13 (£15 weekends & BHs) **Course Designer** Henry Cotton **Prof** Ian MacPherson **Facilities** 🛈 🍴 🏠 🖵 🍴 🥢 🚽

continued

⚐ ◇ ✒ **Conf** facs Corporate Hospitality Days **Location** NE of town centre, signed from A14
Hotel ★★ 72% HL The Brook Hotel, Orwell Road, FELIXSTOWE
☎ 01394 278441 ▤ 01394 278441 25 en suite

FLEMPTON

Map 5 TL86

Flempton IP28 6EQ
☎ 01284 728291

Breckland course with gorse and wooded areas. Very little water but surrounded by woodland and Suffolk Wildlife Trust lakes.

9 Holes, 6184yds, Par 70, SSS 70, Course record 67.
Club membership 260.

Visitors contact club for details. **Green Fees** £40 per day, £35 per 18 holes **Course Designer** J H Taylor **Prof** Kieran Canham
Facilities ⑪ ⑩ ⓛ ◻ ◫ ⋀ ☎ ✒ **Location** 0.5m W on A1101
Hotel ★★★ 82% HL Best Western Priory, Mildenhall Road, BURY ST EDMUNDS ☎ 01284 766181 ▤ 01284 766181 39 en suite

HALESWORTH

Map 5 TM37

Halesworth Bramfield Rd IP19 9XA
☎ 01986 875567 ▤ 01986 874565
e-mail: info@halesworthgc.co.uk
web: www.halesworthgc.co.uk

Situated in the heart of the Suffolk countryside with fine views over the Blyth Valley. Both courses offers golfers of all levels a challenge but the 9 hole Valley course is particularly suitable for the less experienced golfer.

Blyth: 18 Holes, 6512yds, Par 72, SSS 71, Course record 68.
Valley: 9 Holes, 4560yds, Par 66, SSS 66.
Club membership 400.

Visitors Mon-Sun & BHs. Dress code. **Societies** booking advised.
Green Fees £25 per day, £20 per round (£30/£25 weekends & BHs). 9 hole course £7 (£8 weekends) **Course Designer** J W Johnson
Prof Richard Davies **Facilities** ⑪ ⑩ ⓛ ◻ ◫ ⋀ ☎ ⚐
✒ 🍴 ✒ **Conf** facs Corporate Hospitality Days **Location** 0.75m S of town, signed A144 to Bramfield
Hotel ★★★ 81% HL Swan, Market Place, SOUTHWOLD
☎ 01502 722186 ▤ 01502 722186 42 en suite

HAVERHILL

Map 5 TL64

Haverhill Coupals Rd CB9 7UW
☎ 01440 761951 ▤ 01440 761951
e-mail: haverhillgolf@coupalsroad.eclipse.co.uk
web: www.club-noticeboard.co.uk

An 18-hole course lying across two valleys in pleasant parkland. The front nine with undulating fairways is complemented by a saucer-shape back nine, bisected by the River Stour, presenting a challenge to golfers of all standards.

18 Holes, 5986yds, Par 70, SSS 69, Course record 64.
Club membership 750.

Visitors Mon-Sun & BHs. Dress code. **Societies** booking required.
Green Fees phone **Course Designer** P Pilgrem/C Lawrie **Prof** Paul Wilby **Facilities** ⑪ ⑩ ⓛ ◻ ◫ ⋀ ☎ ✒
Leisure chipping green. **Conf** facs **Location** 1m SE off A1017
Hotel ★★★ 82% HL Swynford Paddocks, SIX MILE BOTTOM, Newmarket ☎ 01638 570234 ▤ 01638 570234 15 en suite

WENTWORTH
HOTEL ★★★
Aldeburgh, Suffolk
Tel: (01728) 452312 Fax: (01728) 454343
E-mail: stay@wentworth-aldeburgh.co.uk
Website: www.wentworth-aldeburgh.com

Enjoy the comfort and style of a country house. Two lounges, with open fires and antique furniture, provide ample space to relax. The individually decorated bedrooms, many with sea views, are equipped with a colour TV, radio, hairdryer and tea-making facilities. The Restaurant serves a variety of fresh produce whilst the Bar menu offers a light lunch, and can be eaten outside in the sunken terrace garden. The timeless and unhurried Aldeburgh provides quality shopping, two excellent golf courses within a short distance, long walks and birdwatching at nearby Minsmere Bird Reserve. The internationally famous Snape Malting Concert Hall offers music and the arts and there are miles of beach to sit upon and watch the sea.

HINTLESHAM

Map 5 TM04

Hintlesham IP8 3JG
☎ 01473 652761 ▤ 01473 652750
e-mail: sales@hintleshamgolfclub.com
web: www.hintleshamgolfclub.com

Magnificent championship length course blending harmoniously with the ancient parkland surroundings. Opened in 1991 but seeded two years beforehand, this parkland course has reached a level maturity that allows it to be rivalled in the area only by a few ancient courses. The signature holes are the 4th and 17th, both featuring water at very inconvenient interludes.

18 Holes, 6638yds, Par 72, SSS 72, Course record 63.
Club membership 470.

Visitors Mon-Sun & BHs. Booking required. Handicap certificate. Dress code. **Societies** welcome. **Green Fees** not confirmed **Course Designer** Hawtree & Sons **Prof** Henry Roblin **Facilities** ⑪ ⑩ ⓛ ◻ ◫ ⋀ ⚐ ✒ 🍴 ✒ **Leisure** sauna, gymnasium, spa bath **Conf** Corporate Hospitality Days **Location** in village on A1071
Hotel ★★★★ HL Hintlesham Hall, George Street, HINTLESHAM, Ipswich ☎ 01473 652334 ▤ 01473 652334 33 en suite

IPSWICH
Map 5 TM14

Alnesbourne Priory Priory Park IP10 0JT
☎ 01473 727393   📠 01473 278372
e-mail: golf@priory-park.com
web: www.priory-park.com

A fabulous outlook facing due south across the River Orwell is one of the many good features of this course set in woodland. All holes run among trees with some fairways requiring straight shots. The 8th green is on saltings by the river.

Alnesbourne Priory Golf Course: 9 Holes, 1800yds, Par 30, SSS 30. Club membership 30.

Visitors Mon-Sun & BHs. Dress code. **Societies** booking required. **Green Fees** £10 (£15 weekends & BHs) **Facilities** ⑪ ⑩ 🍴 ☕ 🍺 ⚓ 🏌 **Leisure** practice net **Conf** facs Corporate Hospitality Days **Location** 3m SE off A14
Hotel ★★★★ Salthouse Harbour, No 1 Neptune Quay, IPSWICH ☎ 01473 226789 📠 01473 226789 70 en suite

Fynn Valley IP6 9JA
☎ 01473 785267   📠 01473 785632
e-mail: enquiries@fynn-valley.co.uk
web: www.fynn-valley.co.uk

Undulating parkland alongside a protected river valley. The course has matured into an excellent test of golf enhanced by more than 100 bunkers, 3 water features and protected greens that have tricky slopes and contours.

18 Holes, 6371yds, Par 70, SSS 71, Course record 65. Club membership 680.

Visitors Mon, Tue, Thu-Sat & BHs. Wed & Sun after 10.30am. Dress code. **Societies** booking required. **Green Fees** £36 per day, £26 per 18 holes (£40/£32 weekends & BHs) **Course Designer** Antonio Primavera **Prof** S Dainty/D Barton **Facilities** ⑪ ⑩ 🍴 ☕ 🍺 ⚓ 🏌 🍺 **Leisure** 9 hole par 3 course, practice bunker **Conf** facs Corporate Hospitality Days **Location** 2m N of Ipswich on B1077

Ipswich Purdis Heath IP3 8UQ
☎ 01473 728941   📠 01473 715236
e-mail: neill@ipswichgolfclub.com
web: www.ipswichgolfclub.com

Many golfers are surprised when they hear that Ipswich has, at Purdis Heath, a first-class course. In some ways it resembles some of Surrey's better courses; a beautiful heathland course with two lakes and easy walking.

Purdis Heath: 18 Holes, 6439yds, Par 71, SSS 71, Course record 64.
9 Holes, 1930yds, Par 31, SSS 59. Club membership 926.

Visitors Purdis Heath course Mon-Sun except BHs. Booking required. Handicap certificate. 9 hole pay & play. Dress code for both courses. **Societies** welcome. **Green Fees** 18 hole course £50 per day, £40 per round (£55/£45 weekends). 9 hole course £10 per day (£15 weekends & BHs) **Course Designer** James Braid **Prof** Kevin Lovelock **Facilities** ⑪ ⑩ 🍴 ☕ 🍺 ⚓ 🏌 **Location** 3m E of town centre off A1156
Hotel ★★★ 71% HL Holiday Inn Ipswich - Orwell, 3 The Havens, Ransomes Europark, IPSWICH ☎ 01473 272244 📠 01473 272244 60 en suite

Rushmere Rushmere Heath IP4 5QQ
☎ 01473 725648   📠 01473 273852
e-mail: rushmeregolfclub@btconnect.com
web: www.club-noticeboard.co.uk/rushmere

Heathland course with gorse and prevailing winds. A good test of golf.

18 Holes, 6262yds, Par 70, SSS 70, Course record 66. Club membership 700.

Visitors contact club for details. **Societies** welcome. **Green Fees** £40 per day, £25 per round **Course Designer** James Braid **Prof** K. Vince **Facilities** ⑪ ⑩ 🍴 ☕ 🍺 ⚓ 🏌 **Conf** facs Corporate Hospitality Days **Location** on A1214 Woodbridge road near hospital, signed
Hotel ★★★★ Salthouse Harbour, No 1 Neptune Quay, IPSWICH ☎ 01473 226789 📠 01473 226789 70 en suite

LOWESTOFT
Map 5 TM59

Rookery Park Beccles Rd, Carlton Colville NR33 8HJ
☎ 01502 509190   📠 01502 509191
e-mail: office@rookeryparkgolfclub.co.uk
web: www.club-noticeboard.co.uk

Mature tree lined parkland course over gently undulating ground. The par 3 course is a smaller version of the main course in every respect.

18 Holes, 6714yds, Par 72, SSS 72. Club membership 1000.

Visitors Mon-Sun & BHs. Booking required weekends & BHs. Handicap cerificate. Dress code. **Societies** booking required. **Green Fees** £35 per round (£40 weekends & BHs) **Course Designer** C D Lawrie **Prof** Martin Elsworthy **Facilities** ⑪ ⑩ 🍴 ☕ 🍺 ⚓ 🏌 🍺 ⚓ 🏌 **Leisure** 9 hole par 3 course **Conf** Corporate Hospitality Days **Location** 3.5m SW of Lowestoft on A146

MILDENHALL
Map 5 TL77

West Suffolk Golf Centre New Drove, Beck Row IP28 8RN
☎ 01638 718972   📠 01353 675447
e-mail: golfinsuffolk1@btconnect.com
web: www.club-noticeboard.co.uk

This course has been gradually improved to provide a unique opportunity to play an inland course in all weather conditions. Situated on the edge of the Breckland, the dry nature of the course makes for easy walking with rare flora and fauna.

West Suffolk Golf Centre: 18 Holes, 5487yds, Par 69, SSS 69
Visitors Mon-Sun & BHs. Dress code. **Societies** booking required. **Green Fees** £14 per day (£18 weekends & BHs) **Prof** Duncan Abbott **Facilities** ⑪ 🍴 ☕ 🍺 ⚓ 🏌 🍺 ⚓ 🏌 **Leisure** fishing, pitch and putt practice course **Conf** facs Corporate Hospitality Days **Location** A1101 from Mildenhall to Beck Row, 1st left after Beck Row signed to West Row/Golf Centre, 0.5m on right
Hotel ★★★ 80% HL The Olde Bull Inn, The Street, Barton Mills, MILDENHALL ☎ 01638 711001 📠 01638 711001 14 en suite

NEWMARKET
Map 5 TL66

Links Cambridge Rd CB8 0TG
☎ 01638 663000 📠 01638 661476
e-mail: linksgc@btconnect.com
web: www.clubnoticeboard.co.uk/newmarket
Gently undulating parkland.

18 Holes, 6582yds, Par 72, SSS 72, Course record 66.
Club membership 780.

Visitors contact club for details. **Societies** welcome. **Green Fees** £38
per day, £30 per round (£42/£34 weekends) **Course Designer** Col.
Hotchkin **Prof** John Sharkey **Facilities** ⓣ ⏣ 🍴 ⏣ 🏌 ⛳ 🏠
🏌 🏌 **Location** 1m SW on A1034
Hotel ★★★ 79% HL Rutland Arms, High Street, NEWMARKET
☎ 01638 664251 📠 01638 664251 46 en suite

NEWTON
Map 5 TL94

Newton Green Newton Green CO10 0QN
☎ 01787 377217 & 377501 📠 01787 377549
e-mail: info@newtongreengolfclub.co.uk
web: www.newtongreengolfclub.co.uk
Flat 18-hole course with pond. First nine holes are open with bunkers
and trees. Second nine holes are tight with ditches and gorse.

18 Holes, 5960yds, Par 69, SSS 68. Club membership 500.

Visitors Mon & Wed-Fri. Tue, weekends & BHs pm only. Dress
code. **Societies** booking required. **Green Fees** £23 per round (£27
weekends) **Prof** Tim Cooper **Facilities** ⓣ 🍴 ⏣ ⏣ 🏌 ⛳ 🏠
🏌 **Location** W of village on A134
Hotel ★★★ 78% HL Best Western Stoke by Nayland Hotel, Golf &
Spa, Keepers Lane, Leavenheath, COLCHESTER ☎ 01206 262836
📠 01206 262836 80 en suite

RAYDON
Map 5 TM03

Brett Vale Noakes Rd IP7 5LR
☎ 01473 310718
e-mail: info@brettvalegolf.co.uk
web: www.brettvalegolf.co.uk
Brett Vale course takes you through a nature reserve and on
lakeside walks, affording views over Dedham Vale. The excellent
fairways demand an accurate tee and good approach shots; 1, 2, 3,
8, 10 and 15 are all affected by crosswinds, but once in the valley it
is much more sheltered. Although only 5864yds the course is testing
and interesting at all levels of golf.

18 Holes, 5864yds, Par 70, SSS 69, Course record 65.
Club membership 600.

Visitors Mon-Sun & BHs. Booking required. Dress code.
Societies booking required. **Green Fees** £25 per 18 holes (£30
weekends & BHs) **Course Designer** Howard Swan **Prof** Paul
Bate **Facilities** ⓣ 🍴 ⏣ ⏣ 🏌 ⛳ 🏠 🏌 🏌
Leisure fishing **Conf** facs Corporate Hospitality Days **Location** A12
onto B1070 towards Hadleigh, left at Raydon, by water tower
Hotel ★★★ CHH Maison Talbooth, Stratford Road, DEDHAM
☎ 01206 322367 📠 01206 322367 12 en suite

SOUTHWOLD
Map 5 TM57

Southwold The Common IP18 6TB
☎ 01502 723234
e-mail: mail@southwoldgolfclub.co.uk
Commonland course with fine greens and panoramic views of the sea
and 125 years old in 2009.

9 Holes, 6052yds, Par 70, SSS 69, Course record 67.
Club membership 350.

Visitors Mon-Sun & BHs. Booking required Tue, Wed & Sun. Dress
code. **Societies** booking required **Green Fees** £26 per 18 holes; £13
per 9 holes (£28/£14 weekends). Reduced rate pm **Course Designer** J
Braid **Prof** Brian Allen **Facilities** ⓣ ⏣ ⏣ 🍴 🏌 ⛳ 🏠 🏌 🏌
Conf Corporate Hospitality Days **Location** S of town off A1095
Hotel ★★★ 81% HL Swan, Market Place, SOUTHWOLD
☎ 01502 722186 📠 01502 722186 42 en suite

STOWMARKET
Map 5 TM05

Stowmarket Lower Rd, Onehouse IP14 3DA
☎ 01449 736473 📠 01449 736826
e-mail: mail@stowmarketgolfclub.co.uk
web: www.club-noticeboard.co.uk
Parkland course in rolling countryside with river in play on three holes.
Many majestic trees and fine views of the Suffolk countryside.

18 Holes, 6107yds, Par 69, SSS 69, Course record 65.
Club membership 630.

Visitors Mon, Tue & Thu-Sun except BHs. Booking required. Handicap
certificate. Dress code **Societies** welcome. **Green Fees** £44 per day,
£34 per round (£54/£44 weekends) **Prof** Duncan Burl **Facilities** ⓣ
🍴 ⏣ ⏣ 🍴 🏌 🏠 🏌 🏌 🏌 🏌 🏌 🏌 **Location** 2.5m SW
off B1115
Hotel ★★★ 72% HL Cedars, Needham Road, STOWMARKET
☎ 01449 612668 📠 01449 612668 25 en suite

THORPENESS
Map 5 TM45

Thorpeness Golf Club & Hotel Lakeside Av IP16 4NH
☎ 01728 452176 📠 01728 453868
e-mail: lyn@thorpeness.co.uk
web: www.thorpeness.co.uk

A 6271yd coastal heathland course, designed in 1923 by James
Braid. The quality of his design combined with modern green
keeping techniques has resulted in an extremely challenging course
for golfers at all levels. It is also one of the driest courses in the
region.

continued

Thorpeness Hotel & Golf Club: 18 Holes, 6271yds,
Par 69, SSS 71, Course record 66. Club membership 700.
Visitors Mon-Sun & BHs. **Societies** welcome. **Green Fees** £40
per day/round (£45 weekends & BHs), £25 after 3pm **Course
Designer** James Braid **Prof** Frank Hill **Facilities** ⊕ ⊙ ⓚ ⌑ ⏣
⊟ ⌂ ◇ ⛟ ⚸ **Leisure** hard and grass tennis courts, fishing,
snooker room **Conf** facs Corporate Hospitality Days **Location** off
A1094 to Aldeburgh, signed
Hotel ★★★ 78% HL Thorpeness Hotel, Lakeside Avenue,
THORPENESS ☎ 01728 452176 ▤ 01728 452176 36 en suite

WALDRINGFIELD   Map 5 TM24

Waldringfield Heath Newbourne Rd IP12 4PT
☎ 01473 736768   ▤ 01473 736793
e-mail: patgolf1@aol.com
Easy walking heathland course with long drives on 1st and 13th
(590yds) and some ponds.

Waldringfield Golf Club: 18 Holes, 6057yds, Par 70,
SSS 69, Course record 69. Club membership 550.
Visitors Mon-Sun & BHs. Booking required. Dress code.
Societies booking required. **Green Fees** not confirmed **Course
Designer** Phillip Pilgrem **Prof** Tim Huffer **Facilities** ⊕ ⊙ ⓚ ⌑ ⏣
⊟ ⌂ ⛟ ⚸ **Conf** facs **Location** 1m W of village off A12
Hotel ★★★ 81% HL Seckford Hall, WOODBRIDGE
☎ 01394 385678 ▤ 01394 385678 32 en suite

WOODBRIDGE   Map 5 TM24

Best Western Ufford Park Hotel Golf & Spa Yarmouth Rd,
Ufford IP12 1QW
☎ 0844 4776495   ▤ 0844 4773727
e-mail: mail@uffordpark.co.uk
web: www.uffordpark.co.uk
The 18-hole par 71 course is set in 120 acres of ancient parkland with
12 water features and voted one of the best British winter courses.
The course enjoys excellent natural drainage and a large reservoir
supplements a spring feed pond to ensure ample water for irrigation.
2 storey floodlit driving range and a golf superstore on site.

Best Western Ufford Park Hotel Golf & Spa:
18 Holes, 6312yds, Par 71, SSS 71, Course record 61.
Club membership 400.
Visitors Mon-Sun & BHs. Booking required weekends & BHs. Handicap
certificate. Dress code. **Societies** booking required. **Green Fees** £30
per day, £20 per 18 holes (£40/£30 weekends & BHs) **Course
Designer** Phil Pilgrim **Prof** Stuart Robertson **Facilities** ⊕ ⊙ ⓚ
⌑ ⏣ ⊟ ⌂ ⛟ ◇ ⚸ ⛟ ⚸ **Leisure** heated indoor
swimming pool, sauna, gymnasium, golf academy, health club & spa
Conf facs Corporate Hospitality Days **Location** A12 onto B1438
Hotel ★★★ 78% HL Best Western Ufford Park Hotel Golf &
Spa, Yarmouth Road, Ufford, WOODBRIDGE ☎ 01394 383555
▤ 01394 383555 87 en suite

Seckford Seckford Hall Rd, Great Bealings IP13 6NT
☎ 01394 388000   ▤ 01394 382818
e-mail: info@seckfordgolf.co.uk
web: www.seckfordgolf.co.uk
A challenging course interspersed with young tree plantations,
numerous bunkers, water hazards and undulating fairways, providing
a tough test for all levels of golfer.

18 Holes, 4981yds, Par 68, SSS 65, Course record 62.
Club membership 400.
Visitors dress code. **Societies** welcome. **Green Fees** phone **Course
Designer** J Johnson **Prof** Simon Jay **Facilities** ⊕ ⊙ ⓚ ⌑ ⏣
⌂ ⛟ ◇ ⛟ ⚸ ⚸ **Leisure** heated indoor swimming pool,
fishing, gymnasium **Conf** Corporate Hospitality Days **Location** 1m W of
Woodbridge off A12, next to Seckford Hall Hotel
Hotel ★★★ 81% HL Seckford Hall, WOODBRIDGE
☎ 01394 385678 ▤ 01394 385678 32 en suite

Woodbridge Bromeswell Heath IP12 2PF
☎ 01394 382038   ▤ 01394 382392
e-mail: Info@woodbridgegolfclub.co.uk
web: www.woodbridgegolfclub.co.uk
Courses in a classic heathland setting with fine views. The 18 hole
Heath course requires strategic golfing skill to manoeuvre around
and the Forest is a full length 9 hole course of note.

Heath Course: 18 Holes, 6299yds, Par 70, SSS 70,
Course record 64.
Forest Course: 9 Holes, 3191yds, Par 70, SSS 70.
Club membership 700.
Visitors Heath course Mon-Fri except BHs. Forest course Mon-
Sun & BHs. Handicap certificate for Heath course. Dress code.
Societies booking required. **Green Fees** Heath course £42 per
round, Forest Course £15 per round **Course Designer** James
Braid Davie Grant **Prof** Tim Johnson **Facilities** ⊕ ⊙ by prior
arrangement ⓚ ⌑ ⏣ ⊟ ⌂ ⛟ ◇ ⚸ **Location** 2.5m
NE off A1152
Hotel ★★★ 81% HL Seckford Hall, WOODBRIDGE
☎ 01394 385678 ▤ 01394 385678 32 en suite

WORLINGTON   Map 5 TL67

Royal Worlington & Newmarket Golf Links Rd IP28 8SD
☎ 01638 712216 & 717787   ▤ 01638 717787
web: www.royalworlington.co.uk
Inland links course, renowned as one of the best nine-hole
courses in the world. Well drained, giving excellent winter playing
conditions.

9 Holes, 3123yds, Par 35, SSS 70, Course record 65.
Club membership 330.
Visitors Mon-Sun & BHs. Booking required. Handicap certificate.
Dress code. **Societies** booking required. **Green Fees** £60 per day,
£45 for 18 holes **Course Designer** Tom Dunn **Prof** Richard Beadles
Facilities ⊕ by prior arrangement ⓚ ⌑ ⏣ ⊟ ⌂ ⛟ ◇ ⚸
Location 0.5m SE of Worlington near Mildenhall
Hotel ★★★ 73% HL Riverside Hotel, Bar and Restaurant,
Mill Street, MILDENHALL ☎ 01638 717274 ▤ 01638 717274
22 en suite

SURREY

ADDLESTONE
Map 4 TQ06

New Zealand Woodham Ln KT15 3QD
☎ 01932 345049 📠 01932 342891
e-mail: roger.marrett@nzgc.org
Heathland course set in trees and heather.

18 Holes, 6073yds, Par 68, SSS 69, Course record 66. Club membership 320.

Visitors Mon-Fri except BHs. Booking required. Handicap certificate. Dress code. **Societies** boooking required. **Green Fees** £90 per day **Course Designer** Muir Fergusson/Simpson **Prof** Vic Elvidge **Facilities** ⊕ ⓣ ⓑ ☐ ⓣ ♨ ⓐ ⓥ ♣ ⓔ ♣ **Conf** Corporate Hospitality Days **Location** 1.5m E of Woking **Hotel** ★★★ 77% HL The Ship, Monument Green, WEYBRIDGE ☎ 01932 848364 📠 01932 848364 76 en suite

ASHFORD
Map 4 TQ07

Ashford Manor Fordbridge Rd TW15 3RT
☎ 01784 424644 📠 01784 424649
e-mail: secretary@amgc.co.uk
web: www.amgc.co.uk
Tree-lined parkland course is built on gravel and drains well, never needing temporary tees or greens. A heavy investment in fairway irrigation and an extensive woodland management programme over the past few years have formed a strong future for this course, originally built over a 100 years ago.

18 Holes, 6073yds, Par 70, SSS 70. Club membership 700.
Visitors Mon-Fri except BHs. Booking required. Handicap certificate. Dress code. **Societies** booking required. **Green Fees** £51 per day, £41 per round **Course Designer** Tom Hogg **Prof** Robert Walton **Facilities** ⊕ ⓑ ☐ ⓣ ♨ ⓐ ♣ **Leisure** swing studio with video coaching and club fitting **Conf** facs Corporate Hospitality Days **Location** 2m E of Staines via A308 Staines bypass **Hotel** ★★★ 72% HL Mercure Thames Lodge, Thames Street, STAINES ☎ 01784 464433 📠 01784 464433 79 en suite

BAGSHOT
Map 4 SU96

Pennyhill Park Hotel London Rd GU19 5EU
☎ 01276 471774 📠 01276 473217
e-mail: enquiries@pennyhillpark.co.uk
web: www.exclusivehotels.co.uk
A nine-hole course set in 11 acres of beautiful parkland. It is challenging to even the most experienced golfer.

Pennyhill Park Hotel: 9 Holes, 2055yds, Par 32, SSS 32. Club membership 100.

Visitors contact hotel for details. **Green Fees** complimentary for hotel residents/day visitor using hotel facilities **Facilities** ⊕ ⓣ ⓑ ☐ ⓣ ♨ ⓟ ♦ ♣ **Leisure** hard tennis courts, outdoor and indoor heated swimming pool, sauna, gymnasium, archery, clay pigeon shooting **Conf** facs **Location** off A30 between Camberley and Bagshot **Hotel** ★★★★★ CHH Pennyhill Park Hotel & The Spa, London Road, BAGSHOT ☎ 01276 471774 📠 01276 471774 123 en suite

Windlesham Grove End GU19 5HY
☎ 01276 452220 📠 01276 452290
e-mail: admin@windleshamgolf.com
web: www.windleshamgolf.com
A parkland course with many demanding par 4 holes over 400 yards. Thoughtfully designed by Tommy Horton.

Windlesham Golf Course: 18 Holes, 6650yds, Par 72, SSS 72, Course record 69. Club membership 800.
Visitors Mon-Fri. Weekends & BHs after noon. Handicap certificate. Dress code. **Societies** booking required. **Green Fees** £35 per round (£40 weekends) **Course Designer** Tommy Horton **Prof** Lee Mucklow **Facilities** ⊕ ⓣ ⓑ ☐ ⓣ ♨ ⓐ ♣ ⓔ ♣ **Conf** facs Corporate Hospitality Days **Location** M3 junct 3, on A30 between Sunningdale and Camberley **Hotel** ★★★★★ CHH Pennyhill Park Hotel & The Spa, London Road, BAGSHOT ☎ 01276 471774 📠 01276 471774 123 en suite

BANSTEAD
Map 4 TQ25

Banstead Downs Burdon Ln, Belmont, Sutton SM2 7DD
☎ 020 8642 2284 📠 020 8642 5252
e-mail: secretary@bansteaddowns.com
web: www.bansteaddowns.com
A natural downland course set on a site of botanic interest. A challenging 18 holes with narrow fairways and tight lies.

18 Holes, 6192yds, Par 69, SSS 69, Course record 64. Club membership 877.
Visitors Mon-Thu except BHs. Handicap certificate. Dress code. **Societies** booking required. **Green Fees** £45 before noon. £35 after noon. **Course Designer** J H Taylor/James Braid **Prof** Ian Golding **Facilities** ⊕ ⓣ by prior arrangement ⓑ ☐ ⓣ ♨ ⓐ ♣ **Location** M25 junct 8, A217 N for 6m **Hotel** ★★★ 75% HL Holiday Inn London-Sutton, Gibson Road, SUTTON ☎ 020 8234 1100 & 8234 1104 📠 020 8234 1100 115 en suite

Cuddington Banstead Rd SM7 1RD
☎ 020 8393 0952 📠 020 8786 7025
18 Holes, 6614yds, Par 71, SSS 71, Course record 64.
Course Designer H S Colt **Location** N of Banstead station on A2022 **Telephone for further details**
Hotel ★★★ 75% HL Holiday Inn London-Sutton, Gibson Road, SUTTON ☎ 020 8234 1100 & 8234 1104 📠 020 8234 1100 115 en suite

BLETCHINGLEY
Map 5 TQ35

Bletchingley Church Ln RH1 4LP
☎ 01883 744666 📠 01883 744284
e-mail: info@bletchingleygolf.co.uk
web: www.bletchingleygolf.co.uk
Panoramic views create a perfect backdrop for this course, constructed on rich sandy loam and playable all year round. The course design has made best use of the interesting and undulating land features with a variety of mixed and mature trees providing essential course definition. A mature stream creates several interesting water features.

18 Holes, 6600yds, Par 72, SSS 72, Course record 69. Club membership 500.
Visitors Mon-Sun & BHs. Booking required. Dress code. **Societies** booking required. **Green Fees** £30 (£40 weekends & BHs)

continued

Prof Steven Cookson **Facilities** 🏧 🍴 by prior arrangement 🏌
🏌 🍴 ⛳ 🏌 🏌 **Conf** facs Corporate Hospitality Days
Location A25 onto Church Ln in Bletchingley
Hotel ★★★★ 80% HL Nutfield Priory, Nutfield, REDHILL
☎ 01737 824400 & 0845 072 7485 📄 01737 824400 60 en suite

BRAMLEY   Map 4 TQ04

Bramley GU5 0AL
☎ 01483 892696 📄 01483 894673
e-mail: secretary@bramleygolfclub.co.uk
web: www.bramleygolfclub.co.uk

Parkland course. From the high ground picturesque views of the Wey
valley on one side and the Hog's Back. Full on course irrigation system
with three reservoirs on the course.

18 Holes, 5990yds, Par 69, SSS 69, Course record 61.
Club membership 850.

Visitors Mon-Fri except BHs. Dress code. **Societies** booking required.
Green Fees £50 per 36 holes, £40 per round **Course Designer** Charles
Mayo/James Braid **Prof** Gary Peddie **Facilities** 🏧 🍴 🏌 🏌 🍴
🏌 🏌 🏌 🏌 🏌 🏌 **Conf** facs Corporate Hospitality Days
Location 3m S of Guildford on A281
Hotel BUD Innkeeper's Lodge Godalming, Ockford Road, GODALMING
☎ 0845 112 6102 📄 0845 112 6102 14 en suite

BROOKWOOD   Map 4 SU95

West Hill Bagshot Rd GU24 0BH
☎ 01483 474365 📄 01483 474252
web: www.westhill-golfclub.co.uk
18 Holes, 6343yds, Par 69, SSS 70, Course record 62.
Course Designer C Butchart/W Parke **Location** E of village on A322
Telephone for further details
Hotel ★★★★★ CHH Pennyhill Park Hotel & The Spa, London
Road, BAGSHOT ☎ 01276 471774 📄 01276 471774 123 en suite

CAMBERLEY   Map 4 SU86

Camberley Heath Golf Dr GU15 1JG
☎ 01276 23258 📄 01276 692505
e-mail: info@camberleyheathgolfclub.co.uk
web: www.camberleyheathgolfclub.co.uk

Set in attractive Surrey countryside, a challenging golf course
that features an abundance of pine and heather. A true classic
heathland course with many assets, including the mature fairways.
18 Holes, 6147yds, Par 71, SSS 70, Course record 65.
Club membership 600.

Visitors Mon, Wed & Thu except BHs. Booking required. Handicap
certificate. Dress code. **Societies** booking required. **Green**
Fees £60 per round **Course Designer** Harry S Colt **Prof** Glenn
Ralph **Facilities** 🏧 🍴 🏌 🏌 🍴 🏌 🏌 🏌 🏌 🏌 🏌
Conf facs Corporate Hospitality Days **Location** 1.25m SE of town
centre off A325
Hotel ★★★★★ CHH Pennyhill Park Hotel & The Spa, London
Road, BAGSHOT ☎ 01276 471774 📄 01276 471774 123 en suite

Pine Ridge Old Bisley Rd, Frimley GU16 9NX
☎ 01276 675444 📄 01276 678837
e-mail: pineridge@crown-golf.co.uk
web: www.pineridgegolf.co.uk

Pay and play heathland course cut through a pine forest with
challenging par 3s, deceptively demanding par 4s and several
birdiable par 5s. Easy walking, but gently undulating. Good corporate
or society packages.

18 Holes, 6458yds, Par 72, SSS 71, Course record 65.
Club membership 200.

Visitors Mon-Sun & BHs. Booking required. Dress code.
Societies booking required. **Green Fees** £25 per round (£31
weekends) **Course Designer** Clive D Smith **Prof** Peter Sefton
Facilities 🏧 🍴 🏌 🏌 🍴 🏌 🏌 🏌 🏌 🏌 🏌 🏌
Conf facs Corporate Hospitality Days **Location** off B3015, near A30
Hotel ★★★★ 78% HL Macdonald Frimley Hall Hotel & Spa,
Lime Avenue, CAMBERLEY ☎ 0844 879 9110 📄 0844 879 9110
98 en suite

CATERHAM   Map 5 TQ35

Surrey National Rook Ln, Chaldon CR3 5AA
☎ 01883 344555 📄 01883 344422
e-mail: caroline@surreynational.co.uk
web: www.surreynational.co.uk

Opened in April 1999, this American-style course is set in beautiful
countryside and features fully irrigated greens and fairways. The
setting is dramatic with rolling countryside, thousands of mature trees
and water features. The chalk based sub-soil, computerised irrigation
and buggy paths combine to make the course enjoyable to play at any
time of year.

18 Holes, 6612yds, Par 72, SSS 73, Course record 64.

Visitors Mon-Sun & BHs. Dress code. **Societies** booking
required **Green Fees** £22-£24 per round (£35 weekends) **Course**
Designer David Williams **Prof** David Kent/Matthew Stock **Facilities** 🏧
🍴 by prior arrangement 🏌 🏌 🍴 🏌 🏌 🏌 🏌 🏌 🏌 🏌
Conf facs Corporate Hospitality Days **Location** M25 junct 7, A23/M25
junct 6, A22
Hotel ★★★★ 73% HL Coulsdon Manor, Coulsdon Court
Road, Coulsdon, CROYDON ☎ 020 8668 0414 📄 020 8668 0414
35 en suite

CHERTSEY   Map 4 TQ06

Laleham Laleham Reach KT16 8RP
☎ 01932 564211 📄 01932 564448
e-mail: manager@laleham-golf.co.uk
web: www.laleham-golf.co.uk

Well-bunkered parkland and meadowland course. The prevailing
wind and strategic placement of hazards makes it a fair but testing
challenge. Natural drainage due to the underlying gravel.

continued

18 Holes, 6291yds, Par 70, SSS 70, Course record 65.
Club membership 600.
Visitors Mon-Sun & BHs. Booking required. Dress code.
Societies booking required **Green Fees** phone **Course Designer** Jack
White **Prof** Paul Smith **Facilities** ⚐ 🍴 ⬚ ⊑ 🕤 ⚘ 🏠 🛉 ✦
🛪 ✦ **Conf** facs Corporate Hospitality Days **Location** M25 junct 11,
A320 to Thorpe Park rdbt, exit Penton Marina, club signed
Hotel ★★★ 72% HL Mercure Thames Lodge, Thames Street,
STAINES ☎ 01784 464433 📄 01784 464433 79 en suite

CHIDDINGFOLD — Map 4 SU93

Chiddingfold Petworth Rd GU8 4SL
☎ 01428 685888   📄 01428 685939
e-mail: chiddingfoldgolf@btconnect.com
web: www.chiddingfoldgc.co.uk
With panoramic views across the Surrey hills, this challenging course
offers a unique combination of lakes, mature woodland and wildlife.

*Chiddingfold Golf Course: 18 Holes, 5568yds, Par 70,
SSS 67.*
Visitors contact club for details. **Societies** welcome. **Green Fees** not
confirmed **Course Designer** Johnathan Gaunt **Facilities** ⬚ 🕤 ⚘
🏠 🛉 ✦ **Location** off A283
Hotel ★★★★ 76% HL Lythe Hill Hotel and Spa, Petworth Road,
HASLEMERE ☎ 01428 651251 📄 01428 651251 41 en suite

CHIPSTEAD — Map 4 TQ25

Chipstead How Ln CR5 3LN
☎ 01737 555781   📄 01737 555404
e-mail: office@chipsteadgolf.co.uk
web: www.chipsteadgolf.co.uk
Testing downland course with good views.

*18 Holes, 5504yds, Par 68, SSS 67, Course record 61.
Club membership 475.*
Visitors Mon-Sun except BHs. Booking required. Dress code.
Societies welcome. **Green Fees** £40 per day, £30 per round **Prof** Gary
Torbett **Facilities** ⚐ 🍴 ⬚ ⊑ 🕤 ⚘ 🏠 🛉 ✦ 🛪 ✦
Conf facs Corporate Hospitality Days **Location** 0.5m N of village
Hotel ★★★★ 73% HL Coulsdon Manor, Coulsdon Court Road,
Coulsdon, CROYDON ☎ 020 8668 0414 📄 020 8668 0414 35 en suite

CHOBHAM — Map 4 SU96

Chobham Chobham Rd, Knaphill GU21 2TZ
☎ 01276 855584   📄 01276 855663
e-mail: info@chobhamgolfclub.co.uk
web: www.chobhamgolfclub.co.uk
Designed by Peter Allis and Clive Clark, Chobham course sits among
mature oaks and tree nurseries offering tree-lined fairways, together
with six man-made lakes.

*18 Holes, 5959yds, Par 69, SSS 69, Course record 67.
Club membership 750.*
Visitors Mon-Fri except BHs. Booking required. Handicap certificate.
Dress code. **Societies** booking required. **Green Fees** phone **Course
Designer** Peter Alliss/Clive Clark **Prof** Michael Harrison **Facilities** ⚐
🍴 by prior arrangement ⬚ ⊑ 🕤 ⚘ 🏠 ✦ **Conf** facs
Corporate Hospitality Days **Location** on Chobham road between
Chobham and Knaphill
Hotel ★★★ 78% HL Holiday Inn Woking, Victoria Street, WOKING
☎ 01483 221000 📄 01483 221000 161 en suite

COBHAM — Map 4 TQ16

Silvermere Redhill Rd KT11 1EF
☎ 01932 584300   📄 01932 584301
e-mail: sales@silvermere-golf.co.uk
web: www.silvermere-golf.co.uk
A mixture of light heathland on the first six holes and parkland on
holes 7-16, then two signature water holes at the 17th and 18th,
played over the Silvermere Lake.

18 Holes, 6430yds, Par 71. Club membership 400.
Visitors Mon-Sun & BHs. Booking required weekends & BHs. Dress
code. **Societies** booking required. **Green Fees** £22.50 per 18 holes,
£25 Fri, £37.50 weekends **Course Designer** Neil Coles **Prof** Doug
McClelland **Facilities** ⚐ 🍴 ⬚ ⊑ 🕤 ⚘ 🏠 🛉 ✦ 🛡
Leisure fishing **Conf** facs Corporate Hospitality Days **Location** 0.5m
from M25 junct 10, off A245
Hotel ★★★★ 80% HL Woodlands Park, Woodlands Lane,
STOKE D'ABERNON, Cobham ☎ 01372 843933 📄 01372 843933
57 en suite

CRANLEIGH — Map 4 TQ03

Cranleigh Golf and Leisure Club Barhatch Ln GU6 7NG
☎ 01483 268855   📄 01483 267251
e-mail: info@cranleighgolfandleisure.co.uk
web: www.cranleighgolfandleisure.co.uk
Scenic woodland and parkland at the base of the Surrey hills, easy
walking. The golfer should not be deceived by the length of the course.
Clubhouse in 400-year-old barn.

*Cranleigh Golf and Leisure Club: 18 Holes, 5263yds,
Par 68, SSS 65, Course record 62. Club membership 1400.*
Visitors Mon-Sun & BHs. Booking required. Dress code
Societies booking required. **Green Fees** not confirmed **Prof** Trevor
Longmuir **Facilities** ⚐ ⬚ ⊑ 🕤 ⚘ 🏠 🛉 ✦ 🛪 ✦ 🛡
Leisure hard tennis courts, heated indoor swimming pool, sauna,
gymnasium, steam room, spa bath **Location** 0.5m N of town centre
Hotel ★★★ 79% HL Gatton Manor Hotel & Golf Club, Standon
Lane, OCKLEY, Nr Dorking ☎ 01306 627555 📄 01306 627555
18 en suite

Wildwood Golf & Country Club Horsham Rd, Alfold
GU6 8JE
☎ 01403 753255   📄 01403 752005
e-mail: info@wildwoodgolf.co.uk
web: www.wildwoodgolf.co.uk
Parkland with stands of old oaks dominating several holes, a stream
fed by a natural spring winds through a series of lakes and ponds.
The greens are smooth, undulating and large. Course consists of three
loops of nine holes with a signature hole on each.

*Wildwood Golf & Country Club: 27 Holes, 6655yds, Par 72,
SSS 73, Course record 65. Club membership 600.*
Visitors Mon-Sun & BHs. Dress code. **Societies** welcome. **Green
Fees** phone **Course Designer** Hawtree & Sons **Prof** Phil Harrison
Facilities ⚐ 🍴 ⬚ ⊑ 🕤 ⚘ 🏠 🛉 ✦ 🛪 ✦ 🛡
Leisure gymnasium, par 3 course **Conf** facs Corporate Hospitality
Days **Location** on A281 3m SW of Cranleigh
Hotel ★★★ 79% HL Gatton Manor Hotel & Golf Club, Standon
Lane, OCKLEY, Nr Dorking ☎ 01306 627555 📄 01306 627555
18 en suite

DORKING
Map 4 TQ14

Betchworth Park Reigate Rd RH4 1NZ
☎ 01306 882052   📠 01306 877462
e-mail: manager@betchworthparkgc.co.uk
web: www.betchworthparkgc.co.uk

Established, well presented, parkland course with beautiful views, on the southern side of the North Downs near Boxhill. True test of golf for all levels of golfer.

18 Holes, 6329yds, Par 69, SSS 70, Course record 64.
Club membership 725.

Visitors Mon, Wed-Fri, Sun & BHs. Booking required. Handicap certificate. Dress code. **Societies** welcome. **Green Fees** £45 per round (£55 Fri & Sun) **Course Designer** Harry Colt **Prof** Andy Tocher **Facilities** 🍴 🍺 ☕ 🍷 ⚲ 🏌 🛈 🖊 🚗 🛒 **Conf** facs Corporate Hospitality Days **Location** 1m E of Dorking on A25 towards Reigate, juncts 8/9
Hotel ★★★ 66% HL Mercure White Horse, High Street, DORKING ☎ 0870 400 8282 📠 0870 400 8282 78 en suite

Dorking Chart Park RH5 4BX
☎ 01306 886917
web: www.dorkinggolfclub.co.uk

9 Holes, 5120yds, Par 66, SSS 65, Course record 62.

Course Designer J Braid/Others **Location** 1m S on A24
Telephone for further details
Hotel ★★★★ 74% HL Mercure Burford Bridge, Burford Bridge, Box Hill, DORKING ☎ 01306 884561 📠 01306 884561 57 en suite

EAST HORSLEY
Map 4 TQ05

Drift The Drift KT24 5HD
☎ 01483 284641 & 284772(shop)   📠 01483 284642
web: www.driftgolfclub.com

18 Holes, 6425yds, Par 73, SSS 72, Course record 65.

Course Designer Sir Henry Cotton/Robert Sandow **Location** 0.5m N of East Horsley off B2039
Telephone for further details
Hotel ★★ 65% HL Bookham Grange, Little Bookham Common, Bookham, LEATHERHEAD ☎ 01372 452742 & 459899 📠 01372 452742 27 en suite

EFFINGHAM
Map 4 TQ15

Effingham Guildford Rd KT24 5PZ
☎ 01372 452203   📠 01372 459959
e-mail: secretary@effinghamgolfclub.com
web: www.effinghamgolfclub.com

Easy-walking downland course laid out on 270 acres with tree-lined fairways. It is one of the longest of the Surrey courses with wide subtle greens that provide a provocative but by no means exhausting challenge. Fine views of the London skyline.

18 Holes, 6554yds, Par 71, SSS 71, Course record 64.
Club membership 800.

Visitors Mon-Fri except BHs. Booking required. Handicap certificate. Dress code. **Societies** booking required. **Green Fees** £60 per day, £40 per round after 11am, £25 after 3.30pm **Course Designer** H S Colt **Prof** Steve Hoatson **Facilities** 🍴 🍽 by prior arrangement 🍺 ☕ 🍷 🏌 🛈 🖊 🚗 🖊 **Leisure** hard tennis courts, snooker table **Conf** Corporate Hospitality Days **Location** W of village on A246

Hotel ★★ 65% HL Bookham Grange, Little Bookham Common, Bookham, LEATHERHEAD ☎ 01372 452742 & 459899 📠 01372 452742 27 en suite

ENTON GREEN
Map 4 SU94

West Surrey GU8 5AF
☎ 01483 421275   📠 01483 415419
web: www.wsgc.co.uk

18 Holes, 6482yds, Par 71, SSS 71, Course record 65.

Course Designer Herbert Fowler **Location** S of village
Telephone for further details
Hotel ★★★ 75% HL Mercure Bush, The Borough, FARNHAM ☎ 0870 400 8225 & 01252 715237 📠 0870 400 8225 83 en suite

EPSOM
Map 4 TQ26

Epsom Longdown Lane South KT17 4JR
☎ 01372 721666   📠 01372 817183
web: www.epsomgolfclub.co.uk

18 Holes, 5656yds, Par 69, SSS 67, Course record 63.

Course Designer Willie Dunne **Location** SE of town centre on B288
Telephone for further details
Hotel ★★★★ 80% HL Woodlands Park, Woodlands Lane, STOKE D'ABERNON, Cobham ☎ 01372 843933 📠 01372 843933 57 en suite

Horton Park Golf & Country Club Hook Rd KT19 8QG
☎ 020 8393 8400 & 8394 2626   📠 020 8394 1369
e-mail: mike@hortonparkgolfclub.co.uk
web: www.hortonparkgolfclub.co.uk

Parkland course in picturesque surroundings within a country park with a natural lake. The course offers a challenge to all golfers with dog-legs, water hazards and the 10th at 160yds with an island green. There is also a separate full length par 3 9 hole course.

Millennium: 18 Holes, 6257yds, Par 71, SSS 70.
Club membership 450.

Visitors Mon-Sun & BHs. Booking required. Dress code. **Societies** booking required. **Green Fees** £20 (£26 weekends) **Course Designer** Dr Peter Nicholson **Prof** John Terrell **Facilities** 🍴 🍽 🍺 ☕ 🍷 🏌 🛈 🖊 🚗 🖊 🛒 **Conf** facs Corporate Hospitality Days
Hotel ★★★★ 80% HL Woodlands Park, Woodlands Lane, STOKE D'ABERNON, Cobham ☎ 01372 843933 📠 01372 843933 57 en suite

ESHER
Map 4 TQ16

Moore Place Portsmouth Rd KT10 9LN
☎ 01372 463533
web: www.mooreplacegolf.co.uk

Public course on attractive, undulating parkland, laid out some 80 years ago by Harry Vardon. Examples of most of the trees that thrive in the UK are to be found on the course. Testing short holes at 8th and 9th.

9 Holes, 2103yds, Par 66, SSS 62, Course record 58.
Club membership 150.

Visitors dress code. **Societies** welcome. **Green Fees** not confirmed **Course Designer** H Vardon/D Allen/N Gadd **Prof** Nick Gadd

continued

Facilities 🍴 🍽 🏌 ⛳ 🏑 🏖 🏡 ⛳ ✎ **Conf** facs
Location 0.5m from town centre on A307
Hotel ★★★ 77% HL The Ship, Monument Green, WEYBRIDGE
☎ 01932 848364 📄 01932 848364 76 en suite

Thames Ditton & Esher Portsmouth Rd KT10 9AL
☎ 020 8398 1551

Initially founded in 1892, commonland with public right of way across the course. Although the course is not long, accuracy is essential and wayward shots are normally punished.

18 Holes, 5149yds, Par 66, SSS 65, Course record 61.
Club membership 250.

Visitors Mon-Sat & BHs. Sun pm only. Dress code. **Societies** booking required. **Green Fees** not confirmed **Prof** Mark Rodbard **Facilities** 🍴
🍽 🏌 ⛳ 🏑 🏖 🏡 ✎ **Location** 1m NE on A307, next to Marquis of Granby pub
Hotel ★★★★ 72% HL The Carlton Mitre, Hampton Court Road, HAMPTON COURT ☎ 020 8979 9988 & 8783 3505 📄 020 8979 9988 36 en suite

FARLEIGH   Map 5 TQ36

Farleigh Court Farleigh Common CR6 9PE
☎ 01883 627711 📄 01883 627722
web: www.farleighcourtgolf.com

Members: 18 Holes, 6409yds, Par 72, SSS 70,
Course record 67.
9 Holes, 3281yds, Par 36.

Course Designer John Jacobs **Location** 1.5m from Selsdon
Telephone for further details
Hotel BUD Innkeeper's Lodge Croydon South, 415 Brighton Road, CROYDON ☎ 0845 112 6118 📄 0845 112 6118 30 en suite

FARNHAM   Map 4 SU84

Blacknest Binsted GU34 4QL
☎ 01420 22888 📄 01420 22001
e-mail: office@blacknestgolf.com

Privately owned pay and play golf centre catering for all ages and levels of ability. Facilities include a 15-bay driving range, gymnasium and a challenging 18-hole course featuring water on 14 holes.

18 Holes, 5938yds, Par 69, SSS 69, Course record 64.
Club membership 400.

Visitors Mon-Sun & BHs. Booking required Mon, Thu-Sun & BHs. Dress code. **Societies** booking required. **Green Fees** not confirmed **Course Designer** Mr Nicholson **Facilities** 🍴 🏌 ⛳ 🏑 🏖 🏡 ⛳
✎ 🏖 ✎ ⛳ **Leisure** sauna, gymnasium, 6 hole par 3 academy course. Physiotherapy treatments **Conf** facs Corporate Hospitality Days **Location** 5m SW of Farnham, leave A325 at A31 Bentley
Hotel ★★★ 76% HL Best Western Frensham Pond Hotel, Bacon Lane, CHURT, Farnham ☎ 01252 795161 📄 01252 795161 51 en suite

Farnham The Sands GU10 1PX
☎ 01252 782109 📄 01252 781185
e-mail: farnhamgolfclub@tiscali.co.uk
web: www.farnhamgolfclub.co.uk

A mixture of meadowland and heath with quick drying sandy subsoil. Several of the earlier holes have interesting features.
Farnham Golf Club Ltd: 18 Holes, 6571yds, Par 72,
SSS 71, Course record 66. Club membership 700.

Visitors Mon-Fri. Weekends & BHs by arrangement. Handicap certificate. Dress code **Societies** booking required. **Green Fees** £50 per day, £45 per round **Course Designer** Donald Steel **Prof** Rob Colborne **Facilities** 🍴 🍽 by prior arrangement 🏌 ⛳ 🏑 🏖 🏡 ✎ ✎ **Conf** Corporate Hospitality Days **Location** 3m E off A31
Hotel ★★★ 75% HL Mercure Bush, The Borough, FARNHAM ☎ 0870 400 8225 & 01252 715237 📄 0870 400 8225 83 en suite

GODALMING   Map 4 SU94

Broadwater Park Guildford Rd, Farncombe GU7 3BU
☎ 01483 429955 📄 01483 429955

A par 3 public course with floodlit driving range.
Broadwater Park Golf Club & Driving Range: 9 Holes,
1287yds, Par 54, SSS 50. Club membership 160.

Visitors Mon-Sun & BHs. Booking required weekends & BHs.
Societies welcome. **Green Fees** £6.75 (£8 weekends & BHs) **Course Designer** Kevin Milton **Prof** Kevin D Milton/Nick English **Facilities** 🏌 ⛳ 🏑 🏡 ⛳ ✎ ⛳ **Conf** Corporate Hospitality Days **Location** NE of Godalming on A3100
Hotel ★★★ 79% HL Holiday Inn Guildford, Egerton Road, GUILDFORD ☎ 0870 400 9036 📄 0870 400 9036 168 en suite

Hurtmore Hurtmore Rd, Hurtmore GU7 2RN
☎ 01483 426492 📄 01483 426121
e-mail: general@hurtmore-golf.co.uk
web: www.hurtmore-golf.co.uk

A Peter Alliss and Clive Clark pay and play course with several lakes that come into play more than once. Many well placed bunkers catch any errant shots. The par 5, 15th hole is the longest on the course. A narrow drive, long sweeping fairway, cross bunker and out of bounds to the left provide a daunting challenge to those who are too ambitious.

18 Holes, 5254yds, Par 70, SSS 67, Course record 65.
Club membership 200.

Visitors dress code. **Societies** booking required. **Green Fees** £16 per 18 holes, £12 per 9 holes (£22/£14 weekends). Twilight £12 (£14 weekends) **Course Designer** Peter Alliss/Clive Clark **Prof** Maxine Burton **Facilities** 🍴 🍽 🏌 ⛳ 🏑 🏖 🏡 ⛳ ✎
Leisure practice nets **Conf** Corporate Hospitality Days **Location** 2m NW of Godalming off A3
Hotel ★★★ 79% HL Holiday Inn Guildford, Egerton Road, GUILDFORD ☎ 0870 400 9036 📄 0870 400 9036 168 en suite

GODSTONE   Map 5 TQ35

Godstone Rooks Nest Park RH9 8BZ
☎ 01883 742333 📄 01883 740227
e-mail: admin@godstone-golfclub.co.uk
web: www.godstone-golfclub.co.uk

Designed by David Williams, Godstone offers three tees per hole, making it possible to play the 9 holes twice, with varying tee positions. The three new lakes, linked by a freshwater stream, add interest and a degree of difficulty to the course.

9 Holes, 6068yds, Par 72, SSS 69.

Visitors Mon-Sun & BHs. Booking preferred. Dress code.
Societies booking required. **Green Fees** £18 per 18 holes, £11 per 9 holes (£21/£17 weekends) **Course Designer** David Williams
Facilities 🏌 ⛳ 🏡 🏖 ✎ ⛳ **Location** M25 junct 6, situated on A22 towards Oxted
Hotel ★★★★ 80% HL Nutfield Priory, Nutfield, REDHILL ☎ 01737 824400 & 0845 072 7485 📄 01737 824400 60 en suite

GUILDFORD   Map 4 SU94

Guildford High Path Rd, Merrow GU1 2HL
☎ 01483 563941   📠 01483 453228
e-mail: secretary@guildfordgolfclub.co.uk
web: www.guildfordgolfclub.co.uk

The course is on Surrey downland bordered by attractive woodlands. Situated on chalk, it is acknowledged to be one of the best all-weather courses in the area, and the oldest course in Surrey. Although not a long course, the prevailing winds across the open downs make low scoring difficult. It is possible to see four counties on a clear day.

18 Holes, 6160yds, Par 69, SSS 70, Course record 65. Club membership 700.

Visitors Mon-Fri except BHs. Handicap certificate. Dress code. **Societies** welcome. **Green Fees** £50 per day; £44 per round **Course Designer** J H Taylor/Hawtree **Prof** P G Hollington **Facilities** ⊕ ⯅ ⌺ ⬧ ⬦ **Conf** facs Corporate Hospitality Days **Location** E of town centre off A246
Hotel ★★★ 79% HL Holiday Inn Guildford, Egerton Road, GUILDFORD ☎ 0870 400 9036 📠 0870 400 9036 168 en suite

See advert on opposite page

Merrist Wood Holly Ln, Worplesdon GU3 3PE
☎ 01483 238890   📠 01483 238896
e-mail: merristwood-admin@crowngolf.co.uk
web: merristwood-golfclub.co.uk

More parkland than heathland, Merrist Wood has a bit of everything. Water comes into play on five holes, the bunkering is fierce, the greens slope and the back nine has plenty of trees. Two holes stand out especially: the picturesque par 3 11th with a tee shot through the trees and the dastardly par 4 17th, including a 210yd carry over a lake and ditches either side of the green.

18 Holes, 6600yds, Par 72, SSS 71, Course record 69. Club membership 600.

Visitors Mon-Sun & BHs. Dress code. **Societies** booking required. **Green Fees** not confirmed **Course Designer** David Williams **Prof** Simon Fowler **Facilities** ⊕ ⊗ ⯅ ⌺ ⬧ ⬦ **Leisure** golf tuition academy **Conf** facs Corporate Hospitality Days **Location** 3m from Guildford on A323 to Aldershot
Hotel ★★★ 79% HL Holiday Inn Guildford, Egerton Road, GUILDFORD ☎ 0870 400 9036 📠 0870 400 9036 168 en suite

Milford Station Ln GU8 5HS
☎ 01483 419200   📠 01483 419199
web: www.crowngolf.com/milford
18 Holes, 5960yds, Par 69, SSS 68, Course record 64.

Course Designer Peter Allis **Location** 6m SW Guildford. Off A3 into Milford, E towards station
Telephone for further details
Hotel ★★★ 79% HL Holiday Inn Guildford, Egerton Road, GUILDFORD ☎ 0870 400 9036 📠 0870 400 9036 168 en suite

Roker Park Rokers Farm GU3 3PB
☎ 01483 236677   📠 01483 232324
Roker Park Golf Course: 9 Holes, 3037yds, Par 36, SSS 72.
Course Designer W V Roker **Location** 3m NW of Guildford on A323
Telephone for further details
Hotel ★★★ 79% HL Holiday Inn Guildford, Egerton Road, GUILDFORD ☎ 0870 400 9036 📠 0870 400 9036 168 en suite

HINDHEAD   Map 4 SU83

Hindhead Churt Rd GU26 6HX
☎ 01428 604614   📠 01428 608508
e-mail: secretary@the-hindhead-golf-club.co.uk
web: www.the-hindhead-golf-club.co.uk

A picturesque Surrey heathland course. The front nine holes follow heather lined valleys which give the players a very remote and secluded feel. For the back nine play moves on to a plateau which offers a more traditional game before the tough challenge of the final two finishing holes.

The Hindhead Golf Club: 18 Holes, 6356yds, Par 70, SSS 70, Course record 63. Club membership 610.

Visitors Mon-Sun & BHs after 9.30am. Booking required. Handicap certificate. Dress code. **Societies** booking required. **Green Fees** £70 per day, £60 per round (£80/£70 weekends & BHs) **Course Designer** J H Taylor **Prof** Ian Benson **Facilities** ⊕ ⯅ ⌺ ⬧ ⬦ **Leisure** snooker **Conf** Corporate Hospitality Days **Location** 1.5m NW of Hindhead on A287
Hotel ★★★★ 76% HL Lythe Hill Hotel and Spa, Petworth Road, HASLEMERE ☎ 01428 651251 📠 01428 651251 41 en suite

KINGSWOOD   Map 4 TQ25

Kingswood Golf and Country House Sandy Ln KT20 6NE
☎ 01737 832188   📠 01737 833920
e-mail: sales@kingswood-golf.co.uk
web: www.kingswood-golf.co.uk

Mature parkland course sited on a plateau with delightful views of the Chipstead valley. The course features lush, shaped fairways, testing bunkers positions and true greens. Course improvements ensure it plays every inch of its 6900yds.

Kingswood Golf & Country Club: 18 Holes, 6904yds, Par 72, SSS 73. Club membership 700.

Visitors Mon-Fri. Weekends & BHs after 11am. Booking required. Dress code. **Societies** welcome. **Green Fees** phone **Course Designer** James Braid **Prof** Terry Sims **Facilities** ⯅ ⌺ ⬧ ⬦ **Leisure** squash, 3 snooker tables. **Conf** facs Corporate Hospitality Days **Location** 0.5m S of village off A217
Hotel ★★★ 73% HL Best Western Reigate Manor, Reigate Hill, REIGATE ☎ 01737 240125 📠 01737 240125 50 en suite

Surrey Downs Outwood Ln KT20 6JS
☎ 01737 839090 🖹 01737 839080
e-mail: booking@surreydownsgc.co.uk
web: www.surreydownsgc.co.uk
A challenging downland course with fine views over the Surrey countryside and first class facilities.
18 Holes, 6303yards, Par 71, SSS 70, Course record 64.
Club membership 652.
Visitors Mon-Sun & BHs. Booking required. Dress code.
Societies booking required **Green Fees** £25 per round (£35 weekends & BHs) **Course Designer** Aliss/Clarke **Facilities** ⑪ ⑩ ⓑ ⏛ ⑪ ⓐ 🖿 ❡ 🛒 ❡ ⏌ **Leisure** sauna **Conf** facs Corporate Hospitality Days **Location** off A217 E onto B2032 at Kingswood for 1m, club on right after Eyhurst Park
Hotel ★★★ 73% HL Best Western Reigate Manor, Reigate Hill, REIGATE ☎ 01737 240125 🖹 01737 240125 50 en suite

---

LEATHERHEAD   Map 4 TQ15

Leatherhead Kingston Rd KT22 0EE
☎ 01372 843966 & 843956 🖹 01372 842241
e-mail: sales@lgc-golf.co.uk
web: www.lgc-golf.co.uk
Undulating, 100-year-old parkland course with tree-lined fairways and strategically placed bunkers. Easy walking.
18 Holes, 5795yds, Par 70, SSS 68, Course record 63.
Club membership 450.
Visitors Mon, Tue, Thu & Fri. Wed, weekends & BHs after noon. Dress code. **Societies** welcome. **Green Fees** £38 per round (£40 weekends) **Prof** Timothy Lowe **Facilities** ⑪ ⑩ ⓑ ⏛ ⑪ ⓐ 🖿 🛖 🛒 ❡ ⏌ **Conf** facs Corporate Hospitality Days **Location** 0.25m from junct 9 of M25, on A243
Hotel ★★ 65% HL Bookham Grange, Little Bookham Common, Bookham, LEATHERHEAD ☎ 01372 452742 & 459899 🖹 01372 452742 27 en suite

Pachesham Park Golf Complex Oaklawn Rd KT22 0BP
☎ 01372 843453
e-mail: enquiries@pacheshamgolf.co.uk
web: www.pacheshamgolf.co.uk
An undulating parkland course starting with five shorter but tight holes on one side of the road, followed by four longer more open but testing holes to finish.
Pachesham Park Golf Centre: 9 Holes, 2805yds, Par 70, SSS 67, Course record 67. Club membership 150.
Visitors Mon-Sun & BHs. Booking required. Dress code.
Societies welcome. **Green Fees** £18 per 18 holes; £10 per 9 holes (£20/£14 weekends & BHs) **Course Designer** Phil Taylor **Prof** Philip Taylor **Facilities** ⑪ ⑩ by prior arrangement ⓑ ⏛ ⑪ ⓐ 🖿 🛒 ❡ ⏌ **Leisure** fitting centre **Conf** facs Corporate Hospitality Days **Location** M25 junct 9, 0.5m off A244 or A245
Hotel ★★★★ 80% HL Woodlands Park, Woodlands Lane, STOKE D'ABERNON, Cobham ☎ 01372 843933 🖹 01372 843933 57 en suite

Tyrrells Wood The Drive KT22 8QP
☎ 01372 376025 🖹 01372 360836
web: www.tyrrellswoodgolfclub.com
18 Holes, 6282yds, Par 71, SSS 70, Course record 65.
Course Designer James Braid **Location** M25 junct 9, 2m SE of town off A24
Telephone for further details
Hotel ★★★★ 74% HL Mercure Burford Bridge, Burford Bridge, Box Hill, DORKING ☎ 01306 884561 🖹 01306 884561 57 en suite

---

LIMPSFIELD   Map 5 TQ45

Limpsfield Chart Westerham Rd RH8 0SL
☎ 01883 723405 & 722106
Attractive heathland course on National Trust land, easy walking with tree lined fairways.
9 Holes, 5718yds, Par 70, SSS 68, Course record 64.
Club membership 300.
Visitors Mon-Wed & Fri. Booking required. Dress code.
Societies booking required. **Green Fees** £20 per day, £13 after 3pm **Prof** Mike McLean **Facilities** ⓑ ⏛ ⑪ ⓐ **Conf** Corporate Hospitality Days **Location** M25 junct 6, 1m E on A25
Hotel ★★★ 79% HL Best Western Donnington Manor, London Road, Dunton Green, SEVENOAKS ☎ 01732 462681 🖹 01732 462681 60 en suite

LINGFIELD
Map 5 TQ34

Lingfield Park Lingfield Rd, Racecourse Rd RH7 6PQ
☎ 01342 832659   📠 01342 836077
e-mail: cmorley@lingfieldpark.co.uk
web: www.lingfieldpark.co.uk

Difficult and challenging tree-lined parkland course, set in 210 acres of beautiful Surrey countryside with water features and 60 bunkers.

18 Holes, 6473yds, Par 71, SSS 72, Course record 65. Club membership 700.

Visitors contact club for details. **Societies** booking required. **Green Fees** not confirmed **Prof** Christopher Morley **Facilities** ⑪ ⑪ ㏇ ♨ 🍴 ♨ 🏠 🚩 ♂ ✦ ♂ 🏌 **Leisure** squash, sauna, gymnasium, horse racing **Conf** facs Corporate Hospitality Days **Location** M25 junct 6, signs to racecourse
Hotel ★★★★ 86% HL Felbridge Hotel & Spa, London Road, EAST GRINSTEAD ☎ 01342 337700 📠 01342 337700 120 en suite

NEWDIGATE
Map 4 TQ14

Rusper Rusper Rd RH5 5BX
☎ 01293 871871 (shop)   📠 01293 871456
e-mail: nikki@ruspergolfclub.co.uk
web: www.ruspergolfclub.co.uk

The 18-hole course is set in countryside and offers golfers of all abilities a fair and challenging test. After a gentle start the holes wind through picturesque scenery, tree-lined fairways and natural water hazards.

Rusper Golf Course: 18 Holes, 6724yds, Par 72, SSS 72. Club membership 300.

Visitors Mon-Sun & BHs. Booking required weekends & BHs. Dress code. **Societies** booking required. **Green Fees** £20 per round (£28 weekends & BHs) **Course Designer** A Blunden **Prof** Janice Arnold **Facilities** ⑪ ⑪ ㏇ ♨ 🍴 ♨ 🏠 🚩 ♂ ✦ ♂ 🏌 **Conf** Corporate Hospitality Days **Location** off A24 between Newdigate & Rusper
Hotel ★★★★ 74% HL Mercure Burford Bridge, Burford Bridge, Box Hill, DORKING ☎ 01306 884561 📠 01306 884561 57 en suite

OCKLEY
Map 4 TQ14

Gatton Manor Hotel & Golf Club Standon Ln RH5 5PQ
☎ 01306 627555   📠 01306 627713
e-mail: info@gattonmanor.co.uk
web: www.gattonmanor.co.uk

A mature woodland course, formerly part of the Abinger estate. The challenging course makes imaginative use of the various streams, lakes and woodlands. A good scorecard can be suddenly ruined if the individual challenges each hole presents are not carefully considered.

Gatton Manor Hotel & Golf Club: 18 Holes, 6563yds, Par 72, SSS 72, Course record 68. Club membership 350.

Visitors Mon-Sun & BHs. Booking advised. Dress code. **Societies** booking required **Green Fees** £31 (£41 weekends). Winter £23/£31 **Course Designer** John D Harris **Prof** Ben Lovell **Facilities** ⑪ ⑪ ㏇ ♨ 🍴 ♨ 🏠 🚩 ♦ ✦ ♂ 🏌 **Leisure** fishing, gymnasium **Conf** facs Corporate Hospitality Days **Location** 1.5m SW off A29
Hotel ★★★ 79% HL Gatton Manor Hotel & Golf Club, Standon Lane, OCKLEY, Nr Dorking ☎ 01306 627555 📠 01306 627555 18 en suite

OTTERSHAW
Map 4 TQ06

Foxhills Club and Resort Stonehill Rd KT16 0EL
☎ 01932 704456   📠 01932 875200
e-mail: golf@foxhills.co.uk
web: www.foxhills.co.uk

The Longcross course threads its way through pine trees and is a typical Surrey heathland course. The longer Bernard Hunt course is parkland with several lakes and ponds. The two courses complement each other and offer different challenges.

The Bernard Hunt Course: 18 Holes, 6770yds, Par 73, SSS 72, Course record 65.
Longcross Course: 18 Holes, 6453yds, Par 72, SSS 71.

Visitors Mon-Sun & BHs. Booking required. Dress code **Societies** booking required. **Green Fees** phone **Course Designer** F W Hawtree **Prof** R Summerscales **Facilities** ⑪ ⑪ ㏇ ♨ 🍴 🏠 🚩 ♦ ✦ ♂ 🏌 **Leisure** hard tennis courts, outdoor and indoor heated swimming pool, squash, sauna, gymnasium, par 3 course **Conf** facs Corporate Hospitality Days **Location** 1m NW of Ottershaw. M25 junct 11, signposted
Hotel ★★★★ 79% HL Foxhills Resort & Spa, Stonehill Road, OTTERSHAW ☎ 01932 872050 & 704500 📠 01932 872050 70 en suite

PIRBRIGHT
Map 4 SU95

Goal Farm Gole Rd GU24 0PZ
☎ 01483 473183   📠 01483 473205
web: www.gfgc.co.uk

9 Holes, 1273yds, Par 54, SSS 48, Course record 50.

Course Designer Bill Cox **Location** 1.5m NW on B3012
Telephone for further details
Hotel ★★★ 70% HL Lakeside International, Wharf Road, Frimley Green, CAMBERLEY ☎ 01252 838000 📠 01252 838000 98 en suite

PUTTENHAM
Map 4 SU94

Puttenham Heath Rd GU3 1AL
☎ 01483 810498   📠 01483 810988
e-mail: enquiries@puttenhamgolfclub.co.uk
web: www.puttenhamgolfclub.co.uk

Mixture of heathland and woodland - undulating layout with stunning views across the Hog's Back and towards the South Downs. Sandy subsoil provides free drainage for year round play.

18 Holes, 6220yds, Par 71, SSS 70. Club membership 650.

Visitors Mon-Fri except BHs. Booking required. Dress code. **Societies** booking required, **Green Fees** £50 per day, £38 per round. **Prof** Dean Lintott **Facilities** ⑪ ⑪ by prior arrangement ㏇ ♨ 🍴 ♨ 🏠 ♂ 🏌 **Conf** Corporate Hospitality Days **Location** 1m SE on B3000
Hotel ★★★ 75% HL Mercure Bush, The Borough, FARNHAM ☎ 0870 400 8225 & 01252 715237 📠 0870 400 8225 83 en suite

REDHILL
Map 4 TQ25

Redhill & Reigate Clarence Lodge, Pendelton Rd RH1 6LB
☎ 01737 240777   📠 01737 242117
e-mail: mail@rrgc.net
web: www.rrgc.net

Flat picturesque tree-lined course, well over 100 years old.

continued

WENTWORTH

SURREY - VIRGINIA WATER - MAP 4 TQ06

Wentworth Club, the home of the PGA and World Match Play championships, is a very special venue for any sporting, business or social occasion. The West Course is familiar to millions of television viewers who have followed the championships here. In recent years it was felt that in certain key areas the West course no longer played quite as Colt had intended and so a process of modernisation and restoration was undertaken by Ernie Els involving extensive re-bunkering and lengthening of certain holes, where appropriate. There are two other excellent courses, the East Course and the Edinburgh Course, and a nine-hole par 3 executive course. The courses cross Surrey heathland with woods of pine, oak and birch.

Wentworth Dr GU25 4LS ☎ 01344 842201 🖹 01344 842804
e-mail: reception@wentworthclub.com
web: www.wentworthclub.com
West Course: 18 Holes, 7324yds, Par 73, SSS 74, Course record 63.
East Course: 18 Holes, 6201yds, Par 68, SSS 70, Course record 62.
Edinburgh Course: 18 Holes, 7059yds, Par 72, SSS 74, Course record 67. Club membership 4300.
Visitors Mon-Fri except BHs. Booking required. Handicap certificate. Dress code. **Societies** booking required.
Green Fees West Course from £170-£285, Edinburgh Course from £125-£160, East Course from £110-£130.
Reduced winter rates. **Course Designer** Colt/Jacobs/Gallacher/Player **Prof** Stephen Gibson **Facilities** ⑪ †⊘। ᇈ
🖵 🖺 ﹅ 🖹 ☇ ◇ ✓ 🚗 ⚓ ⚘ **Leisure** hard and grass tennis courts, outdoor and indoor heated swimming pool, fishing, sauna, gymnasium, spa with 6 treatment rooms **Conf** facs Corporate Hospitality Days
Location Main gate directly opposite turning for A329 on main A30
Hotel ★★★★ 78% HL Runnymede Hotel & Spa, Windsor Road, EGHAM ☎ 01784 436171 🖹 01784 436340
180 en suite

18 Holes, 5272yds, Par 68, SSS 66, Course record 65. Club membership 300.

Visitors Mon-Sun & BHs. Booking required weekends. Dress code. **Societies** booking required. **Green Fees** £18 per 18 holes (£21 weekends). Jan-Mar £15/£18 **Course Designer** James Braid **Prof** Darren Peters **Facilities** ⑪ ⑭ by prior arrangement ⌨ 🍴 🏊 🏨 🖑 ♂ **Conf** facs Corporate Hospitality Days **Location** 1m S on A23 **Hotel** ★★★ 73% HL Best Western Reigate Manor, Reigate Hill, REIGATE ☎ 01737 240125 📄 01737 240125 50 en suite

REIGATE   Map 4 TQ25

Reigate Heath Flanchford Rd RH2 8QR
☎ 01737 242610 & 226793
e-mail: manager@reigateheathgolfclub.co.uk
web: www.reigateheathgolfclub.co.uk
Gorse, heather, pine and birch trees abound on this popular nine-hole heathland course. The course is short by modern standards but is a good test of golf. Playing 18 holes from nine greens, the second nine is quite different with changes of angle as well as length.

9 Holes, 5658yds, Par 67, SSS 68, Course record 65. Club membership 630.

Visitors Mon-Sun & BHs. Booking required. Dress code. **Societies** booking required. **Green Fees** £35 per round (£40 weekends). Reduced twilight rate **Prof** Adam Aram **Facilities** ⑪ by prior arrangement ⌨ 🍴 🍴 🏊 🏨 ♂ **Conf** facs Corporate Hospitality Days **Location** 1.5m W off A25 **Hotel** ★★★ 73% HL Best Western Reigate Manor, Reigate Hill, REIGATE ☎ 01737 240125 📄 01737 240125 50 en suite

Reigate Hill Gatton Bottom RH2 0TU
☎ 01737 646070 📄 01737 642650
e-mail: proshop@reigatehillgolfclub.co.uk
web: www.reigatehillgolfclub.co.uk
A challenging course that can be enjoyed by all handicap levels. Tees and greens have been built with USGA specification and can be played all year round. Feature holes include two par fives; the 7th has two parallel fairways and the 14th has a large lake that has to be carried with the approach shot to the green.

18 Holes, 6175yds, Par 72, SSS 70, Course record 63. Club membership 450.

Visitors Mon-Sun & BHs. Booking required. Dress code. **Societies** booking required. **Green Fees** £30 (£40 weekends) **Course Designer** David Williams **Prof** Mike Lovegrove **Facilities** ⑪ ⑭ 🍴 ⌨ 🍴 🏊 🏨 🖑 ♂ **Conf** facs Corporate Hospitality Days **Location** M25 junct 8, 1m **Hotel** ★★★ 73% HL Best Western Reigate Manor, Reigate Hill, REIGATE ☎ 01737 240125 📄 01737 240125 50 en suite

SHEPPERTON   Map 4 TQ06

Sunbury Golf Centre Charlton Ln TW17 8QA
☎ 01932 771414 📄 01932 789300
web: www.crown-golf.co.uk
Sunbury Golf Centre: 18 Holes, 5103yds, Par 68, SSS 65, Course record 60.
Academy: 9 Holes, 2444yds, Par 33, SSS 32.
Course Designer Peter Alliss **Location** M3, junct 1, 1m N off A244 **Telephone for further details** **Hotel** ★★★ 72% HL Mercure Thames Lodge, Thames Street, STAINES ☎ 01784 464433 📄 01784 464433 79 en suite

SOUTH GODSTONE   Map 5 TQ34

Horne Park Croydon Barn Ln, Horne RH9 8JP
☎ 01342 844443 📄 01342 841828
e-mail: info@hornepark.co.uk
web: www.hornepark.co.uk
Set in attractive Surrey countryside with water coming into play in 5 holes. Relatively flat for easy walking. A different set of tees pose an intriguing second 9 holes.

Home Park Golf Club: 9 Holes, 5436yds, Par 68, SSS 66, Course record 62. Club membership 350.

Visitors contact club for details. **Societies** welcome. **Green Fees** £15 per 18 holes, £10.50 per 9 holes (£17/£11.50 weekends) **Course Designer** Howard Swan **Prof** Neil Burke **Facilities** ⑪ ⑭ by prior arrangement 🍴 ⌨ 🍴 🏊 🏨 🖑 ♂ 🏌 ♂ 🏌 **Leisure** swing analysis system, teaching academy **Conf** Corporate Hospitality Days **Location** A22, signposted 3m N of East Grinstead **Hotel** ★★★★ 72% HL Copthorne Hotel and Resort Effingham Park London Gatwick, West Park Road, COPTHORNE ☎ 01342 714994 📄 01342 714994 122 en suite

SUTTON GREEN   Map 4 TQ05

Sutton Green New Ln GU4 7QF
☎ 01483 747898 📄 01483 750289
e-mail: admin@suttongreengc.co.uk
web: www.suttongreengc.co.uk
Set in the Surrey countryside, a challenging course with many water features. Excellent year round conditions with fairway watering. Many testing holes with water surrounding greens and fairways, making accuracy a premium.

18 Holes, 6350yds, Par 71, SSS 70, Course record 64. Club membership 600.

Visitors Mon-Sun & BHs. Booking required. Dress code. **Societies** booking required. **Green Fees** not confirmed **Course Designer** David Walker/Laura Davies **Prof** Paul Tedder **Facilities** ⑪ ⑭ 🍴 ⌨ 🍴 🏊 🏨 🖑 ♂ **Conf** facs Corporate Hospitality Days **Location** off A320 between Woking & Guildford **Hotel** ★★★★★ CHH Pennyhill Park Hotel & The Spa, London Road, BAGSHOT ☎ 01276 471774 📄 01276 471774 123 en suite

TANDRIDGE   Map 5 TQ35

Tandridge RH8 9NQ
☎ 01883 712274 📄 01883 730537
e-mail: secretary@tandridgegolfclub.com
web: www.tandridgegolfclub.com
A parkland course with two loops of nine holes from the clubhouse. The first nine are relatively flat. The second nine undulate with outstanding views of the North Downs.

18 Holes, 6277yds, Par 70, SSS 70, Course record 62. Club membership 750.

Visitors Mon, Wed & Thu except BHs. Booking required. Handicap certificate. Dress code. **Societies** booking required. **Green Fees** £67 per day, £47 after noon. Winter £37 per round **Course Designer** H S Colt **Prof** Chris Evans **Facilities** ⑪ 🍴 ⌨ 🍴 🏊 🏨 🖑 ♂ **Conf** Corporate Hospitality Days **Location** M25 junct 6, 2m SE on A25 **Hotel** ★★★★ 80% HL Nutfield Priory, Nutfield, REDHILL ☎ 01737 824400 & 0845 072 7485 📄 01737 824400 60 en suite

TILFORD
Map 4 SU84

Hankley Common The Club House GU10 2DD
☎ 01252 792493   📄 01252 795699
e-mail: jhay@hankley-commongc.co.uk
web: hankley.co.uk

A natural heathland course subject to wind. Greens are first rate. The 18th, a long par 4, is most challenging, the green being beyond a deep chasm which traps any but the perfect second shot. The 7th is a spectacular one-shotter.

18 Holes, 6702yds, Par 72, SSS 72, Course record 62. Club membership 700.

Visitors contact club for details. **Societies** booking required. **Green Fees** £85 per day, £75 per round **Course Designer** James Braid **Prof** Peter Stow **Facilities** ⊕ ⍾ ▮ ⌂ ⌷ ▵ ⌷ ◢ ⛳ ◢ ⚑ **Location** 0.75m SE of Tilford

Hotel ★★★ 75% HL Mercure Bush, The Borough, FARNHAM ☎ 0870 400 8225 & 01252 715237 📄 0870 400 8225 83 en suite

VIRGINIA WATER
Map 4 TQ06

Wentworth see page 239
Wentworth Dr GU25 4LS
☎ 01344 842201   📄 01344 842804
e-mail: reception@wentworthclub.com
web: www.wentworthclub.com

Hotel ★★★★ 78% HL Runnymede Hotel & Spa, Windsor Road, EGHAM ☎ 01784 436171 📄 01784 436340 180 en suite

See advert on page 241

WALTON-ON-THAMES
Map 4 TQ16

Burhill Burwood Rd KT12 4BL
☎ 01932 227345   📄 01932 267159
e-mail: info@burhillgolf-club.co.uk
web: www.burhillgolf-club.co.uk

The Old Course is a mature tree-lined parkland course with some of the finest greens in Surrey. The New Course, opened in 2001, is a modern course built to USGA specifications has many bunkers and water hazards, including the River Mole.

Old Course: 18 Holes, 6479yds, Par 70, SSS 71, Course record 62.
New Course: 18 Holes, 6597yds, Par 72, SSS 73, Club membership 1100.

Visitors Mon-Fri except BHs. Booking required. Dress code. **Societies** booking required. **Green Fees** £100 per day, £85 per 18 holes Old Course, £70 per 18 holes New Course **Course**

Designer Willie Park/Simon Gidman **Prof** Pip Elson **Facilities** ⊕ ⍾ ▮ ⌂ ⌷ ▵ ⌷ ◢ ⛳ ◢ **Conf** facs Corporate Hospitality Days **Location** M25 junct 10 on to A3 towards London, 1st exit (Painshill junct) towards Byfleet. Follow signs to club.

Hotel ★★★ 77% HL The Ship, Monument Green, WEYBRIDGE ☎ 01932 848364 📄 01932 848364 76 en suite

WALTON-ON-THE-HILL
Map 4 TQ25

Walton Heath see page 243
Deans Ln, Walton-on-the-hill KT20 7TP
☎ 01737 812380   📄 01737 814225
e-mail: secretary@whgc.co.uk
web: www.whgc.co.uk

WEST BYFLEET
Map 4 TQ06

West Byfleet Sheerwater Rd KT14 6AA
☎ 01932 343433
e-mail: admin@wbgc.co.uk
web: www.wbgc.co.uk

An attractive course set against a background of woodland and gorse. The 13th is the famous pond shot with a water hazard and two bunkers fronting the green. No less than six holes of 420yds or more.

18 Holes, 6211yds, Par 70, SSS 70, Course record 62. Club membership 622.

Visitors Mon-Fri except BHs. Booking required. Dress code. **Societies** booking required. **Green Fees** £73 per day, £48.50 per round **Course Designer** C S Butchart **Prof** David Regan **Facilities** ⊕ ⍾ ▮ ⌂ ⌷ ▵ ⌷ ◢ ⛳ ◢ **Conf** facs Corporate Hospitality Days **Location** W of village on A245

Hotel ★★★ 78% HL Holiday Inn Woking, Victoria Street, WOKING ☎ 01483 221000 📄 01483 221000 161 en suite

WEST CLANDON
Map 4 TQ05

Clandon Regis Epsom Rd GU4 7TT
☎ 01483 224888   📄 01483 211781
e-mail: office@clandonregis-golfclub.co.uk
web: www.clandonregis-golfclub.co.uk

High quality parkland course with challenging lake holes on the back nine. European Tour specification tees and greens.

18 Holes, 6485yds, Par 72, SSS 71, Course record 66. Club membership 652.

Visitors contact club for details. **Societies** welcome. **Green Fees** Mon-Fri £50 per day, £40 per 18 holes **Course Designer** David Williams **Prof** Steve Lloyd **Facilities** ⊕ ⍾ ▮ ⌂ ⌷ ▵ ⌷ ◢ **Leisure** sauna **Conf** facs Corporate Hospitality Days **Location** SE of village off A246

Hotel ★★★ 80% HL Ramada Guildford/Leatherhead, Guildford Road, EAST HORSLEY ☎ 01483 280500 📄 01483 280500 87 en suite

WALTON HEATH

SURREY - WALTON-ON-THE-HILL - MAP 4 TQ25

Walton Heath, a traditional member club, has two extremely challenging courses. Enjoying an enviable international reputation, the club was founded in 1903. It has played host to over 60 major amateur and professional championships, including the 1981 Ryder Cup and five European Open Tournaments (1991, 1989, 1987, 1980 and 1977); among the many prestigious amateur events, Walton Heath hosted the English Amateur in 2002. In recent years the club has hosted the European qualification for the U.S. Open Championship. The Old Course is popular with visitors, while the New Course is very challenging, requiring subtle shots to get the ball near the hole. Straying from the fairway brings gorse, bracken and heather to test the golfer.

Deans Ln, Walton-on-the-Hill KT20 7TP ☎ 01737 812380 📠 01737 814225
e-mail: secretary@whgc.co.uk
web: www.whgc.co.uk
Old Course: 18 Holes, 7462yds, Par 72, SSS 74, Course record 65.
New Course: 18 Holes, 7171yds, Par 72, SSS 74. Club membership 1000.
Visitors Mon-Sun & BHs. Booking required. Dress code. **Societies** booking required. **Green Fees** £110 each course, both courses £140 (£140 each course weekends) **Course Designer** Herbert Fowler **Prof** Simon Peaford
Facilities ⑪ 🍴 ⌂ ▯ 🏌 ⛳ ♻ **Conf** Corporate Hospitality Days **Location** M25 junct 8, SE of village off B2032
Hotel ★★★ 78% HL Chalk Lane Hotel, Chalk Lane, Woodcote End, EPSOM ☎ 01372 721179 📠 01372 721179 22 en suite

WEST END

Map 4 SU96

Windlemere Windlesham Rd GU24 9QL
☎ 01276 858727

9 Holes, 2673yds, Par 34, SSS 33, Course record 30.
Course Designer Clive Smith **Location** N of village at junct A319
Telephone for further details
Hotel ★★★★★ CHH Pennyhill Park Hotel & The Spa, London Road, BAGSHOT ☎ 01276 471774 🖺 01276 471774 123 en suite

WEYBRIDGE

Map 4 TQ06

St George's Hill Golf Club Rd, St George's Hill KT13 0NL
☎ 01932 847758   🖺 01932 821564
e-mail: admin@stgeorgeshillgolfclub.co.uk
web: stgeorgeshillgolfclub.co.uk
Comparable and similar to Wentworth, a feature of this course is the number of long and difficult par 4s. To score well it is necessary to place the drive - and long driving pays handsomely. Walking is hard on this undulating, heavily wooded course with plentiful heather and rhododendrons.

Red & Blue: 18 Holes, 6513yds, Par 70, SSS 71, Course record 64.
Green: 9 Holes, 2897yds, Par 35. Club membership 700.
Visitors Wed-Fri except BHs. Booking required. Handicap certificate. Dress code. **Societies** booking required. **Green Fees** not confirmed **Course Designer** H S Colt **Prof** A C Rattue **Facilities** ⑪ ᛅ 🖓 ᛘ 🖻 ᛜ ⚲ **Conf** Corporate Hospitality Days **Location** 2m S off B374
Hotel ★★★ 77% HL The Ship, Monument Green, WEYBRIDGE ☎ 01932 848364 🖺 01932 848364 76 en suite

WOKING

Map 4 TQ05

Hoebridge Golf Centre Old Woking Rd GU22 8JH
☎ 01483 722611   🖺 01483 740369
e-mail: info@hoebridgegc.co.uk
web: www.hoebridgegc.co.uk
The setting encompasses 200 acres of mature parkland and includes 3 golf courses containing 45 holes. The Hoebridge course has tree lined fairways, challenging bunkers and fine views. The testing 9 hole Shey Copse is a par 4/par 3 course which winds around the woodland. The Maybury is an 18 holes par 3 course for beginners or golfers wishing to improve their game.

Hoebridge Golf Centre: 18 Holes, 6549yds, Par 72, SSS 71.
Shey Course: 9 Holes, 2294yds, Par 33.
Maybury Course: 18 Holes, 2181yds, Par 54.
Club membership 750.
Visitors Mon-Sat & BHs. Dress code. **Societies** booking required. **Green Fees** Hoebridge £25 (£33 weekends), Shey £12.50 (£15 weekends), Maybury £11 (£13.50 weekends) **Course Designer** John Jacobs **Prof** Darren Brewer **Facilities** ⑪ 🍴 ᛅ 🖵 ᛘ ᛜ 🖓 ⚲ 🌂 🖻 ⚲ ⚲ **Leisure** sauna, gymnasium, health & fitness club **Conf** facs Corporate Hospitality Days **Location** M25 junct 11, follow signs for Old Woking, then Hoebridge
Hotel ★★★★★ CHH Pennyhill Park Hotel & The Spa, London Road, BAGSHOT ☎ 01276 471774 🖺 01276 471774 123 en suite

Pyrford Warren Ln, Pyrford GU22 8XR
☎ 01483 723555   🖺 01483 729777
e-mail: pyrford@crown-golf.co.uk
web: www.pyrfordgolf.co.uk
This inland links-style course was designed by Peter Alliss and Clive Clark. Set between Surrey woodlands, the fairways weave between 23 acres of water courses while the greens and tees are connected by rustic bridges. The signature hole is the par 5 9th at 595yds, with a dog-leg and final approach over water and a sand shelf. Excellent playing conditions all year round.

18 Holes, 6256yds, Par 72, SSS 70, Course record 64. Club membership 650.
Visitors Mon-Fri. Weekends & BHs after 1pm. Booking required. Handicap certifcate. Dress code. **Societies** booking required. **Green Fees** £40 per round (£45 Fri-Sun & BHs) **Course Designer** Peter Allis & Clive Clark **Prof** Andrew Blackman **Facilities** ⑪ 🍴 ᛅ 🖵 ᛘ 🌂 🖻 🖓 ⚲ ᛜ ᛜ **Conf** facs Corporate Hospitality Days **Location** off A3 Ripley to Pyrford
Hotel ★★★★★ CHH Pennyhill Park Hotel & The Spa, London Road, BAGSHOT ☎ 01276 471774 🖺 01276 471774 123 en suite

Traditions Pyrford Rd GU22 8UE
☎ 01932 350355   🖺 01932 350234
Traditions Golf Course: 18 Holes, 6304yds, Par 71, SSS 70, Course record 67.
Course Designer Peter Alliss **Location** M25 junct 10, A3, signs to RHS Garden Wisley, through Wisley to Pyford, course 0.5m
Telephone for further details
Hotel ★★★★★ CHH Pennyhill Park Hotel & The Spa, London Road, BAGSHOT ☎ 01276 471774 🖺 01276 471774 123 en suite

Woking Pond Rd GU22 0JZ
☎ 01483 760053   🖺 01483 772441
web: www.wokinggolfclub.co.uk
18 Holes, 6340yds, Par 70, SSS 70, Course record 65.
Course Designer Tom Dunn **Location** W of town centre in area of St Johns Heath
Telephone for further details
Hotel ★★★★★ CHH Pennyhill Park Hotel & The Spa, London Road, BAGSHOT ☎ 01276 471774 🖺 01276 471774 123 en suite

Worplesdon Heath House Rd GU22 0RA
☎ 01483 472277
web: www.worplesdon.co.uk
18 Holes, 6431yds, Par 71, SSS 71, Course record 66.
Course Designer J F Abercromby **Location** 1.5m N of village off A322
Telephone for further details
Hotel ★★★★★ CHH Pennyhill Park Hotel & The Spa, London Road, BAGSHOT ☎ 01276 471774 🖺 01276 471774 123 en suite

WOLDINGHAM

Map 5 TQ35

North Downs Northdown Rd CR3 7AA
☎ 01883 652057   🖺 01883 652832
e-mail: manager@northdownsgolfclub.co.uk
web: www.northdownsgolfclub.co.uk
Parkland course, 850ft above sea level, with several testing holes and magnificent views.

continued

18 Holes, 5857yds, Par 69, SSS 68, Course record 64. Club membership 500.

Visitors Mon-Wed, Fri & BHs. Thu & Sun after noon. Booking required Sun. Dress code. **Societies** booking required. **Green Fees** £50 per day; £35 per round (£30 per round Sun) **Course Designer** Pennink **Prof** M Homewood **Facilities** ⓣ ⦿ ⓛ ☐ ⓤ ⚐ ⌂ ✍ **Conf** facs Corporate Hospitality Days **Location** 0.75m S of Woldingham **Hotel** ★★★ 79% HL Best Western Donnington Manor, London Road, Dunton Green, SEVENOAKS ☎ 01732 462681 🖨 01732 462681 60 en suite

Woldingham Halliloo Valley Rd CR3 7HA
☎ 01883 653501   🖨 01883 653502
e-mail: info@woldingham-golfclub.co.uk
web: www.woldingham-golfclub.co.uk

Located in Halliloo Valley and designed by the American architect Bradford Benz, this pleasant course utilises all the contours and features of the valley. The chalk base gives excellent drainage for all year play.

18 Holes, 6393yds, Par 71, SSS 70, Course record 64. Club membership 500.

Visitors Mon-Sun & BHs. Booking required. Dress code. **Societies** welcome. **Green Fees** £44 per day, £32 per round (£35 per round weekends) **Course Designer** Bradford Benz **Facilities** ⓣ ⦿ ⓛ ☐ ⓤ ⚐ ⌂ ⌖ ✍ ✂ **Conf** facs Corporate Hospitality Days **Location** M25 junct 6, A22 N, 1st rdbt onto Woldingham Rd, Valley Rd, on left **Hotel** ★★★ 79% HL Best Western Donnington Manor, London Road, Dunton Green, SEVENOAKS ☎ 01732 462681 🖨 01732 462681 60 en suite

Cooden Beach Hotel

Cooden Beach, Bexhill-on-Sea, TN39 4TT
Tel: 01424 842281 Fax: 01424 846142
Email: rooms@thecoodenbeachhotel.co.uk
Website: www.thecoodenbeachhotel.co.uk

The Cooden Beach Hotel is located directly on the beach with stunning sea views. We are situated next door to Cooden Beach Golf club and have Golf Packages available which include green fees. Hotel facilities include leisure club with indoor pool, beachside Terrace, Restaurant and bars.

SUSSEX, EAST

BEXHILL   Map 5 TQ70

Cooden Beach Cooden Sea Rd TN39 4TR
☎ 01424 842040 & 843938 (Pro Shop)
🖨 01424 842040
e-mail: enquiries@coodenbeachgc.com
web: www.coodenbeachgc.com

Downland links course running alongside the sea but separated by the main rail line. A dry course that plays well throughout the year with some excellent testing holes, particularly the par 4 1st. The 4th and 11th are both played to built up greens and the final three holes required careful club selection.

18 Holes, 6504yds, Par 72, SSS 71, Course record 67. Club membership 850.

Visitors Mon-Fri. Sat & BHs after noon, Sun after 11am. Booking required. Handicap certificate. Dress code. **Societies** booking required. **Green Fees** £46 per day, £40 per round (£46/£49 weekends) **Course Designer** W Herbert Fowler **Prof** Jeffrey Sim **Facilities** ⓣ ⦿ ⓛ ☐ ⓤ ⚐ ⌂ ⌖ ✍ 🛒 ✂ ✍ **Leisure** indoor practice facility **Conf** facs Corporate Hospitality Days **Location** 2m W on A259 **Hotel** ★★★ 80% HL Cooden Beach Hotel, COODEN BEACH, Bexhill-On-Sea ☎ 01424 842281 🖨 01424 842281 41 en suite

See advert on opposite page

Highwoods Ellerslie Ln TN39 4LJ
☎ 01424 212625   🖨 01424 216866
e-mail: highwoods@btconnect.com
web: www.highwoodsgolfclub.co.uk
Undulating parkland with water on six holes.
18 Holes, 6218yds, Par 70, SSS 70, Course record 63. Club membership 750.

continued

Visitors handicap certificate. Dress code. **Societies** welcome. **Green Fees** not confirmed **Course Designer** J H Taylor **Prof** Mike Andrews **Facilities** ⊕ ⦿ 🝙 ⬜ 🍽 🏌 🛋 ⚑ **Conf** facs Corporate Hospitality Days **Location** 1.5m NW

Hotel ★★★ 74% HL Best Western Royal Victoria, Marina, St Leonards-on-Sea, HASTINGS ☎ 01424 445544 📄 01424 445544 50 en suite

BRIGHTON & HOVE   Map 4 TQ30

Brighton & Hove Devils Dyke Rd BN1 8YJ
☎ 01273 556482   📄 01273 554247
e-mail: phil@brightongolf.co.uk
web: www.brightonandhovegolfclub.co.uk

Testing nine-hole course with glorious views over the Downs and the sea. Famous par 3 6th hole considered to be one of the most extraordinary holes in golf.

9 Holes, 5704yds, Par 68, SSS 67, Course record 64.
Club membership 400.

Visitors Mon-Sun & BHs. Booking required weekends & BHs. Dress code. **Societies** booking required **Green Fees** £22 per 18 holes, £14 per 9 holes (£27.50/£17.50 weekends) **Course Designer** James Braid **Prof** Phil Bonsall **Facilities** ⊕ ⦿ 🝙 ⬜ 🍽 🏌 🛋 ⚑ 🛺 ⚑ **Conf** facs Corporate Hospitality Days **Location** 4m NW of Brighton, 1m from A27 & A23

Hotel ★★★ 73% HL Best Western Old Tollgate Restaurant & Hotel, The Street, BRAMBER, Steyning ☎ 01903 879494 📄 01903 879494 38 en suite

> *Dyke* Devils Dyke, Dyke Rd BN1 8YJ
> ☎ 01273 857296(office) & 857260(pro shop)
> 📄 01273 857078
> **e-mail:** office@dykegolfclub.co.uk
> **web:** www.dykegolf.com
>
> Easy draining downland course has some glorious views both towards the sea and inland. The signature hole on the course is probably the 17th; it is one of those tough par 3s of just over 200yds, and is played across a gully to a well protected green. Greens are small, fast and true.
>
> *18 Holes, 6627yds, Par 72, SSS 72, Course record 66.*
> *Club membership 800.*
>
> **Visitors** Mon, Wed-Fri except BHs. Weekends pm only. Booking required weekends. Dress code. **Societies** booking required. **Green Fees** not confirmed **Course Designer** Fred Hawtree **Prof** Mark Stuart-William **Facilities** ⊕ ⦿ 🝙 ⬜ 🍽 🏌 🛋 ⚑ 🛺 ⚑ **Conf** facs Corporate Hospitality Days **Location** 4m N of Brighton, between A23 & A27
> **Hotel** ★★★ 73% HL Best Western Old Tollgate Restaurant & Hotel, The Street, BRAMBER, Steyning ☎ 01903 879494 📄 01903 879494 38 en suite

Hollingbury Park Ditchling Rd BN1 7HS
☎ 01273 552010 (sec) & 500086 (pro)
📄 01273 552010/6
web: www.hollingburyparkgolf.org.uk

18 Holes, 6500yds, Par 72, SSS 71, Course record 65.
Prof Graeme Crompton **Facilities** ⊕ ⬜ 🍽 🏌 🛋 ⚑ 🛺 ⚑
Location 2m N of town centre
Telephone for further details
Hotel ★★★ 64% HL Preston Park Hotel, 216 Preston Road, BRIGHTON ☎ 01273 507853 📄 01273 507853 33 en suite

Waterhall Saddlescombe Rd BN1 8YN
☎ 01273 508658

Hilly downland course with hard walking and open to the wind. Private club playing over municipal course.

18 Holes, 5773yds, Par 69, SSS 68, Course record 66.
Club membership 150.

Visitors Mon-Sun & BHs. Booking required. **Societies** booking required. **Green Fees** phone. **Facilities** ⊕ ⦿ 🝙 ⬜ 🍽 🏌 🛋 ⚑ ⚑ **Conf** facs Corporate Hospitality Days **Location** 2m NE from A27
Hotel ★★★ 73% HL Best Western Old Tollgate Restaurant & Hotel, The Street, BRAMBER, Steyning ☎ 01903 879494 📄 01903 879494 38 en suite

West Hove Badgers Way, Hangleton BN3 8EX
☎ 01273 419738 & 413494 (pro)   📄 01273 439988
e-mail: info@westhovegolfclub.co.uk
web: www.westhovegolfclub.co.uk

Founded in 1910 the course stands in the South Downs, an Area of Outstanding Natural Beauty. Laid out over rolling chalk downland, it is a challenging par 70 and the terrain makes it playable all year.

West Hove Golf Club Ltd: 18 Holes, 6238yds, Par 71,
SSS 70, Course record 62. Club membership 600.

Visitors Mon-Fri & BHs. Weekends after noon. Booking required. Dress code. **Societies** booking required. **Green Fees** £25 per 18 holes (£30 weekends) **Course Designer** Hawtree & Sons **Prof** Darren Cook **Facilities** ⊕ ⦿ 🝙 ⬜ 🍽 🏌 🛋 ⚑ ⚑ 🛺 ⚑ 🏌
Conf facs Corporate Hospitality Days **Location** off A27 N of Brighton
Hotel ★★★ 67% HL The Courtlands Hotel & Conference Centre, 15-27 The Drive, HOVE ☎ 01273 731055 📄 01273 731055 67 en suite

CROWBOROUGH   Map 5 TQ53

Crowborough Beacon Beacon Rd TN6 1UJ
☎ 01892 661511   📄 01892 611988
e-mail: secretary@cbgc.co.uk
web: www.cbgc.co.uk

Standing some 800ft above sea level, this is a testing heathland course where accuracy off the tee rather than distance is paramount. Panoramic views of the South Downs, Eastbourne and even the sea on a clear day.

18 Holes, 6031yds, Par 71, SSS 69, Course record 66.
Club membership 700.

Visitors contact club for details. **Societies** welcome. **Green Fees** £56 per round, £66 per day (£66 per round weekends & BHs) **Prof** Mr D C Newnham **Facilities** ⊕ ⦿ by prior arrangement 🝙 ⬜ 🍽 🏌 🛋 ⚑ 🛺 ⚑ **Conf** Corporate Hospitality Days
Location 9m S of Tunbridge Wells on A26   *continued*

Hotel ★★★★ 77% HL The Spa, Mount Ephraim, TUNBRIDGE WELLS ☎ 01892 520331 📠 01892 520331 72 en suite

Dewlands Manor Cottage Hill, Rotherfield TN6 3JN
☎ 01892 852266 📠 01892 853015

A meadowland course built on land surrounding a 15th-century manor. The short par 4 4th can be played by the brave by launching a driver over the trees; the 7th requires accurate driving on a tight fairway; and the final two holes are sweeping par 5s travelling parallel to each other, a small stream guarding the front of the 9th green.

Dewlands Manor Golf Course: 9 Holes, 3186yds, Par 36, SSS 70. Club membership 400.

Visitors Mon-Sun & BHs. Booking required. Dress code.
Societies welcome. **Green Fees** £17 per 9 holes (£19 weekends & BHs) **Course Designer** R M & N M Godin **Prof** Nick Godin **Facilities** ⑪ 🍴 🗄 🏌 ⛳ 🏪 🚃 🏊 **Leisure** indoor teaching facilities with computer analysis. **Conf** facs Corporate Hospitality Days **Location** 0.5m S of Rotherfield
Hotel ★★★ INN Plough & Horses, Walshes Road, CROWBOROUGH ☎ 01892 652614 📠 01892 652614 15 en suite

---

DITCHLING
Map 5 TQ31

Mid Sussex Spatham Ln BN6 8XJ
☎ 01273 846567 📠 01273 847815
e-mail: admin@midsussexgolfclub.co.uk
web: www.midsussexgolfclub.co.uk

Mature parkland course with many trees, water hazards, strategically placed bunkers and superbly contoured greens. The 14th hole, a spectacular par 5, demands accurate shotmaking to avoid the various hazards along its length.

18 Holes, 6462yds, Par 71, SSS 71, Course record 65. Club membership 650.

Visitors Mon-Sun & BHs. Booking required. Dress code.
Societies booking required. **Green Fees** £30 per round **Course Designer** David Williams **Prof** Neil Plimmer **Facilities** ⑪ 🍴 🗄 🏌 ⛳ 🚃 🏪 **Conf** facs Corporate Hospitality Days **Location** 1m E of Ditchling
Hotel ★★★★ 71% HL Shelleys, 136 High Street, LEWES ☎ 01273 472361 & 483403 📠 01273 472361 19 en suite

---

EASTBOURNE
Map 5 TV69

Eastbourne Downs East Dean Rd BN20 8ES
☎ 01323 720827 📠 01323 412506
e-mail: secretary@ebdownsgolf.co.uk
web: www.ebdownsgolf.co.uk

This downland course has spectacular views over the South Downs and Channel. Situated in an Area of Outstanding Natural Beauty 1m behind Beachy Head. The club celebrated its centenary in 2008.

18 Holes, 6601yds, Par 72, SSS 71, Course record 69. Club membership 600.

Visitors Mon-Sun & BHs. Dress code. **Societies** booking required.
Green Fees £25 per day, £20 per round (£35/£27 weekends & BHs)
Course Designer J H Taylor **Prof** T Marshall **Facilities** ⑪ 🍴 🗄 ⛳ 🚃 🏪 🏊 **Conf** Corporate Hospitality Days **Location** 0.5m W of town centre on A259
Hotel ★★★ 78% HL Best Western Lansdowne, King Edward's Parade, EASTBOURNE ☎ 01323 725174 📠 01323 725174 102 en suite

Royal Eastbourne Paradise Dr BN20 8BP
☎ 01323 744045 📠 01323 744048
e-mail: sec@regc.co.uk
web: www.regc.co.uk

A famous club which celebrated its centenary in 1987. The course plays longer than it measures. Testing holes are the 8th, a par 3 played to a high green and the 16th, a par 5 righthand dog-leg.

Devonshire Course: 18 Holes, 6077yds, Par 70, SSS 69, Course record 62.
Hartington Course: 9 Holes, 2147yds, Par 64, SSS 61. Club membership 800.

Visitors Mon-Sun & BHs. Booking required Mon, weekends & BHs. Handicap certificate. Dress code. **Societies** booking required. **Green Fees** Devonshire £37 per round (£43 weekends & BHs), Hartington £19 per day **Course Designer** Arthur Mayhewe **Prof** Alan Harrison **Facilities** ⑪ 🍴 by prior arrangement 🗄 🏌 ⛳ 🚃 🏪 🏊 **Leisure** snooker table **Conf** facs Corporate Hospitality Days **Location** 0.5m W of town centre
Hotel ★★★ 73% HL New Wilmington, 25 Compton Street, EASTBOURNE ☎ 01323 721219 📠 01323 721219 40 en suite

Willingdon Southdown Rd, Willingdon BN20 9AA
☎ 01323 410981 📠 01323 411510
e-mail: secretary@willingdongolfclub.co.uk
web: www.willingdongolfclub.co.uk

Unique downland course set in an oyster-shaped amphitheatre.

18 Holes, 6118yds, Par 69, SSS 69. Club membership 610.

Visitors Mon-Sun & BHs. Dress code. **Societies** booking required.
Green Fees £24 per round (£35 weekends) **Course Designer** J Taylor/ Dr Mackenzie **Prof** Troy Moore **Facilities** ⑪ 🍴 🗄 🏌 ⛳ 🚃 🏪 🏊 **Location** 0.5m N of town centre off A22
Hotel ★★★ 80% HL Hydro, Mount Road, EASTBOURNE ☎ 01323 720643 📠 01323 720643 84 en suite

---

FOREST ROW
Map 5 TQ43

Ashdown Park Hotel & Country Club Wych Cross RH18 5JR
☎ 01342 824988 📠 01342 826206
e-mail: reservations@ashdownpark.com
web: www.ashdownpark.com

Set in 186 acres of landscaped Sussex countryside at the heart of Ashdown Forest.

Ashdown Park Hotel & Country Club: 18 Holes, 2310yds, Par 54.

Green Fees not confirmed **Facilities** ✧ **Leisure** hard tennis courts, heated indoor swimming pool, sauna, gymnasium **Conf** facs Corporate

continued

Hospitality Days **Location** A264 to East Grinstead, then A22 to Eastbourne, 2m S of Forest Row at Wych Cross traffic lights. left to Hartfied, 0.75m on right
Hotel ★★★★ HL Ashdown Park Hotel and Country Club, Wych Cross, FOREST ROW ☎ 01342 824988 📄 01342 824988 106 en suite

Royal Ashdown Forest Chapel Ln RH18 5LR
☎ 01342 822018 📄 01342 825211
e-mail: office@royalashdown.co.uk
web: www.royalashdown.co.uk

Old Course is on undulating heathland with no bunkers. Long carries off the tees and magnificent views over the Forest. Not a course for the high handicapper. West Course on natural heathland with no bunkers. Less demanding than Old Course although accuracy is at a premium.

Old Course: 18 Holes, 6518yds, Par 72, SSS 71, Course record 67.
West Course: 18 Holes, 5606yds, Par 68, SSS 67, Course record 65. Club membership 450.

Visitors Mon-Sun & BHs. Booking required. Dress code. **Societies** booking required. **Green Fees** not confirmed **Course Designer** Archdeacon Scott **Prof** Martyn Landsborough **Facilities** ⑪ ⑩ by prior arrangement ⛳ ⚑ ⛳ 🍴 👤 🏠 ⚑ 🏌 ⛳ **Leisure** computerised video swing analysis **Conf** Corporate Hospitality Days **Location** on B2110 in Forest Row
Hotel ★★★★ HL Ashdown Park Hotel and Country Club, Wych Cross, FOREST ROW ☎ 01342 824988 📄 01342 824988 106 en suite

HAILSHAM Map 5 TQ50

Wellshurst Golf & Country Club North Street, Hellingly BN27 4EE
☎ 01435 813456 (pro shop) 📄 01435 812444
e-mail: info@wellshurst.com
web: www.wellshurst.com

There are outstanding views of the South Downs and the Weald from this well-manicured, undulating 18-hole course. There are varied features and some water hazards.

Wellshurst Golf & Country Club: 18 Holes, 5992yds, Par 70, SSS 68, Course record 64. Club membership 450.

Visitors contact club for details. **Societies** welcome. **Green Fees** £24 per 18 holes (£28 weekends) **Course Designer** The Golf Corporation **Prof** Richard Holland **Facilities** ⑪ ⑩ ⛳ ⚑ 🍴 👤 🏠 ⚑ ♢ ⚑ 🏌 **Conf** facs Corporate Hospitality Days
Location 2.5m N off A22 junct at Hailsham, on A267
Hotel ★★ 76% HL The Olde Forge Hotel & Restaurant, Magham Down, HAILSHAM ☎ 01323 842893 📄 01323 842893 7 en suite

HASTINGS & ST LEONARDS Map 5 TQ80

Beauport Battle Rd TN37 7BP
☎ 01424 854243 📄 01424 854244
18 Holes, 6248yds, Par 71, SSS 70, Course record 70.
Prof Charles Giddins **Facilities** ⑪ ⑩ ⛳ ⚑ 🍴 👤 🏠 ⚑ ♢ ⚑ 🏌 **Leisure** hard tennis courts, outdoor swimming pool **Conf** Corporate Hospitality Days **Location** 3m N of Hastings on A2100
Telephone for further details
Hotel ★★★ 67% HL High Beech, Eisenhower Drive, Battle Road, St Leonards on Sea, HASTINGS ☎ 01424 851383 📄 01424 851383 17 en suite

HEATHFIELD Map 5 TQ52

Horam Park Chiddingly Rd, Horam TN21 0JJ
☎ 01435 813477 📄 01435 813677
e-mail: angie@horamgolf.com
web: www.horamparkgolf.co.uk

A pretty, woodland course with lakes and quality fast-running greens.

Horam Park Golf Course: 9 Holes, 6128yds, Par 70, SSS 70, Course record 64. Club membership 350.

Visitors Mon-Sun & BHs. Dress code. **Societies** booking required. **Green Fees** £18 per 18 holes; £12 per 9 holes (£20/£13 weekends). Twilight £11 **Course Designer** Glen Johnson **Prof** Giles Velvick **Facilities** ⑪ ⑩ ⛳ ⚑ 🍴 👤 🏠 ⚑ 🏌 ♢ 🏌
Leisure pitch & putt, digital coaching room **Conf** Corporate Hospitality Days **Location** off A267 Hailsham to Heathfield
Hotel ★★★ 74% HL Boship Farm, Lower Dicker, HAILSHAM ☎ 01323 844826 & 442600 📄 01323 844826 47 en suite

HOLTYE Map 5 TQ43

Holtye TN8 7ED
☎ 01342 850635 📄 01342 851139
e-mail: secretary@holtye.com
web: www.holtye.com

Undulating forest and heathland course with tree-lined fairways providing testing golf. Different tees on the back nine.

9 Holes, 5260yds, Par 66, SSS 66, Course record 62. Club membership 300.

Visitors Mon, Tue, Fri & BHs. Wed, Thu & weekends pm only. Booking required Wed, Thu & weekends. Dress code. **Societies** booking required. **Green Fees** £20 per 18 holes; £12 per 9 holes (£24/£15 weekends) **Prof** Kevin Hinton **Facilities** ⑪ ⛳ ⚑ 🍴 👤 🏠 ⚑ ♢ 🏌 ♢ 🏌 **Location** 4m E of East Grinstead on A264
Hotel ★★★★ HL Ashdown Park Hotel and Country Club, Wych Cross, FOREST ROW ☎ 01342 824988 📄 01342 824988 106 en suite

LEWES Map 5 TQ41

Lewes Chapel Hill BN7 2BB
☎ 01273 473245 📄 01273 483474
e-mail: secretary@lewesgolfclub.co.uk
web: www.lewesgolfclub.co.uk

Downland course with undulating fairways. Fine views. Proper greens all-year-round.

18 Holes, 6229yds, Par 71, SSS 70, Course record 64. Club membership 568.

continued

EAST SUSSEX NATIONAL GOLF RESORT & SPA
EAST SUSSEX - UCKFIELD - MAP 5 TQ42

East Sussex National offers two huge courses ideal for big-hitting professionals. The European Open has been staged here and it is home to the European Headquarters of the David Leadbetter Golf Academy, with indoor and outdoor video analysis. Bob Cupp designed the courses using 'bent' grass from tee to green, resulting in an American-style course to test everyone. The greens on both the East and West courses are immaculately maintained. The West Course, with stadium design and chosen for major events, is reserved for members and their guests; visitors are welcome on the East Course, also with stadium design, and which was the venue for the 1993 and 1994 European Open. The complex features a 104-bedroom hotel and a bespoke conference centre capable of seating up to 600 delegates.

Little Horsted TN22 5ES ☎ 01825 880256 📄 01825 880066
e-mail: golf@eastsussexnational.co.uk
web: www.eastsussexnational.co.uk
East Course: 18 Holes, 7138yds, Par 72, SSS 74, Course record 63.
West Course: 18 Holes, 7154yds, Par 72, SSS 74. Club membership 650.
Visitors Mon-Sun & BHs. Booking required. Handicap certificate. Dress code. **Societies** booking required. **Green Fees** Sun-Wed £45, Thu-Sat £60. Twilight £35. Reduced winter rates **Course Designer** Bob Cupp **Prof** Sarah Maclennan/Jack Budgen **Facilities** 🐦 🍽 🏐 🖥 🛱 🏌 🏠 🦶 🟡 🏌 🛢 🏌 🏌 **Leisure** hard tennis courts, heated indoor swimming pool, fishing, sauna, gymnasium, golf academy, health club and spa **Conf** facs Corporate Hospitality Days **Location** 2m S of Uckfield on A22
Hotel ★★★ HL Horsted Place, Little Horsted, UCKFIELD ☎ 01825 750581 📄 01825 750581 20 en suite

Visitors Mon-Sun & BHs. Dress code. Societies booking required.
Green Fees £40 per day, £36 per round, £16 Mon, £15 Twilight
Course Designer Jack Rowe Prof Tony Hilton Facilities ⓣ by prior
arrangement ⓑ ⌶ ⓣ ⌶ ⌶ ⌶ ⌶ Conf Corporate
Hospitality Days Location E of town centre
Hotel ★★★ 82% HL Deans Place, Seaford Road, ALFRISTON,
Polegate ☎ 01323 870248 📄 01323 870248 36 en suite

NEWHAVEN
Map 5 TQ40

Peacehaven Brighton Rd BN9 9UH
☎ 01273 514049 📄 01273 512571
e-mail: ben@golf-academies.com

Downland course, sometimes windy. Testing holes: 1st (par 3), 4th
(par 4), 9th (par 3). Attractive views over the South Downs, the River
Ouse and Newhaven Harbour.

9 Holes, 5488yds, Par 70, SSS 66, Course record 65.
Club membership 270.

Visitors Mon-Sun & BHs. Booking required. Societies booking
required. Green Fees not confirmed Course Designer James
Braid Facilities ⓣ ⓞ ⓑ ⌶ ⓣ ⌶ ⌶ ⌶ ⌶
Leisure gymnasium Conf facs Corporate Hospitality Days
Location 0.75m W on A259
Hotel ★★★ 82% HL Deans Place, Seaford Road, ALFRISTON,
Polegate ☎ 01323 870248 📄 01323 870248 36 en suite

RYE
Map 5 TQ92

Rye New Lydd Rd, Camber TN31 7QS
☎ 01797 225241 📄 01797 225460
e-mail: links@ryegolfclub.co.uk
web: www.ryegolfclub.co.uk

Unique links course with superb undulating greens set among
ridges of sand dunes alongside Rye Harbour. Fine views over
Romney Marsh and towards Fairlight and Dungeness.

Old Course: 18 Holes, 6317yds, Par 68, SSS 71,
Course record 64.
Jubilee Course: 18 Holes, 5848yds, Par 69, SSS 69,
Course record 71. Club membership 1200.

Visitors contact club for details. Green Fees phone Course
Designer H S Colt Prof Michael Lee Facilities ⓣ ⓑ ⌶ ⓣ ⌶
⌶ ⌶ ◇ ⌶ Location 2.75m SE off A259
Hotel ★★★★ 77% HL George in Rye, 98 High Street, RYE
☎ 01797 222114 📄 01797 222114 24 en suite

SEAFORD
Map 5 TV49

Seaford Firle Rd BN25 2JD
☎ 01323 892442 📄 01323 894113
e-mail: secretary@seafordgolfclub.co.uk
web: www.seafordgolfclub.co.uk

The great J H Taylor did not perhaps design as many courses as his
friend and rival, James Braid, but Seaford's original design was
Taylor's. It is a splendid downland course with magnificent views
and some fine holes.

18 Holes, 6546yds, Par 69, SSS 71.
Club membership 600.

Visitors contact club for details. Societies booking required. Green
Fees £40 per 18 holes (£30 winter) Course Designer J H Taylor
Prof Chris Lovis Facilities ⓣ ⓞ by prior arrangement ⓑ ⌶

⌶ ⌶ ⌶ ◇ ⌶ ⌶ ⌶ ⌶ Conf Corporate Hospitality Days
Location turn inland off A259 at war memorial

Seaford Head Southdown Rd BN25 4JS
☎ 01323 890139 📄 01323 894491
e-mail: fraser1974@mac.com
web: www.seafordheadgolfcourse.co.uk

A links type course situated on the cliff edge giving exceptional views
over the Seven Sisters and coastline. The upper level is reached via a
short hole with elevated green - known as the 'Hell Hole' and the 18th
Par 5 tee is on the 'Head' being 300 feet above sea level.

Seaford Head Golf Course: 18 Holes, 5848yds, Par 71,
SSS 68, Course record 62. Club membership 450.

Visitors Mon-Sun & BHs. Booking required. Dress code.
Societies booking required. Green Fees not confirmed Prof Fraser
Morley Facilities ⓣ ⓞ ⓑ ⌶ ⓣ ⌶ ⌶ ⌶ ⌶ ⌶
Conf facs Location E of Seaford on A259
Hotel ★★★ 82% HL Deans Place, Seaford Road, ALFRISTON,
Polegate ☎ 01323 870248 📄 01323 870248 36 en suite

SEDLESCOMBE
Map 5 TQ71

Sedlescombe Kent St TN33 0SD
☎ 01424 871700 📄 01424 871712
web: www.golfschool.co.uk

18 Holes, 6269yds, Par 72, SSS 70.

Prof James Andrews Facilities ⓣ ⓞ ⓑ ⌶ ⓣ ⌶ ⌶
⌶ ◇ ⌶ ⌶ ⌶ Leisure hard tennis courts, golf school
Conf Corporate Hospitality Days Location 4m N of Hastings on A21
Telephone for further details
Hotel ★★★ 75% HL Brickwall Hotel, The Green, Sedlescombe,
BATTLE ☎ 01424 870253 & 870339 📄 01424 870253 25 en suite

TICEHURST
Map 5 TQ63

Dale Hill Hotel & Golf Club TN5 7DQ
☎ 01580 200112 📄 01580 201249
web: www.dalehill.co.uk

Dale Hill: 18 Holes, 6106yds, Par 70, SSS 69.
Ian Woosnam: 18 Holes, 6512yds, Par 71, SSS 71,
Course record 64.

Course Designer Ian Woosnam Location M25 junct 5,A21, B2087
left after 1 mile
Telephone for further details
Hotel ★★★★ 82% HL Dale Hill Hotel & Golf Club, TICEHURST,
Wadhurst ☎ 01580 200112 📄 01580 200112 35 en suite

UCKFIELD
Map 5 TQ42

***East Sussex National Golf Resort* see page 249**
Little Horsted TN22 5ES
☎ 01825 880256   📠 01825 880066
e-mail: golf@eastsussexnational.co.uk
web: www.eastsussexnational.co.uk

Piltdown Piltdown TN22 3XB
☎ 01825 722033   📠 01825 724192
e-mail: info@piltdowngolfclub.co.uk
web: www.piltdowngolfclub.co.uk

A course built on rolling Sussex countryside. The terrain is fairly level
but the narrow fairways, small greens and an abundance of heather
and gorse make for challenging golf. Easy walking and fine views.

18 Holes, 6076yds, Par 68, SSS 69, Course record 64.
Club membership 400.

Visitors Mon-Sun & BHs. Booking required. Dress code.
Societies booking required. **Green Fees** £50 per day, £35 per round,
£30 after 1.30pm, £18 after 4pm **Prof** Jason Partridge **Facilities** ⓣ
🍴 🖥 🛍 🏌 🎯 🏠 ⚑ ✆ 🚗 ✆ ✆ **Conf** facs Corporate
Hospitality Days **Location** 2m W of Uckfield off A272, club signed
Hotel ★★★ HL Horsted Place, Little Horsted, UCKFIELD
☎ 01825 750581 📠 01825 750581 20 en suite

SUSSEX, WEST

ANGMERING
Map 4 TQ00

Ham Manor West Dr BN16 4JE
☎ 01903 783288   📠 01903 850886
e-mail: secretary@hammanor.co.uk
web: www.hammanor.co.uk

Two miles from the sea, this parkland course has fine springy turf
and provides an interesting test in two loops of nine holes each.

18 Holes, 6267yds, Par 70, SSS 70, Course record 64.
Club membership 780.

Visitors Mon-Sun & BHs. Dress code. **Societies** booking required.
Green Fees £35 (£50 weekends) **Course Designer** Harry Colt
Prof Simon Buckley **Facilities** ⓣ 🍴 🖥 🛍 🏌 🎯 🏠 ✆
🚗 ✆ **Conf** facs Corporate Hospitality Days **Location** off A259
Hotel ★★★★ GA Kenmore, Claigmar Road, RUSTINGTON,
Littlehampton ☎ 01903 784634 📠 01903 784634 7 rms
(6 en suite)

ARUNDEL
Map 4 TQ00

Avisford Park Yapton Ln BN18 0LS
☎ 01243 554611   📠 01243 555580

Avisford Park Golf Course: 18 Holes, 5703yds, Par 68,
SSS 66.

Prof K Mann **Facilities** ⓣ 🛍 🖥 🏌 🎯 🏠 ⚑ ◇ ✆ 🚗
✆ **Leisure** outdoor and indoor heated swimming pool **Conf** facs
Location off A27 towards Yapton
Telephone for further details
Hotel ★★★ 75% HL Norfolk Arms, High Street, ARUNDEL
☎ 01903 882101 📠 01903 882101 33 en suite

BOGNOR REGIS
Map 4 SZ99

Bognor Regis Downview Rd, Felpham PO22 8JD
☎ 01243 821929 (Secretary)   📠 01243 860719
e-mail: sec@bognorgolfclub.co.uk
web: www.bognorgolfclub.co.uk

This flattish, well tree-lined, parkland course has more variety
than is to be found on some other south coast courses. The course
is open to the prevailing wind and the River Rife and many water
ditches need negotiation.

18 Holes, 6238yds, Par 70, SSS 70, Course record 64.
Club membership 700.

Visitors Mon, Wed-Sun except BHs. Booking required weekends.
Societies welcome. **Green Fees** £30 **Course Designer** James Braid
Prof Matthew Kirby **Facilities** ⓣ 🍴 🛍 🖥 🏌 🎯 🏠 ✆
🚗 ✆ **Conf** facs Corporate Hospitality Days **Location** 0.5m N at
Felpham lights on A259
Hotel ★★★ 72% HL Beachcroft, Clyde Road, Felpham Village,
BOGNOR REGIS ☎ 01243 827142 📠 01243 827142 35 en suite

BURGESS HILL
Map 4 TQ31

Burgess Hill, Cuckfield Rd RH15 8RE
☎ 01444 258585   📠 01444 247318
e-mail: enquiries@burgesshillgolfcentre.co.uk

Very challenging nine-hole course. Gently undulating layout with trees
and water. Used for PGA short course championships

Burgess Hill Golf Centre: 9 Holes, 1250yds, Par 27.

Visitors Mon-Sun & BHs. **Societies** welcome. **Green Fees** £10 per
9 holes **Course Designer** Donald Steel **Prof** Mark Collins **Facilities** ⓣ
🍴 🛍 🖥 🏌 🎯 🏠 ✆ 🚗 ✆ **Leisure** pitching & chipping
green **Conf** facs Corporate Hospitality Days **Location** N of town on
B2036
Hotel ★★★ 79% CHH Hickstead, Jobs Lane, Bolney, HICKSTEAD
☎ 01444 248023 📠 01444 248023 52 en suite

CHICHESTER
Map 4 SU80

Chichester Hunston Village PO20 1AX
☎ 01243 533833   📠 01243 539922
web: www.chichestergolf.co.uk

Tower Course: 18 Holes, 6175yds, Par 72, SSS 69,
Course record 67.
Cathedral Course: 18 Holes, 6461yds, Par 72, SSS 71,
Course record 65.

Course Designer Philip Saunders **Location** 3m S of Chichester on
B2145
Telephone for further details
Hotel ★★★ 81% HL Crouchers Country Hotel & Restaurant,
Birdham Road, CHICHESTER ☎ 01243 784995 📠 01243 784995
20 en suite

COPTHORNE
Map 5 TQ33

Copthorne Borers Arms Rd RH10 3LL
☎ 01342 712033 & 712508 📠 01342 717682
e-mail: info@copthornegolfclub.co.uk
web: www.copthornegolfclub.co.uk
Despite it having been in existence since 1892, this club remains one of the lesser known Sussex courses. It is hard to know why because it is most attractive with plenty of trees and much variety.

18 Holes, 6435yds, Par 71, SSS 71, Course record 66.
Club membership 550.

Visitors contact club for details. **Societies** welcome. **Green Fees** £40 **Course Designer** James Braid **Prof** Joe Burrell
Facilities ⊗ ⊗ ⊗ ⊗ ⊗ ⊗ ⊗ ⊗ ⊗ **Conf** Corporate Hospitality Days **Location** M23 junct 10, E of village off A264
Hotel ★★★★ 71% HL Copthorne Hotel London Gatwick, Copthorne Way, COPTHORNE ☎ 01342 348800 & 348888
📠 01342 348800 227 en suite

Effingham Park The Copthorne Effingham Park, Hotel, West Park Rd RH10 3EU
☎ 01342 716528 📠 0870 8900 215
web: www.effinghamparkgc.co.uk

Parkland course.
9 Holes, 1822yds, Par 30, SSS 57, Course record 28.
Club membership 230.

Visitors Mon-Sun & BHs. Booking required. Dress code.
Societies welcome. **Green Fees** phone. **Course Designer** Francisco Escario **Prof** Mark Root **Facilities** ⊗ ⊗ ⊗ ⊗ ⊗ ⊗ ⊗ ⊗
◇ ⊗ **Leisure** hard tennis courts, heated indoor swimming pool, sauna, gymnasium **Conf** facs Corporate Hospitality Days **Location** 2m E on B2028
Hotel ★★★★ 72% HL Copthorne Hotel and Resort Effingham Park London Gatwick, West Park Road, COPTHORNE ☎ 01342 714994
📠 01342 714994 122 en suite

CRAWLEY
Map 4 TQ23

Cottesmore Buchan Hill RH11 9AT
☎ 01293 528256 (reception) & 861777 (shop)
📠 01293 522819
web: www.crown-golf.co.uk
Griffin: 18 Holes, 6248yds, Par 71, SSS 70,
Course record 67.
Phoenix: 18 Holes, 5600yds, Par 69, SSS 66.
Course Designer Michael J Rogerson **Location** M23 junct 11, through village of Pease Pottage, 2m on right

Telephone for further details

Cottesmore

Hotel ★★★★ HL Alexander House Hotel & Utopia Spa, East Street, TURNERS HILL ☎ 01342 714914 📠 01342 714914 38 en suite

Ifield Golf & Country Club Rusper Rd, Ifield RH11 0LN
☎ 01293 520222 📠 01293 612973
Parkland course.

Ifield Golf & Country Club: 18 Holes, 6330yds, Par 70,
SSS 70, Course record 64. Club membership 750.
Visitors Mon-Fri except BHs. Booking required except Mon & Thu. Handicap certificate. Dress code. **Societies** booking required. **Green Fees** £27 per day **Course Designer** Hawtree & Taylor **Prof** Jonathan Earl **Facilities** ⊗ ⊗ ⊗ ⊗ ⊗ ⊗ ⊗ ⊗ ⊗
Conf Corporate Hospitality Days **Location** 1m W side of town centre off A23
Hotel ★★★★ HL Alexander House Hotel & Utopia Spa, East Street, TURNERS HILL ☎ 01342 714914 📠 01342 714914 38 en suite

Tilgate Forest Golf Centre Titmus Dr RH10 5EU
☎ 01293 530103 📠 01293 523478
e-mail: tilgate@glendale-services.co.uk
web: www.glendale-golf.com
Designed by former Ryder Cup players Neil Coles and Brian Huggett, the course has been carefully cut through a silver birch and pine forest. It is possibly one of the most beautiful public courses in the country. The 17th is a treacherous par 5 demanding an uphill third shot to a green surrounded by rhododendrons.

Tilgate Forest Golf Centre: 18 Holes, 6359yds, Par 71,
SSS 70, Course record 69. Club membership 200.
Visitors Mon-Sun & BHs. Booking required. Dress code.
Societies welcome. **Green Fees** not confirmed **Course Designer** Neil Coles/Brian Huggett **Prof** William Easdale **Facilities** ⊗ ⊗ ⊗
⊗ ⊗ ⊗ ⊗ ⊗ ⊗ ⊗ **Leisure** par 3 9 hole course
Conf Corporate Hospitality Days **Location** 2m E of town centre
Hotel ★★★★ HL Alexander House Hotel & Utopia Spa, East Street, TURNERS HILL ☎ 01342 714914 📠 01342 714914 38 en suite

EAST GRINSTEAD
Map 5 TQ33

Chartham Park Golf & Country Club Felcourt Rd, Felcourt RH19 2JT
☎ 01342 870340 & 870008 (pro shop) 📠 01342 870719
e-mail: charthampk.retail@theclubcompany.com
web: www.theclubcompany.com
Mature parkland course surrounded by ancient woodland with fine views across the North Downs. The course features an abundance

continued

of mature trees, carp filled lakes and several heathland holes on the back nine. The course has buggy paths and the latest draining features.

Chartham Park Golf & Country Club: 18 Holes, 6680yards, Par 72, SSS 72, Course record 64. Club membership 740.

Visitors booking required. **Societies** welcome. **Green Fees** phone **Course Designer** Neil Coles **Prof** David Hobbs **Facilities** ⑪ ⑩ ⓛ ◫ ⑪ ⌂ 🏠 ⚷ 🚜 ⚷ 🍴 **Leisure** sauna, gymnasium **Conf** Corporate Hospitality Days **Location** 2m N from town centre towards Felcourt, on right

Hotel ★★★ HL Gravetye Manor, EAST GRINSTEAD
☎ 01342 810567 📠 01342 810567 18 en suite

HASSOCKS
Map 4 TQ31

Hassocks London Rd BN6 9NA
☎ 01273 846630 & 846990   📠 01273 846070
e-mail: hassocksgolfclub@btconnect.com
web: www.hassocksgolfclub.co.uk

Set against the backdrop of the South Downs, Hassocks is an 18-hole par 70 course designed and contoured to blend naturally with the surrounding countryside. A friendly and relaxed course, appealing to golfers of all ages and abilities.

18 Holes, 5703yds, Par 70, SSS 68, Course record 66. Club membership 400.

Visitors Mon-Sun & BHs. Booking required. Dress code. **Societies** booking required. **Green Fees** £20 per 18 holes (£25 weekends & BHs) **Course Designer** Paul Wright **Prof** Mike Ovett **Facilities** ⑪ ⑩ ⓛ ◫ ⑪ ⌂ 🏠 ⚷ 🍴 **Conf** facs Corporate Hospitality Days **Location** on A273 between Burgess Hill and Hassocks

Hotel ★★★ 79% CHH Hickstead, Jobs Lane, Bolney, HICKSTEAD
☎ 01444 248023 📠 01444 248023 52 en suite

HAYWARDS HEATH
Map 5 TQ32

Haywards Heath High Beech Ln RH16 1SL
☎ 01444 414457   📠 01444 458319
e-mail: info@haywardsheathgolfclub.co.uk
web: www.haywardsheathgolfclub.co.uk

Pleasant undulating parkland course with easy walking. Several challenging par 4s and 3s.

18 Holes, 6216yds, Par 71, SSS 70, Course record 65. Club membership 770.

Visitors Mon-Sun & BHs. Booking required weekends & BHs. Dress code. **Societies** booking required **Green Fees** £32 per 18 holes (£42 weekends & BHs) **Course Designer** James Braid **Prof** Michael Henning **Facilities** ⑪ ⑩ ⓛ ◫ ⑪ ⌂ 🏠 ⚷ 🍴 **Conf** Corporate Hospitality Days **Location** 1.25m N of Haywards Heath off B2028

Hotel ★★★ 74% HL Best Western The Birch Hotel, Lewes Road, HAYWARDS HEATH ☎ 01444 451565 📠 01444 451565 51 en suite

Lindfield East Mascalls Ln, Lindfield RH16 2QN
☎ 01444 484467   📠 01444 482709
e-mail: info@thegolfcollege.com
web: www.thegolfcollege.com

A downland course in two loops of nine in an Area of Outstanding Natural Beauty. Water hazards on 5th, 13th and 14th holes.

18 Holes, 5957yds, Par 70, SSS 68, Course record 65. Club membership 240.

Visitors contact club for details. **Societies** welcome. **Green Fees** phone **Course Designer** P Tallack **Facilities** ⑪ ⑩ ⓛ ◫ ⑪ ⌂ 🏠 ⚷ 🍴 **Conf** facs Corporate Hospitality Days **Location** 2m NE of Haywards Heath, E of Lindfield off B2011

Hotel ★★★ 74% HL Best Western The Birch Hotel, Lewes Road, HAYWARDS HEATH ☎ 01444 451565 📠 01444 451565 51 en suite

HORSHAM
Map 4 TQ13

See **Slinfold**

Horsham Worthing Rd RH13 7AX
☎ 01403 271525   📠 01403 274528
web: www.horshamgolfandfitness.co.uk

Horsham Golf & Fitness: 9 Holes, 4122yds, Par 33, SSS 30, Course record 55.

Prof Warren Pritchard **Facilities** ⑪ ⑩ ⓛ ◫ ⑪ ⌂ 🏠 ⚷ 🍴 **Leisure** gymnasium **Conf** Corporate Hospitality Days **Location** A24 rdbt onto B2237, by garage
Telephone for further details

Hotel ★★★★★ 89% CHH South Lodge, Brighton Road, LOWER BEEDING ☎ 01403 891711 📠 01403 891711 46 en suite

HURSTPIERPOINT
Map 4 TQ21

Singing Hills, Albourne BN6 9EB
☎ 01273 835353   📠 01273 835444
e-mail: info@singinghills.co.uk
web: www.singinghills.co.uk

Three distinct nines (Lake, River and Valley) can be combined to make a truly varied game. Gently undulating fairways and spectacular waterholes make Singing Hills a test of accurate shot making. The opening two holes of the River nine have long drives, while the second hole on the Lake course is an island green where the tee is also protected by two bunkers. The Valley course demands long, accurate tee shots. The water hazards are picturesque and harbour an abundance of wildlife and golf balls.

Lake: 9 Holes, 3200yds, Par 35.
River: 9 Holes, 2861yds, Par 34.
Valley: 9 Holes, 3362yds, Par 36. Club membership 496.

Visitors Mon-Sun & BHs. Dress code. **Societies** booking required. **Green Fees** £27 per round (£35 weekends & BHs) **Course Designer** M R M Sandow **Prof** Wallace Street **Facilities** ⑪ ⑩ ⓛ ◫ ⑪ ⌂ 🏠 ⚷ 🍴 **Conf** facs Corporate Hospitality Days **Location** A23 onto B2117

Hotel ★★★ 79% CHH Hickstead, Jobs Lane, Bolney, HICKSTEAD
☎ 01444 248023 📠 01444 248023 52 en suite

LITTLEHAMPTON   Map 4 TQ00

Littlehampton 170 Rope Walk, Riverside West BN17 5DL
☎ 01903 717170   📠 01903 726629
e-mail: lgc@talk21.com
web: www.littlehamptongolf.co.uk

A delightful seaside links in an equally delightful setting - and the only links course in the area.

18 Holes, 6226yds, Par 70, SSS 70, Course record 61.
Club membership 600.

Visitors Mon-Sun & BHs. Handicap certificate. Dress code.
Societies booking required. **Green Fees** £50 per 36 holes, £35 per 18 holes (£45 per 18 holes weekends). Twilight after 4.30pm £17.50
Course Designer Hawtree **Prof** Stuart Fallow **Facilities** 🍴 🍽️ 🛍️ 🖥️ 🗄️ ♨️ 🏌️ **Conf** facs Corporate Hospitality Days **Location** 1m W off A259
Hotel BUD Travelodge Littlehampton Rustington, Worthing Road, RUSTINGTON ☎ 08719 846 6045 📠 08719 846 6045 36 en suite

LOWER BEEDING   Map 4 TQ22

Mannings Heath Hotel, Winterpit Ln RH13 6LY
☎ 01403 891191   📠 01403 891499
e-mail: info@manningsheathhotel.com
web: www.manningsheathhotel.com
A nine-hole, 18-tee course with three par 4s set in glorious countryside.

Mannings Heath Hotel: 9 Holes, 1529yds, Par 31.
Club membership 150.

Visitors contact hotel for details. **Societies** welcome. **Green Fees** £7.50 per 18 holes **Prof** Terry Betts **Facilities** 🍴 🍽️ 🛍️ 🖥️ 🗄️ ♨️ ◇ **Leisure** fishing **Conf** facs Corporate Hospitality Days **Location** off A281 S of Horsham
Hotel ★★★★★ 89% CHH South Lodge, Brighton Road, LOWER BEEDING ☎ 01403 891711 📠 01403 891711 46 en suite

MANNINGS HEATH   Map 4 TQ22

Mannings Heath Fullers, Hammerpond Rd RH13 6PG
☎ 01403 210228   📠 01403 270974
e-mail: enquiries@manningsheath.com
web: www.exclusivehotels.co.uk
The Waterfall course is set amid acres of mature deciduous woodland and streams with patchwork fairways. Due to its location on the rolling Sussex Downs, the course is a hybrid mix of heathland, downland and parkland and provides golfers with an exciting and entertaining course holding the interest of the golfer all

the way round. May only be played by members and their guests but is available for corporate golf days. The Kingfisher course may be played by visitors and is suitable for all levels of golfer.

Waterfall: 18 Holes, 6683yds, Par 72, SSS 72,
Course record 63.
Kingfisher: 18 Holes, 6217yds, Par 70, SSS 70.
Club membership 600.

Visitors Mon-Sun & BHs Kingfisher course only. Booking required. Dress code. **Societies** booking required. **Green Fees** Kingfisher £25 per 18 holes **Course Designer** David Williams **Prof** Neil Darnell **Facilities** 🍴 🍽️ 🛍️ 🖥️ 🗄️ ♨️ 🏌️ ◇ 🏌️ **Leisure** hard tennis courts, fishing, sauna, chipping practice area **Conf** facs Corporate Hospitality Days **Location** off A281 on N side of village
Hotel ★★★★★ 89% CHH South Lodge, Brighton Road, LOWER BEEDING ☎ 01403 891711 📠 01403 891711 46 en suite

MIDHURST   Map 4 SU82

Cowdray Park Petworth Rd GU29 0BB
☎ 01730 813599   📠 01730 815900
e-mail: enquiries@cowdraygolf.co.uk
web: www.cowdraygolf.co.uk

Undulating parkland with scenic views of the surrounding countryside, including Elizabethan ruins. The course is in a park designed by 'Capability' Brown in the 18th century.

18 Holes, 6265yds, Par 70, SSS 70, Course record 65.
Club membership 720.

Visitors Mon-Sun & BHs. Booking required. Dress code.
Societies booking required. **Green Fees** £50 per 18 holes, winter £40 **Course Designer** Jack White **Prof** Scott Brown **Facilities** 🍴 🍽️ 🛍️ 🖥️ 🗄️ ◇ 🏌️ 🏌️ **Leisure** clay pigeon shooting **Conf** facs Corporate Hospitality Days **Location** 1m E of Midhurst on A272
Hotel ★★★★ GA Cowdray Park Golf Club, MIDHURST ☎ 01730 813599 📠 01730 813599 6 en suite

PULBOROUGH   Map 4 TQ01

West Sussex Golf Club Ln, Wiggonholt RH20 2EN
☎ 01798 872563   📠 01798 872033
e-mail: secretary@westsussexgolf.co.uk
web: www.westsussexgolf.co.uk
An outstanding beautiful heathland course occupying an oasis of sand, heather and pine in the middle of attractive countryside, which is predominately clay and marsh. The 6th and 13th holes are particularly notable.

continued

18 Holes, 6264yds, Par 68, SSS 70, Course record 61. Club membership 850.
Visitors Mon-Thu except BHs. Weekends by arrangement. Booking required. Handicap certificate. Dress code. **Societies** booking required. **Green Fees** £90 per 36 holes, £70 per 18 holes (£100/£80 weekends) **Course Designer** Campbell/Hutcheson/Hotchkin **Prof** Tim Packham **Facilities** ⓣ ⓑ ⌨ 🍴 ⌴ 🛆 🏠 🍴 🛒 ⌴ 🏌 **Location** 1.5m E of village on A283
Hotel ★★★ 75% HL Best Western Roundabout, Monkmead Lane, WEST CHILTINGTON ☎ 01798 813838 📠 01798 813838 25 en suite

PYECOMBE — Map 4 TQ21

Pyecombe Clayton Hill BN45 7FF
☎ 01273 845372 📠 01273 843338
web: www.pyecombegolfclub.com
18 Holes, 6278yds, Par 71, SSS 70, Course record 65.
Course Designer James Braid **Location** E of village on A273
Telephone for further details
Hotel ★★★ 67% HL The Courtlands Hotel & Conference Centre, 15-27 The Drive, HOVE ☎ 01273 731055 📠 01273 731055 67 en suite

SELSEY — Map 4 SZ89

Selsey Golf Links Ln PO20 9DR
☎ 01243 608935 📠 01243 607101
e-mail: secretary@selseygolfclub.co.uk
web: www.selseygolfclub.co.uk
Fairly difficult links type seaside course, exposed to wind and has natural ditches.
9 Holes, 5834yds, Par 68, SSS 68, Course record 64. Club membership 300.
Visitors Mon-Sat & BHs. Booking required. Dress code. **Societies** booking required. **Green Fees** phone **Course Designer** J H Taylor **Prof** Peter Grindley **Facilities** ⓣ 🍴 ⓑ ⌨ 🍴 🛆 🏠 **Leisure** hard tennis courts **Location** 1m N off B2145
Hotel ★★★ 81% HL Crouchers Country Hotel & Restaurant, Birdham Road, CHICHESTER ☎ 01243 784995 📠 01243 784995 20 en suite

SLINFOLD — Map 4 TQ13

Slinfold Park Golf & Country Club Stane St RH13 0RE
☎ 01403 791555 📠 01403 791465
web: www.slinfoldpark.co.uk
Championship Course: 18 Holes, 6407yds, Par 72, SSS 71, Course record 64.
Academy Course: 9 Holes, 1315yds, Par 28.
Course Designer John Fortune **Location** 4m W on A29
Telephone for further details
Hotel BUD Travelodge Billingshurst Five Oaks, Staines Street, FIVE OAKS ☎ 08719 846 013 📠 08719 846 013 26 en suite

WEST CHILTINGTON — Map 4 TQ01

West Chiltington Broadford Bridge Rd RH20 2YA
☎ 01798 812115 (bookings) & 813574
📠 01798 812631
e-mail: richard@westchiltgolf.co.uk
web: www.westchiltgolf.co.uk
Set in an Area of Outstanding Natural Beauty with panoramic views of the Sussex Downs. The Main Course has well-drained greens and, although quite short, is in places extremely tight. Three large double greens provide an interesting feature to this course. Also a 9-hole short course.
Windmill: 18 Holes, 5967yds, Par 70, SSS 69, Course record 66. Club membership 500.
Visitors Mon-Sun & BHs. Booking required. Dress code. **Societies** booking required **Green Fees** not confirmed **Course Designer** Brian Barnes **Prof** Lorraine Cousins **Facilities** ⓣ ⓑ ⌨ 🍴 🛆 🏠 🍴 🛒 🏌 **Conf** facs Corporate Hospitality Days **Location** N of village
Hotel ★★★ 75% HL Best Western Roundabout, Monkmead Lane, WEST CHILTINGTON ☎ 01798 813838 📠 01798 813838 25 en suite

WORTHING — Map 4 TQ10

Hill Barn Hill Barn Ln BN14 9QF
☎ 01903 237301 📠 01903 217613
web: www.hillbarngolf.com
18 Holes, 6224yds, Par 70, SSS 70, Course record 64.
Course Designer Fred Hawtree **Location** signposted from Grove Lodge roundabout by Norwich Union on A27
Telephone for further details
Hotel ★★★ 71% HL Findon Manor, High Street, Findon, WORTHING ☎ 01903 872733 📠 01903 872733 11 en suite

Worthing Links Rd BN14 9QZ
☎ 01903 260801 📠 01903 694664
e-mail: enquiries@worthinggolf.com
web: www.worthinggolf.co.uk
The Lower Course is considered to be one of the best downland courses in the country with its undulating greens. The Upper Course is shorter than most but compensates with tricky approaches to the green and fine views.
Lower Course: 18 Holes, 6505yds, Par 71, SSS 72, Course record 62.
Upper Course: 18 Holes, 5211yds, Par 66, SSS 65. Club membership 1200.
Visitors Mon-Sun except BHs. Handicap certificate. Dress code. **Societies** welcome. **Green Fees** Lower Course from £35 **Course Designer** H S Colt **Prof** Stephen Rolley **Facilities** ⓣ ⓑ ⌨ 🍴 🛆 🏠 🍴 🛒 🏌 **Conf** facs Corporate Hospitality Days **Location** N of town centre off A27
Hotel ★★★ 80% HL Ardington, Steyne Gardens, WORTHING ☎ 01903 230451 📠 01903 230451 45 en suite

TYNE & WEAR

BIRTLEY
Map 12 NZ25

Birtley Birtley Ln DH3 2LR
☎ 0191 410 2207
e-mail: birtleygolfclub@aol.com
web: www.birtleyportobellogolfclub.co.uk
A nine-hole parkland course. Good test of golf with challenging par 3 and par 4 holes.

9 Holes, 5729yds, Par 67, SSS 67, Course record 63.
Club membership 350.

Visitors contact club for details. **Societies** welcome. **Green Fees** £15 per 18 holes **Facilities** ⬜ ⛳
Hotel BUD Travelodge Washington A1 Northbound, Motorway Service Area, Portobello, BIRTLEY ☎ 0871 984 6270 🖨 0871 984 6270 31 en suite

BOLDON
Map 12 NZ36

Boldon Dipe Ln, East Boldon NE36 0PQ
☎ 0191 536 5360 🖨 0191 537 2270
e-mail: info@boldongolfclub.co.uk
web: www.boldongolfclub.co.uk
Parkland links course, easy walking, distant sea views.

18 Holes, 6362yds, Par 72, SSS 71, Course record 65.
Club membership 700.

Visitors Mon-Sun & BHs. Booking required weekends & BHs. Dress code. **Societies** welcome. **Green Fees** £22.50 per day (£25.50 weekends & BHs) **Course Designer** Harry Vardon **Facilities** ⛽ 🍴
🍺 ⬜ 🍽 ⛳ 🏠 ⛳ 🏌 **Leisure** snooker **Conf** facs Corporate Hospitality Days **Location** S of village off A184
Hotel ★★★★ 75% HL Sunderland Marriott, Queen's Parade, Seaburn, SUNDERLAND ☎ 0191 529 2041 🖨 0191 529 2041 82 en suite

CHOPWELL
Map 12 NZ15

Garesfield NE17 7AP
☎ 01207 561309 🖨 01207 561309
e-mail: garesfieldgc@btconnect.com
web: www.garesfieldgolf.com
The course winds its way through the mature trees which form a natural, tranquil and beautiful setting. All the holes have their own individual challenge and there are fine views of the surrounding counrryside.

18 Holes, 6458yds, Par 72, SSS 70, Course record 68.
Club membership 697.

Visitors Mon-Sun & BHs. Booking required weekends. Dress code. **Societies** welcome. **Green Fees** phone **Course Designer** Harry Fernie **Prof** David Race **Facilities** ⛽ 🍴 🍺 ⬜ 🍽 ⛳ 🏠 🏌 ⛳
🛥 ⛳ **Conf** Corporate Hospitality Days **Location** off B6315 in High Spen at Bute Arms for Chopwell
Hotel ★★★★ 75% HL Close House, HEDDON-ON-THE-WALL ☎ 01661 852255 🖨 01661 852255 19 en suite

FELLING
Map 12 NZ26

Heworth Gingling Gate NE10 8XY
☎ 0191 469 4424 🖨 0191 469 9898
18 Holes, 6422yds, Par 71, SSS 71.

Prof Adrian Marshall **Facilities** ⛽ 🍴 🍺 ⬜ 🍽 ⛳ 🏠 🛥
⛳ **Conf** facs Corporate Hospitality Days **Location** On A195, 0.5m NW of junc with A1(M)
Telephone for further details
Hotel BUD Travelodge Newcastle Whitemare Pool, Wardley, Whitemare Pool, WARDLEY ☎ 0871 984 6165 🖨 0871 984 6165 71 en suite

GATESHEAD
Map 12 NZ26

Ravensworth Angel View, Longbank, Wrekenton NE9 7NE
☎ 0191 487 6014 🖨 0191 487 6014
e-mail: ravensworth.golfclub@virgin.net
web: www.ravensworthgolfclub.co.uk
Moorland and parkland 600ft above sea level with fine views, overlooking the Angel of the North. Testing 5th and 7th holes (par 3s).

18 Holes, 5966yds, Par 70, SSS 70, Course record 63.
Club membership 700.

Visitors Mon-Fri & BHs. Booking required BHs. Dress code.
Societies welcome. **Green Fees** £22 weekdays **Course Designer** J W Fraser **Prof** Shaun Cowell **Facilities** ⛽ 🍴 🍺 ⬜ 🍽 ⛳ 🏠
⛳ **Conf** Corporate Hospitality Days **Location** leave A1(M) at Junction for A167 (Angel of the North) take A1295 for 300 yds
Hotel ★★★ 78% HL Eslington Villa, 8 Station Road, Low Fell, GATESHEAD ☎ 0191 487 6017 & 420 0666 🖨 0191 487 6017 17 en suite

GOSFORTH
Map 12 NZ26

Gosforth Broadway East NE3 5ER
☎ 0191 285 3495 & 285 6710(catering)
🖨 0191 284 6274
e-mail: gosforth.golf@virgin.net
web: www.gosforthgolfclub.com
Easy walking parkland with natural water hazards.

18 Holes, 6031yds, Par 69, SSS 68, Course record 62.
Club membership 500.

Visitors Mon-Sun & BHs. Booking required. Handicap certificate. Dress code. **Societies** booking required. **Green Fees** £30 per day, £25 per round (£32/£28 weekends) **Prof** G Garland **Facilities** ⛽ 🍴 🍺 ⬜
🍽 ⛳ ⛳ **Conf** Corporate Hospitality Days **Location** N of town centre off A6125
Hotel ★★★★ 77% HL Newcastle Marriott Hotel Gosforth Park, High Gosforth Park, Gosforth, NEWCASTLE UPON TYNE ☎ 0191 236 4111 🖨 0191 236 4111 178 en suite

Parklands Gosforth Park Golfing Complex NE3 5HQ
☎ 0191 236 4480 🖨 0191 236 3322
Parklands: 18 Holes, 6013yds, Par 71, SSS 69,
Course record 66.

Prof Brian Rumney **Facilities** ⛽ 🍴 🍺 ⬜ 🍽 ⛳ 🏠 ⛳ 🏌
Conf Corporate Hospitality Days **Location** 3m N at end A1 western bypass
Telephone for further details
Hotel ★★★★ 77% HL Newcastle Marriott Hotel Gosforth Park, High Gosforth Park, Gosforth, NEWCASTLE UPON TYNE ☎ 0191 236 4111 🖨 0191 236 4111 178 en suite

HOUGHTON-LE-SPRING　　　　　Map 12 NZ34

Elemore Elemore Ln, Hetton-le-Hole DH5 0QB
☎ 0191 517 3061　🖷 0191 517 3054

Elemore course tests a player's ability in all aspects of the game, with drives over water as well as wedges. The greens are firm all year round and there are well positioned bunkers.

Elemore Golf Course: 18 Holes, 6003yds, Par 69, Course record 68. Club membership 200.

Visitors contact course for details. **Societies** booking required. **Green Fees** £14 per 18 holes (£18 weekends & BHs) **Course Designer** J Gaunt **Facilities** ⑪ ⛘ 🖵 🍴 ⚐ 🛆 🛎 ⛳ 🚍 ✔ **Location** 4m S of Houghton-le-Spring on A182

Hotel ★★ 74% HL Chilton Country Pub & Hotel, Black Boy Road, Chilton Moor, Fencehouses, HOUGHTON-LE-SPRING ☎ 0191 385 2694 🖷 0191 385 2694　25 en suite

Houghton-le-Spring Copt Hill DH5 8LU
☎ 0191 584 1198 & 584 7421
e-mail: houghton.golf@ntlworld.com
web: www.houghtongolfclub.co.uk

Hilly, downland course with natural slope hazards and excellent greens.

Houghton-Le-Spring Golf Club: 18 Holes, 6381yds, Par 72, SSS 71, Course record 64. Club membership 680.

Visitors Mon-Sat & BHs. Booking required Sat. Dress code. **Societies** welcome. **Green Fees** £20 per 18 holes, £25 Fri pm, Sat £25 **Prof** Graeme Robinson **Facilities** ⑪ 🍴 ⛘ 🖵 🍴 🛆 🛎 ✔ ⚐ ✔ **Conf** facs Corporate Hospitality Days **Location** 0.5m E on B1404

Hotel ★★ 74% HL Chilton Country Pub & Hotel, Black Boy Road, Chilton Moor, Fencehouses, HOUGHTON-LE-SPRING ☎ 0191 385 2694 🖷 0191 385 2694　25 en suite

NEWCASTLE UPON TYNE　　　　Map 12 NZ26

City of Newcastle Three Mile Bridge NE3 2DR
☎ 0191 285 1775　🖷 0191 284 700
e-mail: info@cityofnewcastlegolfclub.com
web: www.cityofnewcastlegolfclub.com

A well-manicured woodland course in the Newcastle suburbs.

18 Holes, 6528yds, Par 72, SSS 71, Course record 64. Club membership 600.

Visitors contact club for details. **Societies** welcome. **Green Fees** £34 per day; £28 per round (£25 per round Sun) **Course Designer** Harry Vardon **Prof** Steve McKenna **Facilities** ⑪ 🍴 ⛘ 🖵 🍴 🛆 🛎 ⚐ ✔ **Conf** facs Corporate Hospitality Days **Location** 3m N on B1318

Hotel ★★★ 70% HL The Caledonian Hotel, Newcastle, 64 Osborne Road, Jesmond, NEWCASTLE UPON TYNE ☎ 0191 281 7881 🖷 0191 281 7881　91 en suite

Newcastle United Ponteland Rd NE5 3JW
☎ 0191 286 9998
web: www.nugc.co.uk

18 Holes, 6617yds, Par 72, SSS 72, Course record 66.

Location 1.25m NW of city centre off A6127
Telephone for further details
Hotel ★★★ 70% HL The Caledonian Hotel, Newcastle, 64 Osborne Road, Jesmond, NEWCASTLE UPON TYNE ☎ 0191 281 7881 🖷 0191 281 7881　91 en suite

Northumberland High Gosforth Park NE3 5HT
☎ 0191 236 2498　🖷 0191 236 2036
e-mail: sec@thengc.co.uk

Predominantly a level heathland style course, the firm, fast greens are a particular feature.

18 Holes, 6683yds, Par 72, SSS 72, Course record 65. Club membership 580.

Visitors Mon-Sun & BHs. Booking required. Handicap certificate. Dress code. **Societies** booking required. **Green Fees** £60 per day, £50 per round (£60 per round weekends) **Course Designer** Colt/Braid **Facilities** ⑪ 🍴 ⛘ 🖵 🍴 🛆 🛎 ✔ **Conf** Corporate Hospitality Days **Location** 4m N of city centre off A1

Hotel ★★★★ 77% HL Newcastle Marriott Hotel Gosforth Park, High Gosforth Park, Gosforth, NEWCASTLE UPON TYNE ☎ 0191 236 4111 🖷 0191 236 4111　178 en suite

Westerhope Whorlton Grange, Westerhope NE5 1PP
☎ 0191 286 7636　🖷 0191 2146287
e-mail: wgc@btconnect.com

Attractive, easy walking parkland with tree-lined fairways. Good open views towards the airport.

18 Holes, 6392yds, Par 72, SSS 71, Course record 64. Club membership 750.

Visitors Mon-Sun & BHs. Dress code. **Societies** booking required. **Green Fees** £34 per day, £28 per round (£30 per round BHs) **Prof** Michael Nesbit **Facilities** ⑪ 🍴 ⛘ 🖵 🍴 🛆 🛎 ⚐ ✔ 🚍 ✔ **Conf** Corporate Hospitality Days **Location** 4.5m NW of city centre off B6324

Hotel ★★★★ 77% HL Newcastle Marriott Hotel Gosforth Park, High Gosforth Park, Gosforth, NEWCASTLE UPON TYNE ☎ 0191 236 4111 🖷 0191 236 4111　178 en suite

RYTON　　　　　　　　　　　　Map 12 NZ16

Ryton Clara Vale NE40 3TD
☎ 0191 413 3253　🖷 0191 413 1642
e-mail: secretary@rytongolfclub.co.uk
web: www.rytongolfclub.co.uk

Parkland course set in the heart of the Tyne Valley and bordered by the river. Tight fairways on some holes add to the challenge.

18 Holes, 6014yds, Par 70, SSS 69, Course record 67. Club membership 400.

Visitors Mon-Fri & BHs. Booking required. Dress code. **Societies** booking required. **Green Fees** £26 per day; £20 per round **Prof** Gary Shipley **Facilities** ⑪ 🍴 ⛘ 🖵 🍴 🛆 **Conf** Corporate Hospitality Days **Location** NW of town centre off A695

Hotel ★★★ 71% HL Gibside, Front Street, WHICKHAM ☎ 0191 488 9292 🖷 0191 488 9292　45 en suite

Tyneside Westfield Ln NE40 3QE
☎ 0191 413 2742　🖷 0191 413 0199
web: www.tynesidegolfclub.co.uk

Open, part hilly parkland course with a water hazard.

Tyneside Golf Club Ltd: 18 Holes, 6103yds, Par 70, SSS 69, Course record 65. Club membership 641.

Visitors Mon-Fri except BHs. Handicap certificate. Dress code. **Societies** booking required. **Green Fees** £30 per day, £25 per round **Course Designer** H S Colt **Prof** Gary Vickers **Facilities** ⑪ 🍴 ⛘ 🖵 🍴 🛆 🛎 ✔ **Conf** Corporate Hospitality Days **Location** NW of town centre off A695

Hotel ★★★ 71% HL Gibside, Front Street, WHICKHAM ☎ 0191 488 9292 🖷 0191 488 9292　45 en suite

SOUTH SHIELDS   Map 12 NZ36

South Shields Cleadon Hills NE34 8EG
☎ 0191 456 8942   📄 0191 456 8942
web: www.ssgc.co.uk

18 Holes, 6174yds, Par 71, SSS 70, Course record 64.
Course Designer McKenzie-Braid **Location** SE of town centre off
A1300
Telephone for further details
Hotel ★★★ 74% HL Best Western Sea, Sea Road, SOUTH SHIELDS
☎ 0191 427 0999 📄 0191 427 0999   37 en suite

Whitburn Lizard Ln NE34 7AF
☎ 0191 529 4944 (Sec)   📄 0191 529 4944
e-mail: wgsec@ukonline.co.uk
web: golf-whitburn.co.uk

Parkland with sea views. Situated on limestone making it rarely
unplayable.

18 Holes, 5899yds, Par 70, SSS 68, Course record 67.
Club membership 700.

Visitors contact club for details. **Societies** booking required. **Green
Fees** not confirmed **Course Designer** Colt, Alison & Morrison **Prof** Neil
Whinham **Facilities** ⑪ 🍴 🍺 ☐ 🛎 ⚂ △ 🔥 ♂
Conf Corporate Hospitality Days **Location** 2.5m SE off A183
Hotel ★★★★ 75% HL Sunderland Marriott, Queen's Parade,
Seaburn, SUNDERLAND ☎ 0191 529 2041 📄 0191 529 2041
82 en suite

SUNDERLAND   Map 12 NZ35

Wearside Coxgreen SR4 9JT
☎ 0191 534 2518   📄 0191 534 6186
web: wearsidegolfclub.com

Open, undulating parkland rolling down to the River Wear beneath
the shadow of the famous Penshaw Monument. Built on the lines of
a Greek temple it is a well-known landmark. Two ravines cross the
course presenting a variety of challenging holes.

18 Holes, 6373yds, Par 71, SSS 70, Course record 63.
Club membership 648.

Visitors Mon-Sun & BHs. Booking required BHs. Handicap
certificate. Dress code. **Societies** booking required. **Green
Fees** phone **Prof** Doug Brolls **Facilities** 🍺 ☐ 🛎 △ 🏠 🚜
♂ **Location** 3.5m W off A183
Hotel ★★★★ 75% HL Sunderland Marriott, Queen's Parade,
Seaburn, SUNDERLAND ☎ 0191 529 2041 📄 0191 529 2041
82 en suite

TYNEMOUTH   Map 12 NZ36

Tynemouth Spital Dene NE30 2ER
☎ 0191 257 4578   📄 0191 259 5193
e-mail: secretary@tynemouthgolfclub.com
web: www.tynemouthgolfclub.com

Well-drained parkland course, not physically demanding but providing
a strong challenge to both low and high handicap players.

18 Holes, 6359yds, Par 70, SSS 70, Course record 65.
Club membership 850.

Visitors Mon-Fri, Sun & BHs. Dress code. **Societies** booking
required. **Green Fees** £30.50 per day, £25.50 per 18 holes **Course**

Designer Willie Park **Prof** J P McKenna **Facilities** ⑪ 🍴 🍺 ☐
🛎 △ 🏠 🔥 ♂ **Location** 0.5m W
Hotel ★★★ 77% HL Grand, Grand Parade, TYNEMOUTH
☎ 0191 293 6666 📄 0191 293 6666   45 en suite

WALLSEND   Map 12 NZ26

Centurion Park Rheydt Av, Bigges Main NE28 8SU
☎ 0191 262 1973

Parkland course, formerly known as Wallsend Golf Club.

*Centurion Park: 18 Holes, 6031yds, Par 70, SSS 69,
Course record 64. Club membership 655.*
Visitors Mon-Sun & BHs. Booking required. Dress code.
Societies welcome. **Green Fees** £24 per round (£26 weekends &
BHs) **Course Designer** A Snowball **Prof** Ken Phillips **Facilities** ⑪
🍴 🍺 ☐ 🛎 △ 🏠 ♂ 🔥 **Conf** Corporate Hospitality Days
Location NW of town centre off A193
Hotel ★★★ 70% HL The Caledonian Hotel, Newcastle, 64
Osborne Road, Jesmond, NEWCASTLE UPON TYNE ☎ 0191 281 7881
📄 0191 281 7881   91 en suite

WASHINGTON   Map 12 NZ25

George Washington Golf & Country Club Stone Cellar Rd,
High Usworth NE37 1PH
☎ 0191 417 8346   📄 0191 415 1166
e-mail: reservations@georgewashington.co.uk
web: www.georgewashington.co.uk

The course is set in 150 acres of rolling parkland. Wide generous
fairways and large greens. Trees feature on most holes, penalising the
wayward shot.

*George Washington Golf & Country Club: 18 Holes,
6604yds, Par 73, SSS 71, Course record 68.
Club membership 550.*

Visitors contact club for details. **Societies** booking required. **Green
Fees** £30 per day, £20 per 18 holes (£35/£25 weekends) **Course
Designer** Eric Watson **Facilities** ⑪ 🍴 🍺 ☐ 🛎 🍴 🍺
◇ ♂ 🚜 ♂ 🔥 **Leisure** heated indoor swimming pool, sauna,
gymnasium, 9 hole par 3 course, hair & beauty salon **Conf** facs
Corporate Hospitality Days **Location** from A195 signed Washington
North take last exit on rdbt, then right at mini-rdbt
Hotel ★★★ 75% HL George Washington Golf & Country Club,
Stone Cellar Road, High Usworth, WASHINGTON ☎ 0191 402 9988
📄 0191 402 9988   103 en suite

WHICKHAM
Map 12 NZ26

Whickham Hollinside Park, Fellside Rd NE16 5BA
☎ 0191 488 1576   📠 0191 488 1577
e-mail: enquiries@whickhamgolfclub.co.uk
web: www.whickhamgolfclub.co.uk

Undulating parkland in the beautiful Derwent valley. Its undulating fairways and subtly contoured greens create an interesting challenge for players of all abilities.

Whickham Golf Club Ltd: 18 Holes, 6542yds, Par 71, SSS 71. Club membership 680.

Visitors Mon-Fri, Sun & BHs. Dress code. **Societies** booking required. **Green Fees** not confirmed **Prof** Simon Williamson **Facilities** ⓑ ⓍⓄⓍ ⓑ ⓐ ⓕⓍ ⓔ ⓕⓍ ⓕ **Location** exit A1 for Whickham. Club is 1m from junct off Front St signed Burnopfield

Hotel ★★★ 71% HL Gibside, Front Street, WHICKHAM
☎ 0191 488 9292 📠 0191 488 9292   45 en suite

WHITLEY BAY
Map 12 NZ37

Whitley Bay Claremont Rd NE26 3UF
☎ 0191 252 0180   📠 0191 297 0030
e-mail: whtglfclb@aol.com
web: www.whitleybaygolfclub.co.uk

An 18-hole links type course, close to the sea, with a stream running through the undulating terrain.

18 Holes, 6579yds, Par 71, SSS 71, Course record 66. Club membership 800.

Visitors Mon, Wed-Fri & BHs. Sun pm only. Booking required. Dress code. **Societies** booking required. **Green Fees** £20 per round (£35 Sun pm) **Prof** Peter Crosby **Facilities** ⓑ ⓍⓄⓍ ⓑ ⓐ ⓕⓍ ⓔ ⓕ **Location** NW of town centre off A1148

Hotel 64% Swallow Gateshead, High West Street, GATESHEAD
☎ 0191 477 1105 📠 0191 477 1105   103 en suite

WARWICKSHIRE

ATHERSTONE
Map 4 SP39

Atherstone The Outwoods CV9 2RL
☎ 01827 713110   📠 01827 715686

Atherstone Golf Club Ltd: 18 Holes, 6006yds, Par 72, SSS 70, Course record 68.

Course Designer Hawtree & Gaunt Mornoch **Location** 0.5m S, A5 onto B4116

Telephone for further details

Hotel BUD Travelodge Tamworth (M42), Moto Service Area, Green Lane, TAMWORTH ☎ 0871 984 6109 & 0800 850950 📠 0871 984 6109
63 en suite

BRANDON
Map 4 SP47

City of Coventry-Brandon Wood Brandon Ln CV8 3GQ
☎ 024 7654 3141   📠 024 7654 5108

18 Holes, 6610yds, Par 72, SSS 71, Course record 68.
Prof Chris Gledhill **Facilities** ⓑ ⓑ ⓐ ⓍⓄ ⓐ ⓕⓍ ⓔ ⓕ
Leisure Pitching area **Location** off A45 S
Telephone for further details

Hotel ★★★ 77% HL Mercure Brandon Hall Hotel & Spa, Main Street, BRANDON ☎ 024 7654 6000 📠 024 7654 6000   120 en suite

COLESHILL
Map 4 SP28

Maxstoke Park Castle Ln B46 2RD
☎ 01675 466743   📠 01675 466185
e-mail: info@maxstokeparkgolfclub.com
web: www.maxstokeparkgolfclub.com

Parkland with easy walking. Numerous trees and a lake form natural hazards and there are several other water features.

18 Holes, 6442yds, Par 71, SSS 71, Course record 64. Club membership 720.

Visitors Mon-Fri except BHs. Dress code. **Societies** booking required. **Green Fees** not confirmed **Prof** Neil McEwan **Facilities** ⓑ ⓍⓄⓍ ⓑ ⓐ ⓕⓍ ⓐ ⓕⓍ ⓔ ⓐ ⓕ **Conf** Corporate Hospitality Days **Location** 3m E of Coleshill, off B4114 for Maxstoke

Hotel ★★★ 71% CHH Grimstock Country House, Gilson Road, Gilson, COLESHILL ☎ 01675 462121 & 462161 📠 01675 462121
44 en suite

HENLEY-IN-ARDEN
Map 4 SP16

Henley Golf & Country Club Birmingham Rd B95 5QA
☎ 01564 793715   📠 01564 795754
web: www.henleygcc.co.uk

Henley Golf & Country Club: 18 Holes, 6933yds, Par 73, SSS 73.

Course Designer N Selwyn Smith **Location** on A3400 just N of Henley-in-Arden
Telephone for further details

Hotel ★★★★ 77% HL Ardencote Manor Hotel, Country Club & Spa, The Cumsey, Lye Green Road, Claverdon, WARWICK
☎ 01926 843111 📠 01926 843111   110 en suite

KENILWORTH
Map 4 SP27

Kenilworth Crewe Ln CV8 2EA
☎ 01926 858517   📠 01926 864453
e-mail: secretary@kenilworthgolfclub.co.uk
web: www.kenilworthgolfclub.co.uk

Parkland course in an open hilly location. Club founded in 1889.

18 Holes, 6400yds, Par 72, SSS 71, Course record 66. Club membership 755.

Visitors Mon-Sun & BHs. Booking required. Handicap certificate. Dress code. **Societies** booking required. **Green Fees** £36 per day **Course Designer** Hawtree **Prof** Steve Yates **Facilities** ⓑ ⓍⓄⓍ ⓑ ⓐ ⓕⓍ ⓐ ⓕ ⓔ ⓕ ⓐ ⓕ **Leisure** Par 3 chipping green **Conf** facs Corporate Hospitality Days **Location** 0.5m NE

Hotel ★★★ 78% HL Best Western Peacock, 149 Warwick Road, KENILWORTH ☎ 01926 851156 & 864500 📠 01926 851156
29 en suite

LEA MARSTON
Map 4 SP29

Lea Marston Hotel Haunch Ln B76 0BY
☎ 01675 470468   📠 01675 470871
e-mail: info@leamarstonhotel.co.uk
web: www.leamarstonhotel.co.uk

The Marston Lakes course was opened in April 2001. The layout includes many water and sand hazards through undulating parkland. While short by modern standards, it is a good test for even low

continued

handicap players, requiring virtually everything in the bag. Tees and greens have been built to championship course specifications.

Marston Lakes: 9 Holes, 2054yds, Par 31, SSS 30, Course record 57. Club membership 330.

Visitors Mon-Sun & BHs. Booking required. Dress code. **Societies** welcome. **Green Fees** £14 per 18 holes, £9 per 9 holes (£18/£12 weekends) **Course Designer** Contour Golf **Prof** Darren Lewis **Facilities** ⚐ ⚑ ⚒ ⚓ ⚔ ⚕ ⚖ ⚗ ⚘ ⚙ ⚚ **Leisure** hard tennis courts, heated indoor swimming pool, sauna, gymnasium, 9 hole par 3 Academy Course, golf simulator, **Conf** facs Corporate Hospitality Days **Location** M42 junct 9, A4097 towards Kingsbury, 1m right

Lea Marston Hotel

Hotel ★★★★ 72% HL Lea Marston Hotel, Haunch Lane, LEA MARSTON, Sutton Coldfield ☎ 01675 470468 ▤ 01675 470468 88 en suite

LEAMINGTON SPA   Map 4 SP36

Leamington & County Golf Ln, Whitnash CV31 2QA
☎ 01926 425961   ▤ 01926 425961
e-mail: office@leamingtongolf.co.uk
web: www.leamingtongolf.co.uk
Undulating parkland with extensive views.

18 Holes, 6418yds, Par 72, SSS 71, Course record 65. Club membership 854.

Visitors Mon-Sun & BHs. Booking required. Handicap certificate. Dress code. **Societies** booking required. **Green Fees** £35 per round (£40 per round weekends). **Course Designer** H S Colt **Prof** Julian Mellor **Facilities** ⚐ ⚑ ⚒ ⚓ ⚔ ⚕ ⚖ ⚗ **Leisure** snooker. **Conf** facs Corporate Hospitality Days **Location** S of town centre **Hotel** ★★★ HL Mallory Court, Harbury Lane, Bishop's Tachbrook, LEAMINGTON SPA ☎ 01926 330214 ▤ 01926 330214   30 en suite

Newbold Comyn Newbold Terrace East CV32 4EW
☎ 01926 421157
e-mail: ian@viscounts.freeserve.co.uk
web: www.warwickdc.gov.uk/golf
Municipal parkland course with a hilly front nine and little room for error. A downhill par 3 of 107 yards is the signature hole here. The back nine is rather flat and slightly more forgiving but includes two par 5s and the par 4 9th which is a 467yd testing hole.

18 Holes, 6315yds, Par 70, SSS 70, Course record 69. Club membership 150.

Visitors dress code. **Societies** welcome. **Green Fees** 18 holes £11.90, 9 holes £8 (£15/£10.60) **Prof** David Playdon/Andy Hicks **Facilities** ⚐ ⚑ ⚒ ⚓ ⚔ ⚕ ⚖ ⚗ **Leisure** heated indoor swimming pool, gymnasium **Location** 0.75m E of town centre off B4099

LEEK WOOTTON   Map 4 SP26

The Warwickshire CV35 7QT
☎ 01926 409409   ▤ 01926 408409
web: www.theclubcompany.com
Kings: 18 Holes, 7000yds, Par 72, SSS 72, Course record 68.
Earls: 18 Holes, 7421yds, Par 74, SSS 73, Course record 70.
Course Designer Karl Litten **Location** S of village off A46
Telephone for further details
Hotel ★★★★ 80% HL Chesford Grange, Chesford Bridge, KENILWORTH ☎ 01926 859331 ▤ 01926 859331   209 en suite

LOWER BRAILES   Map 4 SP33

Brailes Sutton Ln, Lower Brailes OX15 5BB
☎ 01608 685633   ▤ 01608 685205
e-mail: office@brailesgolfclub.co.uk
web: www.brailesgolfclub.co.uk
Undulating meadowland on 105 acres of Cotswold countryside. Sutton Brook passes through the course and must be crossed five times. The par 5 17th offers the most spectacular view of three counties from the tee. Challenging par 3 short holes. Suitable for golfers of all standards.

18 Holes, 6304yds, Par 71, SSS 70, Course record 67. Club membership 600.

Visitors contact club for details. **Societies** welcome. **Green Fees** £40 per day, £25 per round, £35 weekends (winter £18/£25/£25) **Course Designer** R Baldwin **Prof** Mark McGeehan **Facilities** ⚐ ⚑ ⚒ ⚓ ⚔ ⚕ ⚖ ⚗ ⚘ ⚙ **Conf** facs Corporate Hospitality Days **Location** S of Lower Brailes off B4035 **Hotel** ★★★★ INN The Red Lion, Main Street, SHIPSTON ON STOUR ☎ 01608 684221 ▤ 01608 684221   5 en suite

NUNEATON   Map 4 SP39

Nuneaton Golf Dr CV11 6QF
☎ 024 7634 7810   ▤ 024 7632 7563
18 Holes, 6429yds, Par 71, SSS 71.
Prof Craig Phillips **Facilities** ⚐ ⚑ ⚒ ⚓ ⚔ ⚕ ⚖ ⚗ ⚘ **Location** 2m SE off B4114
Telephone for further details
Hotel ★★★ 68% HL Best Western Weston Hall, Weston Lane, Bulkington, NUNEATON ☎ 024 7631 2989 ▤ 024 7631 2989 40 en suite

Oakridge Arley Ln, Ansley Village CV10 9PH
☎ 01676 541389 & 540542   ▤ 01676 542709
e-mail: shane.lovric@golfatoakridge.com
web: www.oakridgegolf.fsnet.co.uk
The water hazards on the back nine add to the natural beauty of the countryside. The undulating course is affected by winter cross winds on several holes. Overall it will certainly test golfing skills.

Oakridge Golf Course: 18 Holes, 6208yds, Par 71, SSS 71. Club membership 500.

Visitors contact course for details. **Societies** welcome. **Green Fees** not confirmed **Course Designer** Algy Jayes **Facilities** ⚐ ⚑ ⚒ ⚓ ⚔ ⚕ ⚖ ⚗ **Conf** Corporate Hospitality Days **Location** 4m W
Hotel ★★★ 68% HL Best Western Weston Hall, Weston Lane, Bulkington, NUNEATON ☎ 024 7631 2989 ▤ 024 7631 2989 40 en suite

Purley Chase Pipers Ln CV10 0RB
☎ 024 7639 3118   🖷 024 7639 8015
web: www.purley-chase.co.uk
18 Holes, 6772yds, Par 72, SSS 72, Course record 64.
Prof Gary Carver **Facilities** ⑪ 🍴 🕭 ⌸ 🎮 🏌 🛄 🏌 🛺
🏌 **Conf facs** Corporate Hospitality Days **Location** 2m NW off B4114
Telephone for further details
Hotel ★★★ 68% HL Best Western Weston Hall, Weston Lane,
Bulkington, NUNEATON ☎ 024 7631 2989 🖷 024 7631 2989
40 en suite

RUGBY   Map 4 SP57

Rugby Clifton Rd CV21 3RD
☎ 01788 542306 (Sec) & 575134 (Pro)
🖷 01788 542306
e-mail: rugbygolfclub@tiscali.co.uk
web: www.rugbygc.co.uk
A short parkland course across the undulating Clifton valley. Clifton
brook runs through the lower level of the course and comes into play
on seven holes. Accuracy is the prime requirement for a good score.
18 Holes, 5457yds, Par 68, SSS 67, Course record 60.
Club membership 700.
Visitors Mon-Sun except BHs. Handicap certificate. Dress code.
Societies booking required. **Green Fees** £25 per day, £50 per week
Prof David Quinn **Facilities** ⑪ 🍴 🕭 ⌸ 🎮 🏌 🛄 🏌 🛺
Conf facs Corporate Hospitality Days **Location** 1m NE on B5414
Hotel ★★★ 62% HL Grosvenor Hotel Rugby, 81-87 Clifton Road,
RUGBY ☎ 01788 535686 🖷 01788 535686   26 en suite

Whitefields London Rd, Thurlaston CV23 9LF
☎ 01788 521800   🖷 01788 521695
e-mail: mail@draycotehotel.co.uk
web: www.draycotehotel.co.uk

Whitefields has superb natural drainage. There are many water
features and the 13th has a stunning dog-leg 442yd par 4 with a
superb view across Draycote Water. The 16th is completely surrounded
by water and is particularly difficult.
*Whitefields Golf Course: 18 Holes, 6289yds, Par 71,
SSS 70, Course record 64. Club membership 400.*
Visitors Mon-Sun & BHs. Booking required. Dress code.
Societies booking required. **Green Fees** £20 (£25 weekends & BHs)
Course Designer Reg Mason **Prof** David Mills **Facilities** ⑪ 🍴
🕭 ⌸ 🎮 🏌 🛄 🏌 🛺 🏌 🏌 **Leisure** gymnasium
Conf facs Corporate Hospitality Days **Location** M45 junct 1, 0.5m on
A45, on left. W of Dunchurch
Hotel ★★★ 72% HL Golden Lion Hotel, Easenhall, RUGBY
☎ 01788 833577 & 832265 🖷 01788 833577   20 en suite

STONELEIGH   Map 4 SP37

Stoneleigh Deer Park The Clubhouse, The Old Deer Park,
Coventry Rd CV8 3DR
☎ 024 7663 9991 & 7663 9912   🖷 024 7651 1533
Parkland course in old deer park with many mature trees. The River
Avon meanders through the course and comes into play on four holes.
Also a nine-hole par 3 course.
*Tantara Course: 18 Holes, 6056yds, Par 71, SSS 69,
Course record 67. Club membership 750.*
Visitors handicap certificate. Dress code. **Societies** booking required.
Green Fees £20 (£22 Fri, £30 weekends & BHs) **Prof** Matt McGuire
Facilities ⑪ 🍴 🕭 ⌸ 🎮 🏌 🛄 🏌 🏌 **Leisure** 9 hole
par 3 Avon Course **Conf facs** Corporate Hospitality Days **Location** 3m
NE of Kenilworth
Hotel ★★★ 68% HL The Chace, London Road, Toll Bar End,
COVENTRY ☎ 0844 736 8607 🖷 0844 736 8607   66 en suite

STRATFORD-UPON-AVON   Map 4 SP25

Ingon Manor Ingon Ln CV37 0QE
☎ 01789 731857   🖷 01789 731657
web: www.ingonmanor.co.uk
Ingon Manor Golf & Country: 18 Holes, 6623yds, Par 72.
Prof Niel Evans **Facilities** ⑪ 🍴 🕭 ⌸ 🎮 🏌 🛄 🏌 🏌
🏌 🏌 **Conf facs** Corporate Hospitality Days
Telephone for further details
Hotel ★★★★ 85% HL Menzies Welcombe Hotel Spa & Golf
Club, Warwick Road, STRATFORD-UPON-AVON ☎ 01789 295252
🖷 01789 295252   78 en suite

Menzies Welcombe Hotel Spa and Golf Club Warwick Rd
CV37 0NR
☎ 01789 413800   🖷 01789 262028
e-mail: welcombe.golfpro@menzies-hotels.co.uk
web: www.menzieshotels.co.uk

Wooded parkland course of great character and boasting superb views
of the River Avon and Stratford. Set within the hotel's 157-acre estate,
it has two lakes and other water features.
*Menzies Welcombe Hotel Spa and Golf Club:
18 Holes, 6288yds, Par 70, SSS 69, Course record 64.
Club membership 450.*
Visitors Mon-Sun & BHs. Booking required. **Societies** booking
required. **Green Fees** not confirmed **Course Designer** Thomas
Macauley **Prof** Dan Hacker **Facilities** ⑪ 🍴 🕭 ⌸ 🎮 🏌 🛄
🏌 🏌 🏌 🏌 🏌 **Leisure** hard tennis courts, heated indoor
swimming pool, fishing, gymnasium **Conf facs** Corporate Hospitality
Days **Location** 1.5m NE off A46
continued

Hotel ★★★★ 85% HL Menzies Welcombe Hotel Spa & Golf Club, Warwick Road, STRATFORD-UPON-AVON, WARWICKSHIRE ☎ 01789 295252 📄 01789 295252 78 en suite

Stratford Oaks Bearley Rd, Snitterfield CV37 0EZ
☎ 01789 731980 📄 01789 731981
e-mail: admin@stratfordoaks.co.uk
web: www.stratfordoaks.co.uk

American-style, level parkland course with some water features designed by Howard Swan.

Stratford Oaks: 18 Holes, 6232yds, Par 71, SSS 70, Course record 61. Club membership 700.

Visitors Mon-Sun & BHs. Booking required. Dress code. **Societies** booking required. **Green Fees** £25 (£30 weekends) **Course Designer** H Swann **Prof** Andrew Dunbar **Facilities** ⊕ 🍴 ⮜ ⌷ 🍴 ⮐ 🛋 🗟 ⚲ ⮐ **Leisure** gymnasium, massage and physiotherapy facility **Conf** Corporate Hospitality Days **Location** 4m N of Stratford-upon-Avon

Hotel ★★★★ 77% HL Stratford Manor, Warwick Road, STRATFORD-UPON-AVON ☎ 01789 731173 📄 01789 731173 104 en suite

Stratford-on-Avon Tiddington Rd CV37 7BA
☎ 01789 205749 📄 01789 414909
e-mail: sec@stratfordgolf.co.uk
web: www.stratfordgolf.co.uk

Beautiful parkland course. The par 3 16th is tricky and the par 5 17th and 18th provide a tough end.

18 Holes, 6274yds, Par 72, SSS 70, Course record 63. Club membership 750.

Visitors contact club for details. **Societies** booking required. **Green Fees** not confirmed **Course Designer** Taylor **Prof** J Dodsworth **Facilities** ⊕ 🍴 ⮜ ⌷ 🍴 ⮐ 🛋 🗟 ⚲ ⮐ ⚲
Location 0.75m E on B4086
Hotel ★★★★ 79% HL Macdonald Alveston Manor, Clopton Bridge, STRATFORD-UPON-AVON ☎ 0844 879 9138 📄 0844 879 9138 113 en suite

TANWORTH IN ARDEN   Map 7 SP17

Ladbrook Park Poolhead Ln B94 5ED
☎ 01564 742264 📄 01564 742909
e-mail: secretary@ladbrookparkgolf.co.uk
web: www.ladbrookparkgolf.co.uk

Parkland course lined with mature trees up to 100 years old.

18 Holes, 6500yds, Par 71, SSS 71, Course record 65. Club membership 700.

Visitors Mon-Fri & BHs. Booking required. Handicap certificate. Dress code. **Societies** booking required. **Green Fees** £45 per 36 holes, £45 per 28 holes, £40 per 18 holes **Course Designer** H S Colt **Prof** Richard Mountford **Facilities** ⊕ 🍴 ⮜ ⌷ 🍴 ⮐ 🛋 🗟 ⚲ 🛋 ⚲
Location M42 junct 3, 2.5m SE
Hotel ★★★ 87% HL Nuthurst Grange Country House & Restaurant, Nuthurst Grange Lane, HOCKLEY HEATH ☎ 01564 783972 📄 01564 783972 19 en suite

WARWICK   Map 4 SP26

Warwick The Racecourse CV34 6HW
☎ 01926 494316

Easy walking parkland. Driving range with floodlit bays.

9 Holes, 2682yds, Par 34, SSS 66, Course record 67. Club membership 150.

Visitors contact club for details. **Societies** welcome. **Green Fees** £7.50 per 9 holes (£8 weekends) **Course Designer** D G Dunkley **Prof** Mario Luca **Facilities** 🍴 ⮜ 🗟 ⮐ ⚲ ⮐ **Location** W of town centre
Hotel ★★★★ 77% HL Ardencote Manor Hotel, Country Club & Spa, The Cumsey, Lye Green Road, Claverdon, WARWICK ☎ 01926 843111 📄 01926 843111 110 en suite

WISHAW   Map 7 SP19

The Belfry see page 263
Wishaw B76 9PR
☎ 01675 470301 📄 01675 470256
e-mail: enquiries@thebelfry.com
web: www.TheBelfry.com

WEST MIDLANDS

ALDRIDGE   Map 7 SK00

Druids Heath Stonnall Rd WS9 8JZ
☎ 01922 455595 (Office) 📄 01922 452887
e-mail: dhgcadmin@talktalkbusiness.net
web: www.druidsheathgc.co.uk

Testing, undulating heathland course. Large greens with subtle slopes. Excellent natural drainage gives good winter play.

18 Holes, 6665yds, Par 72, SSS 73, Course record 68. Club membership 660.

Visitors Mon-Sun except BHs. Booking required. Dress code. **Societies** booking required **Green Fees** £40 per day (£43 weekends pm only)) **Prof** Glenn Williams **Facilities** ⊕ 🍴 ⮜ ⌷ 🍴 ⮜ 🗟 ⚲ **Leisure** snooker **Conf** Corporate Hospitality Days **Location** NE of town centre off A454
Hotel ★★★ 85% HL Fairlawns Hotel & Spa, 178 Little Aston Road, WALSALL ☎ 01922 455122 📄 01922 455122 59 en suite

BIRMINGHAM   Map 7 SP08

Alison Nicholas Golf Academy Host Centre, Queslett Park, Great Barr B42 2RG
☎ 0121 360 7600 📄 0121 360 7603
e-mail: info@ the hostcorporation.com
web: www.thehostcorporation.com

This golf academy consists of a nine-hole short game improvement course, a covered floodlit driving range and teaching and training facilities.

Alison Nicholas Golf Academy: 9 Holes, 905yds, Par 27, SSS 27, Course record 21.

Visitors Mon-Sun & BHs. **Societies** welcome. **Green Fees** phone. **Course Designer** Alison Nicholas/Francis Colella **Prof** Andy Gorman/Alison Nicholas **Facilities** ⮜ ⌷ 🍴 🗟 ⮐ ⚲ **Conf** facs Corporate Hospitality Days **Location** M6 junct 7
Hotel BUD Innkeeper's Lodge Birmingham Sutton Coldfield, Chester Road, Streetley, SUTTON COLDFIELD ☎ 0845 112 6065 📄 0845 112 6065 66 en suite

THE BELFRY

WARWICKSHIRE - WISHAW - MAP 7 SP19

The Belfry is unique as the only venue to have staged the biggest golf event in the world, the Ryder Cup matches, an unprecedented four times, most recently in 2002. The Brabazon is regarded throughout the world as a great championship course with some of the most demanding holes in golf; the 10th (Ballesteros's Hole) and the 18th, with its dangerous lakes and its amphitheatre around the final green, are world famous. Alternatively, you can pit your wits against a new legend in the making, the PGA National Course, which has won plaudits from near and far. The Dave Thomas and Peter Alliss designed course has been used for professional competition and is already established as one of Britain's leading courses. For those who like their golf a little easier or like to get back into the swing gently, The Derby is ideal and can be played by golfers of any standard.

Wishaw B76 9PR ☎ 01675 470301 📄 01675 470256
e-mail: enquiries@thebelfry.com
web: www.TheBelfry.com
The Brabazon: 18 Holes, 7196yds, Par 72, SSS 71.
PGA National: 18 Holes, 7033yds, Par 72.
The Derby: 18 Holes, 6057yds, Par 69, SSS 69. **Club membership 450.**
Visitors Mon-Sun & BHs. Booking required for non-residents. Handicap certificate. Dress code. **Societies** booking required. **Green Fees** Brabazon £140 per round, PGA £70, Derby £40. Reduced winter rates **Course Designer** Dave Thomas/Peter Alliss **Prof** Gary Alliss **Facilities** ⑪ 🍴 📶 🖫 🚡 🏠 ⛳ ◇ 🏌 🛒 ⛳ 🏌
Leisure hard tennis courts, heated indoor swimming pool, squash, sauna, gymnasium, PGA National Golf Academy **Conf** facs Corporate Hospitality Days **Location** M42 junct 9, 4m E on A446
Hotel ★★★★ 72% HL Lea Marston Hotel, Haunch Lane, LEA MARSTON, Sutton Coldfield ☎ 01675 470468 📄 01675 470468 88 en suite

Cocks Moors Woods Alcester Road South B14 4ER
☎ 0121 464 3584   📄 0121 441 1305

18 Holes, 5769yds, Par 69, SSS 68.

Prof Steve Ellis **Facilities** ⊕ ⍩ ⑂ ⌷ ⌷ ⌷ ⌷ ⌷ ⍩ ⌷
Leisure heated indoor swimming pool, gymnasium **Location** M42 junct 3, 4m N on A435
Telephone for further details
Hotel ★★★ 68% HL Corus, Stratford Road, Shirley, SOLIHULL
☎ 0844 736 8605 & 0121 745 0400 📄 0844 736 8605   111 en suite

Edgbaston Church Rd, Edgbaston B15 3TB
☎ 0121 454 1736   📄 0121 454 2395
e-mail: secretary@edgbastongc.co.uk
web: www.edgbastongc.co.uk

Set in 144 acres of woodland, lake and parkland, 2m from the centre of Birmingham, this delightful course utilises the wealth of natural features to provide a series of testing and adventurous holes set in the traditional double loop that starts directly in front of the clubhouse, an imposing Georgian mansion.

18 Holes, 6106yds, Par 69, SSS 69, Course record 63.
Club membership 950.

Visitors Mon-Sun & BHs. Booking required weekends. Handicap certificate. Dress code. **Societies** booking required **Green Fees** £47 per 18 holes (£57 weekends & BHs) **Course Designer** H S Colt
Prof Jamie Cundy **Facilities** ⊕ ⍩ ⑂ ⌷ ⌷ ⌷ ⌷ ⍩ ⌷
⌷ ⋐ ⌷ **Conf** facs Corporate Hospitality Days **Location** 2m S of city centre on B4217, off A38
Hotel ★★★ 80% HL Menzies Strathallan, 225 Hagley Road, Edgbaston, BIRMINGHAM ☎ 0121 455 9777 📄 0121 455 9777
135 en suite

Great Barr Chapel Ln B43 7BA
☎ 0121 358 4376   📄 0121 358 4376
web: www.greatbarrgolfclub.co.uk

18 Holes, 6523yds, Par 72, SSS 72, Course record 67.

Prof Richard Spragg **Facilities** ⊕ ⍩ ⑂ ⌷ ⌷ ⌷ ⍩
Conf Corporate Hospitality Days **Location** 6m N of city centre off A 34
Telephone for further details
Hotel BUD Innkeeper's Lodge Birmingham Sutton Coldfield, Chester Road, Streetley, SUTTON COLDFIELD ☎ 0845 112 6065
📄 0845 112 6065   66 en suite

Handsworth 11 Sunningdale Close, Handsworth Wood B20 1NP
☎ 0121 554 3387   📄 0121 554 6144
e-mail: info@handsworthgolfclub.net

Undulating parkland with some tight fairways and strategic bunkering with a number of well-placed water features.

18 Holes, 6289yds, Par 70, SSS 71, Course record 64.
Club membership 730.

Visitors Mon-Fri except BHs. Dress code. **Societies** booking required. **Green Fees** not confirmed **Course Designer** H. S. Colt
Prof Lee Bashford **Facilities** ⊕ ⍩ ⑂ ⌷ ⌷ ⌷ ⌷ ⍩
⋐ ⌷ **Leisure** squash, fishing **Conf** Corporate Hospitality Days **Location** 3.5m NW of city centre off A4040
Hotel ★★★ 66% HL Great Barr Hotel & Conference Centre, Pear Tree Drive, Newton Road, Great Barr, BIRMINGHAM ☎ 0121 357 1141
📄 0121 357 1141   105 en suite

Harborne 40 Tennal Rd, Harborne B32 2JE
☎ 0121 427 3058   📄 0121 427 4039
e-mail: adrian@harbornegolfclub.org
web: www.harbornegolfclub.co.uk

Parkland course in a hilly location, with a brook running through.

18 Holes, 6230yds, Par 70, SSS 70, Course record 65.
Club membership 600.

Visitors Mon-Fri except BHs. Booking required. Handicap certificate. Dress code. **Societies** welcome. **Green Fees** not confirmed **Course Designer** Harry Colt **Prof** Stewart Mathews **Facilities** ⊕ ⍩ ⑂
⌷ ⑂ ⌷ ⍩ ⌷ **Conf** facs Corporate Hospitality Days
Location 3.5 m SW of city centre off A4040
Hotel ★★★ 80% HL Menzies Strathallan, 225 Hagley Road, Edgbaston, BIRMINGHAM ☎ 0121 455 9777 📄 0121 455 9777
135 en suite

Harborne Church Farm Vicarage Rd B17 0SN
☎ 0121 427 1204   📄 0121 428 3126

9 Holes, 2441yds, Par 66, SSS 64, Course record 62.
Prof Paul Johnson **Facilities** ⊕ ⍩ ⌷ ⌷ ⍩ ⌷
Leisure practice net **Location** 3.5m SW of city centre off A4040
Telephone for further details
Hotel ★★★ 80% HL Menzies Strathallan, 225 Hagley Road, Edgbaston, BIRMINGHAM ☎ 0121 455 9777 📄 0121 455 9777
135 en suite

Hatchford Brook Coventry Rd, Sheldon B26 3PY
☎ 0121 743 9821   📄 0121 743 3420
e-mail: idt@hbgc.freeserve.co.uk
web: golfpro-direct.co.uk

Fairly flat, municipal parkland course.

Hatchford Brook Golf Course: 18 Holes, 6155yds, Par 69, SSS 70. Club membership 280.

Visitors Mon-Sun & BHs. Dress code. **Societies** booking required.
Green Fees not confirmed **Prof** Mark Hampton **Facilities** ⊕ ⑂ ⌷
⑂ ⌷ ⍩ ⌷ **Location** 6m E of city centre on A45
Hotel ★★★ 77% HL Novotel Birmingham Airport, BIRMINGHAM AIRPORT ☎ 0121 782 7000 & 782 4111 📄 0121 782 7000
195 en suite

Hilltop Park Ln, Handsworth B21 8LJ
☎ 0121 554 4463

A good test of golf with interesting layout, undulating fairways and large greens, located in the Sandwell Valley conservation area.

Hilltop Public Golf Course: 18 Holes, 6208yds, Par 71, SSS 70, Course record 65. Club membership 200.

Visitors booking required. **Societies** booking required. **Green Fees** 18 holes £14, 9 holes £8.50 (£16/£8.50 weekends & BHs)
Course Designer Hawtree **Prof** Kevin Highfield **Facilities** ⊕ ⍩ ⑂
⌷ ⑂ ⌷ ⍩ ⌷ ⋐ ⌷ **Conf** facs Corporate Hospitality Days
Location M5 junct 1, 1m on A41
Hotel ★★★ 66% HL Great Barr Hotel & Conference Centre, Pear Tree Drive, Newton Road, Great Barr, BIRMINGHAM ☎ 0121 357 1141
📄 0121 357 1141   105 en suite

Lickey Hills Rosehill, Rednal B45 8RR
☎ 0121 453 3159   📄 0121 457 8779

Undulating parkland course with far reaching views and banks of forest pines.

Lickey Hills Golf Course: 18 Holes, 5835yds, Par 69, SSS 68. Club membership 150.

continued

Visitors Mon-Sun & BHs. Booking required. **Societies** booking required. **Green Fees** £16 per 18 holes, £10 per 9 holes **Prof** Mark Toombs **Facilities** ⓘ 🍴 ⬛ ⌁ 🏠 ⚑ ◇ ✧ **Leisure** hard tennis courts **Conf** facs Corporate Hospitality Days **Location** 10m SW of city centre on B4096
Hotel ★★★ 70% HL The Westmead Hotel, Redditch Road, Hopwood, BIRMINGHAM ☎ 0870 609 6119 📄 0870 609 6119 56 en suite

Moseley Springfield Rd, Kings Heath B14 7DX
☎ 0121 444 4957   📄 0121 441 4662
e-mail: secretary@moseleygolfclub.co.uk
web: www.moseleygolfclub.co.uk

Parkland with a lake, pond and a stream providing natural hazards. The par 3 4th goes through a cutting in woodland to a tree and garden-lined amphitheatre, and the par 4 5th entails a drive over a lake to a dog-leg fairway.

18 Holes, 6300yds, Par 70, SSS 71, Course record 63. Club membership 600.
Visitors Mon-Sun & BHs. Booking required weekends & BHs. Handicap certificate. Dress code. **Societies** booking required. **Green Fees** £40 per round **Course Designer** H S Colt with others **Prof** Martin Griffin **Facilities** ⓘ 🍴 ⬛ ⌁ 🏠 ⚑ ✧ **Conf** facs Corporate Hospitality Days **Location** 4m S of city centre on B4146
Hotel ★★ 75% HL Copperfield House, 60 Upland Road, Selly Park, BIRMINGHAM ☎ 0121 472 8344 📄 0121 472 8344   17 en suite

North Worcestershire Frankley Beeches Rd, Northfield B31 5LP
☎ 0121 475 1047   📄 0121 476 8681
Designed by James Braid and established in 1907, this is a mature parkland course. Tree plantations rather than heavy rough are the main hazards.
North Worcestershire Golf Course: 18 Holes, 5959yds, Par 69, SSS 68, Course record 64. Club membership 600.
Visitors contact course for details. **Societies** welcome. **Green Fees** £37 per day, £25 per round **Course Designer** James Braid **Prof** Dan Cummins **Facilities** ⓘ 🍴 ⬛ ⌁ 🏠 ⚑ 🛒 ✧ **Location** 7m SW of Birmingham city centre, off A38
Hotel ★★★ 70% HL The Westmead Hotel, Redditch Road, Hopwood, BIRMINGHAM ☎ 0870 609 6119 📄 0870 609 6119 56 en suite

Warley Woods The Pavilion, 101 Lightwoods Hill, Smethwick B67 5ED
☎ 0121 429 2440
e-mail: golfshop@warleywoods.org.uk
web: www.warleywoods.org.uk/golf
Municipal parkland course in Warley Woods. New out of bounds areas

and bunkers have tightened the course considerably with further improvement following tree planting. Part of a community trust in liaison with English Heritage.
Warley Woods Golf Course: 9 Holes, 5346yds, Par 66, SSS 66, Course record 64. Club membership 200.
Visitors Mon-Sun & BHs. Booking required weekends & BHs. Dress code. **Societies** welcome **Green Fees** phone **Prof** S Matthews **Facilities** ⓘ 🍴 ⬛ ⌁ 🏠 ⚑ 🛒 ✧ **Leisure** practice nets **Conf** facs Corporate Hospitality Days **Location** 4m W of city centre off A456
Hotel BUD Innkeeper's Lodge Birmingham West (Quinton), 563 Hagley Road West, Quinton, BIRMINGHAM ☎ 0845 112 6066 📄 0845 112 6066   24 en suite

---

COVENTRY   Map 4 SP37

Ansty Golf Centre Brinklow Rd, Ansty CV7 9JL
☎ 024 7662 1341   📄 024 7660 2568
e-mail: info@anstygolfcentre.co.uk
An 18-hole pay and play parkland course of two nine-hole loops. Open all year round.
Ansty Golf Centre: 18 Holes, 6079yds, Par 71, SSS 69, Course record 66.
Visitors Mon-Sun & BHs. Dress code. **Societies** booking required. **Green Fees** £15 per 18 holes (£20 weekends & BHs). Academy £5 (£6 weekends and BHs) **Course Designer** David Morgan **Prof** M Goodwin/L Melling/S Webster **Facilities** ⓘ 🍴 ⬛ ⌁ 🍴 ⌁ 🏠 ⚑ ✧ 🛒 ✧ **Leisure** par 3 course **Conf** facs Corporate Hospitality Days **Location** M6/M69 junct 2, 1m signposted
Hotel ★★★ 72% HL Novotel Coventry, Wilsons Lane, COVENTRY ☎ 024 7636 5000 📄 024 7636 5000   98 en suite

Coventry St Martins Rd, Finham Park CV3 6RJ
☎ 024 7641 4152   📄 024 7669 0131
e-mail: secretary@coventrygolfclub.net
web: www.coventrygolfclub.net
The scene of several major professional events, this undulating parkland course has a great deal of quality. More than that, it usually plays its length, and thus scoring is never easy, as many professionals have found to their cost.
18 Holes, 6601yds, Par 73, SSS 73, Course record 66. Club membership 750.
Visitors Mon-Fri except BHs. Handicap certificate. Dress code. **Societies** booking required **Green Fees** £50 per day **Course Designer** Vardon Bros/Hawtree **Prof** Philip Weaver **Facilities** ⓘ 🍴 ⬛ ⌁ 🍴 ⌁ 🏠 ⚑ 🛒 ✧ **Conf** Corporate Hospitality Days **Location** 3m S of city centre on B4113
Hotel ★★★ 68% HL The Chace, London Road, Toll Bar End, COVENTRY ☎ 0844 736 8607 📄 0844 736 8607   66 en suite

Coventry Hearsall Beechwood Av CV5 6DF
☎ 024 7671 3470   📄 024 7669 1534
Parkland with fairly easy walking. A brook provides an interesting hazard.
18 Holes, 6005yds, Par 70, SSS 69. Club membership 650.
Visitors Mon-Sun & BHs. Booking required. Handicap certificate. Dress code. **Societies** welcome. **Green Fees** not confirmed **Prof** Mike Tarn **Facilities** ⓘ 🍴 ⬛ ⌁ 🏠 ⚑ ◇ ✧ ✧ **Leisure** hard and grass tennis courts, outdoor and indoor heated swimming pool **Location** 1.5m SW of city centre off A429
Hotel ★★★ 68% HL The Chace, London Road, Toll Bar End, COVENTRY ☎ 0844 736 8607 📄 0844 736 8607   66 en suite

Windmill Village Hotel Golf & Leisure Club Birmingham Rd, Allesley CV5 9AL
☎ 024 7640 4041 📠 024 7640 4042
e-mail: leisure@windmillvillagehotel.co.uk
web: www.windmillvillagehotel.co.uk

An attractive 18-hole course over rolling parkland with plenty of trees and two lakes that demand shots over open water. Four challenging par 5 holes.

Windmill Village Golf & Leisure Club:
18 Holes, 5184yds, Par 70, SSS 66, Course record 63.
Club membership 600.

Visitors Mon-Sun & BHs. Booking required Fri-Sun & BHs. Dress code. **Societies** booking required. **Green Fees** £20 (£16 off peak) **Course Designer** Robert Hunter **Prof** Robert Hunter **Facilities** ⓣ ⓘⓞⓘ ⓑ 🖥 🍴 🚶 🏠 ⛳ ◇ ♥ 🚗 ⛳ **Leisure** hard tennis courts, heated indoor swimming pool, sauna, gymnasium, practice nets. **Conf** facs Corporate Hospitality Days **Location** 3m W of Coventry on A45

Hotel ★★★ 70% HL Brooklands Grange Hotel & Restaurant, Holyhead Road, COVENTRY ☎ 024 7660 1601 📠 024 7660 1601 31 en suite

---

DUDLEY   Map 7 SO99

Dudley Turner's Hill, Rowley Regis B65 9DP
☎ 01384 233877 📠 01384 233877
e-mail: secretary@dudleygolfclub.com
web: www.dudleygolfclub.com

A challenging parkland course for the average golfer but rewarding for its fine scenery and sense of achievement.

18 Holes, 5714yds, Par 69, SSS 68, Course record 63.
Club membership 420.

Visitors Mon-Sun & BHs. Booking required weekends & BHs. Handicap certificate. Dress code. **Societies** booking required **Green Fees** £15 per 18 holes (£20 weekends) **Prof** Gary Kilmister **Facilities** ⓣ ⓘⓞⓘ ⓑ 🖥 🍴 🚶 🏠 ♥ 🚗 ⛳ **Leisure** snooker **Conf** facs Corporate Hospitality Days **Location** 2m S of town centre off B4171 **Hotel** ★★★★ 73% HL Copthorne Hotel Merry Hill - Dudley, The Waterfront, Level Street, Brierley Hill, DUDLEY ☎ 01384 482882 📠 01384 482882 138 en suite

Swindon Bridgnorth Rd, Swindon DY3 4PU
☎ 01902 897031 📠 01902 326219
e-mail: admin@swindongolfclub.co.uk
web: www.swindongolfclub.co.uk

Attractive, undulating woodland and parkland with spectacular views.

Old Course: 18 Holes, 6121yds, Par 71, SSS 70.
Club membership 600.

Visitors Mon-Sun & BHs. Booking advisable. Dress code. **Societies** booking required. **Green Fees** not confirmed **Facilities** ⓣ ⓘⓞⓘ ⓑ 🖥 🍴 🚶 🏠 🚗 ♥ ⛳ **Leisure** fishing **Conf** facs Corporate Hospitality Days **Location** 4m W of Dudley on B4176 **Hotel** ★★★ 77% HL Patshull Park Hotel Golf & Country Club, Patshull Park, PATTINGHAM ☎ 01902 700100 📠 01902 700100 49 en suite

---

HALESOWEN   Map 7 SO98

Halesowen The Leasowes, Leasowes Ln B62 8QF
☎ 0121 501 3606 📠 0121 501 3606
e-mail: office@halesowengc.co.uk
web: www.halesowengc..co.uk

Parkland course within the only Grade I listed park in the Midlands.

18 Holes, 5754yds, Par 69, SSS 69, Course record 64.
Club membership 625.

Visitors contact club for details. **Societies** booking required. **Green Fees** £34 per day, £28 per round **Prof** Jon Nicholas **Facilities** ⓣ ⓘⓞⓘ ⓑ 🖥 🍴 🚶 🏠 ⛳ ♥ 🚗 ⛳ **Conf** facs Corporate Hospitality Days **Location** M5 junct 3, 1m E, off Manor Ln **Hotel** ★★★ 71% HL Quality Hotel Dudley, Birmingham Road, DUDLEY ☎ 01384 458070 📠 01384 458070 72 en suite

---

KNOWLE   Map 7 SP17

Copt Heath 1220 Warwick Rd B93 9LN
☎ 01564 731620 📠 01564 731621
e-mail: golf@copt-heath.co.uk
web: coptheathgolf.co.uk

Flat heathland and parkland course designed by H Vardon.

18 Holes, 6190yds, Par 71, SSS 69, Course record 62.
Club membership 700.

Visitors Mon-Sun except BHs. Booking required Tue & weekends. Handicap certificate. Dress code. **Societies** booking required. **Green Fees** £55 per day, £45 per round **Course Designer** H Vardon **Prof** Brian J Barton **Facilities** ⓣ ⓘⓞⓘ ⓑ 🖥 🍴 🚶 🏠 ♥ 🚗 ⛳ **Conf** Corporate Hospitality Days **Location** M42 junct 5, 0.5m S on A4141 **Hotel** ★★★ 77% HL Ramada Solihull/Birmingham, The Square, SOLIHULL ☎ 0121 711 2121 & 0844 815 9011 📠 0121 711 2121 145 en suite

---

MERIDEN   Map 4 SP28

Marriott Forest of Arden Golf & Country Club
see page 267
Maxstoke Ln CV7 7HR
☎ 0870 400 7272 📠 0870 400 7372
web: www.marriotthotels.com/cvtgs

North Warwickshire Hampton Ln CV7 7LL
☎ 01676 522259 (shop) & 522915 (sec)
📠 01676 523004
e-mail: nwgcltd@btconnect.com

Heathland course with easy walking. Very quick drying.

9 Holes, 6390yds, Par 72, SSS 71, Course record 65.
Club membership 425.

Visitors Mon-Sun & BHs. Booking required weekends & BHs. Handicap certificate. Dress code. **Societies** booking required. **Green Fees** £25

continued

MARRIOTT FOREST OF ARDEN

WEST MIDLANDS - MERIDEN - MAP 4 SP28

This is one of the finest golf destinations in the UK, with a range of facilities to impress every golfer. The jewel in the crown is the Arden championship parkland course, set in 10,000 acres of the Packington Estate. Designed by Donald Steel, it presents one of the country's most spectacular challenges and has hosted a succession of international tournaments, including the British Masters and English Open. Beware the 18th hole, which is enough to stretch the nerves of any golfer. The shorter Aylesford Course offers a varied and enjoyable challenge, which golfers of all abilities will find rewarding. Golf events are a speciality, and there is a golf academy and extensive leisure facilities.

Maxstoke Ln CV7 7HR ☎ 0870 400 7272 🖹 0870 400 7372
web: www.marriotthotels.com/cvtgs
Arden Course: 18 Holes, 6707yds, Par 72, SSS 73, Course record 63.
Aylesford Course: 18 Holes, 5801yds, Par 69, SSS 68. Club membership 800.
Visitors Mon-Sun & BHs. Booking required. Handicap certificate. Dress code. **Societies** booking required. **Green Fees** not confirmed **Course Designer** Donald Steele **Prof** Philip Hoye **Facilities** 🏌 🖼 ⛳ ◇ 🏌 🛥 ⛳ 🏌
Leisure hard tennis courts, heated indoor swimming pool, fishing, sauna, gymnasium, croquet lawn, health and beauty salon, steam room, jacuzzi, aerobics studio **Conf** facs Corporate Hospitality Days **Location** M42 junct 6, A45 towards Coventry, straight on at Stonebridge flyover, after 1-5m turn left into Shepherds Lane and follow signs, Hotel 2m on left
Hotel ★★★★ 79% CHH Marriott Forest of Arden Hotel & Country Club, Maxstoke Lane, MERIDEN
☎ 0870 400 7272 🖹 0870 400 7272 214 en suite

per round (£27 weekends & BHs) **Prof** Andrew Bownes **Facilities** ⓣ by prior arrangement ⓞ by prior arrangement 🏌 ⌑ ⛳ 🍴 🛈 ⌒ 📷 🅿
✦ **Location** 1m SW on B4102
Hotel ★★★ 82% HL Manor, Main Road, MERIDEN, Coventry
☎ 01676 522735 🖷 01676 522735 110 en suite

Stonebridge Golf Centre Somers Rd CV7 7PL
☎ 01676 522442 🖷 01676 522447
e-mail: info@stonebridgegolf.co.uk
web: www.stonebridgegolf.co.uk

A parkland course set in 170 acres with towering oak trees, lakes, and the River Blythe on its borders. An additional 9 holes were added in 2007 to make this a 27 hole course, the new holes are very distinctive and blend with the original18 holes. New lakes have been constructed with water coming in to play on three of the new holes.

Stonebridge Golf Club: 27 Holes, 6102yds, Par 70, SSS 70, Course record 67. Club membership 500.

Visitors Mon-Sun & BHs. Dress code. **Societies** booking required. **Green Fees** £19 per 18 holes (£20 Fri, £25 weekends & BHs) **Course Designer** Mark Jones **Prof** Darren Murphy **Facilities** ⓣ ⓞ 🏌 ⌑ 🍴 🛈 ⛳ ✦ 🏌 ✦ **Leisure** fishing, golf academy **Conf** facs Corporate Hospitality Days **Location** M42 junct 6, 3m
Hotel 74% Best Western Stade Court, West Parade, HYTHE
☎ 01303 268263 🖷 01303 268263 42 en suite

SEDGLEY Map 7 SO99

Sedgley Golf Centre Sandyfields Rd DY3 3DL
☎ 01902 880503
e-mail: sedgleygolf@yahoo.co.uk

Public pay and play course. Undulating contours and mature trees with extensive views over surrounding countryside.

Sedgley Golf Centre: 9 Holes, 3147yds, Par 72, SSS 70. Club membership 100.

Visitors Mon-Sun & BHs. **Societies** welcome. **Green Fees** not confirmed **Course Designer** W G Cox **Prof** Garry Mercer **Facilities** ⌑ ⌒ ✦ 🏌 **Location** 0.5m from town centre off A463
Hotel BUD Innkeeper's Lodge Dudley Kingswinford, Swindon Road, KINGSWINFORD ☎ 0845 112 6069 🖷 0845 112 6069 22 en suite

SOLIHULL Map 7 SP17

Olton Mirfield Rd B91 1JH
☎ 0121 704 1936 🖷 0121 711 2010
e-mail: oltongolfclub@tiscali.co.uk
web: www.oltongolf.co.uk

Testing parkland course, over 100 years old, close to the town centre but in a secluded position.

18 Holes, 6230yds, Par 69, SSS 70, Course record 63. Club membership 700.

Visitors Mon-Fri except BHs. Booking required. Handicap certficate. Dress code. **Societies** welcome. **Green Fees** £50 per 36 holes, £45 per 27 holes, £40 per 18 holes **Course Designer** J H Taylor **Prof** Charles Haynes **Facilities** ⓣ ⓞ 🏌 ⌑ 🍴 ⌒ 🛈 ⛳ ✦ 🏌 ✦ **Leisure** snooker **Conf** Corporate Hospitality Days **Location** M42 junct 5, A41 for 1.5m
Hotel ★★★★ 77% HL Holiday Inn Solihull, 61 Homer Road, SOLIHULL ☎ 0870 2255 401 🖷 0870 2255 401 120 en suite

Robin Hood St Bernards Rd B92 7DJ
☎ 0121 706 0061 🖷 0121 700 7502
e-mail: manager@robinhoodgolfclub.co.uk
web: www.robinhoodgolfclub.co.uk

Pleasant parkland with easy walking and good views. Tree-lined fairways and varied holes, culminating in two excellent finishing holes.

18 Holes, 6506yds, Par 72, SSS 72, Course record 68. Club membership 650.

Visitors Mon-Sun & BHs. Booking required. Handicap certificate. Dress code. **Societies** booking required. **Green Fees** £35 per 18 holes **Course Designer** H S Colt **Prof** Alan Harvey **Facilities** ⓣ ⓞ 🏌 ⌑ 🍴 ⌒ 🛈 ⛳ ✦ **Conf** facs Corporate Hospitality Days **Location** 2m W off B4025
Hotel ★★★ 82% HL Best Western Westley, 80-90 Westley Road, Acocks Green, BIRMINGHAM ☎ 0121 706 4312 🖷 0121 706 4312 37 en suite

Shirley Stratford Rd, Monkspath, Shirley B90 4EW
☎ 0121 744 6001 🖷 0121 746 5645
e-mail: shirleygolfclub@btclick.com
web: www.shirleygolfclub.co.uk

Undulating parkland course in the Blythe Valley, with water features and surrounded by woodland.

18 Holes, 6510yds, Par 72, SSS 71, Course record 65. Club membership 600.

Visitors Mon-Fri & BHs. Dress code. **Societies** booking required. **Green Fees** £35 per day **Prof** S Bottrill **Facilities** ⓣ ⓞ 🏌 ⌑ 🍴 ⌒ 🛈 ⛳ ✦ 🏌 ✦ 🏌 **Leisure** halfway house **Conf** facs Corporate Hospitality Days **Location** M42 junct 4, 0.5m N on A34
Hotel ★★★ 68% HL Corus, Stratford Road, Shirley, SOLIHULL ☎ 0844 736 8605 & 0121 745 0400 🖷 0844 736 8605 111 en suite

West Midlands Marsh House Farm Ln, Barston B92 0LB
☎ 01675 444890 🖷 01675 444891
e-mail: bookings@wmgc.co.uk
web: www.wmgc.co.uk

Course built to USGA specification with no temporary greens or tees. The 18th hole is a par 3 to an island green totally surrounded by water. A continuous buggy path allows use of buggies all year round.

18 Holes, 6624yds, Par 72, SSS 72, Course record 65. Club membership 750.

Visitors Mon-Sun & BHs. Dress code. **Societies** booking required. **Green Fees** £25 (£30 weekends) **Course Designer** Nigel & Mark Harrhy/David Griffith **Prof** Alan Roach **Facilities** ⓣ ⓞ 🏌 ⌑ 🍴 ⛳ 🛈 🏌 ✦ **Leisure** fishing **Conf** facs Corporate Hospitality Days **Location** from NEC A45 towards Coventry for 0.5m, onto A452 towards Leamington, club on right behind Mercedes dealership *continued*

Hotel ★★★ 70% HL Arden Hotel & Leisure Club, Coventry Road, Bickenhill, SOLIHULL ☎ 01675 443221 ▤ 01675 443221 216 en suite

Widney Manor Saintbury Dr, Widney Manor B91 3SZ

☎ 0121 704 0704 ▤ 0121 704 7999
e-mail: bookings@wmgc.co.uk
web: www.wmgc.co.uk

Parkland course of medium length, fairly easy walking, it is ideal for beginners and improvers. Other facilities include a driving range, all weather greens built to USGA specification and buggy paths.

18 Holes, 5654yards, Par 71, SSS 66.
Club membership 650.

Visitors Mon-Sun & BHs. Dress code. **Societies** booking required.
Green Fees not confirmed **Course Designer** Nigel & Mark Harrhy **Prof** Tim Atkinson **Facilities** ⑪ ⑨ ⑤ ☐ ⑨ ⑦ △ 🕒 🕒 ⑦
🏌 **Leisure** sauna, gymnasium **Conf** facs Corporate Hospitality Days **Location** M42 junct 4, signs to Monkspath
Hotel ★★★★ 77% HL Holiday Inn Solihull, 61 Homer Road, SOLIHULL ☎ 0870 2255 401 ▤ 0870 2255 401 120 en suite

STOURBRIDGE   Map 7 SO88

Hagley Golf & Country Club Wassell Grove Ln, Hagley DY9 9JW

☎ 01562 883701 ▤ 01562 887518
e-mail: manager@hagleygcc.freeserve.co.uk
web: www.hagleygolfandcountryclub.co.uk

Undulating parkland course beneath the Clent Hills with superb views. Challenging, especially the testing 15th, par 5, 559yds, named Monster or Card Destroyer.

Hagley Golf & Country Club: 18 Holes, 6353yds, Par 72, SSS 72, Course record 66. Club membership 700.

Visitors Mon-Fri except BHs. Dress code. **Societies** welcome. **Green Fees** £36 per day, £31 per 18 holes **Course Designer** Garratt & Co **Prof** Paul Johnson **Facilities** ⑪ ⑨ ⑤ ☐ ⑨ ⑦ △ 🕒 ⑦ ⑦
🏌 **Leisure** squash **Conf** facs Corporate Hospitality Days **Location** 1m E of Hagley off A456. 2m from junct 3 on M5
Hotel ★★★★ 73% HL Copthorne Hotel Merry Hill - Dudley, The Waterfront, Level Street, Brierley Hill, DUDLEY ☎ 01384 482882 ▤ 01384 482882 138 en suite

Stourbridge Worcester Ln, Pedmore DY8 2RB

☎ 01384 395566 ▤ 01384 444660
e-mail: secretary@stourbridge-golf-club.co.uk
web: www.stourbridge-golf-club.co.uk

Parkland course playable all year. Not long by today's standards but accuracy is the key to returning a good score.

18 Holes, 6231yds, Par 70, SSS 69, Course record 67.
Club membership 705.

Visitors Mon-Fri except BHs. Handicap certificate. Dress code **Societies** welcome. **Green Fees** £30 per 18 holes, £37.50 per day **Prof** M Male **Facilities** ⑪ ⑨ ⑤ ☐ ⑨ ⑦ △ 🕒 🕒 ⑦
Conf Corporate Hospitality Days **Location** 2m S from town centre
Hotel ★★★★ 73% HL Copthorne Hotel Merry Hill - Dudley, The Waterfront, Level Street, Brierley Hill, DUDLEY ☎ 01384 482882 ▤ 01384 482882 138 en suite

SUTTON COLDFIELD   Map 7 SP19

Boldmere Monmouth Dr B73 6JL

☎ 0121 354 3379 ▤ 0121 355 4534

Established municipal course with 10 par 3s and a lake coming into play on the 16th and 18th holes.

Boldmere Golf Course: 18 Holes, 4493yds, Par 63, SSS 62, Course record 57. Club membership 300.

Visitors contact course for details. **Societies** welcome **Green Fees** not confirmed **Prof** Trevor Short **Facilities** ⑪ ⑤ ☐ ⑨ ⑦ △ 🕒 ⑦
🏌 **Location** next to Sutton Park
Hotel ★★★★ 74% HL Best Western Premier Moor Hall Hotel & Spa, Moor Hall Drive, Four Oaks, SUTTON COLDFIELD ☎ 0121 308 3751 ▤ 0121 308 3751 82 en suite

Little Aston Roman Rd, Streetly B74 3AN

☎ 0121 353 2942 ▤ 0121 580 8387
e-mail: manager@littleastongolf.co.uk
web: www.littleastongolf.co.uk

This parkland course is set in the rolling countryside of the former Little Aston Hall and there is a wide variety of mature trees. There are three par 3 holes and three par 5 holes and although the fairways are not unduly narrow there are rewards for accuracy - especially from the tee. The course features two lakes. At the par 5 12th the lake cuts into the green and at the par 4 17th the green is partially in the lake.

18 Holes, 6813yds, Par 72, SSS 74, Course record 63.
Club membership 350.

Visitors Mon-Fri, Sun & BHs. Booking required. Handicap certificate. Dress code. **Societies** booking required. **Green Fees** £110 per day, £80 per round **Course Designer** H Vardon **Prof** Brian Rimmer **Facilities** ⑪ ⑨ ⑤ ☐ ⑨ ⑦ △ 🕒 🕒 ⑦ 🏌 **Conf** Corporate Hospitality Days **Location** 3.5m NW of Sutton Coldfield off A454
Hotel ★★★★ 74% HL Best Western Premier Moor Hall Hotel & Spa, Moor Hall Drive, Four Oaks, SUTTON COLDFIELD ☎ 0121 308 3751 ▤ 0121 308 3751 82 en suite

Moor Hall Moor Hall Dr B75 6LN

☎ 0121 308 6130 ▤ 0121 308 9560
e-mail: secretary@moorhallgolfclub.co.uk

Outstanding parkland course with mature trees lining the fairways. The 14th hole is notable and is part of a challenging finish to the round.

18 Holes, 6293yds, Par 70, SSS 70, Course record 64.
Club membership 600.

Visitors Mon-Wed & Fri except BHs. Thu pm only. Dress code. **Societies** booking required. **Green Fees** £60 per day, £45 per round **Course Designer** Hawtree & Taylor **Prof** Cameron Clark **Facilities** ⑪ ⑨ ⑤ ☐ ⑨ ⑦ △ 🕒 ⑦ 🏌 **Conf** Corporate Hospitality Days **Location** 2.5m N of town centre off A453
Hotel ★★★★ 74% HL Best Western Premier Moor Hall Hotel & Spa, Moor Hall Drive, Four Oaks, SUTTON COLDFIELD ☎ 0121 308 3751 ▤ 0121 308 3751 82 en suite

Pype Hayes Eachel Hurst Rd B76 1EP

☎ 0121 351 1014 ▤ 0121 313 0206

18 Holes, 5927yds, Par 71, SSS 69, Course record 65.

Course Designer Bobby Jones **Location** 2.5m S off B4148
Telephone for further details
Hotel ★★★★ 74% HL Best Western Premier Moor Hall Hotel & Spa, Moor Hall Drive, Four Oaks, SUTTON COLDFIELD ☎ 0121 308 3751 ▤ 0121 308 3751 82 en suite

Sutton Coldfield 110 Thornhill Rd, Streetly B74 3ER
☎ 0121 580 7878 📄 0121 353 5503
e-mail: admin@suttoncoldfieldgc.com
web: www.suttoncoldfieldgc.com

A fine natural, all-weather, heathland course, with tight fairways, gorse, heather and trees. A good challenge for all standards of golfer. Co-hosting English Open Amateur Championship in 2010.

18 Holes, 6541yds, Par 72, SSS 71, Course record 65. Club membership 600.

Visitors Mon-Sun & BHs. Booking required Tue, weekends & BHs. Dress code. **Societies** booking required. **Green Fees** £44 per day, £33 per round (£44 weekends) **Course Designer** Dr A McKenzie **Prof** Jerry Hayes **Facilities** 🏧 🍴 🏌 ⛳ 🍷 🏖 📷 🏌 **Conf** facs Corporate Hospitality Days **Location** M6 junct 7, A34 towards Birmingham, 1st lights left onto A4041 Queslett Rd, Thornhill Rd, entrance after 4th left
Hotel ★★★★ 74% HL Best Western Premier Moor Hall Hotel & Spa, Moor Hall Drive, Four Oaks, SUTTON COLDFIELD ☎ 0121 308 3751 📄 0121 308 3751 82 en suite

Walmley Brooks Rd B72 1HR
☎ 0121 373 0029 📄 0121 377 7272
web: www.walmleygolfclub.co.uk

18 Holes, 6585yds, Par 72, SSS 72, Course record 67.
Prof C J Wicketts **Facilities** 🏧 🍴 🏌 ⛳ 🍷 🏖 📷 🏌
Conf Corporate Hospitality Days **Location** 2m S off A5127
Telephone for further details
Hotel ★★★★ 74% HL Best Western Premier Moor Hall Hotel & Spa, Moor Hall Drive, Four Oaks, SUTTON COLDFIELD ☎ 0121 308 3751 📄 0121 308 3751 82 en suite

Wishaw Bulls Ln, Wishaw B76 9QW
☎ 0121 313 2110 📄 0121 313 2110
e-mail: golf@wishawgolfclub.co.uk
web: www.wishawgc.co.uk

Parkland with excellent water features and tight driving holes. Improved by the introduction of 3 new holes in 2008.

18 Holes, 6069yards, Par 70, SSS 69, Course record 67. Club membership 418.

Visitors dress code. **Societies** booking required. **Green Fees** £18 per round (£25 weekends) **Course Designer** R. Wallis **Prof** Alan Partridge **Facilities** 🏧 🍴 🏌 ⛳ 🍷 🏖 📷 🍴 🏌 🚗 🏌 **Conf** facs Corporate Hospitality Days **Location** W of village off A4097
Hotel ★★★★ 77% HL New Hall, Walmley Road, SUTTON COLDFIELD ☎ 0121 378 2442 📄 0121 378 2442 60 en suite

---

WALSALL Map 7 SP09

Bloxwich 136 Stafford Rd, Bloxwich WS3 3PQ
☎ 01922 476593 📄 01922 493449
e-mail: secretary@bloxwichgolfclub.com
web: www.bloxwichgolfclub.com

Undulating parkland with natural hazards and subject to prevailing westerly winds.

18 Holes, 6257yds, Par 71, SSS 71, Course record 63. Club membership 680.

Visitors Mon-Fri except BHs. Dress code. **Societies** welcome. **Green Fees** phone **Prof** Richard J Dance **Facilities** 🏧 🍴 🏌 ⛳ 🍷 🏖 📷 🏌 **Conf** facs Corporate Hospitality Days **Location** M 6 junct 11/M6 (toll) T7, 3m N of town centre on A34

Hotel ★★★ 85% HL Fairlawns Hotel & Spa, 178 Little Aston Road, WALSALL ☎ 01922 455122 📄 01922 455122 59 en suite

Calderfields Aldridge Rd WS4 2JS
☎ 01922 632243 📄 01922 640540
web: www.calderfieldsgolf.com

Calderfields Golf Academy: 18 Holes, 6509yds, Par 73, SSS 71.

Course Designer Roy Winter **Location** on A454
Telephone for further details
Hotel ★★★ 85% HL Fairlawns Hotel & Spa, 178 Little Aston Road, WALSALL ☎ 01922 455122 📄 01922 455122 59 en suite

Walsall The Broadway WS1 3EY
☎ 01922 613512 📄 01922 616460
web: www.walsallgolfclub.co.uk

18 Holes, 6300yds, Par 70, SSS 70, Course record 65.

Course Designer McKenzie **Location** 1m S of town centre off A34
Telephone for further details
Hotel BUD Travelodge Birmingham Walsall, Birmingham Road, WALSALL ☎ 08719 846 323 📄 08719 846 323 96 en suite

---

WEST BROMWICH Map 7 SP09

Dartmouth Vale St B71 4DW
☎ 0121 588 5746 & 588 2131
web: www.dartmouthgolfclub.co.uk

Very tight meadowland course with undulating but easy walking. The 675 yd par 5 1st hole is something of a challenge.

9 Holes, 6055yds, Par 71, SSS 71, Course record 66. Club membership 250.

Visitors Mon-Fri & BHs. Handicap certificate. Dress code. **Societies** booking required **Green Fees** £20 per day **Facilities** 🏧 🏌 ⛳ 🍷 🏖 📷 **Conf** facs Corporate Hospitality Days **Location** E of town centre off A4041
Hotel ★★★ 66% HL Great Barr Hotel & Conference Centre, Pear Tree Drive, Newton Road, Great Barr, BIRMINGHAM ☎ 0121 357 1141 📄 0121 357 1141 105 en suite

Sandwell Park Birmingham Rd B71 4JJ
☎ 0121 553 4637 📄 0121 525 1651
e-mail: secretary@sandwellparkgolfclub.co.uk
web: www.sandwellparkgolfclub.co.uk

A picturesque course wandering over wooded heathland and utilising natural features. Each hole is entirely separate, shielded from the others by either natural banks or lines of trees. A course

continued

that demands careful placing of shots that have been given a great deal of thought. Natural undulating fairways create difficult and testing approach shots to the greens.

Sandwell Park Golf Club Ltd: 18 Holes, 6204yds, Par 71, SSS 71, Course record 65. Club membership 550.

Visitors Mon-Fri except BHs. Handicap certificate. Dress code. **Societies** booking required. **Green Fees** not confirmed **Course Designer** H S Colt **Prof** Nigel Wylie **Facilities** ⊕ ⏁ ⧉ 🍺 🏌 ⛳ 🚶 🏠 ✦ **Leisure** practice chipping area **Conf** facs Corporate Hospitality Days **Location** M5 junct 1, 200yds on A41 **Hotel** ★★★ 66% HL Great Barr Hotel & Conference Centre, Pear Tree Drive, Newton Road, Great Barr, BIRMINGHAM ☎ 0121 357 1141 ⧉ 0121 357 1141 105 en suite

South Staffordshire

WOLVERHAMPTON
Map 7 SO99

Oxley Park Stafford Rd, Bushbury WV10 6DE
☎ 01902 773989 ⧉ 01902 773981
e-mail: secretary@oxleyparkgolfclub.co.uk
web: www.oxleyparkgolfclub.co.uk
Rolling parkland with trees, bunkers and water hazards.

18 Holes, 6226yds, Par 71, SSS 71, Course record 66. Club membership 550.

Visitors Mon, Wed-Fri except BHs. Booking required. Dress code. **Societies** welcome. **Green Fees** not confirmed **Course Designer** H S Colt **Prof** Les Burlison **Facilities** ⊕ ⧉ by prior arrangement 🍺 ⏁ 🍺 🚶 🏠 ✦ **Leisure** snooker **Conf** facs Corporate Hospitality Days **Location** M54 junct 2, 2m S **Hotel** ★★★ 68% HL Holiday Inn Wolverhampton, Dunstall Park, WOLVERHAMPTON ☎ 0870 2200102 ⧉ 0870 2200102 56 en suite

Penn Penn Common, Penn WV4 5JN
☎ 01902 341142 ⧉ 01902 620504
e-mail: secretary@penngolfclub.co.uk
web: www.penngolfclub.co.uk
Heathland course just outside the town.

18 Holes, 6492yds, Par 70, SSS 72, Course record 65. Club membership 650.

Visitors Mon-Fri except BHs. Handicap certificate. Dress code. **Societies** welcome. **Green Fees** £25 per round, £30 per day **Prof** Guy Dean **Facilities** ⊕ ⏁ 🍺 ⧉ 🍺 🚶 🏠 ✦ **Location** SW of town centre off A449 **Hotel** ★★★ 72% HL Best Western Connaught, Tettenhall Road, WOLVERHAMPTON ☎ 01902 424433 ⧉ 01902 424433 90 en suite

South Staffordshire Danescourt Rd, Tettenhall WV6 9BQ
☎ 01902 751065 ⧉ 01902 751159
e-mail: suelebeau@southstaffsgc.co.uk
web: www.southstaffordshiregolfclub.co.uk
A wooded parkland course.

18 Holes, 6521yds, Par 71, SSS 72, Course record 64. Club membership 500.

Visitors Mon-Sun & BHs. Booking required. Handicap certificate. Dress code. **Societies** booking required. **Green Fees** £40 per round **Course Designer** Harry Vardon **Prof** Peter Baker/Shaun Ball **Facilities** ⊕ ⏁ 🍺 ⧉ 🍺 🚶 🏠 🚌 ✦ 🏌 **Conf** Corporate Hospitality Days **Location** 3m NW of town centre, off A41

Hotel ★★★ 68% HL Holiday Inn Wolverhampton, Dunstall Park, WOLVERHAMPTON ☎ 0870 2200102 ⧉ 0870 2200102 56 en suite

Three Hammers Golf Complex Old Stafford Rd, Coven WV10 7PP
☎ 01902 790428 ⧉ 01902 791777
e-mail: info@3hammers.co.uk
web: www.3hammers.co.uk
Well maintained short course designed by Henry Cotton and providing a unique challenge to golfers of all standards.

Three Hammers Golf Complex: 18 Holes, 1438yds, Par 54, SSS 54, Course record 43.

Visitors Mon-Sun & BHs. **Societies** booking required. **Green Fees** £6.95 per round (£7.95 weekends & BHs) **Course Designer** Henry Cotton **Prof** Piers Ward, Andy Proudman **Facilities** ⊕ ⏁ 🍺 ⧉ 🍺 🏠 ✦ **Conf** Corporate Hospitality Days **Location** M54 junct 2, on A449 N **Hotel** 70% Roman Way, Watling Street, CANNOCK ☎ 01543 572121 ⧉ 01543 572121 56 en suite

Wergs Keepers Ln, Tettenhall WV6 8UA
☎ 01902 742225 ⧉ 01902 844553
e-mail: wergs.golfclub@btinternet.com
web: www.wergs.com
Gently undulating parkland with streams and ditches, a mix of evergreen and deciduous trees, large greens and wide fairways.

18 Holes, 6250yds, Par 72, SSS 70. Club membership 100.

Visitors Mon-Sun & BHs. Booking required weekends. Dress code. **Societies** booking required. **Green Fees** £17 per day (£22 weekends & BHs) **Course Designer** C W Moseley **Prof** Steve Weir **Facilities** ⊕ 🍺 ⧉ 🍺 🚶 🏠 ✦ 🏌 **Conf** Corporate Hospitality Days **Location** 3m W of Wolverhampton off A41 **Hotel** ★★★ 68% HL Holiday Inn Wolverhampton, Dunstall Park, WOLVERHAMPTON ☎ 0870 2200102 ⧉ 0870 2200102 56 en suite

WIGHT, ISLE OF

COWES
Map 4 SZ49

Cowes Crossfield Av PO31 8HN
☎ 01983 292303 (secretary) 📠 01983 292303
e-mail: cowesgolfclub@tiscali.co.uk
web: www.cowesgolfclub.co.uk
Fairly level, tight parkland course with difficult par 3s and Solent views.

9 Holes, 5934yds, Par 70, SSS 68, Course record 66.
Club membership 350.

Visitors Mon-Sun & BHs. Booking required. Dress code.
Societies booking required. **Green Fees** £20 (per 18 holes) **Course Designer** Hamilton-Stutt **Facilities** ⑪ ⑩ ⓛ ☐ ⛴ ⚇ ⚒ ⚐ ✇ **Conf** Corporate Hospitality Days **Location** NW of town centre next to Cowes High School
Hotel ★★★ 70% HL Best Western New Holmwood, Queens Road, Egypt Point, COWES ☎ 01983 292508 📠 01983 292508 26 en suite

EAST COWES
Map 4 SZ59

Osborne Osborne House Estate PO32 6JX
☎ 01983 295421 📠 01983 292781
e-mail: osbornegolfclub@tiscali.co.uk
web: www.osbornegolfclub.co.uk
Undulating parkland course in the grounds of Osborne House. Quiet and peaceful situation with outstanding views.

9 Holes, 6398yds, Par 70, SSS 70, Course record 69.
Club membership 450.

Visitors Mon-Sun & BHs. Booking required Tue, Wed, weekends & BHs. Handicap certificate. Dress code. **Societies** booking required. **Green Fees** £25 per day (£30 weekends & BHs) **Prof** Mark Wright **Facilities** ⑪ ⓛ ☐ ⛴ ⚇ ⚑ 🛏 ✇ **Location** E of town centre off A3021, in Osborne House Estate
Hotel ★★★ 70% HL Best Western New Holmwood, Queens Road, Egypt Point, COWES ☎ 01983 292508 📠 01983 292508 26 en suite

FRESHWATER
Map 4 SZ38

Freshwater Bay Afton Down PO40 9TZ
☎ 01983 752955 📠 01983 752955
web: www.isle-of-wight.uk.com/golf
18 Holes, 5725yds, Par 69, SSS 68.
Course Designer J H Taylor **Location** 0.5m E of village off A3055
Telephone for further details
Hotel ★★★ 76% HL Farringford, Bedbury Lane, FRESHWATER BAY ☎ 01983 752500 📠 01983 752500 18 en suite

NEWPORT
Map 4 SZ58

Newport St George's Down PO30 3BA
☎ 01983 525076
web: www.newportgolfclub.co.uk
9 Holes, 5350yds, Par 68, SSS 66.
Course Designer Guy Hunt **Location** 1.5m S off A3020, 200yds past Newport Football Club on left
Telephone for further details
Hotel ★★★ 70% HL Best Western New Holmwood, Queens Road, Egypt Point, COWES ☎ 01983 292508 📠 01983 292508 26 en suite

RYDE
Map 4 SZ59

Ryde Binstead Rd PO33 3NF
☎ 01983 614809 📠 01983 567418
web: www.rydegolf.co.uk
9 Holes, 5587yds, Par 70, SSS 69, Course record 65.
Course Designer Hamilton-Stutt **Location** 1m W from town centre on A3054
Telephone for further details
Hotel ★★★ 74% HL Yelf's, Union Street, RYDE ☎ 01983 564062 📠 01983 564062 40 en suite

SANDOWN
Map 4 SZ58

Shanklin & Sandown The Fairway, Lake PO36 9PR
☎ 01983 403217 (office) & 404424 (pro)
📠 01983 403007 (office)/404424 (pro)
e-mail: club@ssgolfclub.com
web: www.ssgolfclub.com
An 18-hole county championship course, recognised for its natural heathland beauty, spectacular views and challenging qualities. The course demands respect, with accurate driving and careful club selection the order of the day.

18 Holes, 6062yds, Par 70, SSS 69, Course record 63.
Club membership 700.

Visitors dress code. **Societies** booking required. **Green Fees** £36 (£40 weekends & BHs) **Course Designer** Braid **Prof** Peter Hammond **Facilities** ⑪ ⑩ ⓛ ☐ ⛴ ⚇ 🛏 ⚐ ✇ **Conf** Corporate Hospitality Days **Location** from Sandown towards Shanklin past Heights Leisure Centre, 200yds right into Fairway for 1m
Hotel ★★★ 79% HL Melville Hall Hotel & Utopia Spa, Melville Street, SANDOWN ☎ 01983 400500 & 406526 📠 01983 400500 30 en suite

VENTNOR
Map 4 SZ57

Ventnor Steephill Down Rd PO38 1BP
☎ 01983 853326 & 853388 📠 01983 853326
web: www.ventnorgolfclub.co.uk
12 Holes, 5767yds, Par 70, SSS 68, Course record 64.
Facilities ⑪ ⑩ ⓛ ☐ ⛴ ⚇ ⚐ 🛏 ✇ **Leisure** practice nets **Location** 1m NW off B3327, turn at chip shop
Telephone for further details
Hotel ★★★★ 76% HL The Royal Hotel, Belgrave Road, VENTNOR ☎ 01983 852186 📠 01983 852186 54 en suite

WILTSHIRE

BISHOPS CANNINGS
Map 4 SU06

North Wilts SN10 2LP
☎ 01380 860627 📠 01380 860877
e-mail: secretary@northwiltsgolf.com
web: northwiltsgolf.com

Established in 1890 and one of the oldest courses in Wiltshire, North Wilts is situated high on the downlands of Wiltshire, with spectacular views over the surrounding countryside. The chalk base allows free draining and the course provides a challenge to golfers of all abilities.

18 Holes, 6414yds, Par 71, SSS 71, Course record 65.
Club membership 800.

Visitors contact club for details. **Societies** welcome. **Green Fees** £36 per day (£36 per round weekends) **Course Designer** H. S. Colt **Prof** Graham Laing **Facilities** 🍴 🍽 🛒 🖥 🏌 🏌 🏡 ⛳ 🏌 🚜 ⛳ **Conf** Corporate Hospitality Days **Location** 2m NW of Devizes between A4 and A361
Hotel ★★★ 77% HL Bear, Market Place, DEVIZES
☎ 01380 722444 📠 01380 722444 25 en suite

BRADFORD-ON-AVON
Map 3 ST86

Cumberwell Park BA15 2PQ
☎ 01225 863322 📠 01225 868160
e-mail: enquiries@cumberwellpark.com
web: www.cumberwellpark.com

Set within tranquil woodland, parkland, lakes and rolling countryside, this 36 hole course comprises four linked sets of nine holes. A challenge for all levels of golfer.

Red: 9 Holes, 3296yds, Par 35.
Yellow: 9 Holes, 3139yds, Par 36.
Blue: 9 Holes, 3291yds, Par 36.
Orange: 9 Holes, 3061yds, Par 35. Club membership 1300.

Visitors Mon-Sun & BHs. Booking required. Dress code.
Societies welcome. **Green Fees** £55 per 36 holes, £45 per 27 holes, £30 per 18 holes, £18 per 9 holes (£70/£60/£38/£27 weekends & BHs) **Course Designer** Adrian Stiff **Prof** John Jacobs **Facilities** 🍴 🛒 🖥 🏌 🏌 🏡 🚜 ⛳ 🏌 **Conf** facs Corporate Hospitality Days **Location** 1.5m N on A363
Hotel ★★★ 82% HL Woolley Grange, Woolley Green, BRADFORD-ON-AVON ☎ 01225 864705 📠 01225 864705 26 en suite

CALNE
Map 3 ST97

Bowood Hotel, Spa & Golf Resort Derry Hill SN11 9PQ
☎ 01249 822228 📠 01249 822218
e-mail: golfclub@bowood.org
web: www.bowood.org

This Dave Thomas designed course weaves through 200 acres of 'Capability' Brown's mature woodland with cavernous moulded bunkers, skilfully planned hillocks defining the fairways and vast rolling greens. Numerous doglegs, bunkers, tees and lakes will prove a test for any golfer.

Bowood Championship Course: 18 Holes, 7317yds, Par 72, SSS 74, Course record 63. Club membership 500.

Visitors Mon-Sun & BHs. Booking required. Dress code.
Societies booking required. **Green Fees** £49 per round (£60 weekends) **Course Designer** Dave Thomas **Prof** John Hansel **Facilities** 🍴 🍽 🛒 🖥 🏌 🏌 🏡 ⛳ 🏌 🚜 ⛳ **Leisure** heated indoor swimming pool, fishing, sauna, gymnasium **Conf** facs Corporate Hospitality Days **Location** signed from M4 junct 17, 2.5m W of Calne off A4
Hotel ★★★ 66% HL Lansdowne, The Strand, CALNE
☎ 01249 812488 📠 01249 812488 26 en suite

CASTLE COMBE
Map 3 ST87

Manor House Hotel SN14 7JW
☎ 01249 782982 📠 01249 782992
e-mail: enquiries@manorhousegolfclub.co.uk
web: www.exclusivehotels.co.uk

Set in a wonderful location within the wooded estate of the 14th-century Manor House, this course includes five par 5s and some spectacular par 3s. Manicured fairways and hand-cut greens, together with the River Bybrook meandering through the middle make for a picturesque and dramatic course.

The Manor House Hotel & Golf Club: 18 Holes, 6500yds, Par 72, SSS 72. Club membership 450.

Visitors Mon, Tue, Thu, Fri & BHs. Other days pm only. Booking required. Handicap certificate. Dress code. **Societies** booking required. **Green Fees** not confirmed **Course Designer** Peter Alliss/Clive Clark **Prof** P Green/D Tuck/A Ryan **Facilities** 🍴 🍽 🛒 🖥 🏌 🏌 🏡 ⛳ 🏌 🚜 ⛳ 🏌 **Leisure** hard tennis courts, fishing, sauna, croquet **Conf** facs Corporate Hospitality Days **Location** M4 junct 17/18, 5m NW of Chippenham on B4039
Hotel ★★★★ CHH Manor House Hotel and Golf Club, CASTLE COMBE ☎ 01249 782206 📠 01249 782206 48 en suite

CHIPPENHAM
Map 3 ST97

Chippenham Malmesbury Rd SN15 5LT
☎ 01249 652040 📠 01249 446681
e-mail: chippenhamgolf@btconnect.com
web: www.chippenhamgolfclub.com

Easy walking on mixed parkland/heathland course. Nine of the holes will test the best golfer and the remaining holes will give everyone a chance for pars and birdies.

18 Holes, 5783yds, Par 69, SSS 67, Course record 62.
Club membership 650.

Visitors Mon-Sun & BHs. Dress code. **Societies** booking required. **Green Fees** £32 per day, £28 per round (£35 weekends & BHs) **Prof** Bill Creamer **Facilities** 🍴 🍽 🛒 🖥 🏌 🏌 🏡 🚜 🏌

continued

Conf facs Corporate Hospitality Days **Location** 2m S of M4 junct 17, 1m N of Chippenham on A350
Hotel ★★★★ CHH Manor House Hotel and Golf Club, CASTLE COMBE ☎ 01249 782206 📠 01249 782206 48 en suite

CRICKLADE   Map 4 SU09

Cricklade Hotel & Country Club Common Hill SN6 6HA
☎ 01793 750751 📠 01793 751767
e-mail: reception@crickladehotel.co.uk
web: www.crickladehotel.co.uk

A challenging nine-hole course with undulating greens and beautiful views. Par 3 6th (128yds) signature hole from an elevated tee to a green protected by a deep pot bunker.

Cricklade Hotel: 9 Holes, 1830yds, Par 62, SSS 58, Course record 59. Club membership 130.

Visitors Mon-Fri except BHs. Booking required weekends & BHs. Dress code. **Societies** welcome. **Green Fees** £28 per day, £18 for 18 holes **Course Designer** Ian Bolt/Colin Smith **Facilities** ⑨ ⑩| ⓑ ⚑ ⑨|
⚒ ⑨⁺ ◇ ⚐ **Leisure** hard tennis courts, heated indoor swimming pool, gymnasium, snooker, pool, jacuzzi, tennis, steam room **Conf** facs **Location** on B4040 from Cricklade towards Malmesbury
Hotel ★★★ 77% HL Cricklade Hotel, Common Hill, CRICKLADE
☎ 01793 750751 📠 01793 750751 46 en suite

ERLESTOKE   Map 3 ST95

Erlestoke Sands SN10 5UB
☎ 01380 831069 📠 01380 831284
web: www.erlestokesands.co.uk

Erlestoke Sands Golf Course: 18 Holes, 6406yds, Par 73, SSS 71, Course record 66.

Course Designer Adrian Stiff **Location** on B3098 Devizes-Westbury road
Telephone for further details
Hotel ★★★ 77% HL Bear, Market Place, DEVIZES
☎ 01380 722444 📠 01380 722444 25 en suite

GREAT DURNFORD   Map 4 SU13

High Post SP4 6AT
☎ 01722 782356 📠 01722 782674
e-mail: admin@highpostgolfclub.co.uk
web: www.highpostgolfclub.co.uk

A championship downland course which offers summer tees and greens all year. Free draining and easy walking. The opening three holes, usually played with the wind, get you to off to a flying start,

but the closing three provide a tough finish. Peter Alliss has rated the 9th among his dream holes. The club welcomes golfers of all abilities.

18 Holes, 6305yds, Par 70, SSS 70, Course record 64. Club membership 625.

Visitors contact club for details. **Societies** welcome. **Green Fees** £50 per day, £34 per round (£50/£42 weekends) **Course Designer** Hawtree & Ptrs **Prof** Tony Isaacs **Facilities** ⑨ ⑩| ⓑ
⚑ ⑨| ⚒ ⚑ ⑨⁺ ⚐ **Conf** facs Corporate Hospitality Days
Location on A345 between Sailsbury and Amesbury
Hotel ★★★ 63% HL Quality Hotel Andover, Micheldever Road, ANDOVER ☎ 01264 369111 📠 01264 369111 49 en suite

HIGHWORTH   Map 4 SU29

Highworth Community Golf Centre Swindon Rd SN6 7SJ
☎ 01793 766014 📠 01793 766014

Highworth Golf Centre: 9 Holes, 3120yds, Par 35, SSS 35, Course record 29.

Course Designer T Watt/ B Sandry/D Lang **Location** off A361 Swindon-Lechlade road
Telephone for further details
Hotel ★★★ 75% HL Best Western Sudbury House Hotel & Conference Centre, London Street, FARINGDON ☎ 01367 241272
📠 01367 241272 49 en suite

Wrag Barn Golf & Country Club Shrivenham Rd SN6 7QQ
☎ 01793 861327 📠 01793 861325
web: www.wragbarn.com

Wrag Barn Golf & Country Club: 18 Holes, 6633yds, Par 72, SSS 72, Course record 65.

Course Designer Hawtree **Location** on B4000 from Highworth, signed
Telephone for further details
Hotel ★★★ 75% HL Stanton House, The Avenue, Stanton Fitzwarren, SWINDON ☎ 0870 084 1388 📠 0870 084 1388
82 en suite

KINGSDOWN   Map 3 ST86

Kingsdown SN13 8BS
☎ 01225 743472 📠 01225 743472
e-mail: kingsdowngc@btconnect.com
web: www.kingsdowngolfclub.co.uk

Fairly flat, open downland course with very sparse tree cover but surrounding wood. Many interesting holes with testing features.

18 Holes, 6445yds, Par 72, SSS 71, Course record 64. Club membership 750.

Visitors Mon-Fri & BHs. Booking required. Dress code.
Societies booking required. **Green Fees** £36 per day **Prof** Andrew Butler **Facilities** ⑨ ⓑ ⚑ ⑨| ⚒ ⚑ ⑨⁺ ⚐ **Location** W of village between Corsham and Bathford
Hotel ★★★★★ CHH Lucknam Park, COLERNE, Chippenham
☎ 01225 742777 📠 01225 742777 41 en suite

LANDFORD
Map 4 SU21

Hamptworth Golf & Country Club Hamptworth Rd, Hamptworth SP5 2DU
☎ 01794 390155   📠 01794 390022
e-mail: info@hamptworthgolf.co.uk
web: www.hamptworthgolf.co.uk

Hamptworth enjoys ancient woodland and an abundance of wildlife in a beautiful setting on the northern edge of the New Forest. Many holes play alongside or over the Blackwater river with mature forest oaks guarding almost every fairway.

Hamptworth Golf & Country Club: 18 Holes, 6448yds, Par 72, SSS 71, Course record 66. Club membership 750.

Visitors Mon-Sun & BHs. Booking required. Dress code. **Societies** welcome. **Green Fees** Apr-Sep £30 per round, Oct-Mar £25 (£40/£30 weekends) **Course Designer** Philip Sanders/Brian Pierson **Prof** Andy Beal **Facilities** ⊕ ⏐◎⏐ 🛒 ⛽ 🔧 ⚲ 🏌 ♋ 🥈 **Leisure** hard tennis courts, gymnasium, croquet lawns, physiotherapy **Conf** facs Corporate Hospitality Days **Location** 1.5m W of Landford off B3079
Hotel ★★★ 75% HL Bartley Lodge, Lyndhurst Road, CADNAM ☎ 023 8081 2248 📠 023 8081 2248   31 en suite

MARLBOROUGH
Map 4 SU16

Marlborough The Common SN8 1DU
☎ 01672 512147   📠 01672 513164
e-mail: contactus@marlboroughgolfclub.co.uk
web: www.marlboroughgolfclub.co.uk

Undulating downland course with extensive views over the Og valley and the Marlborough Downs.

18 Holes, 6369yds, Par 72, SSS 71, Course record 61. Club membership 800.

Visitors contact club for details. **Societies** booking required. **Green Fees** £42 per day, £30 per round (£55/£40 weekends). **Prof** S Amor **Facilities** ⊕ ⏐◎⏐ 🛒 ⛽ 🔧 ⚲ 🏌 ♋ **Conf** facs Corporate Hospitality Days **Location** N of town centre on A346
Hotel ★★★ 64% HL Ivy House, 43 High Street, MARLBOROUGH ☎ 01672 515333 📠 01672 515333   28 en suite

OGBOURNE ST GEORGE
Map 4 SU27

Ogbourne Downs SN8 1TB
☎ 01672 841327
e-mail: michelle.green@btconnect.com
web: www.ogdgc.co.uk

Downland turf and magnificent greens. Wind and slopes make this one of the most challenging courses in Wiltshire. Extensive views.

18 Holes, 6422yds, Par 71, SSS 71, Course record 65. Club membership 700.

Visitors booking required. Dress code. **Societies** booking required. **Green Fees** £25 per 18 holes (£35 weekends) **Course Designer** J H Taylor **Prof** Robert Ralph/Kevin Pickett **Facilities** ⊕ ⏐◎⏐ 🛒 ⛽ 🔧 ⚲ 🏌 ♋ **Location** N of village on A346
Hotel ★★★ 75% HL Chiseldon House, New Road, Chiseldon, SWINDON ☎ 01793 741010 & 07770 853883 📠 01793 741010   21 en suite

SALISBURY
Map 4 SU12

Salisbury & South Wilts Netherhampton SP2 8PR
☎ 01722 742645   📠 01722 742676
e-mail: mail@salisburygolf.co.uk
web: www.salisburygolf.co.uk

Gently undulating and well-drained parkland courses in country setting with panoramic views of the cathedral and surrounding countryside. Never easy with six excellent opening holes and four equally testing closing holes.

Main Course: 18 Holes, 6485yds, Par 71, SSS 71, Course record 63.
Bibury Course: 9 Holes, 2837yds, Par 34.
Club membership 1000.

Visitors Mon-Sun except BHs. Booking required Mon, Wed, Fri & weekends. Handicap certificate for main course. Dress code. **Societies** booking required. **Green Fees** not confirmed **Course Designer** J H Taylor/S Gidman **Prof** Jon Waring **Facilities** ⊕ ⏐◎⏐ 🛒 ⛽ 🔧 ⚲ 🏌 ♋ **Conf** facs Corporate Hospitality Days **Location** 2m SW of Salisbury on A3094
Hotel ★★★ 68% HL Grasmere House Hotel, Harnham Road, SALISBURY ☎ 01722 338388 📠 01722 338388   38 en suite

SWINDON
Map 4 SU18

Broome Manor Golf Complex Pipers Way SN3 1RG
☎ 01793 532403 (bookings) & 495761 (enquiries)
📠 01793 433255
e-mail: broomegolfshop@swindon.gov.uk

Two courses and a 34-bay floodlit driving range. Parkland with water hazards, open fairways and short cut rough. Walking is easy on gentle slopes.

Broome Manor Golf Complex: 18 Holes, 5989yds, Par 71, SSS 70, Course record 61.
Broome Manor Golf Complex: 9 Holes, 2690yds, Par 33. Club membership 800.

Visitors Mon-Sun & BHs. Booking required. **Societies** welcome. **Green Fees** not confirmed **Course Designer** Hawtree **Prof** Barry Sandry **Facilities** ⊕ 🛒 ⛽ 🔧 ⚲ 🏌 ♋ **Leisure** gymnasium **Conf** facs Corporate Hospitality Days **Location** 1.75m SE of town centre off B4006
Hotel ★★★★ 76% HL Swindon Marriott Hotel, Pipers Way, SWINDON ☎ 01793 512121 📠 01793 512121   156 en suite

TIDWORTH
Map 4 SU24

Tidworth Garrison Bulford Rd SP9 7AF
☎ 01980 842301   📠 01980 842301
e-mail: tidworthgolfclub@btconnect.com
web: www.tidworthgolfclub.co.uk

A breezy, dry downland course with lovely turf, fine trees and views over Salisbury Plain and the surrounding area. The 4th and 12th holes are notable. The 565yd 14th, going down towards the clubhouse, gives the big hitter a chance to let fly.

18 Holes, 6320yds, Par 70, SSS 70, Course record 63. Club membership 750.

Visitors Mon-Sun & BHs. Booking required. Handicap certificate. Dress code. **Societies** booking required. **Green Fees** £30 before noon, £25 after noon **Course Designer** Donald Steel **Prof** Terry

continued

Gosden **Facilities** (⚲) (🍴) 🛌 🖥 📞 🏌 🏠 ⛳ 🚗 ✎
Location W of village off A338
Hotel ★★★ 63% HL Quality Hotel Andover, Micheldever Road, ANDOVER ☎ 01264 369111 📠 01264 369111 49 en suite

---

TOLLARD ROYAL Map 3 ST91

Rushmore SP5 5QB
☎ 01725 516326 📠 01725 516437
e-mail: golf@rushmoreuk.com
web: www.rushmoregolfclub.co.uk

Peaceful and testing parkland course situated on Cranborne Chase with far-reaching views. An undulating course with avenues of trees and well-drained greens. With water on seven out of 18 holes, it will test the most confident of golfers.

Rushmore: 18 Holes, 6131yds, Par 71, SSS 70.
Club membership 650.

Visitors Mon-Sun & BHs. Booking required. Dress code.
Societies booking required. **Green Fees** £27 per round (£32 weekends) **Course Designer** David Pottage/John Jacobs Developments **Prof** Jason Sherman **Facilities** (⚲) (🍴) by prior arrangement 🛌 🖥 📞 🏌 🏠 ⛳ ✎ 🚗 ✎ 🏌 **Conf** facs Corporate Hospitality Days **Location** N off B3081 between Sixpenny Handley & Tollard Royal **Hotel** ★★★ 71% HL Best Western Royal Chase, Royal Chase Roundabout, SHAFTESBURY ☎ 01747 853355 📠 01747 853355 33 en suite

---

UPAVON Map 4 SU15

Upavon Douglas Av SN9 6BQ
☎ 01980 630787 & 630281 📠 01980 635103
e-mail: play@upavongolfclub.co.uk
web: www.upavongolfclub.co.uk

Free-draining course on chalk downland with panoramic views over the Vale of Pewsey and the Alton Barnes White Horse. A fair test of golf with a good mixture of holes including a 602yd par 5 and an excellent finishing hole, a par 3 of 169yds across a valley.

18 Holes, 6402yds, Par 71, SSS 71, Course record 66.
Club membership 600.

Visitors Mon-Sun & BHs. Booking advised. Dress code.
Societies booking required. **Green Fees** £36 per day (£46 weekends) **Course Designer** Richard Blake **Prof** Richard Blake **Facilities** (⚲) (🍴) by prior arrangement 🛌 🖥 📞 🏌 🏠 ✎ 🚗 ✎ **Location** 1.5m SE of Upavon on A342
Hotel ★★★ 77% HL Bear, Market Place, DEVIZES ☎ 01380 722444 📠 01380 722444 25 en suite

---

WARMINSTER Map 3 ST84

West Wilts Elm Hill BA12 0AU
☎ 01985 213133 📠 01985 219809
e-mail: sec@westwiltsgolfclub.co.uk
web: www.westwiltsgolfclub.co.uk

A hilltop chalk downland course among the Wiltshire downs. Free draining, short, but a very good test of accurate iron play. Excellent fairways and greens all year round.

18 Holes, 5754yds, Par 70, SSS 68, Course record 60.
Club membership 570.

Visitors Mon-Fri, Sun & BHs. Booking required Sun. Handicap certificate. Dress code. **Societies** booking required. **Green**

Fees not confirmed **Course Designer** J H Taylor **Prof** Rob Morris
Facilities (⚲) (🍴) by prior arrangement 🛌 🖥 📞 🏌 🏠 ⛳
✎ **Leisure** indoor practice facility **Conf** Corporate Hospitality Days
Location N of town centre, 1m off A350
Hotel ★★★★ 77% HL Bishopstrow House, WARMINSTER
☎ 01985 212312 📠 01985 212312 32 en suite

WOOTTON BASSETT Map 4 SU08

Best Western The Wiltshire Vastern SN4 7PB
☎ 01793 849999 📠 01793 849988
e-mail: reception@the-wiltshire.co.uk
web: www.the-wiltshire.co.uk

A Peter Alliss and Howard Swan design set in rolling Wiltshire downland. A number of lakes add a challenge for both low and high handicappers.

Lakes: 18 Holes, 6519yds, Par 72, SSS 72,
Course record 69.
Garden: 9 Holes, 6112yds, Par 71, SSS 69.
Club membership 450.

Visitors Mon-Sun & BHs. Booking required. Dress code.
Societies booking required. **Green Fees** Lakes £22 per 18 holes (£30 weekends & BHs). Garden £12 per 9 holes (£18 weekends & BHs)
Course Designer Peter Allis & Howard Swan **Prof** Richard Lawless
Facilities (⚲) (🍴) 🛌 🖥 📞 🏌 🏠 ⛳ 🔶 ✎ 🚗 ✎ 🏌
Leisure heated indoor swimming pool, sauna, gymnasium **Conf** facs Corporate Hospitality Days **Location** M4 exit junct 16, off A3102 SW of Wootton Bassett
Hotel ★★★ 78% HL Best Western The Wiltshire, WOOTTON BASSETT, Swindon ☎ 01793 849999 📠 01793 849999 58 en suite

Brinkworth Longmans Farm SN15 5DG
☎ 01666 510277
web: www.woodbridgepark.co.uk

Woodbridge Park Golf Club: 18 Holes, 5884yds, Par 70,
SSS 70.

Course Designer Chris Kane **Location** off B4042 between Malmesbury and Wootton Bassett
Telephone for further details
Hotel ★★★ 73% HL Marsh Farm, Coped Hall, WOOTTON BASSETT ☎ 01793 848044 & 842800 📠 01793 848044 50 en suite

WORCESTERSHIRE

ALVECHURCH
Map 7 SP07

Kings Norton Brockhill Ln, Weatheroak B48 7ED
☎ 01564 826706 & 826789 📠 01564 826955
e-mail: info@kingsnortongolfclub.co.uk
web: www.kingsnortongolfclub.co.uk

Parkland with water hazards. A 27-hole championship venue playing as three combinations of nine holes.

Weatheroak: 18 Holes, 6729yds, Par 72, SSS 72, Course record 65.
Brockhill: 18 Holes, 6645yds, Par 72, SSS 72.
Wythall: 18 Holes, 6600yds, Par 72, SSS 72.
Club membership 1000.

Visitors Mon-Fri except BHs. Dress code. **Societies** booking required. **Green Fees** phone **Course Designer** F Hawtree **Prof** Kevin Hayward **Facilities** ⊕ ⑩ ⓑ ⬛ 🍴 ⚘ 🏖 ⛴ 🚤 ⚘ **Leisure** par 3 course **Conf** facs Corporate Hospitality Days **Location** M42 junct 3, off A435
Hotel ★★★★ 73% HL Holiday Inn Birmingham - Bromsgrove, Kidderminster Road, BROMSGROVE ☎ 01527 576600 & 0871 942 9142 📠 01527 576600 110 en suite

BEWDLEY
Map 7 SO77

Bewdley Pines Habberley Rd DY12 1LY
☎ 01299 404744 & 409098

The course, taking full advantage of the rolling terrain is laid out over sandy, well draining land alongside the scenic Habberley Valley Country Park. The course is free draining and its enviable setting and cunningly enhanced natural hazards ensure that no hole resembles another, each presenting its own test of skill and nerve. Two holes that deserve special mention are the 3rd par 4 367 yds, a 'thread needle' hole onto a sloping fairway which bounces wayward shots out of bounds. The 14th par 3 151 yds has a 30 foot drop from tee to green on to a pocket handkerchief green. Overhanging trees and steep banks ensure a reward only for a well struck tee shot.

18 Holes, 5799yds, Par 69, SSS 67. Club membership 550.
Visitors Mon-Sun & BHs. Booking required. Dress code.
Societies booking required. **Green Fees** £20 per 18 holes, £13 per 9 holes (£25/£15 weekends) **Prof** Mark Slater **Facilities** ⊕ ⑩ ⓑ ⬛ 🍴 ⚘ 🏖 🚤 ⚘ **Conf** Corporate Hospitality Days **Location** A456 past West Midland Safari Park, then take B4190
Hotel ★★★ 79% HL Ramada Hotel Kidderminster, Habberley Road, BEWDLEY, Nr Kidderminster ☎ 01299 406400 📠 01299 406400 44 en suite

Little Lakes Golf and Country Club Lye Head DY12 2UZ
☎ 01299 266385 📠 01299 266398
e-mail: info@little lakes.co.uk
web: www.little-lakes.co.uk

A pleasant undulating 18-hole parkland course. A challenging test of golf with stunning views of the Worcestershire countryside. Well acclaimed for the use of natural features.

Little Lakes Golf and Country Club: 18 Holes, 6298yds, Par 71, SSS 70, Course record 68. Club membership 475.
Visitors Mon-Sun & BHs. Booking required weekends & BHs. Dress code. **Societies** booking required. **Green Fees** £23 (£28 weekends & BHs)) **Course Designer** M Laing **Prof** Mark A Laing **Facilities** ⊕ by prior arrangement ⑩ by prior arrangement ⓑ ⬛ 🍴 ⚘ 🏖

⚘ 🚤 ⚘ **Leisure** hard tennis courts, heated outdoor swimming pool, fishing **Conf** facs Corporate Hospitality Days **Location** 2.25m W of Bewdley off A456
Hotel ★★★ 79% HL Ramada Hotel Kidderminster, Habberley Road, BEWDLEY, Nr Kidderminster ☎ 01299 406400 📠 01299 406400 44 en suite

Wharton Park Longbank DY12 2QW
☎ 01299 405163 📠 01299 405121
e-mail: enquiries@whartonpark.co.uk
web: www.whartonpark.co.uk

An 18-hole championship-standard course set in 200 acres of beautiful Worcestershire countryside, with stunning views. Some long par 5s such as the 9th (594yds) as well as superb par 3 holes at 3rd, 10th and 15th make this a challenging course.

18 Holes, 6435yds, Par 71, SSS 71, Course record 66.
Club membership 500.
Visitors Mon-Sun & BHs. Booking required. Dress code.
Societies booking required. **Green Fees** phone **Course Designer** Howard Swan **Prof** Angus Hoare **Facilities** ⊕ ⑩ ⓑ ⬛ 🍴 ⚘ 🏖 ⚘ 🚤 ⚘ 🏁 **Conf** facs Corporate Hospitality Days **Location** off A456 Bewdley bypass
Hotel ★★★ 79% HL Ramada Hotel Kidderminster, Habberley Road, BEWDLEY, Nr Kidderminster ☎ 01299 406400 📠 01299 406400 44 en suite

BISHAMPTON
Map 3 SO95

Vale Golf Club Hill Furze Rd WR10 2LZ
☎ 01386 462781 📠 01386 462597
e-mail: vale-sales@crown-golf.co.uk
web: www.crown-golf.co.uk

This course offers an American-style layout, with large greens, trees and bunkers and several water hazards. Its rolling fairways provide a testing round, as well as superb views of the Malvern Hills. Picturesque and peaceful.

International Course: 18 Holes, 7174yds, Par 74, SSS 74, Course record 67.
Lenches Course: 9 Holes, 5518yds, Par 70, SSS 66.
Club membership 800.
Visitors Mon-Sun & BHs. Booking required. Dress code.
Societies welcome. **Green Fees** not confirmed **Course Designer** Bob Sandow **Prof** Richard Jenkins **Facilities** ⊕ ⑩ ⓑ ⬛ 🍴 ⚘ 🏖 🚤 ⚘ 🏁 **Conf** facs Corporate Hospitality Days **Location** signed off A44
Hotel ★★★ 80% HL Best Western Salford Hall, ABBOT'S SALFORD, Evesham ☎ 01386 871300 & 0800 212671 📠 01386 871300 33 en suite

BROADWAY
Map 4 SP03

Broadway Willersey Hill WR12 7LG
☎ 01386 853683 📠 01386 858643
e-mail: secretary@broadwaygolfclub.co.uk
web: www.broadwaygolfclub.co.uk

Uniquely located at the edge of the Cotswolds this course lies at an altitude of 850ft above sea level, with extensive views over the Vale of Evesham. The inland links style provides a challenge for golfers of all abilities. It offers holes that with their natural and artificial hazards require drives that are skilfully placed, approaches carefully judged and undulating greens expertly read. The rolling fairways are intersected by Cotswold dry stone walls.

18 Holes, 6228yds, Par 72, SSS 70, Course record 63. Club membership 900.

Visitors Mon-Fri except BHs. Weekends pm. Handicap certificate. Dress code. **Societies** Booking required **Green Fees** £40 per day, £32 per round (£40 weekends & BHs) **Course Designer** James Braid **Prof** Martyn Freeman **Facilities** 🅿 🍽 🍴 🛒 🖥 🛄 ☂ 🏌️ ⚙ 🏌️‍♂️ 🏌️ **Conf** facs Corporate Hospitality Days **Location** 1.5m E on A44, at top of Fish Hill take left turning opposite Broadway Tower signposted Saintbury. After 0.5m turn left as road bends sharply right. Club just past Dormy House Hotel on left
Hotel ★★★★ 77% HL Dormy House, Willersey Hill, BROADWAY
☎ 01386 852711 📠 01386 852711 45 en suite

BROMSGROVE
Map 7 SO97

Blackwell Agmore Rd, Blackwell B60 1PY
☎ 0121 445 1994 📠 0121 445 4911
e-mail: info@blackwellgolfclub.com
web: www.blackwellgolfclub.co.uk

Mature undulating parkland course over a 115 years old, with a variety of trees. Laid out in two nine-hole loops.

The Blackwell Golf Club Ltd: 18 Holes, 6080yds, Par 70, SSS 71, Course record 61. Club membership 338.

Visitors Mon, Wed-Fri except BHs. Booking required. Handicap certificate. Dress code. **Societies** booking required. **Green Fees** £80 per day, £70 per round **Course Designer** Herbert Fowler/Tom Simpson **Prof** Finlay Clark **Facilities** 🅿 by prior arrangement 🍽 by prior arrangement 🛒 🖥 🍴 ☂ 🛄 🏌️ ⚙ 🏌️‍♂️ ⚙ **Conf** Corporate Hospitality Days **Location** 2.5m NE of Bromsgrove off B4096
Hotel ★★★ 78% HL Ladybird Hotel, 2 Finstall Road, Aston Fields, BROMSGROVE ☎ 01527 889900 📠 01527 889900 43 en suite

Bromsgrove Golf Centre Stratford Rd B60 1LD
☎ 01527 575886 & 570505 📠 01527 570964
e-mail: enquiries@bromsgrovegolfcentre.com
web: www.bromsgrovegolfcentre.com

This gently undulating course with superb views over Worcestershire is not to be underestimated. Creative landscaping and a selection of well-defined bunkers ensure that the course delivers a uniquely satisfying experience through a variety of challenging, yet enjoyable, holes.

Bromsgrove Golf Centre: 18 Holes, 5969yds, Par 68, SSS 69. Club membership 900.

Visitors Mon-Sun & BHs. Dress code. **Societies** booking required. **Green Fees** £20.90 per 18 holes (£27.80 weekends) **Course Designer** Hawtree & Son **Prof** Graeme Long/Danny Wall **Facilities** 🅿 🍽 🛒 🖥 🍴 ☂ 🛄 🏌️ 🏌️‍♂️ ⚙ 🏌️ **Conf** facs Corporate

Hospitality Days **Location** 1m from town centre at junct A38/A448, signed

Bromsgrove Golf Centre

Hotel ★★★★ 73% HL Holiday Inn Birmingham - Bromsgrove, Kidderminster Road, BROMSGROVE ☎ 01527 576600 & 0871 942 9142 📠 01527 576600 110 en suite

DROITWICH
Map 3 SO86

Droitwich Golf & Country Club Ford Ln WR9 0BQ
☎ 01905 774344 📠 01905 797290

Droitwich Golf & Country Club: 18 Holes, 5976yds, Par 70, SSS 69, Course record 62.

Course Designer J Braid/G Franks **Location** M5 junct 5, off A38 at Droitwich opposite Chateau Impney Hotel
Telephone for further details
Hotel ★★★ 77% HL Pear Tree Inn & Country Hotel, Smite, WORCESTER ☎ 01905 756565 📠 01905 756565 24 en suite

Gaudet Luce Middle Ln, Hadzor WR9 7DP
☎ 01905 796375 📠 01905 797245
e-mail: info@gaudet-luce.co.uk
web: www.gaudet-luce.co.uk

A challenging 18-hole course with two contrasting 9-hole loops. The front nine are long and fairly open, the back nine are tight and compact requiring good positional and approach play. Water features on several holes.

18 Holes, 6040yds, Par 70, SSS 68. Club membership 600.

Visitors Mon-Sun & BHs. Booking required. Dress code. **Societies** booking required. **Green Fees** £23 per round (£28 weekends & BHs) **Course Designer** M A Laing **Prof** Russel Adams **Facilities** 🅿 🍽 🛒 🖥 🍴 ☂ 🛄 🏌️ ⚙ 🏌️‍♂️ 🏌️ **Leisure** creche **Conf** facs Corporate Hospitality Days **Location** M5 junct 5, left at Tagwell Rd onto Middle Ln, 1st driveway on left
Hotel ★★★ 77% HL Pear Tree Inn & Country Hotel, Smite, WORCESTER ☎ 01905 756565 📠 01905 756565 24 en suite

Ombersley Bishops Wood Rd, Lineholt, Ombersley WR9 0LE
☎ 01905 620747 📠 01905 620047
e-mail: enquiries@ombersleygolfclub
web: www.ombersleygolfclub.co.uk

Undulating course in beautiful countryside high above the edge of the Severn valley. Covered driving range and putting green.

18 Holes, 6139yds, Par 72, SSS 69, Course record 67. Club membership 750.

Visitors Mon-Sun & BHs. Booking advised. Dress code.

continued

Societies booking required. Green Fees £20.50 per 18 holes, £12.35 per 9 holes (£29.10/£17.55 weekends & BHs) Course Designer David Morgan Prof G Glenister/A Dalton Facilities ⊕ ⦿ ⛳ ☐ ⚑ ⬜ ⬜ ⬜ ⛏ ✦ Leisure chipping green & practice bunker Conf facs Corporate Hospitality Days Location 3m W of Droitwich off A449. At Mitre Oak pub A4025 to Stourport, signed 400yds on left Hotel ★★★★ 75% HL Menzies Stourport Manor, 35 Hartlebury Road, STOURPORT-ON-SEVERN ☎ 01299 289955 ▤ 01299 289955 68 en suite

FLADBURY — Map 3 SO94

Evesham Craycombe Links WR10 2QS
☎ 01386 860395 ▤ 01386 861356
web: eveshamgolf.com

9 Holes, 6415yds, Par 72, Course record 65.
Prof Dan Cummins Facilities ⊕ ⦿ ⛳ ☐ ⚑ ⬜ ⬜ ⬜ ⛏ ✦ Location 0.75m N on A4538
Telephone for further details
Hotel ★★★ 79% HL The Evesham, Coopers Lane, Off Waterside, EVESHAM ☎ 01386 765566 & 0800 716969 (Res) ▤ 01386 765566 40 en suite

HOLLYWOOD — Map 7 SP07

Gay Hill Hollywood Ln B47 5PP
☎ 0121 430 8544 & 474 6001 (pro) ▤ 0121 436 7796
e-mail: secretary@ghgc.org.uk
web: www.ghgc.org.uk
Parkland course with some 10,000 trees and a brook running through. Gently undulating so a good test of golf rather than stamina.

Gay Hill Golf Club Ltd: 18 Holes, 6406yds, Par 72, SSS 72, Course record 64. Club membership 700.
Visitors Mon-Sun except BHs. Booking required weekends. Handicap certificate. Societies booking required. Green Fees £35.50 per round (£40.50 weekends) Prof Chris Harrison Facilities ⊕ ⦿ ⛳ ☐ ⚑ ⬜ ⛏ ✦ Location N of village
Hotel ★★★ 68% HL Corus, Stratford Road, Shirley, SOLIHULL ☎ 0844 736 8605 & 0121 745 0400 ▤ 0844 736 8605 111 en suite

KIDDERMINSTER — Map 7 SO87

Churchill and Blakedown Churchill Ln, Blakedown DY10 3NB
☎ 01562 700018 ▤ 0871 242 2049
e-mail: cbgolfclub@tiscali.co.uk
web: www.churchillblakedowngolfclub.co.ukl
Mature hilly course, playable all year round, with good views.

9 Holes, 6488yds, Par 72, SSS 71. Club membership 410.
Visitors Mon-Wed & Fri except BHs. Booking required. Handicap certificate. Dress code. Societies booking required. Green Fees £20 per 18 holes Prof Debbi Garbett Facilities ⊕ ⦿ ⛳ ☐ ⚑ ⬜ ⬜ ⬜ ⬜ ⬜ ⬜ Conf Corporate Hospitality Days Location W of village off A456
Hotel ★★★★ 78% HL Stone Manor, Stone, KIDDERMINSTER ☎ 01562 777555 ▤ 01562 777555 57 en suite

Habberley Low Habberley, Trimpley Rd DY11 5RF
☎ 01562 745756 ▤ 01562 745756
e-mail: dave.mcdermott@blueyonder.co.uk
web: www.habberleygolfclub.co.uk
Wooded, undulating parkland.

9 Holes, 5401yds, Par 69, SSS 67, Course record 62. Club membership 108.
Visitors Handicap certificate. Dress code. Societies booking required. Green Fees not confirmed Facilities ⊕ ⦿ ⛳ ☐ ⚑ ⬜ Location 2m NW of Kidderminster
Hotel ★★★★ 78% HL Stone Manor, Stone, KIDDERMINSTER ☎ 01562 777555 ▤ 01562 777555 57 en suite

Kidderminster Russell Rd DY10 3HT
☎ 01562 822303 ▤ 01562 827866
web: www.kidderminstergolfclub.com
18 Holes, 6422yds, Par 72, SSS 71, Course record 65.
Prof Pat Smith Facilities ⊕ ⦿ ⛳ ☐ ⚑ ⬜ ⬜ ⬜ ⬜ ⬜ ⬜ Conf facs Corporate Hospitality Days Location 0.5m SE of town centre, signed off A449
Telephone for further details
Hotel ★★★★ 78% HL Stone Manor, Stone, KIDDERMINSTER ☎ 01562 777555 ▤ 01562 777555 57 en suite

Wyre Forest Zortech Av DY11 7EX
☎ 01299 822682 ▤ 01299 879433
e-mail: wyreforestgc@hotmail.co.uk
web: www.wyreforestgolf.co.uk
Making full use of the existing contours, this interesting and challenging course is bounded by woodland and gives extensive views over the surrounding area. Well drained fairways and greens give an inland links style.

18 Holes, 6052yds, Par 71, SSS 69, Course record 68. Club membership 397.
Visitors Mon-Sun & BHs. Booking required weekends & BHs. Dress code. Societies booking required. Green Fees £17.40 per 18 holes (£23 weekends) Prof Chris Botterill Facilities ⊕ ⛳ ☐ ⚑ ⬜ ⬜ ⬜ ⬜ ⬜ ⬜ ⬜ ⬜ Conf Corporate Hospitality Days Location on A451 between Kidderminster and Stourport
Hotel ★★★ 80% HL Gainsborough House, Bewdley Hill, KIDDERMINSTER ☎ 01562 820041 ▤ 01562 820041 42 en suite

MALVERN — Map 3 SO74

Worcestershire Wood Farm, Wood Farm Rd WR14 4PP
☎ 01684 575992 ▤ 01684 893334
e-mail: secretary@worcsgolfclub.co.uk
web: www.worcsgolfclub.co.uk
Fairly easy walking on windy downland course with trees, ditches and other natural hazards. Outstanding views of the Malvern Hills and the Severn valley. The 17th hole (par 5) is approached over a small lake.

The Worcestershire Golf Club: 18 Holes, 6455yds, Par 71, SSS 72. Club membership 750.
Visitors Mon-Fri except BHs. Booking required. Handicap certificate. Dress code. Societies booking required. Green Fees £42 per day, £36 per round Course Designer Dr Alistair Mackenzie Prof Richard Lewis Facilities ⊕ ⦿ ⛳ ☐ ⚑ ⬜ ⬜ ⬜ ✦ Leisure indoor teaching facility Conf Corporate Hospitality Days Location 2m S of Gt Malvern on B4209

continued

Hotel ★★★ 85% HL The Cottage in the Wood Hotel, Holywell Road, Malvern Wells, MALVERN ☎ 01684 588860 📄 01684 588860 30 en suite

REDDITCH   Map 7 SP06

Abbey Hotel Golf & Country Club Dagnell End Rd B98 9BE
☎ 01527 406600 & 406500   📄 01527 406514
web: www.theabbeyhotel.co.uk

Abbey Hotel Golf & Country Club: 18 Holes, 6561yds, Par 72, SSS 72.
Course Designer Donald Steele **Location** A441 N from town, onto B4101 signed Beoley, right onto Hither Green Ln
Telephone for further details
Hotel ★★★★ 77% HL Best Western Abbey Hotel Golf & Country Club, Hither Green Lane, Dagnell End Road, Bordesley, REDDITCH
☎ 01527 406600 📄 01527 406600   100 en suite

Pitcheroak Plymouth Rd B97 4PB
☎ 01527 541054   📄 01527 65216
9 Holes, 4561yds, Par 65, SSS 62.
Prof David Stewart **Facilities** ⑪ 🍴 🛦 ⬛ 🍷 🌲 🏠 ☂ ✂
Location SW of town centre off A448
Telephone for further details
Hotel Express by Holiday Inn Redditch, Hewell Road, Enfield, REDDITCH ☎ 01527 584658 📄 01527 584658   100 en suite

Redditch Lower Grinsty, Green Ln, Callow Hill B97 5PJ
☎ 01527 543079 (sec)   📄 01527 547413
e-mail: lee@redditchgolfclub.com
web: www.redditchgolfclub.com
Parkland with many tree-lined fairways, excellent greens, and a particularly tough finish. The par 3s are all long and demanding.

18 Holes, 6671yds, Par 72, SSS 72, Course record 68. Club membership 650.
Visitors Mon-Fri except BHs. Booking required. Dress code.
Societies booking required **Green Fees** £45 per day, £35 per round
Course Designer F Pennick **Prof** David Down **Facilities** ⑪ 🍴 🛦
⬛ 🍷 🌲 🏠 ☂ ✂ 🛒 ✂ **Location** 2m SW
Hotel Express by Holiday Inn Redditch, Hewell Road, Enfield, REDDITCH ☎ 01527 584658 📄 01527 584658   100 en suite

TENBURY WELLS   Map 7 SO56

Cadmore Lodge Hotel & Country Club St Michaels, Berrington Green WR15 8TQ
☎ 01584 810044   📄 01584 810044
e-mail: reception.cadmore@cadmorelodge.com
web: www.cadmorelodge.com

A picturesque 9-hole course in a brook valley. Challenging holes include the 1st and 6th over the lake, 8th over the valley and 9th over hedges.
Cadmore Lodge Hotel & Country Club: 9 Holes, 5132yds, Par 68, SSS 65. Club membership 200.
Visitors Mon-Sun & BHs. Booking required Wed, weekends & BHs. Handicap certificate. Dress code. **Societies** welcome. **Green Fees** not confirmed **Course Designer** G Farr, J Weston **Facilities** ⑪ 🍴 🛦
⬛ 🍷 🌲 ◇ ✂ **Leisure** heated indoor swimming pool, fishing, sauna, gymnasium, pool table **Conf** facs Corporate Hospitality Days **Location** A4112 from Tenbury to Leominster, 2m right for Berrington, 0.75m on left
Hotel ★★ 74% HL Cadmore Lodge Hotel & Country Club, Berrington Green, St Michaels, TENBURY WELLS ☎ 01584 810044
📄 01584 810044   15 en suite

WORCESTER   Map 3 SO85

BW Bank House Hotel Golf & Country Club Bransford WR6 5JD
☎ 01886 833545   📄 01886 832461
e-mail: bransfordgolfclub@brook-hotels.co.uk
web: www.bw-bankhouse.co.uk
The Bransford Course is designed as a Florida-style course with fairways weaving between water courses, 14 lakes and sculpted mounds. The 6172yd course has dog-legs, island greens and tight fairways to challenge all standards of player and comprises 6 par 3's, 6 par 4's and 6 par 5's. The 10th, 16th and 18th (The Devil's Elbow) are particularly tricky.
Bransford Course: 18 Holes, 6172yds, Par 72, SSS 70, Course record 65. Club membership 414.
Visitors Mon-Sun & BHs. Booking required. Dress code. *continued*

Societies welcome. **Green Fees** Summer £22 per 18 holes (£32 weekends) Winter £15 per round (£20 weekends) **Course Designer** Bob Sandow **Prof** Matt Nixon **Facilities** ⓣ ⦿ ⓛ ♿ ⛳ ▲ ▣ ☂ ◇ ♣ ⛳ ♣ ♣ **Leisure** outdoor swimming pool, sauna, gymnasium, vertical sunbed **Conf** facs Corporate Hospitality Days **Location** M5 junct 7, A4103 3m S of Worcester
Hotel ★★★ 67% HL Fownes, City Walls Road, WORCESTER
☎ 01905 613151 ▤ 01905 613151 61 en suite

Perdiswell Park Bilford Rd WR3 8DX
☎ 01905 754668 & 457189
Set in 85 acres of attractive parkland and suitable for all levels of golfer.
Perdiswell Park Golf Course: 18 Holes, 5297yds, Par 68, SSS 66. Club membership 300.
Visitors contact course for details. **Societies** welcome. **Green Fees** £12 per 18 holes, £8 per 9 holes (£16/£10 weekends) **Prof** Mark Woodward **Facilities** ⓣ ⦿ ⓛ ♿ ⛳ ▲ ▣ ☂ ◇ **Leisure** gymnasium **Conf** facs Corporate Hospitality Days **Location** N of city centre off A30
Hotel ★★★ 77% HL Pear Tree Inn & Country Hotel, Smite, WORCESTER ☎ 01905 756565 ▤ 01905 756565 24 en suite

Worcester Golf & Country Club Boughton Park WR2 4EZ
☎ 01905 422555 ▤ 01905 749090
e-mail: worcestergcc@btconnect.com
web: www.worcestergcc.co.uk
Fine parkland course with many varieties of trees, lakes and fine views of the Malvern Hills. Narrow approaches to the greens provide a good test of golf accuracy.
Worcester Golf & Country Club: 18 Holes, 6251yds, Par 70, SSS 70, Course record 64. Club membership 900.
Visitors Mon-Fri & BHs. Booking required. Handicap certificate. Dress code. **Societies** booking required. **Green Fees** £50 per day, £40 per round **Course Designer** Dr A Mackenzie **Prof** Graham Farr **Facilities** ▲ ▣ ◇ **Leisure** hard and grass tennis courts, squash **Conf** facs Corporate Hospitality Days **Location** 1.5m from city centre on A4103
Hotel ★★★ 67% HL Fownes, City Walls Road, WORCESTER
☎ 01905 613151 ▤ 01905 613151 61 en suite

WYTHALL   Map 7 SP07

Fulford Heath Tanners Green Ln B47 6BH
☎ 01564 824758 ▤ 01564 822629
e-mail: secretary@fulfordheathgolfclub.co.uk
web: www.fulfordheathgolfclub.co.uk
A mature parkland course encompassing two classic par 3s. The 11th, a mere 149yds, shoots from an elevated tee through a channel of trees to a well-protected green. The 16th, a 166yd par 3, elevated green, demands a 140yd carry over an imposing lake.
18 Holes, 5959yds, Par 70, SSS 69. Club membership 850.
Visitors handicap certificate. Dress code. **Societies** booking required. **Green Fees** £36 per day **Course Designer** Braid/Hawtree **Prof** Richard Dunbar **Facilities** ⓣ ⦿ ⓛ ♿ ⛳ ▲ ▣ ▦ ◇ **Conf** Corporate Hospitality Days **Location** 1m SE off A435
Hotel ★★★ 68% HL Corus, Stratford Road, Shirley, SOLIHULL
☎ 0844 736 8605 & 0121 745 0400 ▤ 0844 736 8605 111 en suite

YORKSHIRE, EAST RIDING OF

ALLERTHORPE   Map 8 SE85

Allerthorpe Park Allerthorpe Park YO42 4RL
☎ 01759 306686 ▤ 01759 305106
e-mail: enquiries@allerthorpeparkgolfclub.com
web: www.allerthorpeparkgolfclub.com
A picturesque parkland course, maintained to a high standard, with many interesting features, including a meandering beck and the 18th hole over the lake.
Allerthorpe Park Golf Club: 18 Holes, 6430yds, Par 70, SSS 70, Course record 67. Club membership 500.
Visitors Mon-Sun & BHs. Dress code. **Societies** Booking required **Green Fees** £25 per 18 holes, winter £15-£18 **Course Designer** J G Hatcliffe & Partners **Prof** James Drinkall **Facilities** ⓣ ⦿ ⓛ ♿ ⛳ ▲ ▣ ☂ ◇ **Conf** facs Corporate Hospitality Days **Location** 2m SW of Pocklington off A1079
Hotel ★★ 67% HL Feathers, 56 Market Place, POCKLINGTON, York
☎ 01759 303155 ▤ 01759 303155 16 en suite

AUGHTON   Map 8 SE73

Oaks Golf Club & Spa Aughton Common, Long Ln YO42 4PW
☎ 01757 288577 ▤ 01757 288232
e-mail: sheila@theoaksgolfclub.co.uk
web: www.theoaksgolfclub.co.uk

The course is built in harmony with its natural wooded parkland setting, near to the Derwent Ings. The wide green fairways blend and bend with the gentle countryside. Seven lakes come into play.
The Oaks Golf Club & Spa: 18 Holes, 6792yds, Par 72, SSS 72, Course record 65. Club membership 650.
Visitors Mon-Fri excluding BHs. Booking required. Handicap certificate. Dress code.. **Societies** booking required. **Green Fees** not confirmed **Course Designer** Fox Plant **Prof** Graham Walker/Lysa Jones **Facilities** ⓣ ⦿ ⓛ ♿ ⛳ ▲ ▣ ☂ ◇ ♣ ▦ ◇ ♣ **Leisure** heated indoor swimming pool, sauna, gymnasium, self-catering cottage with own putting greens **Conf** facs Corporate Hospitality Days **Location** 1m N of Bubwith on B1228
Hotel ★★★ 78% CHH Parsonage Country House, York Road, ESCRICK ☎ 01904 728111 ▤ 01904 728111 50 en suite

See advert on page 286

BEVERLEY
Map 8 TA03

Beverley & East Riding The Westwood HU17 8RG
☎ 01482 868757   📄 01482 868757
e-mail: golf@beverleygolfclub.karoo.co.uk

Picturesque parkland with some hard walking and natural hazards - trees and gorse bushes. Only two fairways adjoin. Cattle (spring to autumn) and horse-riders are occasional early morning hazards.

Westwood: 18 Holes, 6127yds, Par 69, SSS 69, Course record 64. Club membership 530.

Visitors Mon-Sun & BHs. Booking required weekends. Dress code. **Societies** welcome. **Green Fees** £22 per day; £17 per round (£29/£24 weekends) **Prof** Alex Ashby **Facilities** 🍴 🍽 🍸 💻 🍷 ⛳ 🏌
🚪 🏌 **Conf** Corporate Hospitality Days **Location** 1m SW on B1230
Hotel ★★★ 82% HL Tickton Grange, Tickton, BEVERLEY
☎ 01964 543666 📄 01964 543666   20 en suite

BRANDESBURTON
Map 8 TA14

Hainsworth Park Burton Holme YO25 8RT
☎ 01964 542362

18 Holes, 6362yds, Par 71, SSS 71.

Prof Paul Binnington **Facilities** 🍴 🍽 🍸 💻 🍷 ⛳ 🍴 🏌
◇ 🏌 🛒 🏌 **Location** SW of village on A165
Telephone for further details
Hotel ★★ 72% HL Burton Lodge, BRANDESBURTON
☎ 01964 542847 📄 01964 542847   9 en suite

BRIDLINGTON
Map 8 TA16

Bridlington Belvedere Rd YO15 3NA
☎ 01262 606367
e-mail: enquiries@bridlingtongolfclub.co.uk
web: www.bridlingtongolfclub.co.uk

Parkland alongside Bridlington Bay, with tree-lined fairways and six ponds, comprising two loops of 9 holes. Excellent putting surfaces.

18 Holes, 6638yds, Par 72, SSS 72, Course record 64. Club membership 600.

Visitors Mon-Sun & BHs. Booking required. Dress code. **Societies** welcome. **Green Fees** £32 per day, £25 per round (£40/£32 weekends & BHs) **Course Designer** James Braid **Prof** Anthony Howarth **Facilities** 🍴 🍽 🍸 💻 🍷 ⛳ 🍴 🏌 🏌
Leisure snooker **Conf** facs Corporate Hospitality Days **Location** 1m S off A165
Hotel ★★★ 75% HL Expanse, North Marine Drive, BRIDLINGTON
☎ 01262 675347 📄 01262 675347   47 en suite

Bridlington Links Flamborough Rd, Marton YO15 1DW
☎ 01262 401584   📄 01262 401702
e-mail: info@bridlington-links.co.uk
web: www.bridlington-links.co.uk

Coastal links type course with large greens, numerous water hazards and splendid views towards Flamborough Head. When the wind blows off the sea, the course becomes a challenging test of golf for even the experienced golfer.

Main: 18 Holes, 6719yds, Par 72, SSS 72, Course record 68. Club membership 350.

Visitors Mon-Sun & BHs. Booking required. Handicap certificate & dress code for Main Course. **Societies** booking required. **Green Fees** Summer £20 per round (£25 weekends and BHs). Winter

£12/£15 **Course Designer** Swan **Prof** Steve Raybould **Facilities** 🍴
🍽 🍸 💻 🍷 ⛳ 🍴 🏌 ◇ 🏌 🛒 🏌 🏌 **Conf** facs
Corporate Hospitality Days **Location** on B1255 between Bridlington & Flamborough Head
Hotel ★★★ 75% HL Expanse, North Marine Drive, BRIDLINGTON
☎ 01262 675347 📄 01262 675347   47 en suite

BROUGH
Map 8 SE92

Brough Cave Rd HU15 1HB
☎ 01482 667291   📄 01482 669873
e-mail: gt@brough-golfclub.co.uk
web: www.brough-golfclub.co.uk

Parkland course, where accurate positioning of the tee ball is required for good scoring. Testing for the scratch player without being too difficult for the higher handicap.

18 Holes, 6067yds, Par 68, SSS 69, Course record 61. Club membership 680.

Visitors Mon, Tue, Thu & Fri except BHs. Booking required. Handicap certificate. Dress code. **Societies** booking required. **Green Fees** £50 per day, £35 per round (£70/£55 weekends & BHs) **Prof** Gordon Townhill **Facilities** 🍴 🍽 🍸 💻 🍷 ⛳ 🍴 🏌
Conf Corporate Hospitality Days **Location** 8m W of Hull off A63
Hotel ★★★ 71% HL Cave Castle Hotel & Country Club, Church Hill, SOUTH CAVE ☎ 01430 422245 📄 01430 422245   70 en suite

BURSTWICK
Map 8 TA22

Burstwick Country Golf Ellifoot Ln HU12 9EF
☎ 01964 670112   📄 01964 670116
e-mail: info@burstwickcountrygolf.co.uk
web: www.burstwickcountrygolf.co.uk

An 18 hole course with 72 bunkers, 5 lakes and 4,500 trees set in attractive countryside. Not a long course but very challenging with well-guarded greens, exposed tee shots and sharp dog-legs. A modern yet natural design with each bunker and water feature strategically placed around the landing areas and undulating greens. All greens to full USGA specification.

Burstwick Country Golf: 18 Holes, 5964yds, Par 70, SSS 69, Course record 65. Club membership 400.

Visitors Mon-Sun & BHs. Booking required weekends & BHs. Dress code. **Societies** booking required. **Green Fees** £16 per 18 holes (£22 weekends) **Course Designer** Gaunt Golf Design Ltd **Prof** Mark Richardson **Facilities** 🍴 🍸 💻 🍷 ⛳ 🍴 🏌 🏌 🛒 🏌 🏌
Conf facs Corporate Hospitality Days **Location** 10 miles E of Hull, A63 towards Hull, then A1033 to Hedon. Follow minor roads signed for Burstwick.
Hotel ★★★★ 71% HL Portland, Paragon Street, HULL
☎ 01482 326462 📄 01482 326462   126 en suite

COTTINGHAM
Map 8 TA03

Cottingham Parks Golf & Country Club Woodhill Way HU16 5SW
☎ 01482 846030   📄 01482 845932
e-mail: enquiries@cottinghamparks.co.uk
web: www.cottinghamparks.co.uk

Gently undulating parkland course incorporating many natural features, including lateral water hazards, several ponds on the approach to greens, and rolling fairways.

continued

Cottingham Parks Golf & Leisure Club: 18 Holes, 6453yds, Par 72, SSS 71, Course record 66. Club membership 600.
Visitors booking required. Dress code. **Societies** welcome. **Green Fees** £20 per round (£30 weekends & BHs) **Course Designer** Terry Litten **Prof** Chris Gray **Facilities** ⑪ ⑩ ఉ ఊ 🍴 ⚓ 🏠 ⚑ ◇ 🛒 ✦ ✦ **Leisure** heated indoor swimming pool, sauna, gymnasium, Jacuzzi, Remedial masseur, hair & beauty salon **Conf** facs Corporate Hospitality Days **Location** A164 onto B1233 towards Cottingham, 100yds left onto Woodhill Way

Cottingham Parks Golf & Country Club

Hotel ★★★ 82% HL Best Western Willerby Manor, Well Lane, WILLERBY ☎ 01482 652616 🖷 01482 652616 63 en suite

DRIFFIELD (GREAT) Map 8 TA05

Driffield Sunderlandwick YO25 9AD
☎ 01377 253116 🖷 01377 240599
e-mail: info@driffieldgolfclub.co.uk
web: www.driffieldgolfclub.co.uk
An easy walking, mature parkland course set within the beautiful Sunderlandwick Estate, including numerous water features, one of which is a renowned trout stream.
18 Holes, 6215yds, Par 70, SSS 69, Course record 65. Club membership 693.
Visitors Mon-Sun & BHs. Booking required Tue, weekends & BHs.. Handicap certificate. Dress code. **Societies** booking required. **Green Fees** not confirmed **Prof** Kenton Wright **Facilities** ⑪ ⑩ ఉ ఊ 🍴 ⚓ 🏠 🛒 ✦ ✦ **Leisure** fishing **Conf** facs Corporate Hospitality Days **Location** 0.5m S off A164
Hotel ★★★ 78% HL Best Western Bell, 46 Market Place, DRIFFIELD ☎ 01377 256661 🖷 01377 256661 16 en suite

FLAMBOROUGH Map 8 TA27

Flamborough Head Lighthouse Rd YO15 1AR
☎ 01262 850333 🖷 01262 850279
e-mail: secretary@flamboroughheadgolfclub.co.uk
web: www.flamboroughheadgolfclub.co.uk
Undulating cliff top links type course on the Flamborough headland.
18 Holes, 6189yds, Par 71, SSS 69, Course record 64. Club membership 450.
Visitors Mon-Sat & BHs. Sun pm.Booking required weekends & BHs. Handicap certificate. Dress code. **Societies** welcome. **Green Fees** £32 per day, £22 per round (£31/£38 weekends & BHs) **Prof** C J Feast **Facilities** ⑪ ⑩ ఉ ఊ 🍴 ⚓ 🏠 ✦ 🛒 ✦ **Conf** Corporate Hospitality Days **Location** 2m E off B1259
Hotel ★★ 75% SHL North Star, North Marine Drive, FLAMBOROUGH ☎ 01262 850379 🖷 01262 850379 7 en suite

HORNSEA Map 8 TA14

Hornsea Rolston Rd HU18 1XG
☎ 01964 532020 🖷 01964 532080
web: www.hornseagolfclub.co.uk
Hornsea Golf Club Ltd: 18 Holes, 6685yds, Par 72, SSS 72, Course record 66.
Course Designer Herd/Mackenzie/Braid **Location** 1m S on B1242, signs for Hornsea Freeport
Telephone for further details
Hotel ★★ 72% HL Burton Lodge, BRANDESBURTON ☎ 01964 542847 🖷 01964 542847 9 en suite

HOWDEN Map 8 SE72

Boothferry Spaldington Ln DN14 7NG
☎ 01430 430364 🖷 01430 430567
e-mail: info@boothferrygolfclub.co.uk
web: www.boothferrygolfclub.co.uk
Pleasant, meadowland course in the Vale of York with interesting natural dykes, creating challenges on some holes. The par 5 9th is a test for any golfer with its dyke coming into play on the tee shot, second shot and approach. Easy walking.
18 Holes, 6651yds, Par 73, SSS 72, Course record 64. Eagles: 9 Holes, 2700yds, Par 29, SSS 30. Club membership 370.
Visitors Mon-Sun & BHs. Booking required. Dress code for main course.. **Societies** booking required. **Green Fees** £18 per 18 holes, £13 per 9 holes (£22/£17 weekends). Eagles £8 per 18 holes, £5 per 9 holes **Course Designer** Donald Steel **Prof** Matthew Rumble **Facilities** ⑪ ⑩ ఉ ఊ 🍴 ⚓ 🏠 ⚑ ✦ 🛒 ✦ ✦ **Leisure** 9 hole beginners course **Conf** facs Corporate Hospitality Days **Location** M62 junct 37, 2.5m N of Howden off B1228
Hotel ★★★ 78% CHH Parsonage Country House, York Road, ESCRICK ☎ 01904 728111 🖷 01904 728111 50 en suite

KINGSTON UPON HULL Map 8 TA02

Ganstead Park Longdales Ln, Coniston HU11 4LB
☎ 01482 817754 🖷 01482 817754
e-mail: secretary@gansteadpark.co.uk
web: www.gansteadpark.co.uk
Easy walking parkland with water features.
18 Holes, 6801yds, Par 72, SSS 73, Course record 62. Club membership 500.
Visitors contact club for details. **Societies** welcome. **Green Fees** £27 per day, £20 per round **Course Designer** P Green **Prof** Michael J Smee **Facilities** ⑪ ⑩ ఉ ఊ 🍴 ⚓ 🏠 ⚑ ✦ 🛒 ✦ **Conf** Corporate Hospitality Days **Location** A165 Hull exit, pass Ganstead, right onto B1238 to Bilton, course on right
Hotel ★★★★ 71% HL Portland, Paragon Street, HULL ☎ 01482 326462 🖷 01482 326462 126 en suite

Hull The Hall, 27 Packman Ln HU10 7TJ
☎ 01482 658919 📠 01482 658919
e-mail: secretary@hullgolfclub1921.karoo.co.uk
web: hullgolfclub.com

Attractive mature parkland course.
Hull Golf Club (1921) Ltd: 18 Holes, 6262yds, Par 70, SSS 70, Course record 64. Club membership 693.
Visitors Mon-Sun & BHs. Booking required. Handicap certificate. Dress code. **Societies** booking required. **Green Fees** Nov-Feb £25 per round. Mar-Oct £45 per day, £36 per round (£45 per day/round weekends)
Course Designer James Braid **Prof** David Jagger **Facilities** 🍽 🛒 🏌 🛋 🚗 🎯 🏌 🏌 **Leisure** snooker
Conf Corporate Hospitality Days **Location** 5m W of city off A164
Hotel ★★★ 82% HL Best Western Willerby Manor, Well Lane, WILLERBY ☎ 01482 652616 📠 01482 652616 63 en suite

See advert on this page

Springhead Park Willerby Rd HU5 5JE
☎ 01482 656309
Municipal parkland course with tight, undulating tree-lined fairways.
Springhead Park Golf Club (Municipal): 18 Holes, 6402yds, Par 71, SSS 71. Club membership 200.
Visitors contact club for details. **Societies** welcome. **Green Fees** £12.50 per round (£14.50 weekends) **Facilities** 🛒 🏌 🛋 🏠 🏌 🚗 **Conf** Corporate Hospitality Days **Location** 5m W off A164
Hotel ★★★ 82% HL Best Western Willerby Manor, Well Lane, WILLERBY ☎ 01482 652616 📠 01482 652616 63 en suite

Sutton Park Salthouse Rd HU8 9HF
☎ 01482 374242 📠 01482 701428
18 Holes, 6251yds, Par 70, SSS 69, Course record 67.
Facilities 🎯 by prior arrangement 🍽 by prior arrangement 🛒 🏌 🏠 🏠 🚗 🏌 **Location** 3m NE on B1237, off A165
Telephone for further details
Hotel ★★★★ 71% HL Portland, Paragon Street, HULL
☎ 01482 326462 📠 01482 326462 126 en suite

POCKLINGTON
Map 8 SE84

KP Kilnwick Percy YO42 1UF
☎ 01759 303090 📠 01759 303090
e-mail: info@kpclub.co.uk
web: www.kpclub.co.uk
Attractive parkland course on the edge of the Wolds above Pocklington which has recently undergone a major redevelopment and offers a great golf experience.
The KP Club: 18 Holes, 6218yds, Par 70, SSS 70, Course record 66. Club membership 600.

Visitors Mon-Sun & BHs. Booking required. Dress code.
Societies welcome. **Green Fees** £25 per 18 holes (£30 weekends & BHs) **Course Designer** John Day **Prof** Aaron Pheasant **Facilities** 🎯 🍽 🛒 🏌 🛋 🏠 🚗 🏌 **Conf** facs Corporate Hospitality Days **Location** 1m E of Pocklington off B1246
Hotel ★★ 67% HL Feathers, 56 Market Place, POCKLINGTON, York ☎ 01759 303155 📠 01759 303155 16 en suite

SKIDBY
Map 8 TA03

Skidby Lakes Woodhill Way HU16 5SW
☎ 01482 844270 📠 01482 844269
e-mail: info@skidbylakes.co.uk
web: www.skidbylakes.co.uk
An interesting parkland course with narrow fairways and three large lakes that come into play on several holes whilst playing the well guarded undulating greens.
18 Holes, 6158yds, Par 70, SSS 70, Course record 71.
Visitors Mon-Sun & BHs. Dress code. **Societies** booking required. **Green Fees** £15 per round (£20 weekends & BHs) **Course Designer** Wilf Adamson **Prof** Karl Worby **Facilities** 🎯 🍽 🛒 🏌 🏌 🛋 🏠 🚗 🏌 🏌 **Leisure** heated indoor swimming pool, sauna, gymnasium **Conf** facs Corporate Hospitality Days **Location** from Humber Bridge proceed N on A164 towards Beverley. At Skidby roundabout take B1233 towards Cottingham for 100 yds and turn left into Woodhill Way, entrance 3rd on right
Hotel ★★★ 82% HL Best Western Willerby Manor, Well Lane, WILLERBY ☎ 01482 652616 📠 01482 652616 63 en suite

SOUTH CAVE

Map 8 SE93

Cave Castle Hotel & Country Club Church Hill, South Cave HU15 2EU
☎ 01430 426262 & 426259/421286 📠 01430 421118
e-mail: admin@cavecastlegolf.co.uk
web: www.cavecastlegolf.co.uk
Undulating meadow and parkland at the foot of the Wolds, with superb views.

Cave Castle Hotel & Country Club: 18 Holes, 6524yds, Par 72, SSS 71, Course record 68. Club membership 410.
Visitors Mon-Sun & BHs. Booking required. Dress code.
Societies booking required. **Green Fees** phone **Course Designer** Mrs N Freling **Prof** Stephen MacKinder **Facilities** ⑪ ⑩ 🍴 ⤵ ⌂ ⛴ ⛳
⤴ 🏚 ⛳ ⬡ 🛺 ⛳ **Leisure** heated indoor swimming pool, sauna, gymnasium **Conf** facs Corporate Hospitality Days **Location** 1m from A63
Hotel ★★★ 71% HL Cave Castle Hotel & Country Club, Church Hill, SOUTH CAVE ☎ 01430 422245 📠 01430 422245 70 en suite

WITHERNSEA

Map 8 TA32

Withernsea Chesnut Av HU19 2PG
☎ 01964 612078 & 612258 📠 01964 612078
e-mail: info@withernseagolfclub.co.uk
web: www.withernseagolfclub.co.uk
Exposed seaside links with narrow, undulating fairways, bunkers and small greens.

9 Holes, 6207yds, Par 72, SSS 69. Club membership 200.
Visitors dress code. **Societies** booking required. **Green Fees** £15 per 18 holes **Facilities** ⑪ ⑩ 🍴 ⤵ ⌂ ⛴ ⤴ ⛳ 🛺 **Conf** facs
Corporate Hospitality Days **Location** S of town centre off A1033, signed from Victoria Av
Hotel ★★★★ 71% HL Portland, Paragon Street, HULL
☎ 01482 326462 📠 01482 326462 126 en suite

YORKSHIRE, NORTH

ALDWARK

Map 8 SE46

Aldwark Manor Golf & Spa Hotel YO61 1UF
☎ 01347 838353 📠 01347 833991
e-mail: aldwarkmanorgolf@qhotels.co.uk
web: www.qhotels.co.uk

An easy walking, scenic 18-hole parkland course with holes both sides of the River Ure. The course surrounds the Victorian Aldwark Manor Golf Hotel.

Aldwark Manor Golf & Spa Hotel: 18 Holes, 6187yds, Par 72, SSS 70, Course record 67. Club membership 200.
Visitors Mon-Sun & BHs. Booking required. Dress code.
Societies booking required. **Green Fees** £50 per day, £35 per round (£60/£40 weekends & BHs) **Facilities** ⑪ ⑩ 🍴 ⤵ ⌂ ⛴ ⤴
🛺 ⬡ ⛳ 🏚 ⛳ **Leisure** heated indoor swimming pool, fishing, sauna, gymnasium **Conf** facs Corporate Hospitality Days **Location** 5m SE of Boroughbridge off A1
Hotel ★★★★ 73% HL Aldwark Manor & Spa Hotel, ALDWARK, York ☎ 01347 838146 📠 01347 838146 54 en suite

BEDALE

Map 8 SE28

Bedale Leyburn Rd DL8 1EZ
☎ 01677 422451 (sec) 📠 01677 427143
e-mail: office@bedalegolfclub.com
web: www.bedalegolfclub.com

One of North Yorkshire's most picturesque and interesting courses. The 18-hole course is in parkland with mature trees, water hazards and strategically placed bunkers. Easy walking, no heavy climbs.

Bedale Golf Club Ltd: 18 Holes, 6610yds, Par 72, SSS 72, Course record 68. Club membership 600.
Visitors Mon-Sun & BHs. Dress code. **Societies** welcome. **Green Fees** £32 per day, £25 per round (£36/£32 weekends) **Course Designer** Hawtree **Prof** Tony Johnson **Facilities** ⑪ ⑩ 🍴 ⤵ ⌂
🍴 ⤴ 🏚 ⛳ 🛺 ⛳ **Conf** facs Corporate Hospitality Days
Location A1 onto A684 at Leeming Bar to Bedale
Hotel ★★ 65% HL The White Rose, Bedale Road, LEEMING BAR ☎ 01677 422707 📠 01677 422707 18 en suite

BENTHAM

Map 7 SD66

Bentham Robin Ln LA2 7AG
☎ 015242 62470
e-mail: secretary@benthamgolfclub.co.uk
web: www.benthamgolfclub.co.uk
Moorland course with glorious views and excellent greens.

18 Holes, 6005yds, Par 71, SSS 69, Course record 69. Club membership 500.
Visitors Mon-Sun & BHs. Booking required. Dress code.
Societies booking required. **Green Fees** £35 per day, £30 per round (£35 weekends) **Facilities** ⑪ ⑩ 🍴 ⤵ ⌂ 🍴 ⤴ 🏚 ⛳ 🛺
⛳ **Conf** Corporate Hospitality Days **Location** N side of High Bentham

ENGLAND

The Oaks Golf Club & Spa

Aughton Common, Aughton, YORK YO42 4PW

- ▶ An excellent 18 holes of championship golf
- ▶ First class food and drink served in a warm, friendly environment
- ▶ Bring your partner to The Spa for a very special treat
- ▶ Superb practice and teaching facilities incorporating Golf Monthly Top 25 UK Coach Graham Walker's Golf Academy.

Tel: 01757 288577   **Fax:** 01757 288232
Website: www.theoaksgolfclub.co.uk
www.thespaattheoaks.co.uk

CATTERICK GARRISON
Map 8 SE29

Catterick Leyburn Rd DL9 3QE
☎ 01748 833268 🗎 01748 833268
e-mail: secretary@catterickgolfclub.co.uk
web: www.catterickgolfclub.co.uk

Scenic parkland and moorland course of championship standard, with good views of the Pennines and the Cleveland hills. Testing 1st and 6th holes.

18 Holes, 6329yds, Par 71, SSS 71, Course record 64.
Club membership 500.

Visitors Mon-Sun & BHs. Dress code. **Societies** booking required.
Green Fees £30 per day, £25 per 18 holes (£35/£30 weekends)
Course Designer Arthur Day **Prof** Andy Marshall **Facilities** ⊕
⏣ 🍴 🛒 ⛉ 🎯 🏌 🚶 💺 ♂ 🚗 ♂ **Conf** facs Corporate
Hospitality Days **Location** 0.5m W of Catterick Garrison
Hotel ★★★ 75% HL King's Head, Market Place, RICHMOND
☎ 01748 850220 🗎 01748 850220 30 en suite

COPMANTHORPE
Map 8 SE54

Pike Hills Tadcaster Rd YO23 3UW
☎ 01904 700797 🗎 01904 700797
e-mail: secretary@pikehillsgolfclub.co.uk
web: www.pikehillsgolfclub.co.uk

Parkland course surrounding a nature reserve. Level terrain.

18 Holes, 6146yds, Par 71, SSS 70, Course record 63.
Club membership 750.

Visitors Mon-Fri except BHs. Booking required. Handicap certificate.
Dress code. **Societies** booking required. **Green Fees** £36 per day, £30
per round **Prof** Ian Gradwell **Facilities** ⊕ 🍴 ⏣ 🛒 ⛉ 🏌 🎯
⛉ ♂ 🚗 ♂ **Conf** facs Corporate Hospitality Days **Location** 3m
SW of York on A64
Hotel ★★★★ 76% HL York Marriott, Tadcaster Road, YORK
☎ 01904 701000 🗎 01904 701000 151 en suite

EASINGWOLD
Map 8 SE56

Easingwold Stillington Rd YO61 3ET
☎ 01347 821964 (Pro) & 822474 (Sec)
e-mail: enquiries@easingwoldgolfclub.co.uk
web: www.easingwoldgolfclub.co.uk

Parkland with easy walking. Trees are a major feature and on six holes water hazards come into play.

18 Holes, 6538yds, Par 74, SSS 72. Club membership 650.

Visitors Mon. Wed-Fri except BHs. Handicap certificate. Dress code.
Societies booking required. **Green Fees** £35 per day, £28 per round
Course Designer Hawtree **Prof** John Hughes **Facilities** ⊕ 🍴 ⏣
🛒 ⛉ 🏌 🎯 ⛉ ♂ 🚗 ♂ 🏌 **Conf** Corporate Hospitality
Days **Location** 1m S of Easingwold
Hotel ★★ 75% SHL George, Market Place, EASINGWOLD
☎ 01347 821698 🗎 01347 821698 15 en suite

FILEY
Map 8 TA18

Filey West Av YO14 9BQ
☎ 01723 513293 🗎 01723 514952
e-mail: secretary@fileygolfclub.com
web: www.fileygolfclub.com

Links and parkland course with good views. Stream runs through course. Testing 9th and 13th holes.

18 Holes, 6112yds, Par 70, SSS 69, Course record 64.
Academy Course: 9 Holes, 1513yds, Par 30.
Club membership 800.

Visitors Mon-Sun & BHs. Booking Fri, Sat & BHs. Handicap certificate.
Dress code. **Societies** welcome. **Green Fees** £30 per day (£35 per
round weekends), Academy £7 per round **Course Designer** Braid
Prof Darren Squire **Facilities** ⊕ 🍴 ⏣ 🛒 ⛉ 🏌 🎯 ♂
🚗 ♂ **Location** 0.5m S of Filey

GANTON
Map 8 SE97

Ganton YO12 4PA
☎ 01944 710329 🗎 01944 710922
e-mail: secretary@gantongolfclub.com
web: www.gantongolfclub.com

Championship course, heathland, gorse-lined fairways and heavily bunkered; variable winds. The opening holes make full use of the contours of the land and the approach to the second demands the finest touch. The 4th is considered one of the best holes on the outward half with its shot across a valley to a plateau green, the surrounding gorse punishing anything less than a perfect shot. The finest hole is possibly the 18th, requiring an accurately placed drive to give a clear shot to the sloping, well-bunkered green.

18 Holes, 6724yds, Par 73, SSS 73, Course record 65.
Club membership 500.

Visitors Mon-Sun & BHs. Booking required. Handicap certificate.
Dress code. **Societies** booking required. **Green Fees** £78 per day
(£88 weekends). **Course Designer** Dunn/Vardon/Braid/Colt **Prof** Gary
Brown **Facilities** ⊕ 🍴 ⏣ 🛒 ⛉ 🏌 🎯 ♂ 🚗 ♂
Conf Corporate Hospitality Days **Location** N of village off A64
Hotel ★★★ 73% HL East Ayton Lodge Country House, Moor Lane,
Forge Valley, EAST AYTON ☎ 01723 864227 🗎 01723 864227
27 en suite

HARROGATE
Map 8 SE35

Harrogate Forest Lane Head, Starbeck HG2 7TF
☎ 01423 862999 🗎 01423 860073
e-mail: secretary@harrogate-gc.co.uk
web: www.harrogate-gc.co.uk

Course on fairly flat terrain with MacKenzie-style greens and tree-lined fairways. While not a long course, the layout penalises the golfer who strays off the fairway. Subtly placed bunkers and copses of trees require the golfer to adopt careful thought and accuracy if par is be bettered. The last six holes include five par 4s, of which four exceed 400yds.

18 Holes, 6241yds, Par 69, SSS 70, Course record 63.
Club membership 700.

Visitors Mon, Wed-Fri, Sun & BHs. Tue pm only. Handicap
certificate. Dress code. **Societies** booking required. **Green Fees** £45
per day, £40 per round (£50 Sun) **Course Designer** Sandy Herd

continued

ENGLAND

Prof Gary Stothard, Sam Evison **Facilities** ⊕ ⊙ ▦ ☐ ▦ ⚒ 🏠 ⚑ 🚜 ⚐ **Leisure** snooker **Conf** Corporate Hospitality Days **Location** 2.25m N on A59
Hotel ★★★ 77% HL Best Western Dower House, Bond End, KNARESBOROUGH ☎ 01423 863302 ▤ 01423 863302 31 en suite

Oakdale Oakdale Glen HG1 2LN
☎ 01423 567162   ▤ 01423 536030
e-mail: mikecross@oakdale-golfclub.com
web: www.oakdale-golfclub.com

A pleasant, undulating parkland course which provides a good test of golf for the low handicap player without intimidating the less proficient. A special feature is an attractive stream which comes in to play on four holes. Excellent views from the clubhouse with good facilities.

18 Holes, 6456yds, Par 71, SSS 71, Course record 61. Club membership 975.

Visitors Mon-Sun & BHs. Handicap certificate. Dress code.
Societies booking required. **Green Fees** £49 for 27 holes, £42 per 18 holes (£59 weekends & BHs) **Course Designer** Dr McKenzie
Prof Clive Dell **Facilities** ⊕ ⊙ ▦ ☐ ▦ ⚒ 🏠 ⚑ 🚜 ⚐ **Conf** Corporate Hospitality Days **Location** N of town centre off A61
Hotel ★★★★ 75% HL Barceló Harrogate Majestic Hotel, Ripon Road, HARROGATE ☎ 01423 700300 ▤ 01423 700300 174 en suite

Rudding Park Rudding Park, Follifoot HG3 1JH
☎ 01423 872100   ▤ 01423 872286
e-mail: reservations@ruddingpark.com
web: www.ruddingpark.co.uk

The course runs through 18th century parkland and provides a challenge for the most seasoned golfer with mature trees, attractive lakes and water features. A new 6 hole short course opened in 2008 created to USGA specifications and including a signature island hole based on the notorious 17th at Sawgrass, Florida.

Hawtree Course: 18 Holes, 6883yds, Par 72, SSS 73, Course record 68. Club membership 650.

Visitors Mon-Sun & BHs. Booking required. Handicap certificate. Dress code. **Societies** booking required. **Green Fees** from £12 per 18 holes depending on day/time **Course Designer** Martin Hawtree **Prof** M Moore/N Moore/D Fountain **Facilities** ⊕ ⊙ ▦ ☐ ▦ ⚒ 🏠 ⚑ 🍴 🚜 ⚐ 🏴 **Leisure** 6 hole par 3 short course **Conf** facs Corporate Hospitality Days **Location** 2m SE of Harrogate town centre, off A658, brown tourist signs
Hotel ★★★★ HL Rudding Park Hotel & Golf, Rudding Park, Follifoot, HARROGATE ☎ 01423 871350 ▤ 01423 871350 49 en suite

See advert on opposite page

KIRKBYMOORSIDE Map 8 SE68

Kirkbymoorside Manor Vale YO62 6EG
☎ 01751 430402   ▤ 01751 433190
e-mail: enqs@kirkbymoorsidegolf.co.uk
web: www.kirkbymoorsidegolf.co.uk

Hilly parkland with narrow fairways, gorse and hawthorn bushes. Beautiful views and several interesting holes..

Kirkbymoorside Golf Club Ltd: 18 Holes, 6207yds, Par 69, SSS 69, Course record 65. Club membership 600.

Visitors Mon-Sun & BHs. Booking required. Dress code.
Societies booking required. **Green Fees** not confirmed **Prof** John Hinchliffe **Facilities** ⊕ ⊙ ▦ ☐ ▦ ⚒ 🏠 ⚑ 🚜 ⚐ **Leisure** snooker room **Conf** facs Corporate Hospitality Days **Location** N of village
Hotel ★★ 78% HL Fox & Hounds Country Inn, Main Street, Sinnington, YORK ☎ 01751 431577 ▤ 01751 431577 10 en suite

KNARESBOROUGH Map 8 SE35

Knaresborough Boroughbridge Rd HG5 0QQ
☎ 01423 862690   ▤ 01423 869345
e-mail: secretary@kgc.uk.com
web: www.knaresboroughgolfclub.co.uk

Pleasant and well-presented parkland course in a rural setting. The first 11 holes are tree-lined and are constantly changing direction around the clubhouse. The closing holes head out overlooking the old quarry with fine views.

18 Holes, 6780yds, Par 72, SSS 72, Course record 69. Club membership 720.

Visitors Mon-Fri & Sun except BHs. Handicap certificate. Dress code. **Societies** welcome. **Green Fees** £44 per day, £34 per round (£39 Sun) **Course Designer** Hawtree **Prof** Andrew Turner **Facilities** ⊕ ▦ ☐ ▦ ⚒ 🏠 ⚑ 🚜 ⚐ **Conf** Corporate Hospitality Days **Location** 1.25m N on A6055
Hotel ★★★ 77% HL Best Western Dower House, Bond End, KNARESBOROUGH ☎ 01423 863302 ▤ 01423 863302 31 en suite

MALTON Map 8 SE77

Malton & Norton Welham Park, Norton YO17 9QE
☎ 01653 697912   ▤ 01653 697844
e-mail: maltonandnorton@btconnect.com
web: www.maltonandnortongolfclub.co.uk

Parkland course, consisting of three nine-hole loops, with panoramic views of the moors. Very testing 1st hole (564yd dog-leg, left) on the Welham Course.

continued

Welham Course: 18 Holes, 6456yds, Par 72, SSS 71,
Course record 66.
Park Course: 18 Holes, 6251yds, Par 72, SSS 70,
Course record 67.
Derwent Course: 18 Holes, 6295yds, Par 72, SSS 70,
Course record 66. Club membership 880.

Visitors contact club for details. **Societies** welcome. **Green Fees** £30 per round (£35 weekends & BHs) **Prof** M Brooks **Facilities** ⓘ 🍽 🍺 ☕ 🍴 🛋 🏌 ✦ **Conf** Corporate Hospitality Days **Location** 0.75m from Malton
Hotel ★★★ 82% CHH Burythorpe House Hotel, Burythorpe, MALTON
☎ 01653 658200 📠 01653 658200 13 en suite

MASHAM   Map 8 SE28

Masham Burnholme, Swinton Rd HG4 4NS
☎ 01765 688054 & 689379 📠 01765 688054
e-mail: info@mashamgolfclub.co.uk
web: www.mashamgolfclub.co.uk
Flat parkland crossed by River Burn, which comes into play on six holes.

9 Holes, 6204yds, Par 70, SSS 70, Course record 70.
Club membership 290.

Visitors Mon-Fri except BHs. Weekends pm. Booking required weekends. Dress code. **Societies** booking required. **Green Fees** £25 per day, £20 per 18 holes (£25 per 18 holes weekends) **Facilities** ⓘ by prior arrangement 🍽 by prior arrangement 🍺 ☕ 🍴 🛋 **Conf** Corporate Hospitality Days **Location** SW of Masham centre off A6108
Hotel ★★★★ HL Swinton Park, MASHAM ☎ 01765 680900
📠 01765 680900 30 en suite

MIDDLESBROUGH   Map 8 NZ41

Middlesbrough Brass Castle Ln, Marton TS8 9EE
☎ 01642 311515 📠 01642 319607
e-mail: enquiries@middlesbroughgolfclub.co.uk
web: www.middlesbroughgolfclub.co.uk
Undulating wooded parkland affected by the wind. Testing 6th, 8th and 12th holes.

18 Holes, 6302yds, Par 70, SSS 70, Course record 63.
Club membership 1004.

Visitors Mon, Wed-Fri, Sun & BHs. Booking required. Handicap certificate. Dress code. **Societies** booking required **Green Fees** £59 per round (£44 Sun) **Course Designer** Baird **Prof** Gordon Cattrell **Facilities** ⓘ 🍽 🍺 ☕ 🍴 🛋 🏌 🎯 🏌 ✦ **Leisure** snooker table **Conf** facs Corporate Hospitality Days **Location** 4m S off A172
Hotel ★★★ 79% HL Best Western Parkmore Hotel & Leisure Club, 636 Yarm Road, Eaglescliffe, STOCKTON-ON-TEES ☎ 01642 786815
📠 01642 786815 55 en suite

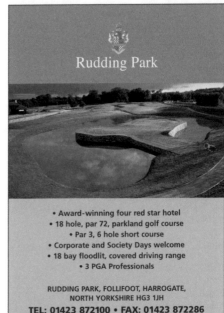

Middlesbrough Municipal Ladgate Ln TS5 7YZ
☎ 01642 315533 📠 01642 300726
e-mail: maurice_gormley@middlesbrough.gov.uk
web: www.middlesbrough.gov.uk

Parkland course with good views. The front nine holes have wide fairways and large, often well-guarded greens while the back nine demand shots over tree-lined water hazards and narrow entrances to subtly contoured greens.

Middlesbrough Municipal Golf Centre: 18 Holes, 6333yds,
Par 71, SSS 70, Course record 67. Club membership 630.

Visitors contact club for details. **Societies** welcome. **Green Fees** not confirmed **Course Designer** Shuttleworth **Prof** Alan Hope **Facilities** 🍺 ☕ 🍴 🛋 🏌 🎯 ✦ 🏌 ✦ 🏌 **Conf** Corporate Hospitality Days **Location** 2m S of Middlesbrough on the A174
Hotel ★★★ 79% HL Best Western Parkmore Hotel & Leisure Club, 636 Yarm Road, Eaglescliffe, STOCKTON-ON-TEES ☎ 01642 786815
📠 01642 786815 55 en suite

NORTHALLERTON
Map 8 SE39

Romanby Yafforth Rd DL7 0PE
☎ 01609 778855   📠 01609 779084
e-mail: richard.boucher@romanby.com
web: www.romanby.com

Set in natural undulating terrain with the River Wiske meandering through the course, it offers a testing round of golf for all abilities. In addition to the river, two lakes come into play on the 2nd, 5th and 11th holes. A 12-bay floodlit driving range.

Romanby Golf & Country Club: 18 Holes, 6663yds, Par 72, SSS 72, Course record 72. Club membership 525.

Visitors dress code. **Societies** welcome. **Green Fees** £25 per round (£30 weekends) **Course Designer** Will Adamson **Prof** Richard Wood **Facilities** ⓉⒾ🅁🄻🄳🄿🄐🄴🄾 **Leisure** 6 hole par 3 academy course **Conf** facs Corporate Hospitality Days **Location** 1m W of Northallerton on B6271
Hotel ★★★ 71% HL Solberge Hall, Newby Wiske, NORTHALLERTON ☎ 01609 779191 📠 01609 779191 24 en suite

PANNAL
Map 8 SE35

Pannal Follifoot Rd HG3 1ES
☎ 01423 872628   📠 01423 870043
e-mail: secretary@pannalgc.co.uk
web: www.pannalgc.co.uk

Fine championship course chosen as a regional qualifying venue for the Open Championship. Moorland turf but well-wooded with trees closely involved with play. Excellent views enhance the course.

18 Holes, 6614yds, Par 72, SSS 72, Course record 62. Club membership 850.

Visitors Mon-Sun & BHs. Booking required. Handicap certificate. Dress code. **Societies** booking required. **Green Fees** £65 per day, £55 per round (£70 weekends & BHs) **Course Designer** Sandy Herd **Prof** David Padgett **Facilities** ⓉⒾ🄻🄳🄿🄐🄴 **Conf** Corporate Hospitality Days **Location** 2m S of Harrogate, E of village off A61
Hotel ★★★ 75% HL Yorkshire, Prospect Place, HARROGATE ☎ 01423 565071 📠 01423 565071 80 en suite

RAVENSCAR
Map 8 NZ90

Raven Hall Hotel Golf Course YO13 0ET
☎ 01723 870353   📠 01723 870072
e-mail: enquiries@ravenhall.co.uk
web: www.ravenhall.co.uk

Opened by the Earl of Cranbrook in 1898, this nine-hole clifftop course is sloping and with good quality small greens. Because of its clifftop position it is subject to strong winds which make it great fun to play, especially the 6th hole.

Raven Hall Hotel Golf Course: 9 Holes, 1894yds, Par 32, SSS 32. Club membership 120.

Visitors Mon-Sun & BHs. **Societies** welcome. **Green Fees** £8 per round **Facilities** ⓉⒾ🄻🄳🄿🄾 **Leisure** hard tennis courts, heated indoor swimming pool, sauna, gymnasium, croquet, bowls **Conf** facs Corporate Hospitality Days **Location** A171 from Scarborough towards Whitby, through Cloughton, right to Ravenscar, hotel on clifftop
Hotel ★★★ 74% HL Raven Hall Country House, RAVENSCAR ☎ 01723 870353 📠 01723 870353 52 en suite

REDCAR
Map 8 NZ62

Cleveland Majuba Rd TS10 5BJ
☎ 01642 471798   📠 01642 471798
e-mail: secretary@clevelandgolfclub.co.uk
web: www.clevelandgolfclub.co.uk

The oldest golf club in Yorkshire playing over the only links championship course in Yorkshire. A true test of traditional golf, especially when windy. Flat seaside links with easy walking.

18 Holes, 6696yds, Par 72, SSS 73, Course record 67. Club membership 480.

Visitors Mon-Fri & Sun except BHs. Booking required. Handicap certificate. Dress code. **Societies** booking required. **Green Fees** £20 (£25 Sun) **Course Designer** Donald Steel (new holes) **Prof** Adam Scott **Facilities** ⓉⒾ🄻🄳🄿🄐🄴🄾🄵 **Conf** Corporate Hospitality Days **Location** 8m E of Middlesborough, at N end of Redcar
Hotel ★★★ 73% HL Rushpool Hall Hotel, Saltburn Lane, SALTBURN-BY-THE-SEA ☎ 01287 624111 📠 01287 624111 21 en suite

Wilton Wilton TS10 4QY
☎ 01642 465265 (Secretary)   📠 01642 465463
e-mail: secretary@wiltongolfclub.co.uk
web: www.wiltongolfclub.co.uk

Parkland with some fine views and an abundance of trees and shrubs.

18 Holes, 6540yds, Par 70, SSS 69, Course record 64. Club membership 650.

Visitors Mon-Fri, Sun & BHs. Dress code. **Societies** booking required **Green Fees** £26 per day (£34 Sun & BHs) **Prof** P D Smillie **Facilities** Ⓣ Ⓘ by prior arrangement 🄻🄳🄿🄾🄴 **Leisure** snooker **Conf** Corporate Hospitality Days **Location** 3m W of Redcar on A174
Hotel ★★★ 73% HL Rushpool Hall Hotel, Saltburn Lane, SALTBURN-BY-THE-SEA ☎ 01287 624111 📠 01287 624111 21 en suite

RICHMOND
Map 7 NZ10

Richmond Bend Hagg DL10 5EX
☎ 01748 823231(Secretary)   📠 01748 821709
e-mail: secretary@richmondyorksgolfclub.co.uk
web: www.richmondyorksgolfclub.co.uk

Undulating parkland. Ideal to play 27 holes, not too testing but very interesting.

18 Holes, 6073yds, Par 71, SSS 69, Course record 63. Club membership 600.

Visitors Mon-Sat & BHs. Booking required Sat & BHs. Handicap certificate. Dress code. **Societies** booking required. **Green Fees** £25 per round (£30 Sat) **Course Designer** F Pennink **Prof** James Cousins **Facilities** ⓉⒾ🄻🄳🄿🄐🄴🄾 **Conf** facs **Location** 0.75m N
Hotel ★★★ 75% HL King's Head, Market Place, RICHMOND ☎ 01748 850220 📠 01748 850220 30 en suite

RIPON
Map 8 SE37

Ripon City Palace Rd HG4 3HH
☎ 01765 603640 📠 01765 692880
e-mail: secretary@riponcitygolfclub.com
web: www.riponcitygolfclub.com
Moderate walking on undulating parkland course; three testing par 3s at 5th, 7th and 14th.

18 Holes, 6084yds, Par 70, SSS 69, Course record 65.
Club membership 600.

Visitors Mon-Fri, Sun & BHs. Booking required. Dress code.
Societies booking required **Green Fees** phone **Course Designer** H Varden **Prof** S T Davis **Facilities** ⑪ ⑩ ⓛ ☐ ⑪ ☒ 🏌 🛒 🏌 🏌 **Conf** facs Corporate Hospitality Days **Location** 1m NW on A6108
Hotel ★★★ 79% HL Best Western Ripon Spa, Park Street, RIPON
☎ 01765 602172 📠 01765 602172 40 en suite

SALTBURN-BY-THE-SEA
Map 8 NZ62

Hunley Hall Golf Club & Hotel Ings Ln TS12 2QQ
☎ 01287 676216 📠 01287 678250
web: www.hunleyhall.co.uk

Morgans: 18 Holes, 6872yds, Par 73, SSS 73, Course record 63.
Millennium: 18 Holes, 5945yds, Par 68, SSS 68, Course record 67.
Jubilee: 18 Holes, 6289yds, Par 71, SSS 70, Course record 65.

Course Designer John Morgan **Location** off A174 in Brotton onto St Margarets Way, 700yds to club
Telephone for further details
Hotel 77% Hunley Hall Golf Club & Hotel, Ings Lane, Brotton, SALTBURN ☎ 01287 676216 📠 01287 676216 28 en suite

Saltburn by the Sea Hob Hill TS12 1NJ
☎ 01287 622812 📠 01287 625988
web: www.saltburngolf.co.uk

18 Holes, 5846yds, Par 70, SSS 68, Course record 62.
Course Designer J Braid **Location** 0.5m S from Saltburn
Telephone for further details
Hotel ★★★ 73% HL Rushpool Hall Hotel, Saltburn Lane, SALTBURN-BY-THE-SEA ☎ 01287 624111 📠 01287 624111 21 en suite

SCARBOROUGH
Map 8 TA08

Scarborough North Cliff North Cliff Av YO12 6PP
☎ 01723 355397 📠 01723 362134
e-mail: info@northcliffgolfclub.co.uk
web: www.northcliffgolfclub.co.uk
Seaside course beginning on clifftop overlooking North Bay and castle winding inland through parkland with stunning views of the North Yorkshire Moors.

18 Holes, 6493yds, Par 72, SSS 71, Course record 65.
Club membership 850.

Visitors Mon-Sun & BHs. Booking required. Handicap certificate. Dress code. **Societies** welcome. **Green Fees** £40 per day, £35 per round (£45/£40 Fri-Sun & BHs). **Course Designer** James Braid **Prof** Simon N Deller **Facilities** ⑪ ⑩ ⓛ ☐ ⑪ ☒ 🏌 🛒 🏌 🛒 🏌
Conf Corporate Hospitality Days **Location** 2m N of town centre off A165
Hotel ★★★★ INN Blacksmiths Arms, High Street, CLOUGHTON
☎ 01723 870244 📠 01723 870244 10 en suite

Scarborough South Cliff Deepdale Av YO11 2UE
☎ 01723 374737 ▤ 01723 374737
e-mail: clubsecretary@southcliffgolf.com
web: www.southcliffgolfclub.com

Parkland and seaside course which falls into two parts, divided from one another by the main road from Scarborough to Filey. On the seaward side of the road lie holes 4 to 10. On the landward side the first three holes and the last eight are laid out along the bottom of a rolling valley, stretching southwards into the hills.

18 Holes, 6432yds, Par 72, SSS 71, Course record 63. Club membership 480.

Visitors Mon-Sun & BHs. Booking required. Handicap certificate. Dress code. **Societies** booking required. **Green Fees** £35 per day, £30 per round (£40/£35 Fri-Sun & BHs) **Course Designer** McKenzie **Prof** Tony Skingle **Facilities** ⊕ ⏐◎⏐ ⮂ ⯭ ⏐⏐ ⏐ ⮂ ⯭ ✔ ⯭ ⚏
Conf Corporate Hospitality Days **Location** 1m S on A165
   Hotel ★★★ 74% HL Palm Court, St Nicholas Cliff,
   SCARBOROUGH ☎ 01723 368161 ▤ 01723 368161 40 en suite

SELBY   Map 8 SE63

Selby Mill Ln, Brayton YO8 9LD
☎ 01757 228622 ▤ 01757 228622
e-mail: selbygolfclub@aol.com
web: www.selbygolfclub.co.uk

Mainly flat, links-type course; prevailing south-west wind. Testing holes including the 3rd, 7th and 16th.

18 Holes, 6374yds, Par 71, SSS 71, Course record 68. Club membership 840.

Visitors contact club for details. **Societies** welcome. **Green Fees** £37 per day, £33 per round **Course Designer** J Taylor & Hawtree **Prof** Nick Ludwell **Facilities** ⊕ ⏐◎⏐ ⮂ ⯭ ⏐⏐ ⏐ ⮂ ⯭ ✔ ⚏
Location off A63 Selby bypass
   Hotel ★★★ 81% CHH Monk Fryston Hall, MONK FRYSTON
   ☎ 01977 682369 ▤ 01977 682369 29 en suite

SETTLE   Map 7 SD86

Settle Buckhaw Brow, Giggleswick BD24 0DH
☎ 01729 825288 & 822858 (sec) ▤ 01729 825288
web: settlegolfclub.com

Picturesque parkland with a stream affecting play on four holes in an Area of Outstanding Natural Beauty.

9 Holes, 6200yds, Par 72, SSS 72, Course record 70. Club membership 160.

Visitors Mon-Sun & BHs. Dress code. **Societies** booking required. **Green Fees** £20 per round **Course Designer** Tom Vardon **Facilities** ⮂ **Location** 1m W of Settle on Kendal Rd

SKIPTON   Map 7 SD95

Skipton Short Lee Ln BD23 3LF
☎ 01756 795657 ▤ 01756 796665
e-mail: enquiries@skiptongolfclub.co.uk
web: www.skiptongolfclub.co.uk

Undulating parkland with some water hazards and panoramic views.

18 Holes, 6049yds, Par 70, SSS 69, Course record 66. Club membership 800.

Visitors Mon-Sun & BHs. Booking required weekends & BHs. Dress code. **Societies** booking required. **Green Fees** not confirmed **Prof** Peter Robinson **Facilities** ⊕ ⏐◎⏐ ⮂ ⯭ ⏐⏐ ⏐ ⮂ ⯭ ⚏
⚏ **Leisure** snooker **Conf** Corporate Hospitality Days **Location** 1m N of Skipton on A59
   Hotel ★★★★ HL The Devonshire Arms Country House Hotel
   & Spa, BOLTON ABBEY, Skipton ☎ 01756 710441 & 718111
   ▤ 01756 710441 40 en suite

TADCASTER   Map 8 SE44

Scarthingwell Scarthingwell LS24 9PF
☎ 01937 557864 (pro) & 557878 (club)
▤ 01937 557909

Scarthingwell Golf Course: 18 Holes, 6771yds, Par 72, SSS 72.

Prof Simon Danby **Facilities** ⊕ ⮂ ⯭ ⏐⏐ ⏐ ⮂ ⯭ ⚏
Leisure snooker **Conf** facs Corporate Hospitality Days **Location** 4m S of Tadcaster on A162 Tadcaster-Ferrybridge road
Telephone for further details

THIRSK   Map 8 SE48

Thirsk & Northallerton Thornton-le-Street YO7 4AB
☎ 01845 525115
e-mail: secretary@tngc.co.uk
web: www.tngc.co.uk

The course has good views of the nearby Hambleton Hills to the east and Wensleydale to the west. Testing course, mainly flat.

Thirsk & Northallerton: 18 Holes, 6533yds, Par 72, SSS 72, Course record 66. Club membership 500.

Visitors contact club for details. **Societies** welcome. **Green Fees** £36 per day, £30 per round (£46/£36 weekends) **Course Designer** ADAS **Prof** Robert Garner **Facilities** ⊕ ⏐◎⏐ ⮂ ⯭ ⏐⏐ ⏐ ⮂ ⯭ ⏐⏐ ⚏
⯭ ⚏ **Location** 2m N on A168

WHITBY   Map 8 NZ81

Whitby Low Straggleton, Sandsend Rd YO21 3SR
☎ 01947 600660 ▤ 01947 600660
e-mail: office@whitbygolfclub.co.uk
web: www.whitbygolfclub.co.uk

Seaside course with four holes along clifftops and over ravines. Good views and a fresh sea breeze.

18 Holes, 6003yds, Par 70, SSS 69, Course record 65. Club membership 450.

Visitors Mon-Sun & BHs. Booking required weekends & BHs.. Handicap certificate. Dress code. **Societies** booking required. **Green Fees** £26 per day (£32 weekends) **Course Designer** Simon Gidman **Prof** Tony Mason **Facilities** ⊕ ⏐◎⏐ ⮂ ⯭ ⏐⏐ ⏐ ⮂ ⯭ ⏐⏐ ⚏
Conf Corporate Hospitality Days **Location** 1.5m NW on A174
   Hotel ★★★ 81% CHH Dunsley Hall, Dunsley, WHITBY
   ☎ 01947 893437 ▤ 01947 893437 26 en suite

YORK   Map 8 SE65

Forest of Galtres Moorlands Rd, Skelton YO32 2RF
☎ 01904 766198   🖩 01904 769400
e-mail: secretary@forestofgaltres.co.uk
web: www.forestofgaltres.co.uk

Level parkland in the heart of the ancient Forest of Galtres, with mature oak trees and interesting water features coming into play on the 6th, 14th and 17th holes. Views of York Minster.

18 Holes, 6534yds, Par 72, SSS 71, Course record 66.
Club membership 450.

Visitors Mon-Sun & BHs. Booking required. Dress code.
Societies booking required. **Green Fees** £32 per day, £25 per round (£42/£32 weekends & BHs) **Course Designer** Simon Gidman
Facilities ⑪ 🍴 by prior arrangement 🏌 ⛳ 🍸 🏖 🏪 🏺 🎯 🏈 **Conf** Corporate Hospitality Days **Location** 0.5m from the York ring road B1237, just off A19 Thirsk road through the village of Skelton

Hotel ★★★★ 72% CHH Fairfield Manor, Shipton Road, Skelton, YORK ☎ 01904 670222 🖩 01904 670222   89 en suite

Forest Park Stockton-on-the-Forest YO32 9UW
☎ 01904 400425
e-mail: admin@forestparkgolfclub.co.uk
web: www.forestparkgolfclub.co.uk

Flat parkland 27-hole course with large greens and narrow tree-lined fairways. The Old Foss beck meanders through the course, creating a natural hazard on many holes.

Old Foss Course: 18 Holes, 6673yds, Par 71, SSS 72, Course record 66.
The West Course: 9 Holes, 3186yds, Par 70, SSS 70.
Club membership 600.

Visitors Mon-Sun & BHs. Dress code. **Societies** booking required.
Green Fees £25 per 18 holes (£30 weekends), £10 per 9 holes (£12)
Facilities ⑪ 🍴 🏌 ⛳ 🍸 🏖 🏪 🏺 🎯 🏈
Conf facs Corporate Hospitality Days **Location** 4m NE of York off A64 York bypass

Fulford Heslington Ln YO10 5DY
☎ 01904 413579 🖩 01904 416918
e-mail: gary@fulfordgolfclub.co.uk
web: www.fulfordgolfclub.co.uk

A flat, parkland and heathland course well-known for the superb quality of its turf, particularly the greens, and famous as the venue for some of the best profeesional golf tournaments in the British Isles in recent years.

Championship Course: 18 Holes, 6775yds, Par 72, SSS 73, Course record 62. Club membership 700.

Visitors Mon-Fri & Sun except BHs. Booking required. Handicap certificate. Dress code. **Societies** booking required **Green Fees** not confirmed **Course Designer** C. MacKenzie **Prof** Guy Wills
Facilities ⑪ 🍴 🏌 ⛳ 🍸 🏖 🏪 🏺 🎯 🏈 🏈 **Conf** facs
Corporate Hospitality Days **Location** 2m S of York off A19
Hotel ★★★ 74% Best Western York Pavilion Hotel, 45 Main Street, Fulford, YORK ☎ 01904 622099 🖩 01904 626939   57 en suite

Heworth Muncaster House YO31 9JY
☎ 01904 422389 🖩 01904 426156
web: www.theheworthgolfclub.co.uk

12 Holes, 6105yds, Par 69, SSS 69, Course record 68.
Course Designer B Cheal **Location** 1.5m NE of city centre on A1036
Telephone for further details
Hotel ★★★ 79% HL Best Western Monkbar, Monkbar, YORK ☎ 01904 638086 🖩 01904 638086   99 en suite

Swallow Hall Crockey Hill YO19 4SG
☎ 01904 448889 🖩 01904 448219
web: www.swallowhall.co.uk

Swallow Hall Golf Course: 18 Holes, 3600yds, Par 57, SSS 56, Course record 58.
Course Designer Brian Henry **Location** off A19 signed Wheldrake
Telephone for further details
Hotel ★★★ 74% HL Best Western York Pavilion, 45 Main Street, Fulford, YORK ☎ 01904 622099 🖩 01904 622099   57 en suite

York Lords Moor Ln, Strensall YO32 5XF
☎ 01904 491840 (Sec) & 490304 (Pro)
🖩 01904 491852
e-mail: secretary@yorkgolfclub.co.uk
web: www.yorkgolfclub.co.uk

A pleasant, well-designed, heathland course with easy walking. The course is of good length but is flat so not too tiring. The course is well bunkered with excellent greens and there are two testing pond holes.

continued

18 Holes, 6301yds, Par 70, SSS 70, Course record 66. Club membership 750.

Visitors Mon-Fri & Sun except BHs. Booking required Sun. Handicap certificate. Dress code. **Societies** welcome. **Green Fees** £52 for 36 holes, £47 for 27 holes, £40 for 18 holes **Course Designer** J H Taylor **Prof** Mark Rogers **Facilities** ⑪ ⁑⑪ ㉝ ⌑ ⑪ ⌁ ⌂ ⁑ ℰ **Conf** facs Corporate Hospitality Days **Location** 6m NE of York, E of Strensall

Hotel ★★★★ 77% HL Best Western Dean Court, Duncombe Place, YORK ☎ 01904 625082 🖥 01904 625082 37 en suite

YORKSHIRE, SOUTH

BARNSLEY
Map 8 SE30

Barnsley Wakefield Rd, Staincross S75 6JZ
☎ 01226 382856 🖥 01226 382856
e-mail: barnsleygolfclub@hotmail.com

Undulating municipal parkland course with easy walking apart from last 4 holes. Testing 8th and 18th holes.

18 Holes, 5951yds, Par 69, SSS 69, Course record 61. Club membership 450.

Visitors Mon-Sun & BHs. Booking required. Dress code. **Societies** welcome. **Green Fees** £15 per 18 holes (£17 weekends) **Prof** Shaun Wyke **Facilities** ⑪ by prior arrangement ⁑⑪ by prior arrangement ㉝ ⌑ ⑪ ⌁ ⌂ ⁑ ℰ ℰ **Conf** Corporate Hospitality Days **Location** 3m N on A61
Hotel ★★★ 79% HL Best Western Ardsley House Hotel, Doncaster Road, Ardsley, BARNSLEY ☎ 01226 309955 🖥 01226 309955 75 en suite

Sandhill Middlecliffe Ln, Little Houghton S72 0HW
☎ 01226 753444 🖥 01226 753444
web: www.sandhillgolfclub.co.uk

Attractive, easy walking parkland with views of the surrounding countryside. Designed with strategically placed bunkers, the 4th hole having a deep bunker directly in front of the green. Very fine views from the 17th tee.

18 Holes, 6309yds, Par 71, SSS 70, Course record 69. Club membership 450.

Visitors Mon-Sun & BHs. Booking required. Dress code. **Societies** welcome. **Green Fees** £17.50 per round (£22.50 weekends & BHs) **Course Designer** John Royston **Facilities** ⑪ ⁑⑪ ㉝ ⌑ ⑪ ⌁ ⌂ ⁑ ℰ **Location** 5m E of Barnsley off A635
Hotel ★★★ 79% HL Best Western Ardsley House Hotel, Doncaster Road, Ardsley, BARNSLEY ☎ 01226 309955 🖥 01226 309955 75 en suite

BAWTRY
Map 8 SK69

Bawtry Cross Ln DN10 6RF
☎ 01302 710841
web: www.bawtrygolfclub.co.uk

18 Holes, 6994yds, Par 73, SSS 73, Course record 67.
Prof Darran Roberts **Facilities** ⑪ ⁑⑪ ㉝ ⌑ ⑪ ⌁ ⌂ ℰ ⌁ ℰ 🏴 **Conf** Corporate Hospitality Days **Location** 2m from Bawtry on A614
Telephone for further details
Hotel ★★★★ 79% HL Best Western Premier Mount Pleasant, Great North Road, DONCASTER ☎ 01302 868696 & 868219 🖥 01302 868696 56 en suite

CONISBROUGH
Map 8 SK59

Crookhill Park Municipal Carr Ln DN12 2AH
☎ 01709 862979 🖥 01709 866455

Crookhill Park Municipal Golf Course: 18 Holes, 5849yds, Par 70, SSS 68, Course record 64.

Prof Richard Swaine **Facilities** ㉝ ⌑ ⑪ ⌁ ⌂ ⁑
Location 1.5m SE on B6094
Telephone for further details
Hotel ★★★ 75% HL Best Western Pastures, Pastures Road, MEXBOROUGH, Rotherham ☎ 01709 577707 🖥 01709 577707 60 en suite

DONCASTER
Map 8 SE50

Doncaster 278 Bawtry Rd, Bessacarr DN4 7PD
☎ 01302 865632 🖥 01302 865994
e-mail: info@doncastergolfclub.co.uk
web: www.doncastergolfclub.co.uk

Pleasant undulating heathland course with wooded surroundings. Quick drying, ideal all year round course.

18 Holes, 6220yds, Par 69, SSS 70, Course record 66. Club membership 500.

Visitors Tue-Fri & Sun except BHs. Booking required Sun. Dress code. **Societies** booking required. **Green Fees** phone **Course Designer** Mackenzie/Hawtree **Prof** Graham Bailey **Facilities** ⑪ ⁑⑪ ㉝ ⌑ ⑪ ⌁ ⌂ ℰ 🏴 ℰ **Conf** Corporate Hospitality Days **Location** 4m SE on A638
Hotel ★★★★ 79% HL Best Western Premier Mount Pleasant, Great North Road, DONCASTER ☎ 01302 868696 & 868219 🖥 01302 868696 56 en suite

Doncaster Town Moor Bawtry Rd, Belle Vue DN4 5HU
☎ 01302 535286 (pro shop) & 533778 (office)
🖥 01302 533778
e-mail: dtmgc@btconnect.com
web: www.doncastertownmoorgolfclub.co.uk

Easy walking, but testing, heathland course with good true greens. Notable hole is 11th (par 4), 464yds. Situated in centre of racecourse.

18 Holes, 6072yds, Par 69, SSS 69, Course record 63. Club membership 520.

Visitors Mon-Sat & BHs. Sun pm only. Booking required. Dress code. **Societies** booking required. **Green Fees** not confirmed **Prof** Steven Shaw **Facilities** ⑪ ⁑⑪ ㉝ ⌑ ⑪ ⌁ ⌂ 🏴 ℰ **Conf** facs Corporate Hospitality Days **Location** 1.5m E at racecourse on A638
Hotel BUD Campanile Doncaster, Doncaster Leisure Park, Bawtry Road, DONCASTER ☎ 01302 370770 🖥 01302 370770 50 en suite

Owston Park Owston Ln, Owston DN6 8EF
☎ 01302 330821
e-mail: michael.parker@foremostgolf.com
web: www.owstonparkgolfcourse.co.uk

A flat easy walking course surrounded by woodland. A lot of mature trees and a few ditches in play. There is also a 9 hole course.

Owston Park Golf Course: 9 Holes, 2866yds, Par 35, SSS 70.

Visitors Mon-Sun & BHs. **Societies** welcome. **Green Fees** phone **Course Designer** M Parker **Prof** Mike Parker **Facilities** ⌑ ⌁ ⌂ ⁑ ℰ 🏴 ℰ **Location** 5m N of Doncaster off A19
Hotel ★★★ 70% HL Danum, High Street, DONCASTER ☎ 01302 342261 🖥 01302 342261 64 en suite

Thornhurst Park Holme Ln, Owston DN5 0LR
☎ 01302 337799   ▤ 01302 721495
e-mail: info.thornhurst@virgin.net
web: www.thornhurst.co.uk
Surrounded by Owston Wood, this scenic parkland course has numerous strategically placed bunkers, and a lake comes into play at the 7th and 8th holes.
18 Holes, 6490yds, Par 72, SSS 72, Course record 72.
Club membership 160.
Visitors contact club for details. **Societies** welcome. **Green Fees** £12 per 18 holes, £7 per 9 holes (£15/£8 weekends & BHs) **Prof** Kevin Pearce **Facilities** ⊕ ⑩ ⓛ 🖵 🍴 🔟 ᕫ 🎒 🚜 ✦ **Conf** facs Corporate Hospitality Days **Location** on A19 between Bentley and Askern
Hotel ★★★ 70% HL Danum, High Street, DONCASTER
☎ 01302 342261 ▤ 01302 342261 64 en suite

Wheatley Armthorpe Rd DN2 5QB
☎ 01302 831655   ▤ 01302 812736
web: www.wheatleygolfclub.co.uk
18 Holes, 6405yds, Par 71, SSS 71, Course record 64.
Course Designer George Duncan **Location** NE of town centre off A18
Telephone for further details
Hotel ★★★ 74% HL Regent, Regent Square, DONCASTER
☎ 01302 364180 & 381960 ▤ 01302 364180 53 en suite

HATFIELD   Map 8 SE60

Kings Wood Thorne Rd DN7 6EP
☎ 01405 741343   ▤ 01705 741343
web: www.kingswoodgolfcentre.co.uk
An undulating course with ditches that come into play on several holes, especially on the testing back nine. Notable holes are the 12th par 4, 16th and par 5 18th. Water is a prominent feature with several large lakes strategically placed.
Kings Wood Golf Course: 18 Holes, 6002yds, Par 71, SSS 69, Course record 67. Club membership 150.
Visitors Mon-Sun & BHs. **Societies** booking required. **Green Fees** £9 per 18 holes, £5.50 per 9 holes (£10/£6 weekends & BHs) **Course Designer** John Hunt **Prof** Chris Mann **Facilities** ⊕ ⑩ ⓛ 🖵 🍴 ᕫ 🎒 ⑨ᵖ ✦ 🚜 ✦ **Conf** facs Corporate Hospitality Days **Location** M180 junct 1, A614 towards Thorne, onto A1146 towards Hatfield for 0.8m
Hotel ★★★ 74% HL Regent, Regent Square, DONCASTER
☎ 01302 364180 & 381960 ▤ 01302 364180 53 en suite

HICKLETON   Map 8 SE40

Hickleton Lidgett Ln DN5 7BE
☎ 01709 896081   ▤ 01709 896083
web: www.hickletongolfclub.co.uk
18 Holes, 6434yds, Par 71, SSS 71, Course record 64.
Course Designer Huggett/Coles **Location** 3m W from A1(M) junct 37, off A635
Telephone for further details
Hotel ★★★ 70% HL Danum, High Street, DONCASTER
☎ 01302 342261 ▤ 01302 342261 64 en suite

HIGH GREEN   Map 8 SK39

Tankersley Park S35 4LG
☎ 0114 246 8247   ▤ 0114 245 7818
e-mail: secretary@tpgc.freeserve.co.uk
web: www.tankersleyparkgolfclub.org.uk
Rolling parkland course that demands accuracy rather than length. Lush fairways. The 18th hole considered to be one of the best last hole tests in Yorkshire.
Tankersley Park Golf Club Ltd: 18 Holes, 6244yds, Par 70, SSS 70, Course record 64. Club membership 634.
Visitors Mon-Fri except BHs. Booking required. Dress code. **Societies** booking required. **Green Fees** £36 per day; £27 per round **Course Designer** Hawtree **Prof** Ian Kirk **Facilities** ⊕ ⑩ ⓛ 🖵 🍴 ᕫ 🎒 🚜 ✦ **Conf** facs Corporate Hospitality Days **Location** A61/M1 onto A616 Stocksbridge bypass
Hotel ★★★★ 75% HL Tankersley Manor, Church Lane, TANKERSLEY ☎ 01226 744700 ▤ 01226 744700 99 en suite

RAWMARSH   Map 8 SK49

Wath Abdy Ln S62 7SJ
☎ 01709 878609   ▤ 01709 877097
e-mail: golf@wathgolfclub.co.uk
web: www.wathgolfclub.co.uk
Parkland course, not easy in spite of its length. Testing course with narrow fairways and small greens. Many dikes crisscross fairways, making playing for position paramount. Strategically placed copses reward the golfer who is straight off the tee. Playing over a pond into a prevailing wind on the 12th hole to a postage stamp size green, will test the most accomplished player.
18 Holes, 6096yds, Par 70, SSS 69, Course record 65.
Club membership 650.
Visitors Mon-Fri & BHs. Sun pm. Booking required Sun & BHs. Dress code. **Societies** welcome. **Green Fees** per 18 holes **Prof** Chris Bassett **Facilities** ⊕ ⑩ ⓛ 🖵 🍴 ᕫ 🎒 ✦ 🚜 ✦ **Conf** facs Corporate Hospitality Days **Location** 2m N of Rotherham on B6089
Hotel ★★★ 77% HL Carlton Park, 102/104 Moorgate Road, ROTHERHAM ☎ 01709 849955 ▤ 01709 849955 80 en suite

ROTHERHAM   Map 8 SK49

Grange Park Upper Wortley Rd S61 2SJ
☎ 01709 559497
Parkland/meadowland course, with panoramic views especially from the back nine. The golf is testing, particularly at the 1st, 4th and 18th holes (par 4), and 8th, 12th and 15th (par 5).
18 Holes, 6421yds, Par 71, SSS 71, Course record 65.
Club membership 214.
Visitors contact club for details. **Societies** booking required. **Green Fees** £18 per 18 holes (£20 weekends) **Course Designer** Fred Hawtree **Prof** Eric Clark **Facilities** ⊕ ⑩ ⓛ 🖵 🍴 ᕫ 🎒 ⑨ᵖ ✦ 🚜 **Conf** facs **Location** 3m NW off A629
Hotel ★★★★ 75% HL Tankersley Manor, Church Lane, TANKERSLEY ☎ 01226 744700 ▤ 01226 744700 99 en suite

Phoenix Pavilion Ln, Brinsworth S60 5PA
☎ 01709 382624
e-mail: secretary@phoenixgolfclub.co.uk
web: www.phoenixgolfclub.co.uk

Easy walking, slightly undulating meadowland course with excellent greens.

18 Holes, 6182yds, Par 71, SSS 70, Course record 65. Club membership 750.

Visitors Mon-Sun & BHs. Handicap certificate. Dress code.
Societies booking required. **Green Fees** Summer £27 per day, £21 per round (£35/£27 Fri-Sun and BHs). Winter £18 per round (£24 Fri-Sun & BHs) **Course Designer** C K Cotton **Prof** M Roberts **Facilities** ⓣ ⓨ ⓵ ☐ ⓥ ⓵ ⓶ ⓷ ⓸ ⓹ ⓺ **Leisure** squash, fishing, gymnasium **Conf** facs Corporate Hospitality Days **Location** SW of Rotherham off A630
Hotel ★★★ 77% HL Carlton Park, 102/104 Moorgate Road, ROTHERHAM ☎ 01709 849955 ▤ 01709 849955 80 en suite

Rotherham Golf Club Ltd Thrybergh Park, Doncaster Rd, Thrybergh S65 4NU
☎ 01709 859500 ▤ 01709 859517
e-mail: manager@rotherhamgolfclub.com
web: www.rotherhamgolfclub.com

Parkland with easy walking along the tree-lined fairways.

Rotherham Golf Club Ltd: 18 Holes, 6324yds, Par 70, SSS 70, Course record 65. Club membership 500.

Visitors Mon, Tue, Thu-Sun except BHs. Booking required. Dress code. **Societies** booking required **Green Fees** not confirmed **Course Designer** Sandy Herd **Prof** Simon Thornhill **Facilities** ⓣ ⓵ ☐ ⓥ ⓵ ⓶ ⓷ **Conf** facs **Location** 3.5m E on A630
Hotel ★★★ 78% HL Best Western Elton, Main Street, Bramley, ROTHERHAM ☎ 01709 545681 ▤ 01709 545681 29 en suite

Sitwell Park Shrogswood Rd S60 4BY
☎ 01709 541046 ▤ 01709 703637
e-mail: secretary@sitwellgolf.co.uk
web: www.sitwellgolf.co.uk

Undulating parkland course designed in 1913 by Dr Alister Mackenzie and retaining many of his greens and complete with its own 'Amen Corner' aptly named 'The Jungle'. Good test of golf for all levels of player.

18 Holes, 5960yds, Par 71, SSS 69. Club membership 500.

Visitors Mon-Fri, Sun & BHs. Booking required. Dress code.
Societies booking required. **Green Fees** £34 per day; £26 per round (£40/£32 Sun). **Course Designer** A MacKenzie **Prof** Nic Taylor **Facilities** ⓣ ⓨ ⓵ ☐ ⓥ ⓵ ⓶ ⓷ ⓸ ⓹ ⓺ **Conf** facs Corporate Hospitality Days **Location** 2m SE of Rotherham centre off A631
Hotel ★★★★ 71% HL Hellaby Hall, Old Hellaby Lane, Hellaby, ROTHERHAM ☎ 01709 702701 ▤ 01709 702701 90 en suite

---

SHEFFIELD   Map 8 SK38

Abbeydale Twentywell Ln, Dore S17 4QA
☎ 0114 236 0763 ▤ 0114 236 0762
e-mail: abbeygolf@btconnect.com
web: www.abbeydalegolfclub.co.uk

Undulating parkland course set in the Beauchief Estate with fine views over Sheffield and the Derbyshire hills.

18 Holes, 6261yds, Par 71, SSS 70, Course record 64. Club membership 725.

Visitors Mon, Tue, Fri, Sun & BHs. Booking required Mon, Tue, Fri, Sun & BHs. Dress code. Handicap certificate. **Societies** booking required **Green Fees** £45 per day, £36 per round (£45 Sun, £35 after 2.30pm). Twilight by arrangement after 4.30pm £20 **Course Designer** Herbert Fowler **Prof** Nigel Perry **Facilities** ⓣ ⓨ ⓵ ☐ ⓥ ⓵ ⓶ ⓷ ⓸ ⓹ ⓺ **Leisure** snooker **Conf** facs Corporate Hospitality Days **Location** 4m SW of city off A621
Hotel ★★★★ 77% HL Sheffield Park, Chesterfield Road South, SHEFFIELD ☎ 0114 282 9988 ▤ 0114 282 9988 95 en suite

Beauchief Public Abbey Ln S8 0DB
☎ 0114 236 7274

Pay and play course with natural water hazards. The rolling land looks west to the Pennines and a 12th-century abbey adorns the course.

Beauchief Golf Course: 18 Holes, 5469yds, Par 67, SSS 66, Course record 65. Club membership 450.

Visitors Mon-Sun & BHs. Booking required. Dress Code **Societies** booking required **Green Fees** £13 per round (£16 Fri-Sun & BHs) **Prof** M C Trippett **Facilities** ⓣ ⓨ ⓵ ☐ ⓥ ⓵ ⓶ ⓷ ⓸ **Conf** facs Corporate Hospitality Days **Location** 4m SW of city off A621
Hotel ★★★★ 77% HL Sheffield Park, Chesterfield Road South, SHEFFIELD ☎ 0114 282 9988 ▤ 0114 282 9988 95 en suite

Birley Wood Birley Ln S12 3BP
☎ 0114 264 7262
web: www.birleywood.com

Fairway course: 18 Holes, 5734yds, Par 69, SSS 67, Course record 64.
Birley Course: 18 Holes, 5037, Par 66, SSS 65.

Prof Peter Ball **Facilities** ⓣ ⓨ ⓵ ☐ ⓥ ⓵ ⓶ ⓷ ⓸ ⓹ ⓺ **Location** 4.5m SE of city off A616
Telephone for further details
Hotel ★★★ 80% HL Best Western Mosborough Hall, High Street, Mosborough, SHEFFIELD ☎ 0114 248 4353 ▤ 0114 248 4353 43 en suite

Concord Park Shiregreen Ln S5 6AE
☎ 0114 257 7378

Hilly municipal parkland course with some fairways wood-flanked, good views, often windy. Seven par 3 holes.

18 Holes, 4872yds, Par 67, SSS 64, Course record 57. Club membership 220.

Visitors contact club for details. **Societies** welcome. **Green Fees** phone **Prof** W Allcroft **Facilities** ⓣ ⓨ ⓵ ☐ ⓥ ⓵ ⓶ ⓷ ⓸ ⓹ ⓺ **Leisure** hard tennis courts, heated indoor swimming pool, squash, sauna, gymnasium **Location** 3.5m N of city on B6086, off A6135

Dore & Totley Bradway Rd, Bradway S17 4QR
☎ 0114 2366 844 ▤ 0114 2366 844
e-mail: dore.totley@btconnect.com
web: www.doreandtotleygolfclub.co.uk

Flat parkland course upgraded with the addition of 5 holes making the course 500 yards longer.

18 Holes, 6763yds, Par 72, SSS 72, Course record 66. Club membership 580.

Visitors Mon-Fri. Sun & BHs pm. Dress code. **Societies** booking required. **Green Fees** £37 per day, £32 per round (£36 Sun) **Prof** Gregg Roberts **Facilities** ⓣ ⓨ ⓵ ☐ ⓥ ⓵ ⓶ ⓷ ⓸ **Leisure** snooker **Conf** facs Corporate Hospitality Days **Location** 7m S of city on B6054, off A61

continued

Hotel ★★★★ 77% HL Sheffield Park, Chesterfield Road South, SHEFFIELD ☎ 0114 282 9988 📄 0114 282 9988 95 en suite

Hallamshire Golf Club Ltd Sandygate S10 4LA
☎ 0114 230 2153 📄 0114 230 5413
e-mail: secretary@hallamshiregolfclub.co.uk
web: www.hallamshiregolfclub.co.uk
Situated on a shelf of land at a height of 850ft. Magnificent views to the west. Moorland turf, long carries over ravine and small and quick greens. Not suitable for high handicap golfers.

Hallamshire Golf Club Ltd: 18 Holes, 6346yds, Par 71, SSS 71, Course record 65. Club membership 600.

Visitors Mon-Fri & Sun except BHs. Booking required. Handicap certificate. Dress code. Societies booking required. Green Fees £45 per day (£60 Sun) Course Designer Harry Colt Prof G R Tickell Facilities ⊕ ⎟⊚⎟ 🍴 🖥 🗄 🔦 ⚲ 🏌 🎏 Conf Corporate Hospitality Days Location off A57 at Crosspool onto Sandygate Rd, clubhouse 0.75m on right
Hotel ★★★ 72% HL Garrison, Hillsborough Barracks, Penistone Road, SHEFFIELD ☎ 0114 249 9555 📄 0114 249 9555 43 en suite

Hillsborough Worrall Rd S6 4BE
☎ 0114 234 9151 (Sec) 📄 0114 229 4105
web: www.hillsboroughgolfclub.co.uk
18 Holes, 6345yards, Par 71, SSS 70, Course record 63.
Prof Lewis Horsman Facilities ⊕ ⎟⊚⎟ 🍴 🖥 🗄 🔦 ⚲ 🏌 🎏 Conf Corporate Hospitality Days Location 3m NW of city off A616
Telephone for further details
Hotel ★★★★ 75% HL Tankersley Manor, Church Lane, TANKERSLEY ☎ 01226 744700 📄 01226 744700 99 en suite

Lees Hall Hemsworth Rd, Norton S8 8LL
☎ 0114 250 7868
e-mail: secretary@leeshallgolfclub.co.uk
web: www.leeshallgolfclub.co.uk
Parkland/meadowland course with panoramic view of city.
18 Holes, 6171yds, Par 71, SSS 70, Course record 63. Club membership 695.
Visitors Mon-Fri, Sun & BHs. Booking required. Dress code.
Societies booking required. Green Fees not confirmed Prof S Berry Facilities ⊕ ⎟⊚⎟ 🍴 🖥 🗄 🔦 ⚲ 🏌 🎏 Conf Corporate Hospitality Days Location 3.5m S of city off A6102
Hotel ★★★★ 77% HL Sheffield Park, Chesterfield Road South, SHEFFIELD ☎ 0114 282 9988 📄 0114 282 9988 95 en suite

Rother Valley Golf Centre Mansfield Rd, Wales Bar S26 5PQ
☎ 0114 247 3000 📄 0114 247 6000
e-mail: rother@jbgolf.co.uk
web: www.jackbarker.com
The challenging Blue Monster parkland course features a variety of water hazards. Notable holes include the 7th, with its island green fronted by water and dominated by bunkers to the rear. Lookout for the water on the par 5 18th.
Rother Valley Golf Centre: 18 Holes, 6602yds, Par 72, SSS 72, Course record 70. Club membership 300.
Visitors Mon-Sun & BHs. Booking required weekends. Dress code.
Societies booking required. Green Fees £16 per 18 holes, £18 Fri, £20.50 weekends and BHs Course Designer Michael Shattock & Mark Roe Prof Jason Ripley Facilities ⊕ ⎟⊚⎟ 🍴 🖥 🗄 🔦 ⚲ 🏌

🍴 🗄 🔦 🏌 Conf facs Corporate Hospitality Days Location M1 junct 31, signs to Rother Valley Country Park
Hotel ★★★ 80% HL Best Western Mosborough Hall, High Street, Mosborough, SHEFFIELD ☎ 0114 248 4353 📄 0114 248 4353 43 en suite

Tinsley Park Municipal Golf High Hazels Park, Darnall S9 4PE
☎ 0114 244 8974
Undulating parkland with plenty of trees and rough. Easy walking. The signature hole is the par 3 17th.
Tinsley Park Municipal Golf Club: 18 Holes, 6064yds, Par 70, SSS 68, Course record 66. Club membership 239.
Visitors Mon-Sun & BHs. Booking required. Dress code.
Societies booking required. Green Fees not confirmed Prof W Yellott Facilities 🖥 🗄 🔦 ⚲ 🏌 Location 4m E of city off A630
Hotel ★★★ 80% HL Best Western Mosborough Hall, High Street, Mosborough, SHEFFIELD ☎ 0114 248 4353 📄 0114 248 4353 43 en suite

SILKSTONE   Map 8 SE20

Silkstone Field Head, Elmhirst Ln S75 4LD
☎ 01226 790328 📄 01226 794902
e-mail: silkstonegolf@hotmail.co.uk
web: www.silkstone-golf-club.co.uk
Parkland and downland course, fine views over the Pennines. Testing golf. Seven new holes opened in 2008 to USGA specifications.
18 Holes, 6648yds, Par 73, SSS 73, Course record 67. Club membership 530.
Visitors Mon-Fri except BHs.. Booking required. Dress code.
Societies booking required. Green Fees £42 per day, £34 per round Course Designer Jonathan Gaunt Prof Kevin Guy Facilities ⊕ ⎟⊚⎟ 🖥 🗄 🔦 ⚲ 🏌 🎏 Conf Corporate Hospitality Days Location M1, junct 37, 1m E off A628
Hotel ★★★ 79% HL Best Western Ardsley House Hotel, Doncaster Road, Ardsley, BARNSLEY ☎ 01226 309955 📄 01226 309955 75 en suite

STOCKSBRIDGE   Map 8 SK29

Stocksbridge & District Royd Ln, Deepcar S36 2RZ
☎ 0114 288 2003 (office) 📄 0114 283 1460
e-mail: stocksbridgegolf@live.co.uk
web: www.stocksbridgegolfclub.co.uk
Hilly moorland course.
18 Holes, 5200yds, Par 65, SSS 65, Course record 60. Club membership 470.
Visitors Mon-Sun & BHs. Booking required weekends & BHs. Dress code. Societies booking required. Green Fees £25 per 18 holes (£37 weekends) Course Designer Dave Thomas Prof Roger Broad Facilities ⊕ ⎟⊚⎟ 🖥 🗄 🔦 ⚲ 🏌 🎏 Location S of town centre
Hotel ★★★ 85% HL Whitley Hall, Elliott Lane, Grenoside, SHEFFIELD ☎ 0114 245 4444 & 246 0456 📄 0114 245 4444 31 en suite

THORNE

Map 8 SE61

Thorne Kirton Ln DN8 5RJ
☎ 01405 812084 📠 01405 741899
web: www.thornegolf.co.uk

Picturesque parkland with 6000 trees. Water hazards on 11th, 14th and 18th holes.

18 Holes, 5366yds, Par 68, SSS 66, Course record 62.
Club membership 300.

Visitors Mon-Sun & BHs. **Societies** booking required. **Green Fees** £12 per round (£13 weekends) **Course Designer** R D Highfield **Prof** Edward Highfield **Facilities** ⊕ ⊚ ⬛ ⬜ ⬜ ⬜ ⬜ ⬜ ⬜ ⬜ ⬜
Conf facs Corporate Hospitality Days **Location** M180 Junct 1, A614 into Thorne, left onto Kirton Ln
Hotel BUD Travelodge Doncaster (M18/M180), DONCASTER
☎ 08719 846 132 📠 08719 846 132 41 en suite

WORTLEY

Map 8 SK39

Wortley Hermit Hill Ln S35 7DF
☎ 0114 288 8469 📠 0114 288 8488
e-mail: wortley.golfclub@btconnect.com
web: www.wortleygolfclub.co.uk

Well-wooded, undulating parkland, sheltered from the prevailing wind. Excellent greens in a totally pastoral setting.

18 Holes, 6028yds, Par 69, SSS 68, Course record 62.
Club membership 600.

Visitors contact club for details. **Societies** Booking required
Green Fees £30 per day (£35 per round Sat & Sun) **Prof** Ian Kirk
Facilities ⊕ ⊚ ⬛ ⬜ ⬜ ⬜ ⬜ **Conf** Corporate Hospitality Days **Location** 0.5m NE of village off A629
Hotel ★★★ 85% HL Whitley Hall, Elliott Lane, Grenoside, SHEFFIELD ☎ 0114 245 4444 & 246 0456 📠 0114 245 4444 31 en suite

YORKSHIRE, WEST

ADDINGHAM

Map 7 SE04

Bracken Ghyll Skipton Rd LS29 0SL
☎ 01943 831207 📠 01943 839453
e-mail: office@brackenghyll.co.uk
web: www.brackenghyll.co.uk

On the edge of the Yorkshire Dales, the course commands superb views over Ilkley Moor and the Wharfe valley. The demanding 18-hole layout is a test of both golfing ability and sensible course management.

18 Holes, 5635yds, Par 68, SSS 67, Course record 66.
Club membership 405.

Visitors Mon-Sun & BHs. Booking required. Dress code.
Societies booking required. **Green Fees** £36 per day, £20 per round (£36/£24 weekends & BHs) **Facilities** ⊕ ⊚ ⬛ ⬜ ⬜ ⬜ ⬜
⬜ **Conf** facs Corporate Hospitality Days **Location** off A65 between Ilkley and Skipton
Hotel ★★★ 83% HL Best Western Rombalds Hotel & Restaurant, 11 West View, Wells Road, ILKLEY ☎ 01943 603201 📠 01943 603201 15 en suite

ALWOODLEY

Map 8 SE24

Alwoodley Wigton Ln LS17 8SA
☎ 0113 268 1680
e-mail: alwoodley@btconnect.com
web: www.alwoodley.co.uk

Natural heathland course with heather, whins and shrubs. Plentifully and cunningly bunkered with undulating and interesting greens.

18 Holes, 6338yds, Par 70, SSS 71.
Club membership 460.

Visitors Mon-Sun & BHs. Booking required. Dress code.
Societies booking required **Green Fees** £75 per day/round (£90 weekends). £40 after 4pm. Winter £55 (£90 weekends) **Course Designer** Dr Alister MacKenzie **Prof** John R Green **Facilities** ⊕ ⊚ ⬛ ⬜ ⬜ ⬜ ⬜ ⬜ **Conf** Corporate Hospitality Days **Location** 5m N off A61
Hotel ★★★ 72% HL Ramada Leeds Parkway, Otley Road, LEEDS ☎ 0844 815 9020 📠 0844 815 9020 118 en suite

BAILDON

Map 7 SE13

Baildon Moorgate BD17 5PP
☎ 01274 584266
e-mail: secretary@baildongolfclub.com
web: www.baildongolfclub.com

Moorland course set out in links style with the outward front nine looping back to clubhouse. Panoramic views with testing short holes in prevailing winds. The 2nd hole has been described as one of Britain's scariest.

18 Holes, 6225yds, Par 70, SSS 70, Course record 63.
Club membership 750.

Visitors Mon-Fri, Sun & BHs. Booking required Tue, Wed, Sun & BHs. Dress code. **Societies** booking required. **Green Fees** £15 per round

continued

Course Designer James Braid Prof Richard Masters Facilities ⓣ
🍽 ⛳ 🖥 🎿 🏌 🏪 🛺 ✆ Leisure snooker tables Conf facs
Corporate Hospitality Days Location 3m N of Bradford off A6038 at
Shipley
Hotel ★★★★ 78% HL Marriott Hollins Hall Hotel & Country Club,
Hollins Hill, Baildon, SHIPLEY ☎ 01274 530053 🖨 01274 530053
122 en suite

BINGLEY
Map 7 SE13

Bingley St Ives Golf Club House, St Ives Estate, Harden
BD16 1AT
☎ 01274 562436 🖨 01274 511788
e-mail: secretary@bingleystivesgc.co.uk
web: www.bingleystivesgc.co.uk

Parkland and moorland course.
*Bingley St Ives Golf Club Ltd: 18 Holes, 6485yds, Par 71,
SSS 71, Course record 69. Club membership 450.*
Visitors contact club for details. Societies booking required Green
Fees phone Course Designer Alastair Mackenzie Prof Nigel Barber
Facilities ⓣ 🍽 ⛳ 🖥 🎿 🏌 🏪 ✆ Conf facs
Corporate Hospitality Days Location 0.75m W off B6429
Hotel ★★ 70% HL Dalesgate, 406 Skipton Road, Utley, KEIGHLEY
☎ 01535 664930 🖨 01535 664930 20 en suite

Shipley Beckfoot Ln BD16 1LX
☎ 01274 568652 (Secretary) 🖨 01274 567739
e-mail: office@shipleygc.co.uk
web: www.shipleygolfclub.com
Well-established parkland course, founded in 1922, featuring six good
par 3s.
*18 Holes, 6220yds, Par 71, SSS 70, Course record 66.
Club membership 600.*
Visitors Mon, Wed-Fri, Sun & BHs. Tue pm only. Booking required.
Dress code. Societies booking required. Green Fees £45 per day, £39
per round, Mon £35/£29 Course Designer Colt, Allison, Mackenzie,
Braid Prof Nathan Stead Facilities ⓣ 🍽 ⛳ 🖥 🎿 🏌 🏪
🛺 ✆ 🍴 ✆ Conf facs Corporate Hospitality Days Location 6m N
of Bradford on A650
Hotel ★★ 70% HL Dalesgate, 406 Skipton Road, Utley, KEIGHLEY
☎ 01535 664930 🖨 01535 664930 20 en suite

BRADFORD
Map 7 SE13

Bradford Moor Scarr Hall BD2 4RW
☎ 01274 771716 & 771693
9 Holes, 5900yds, Par 70, SSS 68, Course record 65.
Facilities 🖥 🎿 🏌 Location 2m NE of city centre off A658
Telephone for further details
Hotel ★★★ 79% HL Midland Hotel, Forster Square, BRADFORD
☎ 01274 735735 🖨 01274 735735 90 en suite

Clayton Thornton View Rd BD14 6JX
☎ 01274 880047
9 Holes, 6300yds, Par 72, SSS 72.
Facilities ⓣ 🍽 ⛳ 🖥 🎿 🏌 Conf Corporate Hospitality Days
Location 2.5m SW of city centre on A647
Telephone for further details
Hotel ★★★ 70% HL Campanile Bradford, 6 Roydsdale Way,
Euroway Estate, BRADFORD ☎ 01274 683683 🖨 01274 683683
130 en suite

East Bierley South View Rd, East Bierley BD4 6PP
☎ 01274 681023 🖨 01274 683666
e-mail: rjwelch@talktalk.net
Hilly moorland course with narrow fairways. Two par 3 holes over
200yds.
*9 Holes, 4700yds, Par 64, SSS 63, Course record 59.
Club membership 300.*
Visitors Handicap certificate. Dress code. Societies booking required.
Green Fees not confirmed Prof J. Whittam Facilities 🖥 🎿 🏌
🏪 Location 4m SE of city centre off A650
Hotel ★★★ 70% HL Campanile Bradford, 6 Roydsdale Way,
Euroway Estate, BRADFORD ☎ 01274 683683 🖨 01274 683683
130 en suite

Headley Headley Ln BD13 3LX
☎ 01274 833481 🖨 01274 833481
web: www.headleygolfclub.co.uk
9 Holes, 4864yds, Par 65, SSS 65, Course record 57.
Facilities ⓣ 🍽 ⛳ 🖥 🎿 🏌 Conf Corporate Hospitality Days
Location 4m W of city centre off B6145 at Thornton
Telephone for further details
Hotel ★★★ 79% HL Midland Hotel, Forster Square, BRADFORD
☎ 01274 735735 🖨 01274 735735 90 en suite

Queensbury Brighouse Rd, Queensbury BD13 1QF
☎ 01274 882155 & 816864 🖨 01274 882155
web: www.queensburygc.co.uk
Undulating woodland and parkland.
*9 Holes, 5008yds, Par 66, SSS 65, Course record 61.
Club membership 350.*
Visitors Mon-Sun & BHs. Booking required weekends. Dress code.
Societies Booking required. Green Fees £16 per 18 holes (£31
weekends, £11 after 4pm) Course Designer Jonathan Gaunt
Prof Graham Murray Facilities ⓣ 🍽 ⛳ 🖥 🎿 🏌 🏪 🛺 ✆
🍴 ✆ Conf Corporate Hospitality Days Location 4m from Bradford
on A647
Hotel ★★★ 79% HL Midland Hotel, Forster Square, BRADFORD
☎ 01274 735735 🖨 01274 735735 90 en suite

ENGLAND

South Bradford Pearson Rd, Odsal BD6 1BH
☎ 01274 673346 (pro shop) & 679195 📄 01274 690643
Hilly course with good greens, trees and ditches. Interesting short 2nd hole (par 3) 200yds, well-bunkered and played from an elevated tee.

9 Holes, 6068yds, Par 70, SSS 68, Course record 65.
Club membership 300.

Visitors contact club for details. **Societies** welcome. **Green Fees** not confirmed **Prof** Paul Cooke **Facilities** ⊕ ⏲ by prior arrangement 🍴 ⏲ 🛒 ⬥ ✎ **Location** 2M S of city centre off A638
Hotel ★★★ 70% HL Campanile Bradford, 6 Roydsdale Way, Euroway Estate, BRADFORD ☎ 01274 683683 📄 01274 683683 130 en suite

West Bradford Chellow Grange Rd, Haworth Rd BD9 6NP
☎ 01274 542767 📄 01274 482079
e-mail: secretary@westbradfordgolfclub.co.uk
web: www.westbradfordgolfclub.co.uk
Parkland course providing a good test for golfers of all abilities with its undulating terrain, tree-lined fairways and demanding par 3 holes.

18 Holes, 5738yds, Par 69, SSS 68, Course record 63.
Club membership 440.

Visitors contact club for details. **Societies** welcome. **Green Fees** not confirmed **Prof** Warren Kemp **Facilities** ⊕ ⏲ 🍴 ⏲ 🛒 ⬥ 🛒 ✎ **Leisure** snooker room **Conf** facs Corporate Hospitality Days **Location** 3.5 m W of city centre off B6144
Hotel ★★★★ 78% HL Marriott Hollins Hall Hotel & Country Club, Hollins Hill, Baildon, SHIPLEY ☎ 01274 530053 📄 01274 530053 122 en suite

BRIGHOUSE
Map 7 SE12

Willow Valley Golf Highmoor Ln, Clifton HD6 4JB
☎ 01274 878624
e-mail: sales@wvgc.co.uk
web: www.wvgc.co.uk

A championship length course offering a unique golfing experience, featuring island greens, shaped fairways and bunkers, and multiple teeing areas. The nine-hole course offers an exciting challenge to less experienced golfers or for a short game. Pine Valley is an intermediate course, suitable for golfers of all abilities.

Willow Valley: 18 Holes, 6496yds, Par 72, SSS 72, Course record 69.
Pine Valley: 18 Holes, 5032yds, Par 67, SSS 64.
Fountain Ridge: 9 Holes, 2039yds, Par 62, SSS 60.
Club membership 350.

Visitors Mon-Sun & BHs. Dress code for Willow Valley & Pine Valley. **Societies** Booking required. **Green Fees** Willow Valley £26 per round, Pine Valley £15 per round, Fountain Ridge £7.50 per round

(£38/£17/£9 weekends & BHs) **Course Designer** Jonathan Gaunt **Prof** Julian Haworth **Facilities** ⊕ ⏲ by prior arrangement 🍴 ⏲ 🍴 ⬥ 🛒 🍴 ✎ ✎ **Leisure** 3 hole floodlit academy course **Conf** Corporate Hospitality Days **Location** M62 junct 25, A644 towards Brighouse, right at rdbt onto A643, course 1m on right
Hotel ★★★ 74% HL Healds Hall, Leeds Road, Liversedge, DEWSBURY ☎ 01924 409112 📄 01924 409112 24 en suite

CLECKHEATON
Map 8 SE12

Cleckheaton & District Bradford Rd BD19 6BU
☎ 01274 851266 📄 01274 871382
e-mail: info@cleckheatongolf.co.uk
web: www.cleckheatongolfclub.co.uk
Parkland with gentle hills and easy walking. Feature holes: 5th, 16th and 17th.

18 Holes, 5706yds, Par 70, SSS 68, Course record 61.
Club membership 550.

Visitors Mon-Fri & Sun except BHs. Booking required Tue, Wed & Sun. Handicap certificate. Dress code. **Societies** welcome. **Green Fees** not confirmed **Course Designer** Dr A MacKenzie **Prof** Warren Lockett **Facilities** ⊕ ⏲ 🍴 ⏲ 🍴 ⬥ 🛒 🍴 ✎ **Conf** facs Corporate Hospitality Days **Location** M62 junct 26, towards Oakenshaw, 100yds on left, signed Low Moor
Hotel ★★★ 78% HL Gomersal Park, Moor Lane, GOMERSAL, Bradford ☎ 01274 869386 📄 01274 869386 100 en suite

DEWSBURY
Map 8 SE22

Hanging Heaton White Cross Rd WF12 7DT
☎ 01924 461606 📄 01924 430100
e-mail: derek.atkinson@hhgc.org
web: www.hhgc.org.uk
Arable land, easy walking, fine views. Testing 4th hole (par 3).

9 Holes, 5836yds, Par 69, SSS 68. Club membership 500.

Visitors Mon-Fri except BHs. Dress code. **Societies** Booking required. **Green Fees** £17 per round **Prof** Gareth Moore **Facilities** ⊕ by prior arrangement ⏲ by prior arrangement 🍴 ⏲ 🍴 ⬥ 🛒 ✎ **Conf** facs Corporate Hospitality Days **Location** 0.75m NE off A653
Hotel ★★★ 74% HL Healds Hall, Leeds Road, Liversedge, DEWSBURY ☎ 01924 409112 📄 01924 409112 24 en suite

ELLAND
Map 7 SE12

Elland Hammerstone, Leach Ln HX5 0TA
☎ 01422 372505 & 374886 (pro)
e-mail: ellandgolfclub@ellandgolfclub.plus.net
web: www.ellandgolfclub.plus.com
Nine-hole parkland course played off 18 tees.

9 Holes, 5498yds, Par 66, SSS 67, Course record 65.
Club membership 450.

Visitors Mon-Wed, Fri & Sun except BHs. Booking required. Handicap certificate. Dress code. **Green Fees** £20 per round/day (£30 Sun & BHs) **Prof** N Krzywicki **Facilities** ⊕ ⏲ 🍴 ⏲ 🍴 ⬥ 🛒 ✎ **Location** M62 junct 24, signs to Blackley
Hotel ★★★ 74% HL Pennine Manor, Nettleton Hill Road, Scapegoat Hill, HUDDERSFIELD ☎ 01484 642368 📄 01484 642368 30 en suite

FENAY BRIDGE   Map 8 SE11

Woodsome Hall HD8 0LQ
☎ 01484 602739   📠 01484 608260
web: www.woodsome.co.uk
18 Holes, 6096yds, Par 70, SSS 69, Course record 67.
Prof M Higginbotton **Facilities** ⓉⓄ 🍴 🏌 💻 🍺 👤 🏠 👝
Location 1.5m SW off A629
Telephone for further details
Hotel ★★★ 74% HL Bagden Hall, Wakefield Road, Scissett,
HUDDERSFIELD ☎ 01484 865330 📠 01484 865330 36 en suite

GARFORTH   Map 8 SE43

Garforth Long Ln LS25 2DS
☎ 0113 286 3308   📠 0113 286 3308
e-mail: garforthgcltd@lineone.net
web: www.garforthgolfclub.co.uk
Gently undulating parkland with fine views and easy walking.
18 Holes, 6304yds, Par 70, SSS 71, Course record 64.
Club membership 600.
Visitors dress code. **Societies** booking required. **Green Fees** £42 per
day, £36 per round. Winter £20 per round **Course Designer** Dr Alister
Mackenzie **Prof** Ken Findlater **Facilities** ⓉⓄ 🍴 🏌 💻 🍺
👤 🏠 👝 👟 🏌 **Conf** Corporate Hospitality Days **Location** 6m E of
Leeds, next to A1/M1 link road between Garforth and Barwick in Elmet
Hotel ★★★ 81% HL Best Western Milford Hotel, A1 Great
North Road, Peckfield, LEEDS ☎ 01977 681800 📠 01977 681800
46 en suite

GUISELEY   Map 8 SE14

Bradford (Hawksworth) Hawksworth Ln LS20 8NP
☎ 01943 875570   📠 01943 875570
web: www.bradfordgolfclub.co.uk
Set in undulating countryside, the course is a moorland links laid out
on the southern slope of a wooded ridge about 650ft above sea level.
The spacious greens with their subtle borrows, together with some
tough and uncompromising par 4s make this a challenging course.
The testing par 4 10th and the par 3 14th require accurate shots to
well-protected greens.
Hawksworth: 18 Holes, 6303yds, Par 71, SSS 71,
Course record 65. Club membership 650.
Visitors Mon-Sun & BHs. Booking required. Handicap certificate. Dress
code. **Societies** booking required **Green Fees** £40 per day (£45 Sun &
BHs) **Course Designer** W H Fowler **Prof** Andrew Hall **Facilities** ⓉⓄ 🍴
🏌 💻 🍺 👤 🏠 👝 🍴 🎯 **Conf** facs Corporate Hospitality
Days **Location** SW of town centre off A6038
Hotel ★★★★ 78% HL Marriott Hollins Hall Hotel & Country Club,
Hollins Hill, Baildon, SHIPLEY ☎ 01274 530053 📠 01274 530053
122 en suite

HALIFAX   Map 7 SE02

Halifax Union Ln, Ogden HX2 8XR
☎ 01422 244171
e-mail: halifax.golfclub@virgin.net
web: www.halifaxgolfclub.co.uk
Moorland course crossed by streams, natural hazards and offering fine
views of wildlife and the surroundings. Testing 172-yd 17th (par 3).
18 Holes, 6037yds, Par 70, SSS 69, Course record 65.
Club membership 600.
Visitors Mon-Fri & BHs. Booking required. Handicap certificate.
Dress code. **Societies** welcome. **Green Fees** not confirmed **Course
Designer** A Herd/J Braid **Prof** David Delaney **Facilities** ⓉⓄ 🍴 🏌
💻 🍺 👤 🏠 👝 🏌 🏌 **Conf** facs Corporate Hospitality Days
Location 4m from Halifax on A629 Halifax-Keighley road
Hotel ★★★ 85% HL Holdsworth House, Holdsworth, HALIFAX
☎ 01422 240024 📠 01422 240024 40 en suite

Lightcliffe Knowle Top Rd, Lightcliffe HX3 8SW
☎ 01422 202459 & 204081
A parkland course where positioning of the drive is as important as
length. Signature hole is a dog-leg with the second shot over a deep
ravine.
9 Holes, 5388mtrs, Par 68, SSS 68. Club membership 460.
Visitors Mon, Tue, Thu, Fri, Sun & BHs. Handicap certificate. Dress
code. **Societies** booking required **Green Fees** £18 per 18 holes (£22
Sun) **Prof** Robert Tickle **Facilities** Ⓣ 🏌 💻 🍺 👤 🏠 👝
Location 3.5m E of Halifax on A58
Hotel ★★★ 85% HL Holdsworth House, Holdsworth, HALIFAX
☎ 01422 240024 📠 01422 240024 40 en suite

West End Paddock Ln, Highroad Well HX2 0NT
☎ 01422 341878   📠 01422 341878
e-mail: westendgc@btinternet.com
web: www.westendgc.co.uk
Semi-moorland course. Tree lined. Two ponds.
West End Golf Club (Halifax) Ltd: 18 Holes, 5951yds,
Par 69, SSS 69, Course record 62. Club membership 650.
Visitors Mon, Wed-Fri, Sun & BHs. Booking required. Handicap
certificate. Dress code. **Societies** welcome. **Green Fees** not confirmed
Prof David Rishworth **Facilities** ⓉⓄ 🍴 🏌 💻 🍺 👤 🏠 👝
🏠 🏌 **Conf** Corporate Hospitality Days **Location** W of town centre
off A646
Hotel ★★★ 85% HL Holdsworth House, Holdsworth, HALIFAX
☎ 01422 240024 📠 01422 240024 40 en suite

HEBDEN BRIDGE   Map 7 SD92

Hebden Bridge Great Mount HX7 8PH
☎ 01422 842896 & 842732
web: www.hebdenbridgegolfclub.co.uk
9 Holes, 5242yds, Par 68, SSS 67, Course record 61.
Facilities ⓉⓄ 🍴 🏌 💻 🍺 👤 🚕 **Location** 1.5m E off A6033
Telephone for further details
Hotel ★★ 71% HL Old White Lion, Main Street, HAWORTH, Keighley
☎ 01535 642313 📠 01535 642313 15 en suite

HOLYWELL GREEN　　　　　　　Map 7 SE01

Halifax Bradley Hall HX4 9AN
☎ 01422 374108

18 Holes, 6138yds, Par 70, SSS 70, Course record 65.
Prof Peter Wood **Facilities** ⊕ ⑩ ⓘ ⬛ ⬜ ⬛ ⬛ ⬛ ✦
Location S on A6112
Telephone for further details
Hotel ★★★ 74% HL Pennine Manor, Nettleton Hill Road,
Scapegoat Hill, HUDDERSFIELD ☎ 01484 642368 🗐 01484 642368
30 en suite

HUDDERSFIELD　　　　　　　Map 7 SE11

Bagden Hall Hotel & Golf Course Wakefield Rd HD8 9LE
☎ 01484 865330　🗐 01484 861001
web: www.bagdenhallhotel.co.uk

*Bagden Hall Hotel & Golf Course: 9 Holes, 3002yds,
Par 56, SSS 55, Course record 60.*

Course Designer F O'Donnell/R Braithwaite **Location** A636 Wakefield-
Denby Dale
Telephone for further details
Hotel ★★★ 74% HL Bagden Hall, Wakefield Road, Scissett,
HUDDERSFIELD ☎ 01484 865330 🗐 01484 865330　36 en suite

Bradley Park Off Bradley Rd HD2 1PZ
☎ 01484 223772　🗐 01484 451613
e-mail: parnellreilly@pgabroadband.com
web: www.bradleyparkgolf.co.uk

Parkland course, challenging with good mix of long and short holes.
Also 14-bay floodlit driving range and a nine-hole par 3 course, ideal
for beginners. Superb views.

*Bradley Park Golf Course: 18 Holes, 6284yds, Par 70,
SSS 70, Course record 300.*

Visitors contact course for details. **Societies** booking required. **Green
Fees** £17 (£19 weekends & BHs) **Course Designer** Cotton/Pennick/
Lowire & Ptnrs **Prof** Parnell E Reilly **Facilities** ⊕ ⑩ ⓘ ⬛ ⬜ ⬛
⬛ ⬛ ⬛ ✦ ⬛ ✦ ✦ **Leisure** 9 hole par 3 course **Conf** facs
Corporate Hospitality Days **Location** M62 junct 25, 2.5m
Hotel ★★★ 80% HL Holiday Inn Leeds-Brighouse, Clifton Village,
BRIGHOUSE ☎ 0870 400 9013 🗐 0870 400 9013　94 en suite

Crosland Heath Felk Stile Rd, Crosland Heath HD4 7AF
☎ 01484 653216　🗐 01484 461079
e-mail: golf@croslandheath.co.uk
web: www.croslandheath.co.uk

Heathland course with fine views over valley.

18 Holes, 6087yds, Par 71, SSS 70. Club membership 650.
Visitors Mon, Tue, Thu, Sun except BHs. Booking required. Handicap
certificate. Dress code. **Societies** welcome. **Green Fees** £37 per day
(£42 Sun) **Course Designer** Dr. McKenzie **Facilities** ⊕ ⑩ ⓘ ⬛ ⬜
⬛ ⬛ ⬛ ✦ **Conf** facs Corporate Hospitality Days **Location** SW
off A62
Hotel ★★★ 74% HL Pennine Manor, Nettleton Hill Road,
Scapegoat Hill, HUDDERSFIELD ☎ 01484 642368 🗐 01484 642368
30 en suite

Huddersfield Fixby Hall HD2 2EP
☎ 01484 426203　🗐 01484 424623
web: www.huddersfield-golf.co.uk

*Huddersfield Golf Club Ltd: 18 Holes, 6466yds, Par 71,
SSS 71, Course record 63.*

Prof Paul Carman **Facilities** ⊕ ⑩ ⓘ ⬛ ⬜ ⬛ ⬛ ⬛ ⬛ ✦
✦ **Conf** facs Corporate Hospitality Days **Location** 2m N off A641
Telephone for further details
Hotel ★★★ 80% HL Holiday Inn Leeds-Brighouse, Clifton Village,
BRIGHOUSE ☎ 0870 400 9013 🗐 0870 400 9013　94 en suite

Longley Park Maple St, Aspley HD5 9AX
☎ 01484 422304　🗐 01484 515280
e-mail: longleyparkgolfclub@12freeukisp.co.uk
Lowland course, surrounded by mature woodland.

*9 Holes, 5212yds, Par 66, SSS 66, Course record 61.
Club membership 440.*

Visitors Mon, Tue & Fri except BHs. Booking required. Dress code.
Societies booking required. **Green Fees** phone **Prof** John Ambler
Facilities ⊕ ⑩ ⓘ ⬛ ⬜ ⬛ ⬛ ⬛ ✦ **Conf** facs Corporate
Hospitality Days **Location** 0.5m SE of town centre off A629
Hotel BUD Innkeeper's Lodge Huddersfield, 36a Penistone Road,
HUDDERSFIELD ☎ 0845 112 6035 🗐 0845 112 6035　23 en suite

ILKLEY　　　　　　　Map 7 SE14

Ben Rhydding High Wood, Ben Rhydding LS29 8SB
☎ 01943 608759
e-mail: secretary@benrhyddinggc.freeserve.co.uk
Moorland and parkland with splendid views over the Wharfe valley. A
compact but testing course.

*9 Holes, 4611yds, Par 65, SSS 63, Course record 64.
Club membership 250.*

Visitors Mon-Sun & BHs. Booking required Tue-Thu, Sun & BHs.
Handicap certificate. Dress code. **Societies** booking required **Green
Fees** £18 per day (£22 weekends & BHs) **Course Designer** William
Dell **Facilities** ⬜ ⬛ **Conf** Corporate Hospitality Days **Location** SE
of town centre. Off Wheatley Ln onto Wheatley Grove, left onto High
Wood, clubhouse on left
Hotel ★★★ 83% HL Best Western Rombalds Hotel & Restaurant,
11 West View, Wells Road, ILKLEY ☎ 01943 603201 🗐 01943 603201
15 en suite

Ilkley Nesfield Rd, Myddleton LS29 0BE
☎ 01943 600214　🗐 01943 816130
e-mail: honsec@ilkleygolfclub.co.uk
web: www.ikleygolfclub.co.uk

A beautiful parkland course in Wharfedale. The Wharfe is a hazard
on the first seven holes - in fact, the 3rd is laid out entirely on an
island in the river.

*18 Holes, 5953yds, Par 69, SSS 70, Course record 64.
Club membership 450.*

Visitors contact club for details. **Societies** welcome. **Green
Fees** £50 (£55 weekends). Reduced winter rates **Course
Designer** Mackenzie **Prof** John L Hammond **Facilities** ⊕ ⑩ ⓘ
⬜ ⬛ ⬛ ⬛ ⬛ ✦ **Leisure** fishing **Conf** facs Corporate
Hospitality Days **Location** W side of town centre off A65
Hotel ★★★ 83% HL Best Western Rombalds Hotel &
Restaurant, 11 West View, Wells Road, ILKLEY ☎ 01943 603201
🗐 01943 603201　15 en suite

KEIGHLEY
Map 7 SE04

Branshaw Branshaw Moor BD22 7ES
☎ 01535 643235 (sec) 📠 01535 648011
18 Holes, 5823yds, Par 69, SSS 68, Course record 64.
Course Designer James Braid **Location** 2m SW on B6149, signed
Oakworth
Telephone for further details
Hotel ★★ 70% HL Dalesgate, 406 Skipton Road, Utley, KEIGHLEY
☎ 01535 664930 📠 01535 664930 20 en suite

Keighley Howden Park, Utley BD20 6DH
☎ 01535 604778 📠 01535 604778
e-mail: manager@keighleygolfclub.com
web: www.keighleygolfclub.com
Parkland course is good quality and has great views down the Aire
valley. The 17th hole has been described as 'one of the most difficult
and dangerous holes in Yorkshire golf'. The club celebrated its
centenary in 2004.
18 Holes, 6141yds, Par 69, SSS 70, Course record 64.
Club membership 650.
Visitors Sun-Fri & BHs. Booking required. Handicap certificate.
Dress code. **Societies** booking required. **Green Fees** £18-£28
depending on day/time **Course Designer** Henry Smith **Prof** Andrew
Rhodes **Facilities** ⓣ ⓞⓘ ⓑ ⓓ ⓟ ⓐ ⓐ ✆ ⓣ ✆
Leisure Snooker table **Conf** facs Corporate Hospitality Days
Location 1m NW of town centre off B6265, turn N at Roebuck pub
Hotel ★★ 70% HL Dalesgate, 406 Skipton Road, Utley, KEIGHLEY
☎ 01535 664930 📠 01535 664930 20 en suite

LEEDS
Map 8 SE33

Brandon Hollywell Ln, Shadwell LS17 8EZ
☎ 0113 273 7471
An 18-hole links type course enjoying varying degrees of rough, water
and sand hazards. Has been extended to include 2 par 5 holes. The
Village/Wike is a 9 hole course with 3 optional extra holes at no extra
charge.
Brandon Golf Course: 18 Holes, 6700yds, Par 72.
The Village/Wike: 12 Holes, 3000yds, Par 34.
Visitors Mon-Sun & BHs. **Societies** booking required. **Green
Fees** £10 per round (£12 weekends & BHs) **Course Designer** William
Binner **Prof** Carl Robinson **Facilities** ⓣ ⓓ ⓐ ⓟ ✆ ✆
Location off A58 into Shadwell, onto Main St, right at Red Lion pub

Cookridge Hall Golf & Country Club Cookridge Ln
LS16 7NL
☎ 0113 2300641 📠 0113 203 0198
e-mail: info@cookridgehall.co.uk
web: www.cookridgehall.co.uk
American-style course designed by Karl Litten. Expect plenty of water
hazards, tees for all standards. Large bunkers and fairways between
mounds and young trees.
Cookridge Hall Golf Club: 18 Holes, 6788yds, Par 72,
SSS 72, Course record 66. Club membership 570.
Visitors Mon-Sun & BHs. Booking required. Dress code.
Societies booking required **Green Fees** £25 per round (£30 weekends
& BHs) **Course Designer** Karl Liiten **Prof** Mark Pinkett **Facilities** ⓣ
ⓞⓘ ⓑ ⓓ ⓟ ⓐ ⓐ ✆ ✆ ✆ ✆ **Leisure** sauna,
gymnasium, chipping and practice bunker **Conf** Corporate Hospitality
Days **Location** 6m NW of Leeds, off A660

De Vere Oulton Hall Rothwell Ln, Oulton LS26 8HN
☎ 0113 282 3152 📠 0113 282 6290
web: www.devere-hotels.com
27 holes of championship standard golf with a state of the art 16 bay
golf academy.
Park Course: 18 Holes, 6500yds, Par 71, SSS 71,
Course record 69.
Hall Course: 9 Holes, 3300yds, Par 36.
Club membership 550.
Visitors Mon-Sun & BHs. Booking required. Handicap certificate.
Dress code. **Societies** booking required **Green Fees** Park £60 per
18 holes (£65 weekends). Hall £20 per 9 holes (£25 weekends)
Course Designer Dave Thomas **Prof** Keith Pickard **Facilities** ⓣ
ⓞⓘ ⓑ ⓓ ⓟ ⓐ ⓐ ⓟ ✆ ✆ **Leisure** heated
indoor swimming pool, sauna, gymnasium, spa **Conf** facs Corporate
Hospitality Days **Location** M62 junct 30, follow signs for Rothwell,
then Oulton. After 1m take first exit at the next 2 rdbts, course on left
Hotel ★★★★ 82% HL De Vere Oulton Hall, Rothwell Lane, Oulton,
LEEDS ☎ 0113 282 1000 📠 0113 282 1000 152 en suite

Gotts Park Armley Ridge Rd LS12 2QX
☎ 0113 231 1896 & 0798 3008044
Municipal parkland course; hilly and windy with narrow fairways.
Some very steep hills to some greens. A challenging course requiring
accuracy rather than length from the tees.
18 Holes, 4960yds, Par 65, SSS 64, Course record 63.
Club membership 200.
Visitors contact club for details. **Societies** welcome. **Green Fees** not
confirmed **Facilities** ⓣ ⓓ ⓟ ⓐ ⓟ ✆ **Location** 3m W of city
centre off A647
Hotel ★★★★ 80% HL The Queens, City Square, LEEDS
☎ 0113 243 1323 📠 0113 243 1323 217 en suite

Headingley Back Church Ln, Adel LS16 8DW
☎ 0113 267 9573 📠 0113 281 7334
e-mail: manager@headingleygolfclub.co.uk
web: www.headingleygolfclub.co.uk
An undulating course with a wealth of natural features offering fine
views from higher ground. Its most striking hazard is the famous
ravine at the 18th. Leeds's oldest course, founded in 1892.
18 Holes, 6608yds, Par 71, SSS 72, Course record 65.
Club membership 700.
Visitors Mon, Fri & BHs. Tue pm only. Handicap certificate. Dress
code. **Societies** booking required. **Green Fees** not confirmed **Course
Designer** Dr Mackenzie **Prof** Neil M Harvey **Facilities** ⓣ ⓞⓘ ⓑ ⓓ
ⓟ ⓐ ⓐ ⓟ ✆ **Location** 5.5m N of city centre. A660 to Skipton,
right at lights junct Farrar Ln and Church Ln, follow Eccup signs

Horsforth Layton Rise, Layton Rd, Horsforth LS18 5EX
☎ 0113 258 6819 📠 0113 258 9336
e-mail: secretary@horsforthgolfclubltd.co.uk
web: www.horsforthgolfclubltd.co.uk
Moorland and parkland course combining devilish short holes with
some more substantial challenges. Extensive views across Leeds and
on a clear day York Minster can be seen from the 14th tee.
18 Holes, 6258yds, Par 71, SSS 71, Course record 65.
Club membership 750.
Visitors Mon-Fri. Sun & BHs. Booking required. Dress code.
Societies booking required. **Green Fees** £42 per day, £36 per
round **Course Designer** Alister MacKenzie **Prof** Dean Stokes/Simon

continued

Booth **Facilities** ⓘ ⓘ ᓕ ☐ ᓗ ⌃ 🏠 ᕃ ✦ **Conf** facs
Corporate Hospitality Days **Location** 6.5m NW of city centre off A65
Hotel BUD Travelodge Leeds Bradford Airport, White House Lane,
LEEDS ☎ 08719 846 248 📄 08719 846 248 48 en suite

Leeds Elmete Ln LS8 2LJ
☎ 0113 265 8786   📄 0113 232 3369
e-mail: secretary@leedsgolfclub.co.uk
web: www.leeds-golf-club.co.uk

Parkland with pleasant views.

18 Holes, 6097yds, Par 69, SSS 69, Course record 63.
Club membership 600.

Visitors Mon-Fri & Sun except BHs. Booking required. Dress code.
Societies booking required. **Green Fees** not confirmed **Course**
Designer Alister McKenzie **Prof** Simon Longster **Facilities** ⓘ ⓘ ᓕ
☐ ᓗ ⌃ 🏠 ᕃ ✦ **Location** 5m NE of city centre on A6120,
off A58

Leeds Golf Centre, Wike Ridge Wike Ridge Ln, Shadwell
LS17 9JW
☎ 0113 288 6000   📄 0113 288 6185
e-mail: info@leedsgolfcentre.com
web: www.leedsgolfcentre.com

The 18-hole Wike Ridge is a traditional heathland course designed
by Donald Steel. The sand-based greens are constructed to USGA
specification and there are an excellent variety of holes with some very
challenging par 5s. The 12-hole, par 3, Oaks is complemented by a
floodlit driving range and other practice facilities. The course is the
home of the Leeds Golf Academy.

Wike Ridge Course: 18 Holes, 6332yds, Par 72, SSS 71,
Course record 64.
Oaks: 12 Holes, 1610yds, Par 36, SSS 35, Course record 29.
Visitors Mon-Sun & BHs. Booking required. Dress code.
Societies booking required. **Green Fees** Wike Ridge: £18.50 (weekends
£25). Oaks £7.50 (weekends £8.50) **Course Designer** Donald Steel
Prof Andrew Herridge/Joe Feather **Facilities** ⓘ ⓘ ᓕ ☐ ᓗ
⌃ 🏠 ᕃ ✦ 🛒 ✦ ✦ **Conf** facs Corporate Hospitality Days
Location 5m N, A58, course on N side of Shadwell

Middleton Park Municipal Middleton Park LS10 3TN
☎ 0113 270 0449   📄 0113 270 0449
18 Holes, 5263yds, Par 68, SSS 66, Course record 63.
Facilities ᓕ ☐ ᓗ ⌃ 🏠 **Location** 3m S off A653
Telephone for further details
Hotel ★★★★ 80% HL The Queens, City Square, LEEDS
☎ 0113 243 1323 📄 0113 243 1323 217 en suite

Moor Allerton Coal Rd, Wike LS17 9NH
☎ 0113 266 1154   📄 0113 268 0589
e-mail: info@magc.co.uk
web: www.magc.co.uk

The Moor Allerton Club, established in 1923, has 27 holes set in
220 acres of undulating parkland, with testing water hazards
and magnificent views extending across the Vale of York. The
championship course was designed by Robert Trent Jones, the
famous American course architect, and provides a challenge to both
high and low handicapped golfers.

Lakes Course: 18 Holes, 6470yds, Par 71, SSS 72.
Blackmoor Course: 18 Holes, 6673yds, Par 71, SSS 73.
High Course: 18 Holes, 6841yds, Par 72, SSS 74.
Club membership 500.

Visitors Mon-Sun & BHs. Handicap certificate. Dress code.
Societies welcome. **Green Fees** £85 per day, £65 per round (£85
weekends) **Course Designer** Robert Trent Jones **Prof** Richard Lane
Facilities ⓘ ⓘ ᓕ ☐ ᓗ ⌃ 🏠 ᕃ ✦ 🛒 ✦ ✦
Leisure sauna **Conf** facs Corporate Hospitality Days **Location** 5.5m
N of city centre on A61
Hotel ★★★ 66% HL Ramada Leeds North, Mill Green View,
Ring Road, Seacroft, LEEDS ☎ 0113 273 2323 & 0844 815 9108
📄 0113 273 2323 102 en suite

Moortown Harrogate Rd, Alwoodley LS17 7DB
☎ 0113 268 6521   📄 0113 268 0986
e-mail: secretary@moortown-gc.co.uk
web: www.moortown-gc.co.uk

Championship course, tough but fair. Springy moorland turf, natural
hazards of heather, gorse and streams, cunningly placed bunkers
and immaculate greens. No winter tees or greens. Home of the Ryder
Cup in 1929.

18 Holes, 6757yds, Par 71, SSS 73, Course record 64.
Club membership 585.

Visitors Mon-Fri, Sun & BHs. Booking required. Handicap certificate.
Dress code. **Societies** welcome. **Green Fees** £80 per day/
round. Reduced winter rates **Course Designer** Alistair Mckenzie
Prof Martin Heggie **Facilities** ⓘ ⓘ ᓕ ☐ ᓗ ⌃ 🏠 ᕃ
✦ 🛒 ✦ ✦ **Conf** facs Corporate Hospitality Days **Location** 6m
N of city centre on A61
Hotel ★★★ 72% HL Ramada Leeds Parkway, Otley Road, LEEDS
☎ 0844 815 9020 📄 0844 815 9020 118 en suite

Roundhay Park Ln LS8 2EJ
☎ 0113 266 2695 & 266 4225

Attractive municipal parkland course, natural hazards, easy walking.

9 Holes, 5223yds, Par 70, SSS 65, Course record 61.
Club membership 240.

Visitors contact club for details **Societies** welcome. **Green Fees** phone
Prof Adrian Newboult **Facilities** ᓕ ☐ ᓗ ⌃ 🏠 ᕃ ✦
Location 4m NE of city centre off A58

Sand Moor Alwoodley Ln LS17 7DJ
☎ 0113 268 5180 📠 0113 266 1105
e-mail: ian.kerr@sandmoorgolf.co.uk
web: www.sandmoorgolf.co.uk
A beautiful, inland course situated next to Eccup reservoir on the north side of Leeds. It has been described as the finest example of golfing paradise being created out of a barren moor. With magnificent views of the surrounding countryside, the course has sandy soil and drains exceptionally well.

18 Holes, 6446yds, Par 71, SSS 71, Course record 63.
Club membership 600.

Visitors Mon-Fri, Sun & BHs. Booking required. Handicap certificate. Dress code. **Green Fees** £55 per day, £45 per round (£55 per round Sun) **Course Designer** Dr A Mackenzie **Prof** Frank Houlgate **Facilities** ⊗ ⏐⊙⏐ ┗ ➴ ⏊ ⎓ 🏛 ⛳ 🏌 🚃 🏌
Conf Corporate Hospitality Days **Location** 5m N of city centre off A61

Hotel ★★★★ 72% HL Cedar Court, Denby Dale Road, WAKEFIELD ☎ 01924 276310 📠 01924 276310 149 en suite

South Leeds Gipsy Ln LS11 5TU
☎ 0113 272 3757
web: www.southleedsgolfclub.co.uk
18 Holes, 5865yds, Par 69, SSS 68, Course record 63.
Course Designer Dr Alister Mackenzie **Location** 3m S of city centre off A653
Telephone for further details
Hotel ★★★★ 80% HL The Queens, City Square, LEEDS
☎ 0113 243 1323 📠 0113 243 1323 217 en suite

Temple Newsam Temple-Newsam Rd LS15 0LN
☎ 0113 264 7362
e-mail: ady@templenewsamgolfcourse.co.uk
web: www.templenewsamgolfcourse.co.uk
Two parkland courses. Long par 3 holes on Lord Irwin course. Testing long 13th (563yds) on second course.

Lord Irwin: 18 Holes, 6460yds, Par 68, SSS 71,
Course record 66.
Lady Dorothy: 18 Holes, 6261yds, Par 70, SSS 70,
Course record 66. Club membership 520.

Visitors Mon-Sun & BHs. Booking required weekends & BHs. **Societies** booking required. **Green Fees** £10.10 per round (£13.10 weekends & BHs) **Course Designer** McKenzie **Prof** Adrian Newboult **Facilities** ⊗ ⏐⊙⏐ by prior arrangement ➴ 🏌 ⏊ 🏛 🏌 🚃
🏌 **Conf** facs Corporate Hospitality Days **Location** 3.5m E of city centre off A63

MARSDEN
Map 7 SE01

Marsden Hemplow Mount Rd HD7 6NN
☎ 01484 844253
e-mail: secretary@marsdengolf.co.uk
web: www.marsdengolf.co.uk
Moorland course with good views, natural hazards, windy.

9 Holes, 5702yds, Par 68, SSS 68, Course record 64.
Club membership 280.

Visitors handicap certificate. Dress code. **Societies** booking required. **Green Fees** £15 per round (£20 Sun & BHs) **Course Designer** Dr McKenzie **Prof** J Crompton **Facilities** ⊗ ⏐⊙⏐ ┗ ➴ 🏌 ⏊
Conf facs Corporate Hospitality Days **Location** S side off A62

MELTHAM
Map 7 SE01

Meltham Thick Hollins Hall HD9 4DQ
☎ 01484 850227 (office) & 851521 (pro)
📠 01484 850227
e-mail: admin@meltham.golf.co.uk
web: www.meltham-golf.co.uk
Parkland setting with moorland views. Tree-lined fairways with natural slopes, true and fast greens.

18 Holes, 6139yds, Par 71, SSS 70, Course record 63.
Club membership 756.

Visitors contact club for details. **Societies** welcome. **Green Fees** £33 per day, £28 per round (£38/£33 weekends & BHs). **Course Designer** Alex Herd **Prof** Paul Davies **Facilities** ⊗ ⏐⊙⏐ ┗ ➴ 🏌
⏊ 🏛 🏌 🏌 **Conf** Corporate Hospitality Days **Location** 0.5m E of Meltham on B6107

MIRFIELD
Map 8 SE21

Dewsbury District Sands Ln WF14 8HJ
☎ 01924 492399 & 496030 📠 01924 491928
e-mail: info@dewsburygolf.co.uk
web: www.dewsburygolf.co.uk
Moorland or parkland terrain with panoramic views. Ponds in middle of 3rd fairway, left of 5th green and 17th green. A challenging test of golf.

18 Holes, 6360yds, Par 71, SSS 71, Course record 64.
Club membership 700.

Visitors Mon-Sun & BHs. Booking required weekends & BHs. Dress code. **Societies** booking required. **Green Fees** £28 per day, £22 per round (£17.50 weekends) **Course Designer** Old Tom Morris/ Peter Alliss **Prof** Nigel P Hirst **Facilities** ⊗ ⏐⊙⏐ by prior arrangement ┗
➴ 🏌 ⏊ 🏛 🏌 🚃 🏌 **Leisure** snooker tables **Conf** facs Corporate Hospitality Days **Location** off A644, 4 m from M62 junct 25 and 6m from M1 junct 40
Hotel ★★★ 74% HL Heals Hall, Leeds Road, Liversedge, DEWSBURY ☎ 01924 409112 📠 01924 409112 24 en suite

MORLEY
Map 8 SE22

Howley Hall Scotchman Ln LS27 0NX
☎ 01924 350100 📠 01924 350104
e-mail: office@howleyhall.co.uk
web: www.howleyhall.co.uk
Easy walking parkland with superb views of the Pennines and the Calder valley.

18 Holes, 6092yds, Par 71, SSS 69, Course record 64.
Club membership 700.

Visitors Mon-Fri, Sun & BHs. Booking required. Dress code. **Societies** booking required. **Green Fees** £36 per day, £30 per round (£40 Sun & BHs). **Course Designer** MacKenzie **Prof** Gary Watkinson **Facilities** ⊗ ⏐⊙⏐ by prior arrangement ┗ ➴ 🏌 ⏊ 🏛 🏌
🚃 🏌 **Conf** facs Corporate Hospitality Days **Location** 1.5m S on B6123
Hotel ★★★ 74% HL Heals Hall, Leeds Road, Liversedge, DEWSBURY ☎ 01924 409112 📠 01924 409112 24 en suite

OSSETT — Map 8 SE22

Low Laithes Parkmill Ln, Flushdyke WF5 9AP
☎ 01924 274667 & 266067 📠 01924 266266
web: www.lowlaithesgolfclub.co.uk
Testing parkland course.

18 Holes, 6463yds, Par 72, SSS 71, Course record 65. Club membership 600.

Visitors Mon-Sun & BHs. Booking required weekends & BHs. Dress code. Handicap certificate. **Societies** booking required. **Green Fees** £30 per day, £25 per round (£36 weekends & BHs) **Course Designer** Dr Mackenzie **Prof** Paul Browning **Facilities** ⑪ ⑩I 🍴 💭 🥤 🏌 🏠 🛒 ♂ **Conf** Corporate Hospitality Days **Location** M1 junct 40, 0.5m on Dewsbury road, signed **Hotel** ★★★ 72% HL Heath Cottage Hotel & Restaurant, Wakefield Road, DEWSBURY ☎ 01924 465399 📠 01924 465399 28 en suite

OTLEY — Map 8 SE24

Otley Off West Busk Ln LS21 3NG
☎ 01943 465329 📠 01943 850387
e-mail: office@otley-golfclub.co.uk
web: www.otley-golfclub.co.uk
An expansive course with magnificent views across Wharfedale. It is well wooded with streams crossing the fairway. The 4th is a fine hole which generally needs two woods to reach the plateau green. The 17th is a good short hole. A test of golf as opposed to stamina.

18 Holes, 6211yds, Par 70, SSS 70, Course record 62. Club membership 700.

Visitors Mon, Wed-Fri. Dress code. **Societies** booking required. **Green Fees** £45 per day, £38 per 18/27 holes **Prof** Steven Tomkinson **Facilities** ⑪ ⑩I 🍴 💭 🥤 🏌 🏠 🍴 ♂ ♂ **Leisure** practice bunker **Conf** facs Corporate Hospitality Days **Location** 1m W of Otley off A6038

OUTLANE — Map 7 SE01

Outlane Slack Ln, Off New Hey Rd HD3 3FQ
☎ 01422 374762 📠 01422 311789
e-mail: secretary@outlanegolfclub.ltd.uk
web: www.outlanegolfclub.ltd.uk
An 18-hole moorland course with undulating fairways. Four par 3 holes with an 8th hole of 249yds and a 15th regarded as the hardest par 3 in Yorkshire. The three par 5s may be reachable on a good day in two strokes but in adverse conditions will take more than three. Smaller than average greens on some holes, which makes for accurate second shots.

Outlane Golf Club Ltd: 18 Holes, 5872yds, Par 71, SSS 69, Course record 67. Club membership 680.

Visitors Mon-Fri, Sun & BHs. Booking required BHs.. Dress code. **Societies** booking required. **Green Fees** £20 per day (£28 Sun) **Prof** David Chapman **Facilities** ⑪ ⑩I 🍴 💭 🥤 🏌 🏠 🍴 🛒 ♂ **Location** M62 junct 23, A640 New Hey Rd through Outlane **Hotel** ★★★ 68% HL The Old Golf House Hotel, New Hey Road, Outlane, HUDDERSFIELD ☎ 0844 736 8609 & 01422 379311 📠 0844 736 8609 52 en suite

PONTEFRACT — Map 8 SE42

Mid Yorkshire Havercroft Ln, Darrington WF8 3BP
☎ 01977 704522 📠 01977 600823
e-mail: admin@midyorkshiregolfclub.com
web: www.midyorkshiregolfclub.com

An 18-hole championship-standard course opened in 1993, and widely considered to be one of the finest new courses in Yorkshire.

18 Holes, 6308yds, Par 70, SSS 70, Course record 68. Club membership 500.

Visitors Mon-Sun & BHs. Booking required. Dress code. **Societies** welcome. **Green Fees** 18 holes £20, £15 am only, £25 pm only (£25 per 18 holes weekends). **Course Designer** Steve Marnoch **Prof** Michael Hessay **Facilities** ⑪ ⑩I 🍴 💭 🥤 🏌 🏠 🍴 ♂ 🛒 ♂ ♂ **Conf** facs Corporate Hospitality Days **Location** on A1 0.5m S junct A1/M62 **Hotel** ★★★★ 75% HL Wentbridge House, Wentbridge, PONTEFRACT ☎ 01977 620444 📠 01977 620444 41 en suite

Pontefract & District Park Ln WF8 4QS
☎ 01977 792241 📠 01977 792241
e-mail: manager@pdgc.co.uk
web: www.pdgc.co.uk
Undulating parkland course with elevated tees.

18 Holes, 6517yds, Par 72, SSS 72, Course record 64. Club membership 800.

Visitors contact club for details **Societies** welcome. **Green Fees** £35 per day, £30 per round.(£37 weekends) **Course Designer** A McKenzie **Prof** Ian Marshall **Facilities** ⑪ ⑩I 🍴 💭 🥤 🏌 🏠 🍴 ♂ **Location** W of Pontefract. A639 onto B6134, club 1m on right **Hotel** ★★★★ 75% HL Wentbridge House, Wentbridge, PONTEFRACT ☎ 01977 620444 📠 01977 620444 41 en suite

PUDSEY — Map 8 SE23

Calverley Golf Club Woodhall Ln LS28 5QY
☎ 0113 256 9244 📠 0113 256 4362
e-mail: calverleygolf@btconnect.com
Gently undulating parkland. The small greens require accurate approach shots.

Calverley Golf Club: 18 Holes, 5590yds, Par 68, SSS 67, Course record 62.
Calverley Golf Club: 9 Holes, 3000yds, Par 36. Club membership 553.

Visitors handicap certificate. Dress code. **Societies** welcome. **Green Fees** £16 per round (£20 weekends) **Prof** Neil Wendel-Jones **Facilities** ⑪ ⑩I 🍴 💭 🥤 🏌 🏠 ♂ 🛒 ♂ **Conf** Corporate Hospitality Days **Location** signed Calverley from A647 *continued*

Hotel BUD Travelodge Bradford, 1 Mid Point, Dick Lane, PUDSEY, Bradford ☎ 08719 846 124 🖹 08719 846 124 48 en suite

Fulneck LS28 8NT
☎ 0113 256 5191
e-mail: fulneck golf@aol.com
web: www.fulneckgolfclub.co.uk
Picturesque parkland course.

9 Holes, 5456yds, Par 66, SSS 67, Course record 65. Club membership 250.

Visitors Mon-Sun & BHs. Booking required weekends & BHs. **Societies** welcome. **Green Fees** not confirmed **Facilities** ⛳ **Location** Pudsey, between Leeds and Bradford
Hotel ★★★ 70% HL Campanile Bradford, 6 Roydsdale Way, Euroway Estate, BRADFORD ☎ 01274 683683 🖹 01274 683683 130 en suite

Woodhall Hills Calverley LS28 5UN
☎ 0113 255 4594 🖹 0113 255 4594
e-mail: whhgolf@tiscali.co.uk

Meadowland course, recently redeveloped with an improved layout and open ditches around the course. A challenging opening hole, a good variety of par 3s and testing holes at the 6th and 11th.

18 Holes, 6184yds, Par 71, SSS 70, Course record 64. Club membership 550.

Visitors dress code. **Societies** booking required. **Green Fees** £26 per round (£30 weekends). £15 Twilight **Prof** Richard Hedley **Facilities** ⓨ ⓧ 🍴 🖥 🏌 ⚑ 🏌 🛍 ⛳ **Conf** facs Corporate Hospitality Days **Location** 1m NW off A647
Hotel BUD Travelodge Bradford, 1 Mid Point, Dick Lane, PUDSEY, Bradford ☎ 08719 846 124 🖹 08719 846 124 48 en suite

RIDDLESDEN   Map 7 SE04

Riddlesden Howden Rough BD20 5QN
☎ 01535 602148

Undulating moorland course with prevailing west winds and beautiful views. Nine par 3 holes and spectacular 6th and 15th holes played over old quarry sites.

18 Holes, 4295yds, Par 63, SSS 61, Course record 59. Club membership 300.

Visitors Mon-Sun & BHs. **Societies** welcome. **Green Fees** not confirmed **Facilities** ⓨ ⓧ 🍴 🖥 🏌 ⛳ **Conf** Corporate Hospitality Days **Location** 1m NW
Hotel ★★ 70% HL Dalesgate, 406 Skipton Road, Utley, KEIGHLEY ☎ 01535 664930 🖹 01535 664930 20 en suite

SCARCROFT   Map 8 SE34

Scarcroft Syke Ln LS14 3BQ
☎ 0113 289 2311 🖹 0113 289 3835
e-mail: secretary@scarcroftgolfclub.com
web: www.scarcroftgolfclub.com

Undulating parkland course with prevailing west wind and easy walking.

18 Holes, 6456yds, Par 71, SSS 69. Club membership 650.

Visitors Mon-Sun & BHs. Booking required. Dress code. **Societies** booking required. **Green Fees** not confirmed **Course Designer** Charles Mackenzie **Prof** David Hughes **Facilities** ⓨ ⓧ 🍴 🖥 🏌 ⚑ 🏌 ⛳ **Location** 0.5m N of village off A58
Hotel ★★★★ CHH Wood Hall, Trip Lane, Linton, WETHERBY ☎ 01937 587271 🖹 01937 587271 44 en suite

SHIPLEY   Map 7 SE13

Marriott Hollins Hall Hotel & Country Club Hollins Hill, Otley Rd BD17 7QW
☎ 01274 534212 🖹 01274 534220
e-mail: mhrs.lbags.golf@marriotthotels.com
web: www.hollinshallgolf.com

Set in 200 acres of natural heathland amongst the beautiful Yorkshire moors and dales. The 6671 yard course offers multiple teeing areas which challenge any standard of golfer and is majestic, challenging and classically designed in the spirit of the game.

Hollins Hall: 18 Holes, 6671yds, Par 71, SSS 71, Course record 65. Club membership 400.

Visitors Mon-Sun & BHs. Booking required. Dress code. **Societies** booking required **Green Fees** £55 per day, £40 per round (£75/£50 Fri-Sun & BHs) **Course Designer** Ross McMurray **Prof** Brian Rumney **Facilities** ⓨ ⓧ 🍴 🖥 🏌 🏌 ⚑ 🛍 ⛳ ⛳ **Leisure** heated indoor swimming pool, sauna, gymnasium, golf academy **Conf** facs Corporate Hospitality Days **Location** 3m N on the A6038
Hotel ★★★★ 78% HL Marriott Hollins Hall Hotel & Country Club, Hollins Hill, Baildon, SHIPLEY ☎ 01274 530053 🖹 01274 530053 122 en suite

Northcliffe High Bank Ln BD18 4LJ
☎ 01274 596731 🖹 01274 584148
e-mail: northcliffegc@hotmail.com
web: www.northcliffegc.org.uk

Parkland with magnificent views of moors. Testing 1st hole, dog-leg left over a ravine. The 18th hole is one of the most picturesque and difficult par 3s in the country, with a green 100feet below the tee and protected by bunkers, water and trees.

18 Holes, 6104yds, Par 71, SSS 70, Course record 64. Club membership 700.

Visitors Mon-Fri, Sun & BHs. Dress code. **Societies** booking required. **Green Fees** £30 per day, £25 per round (£30 per round weekends & BHs). **Course Designer** James Braid **Prof** M Hillas **Facilities** ⓨ ⓧ 🍴 🖥 🏌 ⚑ ⛳ ⛳ **Conf** Corporate Hospitality Days **Location** 1.25m SW of Shipley, off A650
Hotel ★★★★ 78% HL Marriott Hollins Hall Hotel & Country Club, Hollins Hill, Baildon, SHIPLEY ☎ 01274 530053 🖹 01274 530053 122 en suite

SILSDEN
Map 7 SE04

Silsden Brunthwaite Ln, Brunthwaite BD20 0ND
☎ 01535 652998
e-mail: info@silsdengolfclub.co.uk
web: www.silsdengolfclub.co.uk
Tight downland course which can be windy. Good views of the Aire valley.

18 Holes, 5062yds, Par 67, SSS 65, Course record 62.
Club membership 350.

Visitors Mon-Fri, Sun & BHs. Booking required weekends. Dress code.
Societies welcome. **Green Fees** not confirmed **Facilities** ⚒ ⚑ ᛒ
⚐ ⚒ ⚒ ⚒ **Conf** facs Corporate Hospitality Days **Location** E of town off Howden Rd onto Hawber Ln
Hotel ★★ 70% HL Dalesgate, 406 Skipton Road, Utley, KEIGHLEY
☎ 01535 664930 ᛒ 01535 664930 20 en suite

SOWERBY
Map 7 SE02

Ryburn The Shaw, Norland HX6 3QP
☎ 01422 831355
e-mail: secretary@ryburngolfclub.co.uk
web: www.ryburngolfclub.co.uk
Moorland course, easy walking. Panoramic views of the Ryburn and Calder valleys.

9 Holes, 5127yds, Par 66, SSS 65, Course record 64.
Club membership 300.

Visitors Mon-Fri except BHs. Booking required. Handicap certificate.
Dress code. **Societies** booking required. **Green Fees** £20 per round
Facilities ⚒ ⚑ ᛒ ⚐ ⚒ ⚒ **Conf** Corporate Hospitality Days
Location 1m S of Sowerby Bridge off A58
Hotel ★★★ 63% HL Imperial Crown Hotel, 42/46 Horton Street,
HALIFAX ☎ 0844 736 8608 ᛒ 0844 736 8608 56 en suite

TODMORDEN
Map 7 SD92

Todmorden Rive Rocks, Cross Stone Rd OL14 8RD
☎ 01706 812986 ᛒ 01706 812986
e-mail: secretary@todmordengolfclub.co.uk
web: www.todmordengolfclub.co.uk
A tough but fair moorland course with spectacular scenery.

9 Holes, 5874yds, Par 68, SSS 68, Course record 66.
Club membership 240.

Visitors Mon-Wed. Fri, Sun & BHs. Limited play Thu. Booking
required Thu & Sun. Dress code. **Societies** booking required. **Green
Fees** £20 per day (£25 Sun & BHs) **Facilities** ⚒ ᛒ ⚐ ⚒ ⚒
Conf Corporate Hospitality Days **Location** NE off A646
Hotel ★★★ 85% HL Holdsworth House, Holdsworth, HALIFAX
☎ 01422 240024 ᛒ 01422 240024 40 en suite

WAKEFIELD
Map 8 SE32

City of Wakefield Horbury Rd WF2 8QS
☎ 01924 360282
Mature, level parkland course.

18 Holes, 6319yds, Par 72, SSS 70, Course record 64.

Visitors restricted weekends. **Societies** booking required. **Green
Fees** £16 weekends **Course Designer** J S F Morrison **Prof** David Bogg
Facilities ⚒ ⚑ ᛒ ⚐ ⚒ ⚒ ⚒ ⚒ **Location** 1.5m W of
city centre on A642

Hotel ★★★★ 72% HL Best Western Waterton Park, Walton
Hall, The Balk, Walton, WAKEFIELD ☎ 01924 257911 & 249800
ᛒ 01924 257911 65 en suite

Lofthouse Hill Leeds Rd WF3 3LR
☎ 01924 823703 ᛒ 01924 823703
e-mail: lofthousehillgolfclub@fsmail.net
web: www.lofthousehillgolfclub.co.uk
New parkland course.

18 Holes, 5957yds, Par 70, SSS 69.

Visitors Mon-Sun & BHs. Handicap certificate. Dress code.
Societies booking required. **Green Fees** £14 per 18 holes, £7 per
9 holes **Prof** Peter Rishworth/Derek Johnson **Facilities** ⚒ ⚑ ᛒ
⚐ ⚒ ᛒ ⚒ ⚒ ⚒ **Conf** facs Corporate Hospitality Days
Location 2m from Wakefield off A61
Hotel ★★★★ 72% HL Best Western Waterton Park, Walton
Hall, The Balk, Walton, WAKEFIELD ☎ 01924 257911 & 249800
ᛒ 01924 257911 65 en suite

Normanton Hatfield Hall, Aberford Rd WF3 4JP
☎ 01924 377943 ᛒ 01924 200777
web: normantongolf.co.uk
A championship course occupying 145 acres of the Hatfield Hall
Estate. A blend of parkland and elevations, the course incorporates
impressive lakes and benefits from the sympathetic preservation of
long established trees and wildlife. The large undulating greens are
built to USGA standards and are playable all year.

18 Holes, 6205yds, Par 72, SSS 71. Club membership 800.

Visitors Mon-Fri except BHs. Dress code. **Societies** booking required.
Green Fees £28 per 18 holes **Prof** Gary Pritchard **Facilities** ⚒ ⚑
ᛒ ⚐ ⚒ ᛒ ⚒ ⚒ ⚒ **Conf** facs **Location** M62 junct 30,
A642 towards Wakefield, 2m on right
Hotel ★★★★ 82% HL De Vere Oulton Hall, Rothwell Lane, Oulton,
LEEDS ☎ 0113 282 1000 ᛒ 0113 282 1000 152 en suite

Painthorpe House Painthorpe Ln WF4 3HE
☎ 01924 254737 & 255083 ᛒ 01924 252022
Painthorpe House Golf & Country Club: 9 Holes, 4544yds,
Par 62, SSS 62, Course record 63.

Facilities ᛒ **Leisure** bowling green **Location** 2m S off A636
Telephone for further details
Hotel ★★★★ 72% HL Cedar Court, Denby Dale Road, WAKEFIELD
☎ 01924 276310 ᛒ 01924 276310 149 en suite

Wakefield Woodthorpe Ln, Sandal WF2 6JH
☎ 01924 258778 (sec) ᛒ 01924 242752
e-mail: wakefieldgolfclub@woodthorpelane.freeserve.
co.uk
Well-sheltered meadowland and parkland with easy walking and good
views.

18 Holes, 6663yds, Par 72, SSS 72, Course record 67.
Club membership 540.

Visitors contact club for details. **Societies** booking required. **Green
Fees** £37 per day, £32 per round (£40 weekends) **Course Designer** A
McKenzie/S Herd **Prof** Ian M Wright **Facilities** ⚒ ⚑ ᛒ ⚐
⚒ ᛒ ⚒ ⚒ **Conf** Corporate Hospitality Days **Location** 3m S of
Wakefield, off A61
Hotel ★★★ 75% HL Best Western Hotel St Pierre, Barnsley Road,
Newmillerdam, WAKEFIELD ☎ 01924 255596 ᛒ 01924 255596
54 en suite

WETHERBY
Map 8 SE44

Wetherby Linton Ln LS22 4JF
☎ 01937 580089
e-mail: info@wetherbygolfclub.co.uk
web: www.wetherbygolfclub.co.uk

A medium length parkland course renowned for its lush fairways. Particularly memorable holes are the 6th, a par 4 which follows the sweeping bend of the River Wharfe.

18 Holes, 6692yds, Par 72, SSS 72, Course record 70. Club membership 950.

Visitors Mon-Sun & BHs. Booking advised. Handicap certificate. Dress code. **Societies** booking required. **Green Fees** £44 per day, £34 per round (£47 per day, £38 per round weekends) **Prof** Mark Daubney **Facilities** ⑪ ⑩ ⓛ ⏥ ⑪ ⏄ ☎ ⑨ ⋄ 🚗 ⋄ ⅌ **Conf** facs Corporate Hospitality Days **Location** 1m W off A661 **Hotel** ★★★★ CHH Wood Hall, Trip Lane, Linton, WETHERBY ☎ 01937 587271 🖹 01937 587271 44 en suite

WIKE
Map 8 SE34

The Village Golf Course Backstone Gill Ln LS17 9JU
☎ 0113 273 7471 & 07759012364

A 12 hole pay and play course in an elevated position enjoying long panoramic views. The holes are par 3, 4 and 5s and include water hazards and shaped large greens.

The Village Golf Course: 12 Holes, 5780yds, Par 75, SSS 68, Course record 66.

Visitors contact course for details. **Societies** welcome. **Green Fees** not confirmed **Course Designer** William Binner **Prof** Deborah Snowden **Facilities** ⑪ ⏥ ⑨ 🚗 ⋄ **Leisure** fishing **Location** signed, 1m off A61, 2m off A58 **Hotel** ★★★ 73% HL Jurys Inn Leeds, Kendell Street, Brewery Place, Brewery Wharf, LEEDS ☎ 0113 283 8800 🖹 0113 283 8800 248 en suite

WOOLLEY
Map 8 SE31

Woolley Park New Rd WF4 2JS
☎ 01226 380144 🖹 01226 390295
e-mail: woolleyparkgolf@yahoo.co.uk
web: www.woolleyparkgolfclub.co.uk

A demanding course set in a mature wooded parkland. With many water features in play and undulating greens, the course offers a challenge to all golfers.

Woolley Park Golf Course: 18 Holes, 6636yds, Par 71, SSS 72, Course record 70.

Visitors Mon-Sun & BHs. Booking required weekends & BHs. Dress code. **Societies** welcome. **Green Fees** £20 per 18 holes (£28 weekends & BHs). Academy £7.50 **Course Designer** M Shattock **Prof** Jon Baldwin **Facilities** ⑪ ⓛ ⏥ ⑪ ⏄ ☎ ⑨ 🚗 ⋄ **Leisure** 9 hole par 3 course **Conf** Corporate Hospitality Days **Location** M1 junct 38, off A61 between Wakefield and Barnsley **Hotel** ★★★★ 72% HL Cedar Court, Denby Dale Road, WAKEFIELD ☎ 01924 276310 🖹 01924 276310 149 en suite.

CHANNEL ISLANDS

ALDERNEY

ALDERNEY
Map 16

Alderney Route des Carrieres GY9 3YD
☎ 01481 822835

9 Holes, 5006yds, Par 64, SSS 65, Course record 65.
Facilities ⑪ by prior arrangement ⓛ ⏥ ⑪ ⏄ ☎ ⑨ ⋄ **Location** 1m E of St Annes **Telephone for further details** **Hotel** ★★★★ 71% HL Braye Beach, Braye Street, ALDERNEY ☎ 01481 824300 🖹 01481 824300 27 en suite

GUERNSEY

L'ANCRESSE VALE
Map 16

Royal Guernsey GY3 5BY
☎ 01481 246523   🖹 01481 243960
web: www.royalguernseygolfclub.com

18 Holes, 6215yds, Par 70, SSS 70, Course record 64.
Course Designer Mackenzie Ross **Location** 3m N of St Peter Port **Telephone for further details** **Hotel** ★★★ 79% HL St Pierre Park, Rohais, ST PETER PORT ☎ 01481 728282 🖹 01481 728282 131 en suite

CASTEL
Map 16

La Grande Mare Golf & Country Club Vazon Bay GY5 7LL
☎ 01481 253544   🖹 01481 255197
e-mail: golf@lagrandemare.com
web: www.lagrandemare.com

This hotel and golf complex is set in over 120 acres of grounds. The Hawtree designed parkland course opened in 1994 and was originally designed around 14 holes with four double greens. Water hazards on 15 holes.

La Grande Mare Golf & Country Club: 18 Holes, 4755yards, Par 64, SSS 64, Course record 63. Club membership 800.

Visitors Mon-Sun & BHs. Booking required Fri-Sun & BHs. Dress code. **Societies** welcome. **Green Fees** £39 per 18 holes (£45 weekends) **Course Designer** Hawtree **Prof** Matt Groves **Facilities** ⑪ ⑩ ⓛ ⏥ ⑪ ⏄ ☎ ⑨ ⋄ ⋄ ⅌ **Leisure** outdoor and indoor heated swimming pool, fishing, sauna, gymnasium, sports massage **Conf** facs Corporate Hospitality Days **Location** **Hotel** ★★★★ 71% HL La Grande Mare Hotel Golf & Country Club, The Coast Road, Vazon Bay, CASTEL ☎ 01481 256576 🖹 01481 256576 24 en suite

ENGLAND

ST PETER PORT   Map 16

St Pierre Park Golf Club Rohais GY1 1FD
☎ 01481 728282   📄 01481 712041
e-mail: gary.roberts@stpierrepark.co.uk
web: www.stpierrepark.co.uk
Challenging par 3 parkland course in a delightful setting, with lakes, streams and superb greens.

St Pierre Park Golf Club: 9 Holes, 2610yds, Par 54, SSS 50, Course record 52. Club membership 200.
Visitors Mon-Sun & BHs. Booking required. Dress code.
Societies welcome. **Green Fees** not confirmed **Course Designer** Jacklin **Facilities** ⑪ ⑩ 🏐 ⬛ 🍴 ♨ 🛆 🏠 ⛳ ◇
🏌 🏹 **Leisure** hard tennis courts, heated indoor swimming pool, sauna, gymnasium, spa pool **Conf** facs Corporate Hospitality Days
Location 1m W off Rohais Rd
Hotel ★★★ 79% HL St Pierre Park, Rohais, ST PETER PORT
☎ 01481 728282 📄 01481 728282 131 en suite

JERSEY

GROUVILLE   Map 16

Royal Jersey Le Chemin au Greves JE3 9BD
☎ 01534 854416   📄 01534 854684
e-mail: thesecretary@royaljersey.com
web: www.royaljersey.com
A seaside links - its centenary was celebrated in 1978. It is also famous for the fact that Britain's greatest golfer, Harry Vardon, was born in a little cottage on the edge of the course and learned his golf here.

18 Holes, 6100yds, Par 70, SSS 70, Course record 63. Club membership 1234.
Visitors Mon-Sun & BHs. Booking required. Handicap certificate.
Dress code. **Societies** booking required. **Green Fees** not confirmed
Prof David Morgan **Facilities** ⑪ ⑩ 🏐 ⬛ 🍴 ♨ 🛆 🏠 ⛳
🏌 🛒 🏹 **Location** 4m E of St Helier off coast road
Hotel ★★★ 74% HL Old Court House, GOREY, Grouville
☎ 01534 854444 📄 01534 854444 58 en suite

LA MOYE   Map 16

La Moye La Route Orange JE3 8GQ
☎ 01534 743401   📄 01534 747289
e-mail: secretary@lamoyegolfclub.co.uk
web: www.lamoyegolfclub.co.uk
Seaside championship links course (venue for the Jersey Seniors Open) situated in an exposed position on the south western corner of the island overlooking St Ouen's Bay. Offers spectacular views, two start points, full course all year - no temporary greens.

18 Holes, 6664yds, Par 72, SSS 73, Course record 65. Club membership 1500.
Visitors Mon-Sun & BHs. Booking required. Handicap certificate.
Dress code. **Societies** booking required. **Green Fees** £62 per 18 holes (£67 weekends & BHs) **Course Designer** James Braid
Prof Mike Deeley **Facilities** ⑪ 🏐 ⬛ 🍴 ♨ 🛆 🏠 ⛳ 🏌 🛒
🏌 🏹 **Location** W of village off A13
Hotel ★★★★ HL The Atlantic, Le Mont de la Pulente, ST BRELADE ☎ 01534 744101 📄 01534 744101 50 en suite

ST CLEMENT   Map 16

St Clement Jersey Recreation Grounds JE2 6PN
☎ 01534 721938   📄 01534 721012
Very tight moorland course. Impossible to play to scratch. Suitable for middle to high handicaps.

St Clement Golf & Sports Centre: 9 Holes, 2244yds, Par 30, SSS 31, Course record 29. Club membership 500.
Visitors contact centre for details. **Green Fees** £22 per day, £12 per 9 holes. **Prof** Lee Elstone **Facilities** ⑪ ⑩ 🏐 ⬛ 🍴
🏌 🏹 **Leisure** hard tennis courts, squash **Location** E of St Helier on A5
Hotel ★★★★★ HL Longueville Manor, ST SAVIOUR
☎ 01534 725501 📄 01534 725501 30 en suite

ST OUEN   Map 16

Les Mielles Golf & Country Club JE3 7FQ
☎ 01534 482787   📄 01534 485414
e-mail: enquiry@lesmielles.co.je
web: www.lesmielles.com
Challenging championship course with bent grass greens, dwarf rye fairways and picturesque ponds situated in the Island's largest conservation area within St Ouen's Bay.

Les Mielles Golf & Country Club: 18 Holes, 5770yds, Par 70, SSS 68, Course record 60. Club membership 1500.
Visitors Mon-Sun & BHs. Booking required Fri-Sun. Dress code.
Societies welcome. **Green Fees** phone **Course Designer** J Le Brun/R Whitehead **Prof** W Osmand/L Cummins **Facilities** ⑪ ⑩ 🏐 ⬛
🍴 🛆 🏠 ⛳ 🏌 🏹 **Leisure** Laser clay pigeon shooting, 18 hole miniature golf course **Conf** facs Corporate Hospitality Days
Location centre of St Ouen's Bay
Hotel ★★★★ 84% HL L'Horizon Hotel and Spa, St Brelade's Bay, ST BRELADE ☎ 01534 743101 📄 01534 743101 106 en suite

ISLE OF MAN

CASTLETOWN   Map 6 SC26

Castletown Golf Links Fort Island, Derbyhaven IM9 1UA
☎ 01624 822220   📄 01624 829661
e-mail: 1sttee@manx.net
web: www.golfiom.com
Set on the Langness peninsula, this superb championship course is surrounded on three sides by the sea, and holds many surprises from its Championship tees. A bunker redevelopment programme has been completed which has seen 22 additional bunkers added to this historic links course.

Castletown Golf Links: 18 Holes, 6707yds, Par 72, SSS 72, Course record 64. Club membership 500.
Visitors Mon-Sun & BHs. Booking required. Handicap certificate.
Dress code. **Societies** booking required. **Green Fees** not confirmed
Course Designer McKenzie Ross/Old Tom Morris **Prof** Michael Brook **Facilities** ⑪ ⑩ 🏐 ⬛ 🍴 🛆 🏠 ⛳ 🏌 🛒 🏌
Leisure snooker **Conf** Corporate Hospitality Days
Hotel ★★ 67% HL Falcon's Nest, The Promenade, PORT ERIN
☎ 01624 834077 📄 01624 834077 35 en suite

DOUGLAS   Map 6 SC37

Douglas Pulrose Park IM2 1AE
☎ 01624 675952 📠 01624 616865
web: www.isleofmangolf.com
Hilly, parkland and moorland course under the control of Douglas Corporation.

18 Holes, 5937yds, Par 69, SSS 69, Course record 62. Club membership 330.

Visitors contact club for details. **Societies** booking required. **Green Fees** £12 per day (£18 weekends) **Course Designer** Dr A Mackenzie **Facilities** ⑪ ⓑ ☐ 🏐 ⚐ 🏠 ⚑ ✐ 🛒 ✐ **Conf** facs Corporate Hospitality Days **Location** 1m from Douglas on Castletown road on Pulrose Estate
Hotel ★★★★ 78% HL Sefton, Harris Promenade, DOUGLAS ☎ 01624 645500 📠 01624 645500 96 en suite

Mount Murray Hotel & Country Club Mount Murray, Santon IM4 2HT
☎ 01624 661111 📠 01624 611116
e-mail: hotel@mountmurray.com
web: www.mountmurray.com
A challenging course with many natural features, lakes, streams etc. Five par 5s, six par 3s and the rest par 4. Fine views over the whole island.

Mount Murray Hotel & Country Club: 18 Holes, 6356yds, Par 71, SSS 71, Course record 66. Club membership 300.

Visitors Mon-Sun & BHs. Booking required. Dress code. **Societies** booking required. **Green Fees** from £17.50 per round (from £23 weekends) **Course Designer** Bingley Sports Research **Prof** Allyn Laing **Facilities** ⑪ 🏐 ⓑ ☐ 🏐 ⚐ 🏠 ⚑ ◇ ✐ 🛒 ✐ ⚑ **Leisure** heated indoor swimming pool, squash, sauna, gymnasium **Conf** facs Corporate Hospitality Days **Location** 5m from Douglas towards airport
Hotel ★★★★ 75% HL Mount Murray Hotel and Country Club, Santon, DOUGLAS ☎ 01624 661111 📠 01624 661111 100 en suite

ONCHAN   Map 6 SC47

King Edward Bay Golf & Country Club Howstrake IM3 2JR
☎ 01624 672709 & 620430
web: kebgc.com
King Edward Bay Golf Club: 18 Holes, 5492yds, Par 67, SSS 65, Course record 58.
Course Designer Tom Morris **Location** E of town off A11
Telephone for further details
Hotel ★★★★ 78% HL Sefton, Harris Promenade, DOUGLAS ☎ 01624 645500 📠 01624 645500 96 en suite

PEEL   Map 6 SC28

Peel Rheast Ln IM5 1BG
☎ 01624 842227 & 843456 📠 01624 843456
e-mail: peelgc@manx.net
web: www.peelgolfclub.com
Moorland course, with natural hazards and easy walking. Good views. The drop down to the 12th and climb back up to the 13th interrupt an otherwise fairly level course. The long, dog-legged 11th hole is an outstanding par 4, where the gorse must be carried to get a good second shot to the green. Most notable of the short holes are the 10th and 17th where an errant tee shot finds bunker, gorse or thick rough.

18 Holes, 5850yds, Par 69, SSS 69, Course record 64. Club membership 856.

Visitors Mon-Sun & BHs. Booking required. Dress code. Handicap certificate. **Societies** booking required. **Green Fees** £22 per round (£30 weekends) **Course Designer** James Braid **Prof** Paul O'Reilly **Facilities** ⑪ 🏐 ⓑ ☐ 🏐 ⚐ 🏠 ⚑ ✐ **Leisure** snooker **Conf** Corporate Hospitality Days **Location** SE of town centre on A1
Hotel ★★ 67% HL Falcon's Nest, The Promenade, PORT ERIN ☎ 01624 834077 📠 01624 834077 35 en suite

PORT ERIN   Map 6 SC16

Rowany Rowany Dr IM9 6LN
☎ 01624 834108 or 834072 📠 01624 834072
e-mail: rowany@iommail.net
web: www.rowanygolfclub.com
Undulating seaside course with testing later holes, which cut through gorse and rough. However, those familiar with this course maintain that the 7th and 12th holes are the most challenging.

18 Holes, 5840yds, Par 70, SSS 69, Course record 62. Club membership 500.

Visitors contact club for details. **Societies** booking required. **Green Fees** phone **Course Designer** G Lowe **Facilities** ⑪ ⚑ by prior arrangement 🏐 ☐ 🏐 ⚐ 🏠 ⚑ ✐ 🛒 ✐ **Conf** Corporate Hospitality Days **Location** N of village off A32
Hotel ★★ 67% HL Falcon's Nest, The Promenade, PORT ERIN ☎ 01624 834077 📠 01624 834077 35 en suite

PORT ST MARY   Map 6 SC26

Port St Mary Kallow Point Rd IM9 5EJ
☎ 01624 834932
Slightly hilly course with beautiful scenic views over Port St Mary and the Irish Sea.

9 Holes, 5702yds, Par 68, SSS 68, Course record 62. Club membership 324.

Visitors contact club for details. **Societies** welcome. **Green Fees** phone **Course Designer** George Duncan **Facilities** 🏠 ⚑ ✐ **Leisure** hard tennis courts, Croquet lawn **Conf** Corporate Hospitality Days **Location** signed entering Port St Mary, one-way system, 2nd left to end, 1st right
Guesthouse ★★★★★ GH Aaron House, The Promenade, PORT ST MARY ☎ 01624 835702 📠 01624 835702 4 rms (3 en suite)

RAMSEY   Map 6 SC49

Ramsey Brookfield Av IM8 2AH
☎ 01624 812244 📠 01624 815833
e-mail: ramseygolfclub@manx.net
web: www.ramseygolfclub.im
Parkland with easy walking and good views. Testing holes: 1st, par 5; 18th, par 3.

Ramsey Golf Club Ltd: 18 Holes, 5960yds, Par 70, SSS 69, Course record 63. Club membership 700.

Visitors Mon, Wed-Sun & BHs after 10am. Tue after12.30pm. Booking required. Handicap certificate. Dress code. **Societies** booking required. **Green Fees** £28 per day (£38 weekends & BHs). Reduced winter rates **Course Designer** James Braid **Prof** Andrew Dyson **Facilities** ⑪ ⚑ by prior arrangement 🏐 ☐ 🏐 ⚐ 🏠 ⚑ ✐ **Conf** Corporate Hospitality Days **Location** SW of town centre
Hotel ★★★★ 75% HL Mount Murray Hotel and Country Club, Santon, DOUGLAS ☎ 01624 661111 📠 01624 661111 100 en suite

Scotland

ABERDEEN, CITY OF

ABERDEEN
Map 15 NJ90

Auchmill Bonnyview Rd AB16 7FQ
☎ 01224 714577 📠 01224 648693

Auchmill Golf Course: 18 Holes, 5123metres, Par 70, SSS 67, Course record 67.

Course Designer Neil Coles/Brian Hugget **Location** outskirts Aberdeen, A96 Aberdeen-Inverness
Telephone for further details
Hotel ★★★ 77% HL The Craighaar, Waterton Road, Bucksburn, ABERDEEN ☎ 01224 712275 📠 01224 712275 55 en suite

Balnagask St Fitticks Rd AB11 3QT
☎ 01224 876407 📠 01224 648693

Links course with fine views over the harbour and beach. Very hilly with lots of hidden holes.

Balnagask Golf Course: 18 Holes, 5986yds, Par 70, SSS 69.

Visitors Mon-Sun & BHs. **Societies** welcome. **Green Fees** phone **Facilities** 🅿 🍴 ⛳ 🛒 🎯 🏌 ⛳ **Leisure** 9 hole pitch & putt course **Location** 2m E of city centre
Hotel ★★★★ 73% HL Maryculter House Hotel, South Deeside Road, Maryculter, ABERDEEN ☎ 01224 732124 📠 01224 732124 40 en suite

Craibstone Golf Centre Craibstone Estate, Bucksburn AB21 9YA
☎ 01224 716777 📠 01224 711298
e-mail: ballumbie2000@yahoo.com
web: www.craibstone.com

This parkland course is a fair and enjoyable test for all golfers. The course rewards accuracy off the tee, with the difficult 11th, 12th and 13th holes, and true and fast greens.

Craibstone Golf Centre: 18 Holes, 5757yards, Par 69, SSS 69, Course record 66. Club membership 545.

Visitors booking required weekends. Dress code. **Societies** welcome **Green Fees** not confirmed **Facilities** 🅿 🍴 ⛳ 🛒 🎯 🏌 🏠 🎯 🏌 🚌 🏌 **Location** NW of city off A96 Aberdeen-Inverness road. A96 through Bucksburn. Before next rdbt left signed Forrit Brae. At top of road club signed
Hotel ★★★★ 74% HL Aberdeen Marriott Hotel, Overton Circle, Dyce, ABERDEEN ☎ 01224 770011 📠 01224 770011 155 en suite

Deeside Golf Rd, Bieldside AB15 9DL
☎ 01224 869457 📠 01224 861800
e-mail: admin@deesidegolfclub.com
web: www.deesidegolfclub.com

An interesting riverside course with several tree-lined fairways. A stream comes into play at nine of the 18 holes on the main course. In recent years major reconstruction work has taken place to provide a testing course in which only five of the original holes are virtually unchanged. These include the 15th (the old 6th) which bears the name of James Braid who advised the club during previous course alterations. Various water features are incorporated into the course including pools at the 4th, 10th and 17th.

Haughton: 18 Holes, 6286yds, Par 70, SSS 71, Course record 65.
Blairs: 9 Holes, 5042yds, Par 68, SSS 64.
Club membership 1000.

Visitors contact club for details. **Societies** welcome. **Green**

Fees phone **Course Designer** Archie Simpson **Prof** Frank J Coutts **Facilities** 🅿 🍴 ⛳ 🛒 🎯 🏌 🏠 🏌 🏌 **Conf** Corporate Hospitality Days **Location** 3m W of city centre off A93
Hotel ★★★★ 73% HL Mercure Ardoe House Hotel & Spa, South Deeside Road, Blairs, ABERDEEN ☎ 01224 860600 📠 01224 860600 109 en suite

Hazlehead Hazlehead Av AB15 8BD
☎ 01224 321830 📠 01224 810452
e-mail: golf@aberdeencity.gov.uk
web: www.aberdeencity.gov.uk

Three picturesque courses and a pitch and putt course which provide a true test of golfing skills with gorse and woodlands being a hazard for any wayward shots.

No 1 Course: 18 Holes, 6224yds, Par 70, SSS 70.
No 2 Course: 18 Holes, 5764yds, Par 67, SSS 67.

Visitors Mon-Sun & BHs. Handicap certificate. **Societies** booking required. **Green Fees** not confirmed **Prof** C Nelson **Facilities** ⛳ 🛒 🎯 🏠 🏌 **Leisure** 9 hole pitch & putt course **Location** 4m W of city centre off A944
Hotel ★★★★ 73% HL Mercure Ardoe House Hotel & Spa, South Deeside Road, Blairs, ABERDEEN ☎ 01224 860600 📠 01224 860600 109 en suite

Murcar Links Bridge of Don AB23 8BD
☎ 01224 704354 📠 01224 704354
e-mail: golf@murcarlinks.com
web: www.murcarlinks.com

Seaside links course with a prevailing south-west wind. Its main attraction is the challenge of playing round and between gorse, heather and sand dunes. The additional hazards of burns and out of bounds give any golfer a testing round of golf.

Murcar Links: 18 Holes, 6500yds, Par 71, SSS 72, Course record 64.
Strabathie: 9 Holes, 2672yds, Par 70, SSS 71.
Club membership 650.

Visitors handicap certificate. Dress code. **Societies** booking required. **Green Fees** £95 per day, £70 per round (£90 per round weekends). Strabathie £38 per day, £15 per round (£45/£22.50 weekends) **Course Designer** A Simpson/J Braid/G Webster **Prof** Gary Forbes **Facilities** 🅿 🍴 ⛳ 🛒 🎯 🏌 🏠 ⛳ 🏌 🏌 **Location** 5m NE of city centre off A90
Hotel ★★★ 77% HL The Craighaar, Waterton Road, Bucksburn, ABERDEEN ☎ 01224 712275 📠 01224 712275 55 en suite

Royal Aberdeen Links Rd, Balgownie, Bridge of Don AB23 8AT
☎ 01224 702571 📠 01224 826591
e-mail: admin@royalaberdeengolf.com
web: www.royalaberdeengolf.com
Championship genuine links course with undulating dunes. Windy, easy walking.

Balgownie Course: 18 Holes, 6900yds, Par 71, SSS 74, Course record 63.
Silverburn Course: 18 Holes, 4066yds, Par 60, SSS 60. Club membership 500.

Visitors handicap certificate. **Societies** booking required. **Green Fees** £150 per day, £100 per round (£120 per round weekends) **Course Designer** Braid & Simpson **Prof** David Ross **Facilities** ⓦ 🍴 ⛳ 🛒 🎯 🏌 🏠 🐴 🚃 ⚸ **Location** 2.5m N of city centre off A92
Hotel ★★★★ 78% HL Doubletree by Hilton Aberdeen, Beach Boulevard, ABERDEEN ☎ 01224 633339 & 380000 📠 01224 633339 168 en suite

Westhill Westhill Heights, Westhill AB32 6RY
☎ 01224 740159 📠 01224 749124
e-mail: westhillgolf@btconnect.com
web: www.westhillgolfclub.co.uk
A challenging parkland course.

18 Holes, 5921yds, Par 69, SSS 69, Course record 65. Club membership 808.

Visitors Mon-Sun & BHs. Booking required. Dress code. Handicap certificate. **Societies** welcome. **Green Fees** £25 per day, £20 per round (£30/£25 weekends) **Course Designer** Charles Lawrie **Prof** George Bruce **Facilities** ⓦ 🍴 ⛳ 🛒 🎯 🏌 🏠 🐴 ⚸ 🚃 ⚸ **Leisure** snooker table **Conf** facs Corporate Hospitality Days **Location** 7m NW of city centre off A944
Hotel ★★★ 77% HL The Craighaar, Waterton Road, Bucksburn, ABERDEEN ☎ 01224 712275 📠 01224 712275 55 en suite

PETERCULTER   Map 15 NJ80

Peterculter Oldtown, Burnside Rd AB14 0LN
☎ 01224 734994(shop) & 735245(office)
📠 01224 735580
e-mail: info@petercultergolfclub.co.uk
web: www.petercultergolfclub.co.uk
Surrounded by wonderful scenery and bordered by the River Dee, a variety of birds, deer and foxes may be seen on the course, which also has superb views up the Dee Valley.

Peterculter Golf Course: 18 Holes, 6219yds, Par 71, SSS 70, Course record 64. Club membership 1035.

Visitors contact course for details. Handicap certificate. **Societies** welcome **Green Fees** not confirmed **Course Designer** Greens of Scotland **Prof** Dean Vannet **Facilities** ⓦ 🍴 ⛳ 🛒 🎯 🏌 🏠 🐴 ⚸ 🚃 ⚸ **Location** on A93
Hotel ★★★★ 73% HL Maryculter House Hotel, South Deeside Road, Maryculter, ABERDEEN ☎ 01224 732124 📠 01224 732124 40 en suite

ABOYNE   Map 15 NO59

Aboyne Formaston Park AB34 5HP
☎ 013398 86328 📠 013398 87592
e-mail: aboynegolfclub@btconnect.com
web: www.aboynegolfclub.co.uk
Beautiful parkland with outstanding views. Two lochs on course.

18 Holes, 6009yds, Par 68, SSS 69, Course record 62. Club membership 970.

Visitors contact club for details **Societies** welcome. **Green Fees** £40 per day, £28 per round (£45/£32 weekends) **Prof** Stephen Moir **Facilities** ⓦ 🍴 ⛳ 🛒 🎯 🏌 🏠 🐴 🚃 ⚸ **Conf** Corporate Hospitality Days **Location** E side of village, N of A93
Hotel ★★★ 80% HL Loch Kinord, Ballater Road, Dinnet, BALLATER ☎ 013398 85229 📠 013398 85229 20 en suite

ALFORD   Map 15 NJ51

Alford Montgarrie Rd AB33 8AE
☎ 019755 62178 📠 019755 64910
web: www.alford-golf-club.co.uk
18 Holes, 5483yds, Par 69, SSS 65, Course record 64.
Facilities ⓦ 🍴 ⛳ 🛒 🎯 🏌 🏠 🐴 🚃 ⚸ **Conf** Corporate Hospitality Days **Location** in village centre on A944
Telephone for further details
Hotel ★★ 64% HL Gordon Arms Hotel, The Square, HUNTLY ☎ 01466 792288 📠 01466 792288 13 en suite

AUCHENBLAE   Map 15 NO77

Auchenblae AB30 1TX
☎ 01561 320002
e-mail: parks@auchenblae.org.uk
web: www.auchenblae.org.uk/golf
Short but demanding course set in spectacular scenery and renowned for its excellent greens. A mixture of short and long holes, small and large greens add to the challenge and enjoyment of the course.

Auchenblae Golf Course: 9 Holes, 2217yds, Par 32, SSS 61, Course record 61. Club membership 500.

Visitors Mon-Sun & BHs. Handicap certificate. **Societies** booking required. **Green Fees** £13 per day (£16 weekends) **Course Designer** Robin Hiseman **Facilities** ⛳ 🛒 🏌 🐴 ⚸ **Leisure** hard tennis courts **Location** 10m S of Stonehaven off A90
Guesthouse ★★★★ GA Woodside Of Glasslaw, STONEHAVEN ☎ 01569 763799 📠 01569 763799 6 en suite

BALLATER   Map 15 NO39

Ballater Victoria Rd AB35 5LX
☎ 013397 55567
e-mail: sec@ballatergolfclub.co.uk
web: www.ballatergolfclub.co.uk
Heathland course with testing long and short holes and glorious views of the nearby hills.

18 Holes, 5638yds, Par 67, SSS 67, Course record 62. Club membership 750.

Visitors Mon-Sun & BHs. Handicap certificate. **Societies** welcome.

continued

Green Fees £25 per round (£28 weekends) **Prof** Bill Yule **Facilities** ⊕ ⋈ 🍴 🗜 🏌 🌳 ⚑ 🚶 ✦ 🏌 **Leisure** hard tennis courts, fishing, snooker **Conf** facs Corporate Hospitality Days **Location** W side of town

Hotel ★★★ 80% HL Loch Kinord, Ballater Road, Dinnet, BALLATER ☎ 013398 85229 ▤ 013398 85229 20 en suite

---

BALMEDIE   Map 15 NJ91

East Aberdeenshire Golf Centre Millden AB23 8YY
☎ 01358 742111
e-mail: eagc@hotmail.co.uk

Designed as two loops of nine holes each, starting and finishing outside the clubhouse. Skilful use of 130 acres of rolling Buchan farmland has resulted in a challenging course of 6276yds in length. Even in the short history of the course, the par 3 holes have gained the reputation of being equal to any in the north of Scotland.

East Aberdeenshire Golf Centre: 18 Holes, 6276yrds, Par 71, SSS 71, Course record 69. Club membership 400.

Visitors Mon-Sun & BHs. Booking required weekends & BHs. Dress code. **Societies** booking required. **Green Fees** £25 (£31 weekends & BHs) **Facilities** ⊕ ⋈ 🍴 🗜 🏌 🌳 **Conf** Corporate Hospitality Days

Hotel ★★★ 70% HL Udny Arms, Main Street, NEWBURGH ☎ 01358 789444 ▤ 01358 789444 30 en suite

---

BANCHORY   Map 15 NO69

Banchory Kinneskie Rd AB31 5TA
☎ 01330 822365 ▤ 01330 822491
e-mail: info@banchorygolfclub.co.uk
web: www.banchorygolfclub.co.uk

Sheltered parkland beside the River Dee, with easy walking and woodland scenery. Strategically placed bunkers and the "magnetic" River Dee are among the challenges.

18 Holes, 5801yds, Par 69, SSS 68, Course record 63. Club membership 975.

Visitors Mon-Sun & BHs. Handicap certificate. Dress code. **Societies** welcome. **Green Fees** £40 per day, £30 per round (£50/£40 weekends) **Prof** David Naylor **Facilities** ⊕ ⋈ 🍴 🗜 🏌 🌳 ⚑ 🚶 ✦ 🏌 ✦ **Conf** facs **Location** A93, 300yds from W end of High St

Hotel ★★★ 81% CHH Banchory Lodge, BANCHORY ☎ 01330 822625 & 822681 ▤ 01330 822625 22 en suite

---

Inchmarlo Resort & Golf Club Inchmarlo AB31 4BQ
☎ 01330 826424 & 826422 & 826427 ▤ 01330 826425
e-mail: secretary@inchmarlo.com
web: www.inchmarlogolf.com

The Laird's (18-hole course) is laid out on the gentle parkland slopes of the Inchmarlo Estate in the Dee Valley and the designer has taken advantage of the natural contours of the land and its many mature trees. The nine-hole Queen's course is a tricky and testing course with ponds, meadering burns and dry stone dykes combining with the more traditional bunkers to test the skill of even the most accomplished player.

Laird's Course: 18 Holes, 6240yards, Par 71, SSS 71, Course record 63.
Queen's Course: 9 Holes, 2150yds, Par 32, SSS 31. Club membership 900.

Visitors Mon-Fri, Sun & BHs. Sat after 3pm. Booking required.

Dress code. Handicap certificate. **Societies** booking required. **Green Fees** not confirmed **Course Designer** Graeme Webster **Prof** Patrick Lovie **Facilities** ⊕ ⋈ 🍴 🗜 🏌 🌳 ⚑ 🚶 ◇ ✦ 🏌 ✦ 🏌 **Conf** facs Corporate Hospitality Days **Location** 0.5m from A93 Aberdeen-Braemar road

Hotel ★★★ 81% CHH Banchory Lodge, BANCHORY ☎ 01330 822625 & 822681 ▤ 01330 822625 22 en suite

---

BANFF   Map 15 NJ66

Duff House Royal The Barnyards AB45 3SX
☎ 01261 812062 ▤ 01261 812224
e-mail: duff_house_royal@btinternet.com
web: www.theduffhouseroyalgolfclub.co.uk

Well-manicured flat parkland, bounded by woodlands and the River Deveron. Well bunkered and renowned for its large, two-tier greens. The river is a hazard for those who wander off the tee at the 7th, 16th and 17th holes.

Duff House Royal: 18 Holes, 6161yds, Par 68, SSS 70, Course record 62. Club membership 1050.

Visitors Mon-Sun & BHs. Dress code. Handicap certificate. **Societies** welcome. **Green Fees** £40 per day, £30 per round (£50/£36 weekends) **Course Designer** Alistair MacKenzie **Prof** Gary Holland **Facilities** ⊕ ⋈ 🍴 🗜 🏌 🌳 ✦ 🏌 ✦ **Conf** facs Corporate Hospitality Days **Location** 0.5m S on A98

BRAEMAR   Map 15 NO19

Braemar Cluniebank Rd AB35 5XX
☎ 013397 41618 ▤ 013397 41400
e-mail: info@braemargolfclub.co.uk
web: www.braemargolfclub.co.uk

Flat course, set amid beautiful countryside on Royal Deeside, with River Clunie running through several holes. The 2nd hole is one of the most testing in the area.

18 Holes, 5000yds, Par 65, SSS 64, Course record 59. Club membership 450.

Visitors dress code. Handicap certificate. **Societies** booking required. **Green Fees** £25 per day, £20 per round (£30/£25 weekends) **Course Designer** Joe Anderson **Facilities** ⊕ ⋈ 🍴 🗜 🏌 🌳 ⚑ ✦ **Location** 0.5m S

Guesthouse ★★★★ GH Callater Lodge Guest House, 9 Glenshee Road, BRAEMAR ☎ 013397 41275 ▤ 013397 41275 6 en suite

---

CRUDEN BAY   Map 15 NK03

Cruden Bay Aulton Rd AB42 0NN
☎ 01779 812285 ▤ 01779 812945
e-mail: secretary@crudenbaygolfclub.co.uk
web: www.crudenbaygolfclub.co.uk

A typical links course which epitomises the old fashioned style of rugged links golf. The drives require accuracy with bunkers and protecting greens, blind holes and undulating greens. The 10th provides a panoramic view of half the back nine down at beach level, and to the east can be seen the outline of the spectacular ruin of Slains Castle featured in Bram Stoker's Dracula. The figure eight design of the course is quite unusual.

Main Course: 18 Holes, 6395yds, Par 70, SSS 72, Course record 65.

continued

St Olaf Course: 9 Holes, 5106yds, Par 64, SSS 65. Club membership 1100.

Visitors Mon-Sun & BHs. Booking required. Handicap certificate. **Societies** booking required. **Green Fees** £65 per round, £85 per day (£75 per round weekends) **Course Designer** Thomas Simpson **Prof** Robbie Stewart **Facilities** ⊕ ⍩ 🏌 ⌨ 🍴 👤 🛍 ⛳ ✏ 🏴 **Conf** Corporate Hospitality Days **Location** SW side of village on A975

Hotel ★★★ 70% HL Udny Arms, Main Street, NEWBURGH ☎ 01358 789444 📠 01358 789444 30 en suite

ELLON
Map 15 NJ93

McDonald Hospital Rd AB41 9AW
☎ 01358 720576 📠 01358 720001
e-mail: mcdonald.golf@virgin.net
web: www.ellongolfclub.co.uk
Tight, parkland course with streams.

18 Holes, 5986yds, Par 70, SSS 70, Course record 64. Club membership 710.

Visitors Mon-Sun & BHs. Booking required. Dress code. **Societies** booking required. **Green Fees** not confirmed **Prof** Ronnie Urquhart **Facilities** ⊕ ⍩ 🏌 ⌨ 🍴 👤 🛍 ⛳ ✏ **Conf** Corporate Hospitality Days **Location** 0.25m N on A948
Hotel ★★★ 70% HL Udny Arms, Main Street, NEWBURGH ☎ 01358 789444 📠 01358 789444 30 en suite

FRASERBURGH
Map 15 NJ96

Fraserburgh Philorth Links AB43 8TL
☎ 01346 516616 📠 01346 516616
web: www.fraserburghgolfclub.org
Corbie: 18 Holes, 6308yds, Par 70, SSS 71, Course record 63.
Rosehill: 9 Holes, 2416yds, Par 66, SSS 63.

Course Designer James Braid **Location** 1m SE on B9033
Telephone for further details

HUNTLY
Map 15 NJ53

Huntly Cooper Park AB54 4SH
☎ 01466 792643 📠 01466 794574
web: www.huntlygc.com
18 Holes, 5399yds, Par 67, SSS 66.
Facilities ⊕ ⍩ 🏌 ⌨ 🍴 👤 🛍 ⛳ ✏ 🏴 **Location** N side of Huntly, turn off A96 at bypass rdbt
Telephone for further details
Hotel ★★ 64% HL Gordon Arms Hotel, The Square, HUNTLY ☎ 01466 792288 📠 01466 792288 13 en suite

INSCH
Map 15 NJ62

Insch Golf Ter AB52 6JY
☎ 01464 820363 📠 01464 820363
e-mail: administrator@inschgolfclub.co.uk
web: www.inschgolfclub.co.uk
A challenging 18-hole course, a mixture of flat undulating parkland, with trees, stream and pond. The most challenging hole of the course is the 9th, a testing par 5 of 534yds requiring long and accurate play. This follows the par 3 8th, a hole which demands a well-positioned tee

shot played over a large water hazard to a long narrow green. Although a relatively short course, the natural woodland, water hazards and large contoured greens require accurate play.

18 Holes, 5350yds, Par 69, SSS 67. Club membership 400.

Visitors Mon-Sun & BHs. Booking required. Handicap certificate. **Societies** booking required. **Green Fees** £20 per day (£25 weekends). Reductions during winter **Course Designer** Greens of Scotland **Facilities** ⊕ by prior arrangement ⍩ by prior arrangement 🏌 ⌨ 🍴 👤 🛍 ⛳ **Conf** Corporate Hospitality Days **Location** A96
Hotel ★★★★ 74% HL Macdonald Pittodrie House, Chapel of Garioch, Pitcaple, INVERURIE ☎ 0870 1942111 & 01467 681744 📠 0870 1942111 27 en suite

INVERALLOCHY
Map 15 NK06

Inverallochy Whitelink AB43 8XY
☎ 01346 582000
e-mail: inverallochygolf@btconnect.com
web: www.inverallochygolfclub.co.uk
Seaside links course with natural hazards, tricky par 3s and easy walking.

18 Holes, 5351yds, Par 67, SSS 66, Course record 57. Club membership 600.

Visitors Mon-Fri, Sun & BHs. Booking required Sun & BHs. Dress code Handicap certificate. **Societies** booking required. **Green Fees** £25 per day, £20 per round (£30/£25 Sun) **Facilities** ⊕ ⍩ 🏌 ⌨ 🍴 👤 🛍 ⛳ **Leisure** Bowling green **Location** E side of village off B9107

INVERURIE
Map 15 NJ72

Inverurie Davah Wood AB51 5JB
☎ 01467 624080 📠 01467 672869
e-mail: administrator@inveruriegc.co.uk
web: www.inveruriegc.co.uk
Parkland course, part of which is through a wood.

18 Holes, 5711yds, Par 69, SSS 68, Course record 63. Club membership 750.

Visitors Contact club for details. Booking required. Handicap certificate. **Societies** Booking required. **Green Fees** not confirmed **Prof** Steven McLean **Facilities** ⊕ ⍩ 🏌 ⌨ 🍴 👤 🛍 ⛳ 🚜 ✏ **Location** off Blackhall rdbt off A96 bypass
Hotel ★★★★ 74% HL Macdonald Pittodrie House, Chapel of Garioch, Pitcaple, INVERURIE ☎ 0870 1942111 & 01467 681744 📠 0870 1942111 27 en suite

KEMNAY
Map 15 NJ71

Kemnay Monymusk Rd AB51 5RA
☎ 01467 642225 (shop) 📠 01467 643746
e-mail: administrator@kemnaygolfclub.co.uk
web: www.kemnaygolfclub.co.uk
Parkland with stunning views, incorporating tree-lined and open fairways, and a stream crossing four holes. The course is not physically demanding but a challenge is presented to every level of golfer due to the diverse characteristics of each hole.

18 Holes, 6362yds, Par 71, SSS 71, Course record 65. Club membership 800.

Visitors Mon-Sun & BHs. Booking required. **Societies** welcome. **Green Fees** not confirmed **Course Designer** Greens of Scotland **Prof** David

continued

J Brown **Facilities** ⓣ ⑩ ㅂ ⊑ ⑪ ㅅ 🖾 ⑨ ✓ 🛒 ✓
Conf Corporate Hospitality Days **Location** W side of village on B993
Hotel ★★★★ 74% HL Macdonald Pittodrie House, Chapel of
Garioch, Pitcaple, INVERURIE ☎ 0870 1942111 & 01467 681744
📄 0870 1942111   27 en suite

KINTORE   Map 15 NJ71

Kintore Balbithan AB51 0UR
☎ 01467 632631   📄 01467 632995
e-mail: kintoregolfclub@lineone.net
web: www.kintoregolfclub.net

The course covers a large area of ground, from the Don Basin near the
clubhouse, to mature woodland at the far perimeter. The 1st is one
of the toughest opening holes in the North East, and the 7th requires
an accurate drive followed by a second shot over a burn which runs
diagonally across the front of the green. The 11th is the longest hole
on the course, made longer by the fact that it slopes upwards all the
way to the green. The final holes are short, relatively hilly and quite
tricky but offer spectacular views to the Bennachie and Grampian
hills.

*Kintore Golf Course: 18 Holes, 6019yds, Par 70, SSS 69,
Course record 62. Club membership 700.*

Visitors Mon-Fri, Sun & BHs. Dress code **Societies** welcome. **Green
Fees** phone **Facilities** ⓣ ⑩ ㅂ ⊑ ⑪ ㅅ ⑨ 🛒 ✓
Conf Corporate Hospitality Days **Location** 1m from village centre on
B977
Hotel ★★★★ 79% HL Thistle Aberdeen Airport, Aberdeen Airport,
Argyll Road, ABERDEEN ☎ 0871 376 9001 📄 0871 376 9001
147 en suite

MACDUFF   Map 15 NJ76

Royal Tarlair Buchan St AB44 1TA
☎ 01261 832897   📄 01261 833455
e-mail: info@royaltarlair.co.uk
web: www.royaltarlair.co.uk

Seaside clifftop course. Testing 13th, Clivet (par 3).

*18 Holes, 5866yds, Par 71, SSS 68, Course record 62.
Club membership 400.*

Visitors Mon-Sun & BHs. Booking required. Handicap certificate.
Societies booking required. **Green Fees** £25 per day, £20 per round
(£30/£25 weekends) **Facilities** ⓣ ⑩ ㅂ ⊑ ⑪ ㅅ ⑨
🛒 ✓ **Conf** Corporate Hospitality Days **Location** 0.75m E off A98
Hotel ★★★ 62% HL Waterfront, 25 Union Road, MACDUFF
☎ 01261 831661 📄 01261 831661   15 en suite

MINTLAW   Map 15 NJ94

Longside West End AB42 4XJ
☎ 01779 821558   📄 01779 821564

18 Holes, 5225yds, Par 66, SSS 66, Course record 64.
Facilities ⓣ ⑩ ㅂ ⊑ ⑪ ㅅ ✓ **Location** 4m W of Peterhead
on New Pitsligo road
Telephone for further details
Hotel ★★★ 80% HL Palace, Prince Street, PETERHEAD
☎ 01779 474821 📄 01779 474821   64 en suite

NEWBURGH   Map 15 NJ92

Newburgh on Ythan Beach Rd AB41 6BY
☎ 01358 789058 & 789084
e-mail: secretary@newburghgolfclub.co.uk
web: www.newburghgolfclub.co.uk

This seaside course was founded in 1888 and is adjacent to a bird
sanctuary. The course was extended in 1996 and the nine newer
holes, the outward half, are characterised by undulations and hills,
with elevated tees and greens requiring a range of shot making. The
original inward nine demands accurate golf from tee to green. Testing
550yd dog-leg (par 5).

*18 Holes, 6423yds, Par 72, SSS 72, Course record 61.
Club membership 675.*

Visitors Mon-Sun & BHs. Booking required weekends. Dress code..
Societies booking required. **Green Fees** £45 per day, £35 per round
(£55/£45 weekends) **Course Designer** J H Taylor **Prof** Ian Bratton
Facilities ⓣ ⑩ ㅂ ⊑ ⑪ ㅅ 🖾 ⑨ ✓ 🛒 ✓ 🛒
Leisure hard tennis courts, fishing, Indoor swing studio. 6 hole
practice course. **Conf** facs Corporate Hospitality Days **Location** 10m N
of Aberdeen on A975
Hotel ★★★ 70% HL Udny Arms, Main Street, NEWBURGH
☎ 01358 789444 📄 01358 789444   30 en suite

NEWMACHAR   Map 15 NJ81

Newmachar Swailend AB21 7UU
☎ 01651 863002   📄 01651 863055
e-mail: info@newmachargolfclub.co.uk
web: www.newmachargolfclub.co.uk

Hawkshill is a championship-standard parkland course designed by
Dave Thomas. Several lakes affect five of the holes and there are well-
developed birch and Scots pine trees. Swailend is a parkland course,
also designed by Dave Thomas. It provides a test all of its own with
some well-positioned bunkering and testing greens.

*Hawkshill Course: 18 Holes, 6700yds, Par 72, SSS 74,
Course record 67.
Swailend Course: 18 Holes, 6388yds, Par 72, SSS 71,
Course record 64. Club membership 1200.*

Visitors Mon-Sun & BHs. Booking preferred. Dress code. Handicap
certificate. **Societies** booking required. **Green Fees** Hawkshill £65
per day, £45 per round. (£65 per round weekends). Swailend £35 per
day, £25 per round. (£45 per day, £35 per round weekends). **Course
Designer** Dave Thomas/Peter Allis **Prof** Andrew Cooper **Facilities** ⓣ
⑩ ㅂ ⊑ ⑪ ㅅ 🖾 ⑨ ✓ 🛒 ✓ 🛒 **Conf** Corporate
Hospitality Days **Location** 2m N of Dyce, off A947
Hotel ★★★ 74% HL Menzies Dyce Aberdeen Airport, Farburn
Terrace, Dyce, ABERDEEN ☎ 01224 723101 📄 01224 723101
198 en suite

OLDMELDRUM   Map 15 NJ82

Old Meldrum Kirk Brae AB51 0DJ
☎ 01651 872648   📄 01651 873555
e-mail: admin@oldmeldrumgolf.co.uk
web: www.oldmeldrumgolf.co.uk

Parkland with tree-lined fairways and superb views. Challenging
196yd, par 3 11th over two ponds to a green surrounded by bunkers.

*Oldmeldrum Golf Club: 18 Holes, 5988yds, Par 70, SSS 69,
Course record 66. Club membership 850.*

continued

Visitors Mon-Sun & BHs. Dress code. **Societies** welcome. **Green Fees** £24 per round (£30 weekends) **Prof** Hamish Love **Facilities** ⑨ ⑩ 🍴 ♿ 🏌 🛒 ⛳ Ⓦ 🎿 **Location** E side of village off A947
Hotel ★★★ 85% CHH Meldrum House Hotel Golf & Country Estate, OLD MELDRUM ☎ 01651 872294 📠 01651 872294 22 en suite

---

PETERHEAD Map 15 NK14

Peterhead Craigewan Links, Riverside Dr AB42 1LT
☎ 01779 472149 & 480725 📠 01779 480725
e-mail: enquiries@peterheadgolfclub.co.uk
web: www.peterheadgolfclub.co.uk
The Old Course is a natural links course bounded by the sea and the River Ugie. Varying conditions of play depending on wind and weather. The New Course is more of a parkland course.
Old Course: 18 Holes, 6173yds, Par 70, SSS 71,
Course record 64.
New Course: 9 Holes, 2228yds, Par 31.
Club membership 650.
Visitors Mon-Fri, Sun & BHs. Sat by arrangement. Dress code. **Societies** welcome. **Green Fees** Old Course £50 per day, £35 per round (£60/£45 weekends). New Course £18 **Course Designer** W Park/L Auchterconie/J Braid **Prof** Harry Dougal **Facilities** ⑨ ⑩ 🍴 ♿ 🏌 🛒 ⛳ 🎿 **Location** N side of town centre off A90
Hotel ★★★ 80% HL Palace, Prince Street, PETERHEAD
☎ 01779 474821 📠 01779 474821 64 en suite

PORTLETHEN Map 15 NO99

Portlethen Badentoy Rd AB12 4YA
☎ 01224 782575 & 781090 📠 01224 783383
web: www.portlethenclub.com
18 Holes, 6707yds, Par 72, SSS 72, Course record 63.
Course Designer Cameron Sinclair **Location** off A90 S of Aberdeen
Telephone for further details
Hotel ★★★★ 75% HL Norwood Hall, Garthdee Road, Cults, ABERDEEN ☎ 01224 868951 📠 01224 868951 36 en suite

---

STONEHAVEN Map 15 NO88

Stonehaven Cowie AB39 3RH
☎ 01569 762124 📠 01569 765973
e-mail: info@stonehavengolfclub.com
web: www.stonehavengolfclub.com
Challenging meadowland course overlooking sea with three gullies and splendid views.
18 Holes, 5103yds, Par 66, SSS 65, Course record 61.
Club membership 650.
Visitors dress code. Handicap certificate. **Societies** booking required. **Green Fees** £25 per day **Course Designer** C Simpson **Facilities** ⑨ 🍴 🍴 🏌 🛒 ⛳ 🎿 **Leisure** snooker **Location** 1m N off A92
Hotel ★★★★ 73% HL Maryculter House Hotel, South Deeside Road, Maryculter, ABERDEEN ☎ 01224 732124 📠 01224 732124 40 en suite

---

TARLAND Map 15 NJ40

Tarland Aberdeen Rd AB34 4TB
☎ 013398 81000 📠 013398 81000
e-mail: secretary@tarlandgolfclub.co.uk
web: www.tarlandgolfclub.co.uk
Parkland upland course, but easy walking. Some spectacular holes, mainly 4th (par 4) and 5th (par 3) and fine scenery. A challenge to golfers of all abilities.
9 Holes, 5888yds, Par 67, SSS 68, Course record 65.
Club membership 260.
Visitors Mon-Sun & BHs. Dress code. **Societies** welcome. **Green Fees** £18 per day (£24 weekends) **Course Designer** Tom Morris **Facilities** 🍴 🍴 🍴 🏌 🎿 **Conf** Corporate Hospitality Days **Location** E side of village off B9119
Hotel ★★★ 80% HL Loch Kinord, Ballater Road, Dinnet, BALLATER ☎ 013398 85229 📠 013398 85229 20 en suite

---

TORPHINS Map 15 NJ60

Torphins Bog Rd AB31 4JU
☎ 013398 82115
e-mail: stuartmacgregor5@btinternet.com
Heathland and parkland course built on a hill with views of the Cairngorms.
9 Holes, 4800yds, Par 64, SSS 64, Course record 59.
Club membership 310.
Visitors Mon-Sun & BHs. Booking required weekends & BHs. **Societies** welcome. **Green Fees** £15 per day (£16 weekends). £9 per 9 holes **Facilities** 🏌 🎿 **Location** 0.25m W of village off A980
Hotel ★★★ 68% HL Huntly Arms, Charlestown Road, ABOYNE ☎ 01339 886101 📠 01339 886101 49 en suite

---

TURRIFF Map 15 NJ75

Turriff Rosehall AB53 4HD
☎ 01888 562982 📠 01888 568050
e-mail: grace@turriffgolf.sol.co.uk
web: www.turriffgolfclub.com

An inland course with tight fairways, well-paced greens and well-sighted bunkers to test all golfers. The par 5 12th hole sets a challenge for the longest driver while the short par 3 4th, with its green protected by bunkers is a challenge in its own right.
18 Holes, 5664yds, Par 68, SSS 68. Club membership 650.
Visitors Mon-Sun & BHs. Booking required. Dress code. Handicap certificate. **Societies** booking required. **Green Fees** £27 per day, £23

continued

per round (£33/£27 weekends & BHs) **Prof** Gordon Dunn **Facilities** ⓣ ⛻ ⬛ ⬛ ⬛ ⬛ ⬛ ⬛ **Conf** Corporate Hospitality Days **Location** 1m W off B9024

ANGUS

ARBROATH   Map 12 NO64

Arbroath Elliot DD11 2PE
☎ 01241 875837   ▤ 01241 875837
e-mail: arbroathgolf@btinternet.com

A typical links layout, predominately flat, with the prevailing south westerly wind facing for the first seven holes, making a big difference to how certain holes play. When the wind is in a northerly direction the back nine holes are very tough. The greens are well protected by deep riveted pot bunkers. Fast tricky greens make for difficult putting.

Arbroath Golf Course: 18 Holes, 6185yds, Par 70, SSS 69, Course record 64. Club membership 550.

Visitors Mon-Sun & BHs. Booking required weekends & BHs. Dress code. **Societies** welcome. **Green Fees** £35 per day, £30 per round (£45/£35 weekends). £15 per round winter **Course Designer** Braid **Prof** Lindsay Ewart **Facilities** ⓣ ⛻ ⬛ ⬛ ⬛ ⬛ ⬛ ⬛ ⬛ **Location** 1m SW on A92
Hotel ★★★★ 76% HL Carnoustie Golf Hotel & Spa, The Links, CARNOUSTIE ☎ 01241 411999 & 411978 ▤ 01241 411999 85 en suite

Letham Grange Golf Ltd Colliston DD11 4RL
☎ 01241 890373   ▤ 01241 890725
e-mail: lethamgrangegolf@yahoo.co.uk

Often referred to as the 'Augusta of Scotland', the Old Course provides championship standards in spectacular surroundings with attractive lochs and burns. The Glens Course is less arduous and shorter using many natural features of the estate.

Old Course: 18 Holes, 6632yds, Par 73, SSS 73, Course record 66.
Glens Course: 18 Holes, 5528yds, Par 68, SSS 68, Course record 60. Club membership 600.

Visitors Mon-Sun & BHs. Dress code. **Societies** welcome. **Green Fees** not confirmed **Course Designer** G K Smith/Donald Steel **Prof** Scott Graham **Facilities** ⓣ ⛻ ⬛ ⬛ ⬛ ⬛ ⬛ ⬛ ⬛ **Conf** facs Corporate Hospitality Days **Location** 4m N on A933

BARRY   Map 12 NO53

Panmure Burnside Rd DD7 7RT
☎ 01241 855120   ▤ 01241 859737
web: www.panmuregolfclub.co.uk

18 Holes, 6317yds, Par 70, SSS 71, Course record 62.
Course Designer James Braid **Location** S side of village off A930
Telephone for further details
Hotel ★★★★ 76% HL Carnoustie Golf Hotel & Spa, The Links, CARNOUSTIE ☎ 01241 411999 & 411978 ▤ 01241 411999 85 en suite

BRECHIN   Map 15 NO56

Brechin Trinity DD9 7PD
☎ 01356 622383 & 625270   ▤ 01356 625270
e-mail: brechingolfclub@tiscali.co.uk
web: www.brechingolfclub.co.uk

Rolling parkland with easy walking and good views of the Grampian mountains. Set among many tree-lined fairways with excellent greens and lush green fairways. A wide variation of holes with dog legs, long par 3s, tricky par 4s and reachable in two par 5s, where the longer hitters can take a more challenging tee shot.

Brechin Golf & Squash Club: 18 Holes, 6092yds, Par 72, SSS 70, Course record 66. Club membership 850.

Visitors Mon-Sun & BHs. Booking required. Dress code. **Societies** booking required. **Green Fees** £40 per day, £32 per round (£44/£34 weekends) **Course Designer** James Braid (partly) **Prof** Stephen Rennie **Facilities** ⓣ ⛻ ⬛ ⬛ ⬛ ⬛ ⬛ ⬛ ⬛ **Leisure** squash **Conf** Corporate Hospitality Days **Location** 1m N on B966

CARNOUSTIE   Map 12 NO53

Carnoustie Golf Links see page 321
20 Links Pde DD7 7JF
☎ 01241 802270 bookings   ▤ 01241 802271
e-mail: golf@carnoustiegolflinks.co.uk
web: www.carnoustiegolflinks.co.uk

EDZELL   Map 15 NO66

Edzell High St DD9 7TF
☎ 01356 647283 (Secretary)   ▤ 01356 648094
e-mail: secretary@edzellgolfclub.net
web: www.edzellgolfclub.net

This delightful, gentle, flat course is situated in the foothills of the Highlands and provides good golf as well as conveying a feeling of peace and quiet to everyone who plays here. The village of Edzell is one of the most picturesque in Scotland.

18 Holes, 6367yds, Par 71, SSS 71, Course record 63.
West Water: 9 Holes, 2057yds, Par 32, SSS 31.
Club membership 855.

Visitors Mon-Sun & BHs. Handicap certificate. Dress code. **Societies** welcome. **Green Fees** £48 per day, £36 per round (£60/£42 weekends). West Water £16 per 18 holes, £12 per 9 holes **Course Designer** Bob Simpson **Prof** A J Webster **Facilities** ⓣ ⛻ ⬛ ⬛ ⬛ ⬛ ⬛ ⬛ ⬛ **Location** B966 north of Brechin Bypass on A90, 4 miles, club entrance is on left after arch

FORFAR   Map 15 NO45

Forfar Cunninghill DD8 2RL
☎ 01307 463773   ▤ 01307 468495
web: forfargolfclub.com

18 Holes, 6066yds, Par 69, SSS 70, Course record 61.
Course Designer James Braid **Location** 1.5m E of Forfar on A932
Telephone for further details
Hotel ★★★ CHH Castleton House, Castleton of Eassie, GLAMIS ☎ 01307 840340 ▤ 01307 840340 6 en suite

CARNOUSTIE GOLF LINKS

ANGUS - CARNOUSTIE - MAP 12 NO53

This Championship Course has been voted the top course in Britain by many golfing greats and described as Scotland's ultimate golfing challenge. The course developed from origins in the 1560s; James Braid added new bunkers, greens and tees in the 1920s. The Open Championship first came to the course in 1931, and Carnoustie hosted the Scottish Open in 1995 and 1996, was the venue for the 1999 Open Championship, and staged the Championship in 2007. The Burnside Course (6028yds) is enclosed on three sides by the Championship Course and has been used for Open Championship qualifying rounds. The Buddon Course (5420yds) has been extensively remodelled, making it ideal for mid to high handicappers.

20 Links Pde DD7 7JF ☎ 01241 802270 bookings 🖹01241 802271
e-mail: golf@carnoustiegolflinks.co.uk   **web:** www.carnoustiegolflinks.co.uk
Championship: 18 Holes, 6941yds, Par 72, SSS 75, Course record 64.
Burnside: 18 Holes, 6028yds, Par 68, SSS 70, Course record 61.
Buddon Links: 18 Holes, 5420yds, Par 66, SSS 67.
Visitors Mon-Sun & BHs. Booking required. Handicap certificate. Dress code. **Societies** booking required. **Green Fees** Championship course £130, Burnside £35, Buddon £30. Play all 3 courses £150 **Course Designer** James Braid **Prof** Colin Sinclair **Facilities** ⑨ 🍽 🍸 ➡ 🍴 ⚓ 🏠 ⛳ ◇ 🏌 🏳 **Leisure** heated indoor swimming pool, sauna, gymnasium **Conf** facs Corporate Hospitality Days **Location** SW of town centre off A930
Hotel ★★★★ 76% HL Carnoustie Golf Hotel & Spa, The Links, CARNOUSTIE ☎ 01241 411999 & 411978 🖹01241 411999 85 en suite

KIRRIEMUIR
Map 15 NO35

Kirriemuir Shielhill Rd DD8 4LN
☎ 01575 573317 📠 01575 574608
web: www.kirriemuirgolfclub.co.uk
18 Holes, 5553yds, Par 68, SSS 67, Course record 62.
Course Designer James Braid **Location** 1m N off B955
Telephone for further details
Hotel ★★★ CHH Castleton House, Castleton of Eassie, GLAMIS
☎ 01307 840340 📠 01307 840340 6 en suite

MONIFIETH
Map 12 NO43

Monifieth Princes St DD5 4AW
☎ 01382 532767 📠 01382 535816
e-mail: monifiethgolf@freeuk.com
web: www.monifiethgolf.co.uk

The chief of the two courses at Monifieth is the Medal Course. It has been one of the qualifying venues for the Open Championship on more than one occasion. A seaside links, but divided from the sand dunes by a railway which provides the principal hazard for the first few holes. The 10th hole is outstanding, the 17th is excellent and there is a delightful finishing hole. The other course here is the Ashludie, and both are played over by a number of clubs who share the links.
Medal Course: 18 Holes, 6655yds, Par 71, SSS 72, Course record 63.
Ashludie Course: 18 Holes, 5123yds, Par 68, SSS 66.
Club membership 1500.
Visitors handicap certificate. Dress code. **Societies** booking required. **Green Fees** Medal £49 per round (£59 weekends): Ashludie £24 per round (£26 weekends) **Prof** Ian McLeod
Facilities ⊕ ⊺◎⊺ ⅃⅃ ⎁ ⍐⊺ ⅄ 🏠 ⋔⋔ ⚸ **Location** NE side of town on A930
Hotel ★★★★ 76% HL Carnoustie Golf Hotel & Spa, The Links, CARNOUSTIE ☎ 01241 411999 & 411978 📠 01241 411999 85 en suite

MONTROSE
Map 15 NO75

Montrose Golf Links Traill Dr DD10 8SW
☎ 01674 672932 📠 01674 671800
e-mail: secretary@montroselinks.co.uk
web: www.montroselinks.co.uk
The links at Montrose like many others in Scotland are on commonland. The Medal Course at Montrose - the fifth oldest in the world - is typical of Scottish links, with narrow, undulating fairways

and problems from the first hole to the last. In 2007 it was a final qualifying course in the Open Championship. The Broomfield course is flatter and easier.
Medal Course: 18 Holes, 6544yds, Par 71, SSS 72, Course record 62.
Broomfield Course: 18 Holes, 4825yds, Par 66, SSS 63.
Club membership 1300.
Visitors Mon-Sun & BHs. Dress code. Handicap certificate.
Societies welcome. **Green Fees** Medal £62 per day, £49 per round (£70/£54 weekends). Broomfield £20 per round (£22 weekends)
Course Designer W Park/Tom Morris **Prof** Jason J Boyd **Facilities** ⊕ ⊺◎⊺ ⅃⅃ ⎁ ⍐⊺ ⅄ 🏠 ⋔⋔ ⚸ 🚬 ⚸ **Location** NE side of town off A92
Guesthouse ★★★★ RR Gordon's, Main Street, INVERKEILOR, Arbroath ☎ 01241 830364 📠 01241 830364 5 en suite

CARDROSS
Map 10 NS37

Cardross Main Rd G82 5LB
☎ 01389 841754 📠 01389 842162
e-mail: golf@cardross.com
web: www.cardross.com
Undulating, testing parkland course with good views.
18 Holes, 6469yds, Par 71, SSS 72, Course record 64.
Club membership 800.
Visitors Mon-Fri except BHs. Booking required. Dress code.
Societies welcome. **Green Fees** not confirmed **Course Designer** James Braid **Prof** Robert Farrell **Facilities** ⊕ ⊺◎⊺ by prior arrangement ⅃⅃ ⎁ ⍐⊺ ⅄ 🏠 ⋔⋔ ⚸ ⚸ **Conf** Corporate Hospitality Days
Location in village centre on A814
Hotel ★★★★★ 84% HL De Vere Deluxe Cameron House, BALLOCH ☎ 01389 755565 📠 01389 755565 96 en suite

CARRADALE
Map 10 NR83

Carradale, The Arch PA28 6QT
☎ 01583 431321
Pleasant seaside course built on a promontory overlooking the Isle of Arran. Natural terrain and small greens are the most difficult natural hazards. Described as the most sporting nine-hole course in Scotland. Testing 7th hole (240yds), par 3.
9 Holes, 2358yds, Par 65, SSS 62, Course record 62.
Club membership 280.
Visitors Mon-Sun & BHs. **Societies** booking required. **Green Fees** £20 per day, £15 per 9 holes **Facilities** ⅄ ⍐⊺ ⚸ **Location** S side of village, on B842

DALMALLY
Map 10 NN12

Dalmally Old Saw Mill PA33 1AE
☎ 01866 822708
e-mail: dalmallygolfclub@btinternet.com
A nine-hole flat parkland course bounded by the River Orchy and surrounded by mountains. Many water hazards and bunkers.
Dalmally Golf Course: 9 Holes, 2257yds, Par 64, SSS 63, Course record 64. Club membership 130.
Visitors Mon-Fri & BHs. Booking required weekends. Dress code.

continued

Societies booking required. **Green Fees** not confirmed **Course Designer** MacFarlane Barrow Co **Facilities** ⚐ ⛳ ⛳ 🏌 🚶 ⚐
♂ **Location** on A85, 1.5m W of Dalmally
Hotel ★★★ 80% HL Loch Fyne Hotel & Spa, INVERARAY
☎ 0870 950 6270 🖺 0870 950 6270 71 en suite

DUNOON   Map 10 NS17

Cowal Ardenslate Rd PA23 8LT
☎ 01369 705673   🖺 01369 705673
e-mail: secretary@cowalgolfclub.com
web: www.cowalgolfclub.com

Moorland course. Panoramic views of the Clyde estuary and surrounding hills.

18 Holes, 6063yds, Par 70, SSS 70, Course record 63.
Club membership 900.

Visitors Mon-Sun & BHs. Booking required. Dress code.
Societies welcome. **Green Fees** phone **Course Designer** James Braid
Prof Russell Weir **Facilities** ⚐ 🏌 ⛳ ⛳ 🏌 🚶 🏠 ⚐ ♂
Conf Corporate Hospitality Days **Location** 1m N
Hotel ★★ 75% HL Selborne, Clyde Street, West Bay, DUNOON
☎ 01369 702761 🖺 01369 702761 98 en suite

ERISKA   Map 10 NM94

Isle of Eriska PA37 1SD
☎ 01631 720371   🖺 01631 720531
e-mail: gc@eriska-hotel.co.uk
web: www.eriska-hotel.co.uk

This remote and most beautiful course is set around the owners' hotel with stunning views. The signature 5th hole provides a 140yd carry to a green on a hill surrounded by rocks and bunkers.

Isle of Eriska: 9 Holes, 2588yds, Par 35.
Club membership 60.

Visitors Mon-Sun & BHs. Booking required. **Societies** booking required. **Green Fees** £10 per day **Course Designer** H Swan
Facilities ⚐ 🏌 ⛳ 🏌 🚶 ⚐ ◇ ♂ 🚩 **Leisure** hard tennis courts, heated indoor swimming pool, sauna, gymnasium **Conf** facs
Location A828 Connel-Fort William, signed 4m N of Benderloch
Hotel ★★★★★ CHH Isle of Eriska, Eriska, BY OBAN
☎ 01631 720371 🖺 01631 720371 23 en suite

GIGHA ISLAND   Map 10 NR64

Isle of Gigha PA41 7AA
☎ 01583 505242   🖺 01583 505244
e-mail: golf@gigha.net
web: www.gigha.org

A nine-hole course with scenic views of the Sound of Gigha and Kintyre. Ideal for the keen or occasional golfer.

9 Holes, 5042yds, Par 66, SSS 65. Club membership 40.

Visitors contact club for details. **Societies** booking required **Green Fees** £10 per day **Course Designer** Members **Facilities** 🚶 ⚐
Location near ferry landing

HELENSBURGH   Map 10 NS28

Helensburgh 25 East Abercromby St G84 9HZ
☎ 01436 674173   🖺 01436 671170
e-mail: thesecretary@helensburghgolfclub.co.uk
web: www.helensburghgolfclub.co.uk

Testing moorland course with superb views of Loch Lomond and River Clyde.

18 Holes, 5942yds, Par 69, SSS 69, Course record 62.
Club membership 875.

Visitors Mon-Fri except BHs. Booking advised. Dress code.
Societies welcome. **Green Fees** £45 per day, £35 per round. **Course Designer** Old Tom Morris **Prof** Fraser Hall **Facilities** ⚐ 🏌 🚶
⛳ 🏌 🚶 🏠 ⚐ ♂ 🚲 ♂ **Conf** Corporate Hospitality Days
Location NE side of town off B832, turn off Sinclair St into East Abercromby St
Hotel ★★★★★ 84% HL De Vere Deluxe Cameron House,
BALLOCH ☎ 01389 755565 🖺 01389 755565 96 en suite

INNELLAN   Map 10 NS17

Innellan Knockamillie Rd PA23 7SG
☎ 01369 830242 & 830415

Situated above the village of Innellan, this undulating hilltop, parkland course has extensive views of the Firth of Clyde.

Innellan Golf Course: 9 Holes, 4683yds, Par 64, SSS 64,
Course record 63. Club membership 199.

Visitors contact course for details. Handicap certificate.
Societies welcome. **Green Fees** £13 per day, £10 per round. (£15 weekends) **Facilities** 🚶 ⛳ 🏌 ⚐ **Location** 4m S of Dunoon
Hotel ★★ 75% HL Selborne, Clyde Street, West Bay, DUNOON
☎ 01369 702761 🖺 01369 702761 98 en suite

INVERARAY   Map 10 NN00

Inveraray North Cromalt PA32 8XT
☎ 01499 302116

Testing parkland course with beautiful views overlooking Loch Fyne.

Inveraray Golf Course: 9 Holes, 5628yds, Par 70, SSS 69,
Course record 69. Club membership 160.

Visitors Mon-Sun & BHs. Handicap certificate. **Societies** welcome.
Green Fees not confirmed **Facilities** 🚶 ⚐ **Location** 1m S of Inveraray
Hotel ★★★ 80% HL Loch Fyne Hotel & Spa, INVERARAY
☎ 0870 950 6270 🖺 0870 950 6270 71 en suite

LOCHGILPHEAD   Map 10 NR88

Lochgilphead, Blarbuie Rd PA31 8LE
☎ 01546 602340 & 600104

A varied and challenging scenic course with a spectacular par 3 finishing hole.

Lochgilphead Golf Course: 9 Holes, 2242yds, Par 64,
SSS 63, Course record 58. Club membership 250.

Visitors contact course for details. **Societies** welcome **Green Fees** not confirmed **Course Designer** Dr I McCamond **Facilities** 🚶 ⛳ 🏌
🚶 🏠 ⚐ ♂ **Location** next to hospital, signed from village
Hotel ★★★ 77% HL Cairnbaan, Crinan Canal, Cairnbaan,
LOCHGILPHEAD ☎ 01546 603668 🖺 01546 603668 12 en suite

SCOTLAND

MACHRIHANISH
Map 10 NR62

Machrihanish PA28 6PT
☎ 01586 810213   📠 01586 810221
e-mail: secretary@machgolf.com
web: www.machgolf.com

Magnificent natural links of championship status. The 1st hole is the famous drive across the Atlantic. Sandy soil allows for play all year round. Large greens, easy walking, windy.

18 Holes, 6225yds, Par 70, SSS 71, Course record 63. The Pans Course: 9 Holes, 2376yds, Par 34, SSS 69. Club membership 1300.

Visitors contact club for details. **Societies** booking required. **Green Fees** Mon-Fri & Sun £80 per day, £50 per round. (Sat £90/£70). The Pans course £12 per day. **Course Designer** Tom Morris **Prof** Ken Campbell **Facilities** ⑪ ⑩ ⓑ ⌨ ⑨⌨ ⌀ ⓐ ⑨⌨ ⌀ 🚗 ⌀
Location 5m W of Campbeltown on B843
Hotel ★★ 65% HL White Hart, Main Street, CAMPBELTOWN
☎ 01586 552440 📠 01586 552440 19 en suite

OBAN
Map 10 NM83

Glencruitten Glencruitten Rd PA34 4PU
☎ 01631 564604
e-mail: obangolf@btinternet.com
web: www.obangolf.com

There is plenty of space and considerable variety of hole on this parkland course - popular with holidaymakers. In a beautiful, isolated situation, the course is hilly and testing, particularly the 1st and 12th (par 4s) and 10th and 17th (par 3s).

18 Holes, 4452yds, Par 61, SSS 63, Course record 55. Club membership 500.

Visitors Mon-Sun except BHs. Booking required.. Dress code. Handicap certificate. **Societies** booking required. **Green Fees** Mon-Fri £25 per day. (£30 weekends) **Course Designer** James Braid **Facilities** ⑪ ⑩ ⓑ ⌨ ⑨⌨ ⌀ ⓐ ⑨⌨ ⌀ **Location** NE side of town centre off A816
Hotel ★★★ 82% HL Manor House, Gallanach Road, OBAN
☎ 01631 562087 📠 01631 562087 11 en suite

SOUTHEND
Map 10 NR60

Dunaverty PA28 6RW
☎ 01586 830677   📠 01586 830677
e-mail: dunavertygc@aol.com
web: www.dunavertygolfclub.com

Undulating, seaside course with spectacular views of Ireland and the Ayrshire coast.

18 Holes, 4799yds, Par 66, SSS 63, Course record 58. Club membership 400.

Visitors contact club for details **Societies** booking required. **Green Fees** not confirmed **Facilities** ⑪ ⑩ ⓑ ⌨ ⌀ ⓐ ⑨⌨ ⌀
Leisure fishing **Location** 10m S of Campbeltown on B842
Hotel ★★ 65% HL White Hart, Main Street, CAMPBELTOWN
☎ 01586 552440 📠 01586 552440 19 en suite

TARBERT
Map 10 NR86

Tarbert PA29 6XX
☎ 01546 606896

Hilly parkland with views over West Loch Tarbert.

9 Holes, 4460yds, Par 66, SSS 63, Course record 62. Club membership 90.

Visitors Mon-Sun & BHs. **Societies** welcome. **Green Fees** £20 per day, £10 per round. **Location** N 1m W on B8024
Hotel ★★★★ 73% HL Stonefield Castle, TARBERT, Loch Fyne
☎ 01880 820836 📠 01880 820836 32 en suite

TIGHNABRUAICH
Map 10 NR97

Kyles of Bute PA212AB
☎ 01700 811603 (secretary)
web: www.kylesofbutegolfclub.com

Moorland course which is hilly and exposed. Fine mountain and sea views. Heather, whin and burns provide heavy penalties for inaccuracy. Wild life abounds.

9 Holes, 4778yds, Par 66, SSS 64, Course record 62. Club membership 150.

Visitors contact club for details. **Societies** booking required. **Green Fees** £15 per day **Facilities** ⌀ ⑨⌨ ⌀ **Location** 1.25m S off B8000
Hotel ★★★ SHL An Lochan, Shore Road, TIGHNABRUAICH
☎ 01700 811239 📠 01700 811239 11 en suite

CLACKMANNANSHIRE

ALLOA
Map 11 NS89

Alloa Schawpark, Sauchie FK10 3AX
☎ 01259 724476   📠 01259 724476
e-mail: davieherd@btinternet.com
web: alloagolfpage.co.uk

Set in 150 acres of rolling parkland beneath the Ochil Hills, this course will challenge the best golfers while offering great enjoyment to the average player. The challenging finishing holes, 15th to 18th, consist of two long par 3s split by two long and demanding par 4s which will test any golfer's ability. Privacy provided by mature tree-lined fairways.

18 Holes, 6229yds, Par 69, SSS 71, Course record 63. Club membership 910.

Visitors Mon-Fri, Sun & BHs. Booking required. Dress code. **Societies** booking required. **Green Fees** not confirmed **Course Designer** James Braid **Prof** David Herd **Facilities** ⑪ ⑩ ⓑ ⌨ ⑨⌨ ⌀ ⓐ ⌀ **Conf** Corporate Hospitality Days **Location** 1.5m NE on A908
Guesthouse ★★★★ BB Westbourne House, 10 Dollar Road, TILLICOULTRY ☎ 01259 750314 📠 01259 750314 3 rms (2 en suite)

Braehead Cambus FK10 2NT
☎ 01259 725766   📠 01259 214070
e-mail: braehead.gc@btinternet.com
web: www.braeheadgolfclub.co.uk

Attractive parkland at the foot of the Ochil Hills, having spectacular views.

18 Holes, 6053yds, Par 70, SSS 69, Course record 60. Club membership 800.

Visitors Mon-Sun & BHs. Dress code. **Societies** booking required. **Green Fees** £32 per day, £24 per round (£40/£32 weekends) **Course**

continued

Designer Robert Tait **Prof** Jamie Stevenson **Facilities** ⓉⒾ ⚑ ▦ 🍴 🏊 🏠 🏌 ⛳ 🚌 ⛳ **Conf** Corporate Hospitality Days **Location** 1m W on A907
Hotel BUD Express by Holiday Inn Stirling, Springkerse Business Park, STIRLING ☎ 01786 449922 📠 01786 449922 78 en suite

---

ALVA   Map 11 NS89

Alva Beauclerc St FK12 5LD
☎ 01259 760431
e-mail: alva@alvagolfclub.wanadoo.com
web: www.alvagolfclub.com
A nine-hole course at the foot of the Ochil Hills which gives it its characteristic sloping fairways and fast greens.

9 Holes, 2423yds, Par 66, SSS 64, Course record 61.
Club membership 318.

Visitors contact club for details. **Societies** welcome. **Green Fees** phone **Facilities** ⚑ 🍴 ▦ 🏊 **Location** 7m from Stirling, A91 Stirling-St Andrews
Hotel BUD Express by Holiday Inn Stirling, Springkerse Business Park, STIRLING ☎ 01786 449922 📠 01786 449922 78 en suite

---

DOLLAR   Map 11 NS99

Dollar Brewlands House FK14 7EA
☎ 01259 742400 📠 01259 743497
e-mail: info@dollargolfclub.com
web: www.dollargolfclub.com
Compact hillside course with magnificent views along the Ochil Hills.

18 Holes, 5242yds, Par 69, SSS 66, Course record 57.
Club membership 450.

Visitors contact club for details. **Societies** booking required. **Green Fees** phone **Course Designer** Ben Sayers **Facilities** ⓉⒾ 🍴 ⚑ ▦ 🍴 🏊 🏌 ⛳ **Leisure** snooker table **Location** 0.5m N off A91
Hotel ★★★★ INN An Lochan Tormaukin, GLENDEVON
☎ 01259 781252 📠 01259 781252 13 rms (12 en suite)

MUCKHART   Map 11 N000

Muckhart Drumburn Rd FK14 7JH
☎ 01259 781423 & 781493
e-mail: enquiries@muckhartgolf.com
web: www.muckhartgolf.com
Scenic heathland and parkland course comprising 27 holes in three combinations of 18, all of which start and finish close to the clubhouse. Each requires a different approach, demanding tactical awareness and a skilful touch with all the clubs in the bag. There are superb views from the course's many vantage points, including the aptly named Arndean 5th 'Top of the World'.

Arndean/Cowden Course: 18 Holes, 6086yds, Par 71, SSS 70.
Naemoor/Howden Course: 18 Holes, 6485yds, Par 71, SSS 72.
Arndean/Naemoor Course: 18 Holes, 6069yds, Par 70, SSS 70. Club membership 910.

Visitors Mon-Sun & BHs. Booking required. Dress code.
Societies booking required. **Green Fees** £40 per 36 holes, £30 per 18 holes (£45/£35 weekends) **Prof** Keith Salmoni **Facilities** ⓉⒾ 🍴 ⚑ ▦ 🏊 🏠 🏌 **Conf** Corporate Hospitality Days **Location** S of village between A91 & A911

Hotel ★★★ 77% SHL Castle Campbell Hotel, 11 Bridge Street, DOLLAR ☎ 01259 742519 📠 01259 742519 9 en suite

---

TILLICOULTRY   Map 11 NS99

Tillicoultry Alva Rd FK13 6BL
☎ 01259 750124 📠 01259 750124
e-mail: golf@tillygc.freeserve.co.uk
Parkland at foot of the Ochil Hills. Some hard walking but fine views.

9 Holes, 5004metres, Par 68, SSS 67, Course record 64.
Club membership 400.

Visitors Mon-Fri & BHs. By arrangement weekends. Dress code.
Societies welcome. **Green Fees** £12 per 18 holes (£18 weekends & BHs) **Facilities** ▦ 🏊 **Location** A91, 9m E of Stirling
Hotel BUD Express by Holiday Inn Stirling, Springkerse Business Park, STIRLING ☎ 01786 449922 📠 01786 449922 78 en suite

---

DUMFRIES & GALLOWAY

CASTLE DOUGLAS   Map 11 NX76

Castle Douglas Abercromby Rd DG7 1BA
☎ 01556 502801 & 503527 📠 01556 502509
e-mail: cdgolfclub@aol.com
web: www.cdgolfclub.co.uk
The original course was laid out in 1905 and many changes have taken place over the years. The small but fast greens reward accuracy and a good short game is needed. The 359 yard par 4 2nd hole has a green protected by a raised plateau and even the biggest hitters have a tricky second shot. The subtle challenge of the 316 yard 5th, with its up-turned saucer green can leave even the best drive leaving the golfer with a hard job to get par.

9 Holes, 6240yds, Par 68, SSS 68, Course record 61.
Club membership 300.

Visitors contact club for details. Handicap certificate.
Societies booking required. **Green Fees** £18 per day, £12 per 9 holes. **Facilities** ⓉⒾ 🍴 ⚑ ▦ 🍴 🏊 🚌 🏌 **Leisure** pool table **Conf** Corporate Hospitality Days **Location** 0.5m from town centre on A713 Abercrombie road
Hotel ★★ 69% HL Arden House Hotel, Tongland Road, KIRKCUDBRIGHT ☎ 01557 330544 📠 01557 330544 9 en suite

---

COLVEND   Map 11 NX85

Colvend Sandyhills DG5 4PY
☎ 01556 630398 📠 01556 630495
e-mail: thesecretary@colvendgolfclub.co.uk
web: www.colvendgolfclub.co.uk
Picturesque and challenging course on the Solway coast. Superb views.

18 Holes, 5250yds, Par 68, SSS 67, Course record 64.
Club membership 490.

Visitors contact club for details. **Societies** welcome. **Green Fees** £30 per day, £25 per round **Course Designer** Allis & Thomas **Facilities** ⓉⒾ 🍴 ⚑ ▦ 🍴 🏊 🏌 ⛳ 🚌 ⛳ **Location** 6m SE from Dalbeattie on A710
Hotel ★★★ 86% HL Balcary Bay, AUCHENCAIRN
☎ 01556 640217 & 640311 📠 01556 640217 20 en suite

CUMMERTREES

Map 11 NY16

Powfoot DG12 5QE
☎ 01461 204100 🖹 01461 204111
e-mail: info@powfootgolfclub.com
web: www.powfootgolfclub.com

This British Championship course is on the Solway Firth and playing at this delightfully compact semi-links seaside course is a scenic treat. Lovely holes include the 2nd, the 8th and the 11th. The 9th includes a Second World War bomb crater.

18 Holes, 6255yds, Par 69, SSS 69, Course record 63.
Club membership 630.

Visitors Mon-Sun & BHs. Booking required. Handicap certificate. Dress code. Handicap certificate. **Societies** booking required. **Green Fees** £48 per day, £37 per round (£60/£43 weekends) **Course Designer** J Braid **Facilities** ⓣ ⑩ ▸ ⊑ 🍴 ⅄ 🏌 ▰ 🏍 ✦
✦ **Location** 0.5m off B724

Hotel ★★★ 70% HL Best Western Hetland Hall,
CARRUTHERSTOWN ☎ 01387 840201 🖹 01387 840201
32 en suite

DALBEATTIE

Map 11 NX86

Dalbeattie 19 Maxwell Park DG5 4LR
☎ 01556 610666 🖹 01556 612247
web: dalbeattiegc.co.uk

9 Holes, 5710yds, Par 68, SSS 68.

Course Designer Bryan C Moor **Location** signed off B794. Access by Maxwell Park
Telephone for further details
Hotel ★★★ 86% HL Balcary Bay, AUCHENCAIRN
☎ 01556 640217 & 640311 🖹 01556 640217 20 en suite

DUMFRIES

Map 11 NX97

Dumfries & County Nunfield, Edinburgh Rd DG1 1JX
☎ 01387 253585 🖹 01387 253585
e-mail: admin@thecounty.co.uk
web: www.thecounty.org.uk

Parkland alongside the River Nith, with views of the Queensberry Hills. Greens built to USPGA specifications. Nature trails link the fairways and the Burns Walk is incorporated within the course.

Nunfield: 18 Holes, 5918yds, Par 69, SSS 69,
Course record 61. Club membership 800.

Visitors Mon-Fri, Sun & BHs. Booking required. Dress code.
Societies booking required **Green Fees** £45 per day, £40 per 27 holes, £34 per round (£52/£45/£40 Sun & BHs) **Course Designer** William

Fernie **Prof** Stuart Syme **Facilities** ⓣ ⑩ ▸ ⊑ 🍴 ⅄ 📷
🏌 ✦ 🏍 ✦ **Conf** Corporate Hospitality Days **Location** 1m NE of Dumfries on A701
Hotel ★★★ 79% HL Best Western Station, 49 Lovers Walk,
DUMFRIES ☎ 01387 254316 🖹 01387 254316 32 en suite

Dumfries & Galloway 2 Laurieston Av DG2 7NY
☎ 01387 263848 🖹 01387 263848
e-mail: info@dandggolfclub.co.uk
web: www.dandggolfclub.co.uk

Attractive parkland course, a good test of golf but not physically demanding.

18 Holes, 6222yds, Par 70, SSS 71. Club membership 800.

Visitors Mon-Fri, Sun & BHs. Booking required. Handicap certificate. Dress code. Handicap certificate. **Societies** booking required. **Green Fees** £38 per day, £30 per round (£45/£35 Sun) **Course Designer** W Fernie **Prof** Joe Fergusson **Facilities** ⓣ ⑩ ▸ ⊑ 🍴 ⅄ 📷
🏌 ✦ 🏍 ✦ **Location** W of town centre on A780
Hotel ★★★ 79% HL Best Western Station, 49 Lovers Walk,
DUMFRIES ☎ 01387 254316 🖹 01387 254316 32 en suite

Dumfriesshire Golf Centre Lockerbie Rd DG1 3PF
☎ 01387 247444 🖹 01387 249600
e-mail: admin@pinesgolf.com
web: www.pinesgolf.com

A mixture of parkland and woodland with numerous water features and dog-legs. Excellent greens with many subtle undulations. This course cannot be overpowered, so must be played strategically.

Burns Heritage: 18 Holes, 5604yds, Par 68, SSS 68,
Course record 61. Club membership 280.

Visitors Mon-Sun & BHs. **Societies** booking required. **Green Fees** £26 per day, £22 per round **Course Designer** Duncan Gray **Prof** Richard Smith **Facilities** ⓣ ⑩ ▸ ⊑ 🍴 ⅄ 📷 🏌 ◇ ✦ 🏍 ✦
✦ **Conf** Corporate Hospitality Days **Location** off A701 Lockerbie Road, beside A75 Dumfries bypass
Hotel ★★★ 79% HL Best Western Station, 49 Lovers Walk,
DUMFRIES ☎ 01387 254316 🖹 01387 254316 32 en suite

GATEHOUSE OF FLEET

Map 11 NX55

Gatehouse Laurieston Rd DG7 2BE
☎ 01557 814766
e-mail: info@gatehousegolfclub.com
web: www.gatehousegolfclub.com

Set against a background of rolling hills with scenic views of Fleet Bay and the Solway Firth.

9 Holes, 2521yds, Par 66, SSS 66, Course record 62.
Club membership 300.

Visitors Mon-Sat & BHs. Sun after 11.45am. Dress code.
Societies booking required. **Green Fees** £15 per round **Course Designer** Tom Fernie **Facilities** ⅄ **Location** 0.25m N of town
Hotel ★★★★ 74% CHH Cally Palace, GATEHOUSE OF FLEET
☎ 01557 814341 🖹 01557 814341 55 en suite

GLENLUCE
Map 10 NX15

Wigtownshire County Mains of Park DG8 0NN
☎ 01581 300420   📄 01581 300420
e-mail: enquiries@wigtownshirecountygolfclub.com
web: www.wigtownshirecountygolfclub.com

Seaside links course on the shores of Luce Bay, easy walking but affected by winds. The 12th hole, a dog-leg with out of bounds to the right, is named after the course's designer, Gordon Cunningham.

18 Holes, 6104yds, Par 70, SSS 70, Course record 63.
Club membership 450.

Visitors Mon-Sun & BHs. Booking required weekends in summer.
Societies welcome. **Green Fees** £35 per day, £27 per round (£37/£29 weekends) **Course Designer** W Gordon Cunningham **Facilities** ⊕ ⏍ ⏍ 🗗 🖵 🍴 🏖 🛢 🏌 **Conf** Corporate Hospitality Days **Location** 1.5m W off A75, 200yds off A75 on shores of Luce Bay **Hotel** ★★★★ 74% HL North West Castle, STRANRAER
☎ 01776 704413 📄 01776 704413   72 en suite

GRETNA
Map 11 NY36

Gretna Kirtle View DG16 5HD
☎ 01461 338464   📄 01461 337362

9 Holes, 3214yds, Par 72, SSS 71, Course record 71.
Course Designer N Williams **Location** 0.5m W of Gretna on B721, signed
Telephone for further details
Hotel ★★★★ 74% HL Smiths at Gretna Green, Gretna Green, GRETNA ☎ 01461 337007 📄 01461 337007   50 en suite

KIRKCUDBRIGHT
Map 11 NX65

Brighouse Bay Brighouse Bay, Borgue DG6 4TS
☎ 01557 870409   📄 01557 870409
e-mail: admin@brighousebay-golfclub.co.uk
web: www.brighousebay-golfclub.co.uk.

A beautifully situated scenic maritime course on free draining coastal grassland and playable all year. Making use of many natural features - water, gullies and rocks - it provides a testing challenge to golfers of all handicaps.

Brighouse Bay Golf Course & Driving Range: 18 Holes,
6501yds, Par 73, SSS 72. Club membership 170.

Visitors Mon-Sun & BHs. Dress code. **Societies** welcome. **Green Fees** £33 per day, £26 per round (£35/£28 weekends) **Course Designer** D Gray **Facilities** ⊕ ⏍ ⏍ 🗗 🖵 🍴 🏖 🍸 ◇ 🛢 🏌 🍴 **Leisure** heated indoor swimming pool, fishing, sauna, gymnasium, Turkish steam room, jacuzzi, pool tables. **Conf** facs Corporate Hospitality Days **Location** 3m S of Borgue off B727 **Hotel** ★★ 69% HL Arden House Hotel, Tongland Road, KIRKCUDBRIGHT ☎ 01557 330544 📄 01557 330544   9 en suite

Kirkcudbright Stirling Crescent DG6 4EZ
☎ 01557 330314   📄 01557 330314
e-mail: kbtgolfclub@lineone.net
web: www.kirkcudbrightgolf.co.uk

Parkland with exceptional views over the harbour town of Kirkcudbright, the Dee Estuary and the Galloway Hills. This is a challenge for both low and high handicap golfers.

18 Holes, 5717yds, Par 69, SSS 69, Course record 63.
Club membership 500.

Visitors Mon-Sun & BHs. Booking required. Dress code.
Societies booking required. **Green Fees** £30 per day, £25 per round **Course Designer** E. Shamash **Facilities** ⊕ 🍴 ⏍ 🖵 🍴 🏖 🛢 🏌 **Location** NE side of town off A711 **Hotel** ★★ 69% HL Arden House Hotel, Tongland Road, KIRKCUDBRIGHT ☎ 01557 330544 📄 01557 330544   9 en suite

LANGHOLM
Map 11 NY38

Langholm Whitaside DG13 0JR
☎ 07724 875151
e-mail: golf@langholmgolfclub.co.uk
web: www.langholmgolfclub.co.uk

Hillside course with fine views, easy to medium walking.

9 Holes, 6180yds, Par 70, SSS 69, Course record 65.
Club membership 200.

Visitors dress code. **Societies** welcome. **Green Fees** phone **Facilities** ⊕ by prior arrangement 🍴 by prior arrangement ⏍ 🍴 🏖 **Location** E side of village off A7 **Guesthouse** ★★★★★ GA Bessiestown Country Guest House, CATLOWDY, Carlisle ☎ 01228 577219 & 577019 📄 01228 577219 5 en suite

LOCHMABEN
Map 11 NY08

Lochmaben Castlehillgate DG11 1NT
☎ 01387 810552
e-mail: lgc@naims.co.uk
web: www.lochmabengolf.co.uk
Attractive parkland surrounding Kirk Loch. Excellent views from this well-maintained course.

18 Holes, 5933yds, Par 70, SSS 70, Course record 60.
Club membership 850.

Visitors dress code. **Societies** welcome **Green Fees** £38 per day, £30 per round (£43/£33 weekends) **Course Designer** James Braid **Facilities** ⊕ 🍴 ⏍ 🖵 🍴 🏖 🛢 🏌 **Leisure** fishing **Conf** Corporate Hospitality Days **Location** 4m from Lockerbie on A74. S side of village off A709 **Hotel** ★★★★ 75% HL Dryfesdale Country House, Dryfebridge, LOCKERBIE ☎ 01576 202427 📄 01576 202427   28 en suite

LOCKERBIE
Map 11 NY18

Lockerbie Corrie Rd DG11 2ND
☎ 01576 203363   📄 01576 203363
e-mail: enquiries@lockerbiegolf.com
web: www.lockerbiegolf.com
Parkland course with fine views and featuring a pond hole which comes into play at 3 holes.

18 Holes, 5614yds, Par 68, SSS 67, Course record 64.
Club membership 620.

Visitors contact club for details. **Societies** welcome. **Green Fees** £28 per 18 holes (£32 weekends) **Course Designer** James Braid **Facilities** ⊕ ⏍ 🖵 🍴 🏖 🏌 🛢 🏌 **Conf** Corporate Hospitality Days **Location** E side of town centre off B7068 **Hotel** ★★★★ 75% HL Dryfesdale Country House, Dryfebridge, LOCKERBIE ☎ 01576 202427 📄 01576 202427   28 en suite

MOFFAT · Map 11 NT00

Moffat Coatshill DG10 9SB
☎ 01683 220020
e-mail: bookings@moffatgolfclub.co.uk
web: www.moffatgolfclub.co.uk

Scenic moorland course overlooking the town, with panoramic views of southern uplands.

The Moffat Golf Club: 18 Holes, 5276yds, Par 69, SSS 67, Course record 60. Club membership 350.

Visitors Mon-Sun & BHs. Dress code. **Societies** booking required. **Green Fees** £30 per day, £25 per round (£36/£30 weekends and BHs) **Course Designer** Ben Sayers **Facilities** 🍷 🍽 🛍 ⬜ 🍴 🛎 🏡 ⛳ 🛒 ⚸ **Leisure** snooker **Conf** Corporate Hospitality Days **Location** from A74(M) junct 15, take A701 to Moffat, course signposted on left after 30mph limit sign
Hotel ★★★ 73% HL Best Western Moffat House, High Street, MOFFAT ☎ 01683 220039 ▤ 01683 220039 21 en suite

MONREITH · Map 10 NX34

St Medan DG8 8NJ
☎ 01988 700358
e-mail: mail@stmedangolfclub.com
web: www.stmedangolfclub.com

Scotland's most southerly course. This links nestles in Monreith Bay with panoramic views across to the Isle of Man. The testing nine-hole course is a challenge to both high and low handicaps.

9 Holes, 4520yds, Par 64, SSS 64, Course record 60. Club membership 300.

Visitors dress code. **Societies** booking required. **Green Fees** £25 per day, £18 per 18 holes, £12 per 9 holes **Course Designer** James Braid **Facilities** 🛍 ⬜ 🍴 🛎 🏡 ⛳ **Location** 3m S of Port William off A747

NEW GALLOWAY · Map 11 NX67

New Galloway High St DG7 3RN
☎ 01644 420737 & 450685   ▤ 01644 450685
web: www.nggc.com

9 Holes, 5006yds, Par 68, SSS 67, Course record 64.

Course Designer James Braid **Location** S side of town on A762
Telephone for further details

NEWTON STEWART · Map 10 NX46

Newton Stewart Kirroughtree Av, Minnigaff DG8 6PF
☎ 01671 402172   ▤ 01671 402172
e-mail: newtonstewartgc@btconnect.com
web: www.newtonstewartgolfclub.com

A parkland course in a picturesque setting. A good test for all standards of golfer with a variety of shots required. Many mature trees on the course and the five short holes have interesting features.

18 Holes, 5903yds, Par 69, SSS 70, Course record 66. Club membership 380.

Visitors contact club for details. **Societies** welcome. **Green Fees** £28 per round (£32 weekends) **Facilities** 🍷 🍽 🛍 ⬜ 🍴 🏡 ⛳ **Conf** Corporate Hospitality Days **Location** 0.5m N of town centre off A75

Hotel ★★★ HL Kirroughtree House, Minnigaff, NEWTON STEWART ☎ 01671 402141 ▤ 01671 402141 17 en suite

PORTPATRICK · Map 10 NX05

Lagganmore Hotel DG9 9AB
☎ 01776 810499
web: www.lagganmoregolf.co.uk

Lagganmore Hotel: 18 Holes, 5698yds, Par 69, SSS 68, Course record 66.

Course Designer Stephen Hornby **Location** on A77
Telephone for further details
Hotel ★★★ 79% HL Fernhill, Heugh Road, PORTPATRICK ☎ 01776 810220 ▤ 01776 810220 36 en suite

Portpatrick Golf Course Rd DG9 8TB
☎ 01776 810273   ▤ 01776 810811
e-mail: enquiries@portpatrickgolfclub.com
web: www.portpatrickgolfclub.com

Situated on the south-west coast, overlooking the North Channel, Portpatrick benefits from the temperate climate, which allows golf to be played all year round. The two courses are a mix of rolling moorland and seaside heath, and afford some magnificent views.

Dunskey Course: 18 Holes, 5913yds, Par 70, SSS 69, Course record 63.
Club membership 650.

Visitors Mon-Sun & BHs. Booking required. Handicap certificate. Dress code. **Societies** Booking required. **Green Fees** £42.50 per day, £32 per round (£48.50/£37.50 weekends) **Course Designer** Charles Hunter **Facilities** 🍷 🍽 🛍 ⬜ 🍴 🛎 🏡 ⛳ 🛒 ⚸ **Leisure** 9 hole par 3 Dinvin Course **Conf** Corporate Hospitality Days **Location** entering village fork right at war memorial, signed 300yds
Hotel ★★★ 79% HL Fernhill, Heugh Road, PORTPATRICK ☎ 01776 810220 ▤ 01776 810220 36 en suite

SANQUHAR · Map 11 NS70

Sanquhar Euchan Golf Course, Blackaddie Rd DG4 6JZ
☎ 01659 50577
e-mail: tich@rossirence.fsnet.co.uk

Easy walking parkland, fine views. A good test for all standards of golfer.

9 Holes, 5594yds, Par 70, SSS 68, Course record 66. Club membership 200.

Visitors Mon-Sun & BHs. Dress code. **Societies** booking required. **Green Fees** £12 per day (£15 weekends). **Course Designer** Willie Fernie **Facilities** 🍷 by prior arrangement 🍽 by prior arrangement 🛍 ⬜ 🏡 **Leisure** snooker, pool. **Conf** Corporate Hospitality Days **Location** 0.5m SW off A76
Guesthouse ★★★★★ GA Gillbank House, 8 East Morton Street, THORNHILL ☎ 01848 330597 ▤ 01848 330597 6 en suite

SOUTHERNESS · Map 11 NX95

Solway Links Kirkbean DG2 8BE
☎ 01387 880323 & 880623   ▤ 01387 880555
web: www.solwaygolf.co.uk

Solway Links Golf Course: 18 Holes, 5005yds, Par 67.

Course Designer Gordon Gray **Location** On A710 Dumfries to Dalbeattie road.
Telephone for further details

continued

Hotel ★★ CHH Cavens, KIRKBEAN ☎ 01387 880234
🖹 01387 880234 5 en suite

Southerness DG2 8AZ
☎ 01387 880677   🖹 01387 880644
web: www.southernessgolfclub.com

18 Holes, 6105yds, Par 69, SSS 70, Course record 64.

Course Designer McKenzie Ross **Location** 3.5m S of Kirkbean off A710
Telephone for further details
Hotel ★★ CHH Cavens, KIRKBEAN ☎ 01387 880234
🖹 01387 880234 5 en suite

STRANRAER   Map 10 NX06

Stranraer Creachmore DG9 0LF
☎ 01776 870245   🖹 01776 870445
e-mail: stranraergolf@btclick.com
web: www.stranraergolfclub.net

Parkland with beautiful views over Loch Ryan to Ailsa Craig, Arran and
beyond. Several notable holes including the 3rd, where a winding burn
is crossed three times to a green set between a large bunker and a
steep bank sloping down to the burn; the scenic 5th with spectacular
views; the 11th requiring a demanding tee shot with trees and out of
bounds to the left, then a steep rise to a very fast green. The 15th is a
difficult par 3 where accuracy is paramount with ground sloping away
either side of the green.

18 Holes, 6308yds, Par 70, SSS 72, Course record 66.
Club membership 600.

Visitors Mon-Sun & BHs. Booking required. Dress code
Societies booking required. **Green Fees** not confirmed **Course
Designer** James Braid **Facilities** ⓣ ⓞ ▥ ⌑ ⓟ ⚑ 🛆 🖼 ⛿
⚑ 🛺 ⚑ **Location** 2.5m NW on A718 from Stranraer
Hotel ★★★★ 74% HL North West Castle, STRANRAER
☎ 01776 704413 🖹 01776 704413 72 en suite

THORNHILL   Map 11 NX89

Thornhill Blacknest DG3 5DW
☎ 01848 331779 & 330546
e-mail: info@thornhillgolfclub.co.uk
web: www.thornhillgolfclub.co.uk

Moorland and parkland with fine views of the southern uplands.

18 Holes, 6085yds, Par 71, SSS 70, Course record 67.
Club membership 570.

Visitors Mon-Sun & BHs. Booking required. Dress code.
Societies booking required. **Green Fees** not confirmed **Course
Designer** Willie Fernie **Facilities** ⓣ ⓞ ▥ ⌑ ⓟ 🛆 ⛿ 🛺
⚑ **Location** 1m E of town off A76
Guesthouse ★★★★★ GA Gillbank House, 8 East Morton Street,
THORNHILL ☎ 01848 330597 🖹 01848 330597 6 en suite

WIGTOWN   Map 10 NX45

Wigtown & Bladnoch Lightlands Ter DG8 9DY
☎ 01988 403354

Slightly hilly parkland with fine views over Wigtown Bay to the
Galloway Hills.

9 Holes, 5462yds, Par 68, SSS 67, Course record 62.
Club membership 150.

Visitors Mon-Sun & BHs. Booking required. Handicap

certificate. **Societies** booking required. **Green Fees** £20 for 18 holes,
£12 for 9 holes **Course Designer** W Muir **Facilities** ⌑ ⓟ 🛆 ⛿
⚑ **Location** SW on A714
Hotel ★★★ HL Kirroughtree House, Minnigaff, NEWTON STEWART
☎ 01671 402141 🖹 01671 402141 17 en suite

DUNDEE, CITY OF

DUNDEE   Map 11 NO43

Ballumbie Castle 3 Old Quarry Rd DD4 0SY
☎ 01382 730026 (club) & 770028 (pro)
🖹 01382 730008
e-mail: ballumbie2000@yahoo.com
web: www.ballumbiecastlegolfclub.com

Parkland/heathland course built in 2000. No two holes go in the same
direction and every golf club is required. Water comes into play on
4 holes.

Ballumbie Castle Golf Course: 18 Holes, 6157yds, Par 69,
SSS 70, Course record 65. Club membership 550.

Visitors Mon-Sun & BHs. Booking required weekends. Dress code.
Societies welcome. **Green Fees** not confirmed **Prof** Lee Sutherland
Facilities ⓣ ⓞ ▥ ⌑ ⓟ 🛆 ⛿ ⚑
Conf Corporate Hospitality Days **Location** NE outskirts of town, signed
off A90
Hotel ★★★★ 81% HL Apex City Quay Hotel & Spa, 1 West
Victoria Dock Road, DUNDEE ☎ 0845 365 0000 🖹 0845 365 0000
152 en suite

Caird Park Mains Loan DD4 9BX
☎ 01382 438871   🖹 01382 433211
web: www.dundeecity.gov.uk/golf

Caird Park Golf Course: 18 Holes, 6280yds, Par 72, SSS 69,
Course record 65.

Prof J Black **Facilities** ▥ ⓟ 🛆 🖼 ⛿ ⚑ 🛺 ⚑
Leisure sports stadium **Conf** facs Corporate Hospitality Days
Location off A90 Kingsway onto Forfar Rd, left onto Claverhouse Rd,
1st left into Caird Park
Telephone for further details
Hotel ★★★★ 81% HL Apex City Quay Hotel & Spa, 1 West
Victoria Dock Road, DUNDEE ☎ 0845 365 0000 🖹 0845 365 0000
152 en suite

Downfield Turnberry Av DD2 3QP
☎ 01382 825595   🖹 01382 813111
e-mail: downfieldgc@aol.com
web: www.downfieldgolf.co.uk

A 2007 Open Qualifying venue. A course with championship
credentials providing an enjoyable test for all golfers.

18 Holes, 6803yds, Par 73, SSS 73, Course record 65.
Club membership 750.

Visitors Mon-Fri, Sun & BHs. Booking required. Dress code.
Handicap certificate. **Societies** booking required. **Green Fees** £50-
£66 per day, £45-£55 per round **Course Designer** James Braid
Prof Kenny Hutton **Facilities** ⓣ ⓞ ▥ ⌑ ⓟ 🛆 🖼 ⛿
⚑ 🛺 ⚑ **Leisure** snooker room **Conf** Corporate Hospitality Days
Location N of city centre, signed at junct A90
Hotel ★★★★ 81% HL Apex City Quay Hotel & Spa, 1 West
Victoria Dock Road, DUNDEE ☎ 0845 365 0000 🖹 0845 365 0000
152 en suite

SCOTLAND

EAST AYRSHIRE

GALSTON
Map 11 NS53

Loudoun Edinburgh Rd KA4 8PA
☎ 01563 821993 🖹 01563 820011
e-mail: secy@loudoungowfclub.co.uk
web: www.loudoungowfclub.co.uk

Pleasant, fairly flat parkland with many mature trees, in the Irvine valley. Excellent test of golf skills without being too strenuous.

Loudoun Gowf Club: 18 Holes, 6005yds, Par 68, SSS 69, Course record 60. Club membership 850.

Visitors Mon-Fri except BHs. Booking required. Dress code. Handicap certificate. **Societies** booking required. **Green Fees** £40 per day, £30 per 18 holes **Facilities** ⊕ ℉ 🍴 🗅 ♨ 🍺 🛒 ✗ **Conf** Corporate Hospitality Days **Location** NE side of town on A71
Hotel ★★★ 75% HL Best Western Fenwick, Fenwick, KILMARNOCK ☎ 01560 600478 🖹 01560 600478 30 en suite

KILMARNOCK
Map 10 NS43

Annanhill Irvine Rd KA1 2RT
☎ 01563 521644 & 521512 (starter)
Municipal, tree-lined parkland course.

18 Holes, 6269yds, Par 71, SSS 70, Course record 66. Club membership 274.

Visitors Mon-Sun & BHs. Booking required. Handicap certificate. Dress code. **Societies** welcome. **Green Fees** phone **Course Designer** Jack McLean **Facilities** ♨ 🍺 **Location** 1m N on B7081
Hotel ★★★ 75% HL Best Western Fenwick, Fenwick, KILMARNOCK ☎ 01560 600478 🖹 01560 600478 30 en suite

Caprington Ayr Rd KA1 4UW
☎ 01563 523702 & 521915 (Gen Enq)
e-mail: caprington.golf@btconnect.com
Municipal parkland course.

18 Holes, 5810yds, Par 68, SSS 68. Club membership 400.

Visitors Sun-Fri & BHs. Booking required. Dress code. **Societies** booking required. **Green Fees** not confirmed **Facilities** ⊕ by prior arrangement 🍴 🗅 🗅 🍴 ♨ 🗅 ✗ **Location** 1.5m S on B7038
Hotel BUD Travelodge Kilmarnock, Bellfield Interchange, KILMARNOCK ☎ 08719 846 149 🖹 08719 846 149 40 en suite

MAUCHLINE
Map 11 NS42

Ballochmyle Catrine Rd KA5 6LE
☎ 01290 550469
e-mail: ballochmylegolf@btconnect.com
web: www.ballochmylegolfclub.co.uk
Tree lined parkland course with undulating terrain and small tricky greens.

18 Holes, 5972yds, Par 70, SSS 69, Course record 64. Club membership 730.

Visitors Sun-Fri & BHs. Booking required. Handicap certificate. Dress code. **Societies** booking required. **Green Fees** £32.50 per 36 holes, £22.50 per 18 holes (£37.50/£27.50) **Facilities** ⊕ ℉ 🍴 🗅 🍴 ♨ 🗅 ✗ **Leisure** games room **Conf** Corporate Hospitality Days **Location** 1m SE on B705

Hotel BUD Travelodge Kilmarnock, Bellfield Interchange, KILMARNOCK ☎ 08719 846 149 🖹 08719 846 149 40 en suite

PATNA
Map 10 NS41

Doon Valley Hillside Park KA6 7JT
☎ 01292 531607

Established parkland course located on an undulating hillside.

Doon Valley Golf Course: 9 Holes, 5886yds, Par 70, SSS 70, Course record 56. Club membership 100.

Visitors contact club for details. Handicap certificate. **Societies** booking required. **Green Fees** not confirmed **Facilities** ℉ 🗅 **Leisure** fishing, fitness and games hall nearby **Location** 10m S of Ayr on the A713
Hotel ★★★★ Hotel du Vin at One Devonshire Gardens, 1 Devonshire Gardens, GLASGOW ☎ 0141 339 2001 🖹 0141 339 2001 49 en suite

EAST DUNBARTONSHIRE

BALMORE
Map 11 NS57

Balmore Golf Course Rd G64 4AW
☎ 01360 620284 🖹 01360 622742
e-mail: balmoregolf@btconnect.com
web: www.balmoregolfclub.co.uk
Parkland with fine views. Greens to USGA standards.

18 Holes, 5530yds, Par 66, SSS 67, Course record 61. Club membership 700.

Visitors Mon-Fri except BHs. Handicap certificate. Dress code. Handicap certificate. **Societies** Booking required. **Green Fees** not confirmed **Course Designer** Harry Vardon **Prof** Paul Morrison **Facilities** ⊕ ℉ 🍺 🗅 🍴 ♨ 🗅 ♨ ✗ ✗ **Location** N off A807

BEARSDEN
Map 11 NS57

Bearsden Thorn Rd G61 4BP
☎ 0141 586 5300
e-mail: secretary@bearsdengolfclub.com
web: www.bearsdengolfclub.com
Parkland course with 16 greens and 11 teeing grounds. Easy walking and views of city and the Campsie Hills.

9 Holes, 6014yds, Par 68, SSS 69, Course record 64. Club membership 560.

Visitors contact club for details. Handicap certificate. **Societies** booking required. **Green Fees** phone **Facilities** ⊕ ℉ 🍺 🗅 🍴 ♨ **Location** 1m W off A809
Hotel ★★★ 71% HL Best Western Glasgow Pond, Great Western Road, GLASGOW ☎ 0141 334 8161 🖹 0141 334 8161 137 en suite

Douglas Park Hillfoot G61 2TJ
☎ 0141 942 2220 (Clubhouse) 🖹 0141 942 0985
e-mail: secretary@douglasparkgolfclub.co.uk
web: www.douglasparkgolfclub.co.uk
Undulating parkland course with a variety of holes.

18 Holes, 5962yds, Par 69, SSS 69, Course record 64. Club membership 960.

Visitors Mon-Sun & BHs. Booking required. Dress code. Handicap certificate. **Societies** booking required. **Green Fees** not confirmed

continued

Course Designer Willie Fernie **Prof** David Scott **Facilities** ⊕ ⦿ ⓘ ⓘ ⓘ ⓘ ⓘ ⓘ **Location** E side of town on A81
Hotel ★★★ 71% HL Best Western Glasgow Pond, Great Western Road, GLASGOW ☎ 0141 334 8161 ▤ 0141 334 8161 137 en suite

Glasgow Killermont G61 2TW
☎ 0141 942 2011 ▤ 0141 942 0770
e-mail: secretary@glasgowgolfclub.com
web: www.glasgowgolfclub.com
One of the finest parkland courses in Scotland.
Killermont: 18 Holes, 5977yds, Par 70, SSS 69, Course record 64. Club membership 800.
Visitors contact club for details. Handicap certificate.
Societies welcome. **Green Fees** £85 per day, £70 per round **Course Designer** Tom Morris Snr **Prof** J Greaves **Facilities** ⊕ ⦿ ⓘ ⓘ ⓘ ⓘ ⓘ ⓘ ⓘ **Conf** Corporate Hospitality Days **Location** SE side off A81
Hotel ★★★ 71% HL Best Western Glasgow Pond, Great Western Road, GLASGOW ☎ 0141 334 8161 ▤ 0141 334 8161 137 en suite

Windyhill Baljaffray Rd G61 4QQ
☎ 0141 942 2349 ▤ 0141 942 5874
e-mail: secretary@windyhill.co.uk
web: www.windyhillgolfclub.co.uk
Interesting parkland and moorland course with panoramic views of Glasgow and beyond; testing 12th hole.
18 Holes, 6254yds, Par 71, SSS 70, Course record 64. Club membership 800.
Visitors Mon-Fri except BHs. Dress code. Handicap certificate.
Societies booking required. **Green Fees** £25 per round, £35 per day **Course Designer** James Braid **Prof** Chris Duffy **Facilities** ⊕ ⦿ ⓘ ⓘ ⓘ ⓘ ⓘ ⓘ **Conf** Corporate Hospitality Days **Location** 2m NW off B8050, 1.5m from Bearsden cross, just off Drymen road
Hotel ★★★★ 73% HL Beardmore, Beardmore Street, CLYDEBANK ☎ 0141 951 6000 ▤ 0141 951 6000 166 en suite

BISHOPBRIGGS   Map 11 NS67

Bishopbriggs Brackenbrae Rd G64 2DX
☎ 0141 772 1810 & 772 8938 ▤ 0141 762 2532
e-mail: secretarybgc@yahoo.co.uk
web: www.bishopbriggsgolfclub.com
Parkland with views to the Campsie Hills.
18 Holes, 6262yds, Par 71, SSS 70, Course record 63. Club membership 800.
Visitors Mon-Fri & BHs. Booking required. Handicap certificate. Dress code. Handicap certificate. **Societies** booking required. **Green Fees** not confirmed **Course Designer** James Braid **Facilities** ⊕ ⓘ ⓘ ⓘ ⓘ ⓘ ⓘ ⓘ ⓘ ⓘ **Conf** facs Corporate Hospitality Days **Location** 0.5m NW off A803
Hotel ★★★★ 77% HL Glasgow Marriott Hotel, 500 Argyle Street, Anderston, GLASGOW ☎ 0141 226 5577 ▤ 0141 226 5577 300 en suite

Cawder Cadder Rd G64 3QD
☎ 0141 761 1281 ▤ 0141 761 1285
e-mail: secretary@cawdergolfclub.co.uk
web: www.cawdergolfclub.co.uk
Two parkland courses: The Cawdor Course is an excellent test of golfing skill, the 14th and 15th being particularly challenging. The Keir Course shorter and flatter, but the smaller greens make for a challenging short game.
Cawder Course: 18 Holes, 6295yds, Par 70, SSS 70, Course record 63.
Keir Course: 18 Holes, 5877yds, Par 68, SSS 68. Club membership 1150.
Visitors Mon-Fri & BHs. Dress code. **Societies** booking required. **Green Fees** £35 per round/£45 per day **Course Designer** James Braid **Prof** Gordon Stewart **Facilities** ⊕ ⦿ ⓘ ⓘ ⓘ ⓘ ⓘ ⓘ **Conf** Corporate Hospitality Days **Location** 5 m NE off A803
Hotel ★★★★ 77% HL Glasgow Marriott Hotel, 500 Argyle Street, Anderston, GLASGOW ☎ 0141 226 5577 ▤ 0141 226 5577 300 en suite

Littlehill Auchinairn Rd G64 1UT
☎ 0141 772 1916
Littlehill Golf Course: 18 Holes, 6240yds, Par 70, SSS 70.
Facilities ⓘ ⓘ **Location** 3m NE of Glasgow city centre on A803
Telephone for further details
Hotel ★★★★ 77% HL Glasgow Marriott Hotel, 500 Argyle Street, Anderston, GLASGOW ☎ 0141 226 5577 ▤ 0141 226 5577 300 en suite

KIRKINTILLOCH   Map 11 NS67

Hayston Campsie Rd G66 1RN
☎ 0141 776 1244 ▤ 0141 776 9030
e-mail: secretary@haystongolf.com
web: www.haystongolf.com
An undulating, tree-lined course with a sandy subsoil.
18 Holes, 6042yds, Par 70, SSS 70, Course record 60. Club membership 800.
Visitors Mon-Fri except BHs. Handicap certificate. Dress code. **Societies** booking required. **Green Fees** £45 per day, £35 per round **Course Designer** James Braid **Prof** Steven Barnett **Facilities** ⊕ ⦿ ⓘ ⓘ ⓘ ⓘ ⓘ **Conf** facs Corporate Hospitality Days **Location** 1m NW off A803
Hotel ★★★★ 80% HL The Westerwood Hotel & Golf Resort, 1 St Andrews Drive, Westerwood, CUMBERNAULD ☎ 01236 457171 ▤ 01236 457171 148 en suite

Kirkintilloch Todhill G66 1RN
☎ 0141 776 1256 & 775 2387 ▤ 0141 775 2424
web: www.kirkintillochgolfclub.co.uk
18 Holes, 5860yds, Par 70, SSS 69, Course record 64.
Course Designer James Braid **Location** 1m NW off A803
Telephone for further details
Hotel ★★★★ 80% HL The Westerwood Hotel & Golf Resort, 1 St Andrews Drive, Westerwood, CUMBERNAULD ☎ 01236 457171 ▤ 01236 457171 148 en suite

SCOTLAND

LENNOXTOWN — Map 11 NS67

Campsie Crow Rd G66 7HX
☎ 01360 310244 📄 01360 310244
web: www.campsiegolfclub.org.uk

18 Holes, 5507yds, Par 70, SSS 68, Course record 69.
Course Designer W Auchterlonie **Location** 0.5m N on B822
Telephone for further details
Hotel ★★★★ 80% HL The Westerwood Hotel & Golf Resort, 1 St Andrews Drive, Westerwood, CUMBERNAULD ☎ 01236 457171 📄 01236 457171 148 en suite

LENZIE — Map 11 NS67

Lenzie 19 Crosshill Rd G66 5DA
☎ 0141 776 1535 📄 0141 777 7748
e-mail: secretary.lgc@ntlbusiness.com
web: www.lenziegolfclub.co.uk

The course is parkland and prominent features include the old beech trees, which line some of the fairways together with thorn hedges and shallow ditches. Extensive larch and fir plantations have also been created. The course is relatively flat apart from a steep hill to the green at the 5th hole.

18 Holes, 5984yds, Par 69, SSS 69, Course record 64. Club membership 890.

Visitors Mon-Sun & BHs. Booking required. Dress code.
Societies booking required. **Green Fees** not confirmed **Prof** Jim McCallum **Facilities** ⊕ ⊚ ⌨ ⌑ ⍩ ⌲ ⌗ ✦ ✦
Conf facs Corporate Hospitality Days **Location** N of Glasgow, M80 exit Kirkintilloch
Hotel ★★★★ 80% HL The Westerwood Hotel & Golf Resort, 1 St Andrews Drive, Westerwood, CUMBERNAULD ☎ 01236 457171 📄 01236 457171 148 en suite

MILNGAVIE — Map 11 NS57

Clober Craigton Rd G62 7HP
☎ 0141 956 1685 📄 0141 955 1416
e-mail: clobergolfclub@btopenworld.com
web: www.clober.co.uk

Short parkland course that requires skill in chipping with eight par 3s. Testing 5th hole, par 3 with out of bounds left and right and a burn in front of the tee.

18 Holes, 4824yds, Par 66, SSS 65, Course record 61. Club membership 600.

Visitors Mon-Fri. Booking required. Dress code. **Societies** welcome.
Green Fees not confirmed **Course Designer** George Lyle **Prof** Grant McFarlane **Facilities** ⊕ ⊚ ⌨ ⌑ ⍩ ⌲ ⌗ ✦
Location NW side of town
Hotel ★★★★ 73% HL Beardmore, Beardmore Street, CLYDEBANK ☎ 0141 951 6000 📄 0141 951 6000 166 en suite

Esporta, Dougalston Strathblane Rd G62 8HJ
☎ 0141 955 2404 📄 0141 955 2406
web: www.esporta.com

A course of tremendous character set in 300 acres of beautiful woodland dotted with drumlins, lakes and criss-crossed by streams and ditches. The course makes excellent use of the natural features to create mature, tree-lined fairways.

18 Holes, 6120yds, Par 70, SSS 71, Course record 65. Club membership 400.

Visitors Mon-Sun except BHs. Booking required weekends. Handicap certificate. Dress code. **Societies** welcome. **Green Fees** phone **Course Designer** Commander Harris **Prof** Gavin Cooper **Facilities** ⊕ ⊚ ⌨ ⌑ ⍩ ⌲ ⌗ ✦ ⌷ ✦ **Leisure** hard tennis courts, heated indoor swimming pool, sauna, gymnasium **Conf** facs Corporate Hospitality Days **Location** NE side of town on A81
Hotel ★★★ 71% HL Best Western Glasgow Pond, Great Western Road, GLASGOW ☎ 0141 334 8161 📄 0141 334 8161 137 en suite

Hilton Park Auldmarroch Estate G62 7HB
☎ 0141 956 4657 📄 0141 956 1215
web: www.hiltonpark.co.uk

Hilton Course: 18 Holes, 6054yds, Par 70, SSS 70, Course record 65.
Allander Course: 18 Holes, 5487yards, Par 69, SSS 67, Course record 65.

Course Designer James Braid **Location** 3m NW of Milngavie, on A809
Telephone for further details
Hotel ★★★★ 73% HL Beardmore, Beardmore Street, CLYDEBANK ☎ 0141 951 6000 📄 0141 951 6000 166 en suite

EAST LOTHIAN

ABERLADY — Map 12 NT47

Kilspindie EH32 0QD
☎ 01875 870358 📄 01875 870358
e-mail: kilspindie@btconnect.com
web: www.golfeastlothian.com

Traditional Scottish seaside links, short but good challenge of golf and well-bunkered. Situated on the shores of the River Forth with panoramic views.

Kilspindie Golf Club: 18 Holes, 5502yds, Par 69, SSS 66, Course record 59. Club membership 800.

Visitors Mon-Sun & BHs. Booking required. Dress code. Handicap certificate. **Societies** Booking required. **Green Fees** not confirmed **Course Designer** Park & Ross with additions by Braid **Prof** Graham J Sked **Facilities** ⊕ ⊚ ⌨ ⌑ ⍩ ⌲ ⌗ ✦ ⌷ ✦ **Conf** Corporate Hospitality Days **Location** N side of village off A198. Private access at E end of Aberlady
Hotel ★★★★ 82% HL Macdonald Marine Hotel & Spa, Cromwell Road, NORTH BERWICK ☎ 0870 400 8129 📄 0870 400 8129 83 en suite

SCOTLAND

Luffness New EH32 0QA
☎ 01620 843336 🖹 01620 842933
e-mail: secretary@luffnessnew.com
Links course, national final qualifying course for the Open
Championship.
18 Holes, 6328yds, Par 70, SSS 71, Course record 69.
Club membership 750.
Visitors Mon-Fri & BHs. Booking required. Handicap certificate. Dress
code. **Societies** booking required. **Green Fees** not confirmed **Course
Designer** Tom Morris **Facilities** ⑪ ⑩ ♻ 🍽 ♨ 🛆 🖾 ♂
Location 1m E Aberlady on A198
Hotel ★★★★ 82% HL Macdonald Marine Hotel & Spa, Cromwell
Road, NORTH BERWICK ☎ 0870 400 8129 🖹 0870 400 8129
83 en suite

DUNBAR   Map 12 NT67

Dunbar East Links EH42 1LL
☎ 01368 862317 🖹 01368 865202
web: www.dunbar-golfclub.co.uk
18 Holes, 6406yds, Par 71, SSS 71, Course record 62.
Course Designer Tom Morris **Location** 0.5m E off A1087
Telephone for further details
Hotel ★★★★ 82% HL Macdonald Marine Hotel & Spa, Cromwell
Road, NORTH BERWICK ☎ 0870 400 8129 🖹 0870 400 8129
83 en suite

Winterfield North Rd EH42 1AU
☎ 01368 863562
18 Holes, 5155yds, Par 65, SSS 64, Course record 61.
Prof Kevin Phillips **Facilities** ⑪ ⑩ ♻ ♨ 🍽 🛆 🖾 ♂
♨ ♂ **Location** W side of town off A1087
Telephone for further details
Hotel ★★★★ 82% HL Macdonald Marine Hotel & Spa, Cromwell
Road, NORTH BERWICK ☎ 0870 400 8129 🖹 0870 400 8129
83 en suite

GIFFORD   Map 12 NT56

Castle Park Castlemains EH41 4PL
☎ 01620 810733 🖹 01620 810691
e-mail: castleparkgolf@hotmail.com
web: www.castleparkgolfclub.co.uk
Naturally undulating parkland course in beautiful setting with much
wild life. Wide rolling fairways on the first nine with tantalising water
and dyke hazards. The mature back nine is shorter but full of hidden
surprises requiring good golfing strategy when passing Yester Castle.
18 Holes, 6443yds, Par 72, SSS 71, Course record 71.
Club membership 430.
Visitors Mon-Sun & BHs. Booking required. Dress code.
Societies booking required. **Green Fees** £24 per 18 holes, £12 per
9 holes (£32/£16 weekends) **Course Designer** Archie Baird **Prof** Derek
Small **Facilities** ⑪ ⑩ ♻ ♨ 🍽 🛆 ♨ ♂ ♂
Conf Corporate Hospitality Days **Location** off B6355, 2m S of Gifford

Gifford Edinburgh Rd EH41 4JE
☎ 01620 810591
e-mail: secretary@giffordgolfclub.com
web: www.giffordgolfclub.com

One of the oldest clubs in East Lothian. A gently undulating 9 hole
course in the picturesque setting of the Lammermuir Hills, providing a
challenging round of golf in relaxed and peaceful surroundings.
9 Holes, 6057yds, Par 71, SSS 69. Club membership 600.
Visitors contact club for details **Societies** booking required **Green
Fees** not confirmed **Facilities** ♻ ♨ 🍽 🛆 ♨ ♂ ♂
Location 1m SW of village, off B6355

GULLANE   Map 12 NT48

Gullane West Links Rd EH31 2BB
☎ 01620 842255 🖹 01620 842327
e-mail: bookings@gullanegolfclub.com
web: www.gullanegolfclub.com
Gullane is a delightful village and one of Scotland's great golf
centres. The game has been played on the 3 links courses for
over 300 years and was formed in 1882. The first tee of the
Championship No. 1 course (a Final Qualifier when The Open is
played at Muirfield) is literally in the village and the three courses
stretch out along the coast line. All have magnificent views over
the Firth of Forth, standing on the highest point at the 7th tee is
reported as one of the "finest views in golf".
Course No 1: 18 Holes, 6466yds, Par 71, SSS 72,
Course record 65.
Course No 2: 18 Holes, 6244yds, Par 71, SSS 71,
Course record 64.
Course No 3: 18 Holes, 5252yds, Par 68, SSS 66.
Club membership 1200.
Visitors Mon-Sun & BHs. Dress code. Handicap certificate.
Societies welcome. **Green Fees** not confirmed **Prof** Alasdair Good
Facilities ⑪ ⑩ ♻ ♨ 🍽 🛆 🖾 ♨ ♂ 🚗 ♂ ♀
Leisure golf museum **Conf** Corporate Hospitality Days **Location** W
end of village on A198
Hotel ★★★★ 82% HL Macdonald Marine Hotel & Spa, Cromwell
Road, NORTH BERWICK ☎ 0870 400 8129 🖹 0870 400 8129
83 en suite

**Honourable Company of Edinburgh Golfers
see page 335**

Honourable Company of Edinburgh Golfers
Duncur Rd, Muirfield EH31 2EG
☎ 01620 842123   📄 01620 842977
e-mail: hceg@muirfield.org.uk
web: www.muirfield.org.uk

HADDINGTON   Map 12 NT57

Haddington Amisfield Park EH41 4PT
☎ 01620 822727 & 823627   📄 01620 826580
e-mail: info@haddingtongolf.co.uk
web: www.haddingtongolf.co.uk
A slightly undulating parkland course within the grounds of a former
country estate beside the River Tyne. New ponds and bunkers have
been constructed to improve the course in recent years.

*18 Holes, 6335yds, Par 71, SSS 71, Course record 63.
Club membership 850.*

Visitors Mon-Sun & BHs. Booking required. Dress code. Handicap
certificate. **Societies** welcome. **Green Fees** not confirmed **Prof** John
Sandilands **Facilities** 🛈 🍽 🏌 🖥 🏐 🏖 🏌 🛒 🏌
Leisure driving net, practice bunker **Conf** facs Corporate Hospitality
Days **Location** E side of town centre
Hotel ★★★ 77% SHL The Open Arms, DIRLETON ☎ 01620 850241
📄 01620 850241 10 en suite

LONGNIDDRY   Map 12 NT47

Longniddry Links Rd EH32 0NL
☎ 01875 852141   📄 01875 853371
e-mail: secretary@longniddrygolfclub.co.uk
web: www.longniddrygolfclub.co.uk
Undulating seaside links and partial woodland course with no
par 5s. One of the numerous courses which stretch east from
Edinburgh to Dunbar. The inward half is more open than the wooded
outward half, but can be difficult in prevailing west wind.

*Longniddry Golf Club Ltd: 18 Holes, 6260yds, Par 68,
SSS 70, Course record 62. Club membership 1100.*

Visitors Mon-Fri & BHs. Limited play weekends.. Booking required.
Handicap certificate. Dress code. **Societies** booking required.
Green Fees not confirmed **Course Designer** H S Colt **Prof** John
Gray **Facilities** 🛈 🍽 🏌 🖥 🏐 🏖 🏌 🛒 🏌
Conf Corporate Hospitality Days **Location** N side of village off A198
Hotel ★★★ 78% HL Best Western Kings Manor, 100 Milton Road
East, EDINBURGH ☎ 0131 669 0444 & 468 8003 📄 0131 669 0444
95 en suite

MUSSELBURGH   Map 11 NT37

Musselburgh Monktonhall EH21 6SA
☎ 0131 665 2005   📄 0131 665 4435
e-mail: secretary@themusselburghgolfclub.com
web: www.themusselburghgolfclub.com
Testing parkland course with natural hazards including trees and a
burn; easy walking.

*18 Holes, 6725yds, Par 71, SSS 72, Course record 65.
Club membership 1000.*

Visitors contact club for details. **Societies** booking required. **Green**

Fees not confirmed **Course Designer** James Braid **Prof** Fraser
Mann **Facilities** 🛈 🍽 🏌 🖥 🏐 🏖 🏌 🛒 🏌
Conf Corporate Hospitality Days **Location** 1m S on B6415
Hotel ★★★ 78% HL Best Western Kings Manor, 100 Milton Road
East, EDINBURGH ☎ 0131 669 0444 & 468 8003 📄 0131 669 0444
95 en suite

Musselburgh Old Course & Golf Club 10 Balcarres Rd
EH21 7SD
☎ 0131 665 5438 (starter) & 665 6981(club)
📄 0131 653 1770
e-mail: secretary@mocgc.com
web: www.mocgc.com
A delightful nine-hole links course weaving in and out of the famous
Musselburgh Race Course. This course is steeped in the history and
tradition of golf and can lay claim to being the oldest surviving golf
course in the world. Mary Queen of Scots reputedly played golf at the
old course in 1567, but documentary evidence dates back to 1672. The
1st hole is a par 3 and the next three holes play eastward from the
grandstand at the racecourse. The course turns north-west towards
the sea then west for the last four holes. Designed by nature and
defined over the centuries by generations of golfers, the course has
many natural features and hazards.

*Musselburgh Old Course & Golf Club: 9 Holes, 2874yds,
Par 34, SSS 34, Course record 29. Club membership 300.*
Visitors Mon-Sun & BHs. Booking required weekends & BHs. Dress
code **Societies** booking rrequired. **Green Fees** £12 per 9 holes, £24
per 18 holes (£13/£26 weekends) **Prof** Jane Connachan **Facilities** 🛈

continued

MUIRFIELD
(HONOURABLE COMPANY OF EDINBURGH GOLFERS)
EAST LOTHIAN - GULLANE - MAP 12 NT48

The original course at Muirfield was designed by Old Tom Morris in 1891 but the current course was designed by Harry Colt. It is generally considered to be one of the top ten courses in the world. The club itself has an excellent pedigree: it was founded in 1744, making it just 10 years older than the Royal and Ancient but not as old as The Royal Burgess. Muirfield is the only course to have hosted the Open (15 times, the most recent in 2002), the Amateur, the Mid Amateur, the Senior British Open, the Ryder Cup, the Walker Cup and the Curtis Cup. It is consistently ranked as one of the world's most exclusive golf courses.

Duncur Rd, Muirfield EH31 2EG ☎ 01620 842123 📠 01620 842977
e-mail: hceg@muirfield.org.uk **web:** www.muirfield.org.uk
Muirfield Course: 18 Holes, 6673yds, Par 70, SSS 73, Course record 63. Club membership 700.
Visitors Tue & Thu. Booking required. Handicap certificate. Dress code. **Societies** booking required. **Green Fees** £220 per 36 holes, £75 per 18 holes **Course Designer** Harry Colt **Facilities** ⑲ by prior arrangement ♨ 🍴 ♿ ⛳ 🏌 **Location** NE of village, off A198 next to Greywalls Hotel
Hotel ★★★★ 82% HL Macdonald Marine Hotel & Spa, Cromwell Road, NORTH BERWICK ☎ 0870 400 8129 📠 0870 400 8129 83 en suite

🍴 ⅃ ▯ ▥ ⎙ ⚑ ⚑ **Conf** Corporate Hospitality Days
Location 1m E of town off A1
Hotel ★★★ 78% HL Best Western Kings Manor, 100 Milton Road
East, EDINBURGH ☎ 0131 669 0444 & 468 8003 📄 0131 669 0444
95 en suite

NORTH BERWICK
Map 12 NT58

Glen East Links, Tantallon Ter EH39 4LE
☎ 01620 892726   📄 01620 895447
e-mail: secretary@glengolfclub.co.uk
web: www.glengolfclub.co.uk

A popular course with a good variety of holes including the famous
13th, par 3 Sea Hole. The views of the town, the Firth of Forth and the
Bass Rock are breathtaking.

18 Holes, 6321yds, Par 70, SSS 70, Course record 67.
Club membership 650.

Visitors Mon-Sun & BHs. Booking required. Dress code. Handicap
certificate. **Societies** welcome. **Green Fees** £52 per day, £37 per
round (£70/£50 Sat & Sun) **Course Designer** Ben Sayers/James
Braid **Facilities** ⅃ 🍴 ⅃ ▯ ⎙ ⚑ 📄 ⚑ **Conf** facs
Corporate Hospitality Days **Location** A1 onto A198 to North Berwick.
Right at seabird centre, sea-wall road
Hotel ★★★ 77% SHL The Open Arms, DIRLETON ☎ 01620 850241
📄 01620 850241 10 en suite

North Berwick Beach Rd EH39 4BB
☎ 01620 892135   📄 01620 893274
e-mail: secretary@northberwickgolfclub.com
web: www.northberwickgolfclub.com

Another of East Lothian's famous courses, the links at North
Berwick is still popular. A classic championship links, it has many
hazards including the beach, streams, bunkers, light rough and low
walls. The great hole on the course is the 15th, the famous Redan.

West Links: 18 Holes, 6420yds, Par 71, SSS 72,
Course record 63. Club membership 730.

Visitors Mon-Sun & BHs. Booking required. Dress code. Handicap
certificate. **Societies** booking required. **Green Fees** £105 per day,
£75 per round (£95 weekends) **Course Designer** David Strath &
others **Prof** M Huish **Facilities** ⅃ 🍴 ⅃ ▯ ⎙ ⚑ 📄
⚑ **Location** W side of town on A198
Hotel ★★★★ 82% HL Macdonald Marine Hotel & Spa, Cromwell
Road, NORTH BERWICK ☎ 0870 400 8129 📄 0870 400 8129
83 en suite

Whitekirk EH39 5PR
☎ 01620 870300   📄 01620 870330
e-mail: countryclub@whitekirk.com
web: www.whitekirk.com

Scenic coastal course with lush green fairways, gorse covered rocky
banks and stunning views. Natural water hazards and strong sea
breezes make this well-designed course a good test of golf.

Whitekirk Golf & Country Club: 18 Holes, 6526yds,
Par 72, SSS 72, Course record 64.
Club membership 400.

Visitors booking required weekends & BHs. Dress code.
Societies booking required. **Green Fees** £45 per day, £30 per round
(£55/£40 weekends) **Course Designer** Cameron Sinclair **Prof** Paul
Wardell **Facilities** ⅃ 🍴 ⅃ ▯ ⎙ ⚑ 📄 ⚑ ⚑ ⚑
⚑ **Leisure** sauna, gymnasium, health spa **Conf** facs Corporate

Hospitality Days **Location** A198 off A1 to A199, on A198 4m SE of
North Berwick
Hotel Nether Abbey, ☎ 01620 892802 📄 01620 892802 12 en suite

PRESTONPANS
Map 11 NT37

Royal Musselburgh Prestongrange House EH32 9RP
☎ 01875 810276   📄 01875 810276
web: www.royalmusselburgh.co.uk

18 Holes, 6237yds, Par 70, SSS 70, Course record 64.

Course Designer James Braid **Location** W of town centre on B1361 to
North Berwick
Telephone for further details
Hotel ★★★ 78% HL Best Western Kings Manor, 100 Milton Road
East, EDINBURGH ☎ 0131 669 0444 & 468 8003 📄 0131 669 0444
95 en suite

See advert on page 334

EAST RENFREWSHIRE

BARRHEAD
Map 11 NS45

Fereneze Fereneze Av G78 1HJ
☎ 0141 880 7058   📄 0141 881 7149
e-mail: ferenezegc@lineone.net
web: www.ferenezegolfclub.co.uk

Hilly moorland course, with a good view at the end of a hard climb to
the 3rd, then levels out.

18 Holes, 5962yds, Par 71, SSS 69, Course record 65.
Club membership 750.

Visitors Mon-Fri & BHs. Dress code. **Societies** booking required. **Green
Fees** £35 per day, £30 per round **Prof** James Smallwood **Facilities** ⅃
🍴 ⅃ ▯ ⎙ ⚑ 📄 ⚑ ⚑ **Location** NW side of town off
B774
Hotel ★★★ 80% HL Uplawmoor Hotel, Neilston Road, UPLAWMOOR
☎ 01505 850565 📄 01505 850565 14 en suite

CLARKSTON
Map 11 NS55

Cathcart Castle Mearns Rd G76 7YL
☎ 0141 638 9449   📄 0141 638 1201

18 Holes, 5861yds, Par 69, SSS 69.

Prof Stephen Duncan **Facilities** ⅃ 🍴 ⅃ ▯ ⎙ ⚑ 📄 ⚑
⚑ **Location** 0.75m SW off A726
Telephone for further details
Hotel ★★★★ 72% HL Menzies Glasgow, 27 Washington Street,
GLASGOW ☎ 0141 222 2929 & 270 2323 📄 0141 222 2929
141 en suite

EAGLESHAM

Map 11 NS55

Bonnyton Kirktonmoor Rd G76 0QA
☎ 01355 303030 🖹 01355 303151
e-mail: secretarybgc@btconnect.com
web: www.bonnytongolfclub.com

Dramatic moorland course offering spectacular views of beautiful countryside as far as snow-capped Ben Lomond. Tree-lined fairways, plateau greens, natural burns and well-situated bunkers and a unique variety of holes offer golfers both challenge and reward.

18 Holes, 6255yds, Par 72, SSS 71. Club membership 960.
Visitors contact club for details. **Societies** booking required. **Green Fees** £40 per round **Prof** David Andrews **Facilities** ⊕ ⦿ ⓛ ⌷ ⓥ ⌁ 🖻 ⛾ ⛳ ♂ **Conf** facs Corporate Hospitality Days **Location** 0.25m SW off B764
Hotel ★★★★ 72% HL Menzies Glasgow, 27 Washington Street, GLASGOW ☎ 0141 222 2929 & 270 2323 🖹 0141 222 2929 141 en suite

NEWTON MEARNS

Map 11 NS55

East Renfrewshire Pilmuir G77 6RT
☎ 01355 500256 🖹 01355 500323
e-mail: secretary@eastrengolfclub.co.uk
web: www.eastrengolfclub.co.uk

Undulating moorland with loch; prevailing south-west wind. Extensive views of Glasgow and the southern Highlands. Each hole has its own unique challenge.

18 Holes, 6107yds, Par 70, SSS 70, Course record 63. Club membership 900.
Visitors Mon-Fri except BHs.. Booking required. Dress code. Handicap certificate. **Societies** booking required. **Green Fees** £60 per day, £45 per round **Course Designer** James Braid **Prof** Stewart Russell **Facilities** ⊕ ⦿ ⓛ ⌷ ⓥ ⌁ 🖻 ♂ **Conf** Corporate Hospitality Days **Location** 3m SW of Newton Mearns on A77, junct 5
Hotel ★★★ 80% HL Uplawmoor Hotel, Neilston Road, UPLAWMOOR ☎ 01505 850565 🖹 01505 850565 14 en suite

Eastwood Muirshield G77 6RX
☎ 01355 500280 🖹 01355 500333
web: www.eastwoodgolfclub.co.uk

18 Holes, 6071yds, Par 70, SSS 70.
Course Designer Graeme J. Webster/Theodore Moone **Location** 2.5m S of Newton Mearns, on A77
Telephone for further details
Hotel ★★★ 80% HL Uplawmoor Hotel, Neilston Road, UPLAWMOOR ☎ 01505 850565 🖹 01505 850565 14 en suite

UPLAWMOOR

Map 10 NS45

Caldwell G78 4AU
☎ 01505 850366 (Secretary) & 850616 (Pro)
🖹 01505 850604
e-mail: secretary@caldwellgolfclub.co.uk
web: cgc.uplowmoor.net

Parkland course.

18 Holes, 6294yds, Par 71, SSS 71, Course record 62. Club membership 600.
Visitors handicap certificate. Dress code **Societies** booking required. **Green Fees** £25 per round, £35 per day **Course Designer** W. Fernie

Prof Craig Everett **Facilities** ⊕ ⦿ ⓛ ⌷ ⓥ ⌁ 🖻 ♂ **Conf** Corporate Hospitality Days **Location** 5m SW of Barrhead on A736 Irvine road
Hotel ★★★ 80% HL Uplawmoor Hotel, Neilston Road, UPLAWMOOR ☎ 01505 850565 🖹 01505 850565 14 en suite

EDINBURGH, CITY OF

EDINBURGH

Map 11 NT27

Baberton 50 Baberton Av, Juniper Green EH14 5DU
☎ 0131 453 4911 🖹 0131 453 4678
e-mail: manager@baberton.co.uk
web: www.baberton.co.uk

Heathland course offering the golfer a variety of interesting and challenging holes. The outward half follows the boundary of the course and presents some demanding par 3 and 4 holes over the undulating terrain. The inward half has some longer, equally challenging holes contained within the course and presents some majestic views of the Pentland Hills and the Edinburgh skyline.

18 Holes, 6129yds, Par 69, SSS 70, Course record 64. Club membership 900.
Visitors Mon-Fri, Sun & BHs. Dress code. **Societies** welcome. **Green Fees** £42 per day, £32 per round (£35 per round Sun) **Course Designer** Willie Park Jnr **Prof** Ken Kelly **Facilities** ⊕ ⦿ ⓛ ⌷ ⓥ ⌁ 🖻 ⛾ ⛳ ♂ **Leisure** snooker **Conf** Corporate Hospitality Days **Location** 5m W of city centre off A70
Hotel ★★★★ 79% HL Edinburgh Marriott Hotel, 111 Glasgow Road, EDINBURGH ☎ 0131 334 9191 🖹 0131 334 9191 245 en suite

Braid Hills 27 Braid Hills Approach EH10 6JY
☎ 0131 447 6666 🖹 0131 651 2299
web: edinburghleisure.co.uk
Braid Hills Golf Course: 18 Holes, 5345yds, Par 70, SSS 66.
Course Designer Peter McEwan & Bob Ferguson **Location** 2.5m S of city centre off A702
Telephone for further details
Hotel ★★★ 80% HL Best Western Braid Hills, 134 Braid Road, EDINBURGH ☎ 0131 447 8888 🖹 0131 447 8888 67 en suite

See advert on page 339

Bruntsfield Links Golfing Society 32 Barnton Av EH4 6JH
☎ 0131 336 1479 🖹 0131 336 5538
web: www.sol.co.uk/b/bruntsfieldlinks
Bruntsfield Links Golfing Society: 18 Holes, 6428yds, Par 71, SSS 71, Course record 63.
Course Designer Willie Park Jr, A Mackenzie, Hawtree **Location** 4m NW of city centre off A90
continued

337

Telephone for further details
Hotel BUD Travelodge Edinburgh West End, 69 Belford Road, EDINBURGH ☎ 0871 984 6418 📠 0871 984 6418 146 en suite

Carrick Knowe Carrick Knowe EH12 5UZ
☎ 0131 337 1096 📠 0131 651 2299

Carrick Knowe Golf Course: 18 Holes, 5697yds, Par 70, SSS 69.

Facilities ⓣ 🍽 🛍 🖵 🛆 ⛳ ✄ Location 3m W of city centre, S of A8
Telephone for further details
Hotel ★★★ 80% HL Best Western Edinburgh Capital, 187 Clermiston Road, EDINBURGH ☎ 0131 535 9988 📠 0131 535 9988 111 en suite

Craigentinny Fillyside Rd EH7 6RG
☎ 0131 554 7501 📠 0131 651 2299
web: www.edinburghleisure.co.uk

Craigentinny Golf Course: 18 Holes, 5205yds, Par 67, SSS 65, Course record 62.

Facilities 🖵 🛆 🖼 ⛳ ✄ Location NE side of city, between Leith & Portobello
Telephone for further details
Hotel ★★★ 78% HL Best Western Kings Manor, 100 Milton Road East, EDINBURGH ☎ 0131 669 0444 & 468 8003 📠 0131 669 0444 95 en suite

Craigmillar Park 1 Observatory Rd EH9 3HG
☎ 0131 667 0047 📠 0131 662 8091
e-mail: secretary@craigmillarpark.co.uk
web: www.craigmillarpark.co.uk
Parkland with good views.

18 Holes, 5851yds, Par 70, SSS 68, Course record 63. Club membership 850.

Visitors Mon-Fri & BHs. Sun after 3pm. Dress code.
Societies welcome. Green Fees not confirmed Course Designer James Braid Prof Scott Gourlay Facilities ⓣ 🍽 🛍 🖵 🖼 🛆 🖼 ⛳ ✄ Location 2m S of city centre off A7
Hotel ★★★ 80% HL Best Western Braid Hills, 134 Braid Road, EDINBURGH ☎ 0131 447 8888 📠 0131 447 8888 67 en suite

Duddingston Duddingston Road West EH15 3QD
☎ 0131 661 4301 📠 0131 661 4301
e-mail: duddingstonproshop@hotmail.com
web: www.duddingstongolfclub.com
Easy walking parkland with a burn as a natural hazard. Testing 11th hole.

Duddingston Golf Club Ltd: 18 Holes, 6525yds, Par 72, SSS 72, Course record 63. Club membership 700.

Visitors Mon-Sun & BHs. Booking advisable. Dress code
Societies welcome. Green Fees £50 per day, £35 per round. Course Designer Willie Park Jnr Prof Alastair McLean Facilities ⓣ 🍽 🛍 🖵 🖼 🛆 🖼 ⛳ ✄ 🖼 ✄ Conf facs Corporate Hospitality Days Location 2.5m SE of city centre off A1
Hotel ★★★ 78% HL Best Western Kings Manor, 100 Milton Road East, EDINBURGH ☎ 0131 669 0444 & 468 8003 📠 0131 669 0444 95 en suite

Kingsknowe 326 Lanark Rd EH14 2JD
☎ 0131 441 1145 (Sec) 📠 0131 441 2079
e-mail: louis@kingsknowe.com
web: www.kingsknowe.com

Picturesque parkland course set amid gently rolling hills. This course provides a varied and interesting challenge for all levels of golfers.

18 Holes, 5938yds, Par 69, SSS 69, Course record 63. Club membership 930.

Visitors Mon-Fri & BHs. Booking required Fri & BHs. Dress code.
Societies booking required. Green Fees £32 per day, £25 per 18 holes
Course Designer A Herd/James Braid Prof Chris Morris Facilities ⓣ 🍽 🛍 🖵 🖼 🛆 🖼 ⛳ ✄ 🖼 ✄ Leisure indoor teaching/practice facility Conf Corporate Hospitality Days Location 4m SW of city centre on A70
Hotel ★★★★ 77% HL Best Western Bruntsfield, 69 Bruntsfield Place, EDINBURGH ☎ 0131 229 1393 📠 0131 229 1393 67 en suite

Liberton 297 Gilmerton Rd EH16 5UJ
☎ 0131 664 3009 (sec)
e-mail: info@libertongc.co.uk
web: www.libertongc.co.uk
Gentle, undulating, wooded parkland with tight fairways and well guarded greens suitable for all standards of golfer.

18 Holes, 5344yds, Par 67, SSS 66, Course record 62. Club membership 846.

Visitors Mon-Sun & BHs. Booking weekends. Dress code. Handicap certificate. Societies welcome. Green Fees £35 per day, £30 per round (£40 weekends) Prof Iain Seath Facilities ⓣ 🍽 🛍 🖵 🖼 🛆 🖼 ⛳ ✄ Conf facs Corporate Hospitality Days Location 3m SE of city centre on A7
Hotel ★★★ 81% HL Dalhousie Castle and Aqueous Spa, Bonnyrigg, EDINBURGH ☎ 01875 820153 📠 01875 820153 36 en suite

Lothianburn 106A Biggar Rd, Fairmilehead EH10 7DU
☎ 0131 445 2288 📠 0131 445 5067
e-mail: info@lothianburngc.co.uk
web: www.lothianburngc.co.uk
Situated to the south-west of Edinburgh, on the slopes of the Pentland Hills, the course rises from the clubhouse some 300ft to its highest point at the 13th green. There is only one real climb of note, after playing the 2nd shot to the 9th green. The course is noted for its excellent greens, and challenging holes include the 5th, where one drives for position in order to pitch at almost right angles to a plateau green; and the 14th, longest hole on the course, three-quarters of which is downhill with out of bounds on both sides of the fairway.

18 Holes, 5662yds, Par 71, SSS 69, Course record 64. Club membership 500.

continued

Visitors Mon–Sun & BHs. Booking required weekends & BHs. Dress code. **Societies** booking required. **Green Fees** £25 per round (£30 weekends) **Course Designer** J Braid (re-designed 1928) **Prof** Kurt Mungall **Facilities** ⓣ ⑪ 📁 🖥 🍴 👥 🏠 ⛳ ✔ 🚕 🏌
Location 4.5m S of city centre on A702
Hotel ★★★ 80% HL Best Western Braid Hills, 134 Braid Road, EDINBURGH ☎ 0131 447 8888 📠 0131 447 8888 67 en suite

Marriott Dalmahoy Hotel Golf & Country Club
see page 341
Kirknewton EH27 8EB
☎ 0131 335 1845   📠 0131 335 3577
e-mail: mbrs.edigs.golf@marriotthotels.com
web: www.dalmahoygolf.com

Merchants of Edinburgh 10 Craighill Gardens EH10 5PY
☎ 0131 447 1219   📠 0131 446 9833
e-mail: admin@merchantsgolf.com
web: www.merchantsgolf.com
Fairly short but testing hill course with superb views over the city and surrounding countryside.

18 Holes, 4889yds, Par 65, SSS 64, Course record 59.
Club membership 980.
Visitors Mon–Sun & BHs. Booking required weekends. Dress code. **Societies** booking required. **Green Fees** £30 per day, £20 per round **Course Designer** Ben Sayers **Prof** Neil Colquhoun **Facilities** ⓣ
⑪ 📁 🖥 🍴 👥 🏠 ⛳ ✔ **Leisure** snooker room **Conf** facs
Corporate Hospitality Days **Location** 2m SW of city centre off A702
Hotel ★★★ 80% HL Best Western Braid Hills, 134 Braid Road, EDINBURGH ☎ 0131 447 8888 📠 0131 447 8888 67 en suite

Mortonhall 231 Braid Rd EH10 6PB
☎ 0131 447 6974   📠 0131 447 8712
e-mail: clubhouse@mortonhallgc.co.uk
web: www.mortonhallgc.co.uk
Moorland and parkland with views over Edinburgh.

18 Holes, 6551yds, Par 72, SSS 72, Course record 66.
Club membership 525.
Visitors contact club for details. **Societies** booking required. **Green Fees** £60 per day, £45 per round **Course Designer** James Braid/F Hawtree **Prof** Malcolm Leighton **Facilities** ⓣ 📁 🖥 🍴 👥 🏠
⛳ 🚕 ✔ **Location** 3m S of city centre off A702
Hotel ★★★ 80% HL Best Western Braid Hills, 134 Braid Road, EDINBURGH ☎ 0131 447 8888 📠 0131 447 8888 67 en suite

Murrayfield 43 Murrayfield Rd EH12 6EU
☎ 0131 337 3478   📠 0131 313 0721
e-mail: marjorie@murrayfieldgolfclub.co.uk
web: www.murrayfieldgolfclub.co.uk
Parkland on the side of Corstorphine Hill, with fine views.

18 Holes, 5725yds, Par 70, SSS 69. Club membership 815.
Visitors Mon–Sun & BHs. Booking required. Handicap certificate. Dress code. **Societies** booking required. **Green Fees** £50 per day, £40 per round **Prof** Jonnie Cliff **Facilities** ⓣ 📁 🖥 🍴 👥 🏠 ⛳ ✔
Conf Corporate Hospitality Days **Location** 2m W of city centre off A8
Hotel BUD Travelodge Edinburgh West End, 69 Belford Road, EDINBURGH ☎ 0871 984 6418 📠 0871 984 6418 146 en suite

THE BRAID HILLS HOTEL
134 Braid Road, Edinburgh, EH10 6JD
Magnificently situated only two miles from the city centre, yet a world away from the noise and congestion of the centre itself, the Braid Hills Hotel is your ideal choice when visiting Edinburgh. Ample free parking.
To make your reservation in this independently-owned hotel

 Tel: 0131 447 8888
Fax: 0131 452 8477

e-mail: bookings@braidhillshotel.co.uk
www.braidhillshotel.co.uk

Portobello Stanley St EH15 1JJ
☎ 0131 669 4361 & 557 5457(bookings)
📠 0131 557 5170
Portobello Golf Course: 9 Holes, 2252yds, Par 32, SSS 32.
Facilities 📁 👥 🚕 ✔ **Location** 3m E of city centre off A1
Telephone for further details
Hotel ★★★ 78% HL Best Western Kings Manor, 100 Milton Road East, EDINBURGH ☎ 0131 669 0444 & 468 8003 📠 0131 669 0444 95 en suite

Prestonfield 6 Priestfield Road North EH16 5HS
☎ 0131 667 9665   📠 0131 667 9665
e-mail: gavincook@prestonfieldgolfclub.co.uk
web: www.prestonfieldgolfclub.co.uk
Parkland with beautiful views, set under Arthur's Seat, an extinct volcano. The course is a gentle walk, but a challenge for golfers of all levels.

Prestonfield Golf Club Ltd: 18 Holes, 6212yds, Par 70, SSS 70, Course record 66. Club membership 850.
Visitors contact club for details. **Societies** welcome. **Green Fees** £32 per round (£42 per day) **Course Designer** James Braid **Prof** Gavin Cook **Facilities** ⓣ ⑪ 📁 🖥 🍴 👥 🏠 ⛳ ✔ 🚕 ✔
Conf facs Corporate Hospitality Days **Location** 1.5m S of city centre off A68
Hotel ★★★★★ Prestonfield, Priestfield Road, EDINBURGH
☎ 0131 225 7800 📠 0131 225 7800 23 en suite

Ravelston 24 Ravelston Dykes Rd EH4 3NZ
☎ 0131 315 2486   📄 0131 315 2486

Parkland on the north-east side of Corstorphine Hill, overlooking the Firth of Forth.

9 Holes, 5230yds, Par 66, SSS 66, Course record 64. Club membership 610.

Visitors Mon-Fri except BHs. Booking advisable. Handicap certificate. Dress code. **Green Fees** phone **Course Designer** James Braid **Facilities** 🍴 🖵 ⚲ **Location** 3m W of city centre off A90
Hotel ★★★★ 79% HL Edinburgh Marriott Hotel, 111 Glasgow Road, EDINBURGH ☎ 0131 334 9191 📄 0131 334 9191 245 en suite

Royal Burgess 181 Whitehouse Rd, Barnton EH4 6BU
☎ 0131 339 2075   📄 0131 339 3712
e-mail: secretary@royalburgess.co.uk
web: www.royalburgess.co.uk

No mention of golf clubs would be complete without the Royal Burgess, which was instituted in 1735 and is the oldest golfing society in Scotland. Its course is a pleasant parkland, and one with a great deal of variety. A club which anyone interested in the history of the game should visit.

Royal Burgess Golfing Society of Edinburgh: 18 Holes, 6126yds, Par 68, SSS 69, Course record 62. Club membership 635.

Visitors Mon-Fri & BHs. Sat after 2.30pm, Sun after noon. Dress code. **Societies** welcome. **Green Fees** £55 per day (£75 weekends) **Course Designer** Tom Morris **Prof** Steven Brian **Facilities** 🍴 🖵 🍴 ⚲ 📠 ⚲ **Conf** Corporate Hospitality Days **Location** 5m W of city centre off A90
Hotel BUD Travelodge Edinburgh West End, 69 Belford Road, EDINBURGH ☎ 0871 984 6418 📄 0871 984 6418 146 en suite

Silverknowes Silverknowes EH4 5ET
☎ 0131 336 3843
web: www.edinburghleisure.co.uk
Silverknowes Golf Course: 18 Holes, 6070yds, Par 71, SSS 70.

Facilities 🍴 🍴 🍴 🖵 🍴 ⚲ 📠 🍴 ⚲ **Conf** Corporate Hospitality Days **Location** 4m NW of city centre, easy access from city bypass
Telephone for further details
Hotel BUD Travelodge Edinburgh West End, 69 Belford Road, EDINBURGH ☎ 0871 984 6418 📄 0871 984 6418 146 en suite

Swanston Golf 111 Swanston Rd, Fairmilehead EH10 7DS
☎ 0131 445 2239   📄 0131 445 2239
e-mail: stewart.snedden@swanston.co.uk
web: www.swanstongolf.co.uk

The Swanston is a short yet challenging course situated on the lower slopes of the Pentland Hills with fine views over the city of Edinburgh and the Firth of Forth. The course has recently been re-modelled with 6 new holes on the lower level. The Templar is a par 3 short course with features streams, ponds, full sand based USGA specification greens, bunkers and wide fairways.

Swanston Golf: 18 Holes, 5462yds, Par 67, SSS 67. Club membership 800.

Visitors Mon-Fri & BHs. Booking required. Handicap certificate. Dress code. **Societies** booking required **Green Fees** Swanston £22 per round (£34 weekends). Templar £7.50/£9.50 **Course Designer** Herbert More **Prof** Gareth Wright **Facilities** 🍴 🍴 🍴 🖵 🍴 ⚲ 🍴 ◇ ⚲ 📠 ⚲ 🏌 **Leisure** gymnasium, 9 hole par 3 Templar Course.

Fitness suite **Conf** facs Corporate Hospitality Days **Location** 4m S of city centre off B701
Hotel ★★★ 80% HL Best Western Braid Hills, 134 Braid Road, EDINBURGH ☎ 0131 447 8888 📄 0131 447 8888 67 en suite

Torphin Hill Torphin Rd, Colinton EH13 0PG
☎ 0131 441 1100   📄 0131 441 7166
e-mail: torphinhillgc@btconnect.com
web: www.torphin.com

Beautiful hillside, heathland course, with fine views of Edinburgh and the Forth Estuary. From 600 to 700ft above sea level with 14 holes set on a relatively flat plateau.

18 Holes, 5285yds, Par 68, SSS 67, Course record 64. Club membership 450.

Visitors Mon-Sun & BHs. Booking required weekends & BHs. Dress code. **Societies** welcome. **Green Fees** £22 per day, £16 per round (£20 per round weekends) **Prof** Jamie Browne **Facilities** 🍴 🍴 🍴 🖵 🍴 ⚲ 📠 ⚲ **Conf** Corporate Hospitality Days **Location** 5m SW of city centre S of A720
Hotel ★★★ 80% HL Best Western Braid Hills, 134 Braid Road, EDINBURGH ☎ 0131 447 8888 📄 0131 447 8888 67 en suite

Turnhouse 154 Turnhouse Rd EH12 0AD
☎ 0131 339 1014   📄 0131 339 5141
e-mail: secretary@turnhousegc.com
web: www.turnhousegc.com

Challenging tree-lined course with numerous par 4s in excess of 400yds. Large sloping greens give a real challenge and the golfer is virtually guaranteed to use all the clubs in the bag.

18 Holes, 6171yds, Par 69, SSS 70, Course record 62. Club membership 800.

Visitors Mon-Fri & Sun except BHs. Dress code. **Societies** booking required. **Green Fees** £40 per day, £30 per round (£40 per round Sun) **Course Designer** J Braid **Prof** John Murray **Facilities** 🍴 🍴 🖵 🍴 ⚲ 📠 🍴 ⚲ 📠 ⚲ **Conf** facs Corporate Hospitality Days **Location** 6m W of city centre N of A8
Hotel ★★★★ 79% HL Edinburgh Marriott Hotel, 111 Glasgow Road, EDINBURGH ☎ 0131 334 9191 📄 0131 334 9191 245 en suite

---

RATHO   Map 11 NT17

Ratho Park EH28 8NX
☎ 0131 335 0068 & 335 0069   📄 0131 333 1752
e-mail: secretary@rathoparkgolfclub.co.uk
web: www.rathoparkgolfclub.co.uk

Easy walking parkland, with a converted mansion as the clubhouse.

Ratho Park Golf Club Ltd: 18 Holes, 5960yds, Par 69, SSS 68, Course record 62. Club membership 850.

Visitors Mon-Sun & BHs. Booking required. Dress code. **Societies** booking required. **Green Fees** £45 per day, £32 per round (£45 per round weekends) **Course Designer** James Braid **Prof** Alan Pate **Facilities** 🍴 🍴 🍴 🖵 🍴 ⚲ 📠 ⚲ 📠 ⚲ **Conf** Corporate Hospitality Days **Location** 0.75m E, N of A71
Hotel ★★★★ 86% HL Norton House, Ingliston, EDINBURGH ☎ 0131 333 1275 📄 0131 333 1275 83 en suite

MARRIOTT DALMAHOY

CITY OF EDINBURGH - MAP 11 NT27

The Championship East Course has hosted many major events including the Solheim Cup and the Charles Church Seniors PGA Championship of Scotland. The course has long sweeping fairways and generous greens protected by strategic bunkers. Many of the long par 4 holes offer a serious challenge to any golfer. The signature 18th hole has the green set in front of Dalmahoy's historic hotel with a testing approach over a wide ravine. The shorter West Course offers a different test with tighter fairways requiring more accuracy from the tee. The finishing holes incorporate the Gogar burn meandering through the fairway to create a tough finish.

Kirknewton EH27 8EB ☎ 0131 335 1845 📠 0131 335 3577
e-mail: mbrs.edigs.golf@marriotthotels.com **web:** www.dalmahoygolf.com
East Course: 18 Holes, 6814yds, Par 73, SSS 74, Course record 70.
West Course: 18 Holes, 5051yds, Par 68, SSS 65, Course record 60. Club membership 822.
Visitors Mon-Sun & BHs. Booking required. Handicap certificate. Dress code. **Societies** booking required. **Green Fees** East Course £65 per 18 holes (£80 weekends). West £40 (£45 weekends). Reduced winter rates **Course Designer** James Braid **Prof** Scott Dixon **Facilities** 🏦 🍽 🍺 ⬛ 🥤 🏌 🏠 🚩 ◇ 🛒 🏌 ♟ **Leisure** hard tennis courts, heated indoor swimming pool, sauna, gymnasium, fitness studio, golf academy, health salon **Conf** facs Corporate Hospitality Days **Location** 7m W of city on A71
Hotel ★★★★ 81% HL Marriott Dalmahoy Hotel & Country Club, Kirknewton, EDINBURGH ☎ 0131 333 1845 📠 0131 333 1845 215 en suite

SOUTH QUEENSFERRY
Map 11 NT17

Dundas Parks Dundas Estate EH30 9SS
☎ 0131 331 4252
e-mail: cmkwood@btinternet.com
Parkland course situated on the estate of Dundas Castle, with excellent views.

9 Holes, 6100yds, Par 70, SSS 69, Course record 62.
Club membership 500.

Visitors Mon-Fri & BHs. Booking required. Dress code.
Societies booking required. **Green Fees** not confirmed **Facilities** ⛀
Location 0.5m S on A8000
Hotel ★★★ 75% HL The Queensferry Hotel, St Margaret's Head, North Queensferry, INVERKEITHING ☎ 0870 111 2520 ▤ 0870 111 2520 77 en suite

---

FALKIRK

FALKIRK
Map 11 NS88

Falkirk Carmuirs, 136 Stirling Rd, Camelon FK2 7YP
☎ 01324 611061 (club) ▤ 01324 639573 (sec)
e-mail: falkirkgolfclub@btconnect.com
web: www.falkirkgolfclub.co.uk
Parkland with gorse and streams.

Carmuirs: 18 Holes, 6230yds, Par 71, SSS 70,
Course record 65. Club membership 800.

Visitors Sun-Fri & BHs. Dress code. Handicap certificate.
Societies booking required. **Green Fees** £40 per day, £30 per round (£55/£45 Sun) **Course Designer** James Braid **Prof** Stewart Craig
Facilities ⊕ †⊚| ⅃ ☐ ☏ ⅃ ☎ ☕ ✆ ♦ **Conf** Corporate Hospitality Days **Location** 1.5m W on A9
Hotel ★★★★ 72% HL Macdonald Inchyra Grange, Grange Road, POLMONT ☎ 01324 711911 ▤ 01324 711911 98 en suite

LARBERT
Map 11 NS88

Falkirk Tryst 86 Burnhead Rd FK5 4BD
☎ 01324 562054 ▤ 01324 562054

18 Holes, 6053yds, Par 70, SSS 69, Course record 62.
Prof Steven Dunsmore **Facilities** ⊕ ⅃ ☐ ☏ ⅃ ☎ ☕ ✆
✆ **Location** on A88
Telephone for further details
Hotel ★★★★ 72% HL Macdonald Inchyra Grange, Grange Road, POLMONT ☎ 01324 711911 ▤ 01324 711911 98 en suite

Glenbervie Stirling Rd FK5 4SJ
☎ 01324 562605 ▤ 01324 551054
e-mail: secretary@glenberviegolfclub.com
web: www.glenberviegolfclub.com
Parkland course set amidst mature trees with outstanding views of the Ochil Hills

Glenbervie Golf Club Ltd: 18 Holes, 6438yds, Par 71,
SSS 71, Course record 63. Club membership 700.

Visitors Mon-Fri & BHs. Booking advised. Dress code.
Societies booking required. **Green Fees** £50 per day, £35 per round **Course Designer** James Braid **Prof** Steven Rosie **Facilities** ⊕ †⊚|
⅃ ☐ ☏ ⅃ ☎ ♦ **Conf** Corporate Hospitality Days
Location 2m NW on A9
Hotel ★★★★ 72% HL Macdonald Inchyra Grange, Grange Road, POLMONT ☎ 01324 711911 ▤ 01324 711911 98 en suite

POLMONT
Map 11 NS97

Grangemouth Polmont Hill FK2 0YE
☎ 01324 503840 ▤ 01324 503841
e-mail: greg.mcfarlane@falkirk.gov.uk
Windy parkland. Testing holes: 3rd, 4th (par 4s); 5th (par 5); 7th (par 3) 216yds over reservoir (elevated green); 8th, 9th, 18th (par 4s).

18 Holes, 6314yds, Par 71, SSS 71, Course record 65.
Club membership 800.

Visitors Mon-Sun & BHs. Dress code. Handicap certificate.
Societies booking required. **Green Fees** not confirmed **Prof** Greg McFarlane **Facilities** ⊕ †⊚| ⅃ ☐ ☏ ⅃ ☎ ♦ **Location** M9 junct 4, 0.5m N
Hotel ★★★★ 72% HL Macdonald Inchyra Grange, Grange Road, POLMONT ☎ 01324 711911 ▤ 01324 711911 98 en suite

Polmont Manuelrigg, Maddiston FK2 0LS
☎ 01324 711277 ▤ 01324 712504
e-mail: polmontgolfclub@btconnect.com
Hilly parkland with small greens protected by bunkers. Views of the River Forth and the Ochil Hills.

9 Holes, 3073yds, Par 72, SSS 69, Course record 66.
Club membership 300.

Visitors Mon-Fri, Sun & BHs. Booking required Sun. Handicap certificate. Dress code. **Societies** welcome. **Green Fees** £10 per round (Sun £15) **Facilities** ⅃ ☏ ⅃ **Location** A805 from Falkirk, 1st right after fire brigade headquarters
Hotel ★★★★ 72% HL Macdonald Inchyra Grange, Grange Road, POLMONT ☎ 01324 711911 ▤ 01324 711911 98 en suite

---

FIFE

ABERDOUR
Map 11 NT18

Aberdour Seaside Place KY3 0TX
☎ 01383 860080 ▤ 01383 860050
e-mail: manager@aberdourgolfclub.co.uk
web: www.aberdourgolfclub.co.uk
Parkland with lovely views over Firth of Forth.

18 Holes, 5447yds, Par 67, SSS 67, Course record 59.
Club membership 800.

Visitors Mon-Sun & BHs. Booking required. Dress code. Handicap certificate. **Societies** booking required. **Green Fees** Mon-Thu £35 per day, £25 per round, Fri £40/£30, weekends £35/£45 **Prof** David Gemmell **Facilities** ⊕ †⊚| ⅃ ☐ ☏ ⅃ ☎ ☕ ✆ ♦
Location S side of village
Hotel ★★ 67% HL The Cedar Inn, 20 Shore Road, ABERDOUR ☎ 01383 860310 ▤ 01383 860310 9 en suite

---

ANSTRUTHER
Map 12 NO50

Anstruther Marsfield, Shore Rd KY10 3DZ
☎ 01333 310956 ▤ 01333 310956
e-mail: captain@anstruthergolf.co.uk
web: anstruthergolf.co.uk
A tricky links course with some outstanding views of the river Forth. The nine holes consist of four par 4s and five par 3s. The 5th hole is rated one of the hardest par 3s anywhere, measuring 235yds from the medal tees.

continued

SCOTLAND

9 Holes, 2345yds, Par 62, SSS 63, Course record 60. Club membership 550.

Visitors Mon-Fri, Sun & BHs. Dress code Handicap certificate. **Societies** welcome. **Green Fees** £25 per round (free soft drink), £15 per 9 holes **Course Designer** Tom Morris **Facilities** ⊕ ⏺ 🍴 📖 🖵 🍽 ⚖ ⛳ 🚗 ✆ **Location** turn right at Craw's Hotel, SW off A917 **Hotel** ★★ 71% SHL Balcomie Links, Balcomie Road, CRAIL ☎ 01333 450237 ▤ 01333 450237 14 en suite

BURNTISLAND   Map 11 NT28

Burntisland Golf House Club Dodhead KY3 9LQ ☎ 01592 874093 (Office) & 872116 (Golf) ▤ 01592 873247 **web:** www.burntislandgolfhouseclub.co.uk *Burntisland Golf House Club: 18 Holes, 5965yds, Par 70, SSS 70, Course record 62.*

Course Designer Willie Park Jnr **Location** 1m E on B923 **Telephone for further details** **Hotel** ★★★ 73% SHL Inchview Hotel, 65-69 Kinghorn Road, BURNTISLAND ☎ 01592 872239 ▤ 01592 872239 12 en suite

COLINSBURGH   Map 12 NO40

Charleton Charleton KY9 1HG ☎ 01333 340505 ▤ 01333 340583 **e-mail:** clubhouse@charleton.co.uk **web:** www.charleton.co.uk Parkland course with undulating links style greens and wonderful views over the Firth of Forth.

18 Holes, 6443yds, Par 72, SSS 72, Course record 64. Club membership 400.

Visitors Mon-Sun & BHs. Booking required. **Societies** booking required. **Green Fees** £44 per day, £27 per round (£54/£32 weekends) **Course Designer** J Salvesen **Prof** George Finlayson **Facilities** ⊕ ⏺ 📖 🖵 🍽 ⚖ 🏠 🍴 🚗 ✆ ⛳ **Leisure** 9 hole pitch & putt course. **Conf** Corporate Hospitality Days **Location** off B942, NW of Colinsburgh **Hotel** ★★★★ HL Rufflets Country House, Strathkinness Low Road, ST ANDREWS ☎ 01334 472594 ▤ 01334 472594 24 en suite

COWDENBEATH   Map 11 NT19

Cowdenbeath Seco Place KY4 8PD ☎ 01383 511918 **web:** www.cowdenbeath-golfclub.com A parkland-based 18 hole golf course.

Dora Course: 18 Holes, 6300yds, Par 71, SSS 70, Course record 64. Club membership 250.

Visitors contact club for details. **Societies** booking required. **Green Fees** not confirmed **Facilities** ⊕ ⏺ 🖵 🍽 ⚖ 🍴 ✆ **Location** off A92 into Cowdenbeath, 2nd right signed **Hotel** ★★ 67% HL The Cedar Inn, 20 Shore Road, ABERDOUR ☎ 01383 860310 ▤ 01383 860310 9 en suite

CRAIL   Map 12 NO60

Crail Golfing Society Balcomie Clubhouse, Fifeness KY10 3XN ☎ 01333 450686 & 450960 ▤ 01333 450416 **e-mail:** info@crailgolfingsociety.co.uk **web:** www.crailgolfingsociety.co.uk Perched on the edge of the North Sea, the Crail Golfing Society's courses at Balcomie are picturesque and sporting. Crail Golfing Society began its life in 1786 and the course is highly thought of by students of the game both for its testing holes and the standard of its greens. Craighead Links has panoramic seascape and country views. With wide sweeping fairways and USGA specification greens it is a testing but fair challenge.

Balcomie Links: 18 Holes, 5922yds, Par 69, SSS 70, Course record 62.
Craighead Links: 18 Holes, 6722yds, Par 71, SSS 74, Course record 68. Club membership 1600.

Visitors Mon-Sun & BHs. **Societies** welcome. **Green Fees** £70 per day, £51 per round (£90/£63 weekends). Craighead/Balcomie £63 per day (£90 weekends) **Course Designer** Tom Morris **Prof** Graeme Lennie **Facilities** ⊕ ⏺ 🍴 📖 🖵 🍽 ⚖ 🏠 🍴 🚗 ✆ ⛳ **Location** 2m NE off A917 **Hotel** ★★ 71% SHL Balcomie Links, Balcomie Road, CRAIL ☎ 01333 450237 ▤ 01333 450237 14 en suite

CUPAR   Map 11 NO31

Cupar Hilltarvit KY15 5JT ☎ 01334 653549 ▤ 01334 653549 **e-mail:** cupargc@fsmail.net **web:** www.cupargolfclub.co.uk Hilly parkland with fine views over north-east Fife. The 5th/14th hole is most difficult - uphill into the prevailing wind. Said to be the oldest nine-hole club in the UK.

9 Holes, 5153yds, Par 68, SSS 66, Course record 61. Club membership 400.

Visitors Sun-Fri & BHs. Sat pm. Handicap certificate. **Societies** booking required. **Green Fees** £20 per day **Course Designer** Allan Robertson **Facilities** ⊕ 📖 🖵 🍽 ⚖ 🍴 ✆ **Location** 0.75m S off A92 **Hotel** ★★★ 74% HL Fernie Castle, Letham, CUPAR ☎ 01337 810381 ▤ 01337 810381 20 en suite

Elmwood Stratheden KY15 5RS ☎ 01334 658780 ▤ 01334 658781 **e-mail:** clubhouse@elmwood.co.uk **web:** www.elmwoodgc.co.uk A parkland course set in a rural location, offering fine views of the Lomond Hills to the west and the Tarvit Hills to the east. Recently remodelled and lengthened, providing a challenging layout.

Elmwood Golf Course: 18 Holes, 6002yds, Par 70, SSS 68. Club membership 750.

Visitors Mon-Sun & BHs. Handicap certificate. **Societies** booking required. **Green Fees** £24.50 per round (£27.50 weekends & BHs) **Course Designer** John Salveson/Howard Swan **Prof** Graeme McDowall **Facilities** ⊕ ⏺ 📖 🖵 🍽 ⚖ 🏠 🍴 🚗 ✆ ⛳ **Conf** facs Corporate Hospitality Days **Location** M90 junct 8, A91 to St Andrews, 0.5m before Cupar. At Wisemans Dairy right, right at next junct, course 400yds on left **Hotel** ★★★ 74% HL Fernie Castle, Letham, CUPAR ☎ 01337 810381 ▤ 01337 810381 20 en suite

DUNFERMLINE   Map 11 NT08

Canmore Venturefair Av KY12 0PE
☎ 01383 724969   🖹 01383 731649
e-mail: canmoregolfclub@btconnect.com
web: www.canmoregolf.co.uk

Parkland course with excellent turf, moderate in length but a good test of accuracy demanding a good short game. Ideal for 36-hole play, and suitable for all ages.

18 Holes, 5376yds, Par 67, SSS 66, Course record 61.
Club membership 650.

Visitors dress code. **Societies** welcome. **Green Fees** not confirmed **Course Designer** Ben Sayers & others **Prof** Daryn Cochrane **Facilities** ⊕ ⏴⊙⏵ 🐾 ⏄ 🍴 🛆 🖼 ⛽ 🚗 ✦ **Location** 1m N on A823

Hotel ★★★★ 74% HL Best Western Keavil House Hotel, Crossford, DUNFERMLINE ☎ 01383 736258 🖹 01383 736258 73 en suite

Dunfermline Pitfirrane, Crossford KY12 8QW
☎ 01383 723534 & 729061   🖹 01383 723547
e-mail: secretary@dunfermlinegolfclub.com
web: www.dunfermlinegolfclub.com

Gently undulating parkland course with interesting contours. Five par 5s, five par 3s. No water hazards. Centre of the course is a disused walled garden, which is a haven for wildlife.

18 Holes, 6121yds, Par 72, SSS 70, Course record 65.
Club membership 770.

Visitors Mon-Sun & BHs. Dress code. Handicap certificate. **Societies** booking required. **Green Fees** £50 per day, £35 per round,(Sun £40 per round) **Course Designer** J R Stutt **Prof** Chris Nugent **Facilities** ⊕ ⏴⊙⏵ 🐾 ⏄ 🍴 🛆 🖼 ⛽ ✦ 🚗 ✦ **Location** 2m W of Dunfermline on A994

Hotel ★★★★ 74% HL Best Western Keavil House Hotel, Crossford, DUNFERMLINE ☎ 01383 736258 🖹 01383 736258 73 en suite

Forrester Park Pitdinnie Rd, Cairneyhill KY12 8RF
☎ 01383 880505   🖹 01383 882505
e-mail: info@forresterparkresort.co.uk
web: www.forresterparkresort.com

Set in the heart of 350 acres of parkland on what was originally the Keavil Estate. Ponds and streams come into play on 9 holes and all greens have been constructed to USGA specifications giving full play all year.

Forrester Park Golf Course: 18 Holes, 7000yds, Par 72, SSS 74, Course record 69. Club membership 700.

Visitors Mon-Sun & BHs. Booking required. Dress code. **Societies** booking required. **Green Fees** £35 per 18 holes (£45 weekends). Winter £25/£35 **Prof** R Forrester **Facilities** ⊕ ⏴⊙⏵ 🐾 ⏄ 🍴 🛆 🖼 ⛽ ✦ 🚗 ✦ **Conf** facs Corporate Hospitality Days **Location** 2.5m W of Dunfermline in village of Cairneyhill

Hotel ★★★★ 74% HL Best Western Keavil House Hotel, Crossford, DUNFERMLINE ☎ 01383 736258 🖹 01383 736258 73 en suite

Pitreavie Queensferry Rd KY11 8PR
☎ 01383 722591   🖹 01383 722592
web: www.pitreaviegolfclub.co.uk

18 Holes, 6086yds, Par 70, SSS 69, Course record 64.

Course Designer Dr Alister McKenzie **Location** SE side of town on A823
Telephone for further details
Hotel ★★★ 71% HL King Malcolm, Queensferry Road, DUNFERMLINE ☎ 01383 722611 🖹 01383 722611 48 en suite

ELIE   Map 12 NO40

Golf House Club KY9 1AS
☎ 01333 330301   🖹 01333 330895
e-mail: secretary@golfhouseclub.org
web: www.golfhouseclub.org

One of Scotland's most delightful holiday courses with panoramic views over the Firth of Forth. Some of the holes out towards the rocky coastline are splendid. This is the course which has produced many good professionals, including James Braid.

Golf House Club: 18 Holes, 6273yds, Par 70, SSS 70, Course record 62. Club membership 600.

Visitors Mon-Sun & BHs. Booking required. Dress code. Handicap certificate. **Societies** booking required. **Green Fees** £85 per day, £65 per round (£95/£75 weekends) **Prof** Ian Muir **Facilities** ⊕ ⏴⊙⏵ 🐾 ⏄ 🍴 🛆 🖼 ✦ ✦ **Leisure** hard tennis courts **Location** W side of village off A917

Hotel ★★★★ INN The Inn at Lathones, Largoward, ST ANDREWS ☎ 01334 840494 🖹 01334 840494 13 en suite

FALKLAND   Map 11 NO20

Falkland The Myre KY15 7AA
☎ 01337 857404

A flat, well-kept course with excellent greens and views of East Lomond Hill and Falkland Palace.

9 Holes, 4988yds, Par 67, SSS 65, Course record 62.
Club membership 198.

Visitors contact club for details. **Societies** welcome. **Green Fees** £15 per 18 holes **Facilities** ⊕ by prior arrangement 🐾 ⏄ 🍴 🛆 **Location** N side of town on A912

Hotel ★★★★ CHH Balbirnie House, Balbirnie Park, MARKINCH ☎ 01592 610066 🖹 01592 610066 30 en suite

GLENROTHES   Map 11 NO20

Glenrothes Golf Course Rd KY6 2LA
☎ 01592 754561   🖹 01592 754561
web: www.glenrothesgolf.org.uk

18 Holes, 6444yds, Par 71, SSS 71, Course record 67.

Course Designer J R Stutt **Location** W side of town off B921
Telephone for further details
Hotel ★★★★ CHH Balbirnie House, Balbirnie Park, MARKINCH ☎ 01592 610066 🖹 01592 610066 30 en suite

KINCARDINE   Map 11 NS98

Tulliallan Alloa Rd FK10 4BB
☎ 01259 730798   🖹 01259 733950
web: www.tulliallangolf.co.uk

18 Holes, 5965yds, Par 69, SSS 69, Course record 63.

Prof Steven Kelly **Facilities** ⊕ ⏴⊙⏵ 🐾 ⏄ 🍴 🛆 🖼 ✦ ✦ **Conf** facs Corporate Hospitality Days **Location** 1m NW on A977
Telephone for further details
Hotel ★★★★ 78% HL The Grange Manor, Glensburgh, GRANGEMOUTH ☎ 01324 474836 🖹 01324 474836 36 en suite

KINGHORN Map 11 NT28

Kinghorn Macduff Cres KY3 9RE
☎ 01592 890345 & 890978

Municipal course, semi links and parkland, 300ft above sea level with views over the Firth of Forth and the North Sea. Undulating and quite testing.

18 Holes, 5269yds, Par 65, SSS 67, Course record 62. Club membership 190.

Visitors Mon-Fri, Sun & BHs. Booking required. Dress code. Handicap certificate. **Societies** booking required. **Green Fees** £19 per round, £30 per day (£24/£42 Sun) **Course Designer** Tom Morris **Facilities** ⌑ 🏐 ⚐ **Location** S side of town on A921
Hotel ★★★ 78% HL Dean Park, Chapel Level, KIRKCALDY
☎ 01592 261635 📄 01592 261635 46 en suite

KINGSBARNS Map 12 NO51

Kingsbarns Golf Links KY16 8QD
☎ 01334 460860 📄 01334 460877
e-mail: info@kingsbarns.com
web: www.kingsbarns.com

This links site is located in a unique part of East Fife with sandy soil, undulating ridges and hollows, and the Cambo burn running into the sea. Golf was resurrected on Kingsbarns Links at the beginning of the 21st century and is the only Scottish course to be built on links land in over 70 years.

Kingsbarns Golf Links: 18 Holes, 7152yds, Par 72, Course record 62.

Visitors Mon-Sun & BHs. Booking required. Dress code.
Societies booking required. **Green Fees** June-Nov £165, Mar-May £135 **Course Designer** Kyle Phillips **Prof** Alan Purdie **Facilities** ⌑ 🍴 🏐 ⚐ 🏐 ⚐ 🏐 ⚐ 🏐 **Conf** Corporate Hospitality Days
Location from St Andrews take A917 toward Crail, pass through village of Kingsbarns, entrance to Links signposted on left
Hotel ★★★★ HL Rufflets Country House, Strathkinness Low Road, ST ANDREWS ☎ 01334 472594 📄 01334 472594 24 en suite

KIRKCALDY Map 11 NT29

Dunnikier Park Dunnikier Way KY1 3LP
☎ 01592 261599 📄 01592 642541
e-mail: dunnikierparkgolfclub@btinternet.com
web: www.dunnikierparkgolfclub.com

Parkland, rolling fairways, not heavily bunkered, views of the Firth of Forth.

18 Holes, 6036metres, Par 72, SSS 72, Course record 65. Club membership 700.

Visitors Mon-Sun & BHs. Dress code. Handicap certificate.
Societies welcome. **Green Fees** phone **Course Designer** R Stutt **Prof** Gregor Whyte **Facilities** ⌑ 🍴 🏐 ⚐ 🏐 ⚐ 🏐 ⚐
Conf facs **Location** 2m N on B981, next to Kirkcaldy High School
Hotel ★★★ 78% HL Dean Park, Chapel Level, KIRKCALDY
☎ 01592 261635 📄 01592 261635 46 en suite

Kirkcaldy Balwearie Rd KY2 5LT
☎ 01592 205240 & 203258 (Pro Shop)
📄 01592 205240
e-mail: enquiries@kirkcaldygolfclub.co.uk
web: kirkcaldygolfclub.co.uk

A challenging parkland course in countryside, with beautiful views. A burn meanders by five holes. The club celebrated its centenary in 2004.

18 Holes, 6086yds, Par 71, SSS 70, Course record 64. Club membership 892.

Visitors Mon-Sun & BHs. Booking required. Dress code. Handicap certificate. **Societies** booking required. **Green Fees** £44 per day, £34 per round (weekends £54/£44) **Course Designer** Tom Morris **Prof** Anthony Caira **Facilities** ⌑ 🍴 🏐 ⚐ 🏐 ⚐ 🏐 ⚐
🏐 🏐 🏐 **Conf** facs Corporate Hospitality Days **Location** SW side of town off A910
Hotel ★★★ 78% HL Dean Park, Chapel Level, KIRKCALDY
☎ 01592 261635 📄 01592 261635 46 en suite

LADYBANK Map 11 NO30

Ladybank Annsmuir KY15 7RA
☎ 01337 830814 📄 01337 831505
e-mail: info@ladybankgolf.co.uk
web: www.ladybankgolf.co.uk

Picturesque classic heathland course of championship status set among heather, Scots pines and silver birch and comprising two loops of nine holes. The drive at the dog-leg 3rd and 9th holes requires extreme care as do the 15th and 16th on the back nine. The greens are compact and approach shots require precision to find the putting surface. Open qualifying course since 1978 and again in 2010.

18 Holes, 6601yds, Par 71, SSS 72, Course record 63. Club membership 1000.

Visitors Sun-Fri & BHs. Booking required. Handicap certificate. Dress code. **Societies** booking required. **Green Fees** not confirmed **Course Designer** Tom Morris **Prof** Sandy Smith **Facilities** ⌑ 🍴 🏐 ⚐
🏐 🏐 🏐 🏐 🏐 🏐 **Conf** facs Corporate Hospitality Days
Location N of town off A92
Hotel ★★★ 74% HL Fernie Castle, Letham, CUPAR
☎ 01337 810381 📄 01337 810381 20 en suite

LESLIE
Map 11 NO20

Leslie Balsillie Laws KY6 3EZ
☎ 01592 620040

Challenging parkland course.

9 Holes, 4686yds, Par 63, SSS 64, Course record 63. Club membership 230.

Visitors contact club for details. **Societies** welcome. **Green Fees** phone **Course Designer** Tom Morris **Facilities** ⬜ 🍴 ⬚ **Conf** Corporate Hospitality Days **Location** N side of town off A911

Hotel ★★★★ CHH Balbirnie House, Balbirnie Park, MARKINCH ☎ 01592 610066 📠 01592 610066 30 en suite

LEUCHARS
Map 12 NO42

Drumoig Hotel & Golf Course Drumoig KY16 0BE
☎ 01382 541800 (Starter) & 541898 📠 01382 541898
web: www.drumoigleisure.com

Drumoig Hotel & Golf Course: 18 Holes, 6835yds, Par 72, SSS 73, Course record 67.

Facilities 🛈 🍴 🛄 ⬜ 🍴 ⬚ 🍴 🛄 ◇ 🚜 ✂ 🏌
Conf Corporate Hospitality Days **Location** on A914 between St Andrews & Dundee
Telephone for further details

Hotel ★★★★ HL Rufflets Country House, Strathkinness Low Road, ST ANDREWS ☎ 01334 472594 📠 01334 472594 24 en suite

St Michaels KY16 0DX
☎ 01334 839365 & 838666 (office) 📠 01334 838789
e-mail: stmichaelsgc@btclick.com
web: www.stmichaelsgolf.co.uk

Parkland with open views over Fife and Tayside. The undulating course weaves its way through tree plantations. The par 3 15th hole is the signature hole and the short par 4 17th, parallel to the railway and over a pond to a stepped green, poses an interesting challenge.

18 Holes, 5802yds, Par 69, SSS 68, Course record 66. Club membership 350.

Visitors Mon-Sun & BHs. Booking required weekends. Dress code. **Societies** welcome. **Green Fees** £29 per round. **Course Designer** Old Tom Harris **Facilities** 🛈 🍴 by prior arrangement 🛄 ⬜ 🍴 ⬚ 🍴 ✂ 🚜 ✂ **Conf** Corporate Hospitality Days **Location** NW side of village on A919

Hotel ★★★★ HL Rufflets Country House, Strathkinness Low Road, ST ANDREWS ☎ 01334 472594 📠 01334 472594 24 en suite

LEVEN
Map 11 NO30

Leven Links The Promenade KY8 4HS
☎ 01333 428859 & 421390 📠 01333 428859
web: www.leven-links.com

Leven Links Golf Course: 18 Holes, 6506yds, Par 71, SSS 72, Course record 63.

Course Designer Tom Morris **Location** off the A915 Kirkcaldy to St Andrews road
Telephone for further details

Hotel ★★★★ CHH Balbirnie House, Balbirnie Park, MARKINCH ☎ 01592 610066 📠 01592 610066 30 en suite

Scoonie KY8 4SP
☎ 01333 307007 & 423437 (Starter) 📠 01333 307008
web: www.scooniegolfclub.com

Scoonie Golf Course: 18 Holes, 5494mtrs, Par 67, SSS 66, Course record 62.

Facilities 🛈 🛄 ⬜ 🍴 ⬚ **Location** on coastal road to St. Andrews
Telephone for further details

Hotel ★★★★ CHH Balbirnie House, Balbirnie Park, MARKINCH ☎ 01592 610066 📠 01592 610066 30 en suite

LOCHGELLY
Map 11 NT19

Lochgelly Cartmore Rd KY5 9PB
☎ 01592 780174

18 Holes, 5491yds, Par 68, SSS 67, Course record 62.

Course Designer Ian Marchbanks **Location** W side of town off A910
Telephone for further details

Hotel ★★★ 78% HL Dean Park, Chapel Level, KIRKCALDY ☎ 01592 261635 📠 01592 261635 46 en suite

Lochore Meadows Lochore Meadows Country Park, Crosshill, Lochgelly KY5 8BA
☎ 01592 583343 📠 01592 583647
e-mail: info@lochore-meadows.co.uk
web: www.lochore-meadows.co.uk

Lochside course with a stream running through it and woodland nearby. Country park offers many leisure facilities.

Lochore Meadows Country Park Golf Course: 9 Holes, 3207yds, Par 72, SSS 71. Club membership 240.

Visitors contact course for details. Handicap certificate. **Societies** booking required. **Green Fees** £12 per round (weekends £15) **Facilities** 🛈 ⬜ **Leisure** fishing, outdoor education centre, childrens play park **Conf** facs **Location** 0.5m W off B920

Hotel ★★★★ 73% HL The Green Hotel, 2 The Muirs, KINROSS ☎ 01577 863467 📠 01577 863467 46 en suite

ST ANDREWS LINKS

FIFE - ST ANDREWS - MAP 12 NO51

Golf was first played here around 1400 and the Old Course is acknowledged worldwide as the Home of Golf. The Old Course has played host to the greatest golfers in the world and many of golf's most dramatic moments. The New Course (6625yds) was opened in 1895, having been laid out by Old Tom Morris. The Jubilee was opened in 1897 and is 6742yds long from the medal tees. A shorter version of the Jubilee Course is also available, known as the Bronze Course, measuring 5573yds. There is no handicap limit for the shorter course and it is best for lower and middle handicap golfers. The Starthtyrum has a shorter, less testing layout, best for high handicap golfers. The nine-hole Balgrove Course, upgraded and re-opened in 1993, is best for beginners and children. The cliff top Castle Course opened in 2008. The facilities and courses at St Andrews make this the largest golf complex in Europe.

Pilmour House KY16 9SF ☎ 01334 466666 🖷 01334 479555
e-mail: linkstrust@standrews.org.uk **web:** www.standrews.org.uk
Old Course: 18 Holes, 6721yds, Par 72, SSS 73, Course record 64.
New Course: 18 Holes, 6625yds, Par 71, SSS 73, Course record 64.
Jubilee Course: 18 Holes, 6742yds, Par 72, SSS 73, Course record 63.
Eden Course: 18 Holes, 6112yds, Par 70, SSS 70.   Strathtyrum Course: 18 Holes, 5094yds, Par 69, SSS 69.
Balgove Course: 9 Holes, 1530yds, Par 30, SSS 30.   Castle Course: 18 Holes, 7200yds, Par 72.
Visitors Old Course Mon-Sat & BHs. Other courses Mon-Sun & BHs. Handicap certificate required for Old Course. Dress code. **Societies** welcome. **Green Fees** contact course for details. **Prof** Steve North **Facilities** ⑪ ⦿ 🖺 ⏛
🖺 🛋 ⛳ 🛍 ✍ 🏌 **Conf** Corporate Hospitality Days **Location** off A91
Hotel ★★★★★ HL The Old Course Hotel, Golf Resort & Spa, ST ANDREWS ☎ 01334 474371 🖷 01334 474371
144 en suite

LUNDIN LINKS   Map 12 NO40

Lundin, Golf Rd KY8 6BA
☎ 01333 320202   📄 01333 329743
e-mail: secretary@lundingolfclub.co.uk
web: www.lundingolfclub.co.uk

A complex links course with open burns, an internal out of bounds (the old railway line), and strategic bunkering. Lundin presents a challenge for the thinking golfer where position from the tee rather than distance will yield just rewards on the scorecard. Renowned for its beautiful greens and some of the most demanding short par 4's in the game of golf.

18 Holes, 6371yds, Par 71, SSS 71, Course record 63. Club membership 950.

Visitors Mon-Fri & BHs. Restricted play weekends. Booking required. Dress code. **Societies** booking required. **Green Fees** £75 per day, £59 per round (£60 weekends) **Course Designer** James Braid **Prof** Ron Walker **Facilities** ⑪ ⑩ 🏌 🖥 🍽 ⚒ 🏡 ⛳ ♦
Location W side of village off A915
Hotel ★★★★ CHH Balbirnie House, Balbirnie Park, MARKINCH
☎ 01592 610066 📄 01592 610066   30 en suite

Lundin Ladies Woodielea Rd KY8 6AR
☎ 01333 320832 & 320022
e-mail: llgolfclub@tiscali.co.uk

Short, lowland course with Bronze Age standing stones on the second fairway and coastal views.

9 Holes, 2365yds, Par 68, SSS 68, Course record 64. Club membership 325.

Visitors Mon, Tue, Thu-Sun & BHs. Handicap certificate. **Societies** welcome. **Green Fees** £16 per 18 holes, £9 per 9 holes (£18/£10 weekends) **Course Designer** James Braid **Facilities** 🖥 ⚒ ⛳ ♦ **Location** W side of village off A915
Hotel ★★★★ CHH Balbirnie House, Balbirnie Park, MARKINCH
☎ 01592 610066 📄 01592 610066   30 en suite

MARKINCH   Map 11 NO20

Balbirnie Park Balbirnie Park KY7 6NR
☎ 01592 612095 & 752006 (tee times)
📄 01592 612383/752006
e-mail: golfpro@balbirniegolf.com
web: www.balbirniegolf.com

Set in the magnificent Balbirnie Park, a fine example of the best in traditional parkland design, with natural contours the inspiration behind the layout. A course that will suit all standards of golfers.

18 Holes, 6214yds, Par 71, SSS 71, Course record 66. Club membership 900.

Visitors contact club for details. Booking required Fri-Sun & BHs. Dress code. **Societies** welcome. **Green Fees** £40 per round, £50 per day (£45/£60 weekends) **Course Designer** Fraser Middleton **Prof** Craig Donnelly **Facilities** ⑪ ⑩ 🏌 🖥 🍽 ⚒ 🏡 ⛳ ♦ 🛒 🏌
♦ **Conf** facs Corporate Hospitality Days **Location** 2m E of Glenrothes, off A92

Balbirnie Park

Hotel ★★★★ CHH Balbirnie House, Balbirnie Park, MARKINCH
☎ 01592 610066 📄 01592 610066   30 en suite

ST ANDREWS   Map 12 NO51

British Golf Museum

☎ 01334 460046 (situated opposite Royal & Ancient Golf Club)

The museum which tells the history of golf from its origins to the present day, is of interest to golfers and non-golfers alike. Themed galleries and interactive displays explore the history of the major championships and the lives of the famous players, and trace the development of golfing equipment. An audio-visual theatre shows historic golfing moments.

Open Apr-Oct, Mon-Sat 9.30-5, Sun 10-5, Nov-Mar, Mon-Sun 10-4. **Admission** Charged (telephone for details).

The Duke's Craigtoun KY16 8NS
☎ 01334 470214   📄 01334 479456
e-mail: reservations@oldcoursehotel.co.uk
web: www.oldcoursehotel.co.uk

Now owned and managed by the Old Course Hotel, with a spectacular setting above St Andrews, this is one of the finest heathland courses in the UK, and the only one in St Andrews. Five sets of tees are on offer, with something for every ability.

continued

The Duke's Course: 18 Holes, 7512yds, Par 71, SSS 77.
Club membership 300.
Visitors contact course for details. Handicap certificate.
Societies booking required. **Green Fees** £110 per round Jun-Oct,
Winter rates available. **Course Designer** Tim Liddy **Prof** Ayden
Roberts-Jones **Facilities** ⒯ ⓘⓄⓘ ⓛ ⓓ ⓓⓘ ⓐ ⓓ ⓓ
ⓓ ⓓ ⓓ ⓓ ⓕ **Leisure** sauna, gymnasium **Conf** facs
Corporate Hospitality Days **Location** A91 to St Andrews, turn off for
Strathkiness, follow signs to The Duke's, Craigtoun
Hotel ★★★★★ HL The Old Course Hotel, Golf Resort & Spa, ST
ANDREWS ☎ 01334 474371 🖹 01334 474371 144 en suite

Fairmont St Andrews KY16 8PN
☎ 01334 837000 🖹 01334 471115
e-mail: standrews.scotland@fairmont.com
web: www.fairmontgolf.com

Two championship seaside courses overlooking the town and the North
Sea coastline. The Torrance has recently been redeveloped to give one
of the finest new courses in Scotland and is a Open Championship
qualifying course. The Kittocks course, a stunning clifftop course with
unique characteristics, has a new layout, providing a challenge to all
levels of golfer.

Torrance: 18 Holes, 7052yds.
Kittocks: 18 Holes, 7250yds. Club membership 134.
Visitors Mon-Sun & BHs. Dress code. **Societies** booking required.
Green Fees £45-£95 **Course Designer** S Torrance/G Sarazen/B Devlin
Prof Fraser Liston/Gary Slatter **Facilities** ⒯ ⓘⓄⓘ ⓛ ⓓ ⓓⓘ ⓐ
ⓓ ⓓⓘ ⓓ ⓓ ⓓ ⓕ **Leisure** heated indoor swimming pool,
sauna, gymnasium, steam room **Conf** facs Corporate Hospitality Days
Location outskirts of town on Crail road

St Andrews see page 347
Pilmour House KY16 9SF
☎ 01334 466666 🖹 01334 479555
e-mail: linkstrust@standrews.org.uk
web: www.standrews.org.uk

Saline Kinneddar Hill KY12 9LT
☎ 01383 852591 🖹 01383 852591
e-mail: salinegolfclub@btconnect.com
web: www.saline-golf-club.co.uk

Hillside parkland course with excellent turf and panoramic view of the
Forth Valley.

9 Holes, 5384yds, Par 68, SSS 66, Course record 62.
Club membership 300.
Visitors contact club for details. Handicap certificate.
Societies booking required. **Green Fees** £12 per day, £8 per 9 holes
(£15 per day Sun) **Facilities** ⒯ by prior arrangement ⓘⓄⓘ by prior
arrangement ⓛ ⓓ ⓓⓘ ⓐ ⓕ **Location** M90 junct 4, 7m W
following signs for Dollar
Hotel ★★★ 71% HL King Malcolm, Queensferry Road,
DUNFERMLINE ☎ 01383 722611 🖹 01383 722611 48 en suite

Scotscraig Golf Rd DD6 9DZ
☎ 01382 552515 🖹 01382 553130
e-mail: scotscraig@scotscraiggolfclub.com
web: www.scotscraiggolfclub.com

Combined with heather and rolling fairways, the course is part
heathland, part links, with the greens being renowned for being
fast and true.

18 Holes, 6550yds, Par 71, SSS 72, Course record 62.
Club membership 835.
Visitors Mon-Sun & BHs. Booking required. Dress code. Handicap
certificate. **Societies** welcome. **Green Fees** £75 per day, £55 per
round (£100/£70am/£60pm weekends) **Course Designer** James
Braid **Prof** Craig Mackie **Facilities** ⒯ ⓘⓄⓘ ⓛ ⓓ ⓓⓘ ⓐ ⓓ
ⓓⓘ ⓓ ⓓ ⓕ **Conf** Corporate Hospitality Days **Location** S side of
village off B945
Hotel ★★★★ 81% HL Apex City Quay Hotel & Spa, 1 West
Victoria Dock Road, DUNDEE ☎ 0845 365 0000 🖹 0845 365 0000
152 en suite

Thornton Station Rd KY1 4DW
☎ 01592 771111 🖹 01592 774955
e-mail: thorntongolf@btconnect.com
web: www.thorntongolfclub.co.uk

A relatively flat, lightly tree-lined parkland course, bounded on three
sides by a river that comes into play at holes 14 to 16.

18 Holes, 6210yds, Par 70, SSS 70, Course record 61.
Club membership 700.
Visitors Mon-Sun & BHs. Booking required. Dress code. Handicap
certificate. **Societies** booking required. **Green Fees** £35 per day, £25
per round (£50/£35 weekends) **Facilities** ⒯ ⓘⓄⓘ ⓛ ⓓ ⓓⓘ ⓐ
ⓓ ⓕ **Conf** Corporate Hospitality Days **Location** 1m E of town off A92
Hotel ★★★★ CHH Balbirnie House, Balbirnie Park, MARKINCH
☎ 01592 610066 🖹 01592 610066 30 en suite

GLASGOW, CITY OF

Alexandra Alexandra Park, Alexandra Pde G31 8SE
☎ 0141 276 0600

Hilly parkland with some woodland. Many bunkers and a barrier of
trees between 1st and 9th fairway.

9 Holes, 2800yds, Par 31, SSS 25.
Club membership 85.
Visitors Mon-Sun & BHs. **Societies** welcome. **Green Fees** phone
Course Designer G McArthur **Facilities** ⓐ **Leisure** bowling green
Location 2m E of city centre off M8/A8
Hotel ★★★ 80% HL Holiday Inn, 161 West Nile Street, GLASGOW
☎ 0141 352 8300 🖹 0141 352 8300 113 en suite

SCOTLAND

Cowglen Barrhead Rd G43 1AU
☎ 0141 632 0556 📠 01505 503000
e-mail: r.jamieson-accountants@rsmail.net
web: www.cowglengolfclub.co.uk

Undulating and challenging parkland course with good views over the Clyde valley to the Campsie Hills. Club and line selection is most important on many holes due to the strategic placing of copses on the course.

18 Holes, 6053yds, Par 70, SSS 70, Course record 64.
Club membership 805.

Visitors Mon-Fri & BHs, Sun pm only. Booking required Sun. Handicap certificate. Dress code **Societies** booking required. **Green Fees** not confirmed **Course Designer** David Adams/James Braid **Prof** Simon Payne **Facilities** ⑪ ⑥ ⓛ ⓛ ⓛ ⓛ ⓛ ⓛ ⓛ **Conf** facs Corporate Hospitality Days **Location** M77 S from Glasgow, Pollok/Barrhead slip road, left at lights, club 0.5m right
Hotel BUD Travelodge Glagow Paisley Road, 251 Paisley Road, GLASGOW ☎ 08719 846 142 📠 08719 846 142 75 en suite

Haggs Castle 70 Dumbreck Rd, Dumbreck G41 4SN
☎ 0141 427 1157 📠 0141 427 1157
e-mail: secretary@haggscastlegolfclub.com
web: www.haggscastlegolfclub.com
Wooded, parkland course where Scottish National Championships and the Glasgow and Scottish Open have been held.

18 Holes, 6426yds, Par 72, SSS 71, Course record 63.
Club membership 900.

Visitors dress code. **Societies** booking required. **Green Fees** £40 per round, £50 per day **Course Designer** Dave Thomas (1998) **Prof** Campbell Elliott **Facilities** ⑪ ⑥ ⓛ ⓛ ⓛ ⓛ ⓛ ⓛ ⓛ **Conf** Corporate Hospitality Days **Location** M77 junct 1, 2.5m SW of city centre
Hotel ★★★★ 72% HL Menzies Glasgow, 27 Washington Street, GLASGOW ☎ 0141 222 2929 & 270 2323 📠 0141 222 2929 141 en suite

Kirkhill Greenless Rd, Cambuslang G72 8YN
☎ 0141 641 8499 📠 0141 641 8499
e-mail: carol.downes@btconnect.com
web: www.kirkhillgolfclub.org.uk
Meadowland course designed by James Braid.

18 Holes, 6030yds, Par 70, SSS 70, Course record 63.
Club membership 650.

Visitors Mon-Fri. Booking required. Handicap certificate. Dress code. **Societies** booking required. **Green Fees** not confirmed **Course Designer** J Braid **Prof** Duncan Williamson **Facilities** ⑪ ⑥ ⓛ ⓛ ⓛ ⓛ ⓛ ⓛ **Location** 5m SE of city centre off A749

Hotel ★★★ 79% HL Bothwell Bridge, 89 Main Street, BOTHWELL ☎ 01698 852246 📠 01698 852246 90 en suite

Knightswood Lincoln Av G13 5QZ
☎ 0141 959 6358
9 Holes, 5586yds, Par 68, SSS 67.
Facilities ⓛ **Location** 4m W of city centre off A82
Telephone for further details
Hotel ★★★ 71% HL Best Western Glasgow Pond, Great Western Road, GLASGOW ☎ 0141 334 8161 📠 0141 334 8161 137 en suite

Lethamhill 1240 Cumbernauld Rd G33 1AH
☎ 0141 770 6220 & 0141 770 7135 📠 1041 770 0520
18 Holes, 5859yds, Par 70, SSS 69.
Facilities ⓛ **Location** 3m NE of city centre on A80
Telephone for further details
Hotel ★★★★ 74% HL Millennium Hotel Glasgow, George Square, GLASGOW ☎ 0141 332 6711 📠 0141 332 6711 116 en suite

Linn Park Simshill Rd G44 5EP
☎ 0141 633 0377
Municipal parkland/woodland course with six par 3s in outward half.
18 Holes, 5132yds, Par 67, SSS 66, Course record 61.
Club membership 83.
Visitors Mon-Sun & BHs. Booking required. **Societies** booking required. **Green Fees** £10.30 per round summer, £9.30 winter. **Facilities** ⓛ **Location** 4m S of city centre off B766, between Castle Milk and Cathcart
Hotel ★★★ 73% HL Jurys Inn Glasgow, 80 Jamaica Street, GLASGOW ☎ 0141 314 4800 📠 0141 314 4800 321 en suite

Pollok 90 Barrhead Rd G43 1BG
☎ 0141 632 4351 📠 0141 649 1398
e-mail: secretary@pollokgolf.com
web: www.pollokgolf.com
Parkland with woods and river. Gentle walking until the 18th hole.
18 Holes, 6358yds, Par 71, SSS 71, Course record 62.
Club membership 620.
Visitors contact club for details. Dress code. **Societies** welcome. **Green Fees** not confirmed **Course Designer** J Douglas & Alistair McKenzie **Facilities** ⑪ ⓛ ⓛ ⓛ ⓛ ⓛ ⓛ ⓛ **Conf** facs Corporate Hospitality Days **Location** M77 junct 2, S to A762 Barrhead Rd, 1m E
Hotel ★★★★ 72% HL Menzies Glasgow, 27 Washington Street, GLASGOW ☎ 0141 222 2929 & 270 2323 📠 0141 222 2929 141 en suite

Williamwood Clarkston Rd G44 3YR
☎ 0141 637 1783 📠 0141 571 0166
18 Holes, 5878yds, Par 68, SSS 69, Course record 61.
Course Designer James Braid **Location** 5m S of city centre on B767
Telephone for further details
Hotel ★★★★ 72% HL Menzies Glasgow, 27 Washington Street, GLASGOW ☎ 0141 222 2929 & 270 2323 📠 0141 222 2929 141 en suite

HIGHLAND

ALNESS
Map 14 NH66

Alness Ardross Rd IV17 0QA
☎ 01349 883877
web: www.alness-golfclub.co.uk
18 Holes, 4886yds, Par 67, SSS 64, Course record 62.
Prof Gary Lister **Facilities** ⓣ ⑩ ⓑ ⌺ ⚑ ⚑ ⚓ ⚐ ⚐
🛶 ⚐ 🎣 **Leisure** fishing **Conf** facs Corporate Hospitality Days
Location 0.5m N off A9
Telephone for further details
Hotel ★★★★ 78% CHH Kincraig House, INVERGORDON
☎ 01349 852587 📠 01349 852587 15 en suite

ARISAIG
Map 13 NM68

Traigh Traigh PH39 4NT
☎ 01687 450337 📠 01678 450293
web: www.traighgolf.co.uk
According to at least one newspaper Traigh is 'probably the most
beautifully sited nine-hole golf course in the world'. True or not,
Traigh lies alongside sandy beaches with views to Skye and the Inner
Hebrides. The feature of the course is a line of grassy hills, originally
sand dunes, that rise to some 60ft, and provide a challenge to the
keenest golfer.
*Traigh Golf Course: 9 Holes, 2456yds, Par 68, SSS 65,
Course record 67. Club membership 150.*
Visitors contact club for details. **Societies** booking required. **Green
Fees** £16 per day **Course Designer** John Salvesen 1994 **Facilities** ⌺
⚓ ⚐ ⚐ **Location** A830 to Arisaig, signed onto B8008, 2m N of
Arisaig
Hotel ★★ 72% HL West Highland, MALLAIG ☎ 01687 462210
📠 01687 462210 34 en suite

AVIEMORE
Map 14 NH81

Spey Valley Aviemore Highland Resort PH22 1PJ
☎ 01479 815100 📠 01479 812128
web: www.macdonaldhotels.co.uk
Spey Valley Golf Course: 18 Holes, 7153yds, Par 72.
Course Designer Dave Thomas **Location** leave A9 signposted
Aviemore on B970. Follow road to village then turn off for Dalfaber and
follow signs for golf course.
Telephone for further details
Guesthouse ★★★★ GH Ravenscraig, Grampian Road, AVIEMORE
☎ 01479 810278 📠 01479 810278 12 en suite

BOAT OF GARTEN
Map 14 NH91

Boat of Garten PH24 3BQ
☎ 01479 831282 📠 01479 831523
e-mail: office@boatgolf.com
web: www.boatgolf.com
In the heart of the Cairngorm National Park, this prime example
of James Braid's design genius is cut through moorland and
birch forest, maximising the natural landscape. A beautiful and
challenging course set amid stunning scenery.
*18 Holes, 5876yds, Par 70, SSS 69, Course record 67.
Club membership 650.*

Visitors handicap certificate. Dress code. **Societies** booking
required. **Green Fees** £44 per day, £34 per round (£49/£39
weekends) **Course Designer** James Braid **Prof** Ross Harrower
Facilities ⓣ ⑩ ⓑ ⌺ ⚑ ⚓ ⚐ ⚐ ⚐ ⚐
Leisure hard tennis courts **Conf** Corporate Hospitality Days
Location E side of village

Boat of Garten

Hotel ★★★ 82% HL Boat, BOAT OF GARTEN ☎ 01479 831258
& 831696 📠 01479 831258 34 en suite

BONAR BRIDGE
Map 14 NH69

Bonar Bridge-Ardgay Migdale Rd IV24 3EJ
☎ 01863 766199
e-mail: bonar-ardgay-golf@tiscali.co.uk
Wooded moorland course with picturesque views of hills and loch.
*Bonar Bridge/Ardgay Golf Club: 9 Holes, 5162yds, Par 68,
SSS 65. Club membership 250.*
Visitors contact club for details. **Societies** booking required. **Green
Fees** £18 per day **Facilities** ⓣ ⓑ ⌺ ⚓ ⚐ ⚐ **Location** 0.5m
E
Guesthouse ★★★ GA Kyle House, Dornoch Road, BONAR BRIDGE
☎ 01863 766360 📠 01863 766360 5 rms (3 en suite)

BRORA
Map 14 NC90

Brora Golf Rd KW9 6QS
☎ 01408 621417 📠 01408 622157
e-mail: secretary@broragolf.co.uk
web: www.broragolf.co.uk
Natural seaside links with little rough and fine views. Some testing
holes including the 17th Tarbatness, so called because of the
lighthouse which gives the line; the elevated tee is one of the best
driving holes in Scotland.
*18 Holes, 6110yds, Par 69, SSS 70, Course record 61.
Club membership 700.*
Visitors contact club for details. **Societies** Booking required. **Green
Fees** not confirmed **Course Designer** James Braid **Prof** Brian
Anderson **Facilities** ⓣ ⑩ ⓑ ⌺ ⚑ ⚓ ⚐ ⚐ ⚐ 🛶 ⚐
Location E side of village, signs to Beach Car Park
Hotel ★★★★ 75% HL Royal Marine, Golf Road, BRORA
☎ 01408 621252 📠 01408 621252 21 en suite

CARRBRIDGE
Map 14 NH92

Carrbridge Inverness Rd PH23 3AU
☎ 08444 141415 📠 0871 288 1014
e-mail: katie@carrbridgegolf.co.uk
web: www.carrbridgegolf.com

Challenging part-parkland, part-moorland course with magnificent views of the Cairngorms, this is a fine 9-hole course that is a challenge for more experienced golfers, and loads of fun for the less experienced.

9 Holes, 5402yds, Par 71, SSS 68, Course record 63. Club membership 450.

Visitors Mon-Sun & BHs. Booking required. Dress code. Handicap certificate. **Societies** booking required. **Green Fees** not confirmed **Facilities** ⑪ ⑩ by prior arrangement 🏌 ⬚ 🏊 🏠 ⛳ ✎ **Conf** Corporate Hospitality Days **Location** N side of village **Hotel** ★★★ 74% SHL Dalrachney Lodge, CARRBRIDGE
☎ 01479 841252 📠 01479 841252 11 en suite

DORNOCH
Map 14 NH78

Royal Dornoch see page 353
Golf Rd IV25 3LW
☎ 01862 810219 ext.1 📠 01862 810792
e-mail: bookings@royaldornoch.com
web: www.royaldornoch.com

DURNESS
Map 14 NC46

Durness Balnakeil IV27 4PG
☎ 01971 511364 📠 01971 511321
e-mail: lucy@durnessgolfclub.org
web: www.durnessgolfclub.org

A nine-hole course set in tremendous scenery overlooking Balnakeil Bay. Part links and part inland with water hazards. Off alternative tees for second nine holes giving surprising variety. Tremendous last hole played over a deep gully to the green over 100yds away.

9 Holes, 5555yds, Par 70, SSS 67, Course record 69. Club membership 150.

Visitors Mon-Sat & BHs. **Societies** booking required. **Green Fees** £20 per day, £18 per 18 holes, £15 per 9 holes **Course Designer** F Keith/L Ross/I Morrison **Facilities** ⑪ ⬚ 🏊 ⛳ ✎ **Leisure** fishing **Conf** Corporate Hospitality Days **Location** 1m W of village overlooking Balnakeil Bay

FORT AUGUSTUS
Map 14 NH30

Fort Augustus Markethill PH32 4DS
☎ 01320 366660
e-mail: fortaugustusgc@aol.com
web: www.fortaugustusgc.webeden.co.uk

Fort Augustus is a traditional heathland course, which many consider the most challenging 9 hole in Scotland. The dense gorse and heather that line the long narrow fairways demand accurate driving. The course is also bordered by the tree-lined Caledonian canal.

9 Holes, 5379yds, Par 67, SSS 67, Course record 67. Club membership 136.

Visitors Mon-Sun & BHs. Booking required weekends & BHs. **Societies** booking required. **Green Fees** £20 per day, £15 per round **Course Designer** Colt **Facilities** 🏌 ⬚ 🏊 🏠 ⛳ ✎ **Location** 1m SW on A82 **Hotel** ★★★ 86% HL Lovat Arms, Loch Ness Side, FORT AUGUSTUS
☎ 0845 450 1100 & 01456 459250 📠 0845 450 1100 29 en suite

FORTROSE
Map 14 NH75

Fortrose & Rosemarkie Ness Road East IV10 8SE
☎ 01381 620529 📠 01381 621328
e-mail: secretary@fortrosegolfclub.co.uk
web: www.fortrosegolfclub.co.uk

Links set on a peninsula with the sea on three sides. Easy walking, good views. Designed by James Braid. The club was formed in 1888.

18 Holes, 5890yds, Par 71, SSS 69, Course record 63. Club membership 770.

Visitors Mon-Sun & BHs. Booking required. **Societies** welcome. **Green Fees** not confirmed **Course Designer** James Braid **Facilities** ⑪ ⑩ 🏌 ⬚ 🏊 🏠 ⛳ ✎ **Conf** Corporate Hospitality Days **Location** A9 N over Kessock Bridge, signs to Munlochy **Hotel** ★★★★ 74% HL Kingsmills, Culcabock Road, INVERNESS
☎ 01463 237166 & 257100 📠 01463 237166 77 en suite

FORT WILLIAM
Map 14 NN17

Fort William Torlundy PH33 6SN
☎ 01397 704464
e-mail: fwgolf41@msn.com
web: www.fortwilliamgolf.co.uk

Spectacular moorland location looking onto the north face of Ben Nevis.

18 Holes, 6217yds, Par 72, SSS 71, Course record 67. Club membership 420.

Visitors Mon-Sun & BHs. Booking required weekends & BHs. Dress code. **Societies** booking required. **Green Fees** not confirmed **Course Designer** Hamilton Stutt **Facilities** 🏌 ⬚ 🏊 🏠 ⛳ ✎ **Conf** Corporate Hospitality Days **Location** 3m NE on A82 **Hotel** ★★★ 80% HL Moorings, Banavie, FORT WILLIAM
☎ 01397 772797 📠 01397 772797 27 en suite

GAIRLOCH
Map 14 NG87

Gairloch IV21 2BE
☎ 01445 712407 📠 01445 712865
e-mail: gairlochgolfclub@hotmail.co.uk
web: www.gairlochgolfclub.co.uk

Fine seaside links course running along Gairloch Sands with good views over the sea to Skye. In windy conditions each hole is affected. Founded in 1898, the course, although short is challenging for all golfers.

9 Holes, 4108yds, Par 62, SSS 62, Course record 57. Club membership 275.

Visitors contact club for details. **Societies** welcome. **Green Fees** phone **Course Designer** Capt Burgess **Facilities** ⑪ 🏌 ⬚ 🏊 🏠 ⛳ ✎ **Conf** Corporate Hospitality Days **Location** 1m S on A832 **Hotel** ★★★ SHL Pool House Hotel, POOLEWE, Wester Ross
☎ 01445 781272 📠 01445 781272 7 en suite

ROYAL DORNOCH

HIGHLAND - DORNOCH - MAP 14 NH78

The championship course was recently rated 3rd among the world's top courses outside the USA, and is a links of rare subtlety. It appears amicable but proves very challenging in play with stiff breezes and tight lies. It is wild and isolated with a pure white sandy beach dividing it from the Dornoch Firth and has hosted golfers since 1616. It was granted a royal charter by King Edward VII in 1906. The unique features of the links land have been used to create a magical golfing experience. The 18-hole Struie links course provides, in a gentler style, an enjoyable test of a golfer's accuracy for players of all abilities. Every golfer should make at least one pilgrimage to this superb setting.

Golf Rd IV25 3LW ☎ 01862 810219 ext.1 📠 01862 810792
e-mail: bookings@royaldornoch.com **web:** www.royaldornoch.com
Championship: 18 Holes, 6595yds, Par 70, SSS 73, Course record 65.
Struie Course: 18 Holes, 6276yds, Par 72, SSS 70, Course record 68. Club membership 1700.
Visitors Mon-Sun & BHs. Booking advisable. **Societies** booking required. **Green Fees** Championship course £82 per round (£92 weekends), Struie course £35 all week. **Course Designer** Tom Morris **Prof** A Skinner **Facilities** ⊕ 🍴 🍺 🖥 🐟 🛆 🏠 ⛳ ✦ 🛺 ✦ **Leisure** hard tennis courts **Conf** facs Corporate Hospitality Days **Location** E side of town
Hotel ★★★ 74% HL Dornoch Castle Hotel, Castle Street, DORNOCH ☎ 01862 810216 📠 01862 810216 21 en suite

GOLSPIE
Map 14 NH89

Golspie Ferry Rd KW10 6ST
☎ 01408 633266
e-mail: info@golspie-golf-club.co.uk
web: www-golspie-golf-club.co.uk
Founded in 1889, laid out by Archibald Simpson in 1908 and redesigned in 1926 by James Braid, Golspie's seaside links course offers easy walking and natural hazards including beach, heather, and woodland. Spectacular scenery.

18 Holes, 5980yds, Par 69, SSS 69, Course record 64. Club membership 300.

Visitors Mon-Sun & BHs. Booking advisable. **Societies** booking required. **Green Fees** £45 per day, £35 per round **Course Designer** Archibald Simpson/James Braid **Facilities** ⑪ ℐ◎ℐ ⓛ ⌂ ⸼ ⌘ ☖ ⌐ ⌖ ◇ ✎ ⌖ **Location** 0.5m S off A9 at S entry to Golspie

Hotel ★★★★ 75% HL Royal Marine, Golf Road, BRORA
☎ 01408 621252 📠 01408 621252 21 en suite

GRANTOWN-ON-SPEY
Map 14 NJ02

Craggan Craggan PH26 3NT
☎ 01479 873283 📠 01479 872325
e-mail: fhglaing@btopenworld.com
web: www.cragganforleisure.co.uk
A golf course in miniature set in stunning scenery on the edge of the Cairngorms National Park.

Craggan Golf Course: 18 Holes, 2400yds, Par 54, SSS 54, Course record 52. Club membership 400.

Visitors Mon-Sun & BHs. **Societies** booking required. **Green Fees** not confirmed **Course Designer** Bill Mitchel **Facilities** ⑪ ⓛ ⌂ ⌐ ⌖ ☖ ⌐ ✎ **Leisure** fishing, biking **Conf** Corporate Hospitality Days **Location** off A95, 1m S of Grantown-on-Spey

Hotel ★★ 85% SHL Culdearn House, Woodlands Terrace,
GRANTOWN ON SPEY ☎ 01479 872106 📠 01479 872106 7 en suite

Grantown-on-Spey Golf Course Rd PH26 3HY
☎ 01479 872079 📠 01479 873725
e-mail: secretary@grantownonspeygolfclub.co.uk
web: www.grantownonspeygolfclub.co.uk

Parkland and woodland course. Part easy walking, remainder hilly. The 7th to 13th holes really sort out the golfers.

18 Holes, 5710yds, Par 70, SSS 68, Course record 60. Club membership 800.

Visitors Mon-Sun & BHs. Booking advisable. Dress code. **Societies** booking required. **Green Fees** £26 per day, £29 per round (£41/£34 weekends) **Course Designer** A Brown/W Park/J Braid

Facilities ⑪ ℐ◎ℐ by prior arrangement ⓛ ⌂ ⌐ ⌖ ☖ ⌐ ✎ ⌘ ✎ **Conf** Corporate Hospitality Days **Location** NE side of town centre

Hotel ★★ 85% SHL Culdearn House, Woodlands Terrace,
GRANTOWN ON SPEY ☎ 01479 872106 📠 01479 872106 7 en suite

HELMSDALE
Map 14 ND01

Helmsdale Golf Rd KW8 6JL
☎ 01431 821063
web: www.helmsdale.org
Sheltered, undulating course following the line of the Helmsdale River.

9 Holes, 1860yds, Par 60, SSS 60. Club membership 58.

Visitors Mon-Sun & BHs. **Societies** booking required. **Green Fees** £15 per 18 holes **Facilities** ⌂ **Location** NW side of town on A896

Hotel ★★★★ 75% HL Royal Marine, Golf Road, BRORA
☎ 01408 621252 📠 01408 621252 21 en suite

INVERGORDON
Map 14 NH76

Invergordon King George St IV18 0BD
☎ 01349 852715
e-mail: invergordongolf@tiscali.co.uk
web: www.invergordongolf.co.uk
A windy 18-hole parkland course, with woodland and good views over Cromarty Firth to the distant mountains. Very good greens and a fair challenge for all golfers, especially if the wind is from the south west. Four par 3s and one par 5.

18 Holes, 6030yds, Par 69, SSS 69, Course record 63. Club membership 266.

Visitors Mon-Sun & BHs. Booking required Sat. **Societies** booking required. **Green Fees** £25 per day, £20 per round. **Course Designer** A Rae **Facilities** ⑪ ⓛ ⌂ ⌐ ⌖ ☖ ⌐ ✎ **Conf** Corporate Hospitality Days **Location** from A9 take B817 for 2m entering town via High St, after approx 300 yds turn left into Albany Rd and left again over railway bridge. Continue for 0.6m into club car park).

Hotel ★★★★ 78% CHH Kincraig House, INVERGORDON
☎ 01349 852587 📠 01349 852587 15 en suite

INVERNESS
Map 14 NH64

Inverness Culcabock IV2 3XQ
☎ 01463 239882 📠 01463 240616
e-mail: igc@freeuk.com
web: www.invernessgolfclub.co.uk
A parkland course with tree lined fairways. The Mill burn meanders through the course, posing a challenge at several holes. The 313 yd 6th hole requires caution from the tee as a long drive may reach the burn that guards the green. The 14th (Midmills)is a hole of exceptional quality with a dog leg to the right which obscures a view of the green with a wayward shot. At 461 yds the long par 4 18th is a demanding finish, especially into a north east breeze.

18 Holes, 6256yds, Par 69, SSS 70, Course record 61. Club membership 1250.

Visitors Mon-Sun & BHs. Booking required weekends Handicap certificate. Dress code. **Societies** booking required. **Green Fees** £52 per day, £38 per round **Course Designer** J Fraser/G Smith **Prof** Alistair P Thomson **Facilities** ⑪ ℐ◎ℐ ⓛ ⌂ ⌐ ⌖ ☖ ⌐ ✎ **Leisure** chipping green **Conf** Corporate Hospitality Days **Location** A96 towards Inverness. Pass retail park on left and straight on at rdbt.

continued

At next rdbt take 2nd exit (B865), then at next rdbt take first exit (B9006). At next rdbt take 2nd exit into Culcabock Rd, golf club 200 yds on left
Hotel ★★★★ 74% HL Kingsmills, Culcabock Road, INVERNESS
☎ 01463 237166 & 257100 📄 01463 237166 77 en suite

Loch Ness Fairways, Castle Heather IV2 6AA
☎ 01463 713335 📄 01463 712695
e-mail: info@golflochness.com
web: www.golflochness.com

Course with two 18 hole options and a 9 hole family course with seven par 3's and two par 4's and small undulating greens and deep bunkers to test short game skills. The New and Old courses combine several holes giving a great variety from the 550 yard 2nd hole to the 76 yard hole called Chance which is played over a deep gully.
Old Course: 18 Holes, 6772yds, Par 73, SSS 72,
Course record 67.
New Course: 18 Holes, 5907yds, Par 70, SSS 69,
Course record 68.
Family Course: 9 Holes, 1440yds, Par 29.
Club membership 600.
Visitors Mon-Sun & BHs. Dress code. **Societies** welcome. **Green Fees** £45-£55 per day, £30-£35 per round. Family Course £10 **Course Designer** Caddies Golf Course Design **Prof** Martin Piggot **Facilities** ⊕ ⊘ ⊫ ⊔ ⊪ ⊿ 🏠 ⊓ ◇ ✍ 🏌 ✍ ✦ **Leisure** sports injury clinic, indoor bowls. **Conf** facs Corporate Hospitality Days **Location** SW outskirts of Inverness, along bypass
Hotel 66% Loch Ness House, Glenurquhart Road, INVERNESS
☎ 01463 231248 📄 01463 231248 21 en suite

Torvean Glenurquhart Rd IV3 8JN
☎ 01463 225651 (Office) 📄 01463 711417
e-mail: sarah@torveangolfclub.com
web: www.torveangolfclub.co.uk
Public parkland course, easy walking, good views. One of the longest par 5s in the north at 565yds. Three ponds come into play at the 8th, 15th and 17th holes.
18 Holes, 5799yds, Par 69, SSS 68, Course record 63.
Club membership 800.
Visitors contact club for details. **Societies** welcome **Green Fees** not confirmed **Course Designer** Hamilton **Facilities** ⊕ ⊘ ⊫ ⊔ ⊪ ⊿ 🏠 ⊓ ✍ **Conf** Corporate Hospitality Days **Location** 1.5m SW on A82
Hotel ★★★ 77% HL Royal Highland, Station Square, Academy Street, INVERNESS ☎ 01463 231926 & 251451 📄 01463 231926 85 en suite

KINGUSSIE
Map 14 NH70

Kingussie Gynack Rd PH21 1LR
☎ 01540 661600 📄 01540 662066
e-mail: sec@kingussie-golf.co.uk
web: www.kingussie-golf.co.uk
Upland course with natural hazards and magnificent views. Stands about 1000ft above sea level at its highest point, and the River Gynack, which runs through the course, comes into play on five holes. Golf has been played here for over 100years and some tight fairways and deceptive par threes make the course a challenge for all golfers.
18 Holes, 5500yds, Par 67, SSS 68, Course record 61.
Club membership 650.
Visitors contact club for details. **Societies** welcome. **Green Fees** not confirmed **Course Designer** Vardon **Facilities** ⊕ ⊘ ⊫ ⊔ ⊪ ⊿ 🏠 ⊓ 🏌 ✍ **Location** 0.25m N off A86

LOCHCARRON
Map 14 NG83

Lochcarron IV54 8YS
☎ 01599 577219
web: www.lochcarrongolf.co.uk
9 Holes, 3575yds, Par 60, SSS 60, Course record 58.
Facilities ⊕ ⊫ ⊔ ⊿ ⊓ **Location** 1m E of Lochcarron by A896
Telephone for further details
Hotel ★★★ 75% SHL The Plockton, 41 Harbour Street, PLOCKTON
☎ 01599 544274 📄 01599 544274 15 en suite

LYBSTER
Map 15 ND23

Lybster Main St KW3 6AE
☎ 01593 721486 & 721316
web: www.lybstergolfclub.co.uk
Picturesque, short heathland course, easy walking.
9 Holes, 2002yds, Par 62, SSS 61, Course record 57.
Club membership 140.
Visitors contact club for details. **Societies** welcome. **Green Fees** £10 per day **Facilities** ⊿ **Location** E side of village
Hotel ★★★ 75% HL Mackay's, Union Street, WICK
☎ 01955 602323 📄 01955 602323 30 en suite

MUIR OF ORD
Map 14 NH55

Muir of Ord Great North Rd IV6 7SX
☎ 01463 870825 📄 01463 871867
e-mail: muir.golf@btconnect.com
web: www.muirofordgolfclub.com
Long-established (1875) heathland course with tight fairways and easy walking. Playable all year.
18 Holes, 5542yds, Par 68, SSS 68, Course record 61.
Club membership 750.
Visitors Mon-Sun & BHs. Booking required. Dress code.
Societies booking required **Green Fees** £31 per day, £27 per round (weekends £42/£38) **Course Designer** James Braid **Facilities** ⊕ by prior arrangement 🏌 by prior arrangement ⊫ ⊔ ⊪ ⊿ 🏠 ✍ 🏌 ✍ **Conf** Corporate Hospitality Days **Location** S side of village on A862
Hotel ★★★ 74% HL Priory, The Square, BEAULY ☎ 01463 782309 📄 01463 782309 37 en suite

NAIRN — Map 14 NH85

Nairn Seabank Rd IV12 4HB
☎ 01667 453208 📠 01667 456328
e-mail: bookings@nairngolfclub.co.uk
web: www.nairngolfclub.co.uk
Championship, seaside links founded in 1887 and created from a wilderness of heather and whin. Designed by Archie Simpson, Old Tom Morris and James Braid. Opening holes stretch out along the shoreline with the turn for home at the 10th. The Nairn will be the 2012 Curtis Cup venue.

The Nairn Golf Club: 18 Holes, 6430yds, Par 71, SSS 73, Course record 64.
Newton: 9 Holes, 3542yds, Par 58, SSS 57.
Club membership 1150.

Visitors contact club for details. **Societies** booking required. **Green Fees** not confirmed **Course Designer** A Simpson/Old Tom Morris/James Braid **Prof** Robin P Fyfe **Facilities** ⑪ ⑩ 🍴 ☕ ☂ ⚲ 🏠 ☂ ⚲ 🏌 **Leisure** snooker **Location** 16m E of Inverness on A96
Hotel ★★★★ 74% HL Golf View Hotel & Leisure Club, The Seafront, NAIRN ☎ 01667 452301 📠 01667 452301   42 en suite

Nairn Dunbar Lochloy Rd IV12 5AE
☎ 01667 452741 📠 01667 456897
e-mail: secretary@nairndunbar.com
web: www.nairndunbar.com
Links course with sea views and testing gorse and whin-lined fairways. Testing hole: Long Peter (527yds).

18 Holes, 6765yds, Par 72, SSS 74, Course record 64.
Club membership 1200.

Visitors Mon-Sun & BHs. Booking required. Dress code.
Societies booking required. **Green Fees** £55 per day, £42 per round (£70/£50 weekends) **Prof** David Torrance **Facilities** ⑪ ⑩ 🍴 ☕ 🏌 ☂ ⚲ 🏠 ☂ ⚲ **Conf** facs Corporate Hospitality Days **Location** E side of town off A96
Hotel ★★ 61% HL Alton Burn, Alton Burn Road, NAIRN ☎ 01667 452051 & 453325 📠 01667 452051   23 en suite

NETHY BRIDGE — Map 14 NJ02

Abernethy PH25 3EB
☎ 01479 821305 📠 01479 821305
e-mail: info@abernethygolfclub.com
web: www.abernethygolfclub.com
Traditional Highland course built on moorland surrounded by pine trees and offering a great variety of shot making for the low handicapped or casual visitor. The 2nd hole, although very short is played across bogland and a B road to a two-tiered green. The small and fast greens are the most undulating and tricky in the valley. The Abernethy forest lies on the boundary and from many parts of the course there are splendid views of Strathspey.

9 Holes, 2526yds, Par 66, SSS 66. Club membership 400.
Visitors Mon-Sun & BHs. Booking advisable. **Societies** booking required. **Green Fees** £18 per day (£20 weekends), late day £10 (£12 weekends) **Facilities** ⑪ ⑩ 🍴 ☕ ☂ 🏠 ☂ ⚲ **Conf** Corporate Hospitality Days **Location** N side of village on B970
Hotel ★★ 78% HL The Mountview Hotel, Grantown Road, NETHY BRIDGE ☎ 01479 821248 📠 01479 821248   12 en suite

NEWTONMORE — Map 14 NN79

Newtonmore Golf Course Rd PH20 1AT
☎ 01540 673878 📠 01540 673878
web: www.newtonmoregolf.com
18 Holes, 6031yds, Par 70, SSS 69, Course record 64.
Prof Robert Henderson **Facilities** ⑪ ⑩ 🍴 ☕ 🏌 ☂ 🏠 ☂ ⚲ 🏌 **Location** E side of town off A9
Telephone for further details

REAY — Map 14 NC96

Reay KW14 7RE
☎ 01847 811288 📠 01847 894189
web: www.reaygolfclub.co.uk
18 Holes, 5831yds, Par 69, SSS 69, Course record 64.
Course Designer Braid **Location** 11m W of Thurso on A836
Telephone for further details

STRATHPEFFER — Map 14 NH45

Strathpeffer Spa IV14 9AS
☎ 01997 421219 & 421011 📠 01997 421011
e-mail: mail@strathpeffergolf.co.uk
web: www.strathpeffergolf.co.uk
Beautiful, testing upland course in this historic village. Many natural hazards alongside eight sand bunkers on the course and the course's claim to fame is the 1st hole which features the longest drop from tee to green in Scotland. Stunning views.

18 Holes, 4956yds, Par 67, SSS 65, Course record 62.
Club membership 400.
Visitors Mon-Sun & BHs. Booking required Tue, Wed, weekends & BHs. Dress code. **Societies** booking required. **Green Fees** not confirmed **Course Designer** Willie Park/Tom Morris **Facilities** ⑪ 🍴 ☕ 🏌 ☂ 🏠 ☂ 🏌 ⚲ **Conf** Corporate Hospitality Days **Location** 0.25m N of village off A834, signed
Hotel ★★★ 73% SHL Achilty, CONTIN ☎ 01997 421355 📠 01997 421355   11 en suite

TAIN — Map 14 NH78

Tain Chapel Rd IV19 1JE
☎ 01862 892314 📠 01862 892099
e-mail: info@tain-golfclub.co.uk
web: www.tain-golfclub.co.uk

Links course with river affecting three holes; easy walking, fine views. Many of the original Old Tom Morris-designed holes are still in play.

continued

18 Holes, 6404yds, Par 70, SSS 72, Course record 64.
Club membership 600.

Visitors Mon-Sun & BHs. **Societies** welcome. **Green Fees** £55 per day, £40 per round (£60/£45 weekends) **Course Designer** Old Tom Morris **Facilities** ⊕ ⊙ ⓘ ⓛ ⊡ ⓡ ⓐ ⓔ ⓟ ✦ ⓜ ✦ **Leisure** 3 practice nets, 3 bay driving unit, short game area **Conf** Corporate Hospitality Days **Location** E side of town centre off B9174
Hotel ★★★ 74% HL Dornoch Castle Hotel, Castle Street, DORNOCH
☎ 01862 810216 📄 01862 810216 21 en suite

THURSO   Map 15 ND16

Thurso Newlands of Geise KW14 7XD
☎ 01847 893807
web: europgolf.com

Parkland course, windy, but with fine views of Dunnet Head and the Orkney Islands. Tree-lined fairways but 4th and 16th holes are testing into the prevailing wind. The 13th is a short par 4 but has a testing drive over a burn with heather on left and punishing rough on right.

18 Holes, 5853yds, Par 69, SSS 69, Course record 61.
Club membership 320.

Visitors Mon-Sun & BHs. Booking required weekends.
Societies welcome. **Green Fees** £20 per day **Course Designer** W S Stewart **Facilities** ⊡ ⓡ ⓐ ⓟ ✦ **Conf** Corporate Hospitality Days **Location** 2m SW of Thurso on B874

ULLAPOOL

Ullapool The Clubhouse, North Rd, Morefield IV26 2TH
☎ 01854 613323
web: www.ullapool-golf.co.uk
Seaside/parkland course with fine views.

Ullapool Golf Course: 9 Holes, 5281yds, Par 70, SSS 67, Course record 71. Club membership 140.

Visitors Mon-Fri & BHs. **Societies** booking required. **Green Fees** £20 per day, £15 per 9 holes **Course Designer** Souters **Facilities** ⊡ ⓡ ⓐ ⓔ ⓟ ✦ **Conf** Corporate Hospitality Days **Location** on A835 at N end of village

WICK   Map 15 ND35

Wick Reiss KW1 4RW
☎ 01955 602726
web: www.wickgolfclub.com
18 Holes, 6123yds, Par 69, SSS 71, Course record 63.
Facilities ⓛ ⊡ ⓡ ⓐ ⓟ ✦ **Location** 3.5m N off A9
Telephone for further details
Hotel ★★★ 75% HL Mackay's, Union Street, WICK
☎ 01955 602323 📄 01955 602323 30 en suite

INVERCLYDE

GOUROCK   Map 10 NS27

Gourock Cowal View PA19 1HD
☎ 01475 631001 & 636834 (pro) 📄 01475 638307
e-mail: secretary@gourockgolfclub.com
web: wwww.gourockgolfclub.com

Moorland course with hills and dells. Testing 8th hole, par 5 and a fine finishing hole. Magnificent views over Firth of Clyde.

18 Holes, 6408yds, Par 73, SSS 72, Course record 64.
Club membership 803.

Visitors Mon, Tue, Thu, Fri & Sun except BHs. Sat after 3pm. Dress code. **Societies** booking required. **Green Fees** £40 per day, £30 per round (£52/£38 weekends) **Course Designer** J Braid/H Cotton **Prof** Derek Watters **Facilities** ⊕ ⊙ ⓘ ⓛ ⊡ ⓡ ⓐ ⓔ ⓟ ✦ ⓜ ✦ **Conf** Corporate Hospitality Days **Location** SW side of town off A770
Hotel ★★ 75% HL Selborne, Clyde Street, West Bay, DUNOON
☎ 01369 702761 📄 01369 702761 98 en suite

GREENOCK   Map 10 NS27

Greenock Forsyth St PA16 8RE
☎ 01475 720793 📄 01475 791912
e-mail: secretary@greenockgolfclub.co.uk
web: www.greenockgolfclub.co.uk
Testing moorland courses with panoramic views of Clyde Estuary.

18 Holes, 5838yds, Par 69, SSS 69.
9 Holes, 2160yds, Par 32, SSS 32. Club membership 700.
Visitors Mon, Tue, Thu, Fri & Sun except BHs. Dress code.
Societies booking required. **Green Fees** phone **Course Designer** James Braid **Facilities** ⊕ ⊙ ⓘ ⓛ ⊡ ⓡ ⓐ ⓔ ⓟ ✦ ⓜ ✦ **Conf** Corporate Hospitality Days **Location** SW side of town off A770
Hotel ★★★ 79% SHL Knockderry House, Shore Road, COVE, Helensborough ☎ 01436 842283 📄 01436 842283 9 en suite

Greenock Whinhill Beith Rd PA16 9LN
☎ 01475 724694 (evenings & weekends only)
18 Holes, 5504yds, Par 68, SSS 67, Course record 64.
Course Designer William Fernie **Location** 1.5m SW off B7054
Telephone for further details
Hotel BUD Express by Holiday Inn Greenock, Cartsburn, GREENOCK
☎ 01475 786666 📄 01475 786666 71 en suite

KILMACOLM   Map 10 NS36

Kilmacolm Porterfield Rd PA13 4PD
☎ 01505 872139 📄 01505 874007
web: www.kilmacolmgolfclub.com
18 Holes, 5961yds, Par 69, SSS 69, Course record 64.
Course Designer Willie Campbell **Location** SE side of town off A761
Telephone for further details
Hotel ★★★ 79% HL Best Western Gleddoch House, LANGBANK
☎ 01475 540711 📄 01475 540711 70 en suite

PORT GLASGOW   Map 10 NS37

Port Glasgow Devol Rd PA14 5XE
☎ 01475 704181
web: www.portglasgowgolfclub.com
18 Holes, 5712yds, Par 68, SSS 68.
Facilities ⊕ ⊙ ⓘ ⓛ ⊡ ⓡ ⓐ **Location** 1m S
Telephone for further details
Hotel ★★★ 79% HL Best Western Gleddoch House, LANGBANK
☎ 01475 540711 📄 01475 540711 70 en suite

MIDLOTHIAN

BONNYRIGG
Map 11 NT36

Broomieknowe 36 Golf Course Rd EH19 2HZ
☎ 0131 663 9317 ▤ 0131 663 2152
web: www.broomieknowe.com
18 Holes, 6150yds, Par 70, SSS 70, Course record 65.
Course Designer Ben Sayers/Hawtree **Location** 0.5m NE off B704
Telephone for further details
Hotel ★★★ 81% HL Dalhousie Castle and Aqueous Spa, Bonnyrigg,
EDINBURGH ☎ 01875 820153 ▤ 01875 820153 36 en suite

DALKEITH
Map 11 NT36

Newbattle Abbey Rd EH22 3AD
☎ 0131 663 2123 & 0131 663 1819 ▤ 0131 654 1810
e-mail: mail@newbattlegolfclub.com
web: www.newbattlegolfclub.com
Gently undulating parkland course, dissected by the South Esk river
and surrounded by woods.
18 Holes, 6025yds, Par 69, SSS 69, Course record 61.
Club membership 700.
Visitors Mon-Fri & BHs. Sun pm. Dress code. **Societies** welcome.
Green Fees £40 per day, £30 per round **Course Designer** S Colt
Prof Scott McDonald **Facilities** ⑪ ⑩ ⓛ ⬚ 🥂 ⚊ 🛇 🛏
⛳ **Location** SW side of town off A68
Hotel ★★★ 81% HL Dalhousie Castle and Aqueous Spa,
Bonnyrigg, EDINBURGH ☎ 01875 820153 ▤ 01875 820153
36 en suite

GOREBRIDGE
Map 11 NT36

Vogrie Vogrie Estate Country Park EH23 4NU
☎ 01875 821716 ▤ 01875 823958
web: www.midlothian.gov.uk
Vogrie Golf Course: 9 Holes, 2530yds, Par 33.
Facilities ⑪ ⓛ ⬚ 🥂 ⛳ **Location** off B6372
Telephone for further details
Hotel ★★★ 81% HL Dalhousie Castle and Aqueous Spa,
Bonnyrigg, EDINBURGH ☎ 01875 820153 ▤ 01875 820153
36 en suite

LASSWADE
Map 11 NT36

Kings Acre EH18 1AU
☎ 0131 663 3456 ▤ 0131 663 7076
e-mail: info@kings-acregolf.com
web: www.kings-acregolf.com
Parkland course set in countryside location and making excellent use
of the natural contours of the land with strategically placed water
hazards and over 50 bunkers leading to large undulating greens. The
naturally sandy based soil ensures excellent play all year.
Kings Acre Golf Course & Academy: 18 Holes, 6031yds,
Par 70, SSS 69. Club membership 300.
Visitors Mon-Sun & BHs. Dress code. **Societies** welcome. **Green**
Fees £36 per day, £26 per 18 holes (£36 weekends) **Course**
Designer Graeme Webster **Prof** Alan Murdoch **Facilities** ⑪ ⑩
ⓛ ⬚ 🥂 🥢 🛇 🔷 ⚡ 🛏 ⛳ **Conf** facs Corporate
Hospitality Days **Location** off A720, City of Edinburgh bypass road

Hotel ★★★ 77% HL Melville Castle, Melville Gate, Gilmerton Road,
EDINBURGH ☎ 0131 654 0088 ▤ 0131 654 0088 32 en suite

PENICUIK
Map 11 NT25

Glencorse Milton Bridge EH26 0RD
☎ 01968 677189 & 676481 ▤ 01968 674399
e-mail: glencorsegc@btconnect.com
web: www.glencorsegolfclub.com
Picturesque parkland with a burn affecting 10 holes. Testing 5th hole
(237yds) par 3.
18 Holes, 5217yds, Par 64, SSS 66, Course record 60.
Club membership 700.
Visitors Mon-Fri & BHs. Sun pm. Booking required. Dress code.
Societies booking required. **Green Fees** £32 per day, £25 per round
(BHs £32 per round) **Course Designer** Willie Park **Prof** Cliffe Jones
Facilities ⑪ ⑩ ⓛ ⬚ 🥂 🥢 ⚊ 🛇 🛏 ⛳ **Location** 9m S
of Edinburgh on A701 Peebles Road

MORAY

BALLINDALLOCH
Map 15 NJ13

Ballindalloch Castle Lagmore AB37 9AA
☎ 01807 500305 ▤ 01807 500226
e-mail: golf@ballindallochcastle.co.uk
web: www.ballindallochcastle.co.uk
Course nestling among mature trees on the banks of the river Avon
with fine views of the surrounding hills and woods.
Ballindalloch Castle Golf Course: 9 Holes, 6495yds, Par 72,
SSS 71, Course record 64.
Visitors Mon-Sun & BHs. **Societies** welcome. **Green Fees** £20 per
18 holes, £15 per 9 holes **Course Designer** Donald Steel **Facilities** ⓛ
⬚ 🥢 🥂 🔷 🛏 ⛳ **Conf** Corporate Hospitality Days
Location off A95 13m NE of Grantown-on-Spey

BUCKIE
Map 15 NJ46

Buckpool Barhill Rd, Buckpool AB56 1DU
☎ 01542 832236 ▤ 01542 832236
e-mail: golf@buckpoolgolf.com
web: www.buckpoolgolf.com
Links course with superlative view over Moray Firth, easy walking.
18 Holes, 6097yds, Par 70, SSS 69, Course record 63.
Club membership 430.
Visitors Mon-Sun & BHs. **Societies** booking required. **Green Fees** £28
per day, £22 per round **Course Designer** J H Taylor **Facilities** ⑪ by
prior arrangement ⑩ by prior arrangement ⓛ ⬚ 🥂 🥂 ⛳
⛳ **Leisure** squash, snooker **Location** off A98
Hotel ★★★ 75% SHL Cullen Bay Hotel, A98, CULLEN
☎ 01542 840432 ▤ 01542 840432 14 en suite

Strathlene Buckie Portessie AB56 2DJ
☎ 01542 831798 ▤ 01542 831798
e-mail: strathgolf@ukonline.co.uk
web: www.strathlenegolfclub.co.uk
Raised seaside links course with magnificent view. A special feature
of the course is approach shots to raised greens (holes 4, 5, 6 and 13).
18 Holes, 5980yds, Par 69, SSS 69, Course record 64.

continued

SCOTLAND

Visitors Mon-Sun & BHs. **Societies** booking required. **Green Fees** not confirmed **Course Designer** George Smith **Facilities** 🏊 ♨ 🍽 🏌 🛶 ♨ 🏌 **Conf** Corporate Hospitality Days **Location** 2m E of Buckie on A942

Hotel ★★★ 75% SHL Cullen Bay Hotel, A98, CULLEN
☎ 01542 840432 📠 01542 840432 14 en suite

CULLEN Map 15 NJ56

Cullen The Links AB56 4WB
☎ 01542 840685
e-mail: cullengolfclub@btinternet.com
web: www.cullengolfclub.co.uk

Interesting links on three levels with rocks and ravines offering some challenging holes. Spectacular scenery.

18 Holes, 4610yds, Par 63, SSS 62, Course record 55. Club membership 400.

Visitors Mon-Sun & BHs. **Societies** welcome. **Green Fees** not confirmed **Course Designer** Tom Morris/Charlie Neaves **Facilities** 🛎 🍴 🏊 ♨ 🍽 🛶 ♨ 🏌 **Conf** Corporate Hospitality Days **Location** 0.5m W off A98

Hotel ★★★ 75% SHL Cullen Bay Hotel, A98, CULLEN
☎ 01542 840432 📠 01542 840432 14 en suite

DUFFTOWN Map 15 NJ34

Dufftown Tomintoul Rd AB55 4BS
☎ 01340 820325 📠 01340 820325
e-mail: admin@dufftowngolfclub.com
web: www.dufftowngolfclub.com

A short and undulating inland course with spectacular views. The tee of the highest hole, the 9th, is over 1200ft above sea level.

18 Holes, 5308yds, Par 67, SSS 67, Course record 64. Club membership 350.

Visitors Mon-Sun & BHs. Booking required. **Societies** booking required. **Green Fees** £20 per day/round **Course Designer** Members **Facilities** 🛎 by prior arrangement 🍴 by prior arrangement 🏊 🍽 🛶 ♨ 🍴 🚐 🏌 **Conf** facs Corporate Hospitality Days **Location** 0.75m SW off B9009

Hotel ★★★ 81% HL Craigellachie, CRAIGELLACHIE
☎ 01340 881204 📠 01340 881204 26 en suite

ELGIN Map 15 NJ26

Elgin Hardhillock, Birnie Rd, New Elgin IV30 8SX
☎ 01343 542884 📠 01343 542341
e-mail: secretary@elgingolfclub.com
web: www.elgingolfclub.com

Possibly the finest inland course in the north of Scotland, with undulating greens and compact holes that demand the highest accuracy. There are 13 par 4s and one par 5 hole on its parkland layout, eight of the par 4s being over 400yds long.

Hardhillock: 18 Holes, 6416yds, Par 68, SSS 69, Course record 63. Club membership 1000.

Visitors handicap certificate. Dress code. **Societies** booking required. **Green Fees** £47 per day, £37 per round (weekends £49/£39) **Course Designer** John Macpherson **Prof** Kevin Stables **Facilities** 🛎 🍴 🏊 🍽 🛶 🏌 🚐 ♨ 🍴 🏌 🏌 **Conf** facs Corporate Hospitality Days **Location** 1m S on A941

Elgin

Hotel ★★★ 74% HL Mansion House, The Haugh, ELGIN
☎ 01343 548811 📠 01343 548811 23 en suite

FORRES Map 14 NJ05

Forres Muiryshade IV36 2RD
☎ 01309 672250 📠 01309 672250
e-mail: sandy@forresgolf.demon.co.uk
web: www.forresgolfclub.co.uk

An all-year parkland course laid on light, well-drained soil in wooded countryside. Walking is easy despite some hilly holes. A test for the best golfers.

Forres Golf Course: 18 Holes, 6240yds, Par 70, SSS 70, Course record 60. Club membership 800.

Visitors contact course for details. **Societies** welcome. **Green Fees** £45 per day, £34 per round **Course Designer** James Braid/Willie Park **Prof** Sandy Aird **Facilities** 🍴 🍴 🏊 🍽 🛶 🏊 🚐 ♨ 🍴 🏌 🏌 **Conf** Corporate Hospitality Days **Location** SE side of town centre off B9010

Hotel ★★★ 75% HL Ramnee, Victoria Road, FORRES
☎ 01309 672410 📠 01309 672410 19 en suite

GARMOUTH Map 15 NJ36

Garmouth & Kingston Spey St IV32 7NJ
☎ 01343 870388 📠 01343 870388
e-mail: garmouthgolfclub@aol.com
web: www.garmouthkingstongolfclub.com

Flat seaside course with several parkland holes and tidal waters. The 8th hole measures only 328yds from the medal tee but the fairway is bounded by a ditch on either side, the left hand one being out of bounds for the entire length of the hole. The par 5 17th Whinny Side has gorse bordering on both sides of the fairway which can be intimidating to any level of golfer.

18 Holes, 5545yds, Par 69, SSS 67. Club membership 500.

Visitors Mon-Sun & BHs. Booking required Tue, Wed & weekends.. **Societies** booking required. **Green Fees** £25 per day, £20 per round (£28/£25 weekends) **Course Designer** George Smith **Facilities** 🍴 by prior arrangement 🍴 by prior arrangement 🏊 🍽 🛶 🏊 🚐 🏌 **Conf** Corporate Hospitality Days **Location** In village on B9015

Hotel ★★★ 74% HL Mansion House, The Haugh, ELGIN
☎ 01343 548811 📠 01343 548811 23 en suite

SCOTLAND

HOPEMAN
Map 15 NJ16

Hopeman Clubhouse IV30 5YA
☎ 01343 830578   📠 01343 830152
e-mail: hopemangc@aol.com
web: www.hopemangc.co.uk

Links-type course with beautiful views over the Moray Firth. The 12th hole, called the Priescach, is a short hole with a drop of 100ft from tee to green. It can require anything from a wedge to a wood depending on the wind.

18 Holes, 5624yds, Par 68, SSS 68. Club membership 700.

Visitors Mon-Sun & BHs. Booking required Sat. **Societies** welcome.
Green Fees £22 per round (£28 weekends) **Facilities** 🛈 🍽 ⛳ 🛒
🏌 🏖 🏪 ⛳ ⚑ ⚑ **Location** E side of village off B9040
Hotel ★★★ 74% HL Mansion House, The Haugh, ELGIN
☎ 01343 548811 📠 01343 548811 23 en suite

KEITH
Map 15 NJ45

Keith Fife Park AB55 5DF
☎ 01542 882469
e-mail: secretary@keithgolfclub.org.uk
web: www.keithgolfclub.org.uk

Parkland course, with natural hazards over first 9 holes. Testing 7th hole, 232 yds, par 3.

18 Holes, 5767yds, Par 69, SSS 68, Course record 65.
Club membership 500.

Visitors contact club for details. **Societies** welcome. **Green Fees** £15 per day (£20 weekends) **Course Designer** Roy Phimister **Facilities** 🛈
🍽 🛒 🏪 🏖 ⚑ **Location** NW of town centre, A96 onto B9014 right
Hotel ★★★ 81% HL Craigellachie, CRAIGELLACHIE
☎ 01340 881204 📠 01340 881204 26 en suite

LOSSIEMOUTH
Map 15 NJ27

Moray Stotfield Rd IV31 6QS
☎ 01343 812018   📠 01343 815102
e-mail: secretary@moraygolf.co.uk
web: www.moraygolf.co.uk

Two fine Scottish Championship links courses, known as Old and New (Moray), and situated on the Moray Firth where the weather is unusually mild. The Old course was designed by Old Tom Harris, and includes seven par fours over 400 yards. The New course is the work of Henry Cotton, who has designed a tighter and smaller course.

Old Course: 18 Holes, 6687yds, Par 71, SSS 73,
Course record 65.
New Course: 18 Holes, 6008yds, Par 69, SSS 69,
Course record 61. Club membership 1550.

Visitors Mon-Sun & BHs. Handicap certificate. Dress code.
Societies welcome. **Green Fees** Old course Mon-Fri £45 (weekends & BHs £55). New course Mon-Fri £20 (weekends & BHs £25)
Course Designer Tom Morris & Henry Cotton **Prof** Alistair Thomson
Facilities 🛈 🍽 ⛳ 🛒 🏪 🏖 🏪 ⛳ ⚑ 🚗 ⚑
Conf Corporate Hospitality Days **Location** N side of town
Hotel ★★★ 74% HL Mansion House, The Haugh, ELGIN
☎ 01343 548811 📠 01343 548811 23 en suite

ROTHES
Map 15 NJ24

Rothes Blackhall AB38 7AN
☎ 01340 831443 (evenings)   📠 01340 831443
web: www.rothesgolfclub.co.uk
9 Holes, 4972yds, Par 68, SSS 64.

Course Designer John Souter **Location** on A941 10m S of Elgin
Telephone for further details
Hotel ★★★ 81% HL Craigellachie, CRAIGELLACHIE
☎ 01340 881204 📠 01340 881204 26 en suite

SPEY BAY
Map 15 NJ36

Spey Bay IV32 7PJ
☎ 01343 820424   📠 01343 829282
web: www.speybay.com
Spey Bay Golf Course: 18 Holes, 6182yds, Par 70, SSS 70,
Course record 65.

Course Designer Ben Sayers **Location** 4.5m N of Fochabers on B9104
Telephone for further details

NORTH AYRSHIRE

BEITH
Map 10 NS35

Beith Threepwood Rd KA15 2JR
☎ 01505 503166 & 506814   📠 01505 506814
e-mail: beith_secretary@btconnect.com
web: www.beithgolfclub.co.uk

Hilly course, with panoramic views over seven counties.

18 Holes, 5616yds, Par 68, SSS 68. Club membership 487.

Visitors Mon-Sun & BHs. Booking required weekends & BHs. Dress code. **Societies** booking required. **Green Fees** £20 per round, £28 per day (weekend £25 per round) **Course Designer** Members **Facilities** 🛈
🍽 ⛳ 🛒 🏪 🏖 **Conf** Corporate Hospitality Days **Location** 1st left on Beith bypass, S on A737

GREAT CUMBRAE ISLAND (MILLPORT)
Map 10 NS15

Millport Golf Rd KA28 0HB
☎ 01475 530306   📠 01475 530306
e-mail: secretary@millportgolfclub.co.uk
web: www.millportgolfclub.co.uk

Pleasantly situated on the west side of Cumbrae looking over Bute to Arran and the Mull of Kintyre. Exposed, so conditions can vary according to wind strength and direction. A typical seaside resort course welcoming visitors.

18 Holes, 5828yds, Par 68, SSS 69, Course record 64.
Club membership 460.

Visitors contact club for details. **Societies** welcome. **Green Fees** phone **Course Designer** James Braid **Facilities** 🛈 🍽 ⛳
🛒 🏪 🏖 🏪 ⛳ ⚑ 🔧 **Conf** Corporate Hospitality Days
Location 4m from ferry slip
Hotel ★★★ 74% HL Willowbank, 96 Greenock Road, LARGS
☎ 01475 672311 & 675435 📠 01475 672311 30 en suite

IRVINE
Map 10 NS34

Glasgow Gailes KA11 5AE
☎ 0141 942 2011   📄 0141 942 0770
web: www.glasgowgailes-golf.com
Glasgow: 18 Holes, 6535yds, Par 71, SSS 72,
Course record 63.
Course Designer W Park Jnr **Location** off A78 at Newhouse junct,
S of Irvine
Telephone for further details

Irvine Bogside KA12 8SN
☎ 01294 275979   📄 01294 278209
e-mail: secretary@theirvinegolfclub.co.uk
web: www.theirvinegolfclub.co.uk
Testing links course; only two short holes.
18 Holes, 6400yds, Par 71, SSS 73, Course record 65.
Club membership 450.
Visitors contact club for details. **Societies** welcome. **Green**
Fees phone **Course Designer** James Braid **Prof** Jim McKinnon
Facilities ⊕ ⑩ ⓘ ⬚ ⬚ ⬚ ⬚ ⬚ ⬚ **Location** N side of town
off A737

Irvine Ravenspark 13 Kidsneuk Ln KA12 8SR
☎ 01294 271293
web: www.irgc.co.uk
18 Holes, 6457yds, Par 71, SSS 71, Course record 65.
Prof Peter Bond **Facilities** ⊕ ⑩ ⓘ ⬚ ⬚ ⬚ ⬚ ⬚
Location N side of town on A737
Telephone for further details

Western Gailes Gailes by Irvine KA11 5AE
☎ 01294 311649   📄 01294 312312
e-mail: enquiries@westerngailes.com
web: www.westerngailes.com
A magnificent seaside links with glorious turf and wonderful greens.
The view is open across the Firth of Clyde to the neighbouring
islands. It is a well-balanced course crossed by three burns. There
are two par 5s, the 6th and 14th, and the 11th is a testing 445yd
par 4 dog-leg.
18 Holes, 6639yds, Par 71, SSS 74, Course record 65.
Club membership 475.
Visitors Mon, Wed, Fri except BHs. Sun pm. Sat twilight in summer.
Booking required. Dress code. **Societies** booking required. **Green**
Fees £115 per 18 holes, £165 per 36 holes (both including lunch).
£125 Sun (no lunch), Sat twilight £100 (no food) **Facilities** ⊕ ⑩
by prior arrangement ⓘ ⬚ ⬚ ⬚ ⬚ ⬚ **Location** 2m
S off A737

KILBIRNIE
Map 10 NS35

Kilbirnie Place Largs Rd KA25 7AT
☎ 01505 684444 & 683398
e-mail: kilbirnie.golfclub@tiscali.co.uk
web: www.kilbirniegolfclub.co.uk
Easy walking parkland. The fairways are generally narrow and burns
come into play on five holes and the greens are generally small with
fairly tricky borrows. Two par 5 holes, both 500 yds.
18 Holes, 5543yds, Par 69, SSS 67, Course record 65.
Club membership 578.
Visitors Sun-Fri & BHs. Booking required Sun. Dress code.
Societies booking required. **Green Fees** £25 per round (£35 Sun)
Facilities ⊕ ⑩ ⓘ ⬚ ⬚ ⬚ **Location** 1m W from Kilbirnie
Cross on A760
Hotel ★★★ 74% HL Willowbank, 96 Greenock Road, LARGS
☎ 01475 672311 & 675435 📄 01475 672311 30 en suite

LARGS
Map 10 NS25

Largs Irvine Rd KA30 8EU
☎ 01475 673594   📄 01475 673594
web: www.largsgolfclub.co.uk
18 Holes, 6140yds, Par 70, SSS 71, Course record 63.
Course Designer H Stutt **Location** 1m S of town centre on A78
Telephone for further details
Hotel ★★★ 74% HL Willowbank, 96 Greenock Road, LARGS
☎ 01475 672311 & 675435 📄 01475 672311 30 en suite

Routenburn Routenburn Rd KA30 8QA
☎ 01475 686475   📄 01475 687240
Heathland course with panoramic views over the Firth of Clyde and the
Argyll peninsula to the Isle of Aran.
18 Holes, 5675yds, Par 68, SSS 68, Course record 63.
Club membership 300.
Visitors Mon-Sun & BHs. Booking required Wed, weekends & BHs.
Societies booking required. **Green Fees** phone **Course Designer** J
Braid **Prof** J Grieg McQueen **Facilities** ⊕ by prior arrangement
ⓘ ⬚ ⬚ ⬚ ⬚ ⬚ **Conf** Corporate Hospitality Days
Location 1m N off A78
Hotel ★★★ 74% HL Willowbank, 96 Greenock Road, LARGS
☎ 01475 672311 & 675435 📄 01475 672311 30 en suite

SKELMORLIE
Map 10 NS16

Skelmorlie Beithglass PA17 5ES
☎ 01475 520152
e-mail: sgcsec@yahoo.co.uk
web: www.skelmorliegolf.co.uk
Parkland and moorland course with magnificent views over the Firth
of Clyde.
18 Holes, 5030yds, Par 65, SSS 65, Course record 63.
Club membership 450.
Visitors Mon-Fri except BHs. Dress code. **Societies** booking required.
Green Fees £27 per day, £22 per round (£32/£27 weekends) **Course**
Designer James Braid **Facilities** ⊕ by prior arrangement ⑩ by prior
arrangement ⓘ ⬚ ⬚ ⬚ ⬚ **Conf** Corporate Hospitality Days
Location E side of village off A78
Hotel ★★★ 74% HL Willowbank, 96 Greenock Road, LARGS
☎ 01475 672311 & 675435 📄 01475 672311 30 en suite

SCOTLAND

STEVENSTON

Map 10 NS24

Ardeer Greenhead KA20 4LB
☎ 01294 464542 📄 01294 464542
e-mail: info@ardeergolf.co.uk
web: www.ardeergolfclub.co.uk
Parkland with natural hazards, including several water features.

18 Holes, 6401yds, Par 72, SSS 71, Course record 66.
Club membership 650.

Visitors Sun-Fri & BHs. Booking required Sun & BHs..
Societies welcome. **Green Fees** £40 per day, £25 per round (£50/£35 Sun) **Course Designer** Stutt **Facilities** 🏵 🍴 🛏 🖵 🍷 🎿 🏠 🛍
⛳ **Leisure** snooker **Conf** Corporate Hospitality Days **Location** 0.5m N off A78

WEST KILBRIDE

Map 10 NS24

West Kilbride 33-35 Fullerton Dr, Seamill KA23 9HT
☎ 01294 823911 📄 01294 829573
e-mail: golf@westkilbridegolfclub.com
web: www.westkilbridegolfclub.com
Seaside links course on the Firth of Clyde, with fine views of Isle of Arran from every hole.

The West Kilbride Golf Club: 18 Holes, 5974yds, Par 70, SSS 70, Course record 63. Club membership 840.

Visitors Mon-Fri except BHs. Booking required. Handicap certificate. Dress code. **Societies** welcome. **Green Fees** phone **Course Designer** James Braid **Prof** Iain Darroch **Facilities** 🏵 🍴 🛏 🖵
🍷 🎿 🏠 🏴 🛍 ⛳ **Location** W side of town off A78
Hotel ★★★ 74% HL Willowbank, 96 Greenock Road, LARGS
☎ 01475 672311 & 675435 📄 01475 672311 30 en suite

NORTH LANARKSHIRE

AIRDRIE

Map 11 NS76

Airdrie Rochsoles ML6 0PQ
☎ 01236 762195 📄 01236 760584

18 Holes, 6004yds, Par 69, SSS 68, Course record 61.
Course Designer J Braid **Location** 1m N on B802
Telephone for further details
Hotel ★★★★ 80% HL The Westerwood Hotel & Golf Resort, 1 St Andrews Drive, Westerwood, CUMBERNAULD ☎ 01236 457171
📄 01236 457171 148 en suite

Easter Moffat Mansion House, Station Rd, Plains ML6 8NP
☎ 01236 842878 📄 01236 842904
e-mail: secretary@emgc.org.uk
A challenging moorland and parkland course which enjoys good views of the Campsie and Ochil hills. Although fairways are generous, accurate placement from the tee is essential on most holes. The signature hole on the course, the 18th is a truly memorable par 3, played from an elevated tee, to a receptive green in front of the clubhouse.

18 Holes, 6221yds, Par 72, SSS 70, Course record 66.
Club membership 500.

Visitors Mon-Fri & BHs. Dress code. **Societies** welcome. **Green Fees** £35 per day, £23 per round **Prof** Graham King **Facilities** 🏵 🍴
🛏 🖵 🍷 🎿 🏠 ⛳ **Location** 2m E of Airdrie on A89
Hotel ★★★★ 80% HL The Westerwood Hotel & Golf Resort, 1

St Andrews Drive, Westerwood, CUMBERNAULD ☎ 01236 457171
📄 01236 457171 148 en suite

BELLSHILL

Map 11 NS76

Bellshill Community Rd, Orbiston ML4 2RZ
☎ 01698 745124 📄 01698 292576
e-mail: info@bellshillgolfclub.com
web: www.bellshillgolfclub.com
Tree-lined 18 holes situated in the heart of Lanarkshire near Strathclyde Park. First opened for play in 1905 and extended in 1970. The 2nd hole has been redesigned by Mark James and Andrew Mair. The first five holes are extremely demanding but are followed by the gentler birdie alley where shots can be recovered. The signature hole is the 17th, a par 3 which involves a tricky tee shot from an elevated tee to a small well-bunkered green with out of bounds on the right.

18 Holes, 6272yds, Par 70, SSS 69. Club membership 700.
Visitors contact club for details. **Societies** booking required. **Green Fees** Summer £32 per day, £20 per round. Winter reduced rates
Facilities 🏵 🍴 🛏 🖵 🍷 🎿 **Location** 1m SE off A721

COATBRIDGE

Map 11 NS76

Drumpellier Drumpellier Av ML5 1RX
☎ 01236 424139 📄 01236 428723
e-mail: administrator@drumpelliergolfclub.com
web: www.drumpelliergolfclub.com

Parkland with rolling fairways and fast greens.

18 Holes, 6227yds, Par 71, SSS 70, Course record 62.
Club membership 827.

Visitors Mon-Fri & BHs. Booking required. Handicap certificate. Dress code. **Societies** booking required. **Green Fees** £50 per day, £35 per round **Course Designer** W Fernie **Prof** Ian Taylor **Facilities** 🏵
🍴 🛏 🖵 🍷 🎿 🏠 🏴 ⛳ 🛍 ⛳ **Conf** facs Corporate Hospitality Days **Location** 0.75m W off A89
Hotel ★★★ 79% HL Bothwell Bridge, 89 Main Street, BOTHWELL
☎ 01698 852246 📄 01698 852246 90 en suite

CUMBERNAULD

Map 11 NS77

Dullatur 1A Glen Douglas Dr G68 0DW
☎ 01236 723230 📄 01236 727271
web: www.dullaturgolf.com

Carrickstone: 18 Holes, 6204yds, Par 70, SSS 70, Course record 68.
Antonine: 18 Holes, 5875yds, Par 69, SSS 68.

continued

Course Designer James Braid **Location** 1.5m N of A80 at Cumbernauld
Telephone for further details
Hotel ★★★★ 80% HL The Westerwood Hotel & Golf Resort, 1 St Andrews Drive, Westerwood, CUMBERNAULD ☎ 01236 457171 🖹 01236 457171 148 en suite

Palacerigg Palacerigg Country Park G67 3HU
☎ 01236 734969 & 721461 🖹 01236 721461
e-mail: palacerigg-golfclub@lineone.net
web: www.palaceriggolfclub.co.uk

Well-wooded parkland course set in Palacerigg Country Park, with good views to the Campsie Hills.

18 Holes, 6444yds, Par 72, SSS 72, Course record 65. Club membership 300.

Visitors Mon-Sun & BHs. Booking required. Dress code.
Societies booking required. **Green Fees** £12 per day, £8 per round (weekend £10 per round) **Course Designer** Henry Cotton **Facilities** ⊕ ⏱ ⛾ ⏱ ⛾ ⏱ ☎ ⏱ ⛾ **Conf** Corporate Hospitality Days **Location** 2m S of Cumbernauld on Palacerigg road off Lenziemill road B8054, within Palacerigg Country Park
Hotel ★★★★ 80% HL The Westerwood Hotel & Golf Resort, 1 St Andrews Drive, Westerwood, CUMBERNAULD ☎ 01236 457171 🖹 01236 457171 148 en suite

Westerwood Hotel & Golf Resort 1 St Andrews Dr, Westerwood G68 0EW
☎ 01236 725281 🖹 01236 738478
e-mail: westerwoodgolf@qhotels.co.uk
web: www.qhotels.co.uk

Undulating parkland and woodland course designed by Dave Thomas and Seve Ballesteros. Holes meander through silver birch, firs, heaths and heather, and the spectacular 15th, The Waterfall, has its green set against a 40ft rockface. Buggie track.

The Westerwood Hotel & Golf Resort: 18 Holes, 6557yds, Par 72, SSS 72, Course record 65. Club membership 400.

Visitors contact hotel for details. **Societies** welcome. **Green Fees** Apr-Oct £35 per round (£40 weekends). Nov-Mar £20 **Course Designer** Seve Ballesteros/Dave Thomas **Prof** Vincent Brown
Facilities ⊕ ⏱ ⛾ ⏱ ⛾ ⏱ ☎ ⛾ ⛾ ⛾
Leisure hard tennis courts, heated indoor swimming pool, sauna, gymnasium, Beauty salon **Conf** facs Corporate Hospitality Days **Location** by A80, 14m from Glasgow
Hotel ★★★★ 80% HL The Westerwood Hotel & Golf Resort, 1 St Andrews Drive, Westerwood, CUMBERNAULD ☎ 01236 457171 🖹 01236 457171 148 en suite

GARTCOSH
Map 11 NS66

Mount Ellen Johnston Rd G69 8BD
☎ 01236 872277 🖹 01236 872249
e-mail: secretary@mountellengolfclub.co.uk
web: www.mountellengolfclub.co.uk

Downland course with 73 bunkers. Testing 10th (Bedlay), 156yds, par 3.

18 Holes, 5525yds, Par 68, SSS 67, Course record 61. Club membership 500.

Visitors Mon-Fri & BHs. Booking required. Dress code.
Societies booking required. **Green Fees** phone **Prof** Iain Bilsborough **Facilities** ⊕ ⏱ ⛾ ⏱ ⛾ ⏱ ☎ ⛾ ⛾ ⛾ **Conf** Corporate Hospitality Days **Location** 0.75m N off A752
Hotel ★★★★ 74% HL Millennium Hotel Glasgow, George Square, GLASGOW ☎ 0141 332 6711 🖹 0141 332 6711 116 en suite

KILSYTH
Map 11 NS77

Kilsyth Lennox Tak Ma Doon Rd G65 0RS
☎ 01236 824115 🖹 01236 823089
e-mail: admin@kilsythlennox.com
web: www.kilsythlennox.com

Over the last 20 years all the greens and tees at this course have been rebuilt to USGA specifications, with much of the redesign carried out by renowned architect Rocky Roquemore. The course enjoys some magnificent views of the Kelvin valley.

18 Holes, 6612yds, Par 71, SSS 71, Course record 66. Club membership 667.

Visitors Sun-Fri & BHs. Booking required Sun. Dress code.
Societies welcome. **Green Fees** £25 per 18 holes (£30 Sun) **Course Designer** Rocky Roquemore **Prof** William Erskine **Facilities** ⊕ ⏱ ⛾ ⏱ ⛾ ⏱ ☎ ⛾ **Conf** Corporate Hospitality Days **Location** N side of town off A803
Hotel ★★★★ 80% HL The Westerwood Hotel & Golf Resort, 1 St Andrews Drive, Westerwood, CUMBERNAULD ☎ 01236 457171 🖹 01236 457171 148 en suite

MOTHERWELL
Map 11 NS75

Colville Park New Jerviston House ML1 4UG
☎ 01698 265779 (pro) 🖹 01698 230418

18 Holes, 6250yds, Par 71, SSS 70, Course record 63.

Course Designer James Braid **Location** 1.25m NE of Motherwell town centre on A723
Telephone for further details
Hotel ★★★ 79% HL Bothwell Bridge, 89 Main Street, BOTHWELL ☎ 01698 852246 🖹 01698 852246 90 en suite

SCOTLAND

MUIRHEAD
Map 11 NS66

Crow Wood Garnkirk House, Cumbernauld Rd G69 9JF
☎ 0141 779 2011   📠 0141 779 4873
e-mail: secretary@crowwood-golfclub.co.uk
web: www.crowwood-golfclub.co.uk
Parkland course.

18 Holes, 6261yds, Par 71, SSS 71, Course record 62.
Club membership 800.

Visitors Mon-Fri except BHs. Booking required. Handicap certificate. Dress code. **Societies** booking required. **Green Fees** £40 per day, £30 per round **Course Designer** James Braid **Prof** Brian Moffat **Facilities** ⑪ ⑩ ⓛ ⛳ 🐴 ⚑ 🏌 🏠 ✪ **Leisure** snooker, pool **Conf** facs Corporate Hospitality Days **Location** N of Glasgow, first left off A80 immediately after end of M80 Stepps bypass towards Stirling. **Hotel** ★★★ 83% HL Malmaison Glasgow, 278 West George Street, GLASGOW ☎ 0141 572 1000 📠 0141 572 1000   72 en suite

SHOTTS
Map 11 NS86

Shotts Blairhead ML7 5BJ
☎ 01501 822658   📠 01501 822650
web: www.shottsgolfclub.co.uk
Moorland course with fine panoramic views. A good test for all abilities.

18 Holes, 6205yds, Par 70, SSS 70, Course record 63.
Club membership 800.

Visitors Mon-Fri & BHs. Sat-Sun after 4pm. Dress code. **Societies** welcome. **Green Fees** not confirmed **Course Designer** James Braid **Prof** John Strachan **Facilities** ⑪ ⑩ ⓛ ⛳ 🐴 ⚑ 🏠 ✪ 🐴 ✪ **Location** 2m from M8 off Benhar Road **Hotel** ★★★ 78% HL Best Western Hilcroft, East Main Street, WHITBURN ☎ 01501 740818 & 743372 📠 01501 740818 32 en suite

WISHAW
Map 11 NS75

Wishaw 55 Cleland Rd ML2 7PH
☎ 01698 372869 (club house) & 357480 (admin)
📠 01698 356930
e-mail: jwdouglas@btconnect.com
web: www.wishawgolfclub.com
Parkland with many tree-lined fairways. Bunkers protect 17 of the 18 greens.

18 Holes, 5999yds, Par 69, SSS 69, Course record 62.
Club membership 984.

Visitors Mon-Fri, Sun & BHs. Booking required Sun & BHs. Dress code. **Societies** booking required. **Green Fees** £36 per day, £26 per round (£40/£30 Sun) **Course Designer** James Braid **Prof** Stuart Adair **Facilities** ⑪ ⑩ ⓛ ⛳ 🐴 ⚑ 🏠 ✪ 🐴 ✪ **Location** NW side of town off A721

PERTH & KINROSS

ABERFELDY
Map 14 NN84

Aberfeldy Taybridge Rd PH15 2BH
☎ 01887 820535   📠 01887 820535
e-mail: abergc@tiscali.com.uk
web: www.aberfeldygolf.co.uk
Founded in 1895, this flat, parkland course is situated by the River Tay near the famous Wade Bridge and Black Watch Monument, and enjoys some splendid scenery. The layout will test the keen golfer.

18 Holes, 5283yds, Par 68, SSS 66, Course record 67.
Club membership 140.

Visitors Mon-Sun & BHs. Booking required weekkends. Dress code. **Societies** booking required. **Green Fees** phone **Course Designer** Soutars **Facilities** ⑪ ⑩ ⓛ ⛳ 🐴 ⚑ 🏠 ✪ **Conf** Corporate Hospitality Days **Location** N side of town centre

ALYTH
Map 15 NO24

Alyth Pitcrocknie PH11 8HF
☎ 01828 632268   📠 01828 633491
e-mail: enquiries@alythgolfclub.co.uk
web: www.alythgolfclub.co.uk
Windy, heathland course with easy walking.

The Alyth Golf Club 1894: 18 Holes, 6205yds, Par 71,
SSS 71, Course record 64. Club membership 1000.

Visitors contact club for details. **Societies** welcome. **Green Fees** not confirmed **Course Designer** James Braid **Prof** Tom Melville **Facilities** ⑪ ⑩ ⓛ ⛳ 🐴 ⚑ 🏠 🐴 ✪ 🐴 ✪ **Location** 1m E on B954

Strathmore Golf Centre Leroch PH11 8NZ
☎ 01828 633322   📠 01828 633533
e-mail: enquiries@strathmoregolf.com
web: www.strathmoregolf.com

The Rannaleroch Course is set on rolling parkland and heath with splendid views over Strathmore. It is generous off the tee but beware of the udulating, links-style greens. Among the challenging holes is the 480yd 5th with a 180yd carry over water from a high tee position. The nine-hole Leitfie Links has been specially designed with beginners, juniors and older golfers in mind.

Rannaleroch Course: 18 Holes, 6454yds, Par 72, SSS 72,
Course record 65.
Leitfie Links: 9 Holes, 1666yds, Par 29, SSS 29.
Club membership 580.

Visitors Mon-Sun & BHs. **Societies** booking required. **Green Fees** £30
continued

GLENEAGLES HOTEL

PERTH & KINROSS - AUCHTERARDER - MAP 11 NN91

The PGA Centenary Course, created by Jack Nicklaus, and launched in style in May 1993, has an American-Scottish layout with many water hazards, elevated tees and raised contoured greens. It is the selected venue for the Ryder Cup 2014. It has a five-tier tee structure making it both the longest and shortest playable course, as well as the most accommodating to all standards of golfer. The King's Course, with its abundance of heather, gorse, raised greens and plateau tees, is set within the valley of Strathearn with the Grampian mountains spectacularly in view to the north. The shorter Queen's Course, with fairways lined with Scots pines and water hazards, is set within a softer landscape and is considered an easier test of golf. You can improve your game at the golf academy at Gleneagles where the philosophy that golf should be fun and fun in golf comes from playing better. A complete corporate golf package is available.

PH3 1NF ☎ 01764 662231 📠 01764 662134
e-mail: resort.sales@gleneagles.com **web:** www.gleneagles.com
King's Course: 18 Holes, 6471yds, Par 70, SSS 73, Course record 60.
Queen's Course: 18 Holes, 5965yds, Par 68, SSS 70, Course record 61.
PGA Centenary Course: 18 Holes, 6815yds, Par 73, SSS 74, Course record 65. Club membership 600.
Visitors Mon-Sun & BHs. Booking required. Dress code. **Societies** booking required. **Green Fees** May-Sept £155. Reduced rates rest of the year **Course Designer** James Braid/Jack Nicklaus **Prof** Russell Smith **Facilities** **Leisure** hard tennis courts, heated indoor swimming pool, fishing, sauna, gymnasium, halfway house, golf academy, horse riding, shooting, falconry, off road driving, **Conf** facs Corporate Hospitality Days **Location** 2m SW of A823
Hotel ★★★★★ HL The Gleneagles Hotel, AUCHTERARDER ☎ 01764 662231 📠 01764 662231 232 en suite
Hotel ★★★ HL Best Western Huntingtower Hotel, Crieff Road, PERTH ☎ 01738 583771 📠 01738 583777 34 en suite

per round. Leitfie £12 per round (£36/£14 weekends) **Course Designer** John Salvesen **Prof** Andy Lamb/Gareth Couzens **Facilities** ⑪ ⭘⑃ ⓘ ⭙ ⑃ ⑃ ⭙ ⭙ ⭙ **Conf** Corporate Hospitality Days **Location** 2m SE of Alyth, B954 at Meigle onto A926, signed from Blairgowrie

AUCHTERARDER   Map 11 NN91

Auchterarder Orchil Rd PH3 1LS
☎ 01764 662804 (Sec)   📄 01764 664423 (Sec)
e-mail: secretary@auchterardergolf.co.uk
web: www.auchterardergolf.co.uk

Flat parkland course, part woodland with pine, larch and silver birch. It may be short but tricky with cunning dog-legs and guarded greens that require accuracy rather than sheer power. The 14th Punchbowl hole is perhaps the trickiest. A blind tee shot needs to be hit accurately over the left edge of the cross bunker to a long and narrow green - miss and you face a difficult downhill chip shot from deep rough.

18 Holes, 5775yds, Par 69, SSS 68, Course record 61.
Club membership 820.

Visitors Mon-Sun & BHs. Booking required Wed, weekends & BHs.. Handicap certificate. Dress code. **Societies** welcome. **Green Fees** £42 per day, £30 per round (weekends £50/£35) **Course Designer** Ben Sayers **Prof** Gavin Baxter **Facilities** ⑪ ⭘⑃ ⓘ ⭙ ⑃ ⑃ ⑃ ⭙ **Conf** Corporate Hospitality Days **Location** 0.75m SW on A824
Hotel ★★★★★ HL The Gleneagles Hotel, AUCHTERARDER
☎ 01764 662231 📄 01764 662231 232 en suite

Gleneagles Hotel   see page 365

PH3 1NF
☎ 01764 662231   📄 01764 662134
e-mail: resort.sales@gleneagles.com
web: www.gleneagles.com
Hotel ★★★★★ HL The Gleneagles Hotel, AUCHTERARDER
☎ 01764 662231 📄 01764 662231 232 en suite
Hotel ★★★ HL Best Western Huntingtower Hotel, Crieff Road, PERTH ☎ 01738 583771 📄 01738 583777 34 en suite

BLAIR ATHOLL   Map 14 NN86

Blair Atholl Invertilt Rd PH18 5TG
☎ 01796 481407   📄 01796 481292
Easy walking parkland with a river alongside three holes.

9 Holes, 5816yds, Par 70, SSS 68, Course record 65.
Club membership 309.

Visitors dress code. **Societies** welcome. **Green Fees** £22 per day (£24 weekends) **Course Designer** Tom Morriss **Facilities** ⑪ ⭘⑃ ⓘ ⭙ ⑃ ⑃ ⭙ ⭙ **Location** 0.5m S off B8079

Hotel ★★★ 74% HL Atholl Arms, Old North Road, BLAIR ATHOLL
☎ 01796 481205 📄 01796 481205 30 en suite

BLAIRGOWRIE   Map 15 NO14

Blairgowrie Golf Course Rd, Rosemount PH10 6LG
☎ 01250 872622   📄 01250 875451
e-mail: office@theblairgowriegolfclub.co.uk
web: www.theblairgowriegolfclub.co.uk

Two 18-hole championship heathland/woodland courses, also a nine-hole course.

Rosemount Course: 18 Holes, 6630yds, Par 72, SSS 72, Course record 64.
Lansdowne Course: 18 Holes, 6834yds, Par 72, SSS 73, Course record 66.
Wee Course: 9 Holes, 2352yds, Par 32.
Club membership 1724.

Visitors Mon-Sun & BHs. Booking required. Handicap certificate. Dress code. **Societies** booking required. **Green Fees** phone **Course Designer** J Braid/P Allis/D Thomas/Old Tom Morris **Prof** Charles Dernie **Facilities** ⑪ ⭘⑃ ⓘ ⭙ ⑃ ⑃ ⑃ ⭙ ⭙ ⭙ **Conf** Corporate Hospitality Days **Location** off A93 Rosemount

COMRIE   Map 11 NN72

Comrie Laggan Braes PH6 2LR
☎ 01764 670055
e-mail: enquiries@comriegolf.co.uk
web: www.comriegolf.co.uk

Challenging 9-hole course with two tricky par 3s. Good views of highland scenery from most holes.

9 Holes, 6040yds, Par 70, SSS 70, Course record 61.
Club membership 350.

Visitors Mon-Sun & BHs. Booking required Mon-Tue. Dress code. **Societies** booking required. **Green Fees** not confirmed **Course Designer** Col. Williamson **Facilities** ⑪ ⭘⑃ ⭙ ⑃ ⑃ ⭙ ⭙ **Location** E side of village off A85
Hotel ★★★ 83% HL The Four Seasons Hotel, Loch Earn, ST FILLANS
☎ 01764 685333 📄 01764 685333 18 en suite

CRIEFF
Map 11 NN82

Crieff Ferntower, Perth Rd PH7 3LR
☎ 01764 652909 📠 01764 653803
e-mail: bookings@crieffgolf.co.uk
web: www.crieffgolf.co.uk

Set in dramatic countryside, Crieff Golf Club was established in 1891. The Ferntower championship course has magnificent views over the Strathearn valley and offers all golfers an enjoyable round. The short nine-hole Dornoch course, which incorporates some of the James Braid designed holes from the original 18 holes, provides an interesting challenge for juniors, beginners and others short of time.

Ferntower Course: 18 Holes, 6502yds, Par 71, SSS 72, Course record 63.
Dornoch Course: 9 Holes, 2372yds, Par 32, SSS 63.
Club membership 720.

Visitors handicap certificate. Dress code. **Societies** welcome. **Green Fees** Ferntower £34 May & Oct, £36 Jun-Sep (£38/£44 weekends). Dornock £12 for 9 holes, £16 for 18 holes **Course Designer** James Braid **Prof** David Murchie **Facilities** ⊕ †◎† 🍴 🖵 ☕ ⚒ 🖺 ⚲ 🛒 **Conf** Corporate Hospitality Days **Location** 0.5m NE on A85
Hotel ★★★ 83% HL Royal, Melville Square, COMRIE
☎ 01764 679200 📠 01764 679200 13 en suite

DUNKELD
Map 11 NO04

Dunkeld & Birnam Fungarth PH8 0ES
☎ 01350 727524 📠 01350 728660
e-mail: secretary-dunkeld@tiscali.co.uk
web: dunkeldandbirnamgolfclub.co.uk

Interesting and challenging course with spectacular views of the surrounding countryside. The original nine-hole heathland course is now augmented by an additional nine holes of parkland character close to the Loch of the Lowes.

18 Holes, 5511yds, Par 69, SSS 67, Course record 63.
Club membership 600.
Visitors contact club for details. Handicap certificate.
Societies welcome. **Green Fees** phone **Course Designer** D A Tod **Facilities** ⊕ †◎† 🍴 🖵 ☕ 🖺 ⚲ ⚒ 🛒 🛒
Conf Corporate Hospitality Days **Location** 1m N of village on A923
Hotel ★★★★ HL Kinnaird, Kinnaird Estate, DUNKELD
☎ 01796 482440 📠 01796 482440 9 en suite

DUNNING
Map 11 NO01

Dunning Rollo Park, Station Rd PH2 0QX
☎ 01764 684747
e-mail: secretary@dunninggolfclub.co.uk
web: www.dunninggolfclub.co.uk

A pleasant parkland course with some testing holes, complicated by the burn which is a feature of four of the nine holes.

9 Holes, 4894yds, Par 66, SSS 64, Course record 62.
Club membership 480.
Visitors contact course for details. **Societies** booking required.
Green Fees £20 per 18 holes, £10 per 9 holes **Prof** Stuart Barker **Facilities** 🖵 🖺 ⚒ 🛒 **Location** 4m N of Auchterarder, 1.5m off A9 on B9141
Hotel ★★★ 74% HL Lovat, 90 Glasgow Road, PERTH
☎ 01738 636555 📠 01738 636555 30 en suite

Whitemoss Whitemoss Rd PH2 0QX
☎ 01738 730300 📠 01738 730490
web: www.whitemossgolf.com

Whitemoss Golf Course: 18 Holes, 5595yds, Par 68, SSS 68, Course record 63.
Course Designer Whitemoss Leisure **Location** off A9 at Whitemoss Rd junct, 3m N of Gleneagles
Telephone for further details

GLENSHEE (SPITTAL OF)
Map 15 NO17

Dalmunzie Dalmunzie Estate PH10 7QE
☎ 01250 885226
e-mail: enquiries@dalmunziecottages.com
web: www.dalmunziecottages.com

Well-maintained highland course. Testing short course with small but good greens. One of the highest courses in Britain at 1200ft.

9 Holes, 2099yds, Par 30, Course record 29.
Club membership 90.
Visitors Mon-Sun & BHs. **Societies** welcome. **Green Fees** £14 per day
Course Designer Alistair Campbell **Facilities** ⊕ †◎† 🖺 🖵 🍴

continued

SCOTLAND

🏠 ⛳ 🔷 **Leisure** hard tennis courts, fishing, mountain bikes, clay target shooting **Conf** facs Corporate Hospitality Days **Location** 2m NW of Spittal of Glenshee
Hotel ★★★ 81% CHH Dalmunzie Castle, SPITTAL OF GLENSHEE
☎ 01250 885224 📄 01250 885224 17 en suite

KENMORE
Map 14 NN74

Kenmore PH15 2HN
☎ 01887 830226   📄 01887 830775
e-mail: info@taymouth.co.uk
web: www.taymouth.co.uk

Testing course in mildly undulating natural terrain. Beautiful views in tranquil setting by Loch Tay. The par 5 4th is 560yds and only one of the par 4s, the 2nd, is under 400yds - hitting from the tee out of a mound of trees down a snaking banking fairway which encourages the ball to stay on the fairway. The slightly elevated green is surrounded by banks to help hold the ball on the green. The fairways are generous and the rough short, which tends to encourage an unhindered round.

Kenmore Golf Course: 9 Holes, 6052yds, Par 70, SSS 69, Course record 67. Club membership 200.

Visitors Mon-Sun & BHs. **Societies** booking required. **Green Fees** £30 per day, £20 per 18 holes, £15 per 9 holes (£35/£25/£17 weekends) **Course Designer** Robin Menzies **Facilities** 🍸 🍴 🛒 🖥 📞 ⛳ 🏠 ⛳ 🔷 🛵 🚌 ⛳ **Leisure** fishing **Conf** Corporate Hospitality Days **Location** on A827, beside Kenmore Bridge
Hotel ★★★ 74% HL Kenmore Hotel, The Square, KENMORE
☎ 01887 830205 📄 01887 830205 40 en suite

KINROSS
Map 11 NO10

Kinross The Green Hotel, 2 The Muirs KY13 8AS
☎ 01577 863407   📄 01577 863180
e-mail: bookings@golfkinross.com
web: www.golfkinross.com

Two interesting and picturesque parkland courses, with easy walking. Many of the fairways are bounded by trees and plantations. A number of holes have views over Loch Leven to the hills beyond. The more challenging of the two is the Montgomery which has been enhanced by the addition of a pond in front of the 11th green and 19 extra bunkers. The Bruce is slightly shorter but still provides a stern test of golf with notable features being the 6th Pond Hole and the run of four par 5s in six holes on the front nine.

*Bruce: 18 Holes, 6231yds, Par 73, SSS 72, Course record 66.
Montgomery: 18 Holes, 6452yds, Par 71, SSS 72, Course record 68. Club membership 600.*

Visitors Mon-Sun & BHs. Dress code. **Societies** booking required.

Green Fees The Bruce £40 per day, £28 per round (£50/£38 weekends). The Montgomery £50 per day, £33 per round (£60/£43 weekends) **Course Designer** Sir David Montgomery **Prof** Greig McSporran **Facilities** 🍸 🍴 🛒 🖥 📞 🛵 🏠 ⛳ 🔷 🚌 ⛳
Leisure heated indoor swimming pool, fishing, sauna, gymnasium, 4 sheet curling rink, croquet **Conf** facs Corporate Hospitality Days **Location** M90 junct 6, NE side of town on B996
Hotel ★★★★ 73% HL The Green Hotel, 2 The Muirs, KINROSS
☎ 01577 863467 📄 01577 863467 46 en suite

MILNATHORT
Map 11 NO10

Milnathort South St KY13 9XA
☎ 01577 864069
e-mail: milnathort.gc@btconnect.com

Undulating inland course with lush fairways and excellent greens for most of the year. Strategically placed copses require accurate tee shots. Different tees and greens for some holes will make for more interesting play.

9 Holes, 5969yds, Par 71, SSS 69, Course record 62. Club membership 575.

Visitors Sun-Fri & BHs. Booking required. Dress code.
Societies booking required. **Green Fees** Weekdays £22 per day, £15 per round (weekends £25/£17) **Facilities** 🍸 🍴 🛒 🖥 📞 ⛳ ⛳ 🏴 **Conf** Corporate Hospitality Days **Location** S side of town on A922
Hotel ★★★★ 73% HL The Green Hotel, 2 The Muirs, KINROSS
☎ 01577 863467 📄 01577 863467 46 en suite

MUTHILL
Map 11 NN81

Muthill Peat Rd PH5 2DA
☎ 01764 681523   📄 01764 681557
web: muthillgolfclub.co.uk

9 Holes, 4700yds, Par 66, SSS 63, Course record 62.

Course Designer Members **Location** W side of village off A822
Telephone for further details

PERTH
Map 11 NO12

Craigie Hill Cherrybank PH2 0NE
☎ 01738 622644 (pro)   📄 01738 620829
e-mail: admin@craigiehill.co.uk
web: www.craigiehill.com

Slightly hilly, heathland course. Panoramic views of Perth and the surrounding hills.

18 Holes, 5386yds, Par 66, SSS 67, Course record 60. Club membership 600.

Visitors Mon-Sun & BHs. Booking required Wed, Thu & weekends. Dress code. **Societies** booking required. **Green Fees** £30 per day; £20 per round (£30/£25 weekends) **Course Designer** Fernie/Anderson **Prof** Niall McGill **Facilities** 🍸 🍴 🛒 🖥 📞 🛵 🏠 ⛳ ⛳ **Conf** facs Corporate Hospitality Days **Location** 1m SW of city centre off A952
Hotel ★★★ 75% HL Best Western Queens Hotel, Leonard Street, PERTH ☎ 01738 442222 📄 01738 442222 50 en suite

King James VI Moncreiffe Island PH2 8NR
☎ 01738 445132 (Sec) & 632460 (Pro)
🖷 01738 445132
e-mail: mansec@kingjamesvi.com
web: www.kingjamesvi.com
Parkland course on island in the River Tay. Easy walking.

18 Holes, 6038yds, Par 70, SSS 69, Course record 62.
Club membership 650.

Visitors dress code. **Societies** welcome. **Green Fees** £32 per day, £24
per round (£34/£26 weekends) **Course Designer** Tom Morris **Prof** Allan
Knox **Facilities** ⊕ ⑩ ᳖ ☐ 🎣 ᙏ 🏠 ⛳ ⚙ 🚗 ⚙
Location SE side of city centre
Hotel ★★★ 75% HL Best Western Queens Hotel, Leonard Street,
PERTH ☎ 01738 442222 🖷 01738 442222 50 en suite

Murrayshall Country House Hotel Murrayshall, Scone
PH2 7PH
☎ 01738 552784 & 551171 🖷 01738 552595
e-mail: info@murrayshall.com
web: www.murrayshall.com
Set within 350 acres of undulating parkland, Murrayshall offers
36 holes of outstanding golf. The original championship course is
set out within the parkland estate and the Lynedoch is a woodland-
style course, full of natural features. Many of the fairways are lined
by majestic trees while white sand bunkers and water hazards with
natural stone bridges protect the generous greens.

Murrayshall Course: 18 Holes, 6441yds, Par 73, SSS 72.
Lynedoch Course: 18 Holes, 5800yds, Par 69.
Club membership 350.

Visitors booking required. **Societies** booking required. **Green**
Fees not confirmed **Course Designer** Hamilton Stutt **Prof** Alan Reid
Facilities ⊕ ⑩ ᳖ ☐ 🎣 ᙏ 🏠 ⛳ ◇ ⚙ 🚗 ⚙ ⚘
Leisure hard tennis courts **Conf** facs Corporate Hospitality Days
Location E side of village off A94
Hotel ★★★★ 76% HL Murrayshall House Hotel & Golf Course,
New Scone, PERTH ☎ 01738 551171 🖷 01738 551171 41 en suite

North Inch North Inch PH1 5PH
☎ 01738 636481
North Inch Golf Course: 18 Holes, 5442yds, Par 68, SSS 66,
Course record 62.

Course Designer Tom Morris **Location** N of City
Telephone for further details
Hotel ★★★ 75% HL Best Western Queens Hotel, Leonard Street,
PERTH ☎ 01738 442222 🖷 01738 442222 50 en suite

PITLOCHRY

Map 14 NN95

Pitlochry Golf Course Rd PH16 5QY
☎ 01796 472792 🖷 01796 473947
e-mail: pro@pitlochrygolf.co.uk
web: www.pitlochrygolf.co.uk
A varied and interesting heathland course with fine views
and posing many problems. Its SSS permits few errors in its
achievement.

Pitlochry Golf Course Ltd: 18 Holes, 5681yds, Par 69,
SSS 69, Course record 60. Club membership 400.

Societies booking required. **Green Fees** £40 per day, £30 per round
(£48/£38 weekends). Reduced winter rates **Course Designer** Willy
Fernie **Prof** Mark Pirie **Facilities** ⊕ ⑩ ᳖ ☐ 🎣 ᙏ 🏠 ⛳

⚙ ⚙ **Location** off A924 onto Larchwood Rd
Hotel ★★★ 73% SHL Moulin Hotel, 11-13 Kirkmichael
Road, Moulin, PITLOCHRY ☎ 01796 472196 🖷 01796 472196
15 en suite

ST FILLANS

Map 11 NN62

St Fillans South Loch Earn Rd PH6 2NJ
☎ 01764 685312 🖷 01764 685312
e-mail: stfillansgolf@aol.com
web: www.stfillans-golf.com
Fairly flat, beautiful parkland course. Beside the river Earn and set
amongst the Perthshire hills. Wonderfully rich in flora, animal and bird
life. Easy to play but hard to score.

9 Holes, 6054yds, Par 69, SSS 69, Course record 73.
Club membership 400.

Visitors Mon-Sun & BHs. Booking required Sat. Dress code.
Societies booking required. **Green Fees** phone **Course Designer** W
Auchterlonie **Facilities** ⊕ ⑩ ᳖ ☐ 🎣 ᙏ 🏠 ⛳ ⚙ 🚗
⚙ **Conf** Corporate Hospitality Days **Location** E side of village off A85
Hotel ★★★ 83% HL The Four Seasons Hotel, Loch Earn, ST FILLANS
☎ 01764 685333 🖷 01764 685333 18 en suite

STRATHTAY

Map 14 NN95

Strathtay Upper Derculich PH9 0LR
☎ 01887 840373 🖷 01887 840777
e-mail: aivr@aol.com
web: www.strathtaygolfclub.com
Very attractive highland course in a charming location. Steep in
places but with fine views of surrounding hills and the Tay valley. New
tees in operation give a different and challenging perspective.

9 Holes, 4082yds, Par 63, SSS 61, Course record 61.
Club membership 212.

Visitors Mon-Sun & BHs. Booking required Sun. **Societies** welcome.
Green Fees £15 per day (£20 weekends & BHs) **Facilities** ᙏ ⚙
Location E of village centre off A827

RENFREWSHIRE

SCOTLAND

BISHOPTON
Map 10 NS47

Erskine PA7 5PH
☎ 01505 862108 📠 01505 862302
e-mail: peter@erskinegc.wanadoo.co.uk
Parkland on the south bank of the River Clyde, with views of the hills beyond.

18 Holes, 6372yds, Par 71, SSS 71. Club membership 800.

Visitors Mon-Fri & BHs. Booking required. Dress code. Handicap certificate. **Societies** welcome **Green Fees** £45 per day, £35 per round **Prof** Peter Thomson **Facilities** ⓣ ⎿⎬ ⌷ ⌷ ⌷ ⤴ ⌷ ⌷ ⌷ ⌷ **Conf** Corporate Hospitality Days **Location** 0.75 NE off B815

BRIDGE OF WEIR
Map 10 NS36

Old Course Ranfurly Ranfurly Place PA11 3DE
☎ 01505 613612 📠 01505 613214
web: www.oldranfurly.com

18 Holes, 6061yds, Par 70, SSS 70, Course record 63.

Course Designer W Park **Location** 6m S of Glasgow Airport
Telephone for further details

Ranfurly Castle The Clubhouse, Golf Rd PA11 3HN
☎ 01505 612609 📠 01505 610406
e-mail: secretary@ranfurlycastlegolfclub.co.uk
web: www.ranfurlycastlegolfclub.co.uk
A picturesque, highly challenging 240-acre moorland course.

18 Holes, 6261yds, Par 70, SSS 71, Course record 65. Club membership 824.

Visitors Mon. Tue, Thu & Fri. Booking required. Handicap certificate. Dress code. **Societies** booking required. **Green Fees** £45 per day, £35 per round **Course Designer** A Kirkcaldy/W Auchterlomie **Prof** Tom Eckford **Facilities** ⓣ ⎿⎬ ⌷ ⌷ ⌷ ⤴ ⌷ ⌷ **Location** 5m NW of Johnstone

JOHNSTONE
Map 10 NS46

Cochrane Castle Scott Av, Craigston PA5 0HF
☎ 01505 328465 📠 01505 325338
web: www.cochranecastle.com
Fairly hilly parkland, wooded with two small streams running through.

18 Holes, 6194yds, Par 71, SSS 71, Course record 63. Club membership 721.

Visitors Mon-Fri & BHs. Booking required. Handicap certificate. Dress code. **Societies** booking required. **Green Fees** £35 per day, £25 per round **Course Designer** J Hunter **Prof** Alan J Logan **Facilities** ⓣ ⎿⎬ ⌷ ⌷ ⌷ ⌷ ⤴ ⌷ ⌷ **Location** 1m from town centre, off Beith Rd

Elderslie 63 Main Rd, Elderslie PA5 9AZ
☎ 01505 320032
e-mail: eldersliegolfclub@btconnect.com
web: www.eldersliegolfclub.net
Undulating parkland with good views.

18 Holes, 6175yds, Par 70, SSS 70, Course record 61. Club membership 940.

Visitors Mon-Fri except BHs. Booking required. Handicap certificate. Dress code. **Societies** booking required. **Green Fees** £50 per day, £30 per round **Course Designer** J Braid **Prof** Richard Bowman

Facilities ⓣ ⎿⎬ ⌷ ⌷ ⌷ ⤴ ⌷ ⌷ **Leisure** snooker table
Conf Corporate Hospitality Days **Location** E side of town on A737

LANGBANK
Map 10 NS37

Gleddoch Golf and Country Club PA14 6YE
☎ 01475 540304 📠 01475 540201
web: www.gleddochgolf.co.uk

Gleddoch Golf and Country Club: 18 Holes, 6330yds, Par 71, SSS 71, Course record 64.

Course Designer Hamilton Strutt **Location** B789-Old Greenock Road
Telephone for further details
Hotel ★★★ 79% HL Best Western Gleddoch House, LANGBANK
☎ 01475 540711 📠 01475 540711 70 en suite

LOCHWINNOCH
Map 10 NS35

Lochwinnoch Burnfoot Rd PA12 4AN
☎ 01505 842153 & 01505 843029 📠 01505 843668
e-mail: admin@lochwinnochgolf.co.uk
web: www.lochwinnochgolf.co.uk

Well-maintained parkland course incorporating natural burns. Throughout the course the majority of fairways are wide with tricky greens, but always in good condition. Very scenic with lots of bunkers.

18 Holes, 6243yds, Par 71, SSS 71, Course record 63. Club membership 650.

Visitors dress code. **Societies** welcome **Green Fees** £25 per round, £35 per day **Prof** Gerry Reilly **Facilities** ⓣ ⎿⎬ ⌷ ⌷ ⌷ ⤴ ⌷ ⌷ ⌷ ⌷ **Conf** facs Corporate Hospitality Days **Location** W side of town off A760

PAISLEY
Map 11 NS46

Barshaw Barshaw Park PA1 3TJ
☎ 0141 889 2908

18 Holes, 5703yds, Par 68, SSS 67, Course record 63.

Course Designer J R Stutt **Location** 1m E off A737
Telephone for further details
Hotel ★★★ 79% HL Glynhill Hotel & Leisure Club, Paisley Road, RENFREW ☎ 0141 886 5555 📠 0141 886 5555 145 en suite

Paisley Braehead Rd PA2 8TZ
☎ 0141 884 3903 & 884 2292 📠 0141 884 3903
e-mail: paisleygolfclub@btconnect.com
web: www.paisleygolfclub.co.uk

Moorland course with good views which suits all handicaps. The course has been designed in two loops of nine holes. Holes feature trees and gorse.

18 Holes, 6466yds, Par 71, SSS 72, Course record 64. Club membership 810.

Visitors Mon-Fri & Sun except BHs. Booking required Fri & Sun. Handicap certificate. Dress code. **Societies** booking required. **Green Fees** £40 per day, £30 per round **Course Designer** John Stutt **Prof** David Gordon **Facilities** ⓣ ⎿⎬ ⌷ ⌷ ⌷ ⤴ ⌷ ⌷ ⌷ ⌷ **Conf** facs **Location** Exit M8 junct 27, Renfrew Rd and continue through lights. Left at Causeyside St, right before Gleniffer Hotel, left at rdbt, at top of hill
Hotel ★★★ 79% HL Glynhill Hotel & Leisure Club, Paisley Road, RENFREW ☎ 0141 886 5555 📠 0141 886 5555 145 en suite

Ralston Strathmore Av, Ralston PA1 3DT
☎ 0141 882 1349 🖷 0141 883 9837
e-mail: thesecretary@ralstongolf.co.uk
web: www.ralstongolfclub.co.uk
Parkland course.
18 Holes, 6071yds, Par 70, SSS 69, Course record 62.
Club membership 750.
Visitors Mon-Fri except BHs. Booking required. Handicap certificate.
Dress code. **Societies** booking required. **Green Fees** £42 per day, £27
per round **Course Designer** J Braid **Prof** Colin Munro **Facilities** ⊕
🏴 🍴 🔁 ♿ 🦽 / / **Conf** facs Corporate Hospitality
Days **Location** 2m E of Paisley town centre on A761

RENFREW   Map 11 NS46

Renfrew Blythswood Estate, Inchinnan Rd PA4 9EG
☎ 0141 886 6692 🖷 0141 886 1808
e-mail: secretary@renfrewgolfclub.co.uk
web: www.renfrewgolfclub.co.uk
A tree-lined parkland course.
18 Holes, 6818yds, Par 72, SSS 73, Course record 65.
Club membership 800.
Visitors Mon, Tue, Thu & Fri except BHs. Booking required. Dress code.
Handicap certificate. **Societies** Booking required. **Green Fees** £45 per
day, £35 per round **Course Designer** Commander Harris **Facilities** ⊕
🏴 🍴 🔁 ♿ 🦽 / **Location** 0.75m W off A8
Hotel ★★★ 79% HL Glynhill Hotel & Leisure Club, Paisley Road,
RENFREW ☎ 0141 886 5555 🖷 0141 886 5555 145 en suite

SCOTTISH BORDERS

ASHKIRK   Map 12 NT42

Woll New Woll Estate TD7 4PE
☎ 01750 32711
e-mail: wollclubhouse@tiscali.co.uk
web: www.wollgolf.co.uk
Flat parkland course with mature trees and a natural burn and ponds.
The course is gentle but testing for all standards of golfer. Set in
outstanding countryside in the Ale valley.
Woll Golf Course: 18 Holes, 6051yds, Par 70, SSS 70,
Course record 70. Club membership 500.
Visitors Mon-Sun & BHs. Dress code. **Societies** booking required.
Green Fees £40 per day, £28 per 18 holes. (weekend £32 per
18 holes) **Course Designer** Alec Cleghorn **Prof** Murray Cleghorn
Facilities ⊕ 🏴 🍴 🔁 ♿ 🦽 / ◇ / 🛒 /
Leisure sauna **Conf** facs Corporate Hospitality Days **Location** off A7
at village of Ashkirk
Hotel ★★★ 75% HL Kingsknowes, Selkirk Road, GALASHIELS
☎ 01896 758375 🖷 01896 758375 12 en suite

COLDSTREAM   Map 12 NT83

Hirsel Kelso Rd TD12 4NJ
☎ 01890 882678 🖷 01890 882233
e-mail: bookings@hirselgc.co.uk
web: www.hirselgc.co.uk
A beautifully situated parkland course set in the Hirsel Estate, with
panoramic views of the Cheviot Hills. Each hole offers a different
challenge especially the 7th, a 170yd par 3 demanding accuracy of
flight and length from the tee to ensure achieving a par.
18 Holes, 6024yds, Par 70, SSS 70, Course record 65.
Club membership 680.
Visitors contact club for details. **Societies** welcome. **Green Fees** £34
per day **Facilities** ⊕ 🏴 🔁 ♿ 🦽 🍴 🛒 / /
Location on A697 at W end of Coldstream
Guesthouse ★★★★ RR Wheatsheaf at Swinton, SWINTON
☎ 01890 860257 🖷 01890 860257 10 en suite

DUNS   Map 12 NT75

Duns Hardens Rd TD11 3NR
☎ 01361 882194 🖷 01361 883599
e-mail: secretary@dunsgolfclub.com
web: www.dunsgolfclub.com
Interesting upland course, with natural hazards of water and hilly
slopes. Views south to the Cheviot Hills. A burn comes into play at
seven of the holes.
18 Holes, 6298yds, Par 71, SSS 70, Course record 67.
Club membership 426.
Visitors Mon-Sun & BHs. Booking required. Dress code.
Societies Booking details. **Green Fees** not confirmed **Course**
Designer A H Scott **Facilities** ⊕ 🏴 🔁 ♿ 🍴 🛒 🦽 🚜
/ **Conf** Corporate Hospitality Days **Location** 1m W off A6105
Hotel ★★★ 70% CHH Marshall Meadows Country House,
BERWICK-UPON-TWEED ☎ 01289 331133 🖷 01289 331133
19 en suite

EYEMOUTH   Map 12 NT96

Eyemouth Gunsgreen Hill TD14 5SF
☎ 01890 750551 (clubhouse) & 750004 (pro)
e-mail: eyemouth@gxn.co.uk
web: www.eyemouthgolfclub.co.uk
A superb course set on the coast, containing interesting and
challenging holes, in particular the intimidating 6th hole, a
formidable par 3 across a vast gully with the waves crashing below
and leaving little room for error. Unsurprisingly, this has been voted
Britain's Must Extraordinary Golf Hole. The clubhouse overlooks the
picturesque fishing village of Eyemouth and provides panoramic views
over the course and the North Sea.
18 Holes, 6520yds, Par 72, SSS 72, Course record 66.
Club membership 400.
Visitors Mon-Sun & BHs. Dress code. Handicap certificate.
Societies booking required. **Green Fees** not confirmed **Course**
Designer J R Bain **Prof** Michael Hackett **Facilities** ⊕ 🏴 🔁 🍴
♿ 🦽 🛒 / 🚜 / **Conf** Corporate Hospitality Days **Location** E
side of town, 8m N of Berwick and 2m off A1
Hotel ★★★ 70% CHH Marshall Meadows Country House,
BERWICK-UPON-TWEED ☎ 01289 331133 🖷 01289 331133
19 en suite

GALASHIELS
Map 12 NT43

Galashiels Ladhope Recreation Ground TD1 2NJ
☎ 01896 753724
e-mail: secretary@galashiels-golfclub.co.uk
web: www.galashiels-golfclub.co.uk
Hillside course with superb views from the top, recently redeveloped.
9 Holes, 5424yds, Par 68. Club membership 186.
Visitors Mon-Sun & BHs. Booking required Fri-Sun. **Societies** booking required. **Green Fees** £30 per 36 holes, £25 per 27 holes, £20 per 18 holes, £10 per 9 holes **Course Designer** James Braid **Facilities** ⊕ by prior arrangement ⊖ by prior arrangement ⌷ ⎁ ⌷ ⌷
⌂ **Location** N side of town centre off A7, opposite Ladhope Inn
Hotel ★★★ 75% HL Kingsknowes, Selkirk Road, GALASHIELS
☎ 01896 758375 ▤ 01896 758375 12 en suite

Torwoodlee Edinburgh Rd TD1 2NE
☎ 01896 752260 ▤ 01896 752306
e-mail: thesecretary@torwoodleegolfclub.org.uk
web: www.torwoodleegolfclub.org.uk
A picturesque course flanked by the River Gala and set among a mix of mature woodland and rolling parkland.
18 Holes, 6021yds, Par 69, SSS 70, Course record 63.
Club membership 550.
Visitors Mon-Sun & BHs. Booking required. Dress code.
Societies booking required. **Green Fees** £40 per day, £30 per round
Course Designer Willie Park **Facilities** ⊕ ⊖ ⌷ ⎁ ⌷ ⌷ ⌷
⌂ **Conf** Corporate Hospitality Days **Location** 1.75m NW of Galashiels off A7
Hotel ★★★ 75% HL Kingsknowes, Selkirk Road, GALASHIELS
☎ 01896 758375 ▤ 01896 758375 12 en suite

HAWICK
Map 12 NT51

Hawick Vertish Hill TD9 0NY
☎ 01450 372293
e-mail: thesecretary@hawickgolfclub.com
web: www.hawickgolfclub.com
Hill course with good views.
18 Holes, 5933yds, Par 68, SSS 69, Course record 61.
Club membership 600.
Visitors Mon-Sun & BHs. Booking required. Dress code. Handicap certificate. **Societies** booking required. **Green Fees** £36 per day, £30 per round **Facilities** ⊕ ⊖ ⌷ ⎁ ⌷ ⌷ ⌷ ⌷ ⌷ ⌷
Conf Corporate Hospitality Days **Location** SW side of town
Guesthouse ★★★ RR Mosspaul, Teviothead, HAWICK
☎ 01450 850245 ▤ 01450 850245 5 en suite

INNERLEITHEN
Map 11 NT33

Innerleithen Leithen Water, Leithen Rd EH44 6NL
☎ 01896 830951
Moorland course, with easy walking. Burns and rivers are natural hazards. Holes of note are the 1st (175yd par 3), the 3rd (474yd par 4), the 5th (100yd par 3) and the 6th (485yd par 5).
9 Holes, 6066yds, Par 70, SSS 69, Course record 64.
Club membership 280.
Visitors Mon-Fri except BHs. Handicap certificate. **Societies** booking required. **Green Fees** £30 per day, £20 per 18 holes, £10 per

9 holes **Course Designer** Willie Park **Facilities** ⌷ ⎁ ⌷ ⌷
Location 1.5m N on B709
Hotel ★★★★ 75% HL Peebles Hotel Hydro, PEEBLES
☎ 01721 720602 ▤ 01721 720602 132 en suite

JEDBURGH
Map 12 NT62

Jedburgh Dunion Rd TD8 6TA
☎ 01835 863587
e-mail: info@jedburghgolfclub.co.uk
web: www.jedburghgolfclub.co.uk
Mature, undulating parkland course with great views. Some unusual square greens.
Dunion Course: 18 Holes, 5819yds, Par 69, SSS 69,
Course record 70. Club membership 220.
Visitors Mon-Sun & BHs. Booking required. Dress code.
Societies booking required. **Green Fees** £30 per day, £25 per round (weekend £35/£28) **Course Designer** William Park **Facilities** ⊕
⊖ ⌷ ⎁ ⌷ ⌷ ⌷ ⌷ **Conf** Corporate Hospitality Days
Location 1m W on B6358
Hotel ★★★ 85% CHH The Roxburghe Hotel & Golf Course, Heiton, KELSO ☎ 01573 450331 ▤ 01573 450331 22 en suite

KELSO
Map 12 NT73

Kelso Racecourse Rd TD5 7SL
☎ 01573 223009 ▤ 01573 228490
18 Holes, 6046yds, Par 70, SSS 69, Course record 64.
Course Designer James Braid **Location** N side of town centre off B6461
Telephone for further details
Hotel ★★★ 73% HL Cross Keys, 36-37 The Square, KELSO
☎ 01573 223303 ▤ 01573 223303 27 en suite

Roxburghe Heiton TD5 8JZ
☎ 01573 450 333 ▤ 01573 450611
e-mail: hotel@roxburghe.net
web: www.roxburghe.net

An exceptional parkland layout designed by Dave Thomas and opened in 1997. Surrounded by natural woodland on the banks of the River Teviot. Owned by the Duke of Roxburghe, this course has numerous bunkers, wide rolling and sloping fairways and strategically placed water features. The signature hole is the 14th.
The Roxburghe Golf Course: 18 Holes, 6925yds, Par 72,
SSS 74, Course record 66. Club membership 300.
Visitors Mon-Sun & BHs. Handicap certificate. Dress code.
Societies booking required. **Green Fees** £90 per day, £70 per

continued

round **Course Designer** Dave Thomas **Prof** Craig Montgomerie
Facilities ⑪ ⑩ ⅃ ⌱ ⌁ ⌰ ⍁ ◇ ✦ 🛒 ✦ ✦
Leisure fishing, Clay pigeon shooting, falconry, archery, mountain
bikes **Conf** facs Corporate Hospitality Days **Location** 2m W of Kelso
on A698
Hotel ★★★ 85% CHH The Roxburghe Hotel & Golf Course,
Heiton, KELSO ☎ 01573 450331 🖹 01573 450331 22 en suite

LAUDER   Map 12 NT54

Lauder Galashiels Rd TD2 6RS
☎ 01578 722240   🖹 01578 722526
e-mail: secretary@laudergolfclub.org.uk
web: www.laudergolfclub.org.uk
Inland course and practice area on gently sloping hill with stunning
views of the Lauderdale district. The signature holes are The Wood, a
dog-leg par 4 played round the corner of a wood which is itself out of
bounds, and The Quarry, a 150yd par 3 played over several old quarry
holes into a bowl shaped green.
Lauder Golf Course: 9 Holes, 6050yds, Par 72, SSS 69,
Course record 66. Club membership 220.
Visitors Mon-Sun & BHs. Booking required Sun & BHs. Dress code.
Handicap certificate. **Societies** booking required. **Green Fees** £15
per day **Course Designer** Willie Park Jnr **Facilities** ⅃ ⌱ ⌰
Conf Corporate Hospitality Days **Location** off A68, 0.5m from Lauder,
on Galashiels Road
Hotel ★★ 74% HL Lauderdale, 1 Edinburgh Road, LAUDER
☎ 01578 722231 🖹 01578 722231 10 en suite

MELROSE   Map 12 NT53

Melrose Dingleton TD6 9HS
☎ 01896 822855   🖹 01896 822855
e-mail: melrosegolfclub@tiscali.co.uk
Undulating tree-lined fairways with splendid views. Many bunkers.
Ponds and streams cross and border four of the holes.
9 Holes, 5562yds, Par 70, SSS 68, Course record 64.
Club membership 400.
Visitors Mon-Sun & BHs. Booking required Wed & Sat. Handicap
certificate. **Societies** welcome. **Green Fees** £25 per day. Reductions
for 9 holes. **Course Designer** James Braid **Facilities** ⌱ ⍁ ⌰ ✦
Location S side of town centre on B6359
Hotel ★★★ 75% HL Burt's, Market Square, MELROSE
☎ 01896 822285 🖹 01896 822285 20 en suite

MINTO   Map 12 NT52

Minto TD9 8SH
☎ 01450 870220   🖹 01450 870126
e-mail: pat@mintogolfclub.freeserve.co.uk
web: mintogolf.co.uk
Pleasant, undulating parkland, featuring mature trees and panoramic
views of the border country. Short but quite testing course.
18 Holes, 5542yds, Par 69, SSS 67, Course record 63.
Club membership 500.
Visitors Mon-Sun & BHs. Booking required. Dress code. Handicap
certificate. **Societies** Booking required. **Green Fees** not confirmed
Course Designer Thomas Telford **Facilities** ⑪ ⑩ ⅃ ⌱ ⌁
⌰ 🛒 ✦ **Conf** Corporate Hospitality Days **Location** 5m NE from
Hawick off B6405

Hotel ★★★★ 73% CHH Dryburgh Abbey Hotel, ST BOSWELLS
☎ 01835 822261 🖹 01835 822261 38 en suite

NEWCASTLETON   Map 12 NY48

Newcastleton Holm Hill TD9 0QD
☎ 01387 375608
Hilly course with scenic views over the Liddesdale valley and
Newcastleton.
9 Holes, 5491yds, Par 69, SSS 70, Course record 67.
Club membership 100.
Visitors contact club for details. Handicap certificate.
Societies Booking required. **Green Fees** not confirmed **Course
Designer** J Shade **Facilities** ⌰ ⍀ **Leisure** fishing **Location** W side
of village
Hotel ★★★ 73% HL Garden House, Sarkfoot Road, GRETNA
☎ 01461 337621 🖹 01461 337621 38 en suite

PEEBLES   Map 11 NT24

Macdonald Cardrona Hotel, Golf & Country Club
Cardrona EH45 8NE
☎ 01896 833600   🖹 01896 831166
e-mail: golf.cardrona@macdonald-hotels.co.uk
web: www.macdonaldhotels.co.uk
Opened for play in 2001 and already a settled and inspiring test. The
terrain is a mixture of parkland, heathland and woodland with an
additional 20,000 trees planted. The USPGA specification greens are
mostly raised and mildly contoured with no two being the same shape.
Macdonald Cardrona Hotel, Golf & Country Club:
18 Holes, 6856yds, Par 72, SSS 74, Course record 64.
Club membership 200.
Visitors contact for details. **Societies** welcome. **Green Fees** £45 per
round (£55 weekends) **Course Designer** Dave Thomas **Facilities** ⑪
⑩ ⅃ ⌱ ⌁ ⌰ ⍁ ◇ ✦ 🛒 ✦ ✦ **Leisure** heated
indoor swimming pool, fishing, sauna, gymnasium **Conf** facs
Corporate Hospitality Days **Location** off A72, 3m S of Peebles
Hotel ★★★★ 77% HL Macdonald Cardrona Hotel Golf & Country
Club, Cardrona Mains, PEEBLES ☎ 01896 833600 🖹 01896 833600
99 en suite

Peebles Kirkland St EH45 8EU
☎ 01721 720197
e-mail: secretary@peeblesgolfclub.co.uk
web: peeblesgolfclub.co.uk
This parkland course is one of the most picturesque courses in
Scotland, shadowed by the rolling border hills and Tweed valley and
set high above the town. The tough opening holes are balanced by
a more generous stretch through to the 14th hole but from here the
closing five prove a challenging test.
18 Holes, 6160yds, Par 70, SSS 70, Course record 63.
Club membership 750.
Visitors Mon-Fri, Sun & BHs. Dress code. Handicap certificate.
Societies welcome. **Green Fees** £55 per day, £40 per round. **Course
Designer** H S Colt **Prof** Craig Imlah **Facilities** ⑪ ⑩ ⅃ ⌱ ⌁
⌰ ⍁ ⍀ ✦ 🛒 ✦ **Conf** Corporate Hospitality Days **Location** W
side of town centre off A72
Hotel ★★★★ 75% HL Peebles Hotel Hydro, PEEBLES
☎ 01721 720602 🖹 01721 720602 132 en suite

ST BOSWELLS
Map 12 NT53

St Boswells Braeheads TD6 0DE
☎ 01835 823527 📄 01835 823527
e-mail: secretary@stboswellsgolfclub.co.uk
web: www.stboswellsgolfclub.co.uk
Attractive, easy walking parkland by the River Tweed.

9 Holes, 5274yds, Par 68, SSS 66. Club membership 350.
Visitors Mon-Sun & BHs. Booking advisable May-Sep Handicap certificate. **Societies** booking required. **Green Fees** not confirmed **Course Designer** W Park **Facilities** ⌑ ⚐ **Location** 500yds off A68 east end of village
Hotel ★★★★ 73% CHH Dryburgh Abbey Hotel, ST BOSWELLS
☎ 01835 822261 📄 01835 822261 38 en suite

SELKIRK
Map 12 NT42

Selkirk Selkirk Hill TD7 4NW
☎ 01750 20621
e-mail: secretary@selkirkgolfclub.co.uk
web: www.selkirkgolfclub.co.uk
Pleasant moorland course with gorse and heather, set around Selkirk Hill. A testing course for all golfers. Unrivalled views.

9 Holes, 5620yds, Par 68, SSS 68, Course record 61. Club membership 300.
Visitors Mon-Wed & Fri except BHs. Handicap certificate. Dress code. **Societies** booking required. **Green Fees** £22 per 18 holes, £12 per 9 holes **Facilities** ⚐ ⚐ **Location** 1m S on A7
Hotel ★★★ 75% HL Burt's, Market Square, MELROSE
☎ 01896 822285 📄 01896 822285 20 en suite

WEST LINTON
Map 11 NT15

Rutherford Castle Golf Club EH46 7AS
☎ 01968 661233 📄 01968 661233
Rutherford Castle Golf Club: 18 Holes, 6525yds, Par 72, SSS 71.
Course Designer Bryan Moore **Location** on A702 towards Carlisle **Telephone for further details**
Hotel ★★★★ 75% HL Peebles Hotel Hydro, PEEBLES
☎ 01721 720602 📄 01721 720602 132 en suite

West Linton EH46 7HN
☎ 01968 660970 📄 01968 660622
e-mail: secretarywlgc@btinternet.com
web: www.wlgc.co.uk
Moorland course with beautiful views of Pentland Hills. This well-maintained course offers a fine challenge to all golfers with ample fairways and interesting layouts. The wildlife and natural scenery give added enjoyment.

18 Holes, 6161yds, Par 69, SSS 70, Course record 63. Club membership 1000.
Visitors Mon-Sun & BHs. Booking required. Dress code. Handicap certificate. **Societies** welcome. **Green Fees** £40 per day, £30 per round (£40 per round weekends) **Course Designer** Millar/Braid/Fraser **Prof** Ian Wright **Facilities** ⚐ ⚐ ⚐ ⚐ ⚐ ⚐ ⚐ **Conf** Corporate Hospitality Days **Location** NW side of village off A702
Hotel ★★★★ 75% HL Peebles Hotel Hydro, PEEBLES
☎ 01721 720602 📄 01721 720602 132 en suite

SOUTH AYRSHIRE

AYR
Map 10 NS32

Belleisle Belleisle Park KA7 4DU
☎ 01292 441258 📄 01292 442632
web: www.golfsouthayrshire.com
Belleisle Course: 18 Holes, 6431yds, Par 71, SSS 72, Course record 63.
Seafield Course: 18 Holes, 5498yds, Par 68, SSS 67.
Course Designer James Braid **Location** 2m S of Ayr on A719 **Telephone for further details**
Hotel ★★★ 79% HL Savoy Park, 16 Racecourse Road, AYR
☎ 01292 266112 📄 01292 266112 15 en suite

Dalmilling Westwood Av KA8 0QY
☎ 01292 263893 📄 01292 610543
web: www.golfsouthayrshire.com/dalmilling.html
Meadowland course, with easy walking. Tributaries of the River Ayr add interest to early holes.

18 Holes, 5724yds, Par 69, SSS 68, Course record 61. Club membership 260.
Visitors contact club for details. Handicap certificate. **Societies** booking required. **Green Fees** not confirmed **Prof** Philip Cheyney **Facilities** ⚐ ⚐ ⚐ ⚐ ⚐ ⚐ ⚐ ⚐ **Location** 1.5m E of town centre off A77
Hotel ★★★★ 78% HL Fairfield House, 12 Fairfield Road, AYR
☎ 01292 267461 📄 01292 267461 44 en suite

BARASSIE
Map 10 NS33

Kilmarnock (Barassie) 29 Hillhouse Rd KA10 6SY
☎ 01292 313920 📄 01292 318300
e-mail: secretary@kbgc.co.uk
web: www.kbgc.co.uk
The club has a 27-hole layout. Magnificent seaside links, relatively flat with much heather and small, undulating greens.

18 Holes, 6817yds, Par 72, SSS 74, Course record 63.
Hillhouse Course: 9 Holes, 2756yds, Par 34, SSS 34. Club membership 600.
Visitors Mon-Sun & BHs. Booking required. Dress code. Handicap certificate. **Societies** booking required. **Green Fees** £75 per 36 holes, £50 per round (£60 per round weekends) **Course Designer** Theodore Moone **Prof** Gregor Howie **Facilities** ⚐ ⚐ ⚐ ⚐ ⚐ ⚐ ⚐ ⚐ **Conf** Corporate Hospitality Days **Location** E side of village on B746, 2m N of Troon
Hotel ★★★★ 72% HL Barceló Troon Marine Hotel, Crosbie Road, TROON ☎ 01292 314444 📄 01292 314444 89 en suite

ROYAL TROON

SOUTH AYRSHIRE - TROON - MAP 10 NS33

Troon was founded in 1878 with just five holes on linksland. In its first decade it grew from five holes to six, then 12, and finally 18 holes. It became Royal Troon in 1978 on its 100th anniversary. Royal Troon's reputation is based on its combination of rough and sandy hills, bunkers, and a severity of finish that has diminished the championship hopes of many. The most successful players have relied on an equal blend of finesse and power. The British Open Championship has been played at Troon eight times - in 1923, 1950, 1962, 1973, 1982, 1989, 1997, and lastly in 2004 when it hosted the 133rd tournament. It has the shortest hole of courses hosting the Open. It is recommended that you apply to the course in advance for full visitor information.

Craigend Rd KA10 6EP ☎ 01292 311555 📠 01292 318204
e-mail: bookings@royaltroon.com **web:** www.royaltroon.com
Old Course: 18 Holes, 6641yds, Par 71, SSS 73, Course record 64.
Portland: 18 Holes, 6289yds, Par 71, SSS 71.
Craigend: 9 Holes, 1539yds, Par 29. Club membership 800.
Visitors Mon-Tue & Thu. Booking required. Handicap certificate. Dress code. **Societies** booking required. **Green Fees** £220 per day including coffee/lunch, 1 round over Old & 1 round over Portland. **Course Designer** C Hunter/G Strath/W Fernie **Prof** Kieron Stevenson **Facilities** ⑪ 🍴 🝙 🖵 🍽 ⚓ 🛎 ⛳ 🏌 🏹 **Location** S of town on B749. 3m from Prestwick airport
Hotel ★★★★ 72% HL Barceló Troon Marine Hotel, Crosbie Road, TROON ☎ 01292 314444 📠 01292 314444 89 en suite

GIRVAN
Map 10 NX19

Brunston Castle Golf Course Rd, Dailly KA26 9GD
☎ 01465 811471 & 811825 ▤ 01465 811545
e-mail: golf@brunstoncastle.co.uk
web: www.brunstoncastle.co.uk

Sheltered inland parkland course. A championship design by Donald Steel, the course is bisected by the River Girvan and shaped to incorporate all the natural surroundings. Lined with mature trees and incorporating a number of water features in addition to the river.

Burns: 18 Holes, 6662yds, Par 72, SSS 72, Course record 63. Club membership 400.

Visitors Mon-Sun & BHs. Dress code. **Societies** welcome. **Green Fees** not confirmed **Course Designer** Donald Steel **Prof** Stuart Smith **Facilities** ⑪ ⑩ ⥾ ⌨ ⑪ ⌦ ⌂ ⚑ ✿ ⌂ ✿ **Conf** facs Corporate Hospitality Days **Location** 5m E of Girvan
Hotel ★★★ 82% HL Malin Court, TURNBERRY ☎ 01655 331457 ▤ 01655 331457 18 en suite

Girvan Golf Course Rd KA26 9HW
☎ 01465 714346 ▤ 01465 714272

18 Holes, 5098yds, Par 64, SSS 65, Course record 61.

Course Designer D Kinnell/J Braid **Location** N side of town off A77
Telephone for further details
Hotel ★★★ 82% HL Malin Court, TURNBERRY ☎ 01655 331457 ▤ 01655 331457 18 en suite

MAYBOLE
Map 10 NS20

Maybole Municipal Memorial Park KA19 7DX
☎ 01655 889770

9 Holes, 2635yds, Par 33, SSS 65, Course record 64.

Leisure heated indoor swimming pool, bowling green **Location** off A77 S of town
Telephone for further details

PRESTWICK
Map 10 NS32

Prestwick 2 Links Rd KA9 1QG
☎ 01292 477404 ▤ 01292 477255
e-mail: bookings@prestwickgc.co.uk
web: www.prestwickgc.co.uk

Seaside links with natural hazards, tight fairways and difficult fast undulating greens.

18 Holes, 6544yds, Par 71, SSS 73, Course record 67. Club membership 575.

Visitors Mon-Sun & BHs. Booking required. Handicap certificate. Dress code. **Societies** booking required. **Green Fees** £175 per day, £120 per round (weekends £145 per round) **Course Designer** Tom Morris **Prof** D A Fleming **Facilities** ⑪ ⥾ ⌨ ⑪ ⌂ ⚑ ✿ **Conf** Corporate Hospitality Days **Location** in town centre off A79
Hotel ★★★ 77% HL Parkstone, Esplanade, PRESTWICK ☎ 01292 477286 ▤ 01292 477286 30 en suite

Prestwick St Cuthbert East Rd KA9 2SX
☎ 01292 477101 ▤ 01292 671730
e-mail: secretary@stcuthbert.co.uk
web: www.stcuthbert.co.uk

Parkland with easy walking and natural hazards. Tree-lined fairways, nine doglegs and well bunkered.

18 Holes, 6470yds, Par 71, SSS 71, Course record 64. Club membership 884.

Visitors Sun-Fri & BHs. Booking required Sun. Dress code. Handicap certificate. **Societies** booking required. **Green Fees** £48 per day, £35 per round. **Course Designer** Stutt & Co **Facilities** ⑪ ⑩ ⥾ ⌨ ⑪ ⌦ ⌂ ⚑ ✿ **Conf** Corporate Hospitality Days **Location** 0.5m E of town centre off A77
Hotel ★★★ 77% HL Parkstone, Esplanade, PRESTWICK ☎ 01292 477286 ▤ 01292 477286 30 en suite

Prestwick St Nicholas Grangemuir Rd KA9 1SN
☎ 01292 477608 ▤ 01292 473900
web: www.prestwickstnicholas.com

18 Holes, 5952yds, Par 69, SSS 69, Course record 63.

Course Designer Charles Hunter **Location** S side of town off A79
Telephone for further details
Hotel ★★★ 77% HL Parkstone, Esplanade, PRESTWICK ☎ 01292 477286 ▤ 01292 477286 30 en suite

TROON
Map 10 NS33

Royal Troon see page 375
Craigend Rd KA10 6EP
☎ 01292 311555 ▤ 01292 318204
e-mail: bookings@royaltroon.com
web: www.royaltroon.com

Troon Municipal Harling Dr KA10 6NE
☎ 01292 312464 ▤ 01292 312578
web: www.golfsouthayrshire.com

Lochgreen Course: 18 Holes, 6820yds, Par 74, SSS 73. Darley Course: 18 Holes, 6360yds, Par 71, SSS 63. Fullarton Course: 18 Holes, 4870yds, Par 66, SSS 64.

Prof Gordon McKinlay **Facilities** ⑪ ⑩ ⥾ ⌨ ⑪ ⌂ ⚑ ✿ **Location** 100yds from railway station
Telephone for further details
Hotel ★★★★ 72% HL Barceló Troon Marine Hotel, Crosbie Road, TROON ☎ 01292 314444 ▤ 01292 314444 89 en suite

TURNBERRY
Map 10 NS20

Turnberry Resort see page 377
Maidens Rd KA26 9LT
☎ 01655 331000 ▤ 01655 331069
web: www.turnberry.co.uk

TURNBERRY RESORT

SOUTH AYRSHIRE - TURNBERRY - MAP 10 NS20

For thousands of players of all nationalities, Turnberry is one of the finest of all golf destinations, where some of the most remarkable moments in Open history have taken place. The legendary Ailsa Course is complemented by the highly acclaimed Kintyre Course, while the nine-hole Arran Course, created by Donald Steel and Colin Montgomerie, has similar challenges such as undulating greens, tight tee shots, pot bunkers and thick Scottish rough. With the famous hotel on the left and the magnificent Ailsa Craig away to the right, there are few vistas in world golf to match the 1st tee here. To help you prepare for your game the Colin Montgomerie Links Golf Academy, alongside the luxurious and extensive clubhouse, was opened in April 2000; it features 12 driving bays, four short-game bays, two dedicated teaching rooms and a group teaching room. The Open returned to the Ailsa in 2009.

Maidens Rd KA26 9LT ☎ 01655 331000 📄 01655 331069
web: www.turnberry.co.uk
Ailsa Course: 18 Holes, 6520yds, Par 69, SSS 73, Course record 63.
Kintyre Course: 18 Holes, 6452yds, Par 72, SSS 72, Course record 63.
Arran Course: 9 Holes, 1996yds, Par 31, SSS 31.
Visitors Mon-Sun & BHs. Booking required. Dress code. Handicap certificate. **Societies** booking required. **Green Fees** Ailsa £176 per round (£215 weekends). Kintyre £117 per 18 holes **Course Designer** Mackenzie Ross/Donald Steel **Prof** Richard Hall **Facilities** ⑪ 🍽 🍺 🖳 🎣 👤 📷 ⛳ ◇ 🛵 ✗ 🏴 **Leisure** hard tennis courts, heated indoor swimming pool, fishing, sauna, gymnasium, Colin Montgomerie Links Golf Academy **Conf** facs Corporate Hospitality Days **Location** 15m SW of Ayr on A77
Hotel ★★★★★ HL Westin Turnberry Resort, TURNBERRY ☎ 01655 331000 📄 01655 331000 207 en suite

SCOTLAND

SOUTH LANARKSHIRE

BIGGAR
Map 11 NT03

Biggar The Park ML12 6AH
☎ 01899 220618(club) & 220319(course)
18 Holes, 5600yds, Par 68, SSS 67, Course record 61.
Course Designer W Park Jnr **Location** S side of town
Telephone for further details
Hotel ★★★★ 71% CHH Shieldhill Castle, Quothquan, BIGGAR
☎ 01899 220035 📄 01899 220035 26 en suite

BOTHWELL
Map 11 NS75

Bothwell Castle Uddingston Rd G71 8TD
☎ 01698 801971 & 801972 📄 01698 801971
e-mail: matchsecretary@bcgolf.co.uk
web: www.bcgolf.co.uk
Flattish tree-lined parkland course in a residential area.
18 Holes, 6220yds, Par 70, SSS 70, Course record 62.
Club membership 1000.
Visitors Mon-Fri except BHs. Booking required. Handicap certificate.
Dress code. **Societies** booking required. **Green Fees** £50 per day, £36
per round **Prof** Alan McCloskey **Facilities** ⊕ ⊖ ⛳ 🖥 ☂ 🏌 ⚲
🍴 ✦ **Conf** facs Corporate Hospitality Days **Location** NW of village
off B7071
Hotel ★★★ 79% HL Bothwell Bridge, 89 Main Street, BOTHWELL
☎ 01698 852246 📄 01698 852246 90 en suite

BURNSIDE
Map 11 NS65

Blairbeth Fernbrae Av, Fernhill G73 4SF
☎ 0141 634 3355 & 634 3325
e-mail: bcg1910@yahoo.co.uk
web: www.blairbethgolfclub.co.uk
Parkland with some small elevated greens and views over Glasgow
and the Clyde valley.
18 Holes, 5537yds, Par 70, SSS 68, Course record 63.
Club membership 280.
Visitors Mon-Sun & BHs. Booking required weekends. Dress code.
Handicap certificate. **Societies** welcome. **Green Fees** £25 per
day, £18 per round. **Facilities** ⊕ ⊖ ⛳ 🖥 🏌 ⚲ 🍴 ✦
Conf Corporate Hospitality Days **Location** 2m S of Rutherglen off
Burnside Rd

Cathkin Braes Cathkin Rd G73 4SE
☎ 0141 634 6605
e-mail: secretary@cathkinbraesgolfclub.co.uk
web: www.cathkinbraesgolfclub.co.uk
Moorland course, 600ft above sea level but relatively flat with a
prevailing westerly wind and views over Glasgow. A small loch hazard
at 5th hole. Very strong finishing holes.
18 Holes, 6200yds, Par 71, SSS 71, Course record 62.
Club membership 1020.
Visitors contact club for details. Handicap certificate.
Societies booking required. **Green Fees** £45 per day, £35 per round
Course Designer James Braid **Prof** Stephen Bree **Facilities** ⊕ ⊖
⛳ 🖥 🏌 ⚲ 🍴 ✦ 🍴 ✦ **Conf** Corporate Hospitality
Days **Location** 1m S on B759

CARLUKE
Map 11 NS85

Carluke, Mauldslie Rd, Hallcraig ML8 5HG
☎ 01555 770574 & 771070
e-mail: carlukegolfsecy@tiscali.co.uk
web: www.carlukegolfclub.com/
Parkland course with views over the Clyde Valley. Testing 11th hole,
par 3.
18 Holes, 5919yds, Par 70, SSS 69, Course record 63.
Club membership 750.
Visitors Mon-Fri & BHs. Handicap certificate. Dress code.
Societies booking required **Green Fees** £35 per day, £25 per round
Prof Craig Ronald **Facilities** ⊕ ⊖ ⛳ 🖥 🏌 ⚲ 🍴 ✦ ✦
Location 1m W off A73

CARNWATH
Map 11 NS94

Carnwath 1 Main St ML11 8JX
☎ 01555 840251 📄 01555 841070
e-mail: carnwathgc@hotmail.co.uk
web: www.carnwathgc.co.uk
Picturesque parkland, slightly hilly, panoramic views. The small
greens call for accuracy.
18 Holes, 5222yds, Par 66, SSS 66, Course record 63.
Club membership 586.
Visitors Mon-Fri & Sun except BHs. Booking required. Dress code.
Handicap certificate. **Societies** booking required. **Green Fees** £35 per
day, £25 per round (£40/£30 Sun) **Facilities** ⊕ ⊖ ⛳ 🖥 🏌
⚲ ✦ **Location** W side of village on A70
Hotel ★★★ 75% CHH Best Western Cartland Bridge, Glasgow
Road, LANARK ☎ 01555 664426 📄 01555 664426 20 en suite

EAST KILBRIDE
Map 11 NS65

East Kilbride Chapelside Rd, Nerston G74 4PF
☎ 01355 247728 📄 01355 247728
e-mail: secretary@ekgolfclub.co.uk
web: www.ekgolfclub.co.uk
Parkland course of variable topography. Generous fairways and greens
but a challenging test of golf.
18 Holes, 6419yds, Par 71, SSS 71, Course record 64.
Club membership 850.
Visitors Mon-Fri & BHs.. Booking required. Dress code.
Societies booking required. **Green Fees** £40 per day; £30 per round
Course Designer Charles Hawtree **Prof** Paul McKay **Facilities** ⊕
⊖ ⛳ 🖥 🏌 ⚲ 🍴 ✦ ✦ **Leisure** pool room **Conf** facs
Corporate Hospitality Days **Location** 0.5m N off A749, adjacent to
Nerston village

Torrance House Calderglen Country Park, Strathaven Rd
G75 0QZ
☎ 01355 248638 📄 01355 570916
A mature parkland course which has undergone major renovations in
preparation for 2010 Open Qualifying.
*Torrance House Golf Course: 18 Holes, 6476yds, Par 72,
SSS 69, Course record 71. Club membership 700.*
Visitors contact course for details. **Societies** welcome. **Green Fees** not
confirmed **Course Designer** Hawtree & Son **Facilities** ⊕ ⊖ ⛳ 🖥
🏌 ⚲ 🍴 ✦ **Conf** Corporate Hospitality Days **Location** 1.5m
SE of East Kilbride on A726

HAMILTON
Map 11 NS75

Hamilton Carlisle Rd, Ferniegair ML3 7UE
☎ 01698 282872   🖷 01698 204650
e-mail: secretary@hamiltongolfclub.co.uk
Beautiful parkland.

18 Holes, 6498yds, Par 70, SSS 70, Course record 62.

Visitors Mon-Fri & Sun. Booking required. Handicap certificate. Dress code. **Societies** booking required. **Green Fees** not confirmed **Course Designer** James Braid **Prof** Derek Wright **Facilities** ⓣ 🍴 🍺 ⌂ 🏌 ⅄ 🖿 ⚅ ⚅ **Location** 1.5m SE on A72

Strathclyde Park Mote Hill ML3 6BY
☎ 01698 429350

Municipal wooded parkland course with views of the Strathclyde Park sailing loch. With its undulating fairways, every shot in the book is required. Surrounded by a nature reserve and Hamilton racecourse.

9 Holes, 3113yds, Par 36, SSS 70, Course record 68.
Club membership 120.

Visitors Mon-Sun & BHs. Booking required. Dress code. Handicap certificate. **Societies** booking required. **Green Fees** £3.55 per 9 holes **Prof** William Walker **Facilities** ⌂ ⅄ 🖿 ⚅ 🏌 **Location** N side of town off B7071

LANARK
Map 11 NS84

Lanark The Moor, Whitelees Rd ML11 7RX
☎ 01555 663219 & 661456   🖷 01555 663219
e-mail: lanarkgolfclub@supanet.com
web: www.lanarkgolfclub.co.uk

Lanark is renowned for its smooth fast greens, natural moorland fairways and beautiful scenery. The course is built on a substrata of glacial sands, providing a unique feeling of tackling a links course at 600ft above sea level. The par of 70 can be a real test when the prevailing wind blows.

Old Course: 18 Holes, 6306yds, Par 70, SSS 71,
Course record 62.
Wee Course: 9 Holes, 1489yds, Par 28.
Club membership 880.

Visitors Mon-Fri & BHs. Booking required. Dress code. Handicap certificate. **Societies** booking required. **Green Fees** £50 per day, £40 per round. Wee Course £8 per day **Course Designer** Tom Morris **Prof** Alan White **Facilities** ⓣ 🍴 🍺 ⌂ 🍴 ⅄ 🖿 ⚅ 🚍 ⚅ **Conf** Corporate Hospitality Days **Location** E side of town centre off A73

Hotel ★★★ 75% CHH Best Western Cartland Bridge, Glasgow Road, LANARK ☎ 01555 664426 🖷 01555 664426 20 en suite

LARKHALL
Map 11 NS75

Larkhall Burnhead Rd ML9 3AA
☎ 01698 889597 & 881113 (bookings)
Small, inland parkland course.

9 Holes, 6234yds, Par 70, SSS 70, Course record 69.
Club membership 130.

Visitors Mon-Fri, Sun & BHs. Sat Nov-Mar only. Booking required. Dress code. **Societies** booking required. **Green Fees** not confirmed **Facilities** ⌂ 🍴 ⅄ ⚅ **Location** E side of town on B7019

LEADHILLS
Map 11 NS81

Leadhills 51 Main St ML12 6XP
☎ 01659 74456
e-mail: harry@glenfranka.fsnet.co.uk
A testing, hilly course. At 1500ft above sea level it is the highest golf course in Scotland.

9 Holes, 4354yds, Par 66, SSS 64. Club membership 80.

Visitors Mon-Sun & BHs. Handicap certificate. **Societies** booking required. **Green Fees** £10 per day **Facilities** by prior arrangement by prior arrangement **Location** E side of village off B797
Hotel 67% Blackaddie House Hotel, Blackaddie Road, SANQUHAR ☎ 01695 50270 🖷 01695 50270 14 en suite

LESMAHAGOW
Map 11 NS83

Hollandbush Acretophead ML11 0JS
☎ 01555 893484 & 893646
e-mail: mail@hollandbushgolfclub.co.uk
web: www.hollandbushgolfclub.co.uk
Fairly difficult, tree-lined municipal parkland and moorland course. 1st half is relatively flat, while 2nd half is hilly.

18 Holes, 6246yds, Par 71, SSS 70, Course record 63.
Club membership 400.

Visitors Mon-Sun & BHs. Booking required. Dress code. **Societies** welcome. **Green Fees** phone. **Course Designer** J Lawson/K Pate **Facilities** ⓣ 🍴 🍺 ⌂ 🍴 ⅄ 🖿 ⚅ **Location** 3m S of Lesmahagow on Coalburn Rd

RIGSIDE
Map 11 NS83

Douglas Water, Ayr Rd ML11 9NP
☎ 01555 880361   🖷 01555 880361
A 9-hole course with good variety and some hills and spectacular views. An interesting course with a challenging longest hole of 564 yards but, overall, not too testing for average golfers.

9 Holes, 5890yds, Par 72, SSS 69, Course record 63.
Club membership 150.

Visitors contact club for details. **Societies** welcome. **Green Fees** £10 per day (£12 weekends) **Facilities** ⌂ ⅄ **Location** on A70
Hotel ★★★ 75% CHH Best Western Cartland Bridge, Glasgow Road, LANARK ☎ 01555 664426 🖷 01555 664426 20 en suite

STRATHAVEN
Map 11 NS74

Strathaven Glasgow Rd ML10 6NL
☎ 01357 520421   🖷 01357 520539
e-mail: info@strathavengc.com
web: www.strathavengc.com
Gently undulating, tree-lined, championship parkland course with views over the town and the Avon valley.

18 Holes, 6265yds, Par 71, SSS 71, Course record 65.
Club membership 1050.

Visitors handicap certificate. Dress code. **Societies** welcome. **Green Fees** £45 per day, £35 per round **Course Designer** Willie Fernie/J Stutt **Prof** Stuart Kerr **Facilities** ⓣ 🍴 🍺 ⌂ 🍴 ⅄ 🖿 ⚅ 🚍 ⚅ **Location** NE side of town on A726

UDDINGSTON   Map 11 NS66

Calderbraes 57 Roundknowe Rd G71 7TS
☎ 01698 813425

Parkland with good views of Clyde valley. Testing 4th hole (par 4), hard uphill.

9 Holes, 5046yds, Par 66, SSS 67, Course record 65.
Club membership 230.

Visitors Mon-Fri & BHs. Weekends by arrangement. Dress code. Handicap certificate. **Societies** booking required. **Green Fees** £15 per day **Facilities** ⑪ ⑩ ⓑ ⵏ ⵎ ⵏ ⵏ **Location** 1.5m NW off A74 **Hotel** ★★★ 79% HL Bothwell Bridge, 89 Main Street, BOTHWELL ☎ 01698 852246 ◻ 01698 852246 90 en suite

STIRLING

ABERFOYLE   Map 11 NN50

Aberfoyle Braeval FK8 3UY
☎ 01877 382493
e-mail: secretary@aberfoylegolf.co.uk
web: www.aberfoylegolf.co.uk

Scenic heathland course with mountain views, sitting at the foot of the Monteith Hills, on the southern border of Loch Lomond and the Trossachs.

18 Holes, 5210yds, Par 66, SSS 66, Course record 64.
Club membership 520.

Visitors Mon-Sun & BHs. Booking required weekends & BHs. Handicap certificate. **Societies** booking required. **Green Fees** £24 per day, £20 per round (£30/24 weekends) **Facilities** ⑪ ⑩ ⓑ ⵏ ⵎ ⵏ
ⵏ ⵏ ⵏ ⵏ **Conf** Corporate Hospitality Days **Location** 1m E on A81
Hotel ★★★★ 74% HL Macdonald Forest Hills Hotel & Resort, Kinlochard, ABERFOYLE ☎ 0844 879 9057 & 01877 389500 ◻ 0844 879 9057 49 en suite

BANNOCKBURN   Map 11 NS89

Brucefields Family Golf Centre Ltd Pirnhall Rd FK7 8EH
☎ 01786 818184 ◻ 01786 817770
e-mail: info@brucefields.co.uk
web: www.brucefields.co.uk

Gently rolling parkland with fine views. Most holes can be played without too much difficulty with the exception of the 2nd which is a long and tricky par 4 and the 6th, a par 3, which requires exact club selection and a straight shot.

Main Course: 9 Holes, 2513yds, Par 68, SSS 68, Course record 66. Club membership 300.

Visitors dress code. Handicap certificate. **Societies** Booking required. **Green Fees** £18 per 18 holes, £11 per 9 holes (£20/£12 weekends) **Course Designer** Souters Sportsturf **Facilities** ⑪ ⑩
ⓑ ⵏ ⵏ ⵏ ⵏ ⵏ ⵏ **Leisure** golf academy, par 3 9 hole course **Conf** facs Corporate Hospitality Days **Location** M80/M9 junct 9, A91, 1st left signed
Hotel ★★★★ 75% HL Barceló Stirling Highland Hotel, Spittal Street, STIRLING ☎ 01786 272727 ◻ 01786 272727 96 en suite

BRIDGE OF ALLAN   Map 11 NS79

Bridge of Allan Sunnylaw FK9 4LY
☎ 01786 832332
e-mail: secretary@bofagc.com
web: www.bofagc.co.uk

Very hilly parkland with good views of Stirling Castle and beyond to the Trossachs. Testing par 3 1st hole, 221yds uphill, with a 6ft wall 25yds before green.

9 Holes, 4932yds, Par 66, SSS 66, Course record 59.
Club membership 400.

Visitors Mon-Fri & Sun except BHs. Dress code. Handicap certificate. **Societies** welcome. **Green Fees** phone **Course Designer** Tom Morris **Facilities** ⓑ ⵏ ⵏ ⵏ **Location** 0.5m N off A9
Hotel ★★★★ 75% HL Barceló Stirling Highland Hotel, Spittal Street, STIRLING ☎ 01786 272727 ◻ 01786 272727 96 en suite

CALLANDER   Map 11 NN60

Callander Aveland Rd FK17 8EN
☎ 01877 330090 & 330975 ◻ 01877 330062
web: www.callandergolfclub.co.uk

18 Holes, 5151yds, Par 66, SSS 65, Course record 61.

Course Designer Morris/Fernie **Location** E side of town off A84
Telephone for further details
Hotel ★★★ 86% CHH Roman Camp Country House, CALLANDER ☎ 01877 330003 ◻ 01877 330003 15 en suite

DRYMEN   Map 11 NS48

Buchanan Castle G63 0HY
☎ 01360 660307 ◻ 01360 660993
web: www.buchanancastlegolfclub.com
18 Holes, 6059yds, Par 70, SSS 69.

Course Designer James Braid **Location** 1m W
Telephone for further details
Hotel ★★★ 75% HL Best Western Winnock, The Square, DRYMEN ☎ 01360 660245 ◻ 01360 660245 73 en suite

Strathendrick G63 0AA
☎ 01360 660695
e-mail: melvinquyn@hotmail.com

Hillside course with breathtaking views of the Campsie and Luss Hills and Ben Lomond. Mainly natural hazards with few bunkers. Greens are comparatively small but in immaculate condition.

9 Holes, 4982yards, Par 66, SSS 64, Course record 60.
Club membership 470.

Visitors Mon-Fri except BHs. Dress code. **Societies** booking required. **Green Fees** £15 per 18 holes **Facilities** ⵏ ⵏ ⵏ **Leisure** hard tennis courts, driving net **Location** 0.5m S of Drymen via access lane E of A811
Hotel ★★★★★ 84% HL De Vere Deluxe Cameron House, BALLOCH ☎ 01389 755565 ◻ 01389 755565 96 en suite

SCOTLAND

DUNBLANE
Map 11 NN70

Dunblane New Golf Club Perth Rd FK15 0LJ
☎ 01786 821521 📠 01786 825066
e-mail: secretary@dngc.co.uk
web: www.dngc.co.uk
Well-maintained parkland course. Testing par 3 holes.
Dunblane New Golf Club Ltd: 18 Holes, 5930yds, Par 69, SSS 69. Club membership 1000.
Visitors Mon-Fri, Sun & BHs. Booking required. Dress code.
Societies Booking required. **Green Fees** not confirmed **Course Designer** James Braid **Prof** Bob Jamieson **Facilities** ⓣ ⑪ ⌱ ⌂ 🍴 ⌲ 🏠 ⚑ ✆ **Conf** facs Corporate Hospitality Days
Location Off fourways rdbt in town centre
Hotel ★★★★ 75% HL Barceló Stirling Highland Hotel, Spittal Street, STIRLING ☎ 01786 272727 📠 01786 272727 96 en suite

KILLIN
Map 11 NN53

Killin FK21 8TX
☎ 01567 820312 📠 01567 820312
e-mail: info@killingolfclub.co.uk
web: www.killingolfclub.co.uk
Parkland course at the west end of Loch Tay with outstanding views. Challenging nine-hole course with 14 different tees.
9 Holes, 2600yds, Par 66, SSS 65, Course record 61. Club membership 200.
Visitors Mon-Sun & BHs. Dress code. Handicap certificate.
Societies booking required. **Green Fees** £27 per day, £20 per 18 holes, £12 per 9 holes (£30/£24/£14 weekends) **Course Designer** John Duncan/J Braid **Facilities** ⓣ ⌱ 🍴 ⌲ ⚑ ✆ 🛒 ✆ **Location** 0.5m N of village centre on A827
Hotel ★★★ 83% HL The Four Seasons Hotel, Loch Earn, ST FILLANS ☎ 01764 685333 📠 01764 685333 18 en suite

STIRLING
Map 11 NS79

Stirling Queens Rd FK8 3AA
☎ 01786 464098 📠 01786 460090
web: www.stirlinggolfclub.com
Undulating parkland with magnificent views of Stirling Castle and the Grampian Mountains. Testing 15th, Cotton's Fancy, 384yds (par 4).
18 Holes, 6438yds, Par 72, SSS 71, Course record 64. Club membership 1100.
Visitors Mon-Fri, Sun & BHs. Booking required. Dress code. Handicap certificate. **Societies** booking required. **Green Fees** £45 per day, £30 per round **Course Designer** Henry Cotton **Prof** Ian Collins **Facilities** ⓣ ⑪ ⌱ ⌂ 🍴 ⌲ 🏠 ⚑ ✆ ✆ **Conf** Corporate Hospitality Days **Location** W side of town on B8051
Hotel ★★★★ 75% HL Barceló Stirling Highland Hotel, Spittal Street, STIRLING ☎ 01786 272727 📠 01786 272727 96 en suite

WEST DUNBARTONSHIRE

BALLOCH
Map 10 NS48

The Carrick on Loch Lomond, Loch Lomond G83 8RE
☎ 01389 713655
e-mail: colin.white@cameronhouse.co.uk
web: www.devere.co.uk
The Carrick at Cameron House, opened 2007. The front 9 holes are in the lowlands, but the back 9 are in the highlands.The stunning views of Loch Lomond create an amazing backdrop.
The Carrick on Loch Lomond: 18 Holes, 7082yds, Par 71, SSS 74.
Wee Demon: 9 Holes, 3200yds, Par 29.
Club membership 250.
Visitors Mon-Sun & BHs. Booking required. Dress code.
Societies booking required. **Green Fees** Carrick £125 per round, Wee Demon £25 per day, £15 per 9 holes **Course Designer** Doug Carrick **Prof** Colin White **Facilities** ⓣ ⑪ ⌱ ⌂ 🍴 ⌲ 🏠 ⚑ ◇ ✆ ✆ ♟ **Leisure** hard tennis courts, heated indoor swimming pool, squash, fishing, sauna, gymnasium, spa **Conf** facs Corporate Hospitality Days **Location** M8 (W) junct 30 for Erskine Bridge, then A82 for Crainlarich. Course 1m past Balloch roundabout
Hotel ★★★★★ 84% HL De Vere Deluxe Cameron House, BALLOCH ☎ 01389 755565 📠 01389 755565 96 en suite

BONHILL
Map 10 NS37

Vale of Leven North Field Rd G83 9ET
☎ 01389 752351 📠 0870 749 8950
e-mail: rbarclay@volgc.org
web: www.volgc.org
Moorland course, tricky with many natural hazards - gorse, burns, trees. Overlooks Loch Lomond.
18 Holes, 5277yds, Par 67, SSS 67, Course record 62. Club membership 750.
Visitors Mon-Fri, Sun & BHs. Booking required Fri & Sun. Dress code. **Societies** booking required. **Green Fees** £32 per day, £22 per round (£39.50/£27 Sun) **Prof** Barry Campbell **Facilities** ⓣ ⑪ ⌱ ⌂ 🍴 ⌲ 🏠 ⚑ ✆ **Conf** facs Corporate Hospitality Days **Location** E side of town off A813
Hotel ★★★★★ 84% HL De Vere Deluxe Cameron House, BALLOCH ☎ 01389 755565 📠 01389 755565 96 en suite

CLYDEBANK
Map 11 NS56

Clydebank & District Glasgow Rd, Hardgate G81 5QY
☎ 01389 383831 & 383833 📠 01389 383831
e-mail: clydebankanddgc@yahoo.com
An undulating parkland course established in 1905, overlooking Clydebank.
18 Holes, 5825yds, Par 68, SSS 69, Course record 63. Club membership 850.
Visitors contact club for details. **Societies** welcome. **Green Fees** £35 per day, £20 per round **Course Designer** Members **Prof** A Waugh **Facilities** ⓣ ⑪ ⌱ ⌂ 🍴 ⌲ 🏠 ✆ **Location** 2m E of Erskine Bridge

SCOTLAND

SCOTLAND

Clydebank Municipal Overtoun Rd, Dalmuir G81 3RE
☎ 0141 952 6372 📠 0141 9526372
e-mail: dalmuirgolf@tiscali.co.uk
Hilly, compact parkland course with tough finishing holes.
Clydebank Municipal Golf Course: 18 Holes, 5349yds,
Par 67, SSS 66, Course record 61.
Visitors Mon-Sun & BHs. Booking required Wed, Fri-Sun & BHs.
Societies welcome. **Green Fees** not confirmed **Prof** Stewart Savage
Facilities ⊕ ⊑ ⌳ 🖾 ⌁ ⚡ **Location** 2m NW of town centre
Hotel ★★★★ 73% HL Beardmore, Beardmore Street, CLYDEBANK
☎ 0141 951 6000 📠 0141 951 6000 166 en suite

DUMBARTON   Map 10 NS37

Dumbarton Broadmeadow G82 2BQ
☎ 01389 732830 & 765995
e-mail: secretary@dumbartongolfclub.co.uk
web: www.dumbartongolfclub.co.uk
Flat parkland with many trees.
18 Holes, 5905yds, Par 71, SSS 69, Course record 64.
Club membership 800.
Visitors Mon-Fri except BHs. Dress code. **Societies** booking required.
Green Fees £32 per day, £22 per round **Facilities** ⊕ ⓃⓄⓁ ⓁⓁ ⊑
⌁ ⌳ 🖾 ⚡ **Conf** Corporate Hospitality Days **Location** 0.25m N
off A814
Guesthouse ★★★★★ GA Kirkton House, Darleith Road,
CARDROSS ☎ 01389 841951 📠 01389 841951 6 en suite

WEST LOTHIAN

BATHGATE   Map 11 NS96

Bathgate Edinburgh Rd EH48 1BA
☎ 01506 630553 & 652232/630505
e-mail: bathgate.golfclub@lineone.net
web: www.bathgategolfclub.co.uk
Moorland course. Easy walking. Testing 11th hole, par 3.
18 Holes, 6328yds, Par 71, SSS 71, Course record 58.
Club membership 900.
Visitors Mon-Sat except BHs.. Booking required. Dress code.
Societies booking required. **Green Fees** £30 per day, £25 per
round (£40/£30 Sat) **Course Designer** W Park **Prof** Stuart Callan
Facilities ⊕ ⓃⓄⓁ ⓁⓁ ⊑ ⌁ ⌳ 🖾 ⌁ ⚡ ⚡
Conf Corporate Hospitality Days **Location** E side of town off A89
Hotel ★★★ 78% HL Best Western Hilcroft, East Main Street,
WHITBURN ☎ 01501 740818 & 743372 📠 01501 740818
32 en suite

BROXBURN   Map 11 NT07

Niddry Castle Castle Rd EH52 6RQ
☎ 01506 891097 📠 01506 891097
web: www.niddrycastlegc.co.uk
18 Holes, 5914yds, Par 70, SSS 69, Course record 63.
Course Designer A Scott **Location** 9m W of Edinburgh on B9080
Telephone for further details
Hotel ★★★★ 78% HL Macdonald Houstoun House, UPHALL
☎ 0844 879 9043 📠 0844 879 9043 71 en suite

FAULDHOUSE   Map 11 NS96

Greenburn 6 Greenburn Rd EH47 9HJ
☎ 01501 770292 📠 01501 772615
e-mail: administrator@greenburngolfclub.co.uk
web: www.greenburngolfclub.co.uk
A testing course, with a mixture of parkland and moorland. Water
features on 14 of the 18 holes, with a burn crossing most of the holes
on the back 9.
18 Holes, 6067yds, Par 71, SSS 70, Course record 63.
Club membership 750.
Visitors Mon-Sun & BHs. Booking required. Dress code.
Societies booking required. **Green Fees** £32 per day, £24 per round
(weekends £40/£32) **Prof** Scott Catlin **Facilities** ⊕ ⓃⓄⓁ ⓁⓁ ⊑ ⌁
⌳ 🖾 ⚡ **Location** 3m SW of Whitburn
Hotel ★★★ 78% HL Best Western Hilcroft, East Main Street,
WHITBURN ☎ 01501 740818 & 743372 📠 01501 740818
32 en suite

LINLITHGOW   Map 11 NS97

Linlithgow Braehead EH49 6QF
☎ 01506 844356 (pro) & 842585 (sec)
📠 01506 842764
e-mail: info@linlithgowgolf.co.uk
web: www.linlithgowgolf.co.uk
A short but testing undulating parkland course with panoramic views
of the Forth valley.
18 Holes, 5800yds, Par 70, SSS 68, Course record 64.
Club membership 450.
Visitors contact club for details. **Societies** booking required. **Green
Fees** £35 per day, £25 per round (£40/£30 Sun) **Course Designer** R
Simpson of Carnoustie **Prof** Graeme Bell **Facilities** ⊕ ⓃⓄⓁ ⓁⓁ ⊑
⌁ ⌳ 🖾 ⚡ ⚡ **Conf** Corporate Hospitality Days **Location** 1m
S off A706
Hotel ★★★★ 72% HL Macdonald Inchyra Grange, Grange Road,
POLMONT ☎ 01324 711911 📠 01324 711911 98 en suite

West Lothian Airngath Hill EH49 7RH
☎ 01506 825060 📠 01506 826462
web: www.thewestlothiangolfclub.co.uk
18 Holes, 6249yds, Par 71, SSS 70.
Course Designer Fraser Middleton **Location** 1m N off A706
Telephone for further details
Hotel ★★★★ 72% HL Macdonald Inchyra Grange, Grange Road,
POLMONT ☎ 01324 711911 📠 01324 711911 98 en suite

LIVINGSTON   Map 11 NT06

Deer Park Golf & Country Club Golf Course Rd EH54 8AB
☎ 01506 446699 📠 01506 435608
e-mail: deerpark@muir-group.co.uk
web: www.deer-park.co.uk
Home of the Scottish PGA Deer Park Masters, this is a championship
standard course, with panoramic views over the Pentlands.
Deer Park Golf & Country Club: 18 Holes, 6737yds,
Par 72, SSS 72, Course record 65. Club membership 1700.
Visitors Mon-Sun & BHs. Dress code. **Societies** welcome. **Green
Fees** £30 per 18 holes (£40 weekends) **Course Designer** Alliss/

continued

Thomas **Prof** Sandy Strachan **Facilities** ⑪ ⑩ 🍴 ⬛ ⬜ 🍽️ ⛳ 🏌 🍴 ⛳ **Leisure** heated indoor swimming pool, squash, sauna, gymnasium, snooker table, ten pin bowling **Conf** facs Corporate Hospitality Days **Location** M8 junct 3, to N side of town

Pumpherston Drumshoreland Rd, Pumpherston EH53 0LH
☎ 01506 433336 (office) & 433337 (pro)
🖷 01506 438250
e-mail: sheena.corner@tiscali.co.uk
web: www.pumpherstongolfclub.co.uk
Undulating, well-bunkered parkland course with very testing 2nd and 15th holes. The course has water features at five holes and has won several environmental awards. Panoramic views of Edinburgh and the Pentland Hills.
18 Holes, 6006yds, Par 70, SSS 72. Club membership 800.
Visitors Mon-Sun & BHs. Booking required. Handicap certificate. Dress code. **Societies** booking required. **Green Fees** phone. **Course Designer** G Webster **Facilities** ⑪ ⑩ by prior arrangement 🍴 ⬜ 🍽️ ⛳ 🏌 🍴 🏌 **Location** 1m E of Livingston off B8046

UPHALL Map 11 NT07

Uphall EH52 6JT
☎ 01506 856404 🖷 01506 855358
web: www.uphallgolfclub.com
18 Holes, 5588yds, Par 69, SSS 67, Course record 61.
Prof Gordon Law **Facilities** ⑪ ⑩ 🍴 ⬛ ⬜ 🍽️ 🍴 🏌 ⛳
Conf facs Corporate Hospitality Days **Location** W side of village on A899
Telephone for further details
Hotel ★★★★ 78% HL Macdonald Houstoun House, UPHALL
☎ 0844 879 9043 🖷 0844 879 9043 71 en suite

WEST CALDER Map 11 NT06

Harburn EH55 8RS
☎ 01506 871131 & 871256 🖷 01506 870286
e-mail: info@harburngolfclub.co.uk
web: www.harburngolfclub.co.uk
Parkland with a variety of beech, oak and pine trees. The 11th and 12th holes were extended in 2004. Fine views of the Pentlands
18 Holes, 6125yds, Par 71, SSS 70, Course record 64. Club membership 870.
Visitors Mon-Sun & BHs. Booking required. Handicap certificate. Dress code. **Societies** Booking required. **Green Fees** not confirmed **Prof** Stephen Mills **Facilities** ⑪ ⑩ 🍴 ⬜ 🍽️ 🍴 ⬛ ⛳ **Conf** facs Corporate Hospitality Days **Location** 2m S of West Calder on B7008
Hotel ★★★ 78% HL Best Western Hilcroft, East Main Street, WHITBURN ☎ 01501 740818 & 743372 🖷 01501 740818 32 en suite

WHITBURN Map 11 NS96

Polkemmet Country Park EH47 0AD
☎ 01501 743905 🖷 01506 846256
e-mail: mail@beecraigs.com
web: www.beecraigs.com
Public parkland course surrounded by mature woodland and rhododendron bushes and bisected by a river. Interesting and demanding last hole.

Polkemmet Country Park: 9 Holes, 2946mtrs, Par 37.
Visitors contact for details. Handicap certificate. **Societies** welcome.
Green Fees £9.85 per 18 holes, £5.65 per 9 holes (£11.65/£6.75 weekends & BHs) **Facilities** ⑪ ⑩ 🍴 ⬛ ⬜ 🍽️ 🍴 🏌 ⛳ 🏌 **Leisure** bowling green **Location** 2m W of Whitburn on B7066
Hotel ★★★ 78% HL Best Western Hilcroft, East Main Street, WHITBURN ☎ 01501 740818 & 743372 🖷 01501 740818 32 en suite

SCOTTISH ISLANDS

ARRAN, ISLE OF

BLACKWATERFOOT Map 10 NR92

Shiskine Shore Rd KA27 8HA
☎ 01770 860226 🖷 01770 860205
e-mail: info@shiskinegolf.com
web: www.shiskinegolf.com
Unique 12-hole links course with gorgeous outlook to the Mull of Kintyre. The course is crossed by two burns and includes the longest par 5 on the island at 509yds. There are several blind holes at which various signals indicate when the green is clear and it is safe to play.
12 Holes, 2990yds, Par 42, SSS 42, Course record 38. Club membership 751.
Visitors Mon-Sun & BHs. Booking required. **Societies** Booking required. **Green Fees** not confirmed **Course Designer** W Fernie **Facilities** ⑪ ⑩ by prior arrangement 🍴 ⬜ 🍴 🏌 ⛳ 🏌 **Leisure** hard tennis courts, bowling green, golf practice nets **Conf** Corporate Hospitality Days **Location** W side of village off A841
Hotel ★★★ CHH Kilmichael Country House, Glen Cloy, BRODICK ☎ 01770 302219 🖷 01770 302219 8 en suite

BRODICK Map 10 NS03

Brodick KA27 8DL
☎ 01770 302349 🖷 01770 302349
web: www.brodickgolfclub.org
18 Holes, 4747yds, Par 65, SSS 64, Course record 60.
Course Designer Location N side of village, 0.5m N of Brodick Ferry Terminal
Telephone for further details
Hotel ★★★★ 77% HL Auchrannie House, BRODICK ☎ 01770 302234 🖷 01770 302234 28 en suite

LAMLASH Map 10 NS03

Lamlash KA27 8JU
☎ 01770 600296 & 600196 (starter) 🖷 01770 600296
e-mail: lamlashgolfclub@btconnect.com
web: www.lamlashgolfclub.co.uk
Undulating heathland course with magnificent views of the mountains and sea.
18 Holes, 4510yds, Par 64, SSS 64, Course record 58. Club membership 450.
Visitors Mon-Sun & BHs. Booking required. **Societies** welcome. **Green Fees** phone **Course Designer** Auchterlonie **Facilities** ⑪ ⑩ 🍴 ⬜ 🍽️ 🍴 🏌 ⛳ 🏌 **Location** 0.75m N of Lamlash on A841
Hotel ★★★★ 77% HL Auchrannie House, BRODICK ☎ 01770 302234 🖷 01770 302234 28 en suite

SCOTLAND

LOCHRANZA
Map 10 NR95

Lochranza KA27 8HL
☎ 01770 830273
e-mail: office@lochgolf.demon.co.uk
web: www.lochranzagolf.com

This course is mainly on the level, set amid spectacular scenery where the fairways are grazed by wild red deer, while overhead buzzards and golden eagles may be seen. There are water hazards including the river which is lined by mature trees. The final three holes, nicknamed the Bermuda Triangle, provide an absorbing finish right to the 18th hole - a 530yd dogleg through trees and over the river. The large greens, six single and six double, are played off 18 tees.

Lochranza Golf: 18 Holes, 5033mtrs, Par 70, SSS 67, Course record 72.

Visitors Mon-Sun & BHs. **Societies** welcome. **Green Fees** £24 per day, £18 per 18 holes, £12 per 9 holes **Course Designer** relaid 1991 by I Robertson **Facilities** ⊕ ⓑ ☐ ⚲ 📷 ⚑ ✆ **Location** in Lochranza village
Hotel ★★★ CHH Kilmichael Country House, Glen Cloy, BRODICK
☎ 01770 302219 📄 01770 302219 8 en suite

MACHRIE
Map 10 NR83

Machrie Bay KA27 8DZ
☎ 01770 840259 📄 01770 840266
web: www.dougarie.com

Machrie Bay Golf Course: 9 Holes, 4556yds, Par 66, SSS 63, Course record 63.

Course Designer W Fernie **Location** 9m W of Brodick via String Rd **Telephone for further details**
Hotel ★★★ CHH Kilmichael Country House, Glen Cloy, BRODICK
☎ 01770 302219 📄 01770 302219 8 en suite

SANNOX
Map 10 NS04

Corrie KA27 8JD
☎ 01770 810223 & 810606

A heathland course on the coast with beautiful mountain scenery. An upward climb to 6th hole then a descent from the 7th. All these holes are subject to strong winds in bad weather.

9 Holes, 1948yds, Par 62, SSS 61, Course record 56. Club membership 300.

Visitors contact club for details. **Societies** booking required. **Green Fees** not confirmed **Course Designer Facilities** ⊕ ⓣ ☐ ⚲ **Location** 6m N of A841
Hotel ★★★★ 77% HL Auchrannie House, BRODICK
☎ 01770 302234 📄 01770 302234 28 en suite

WHITING BAY
Map 10 NS02

Whiting Bay KA27 8QT
☎ 01770 700487

Heathland course.

18 Holes, 4405yds, Par 63, SSS 63, Course record 59. Club membership 350.

Visitors Mon-Sun & BHs. Booking required weekends & BHs. **Societies** booking required. **Green Fees** £24 per day, £19 per round **Course Designer Facilities** ⓑ ☐ ⚲ 📷 ⚑ ✆ 🚻 ✆ **Location** NW side of village off A841

Hotel ★★★ CHH Kilmichael Country House, Glen Cloy, BRODICK
☎ 01770 302219 📄 01770 302219 8 en suite

BUTE, ISLE OF

PORT BANNATYNE
Map 10 NS06

Port Bannatyne Bannatyne Mains Rd PA20 0PH
☎ 01700 505142
web: www.portbannatynegolf.co.uk

Seaside hill course with panoramic views. Almost unique in having 13 holes, with the first five being played again before a separate 18th. Difficult 4th (par 3).

13 Holes, 5085yds, Par 68, SSS 65, Course record 61. Club membership 170.

Visitors Mon-Sun & BHs. Handicap certificate. **Societies** booking required **Green Fees** £17 per day, £12 per round. (£22/£18 weekends) **Course Designer** Peter Morrison **Facilities** ⊕ ⓑ ☐ ⚲ **Location** W side of village off A886
Hotel ★★★ SHL An Lochan, Shore Road, TIGHNABRUAICH
☎ 01700 811239 📄 01700 811239 11 en suite

ROTHESAY
Map 10 NS06

Rothesay Canada Hill PA20 9HN
☎ 01700 503554 📄 01700 503554
e-mail: thepro@rothesaygolfclub.com
web: www.rothesaygolfclub.com

A scenic island course designed by James Braid and Ben Sayers. The course is fairly hilly, with views of the Firth of Clyde, Rothesay Bay or the Kyles of Bute from every hole. Winds make the two par 5 holes extremely challenging.

18 Holes, 5419yds, Par 69, SSS 66, Course record 62. Club membership 400.

Visitors Mon-Sun & BHs. Booking required weekends. Dress code. **Societies** booking required. **Green Fees** phone **Course Designer** James Braid & Ben Sayers **Prof** James M Dougal **Facilities** ⊕ ⓣ ⓑ ☐ ⚲ 📷 ⚑ ✆ ✆ **Leisure** golf nets **Conf** Corporate Hospitality Days **Location** 500yds SE from main ferry terminal
Hotel ★★★ SHL An Lochan, Shore Road, TIGHNABRUAICH
☎ 01700 811239 📄 01700 811239 11 en suite

KINGARTH
Map 10 NS05

Bute St Ninians, 32 Marine Place, Ardbeg, Rothesay PA20 0LF
☎ 01700 503091
e-mail: administrator@butegolfclub.com
web: www.butegolfclub.com

Flat seaside course with good fenced greens and fine views over the Sound of Bute to Isle of Arran. Challenging par 3 along sea.

9 Holes, 2582yds, Par 68, SSS 64, Course record 61. Club membership 200.

Visitors Mon-Sun & BHs. Handicap certificate. **Societies** booking required. **Green Fees** £10 per day **Course Designer Facilities** ⚲ **Location** 6m from Rothesay pier on A845
Hotel ★★★ SHL An Lochan, Shore Road, TIGHNABRUAICH
☎ 01700 811239 📄 01700 811239 11 en suite

COLONSAY, ISLE OF

SCALASAIG Map 10 NR39

Colonsay Machrins Farm PA61 7YR
☎ 01951 200290 🖹 01951 200290

18 Holes, 4775yds, Par 72, SSS 72.
Course Designer Location 2m W on A870
Telephone for further details

ISLAY, ISLE OF

PORT ELLEN Map 10 NR34

Machrie Hotel Machrie PA42 7AN
☎ 01496 302310 🖹 01496 302404
e-mail: machrie@machrie.com
web: www.machrie.com
Championship links course opened in 1891, where golf's first £100 Open Championship was played in 1901. Fine turf and many blind holes.

Machrie Hotel & Golf Links: 18 Holes, 6324yds, Par 71, SSS 71, Course record 66. Club membership 340.

Visitors dress code **Societies** booking required. **Green Fees** £80 per day, £55 per round **Course Designer** W Campbell **Prof** Ron Goudie **Facilities** ⓣ 🍴 🍽 🏌 🖥 🍴 ◇ 🏌 🛒
🏌 **Leisure** fishing, snooker, table tennis **Conf** facs Corporate Hospitality Days **Location** 4m N off A846
Hotel ★★★★★ RR The Harbour Inn and Restaurant,
BOWMORE ☎ 01496 810330 🖹 01496 810330 7 en suite

LEWIS, ISLE OF

STORNOWAY Map 13 NB43

Stornoway Lady Lever Park HS2 0XP
☎ 01851 702240
e-mail: admin@stornowaygolfclub.co.uk
web: www.stornowaygolfclub.co.uk
A short but tricky undulating parkland course set in the grounds of Lewis Castle with fine views over the Minch to the mainland. The terrain is peat based and there has been substantial investment in drainage works.

18 Holes, 5252yds, Par 68, SSS 67, Course record 61. Club membership 500.

Visitors contact club for details. Handicap certificate.
Societies welcome. **Green Fees** £30 per day, £25 per round **Course Designer** J & R Stutt **Facilities** ⓣ by prior arrangement 🏌 🖥 🍽
🏌 🛒 🍴 🏌 **Conf** facs **Location** 0.5m from town centre off A857

MULL, ISLE OF

CRAIGNURE Map 10 NM73

Craignure Scallastle PA65 6BA
☎ 01680 812370
A natural links course designed round the estuary of the Scallastle Burn that flows into the Sound of Mull. Continual improvements have provided 18 teeing areas for the 9-hole layout.

9 Holes, 5357yds, Par 69, SSS 66, Course record 72. Club membership 104.

Visitors contact club for details. **Societies** welcome. **Green Fees** £15 per day/round **Course Designer Facilities** 🏌 🍽 🏌 **Location** 1.5m N of Craignure A849
Hotel ★★★ 74% HL Isle of Mull Hotel, CRAIGNURE
☎ 0870 950 6267 🖹 0870 950 6267 86 en suite

TOBERMORY Map 13 NM55

Tobermory PA75 6PG
☎ 01688 302743 🖹 0870 052 3091
e-mail: enquiries@tobermorygolfclub.com
web: www.tobermorygolfclub.com
A beautifully maintained hilltop course with superb views over the Sound of Mull. Testing 7th hole (par 3).

9 Holes, 4912yds, Par 64, SSS 64, Course record 65. Club membership 150.

Visitors Mon-Fri & BHs. Limited play weekends. **Societies** welcome. **Green Fees** not confirmed **Course Designer** David Adams **Facilities** 🏌 🖥 🍽 🏌 🛒 ◇ 🏌 **Location** 0.5m N off A848
Hotel ★★★ SHL Highland Cottage, Breadalbane Street,
TOBERMORY ☎ 01688 302030 🖹 01688 302030 6 en suite

ORKNEY

KIRKWALL Map 16 HY41

Orkney Grainbank KW15 1RB
☎ 01856 872457
e-mail: orkneygolfclub@grainbank.freeserve.co.uk
web: www.orkneygolfclub.co.uk
Open parkland course with few hazards and superb views over Kirkwall and Islands. Very exposed to the elements which can make play tough.

18 Holes, 5411yds, Par 70, SSS 67, Course record 63. Club membership 350.

Visitors contact club for details. Handicap certificate.
Societies welcome. **Green Fees** £25 per day **Course Designer Facilities** 🏌 🖥 🍽 🏌 🏌 **Location** 0.5m W off A965

STROMNESS Map 16 HY20

Stromness, Ness KW16 3DW
☎ 01856 850772
e-mail: sgc@stromnessgc.co.uk
web: www.stromnessgc.co.uk
Testing parkland and seaside course with easy walking. Magnificent views of Scapa Flow.

18 Holes, 4762yds, Par 65, SSS 64, Course record 61. Club membership 350.

Visitors Mon-Sun & BHs. **Societies** welcome. **Green Fees** not confirmed **Course Designer Facilities** 🖥 🍽 🏌 🏌 🏌
Leisure hard tennis courts, Bowling **Location** S side of town centre off A965

SCOTLAND

SHETLAND

LERWICK
Map 16 HU44

Shetland Dale Golf Course, Gott ZE2 9SB
☎ 01595 840369 🖹 01595 840369
e-mail: shetlandgolfclub@btopenworld.com
web: www.shetlandgolfclub.co.uk

Challenging moorland course, hard walking. A burn runs the full length of the course and provides a natural hazard. Testing holes include the 4th (par 4), 7th (par 4), 14th (par 3) and 15th (par 4). Every hole provides a new and varied challenge with no two holes similar in layout or appearance.

Dale Course: 18 Holes, 5562yds, Par 68, SSS 68, Course record 68. Club membership 430.

Visitors contact course for details. **Societies** booking required. **Green Fees** not confirmed **Course Designer** Fraser Middleton **Facilities** 🍴 ☕ 🍷 ⛳ 🏌 ♂ **Conf** facs Corporate Hospitality Days
Location 4m N on A970
Hotel ★★★ 73% HL Lerwick, 15 South Road, LERWICK
☎ 01595 692166 🖹 01595 692166   34 en suite

WHALSAY, ISLAND OF
Map 16 HU56

Whalsay Skaw Taing ZE2 9AA
☎ 01806 566450 & 566481

The most northerly golf course in Britain, with a large part of it running round the coastline, offering spectacular holes in an exposed but highly scenic setting and wildlife in abundance. Signature hole is the par 4 16th. Preferred lies in operation all year round.

18 Holes, 6140yds, Par 71, SSS 69, Course record 69. Club membership 205.

Visitors contact club for details. Handicap certificate.
Societies booking required. **Green Fees** £20 per 18 holes **Course Designer Facilities** ⓣ by prior arrangement ☕ 🍷 ⛳ ♂
Location 5m N from Symbister ferry terminal

SKYE, ISLE OF

SCONSER
Map 13 NG53

Isle of Skye IV48 8TD
☎ 01478 650414
web: www.isleofskyegolfclub.co.uk

18 Holes, 4677yds, Par 66, SSS 64, Course record 62.

Course Designer Location on A87 between Broadford
Telephone for further details
Hotel ★★★ 73% HL Rosedale, Beaumont Crescent, PORTREE
☎ 01478 613131 🖹 01478 613131   18 en suite

SCOTLAND

Wales

ANGLESEY, ISLE OF

AMLWCH
Map 6 SH49

Bull Bay LL68 9RY
☎ 01407 830960 📠 01407 832612
e-mail: info@bullbaygc.co.uk
web: ww.bullbaygc.co.uk

Wales's northernmost course, Bull Bay is a pleasant coastal, heathland course with natural rock, gorse and wind hazards. Views from several tees across the Irish Sea to the Isle of Man, and across Anglesey to Snowdonia.

18 Holes, 6217yds, Par 70, SSS 72, Course record 60.
Club membership 700.

Visitors contact club for details. Handicap certificate.
Societies welcome. **Green Fees** £45 per day, £33 per round (£50/£36 weekends & BHs) **Course Designer** W H Fowler **Prof** John Burns **Facilities** 🍷 🍴 🍸 🛒 🏌 🏑 🛍 ⛳ 🏌 🏌 🚕 🏌
Conf Corporate Hospitality Days **Location** 1m W of Amlwch on A5025

BEAUMARIS
Map 6 SH67

Baron Hill LL58 8YW
☎ 01248 810231 📠 01248 810231
e-mail: golf@baronhill.co.uk
web: www.baronhill.co.uk

Undulating course with natural hazards of rock and gorse. Testing 3rd and 4th holes (par 4s). Hole 5/14 plays into the prevailing wind with an elevated tee across two streams. The hole is between two gorse covered mounds and considered one of the best par 3 holes in North Wales.

9 Holes, 5572yds, Par 68, SSS 68, Course record 65.
Club membership 350.

Visitors Mon, Wed, Fri, Sat & BHs. Tue & Thu pm only. Booking advisable. Dress code. Handicap certificate. **Societies** welcome.
Green Fees £20 per day, £12.50 per 9 holes **Course Designer** R Dawson **Facilities** 🍷 🍴 🍸 🛒 🏌 🏑 🛍 ⛳ **Conf** Corporate Hospitality Days **Location** A545 from Menai Bridge to Beaumaris, course signed on approach to town
Hotel ★★ 85% SHL Bishopsgate House, 54 Castle Street, BEAUMARIS ☎ 01248 810302 📠 01248 810302 9 en suite

Henllys Henllys Hall LL58 8HU
☎ 01248 811717 📠 01248 811511
e-mail: hg@hpb.co.uk
web: www.henllysgolfclub.co.uk

The Menai Straits and the Snowdonia mountains form a magnificent backdrop to the course. Full use has been made of the mature parkland trees and natural water hazards to provide a really testing and enjoyable game of golf.

18 Holes, 6062yards, Par 71, SSS 69, Course record 65.
Club membership 300.

Visitors Mon-Sun & BHs. Booking required. Dress code.
Societies booking required. **Green Fees** not confirmed **Course Designer** Roger Jones **Prof** Peter Maton & David Gadsby
Facilities 🍷 🍴 🍸 🛒 🏌 🏑 🛍 ⛳ 🏌
Location A545 through Beaumaris, 0.25m Henllys Hall signed on left
Hotel ★★★ 77% HL Best Western Bulkeley Hotel, Castle Street, BEAUMARIS ☎ 01248 810415 📠 01248 810415 43 en suite

HOLYHEAD
Map 6 SH28

Holyhead Lon Garreg Fawr, Trearddur Bay LL65 2YL
☎ 01407 763279 📠 01407 763279
e-mail: holyheadgolfclub@tiscali.co.uk
web: www.holyheadgolfclub.co.uk

Treeless, undulating seaside course which provides a varied and testing game, particularly in a south wind. The fairways are bordered by gorse, heather and rugged outcrops of rock. Accuracy from most tees is paramount as there are 43 fairway and greenside bunkers and lakes. Designed by James Braid.

18 Holes, 6058yds, Par 70, SSS 70, Course record 64.
Club membership 962.

Visitors Mon-Sun & BHs. Booking required. Handicap certificate. Dress code. **Societies** booking required **Green Fees** £35 per day (£40 weekends) **Course Designer** James Braid **Prof** Stephen Elliott **Facilities** 🍷 🍴 🍸 🛒 🏌 🏑 🛍 ⛳ 🏌 🏌 🚕 🏌
Conf facs Corporate Hospitality Days **Location** A55 to rdbt at Holyhead, left onto B4545 to Trearddur Bay 1m
Hotel ★★★ 80% HL Trearddur Bay, TREARDDUR BAY ☎ 01407 860301 📠 01407 860301 40 en suite

RHOSNEIGR
Map 6 SH37

Anglesey Station Rd LL64 5QX
☎ 01407 811127 & 811202 📠 01407 811127
e-mail: info@theangleseygolfclub.com
web: www.theangleseygolfclub.co.uk

An interesting 18-hole links course set among sand dunes and heather, renowned for its excellent greens and numerous streams. The whole course has an abundance of wildlife and is an important conservation area.

18 Holes, 6330yds, Par 70, SSS 71, Course record 64.
Club membership 500.

Visitors contact club for details. **Societies** booking required.
Green Fees phone **Course Designer** H Hilton **Prof** Mr Matthew Parry **Facilities** 🍷 🍴 🍸 🛒 🏌 🏑 🛍 ⛳ 🏌 🚕 🏌
Location NE side of village on A4080
Hotel ★★★ 80% HL Trearddur Bay, TREARDDUR BAY ☎ 01407 860301 📠 01407 860301 40 en suite

BLAENAU GWENT

NANTYGLO   Map 3 SO11

West Monmouthshire Golf Rd, Winchestown NP23 4QT
☎ 01495 310233
e-mail: care@westmongolfclub.co.uk
web: www.westmongolfclub.co.uk
Established in 1906, this mountain and heathland course was
officially designated by the Guinness Book of Records as being the
highest above sea level, with the 14th tee at a height of 1513ft. The
course has plenty of picturesque views, hard walking and natural
hazards. Testing 3rd hole, par 5, and 7th hole, par 4.

18 Holes, 6300yds, Par 71, SSS 69, Course record 65.
Club membership 350.

Visitors Mon-Fri except BHs. Booking required. Dress code. Handicap
certificate. **Societies** booking required. **Green Fees** £15 per day (£18
weekends) **Course Designer** Ben Sayers **Facilities** ⊕ ⊖ ┗ ▱
┱ ⩗ ⛏ ✦ ☂ **Conf** facs **Location** 0.25m W off A467
Hotel ★★ 79% HL Llanwenarth Hotel & Riverside Restaurant,
Brecon Road, ABERGAVENNY ☎ 01873 810550 🖹 01873 810550
17 en suite

TREDEGAR   Map 3 SO10

Tredegar and Rhymney Cwmtysswg, Rhymney NP22 5HA
☎ 01685 840743 (club)
e-mail: tandrgc@googlemail.com
web: www.tandrgc.co.uk
Mountain course with lovely views. The course has now been developed
into an 18-hole course with easy walking.

18 Holes, 6250yds, Par 67, SSS 67, Course record 68.
Club membership 194.

Visitors contact club for details. Handicap certificate.
Societies welcome. **Green Fees** £15 per day **Facilities** ⊕ ⊖
┗ ▱ ┱ ⩗ ⛏ **Conf** facs Corporate Hospitality Days
Location 1.75m SW on B426
Hotel ★★★ 72% CHH Maes Manor, BLACKWOOD
☎ 01495 220011 🖹 01495 220011 28 en suite

BRIDGEND

BRIDGEND   Map 3 SS97

Coed-Y-Mwstwr The Clubhouse, Bryn Rd, Coychurch
CF35 6AF
☎ 01656 864934 🖹 01656 864934
e-mail: secretary@coed-y-mwstwr.co.uk
web: www.coed-y-mwstwr.co.uk
Course extended to 18 holes during 2005 and the new holes are now
fully bedded in. The 2nd hole, a 212 yard par 3 to a well guarded green
is a real tester. The fairways are lush and generous fairways allow the
golfer to open their shoulders but the surrounding woodland is a trap
for the wayward drive. A conservatory gives fine views over the course
and surrounding hills.

18 Holes, 5703yds, Par 69, SSS 68, Course record 69.
Club membership 300.

Visitors Mon-Sun & BHs. Booking required weekends & BHs. Handicap
certificate. Dress code. **Societies** booking required. **Green Fees** £22
per 18 holes (£26.50 weekends & BHs) **Course Designer** Chapman/

Warren **Prof** Paul Thomas **Facilities** ⊕ ┗ ▱ ┱ ⩗ ⛏ ☂
⩗ **Conf** facs Corporate Hospitality Days **Location** M4 junct 35, A473
into Coychurch, course 1m N
Hotel ★★★ 76% CHH Coed-Y-Mwstwr, Coychurch, BRIDGEND
☎ 01656 860621 🖹 01656 860621 28 en suite

Southerndown Ogmore By Sea CF32 0QP
☎ 01656 880476 🖹 01656 880317
e-mail: admin@southerndowngolfclub.com
web: www.southerndowngolfclub.co.uk
Downland-links championship course with rolling fairways and
fast greens. Golfers who successfully negotiate the four par 3s still
face a testing finish with three of the last four holes played into
the prevailing wind. The par 3 5th is played across a valley and the
18th, with its split-level fairway, is a demanding finishing hole.
Superb views.

18 Holes, 6449yds, Par 70, SSS 72, Course record 63.
Club membership 710.

Visitors Mon-Sun & BHs. Booking required. Handicap certificate.
Dress code. **Societies** booking required. **Green Fees** £55 per
18 holes, £45 pm & £15 extra holes (£75/£65 & £20 extra holes
weekends) **Course Designer** W Park/W Fernie & others **Prof** D G
McMonagle **Facilities** ⊕ ⊖ ┗ ▱ ┱ ⩗ ⛏ ☂ ⩗
🛒 ⩗ ☂ **Conf** Corporate Hospitality Days **Location** 3m SW of
Bridgend on B4524
Hotel ★★★ 73% HL Best Western Heronston, Ewenny Road,
BRIDGEND ☎ 01656 668811 & 666085 🖹 01656 668811
75 en suite

MAESTEG   Map 3 SS89

Maesteg Mount Pleasant, Neath Rd CF34 9PR
☎ 01656 734106 🖹 01656 731822
e-mail: ijm@fsmail.net
web: www.maesteg-golf.co.uk
Reasonably flat hill-top course with scenic views.

18 Holes, 5929yds, Par 70, SSS 69, Course record 69.
Club membership 789.

Visitors Mon-Sun & BHs. Booking required weekends & BHs. Handicap
certificate. Dress code. **Societies** welcome. **Green Fees** not confirmed
Course Designer James Braid **Facilities** ⊕ ⊖ by prior arrangement
┗ ▱ ┱ ⩗ ⛏ ⩗ **Conf** facs Corporate Hospitality Days
Location 0.5m W off B4282
Hotel ★★★ 75% HL Best Western Aberavon Beach, Neath, PORT
TALBOT ☎ 01639 884949 🖹 01639 884949 52 en suite

PENCOED   Map 3 SS98

St Mary's Hotel & Country Club St Mary Hill CF35 5EA
☎ 01656 868900 🖹 01656 863400
e-mail: stmarys.reception@btopenworld.com
web: www.stmaryshotel.com
A parkland course with many American-style features. The par 3 10th,
called Alcatraz, has a well-deserved reputation.

St Mary's Course: 18 Holes, 5291yds, Par 68, SSS 66,
Course record 65.
Kingfisher: 12 Holes, 3125yds, Par 35.
Club membership 600.

Visitors Mon-Sun & BHs. Booking required. Handicap certificate
for St Mary's course. Dress code. **Societies** booking required **Green**

continued

WALES

Fees not confirmed **Course Designer** Peter Johnson **Prof** Leighton Janes **Facilities** ⊕ ⓘⓄⓘ ⓑ ⓛ ⓜ ⓝⓘ ⚄ ⓐ ⓥⓘ ◇ ⚲ ⚑ **Conf** facs Corporate Hospitality Days **Location** M4 junct 35, 5m **Hotel** ★★★ 73% HL St Mary's Hotel & Country Club, St Marys Golf Club, PENCOED ☎ 01656 861100 📠 01656 861100 24 en suite

PORTHCAWL Map 3 SS87

Royal Porthcawl Rest Bay CF36 3UW
☎ 01656 782251 📠 01656 771687
e-mail: office@royalporthcawl.com
web: www.royalporthcawl.com
One of the great links courses, Royal Porthcawl is unique in that the sea is in full view from every single hole. The course enjoys a substantial reputation with heather, broom, gorse and a challenging wind demanding a player's full skill and attention.

18 Holes, 6578yds, Par 72, SSS 73.
Club membership 800.

Visitors Mon, Tue, Thu, Fri & Sun except BHs. Booking required. Handicap certificate. Dress code. **Societies** booking required. **Green Fees** £140 per day, £95 per round (£175/£120 weekends). All rates include lunch **Course Designer** Ramsey Hunter **Prof** Peter Evans **Facilities** ⊕ ⓘⓄⓘ ⓑ ⓛ ⓜ ⓝⓘ ⚄ ⓐ ⓥⓘ ◇ ⚲ ⚑ **Conf** Corporate Hospitality Days **Location** M4 junct 37, proceed to Rest Bay
Hotel ★★★ 66% HL Seabank, The Promenade, PORTHCAWL
☎ 01656 782261 📠 01656 782261 67 en suite

PYLE Map 3 SS88

Pyle & Kenfig Waun-Y-Mer CF33 4PU
☎ 01656 783093 📠 01656 772822
e-mail: secretary@pandkgolfclub.co.uk
web: www.pandkgolfclub.co.uk
Links and downland course, with dunes. Easy walking.

18 Holes, 6776yds, Par 71, SSS 73, Course record 61.
Club membership 933.

Visitors Mon-Fri except BHs.. Booking required. Handicap certificate. Dress code. **Societies** welcome. **Green Fees** not confirmed **Course Designer** Colt **Prof** Robert Evans **Facilities** ⊕ ⓘⓄⓘ ⓑ ⓛ ⓜ ⓝⓘ ⚄ ⓐ ⓥⓘ ⚲ ⚑ **Conf** facs Corporate Hospitality Days **Location** M4 junct 37, S side of Pyle off A4229
Hotel ★★★ 66% HL Seabank, The Promenade, PORTHCAWL
☎ 01656 782261 📠 01656 782261 67 en suite

CAERPHILLY

BARGOED Map 3 ST19

Bargoed Heolddu CF81 9GF
☎ 01443 836179
Mountain parkland course, a challenging par 70 with panoramic views. Easy walking.

18 Holes, 6049yds, Par 70, SSS 70, Course record 64.
Club membership 600.

Visitors Mon-Fri & BHs. Sat pm only. Dress code. **Societies** booking required. **Green Fees** £17.50 per round **Prof** Craig Easton **Facilities** ⊕ ⓘⓄⓘ ⓑ ⓛ ⓜ ⓝⓘ ⚄ ⓐ ⚲ ⚑ **Conf** facs Corporate Hospitality Days **Location** NW side of town
Hotel ★★★ 72% CHH Maes Manor, BLACKWOOD
☎ 01495 220011 📠 01495 220011 28 en suite

BLACKWOOD Map 3 ST19

Blackwood Cwmgelli NP12 1BR
☎ 01495 222121 (Office) & 223152 (Club)
9 Holes, 5332yds, Par 67, Course record 62.
Facilities ⊕ ⓑ ⓛ ⓜ ⓝⓘ ⚄ **Location** 0.25m N of Blackwood, off A4048
Telephone for further details
Hotel ★★★ 72% CHH Maes Manor, BLACKWOOD
☎ 01495 220011 📠 01495 220011 28 en suite

CAERPHILLY Map 3 ST18

Caerphilly Pencapel CF83 1HJ
☎ 029 2088 3481 & 2086 3441 📠 029 2086 3441
18 Holes, 5732yds, Par 71, SSS 69.
Prof Joel Hill **Facilities** ⓑ ⓛ ⓜ ⓝⓘ ⚄ ⓐ ⚑ **Location** 0.5m S on A469
Telephone for further details
Hotel ★★★ 73% HL Manor Parc Country Hotel & Restaurant, Thornhill Road, Thornhill, CARDIFF ☎ 029 2069 3723 📠 029 2069 3723 21 en suite

Mountain Lakes & Castell Heights Blaengwynlais CF83 1NG
☎ 029 2086 1128 & 2088 6666 📠 029 2086 3243
e-mail: sales@golfclub.co.uk
web: www.golfclub.co.uk
The nine-hole Castell Heights course within the Mountain Lakes complex was established in 1982 on a 45-acre site. In 1988 a further 18-hole course, Mountain Lakes was designed by Bob Sandow to take advantage of 160 acres of mountain heathland, combining both mountain-top golf and parkland. Most holes are tree-lined and there are 20 lakes as hazards. Host to major PGA tournaments.

Mountain Lakes Course: 18 Holes, 6046mtrs, Par 74, SSS 73, Course record 69.
Castell Heights Course: 9 Holes, 2751mtrs, Par 35, SSS 32, Course record 32. Club membership 500.

Visitors contact club for details. **Societies** welcome. **Green Fees** not confirmed **Course Designer** Bob Sandow **Prof** Sion Bebb **Facilities** ⊕ ⓑ ⓛ ⓜ ⓝⓘ ⚄ ⓐ ⚲ ⚑ **Conf** facs Corporate Hospitality Days **Location** M4 junct 32, near Black Cock Inn, Caerphilly Mountain
Hotel ★★★ 73% HL Manor Parc Country Hotel & Restaurant, Thornhill Road, Thornhill, CARDIFF ☎ 029 2069 3723 📠 029 2069 3723 21 en suite

MAESYCWMMER Map 3 ST19

Bryn Meadows Golf & Country Hotel CF82 7FN
☎ 01495 225590 📠 01495 228272
e-mail: information@brynmeadows.co.uk
web: www.brynmeadows.com
Heavily wooded parkland with panoramic views of the Brecon Beacons.
Bryn Meadows Golf, Hotel Spa: 18 Holes, 6021yds, Par 71, SSS 70, Course record 68. Club membership 540.

Visitors Mon-Sun & BHs. Dress code. **Societies** welcome. **Green Fees** not confirmed **Course Designer** Mayo/Jeffries **Prof** Martin Sanders **Facilities** ⊕ ⓘⓄⓘ ⓑ ⓛ ⓜ ⓝⓘ ⚄ ⓐ ⓥⓘ ◇ ⚲ 🚗 ⚑ **Leisure** heated indoor swimming pool, sauna, gymnasium **Conf** facs Corporate Hospitality Days **Location** on A4048 Blackwood-Ystrad Mynach road *continued*

WALES

Hotel ★★★ 72% CHH Maes Manor, BLACKWOOD
☎ 01495 220011 ▤ 01495 220011 28 en suite

NELSON   Map 3 ST19

Whitehall The Pavilion CF46 6ST
☎ 01443 740245
web: www.whitehallgolfclub1922.co.uk
9 Holes, 5666yds, Par 69, SSS 68, Course record 63.
Facilities ⑪ ⑩ ᵇ ▱ ⑪ ᷓ **Leisure** snooker **Conf** facs
Corporate Hospitality Days **Location** 1m SW of Nelson off A4054
Telephone for further details
Hotel ★★★ 75% CHH Llechwen Hall, Llanfabon, PONTYPRIDD
☎ 01443 742050 & 743020 ▤ 01443 742050 20 en suite

OAKDALE   Map 3 ST19

Oakdale Llwynon Ln NP12 0NF
☎ 01495 220044 & 220440
A challenging parkland course for players of all abilities. Well-
maintained mature greens.
Oakdale Golf Course: 9 Holes, 1344yds, Par 28,
Course record 27.
Visitors contact club for details. **Societies** welcome. **Green Fees** not
confirmed **Course Designer** Ian Goodenough **Facilities** ᵇ ▱ ⑪
ᷓ ᷛ ᵉ ᵍ ᵉ **Leisure** fishing, snooker tables. **Location** off
B4251 at Oakdale
Hotel ★★★ 72% CHH Maes Manor, BLACKWOOD
☎ 01495 220011 ▤ 01495 220011 28 en suite

Cottrell Park Golf Resort

- 36 Hole Championship Venue
- Only 15 Minutes from Cardiff City Centre
- Driving Range with Power Tee Technology
- Friendly Golf Service Reception
- Clubhouse serving Meals Daily
- Buggies and Trolley's for Hire

Cottrell Park Golf Resort
St Nicholas, Cardiff CF5 6SJ
Tel: 01446 781781 **Email:** sales@golfwithus.com
w w w . g o l f w i t h u s . c o m
COTTRELL PARK
GOLF RESORT

WALES

CARDIFF

CARDIFF   Map 3 ST17

Cardiff Sherborne Av, Cyncoed CF23 6SJ
☎ 029 2075 3320 ▤ 029 2068 0011
e-mail: cardiff.golfclub@virgin.net
web: www.cardiffgc.co.uk
Parkland where trees form natural hazards. Interesting variety of
holes, mostly bunkered. A stream flows through course and comes
into play on nine separate holes.
18 Holes, 6116yds, Par 70, SSS 70, Course record 66.
Club membership 900.
Visitors Mon-Fri, Sun & BHs. Booking required. Handicap certificate.
Dress code. Handicap certificate. **Societies** booking required. **Green
Fees** £50 per round **Prof** Terry Hanson **Facilities** ⑪ ⑩ ᵇ ▱
⑪ ᷓ ᵉ ᵍ **Leisure** snooker **Conf** facs Corporate Hospitality
Days **Location** 3m N of city centre
Hotel BUD Ibis Cardiff Gate, Malthouse Avenue, Cardiff Gate
Business Park, Pontprennau, CARDIFF ☎ 029 2073 3222
▤ 029 2073 3222 78 en suite

Llanishen Cwm Lisvane CF14 9UD
☎ 029 2075 5078 ▤ 029 2076 5253
web: www.llanishengc.co.uk
18 Holes, 5338yds, Par 68, SSS 67, Course record 63.
Prof Adrian Jones **Facilities** ⑪ ⑩ ᵇ ▱ ⑪ ᷓ ᵉ ᵍ
Conf Corporate Hospitality Days **Location** 5m N of city off A469
Telephone for further details

Wales' sweet spot

The Vale Resort
- 143 bedroom 4* hotel
- Two championship courses
- Driving range
- Coaching academy
- Video analysis
- Custom fit golf centre
- Pro-shop
- Only 15 minutes from Cardiff

Hensol Park, Hensol, nr Cardiff, Vale of Glamorgan CF72 8JY
Tel: 01443 667800   www.vale-hotel.com

Vale RESORT ★★★★

continued

Hotel ★★★ 73% HL Manor Parc Country Hotel & Restaurant, Thornhill Road, Thornhill, CARDIFF ☎ 029 2069 3723 🖷 029 2069 3723 21 en suite

Peterstone Lakes Peterstone, Wentloog CF3 2TN
☎ 01633 680009 & 680075 (pro) 🖷 01633 680563
e-mail: peterstone_lakes@yahoo.com
web: www.peterstonelakes.com
Parkland course with abundant water features and several long drives (15th, 601yds).

18 Holes, 6569yds, Par 72. Club membership 450.
Visitors Mon-Sun & BHs. Booking advised. Dress code. Handicap certificate. **Societies** booking required. **Green Fees** £26 (£29.50 weekends) **Course Designer** Bob Sandow **Prof** Paul Glynn **Facilities** 🖥 ⬝ 🖭 🛆 🖴 ♦ 🚜 ♦ **Conf** facs Corporate Hospitality Days **Location** 3m from Castleton off A48
Hotel ★★★ 72% HL Best Western St Mellons Hotel & Country Club, Castleton, CARDIFF ☎ 01633 680355 🖷 01633 680355 41 en suite

Radyr The Clubhouse, Drysgol Rd, Radyr CF15 8BS
☎ 029 2084 2408 🖷 029 2084 3914
e-mail: manager@radyrgolf.co.uk
web: www.radyrgolf.co.uk
Parkland course that celebrated its centenary in 2002. Good views. Venue for many county and national championships.

18 Holes, 6078yds, Par 69, SSS 70, Course record 62. Club membership 935.
Visitors Mon-Fri & BHs. Booking required Fri. Dress code. **Societies** booking required. **Green Fees** not confirmed **Course Designer** Colt **Prof** Simon Swales **Facilities** 🖥 🍽 🖭 ⬝ 🖭 🛆 🖴 🏮 ♦ 🏐 **Leisure** Table tennis **Conf** facs Corporate Hospitality Days **Location** M4 junct 32, 4.5m NW of city off A4119
Hotel ★★★ 73% HL Manor Parc Country Hotel & Restaurant, Thornhill Road, Thornhill, CARDIFF ☎ 029 2069 3723 🖷 029 2069 3723 21 en suite

St Mellons St Mellons CF3 2XS
☎ 01633 680408 🖷 01633 681219
e-mail: stmellons@golf2003.fsnet.co.uk
web: www.stmellonsgolfclub.co.uk
Opened in 1936, St Mellons is a parkland course on the eastern edge of Cardiff. The course is laid out in the shape of a clover leaf and provides one of the best tests of golf in south Wales. The course comprises three par 5s, five par 3s and 10 par 4s. The par 3s will make or break your card but the two finishing par 4 holes are absolutely superb.

18 Holes, 6275yds, Par 70, SSS 70, Course record 63. Club membership 700.
Visitors contact club for details. Handicap certificate. **Societies** booking required. **Green Fees** £45 per day, £40 per round **Course Designer** Colt & Morrison **Prof** Barry Thomas **Facilities** 🖥 🍽 🖭 ⬝ 🖭 🛆 🖴 🏮 🚜 ♦ **Conf** Corporate Hospitality Days **Location** M4 junct 30, 2m E off A48
Hotel ★★★ 72% HL Best Western St Mellons Hotel & Country Club, Castleton, CARDIFF ☎ 01633 680355 🖷 01633 680355 41 en suite

Whitchurch Pantmawr Rd, Whitchurch CF14 7TD
☎ 029 2062 0985 🖷 029 2052 9860
e-mail: secretary@whitchurchcardiffgolfclub.com
web: www.whitchurchcardiffgolfclub.com
This undulating parkland course is an urban oasis and offers panoramic views of the city. It is an easy walk and always in good condition with excellent drainage and smooth, quick greens.

Whitchurch (Cardiff) Golf Club: 18 Holes, 6278yds, Par 71, SSS 71, Course record 63. Club membership 750.
Visitors handicap certificate. Dress code. **Societies** booking required. **Green Fees** £50 per day (£60 per round weekends) **Course Designer** F Johns **Prof** Rhys Davies **Facilities** 🖥 🍽 🖭 ⬝ 🖭 🛆 🖴 ♦ **Conf** Corporate Hospitality Days **Location** M4 junct 32, 0.5m S on A470
Hotel ★★★ 73% HL Manor Parc Country Hotel & Restaurant, Thornhill Road, Thornhill, CARDIFF ☎ 029 2069 3723 🖷 029 2069 3723 21 en suite

CREIGIAU (CREIYIAU) — Map 3 ST08

Creigiau Llantwit Rd CF15 9NN
☎ 029 2089 0263 🖷 029 2089 0706
e-mail: creigiaugolfclub@btconnect.com
web: www.creigiaugolf.co.uk
Downland course, with small greens and many interesting water hazards.

18 Holes, 6063yds, Par 71, SSS 70, Course record 64. Club membership 800.
Visitors Mon-Fri except BHs. Handicap certificate. Dress code. **Societies** welcome. **Green Fees** £40 per day **Prof** Iain Luntz **Facilities** 🖥 🍽 🖭 ⬝ 🖭 🛆 🖴 🏮 🚜 ♦ **Location** 6m NW of Cardiff on A4119
Hotel ★★★★ 75% CHH Miskin Manor Country Hotel, Pendoylan Road, MISKIN ☎ 01443 224204 🖷 01443 224204 43 en suite

CARMARTHENSHIRE

AMMANFORD — Map 3 SN61

Glynhir Glynhir Rd, Llandybie SA18 2TF
☎ 01269 851365 🖷 01269 851365
e-mail: glynhir.golfclub@virgin.net
web: www.glynhirgolfclub.co.uk
Parkland with good views. Last holes close to Upper Loughor River and the 14th is a 394yd dog-leg.

18 Holes, 5917yds, Par 69, SSS 70, Course record 66. Club membership 450.
Visitors Mon-Sun & BHs. Booking required Wed, Fri-Sun & BHs. Handicap certificate. Dress code. **Societies** booking required. **Green Fees** Winter £13, Summer £20 (£16/£25 weekends) **Course Designer** F Hawtree **Prof** Richard Herbert **Facilities** 🖥 🍽 🖭 ⬝ 🖭 🛆 🖴 🏮 ◇ 🚜 ♦ 🏐 **Conf** facs Corporate Hospitality Days **Location** 2m N of Ammanford
Hotel ★★★ 83% HL The Plough Inn, Rhosmaen, LLANDEILO ☎ 01558 823431 🖷 01558 823431 14 en suite

BURRY PORT
Map 2 SN40

Ashburnham Cliffe Ter SA16 0HN
☎ 01554 832269 & 833846 🖨 01554 836974
e-mail: golf@ashburnhamgolfclub.co.uk
web: www.ashburnhamgolfclub.co.uk

This course has a lot of variety. In the main it is of the seaside type although the holes in front of the clubhouse are of an inland character. The front nine are played in a westerly direction into the prevailing wind, which can vary from a mild breeze to a near gale, the 1st and 9th being particularly tough. The second nine, usually wind assisted, opens with a long par 5 and has a testing last few holes finishing with an elevated treacherous green at the 18th.

18 Holes, 6950yds, Par 72, SSS 74, Course record 66.
Club membership 650.

Visitors Mon-Fri, Sun & BHs. Sat pm only. Booking required. Handicap certificate. Dress code **Societies** booking required. **Green Fees** not confirmed **Course Designer** J H Taylor **Prof** Martin Stimson **Facilities** ⊕ by prior arrangement ⑧ by prior arrangement ⛳ ⌨ 🍸 ⚲ 🏠 🏌 ⛳ 🚗 ⚑ **Conf** facs Corporate Hospitality Days **Location** W of town centre on A484
Hotel ★★ 74% HL Ashburnham, Ashburnham Road, Pembrey, LLANELLI ☎ 01554 834343 & 834455 🖨 01554 834343 13 en suite

CARMARTHEN
Map 2 SN42

Carmarthen Blaenycoed Rd SA33 6EH
☎ 01267 281588 🖨 01267 281493
e-mail: carmarthengolfclub@btinternet.com
web: www.carmarthengolfclub.com

A well maintained heathland course with tricky greens. Magnificent clubhouse and scenery.

18 Holes, 6245yds, Par 71, SSS 71, Course record 66.
Club membership 450.

Visitors contact club for details. Handicap certificate. **Societies** welcome. **Green Fees** £25 (£30 weekends) **Course Designer** J H Taylor **Prof** Jon Hartley **Facilities** ⊕ ⑧ ⛳ ⌨ 🍸 ⚲ 🏠 🏌 🚗 ⚑ **Conf** facs Corporate Hospitality Days **Location** 4m N of town
Hotel ★★ 76% HL Falcon, Lammas Street, CARMARTHEN ☎ 01267 234959 & 237152 🖨 01267 234959 16 en suite

Derllys Court Llysonnen Rd, Bancyfelin SA33 5DT
☎ 01267 211575 🖨 01267 211575
e-mail: derllys@hotmail.com
web: www.derllyscourtgolfclub.com

The back and front halves provide an interesting contrast. The greens on the front 9 are extremely undulating as opposed to the relatively flat greens of the back 9. Water hazards and bunkers come into play providing an interesting challenge. Fine views.

18 Holes, 5847yds, Par 70, SSS 68, Course record 69.
Club membership 300.

Visitors dress code. Handicap certificate. **Societies** welcome. **Green Fees** Phone **Course Designer** Peter Johnson/Stuart Finney **Facilities** ⊕ ⛳ ⌨ 🍸 ⚲ 🏠 🚗 ⚑ **Conf** Corporate Hospitality Days **Location** off A40 between Carmarthen and St Clears
Hotel ★★ 76% HL Falcon, Lammas Street, CARMARTHEN ☎ 01267 234959 & 237152 🖨 01267 234959 16 en suite

GARNANT
Map 3 SN61

Garnant Park Dinefwr Rd SA18 1NP
☎ 01269 823365
web: www.parcgarnantgolf.co.uk

18 Holes, 6670yds, Par 72, SSS 72, Course record 69.

Course Designer Roger Jones **Location** M4 junct 48, off A474 in village of Garnant, signed
Telephone for further details
Hotel ★★ 71% HL White Hart Inn, 36 Carmarthen Road, LLANDEILO ☎ 01558 823419 🖨 01558 823419 11 en suite

KIDWELLY
Map 2 SN40

Glyn Abbey Trimsaran SA17 4LB
☎ 01554 810278 🖨 01554 810889
e-mail: course-enquiries@glynabbey.co.uk
web: www.glynabbey.co.uk

Beautiful parkland course with spectacular views of the Gwendraeth valley, set in 200 acres with mature wooded backdrops. USGA greens and tees.

Abbey: 18 Holes, 6173yds, Par 70, SSS 70,
Course record 68. Club membership 420.

Visitors Mon-Sun & BHs. Dress code. Handicap certificate. **Societies** booking required. **Green Fees** £20 per round (£25 weekends & BHs), par 3 course £5 per round **Course Designer** Hawtree **Prof** Darren Griffiths **Facilities** ⊕ ⑧ ⛳ ⌨ 🍸 ⚲ 🏠 🏌 🛆 🏌 🚗 ⚑ 🏌 **Leisure** gymnasium, 9 hole par 3 course **Conf** facs Corporate Hospitality Days **Location** E of Kidwelly on B4317 between Trimsaran & Carway
Hotel ★★ 74% HL Ashburnham, Ashburnham Road, Pembrey, LLANELLI ☎ 01554 834343 & 834455 🖨 01554 834343 13 en suite

LLANELLI
Map 3 SS59

Machynys Peninsula Golf & Country Club Nicklaus Av SA15 2DG
☎ 01554 744888 🖨 01554 744680
web: www.machynys.com

Machynys Peninsula Golf & Country Club: 18 Holes,
7051yds, Par 72, SSS 75.

Course Designer Gary Nicklaus **Location** M4 junct 47/48, follow directions for Llanelli. Take B4034 to Machynys, golf club on left
Telephone for further details
Hotel ★★★ 77% HL Best Western Diplomat Hotel, Felinfoel, LLANELLI ☎ 01554 756156 🖨 01554 756156 50 en suite

RHOS
Map 2 SN44

Saron Saron, Penwern SA44 5EL
☎ 01559 370705 🖨 01559 370705
e-mail: c9mbl@sarongolf.freeserve.co.uk
web: www.saron-golf.com

Set in 50 acres of mature parkland with large trees and magnificent Teifi valley views. Numerous water hazards and bunkers.

Saron Golf Course: 9 Holes, 2091yds, Par 32,
Course record 34.

Visitors Mon-Sun & BHs. Handicap certificate. **Societies** welcome. **Green Fees** £12 per 18 holes, £9 per 9 holes **Course Designer** Adas

continued

WALES

Facilities ⚑ ◇ ✔ **Location** off A484 at Saron, between Carmarthen and Newcastle Emlyn
Hotel ★★★ 80% HL The Penrallt, ABERPORTH ☎ 01239 810127 & 810927 📠 01239 810227 26 en suite

CEREDIGION

ABERYSTWYTH   Map 6 SN58

Aberystwyth Brynmor Rd SY23 2HY
☎ 01970 615104   📠 01970 626622
e-mail: aberystwythgolf@talk21.com
web: www.aberystwythgolfclub.com

Undulating meadowland course. Testing holes: 16th (The Loop), par 3; 17th, par 4; 18th, par 3. Good views over Cardigan Bay.

18 Holes, 5801yds, Par 70, SSS 69. Club membership 337.

Visitors Mon-Sun & BHs. Booking required. Dress code. Handicap certificate. **Societies** booking required. **Green Fees** £25 per round (£30 weekends & BHs). £10 per round Mon & Thu am. **Course Designer** Harry Vardon **Prof** Jim McLeod **Facilities** ⑪ ⛶ 🍴 ⇤ 🖵 🏌 🧍 🏠 ⚑ 🛒 ✔ ✔ **Leisure** 6 hole par 3 course **Conf** facs Corporate Hospitality Days **Location** N side of town near Constitution Hill and Cliff Railway

Hotel ★★★ 75% HL Belle Vue Royal, Marine Terrace, ABERYSTWYTH ☎ 01970 617558 & 639240 📠 01970 617558 34 en suite

BORTH   Map 6 SN69

Borth & Ynyslas SY24 5JS
☎ 01970 871202   📠 01970 871202
e-mail: secretary@borthgolf.co.uk
web: www.borthgolf.co.uk

Traditional championship links course with superb scenery. Provides a true test of golf for all standards of player.

18 Holes, 6116yds, Par 70, SSS 70, Course record 63. Club membership 500.

Visitors contact club for details. Handicap certificate.
Societies booking required. **Green Fees** winter £30 per round, summer £40 **Course Designer** Harry Colt **Prof** J G Lewis **Facilities** ⑪ 🍴 by prior arrangement ⇤ 🖵 🏌 🧍 🏠 ⚑ 🛒 ✔ **Location** 0.5m N on B4353

Hotel ★★★ CHH Ynyshir Hall, EGLWYS FACH, Machynlleth ☎ 01654 781209 & 781268 📠 01654 781209 9 en suite

CARDIGAN   Map 2 SN14

Cardigan Gwbert-on-Sea SA43 1PR
☎ 01239 621775 & 612035   📠 01239 621775
e-mail: golf@cardigan.fsnet.co.uk
web: www.cardigangolf.co.uk

A links course, very dry in winter, with wide fairways, light rough and gorse. Every hole overlooks the sea.

18 Holes, 6687yds, Par 72, SSS 73, Course record 66. Club membership 600.

Visitors Mon-Sun & BHs. Booking required. Dress code. Handicap certificate. **Societies** booking required. **Green Fees** £27.50 per day (£35 weekends & BHs) **Course Designer** Grant/Hawtree **Prof** Steve Parsons **Facilities** ⑪ 🍴 ⇤ 🖵 🏌 🧍 🏠 ⚑ ✔ 🛒 ✔ **Leisure** squash, squash courts **Location** 3m N off A487

Hotel ★★★ 77% HL The Cliff, GWBERT-ON-SEA, Cardigan ☎ 01239 613241 📠 01239 613241 70 en suite

GWBERT ON SEA   Map 2 SN15

Cliff Hotel SA43 1PP
☎ 01239 613241   📠 01239 615391
e-mail: reservations@cliffhotel.com
web: www.cliffhotel.com

This is a short course with two par 4s and the remainder are challenging par 3s. Particularly interesting holes are played across the sea on to a small island.

Cliff Hotel Golf Course: 9 Holes, 1545yds, Par 29.

Visitors Mon-Sun & BHs. Handicap certificate. **Societies** welcome. **Green Fees** from £7 **Facilities** ⑪ 🍴 ⇤ 🖵 🏌 ⚑ ◇ 🛒 ✔ **Leisure** outdoor and indoor heated swimming pool, fishing, sauna, gymnasium, spa facility **Conf** facs Corporate Hospitality Days **Location** 3m N of Cardigan off B4548

Hotel ★★★ 77% HL The Cliff, GWBERT-ON-SEA, Cardigan ☎ 01239 613241 📠 01239 613241 70 en suite

LLANRHYSTUD   Map 6 SN56

Penrhos Golf & Country Club SY23 5AY
☎ 01974 202999   📠 01974 202100
e-mail: info@penrhosgolf.co.uk
web: www.penrhosgolf.co.uk

Beautifully scenic course incorporating lakes and spectacular coastal and inland views.

Championship: 18 Holes, 6660yds, Par 72, SSS 73, Course record 70.

Academy: 9 Holes, 1784yds, Par 31. Club membership 300.

Visitors Mon-Sun & BHs. Booking required for Championship course. Dress code. Handicap certificate. **Societies** booking required. **Green Fees** Championship £25 (£35 weekends). Academy £6 **Course Designer** Jim Walters **Prof** Paul Diamond **Facilities** ⑪ 🍴 ⇤ 🖵 🏌 🧍 🏠 ⚑ ◇ 🛒 ✔ ✔ **Leisure** hard tennis courts, heated indoor swimming pool, sauna, gymnasium, bowling green **Conf** facs Corporate Hospitality Days **Location** A487 onto B4337 in Llanrhystud, course 0.25m on left

Hotel ★★★ 83% CHH Conrah, Ffosrhydygaled, Chancery, ABERYSTWYTH ☎ 01970 617941 📠 01970 617941 17 en suite

WALES

CONWY

Empire Hotel & Spa
Church Walks, Llandudno, LL30 2HE

Award winning 4 star popular family run hotel.
Central location near to promenade and shops.
Convenient to three good local golf clubs.
Spa with pool, sauna, steam room, fitness suite
also beauty treatments. Small outdoor pool and terrace.
Free wireless broadband. Free Car Parks. Mini breaks all year.

AA ★★★★ Hotel

Tel: 01492 860555
Fax: 01492 860791
Website: www.empirehotel.co.uk
Email: reservations@empirehotel.co.uk

Cymru Wales Guest Hotel ★★★★

ABERGELE
Map 6 SH97

Abergele Tan-y-Gopa Rd LL22 8DS
☎ 01745 824034 📠 01745 824772
web: abergelegolfclub.co.uk
18 Holes, 6520yds, Par 72, SSS 71, Course record 66.
0 Holes, 0.
Course Designer Hawtree **Location** 0.5m W off A547
Telephone for further details
Hotel ★★★ 73% HL Kinmel Manor, St George's Road, ABERGELE
☎ 01745 832014 📠 01745 832014 51 en suite

BETWS-Y-COED
Map 6 SH75

Betws-y-Coed LL24 0AL
☎ 01690 710556
e-mail: info@betws-y-coed.co.uk
web: www.betws-y-coedgolfclub.co.uk
Attractive flat meadowland course set between two rivers in
Snowdonia National Park, known as the Jewel of the Nines.
9 Holes, 4998yds, Par 64, SSS 64, Course record 63.
Club membership 300.
Visitors dress code. Handicap certificate. **Societies** welcome. **Green Fees** Summer £20 per round (£25 weekends) **Facilities** 🎯 🍽 🛒 🍺 🥤 🏌 **Location** NE side of village off A5
Hotel ★★★ 83% HL Royal Oak, Holyhead Road, BETWS-Y-COED
☎ 01690 710219 📠 01690 710219 27 en suite

COLWYN BAY
Map 6 SH87

Old Colwyn Woodland Av LL29 9NL
☎ 01492 515581
web: www.oldcolwyngolfclub.co.uk
9 Holes, 5243yds, Par 68, SSS 66, Course record 62.
Course Designer James Braid **Location** E of town centre on B5383
Telephone for further details
Hotel ★★ 74% HL Lyndale, 410 Abergele Road, Old Colwyn,
COLWYN BAY ☎ 01492 515429 📠 01492 515429 14 en suite

CONWY
Map 6 SH77

Conwy (Caernarvonshire) Beacons Way, Morfa
LL32 8ER
☎ 01492 592423 📠 01492 593363
e-mail: secretary@conwygolfclub.com
web: www.conwygolfclub.com
Founded in 1890, Conwy has hosted national and international
championships since 1898. Set among sand hills, possessing true
links greens and a profusion of gorse on the latter holes, especially
the 16th, 17th and 18th. This course provides the visitor with real
golfing enjoyment in stunning scenery. In 2006 the course became
the first in Wales to stage the final qualifying rounds for the Open
Championship.
18 Holes, 6647yds, Par 72, SSS 75, Course record 64.
Club membership 1050.
Visitors Mon-Sun & BHs. Booking required. Handicap certificate.
Dress code. **Societies** welcome. **Green Fees** £50 per day, £45 per
round (£50 weekends & BHs) **Prof** Peter Lees **Facilities** 🎯 🍽 🛒 🍺 🥤 🏌 **Leisure** snooker tables
Conf facs Corporate Hospitality Days **Location** 1m W of town centre
on A55, junct 17
Hotel ★★★★ 73% HL Empire, Church Walks, LLANDUDNO
☎ 01492 860555 📠 01492 860555 54 en suite

See advert on this page

LLANDUDNO
Map 6 SH78

Llandudno (Maesdu) Hospital Rd LL30 1HU
☎ 01492 876450 📠 01492 876450
e-mail: secretary@maesdugolfclub.co.uk
web: www.maesdugolfclub.co.uk
Part links, part parkland, this championship course starts and
finishes on one side of the main road, the remaining holes, more
seaside in nature, being played on the other side. The holes are
pleasantly undulating and present a pretty picture when the gorse

continued

WALES

is in bloom. Often windy, this varied and testing course is not for beginners.

18 Holes, 6545yds, Par 72, SSS 72, Course record 62. Club membership 1120.

Visitors contact club for details. **Societies** welcome. **Green Fees** £35 per day, £25 per round (£40/£30 weekends) **Prof** Simon Boulden **Facilities** ⊕ ⊚ ☒ ☐ ☒ ☒ ☒ ☒ ☒ **Leisure** snooker **Location** S of town centre on A546
Hotel ★★★★ 76% HL Imperial, The Promenade, LLANDUDNO ☎ 01492 877466 ☷ 01492 877466 98 en suite

North Wales 72 Bryniau Rd, West Shore LL30 2DZ
☎ 01492 875325 ☷ 01492 873355
e-mail: enquiries@northwalesgolfclub.co.uk
web: www.northwalesgolfclub.co.uk

Challenging seaside links of championship standard with superb views of Anglesey and Snowdonia. It possesses hillocky fairways, awkward stances and the occasional blind shot. Heather and gorse lurk beyond the fairways and several of the greens are defended by deep bunkers.

18 Holes, 6287yds, Par 71, SSS 71, Course record 66. Club membership 670.

Visitors Mon-Sun & BHs. Booking required. Dress code. Handicap certificate. **Societies** booking required. **Green Fees** £23-£35 per round (£35-£42 weekends and BHs), £10 after 3pm **Course Designer** Tancred Cummins **Prof** Richard Bradbury **Facilities** ⊕ ⊚ ☒ ☐ ☒ ☒ ☒ ☒ ☒ ☒ **Leisure** snooker **Conf** facs Corporate Hospitality Days **Location** W side of town on A546
Hotel ★★★ HL St Tudno Hotel and Restaurant, The Promenade, LLANDUDNO ☎ 01492 874411 ☷ 01492 874411 18 en suite

Rhos-on-Sea Penryhn Bay LL30 3PU
☎ 01492 548115 (pro) & 549641 (clubhouse)
☷ 01492 549100
e-mail: info@rhosgolf.co.uk
web: www.rhosgolf.co.uk

Seaside course, with easy walking and panoramic views.
18 Holes, 6064yds, Par 69, SSS 69, Course record 68. Club membership 400.

Visitors contact club for details. **Societies** welcome. **Green Fees** not confirmed **Course Designer** J J Simpson **Prof** Jon Kelly **Facilities** ⊕ ⊚ ☒ ☐ ☒ ☒ ☒ ☒ ☒ **Conf** Corporate Hospitality Days **Location** 0.5m W of Llandudno off A55
Hotel ★★★★ 76% HL Imperial, The Promenade, LLANDUDNO ☎ 01492 877466 ☷ 01492 877466 98 en suite

LLANFAIRFECHAN
Map 6 SH67

Llanfairfechan Llannerch Rd LL33 0ES
☎ 01248 680144 & 680524
e-mail: llangolf@hotmail.com

Hillside course with panoramic views of the Menai Strait and Anglesey. 9 hole course with 11 greens and 18 tees. 11 holes over 200 yds. Deceptive and challenging to play to standard scratch score.

9 Holes, 3119yds, Par 54, SSS 57, Course record 53. Club membership 191.

Visitors Mon-Fri except BHs. Handicap certificate. Dress code. **Societies** booking required. **Green Fees** £15 per day **Facilities** ☒ **Leisure** practice net **Location** W side of town on A55
Hotel ★★★ 77% HL Best Western Bulkeley Hotel, Castle Street, BEAUMARIS ☎ 01248 810415 ☷ 01248 810415 43 en suite

PENMAENMAWR
Map 6 SH77

Penmaenmawr Conway Old Rd LL34 6RD
☎ 01492 623330 ☷ 01492 622105
e-mail: clubhouse@pengolfclub.co.uk
web: www.pengolf.co.uk

Hilly course with magnificent views across the bay to Llandudno and Anglesey. Drystone wall hazards.

9 Holes, 5350yds, Par 67, SSS 66, Course record 62. Club membership 600.

Visitors booking required weekends & BHs. Handicap certificate. **Societies** welcome. **Green Fees** not confirmed **Facilities** ⊕ ☒ ☐ ☒ ☒ ☒ ☒ **Conf** Corporate Hospitality Days **Location** 1.5m NE off A55
Hotel ★★★★ Castle Hotel Conwy, High Street, CONWY ☎ 01492 582800 ☷ 01492 582800 28 en suite

DENBIGHSHIRE

BODELWYDDAN
Map 6 SJ07

Kimnel Park LL18 5SR
☎ 01745 833548 ☷ 01745 833544
Kimnel Park Golf Course: 9 Holes, 3100, Par 58, SSS 58.
Prof Andrew Barnett **Facilities** ☒ ☐ ☒ ☒ ☒ ☒ ☒ **Leisure** golf academy
Telephone for further details
Hotel ★★★ 81% HL The Oriel, Upper Denbigh Road, ST ASAPH ☎ 01745 582716 ☷ 01745 582716 33 en suite

DENBIGH
Map 6 SJ06

Bryn Morfydd Hotel LL16 4NP
☎ 01745 589090 ☷ 01745 589093
web: www.byrnmorfyddhotelgolf.co.uk

Dukes Course: 18 Holes, 5650yds, Par 70, SSS 67, Course record 74.
Duchess Course: 9 Holes, 2098yds, Par 27.

Course Designer Peter Allis **Location** on A525 between Denbigh and Ruthin
Telephone for further details
Hotel ★★★ 85% HL Ruthin Castle, RUTHIN ☎ 01824 702664 & 703435 ☷ 01824 702664 61 en suite

Denbigh Henllan Rd LL16 5AA
☎ 01745 814159 & 816669 📠 01745 814888
e-mail: denbighgolfclub@aol.com
web: www.denbighgolfclub.co.uk
Parkland course, giving a testing and varied game. Good views.
18 Holes, 5712yds, Par 69, SSS 68, Course record 64.
Club membership 615.
Visitors Mon-Sun & BHs. Dress code. Handicap certificate.
Societies welcome. **Green Fees** £32 per 27 holes, £26 per round
(£37/£32 weekends) **Course Designer** John Stockton **Prof** Mike Jones
Facilities ⊕ ⏐◎⏐ ⑃ ⌂ 🍴 ⚐ ☖ ⛳ ⚐ **Conf** Corporate
Hospitality Days **Location** 1.5m NW on B5382
Hotel ★★★ 81% HL The Oriel, Upper Denbigh Road, ST ASAPH
☎ 01745 582716 📠 01745 582716 33 en suite

St Melyd The Paddock, Meliden Rd LL19 8NB
☎ 01745 854405 📠 01745 856908
e-mail: info@stmelydgolf.co.uk
web: www.stmelydgolf.co.uk
Parkland with good views of mountains and the Irish Sea. Testing 1st
hole (423yds) par 4.
9 Holes, 5829yds, Par 68, SSS 68, Course record 65.
Club membership 400.
Visitors Contact club for details. **Societies** welcome. **Green Fees** not
confirmed **Prof** Andrew Barnett **Facilities** ⊕ ⏐◎⏐ ⑃ ⌂ 🍴
⑃ ☖ ⚐ **Leisure** snooker **Conf** Corporate Hospitality Days
Location 0.5m S on A547
Hotel ★★★ 81% HL The Oriel, Upper Denbigh Road, ST ASAPH
☎ 01745 582716 📠 01745 582716 33 en suite

LLANGOLLEN   Map 7 SJ24

Vale of Llangollen Holyhead Rd LL20 7PR
☎ 01978 860906
e-mail: info@vlgc.co.uk
web: www.vlgc.co.uk
Parkland in superb scenery by the River Dee.
18 Holes, 6705yds, Par 72, SSS 73, Course record 66.
Club membership 800.
Visitors Mon-Sun & BHs. Booking required Fri-Sun & BHs. Handicap
certificate. **Societies** booking required. **Green Fees** £35 per round
(£40 weekends) **Prof** David Vaughan **Facilities** ⊕ ⑃ ⌂ 🍴 ⑃
☖ ⚐ ☖ ⚐ **Location** 1.5m E on A5
Hotel ★★★ 75% HL Golden Pheasant Country Hotel & Inn,
Llwynmawr, GLYN CEIRIOG ☎ 01691 718281 📠 01691 718281
20 en suite

PRESTATYN   Map 6 SJ08

Prestatyn Marine Road East LL19 7HS
☎ 01745 854320 📠 01745 854320
e-mail: prestatyngcmanager@freenet.co.uk
web: www.prestatyngolfclub.co.uk
Set besides rolling sand dunes and only a few hundred yards from the
sea, this course enjoys a temperate climate and its seaside location
ensures that golfers can play on superb greens all year round. Some
holes of note are the par 5 3rd with out of bounds on the left dog-leg
followed by the Ridge, a par 4 of 468yds normally played with the
prevailing wind. The pretty 9th is surrounded by a moat where birdies
and double bogies are common followed by the challenging par 4
450yd 10th.
18 Holes, 6568yds, Par 72, SSS 72, Course record 65.
Club membership 673.
Visitors Mon-Fri & Sun except BHs. Dress code. Handicap certificate.
Societies welcome. **Green Fees** not confirmed **Course Designer** S
Collins **Prof** David Ames **Facilities** ⊕ ⏐◎⏐ ⑃ ⌂ 🍴 ⑃ ☖
⚐ ⚐ ⚐ **Leisure** snooker **Conf** facs Corporate Hospitality Days
Location 0.5m N off A548
Guesthouse ★★★★ RR Barratt's at Ty'n Rhyl, Ty'n Rhyl, 167 Vale
Road, RHYL ☎ 01745 344138 & 0773 095 4994 📠 01745 344138
3 en suite

RHUDDLAN   Map 6 SJ07

Rhuddlan Meliden Rd LL18 6LB
☎ 01745 590217 (Sec) & 590898(Pro) 📠 01745 590472
e-mail: secretary@rhuddlangolfclub.co.uk
web: www.rhuddlangolfclub.co.uk

Attractive, gently undulating parkland with good views. Well bunkered
with trees and water hazards. The 476yd 8th and 431yd 11th require
both length and accuracy.
18 Holes, 6471yds, Par 71, SSS 71, Course record 66.
Club membership 1133.
Visitors Mon-Sat & BHs. Handicap certificate. Dress code.
Societies welcome. **Green Fees** £32.50 per day, £27.50 per
round (£35/30 Sat) **Course Designer** Hawtree & Son **Prof** Andrew
Carr **Facilities** ⊕ ⏐◎⏐ ⑃ ⌂ 🍴 ⑃ ☖ ⚐ ⚐ ⚐
Conf Corporate Hospitality Days **Location** from A55 take Rhyl
junct and follow dual carriageway to rdbt, take 3rd exit into Rhuddlan.
Follow A547, club on right
Hotel ★★★ 73% HL Kinmel Manor, St George's Road, ABERGELE
☎ 01745 832014 📠 01745 832014 51 en suite

RHYL   Map 6 SJ08

Rhyl Coast Rd LL18 3RE
☎ 01745 353171 📠 01745 360007
web: www.rhylgolfclub.co.uk
9 Holes, 6220yds, Par 71, SSS 70, Course record 64.
Course Designer James Braid **Location** 1m E on A548
Telephone for further details
Guesthouse ★★★★ RR Barratt's at Ty'n Rhyl, Ty'n Rhyl, 167 Vale
Road, RHYL ☎ 01745 344138 & 0773 095 4994 📠 01745 344138
3 en suite

WALES

RUTHIN
Map 6 SJ15

Ruthin-Pwllglas Pwllglas LL15 2PE
☎ 01824 702296 & 07831388488
e-mail: neillroberts@aol.com
web: www.ruthinpwllglasgc.co.uk

Parkland course established in 1905 with panoramic views of the Vale of Clwyd. Three testing par 3 holes.

10 Holes, 5362yds, Par 66, SSS 66, Course record 62. Club membership 380.

Visitors Mon-Sun & BHs. Dress code. Handicap certificate. **Societies** booking required. **Green Fees** £16 per day (£22 weekends & BHs) **Course Designer** Dai Rees **Prof** Richard Heginbotham **Facilities** ⑪ ⑩ ⓵ ☐ ♦ ⚒ ♣ ⚑ **Conf** Corporate Hospitality Days **Location** 2.5m S off A494
Hotel ★★★ 85% HL Ruthin Castle, RUTHIN ☎ 01824 702664 & 703435 📄 01824 702664 61 en suite

ST ASAPH
Map 6 SJ07

Llannerch Park North Wales Golf Range LL17 0BD
☎ 01745 730805
web: www.parkgolf.co.uk

Llannerch Park Golf Course: 9 Holes, 1587yds, Par 30, Course record 27.

Course Designer B Williams **Location** 200yds S off A525
Telephone for further details
Hotel ★★ 74% SHL Plas Elwy Hotel & Restaurant, The Roe, ST ASAPH ☎ 01745 582263 & 582089 📄 01745 582263 13 en suite

FLINTSHIRE

BRYNFORD
Map 7 SJ17

Holywell Brynford CH8 8LQ
☎ 01352 710040
web: www.hoywellgc.co.uk

Links type course on well-drained mountain turf, with bracken and gorse flanking undulating fairways. 720ft above sea level.

18 Holes, 6100yds, Par 70, SSS 70, Course record 67. Club membership 400.

Visitors Mon-Fri, Sun & BHs. Dress code. Handicap certificate. **Societies** booking required. **Green Fees** £25 per round (£30 weekends & BHs) **Prof** Matt Parsley **Facilities** ⑪ ⑩ ⓵ ☐ ⚑ ♦ ⚒ ♣ **Leisure** snooker **Conf** Corporate Hospitality Days **Location** 1.25m SW off B5121
Hotel ★★ 72% HL Stamford Gate, Halkyn Road, HOLYWELL ☎ 01352 712942 📄 01352 712942 12 en suite

FLINT
Map 7 SJ27

Flint Cornist Park CH6 5HJ
☎ 01352 735645
e-mail: secretary@flintgolfclub.co.uk
web: www.flintgolfclub.co.uk

Parkland incorporating woods and streams. Excellent views of Dee estuary and the Welsh hills.

9 Holes, 6984yds, Par 70, SSS 69, Course record 65. Club membership 200.

Visitors Contact club for details. Handicap certificate.

Societies welcome. **Green Fees** not confirmed **Course Designer** H G Griffith **Facilities** ⑪ ⑩ ⓵ ☐ ⚑ ♣ **Location** 1m W of Flint, signs for Cornist Hall Golf Club
Hotel ★★★ 77% HL Northop Hall Country House, Chester Road, NORTHOP HALL ☎ 01244 816181 📄 01244 816181 39 en suite

HAWARDEN
Map 7 SJ36

Hawarden Groomsdale Ln CH5 3EH
☎ 01244 531447 & 520809 📄 01244 536901
e-mail: secretary@hawardengolfclub.co.uk
web: www.hawardengolfclub.co.uk

Parkland course with comfortable walking and good views.

18 Holes, 5842yds, Par 69, SSS 69. Club membership 500.

Visitors Sun-Fri & BHs. Booking required. Dress code. Handicap certificate. **Societies** booking required. **Green Fees** £20 (£25 Sun). Mon/Tue pm £14 **Prof** Alex Rowland **Facilities** ⑪ ⑩ ⓵ ☐ ⚑ ♣ **Location** W side of town off B5125
Hotel ★★★★ 74% HL De Vere St David's Park, St Davids Park, EWLOE ☎ 01244 520800 📄 01244 520800 147 en suite

MOLD
Map 7 SJ26

Old Padeswood Station Ln, Padeswood CH7 4JL
☎ 01244 547401 & 547701 📄 01244 545082
e-mail: oldpad@par72.fsbusiness.co.uk
web: www.oldpadeswoodgolfclub.co.uk

Situated in the beautiful Alyn valley, part bounded by the River Alyn, this challenging course suits all categories of golfers. Nine holes are flat and nine are gently undulating. The signature hole is the 18th, a par 3 that needs a carry to the green as a valley waits below.

18 Holes, 6685yds, Par 72, SSS 72, Course record 66. Club membership 600.

Visitors Contact club for details. Handicap certificate. **Societies** booking required. **Green Fees** not confirmed **Course Designer** Jeffries **Prof** Tony Davies **Facilities** ⑪ ⑩ ⓵ ☐ ⚑ ♣ ⚒ ♦ ⚑ **Conf** facs Corporate Hospitality Days **Location** 3m SE off A5118
Hotel ★★★ 74% HL Beaufort Park Hotel, Alltami Road, New Brighton, MOLD ☎ 01352 758646 📄 01352 758646 106 en suite

Padeswood & Buckley The Caia, Station Ln, Padeswood CH7 4JD
☎ 01244 550537 📄 01244 541600
e-mail: admin@padeswoodgolf.plus.com
web: www.padeswoodgolfclub.com

Bounded by the banks of the River Alyn, gently undulating parkland with natural hazards and good views of the Welsh hills.

18 Holes, 6042yds, Par 70, SSS 69. Club membership 800.

Visitors Mon-Fri except BHs. Limited play Sat. Booking required. Dress code. Handicap certificate. **Societies** booking required. **Green Fees** £28 per round (£32 Sat) **Course Designer** Williams Partnership **Prof** David Ashton **Facilities** ⑪ ⑩ ⓵ ☐ ⚑ ♣ ⚒ ♦ ⚑ ♦ **Leisure** snooker tables **Conf** Corporate Hospitality Days **Location** 3m SE off A5118
Hotel ★★★ 74% HL Beaufort Park Hotel, Alltami Road, New Brighton, MOLD ☎ 01352 758646 📄 01352 758646 106 en suite

NORTHOP
Map 7 SJ26

Northop Golf & Country Club CH7 6WA
☎ 01352 840440 📠 01352 840445
e-mail: john@northoppark.co.uk
web: www.northoppark.co.uk

Designed by former British Ryder Cup captain, John Jacobs, the parkland course gives the impression of having been established for many years. No two holes are the same and design allows all year play.

Northop Golf & Country Club: 18 Holes, 6750yds, Par 72, SSS 73, Course record 64. Club membership 600.

Visitors Mon-Sun & BHs. Handicap certificate. Dress code. **Societies** welcome. **Green Fees** £40 **Course Designer** John Jacobs **Prof** John Nolan **Facilities** Ⓣ 🍴 🍺 ⬛ 🍴 🏌 ✍ ✏ **Leisure** hard tennis courts, sauna, gymnasium **Conf** facs Corporate Hospitality Days **Location** 150yds from Connahs Quay turning on A55
Hotel ★★★★ 74% HL De Vere St David's Park, St Davids Park, EWLOE ☎ 01244 520800 📠 01244 520800 147 en suite

PANTYMWYN
Map 7 SJ16

Mold Cilcain Rd CH7 5EH
☎ 01352 741513 📠 01352 741517
e-mail: info@moldgolfclub.co.uk
web: www.moldgolfclub.co.uk

Meadowland course with some hard walking and natural hazards. Fine views.

18 Holes, 5603yds, Par 68, SSS 67, Course record 63. Club membership 700.

Visitors Mon-Sun & BHs. Booking required. Handicap certificate. Dress code. **Societies** welcome. **Green Fees** winter: £15 per day (£25 weekends & BHs), £22 per round. Summer £27.50 per day (£33 weekends & BHs), £25 per round **Course Designer** Hawtree **Prof** Mark Jordan **Facilities** Ⓣ 🍴 🍺 ⬛ 🍴 🏌 🛒 ✍ ✏ **Conf** facs Corporate Hospitality Days **Location** E side of village
Hotel ★★★ 74% HL Beaufort Park Hotel, Alltami Road, New Brighton, MOLD ☎ 01352 758646 📠 01352 758646 106 en suite

WHITFORD
Map 6 SJ17

Pennant Park CH8 9AE
☎ 01745 563000
e-mail: enquiries@pennant-park.co.uk
web: www.pennant-park.co.uk

Parkland course set in rolling countryside with fine quality greens and spectacular views.

18 Holes, 6059yds, Par 70, SSS 70, Course record 66. Club membership 319.

Visitors contact club for details. **Societies** welcome. **Green Fees** £20 per round (£25 weekends) **Course Designer** Roger Jones **Prof** Matthew Pritchard **Facilities** Ⓣ 🍴 🍺 ⬛ 🍴 🏌 🛒 ✍ ✏ 🏌 **Leisure** 3 hole academy course **Conf** facs Corporate Hospitality Days **Location** from Chester take A55 towards Holyhead. Exit at junct 32 to Holywell, follow signs for Pennant Park
Hotel ★★ 72% HL Stamford Gate, Halkyn Road, HOLYWELL ☎ 01352 712942 📠 01352 712942 12 en suite

GWYNEDD

— Clwb Golf Abersoch —

Located at Abersoch on the Llyn Peninsula in Gwynedd, Wales, UK – Clwb Golff Abersoch / Abersoch Golf Club offers-18 holes of links and parkland golf.

Designed by Harry Varden in 1907, the original 9 hole links course opened in 1908. Today we offer a full 18 holes of links and parkland golf. The sandy soil and the unique microclimate ensures golf for 365-days a year.

We pride ourselves in the condition of the course and the warm welcome extended to members and visitors alike.

Please browse the website for all the latest information, green fees and facilities offered, then visit the local www.abersoch.co.uk website for further details about the resort's surrounding area.

Clwb Golf Abersoch	Tel: Admin 01758 712636
Abersoch	Email: admin@abersochgolf.co.uk
Pwllheli	Web: www.abersochgolf.co.uk
Gwynedd	Pro: Tel: 01758 712622
LL53 7NN	Email: pro@abersochgolf.co.uk

ABERDYFI
Map 6 SN69

Aberdovey see page 401
LL35 0RT
☎ 01654 767493 📠 01654 767027
e-mail: sec@aberdoveygolf.co.uk
web: www.aberdoveygolf.co.uk

ABERSOCH
Map 6 SH32

Abersoch LL53 7EY
☎ 01758 712622(shop) & 712636(office)
📠 01758 712777
web: www.abersochgolf.co.uk

18 Holes, 5819yds, Par 69, SSS 68, Course record 66.
continued

WALES

Course Designer Harry Vardon **Location** S side of village
Telephone for further details
Hotel ★★ 81% HL Neigwl, Lon Sarn Bach, ABERSOCH
☎ 01758 712363 📄 01758 712363 9 en suite

See advert on page 397

BALA
Map 6 SH93

Bala Penlan LL23 7YD
☎ 01678 520359 & 521361   📄 01678 521361
e-mail: balagolfclub@one-tel.com
web: www.balagolf.co.uk

Upland course with natural hazards. All holes except first and last
affected by wind. First hole is a most challenging par 3. Irrigated
greens and spectacular views of surrounding countryside.

10 Holes, 4962yds, Par 66, SSS 64, Course record 64.
Club membership 235.

Visitors Mon-Sun & BHs. Booking required weekends & BHs. Handicap
certificate. **Societies** welcome. **Green Fees** £15 (£20 weekends & BHs)
Course Designer Syd Collins **Facilities** ⊕ by prior arrangement 🍽️
by prior arrangement 🍺 ⛳ 🍴 ▲ 🏠 ❖ 🏌️ **Conf** Corporate
Hospitality Days **Location** 0.5m SW off A494

BANGOR
Map 6 SH57

St Deiniol Penybryn LL57 1PX
☎ 01248 353098   📄 01248 370792
e-mail: secretary@st-deiniol.co.uk
web: www.st-deiniol.co.uk

Elevated parkland course with panoramic views of Snowdonia, the
Menai Strait and Anglesey. Designed by James Braid in 1906 this
course is a test test of accuracy and course management. The 3rd
has a narrow driving area and a shot to an elevated green. The 4th,
one of six par 3s, provides a choice of pitching the green or utilising
the contours, making it one of the most difficult holes on the course.
The 13th, a dog-leg par 4, is the last hole of the course's own Amen
Corner with its out of bounds to the right and left. Centenary in
2006.

18 Holes, 5421yds, Par 68, SSS 67, Course record 61.
Club membership 300.

Visitors Mon-Sun & BHs. Booking required. Dress code Handicap
certificate. **Societies** booking required. **Green Fees** not confirmed
Course Designer James Braid **Facilities** ⊕ 🍽️ 🍺 ⛳ 🍴 ▲
🏠 🍴 🚂 🏌️ **Location** A55 junct 11, E of town centre off A5122
Hotel ★★ 85% SHL Bishopsgate House, 54 Castle Street,
BEAUMARIS ☎ 01248 810302 📄 01248 810302 9 en suite

CAERNARFON
Map 6 SH46

Caernarfon, Llanfaglan LL54 5RP
☎ 01286 673783   📄 01286 673783
e-mail: secretary@caernarfongolfclub.co.uk
web: www.caernarfongolfclub.co.uk

Parkland with gentle gradients. Immaculately kept course with
excellent greens and tree-lined fairways.

Royal Town of Caernarfon Golf Club: 18 Holes, 5941yds,
Par 69, SSS 68, Course record 63. Club membership 600.
Visitors Mon-Sun & BHs. Booking required weekends & BHs. Dress
code. Handicap certificate. **Societies** welcome. **Green Fees** £35
per day, £30 per round (£35 per round weekends) **Prof** Aled Owen

Facilities ⊕ 🍽️ 🍺 ⛳ 🍴 ▲ 🏠 🏌️ 🚂 🏌️ **Conf** facs
Corporate Hospitality Days **Location** 1.75m SW
Hotel ★★★ 79% HL Celtic Royal Hotel, Bangor Street,
CAERNARFON ☎ 01286 674477 📄 01286 674477 110 en suite

CRICCIETH
Map 6 SH43

Criccieth Ednyfed Hill LL52 0PH
☎ 01766 522154
web: www.cricciethgolfclub.co.uk
18 Holes, 5787yds, Par 69, SSS 68.
Facilities ⊕ 🍽️ 🍺 ⛳ 🍴 ▲ 🏠 🏌️ **Location** 1m NE
Telephone for further details
Hotel ★★★ 86% CHH Bron Eifion Country House, CRICCIETH
☎ 01766 522385 📄 01766 522385 19 en suite

DOLGELLAU
Map 6 SH71

Dolgellau Pencefn Rd LL40 2ES
☎ 01341 422603   📄 01341 422603
e-mail: richard@dolgellaugolfclub.com
web: www.dolgellaugolfclub.com

Undulating parkland course set on former hunting grounds of the
last Welsh prince, with ancient oak and holly trees. Good views of
mountains and the Mawddach estuary.

9 Holes, 4671yds, Par 66, SSS 63, Course record 62.
Club membership 300.

Visitors Mon-Sun & BHs. Booking required weekends & BHs. Dress code.
Societies booking required. **Green Fees** £18 per day (£22.50 weekends
& BHs) **Course Designer** Jack Jones **Facilities** ⊕ 🍽️ 🍺 ⛳ 🍴
▲ 🍴 🏌️ 🚂 🏌️ **Conf** facs **Location** 0.5m N, near Town Bridge
Hotel ★★★ CHH Penmaenuchaf Hall, Penmaenpool, DOLGELLAU
☎ 01341 422129 📄 01341 422129 14 en suite

FFESTINIOG
Map 6 SH93

Ffestiniog Y Cefn LL41 4LS
☎ 01766 762637
e-mail: info@ffestinioggolf.org
web: www.ffestiniog.org
Moorland course set in Snowdonia National Park.

9 Holes, 4570yds, Par 68, SSS 66. Club membership 150.
Visitors contact club for details. Handicap certificate.
Societies welcome. **Green Fees** £10 per day **Facilities** ▲
Location 1m E of Ffestiniog on B4391

HARLECH
Map 6 SH53

Royal St Davids LL46 2UB
☎ 01766 780361   📄 01766 781110
e-mail: secretary@royalstdavids.co.uk
web: www.royalstdavids.co.uk

Championship links with easy walking. Natural hazards demand
strength and accuracy. Under the gaze of Harlech Castle, with a
magnificent backdrop of the Snowdonia mountains.

18 Holes, 6225yds, Par 69, SSS 71, Course record 61.
Club membership 900.

Visitors Mon-Sun & BHs. Booking required. Handicap certificate.
Dress code. **Societies** booking required. **Green Fees** £65 per

continued

WALES

ABERDOVEY
GWYNEDD - ABERDYFI - MAP 6 SN69

Golf was first played at Aberdovey in 1886, with the club founded six years later. The links has since developed into one of the finest championship courses in Wales. The club has hosted many prestigious events over the years, and is popular with golfing societies and clubs who regularly return here. Golfers can enjoy spectacular views and easy walking alongside the dunes of this characteristic seaside links. Fine holes include the 3rd, 11th and a good short hole at the 12th. The late Bernard Darwin, a former president and captain at the club, was a golf correspondent for the Times. Many of his writings feature the course, which he referred to as "the course that my soul loves best of all the courses in the world."

LL35 0RT ☎ 01654 767493 📠 01654 767027
e-mail: sec@aberdoveygolf.co.uk **web:** www.aberdoveygolf.co.uk
18 Holes, 6615yds, Par 71, SSS 72, Course record 66. Club membership 1000.
Visitors Mon-Sun & BHs. Booking required. Handicap certificate. Dress code. **Societies** welcome. **Green Fees** £60 per day, £45 per round **Course Designer** J Braid **Prof** John Davies **Facilities** ⑪ 🍴 🛍 ⛶ 🚩 ⚒ 🏠 ◇ 🏌 🛒 🏌 **Conf** facs Corporate Hospitality Days **Location** 0.5m W on A493

day, £50 per round, £30 after 3pm (weekends £75/£60/£36 after 2pm) **Course Designer** Harold Finch-Hatton **Prof** John Barnett **Facilities** ⑪ ⑧ ⓛ ⓛ ⑪ ⑪ ⑪ ⑪ ⑪ ⑪ ⑪ ⑪ ⑪ **Conf** facs Corporate Hospitality Days **Location** W side of town on A496

Hotel ★★ 71% SHL Ty Mawr, LLANBEDR ☎ 01341 241440 📠 01341 241440 10 en suite

MORFA NEFYN   Map 6 SH24

Nefyn & District LL53 6DA
☎ 01758 720966   📠 01758 720476
web: nefyn-golf-club.co.uk
Old Course: 18 Holes, 6201yds, Par 71, SSS 71, Course record 67.
New Course: 18 Holes, 6317yds, Par 71, SSS 71, Course record 66.
Course Designer James Braid **Location** 0.75m NW
Telephone for further details
Hotel ★★★ 86% CHH Bron Eifion Country House, CRICCIETH ☎ 01766 522385 📠 01766 522385 19 en suite

PORTHMADOG   Map 6 SH53

Porthmadog Morfa Bychan LL49 9UU
☎ 01766 514124   📠 01766 514124
e-mail: secretary@porthmadog-golf-club.co.uk
web: www.porthmadog-golf-club-co.uk
Seaside links, very interesting but with easy walking and good views.
18 Holes, 6322yds, Par 71, SSS 71. Club membership 900.
Visitors Mon-Sun & BHs. Booking required. Handicap certificate. Dress code. **Societies** booking required. **Green Fees** £45 per day, £35 per round (£50/£40 weekends & BHs) **Course Designer** James Braid **Prof** Peter L Bright **Facilities** ⑪ ⑧ ⓛ ⓛ ⑪ ⑪ ⑪ ⑪ ⑪ **Leisure** snooker **Conf** Corporate Hospitality Days **Location** 1.5m SW of Porthmadog
Hotel ★★★ 86% CHH Bron Eifion Country House, CRICCIETH ☎ 01766 522385 📠 01766 522385 19 en suite

PWLLHELI   Map 6 SH33

Pwllheli Golf Rd LL53 5PS
☎ 01758 701644   📠 01758 701644
e-mail: admin@pwllheligolfclub.co.uk
web: www.pwllheligolfclub.co.uk
Easy walking on flat seaside course, 9 holes links, 9 holes parkland. Outstanding views of Snowdon, Cader Idris and Cardigan Bay.
18 Holes, 6091yds, Par 69, SSS 70, Course record 66. Club membership 880.
Visitors Mon-Sun & BHs. Dress code. Handicap certificate. **Societies** booking required. **Green Fees** not confirmed **Course Designer** Tom Morris **Prof** Stuart Pilkington **Facilities** ⑪ ⑧ ⓛ ⓛ ⑪ ⑪ ⑪ ⑪ ⑪ **Location** 0.5m SW off A497
Hotel ★★★ 80% CHH Porth Tocyn, Bwlch Tocyn, ABERSOCH, Pwllheli ☎ 01758 713303 & 07789994942 📠 01758 713303 17 en suite

MERTHYR TYDFIL

MERTHYR TYDFIL   Map 3 SO00

Merthyr Tydfil Cilsanws Mountain, Cefn Coed CF48 2NT
☎ 01685 723308
Mountain-top course in the Brecon Beacons National Park with beautiful views of the surrounding area. The course plays longer than its card length and requires accuracy off the tee.
18 Holes, 5625yds, Par 69, SSS 68, Course record 65. Club membership 160.
Visitors Mon-Sun & BHs. Dress code. **Societies** welcome. **Green Fees** not confirmed **Course Designer** V Price/R Mathias **Facilities** ⑪ by prior arrangement ⑧ by prior arrangement ⓛ ⓛ ⑪ ⑪ **Location** off A470 at Cefn Coed

Morlais Castle Pant CF48 2UY
☎ 01685 722822
e-mail: morlaiscastle.golfclub@surfwise.co.uk
web: www.morlaiscastlegolf.co.uk
Beautiful moorland course with excellent views of the Brecon Beacons and surrounding countryside. The interesting layout makes for a testing game.
18 Holes, 6320yds, Par 71, SSS 71, Course record 64. Club membership 600.
Visitors handicap certificate. Dress code. **Societies** booking required. **Green Fees** £18 (£22 weekends) **Course Designer** Donald Steel **Prof** H Jarrett **Facilities** ⑪ ⑧ ⓛ ⓛ ⑪ ⑪ ⑪ ⑪ **Conf** facs Corporate Hospitality Days **Location** 2.5m N off A465. Follow signs for Mountain Railway. Course entrance opposite railway car park

MONMOUTHSHIRE

ABERGAVENNY   Map 3 SO21

Monmouthshire Gypsy Ln, LLanfoist NP7 9HE
☎ 01873 852606   📠 01873 850470
e-mail: monmouthshiregc@btconnect.com
web: www.monmouthshiregolfclub.co.uk
This parkland course is very picturesque, with the beautifully wooded River Usk running alongside. There are a number of par 3 holes and a testing par 4 at the 15th.
18 Holes, 5776yds, Par 70, SSS 69, Course record 65. Club membership 600.
Visitors Mon-Fri except BHs. Booking required. Handicap certificate. Dress code. **Societies** booking required. **Green Fees** phone **Course Designer** James Braid **Prof** B Edwards **Facilities** ⑪ ⑧ by prior arrangement ⓛ ⓛ ⑪ ⑪ ⑪ ⑪ **Conf** Corporate Hospitality Days **Location** 2m S off B4269
Hotel ★★ 79% HL Llanwenarth Hotel & Riverside Restaurant, Brecon Road, ABERGAVENNY ☎ 01873 810550 📠 01873 810550 17 en suite

Wernddu Golf Centre Old Ross Rd NP7 8NG
☎ 01873 856223   📠 01873 852177
e-mail: info@wernddu-golf-club.co.uk
web: www.wernddu-golf-club.co.uk
A parkland course with magnificent views, wind hazards on several holes in certain conditions, and water hazards on four holes. This

continued

MARRIOTT ST PIERRE HOTEL

MONMOUTHSHIRE - CHEPSTOW - MAP 3 ST59

Set in 400 acres of beautiful parkland, Marriott St Pierre offers two 18-hole courses. The Old Course is one of the finest in the country and has played host to over 14 European Tour events. The par 3 18th hole is famous for its tee shot over the lake to an elevated green. The Mathern has its own challenges and is highly enjoyable for golfers of all abilities.

St Pierre Park NP16 6YA ☎ 01291 625261 📠 01291 627977
e-mail: will.hewitt@marriotthotels.com **web:** www.stpierregolf.com
Old Course: 18 Holes, 6733yds, Par 71, SSS 72, Course record 64.
Mathern Course: 18 Holes, 5700yds, Par 68, SSS 68, Course record 65. Club membership 800.
Visitors Mon-Sun & BHs. Booking required. Dress code. **Societies** booking required. **Green Fees** Old from £68, Mathern from £37. Winter Old from £32, Mathern from £25 **Course Designer** H Cotton **Prof** Craig Dun
Facilities ⑪ ⑩ 🍴 🏌 🛒 🍽 ⚑ 🏧 ♿ 🚗 ♣ 🏁 **Leisure** hard tennis courts, heated indoor swimming pool, fishing, sauna, gymnasium, halfway house on Old Course, health & beauty suite, chipping green. **Conf** facs Corporate Hospitality Days **Location** M48 junct 2, A466 towards Chepstow, at 2nd rdbt take exit for Caerwent. Hotel after 2m
Hotel ★★★★ 80% HL Marriott St Pierre Hotel & Country Club, St Pierre Park, CHEPSTOW ☎ 01291 625261 📠 01291 625261 148 en suite

gently undulating course has a long front nine and a shorter back nine, while the final hole, a par 3, is an outstanding finish.

Wernddu Golf Centre: 18 Holes, 5572yds, Par 69, SSS 67, Course record 63. Club membership 550.

Visitors Mon-Sun & BHs. Booking required weekends & BHs. Dress code. **Societies** booking required. **Green Fees** £18 per round **Course Designer** G Watkins **Prof** Tina Tetley **Facilities** ⓦ ▤ ▱ ▥ ⚲ ▦ ▰ ◔ ✦ **Leisure** 9 hole pitch & putt course **Location** 1.5m NE on B4521

Hotel ★★★ 80% CHH Llansantffraed Court, Llanvihangel Gobion, Clytha, ABERGAVENNY ☎ 01873 840678 ▤ 01873 840678 21 en suite

BETTWS NEWYDD   Map 3 SO30

Alice Springs Kemeys Commander NP15 1JU
☎ 01873 880708   ▤ 01873 881381
e-mail: alice_springs@btconnect.com
web: www.alicespringsgolfclub.co.uk

Two 18-hole undulating parkland courses set back to back with magnificent views of the Usk Valley. The Monow course has testing 7th and 15th holes, the Usk 3rd, 12th and 13th.

Monow Course: 18 Holes, 5544yds, Par 69, SSS 69.
Usk Course: 18 Holes, 5934, Par 70, SSS 70.
Club membership 450.

Visitors Mon-Sun & BHs. Booking required weekends & BHs. Dress code. **Societies** booking required. **Green Fees** not confirmed **Course Designer** Keith R Morgan **Prof** Stuart Steel **Facilities** ⓦ ▤ ▥ ▱ ▦ ▰ ◔ ▦ ◗ ⚲ ◔ ✦ **Conf** facs Corporate Hospitality Days **Location** N of Usk on B4598

CAERWENT   Map 3 ST49

Dewstow NP26 5AH
☎ 01291 430444   ▤ 01291 425816
e-mail: info@dewstow.com
web: www.dewstow.co.uk

Two picturesque parkland courses with easy walking and spectacular views over the Severn estuary towards Bristol. Testing holes include the par 3 7th, Valley Course, which is approached over water, some 50ft lower than the tee, and the par 4 15th, Park Course, which has a 50ft totem pole in the middle of the fairway, a unique feature. There is also a 26-bay floodlit driving range.

Valley Course: 18 Holes, 6110yds, Par 72, SSS 70, Course record 64.
Park Course: 18 Holes, 6226yds, Par 69, SSS 69, Course record 67. Club membership 800.

Visitors Mon-Sun & BHs. Booking required. Dress code.

Societies booking required. **Green Fees** £25 per 18 holes, £13 per 9 holes **Prof** Steve Truman **Facilities** ⓦ ▥ ▤ ▱ ▦ ◗ ⚲ ▦ ▰ ◔ ◗ **Conf** facs Corporate Hospitality Days **Location** 0.5m S of Caerwent

Hotel BUD Travelodge Newport Magor, Magor Service Area, MAGOR ☎ 0871 984 6336 ▤ 0871 984 6336 43 en suite

CHEPSTOW   Map 3 ST59

Marriott St Pierre Hotel Country Club see page 403
St Pierre Park NP16 6YA
☎ 01291 625261   ▤ 01291 627977
e-mail: will.hewitt@marriotthotels.com
web: www.stpierregolf.com

MONMOUTH   Map 3 SO51

Monmouth Leasbrook Ln NP25 3SN
☎ 01600 712212 (clubhouse)   ▤ 01600 772399
e-mail: sec@monmouthgolfclub.co.uk
web: www.monmouthgolfclub.co.uk

Parkland on high undulating land with beautiful views. The 8th hole, Cresta Run, is renowned as one of Britain's most extraordinary golf holes.

18 Holes, 5698yds, Par 69, SSS 69, Course record 67. Club membership 484.

Visitors contact club for details. **Societies** booking required. **Green Fees** £30 per day, £20 per round (£32/£24 weekends & BHs) **Course Designer** George Walden **Prof** Richard Ballard **Facilities** ⓦ ▥ ▤ ▱ ▦ ◗ ▰ ◔ ▦ ⚲ **Conf** Corporate Hospitality Days **Location** turn into Leasbrook Lane, 150 yds past Dixon rdbt on Monmouth to Ross on Wye dual carriageway. Club 0.5m up lane on right

Rolls of Monmouth The Hendre NP25 5HG
☎ 01600 715353   ▤ 01600 713115
e-mail: sandra@therollsgolfclub.co.uk
web: www.therollsgolfclub.co.uk

A hilly and challenging parkland course encompassing several lakes and ponds and surrounded by woodland. Set within a beautiful private estate complete with listed mansion and panoramic views towards the Black Mountains. The short 4th has a lake beyond the green and both the 17th and 18th holes are magnificent holes with which to end your round.

The Rolls of Monmouth Golf Club: 18 Holes, 6733yds, Par 72, SSS 73, Course record 69. Club membership 160.
Visitors Mon-Sun & BHs. Booking required. Dress code.

continued

WALES

Societies booking required. Green Fees £42 per day (£46 weekends) Facilities ⑪ ⑂ ☖ ☐ ☜ ⚐ ☜ ◇ ☜ ✦ Conf Corporate Hospitality Days Location 4m W on B4233

RAGLAN — Map 3 SO40

Raglan Parc Parc Lodge NP5 2ER
☎ 01291 690077

18 Holes, 6604yds, Par 72, SSS 73, Course record 67.
Facilities ⑪ ⑂ ☖ ☐ ☜ ⚐ ☜ Location off junct A449
Telephone for further details
Hotel ★★★ 80% CHH Llansantffraed Court, Llanvihangel Gobion, Clytha, ABERGAVENNY ☎ 01873 840678 📄 01873 840678 21 en suite

NEATH PORT TALBOT

GLYNNEATH — Map 3 SN80

Glynneath Pen-y-graig, Pontneathvaughan SA11 5UH
☎ 01639 720452 & 720872   📄 01639 720452
e-mail: enquiries@glynneathgolfclub.co.uk
web: www.glynneathgolfclub.co.uk

Attractive hillside golf overlooking the Vale of Neath in the foothills of the Brecon Beacons National Park. Reasonably level parkland and wooded course.

18 Holes, 6211yds, Par 71, SSS 70, Course record 69.
Club membership 603.

Visitors Mon-Sun & BHs. Booking required Wed & weekends. Dress code. Societies booking required. Green Fees £16 per day (£22 weekends and BHs). £11 Monday Course Designer Cotton/Pennick/Lawrie/williams Prof Shane McMenamin Facilities ⑪ ⑂ ☖ ☐ ☜ ⚐ ✦ ☜ ✦ Leisure Snooker Conf facs Corporate Hospitality Days Location 2m NE of Glynneath on B4242 then take Pontneath Vaughan Rd
Hotel ★★★ 70% HL Castle Hotel, The Parade, NEATH ☎ 01639 641119 📄 01639 641119 29 en suite

MARGAM — Map 3 SS78

Lakeside Water St SA13 2PA
☎ 01639 899959
web: www.lakesidegolf.co.uk

Lakeside Golf Course: 18 Holes, 4550yds, Par 63, SSS 63, Course record 65.

Course Designer Matthew Wootton Location M4 junct 38, off B4283
Telephone for further details
Hotel ★★★ 75% HL Best Western Aberavon Beach, Neath, PORT TALBOT ☎ 01639 884949 📄 01639 884949 52 en suite

NEATH — Map 3 SS79

Earlswood Jersey Marine SA10 6JP
☎ 01792 321578

Earlswood is a hillside course offering spectacular scenic views over Swansea Bay. The terrain is gently undulating downs with natural hazards and is designed to appeal to both the new and the experienced golfer.

Earlswood Golf Course: 18 Holes, 5084yds, Par 68, SSS 68.
Visitors contact course for details. Societies welcome. Green

Fees £10 per round Course Designer Gorvett Estates Prof Mike Day Facilities ☖ ☐ ☜ ☜ ⚐ ✦ Location 4m E of Swansea, off A483
Hotel ★★★ 70% HL Castle Hotel, The Parade, NEATH ☎ 01639 641119 📄 01639 641119 29 en suite

Neath Cadoxton SA10 8AH
☎ 01639 643615 (clubhouse) & 632759
📄 01639 632759
e-mail: neathgolf@btconnect.com
web: www.neathgolfclub.com

Mountain course, with spectacular views of the Brecon Beacons to the north and the Bristol Channel to the south.

18 Holes, 6490yds, Par 72, SSS 72, Course record 66.
Club membership 700.

Visitors Mon-Fri except BHs. Societies welcome. Green Fees Apr-Sep £25 (£30 weekends), Oct & Mar £17, Nov & Feb £15, Dec & Jan £11 Course Designer James Braid Facilities ⑪ ⑂ ☖ ☐ ☜ ☖ ☜ ⚐ ☜ ✦ Leisure snooker Location 2m NE off A4230
Hotel ★★★ 70% HL Castle Hotel, The Parade, NEATH ☎ 01639 641119 📄 01639 641119 29 en suite

Swansea Bay Jersey Marine SA10 6JP
☎ 01792 812198 & 814153

Fairly level seaside links with part dunes.

18 Holes, 6459yds, Par 72, SSS 71, Course record 69.
Club membership 500.

Visitors Mon-Sun & BHs. Dress code. Societies booking required. Green Fees £18 per round (£26 weekends & BHs). Prof Mike Day Facilities ⑪ ⑂ ☖ ☐ ☜ ⚐ ☜ ☜ ✦ Leisure indoor bowls Conf facs Corporate Hospitality Days Location M4 junct 42, onto A483, 1st right onto B4290 towards Jersey Marine, 1st right to clubhouse
Hotel ★★★ 75% HL Best Western Aberavon Beach, Neath, PORT TALBOT ☎ 01639 884949 📄 01639 884949 52 en suite

PONTARDAWE
Map 3 SN70

Pontardawe Cefn Llan SA8 4SH
☎ 01792 863118   📄 01792 830041
e-mail: enquiries@pontardawegolfclub.com
web: www.pontardawegolfclub.co.uk

Meadowland course situated on plateau 600ft above sea level with good views of the Bristol Channel and the Brecon Beacons.

18 Holes, 6101yds, Par 70, SSS 70, Course record 64. Club membership 500.

Visitors contact club for details. **Societies** welcome. **Green Fees** £22 per day **Prof** Danny Evans **Facilities** ⓦ ⏐⊚⏐ 🏌 ☕ 🍴 🏌 ⚒ 🛒 🏌 **Leisure** snooker & pool rooms **Conf** Corporate Hospitality Days **Location** M4 junct 45, off A4067 N of town centre
Hotel ★★★ 70% HL Castle Hotel, The Parade, NEATH
☎ 01639 641119 📄 01639 641119 29 en suite

PORT TALBOT
Map 3 SS78

British Steel Port Talbot, Sports & Social Club, Margam SA13 2NF
☎ 01639 793194

A 9 hole course with two lakes. All the holes are affected by crosswinds and the 7th, Par 3, is alongside a deep stream, so is very tight.

British Steel Port Talbot Golf Course: 9 Holes, 4726yds, Par 62, SSS 63, Course record 60. Club membership 100.

Visitors Mon-Sat except BHs. Booking required Sat. **Societies** booking required. **Green Fees** £10 (£12 Sat) **Facilities** ⓦ ⏐⊚⏐ 🏌 ☕ 🍴 ⚒ **Leisure** hard tennis courts, fishing **Conf** facs Corporate Hospitality Days **Location** M4 junct 40
Hotel ★★★ 75% HL Best Western Aberavon Beach, Neath, PORT TALBOT ☎ 01639 884949 📄 01639 884949 52 en suite

YSTRADGYNLAIS
Map 3 SN71

Palleg and Swansea Valley Lower Cwmtwrch SA9 2QQ
☎ 01639 842193   📄 01639 845661
e-mail: gc.gcgs@btinternet.com
web: www.palleg-golf.com

Meadowland course set in 120 acres with spectacular views of the Black Mountains and Swansea Valley situated at the foot of the Brecon Beacons. An attractive ravine runs through the back nine holes.

18 Holes, 5902yds, Par 72, SSS 70. Club membership 320.

Visitors dress code. **Societies** booking required. **Green Fees** £24 per day, £18 per round **Course Designer** C H Cotton **Prof** Graham Coombe **Facilities** ⓦ ⏐⊚⏐ 🏌 ☕ 🍴 ⚒ 🏌 🛒 ⚒ 🏌 **Leisure** practice nets **Conf** facs Corporate Hospitality Days **Location** M4 junct 45, N on A4067 towards Brecon. At 6th roundabout (Powys sign) turn left to Cwmtwrch for 500 yds. Turn right at mini roundabout, up hill into Palleg Rd. Course 1m on left
Hotel ★★★ 70% HL Castle Hotel, The Parade, NEATH
☎ 01639 641119 📄 01639 641119 29 en suite

NEWPORT

CAERLEON
Map 3 ST39

Caerleon NP6 1AY
☎ 01633 420342   📄 01633 420342

Caerleon Golf Course: 9 Holes, 2900yds, Par 34, SSS 34, Course record 29.

Course Designer Steel **Location** M4 junct 24, B4236 to Caerleon, 1st left after Priory Hotel, follow road to bottom
Telephone for further details
Hotel ★★★★★ 85% HL The Celtic Manor Resort, Coldra Woods, NEWPORT ☎ 01633 413000 📄 01633 413000 400 en suite

LLANWERN
Map 3 ST38

Llanwern Tennyson Av NP18 2DY
☎ 01633 412029 (sec) & 413233 (pro)
📄 01633 412029
e-mail: llanwerngolfclub@btconnect.com
web: www.llanwerngolfclub.co.uk

Established in 1928, a mature, parkland course in a picturesque village setting.

18 Holes, 6177yds, Par 70, SSS 70, Course record 66. Club membership 500.

Visitors contact club for details. **Societies** welcome. **Green Fees** £35 per day, £25 per round (£40/£30 Sat) **Prof** Stephen Price **Facilities** ⓦ ⏐⊚⏐ 🏌 ☕ 🍴 ⚒ 🏌 🛒 ⚒ 🏌 **Conf** Corporate Hospitality Days **Location** 0.5m S off A455, signed
Hotel ★★★★★ 85% HL The Celtic Manor Resort, Coldra Woods, NEWPORT ☎ 01633 413000 📄 01633 413000 400 en suite

NEWPORT
Map 3 ST38

Celtic Manor Resort see page 407
Coldra Woods NP18 1HQ
☎ 01633 413000   📄 01633 410269
e-mail: postbox@celtic-manor.com
web: www.celtic-manor.com

Newport Great Oak, Rogerstone NP10 9FX
☎ 01633 892643   📄 01633 896676
e-mail: secretary@newportgolfclub.org.uk
web: newportgolfclub.org.uk

Undulating parkland on an inland plateau 300ft above sea level, with views over the surrounding wooded countryside. There are no blind holes, but plenty of natural hazards and bunkers.

18 Holes, 6500yds, Par 72, SSS 71, Course record 63. Club membership 800.

Visitors Mon, Wed-Fri & Sun except BHs. Handicap certificate. Dress code. **Societies** booking required. **Green Fees** not confirmed **Course Designer** W Fernie **Prof** Paul Mayo **Facilities** ⓦ ⏐⊚⏐ 🏌 ☕ 🍴 ⚒ 🛒 ⚒ 🏌 **Conf** Corporate Hospitality Days **Location** M4 junct 27, 1m NW on B4591
Hotel ★★★★★ 85% HL The Celtic Manor Resort, Coldra Woods, NEWPORT ☎ 01633 413000 📄 01633 413000 400 en suite

WALES

CELTIC MANOR RESORT
NEWPORT - MAP 3 ST38

This relatively new resort has quickly become a world-renowned venue for golf, set in 1400 acres of beautiful, unspoiled parkland at the southern gateway to Wales. Boasting three championship courses, Celtic Manor offers a challenge for all levels of play, complemented by a golf school and one of the largest clubhouses in Europe, as well as extensive leisure facilities. In 2010, The Celtic Manor Resort hosts the 38th Ryder Cup on the world's first ever course to be specifically designed for this prestigious tournament. The new course opened in spring 2007, featuring nine holes from the original Wentwood Hills course and nine spectacular new holes in the valley of the River Usk.

Coldra Woods NP18 1HQ ☎ 01633 413000 🖷 01633 410269
e-mail: postbox@celtic-manor.com **web:** www.celtic-manor.com
Roman Road: 18 Holes, 6515yds, Par 70, SSS 72, Course record 60.
Montgomerie: 18 Holes, 6294yds, Par 69, SSS 71.
Twenty Ten Course: 18 Holes, 7008yds, Par 71, SSS 75. Club membership 720.
Visitors Mon-Sun & BHs. Booking required. Dress code. **Societies** booking required. **Green Fees** Twenty Ten from £110 per 18 holes, Roman Road/Montgomerie from £50 **Course Designer** Robert Trent Jones **Prof** Lee Jay Barnes
Facilities ⊕ ◯ ⌫ ⌨ ⊞ ⌷ ⌸ ♢ ⌑ ⌥ ⌦ ⌧ **Leisure** hard tennis courts, heated indoor swimming pool, fishing, sauna, gymnasium, Health spa, Golf Academy with 18 hole course, Shooting school **Conf** facs Corporate Hospitality Days **Location** M4 junct 24, B4237 towards Newport, 300yds right
Hotel ★★★★★ 85% HL The Celtic Manor Resort, Coldra Woods, NEWPORT ☎ 01633 413000 🖷 01633 413000 400 en suite

Parc Church Ln, Coedkernew NP10 8TU
☎ 01633 680933   📠 01633 681011
web: www.parcgolf.co.uk

A challenging but enjoyable 18-hole course with water hazards and accompanying wildlife. The 38-bay driving range is floodlit until 10pm.

Parc Golf Course: 18 Holes, 5619yds, Par 70, SSS 68, Course record 66. Club membership 400.

Visitors Mon-Sun & BHs. Dress code. **Societies** welcome. **Green Fees** Weekdays £15 (£20 weekends & BHs) **Prof** R Dinsdale/J Wills/N Humphries **Facilities** ⓨ 🍴 🍺 🖥 🎣 👥 🏠 ☂ 🏌 🛥 🔧 **Leisure** 9 hole astra turf short course **Conf** facs Corporate Hospitality Days **Location** 3m SW of Newport, off A48

Tredegar Park Parc-y-Brain Rd NP10 9TG
☎ 01633 894433   📠 01633 897152
web: www.tredegarparkgolfclub.co.uk
18 Holes, 6545yds, Par 72, SSS 72.

Course Designer R Sandow **Location** M4 junct 27, B4591 N, club signed
Telephone for further details

PEMBROKESHIRE

HAVERFORDWEST   Map 2 SM91

Haverfordwest Arnolds Down SA61 2XQ
☎ 01437 764523 & 768409   📠 01437 764143
e-mail: haverfordwestgc@btconnect.com
web: www.haverfordwestgolfclub.co.uk

Fairly flat parkland course, a good challenge for golfers of all handicaps. Set in attractive surroundings with fine views over the Preseli Hills.

18 Holes, 6002yds, Par 70, SSS 69, Course record 63. Club membership 770.

Visitors Mon-Sun & BHs. Booking required. Dress code. **Societies** booking required. **Green Fees** phone **Prof** Alex Pile **Facilities** ⓨ 🍴 🍺 🖥 🎣 👥 🏠 ☂ 🏌 🔧 **Conf** facs Corporate Hospitality Days **Location** 1m E on A40
Hotel ★★ 71% HL Hotel Mariners, Mariners Square, HAVERFORDWEST ☎ 01437 763353 📠 01437 763353 28 en suite

LETTERSTON   Map 2 SM92

Priskilly Forest Castlemorris SA62 5EH
☎ 01348 840276   📠 01348 840276
e-mail: jevans@priskilly-forest.co.uk
web: www.priskilly-forest.co.uk

Challenging parkland course with panoramic views and a stunning 18th hole. Immaculate greens and fairways surrounded by rhododendrons, established shrubs and trees. Testing lies.

9 Holes, 5874yds, Par 70, SSS 68, Course record 73. Club membership 180.

Visitors contact club for details. **Societies** welcome. **Green Fees** £24 per day, £20 per 18 holes, £14 per 9 holes **Course Designer** J Walters **Prof** S Parsons **Facilities** ⓨ 🍴 🍺 🖥 🎣 👥 🏠 ☂ ◇ 🔧 🛥 🔧 **Leisure** fishing **Conf** facs Corporate Hospitality Days **Location** 2 miles off the A40 at Letterston off B4331

Hotel ★★★ 78% CHH Wolfscastle Country Hotel, WOLF'S CASTLE ☎ 01437 741688 & 741225 📠 01437 741688 22 en suite

MILFORD HAVEN   Map 2 SM90

Milford Haven Woodbine House, Hubberston SA73 3RX
☎ 01646 697762   📠 01646 697870
e-mail: milfordgolfclub@aol.com
web: www.mhgc.co.uk

Parkland course with excellent greens and views of the Milford Haven waterway.

18 Holes, 6112yds, Par 71, SSS 70, Course record 64. Club membership 450.

Visitors Mon-Sun & BHs. Dress code. **Societies** booking required. **Green Fees** £10 Mon, Wed & Fri. Other days £15 **Course Designer** David Williams **Prof** Alex Pile **Facilities** ⓨ 🍴 🍺 🖥 🎣 👥 🏠 ☂ 🏌 🔧 **Conf** Corporate Hospitality Days **Location** 1.5m W of Milford Haven
Hotel ★★★ 75% HL Cleddau Bridge, Essex Road, PEMBROKE DOCK ☎ 01646 685961 📠 01646 685961 40 en suite

NEWPORT (PEMBROKESHIRE)   Map 2 SN03

Newport Links Newport Links Golf Club SA42 0NR
☎ 01239 820244   📠 01239 820085
e-mail: info@newportlinks.co.uk
web: www.newportlinks.co.uk

Seaside links course situated in a National Park, with easy walking and good view of the Preselli Hills and Newport Bay.

18 Holes, 6100yds, Par 70, SSS 69, Course record 64. Club membership 500.

Visitors Mon-Sun & BHs. Booking required. Dress code. **Societies** booking required **Green Fees** £28 per round (£32 weekends & BHs) **Course Designer** James Braid **Prof** Alun Evans **Facilities** ⓨ 🍴 🍺 🖥 🎣 👥 🏠 ☂ ◇ 🔧 🛥 🔧 ☂ **Conf** facs Corporate Hospitality Days **Location** 1.25m N of Newport off A487

PEMBROKE DOCK   Map 2 SM90

South Pembrokeshire Military Rd SA72 6SE
☎ 01646 621453   📠 01646 621453
e-mail: spgc06@tiscali.co.uk
web: www.southpembsgolf.co.uk

A hillside course on an elevated site overlooking the Cleddau and Haven waterway.

18 Holes, 6279yds, Par 70, SSS 69, Course record 65. Club membership 350.

Visitors Mon-Sun & BHs. Booking required. Dress code. **Societies** booking required **Green Fees** phone **Course Designer** Committee **Facilities** ⓨ 🍴 🍺 🖥 🎣 👥 ☂ 🛥 🔧 **Conf** facs Corporate Hospitality Days **Location** SW of town centre off B4322

TENBY — Map 2 SN10

Tenby The Burrows SA70 7NP
☎ 01834 844447 & 842978 📠 01834 842978
e-mail: tenbygolfclub@uku.co.uk
web: www.tenbygolf.co.uk
The oldest club in Wales, this fine seaside links, with sea views and natural hazards, provides good golf all the year round.
18 Holes, 6224yds, Par 69, SSS 71, Course record 65. Club membership 700.
Visitors contact club for details. **Societies** welcome. **Green Fees** not confirmed **Course Designer** James Braid **Prof** Rhys Harry **Facilities** ⓦ ⓧ 🍴 🏌 ▯ 🏐 ⛳ 🛒 ⛳ **Conf** Corporate Hospitality Days **Location** near railway station
Hotel ★★★ 78% HL Atlantic, The Esplanade, TENBY ☎ 01834 842881 📠 01834 842881 42 en suite

Trefloyne Golf, Bar & Restaurant Trefloyne Park, Penally SA70 7RG
☎ 01834 842165 📠 01834 844288
e-mail: enquiries@trefloyne.com
web: www.trefloyne.com
Idyllic parkland course with backdrop of mature mixed woodlands and distant views of Tenby, Carmarthen Bay and Caldey Island. Natural features and hazards such as the Old Quarry make for exciting and challenging golf.
Trefloyne Golf, Bar & Restaurant: 18 Holes, 6635yds, Par 71, SSS 73. Club membership 400.
Visitors Mon-Sun & BHs. Booking required Sat. Dress code. **Societies** booking required. **Green Fees** £27 per day **Course Designer** F H Gillman **Facilities** ⓦ 🍴 🏌 ▯ 🏐 ⛳ 🛒 ⛳ **Location** in Trefloyne Park, just W of Tenby
Hotel ★★★ 75% HL Fourcroft, North Beach, TENBY ☎ 01834 842886 📠 01834 842886 40 en suite

POWYS

BRECON — Map 3 S002

Brecon Newton Park LD3 8PA
☎ 01874 622004
e-mail: info@brecongolfclub.co.uk
web: www.brecongolfclub.co.uk
Easy walking parkland. Natural hazards include two rivers on the boundary. Good river and mountain scenery.
9 Holes, 6080yds, Par 70, SSS 70, Course record 66. Club membership 280.
Visitors Mon-Sat & BHs. Booking required Thu . Dress code. **Societies** booking required. **Green Fees** £15 per day/per round (£18 Sat & BHs) **Course Designer** James Braid **Facilities** ⓦ 🍴 🏌 ▯ 🏐 ⛳ **Location** 0.75m W of town centre on A40

Cradoc Penoyre Park, Cradoc LD3 9LP
☎ 01874 623658 📠 01874 611711
e-mail: secretary@cradoc.co.uk
web: www.cradoc.co.uk
Parkland with wooded areas, ponds and spectacular views over the Brecon Beacons. Challenging golf.
18 Holes, 6188yds, Par 71, SSS 71, Course record 65. Club membership 700.

Visitors Mon-Sun & BHs. Booking required except Mon & Thu. Handicap certificate. Dress code. **Societies** booking required. **Green Fees** £26 per day (£32 weekends & BHs) **Course Designer** C K Cotton **Prof** Richard Davies **Facilities** ⓦ 🍴 🏌 ▯ 🏐 ⛳ 🛒 ⛳ 🚜 ⛳ 🏁 **Location** 2m N of Brecon off B4520

BUILTH WELLS — Map 3 S005

Builth Wells Golf Links Rd LD2 3NF
☎ 01982 553296 📠 01982 551064
e-mail: info@builthwellsgolf.co.uk
web: www.builthwellsgolf.co.uk
Well-guarded greens and a stream running through the centre of the course add interest to this 18-hole undulating parkland course. The clubhouse is a converted 15th-century Welsh longhouse.
18 Holes, 5424yds, Par 66, SSS 67, Course record 62. Club membership 380.
Visitors Mon-Sun & BHs. Booking required. Handicap certificate. Dress code. **Societies** booking required. **Green Fees** £30 per day, £23 per round (£32/£27 weekends & BHs) **Prof** Simon Edwards **Facilities** ⓦ 🍴 🏌 ▯ 🏐 ⛳ 🚜 ⛳ **Conf** Corporate Hospitality Days **Location** N of A483
Guesthouse ★★★★ 75% RR Lasswade Country House, Station Road, LLANWRTYD WELLS ☎ 01591 610515 📠 01591 610515

KNIGHTON — Map 7 S027

Knighton Ffrydd Wood LD7 1DL
☎ 01547 528046 (Sec)
Upland course with some hard walking. Fine views over the England border.
9 Holes, 5362yds, Par 68, SSS 66, Course record 65. Club membership 150.
Visitors Mon-Sat & BHs. Booking required Tue, Wed & Sat. Dress code. **Societies** booking required. **Green Fees** not confirmed **Course Designer** Harry Vardon **Facilities** ⓦ by prior arrangement 🏌 ▯ 🏐 🏌 **Location** 0.5m S off B4355
Hotel ★★★ 79% CHH Milebrook House, Milebrook, KNIGHTON ☎ 01547 528632 📠 01547 528632 10 en suite

LLANDRINDOD WELLS — Map 3 S006

Llandrindod Wells The Clubhouse LD1 5NY
☎ 01597 823873 (sec) 📠 01597 823873
e-mail: secretary@lwgc.co.uk
web: www.lwgc.co.uk
An upland links course, designed by Harry Vardon, with easy walking and panoramic views.
18 Holes, 5759yds, Par 69, SSS 69, Course record 65. Club membership 465.
Visitors Mon-Sun & BHs. Booking required Fri-Sun & BHs. Dress code. **Societies** welcome. **Green Fees** not confirmed **Course Designer** H Vardon **Prof** Philip Davies **Facilities** ⓦ 🍴 🏌 ▯ 🏐 ⛳ 🛒 ⛳ 🚜 ⛳ 🏁 **Conf** facs Corporate Hospitality Days **Location** 1m SE off A483
Hotel ★★★ 82% HL The Metropole, Temple Street, LLANDRINDOD WELLS ☎ 01597 823700 📠 01597 823700 120 en suite

WALES

LLANGATTOCK
Map 3 SO21

Old Rectory NP8 1PH
☎ 01873 810373   🖹 018373 810373
web: www.rectoryhotel.co.uk

9 Holes, 2200yds, Par 54, SSS 59, Course record 53.
Facilities Ⓣ Ⓚ Ⓚ ⊑ Ⓚ ⌿ ⋈ ◇**Leisure** fishing
Conf facs Location SW of village
Telephone for further details
Hotel ★★★ 81% CHH Gliffaes Country House Hotel, CRICKHOWELL
☎ 01874 730371🖹 01874 730371   23 en suite

LLANIDLOES
Map 6 SN98

St Idloes Penrallt SY18 6LG
☎ 01686 412559
web: www.stidloesgolfclub.co.uk

Hill-course, slightly undulating but walking is easy. Good views, partly lined with trees. Sand and grass bunkers.

9 Holes, 5540yds, Par 66, SSS 66, Course record 61.
Club membership 339.

Visitors Mon-Sun & BHs. Booking advised Sun. **Societies** booking required. **Green Fees** not confirmed **Facilities** Ⓣ by prior arrangement Ⓚby prior arrangement ⓀⓀ ⊑ ⓀⓀ ⋈ ⌿
Conf facs Location 1m N off B4569
Hotel ★★★ INN Mount, China Street, LLANIDLOES
☎ 01686 412247🖹 01686 412247   9 en suite

LLANYMYNECH
Map 7 SJ22

Llanymynech SY10 8LB
☎ 01691 830983 & 830542   🖹 01691 839184
e-mail: secretary@llanymynechgolfclub.co.uk
web: www.llanymynechgolfclub.co.uk

Upland course on the site of a prehistoric hill fort with far-reaching views. With 15 holes in Wales and three in England, drive off in Wales and putt out in England on 4th hole. A quality mature course with a tremendous variety of holes.

18 Holes, 6114yds, Par 70, SSS 69, Course record 64.
Club membership 750.

Visitors Mon-Fri & Sun except BHs. Booking required. Dress code. **Societies** booking required. **Green Fees** £42 per day, £32 per round (£42 Sun) **Prof** Andrew P Griffiths **Facilities** Ⓣ Ⓚ Ⓚ ⊑ ⓀⓀ ⋈ ⓐ ⌿ ⓴ ⌿ **Conf** Corporate Hospitality Days **Location** 6m S of Oswestry, off A483 in Pant at Cross Guns Inn
Hotel ★★★★ 80% HL Wynnstay, Church Street, OSWESTRY
☎ 01691 655261🖹 01691 655261   34 en suite

MACHYNLLETH
Map 6 SH70

Machynlleth SY20 8UH
☎ 01654 702000   🖹 01654 702928
e-mail: machgolf2@tiscali.co.uk
web: www.machynllethgolf.co.uk

A heathland course surrounded by hills. The course is at its best in spring and summer with colour from the gorse and rhododendrons. Elevated tees on the 5th and 8th holes give wonderful views of the surrounding countryside.

9 Holes, 5726yds, Par 68, SSS 68, Course record 65.
Club membership 200.

Visitors contact club for details. **Societies** booking required. **Green Fees** £20 per day **Course Designer** James Braid **Facilities** Ⓣ Ⓚ ⓀⓀ ⊑ ⓀⓀ ⋈ ⌿⌿ **Leisure** 3 hole par 3 course **Location** 0.5m E off A489

NEWTOWN
Map 6 SO19

St Giles Pool Rd SY16 3AJ
☎ 01686 625844   🖹 01686 625844
web: www.stgilesgolf.co.uk

9 Holes, 6012yds, Par 70, SSS 70, Course record 67.
Prof D P Owen **Facilities** Ⓣ by prior arrangement Ⓚ by prior arrangement ⓀⓀ ⊑ ⋈ ⌿ **Location** 0.5m NE on A483
Telephone for further details

WELSHPOOL
Map 7 SJ20

Welshpool Golfa Hill SY21 9AQ
☎ 01938 850249   🖹 01938 850249
e-mail: welshpool.golfclub@btconnect.com
web: www.welshpoolgolfclub.co.uk

Undulating, hilly, heathland course with bracing air. Testing holes are 2nd (par 5), 14th (par 3), 17th (par 3) and a memorable 18th.

18 Holes, 5846yds, Par 71, SSS 69, Course record 68.
Club membership 400.

Visitors dress code. **Societies** welcome. **Green Fees** £15.50 per day (£25.50 weekends, £15.50 winter months) **Course Designer** James Braid **Facilities** Ⓣ Ⓚ ⓀⓀ ⊑ ⓀⓀ ⋈ ⓐ ⌿ ⌿ ⓴ ⌿ **Conf** Corporate Hospitality Days **Location** 3m W off A458
Hotel ★★★ 78% HL Royal Oak, The Cross, WELSHPOOL
☎ 01938 552217🖹 01938 552217   25 en suite

RHONDDA CYNON TAFF

ABERDARE
Map 3 SO00

Aberdare Abernant CF44 0RY
☎ 01685 872797   🖹 01685 872797
e-mail: sec-age@tiscali.co.uk
web: www.aberdaregolfclub.co.uk

Mountain course with parkland features overlooking the Brecon Beacons. Tree-lined with many mature oaks.

18 Holes, 5875yds, Par 69, SSS 69, Course record 64.
Club membership 550.

Visitors Mon-Sun & BHs. Booking required. Dress code. **Societies** booking required. **Green Fees** £17 per day (£21 weekends & BHs) **Prof** Catherine & David Price **Facilities** Ⓣ Ⓚ ⓀⓀ ⊑ ⓀⓀ ⋈ ⓐ ⌿ ⓴ ⌿ **Leisure** 3 practice nets **Conf** facs Corporate Hospitality Days **Location** 1m NE of town centre. Past hospital, 400yds on right

MOUNTAIN ASH
Map 3 ST09

Mountain Ash Cefnpennar CF45 4DT
☎ 01443 479459 🖹 01443 479628
e-mail: sec@magc.fsnet.co.uk
web: www.mountainash.co.uk
Mountain moorland course with panoramic views of the Brecon Beacons. Not long but testing and demands accuracy from the opening hole, a 390yd par 4 that rises up halfway down its length with woodland on the left and out of bounds on the right. The 10th hole is the highest point, hitting from an elevated platform with woodland on the left below. The 18th is a dramatic finale in the form of a 510yd, par 5, with a carry over gorse, a ditch crossing the fairway and bunkers and sand traps protecting the green.
18 Holes, 5553yds, Par 69, SSS 67, Course record 60.
Club membership 560.

Visitors contact club for details. **Societies** welcome. **Green Fees** not confirmed **Prof** Darren Clark **Facilities** ⑪ ⑩ 🍴 ⌷ 🍴 🧍 📷 🚗 **Conf** facs Corporate Hospitality Days **Location** 1m NW off A4059 **Hotel** ★★★ 75% CHH Llechwen Hall, Llanfabon, PONTYPRIDD ☎ 01443 742050 & 743020 🖹 01443 742050 20 en suite

PENRHYS
Map 3 ST09

Rhondda Golf Club House CF43 3PW
☎ 01443 441384 🖹 01443 441384
18 Holes, 6205yds, Par 70, SSS 71, Course record 67.
Facilities ⑪ by prior arrangement ⑩ by prior arrangement 🍴 ⌷ 🍴 🧍 📷 🚗 ⚑ **Conf** facs Corporate Hospitality Days
Location 0.5m W off B4512
Telephone for further details

PONTYPRIDD
Map 3 ST08

Pontypridd Ty Gwyn Rd CF37 4DJ
☎ 01443 409904 🖹 01443 491622
e-mail: secretary.pontypriddgc@virgin.net
web: www.pontypriddgolfclub.co.uk
Well-wooded mountain course with springy turf. Fine views of the Rhondda and Taff valleys and coast. Challenging but rewarding course.
18 Holes, 5721yds, Par 69, SSS 68, Course record 65.
Club membership 650.

Visitors Mon-Fri except BHs. Handicap certificate. Dress code. **Societies** booking required **Green Fees** £20 per 18 holes **Prof** Wade Walters **Facilities** ⑪ ⑩ 🍴 ⌷ 🍴 🧍 📷 🚗 🚙 **Conf** Corporate Hospitality Days **Location** E of town centre off A470

TALBOT GREEN
Map 3 ST08

Llantrisant & Pontyclun Off Ely Valley Rd CF72 8AL
☎ 01443 228169
e-mail: llantrisantgolf@btconnect.com
web: www.llantrisantgolfclub.co.uk
Scenic, undulating parkland.
18 Holes, 5328yds, Par 68, SSS 66, Course record 62.
Club membership 400.

Visitors Mon-Sat except BHs. Booking required. Handicap certificate. Dress code. **Societies** booking required. **Green Fees** £20 (£25 Sat) **Prof** Andrew Bowen **Facilities** ⑪ ⑩ 🍴 ⌷ 🍴 🧍 📷 🚗 ⚑ **Conf** facs Corporate Hospitality Days **Location** M4 junct 34, A4119 to Llantrisant, over 1st rdbt, left at 2nd lights to Talbot Green, right at minirdbt, club 50yds on left
Hotel ★★★★ 75% CHH Miskin Manor Country Hotel, Pendoylan Road, MISKIN ☎ 01443 224204 🖹 01443 224204 43 en suite

SWANSEA

CLYDACH
Map 3 SN60

Inco SA6 5QR
☎ 01792 842929
Flat meadowland course bordered by meandering River Tawe and the Swansea valley.
18 Holes, 6064yds, Par 70, SSS 69, Course record 68.
Club membership 450.

Visitors contact club for details. **Societies** booking required. **Green Fees** £20 per round (£25 weekends) **Facilities** ⑪ ⑩ 🍴 ⌷ 🍴 🧍 ⚑ **Leisure** outdoor bowling green **Conf** Corporate Hospitality Days **Location** M4 junct 45, 1.5m NE on A4067
Hotel ★★★ 77% HL Ramada Swansea, Phoenix Way, Swansea Enterprise Park, SWANSEA ☎ 01792 310330 🖹 01792 310330 119 en suite

PONTLLIW
Map 2 SS69

Allt-y-Graban Allt-y-Graban Rd SA4 1DT
☎ 01792 885757
Allt-y-Graban Golf Course: 9 Holes, 2210yds, Par 66, SSS 66, Course record 63.
Course Designer F G Thomas **Location** M4 junct 47, A48 towards Pontardulais, left after Glamorgan Arms
Telephone for further details
Hotel BUD Travelodge Swansea (M4), Penllergaer, SWANSEA ☎ 0871 9846055 🖹 0871 9846055 51 en suite

WALES

SOUTHGATE Map 2 SS58

Pennard 2 Southgate Rd SA3 2BT
☎ 01792 233131 & 233451   ▤ 01792 235125
e-mail: sec@pennardgolfclub.com
web: www.pennardgolfclub.com

Undulating, cliff-top seaside links with good coastal views. At first sight it can be intimidating with steep hills that make club selection important - there are a few blind shots to contend with. The difficulties are not insurmountable unless the wind begins to blow in calm weather. Greens are slick and firm all year.

18 Holes, 6265yds, Par 71, SSS 72, Course record 69.
Club membership 1020.

Visitors Mon-Wed & Fri except BHs. Booking required Tue. Handicap certificate. Dress code. **Societies** welcome. **Green Fees** £50 per 18 holes **Course Designer** James Braid **Prof** M V Bennett **Facilities** ⊕ ⓘⓞⓘ ⓑ ▱ ⓟ ⚑ ⚑ ⓐ ⓒ ⚑ ⚑ **Conf** facs **Location** 8m W of Swansea by A4067 and B4436

Hotel ★★ 68% HL Winston, 11 Church Lane, BISHOPSTON
☎ 01792 232074 ▤ 01792 232074   17 en suite

SWANSEA Map 3 SS69

Clyne 120 Owls Lodge Ln, The Mayals, Blackpill SA3 5DP
☎ 01792 401989   ▤ 01792 401078
e-mail: clynegolfclub@supanet.com
web: www.clynegolfclub.com

Challenging moorland course with excellent greens and scenic views of Swansea Bay and the Gower. Many natural hazards with a large number of bunkers and gorse and bracken in profusion.

18 Holes, 6323yds, Par 70, SSS 72, Course record 64.
Club membership 800.

Visitors contact club for details. **Societies** booking required. **Green Fees** £30 per round (£40 weekends & BHs), Winter £20 including bar meal **Course Designer** H S Colt & Harries **Prof** Jonathan Clewett **Facilities** ⊕ ⓘⓞⓘ ⓑ ▱ ⓟ ⚑ ⓐ ⓒ ⓟ ⚑ ⚑ **Leisure** chipping green,driving nets,indoor practice net **Conf** facs Corporate Hospitality Days **Location** 3.5m SW on B4436

Hotel ★★★★ 78% HL Swansea Marriott Hotel, The Maritime Quarter, SWANSEA ☎ 0870 400 7282 ▤ 0870 400 7282   122 en suite

Langland Bay Langland Bay SA3 4QR
☎ 01792 361721   ▤ 01792 361082
e-mail: info@langlandbaygolfclub.com
web: www.langlandbaygolfclub.com

Parkland situated on cliff tops and land between Caswell and Langland Bay. The par 4 6th is an uphill dog-leg open to the wind, and the par 3 16th (151yds) is aptly named Death or Glory.

18 Holes, 5857yds, Par 70, SSS 70, Course record 63.
Club membership 850.

Visitors Handicap certificate. Dress code. **Societies** booking required. **Green Fees** £40 per day (£50 weekends & BHs) **Prof** Mark Evans **Facilities** ⊕ ⓘⓞⓘ ⓑ ▱ ⓟ ⚑ ⓐ ⓟ ⚑ **Location** 6m SW off B4593

Hotel ★★★★ 78% HL Swansea Marriott Hotel, The Maritime Quarter, SWANSEA ☎ 0870 400 7282 ▤ 0870 400 7282   122 en suite

Morriston 160 Clasemont Rd, Morriston SA6 6AJ
☎ 01792 796528   ▤ 01792 796528
e-mail: morristongolf@btconnect.com
web: www.morristongolfclub.co.uk

Pleasant parkland course with a very difficult par 3 15th hole, one of the most challenging short holes in Wales. The 17th is aptly nicknamed Temple of Doom.

18 Holes, 5708yds, Par 68, SSS 68, Course record 61.
Club membership 650.

Visitors Mon-Sun & BHs. Booking required. Handicap Certificate. Dress code. **Societies** booking required. **Green Fees** £25 per day (£35 weekends & BHs) **Prof** M. Govier **Facilities** ⊕ ⓘⓞⓘ ⓑ ▱ ⓟ ⓐ ⓟ ⚑ ⚑ ⚑ **Conf** facs Corporate Hospitality Days **Location** M4 junct 46, 1m E on A48

Hotel ★★★ 77% HL Ramada Swansea, Phoenix Way, Swansea Enterprise Park, SWANSEA ☎ 01792 310330 ▤ 01792 310330   119 en suite

THREE CROSSES Map 2 SS59

Gower Cefn Goleu SA4 3HS
☎ 01792 872480   ▤ 01792 875535
web: www.gowergolf.co.uk

18 Holes, 6441yds, Par 71, SSS 72, Course record 66.

Course Designer Donald Steel **Location** off A4118 Swansea to Gower, signed from Three Crosses
Telephone for further details

UPPER KILLAY Map 2 SS59

Fairwood Park Blackhills Ln SA2 7JN
☎ 01792 297849   ▤ 01792 297849
e-mail: info@fairwoodpark.com
web: www.fairwoodpark.com

Parkland championship course on the beautiful Gower peninsula, being both the flattest and the longest course in Swansea. Surrounded by vast areas of woodland on all sides, each fairway is well defined with lakes and bunkers to test the nerve of any golfer.

18 Holes, 6650yds, Par 73, SSS 73, Course record 68.
Club membership 500.

Visitors Mon-Sun & BHs. Booking required. Dress code. **Societies** booking required. **Green Fees** £27 per round, (£34 Fri-Sun) **Course Designer** Hawtree **Prof** Gary Hughes **Facilities** ⊕ ⓘⓞⓘ ⓑ ▱ ⓟ ⚑ ⓐ ⓟ ◇ ⚑ ⚑ ⚑ **Conf** facs Corporate Hospitality Days **Location** 1.5m S off A4118

Hotel ★★★★ 78% HL Swansea Marriott Hotel, The Maritime Quarter, SWANSEA ☎ 0870 400 7282 ▤ 0870 400 7282   122 en suite

TORFAEN

CWMBRAN
Map 3 ST29

Green Meadow Golf & Country Club, Treherbert Rd, Croesyceiliog NP44 2BZ
☎ 01633 869321 & 862626 📠 01633 868430
e-mail: info@greenmeadowgolf.com
web: www.greenmeadowgolf.com
Undulating parkland with panoramic views. Tree-lined fairways, water hazards and pot bunkers. The greens are excellent and are playable all year round.
Green Meadow Golf & Country Club: 18 Holes, 6029yds, Par 70, SSS 70, Course record 64. Club membership 400.
Visitors contact club for details. **Societies** booking required. **Green Fees** £22 per round (£19 Mon, £27 weekends & BHs) **Course Designer** Peter Richardson **Prof** Dave Woodman **Facilities** ⊕ ⊚ 🏐 ♥ 🏋 🛒 🚶 🏌 **Leisure** hard tennis courts, sauna, gymnasium **Conf** facs Corporate Hospitality Days **Location** NE of town off A4042
Hotel ★★★★ 78% HL Best Western Parkway, Cwmbran Drive, CWMBRAN ☎ 01633 871199 📠 01633 871199 70 en suite

Pontnewydd Maesgwyn Farm, Upper Cwmbran NP44 1AB
☎ 01633 482170 📠 01633 838598
e-mail: ct.phillips@virgin.net
web: www.pontnewyddgolf.co.uk.
Meadowland course with good views across the Severn estuary. Oldest golf course in Wales, established 1875.
11 Holes, 5278yds, Par 68, SSS 67, Course record 61. Club membership 502.
Visitors Mon-Sun & BHs. Booking required Wed, Sat & BHs. Handicap certificate. Dress code. **Societies** booking required **Green Fees** £15 per round **Prof** Gavin Evans **Facilities** ⊕ ⊚ 🏐 ♥ 🏋 🛒 🚶 **Conf** Corporate Hospitality Days **Location** N of town centre
Hotel ★★★★ 78% HL Best Western Parkway, Cwmbran Drive, CWMBRAN ☎ 01633 871199 📠 01633 871199 70 en suite

PONTYPOOL
Map 3 SO20

Pontypool Lasgarn Ln, Trevethin NP4 8TR
☎ 01495 763655 📠 01495 755564
e-mail: pontypoolgolf@btconnect.com
web: pontypoolgolf.co.uk
Undulating mountain course with magnificent views of the Bristol Channel.
18 Holes, 5963yds, Par 69, SSS 69, Course record 64. Club membership 638.
Visitors Mon-Fri & Sun. Booking required. Handicap certificate. Dress code. **Societies** booking required. **Green Fees** not confirmed **Prof** Neil Matthews **Facilities** ⊕ ⊚ 🏐 ♥ 🏋 🛒 🚶 🏌 **Leisure** indoor teaching academy with video analysis **Conf** Corporate Hospitality Days **Location** 1.5m N off A4043
Hotel ★★★ 79% HL Glen-yr-Afon House, Pontypool Road, USK ☎ 01291 672302 & 673202 📠 01291 672302 27 en suite

Woodlake Park Golf & Country Club Glascoed NP4 0TE
☎ 01291 673933 📠 01291 673811
e-mail: golf@woodlake.co.uk
web: www.woodlake.co.uk
Undulating parkland with magnificent views over the Llandegfedd Reservoir. Superb greens constructed to USGA specification. Holes 4, 7 and 16 are par 3s, which are particularly challenging. Holes 6 and 17 are long par 4s, which can be wind affected.
Woodlake Park Golf & Country Club: 18 Holes, 6278yds, Par 71, SSS 72, Course record 67. Club membership 500.
Visitors Mon-Sun & BHs. Booking required. Handicap certificate. Dress code. **Societies** booking required. **Green Fees** £35 per day, £25 per round (£42/£32 Fri-Sun & BHs) **Prof** Leon Lancey **Facilities** ⊕ ⊚ 🏐 ♥ 🏋 🛒 🚶 🚗 🏌 **Leisure** fishing **Conf** facs Corporate Hospitality Days **Location** overlooking Llandegfedd Reservoir
Hotel ★★★ 79% HL Glen-yr-Afon House, Pontypool Road, USK ☎ 01291 672302 & 673202 📠 01291 672302 27 en suite

VALE OF GLAMORGAN

BARRY
Map 3 ST16

Brynhill Port Rd CF62 8PN
☎ 01446 720277 📠 01446 740422
e-mail: postbox@brynhillgolfclub.co.uk
web: www.brynhillgolfclub.co.uk
Picturesque parkland course with some hard walking and a prevailing west wind.
18 Holes, 6516yds, Par 72, SSS 71. Club membership 750.
Visitors Mon-Sun & BHs. Booking required Tue, weekends & BHs. Handicap certificate. Dress code. **Societies** booking required. **Green Fees** £30 per 18 holes (£35 weekends) **Course Designer** David Thomas **Prof** Duncan Prior **Facilities** ⊕ ⊚ 🏐 ♥ 🏋 🛒 🚗 🏌 **Conf** facs Corporate Hospitality Days **Location** 1.25m N on B4050
Hotel ★★★ 74% HL Best Western Mount Sorrel, Porthkerry Road, BARRY ☎ 01446 740069 📠 01446 740069 42 en suite

RAF St Athan Clive Rd CF62 4JD
☎ 01446 751043 📠 01446 751862
9 Holes, 6480yds, Par 72, SSS 72.
Course Designer the members **Location** between Barry & Llantwit Major
Telephone for further details
Hotel ★★★★ 81% CHH Egerton Grey Country House, Porthkerry, BARRY ☎ 01446 711666 📠 01446 711666 10 en suite

St Andrews Major Coldbrook Road East, Cadoxton CF63 1BL
☎ 01446 722227 📠 01446 748953
e-mail: info@standrewsmajorgolfclub.com
web: www.standrewsmajorgolfclub.com
A scenic 18-hole parkland course, suitable for all standards of golfer. The greens are designed to US specifications. The course provides excellent challenges to all levels of golfers without being physically exerting.
St Andrews Major Golf Course: 18 Holes, 5300yds, Par 69, SSS 70, Course record 65. Club membership 400.
Visitors Mon-Sun & BHs. Dress code. **Societies** welcome. **Green Fees** £18 per round (£20 weekends) **Course Designer** Richard Hurd

continued

Prof John Hastinggs **Facilities** ⊕ ⑩ 🝙 ⬜ 🍴 👤 🗑 🛇 🛴 🛇 🕭 **Conf** facs Corporate Hospitality Days **Location** M4 junct 33, follow signs for Cardiff Wales Airport, take A4231 and follow signs for golf club
Hotel ★★★★ 81% CHH Egerton Grey Country House, Porthkerry, BARRY ☎ 01446 711666 📄 01446 711666 10 en suite

DINAS POWYS Map 3 ST17

Dinas Powis High Walls Av CF64 4AJ
☎ 029 2051 2727 📄 029 2051 2727
e-mail: dinaspowisgolfclub@yahoo.co.uk
web: www.dpgc.co.uk

Parkland/downland course with dramatic views over the Bristol Channel and the Vale of Glamorgan. Open all year with fine natural drainage.

18 Holes, 5595yds, Par 68, SSS 67, Course record 67.
Club membership 550.

Visitors Mon-Fri, Sun & BHs. Booking required Sun. Handicap certificate. Dress code. **Societies** booking required **Green Fees** £25 per round summer, £15 winter (£35/£25 Sun) **Course Designer** James Braid **Prof** Gareth Bennett **Facilities** ⊕ ⑩ 🝙 ⬜ 🍴 👤 🗑 🛴 🛇 🕭 **Conf** facs Corporate Hospitality Days **Location** NW side of village, turning opposite cenotaph
Hotel ★★★ 74% HL Best Western Mount Sorrel, Porthkerry Road, BARRY ☎ 01446 740069 📄 01446 740069 42 en suite

HENSOL Map 3 ST07

Vale Hotel Golf & Spa Resort Hensol Park CF72 8JY
☎ 01443 667800 📄 01443 222220
web: www.vale-hotel.com

Lake: 18 Holes, 6426yds, Par 72, SSS 71.
Wales National: 18 Holes, 7414yds, Par 73, SSS 73, Course record 64.
Course Designer Peter Johnson & Terry Jones **Location** M4 junct 34, signed
Telephone for further details
Hotel ★★★★ 82% HL Vale Hotel Golf & Spa Resort, Hensol Park, HENSOL ☎ 01443 667800 📄 01443 667800 143 en suite

See advert on page 389

PENARTH Map

Glamorganshire Lavernock Rd CF64 5UP
☎ 029 2070 1185 📄 029 2070 1185
e-mail: glamgolf@btconnect.com
web: www.glamorganshiregolfclub.co.uk

Parkland overlooking the Bristol Channel.

18 Holes, 6184yds, Par 70, SSS 70, Course record 64
Club membership 1000.

Visitors Mon, Wed-Fri, Sun except BHs. Booking required. Hand certificate. Dress code **Societies** booking required. **Green Fees** per day (£45 Sun & BHs) **Course Designer** James Braid **Prof** A Kerr-Smith **Facilities** ⊕ ⑩ 🝙 ⬜ 🍴 👤 🗑 🛇 🛴 🛇 **Location** S of town centre on B4267
Hotel ★★★ 74% HL Best Western Mount Sorrel, Porthkerry BARRY ☎ 01446 740069 📄 01446 740069 42 en suite

ST NICHOLAS Map

Cottrell Park Golf Resort Cottrell Park CF5 6SJ
☎ 01446 781781 📄 01446 781187
e-mail: admin@golfwithus.com
web: www.golfwithus.com

Two well-designed courses situated in historic parkland with spectacular views across the Brecon Beacons to the Mendips Bristol Channel. An enjoyable yet testing game of golf for play all abilities.

Mackintosh: 18 Holes, 6052yds, Par 72, SSS 69, Course record 66.
Button Gwinnett: 18 Holes, 5777yds, Par 71, SSS 68
Club membership 1217.

Visitors Mon-Sun & BHs. Booking required. Dress code. Handi certificate. **Societies** booking required. **Green Fees** £30 per 1 (£40 Fri-Sun) **Course Designer** MRM Sandow **Prof** Steve Birch Hastings **Facilities** ⊕ ⑩ 🝙 ⬜ 🍴 👤 🗑 🛴 🛇 🕭 **Conf** facs Corporate Hospitality Days **Location** M4 junct 33 W of Cardiff off A48, NW of St Nicholas
Hotel ★★★★ 72% HL Copthorne Hotel Cardiff-Caerdydd, Copthorne Way, Culverhouse Cross, CARDIFF ☎ 029 2059 91 📄 029 2059 9100 135 en suite

See advert on pa

WREXHAM

CHIRK
Map 7 SJ23

Chirk Golf Club LL14 5AD
☎ 01691 774407 📠 01691 773878
web: www.jackbarker.com

Chirk Golf Club: 18 Holes, 7045yds, Par 72, SSS 73, Course record 69.

Prof M Maddison **Facilities** ⊕ ⍥ 🛏 ☐ 🍽 👤 🏠 🏴 ✂ 🛺 ✂ 🎏 **Leisure** 9 hole par 3 course **Conf** facs **Location** 1m NW of Chirk, near Chirk Castle
Telephone for further details
Hotel ★★★ 75% HL Moreton Park Lodge, Moreton Park, Gledrid, CHIRK ☎ 01691 776666 📠 01691 776666 46 en suite

EYTON
Map 7 SJ34

Plassey Oaks Golf Complec LL13 0SP
☎ 01978 780020 📠 01978 781397
e-mail: hjones@plasseygolf.com
web: www.plasseygolf.com

Picturesque nine-hole course in undulating parkland.

Plassey Oaks Golf Complex: 9 Holes, 5002yds, Par 68, SSS 66, Course record 62. Club membership 222.

Visitors dress code. **Societies** booking required. **Green Fees** not confirmed **Course Designer** Welsh Golf Union **Facilities** ⊕ ⍥ 🛏 ☐ 🍽 👤 🏠 🏴 ✂ 🛺 ✂ 🎏 **Leisure** fishing **Conf** facs Corporate Hospitality Days **Location** 4m S of Wrexham off B5426, signed
Hotel ★★★ 75% HL Best Western Cross Lanes Hotel & Restaurant, Cross Lanes, Bangor Road, Marchwiel, WREXHAM ☎ 01978 780555 📠 01978 780555 16 en suite

WREXHAM
Map 7 SJ35

Clays Bryn Estyn Rd, Llan-y-Pwll LL13 9UB
☎ 01978 661406 📠 01978 661406
e-mail: sales@claysgolf.co.uk
web: www.claysgolf.co.uk

Gently undulating parkland course in countryside with views of the Welsh mountains. Noted for its difficult par 3s.

Clays Golf Centre: 18 Holes, 6100yds, Par 69, SSS 69, Course record 62. Club membership 500.

Visitors Mon-Sun & BHs. Booking required. Dress code. **Societies** booking required. **Green Fees** £20 per round (£26 weekends) **Course Designer** R D Jones **Prof** David Larvin **Facilities** ⊕ ⍥ 🛏 ☐ 🍽 👤 🏠 🏴 ✂ 🚗 🛺 ✂ 🎏 **Conf** facs Corporate Hospitality Days **Location** off A534

Wrexham Holt Rd LL13 9SB
☎ 01978 364268 📠 01978 362168
e-mail: info@wrexhamgolfclub.co.uk
web: www.wrexhamgolfclub.co.uk

Inland, sandy course with easy walking. Testing dog-leg 7th hole (par 4), and short 14th hole (par 3) with full carry to green.

18 Holes, 6233yds, Par 70, SSS 70, Course record 64. Club membership 680.

Visitors Mon-Sun & BHs. Booking required weekends & BHs.. Handicap certificate. Dress code. **Societies** welcome. **Green Fees** phone **Course Designer** James Braid **Prof** Paul Williams **Facilities** ⊕ ⍥ 🛏 ☐ 🍽 👤 🏠 🛺 ✂ **Conf** facs Corporate Hospitality Days **Location** 2m NE on A534

WALES

Ireland

NORTHERN IRELAND

CO ANTRIM

ANTRIM
Map 1 D5

Massereene 51 Lough Rd BT41 4DQ
☎ 028 9442 8096   📠 028 9448 7661
e-mail: info@massereene.com
web: www.massereene.com

The first nine holes are parkland, while the second, adjacent to the shore of Lough Neagh, have more of a links character with sandy ground.

18 Holes, 6602yds, Par 72, SSS 72, Course record 63. Club membership 1050.

Visitors Mon-Fri, Sun & BHs. Booking required. Dress code. **Societies** booking required. **Green Fees** £25 per round (£35 weekends) **Course Designer** F Hawtree/H Swan **Prof** Jim Smyth **Facilities** ⑪ ⑪ ㄴ ㅁ ㅁ ㅅ ⊟ ⊓ ⌀ **Conf** facs Corporate Hospitality Days **Location** 1m SW of town **Hotel** ★★★★ 82% HL Galgorm Resort & Spa, BALLYMENA, Co Antrim ☎ 028 2588 1001 📠 028 2588 1001 75 en suite

BALLYCASTLE
Map 1 D6

Ballycastle Cushendall Rd BT54 6QP
☎ 028 2076 2536   📠 028 2076 9909
e-mail: info@ballycastlegolfclub.com
web: www.ballycastlegolfclub.com

An unusual mixture of terrain beside the sea, lying at the foot of one of the nine glens of Antrim, with magnificent views from all parts. The first five holes are parkland with natural hazards; the middle holes are links type and the rest on adjacent upland. Accurate iron play is essential for good scoring while the undulating greens will test putting skills.

18 Holes, 5927yds, Par 71, SSS 70, Course record 64. Club membership 806.

Visitors contact club for details. **Societies** booking required. **Green Fees** £25 per round (£35 weekends & BHs) **Prof** Ian McLaughlin **Facilities** ⑪ ⑪ ㄴ ㅁ ㅁ ㅅ ⊟ ⊓ ⌀ **Conf** facs Corporate Hospitality Days **Location** between Portrush & Cushendall (A2)

BALLYCLARE
Map 1 D5

Ballyclare 23 Springdale Rd BT39 9JW
☎ 028 9332 2696   📠 028 9332 2696
web: www.ballyclaregolfclub.com

18 Holes, 5745mtrs, Par 71, SSS 71, Course record 66.
Course Designer T McCauley **Location** 1.5m N of Ballyclare
Telephone for further details
Hotel ★★★★ 82% HL Galgorm Resort & Spa, BALLYMENA, Co Antrim ☎ 028 2588 1001 📠 028 2588 1001 75 en suite

Greenacres 153 Ballyrobert Rd BT39 9RT
☎ 028 9335 4111   📠 028 9335 4166
e-mail: info@greenacresgolfcentre.co.uk
web: www.greenacresgolfcentre.co.uk

Designed and built into the rolling countryside, and with the addition of lakes at five of the holes, provides a challenge for both the seasoned golfer and the higher-handicapped player.

Greenacres Golf Course: 18 Holes, 6031yds, Par 71, SSS 69. Club membership 520.

Visitors Mon-Fri. Par 3 course Mon-Sun & BHs. Dress code **Societies** booking required. **Green Fees** not confirmed **Prof** John Foster **Facilities** ⑪ ⑪ ㄴ ㅁ ㅁ ㅅ ⊓ ⌀ ⌀ **Leisure** 18 hole mini golf & 9 hole par 3 course. **Conf** Corporate Hospitality Days **Location** 12m from Belfast city centre **Hotel** ★★★ 74% HL Headfort Arms, Headfort Place, KELLS, Co Meath ☎ 046 9240063 📠 046 9240063 45 en suite

BALLYGALLY
Map 1 D5

Cairndhu 192 Coast Rd BT40 2QG
☎ 028 2858 3954   📠 028 2858 3324
e-mail: cairndhugc@btconnect.com
web: www.cairndhugolfclub.co.uk

Built on a hilly headland, this course is both testing and scenic, with wonderful coastal views. The par 3 second hole can require anything from a 9 to a 3 iron depending on the wind, while the 3rd has a carry of 165 metres over a headland to the fairway. The 10th, 11th and 12th holes constitute Cairndhu's Amen Corner, feared and respected by any standard of golfer.

18 Holes, 6120yds, Par 70, SSS 69, Course record 64. Club membership 905.

Visitors Mon-Fri, Sun & BHs. Booking required. Dress code. **Societies** booking required. **Green Fees** not confirmed **Course Designer** Mr Morrison **Prof** Stephen Hood **Facilities** ⑪ ⑪ ㄴ ㅁ ㅁ ㅅ ⊓ ⌀ ⌀ ⌀ **Conf** facs **Location** 4m N of Larne on coast road **Guesthouse** ★★★★ GH Manor, 23 Older Fleet Road, Harbour Highway, LARNE, Co Antrim ☎ 028 2827 3305 📠 028 2827 3305 8 en suite

BALLYMENA
Map 1 D5

Ballymena 128 Raceview Rd BT42 4HY
☎ 028 2586 1487   📠 028 2586 1487

18 Holes, 5299mtrs, Par 68, SSS 67, Course record 62.
Prof Ken Revie **Facilities** ⑪ ⑪ ㄴ ㅁ ㅁ ㅅ ⊟ ⊓ ⌀ **Location** 2m E on A42
Telephone for further details
Hotel ★★★★ 82% HL Galgorm Resort & Spa, BALLYMENA, Co Antrim ☎ 028 2588 1001 📠 028 2588 1001 75 en suite

Galgorm Castle Golf & Country Club Galgorm Rd BT42 1HL
☎ 028 2564 6161   📠 028 2565 1151
e-mail: golf@galgormcastle.com
web: www.galgormcastle.com

An 18-hole USGA championship course set in 220 acres of mature parkland in the grounds of one of Ireland's most historic castles. The course is bordered by two rivers which come into play and includes five lakes. A course of outstanding beauty offering a challenge to both the novice and low handicapped golfer.

Galgorm Castle Golf & Country Club: 18 Holes, 6736yds, Par 72, SSS 72, Course record 67. Club membership 600.

Visitors Mon-Sun & BHs. Booking required. Dress code. **Societies** welcome. **Green Fees** £33 per round Mon-Thu, £35 Fri (£45 weekends & BHs) **Course Designer** Simon Gidman **Prof** Phil Collins **Facilities** ⑪ ⑪ ㄴ ㅁ ㅁ ㅅ ⊟ ⊓ ⌀ ⌀ ⌀

continued

IRELAND

ROYAL PORTRUSH

CO ANTRIM · PORTRUSH · MAP 1 C6

This course, designed by Harry S Colt, is considered to be among the best six in the UK. Founded in 1888, it was the venue of the first professional golf event in Ireland, held in 1895, when Sandy Herd beat Harry Vardon in the final. Royal Portrush is spectacular and breathtaking, one of the tightest driving courses known to golfers. On a clear day there's a fine view of Islay and the Paps of Jura from the 3rd tee, and the Giant's Causeway from the 5th. While the greens have to be 'read' from the start, there are fairways up and down valleys, and holes called Calamity Corner and Purgatory (for good reason). The 2nd hole, Giant's Grave, is 509yds, but the 17th is even longer. The 6867 yard course is currently being extended.

Dunluce Rd BT56 8JQ ☎ 028 7082 2311 📄 028 7082 3139
e-mail: info@royalportrushgolfclub.com **web:** www.royalportrushgolfclub.com
Dunluce: 18 Holes, 6867yds, Par 72.
Valley: 18 Holes, 6304yds, Par 70. Club membership 1300.
Visitors Mon-Sun & BHs. Booking required. Handicap certificate. Dress code. **Societies** welcome. **Green Fees** Dunluce: £125 per round (£140 weekends). Valley: £35 per round (£40 weekends). Nov-Mar, Dunluce £60 per round, Valley £25 per round **Course Designer** Harry Colt **Prof** Gary McNeill **Facilities** ⑪ ◎ ☕ ☐ ☜ ⚐ ☜ ☕ ☜ **Conf** Corporate Hospitality Days **Location** 0.8km from Portrush on Bushmills road

Leisure fishing, PGA staffed Academy Conf facs Corporate Hospitality Days Location 1m S of Ballymena on A42
Hotel ★★★★ 82% HL Galgorm Resort & Spa, BALLYMENA, Co Antrim ☎ 028 2588 1001 📄 028 2588 1001 75 en suite

BALLYMONEY · Map 1 D6

Gracehill 141 Ballinlea Rd, Stranocum BT53 8PX
☎ 028 2075 1209 📄 028 2075 1074
e-mail: info@gracehillgolfclub.co.uk
web: www.gracehillgolfclub.co.uk

Challenging parkland course with some holes played over water and many mature trees coming into play.

Gracehill Golf Course: 18 Holes, 6553yds, Par 72, SSS 73, Course record 69. Club membership 400.

Visitors Mon-Sun & BHs. Booking required weekends & BHs. **Societies** welcome. **Green Fees** £27.50 per round (£32.50 weekends) **Course Designer** Frank Ainsworth **Facilities** ⊕ 🍴 🖥 ⚑ 🖥 ⚐ 🚶 ⛳ ⛳ **Conf** Corporate Hospitality Days **Location** M2 N from Belfast, onto A26 N to Ballymoney, signs for Coleraine. At Ballymoney bypass onto B147/A2 to Sranocum/Ballintoy

Hotel ★★ 76% HL Brown Trout Golf & Country Inn, 209 Agivey Road, AGHADOWEY, Co Londonderry ☎ 028 7086 8209 📄 028 7086 8209 15 en suite

CARRICKFERGUS · Map 1 D5

Carrickfergus 35 North Rd BT38 8LP
☎ 028 9336 3713 📄 028 9336 3023
e-mail: carrickfergusgc@btconnect.com

Parkland course, fairly level but nevertheless demanding, with a notorious water hazard at the 1st. Well-maintained, with an interesting in-course riverway and fine views across Belfast Lough.

18 Holes, 5768yds, Par 68, SSS 68. Club membership 980.

Visitors dress code. **Societies** welcome. **Green Fees** £19 per day, £13 per round (£25/£16 weekends & BHs) **Prof** Gary Mercer **Facilities** ⊕ 🍴 🖥 ⚑ 🖥 🚶 📧 ⛳ **Conf** facs Corporate Hospitality Days **Location** 9m NE of Belfast on A2
Hotel ★★ 65% HL Dobbins Inn, 6-8 High Street, CARRICKFERGUS, Co Antrim ☎ 028 9335 1905 📄 028 9335 1905 15 en suite

Greenisland 156 Upper Rd, Greenisland BT38 8RW
☎ 028 9086 2236
e-mail: greenislandgolf@btconnect.com
web: greenislandgolfclub.co.uk

A parkland course nestling at the foot of Knockagh Hill, with scenic views over Belfast Lough.

9 Holes, 6090yds, Par 71, SSS 69, Course record 66. Club membership 600.

Visitors Mon-Wed, Fri, Sun & BHs. Sat after 5pm. Dress code. **Societies** booking required. **Green Fees** £15 (£20 weekends) **Facilities** ⊕ 🍴 🖥 ⚑ 🖥 🚶 **Location** N of Belfast, close to Carrickfergus
Hotel ★★ 65% HL Dobbins Inn, 6-8 High Street, CARRICKFERGUS, Co Antrim ☎ 028 9335 1905 📄 028 9335 1905 15 en suite

CUSHENDALL · Map 1 D6

Cushendall 21 Shore Rd BT44 0NG
☎ 028 2177 1318
e-mail: cushendallgc@btconnect.com

Scenic course with spectacular views over the Sea of Moyle and Red Bay to the Mull of Kintyre. The River Dall winds through the course, coming into play in seven of the nine holes. This demands a premium on accuracy rather than length. The signature hole is the par 3 2nd, requiring a tee shot across the river to a plateau green with a steep slope in front and out of bounds behind.

9 Holes, 4386mtrs, Par 66, SSS 63, Course record 59. Club membership 680.

Visitors Mon-Sun & BHs. Booking required Thu & weekends. Dress code. **Societies** booking required. **Green Fees** £15 per day (£20 BHs) **Course Designer** D Delargy **Facilities** ⊕ 🍴 🖥 ⚑ 🖥 🚶 ⛳ **Conf** facs **Location** in Cushendall beside beach on Antrim coast road

LARNE · Map 1 D5

Larne 54 Ferris Bay Rd, Islandmagee BT40 3RT
☎ 028 9338 2228 📄 028 9338 2088
e-mail: info@larnegolfclub.co.uk
web: www.larnegolfclub.co.uk

An exposed part links, part heathland course offering a good test, particularly on the last three holes along the sea shore.

Larne Golf Club Ltd: 9 Holes, 6686yds, Par 70, SSS 70, Course record 64. Club membership 430.

Visitors Mon, Tue,Thu, Sun & BHs. Dress code. **Societies** booking required. **Green Fees** £15 per day (£20 weekends & BHs) **Course Designer** G L Bailie **Facilities** ⊕ 🍴 🖥 ⚑ 🖥 🚶 **Location** 6m N of Whitehead on Browns Bay road

LISBURN · Map 1 D5

Aberdelghy Bell's Ln, Lambeg BT27 4QH
☎ 028 9266 2738 📄 028 9260 3432
e-mail: info@customprogolf.co.uk
web: customprogolf.co.uk

This parkland course has no bunkers. The hardest hole on the course is the 340-metre 3rd, a dog-leg through trees to a green guarded by water. The par 3 12th high on the hill and the 14th hole over the dam provide a challenge. The par 4 15th hole is a long dog-leg.

Aberdelghy Golf Course: 18 Holes, 4139mtrs, Par 66, SSS 62, Course record 64. Club membership 200.

Visitors Mon-Sun & BHs. **Societies** booking required. **Green Fees** £12 per 18 holes (£14.50 weekends & BHs) **Course Designer** Alec Blair **Prof** Ed Morrison **Facilities** 🖥 🚶 📧 🔧 ⛳ **Location** 1.5m N of Lisburn off A1
Hotel ★★★★ 73% HL Malone Lodge, 60 Eglantine Avenue, BELFAST ☎ 028 9038 8000 📄 028 9038 8000 46 en suite

Lisburn 68 Eglantine Rd BT27 5RQ
☎ 028 9267 7216 📄 028 9260 3608
web: www.lisburngolfclub.com

18 Holes, 6647yds, Par 72, SSS 72, Course record 67.

Course Designer Hawtree **Location** 2m from town on A1
Telephone for further details
Hotel ★★★★ 73% HL Malone Lodge, 60 Eglantine Avenue, BELFAST ☎ 028 9038 8000 📄 028 9038 8000 46 en suite

MAZE — Map 1 D5

Down Royal Park 6 Dunygarton Rd BT27 5RT
☎ 028 9262 1339 📠 028 9262 1339

Located in the Lagan Valley near Lisburn. The 18 hole course is one of the longest courses in Northern Ireland. The par 4 holes are made up of wide open fairways with few bunkers to present any danger but the par 3's are more challenging. The par 5 2nd is a dog-leg left with out of bounds at 220 yds straight ahead from the tee and a stream to carry. The 9 hole Valley course ia a challenging course for beginners or for those wanting to play a quick round.

Down Royal Park Golf Course: 18 Holes, 6940yds, Par 72, SSS 72, Course record 69.
Valley Course: 9 Holes, 2019, Par 33.
Club membership 120.

Visitors Mon-Sun & BHs. Dress code. **Societies** welcome. **Green Fees** phone **Prof** Mervyn McMaster **Facilities** Ⓣ by prior arrangement 🍴 🍺 🖥 🍽 🏌 🏠 ⛳ 🏌 ⛳ 🏌 **Conf** facs Corporate Hospitality Days **Location** inside Down Royal Race Course
Hotel ★★★★ 73% HL Malone Lodge, 60 Eglantine Avenue, BELFAST ☎ 028 9038 8000 📠 028 9038 8000 46 en suite

PORTBALLINTRAE — Map 1 C6

Bushfoot 50 Bushfoot Rd, Portballintrae BT57 8RR
☎ 028 2073 1317 📠 028 2073 1852
e-mail: bushfootgolfclub@btconnect.com

A seaside links course with superb views in an area of outstanding beauty. A challenging par 3 7th is ringed by bunkers with out of bounds beyond, while the 3rd has a blind approach. Also a putting green and pitch and putt course.

Bushfoot Golf Club Ltd: 9 Holes, 6075yds, Par 70, SSS 68, Course record 65. Club membership 850.

Visitors Mon, Wed-Fri, Sun & BHs. Handicap certificate. Dress code. **Societies** welcome. **Green Fees** £16 per round (£20 weekends & BHs) **Facilities** ⓉⓉ 🍴 🍺 🖥 🍽 🏌 **Location** off Ballaghmore road

PORTRUSH — Map 1 C6

Royal Portrush see page 419
Dunluce Rd BT56 8JQ
☎ 028 7082 2311 📠 028 7082 3139
e-mail: info@royalportrushgolfclub.com
web: www.royalportrushgolfclub.com

WHITEHEAD — Map 1 D5

Bentra Slaughterford Rd BT38 9TG
☎ 028 9337 8996 📠 028 9337 8996

A mature course designed with the experienced golfer and novice in mind with wide fairways and some particularly long holes.

Bentra Golf Course: 9 Holes, 5952yds, Par 37, SSS 35.

Visitors Mon-Sun & BHs. Booking required weekends & BHs. Dress code. **Societies** welcome. **Green Fees** not confirmed **Facilities** 🖥 🏌 🏠 🍽 ⛳ **Leisure** restaurant on site **Location** 6m from Carrickfergus

Bentra

Hotel ★★ 65% HL Dobbins Inn, 6-8 High Street, CARRICKFERGUS, Co Antrim ☎ 028 9335 1905 📠 028 9335 1905 15 en suite

Whitehead McCrae's Brae BT38 9NZ
☎ 028 9337 0820 & 9337 0822 📠 028 9337 0825
web: www.whiteheadgolfclub.com

18 Holes, 5952yds, Par 70, SSS 69, Course record 65.

Course Designer A B Armstrong **Location** 1m from town
Telephone for further details
Hotel ★★ 65% HL Dobbins Inn, 6-8 High Street, CARRICKFERGUS, Co Antrim ☎ 028 9335 1905 📠 028 9335 1905 15 en suite

CO ARMAGH

ARMAGH — Map 1 C5

County Armagh The Demesne, Newry Rd BT60 1EN
☎ 028 3752 5861 📠 028 3752 8768
e-mail: lynne@golfarmagh.co.uk
web: www.golfarmagh.co.uk

Mature parkland course with excellent views of Armagh city and its surroundings.

18 Holes, 6212yds, Par 70, SSS 69, Course record 63.
Club membership 1300.

Visitors Mon-Wed, Fri, Sun & BHs. Booking required Thu & Sun. Handicap certificate. Dress code. **Societies** welcome. **Green Fees** not confirmed **Prof** Alan Rankin **Facilities** Ⓣ 🍴 🍺 🖥 🏌 🏠 ⛳ 🚜 ⛳ **Leisure** snooker **Conf** Corporate Hospitality Days **Location** on Newry Rd
Hotel ★★ 69% HL Cohannon Inn & Autolodge, 212 Ballynakilly Road, DUNGANNON, Co Tyrone ☎ 028 8772 4488 📠 028 8772 4488 42 en suite

CULLYHANNA — Map 1 C5

Ashfield 44 Cregganduff Rd BT35 0JJ
☎ 028 3086 8611

Parkland with lakes. The course has seen continuous improvement over the years with thousands of trees planted from a wide variety of species.

18 Holes, 5840yds, Par 69.

Visitors Mon-Sun & BHs. Dress code. **Societies** welcome. **Green Fees** £16 (£22 weekends) **Course Designer** Frank Ainsworth **Prof** Dougie Bell **Facilities** Ⓣ 🍴 🍺 🖥 🍽 🏌 🏠 ⛳ 🚜 ⛳ 🏌
Hotel ★★ 69% SHL Enniskeen House, 98 Bryansford Road, NEWCASTLE, Co Down ☎ 028 4372 2392 📠 028 4372 2392 12 en suite

IRELAND

LURGAN

Map 1 D5

Craigavon Golf & Ski Centre Turmoyra Ln, Silverwood BT66 6NG

☎ 028 3832 6606   🖷 028 3834 7272
e-mail: michael.stanford@craigavon.gov.uk
web: www.craigavon.gov.uk

Mature tree lined parkland course with a lake and stream providing water hazards. Playable all year round.

Silverwood: 18 Holes, 6496yds, Par 72, SSS 72, Course record 67. Club membership 400.

Visitors Mon-Sun & BHs. Booking required Sun. Dress code. **Societies** booking required **Green Fees** not confirmed **Prof** Michael Stanford **Facilities** ⓦ 🖵 👤 ⛳ ✦ 🏌 **Leisure** Ski slope **Conf** facs Corporate Hospitality Days **Location** 2m N at Silverwood off M1

Lurgan The Demesne BT67 9BN

☎ 028 3832 2087   🖷 028 3831 6166
e-mail: lurgangolfclub@btconnect.com
web: www.lurgangolfclub.com

Testing parkland course bordering Lurgan Park Lake with a need for accurate shots. Drains well in wet weather and suits a long straight hitter.

18 Holes, 6257yds, Par 70, SSS 70, Course record 66. Club membership 903.

Visitors Mon-Fri, Sun & BHs. Booking required Tue, Wed, Fri, Sun & BHs. Dress code. **Societies** booking required. **Green Fees** £20 (£25 weekends & BHs) **Course Designer** A Pennink **Prof** Des Paul **Facilities** ⓦ 🍴 👤 🖵 ⛳ 🏌 👤 🖻 ✦ **Conf** facs **Location** 0.5m from town centre near Lurgan Park

PORTADOWN

Map 1 D5

Portadown 192 Gilford Rd BT63 5LF

☎ 028 3835 5356   🖷 028 3839 1394
e-mail: info@portadowngolfclub.co.uk
web: www.portadowngolfclub.co.uk

Well-wooded parkland on the banks of the River Bann, nestled in the heart of Orchard County since 1900. A signature hole is the 9th, where players are required to drive over the river.

18 Holes, 6130yds, Par 70, SSS 69, Course record 65. Club membership 800.

Visitors Mon-Sun & BHs. Booking required Tue-Thu & Sat.. Dress code. **Societies** welcome **Green Fees** £18 (£22 weekends & BHs) **Prof** Paul Stevenson **Facilities** ⓦ 🍴 👤 🖵 ⛳ 👤 🖻 ⛳ ✦ **Leisure** squash **Conf** facs Corporate Hospitality Days **Location** A50 towards Banbridge from Portadown

Hotel ★★ 69% HL Cohannon Inn & Autolodge, 212 Ballynakilly Road, DUNGANNON, Co Tyrone ☎ 028 8772 4488 🖷 028 8772 4488 42 en suite

TANDRAGEE

Map 1 D5

Tandragee Markethill Rd BT62 2ER

☎ 028 3884 1272   🖷 028 3884 0664
e-mail: office@tandragee.co.uk
web: www.tandragee.co.uk

Pleasant parkland course, the signature hole is the demanding par 3 16th known as 'The Quarry Hole'; the real strength of Tandragee is

in the short holes. Pleasant views with the Mourne mountains in distance.

18 Holes, 5747mtrs, Par 71, SSS 70, Course record 6 Club membership 1018.

Visitors Mon-Fri & Sun. Dress code. **Societies** welcome. **Green Fees** not confirmed **Course Designer** John Stone **Prof** Dympna Keenan **Facilities** ⓦ 🍴 👤 🖵 ⛳ 👤 🖻 ⛳ ✦ **Leisure** snooker **Conf** facs Corporate Hospitality Days **Location** from Tandragee towards Markethill

CO BELFAST

BELFAST

Ma

See also **The Royal Belfast, Holywood, Co Down.**

Balmoral 518 Lisburn Rd BT9 6GX

☎ 028 9038 1514   🖷 028 9066 6759
web: www.balmoralgolf.com

18 Holes, 6276yds, Par 69, SSS 70, Course record 64

Prof Geoff Bleakley **Facilities** ⓦ 🍴 👤 🖵 ⛳ 👤 🖻 **Leisure** snooker **Conf** facs Corporate Hospitality Days **Location** next to Kings Hall
Telephone for further details
Hotel ★★★★ 73% HL Malone Lodge, 60 Eglantine Avenue BELFAST ☎ 028 9038 8000 🖷 028 9038 8000 46 en suite

Cliftonville 44 Westland Rd BT14 6NH

☎ 028 9074 4158 & 9022 8585
web: www.cliftonvillegolfclub.com

9 Holes, 6242yds, Par 70, SSS 70, Course record 65.

Prof R Duckett **Facilities** ⓦ 👤 🖵 ⛳ 👤 🖻 ✦ **Location** between Cavehill Rd & Cliftonville Circus
Telephone for further details
Hotel ★★★ 71% HL Jurys Inn Belfast, Fisherwick Place, Gre Victoria Street, BELFAST ☎ 028 9053 3500 🖷 028 9053 3500 190 en suite

Dunmurry 91 Dunmurry Ln BT17 9JS

☎ 028 9061 0834   🖷 028 9060 2540
web: www.dunmurrygolfclub.co.uk

18 Holes, 6156yds, Par 70, SSS 69, Course record 65

Prof John Dolan **Facilities** ⓦ 🍴 👤 🖵 ⛳ 👤 🖻 ⛳ **Telephone for further details**
Hotel ★★★★ 73% HL Malone Lodge, 60 Eglantine Avenue BELFAST ☎ 028 9038 8000 🖷 028 9038 8000 46 en suite

Fortwilliam 8A Downview Ave BT15 4EZ

☎ 028 9037 0770 (Office) & 9077 0980 (Pro)
🖷 028 9078 1891
e-mail: admin@fortwilliam.co.uk
web: www.fortwilliam.co.uk

Parkland course in most attractive surroundings. The course is bisected by a lane.

18 Holes, 5692yds, Par 70, SSS 68, Course record 63
Club membership 1000.

Visitors Mon-Fri, Sun & BHs. Booking required Wed, Fri, Sun & Handicap certificate. Dress code. **Societies** booking required. **Fees** not confirmed **Prof** Peter Hanna **Facilities** ⓦ 🍴 👤 👤 🖻 ⛳ ✦ 🏌 ✦ 🏌 **Conf** facs Corporate Hospitality **Location** off Antrim road

CO

IRELAND

Hotel ★★★ 71% HL Jurys Inn Belfast, Fisherwick Place, Great Victoria Street, BELFAST ☎ 028 9053 3500 ▤ 028 9053 3500 190 en suite

Malone 240 Upper Malone Rd BT17 9LB
☎ 028 9061 2758 (Office) & 9061 4917 (Pro)
▤ 028 9043 1394
web: www.malonegolfclub.co.uk

Main Course: 18 Holes, 6706yds, Par 71, SSS 72, Course record 65.
Edenderry: 9 Holes, 6320yds, Par 72, SSS 70.
Course Designer C K Cotton **Location** 4.5m S opposite Lady Dixon Park
Telephone for further details
Hotel ★★★★ 73% HL Malone Lodge, 60 Eglantine Avenue, BELFAST ☎ 028 9038 8000 ▤ 028 9038 8000 46 en suite

Mount Ober Golf & Country Club 24 Ballymaconaghy Rd BT8 6SB
☎ 028 9040 1811 & 9079 5666 ▤ 028 9070 5862
e-mail: mt.ober@ukonline.co.uk
web: www.mountober.com
Inland parkland course which is a great test of golf for all handicaps.
Mount Ober Golf & Country Club: 18 Holes, 5022yds, Par 67, SSS 66, Course record 67. Club membership 400.
Visitors Mon-Fri, Sun & BHs. Dress code. **Societies** booking required.
Green Fees £18 per round (£20 Sun & BHs) **Prof** Wesley Ramsay
Facilities ⓘ ⓘ ▤ ⌨ ⌨ ⌨ ⌨ ⌨ ⌨ **Leisure** American billiards & snooker **Conf** facs Corporate Hospitality Days **Location** off Saintfield road
Hotel ★★★ 75% HL The Crescent Townhouse, 13 Lower Crescent, BELFAST ☎ 028 9032 3349 ▤ 028 9032 3349 17 en suite

Ormeau 50 Park Rd BT7 2FX
☎ 028 9064 0700 ▤ 028 9064 6250
web: www.ormeaugolfclub.co.uk
Ormeau Golf Course: 9 Holes, 2688yds, Par 68, SSS 66.
Prof Mr Stephen Rourke **Facilities** ⓘ ⓘ ▤ ⌨ ⌨ ⌨ ⌨
⌨ ⌨ **Conf** facs Corporate Hospitality Days **Location** S of city centre between Ravenhill & Ormeau roads
Telephone for further details
Hotel ★★★ 75% HL The Crescent Townhouse, 13 Lower Crescent, BELFAST ☎ 028 9032 3349 ▤ 028 9032 3349 17 en suite

Shandon Park 73 Shandon Park BT5 6NY
☎ 028 9080 5030
e-mail: shandonpark@btconnect.com
Fairly level parkland with excellent greens, offering a pleasant challenge.
18 Holes, 6261yds, Par 70, SSS 70. Club membership 1100.
Visitors Mon-Fri, Sun & BHs. Booking required. Dress code.
Societies booking required. **Green Fees** £27.50 per round (£35 weekends) **Prof** Barry Wilson **Facilities** ⓘ ⓘ ▤ ⌨ ⌨ ⌨
⌨ ⌨ ⌨ ⌨ ⌨ **Conf** facs Corporate Hospitality Days **Location** off Knock road
Hotel ★★★ 75% HL The Crescent Townhouse, 13 Lower Crescent, BELFAST ☎ 028 9032 3349 ▤ 028 9032 3349 17 en suite

DUNDONALD   Map 1 D5

Knock Summerfield BT16 2QX
☎ 028 9048 3251 ▤ 028 9048 7277
e-mail: knockgolfclub@btconnect.com
web: www.knockgolfclub.co.uk
Parkland course with huge trees, deep bunkers and a river cutting across several fairways. This is a hard but fair course and will test the best of golfers.
18 Holes, 6435yds, Par 70, SSS 71, Course record 65. Club membership 920.
Visitors Mon, Thu, Fri, Sun & BHs. booking required. Handicap certificate. Dress code. **Societies** booking required. **Green Fees** £26 per day (£55 weekends & BHs) **Course Designer** Colt, Allison & McKenzie **Prof** Richard Whitford **Facilities** ⓘ ⓘ ▤ ⌨ ⌨ ⌨
⌨ ⌨ ⌨ ⌨ ⌨ **Conf** Corporate Hospitality Days **Location** 5m E of Belfast
Hotel ★★★★ 74% HL The Old Inn, 15 Main Street, CRAWFORDSBURN ☎ 028 9185 3255 ▤ 028 9185 3255 31 en suite

NEWTOWNBREDA   Map 1 D5

Belvoir Park 73 Church Rd BT8 7AN
☎ 028 9049 1693 ▤ 028 9064 6113
e-mail: info@belvoirparkgolfclub.com
web: www.belvoirparkgolfclub.com
This undulating parkland course is not strenuous to walk, but is certainly a test of your golf, with tree-lined fairways and a particularly challenging finish at the final four holes.
18 Holes, 6516yds, Par 71, SSS 71, Course record 65. Club membership 1220.
Visitors Mon, Tue & Thu except BHs. Booking required. Handicap certificate. Dress code. **Societies** booking required. **Green Fees** £65
Course Designer H. S. Colt **Prof** Michael McGivern **Facilities** ⓘ
⌨ ⌨ ▤ ⌨ ⌨ ⌨ ⌨ ⌨ ⌨ ⌨ **Conf** facs **Location** 2m from city centre off Saintfield-Newcastle road
Hotel ★★★★ 78% HL Clandeboye Lodge, 10 Estate Road, Clandeboye, BANGOR ☎ 028 9185 2500 ▤ 028 9185 2500
43 en suite

IRELAND

CO DOWN

ARDGLASS
Map 1 D5

Ardglass Castle Place BT30 7TP
☎ 028 4484 1219   📠 028 4484 1841
web: www.ardglassgolfclub.com

18 Holes, 6268yds, Par 70, SSS 69, Course record 65.
Course Designer David Jones **Location** 7m from Downpatrick on the B1
Telephone for further details
Hotel ★★ 69% SHL Enniskeen House, 98 Bryansford Road, NEWCASTLE, Co Down ☎ 028 4372 2392 📠 028 4372 2392 12 en suite

BALLYNAHINCH
Map 1 D5

Spa 20 Grove Rd BT24 8PN
☎ 028 9756 2365   📠 028 9756 4158
e-mail: spagolfclub@btconnect.com
web: www.spagolfclub.net

Parkland course with tree-lined fairways and scenic views of the Mourne Mountains. A long and demanding course and feature holes include the par 3 2nd and 405yd par 4 11th.

18 Holes, 6003mtrs, Par 72, SSS 72, Course record 65.
Club membership 922.
Visitors booking required. Dress code. **Societies** welcome. **Green Fees** £20 per round (£25 Sun & BHs) **Course Designer** F Ainsworth/T Magee/R Wallace **Facilities** ⓨ ⑩ 🍴 ⚐ 🏌 🛒 🏧 🚆 ∜ **Leisure** gymnasium, outdoor bowls **Conf** facs Corporate Hospitality Days **Location** 1m S
Hotel ★★ 69% SHL Enniskeen House, 98 Bryansford Road, NEWCASTLE, Co Down ☎ 028 4372 2392 📠 028 4372 2392 12 en suite

BANBRIDGE
Map 1 D5

Banbridge 116 Huntly Rd BT32 3UR
☎ 028 4066 2211   📠 028 4066 9400
e-mail: info@banbridgegolfclub.net
web: www.banbridgegolfclub.net

A mature parkland course with excellent views of the Mourne mountains. The holes are not long, but are tricky. Signature holes are the 6th with its menacing pond and the par 3 10th where playing for a safe 4 is usually the best option.

18 Holes, 5003mtrs, Par 69, SSS 67, Course record 61.
Club membership 800.

Visitors Mon-Sun & BHs. Booking advised. Dress code.
Societies booking required. **Green Fees** £18 (£24 Sun). Winter £10/£12 **Course Designer** F Ainsworth **Prof** Jason Greenaway
Facilities ⓨ ⑩ 🍴 ⚐ 🏌 🛒 🏧 🚆 ∜ **Conf** facs
Location 0.5m along Huntly Rd

BANGOR
Map 1 D5

Bangor Broadway BT20 4RH
☎ 028 9127 0922   📠 028 9145 3394
e-mail: office@bangorgolfclubni.co.uk
web: www.bangorgolfclubni.co.uk

Undulating parkland course in the town. It is well maintained and pleasant and offers a challenging round, particularly at the 5th. Scenic views to Scotland on a clear day.

18 Holes, 6410yds, Par 71, SSS 71, Course record 62.
Club membership 1122.
Visitors Mon, Wed-Fri, Sun & BHs. Handicap certificate. Dress code. **Societies** booking required. **Green Fees** phone **Course Designer** James Braid **Prof** Michael Bannon **Facilities** ⓨ ⑩ 🍴 ⚐ 🏌 🛒 🏧 🚆 🏧 ∜ **Location** 1m from town centre, 300yds off Donaghadee Rd
Hotel ★★★ 61% HL Royal, Seafront, BANGOR, Co Down ☎ 028 9127 1866 📠 028 9127 1866 49 en suite

Blackwood Golf Centre 150 Crawfordsburn Rd, Clandeboye BT19 1GB
☎ 028 9185 2706   📠 028 9185 3785
web: www.blackwoodgolfcentre.com

The golf centre is a pay and play development with a computerised booking system for the 18-hole championship-standard Hamilton Course. The course is built on mature woodland with man-made lakes that come into play on five holes. The Temple course is an 18-hole par 3 course with holes ranging from the 75yd 1st to the 185yd 10th, which has a lake on the right of the green. Banked by gorse with streams crossing throughout, this par 3 course is no pushover.

Hamilton Course: 18 Holes, 6392yds, Par 71, SSS 70, Course record 62.
Temple Course: 18 Holes, 2492yds, Par 54.
Visitors Contact club for details. **Societies** welcome. **Green Fees** not confirmed **Course Designer** Simon Gidman **Prof** Debbie Hanna **Facilities** ⓨ ⑩ 🍴 ⚐ 🏌 🛒 🏧 ∜ **Location** 2m from Bangor off A2 to Belfast
Hotel ★★★★ 78% HL Clandeboye Lodge, 10 Estate Road, Clandeboye, BANGOR ☎ 028 9185 2500 📠 028 9185 2500 43 en suite

Carnalea Station Rd BT19 1EZ
☎ 028 9127 0368   📠 028 9127 3989

A scenic course on the shores of Belfast Lough.

18 Holes, 5647yds, Par 69, SSS 67, Course record 63.
Club membership 1354.
Visitors Mon-Fri, Sun & BHs. Dress code. **Societies** welcome. **Green Fees** £17.50 (£22 Sun) **Prof** Tom Loughran **Facilities** ⓨ ⑩ 🍴 ⚐ 🏌 🛒 🏧 ∜ **Location** 2m W next to railway station
Hotel ★★★★ 74% HL The Old Inn, 15 Main Street, CRAWFORDSBURN ☎ 028 9185 3255 📠 028 9185 3255 31 en suite

IRELAND

Clandeboye Tower Rd, Conlig, Newtownards BT23 3PN
☎ 028 9127 1767   ≣ 028 9147 3711
e-mail: cgc-ni@btconnect.com
web: www.cgc-ni.com

Parkland and heathland courses. The Dufferin is the championship course and offers a tough challenge demanding extreme accuracy, with gorse, bracken and strategically placed trees that flank every hole. Errors will be punished. The Ava compliments the Dufferin perfectly. Accuracy is the key on this course with small targets and demanding tee shots. Outstanding panoramic views.

Dufferin Course: 18 Holes, 6559yds, Par 71, SSS 71.
Ava Course: 18 Holes, 5755yds, Par 70, SSS 68.
Club membership 1450.

Visitors contact club for details. **Societies** welcome. **Green Fees** not confirmed **Course Designer** Von Limburger/Allis/Thomas **Prof** Peter Gregory **Facilities** ⑪ ⚑ ⬛ ⬜ ⚒ ⚐ ⚑ ⛏ ⚐ **Leisure** snooker, table tennis, indoor bowls **Conf** facs Corporate Hospitality Days **Location** 2m S on A1 between Bangor & Newtownards **Hotel** ★★★ 61% HL Royal, Seafront, BANGOR, Co Down ☎ 028 9127 1866 ≣ 028 9127 1866 49 en suite

Helen's Bay Golf Rd BT19 1TL
☎ 028 9185 2815 & 9185 2601   ≣ 028 9185 2660
web: www.helensbaygc.com

9 Holes, 5644yds, Par 68, SSS 67, Course record 67.
Facilities ⑪ ⚑ ⬛ ⬜ ⚒ ⚐ ⛏ ⚐ **Conf** facs
Location A2 from Belfast
Telephone for further details
Hotel ★★★★ 74% HL The Old Inn, 15 Main Street, CRAWFORDSBURN ☎ 028 9185 3255 ≣ 028 9185 3255 31 en suite

CARRYDUFF   Map 1 D5

Rockmount 28 Drumalig Rd, Carryduff BT8 8EQ
☎ 028 9081 2279   ≣ 028 9081 5851
e-mail: rockmountgc@btconnect.com
web: www.rockmountgolfclub.co.uk

A cleverly designed course incorporating natural features with water coming into play as streams with a lake at the 11th and 14th.

18 Holes, 6373yds, Par 71, SSS 71, Course record 68.
Club membership 750.

Visitors contact club for details. **Societies** welcome. **Green Fees** not confirmed **Course Designer** Robert Patterson **Facilities** ⑪ ⚑ ⬛ ⬜ ⚒ ⚐ ⛏ ⚐ **Conf** facs **Location** 10m S of Belfast **Hotel** ★★★ 81% HL Malmaison Belfast, 34 - 38 Victoria Street, BELFAST ☎ 028 9022 0200 ≣ 028 9022 0200 64 en suite

CLOUGHEY   Map 1 D5

Kirkistown Castle 142 Main Rd, Cloughey BT22 1JA
☎ 028 4277 1233   ≣ 028 4277 1699
e-mail: kirkistown@supanet.com
web: www.linksgolfkirkistown.com

A seaside part-links, designed by James Braid, popular with visiting golfers because of its quiet location. The course is exceptionally dry and remains open when others in the area have to close. The short but treacherous par 4 15th hole was known as Braid's Hole. The 2nd and 10th holes are long par 4s with elevated greens, which are a feature of the course. The 10th is particularly distinctive with a long drive and a slight dog-leg to a raised green with a gorse covered motte waiting

for the wayward approach shot. It has the reputation of being one of the hardest par 4s in Ireland.

18 Holes, 6167yds, Par 69, SSS 70, Course record 65.
Club membership 1012.

Visitors Mon-Fri except BHs. Booking required. Dress code. Handicap certificate. **Societies** booking required. **Green Fees** £25 per day **Course Designer** James Braid **Prof** Neil Graham **Facilities** ⑪ ⚑ ⬛ ⬜ ⚒ ⚐ ⛏ ⚐ ⛏ **Leisure** snooker room **Conf** facs Corporate Hospitality Days **Location** 16m from Newtownards on A2 **Hotel** ★★★★ 74% HL The Old Inn, 15 Main Street, CRAWFORDSBURN ☎ 028 9185 3255 ≣ 028 9185 3255 31 en suite

COMBER   Map 1 D5

Mahee Island 14 Mahee Island, Comber BT23 6EP
☎ 028 9754 1234
e-mail: mahee_gents@hotmail.com

An undulating parkland course, almost surrounded by water, with magnificent views of Strangford Lough and its islands, with Scrabo Tower in the background. Undulating fairways and tricky greens make this a good test of golf.

9 Holes, 5324mtrs, Par 71, SSS 68, Course record 66.
Club membership 600.

Visitors Mon-Fri, Sun & BHs. Dress code Handicap certificate. **Societies** booking required. **Green Fees** £13 per round, £9 per 9 holes (£18/£12 Sun & BHs) **Course Designer** Mr Robinson **Facilities** ⑪ by prior arrangement ⚑ by prior arrangement ⬜ ⚒ ⚐ ⛏ ⚐ **Location** off Comber-Killyleagh road, 0.5m from Comber **Hotel** ★★★★ 78% HL Clandeboye Lodge, 10 Estate Road, Clandeboye, BANGOR ☎ 028 9185 2500 ≣ 028 9185 2500 43 en suite

DONAGHADEE   Map 1 D5

Donaghadee Warren Rd BT21 0PQ
☎ 028 9188 3624   ≣ 028 9188 8891

18 Holes, 5616mtrs, Par 71, SSS 69, Course record 64.
Prof Gordon Drew **Facilities** ⑪ ⚑ ⬛ ⬜ ⚒ ⚐ ⛏ ⚐ ⛏ ⚐ **Conf** facs Corporate Hospitality Days **Location** 5m S of Bangor on Coast Rd
Telephone for further details
Hotel ★★★★ 74% HL The Old Inn, 15 Main Street, CRAWFORDSBURN ☎ 028 9185 3255 ≣ 028 9185 3255 31 en suite

DOWNPATRICK   Map 1 D5

Bright Castle 14 Coniamstown Rd BT30 8LU
☎ 028 44841319

18 Holes, 7300yds, Par 74, SSS 74, Course record 69.
Course Designer Mr Ennis Snr **Location** 5m S
Telephone for further details
Hotel ★★ 69% SHL Enniskeen House, 98 Bryansford Road, NEWCASTLE, Co Down ☎ 028 4372 2392 ≣ 028 4372 2392 12 en suite

Downpatrick 43 Saul Rd BT30 6PA
☎ 028 44615947 🖷 028 44617502
e-mail: office@downpatrickgolfclub.org.uk
web: www.downpatrickgolfclub.org.uk

A classic parkland course with most holes boasting spectacular views of Co Down, Strangford Lough and even the Isle of Man, on a clear day. Undulating fairways, strategically placed sand traps and quick but true greens make the course a testing yet pleasurable challenge to golfers of all abilities.

18 Holes, 6100yds, Par 69, SSS 69, Course record 66. Club membership 960.

Visitors Mon-Sun & BHs. Dress code. **Societies** welcome. **Green Fees** £23 per day (£28 weekends & BHs) **Course Designer** Hawtree & Son **Prof** Robert Hutton **Facilities** ⑪ ⑩ ⒧ ⌹ ⒨ ⎁ 🖀 ⍾ ⍻ 🖥 ⍾ **Conf** facs **Location** 1.5m from town centre
Hotel ★★ 69% SHL Enniskeen House, 98 Bryansford Road, NEWCASTLE, Co Down ☎ 028 4372 2392 🖷 028 4372 2392 12 en suite

HOLYWOOD   Map 1 D5

Holywood Nuns Walk, Demesne Rd BT18 9LE
☎ 028 9042 3135 🖷 028 9042 5040
e-mail: mail@holywoodgolfclub.co.uk
web: www.holywoodgolfclub.co.uk

Hilly parkland course, providing some fine views and an interesting game. Several feature holes, including the short 6th 'Nuns Walk', fondly remembered by the many who have 'holed out in one'. In contrast, the treacherous 12th 'White House' is a most difficult par 4. The tee shot must be placed precisely on the fairway to allow the long approach to a green which is protected out of bounds to the right and a perilous drop to the left.

18 Holes, 5480mtrs, Par 69, SSS 68, Course record 64. Club membership 950.

Visitors Mon-Wed, Fri, Sun & BHs. Booking required. Dress code. **Societies** booking required. **Green Fees** phone **Prof** Stephen Crooks **Facilities** ⑪ ⑩ ⒧ ⌹ ⒨ ⎁ ⍾ 🖀 ⍾ **Conf** Corporate Hospitality Days **Location** off Bangor dual carriageway
Hotel ★★★★ 74% HL The Old Inn, 15 Main Street, CRAWFORDSBURN ☎ 028 9185 3255 🖷 028 9185 3255 31 en suite

The Royal Belfast Station Rd, Craigavad BT18 0BP
☎ 028 9042 8165 🖷 028 9042 1404
e-mail: royalbelfastgc@btconnect.com
web: www.royalbelfast.com

On the shores of Belfast Lough, this attractive course consists of wooded parkland on undulating terrain which provides a pleasant, challenging game.

18 Holes, 6185yds, Par 70, SSS 69. Club membership 1200.

Visitors Mon, Tue, Thu, Fri, Sun & BHs. Booking required. Handicap certificate. Dress code **Societies** booking required. **Green Fees** not confirmed **Course Designer** H C Colt **Prof** Andrew Ferguson **Facilities** ⑪ ⑩ ⒧ ⌹ ⒨ ⎁ 🖀 ⍾ ⍻ 🖥 ⍾ **Leisure** hard tennis courts, squash **Location** 2m E on A2
Hotel ★★★★ 74% HL The Old Inn, 15 Main Street, CRAWFORDSBURN ☎ 028 9185 3255 🖷 028 9185 3255 31 en suite

KILKEEL   Map 1 D5

Kilkeel Mourne Park BT34 4LB
☎ 028 4176 5095 🖷 028 4176 5579
e-mail: kilkeelgolfclub@gmail.com

Picturesquely situated at the foot of the Mourne Mountains. Eleven holes have tree-lined fairways with the remainder in open parkland. The 13th hole is testing and a well-positioned tee shot is essential.

18 Holes, 6579yds, Par 72, SSS 72, Course record 67. Club membership 750.

Visitors Mon-Fri, Sun & BHs. Booking required Sun & BHs. Dress code. **Societies** welcome. **Green Fees** not confirmed **Course Designer** Babington/Hackett **Facilities** ⑪ ⑩ ⒧ ⌹ ⒨ ⎁ 🖀 ⍾ 🖥 ⍾ **Conf** facs Corporate Hospitality Days **Location** 3m from Kilkeel on Newry road
Hotel ★★ 69% SHL Enniskeen House, 98 Bryansford Road, NEWCASTLE, Co Down ☎ 028 4372 2392 🖷 028 4372 2392 12 en suite

KILLYLEAGH   Map 1 D5

Ringdufferin Golf Course, 31 Ringdufferin Rd, Toye BT30 9PH
☎ 028 4482 8812 🖷 028 4482 8972
e-mail: country-club@btconnect.com
web: www.ringdufferin.com

The course overlooks Strangford Lough.

Ringdufferin Golf Course: 18 Holes, 5093mtrs, Par 68, SSS 66. Club membership 300.

Visitors contact club for details. Handicap certificate. **Societies** welcome. **Green Fees** not confirmed **Course Designer** Frank Ainsworth **Prof** Maruyn McMaster **Facilities** ⑪ ⒧ ⌹ ⒨ ⎁ 🖀 ⍻ ⍾ 🖐 **Leisure** fishing, gymnasium **Conf** facs **Location** 2m N of Killyleagh
Hotel ★★★★ 84% CHH Ballynahinch Castle, Recess, Connemara, BALLYNAHINCH, Co Galway ☎ 095 31006 🖷 095 31006 40 en suite

MAGHERALIN   Map 1 D5

Edenmore Golf & Country Club Edenmore House, 70 Drumnabreeze Rd BT67 0RH
☎ 028 9261 9241 🖷 028 9261 3310
e-mail: info@edenmore.com
web: www.edenmore.com

Set in mature parkland with gently rolling slopes. The front nine holes provide an interesting contrast to the back nine with more open play involved. Many paths and features have been added. The 13th hole, Edenmore, is the most memorable hole with a small lake protecting a contoured green.

Edenmore Golf & Country Club: 18 Holes, 6278yds, Par 71, SSS 70, Course record 70. Club membership 600.

Visitors Mon-Sun & BHs. Booking required weekends & BHs. Dress code. **Societies** booking required. **Green Fees** £20 (£25 weekends & BHs) **Course Designer** F Ainsworth **Prof** Andrew Manson **Facilities** ⑪ ⑩ ⒧ ⌹ ⒨ ⎁ 🖀 ⍻ ◇ ⍾ 🖥 ⍾ **Leisure** sauna, gymnasium **Conf** facs Corporate Hospitality Days **Location** M1 Moira exit, through Moira towards Lurgan. Turn off in Magheralin signed
Hotel ★★★★ 74% HL The Old Inn, 15 Main Street, CRAWFORDSBURN ☎ 028 9185 3255 🖷 028 9185 3255 31 en suite

ROYAL COUNTY DOWN
CO DOWN - NEWCASTLE - MAP 1 D5

The Championship Course is consistently rated among the world's top ten courses. Laid out beneath the imperious Mourne Mountains, the course has a magnificent setting as it stretches out along the shores of Dundrum Bay. As well as being one of the most-beautiful courses, it is also one of the most challenging, with great swathes of heather and gorse lining fairways that tumble beneath vast sand hills, and wild tussock-faced bunkers defending small, subtly contoured greens. The Annesley Links offers a less formidable yet extremely characterful game, played against the same incomparable backdrop. Substantially revised under the direction of Donald Steel, the course begins quite benignly before charging headlong into the dunes. Several charming and one or two teasing holes have been carved out amid the gorse, heather and bracken.

---

36 Golf Links Rd BT33 0AN ☎ 028 43723314 📄 028 43726281
e-mail: golf@royalcountydown.org **web:** www.royalcountydown.org
Championship Course: 18 Holes, 7181yds, Par 71, SSS 74, Course record 66.
Annesley: 18 Holes, 4681yds, Par 66, SSS 63. Club membership 450.
Visitors Mon, Tue, Thu, Fri, Sun & BHs. Booking required. Handicap certificate. **Societies** booking required.
Green Fees Championship Course £160, £145 pm (£180 Sun) **Course Designer** Tom Morris **Prof** Kevan Whitson
Facilities ⑨ by prior arrangement 🍴 💷 🍺 🧴 🏠 ⛳ 🏌 **Location** N of town centre off A24
Hotel ★★ **69%** SHL Enniskeen House, 98 Bryansford Road, NEWCASTLE, Co Down ☎ 028 4372 2392
📄 028 4372 2392 12 en suite

NEWCASTLE
Map 1 D5

Royal County Down see page 427
36 Golf Links Rd BT33 0AN
☎ 028 43723314 📄 028 43726281
e-mail: golf@royalcountydown.org
web: www.royalcountydown.org

NEWTOWNARDS
Map 1 D5

Scrabo 233 Scrabo Rd BT23 4SL
☎ 028 9181 2355 📄 028 9182 2919
e-mail: admin.scrabogc@btconnect.com
web: www.scrabo-golf-club.org
Hilly and picturesque, this heathland course stands on a 150-metre hill with rocky outcrops. The matured course has a totally natural layout with stunning views over the surrounding countryside.
18 Holes, 5722mtrs, Par 71, SSS 71, Course record 65. Club membership 1002.
Visitors Mon-Sun & BHs. Booking required weekends. Dress code. **Societies** welcome. **Green Fees** £19 (£24 Sun) **Facilities** ⑪ ⑩ 🏌 🖵 🍴 👤 🏠 ♂ 🛺 ♂ **Conf** facs Corporate Hospitality Days **Location** outskirts of Newtownards on Ards peninsula, signs for Scrabo Country Park
Hotel ★★★★ 78% HL Clandeboye Lodge, 10 Estate Road, Clandeboye, BANGOR ☎ 028 9185 2500 📄 028 9185 2500 43 en suite

WARRENPOINT
Map 1 D5

Warrenpoint Lower Dromore Rd BT34 3LN
☎ 028 4175 3695 📄 028 4175 2918
e-mail: office@warrenpointgolf.com
web: www.warrenpointgolf.com
Parkland course with marvellous views and a need for accurate shots.
18 Holes, 6108yds, Par 71, SSS 70, Course record 61. Club membership 1460.
Visitors Mon, Thu, Fri, Sun & BHs. Booking required. Handicap certificate. Dress code. **Societies** welcome. **Green Fees** £30 per round (£34 Sun & BHs) **Course Designer** Tom Craddock/Pat Ruddy **Prof** Nigel Shaw **Facilities** ⑪ ⑩ 🏌 🖵 🍴 👤 🏠 🍴 🛺 ♂ **Leisure** 9 hole par 3 academy course **Conf** facs Corporate Hospitality Days **Location** 1m W
Hotel ★★ 69% SHL Enniskeen House, 98 Bryansford Road, NEWCASTLE, Co Down ☎ 028 4372 2392 📄 028 4372 2392 12 en suite

CO FERMANAGH

ENNISKILLEN
Map 1 C5

Ashwoods Golf Centre Sligo Rd BT74 7JY
☎ 028 6632 5321 & 6632 2908 📄 028 6632 9411
Only one mile from Enniskillen, this course is in open meadowland. It has been well planted with many young trees.
Ashwoods Golf Centre: 14 Holes, 1930yds, Par 42.
Visitors contact centre for details. **Societies** booking required. **Green Fees** phone. **Course Designer** P Loughran **Prof** L McCool **Facilities** ⑪ ⑩ by prior arrangement 🏌 🖵 👤 🏠 🍴 ♢ ♂ 🏹

10th Hole - Emerald Isle

THE FALDO COURSE...
THE ULTIMATE GOLF DESTINATION

Book your Tee Time
Online now or call
the Golf Office on
T. +44 (0)28 6634 5725

LOUGH
ERNE
GOLF RESORT
★ ★ ★ ★ ★

www.loughernegolfresort.com

Conf facs Corporate Hospitality Days **Location** 1.5m W of Enniskillen on Sligo road
Hotel ★★★★ 77% HL Killyhevlin, ENNISKILLEN, Co Fermanagh ☎ 028 6632 3481 📄 028 6632 3481 70 en suite

Castle Hume Castle Hume, Belleek Rd BT93 7ED
☎ 028 6632 7077 📄 028 6632 7076
e-mail: info@castlehumegolf.com
web: www.castlehumegolf.com
Castle Hume is a particularly scenic and challenging course. Set in undulating parkland with large rolling greens, rivers, lakes and water hazards all in play on a championship standard course.
Castle Hume Golf Course: 18 Holes, 5770mtrs, Par 72, SSS 70, Course record 69. Club membership 350.
Visitors Mon-Sun & BHs. Booking required. Dress code. Handicap certificate. **Societies** booking required. **Green Fees** £25/35 per 18 holes (£35/50 weekends and BHs) **Course Designer** B Browne **Facilities** ⑪ ⑩ 🏌 🖵 🍴 👤 🏠 🍴 🛺 ♂ **Leisure** fishing, sauna, gymnasium **Conf** facs Corporate Hospitality Days **Location** 4m from Enniskillen on A46 Belleek-Donegal road
Hotel ★★★★ 77% HL Killyhevlin, ENNISKILLEN, Co Fermanagh ☎ 028 6632 3481 📄 028 6632 3481 70 en suite

Enniskillen Castlecoole BT74 6HZ
☎ 028 6632 5250 📄 028 6632 5250
e-mail: enniskillengolfclub@mail.com
web: www.enniskillengolfclub.com
Tree lined parkland course offering panoramic views of Enniskillen town and the surrounding lakeland area. Situated beside the National Trust's Castlecoole Estate.

continued

IRELAND

18 Holes, 6230yds, Par 71, SSS 69, Course record 67. Club membership 550.
Visitors Mon-Sun & BHs. Booking required weekends & BHs. Dress code. **Societies** welcome. **Green Fees** £20 per day (£25 weekends & BHs) **Facilities** ⑪ by prior arrangement ⑩ by prior arrangement ⓛ ▯ ⑩ ⚲ ⑨ ⚲ 🏎 ✧ **Conf** facs Corporate Hospitality Days **Location** 1m E of town centre
Hotel ★★★★ 77% HL Killyhevlin, ENNISKILLEN, Co Fermanagh ☎ 028 6632 3481 ▤ 028 6632 3481 70 en suite

Lough Erne Golf Resort Belleek Rd BT93 7ED
☎ 028 6632 3230 ▤ 028 6634 5758
e-mail: info@loughernegolfresort.com
web: www.loughernegolfresort.com

The first course designed by Nick Faldo in Ireland, set in a beautiful lakeland setting. It rests on its own secluded island nestling between Lower Lough Erne and Castle Hume Lough. Challenging for all levels of golfer.
Faldo Championship Course: 18 Holes, 7216yds, Par 72. Club membership 225.
Visitors Mon-Sun & BHs. Booking required. Dress code. **Societies** booking required. **Green Fees** £95 July-Sept. Reduced rates low season. **Course Designer** Nick Faldo **Facilities** ⑪ ⑩ ⓛ ▯ ⑩ ⚲ ⑩ ⚲ ◇ ⑨ 🏎 ✧ **Leisure** heated indoor swimming pool, fishing, sauna, gymnasium, Thai spa **Conf** facs Corporate Hospitality Days **Location** 4m N of Enniskillen on Enniskillen to Donegal road.
Hotel ★★★★★ 86% HL Lough Erne Golf Resort, Belleek Road, ENNISKILLEN ☎ 028 6632 3230 ▤ 028 6632 3230 120 en suite

See advert on opposite page

CO LONDONDERRY

AGHADOWEY   Map 1 C6

Brown Trout Golf & Country Inn 209 Agivey Rd BT51 4AD
☎ 028 7086 8209 ▤ 028 7086 8878
e-mail: bill@browntroutinn.com
web: www.browntroutinn.com
A challenging course with two par 5s. During the course of the nine holes, players have to negotiate water seven times and all the fairways are lined with densely packed fir trees.
Brown Trout Golf & Country Inn: 9 Holes, 5510yds, Par 70, SSS 68, Course record 64. Club membership 100.
Visitors contact inn for details. **Societies** booking required. **Green Fees** £10 per day (£15 weekends) **Course Designer** Bill O'Hara Snr **Prof** Ken Revie **Facilities** ⑪ ⑩ ⓛ ▯ ⑩ ⚲ ⓛ ⚲ ◇ ⚲ **Leisure** fishing, gymnasium **Conf** facs **Location** junct A54, 7m S of Coleraine

Hotel ★★ 76% HL Brown Trout Golf & Country Inn, 209 Agivey Road, AGHADOWEY, Co Londonderry ☎ 028 7086 8209 ▤ 028 7086 8209 15 en suite

CASTLEDAWSON   Map 1 C5

Moyola Park 15 Curran Rd BT45 8DG
☎ 028 7946 8468 & 7946 8830 (Prof) ▤ 028 7946 8626
e-mail: moyolapark@btconnect.com
web: www.moyolapark.com
Parkland championship course with some difficult shots, calling for length and accuracy. The Moyola River provides a water hazard at the 8th. Newly designed par 3 17th demands good shot placement to a green on an island in the Moyola river, when players' capabilities will be tested by the undulating green.
18 Holes, 6519yds, Par 71, SSS 71, Course record 67. Club membership 800.
Visitors Mon-Sun & BHs. Booking required. Dress code. **Societies** booking required. **Green Fees** Mon-Thu £24 per 18 holes (Fri-Sun £30) **Course Designer** Don Patterson **Prof** Bob Cockcroft **Facilities** ⑪ ⑩ ⓛ ▯ ⑩ ⚲ ⓛ ⚲ ◇ 🏎 ✧ **Conf** facs Corporate Hospitality Days **Location** club signed
Hotel ★★★★ 82% HL Galgorm Resort & Spa, BALLYMENA, Co Antrim ☎ 028 2588 1001 ▤ 028 2588 1001 75 en suite

CASTLEROCK   Map 1 C6

Castlerock 65 Circular Rd BT51 4TJ
☎ 028 7084 8314 ▤ 028 7084 9440
e-mail: admin@castlerockgc.co.uk
web: www.castlerockgc.co.uk
A most exhilarating course with three superb par 4s, four testing short holes and five par 5s. After an uphill start, the hazards are many, including the river and a railway, and both judgement and accuracy are called for. The signature hole is the 4th, Leg of Mutton. A challenge in calm weather, any trouble from the elements will test your golf to the limits.
Mussenden Course: 18 Holes, 6499yds, Par 73, SSS 71, Course record 64.
Bann Course: 9 Holes, 4892yds, Par 68, SSS 66, Course record 64. Club membership 1220.
Visitors Mon-Sun & BHs. Booking required. Dress code. Handicap certificate. **Societies** booking required. **Green Fees** £65 per day (£80 weekends & BHs) **Course Designer** Ben Sayers **Prof** Thomas Johnston **Facilities** ⑪ ⑩ ⓛ ▯ ⑩ ⚲ ⓛ ⚲ ◇ ⚲ 🏎 ⚲ **Location** 6m from Coleraine on A2
Guesthouse ★★★★★ FH Greenhill House, 24 Greenhill Road, Aghadowey, COLERAINE ☎ 028 7086 8241 ▤ 028 7086 8241 6 en suite

KILREA   Map 1 C5

Kilrea 47a Lisnagrot Rd BT51 5TB
☎ 028 2954 0044
Kilrea Golf Course: 9 Holes, 5578yds, Par 68, SSS 68, Course record 66.
Facilities ⑪ ⑩ ⓛ ▯ ⑩ ⚲ ⓛ
Telephone for further details
Hotel ★★ 76% HL Brown Trout Golf & Country Inn, 209 Agivey Road, AGHADOWEY, Co Londonderry ☎ 028 7086 8209 ▤ 028 7086 8209 15 en suite

IRELAND

LIMAVADY
Map 1 C6

Benone 53 Benone Ave BT49 0LQ
☎ 028 7775 0555 📄 028 7775 0919

Beside a beach, a delightful mix of parkland quite testing for the short game. Nestling at the foot of the Binevenagh mountains with picturesque views.

Benone Tourist Complex: 9 Holes, 1459yds, Par 27. Club membership 100.

Visitors Mon-Sun & BHs. Booking required. **Societies** booking required. **Green Fees** not confirmed **Facilities** ⛳ 🏌 **Leisure** hard tennis courts, heated outdoor swimming pool, bowling green **Location** between Coleraine & Limavady on A2
Hotel ★★★★ 76% HL Radisson SAS Roe Park Resort, LIMAVADY, Co Londonderry ☎ 028 7772 2222 📄 028 7772 2222 118 en suite

Radisson SAS Roe Park Resort, Roe Park BT49 9LB
☎ 028 7772 2222 📄 028 7772 2313
e-mail: sales@radissonroepark.com
web: www.radissonroepark.com

A parkland course opened in 1992 on an historic Georgian estate. The course surrounds the original buildings and a driving range has been created in the old walled garden. Final holes 15-18 are particularly memorable with water, trees and out-of-bounds to provide a testing finish.

Radisson SAS Roe Park Resort: 18 Holes, 6283yds, Par 70, SSS 70, Course record 67. Club membership 600.

Visitors Mon-Sun & BHs. Booking required. Dress code. Handicap certificate. **Societies** booking required. **Green Fees** not confirmed **Course Designer** Frank Ainsworth **Prof** Shaun Devenney **Facilities** ⛳ 🍴 🍸 🛒 🛍 🏌 🏠 ⛳ 🔧 🏸 🎿 🏌 **Leisure** heated indoor swimming pool, fishing, sauna, gymnasium, indoor golf academy **Conf** facs Corporate Hospitality Days **Location** just outside Limavady on A2 Ballykelly-Londonderry road
Hotel ★★★★ 76% HL Radisson SAS Roe Park Resort, LIMAVADY, Co Londonderry ☎ 028 7772 2222 📄 028 7772 2222 118 en suite

LONDONDERRY
Map 1 C5

City of Derry 49 Victoria Rd BT47 2PU
☎ 028 7134 6369 📄 028 7131 0008
e-mail: info@cityofderrygolfclub.com
web: cityofderrygolfclub.com

Two parkland courses on undulating parkland with good views and lots of trees, occupying a magnificent setting on the banks of the river Foyle. The nine-hole course will particularly suit novices.

Prehen Course: 18 Holes, 6406yds, Par 71, SSS 71, Course record 68.
Dunhugh Course: 9 Holes, 2354yds, Par 66, SSS 66. Club membership 700.

Visitors Sun-Fri & BHs. Dress code. Handicap certificate. **Societies** booking required. **Green Fees** not confirmed **Prof** Michael Doherty **Facilities** ⛳ 🍴 🍸 🛒 🛍 🏌 🏠 🔧 **Conf** facs Corporate Hospitality Days **Location** 2m S
Hotel ★★★ 79% HL Beech Hill Country House Hotel, 32 Ardmore Road, LONDONDERRY, Northern Ireland ☎ 028 7134 9279 📄 028 7134 9279 27 en suite

Foyle International Golf Centre 12 Alder Rd BT48 8DB
☎ 028 7135 2222 📄 028 7135 3967
e-mail: mail@foylegolf.club24.co.uk
web: www.foylegolfcentre.co.uk

Foyle International has a championship course, a nine-hole par 3 course and a driving range. It is a fine test of golf with water coming into play on the 3rd, 10th and 11th holes. The 6th green overlooks the Amelia Earhart centre.

Earhart: 18 Holes, 6639yds, Par 71, SSS 71, Course record 70.
Woodlands: 9 Holes, 1349yds, Par 27. Club membership 320.

Visitors contact centre for details. Handicap certificate. **Societies** booking required. **Green Fees** £17 (£20 weekends) **Course Designer** Frank Ainsworth **Prof** Derek Morrison & Sean Young **Facilities** ⛳ 🍴 🛒 🛍 🏌 🏠 🏌 🔧 🏸 **Leisure** 9 hole par 3 course **Conf** facs Corporate Hospitality Days **Location** 1.5m from Foyle Bridge towards Moville
Hotel ★★★★ 73% HL City Hotel, Queens Quay, LONDONDERRY ☎ 028 7136 5800 📄 028 7136 5800 146 en suite

PORTSTEWART
Map 1 C6

Portstewart 117 Strand Rd BT55 7PG
☎ 028 7083 2015 & 7083 3839 📄 028 7083 4097
web: www.portstewartgc.co.uk

Strand Course: 18 Holes, 6784yds, Par 72, SSS 72, Course record 67.
Old Course: 18 Holes, 4733yds, Par 64, SSS 62.
Riverside: 9 Holes, 2622yds, Par 32.

Course Designer Des Giffin **Location**
Telephone for further details

CO TYRONE

COOKSTOWN
Map 1 C5

Killymoon 200 Killymoon Rd BT80 8TW
☎ 028 8676 3762 & 8676 2254 📄 028 8676 3762
e-mail: killymoongolf@btconnect.com
web: www.killymoongolfclub.com

Parkland course on elevated, well-drained land. The signature hole is the aptly named 10th hole - the Giant's Grave. Accuracy is paramount here and a daunting tee shot into a narrow-necked fairway will challenge even the most seasoned golfer. The enclosing influence of the trees continues the whole way to the green.

18 Holes, 6202yds, Par 70, SSS 70, Course record 64. Club membership 830.

Visitors Mon-Fri, Sun & BHs. Booking required. Dress code. Handicap certificate. **Societies** booking required. **Green Fees** £16 per round Mon, £22 Tue-Fri (£28 weekends) **Course Designer** John Nash **Prof** Gary Chambers **Facilities** ⛳ 🍴 🛒 🛍 🏌 🏠 🏌 **Leisure** snooker **Conf** facs Corporate Hospitality Days **Location** S of Cookstown
Hotel ★★ 69% HL Cohannon Inn & Autolodge, 212 Ballynakilly Road, DUNGANNON, Co Tyrone ☎ 028 8772 4488 📄 028 8772 4488 42 en suite

IRELAND

DUNGANNON   Map 1 C5

Dungannon 34 Springfield Ln BT70 1QX
☎ 028 8772 2098 📱 028 8772 7338
e-mail: dungannon.golfclub@btopenworld.com
web: www.dungannongolfclub.com
Parkland course with five par 3s and tree-lined fairways.

18 Holes, 6046yds, Par 72, SSS 69, Course record 62.
Club membership 1100.

Visitors Mon-Sun & BHs. Booking required weekends & BHs. Dress code. Handicap certificate. **Societies** booking required. **Green Fees** not confirmed **Course Designer** Sam Bacon **Facilities** ⊕ 🍴 🛍 🖵 🏌 🛒 Location 0.5m outside town on Donaghmore road
Hotel ★★ 69% HL Cohannon Inn & Autolodge, 212 Ballynakilly Road, DUNGANNON, Co Tyrone ☎ 028 8772 4488 📱 028 8772 4488 42 en suite

FINTONA   Map 1 C5

Fintona Ecclesville Demesne BT78 2BJ
☎ 028 8284 1480 & 8284 0777 (office)
📱 028 8284 1480

Fintona Golf Course: 9 Holes, 5765mtrs, Par 72, SSS 70.
Prof Paul Leonard **Facilities** ⊕ by prior arrangement 🍴 by prior arrangement 🛍 🖵 🍴 🏌 **Location** 8m S of Omagh
Telephone for further details
Hotel ★★★ 70% HL Mahons, Mill St, IRVINESTOWN, Co Fermanagh ☎ 028 6862 1656 & 6862 1657 📱 028 6862 1656 24 en suite

NEWTOWNSTEWART   Map 1 C5

Newtownstewart 38 Golf Course Rd BT78 4HU
☎ 028 8166 1466 📱 028 8166 2506
e-mail: newtown.stewart@lineone.net
web: www.newtownstewartgolfclub.com
Parkland course bisected by a stream. Deer and pheasant are present on the course.

18 Holes, 5320mtrs, Par 70, SSS 69, Course record 65.
Club membership 550.

Visitors Mon-Sun & BHs. Booking required weekends & BHs. Handicap certificate. Dress code. **Societies** booking required. **Green Fees** £18 per 18 holes (£25 weekends & BHs) **Course Designer** Frank Pennick **Facilities** 🖵 🍴 🏌 🏠 🍴 🛒 **Leisure** snooker **Conf** facs Corporate Hospitality Days **Location** 2m SW on B84

OMAGH   Map 1 C5

Omagh 83a Dublin Rd BT78 1HQ
☎ 028 8224 3160 📱 028 8224 3160
web: www.omaghgolfclub.co.uk
Undulating parkland course beside the River Drumnagh, with the river coming into play on 4 of the holes.

18 Holes, 5683mtrs, Par 71, SSS 70, Course record 65.
Club membership 850.

Visitors Mon-Sun & BHs. Booking required weekends. Handicap certificate. Dress code. **Societies** welcome. **Green Fees** not confirmed **Course Designer** Don Patterson **Facilities** ⊕ by prior arrangement 🍴 by prior arrangement 🛍 🖵 🍴 🏌 🏠 **Conf** Corporate Hospitality Days **Location** S outskirts of town

STRABANE   Map 1 C5

Strabane Ballycolman Rd BT82 9HY
☎ 028 7138 2271 & 7138 2007 📱 028 7188 6514
18 Holes, 5537mtrs, Par 69, SSS 69, Course record 62.
Course Designer Eddie Hackett/P Jones **Location** 1m from Strabane on Dublin road
Telephone for further details

REPUBLIC OF IRELAND

CO CARLOW

BORRIS   Map 1 C3

Borris Deerpark
☎ 059 9773310 📱 059 9773750
9 Holes, 5680mtrs, Par 70, SSS 69, Course record 66.
Facilities ⊕ 🍴 🛍 🖵 🍴 🏌 🛒
Telephone for further details
Hotel ★★★★ CHH Mount Juliet Conrad, THOMASTOWN, Co Kilkenny ☎ 056 7773000 📱 056 7773000 57 en suite

CARLOW   Map 1 C3

Carlow Deerpark
☎ 059 9131695 📱 059 9140065
e-mail: carlowgolfclub@eircom.net
web: www.carlowgolfclub.com
Created in 1922 to a design by Cecil Barcroft, this testing and enjoyable course is set in a wild deer park, with beautiful dry terrain and a varied character. With sandy subsoil, the course is playable all year round. There are water hazards at the 2nd, 10th and 11th and only two par 5s, both offering genuine birdie opportunities.

18 Holes, 6025mtrs, Par 70, SSS 71, Course record 63.
Oakpark: 9 Holes, 2564mtrs, Par 35, SSS 35,
Course record 67. Club membership 1200.

Visitors Mon-Sat except BHs. Booking required. Handicap certificate. Dress code. **Societies** booking required. **Green Fees** €60 per round (€70 Sat). Oakpark: €20 per 9/18 holes **Course Designer** Cecil Barcroft/Tom Simpson **Prof** Andrew Gilbert **Facilities** ⊕ 🍴 🛍 🖵 🍴 🏌 🏠 🍴 🛒 **Location** 3km N of Carlow on N9
Hotel ★★★ 78% HL Seven Oaks, Athy Road, CARLOW, Co Carlow ☎ 059 9131308 📱 059 9131308 89 en suite

TULLOW   Map 1 C3

Mount Wolseley Hotel, Spa, Golf & Country Club
☎ 059 9180100 📱 059 9152123
e-mail: sales@mountwolseley.ie
web: www.mountwolseley.ie
A magnificent setting, a few hundred yards from the banks of the River Slaney with its mature trees and lakes set against the backdrop of the East Carlow and Wicklow mountains. With wide landing areas the only concession for demanding approach shots to almost every green. There is water in play on 11 holes, with the 11th an all-water

continued

IRELAND

carry off the tee of 207yds. The 18th is a fine finishing hole - a fairway lined with mature oak trees, then a second shot uphill across a water hazard to a green.

Mount Wolseley Hotel,Spa, Golf & Country Club: 18 Holes, 6558metres, Par 72, SSS 74, Course record 68. Club membership 300.

Visitors booking required weekends.. **Societies** booking required. **Green Fees** from €40 low season to €80 high season **Course Designer** Christy O'Connor Jnr **Facilities** ⑪ ⑩ ⒧ ⊡ ⑩ ⚖ 🏠 ⑩ ◇ ✦ 🛒 ✦ **Leisure** heated indoor swimming pool, sauna, gymnasium, spa **Conf** facs Corporate Hospitality Days **Location** from Dublin take N7, then N9. At Castledermos take left **Hotel** ★★★ 78% HL Seven Oaks, Athy Road, CARLOW, Co Carlow ☎ 059 9131308 ▤ 059 9131308 89 en suite

CO CAVAN

BALLYCONNELL
Map 1 C4

Slieve Russell Hotel Golf & Country Club ☎ 049 9525090 ▤ 049 9526640 **web:** www.quinnhotels.com *Slieve Russell Hotel Golf and Country Club: 18 Holes, 6048mtrs, Par 72, SSS 72, Course record 65.*

Course Designer Paddy Merrigan **Location** 4km E of Ballyconnell **Telephone for further details**

BELTURBET
Map 1 C4

Belturbet Erne Hill ☎ 049 9522287 & 9524044 *9 Holes, 5011metres, Par 68, SSS 65, Course record 64.* **Course Designer** Eddie Hackett **Location** 0.8km N of town off N3 **Telephone for further details**

BLACKLION
Map 1 C5

Blacklion Toam ☎ 072 53024 & 53418 ▤ 072 53418 *9 Holes, 5614mtrs, Par 72, SSS 69.* **Course Designer** Eddie Hackett **Telephone for further details** **Hotel** ★★★ 79% HL Sligo Park, Pearse Road, SLIGO, Co Sligo ☎ 071 9190400 ▤ 071 9190400 137 en suite

CAVAN
Map 1 C4

County Cavan Drumelis ☎ 049 4331541 & 4371313 ▤ 049 31541 **e-mail:** info@cavangolf.ie **web:** www.cavangolf.ie

Parkland course with number of mature trees, some over 100 years old. The closing six holes are an exacting challenge for both the handicap and professional golfer alike.

County Cavan Golf Course: 18 Holes, 5634mtrs, Par 70, SSS 69, Course record 64. Club membership 830.

Visitors dress code. **Societies** welcome. **Green Fees** €30 per round (€35 weekends) **Course Designer** Eddie Hackett, Arthur Spring **Prof** Bill Noble **Facilities** ⒧ ⊡ ⑩ ⚖ 🏠 ⑩ 🛒 ✦ 🏹 **Location** on road towards Killeshandra

Hotel ★★★ 79% HL Kilmore, Dublin Road, CAVAN, Co Cavan ☎ 049 4332288 ▤ 049 4332288 38 en suite

VIRGINIA
Map 1 C4

Virginia ☎ 049 47235 & 48066 *Virginia Golf Course: 9 Holes, 4139mtrs, Par 64, SSS 62, Course record 57.*

Facilities ⚖ ⑩ ◇ **Leisure** fishing **Location** by Lough Ramor **Telephone for further details** **Hotel** ★★★ 71% HL The Park Hotel, Virginia Park, VIRGINIA, Co Cavan ☎ 049 8546100 ▤ 049 8546100 26 en suite

CO CLARE

BODYKE
Map 1 B3

East Clare ☎ 061 921322 ▤ 061 921717 **web:** www.eastclare.com *18 Holes, 5415metres, Par 71, SSS 71.* **Course Designer** Dr Arthur Spring **Telephone for further details** **Hotel** ★★★ 78% HL Temple Gate, The Square, ENNIS, Co Clare ☎ 065 6823300 ▤ 065 6823300 70 en suite

ENNIS
Map 1 B3

Ennis Drumbiggle ☎ 065 6824074 & 6865415 ▤ 065 6841848 **e-mail:** info@ennisgolfclub.com **web:** www.ennisgolfclub.com

On rolling hills, this immaculately manicured course presents an excellent challenge to both casual visitors and aspiring scratch golfers, with tree-lined fairways and well-protected greens.

18 Holes, 5706mtrs, Par 70, SSS 70, Course record 65. Club membership 1370.

Visitors Mon-Sat & BHs. Booking required Wed, Fri, Sat & BHs. Dress code. **Societies** welcome. **Green Fees** €35 per round (€40 Sat) **Facilities** ⑪ ⑩ by prior arrangement ⒧ ⊡ ⑩ ⚖ 🏠 ⑩ 🛒 ✦ **Location** signed near town **Hotel** ★★★ 78% HL Temple Gate, The Square, ENNIS, Co Clare ☎ 065 6823300 ▤ 065 6823300 70 en suite

Woodstock Golf and Country Club Shanaway Rd ☎ 065 6829463 & 6842406 ▤ 065 6820304 **e-mail:** proshopwoodstock@eircom.net **web:** www.woodstockgolfclub.com

This parkland course is set in 63 hectares and includes four holes where water is a major hazard. The sand-based greens offer a consistent surface for putting. The layout takes in beautiful views of the surrounding countryside and the lake feature at the 7th hole is challenging.

Woodstock Golf and Country Club: 18 Holes, 5864mtrs, Par 71, SSS 71. Club membership 350.

Visitors Mon-Sun and BHs. Booking required weekends & BHs. Handicap certificate. Dress code. Handicap certificate. **Societies** booking required. **Green Fees** €45 per 18 holes (€48

continued

IRELAND

weekends & BHs), €15 per 9 holes **Course Designer** Arthur Spring **Facilities** ⊕ ⍩ ▤ ⊑ ▦ ⋏ ⊟ ⊹ ◇ ⛟ ✧ **Leisure** sauna, gymnasium **Conf** Corporate Hospitality Days **Location** off N85

KILKEE   Map 1 B3

Kilkee East End
☎ 065 9056048   ▤ 065 9656977
e-mail: kilkeegolfclub@eircom.net
web: www.kilkeegolfclub.ie

Well-established course on the cliffs of Kilkee Bay. Mature championship course with a great variety of challenges - seaside holes, clifftop holes and holes that feature well-positioned water hazards. The spectacular 3rd hole hugs the cliff top. The ever present Atlantic breeze provides golfers with a real test.

18 Holes, 5555mtrs, Par 70, SSS 69, Course record 68. Club membership 770.

Visitors Mon-Sun & BHs. Booking required. Dress code. **Societies** booking required. **Green Fees** not confirmed **Course Designer** Eddie Hackett **Facilities** ⊕ ⍩ ▤ ▤ ⊑ ▦ ⋏ ⊟ ⊹ ⛟ ▤ ✧
Hotel ★★ 64% HL Halpins Town House, Erin Street, KILKEE, Co Clare ☎ 065 9056032 ▤ 065 9056032 12 en suite

KILRUSH   Map 1 B3

Kilrush Parknamoney
☎ 065 9051138   ▤ 065 9052633
web: www.kilrushgolfclub.com

Kilrush Golf Course: 18 Holes, 5474metres, Par 70, SSS 70, Course record 68.

Course Designer Arthur Spring **Location** 0.8km from Kilrush towards Ennis
Telephone for further details
Hotel ★★ 64% HL Halpins Town House, Erin Street, KILKEE, Co Clare ☎ 065 9056032 ▤ 065 9056032 12 en suite

LAHINCH   Map 1 B3

Lahinch
☎ 065 7081003   ▤ 065 7081592
e-mail: info@lahinchgolf.com
web: www.lahinchgolf.com

Originally designed by Tom Morris and later modified by Dr Alister MacKenzie, Lahinch has hosted every important Irish amateur fixture and the Home Internationals. The par five 4th - The Klondike - is played along a deep valley and over a huge dune; the par three 5th may be short, but calls for a blind shot over the ridge of a hill to a green hemmed in by hills on three sides.

Old Course: 18 Holes, 6355metres, Par 72, SSS 73. Castle Course: 18 Holes, 5080metres, Par 70, SSS 70. Club membership 1840.

Visitors Mon-Sun except BHs. Booking required. Handicap certificate. Dress code. **Societies** booking required. **Green Fees** Old Course €165, Castle Course €55 **Course Designer** Alister MacKenzie **Prof** R McCavery **Facilities** ⊕ ⍩ ▤ ⊑ ▦ ⋏ ⊟ ⊹ ✧ **Location** 3km W of Ennistymon on N67
Hotel ★★★ 68% HL Aran View House, Coast Road, DOOLIN, Co Clare ☎ 065 7074061 & 7074420 ▤ 065 7074061 19 en suite

MILLTOWN MALBAY   Map 1 B3

Spanish Point
☎ 065 7084198   ▤ 065 7084263
web: spanish-point.com

A nine-hole links course overlooking Spanish Point beach, with three elevated greens and four elevated tees. Holes comprise a par 5, 5 par 4's and 3 par 3's.

9 Holes, 4950mtrs, Par 68, SSS 66, Course record 59. Club membership 600.

Visitors Mon-Sun & BHs. Booking required Sun & BHs. **Societies** booking required. **Green Fees** €25 per 18 holes (€30 weekends & BHs) **Facilities** ▤ ⊑ ▦ ⋏ ⊟ ⊹ ✧ **Location** 3km SW of Miltown Malbay on N67
Hotel ★★ 64% HL Halpins Town House, Erin Street, KILKEE, Co Clare ☎ 065 9056032 ▤ 065 9056032 12 en suite

NEWMARKET-ON-FERGUS   Map 1 B3

Dromoland Castle Golf & Country Club
☎ 061 368444 & 368144   ▤ 061 363355/368498
web: www.dromoland.ie

Dromoland Castle Golf & Country Club: 18 Holes, 6240mtrs, Par 72, SSS 72, Course record 65.

Course Designer Ron Kirby & J. B. Carr **Location** 3km N on Limerick-Galway road
Telephone for further details
Hotel ★★★★★ HL Dromoland Castle, NEWMARKET-ON-FERGUS, Co Clare ☎ 061 368144 ▤ 061 368144 99 en suite

CO CORK

BANDON   Map 1 B2

Bandon Castlebernard
☎ 023 41111   ▤ 023 44690
e-mail: enquiries@bandongolfclub.com
web: www.bandongolfclub.com

Lovely parkland in pleasant countryside. Hazards of water, sand and trees. The course has been extended around the picturesque ruin of Castle Barnard.

18 Holes, 5854mtrs, Par 71, SSS 71. Club membership 900.

Visitors booking required Wed, weekends & BHs. Dress code. **Societies** booking required **Green Fees** not confirmed **Prof** Paddy O'Boyle **Facilities** ⊕ ⍩ ▤ ⊑ ▦ ⋏ ⊟ ⊹ ✧ ⛟ ✧ **Leisure** hard tennis courts **Location** 2.5km W
Guesthouse ★★★★ BB Glebe Country House, Ballinadee, BANDON, Co Cork ☎ 021 4778294 ▤ 021 4778294 4 en suite

BANTRY   Map 1 B2

Bantry Bay Donemark
☎ 027 50579   ▤ 027 53790
e-mail: info@bantrygolf.com
web: www.bantrygolf.com

Designed by Christy O'Connor Jnr, this challenging and rewarding course is idyllically set at the head of Bantry Bay. Testing holes include the par 5 of 487 metres and the little par 3 of 127 metres where accuracy is all-important.

continued

IRELAND

18 Holes, 6117mtrs, Par 71, SSS 72, Course record 71.
Club membership 600.

Visitors Mon-Sat & BHs. Booking required Mon, Fri, Sat & BHs.
Societies booking required. **Green Fees** not confirmed **Course**
Designer Christy O'Connor Jnr/Eddie Hackett **Facilities** ⑪ 🍴 🔟
🍺 🍷 🛒 🏡 ⛳ ✒ ⛳ **Conf** Corporate Hospitality Days
Location 3km N of town on N71
Hotel ★★★ 71% HL Westlodge, BANTRY, Co Cork ☎ 027 50360
📠 027 50360 90 en suite

BLACKROCK   Map 1 B2

Mahon Clover Hill
☎ 021 4294280

Mahon Golf Course: 18 Holes, 4862metres, Par 70, SSS 67,
Course record 64.

Course Designer Eddie Hackett
Telephone for further details
Hotel ★★★★ 78% HL Rochestown Park Hotel, Rochestown
Road, Douglas, CORK, Co Cork ☎ 021 4890800 📠 021 4890800
160 en suite

BLARNEY   Map 1 B2

Blarney Golf Resort Tower
☎ 021 4384477 📠 021 4516453
e-mail: reservations@blarneygolfresort.com
web: www.blarneygolfresort.com

You will come across some of the best greens in Ireland as you
wind your way along the course. Its location nestled in the stunning
Shournagh Valley creates a great atmosphere with breathtaking
views. The 601 yard par 5 has the signature of the designer, John Daly,
written all over it.

The Blarney Golf Resort: 18 Holes, 6712yds, Par 71,
Course record 69.

Visitors Mon-Sun & BHs. Booking required. Handicap certificate. Dress
code. **Societies** booking required. **Green Fees** not confirmed **Course**
Designer John Daly **Prof** Alan O'Meara **Facilities** ⑪ 🍴 🔟 🍺
🍷 🏡 ⛳ ◇ ✒ 🛒 ⛳ **Leisure** heated indoor swimming
pool, sauna, gymnasium **Conf** facs Corporate Hospitality Days
Hotel ★★★★ 76% HL Blarney Golf Resort, Tower, BLARNEY, Co
Cork ☎ 021 4384477 📠 021 4384477 117 en suite

CASTLETOWNBERE   Map 1 A2
(CASTLETOWN BEARHAVEN)

Berehaven Millcove
☎ 027 70700 📠 027 71957
e-mail: info@berehavengolf.com
web: www.berehavengolf.com

Scenic seaside links founded in 1902. Moderately difficult with four
holes over water. Testing nine-hole course with different tee positions
for the back nine. Water is a dominant feature and comes into play
at every hole.

9 Holes, 2624mtrs, Par 68, SSS 67, Course record 63.
Club membership 200.

Visitors Mon-Sun & BHs. **Societies** booking required. **Green Fees** not
confirmed **Course Designer** Royal Navy **Facilities** ⑪ 🍴 🔟 🍷
🍺 🏡 ⛳ ✒ **Leisure** hard tennis courts, sauna **Conf** facs
Corporate Hospitality Days **Location** 3km E from Castletownbere on
R572
Hotel ★★★ HL Sea View House Hotel, BALLYLICKEY, Co Cork
☎ 027 50073 & 50462 📠 027 50073 25 en suite

CHARLEVILLE   Map 1 B2

Charleville
☎ 063 81257 & 81515 📠 063 81274
e-mail: info@charlevillegolf.com
web: www.charlevillegolf.com

Wooded parkland course offering not too strenuous walking. Enjoyable
test of a golfer's ability with the emphasis on course management
rather than length from the tee.

West Course: 18 Holes, 5680metres, Par 71, SSS 69,
Course record 65.
East Course: 9 Holes, 6128metres, Par 72, SSS 72.
Club membership 1000.

Visitors Mon-Sun & BHs. Booking required Sun & BHs. Dress code
Societies booking required. **Green Fees** €25 (€35 weekends & BHs)
Course Designer Murphy/Barry (West)/Connaughton (East) **Prof** Jamie
O'Sullivan **Facilities** ⑪ 🍴 🔟 🍺 🍷 🍺 🏡 ⛳ ✒ 🛒 ⛳
⛳ **Conf** Corporate Hospitality Days **Location** 3km W of town centre
Hotel ★★★ CHH Longueville House, MALLOW, Co Cork
☎ 022 47156 & 47306 📠 022 47156 20 en suite

CLONAKILTY   Map 1 B2

Dunmore
☎ 023 33352

Dunmore Golf Course: 9 Holes, 4082metres, Par 64,
SSS 61, Course record 57.

Course Designer E Hackett **Location** 5.5km S of Clonakilty
Telephone for further details
Hotel ★★★★ 83% HL Inchydoney Island Lodge & Spa,
CLONAKILTY, Co Cork ☎ 023 33143 📠 023 33143 67 en suite

IRELAND

CORK
Map 1 B2

Cork Little Island
☎ 021 4353451 📠 021 4353410
e-mail: info@corkgolfclub.ie
web: www.corkgolfclub.ie

This championship-standard course is kept in superb condition and is playable all year round. Memorable and distinctive features include holes at the water's edge and in a disused quarry. The 4th hole is considered to be among the most attractive and testing holes in Irish golf.

18 Holes, 5910mtrs, Par 72, SSS 72, Course record 67. Club membership 750.

Visitors booking required. Handicap certificate. Dress code. **Societies** booking required. **Green Fees** €85 (€95 weekends) **Course Designer** Alister Mackenzie **Prof** Peter Hickey **Facilities** ⑪ ⍩⍩⍩⍩⍩⍩⍩⍩⍩⍩⍩⍩ **Conf** Corporate Hospitality Days **Location** 8km E of Cork on N25 **Hotel** ★★★ 74% HL Fitzgeralds Vienna Woods, GLANMIRE, CO CORK ☎ 021 4556800 & 021 4821146 📠 021 4556800 80 en suite

See advert on this page

Fota Island Resort see page 437
Fota Island
☎ 021 4883700 📠 021 4883713
e-mail: reservations@fotaisland.ie
web: www.fotaisland.ie

Muskerry Carrigrohane
☎ 021 4385297 📠 021 4516860
e-mail: muskgc@eircom.net
web: www.muskerrygolfclub.ie
An adventurous game is guaranteed at this course, with its wooded hillsides and the meandering Shournagh River coming into play at a number of holes. The 15th is a notable hole - not long, but very deep - and after that all you need to do to get back to the clubhouse is stay out of the water.

18 Holes, 5520mtrs, Par 71, SSS 70. Club membership 851.

Visitors Mon & Tue, Wed & Thu am. Sat & Sun pm. Booking required. Handicap certificate. Dress code. **Societies** booking required. **Green Fees** €40 per round (€50 weekends) **Course Designer** Dr A McKenzie **Prof** W M Lehane **Facilities** ⑪ ⍩⍩⍩⍩⍩ ⍩ ⍩ **Location** 4km W of Blarney

CORK GOLF CLUB
FOUNDED 1888 & REDESIGNED IN 1927 BY ALISTER MACKENZIE

Founded in 1888 and redesigned in 1927 by Alister Mackenzie, this championship parkland course is as graceful and mature as its age would suggest. Situated in the scenic Cork Harbour, the club has played host to major Amateur and Professional Championships over the years, including the Irish Open, Irish Professional Championships, Irish Close Championships and the National Finals.

Cork Golf Club, Little Island, Co. Cork
Tel: +353 21 4353 451
Fax: +353 21 4353 410
Email: info@corkgolfclub.ie

Hotel ★★★ 73% HL Blarney Castle, The Village Green, BLARNEY, Co Cork ☎ 021 4385116 📠 021 4385116 13 en suite

The Ted McCarthy Municipal Golf Course Blackrock
☎ 021 4292543 📠 021 4292604
web: www.mahongolfclub.com
The Ted McCarthy Municipal Course: 18 Holes, 5033mtrs, Par 70, SSS 66, Course record 65.

Course Designer E Hackett **Location** 3km from city centre **Telephone for further details** **Hotel** ★★★★ 78% HL Silver Springs Moran, Tivoli, CORK ☎ 021 4507533 📠 021 4507533 109 en suite

DONERAILE   Map 1 B2

Doneraile
☎ 022 24137 & 24379

Doneraile Golf Course: 9 Holes, 5055metres, Par 68, SSS 67, Course record 61.

Facilities ⑪ by prior arrangement ◎ by prior arrangement ▯ ▭ ▯ ▵ ✧ **Leisure** Doneraile National Heritage Park **Conf** Corporate Hospitality Days **Location** N of town centre
Telephone for further details
Hotel ★★★ 72% HL Springfort Hall Country House Hotel, MALLOW, Co Cork ☎ 022 21278 🗎 022 21278 49 en suite

DOUGLAS   Map 1 B2

Douglas
☎ 021 4895297 🗎 021 4367200
e-mail: admin@douglasgolfclub.ie
web: www.douglasgolfclub.ie

Well-maintained, relatively flat parkland course with panoramic views from the clubhouse. All tees and greens constructed to full USGA specifications.

18 Holes, 5607mtrs, Par 72, SSS 69. Club membership 900.

Visitors Mon, Thu, Fri & BHs. Weekends pm only. Booking required Thu & Fri. Dress code. **Societies** booking required. **Green Fees** €45 per round (€50 weekends and BHs) **Course Designer** Peter McEvoy **Prof** Gary Nicholson **Facilities** ⑪ ◎ ▯ ▭ ▯ ▵ ᵀ ✧ ✦ **Location** 6km S of Cork
Hotel ★★★★ 78% HL Rochestown Park Hotel, Rochestown Road, Douglas, CORK, Co Cork ☎ 021 4890800 🗎 021 4890800 160 en suite

FERMOY   Map 1 B2

Fermoy Corrin Cross
☎ 025 32694 (office) & 31472 (shop) 🗎 025 33072
web: www.fermoygolfclub.com

18 Holes, 5596mtrs, Par 70, SSS 69, Course record 66.

Course Designer John Harris **Location** S of town off N8, signed
Telephone for further details
Hotel ★★★ CHH Longueville House, MALLOW, Co Cork ☎ 022 47156 & 47306 🗎 022 47156 20 en suite

GLENGARRIFF   Map 1 B2

Glengarriff
☎ 027 63150 🗎 027 63575

Glengarriff Golf Course: 9 Holes, 2042metres, Par 66, SSS 62.

Facilities ▵ ᵀ ✧ **Location** on N71
Telephone for further details
Hotel ★★★ 71% HL Westlodge, BANTRY, Co Cork ☎ 027 50360 🗎 027 50360 90 en suite

KANTURK   Map 1 B2

Kanturk Fairyhill
☎ 029 50534 🗎 029 20951
e-mail: kanturkgolfclub@eircom.net

Scenic parkland course set in the heart of the Duhallow region with superb mountain views. It provides a good test of skill for golfers of all standards, with tight fairways requiring accurate driving and precise approach shots to small and tricky greens.

18 Holes, 5721mtrs, Par 71, SSS 69, Course record 64. Club membership 600.

Visitors Mon-Sun & BHs. Booking required Fri-Sun & BHs. Dress code. **Societies** booking required **Green Fees** not confirmed **Course Designer** Richard Barry **Facilities** ⑪ by prior arrangement ◎ by prior arrangement ▯ ▭ ▯ ▵ ᵇ✦ ✧ ✦ **Location** 1.6km SW of Kanturk
Hotel ★★★ CHH Longueville House, MALLOW, Co Cork ☎ 022 47156 & 47306 🗎 022 47156 20 en suite

KINSALE   Map 1 B2

Kinsale Farrangalway
☎ 021 4774722 🗎 021 4773114
e-mail: office@kinsalegolf.com
web: www.kinsalegolf.com

Set in farmland surrounded by rolling countryside. A stiff yet fair challenge to be enjoyed by all standards of golfers.

Farrangalway: 18 Holes, 6043metres, Par 71, SSS 71, Course record 70.
Ringenane: 9 Holes, 4936metres, Par 70, SSS 66. Club membership 880.

Visitors Mon-Sun & BHs. Booking required weekends & BHs. Dress code. Handicap certificate. **Societies** booking required. **Green Fees** €35 (€40 Fri-Sun) **Course Designer** Jack Kenneally **Prof** Ger Broderick **Facilities** ⑪ ◎ ▯ ▭ ▯ ▵ ᵇ✦ ᵀ ✧ ᵇ✦ ✧ **Location** Farrangalway course N off R607, Ringenane course N off R600
Hotel ★★★★ 73% HL Trident, Worlds End, KINSALE, Co Cork ☎ 021 4779300 🗎 021 4779300 75 en suite

Old Head
☎ 021 4778444 🗎 021 4778022
e-mail: info@oldhead.com
web: www.oldhead.com

Spectacular location on a promontory jutting out into the Atlantic. As well as bringing the sea and cliffs into play, you have to contend with strong prevailing winds - a fine test for serious golfers.

Old Head Golf Links: 18 Holes, 6583meters, Par 72, SSS 73. Club membership 350.

Visitors Mon-Sun & BHs. Booking required. Handicap certificate. Dress code. **Societies** booking required. **Green Fees** not confirmed **Course Designer** R Kirby/J Carr/P Merrigan/E Hackett **Prof** Danny Brassil **Facilities** ⑪ ◎ ▯ ▭ ▯ ▵ ᵇ✦ ᵀ ◇ ✧ ᵇ✦ ✦ **Leisure** sauna, gymnasium, spa & beauty treatment rooms **Conf** facs Corporate Hospitality Days **Location** On R600 towards Cork, signed
Hotel ★★★ 73% HL Blue Haven, 3 Pearse Street, KINSALE, Co Cork ☎ 021 4772209 🗎 021 4772209 17 en suite

FOTA ISLAND RESORT

CO CORK - CORK - MAP 1 B2

The landscape of this attractive course, set on a 780 acre island in Cork harbour, is magnificent. The Deerpark Course was designed in 1993 by Christy O'Connor and Peter McEvoy and upgraded in 1999 under the direction of the Canadian designer, Jeff Howes. It hosted the 2001 and 2002 Irish Open Championships and has recently been transformed by the addition of nine new holes. These have been incorporated into the original design, with the result that three courses have now been created, depending on how the new holes are combined with the existing ones. In addition to this innovative development, there is a hi-tech golf academy where computer systems can analyse your swing, either on the spot, or by e-mail! All this, coupled with the luxurious clubhouse and hotel complex, make this course akin to an American style country club.

Fota Island ☎ 021 4883700 📠 021 4883713
e-mail: reservations@fotaisland.ie **web:** www.fotaisland.ie
Deerpark: 18 Holes, 6334mtrs, Par 71, SSS 73, Course record 63.
Belvelly: 18 Holes, 6511mtrs, Par 72.
Barryscourt: 18 Holes, 6732mtrs, Par 73. Club membership 600.
Visitors Mon-Sun & BHs. Booking required. Dress code. **Societies** welcome. **Green Fees** from €60 per round
Course Designer Jeff Howes **Prof** Kevin Morris **Facilities** ⊕ ↿◯⫞ ╚ ⌷ ⫞⎕ ⅄ ⌂ ⫪ ◇ ⌀ 🛍 ⌀ 🏌
Leisure heated indoor swimming pool, sauna, gymnasium, golf academy, spa treatments **Conf** facs Corporate
Hospitality Days **Location** E of Cork. N25 exit for Cobh, 500 metres on right
Hotel ★★★ 79% HL Midleton Park Hotel & Spa, MIDLETON, Co Cork ☎ 021 4631767 📠 021 4631767
40 en suite

LITTLE ISLAND
Map 1 B2

Harbour Point Clash Rd
☎ 021 4353094 🖷 021 4354408
18 Holes, 5883metres, Par 72, SSS 71, Course record 71.
Course Designer Patrick Merrigan **Location** 8km E of Cork on Rosslare road
Telephone for further details
Hotel ★★★★ 78% HL Silver Springs Moran, Tivoli, CORK
☎ 021 4507533 🖷 021 4507533 109 en suite

MACROOM
Map 1 B2

Macroom, Lackaduve
☎ 026 41072 & 42615   🖷 026 41391
e-mail: mcroomgc@iol.ie
web: macroomgolfclub.com
A particularly scenic parkland course located on undulating ground along the banks of the River Sullane. Bunkers and mature trees make a variable and testing course and the 12th has a 73-metre carry over the river to the green.
18 Holes, 5574mtrs, Par 71, SSS 69, Course record 65.
Club membership 750.
Visitors booking required Wed, Fri-Sun & BHs. Dress code.
Societies booking required. **Green Fees** not confirmed **Course Designer** Jack Kenneally/Eddie Hackett **Facilities** ⑪ ⑩ ⓑ ☖ ⑴ ⚐ ⎙ 🔩 ✐ **Location** through castle entrance in town square
Hotel ★★★ 78% HL Castle, Main Street, MACROOM, Co Cork
☎ 026 41074 🖷 026 41074 58 en suite

MALLOW
Map 1 B2

Mallow Ballyellis
☎ 022 21145   🖷 022 42501
web: www.mallowgolfclub.net

18 Holes, 5769mtrs, Par 72, SSS 71, Course record 66.
Course Designer D W Wishart **Location** 1.6km E of Mallow
Telephone for further details
Hotel ★★★ CHH Longueville House, MALLOW, Co Cork
☎ 022 47156 & 47306 🖷 022 47156 20 en suite

MIDLETON
Map 1 C2

East Cork Gortacrue
☎ 021 4631687 & 4631273   🖷 021 4613695
e-mail: eastcorkgolfclub@eircom.net
web: eastcorkgolfclub.com
A well-wooded course calling for accuracy of shots.
18 Holes, 5152mtrs, Par 69, SSS 66, Course record 64.
Club membership 820.
Visitors Mon-Sun & BHs. Booking required weekends & BHs.
Societies booking requested **Green Fees** not confirmed **Course Designer** E Hackett **Prof** Don MacFarlane **Facilities** ⑪ ⑩ ⓑ ☖ ⑴ ⚐ ⎙ ⋔ ✐ ⚑ **Location** 3km N of Midleton on A626
Hotel ★★★ 79% HL Midleton Park Hotel & Spa, MIDLETON, Co Cork
☎ 021 4631767 🖷 021 4631767 40 en suite

Water Rock Water Rock
☎ 021 4613499
e-mail: waterrock@eircom.net
web: www.waterrockgolfcourse.com
A pay and play parkland course on the banks of the Owencurra river, employing international standards and construction including mildly contoured sand based greens. The course comprises five par 3s and three par 5s in two loops. The signature hole is known as Swan Lake, the 240yd 12th par 3, plays over water to a contoured green.
Water Rock Golf Course: 18 Holes, 6223yds, Par 70, SSS 70.
Visitors Mon-Sun & BHs. Booking required Fri, weekends & BHs.
Societies welcome. **Green Fees** €32 (€38 weekends & BHs) **Course Designer** Patrick Merrigan **Facilities** ⑪ ⑩ ⓑ ☖ ⑴ ⚐ ⋔ 🔩 ✐ **Location** next to N25 on outskirts of Midleton
Hotel ★★★ 79% HL Midleton Park Hotel & Spa, MIDLETON, Co Cork
☎ 021 4631767 🖷 021 4631767 40 en suite

MITCHELSTOWN
Map 1 B2

Mitchelstown Limerick Rd
☎ 025 24072 & 086 8263089   🖷 025 86631
e-mail: info@mitchelstown-golf.com
web: www.mitchelstown-golf.com
Attractive, gently undulating parkland course set in the Golden Vale, noted for the quality of the greens, the magnificent views of the Galtee Mountains and its friendly atmosphere. Strategically placed sand bunkers will need accurate play. The course offers woodland and water in a undulating parkland setting.
18 Holes, 5773mtrs, Par 71, SSS 71. Club membership 850.
Visitors Mon-Sun & BHs. Booking required weekends & BHs.. Dress code. **Societies** booking required. **Green Fees** €20 per round (€25 weekends) **Course Designer** David Jones **Facilities** ⑪ ⓑ ☖ ⑴ ⚐ ✐ 🔩 ✐ ⚑ **Location** 1km from Mitchelstown
Hotel ★★★ CHH Longueville House, MALLOW, Co Cork
☎ 022 47156 & 47306 🖷 022 47156 20 en suite

IRELAND

MONKSTOWN — Map 1 B2

Monkstown Parkgariffe, Monkstown
☎ 021 4841376
e-mail: office@monkstowngolfclub.com
web: www.monkstowngolfclub.com

Undulating parkland with five tough finishing holes.
18 Holes, 5441mtrs, Par 70, SSS 68, Course record 66.
Club membership 960.

Visitors Mon & Thu-Sun except BHs. Dress code. Handicap certificate. **Societies** booking required. **Green Fees** €43 per day (€50 weekends) **Course Designer** Peter O'Hare & Tom Carey **Prof** Batt Murphy **Facilities** ⚐ ⏐◎⏐ ⓛ ⊑ ⏛ ⅄ 🏠 ⛾ ⚡ 🚗 ⚡ ⏛ **Conf** Corporate Hospitality Days **Location** 0.8km SE of Monkstown
Hotel ★★★★ 77% HL Carrigaline Court Hotel, CARRIGALINE, Co. Cork ☎ 021 4852100 ▤ 021 4852100 91 en suite

SKIBBEREEN — Map 1 B2

Skibbereen & West Carbery Licknavar
☎ 028 21227 ▤ 028 22994
web: www.skibbgolf.com
18 Holes, 5490mtrs, Par 71, SSS 69, Course record 66.
Course Designer Jack Kenneally **Location** 1.6km SW on R595
Telephone for further details

YOUGHAL — Map 1 C2

Youghal Knockaverry
☎ 024 92787 & 92861 ▤ 024 92641
e-mail: youghalgolfclub@eircom.net
web: www.youghalgolfclub.ie
Youghal offers a good test of golf and is well maintained for year-round play. There are panoramic views of Youghal Bay and the Blackwater estuary.
18 Holes, 5976mtrs, Par 71, SSS 71, Course record 66.
Club membership 1050.

Visitors dress code. Handicap certificate. **Societies** booking required. **Green Fees** not confirmed **Course Designer** Jeff Howes Golf Design **Prof** Liam Burns **Facilities** ⚐ ⏐◎⏐ ⓛ ⊑ ⏛ ⅄ 🏠 ⛾ ⚡ ⚡ **Conf** facs Corporate Hospitality Days **Location** off N25
Hotel ★★★ 72% HL Quality Hotel Youghal, Redbarn, YOUGHAL, CO CORK ☎ 024 93050 ▤ 024 93050 25 en suite

CO DONEGAL

BALLYBOFEY — Map 1 C5

Ballybofey & Stranorlar Stranorlar
☎ 074 9131093 ▤ 074 9130158
e-mail: info@ballybofeyandstranorlar
web: www.ballybofeyandstranorlargolfclub.com
A most scenic course incorporating pleasant valleys backed by mountains with three of its holes bordered by a lake. There are three par 3s on the first nine and two on the second. The most difficult hole is the long uphill par 4 16th. The only par 5 is the 7th.
18 Holes, 5366mtrs, Par 68, SSS 68, Course record 64.
Club membership 648.

Visitors Mon-Sun & BHs. Booking required Tue, weekends & BHs. **Societies** welcome. **Green Fees** €25 (€30 weekends) **Course Designer** P C Carr **Facilities** ⚐ ⏐◎⏐ ⓛ ⊑ ⏛ ⅄ 🏠 ⛾ ⚡ ⚡ **Conf** facs **Location** 0.4km E of Stranorlar

BALLYLIFFIN — Map 1 C6

Ballyliffin
☎ 074 9376119 ▤ 074 9376672
e-mail: info@ballyliffingolfclub.com
web: www.ballyliffingolfclub.com
The Old links is a traditional course with rolling fairways, surrounded by sand dunes and bounded on one side by the ocean and has been upgraded by Nick Faldo. The 18-hole Glashedy course offers a modern championship test and has hosted the European Tour Irish Seniors Open.
Old Links: 18 Holes, 6273metres, Par 71, SSS 72,
Course record 67.
Glashedy Links: 18 Holes, 7135yds, Par 72, SSS 74,
Course record 68. Club membership 1400.

Visitors Mon-Sun & BHs. Booking required. Handicap certificate. Dress code. **Societies** welcome. **Green Fees** not confirmed **Course Designer** Nick Faldo/Tom Craddock/Pat Ruddy **Prof** John P Dolan **Facilities** ⚐ ⏐◎⏐ ⓛ ⊑ ⏛ ⅄ 🏠 ⛾ ⚡ ⚡ **Conf** facs Corporate Hospitality Days **Location** off R238
Guesthouse ★★★★ BB Mount Royd Country Home, CARRIGANS, Co Donegal ☎ 074 914 0163 ▤ 074 914 0163 4 en suite

BUNCRANA — Map 1 C6

Buncrana Railway Rd, Ballymacarry
☎ 074 9362279 & 074 9320749
e-mail: buncranagc@eircom.net
A nine-hole course with a very challenging par 3 3rd hole with all carry out of bounds on either side. Situated on the banks of The White Strand, overlooking the beautiful Lough Swilly. The 9 hole course offers a challenge to golfers of all ability.
9 Holes, 1969mtrs, Par 62, SSS 60, Course record 59.
Club membership 200.

Visitors Mon-Sun & BHs. Booking required weekends. Handicap certificate. **Societies** booking required. **Green Fees** not confirmed **Prof** Jim Doherty **Facilities** ⊑ ⅄ 🏠 ⚡ **Conf** facs
Guesthouse ★★★★ BB Mount Royd Country Home, CARRIGANS, Co Donegal ☎ 074 914 0163 ▤ 074 914 0163 4 en suite

North West Lisfannon
☎ 074 9361715   📄 074 9363284
web: www.northwestgolfclub.com
18 Holes, 5457mtrs, Par 70, SSS 70, Course record 64.
Course Designer Thompson Davy **Location** 1.6km S of Buncrana on R238
Telephone for further details
Guesthouse ★★★★ BB Mount Royd Country Home, CARRIGANS, Co Donegal ☎ 074 914 0163 📄 074 914 0163   4 en suite

BUNDORAN   Map 1 B5

Bundoran
☎ 071 9841302   📄 071 9842014
web: www.bundorangolfclub.com
18 Holes, 5688metres, Par 70, SSS 70, Course record 67.
Course Designer Harry Vardon **Location** off Main St onto Sligo-Derry road
Telephone for further details
Hotel ★★★ HL Sandhouse, ROSSNOWLAGH, Co Donegal
☎ 071 9851777 📄 071 9851777   55 en suite

CRUIT ISLAND (AN CHRUIT)   Map 1 B5

Cruit Island Kincasslagh
☎ 074 9543296   📄 074 9548028
Cruit Island Golf Course: 9 Holes, 4833mtrs, Par 68, SSS 66, Course record 62.
Course Designer Michael Doherty **Location** 8km N of Dungloe
Hotel ★★★ 73% HL Arnold's, DUNFANAGHY, Co Donegal
☎ 074 9136208 📄 074 9136208   30 en suite

DUNFANAGHY   Map 1 C6

Dunfanaghy Kill
☎ 074 9136335   📄 074 9136684
e-mail: dunfanaghygolf@eircom.net
web: www.dunfanaghygolfclub.com
Overlooking Sheephaven Bay, the course has a flat central area with three difficult streams to negotiate. At the Port-na-Blagh end there are five marvellous holes, including one across the beach, while at the Horn Head end, the last five holes are a test for any golfer.
18 Holes, 5247mtrs, Par 68, SSS 66, Course record 63. Club membership 335.
Visitors Mon-Sun & BHs. Booking required Wed, weekends & BHs. Handicap certificate. Dress code. **Societies** booking required. **Green Fees** not confirmed **Course Designer** Harry Vardon **Facilities** 🍺 🍽 🛗 🚻 🛒 🏌 🚜 🏊 🏆 **Conf** facs **Location** 30m W of Letterkenny on N56
Hotel ★★★ 73% HL Arnold's, DUNFANAGHY, Co Donegal
☎ 074 9136208 📄 074 9136208   30 en suite

GREENCASTLE   Map 1 C6

Greencastle Greencastle
☎ 074 9381013   📄 074 9381015
e-mail: info@greencastlegolfclub.net
web: ww.greencastlegolfclub.net
A links course along the shores of Lough Foyle, surrounded by rocky headlands and sandy beaches.
18 Holes, 5334mtrs, Par 69, SSS 67, Course record 65. Club membership 750.
Visitors Mon-Sun & BHs. Dress code. **Societies** booking required
Green Fees €30 per day, €25 per round (€40/€30 weekends & BHs)
Course Designer E Hackett/D Jones **Facilities** 🍺 🍽 🛗 🚻 🛒 🏊 🏌 🏆 🚜 🏌

LETTERKENNY   Map 1 C5

Letterkenny Barnhill
☎ 074 9121150   📄 074 9121175
e-mail: info@letterkennygolfclub.com
web: www.letterkennygolfclub.com
The fairways are wide and generous, but the rough, when you find it, is short, tough and mean. The flat and untiring terrain on the shores of Lough Swilly provides good holiday golf. The first 11 holes incorporate 7 lakes and 5 greens and bunkers on all holes. The next 7 holes have been redesigned with bunkers and fairway mounding and 2 new greens
18 Holes, 5705mtrs, Par 72, SSS 71, Course record 65. Club membership 700.
Visitors dress code. **Societies** booking required **Green Fees** phone
Course Designer Eddie Hacket **Facilities** 🍺 🍽 🛗 🚻 🛒 🏊 🏠 🏌 🏆 🚜 🏌 **Conf** facs Corporate Hospitality Days
Location 3km NE of town on R245
Hotel ★★★ 70% HL Downings Bay, Downings, LETTERKENNY, Co Donegal ☎ 074 9155586 & 9155770 📄 074 9155586   40 en suite

MOVILLE   Map 1 C6

Redcastle
☎ 074 9385555   📄 074 9385444
web: www.carltonredcastlehotel.ie
Redcastle Golf Course: 9 Holes, 2846mtrs, Par 35.
Prof James Gallagher **Facilities** 🍺 🍽 🛗 🚻 🛒 🏊 🏠 🏌 ◇ 🏌 🚜 🏌 **Leisure** gymnasium **Conf** facs Corporate Hospitality Days
Location 6km SW on R238
Telephone for further details
Hotel ★★ 67% HL Malin, Malin Town, INISHOWEN, Co Donegal
☎ 074 9370606 📄 074 9370606   18 en suite

NARIN (NARAN)   Map 1 B5

Narin & Portnoo
☎ 074 9545107   📄 074 9545994
e-mail: narinportnoo@eircom.net
web: www.narinportnoogolfclub.ie
Seaside links with every hole presenting its own special feature, the signature hole being the chasm-crossing 8th. One of the few natural links layouts remaining, with undulating fairways and greens. Fine views of Gweebarra Bay are visible from the course with an adjacent award winning beach. The links will test a player's iron play, with raised greens a common feature. *continued*

18 Holes, 6269mtrs, Par 73, SSS 74, Course record 68. Club membership 700.

Visitors Mon-Sat except BHs. **Societies** booking required. **Green Fees** €55 per day (€60 Sat) **Course Designer** Leo Wallace/Hugh McNeill **Facilities** 🕦 🍴 🏓 🖵 ⛴ 🛄 🖼 🏌 🛺 🏌 **Conf** Corporate Hospitality Days **Location** off R261 **Hotel** ★★★ HL Sandhouse, ROSSNOWLAGH, Co Donegal ☎ 071 9851777 📄 071 9851777 55 en suite

PORTSALON
Map 1 C6

Portsalon
☎ 074 9159459 📄 074 9159919
e-mail: portsalongolfclub@eircom.net
web: www.portsalongolfclub.ie

Another course blessed by nature. The golden beaches of Ballymastocker Bay lie at one end, while the beauty of Lough Swilly and the Inishowen Peninsula beyond is a distracting but pleasant feature to the west. Situated on the Fanad Peninsula, this lovely links course provides untiring holiday golf at its best.

18 Holes, 6185mtrs, Par 72, SSS 72, Course record 71. Club membership 500.

Visitors booking required. Handicap certificate. Dress code. **Societies** booking required. **Green Fees** not confirmed **Course Designer** Pat Ruddy **Facilities** 🕦 🍴 🏓 🖵 ⛴ 🛄 🛺 🏌 **Conf** Corporate Hospitality Days **Location** 22m N of Letterkenny on R246 **Hotel** ★★★ 80% HL Fort Royal Hotel, Fort Royal, RATHMULLAN, Co Donegal ☎ 074 9158100 📄 074 9158100 15 en suite

RATHMULLAN
Map 1 C6

Otway Whiteleas, Ramelton
☎ 074 9158319
e-mail: otway_golf_club@eircom.net

One of the oldest courses in Ireland, created in 1861 by British military personnel as a recreational facility.

Otway Golf Course: 9 Holes, 3872mtrs, Par 64, SSS 60, Course record 60. Club membership 112.

Visitors dress code. Handicap certificate. **Societies** booking required. **Green Fees** €15 per day (€20 weekends) **Facilities** 🍴 🖵 🛄 **Conf** Corporate Hospitality Days **Location** in Rathmullan, turn left at Mace convenience store, head for Knockalla coast Rd. 2m signed **Hotel** ★★★ 80% HL Fort Royal Hotel, Fort Royal, RATHMULLAN, Co Donegal ☎ 074 9158100 📄 074 9158100 15 en suite

ROSEPENNA
Map 1 C6

Rosapenna Downings
☎ 074 9155301 & 9155000 📄 074 9155128
e-mail: golf@rosapenna.ie
web: www.rosapenna.ie

Dramatic links courses offering a challenging round. Originally designed by Tom Morris and later modified by James Braid and Harry Vardon, it includes features such as bunkers in mid-fairway. The best part of the links runs in the low valley along the ocean. The Sandy Hills links course is newer, having opened in 2003. Both courses are considered among the best in Ireland.

Old Tom Morris: 18 Holes, 5734mtrs, Par 70, SSS 71. Sandy Hills Links: 18 Holes, 5812metres, Par 71. Club membership 400.

Visitors contact club for details. **Societies** booking required **Green Fees** Old Tom Morris €45 per round (€50 weekends & €60 BHs). Sandy Hills Links €60/€80 **Course Designer** Old Tom Morris **Prof** Brian Patterson **Facilities** 🕦 🍴 🏓 🖵 ⛴ 🛄 🖼 🛺 🏌 🛺 🏌 **Leisure** hard tennis courts, heated indoor swimming pool **Conf** facs **Location** NE of village off R248 **Hotel** ★★★ 70% HL Downings Bay, Downings, LETTERKENNY, CO DONEGAL ☎ 074 9155586 & 9155770 📄 074 9155586 40 en suite

GWEEDORE
Map 1 B6

Gweedore Derrybeg
☎ 074 9531140
e-mail: eugenemccafferty@hotmail.com
web: www.gweedoregolfclub.com

With breath taking scenery, this 9-hole links course provides plenty of challenge with two subtle par 3s and the par 5 5th/14th at 556yards into the prevailing west wind is a monster.

Gweedore Golf Course: 9 Holes, 5699mtrs, Par 71, SSS 68, Course record 65. Club membership 150.

Visitors Mon-Sun & BHs. Booking required. Dress code. **Societies** booking required. **Green Fees** €20 per day **Facilities** 🏓 🖵 ⛴ 🛄 🏌 🏌 **Location** 37m NW of Letterkenny on N56 **Hotel** ★★★ 70% HL Ostan Na Rosann, Mill Road, DUNGLOE, Co Donegal ☎ 074 9522444 📄 074 9522444 48 en suite

CO DUBLIN

BALBRIGGAN
Map 1 D4

Balbriggan Blackhall
☎ 01 8412229 📄 01 8413927
e-mail: balbriggangolfclub@eircom.net
web: www.balbriggangolfclub.com

A parkland course with great variations and good views of the Mourne and Cooley mountains.

18 Holes, 5922mtrs, Par 71, SSS 72, Course record 67. Club membership 750.

Visitors Mon-Sun & BHs. Booking required weekends & BHs. Dress code. **Societies** booking required. **Green Fees** not confirmed **Course Designer** E. Connaughton **Prof** Nigel Howley **Facilities** 🕦 🍴 🏓 🖵 ⛴ 🛄 🛺 🏌 **Location** 1km S of Balbriggan on N1 **Hotel** ★★★ 70% HL Boyne Valley Hotel & Country Club, Stameen, Dublin Road, DROGHEDA, Co Louth ☎ 041 9837737 📄 041 9837737 73 en suite

IRELAND

BALLYBOGHILL · Map 1 D4

Hollywood Lakes
☎ 01 8433406 📠 01 8433002
web: www.hollywoodlakesgolfclub.com

18 Holes, 6246mtrs, Par 72, SSS 72, Course record 67.
Course Designer Mel Flanagan **Location** N of village on R108
Telephone for further details
Hotel ★★★ 71% HL Waterside House, DONABATE, Co Dublin
☎ 01 8436153 📠 01 8436153 35 en suite

BRITTAS · Map 1 D4

Slade Valley Lynch Park
☎ 01 4582183 & 4582739 📠 01 4582784
e-mail: info@sladevalleygolfclub.ie
web: www.sladevalleygolfclub.ie

This is a course for a relaxing game, being fairly easy and in pleasant surroundings.

18 Holes, 5388mtrs, Par 69, SSS 68, Course record 65.
Club membership 954.

Visitors Mon-Fri, Sun & BHs. Booking required Sun & BHs. Dress code.
Societies welcome. **Green Fees** not confirmed **Course Designer** W
Sullivan & D O Brien **Prof** John Dignam **Facilities** ⊕ ⑩ ⓛ ♤
⬚ ⚑ ⌀ 🛒 ⚬ **Location** off N81

CASTLEKNOCK · Map 1 D4

Elm Green
☎ 01 8200797 📠 01 8226668
e-mail: elmgreen@golfdublin.com
web: www.golfdublin.com

Located a short distance from Dublin, beside Phoenix Park, with a fine layout, tricky greens and year round playability.

Elm Green Golf Course: 18 Holes, 5300mtrs, Par 71, SSS 66, Course record 65. Club membership 800.

Visitors Mon-Sat & BHs. Booking required. **Societies** booking required. **Green Fees** not confirmed **Course Designer** Eddie Hackett **Prof** Paul McGahan & Karl Kelly **Facilities** ⊕ ⑩ ⓛ ⬚ ♤ ⬚ ⚑ ⌀ 🛒 ⚬ 🏴 **Leisure** pitch and putt course. **Conf** facs Corporate Hospitality Days **Location** off N3
Hotel ★★★ 77% HL Finnstown Country House Hotel, Newcastle Road, LUCAN, Co Dublin ☎ 01 6010700 📠 01 6010700 81 en suite

Luttrellstown Castle Dublin15
☎ 01 8089988 📠 01 8089989
e-mail: golf@luttrellstown.ie
web: www.luttrellstown.ie

Set in the grounds of the magnificent 560-acre Luttrellstown Castle estate, this championship course has been re-designed to enhance the golfing experience. The layout respects and retains the integrity of the mature and ancient parkland. The course is renowned for the quality of its greens and facilities.

Luttrellstown Castle Golf & Country Club: 18 Holes, 6378metres, Par 72, SSS 73, Course record 66. Club membership 400.

Visitors Mon-Sun & BHs. Booking required. Dress code. Handicap certificate. **Societies** booking required. **Green Fees** not confirmed **Course Designer** Donald Steele **Prof** Edward Doyle **Facilities** ⊕ ⑩

ⓛ ⬚ ⚑ ♤ ⬚ ⚑ ⌀ 🛒 ⚬ 🏴 **Leisure** fishing, clay shooting **Conf** facs Corporate Hospitality Days **Location** W of town off R121
Hotel ★★★ 77% HL Finnstown Country House Hotel, Newcastle Road, LUCAN, Co Dublin ☎ 01 6010700 📠 01 6010700 81 en suite

CLOGHRAN · Map 1 D4

Forrest Little
☎ 01 8401183 & 8401763 📠 01 8908499
e-mail: margaret@forrestlittle.ie
web: www.forrestlittle.ie

A well-manicured and mature parkland with many water features, large sand based greens and undulating fairways, playable all year.

18 Holes, 5902mtrs, Par 71, SSS 72, Course record 68.
Club membership 1000.

Visitors Mon, Tue, Thu & Fri. Booking required Wed. Dress code. Handicap certificate. **Societies** booking required. **Green Fees** €50 per 18 holes **Course Designer** Mr Hawtree snr **Prof** Tony Judd **Facilities** ⊕ ⑩ ⓛ ⬚ ⚑ ♤ ⬚ ⚑ ⌀ 🛒 ⚬ **Location** N of Dublin Airport off R132
Hotel ★★★ 71% HL Waterside House, DONABATE, CO DUBLIN ☎ 01 8436153 📠 01 8436153 35 en suite

DONABATE · Map 1 D4

Balcarrick Corballis
☎ 01 8436957 📠 01 8436228
e-mail: balcarr@iol.ie
web: www.balcarrickgolfclub.com

Splendid 18-hole estuary course with many challenging holes, located close to the sea and exposed to the elements.

18 Holes, 6273mtrs, Par 73, SSS 71. Club membership 750.
Visitors Mon-Sun & BHs. Booking required Thu, weekends & BHs. Dress code. **Societies** booking required **Green Fees** not confirmed **Course Designer** Roger Jones **Prof** Stephen Rayfus **Facilities** ⊕ ⑩ ⓛ ⬚ ⚑ ♤ ⬚ ⚬ 🛒 ⚬ **Location** off R126
Hotel ★★★ 74% HL Deer Park Hotel, Golf & Spa, HOWTH, Co Dublin ☎ 01 8322624 📠 01 8322624 75 en suite

Donabate, Balcarrick
☎ 01 8436346 📠 01 8434488
e-mail: info@donabategolfclub.com
web: www.donabategolfclub.com

A challenging 27 hole golf course with mature tree lined fairways which has been rebuilt to USGA specifications. All greens are sand based and the course is playable all year round.

27 Holes, 6068mtrs, Par 72, SSS 73, Course record 66.
Club membership 1200.

Visitors Mon, Tue, Thu-Sun & BHs. Booking required weekends & BHs. Dress code. Handicap certificate. **Societies** welcome. **Green Fees** not confirmed **Course Designer** Pat Suttle **Prof** Hugh Jackson **Facilities** ⊕ ⑩ ⓛ ⬚ ⚑ ♤ ⬚ ⚑ ⌀ 🛒 ⚬ **Conf** Corporate Hospitality Days **Location** E of town off R126
Hotel ★★★ 74% HL Deer Park Hotel, Golf & Spa, HOWTH, Co Dublin ☎ 01 8322624 📠 01 8322624 75 en suite

Island Corballis
☎ 01 8436205 🖨 01 8436860
e-mail: info@theislandgolfclub.com
web: www.theislandgolfclub.com

An old links course surrounded by the Irish Sea, Donabate beach and the Broadmeadow estuary, nestling between the highest sand dunes of any links course in Ireland. The rugged beauty cannot fail to impress. An Irish qualifying course for the Open Championship from 2005.

The Island Golf Club: 18 Holes, 6206mtrs, Par 71, SSS 63. Club membership 1100.

Visitors Mon, Tue & Fri except BHs. Booking required. Dress code. **Societies** booking required. **Green Fees** €135 per 18 holes **Course Designer** Martin Hawtree **Prof** Marcus Casey **Facilities** ⓣ ⦿ 🖳 ⛳ 🍴 ⚏ 🏠 ⬚ 🏌 🛒 ⚐ **Conf** facs Corporate Hospitality Days **Location** off R126
Hotel ★★★ 74% HL Deer Park Hotel, Golf & Spa, HOWTH, Co Dublin ☎ 01 8322624 🖨 01 8322624 75 en suite

Turvey Golf Club & Hotel Turvey Av
☎ 01 8435169 🖨 01 8435179
e-mail: turveygc@eircom.net
web: www.turveygolfclub.com

A mature parkland course with oak trees over 220 years old. A test of golf for all levels of golfer.

Turvey Golf Club & Hotel: 18 Holes, 6068mtrs, Par 71, SSS 72, Course record 64. Club membership 500.

Visitors Mon-Sun & BHs. Booking required weekends & BHs. Dress code. Handicap certificate. **Societies** booking required. **Green Fees** not confirmed **Course Designer** P McGurk **Facilities** ⓣ ⦿ 🖳 ⛳ 🍴 ⚏ ◇ 🏠 🛒 ⚐ 🏌 **Conf** facs Corporate Hospitality Days **Location** M1, 1st junct N after Dublin airport, 1m on N1 Turvey signed on right
Hotel ★★★ 74% HL Deer Park Hotel, Golf & Spa, HOWTH, Co Dublin ☎ 01 8322624 🖨 01 8322624 75 en suite

---

DUBLIN
Map 1 D4

Carrickmines Carrickmines
☎ 01 2955972

Meadowland and partly hilly gorseland course.

The Carrickmines Golf Club: 9 Holes, 4644mtrs, Par 71, SSS 69. Club membership 600.

Visitors Mon, Tue, Thu, Fri & Sun except BHs. Handicap certificate. Dress code. Handicap certificate. **Green Fees** phone **Facilities** ⚏ 🍴 ⛳ 🏌 **Location** 11km SE of city centre off N11
Hotel ★★★ 72% HL Bewleys Hotel Leopardstown, Central Park, Leopardstown, DUBLIN 18 ☎ 01 2935000 & 2935001 🖨 01 2935000 352 en suite

Castle Woodside Dr
☎ 01 4904207 🖨 01 4920264
web: www.castlegc.ie
18 Holes, 5732mtrs, Par 70, SSS 71, Course record 66.
Course Designer Harry Colt **Location** off Dodder Park Rd
Telephone for further details
Hotel ★★★★ 79% HL Clarion Hotel Dublin, IFSC, DUBLIN 1
☎ 01 4338800 🖨 01 4338800 176 en suite

Clontarf Donnycarney House, Malahide Rd
☎ 01 8331892 & 8331520 🖨 01 8331933
e-mail: info@clontarfgolfclub.ie
web: clontarfgolfclub.ie

The nearest golf course to Dublin city, with a historic building as a clubhouse, Clontarf is a parkland type course bordered on one side by a railway line. Although a relatively short course, its narrow fairways and punitive rough call for accuracy off the tee and will test players' golfing skill. There are several challenging holes including the 12th, which involves playing over a pond and a quarry.

18 Holes, 5317metres, Par 69, SSS 68, Course record 64. Club membership 1150.

Visitors dress code. **Societies** booking required. **Green Fees** not confirmed **Course Designer** Harry Colt **Prof** Eamon Brady **Facilities** ⓣ ⦿ 🖳 ⛳ 🍴 ⚏ 🏠 ⬚ ◇ 🛒 ⚐ **Leisure** bowling green, snooker room, golf teaching by pro **Conf** facs Corporate Hospitality Days **Location** 4km NE of city centre via Fairview
Hotel ★★★★ 77% HL Clontarf Castle, Castle Avenue, Clontarf, DUBLIN 3 ☎ 01 8332321 & 8534336 🖨 01 8332321 111 en suite

Corrstown Corrstown
☎ 01 8640533 & 8640534 🖨 01 8640537
web: www.corrstowngolfclub.com
River Course: 18 Holes, 6077mtrs, Par 72, SSS 71, Course record 69.
Orchard Course: 9 Holes, 2792metres, Par 35, SSS 69.
Course Designer Eddie Connaughton **Location** 10km N of city centre via St Margarets
Telephone for further details
Hotel ★★★ 74% HL Grand Canal Hotel, Upper Grand Canal Street, Ballsbridge, DUBLIN 4 ☎ 01 6461000 🖨 01 6461000 142 en suite

Edmondstown Edmondstown Rd, Edmondstown
☎ 01 4931082 & 4932461 📄 01 4933152
e-mail: info@edmondstowngolfclub.ie
web: www.edmondstowngolfclub.ie

A popular and testing parkland course situated at the foot of the Dublin Mountains in the suburbs of the city. Now completely renovated and redesigned. All greens are now sand based to the highest standard. An attractive stream flows in front of the 4th and 6th greens calling for an accurate approach shot. The par 3 17th will test the best golfers and the 5th and 12th require thoughtful club selection to the green.

18 Holes, 6011mtrs, Par 71, SSS 73, Course record 66. Club membership 750.

Visitors Mon, Tue,Thu-Sat & BHs. Booking required. Dress code. **Societies** booking required **Green Fees** €55 per round (€65 Sat & BHs) **Course Designer** McEvoy/Cooke **Prof** Gareth McShea **Facilities** ⑪ ⑩ 🛄 ⚏ 🍴 ⚱ 🏠 ⛳ ♥ 🛺 ♥ **Conf** facs Corporate Hospitality Days **Location** M50 junct 12, follow signs to Edmondstown

Hotel ★★★ 74% HL Montrose, Stillorgan Road, DUBLIN 4 ☎ 01 2693311 📄 01 2693311 180 en suite

Elm Park Golf & Sports Club Nutley House, Nutley Ln, Donnybrook
☎ 01 2693438 📄 01 2694505
e-mail: office@elmparkgolfclub.ie
web: elmparkgolfclub.ie

Interesting parkland course requiring a degree of accuracy, particularly as half of the holes involve crossing the stream.

Elm Park Golf & Sports Club: 18 Holes, 5380mtrs, Par 69, SSS 69, Course record 64. Club membership 1900.

Visitors contact club for details. **Societies** welcome. **Green Fees** not confirmed **Course Designer** Patrick Merrigan **Prof** Seamus Green **Facilities** ⑪ ⑩ 🛄 ⚏ 🍴 ⚱ 🏠 ⛳ 🛺 ♥ **Leisure** hard and grass tennis courts **Conf** facs **Location** 5km SE of city centre off N11

Hotel ★★★ 74% HL Mount Herbert Hotel, Herbert Road, Sandymount, DUBLIN 4 ☎ 01 6142000 📄 01 6142000 168 en suite

Hollystown Hollystown
☎ 01 8207444 📄 01 8207447
web: www.hollystown.com

Red/Yellow: 18 Holes, 5829yds, Par 70, SSS 69.
Yellow/Blue: 18 Holes, 6216yds, Par 71, SSS 69.
Blue/Red: 18 Holes, 6201yds, Par 71, SSS 69.

Course Designer Eddie Hackett **Location** 8m off N3 Dublin-Cavan road at Mulhuddart or off the N2 Dublin-Ashbourne road at Ward **Telephone for further details**

Hotel BUD Travelodge Dublin Castleknock, Auburn Avenue Roundabout, Navan Road, Castleknock, DUBLIN 15 ☎ 01 8202626 📄 01 8202626 100 en suite

Howth, Carrickbrack Rd, Sutton
☎ 01 8323055 📄 01 8321793
e-mail: secretary@howthgolfclub.ie
web: www.howthgolfclub.ie

A hilly heathland course with scenic views of Dublin Bay. A good challenge to the novice or expert golfer.

18 Holes, 5618mtrs, Par 72, SSS 71. Club membership 1400.

Visitors Mon-Sat. Dress code. **Societies** booking required **Green Fees** not confirmed **Course Designer** James Braid **Prof** John McGuirk **Facilities** ⑪ by prior arrangement ⑩ by prior arrangement 🛄 ⚏ 🍴 ⚱ 🏠 ⛳ ♥ 🛺 ♥ **Conf** facs Corporate Hospitality Days **Location** 14.5km NE of city

Hotel ★★★ 74% HL Deer Park Hotel, Golf & Spa, HOWTH, Co Dublin ☎ 01 8322624 📄 01 8322624 75 en suite

Milltown Lower Churchtown Rd
☎ 01 4976090 📄 01 4976008
e-mail: info@milltowngolfclub.ie
web: www.milltowngolfclub.ie.

Level parkland three miles from Dublin City Centre. Greens recently reconstructed to USGA specification.

18 Holes, 5638mtrs, Par 71, SSS 70, Course record 64. Club membership 1400.

Visitors Mon, Thu & Fri except BHs.. Booking required. Handicap certificate. Dress code. **Societies** booking required. **Green Fees** €85 per 18 holes **Course Designer** Freddie Davis **Prof** John Harnett **Facilities** ⑪ ⑩ 🛄 ⚏ 🍴 ⚱ 🏠 ⛳ ♥ ♥ **Conf** facs Corporate Hospitality Days

Hotel ★★★★ 79% HL Clarion Hotel Dublin, IFSC, DUBLIN 1 ☎ 01 4338800 📄 01 4338800 176 en suite

Newlands Clondalkin
☎ 01 4593157 & 4593498 📄 01 4593498
web: www.newlandsgolfclub.com

18 Holes, 5982mtrs, Par 71, SSS 70.

Course Designer James Braid **Location** 6m SW of Dublin at Newlands Cross N7
Telephone for further details

Rathfarnham Newtown
☎ 01 4931201 & 4931561 📄 01 4931561

14 Holes, 5815mtrs, Par 71, SSS 70, Course record 69.

Course Designer John Jacobs **Location** 5km S of city centre off N81
Telephone for further details

Royal Dublin North Bull Island Reserve, Dollymount
☎ 01 8336346 📄 01 8336504
e-mail: info@theroyaldublingolfclub.com
web: www.theroyaldublingolfclub.com

A popular course with visitors, for its design subtleties, the condition of the links and the friendly atmosphere. Founded in 1885, the club moved to its present site in 1889 and received its Royal designation in 1891. A notable former club professional was Christy O'Connor, who was appointed in 1959 and immediately made his name. Along with its many notable holes, Royal Dublin has a fine

continued

IRELAND

and testing finish. The 18th is a sharp dog-leg par 4, with out of bounds along the right-hand side. The decision to try the long carry over the 'garden' is one many visitors have regretted.

The Royal Dublin Golf Club: 18 Holes, 6316mtrs, Par 72, SSS 74, Course record 66. Club membership 1250.

Visitors Mon, Tue, Thu, Fri & Sun except BHs. Limited play Sat. Booking required. Handicap certificate. Dress code. **Societies** booking required. **Green Fees** €170 per round **Course Designer** H S Colt **Prof** Leonard Owens **Facilities** ⒲ †⦿ ⓛ ⌨ ▯ ⌨ ⌂ ⇑ ⌁ ⛟ ⌁ ⏃ **Conf** facs Corporate Hospitality Days **Location** 5.5km NE of city centre **Hotel** ★★★★ 77% HL Clontarf Castle, Castle Avenue, Clontarf, DUBLIN 3 ☎ 01 8332321 & 8534336 🖹 01 8332321 111 en suite

St Margaret's Golf & Country Club St Margaret's
☎ 01 8640400 🖹 01 8640408
e-mail: reservations@stmargaretsgolf.com
web: www.stmargaretsgolf.com

A championship standard course which measures nearly 7,000 yards off the back tees, but flexible teeing offers a fairer challenge to the middle and high handicap golfer. The modern design makes wide use of water hazards and mounding. Ryder Cup player, Sam Torrance, has described the 18th as 'possibly the strongest and most exciting in the world'. Has hosted many international tournaments.

St Margaret's Golf & Country Club: 18 Holes, 6325metres, Par 73, SSS 73, Course record 69. Club membership 260.

Visitors dress code. Handicap certificate. **Societies** welcome. **Green Fees** Low season €40-€60, high season €50-€80 **Course**

Designer Craddock/Ruddy **Prof** Gary Kearney **Facilities** ⒲ †⦿ ⓛ ▯ ⌨ ⌂ ⇑ ⌁ ⛟ ⌁ ⏃ **Leisure** golf academy **Conf** facs Corporate Hospitality Days **Location** 9km N of city centre off R122
Hotel ★★★ 74% HL Grand Canal Hotel, Upper Grand Canal Street, Ballsbridge, DUBLIN 4 ☎ 01 6461000 🖹 01 6461000 142 en suite

Stackstown Kellystown Rd, Rathfarnham
☎ 01 4942338 & 4941993 🖹 01 4933934
e-mail: stackstowngc@eircom.net
web: stackstowngolfclub.com

Pleasant course in the foothills of the Dublin mountains, affording breathtaking views of Dublin city and bay. Mature woodland borders every hole and premium is placed on accuracy off the tee. The mountain streams which run through the course come into play and provide attractive on-course water features.

18 Holes, 5625mtrs, Par 72, SSS 72, Course record 63. Club membership 1092.

Visitors contact club for details. **Societies** booking required. **Green Fees** not confirmed **Course Designer** Shaftrey **Prof** Michael Kavanagh **Facilities** ⒲ †⦿ ⓛ ▯ ⌨ ⌂ ⇑ ⌁ ⛟ ⌁ **Conf** facs Corporate Hospitality Days **Location** 9km S of city centre. M50 junct 13, signs for Rathfarnham, 3rd lights left for Leopardstown, next lights follow road under M50, club 300 metres
Hotel ★★★ 74% HL Montrose, Stillorgan Road, DUBLIN 4 ☎ 01 2693311 🖹 01 2693311 180 en suite

DUN LAOGHAIRE Map 1 D4

Dun Laoghaire Eglinton Park
☎ 01 2803916 🖹 01 2804868
web: www.dunlaoghairegolfclub.ie
18 Holes, 5313mtrs, Par 69, SSS 68, Course record 63.
Course Designer Harry Colt **Location** 1.2km from town centre port
Telephone for further details
Hotel ★★★ 72% HL Bewleys Hotel Leopardstown, Central Park,
Leopardstown, DUBLIN 18 ☎ 01 2935000 & 2935001 🖹 01 2935000
352 en suite

HOWTH Map 1 D4

Deer Park Hotel, Golf & Spa D13
☎ 01 8322624 🖹 01 8392405
web: www.deerpark-hotel.ie

St Fintans: 9 Holes, 3084metres, Par 37.
Deer Park: 18 Holes, 6245metres, Par 72.
Grace O'Malley: 9 Holes, 2862metres, Par 35.
Short Course: 12 Holes, 1655metres, Par 36.
Course Designer Fred Hawtree **Location** 14.5km NE of city centre, off
coast road 0.8km before Howth Harbour
Telephone for further details
Hotel ★★★ 74% HL Deer Park Hotel, Golf & Spa, HOWTH, Co
Dublin ☎ 01 8322624 🖹 01 8322624 75 en suite

See advert on page 443

KILLINEY Map 1 D4

Killiney Ballinclea Rd
☎ 01 2852823 🖹 01 2852861
9 Holes, 5655mtrs, Par 70, SSS 70.
Prof P O'Boyle **Facilities** 🏌 🖳 🍴 🍸 ⌂ ☂ 🛺 ⚑
Telephone for further details
Hotel ★★★★ 80% HL Fitzpatrick Castle, KILLINEY, Co Dublin
☎ 01 2305400 🖹 01 2305400 113 en suite

LUCAN Map 1 D4

Hermitage Ballydowd
☎ 01 6268491 🖹 01 6238881
e-mail: hermitagegolf@eircom.net
web: www.hermitagegolf.ie
Part level, part undulating course bordered by the River Liffey and
offering some surprises.

Malahide Golf Club

Golfers visiting this 27-hole parkland course will find a scenically beautiful course, consistently maintained to the highest standards.

The motto of the club is "A light heart and a cheerful spirit", also reflected in the warmth of our welcome both to individuals and Societies, which sees many returning year after year.

For beginner or established players, our friendly Golf Professional John Murray is on hand to offer advice or lessons to improve your game.

From the Clubhouse there are breath-taking views of Howth Head and the Wicklow Mountains, matched by the hospitality cuisine found in out Restaurant and bar.

Beechwood, The Grange, Malahide, Co. Dublin
For bookings please contact Mark Gannon, General Manager
Email: manager@malahidegolfclub.ie
Tel: +353 (01) 846-1611   Fax: +353 (01) 846-1270
Website: www.malahidegoldclub.ie

---

18 Holes, 6034mtrs, Par 71, SSS 71.
Club membership 1100.
Visitors Mon, Thu & Fri. Booking required. Dress code. Handicap
certificate. **Societies** booking required. **Green Fees** not confirmed
Course Designer J McKenna **Prof** Simon Byrne **Facilities** 🕐 🍴 🖳
🖳 🍸 ⌂ 🏠 ☂ 🛺 ⚑ **Conf** facs Corporate Hospitality Days
Location On N4
Hotel ★★★ 77% HL Finnstown Country House Hotel, Newcastle
Road, LUCAN, Co Dublin ☎ 01 6010700 🖹 01 6010700 81 en suite

Lucan Celbridge Rd
☎ 01 6282106 🖹 01 6282929
e-mail: luncangolf@eircom.net
web: lucangolfclub.ie
Founded in 1897 as a nine-hole course and extended to 18 holes in
1988, Lucan involves playing over a lane which bisects the 1st and
7th holes. The front nine is undulating while the back nine is flatter
and features water hazards and a 531-metre par 5 18th hole.
18 Holes, 5958mtrs, Par 71, SSS 71, Course record 67.
Club membership 920.
Visitors Mon, Tue, Fri-Sun & BHs. Booking required. Dress code.
Societies booking required. **Green Fees** not confirmed **Course
Designer** Eddie Hackett **Facilities** 🕐 🍴 🏌 🖳 🍸 ⌂ ⚑ 🛺
⚑ **Location** W of town towards Celbridge
Hotel ★★★ 67% HL Lucan Spa, LUCAN, Co Dublin ☎ 01 6280494
🖹 01 6280494 71 en suite

PORTMARNOCK
CO DUBLIN - PORTMARNOCK - MAP 1 D4

Universally acknowledged as one of the truly great links courses, Portmarnock has hosted many great events from the British Amateur Championships of 1949 and the Canada Cup in 1960, to 12 stagings of the revised Irish Open. Founded in 1894, the serpentine championship course offers a classic challenge: surrounded by water on three sides, no two successive holes play in the same direction. Unlike many courses that play nine out and nine home, Portmarnock demands a continual awareness of wind direction. Extraordinary holes include the 14th, which Henry Cotton regarded as the best hole in golf; the 15th, which Arnold Palmer regards as the best par 3 in the world; and the 5th, regarded as the best on the course by the late Harry Bradshaw. Bradshaw was for 40 years Portmarnock's golf professional and runner-up to AD Locke in the 1949 British Open, playing his ball from an empty bottle of stout.

☎ 01 8462968   📄 01 8462601
web: www.portmarnockgolfclub.ie
Old Course: 18 Holes, 6567metres, Par 72, SSS 73.
New Course: 9 Holes, 3082metres, Par 37. Club membership 1100.
Visitors booking required. Handicap certificate. Dress code. **Societies** booking required. **Green Fees** phone
Course Designer W Pickeman **Prof** Joey Purcell **Facilities** ⑪ 🍴 by prior arrangement 🏌 🖵 🏌 ⛳ 🏠 ⛳ ⛳
🚗 ⛳ **Conf** Corporate Hospitality Days **Location** S of town off R106
Hotel ★★★★ HL Portmarnock Hotel & Golf Links, Strand Road, PORTMARNOCK, Co Dublin ☎ 01 8460611
📄 01 8460611 138 en suite

MALAHIDE　　　　　　　　　　　Map 1 D4

Malahide Beechwood
☎ 01 8461611　📄 01 8461270
web: www.malahidegolfclub.ie

Main Course: 18 Holes, 6066mtrs, Par 71.

Course Designer E Hackett **Location** 1.6km from R106 coast road at Portmarnock
Telephone for further details
Hotel ★★★★ HL Portmarnock Hotel & Golf Links, Strand Road, PORTMARNOCK, Co Dublin ☎ 01 8460611 📄 01 8460611 138 en suite

See advert on page 444

PORTMARNOCK　　　　　　　　　Map 1 D4

Portmarnock see page 447
☎ 01 8462968　📄 01 8462601
web: www.portmarnockgolfclub.ie

Portmarnock Hotel & Golf Links Strand Rd
☎ 01 8460611　📄 01 8462442
web: www.portmarnock.com

Portmarnock Hotel & Golf Links: 18 Holes, 5992metres, Par 71, SSS 72, Course record 67.

Course Designer Bernhard Langer **Location** from Dublin Airport, N1, rdbt 1st exit, 2nd rdbt 2nd exit, next rdbt 3rd exit, left at T-junct, over x-rds. Hotel on left past Strand
Telephone for further details
Hotel ★★★★ HL Portmarnock Hotel & Golf Links, Strand Road, PORTMARNOCK, Co Dublin ☎ 01 8460611 📄 01 8460611 138 en suite

RATHCOOLE　　　　　　　　　　Map 1 D4

Beech Park Johnstown
☎ 01 4580522　📄 01 4588365
e-mail: info@beechpark.ie
web: www.beechpark.ie

Undulating flat parkland course with heavily wooded fairways. Famous for its Amen Corner (holes 9 to 13).

18 Holes, 5753metres, Par 72, SSS 70, Course record 67. Club membership 1050.

Visitors Mon, Thu & Fri except BHs. Booking required. Dress code. **Societies** booking required. **Green Fees** €40 per 18 holes **Course Designer** Eddie Hackett **Facilities** ⓣ ⚟ ⌾ ⧠ ⛳ ⚒ 🏌 ⚑

♦ Conf Corporate Hospitality Days **Location** From N7, take exit signed Rathcoole North. Follow local signs.
Hotel ★★★ 77% HL Finnstown Country House Hotel, Newcastle Road, LUCAN, Co Dublin ☎ 01 6010700 📄 01 6010700 81 en suite

RUSH　　　　　　　　　　　　　Map 1 D4

Rush
☎ 01 8438177 (Office) & 8437548　📄 01 8438177
e-mail: info@rushgolfclub.com

Seaside borders three fairways on this links course. There are 28 bunkers and undulating fairways to add to the challenge of the variable and strong winds that blow at all times and change with the tides. There are no easy holes.

9 Holes, 5598mtrs, Par 70, SSS 69. Club membership 500.

Visitors Mon, Tue, Thu & Fri except BHs. Booking required. Dress code. **Societies** booking required. **Green Fees** €36 per 18 holes **Facilities** ⓣ ⚟ ⌾ ⧠ 🏌 ⚑ **Location** SW of town

SAGGART　　　　　　　　　　　Map 1 D4

Citywest Hotel
☎ 01 4010500 & 4010878 (shop)　📄 01 4588565
e-mail: proshop@citywesthotel.com
web: www.citywesthotel.com

Course west of Dublin comprising 142 acres at the foothills of the Dublin mountains and built on fine parkland. Well wooded and enjoys natural drainage. The Lakes course is fairly short but a good test of golf with fine greens and fairways.

Championship: 18 Holes, 5312metres, Par 68, SSS 70, Course record 65.
Lakes: 18 Holes, 4713metres, Par 65, SSS 69.

Visitors Mon-Sun & BHs. Booking required. Dress code. Handicap certificate. **Societies** booking required. **Green Fees** Jan-Mar, Championship €35 per round, Lakes €30. Apr-Oct €50/ €35
Course Designer Christy O'Connor Jnr **Facilities** ⓣ ⚟ ⌾ ⧠ ⛳ 🏌 ⚑ ♦ ⚒ ⛳ ⚑ **Leisure** heated indoor swimming pool, fishing, sauna, gymnasium **Conf** facs Corporate Hospitality Days **Location** off N7 S to village
Hotel ★★★ 71% HL Bewleys Hotel Newlands Cross, Newlands Cross, Naas Rd, DUBLIN 22 ☎ 01 4640140 & 4123301 📄 01 4640140 299 en suite

SKERRIES　　　　　　　　　　　Map 1 D4

Skerries Hacketstown
☎ 01 8491567　📄 01 8491591
e-mail: admin@skerriesgolfclub.ie
web: www.skerriesgolfclub.ie

Tree-lined parkland course on gently rolling countryside, with sea views from some holes. The 1st and 18th are particularly challenging.

18 Holes, 6081mtrs, Par 73, SSS 72, Course record 67. Club membership 1200.

Visitors Mon, Tue, Thu & Fri except BHs. Booking required Fri. Dress code. **Societies** booking required **Green Fees** €40 per round **Prof** Bobby Kinsella **Facilities** ⓣ ⚟ ⌾ ⧠ ⛳ 🏌 ⚑ ♦ **Location** S of town off R127
Hotel ★★★ 70% HL Boyne Valley Hotel & Country Club, Stameen, Dublin Road, DROGHEDA, Co Louth ☎ 041 9837737 📄 041 9837737 73 en suite

SWORDS
Map 1 D4

Swords Open Golf Course Balheary Av, Swords
☎ 01 8409819 & 8901030 📄 01 8409819
e-mail: info@swordsopengolfcourse.com
web: www.swordsopengolfcourse.com
Parkland beside the River Broadmeadow, in countryside, easily accessible from Dublin Airport.

Swords Open Golf Course: 18 Holes, 5612metres, Par 71, SSS 69, Course record 73. Club membership 500.
Visitors Mon-Sun & BHs. Booking required. Dress code.
Societies booking required. **Green Fees** €20 per 18 holes (€25 weekends & BHs) **Course Designer** T Halpin **Facilities** 🏳 ⛳ ♿ ✿
Location from M1 take Donabate/Skerries exit towards Swords Turn right at Estuary rdbt, right at lights, then second turning left, course 2m on left
Hotel ★★★ 73% HL Bewleys Hotel Dublin Airport, Baskin Lane, Swords, CO DUBLIN ☎ 01 8711000 📄 01 8711000 466 en suite

TALLAGHT
Map 1 D4

Dublin City Ballinascorney
☎ 01 4516430 📄 01 4598445
web: www.dublincitygolf.com

18 Holes, 5061metres, Par 69, SSS 67, Course record 63.
Course Designer Eddie Hackett **Location** 12km SW of city centre on R114
Telephone for further details

CO GALWAY

BALLINASLOE
Map 1 B4

Ballinasloe Rosglos
☎ 090 9642126 📄 090 9642538
web: www.ballinasloegolfclub.com
18 Holes, 5865mtrs, Par 72, SSS 70, Course record 69.
Course Designer E Hackett/E Connaughton **Location** 3km S on R355
Telephone for further details

BALLYCONNEELY
Map 1 A4

Connemara
☎ 095 23502 & 23602 📄 095 23662
e-mail: info@connemaragolflinks.net
web: www.connemaragolflinks.com

This championship links course has a spectacular setting by the Atlantic Ocean, with the Twelve Bens Mountains in the background.

Established in 1973, it is a tough challenge, due in no small part to its exposed location, with the back nine the equal of any in the world. The last six holes are exceptionally long and offer a great challenge to golfers of all abilities. When the wind blows, club selection is crucial. Notable holes are the 13th (200yd par 3), the long par 5 14th, the 15th with a green nestling in the hills, the 16th guarded by water and the 17th and 18th, both par 5s over 500yds long.

Championship: 18 Holes, 6095mtrs, Par 72, SSS 73, Course record 64.
New: 9 Holes, 2606mtrs, Par 35, SSS 36.
Club membership 970.
Visitors Mon-Sat & BHs. Sun pm only. Booking preferred. Dress code. Handicap certificate. **Societies** booking required. **Green Fees** €65 per round (€75 Fri-Sun) **Course Designer** Eddie Hackett **Prof** Hugh O'Neill **Facilities** 🏌 🍴 🛒 🏳 🥤 ⛳ 🏠 ♿ ✿ 🍺 ✿ 🚩 **Conf** Corporate Hospitality Days **Location** from Clifden take R341 to Bally Conneely, then fork right in village after Keogh's public house
Hotel ★★★★ 80% HL Abbeyglen Castle, Sky Road, CLIFDEN, CO GALWAY ☎ 095 21201 📄 095 21201 45 en suite

BEARNA
Map 1 B3

Bearna Golf and Country Club Corboley
☎ 091 592677 📄 091 592674
e-mail: info@bearnagolfclub.com
web: www.bearnagolfclub.com

Set amid the beautiful landscape of the west of Ireland and enjoying commanding views of Galway Bay, the course covers more than 100 hectares. This has resulted in generously proportioned fairways, many elevated tees and some splendid carries. Water comes into play at thirteen holes and the final four holes provide a memorable finish. Lakes on 6th, 7th and 10th holes.

Bearna Golf and Country Club: 18 Holes, 5746metres, Par 72, SSS 72, Course record 68. Club membership 600.
Visitors Mon-Sun & BHs. Booking required. Dress code.
Societies booking required. **Green Fees** €35 per round Mon-Thu (€40 Fri, €50 weekends & BHs) **Course Designer** Robert J Brown **Prof** Declan Cunningham **Facilities** 🏌 🍴 🛒 🏳 🥤 🏠 ♿ 🚩 🍺 ✿ **Conf** facs Corporate Hospitality Days **Location** 3.5km N of Bearna, off R336
Hotel ★★★★ 78% HL Galway Bay Hotel Conference & Leisure Centre, The Promenade, Salthill, GALWAY, Co Galway ☎ 091 520520 📄 091 520520 153 en suite

GALWAY   Map 1 B4

Galway Blackrock, Salthill
☎ 091 522033   🖷 091 529783
e-mail: galwaygolf@eircom.net
web: galwaygolf.com

Designed by Dr A McKenzie, this course is inland by nature,
although some of the fairways run close to the ocean. The terrain
is of gently sloping hillocks with plenty of trees and furze bushes
to catch out the unwary. Although not a long course it continues to
delight visiting golfers.

18 Holes, 5995metres, Par 70, SSS 71, Course record 67.
Club membership 1238.

Visitors Mon, Wed-Sat & BHs. Booking required. Handicap
certificate. Dress code. **Societies** booking required. **Green
Fees** not confirmed **Course Designer** McKenzie **Prof** Don Wallace
Facilities ⑪ ⑩ 🍴 ⌨ 🛥 ⚲ 🏺 ⛳ 🥢 🚶 🛒 🥢
Conf Corporate Hospitality Days **Location** 3km W in Salthill
Hotel ★★★ 79% HL Claregalway, Claregalway Village,
GALWAY, CO GALWAY ☎ 091 738300 & 738302 🖷 091 738300
48 en suite

GORT   Map 1 B3

Gort, Castlequarter
☎ 091 632244   🖷 091 632387
e-mail: info@gortgolf.com
web: www.gortgolf.com

Set in 65 hectares of picturesque parkland. The 515-metre 9th and
the 472-metre 17th are played into a prevailing wind and the par 4
dog-leg 7th will test the best.

18 Holes, 5705mtrs, Par 71, SSS 69, Course record 67.
Club membership 978.

Visitors Mon-Fri & BHs. Limited play weekends. Booking required.
Dress code. **Societies** booking required. **Green Fees** €30 per
18 holes (€35 weekends & BHs) **Course Designer** Christy O'Connor
Jnr **Facilities** ⑪ ⑩ 🍴 ⌨ 🍴 🛥 🏺 ⛳ 🥢 🛒 🥢
Location located at Castlequarter, approx 2 miles W of Gort

LOUGHREA   Map 1 B3

Loughrea Bullaun Rd
☎ 091 841049   🖷 091 847472

18 Holes, 5825mtrs, Par 71, SSS 70, Course record 68.
Course Designer Eddie Hackett **Location** Follow signs from bypass for
Mountbellew/New Inn. 1.5m N of town.
Telephone for further details

Guesthouse ★★★★★ GH St Clerans Manor House, CRAUGHWELL,
CO GALWAY ☎ 091 846555 🖷 091 846555 12 en suite

MOUNTBELLEW   Map 1 B4

Mountbellew
☎ 0905 79259   🖷 0905 79274

Mountbellew Golf Course: 9 Holes, 5143mtrs, Par 69,
SSS 66, Course record 63.

Facilities 🛥 ⌨ 🍴 🛥 🥢 ⛳ **Conf** Corporate Hospitality Days
Location off N63
Telephone for further details

ORANMORE   Map 1 B3

Athenry Palmerstown
☎ 091 794466   🖷 091 794971
e-mail: athenrygc@eircom.net
web: athenrygolfclub.com

A mixture of parkland and heathland built on a limestone base
against the backdrop of a large pine forest. The par 3 holes are
notable with a feature hole at the 12th - from an elevated tee played
between beech and pine trees.

18 Holes, 5687metres, Par 70, SSS 70, Course record 67.
Club membership 1000.

Visitors Mon-Sat & BHs. Booking required. Dress code.
Societies booking required. **Green Fees** not confirmed **Course
Designer** Eddie Hackett **Prof** Raymond Ryan **Facilities** ⑪ ⑩ 🛥
⌨ 🍴 🛥 🏺 ⛳ 🥢 🛒 🥢 **Conf** Corporate Hospitality
Days **Location** 6km E on R348
Hotel ★★★ 70% HL Maldron Hotel Galway, ORANMORE, Co Galway
☎ 091 792244 🖷 091 792244 113 en suite

Galway Bay Golf Resort
☎ 091 790711   🖷 091 792510
web: www.galwaybaygolfresort.com

Galway Bay Golf Resort: 18 Holes, 6533metres, Par 72,
SSS 73, Course record 68.

Course Designer Christy O'Connor Jnr **Location** 5km SW of village
Telephone for further details
Hotel ★★★ 70% HL Maldron Hotel Galway, ORANMORE, Co
Galway ☎ 091 792244 🖷 091 792244 113 en suite

PORTUMNA   Map 1 B3

Portumna
☎ 090 9741059   🖷 090 9741798
web: www.portumnagolfclub.ie.

18 Holes, 6225mtrs, Par 72, SSS 72.

Course Designer E Connaughton **Location** 4km W of town on R352
Telephone for further details
Hotel ★★★ 75% HL Shannon Oaks Hotel & Country Club, St Joseph
Road, PORTUMNA, Co Galway ☎ 090 9741777 🖷 090 9741777
109 en suite

RENVYLE
Map 1 A4

Renvyle House Hotel
☎ 095 43511   🖹 095 43515
web: www.renvyle.com
Pebble Beach: 9 Holes, 3200metres, Par 36,
Course record 34.
Facilities 🛈 🍴 🗲 🍺 🍷 🏖 🛗 ◇ ⛳ **Leisure** hard tennis
courts, heated outdoor swimming pool, fishing **Conf** facs Corporate
Hospitality Days **Location** Renvyle 6km off N59, course NW of village
Telephone for further details
Hotel ★★★ 75% HL Renvyle House Hotel, RENVYLE, Co Galway
☎ 095 43511 🖹 095 43511 73 en suite

TUAM
Map 1 B4

Tuam Barnacurragh
☎ 093 28993   🖹 093 26003
18 Holes, 5513mtrs, Par 72, SSS 69.
Course Designer Eddie Hackett **Location** 1km S of town on R347
Telephone for further details
Guesthouse ★★★★★ GH The Beach Guest House, Lower Village,
Dunmore East, Waterford ☎ 051 383316 🖹 051 383316 7 en suite

CO KERRY

BALLYBUNION
Map 1 A3

Ballybunion see page 453
Sandhill Rd
☎ 068 27146   🖹 068 27387
e-mail: bbgolfgc@ioe.ie
web: www.ballybuniongolfclub.ie

BALLYFERRITER
Map 1 A2

Dingle Links
☎ 066 9156255   🖹 066 9156409
e-mail: dinglegc@iol.ie
web: www.dinglelinks.com

This most westerly course in Europe has a magnificent scenic location.
It is a traditional links course with beautiful turf, many bunkers, a
stream that comes into play on 14 holes and, usually, a prevailing wind.
18 Holes, 6126metres, Par 72, SSS 71, Course record 72.
Club membership 432.
Visitors contact club for details. **Societies** welcome. **Green Fees** Nov-
Feb €40 per 18 holes (weekends €40), Mar,Apr,Oct €50 (€60); May-

Sep €65 (€75) **Course Designer** Hackett/O'Connor Jnr **Facilities** 🛈
🍴 🗲 🍺 🍷 🏖 ⛳ **Leisure** buggies for hire
May-Oct **Location** 2.5km NW of village off R559
Guesthouse ★★★★★ GH Gormans Clifftop House & Restaurant,
Glaise Bheag, Ballydavid, DINGLE, Co Kerry ☎ 066 9155162
🖹 066 9155162 9 en suite

CASTLEGREGORY
Map 1 A2

Castlegregory Stradbally
☎ 066 7139444   🖹 066 7139958
e-mail: castlegregorygolf@oceanfree.net
web: www.castlegregorygolflinks.com
A links course sandwiched between the sea and a freshwater lake and
mountains on two sides. The 3rd hole is visually superb with a 234-
metre drive into the wind.
Castlegregory Golf Course: 9 Holes, 2569mtrs, Par 68,
SSS 68, Course record 67. Club membership 426.
Visitors Mon-Sun & BHs. Booking required weekends & BHs. Dress
code. **Societies** booking required. **Green Fees** €38 per 18 holes, €20
per 9 holes **Course Designer** Dr Arthur Spring **Facilities** 🗲 🏖 🍷
⛳ **Leisure** fishing **Conf** Corporate Hospitality Days **Location** 3km W of
town near Stradbally
Guesthouse ★★★★ BB Sea-Mount House, Cappatigue,
Conor Pass Road, CASTLEGREGORY, Co Kerry ☎ 066 7139229
🖹 066 7139229 3 en suite

GLENBEIGH
Map 1 A2

Dooks
☎ 066 9768205   🖹 066 9768476
e-mail: office@dooks.com
web: dooks.com
Long-established course on the shore between the Kerry mountains
and Dingle Bay. Sand dunes are a feature (the name Dooks is a
derivation of the Gaelic word for sand bank) and the course offers a
fine challenge in a superb Ring of Kerry location.
Dooks Golf Links: 18 Holes, 5944mtrs, Par 71, SSS 70,
Course record 70. Club membership 1000.
Visitors contact links for details. **Societies** booking required.
Green Fees €85 per 18 holes **Course Designer** Martin Hawtree
Facilities 🛈 🍴 🗲 🍺 🍷 🏖 🛗 🍷 ⛳ 🚗 ⛳
Conf Corporate Hospitality Days **Location** NE of village off on N70
Hotel ★★★ 74% HL Gleneagle, Muckross Road, KILLARNEY, Co
Kerry ☎ 064 6636000 🖹 064 6636000 245 en suite

KENMARE
Map 1 B2

Ring of Kerry Golf & Country Club Templenoe
☎ 064 6642000   🖹 064 6642533
e-mail: reservations@ringofkerrygolf.com
web: www.ringofkerrygolf.com
A world class golf facility with spectacular views across Kenmare
Bay. Opened in 1998, the club has gone from strength to strength and
is fast becoming a must-play course for golfers visiting the
area. Every hole is memorable.
Ring of Kerry Golf & Country Club: 18 Holes, 6353mtrs,
Par 72, SSS 73, Course record 68. Club membership 275.
Visitors Mon-Sun & BHS. Dress code. **Societies** booking required.

continued

IRELAND

Green Fees €60 per 18 holes **Course Designer** Eddie Hackett **Prof** Adrian Whitehead **Facilities** **Conf** facs Corporate Hospitality Days **Location** 6.5km W of Kenmare

Reing of Kerry Golf & Country Club

Hotel ★★★★★ **90%** CHH Sheen Falls Lodge, KENMARE, Co Kerry ☎ 06466 41600 🖹 06466 41600 66 en suite

KILLARNEY Map 1 B2

Beaufort Golf Resort Churchtown, Beaufort
☎ 064 6644440 🖹 064 6644752
e-mail: info@beaufortgolfresort.com
web: www.beaufortgolfresort.com

A championship-standard parkland course designed by Dr Arthur Spring. This course is in the centre of south-west Ireland's golfing mecca. Ruins of a medieval castle dominate the back nine and the whole course is overlooked by the MacGillycuddy Reeks. The par 3 8th and par 4 11th are two of the most memorable holes.

Beaufort Golf Resort: 18 Holes, 6035mtrs, Par 71, SSS 72, Course record 68. Club membership 350.

Visitors Mon-Sun & BHs. Booking required. Dress code. **Societies** booking required. **Green Fees** €65 per round (€80 weekends) **Course Designer** Arthur Spring **Facilities** **Conf** Corporate Hospitality Days **Location** 11km W of Killarney off N72
Hotel ★★★ **79%** HL Castlerosse Hotel & Golf Resort, KILLARNEY, Co Kerry ☎ 064 6631144 🖹 064 6631144 120 en suite

Castlerosse Hotel & Golf Resort
☎ 064 6631144 🖹 064 6631031
e-mail: res@castlerosse.ie
web: www.castlerosse.com

Set in mature parkland, the course commands stunning views and has fully irrigated USGA standard greens plus a practice green.

Castlerosse Hotel: 9 Holes, 2761metres, Par 36. Club membership 140.

Visitors contact hotel for details. Handicap certificate. **Societies** welcome. **Green Fees** €32 for 18 holes, €20 for 9 holes **Course Designer** H Wallace **Facilities** **Leisure** hard tennis courts, heated indoor swimming pool, sauna, gymnasium **Conf** facs **Location** 2km from Killarney, off the Ring of Kerry road
Hotel ★★★ **79%** HL Castlerosse Hotel & Golf Resort, KILLARNEY, Co Kerry ☎ 064 6631144 🖹 064 6631144 120 en suite

Killarney Golf & Fishing Club Mahony's Point
☎ 06466 31034 🖹 06466 33065
e-mail: reservations@killarney-golf.com
web: www.killarney-golf.com

The three courses are lakeside with tree-lined fairways; many bunkers and small lakes provide no mean challenge. Mahoney's Point Course has a particularly testing par 5, 4, 3 finish and the courses call for great skill from the tee. Killarney has been the venue for many important events and is a favourite of many famous golfers.

Mahony's Point: 18 Holes, 5826mtrs, Par 72, SSS 72, Course record 64.
Killeen: 18 Holes, 6047mtrs, Par 72, SSS 72, Course record 68.
Lackabane: 18 Holes, 6011mtrs, Par 72, SSS 72, Course record 64. Club membership 1600.

Visitors dress code. Handicap certificate. **Societies** welcome. **Green Fees** not confirmed **Course Designer** H Longhurst/Sir Guy Campbell **Prof** David Keating **Facilities** **Leisure** sauna, gymnasium **Conf** Corporate Hospitality Days **Location** 3.5km W on N72
Hotel ★★★★★ HL Aghadoe Heights Hotel & Spa, KILLARNEY, Co Kerry ☎ 064 6631766 🖹 064 6631766 74 en suite

IRELAND

BALLYBUNION

CO KERRY - BALLYBUNION - MAP 1 A3

Having excellent links, Ballybunion is recognised for its fine development of the natural terrain. Mr Murphy built the Old Course in 1906. With large sand dunes and an Atlantic backdrop, Ballybunion offers the golfer an exciting round of golf in a scenic location. But be warned, the Old course is difficult to play in the wind. President Clinton played Ballybunion on his historic visit to Ireland in 1998. Although overshadowed by the Old Course, the Cashen Course designed by Robert Trent Jones is also world class, characterised by narrow fairways, small greens and large dunes.

Sandhill Rd ☎ 068 27146 🖷 068 27387
e-mail: bbgolfgc@ioe.ie **web:** www.ballybuniongolfclub.ie
Old Course: 18 Holes, 6083mtrs, Par 71, SSS 72, Course record 67.
Cashen: 18 Holes, 0yds, Par 72, SSS 71, Course record 69. Club membership 1500.
Visitors Mon-Fri except BHs. Booking required. Handicap certificate. Dress code. **Societies** welcome. **Green Fees** Old Course: €180 per round; Cashen Course: €110 per round; Both courses: €265 **Course Designer** Simpson **Prof** Brian O'Callaghan **Facilities** ⑪ ⑩ 🖢 ⬚ 🖫 ⛲ 🏠 ♞ ♟ ✔ 🚜 ✔ ⚑ **Leisure** sauna
Location 2km S of town
Guesthouse ★★★★★ GH Cashen Course House, Golf Links Road, Ballybunion, CO KERRY ☎ 068 27351 🖷 068 27351 9 en suite

KILLORGLIN   Map 1 A2

Killorglin Stealroe
☎ 066 9761979   📄 066 9761437
web: killorglingolf.ie
18 Holes, 5941metres, Par 72, SSS 71, Course record 68.
Course Designer Eddie Hackett **Location** 3km NE on N70
Telephone for further details
Guesthouse ★★★★ GH Grove Lodge, Killarney Road, KILLORGLIN,
Co Kerry ☎ 066 9761157 & 08720 73238 📄 066 9761157
10 en suite

PARKNASILLA   Map 1 A2

Parknasilla
☎ 064 45122   📄 064 45323
9 Holes, 5400mtrs, Par 70, SSS 69.
Course Designer Arthur Spring **Location** near village off N70
Telephone for further details
Hotel ★★★★ 81% HL Parknasilla, PARKNASILLA, Co Kerry
☎ 064 45122 📄 064 45122   83 en suite

TRALEE   Map 1 A2

Tralee West Barrow
☎ 066 7136379   📄 066 7136008
e-mail: info@traleegolfclub.com
web: www.traleegolfclub.com

The first Arnold Palmer designed course in Europe, this magnificent 18-hole links is set in spectacular scenery on the Barrow peninsula, surrounded on three sides by the sea. Perhaps the most memorable hole is the par 4 17th which plays from a high tee, across a deep gorge to a green perched high against a backdrop of mountains. The back nine is very difficult and challenging. Not suitable for beginners.
18 Holes, 5970mtrs, Par 71, SSS 71, Course record 66.
Club membership 1306.
Visitors contact club for details. **Green Fees** €180 per round
Course Designer Arnold Palmer **Prof** David Power **Facilities** 🕙
🍴 🍷 🖥 🛒 👤 🏪 🛺 ✏ 🏌 **Location** 13km NW of
Tralee off R558
Hotel ★★★★ 73% HL Meadowlands Hotel, Oakpark, TRALEE,
Co Kerry ☎ 066 7180444 📄 066 7180444   57 en suite

WATERVILLE (AN COIREÁN)   Map 1 A2

Waterville House & Golf Links
☎ 066 9474102   📄 066 9474482
e-mail: wvgolf@iol.ie
web: www.watervillegolflinks.ie

On the western tip of the Ring of Kerry, this course is highly regarded by many top golfers. The feature holes are the par 5 11th, which runs along a rugged valley between towering dunes, and the par 3 17th, which features an exceptionally elevated tee. Needless to say, the surroundings are beautiful.
Waterville House & Golf Links: 18 Holes, 6202mtrs, Par 72, SSS 72, Course record 65.
Visitors Mon-Sun & BHs. Booking required. Dress code.
Societies booking required **Green Fees** not confirmed
Course Designer Eddie Hackett/Tom Fazio **Prof** Liam Higgins
Facilities 🕙 🍴 🖥 🛒 🍷 👤 🏪 🛺 🏌 ✏ 🏌
✏ 🏌 **Leisure** fishing, sauna, gymnasium, short game area
Location 0.5km from Waterville on N70
Hotel ★★★ 73% HL Derrynane, CAHERDANIEL, Co Kerry
☎ 066 9475136 📄 066 9475136   70 en suite

CO KILDARE

ATHY   Map 1 C3

Athy Geraldine
☎ 059 8631729   📄 059 8634710
web: www.athygolfclub.com
18 Holes, 5921metres, Par 72, SSS 71.
Course Designer Jeff Howes **Location** 1.6km NE of town on N78
Telephone for further details
Hotel ★★★★ 73% HL Clanard Court, Dublin Road, ATHY, Co
Kildare ☎ 059 8640666 📄 059 8640666   38 en suite

CARBURY   Map 1 C4

Highfield Golf & Country Club
☎ 046 9731021   📄 046 9731021
e-mail: highfieldgolf@eircom.ie
web: www.highfield-golf.ie

Environmentally friendly parkland course with interesting undulations, enhanced by the fast stream that runs through many holes. Many innovative water features and mature trees with naturally built greens. The 4th dog-legs over the lake, the 7th is a great par 5 with a challenging green, the 10th par 3 is over rushes onto a plateau green

continued

IRELAND

THE K CLUB
CO KILDARE - STRAFFAN - MAP 1 D4

The K Club was the venue for the Ryder Cup in 2006, the first time that Ireland has hosted the event. The course reflects the personality of its architect, Arnold Palmer, covering 220 acres of Kildare woodland, with 14 man-made lakes and the River Liffey providing the water hazards. From the instant you arrive at the 1st tee, you are enveloped by a unique atmosphere: the courses are both cavalier and charismatic. The Palmer Course is one of Europe's most spectacular courses, charming, enticing, and invariably bringing out the very best in your game. The best way to describe the Smurfit Course is that of an inland links but its attributes do not stop there. The course has many dramatic landscapes with dunes moulding throughout, while some 14 acres of water have been worked in to the design, especially through the holes 13-18; a watery grave awaits many on the home stretch. The course is entirely different from the Palmer Course located just across the River Liffey.

☎ 01 6017200 📄 01 6017297
e-mail: resortsales@kclub.ie **web:** www.kclub.ie
Palmer Course: 18 Holes, 6526mtrs, Par 74, SSS 72, Course record 65.
Smurfit Course: 18 Holes, 6636mtrs, Par 72, SSS 72. Club membership 540.
Visitors booking required. **Societies** booking required. **Green Fees** phone **Course Designer** Arnold Palmer
Prof Lynn McCool **Facilities** ⑪ 🍴 🍺 ☕ 🍷 🏌 🏠 ⛳ ◇ 🏌 🛒 🏌 🏴 **Leisure** heated indoor swimming pool, fishing, sauna, gymnasium **Conf** facs Corporate Hospitality Days **Location** W of village off R403
Hotel ★★★★★ CHH The K Club, STRAFFAN, Co Kildare ☎ 01 6017200 📄 01 6017200 79 en suite

(out of bounds on left). The 1st tee is situated on top of the cedar log clubhouse, which provides a spectacular starting point.

Highfield Golf & Country Club: 18 Holes, 5493mtrs, Par 70, SSS 69. Club membership 500.

Visitors Mon-Sun & BHs. Booking required weekends. Dress code.. Handicap certificate. **Societies** welcome. **Green Fees** €30-€40 **Course Designer** Alan Duggan **Facilities** ⓣ 🍽 ⮕ 🛒 🐱 ⛳ 🏌 🍸 ◇ 🏌 🛺 🏌 👤 **Leisure** hard tennis courts, gymnasium **Conf** facs Corporate Hospitality Days **Location** 4.5km NW of village off R402
Hotel ★★★★ 81% HL Keadeen, NEWBRIDGE, Co Kildare ☎ 045 431666 📄 045 431666 75 en suite

CASTLEDERMOT
Map 1 C3

Kilkea Castle
☎ 059 49145156
web: www.kilkeacastle.ie

18 Holes, 6200mtrs, Par 71, SSS 71.

Facilities 👤 🏠 🍸 👤 **Leisure** hard tennis courts, heated indoor swimming pool, fishing, sauna, gymnasium **Location** from Dublin take M9 S, take exit for High Cross Inn. Left after pub, hotel 3m on right
Telephone for further details
Hotel ★★★ 78% HL Seven Oaks, Athy Road, CARLOW, Co Carlow ☎ 059 9131308 📄 059 9131308 89 en suite

DONADEA
Map 1 C4

Knockanally Golf & Country Club
☎ 045 869322 📄 045 869322
e-mail: golf@knockanally.com
web: www.knockanally.com
Home of the Irish International Professional Matchplay championship, this parkland course is set in a former estate, with a Palladian-style clubhouse.

Knockanally Golf & Country Club: 18 Holes, 5930mtrs, Par 72, SSS 72, Course record 66. Club membership 500.
Visitors Mon-Sun & BHs. Booking required. Dress code.
Societies booking required. **Green Fees** €35 per round (€45 weekends) **Course Designer** Noel Lyons **Prof** Martin Darcy
Facilities ⓣ 🍽 ⮕ 🛒 🐱 👤 🏠 🍸 ◇ 🛺 🏌 **Leisure** fishing **Conf** Corporate Hospitality Days **Location** 6km NW of village off M4
Hotel ★★★ 73% HL The Hamlet Court Hotel, Johnstownbridge, ENFIELD, Co Meath ☎ 046 9541200 📄 046 9541200 30 en suite

KILDARE
Map 1 C3

Cill Dara Cill Dara, Little Curragh
☎ 045 521295 & 521433
e-mail: cilldaragolfclub@ireland.com
Only 1 mile from the famous Curragh racecourse, this 9-hole parkland course is unusual in having links type soil as well as plenty of trees.

Cill Dara Golf Course: 9 Holes, 5852mtrs, Par 71, SSS 70, Course record 64. Club membership 800.
Visitors Mon, Tue, Thu, Fri & BHs. Booking required Wed. Dress code.
Societies welcome. **Green Fees** €20 **Facilities** ⓣ 🍽 ⮕ 🛒 🐱 👤 🏠 🍸 🛺 🏌 **Leisure** snooker room, darts and pool room **Location** 1.6km E of town
Hotel ★★★★ 81% HL Keadeen, NEWBRIDGE, Co Kildare ☎ 045 431666 📄 045 431666 75 en suite

The Curragh Curragh
☎ 045 441238 & 441714 📄 045 442476
e-mail: curraghgolf@eircom.net
web: www.curraghgolf.com
A particularly challenging course, well wooded and with lovely scenery all around.

18 Holes, 6035mtrs, Par 72, SSS 71, Course record 63. Club membership 1040.
Visitors Mon & Wed-Sat. Booking required. Handicap certificate. Dress code. **Societies** welcome. **Green Fees** €35 per 18 holes **Prof** Gerry Burke **Facilities** ⓣ 🍽 ⮕ 🛒 🐱 🍸 👤 🏠 🍸 ◇ 🛺 🏌 👤 **Location** N7 junct 12, follow R413 E towards Kilcullen, turn right at crossroads
Hotel ★★★★ 81% HL Keadeen, NEWBRIDGE, Co Kildare ☎ 045 431666 📄 045 431666 75 en suite

KILL
Map 1 D4

Killeen
☎ 045 866003 📄 045 875881
18 Holes, 5561mtrs, Par 71, SSS 71, Course record 70.
Course Designer Pat Ruddy/M Kelly **Location** signed off N7 at Kill
Telephone for further details
Hotel ★★★★ 80% HL Barberstown Castle, STRAFFAN, Co Kildare ☎ 01 6288157 📄 01 6288157 58 en suite

MAYNOOTH
Map 1 D4

Carton House
☎ 01 5052000 📄 01 6286555
web: www.cartonhouse.com
O'Meara: 18 Holes, 6042metres, Par 72, SSS 72.
Montgomerie: 18 Holes, 6237metres, Par 72, SSS 73, Course record 68.
Course Designer O'Meara/Lobb & Montgomerie/Edy **Location** N4 W from Dublin, exit Leixlip West, signed
Telephone for further details
Hotel ★★★ 79% HL Leixlip House, Captains Hill, LEIXLIP, Co Kildare ☎ 01 6242268 📄 01 6242268 19 en suite

MOUNT JULIET HOTEL

CO KILKENNY - THOMASTOWN - MAP 1 C3

Mount Juliet's superb 18-hole course was designed by Jack Nicklaus. It has hosted many prestigious events including the Irish Open on three occasions. The course has a cleverly concealed drainage and irrigation system, perfect even when inclement weather would otherwise halt play. It takes advantage of the estate's mature landscape to provide a world-class 72-par challenge for professionals and high-handicap golfers alike. A unique three-hole golfing academy has been added to allow novice and experienced players ample opportunity to improve their game, while an 18-hole putting course provides an extra dimension of golfing pleasure and is the venue for the National Putting Championship.

☎ 056 7773064 📠 056 7773078

e-mail: golfreservations@mountjuliet.ie **web:** www.mountjuliet.ie

Mount Juliet Golf Club: 18 Holes, 6639metres, Par 72, SSS 75, Course record 62. Club membership 500.

Visitors Mon-Sun & BHs. Booking required weekends. Dress code. Handicap certificate. **Societies** booking required. **Green Fees** Apr-Oct Mon/Tue €90 per round, Wed/Thu/Sun €100, Fri/Sat €120. Nov-Dec €80/€90/€100 **Course Designer** Jack Nicklaus **Prof** Sean Cotter **Facilities** 🍽️ 🍴 🛏️ 🛒 🚻 🧖 🏠 ⛳ ♻️ 🏌️ 🏌️ 🚶 **Leisure** hard tennis courts, heated indoor swimming pool, fishing, sauna, gymnasium, Archery/clay shooting/equestrian **Conf** facs Corporate Hospitality Days **Location** 4km S of town off N9

Hotel ★★★★ CHH Mount Juliet Conrad, THOMASTOWN, Co Kilkenny ☎ 056 7773000 📠 056 7773000 57 en suite

NAAS
Map 1 D4

Craddockstown Blessington Rd
☎ 045 897610 📠 045 896968
web: www.craddockstown.com

18 Holes, 5748mtrs, Par 72, SSS 72, Course record 66.
Course Designer A Spring & R Jones **Location** SE of town off R410
Telephone for further details
Hotel ★★★ 79% HL Maudlins House, Dublin Road, NAAS, CO
KILDARE ☎ 045 896999 📠 045 896999 25 en suite

Naas Kerdiffstown
☎ 045 897509 & 874644 📠 045 896109
web: naasgolfclub.com

18 Holes, 5663mtrs, Par 71, SSS 69, Course record 65.
Course Designer E Hackett/A Spring/J Howes **Location** NE of town, off
N7 onto Johnstown-Sallins road
Telephone for further details
Hotel ★★★ 79% HL Maudlins House, Dublin Road, NAAS, CO
KILDARE ☎ 045 896999 📠 045 896999 25 en suite

STRAFFAN
Map 1 D4

Castlewarden
☎ 01 4589254 📠 01 4588972
e-mail: info@castlewardengolfclub.com
web: www.castlewardengolfclub.com
Founded in 1990, Castlewarden is maturing into a delightful parkland
course with water features and excellent greens.

*Castlewarden Golf & Country Club: 18 Holes, 5940metres,
Par 72, SSS 70. Club membership 765.*

Visitors dress code. **Societies** booking required. **Green Fees** €35-
€45 **Course Designer** Tommy Halpin **Prof** Brian O'Brien **Facilities** ⑪
🍽 🍺 ⌂ 🎯 👤 🛍 🛒 🏌 **Location** 6km S of village off N7
Hotel ★★★★ 80% HL Barberstown Castle, STRAFFAN, Co Kildare
☎ 01 6288157 📠 01 6288157 58 en suite

The K Club see page 455
☎ 01 6017200 📠 01 6017297
e-mail: resortsales@kclub.ie
web: www.kclub.ie

CO KILKENNY

CALLAN
Map 1 C3

Callan Geraldine
☎ 056 7725136 & 7725949 📠 056 7755155
web: www.callangolfclub.com
Meadowland course with well positioned spinneys and water hazards.
Not difficult walking and a good test for golfers of all standards.

*Callan Golf Course: 18 Holes, 5872metres, Par 72, SSS 70,
Course record 66. Club membership 1100.*

Visitors Mon-Sun & BHs. Booking required. Handicap certificate. Dress
code. **Societies** booking required. **Green Fees** Apr-Oct: €30 per round
(€35 weekends & BHs), Nov-Mar €25 (€30) **Course Designer** B
Moore/J Power **Prof** Michael O'Shea **Facilities** ⑪ 🍽 🍺 ⌂ 🎯
👤 🛍 🏌 🛒 🏌 **Leisure** fishing **Location** 1.6km SE of village
on R699
Hotel ★★★★ 78% HL Newpark, KILKENNY, Co Kilkenny
☎ 056 7760500 📠 056 7760500 129 en suite

KILKENNY
Map 1 C3

Kilkenny Glendine
☎ 056 7765400 📠 056 7723593
e-mail: enquiries@kilkennygolfclub.com
web: www.kilkennygolfclub.com
One of Ireland's most pleasant inland courses, noted for its tricky
finishing holes and its par 3s. Features of the course are its long
11th and 13th holes and the challenge increases year by year
as thousands of trees planted over the last 30 years or so are
maturing. As host of the Kilkenny Scratch Cup annually, the course
is permanently maintained in championship condition. Sand based
greens make the course playable all year round.

*18 Holes, 5925mtrs, Par 71, SSS 70, Course record 68.
Club membership 1380.*

Visitors Mon-Sat & BHs. Booking required Fri, Sat & BHs. Dress
code. **Societies** booking required. **Green Fees** Apr-Oct: Mon-Thu
€35, Fri €40 (Sat €45); Nov-Mar: €30 (€35 Sat) **Prof** Jimmy
Bolger **Facilities** ⑪ 🍽 🍺 ⌂ 🎯 👤 🛍 🛒 🏌 🛒
🏌 🏌 **Leisure** snooker & pool **Conf** Corporate Hospitality Days
Location 1.6km N of town on N77
Hotel ★★★ 71% HL The Kilkenny Inn Hotel, 15/16 Vicar
Street, KILKENNY, CO KILKENNY ☎ 056 7772828 & 7722821
📠 056 7772828 30 en suite

THOMASTOWN
Map 1 C3

Mount Juliet Hotel & Golf Club see page 457
☎ 056 7773064 📠 056 7773078
e-mail: golfreservations@mountjuliet.ie
web: www.mountjuliet.ie

CO LAOIS

ABBEYLEIX
Map 1 C3

Abbeyleix Rathmoyle
☎ 057 8731450
web: www.abbeyleixgolfclub.ie
*Abbeyleix Golf Course: 18 Holes, 5557mtrs, Par 72,
SSS 70.*

Course Designer Mel Flanagan **Location** 0.6km from Abbeyleix on
Ballyroan road
Telephone for further details
Hotel ★★★★ 78% HL Newpark, KILKENNY, Co Kilkenny
☎ 056 7760500 📠 056 7760500 129 en suite

MOUNTRATH
Map 1 C3

Mountrath Knockanina
☎ 057 8732558 📠 057 8732643
web: www.mountrathgolfclub.com
18 Holes, 5732mtrs, Par 71, SSS 70, Course record 68.
Facilities ⑪ 🍽 🍺 ⌂ 🎯 👤 🏌 🛒 🏌 **Conf** Corporate
Hospitality Days **Location** 2.5km SW of town off N7
Telephone for further details
Hotel ★★★★ 81% HL Keadeen, NEWBRIDGE, Co Kildare
☎ 045 431666 📠 045 431666 75 en suite

IRELAND

PORTARLINGTON Map 1 C3

Portarlington Garryhinch
☎ 057 8623115 ▤ 057 8623044
e-mail: portalingtongc@eircom.net
web: www.portalingtongolf.com

Lovely parkland course designed around woodland with flat terrain. It is bounded on the 16th and 17th by the River Barrow which makes the back 9 very challenging. Club celebrated its centenary in 2008.

18 Holes, 5723mtrs, Par 70, SSS 70, Course record 66. Club membership 1080.

Visitors Mon-Fri. Weekends & BHs by arrangement. Dress code. **Societies** booking required. **Green Fees** €35 per round (€40 weekends) **Course Designer** Eddie Hackett **Facilities** ⑪ ⑩ ᗷ ⌸ ᵮ⌶ ⚲ 🖅 ⚷ 🛒 ⚷ **Conf** facs Corporate Hospitality Days **Location** 6.5km SW of town on R423
Hotel ★★★★ 81% HL Keadeen, NEWBRIDGE, Co Kildare
☎ 045 431666 ▤ 045 431666 75 en suite

PORTLAOISE Map 1 C3

The Heath
☎ 057 8646533 ▤ 057 8646735
e-mail: info@theheathgc.ie
web: www.theheathgc.ie

Course noted for its rough heather and gorze furze and scenic views of the rolling hills of Co Laois. Remarkably dry conditions all year round.

18 Holes, 5857mtrs, Par 71, SSS 50, Course record 67. Club membership 850.

Visitors Mon-Sat except BHs. Booking required Sat. **Societies** booking required. **Green Fees** €25 per round (€35 Sat) **Course Designer** Jeff Howes **Prof** Mark O'Boyle **Facilities** ⑪ ⑩ ᗷ ⌸ ᵮ⌶ ⚲ 🖅 🖳 ⚷ 🛒 ⚷ **Location** 6.5km N on N7
Hotel ★★★★ 81% HL Keadeen, NEWBRIDGE, Co Kildare
☎ 045 431666 ▤ 045 431666 75 en suite

RATHDOWNEY Map 1 C3

Rathdowney
☎ 0505 46170 ▤ 0505 46065
e-mail: rathdowneygolf@eircom.net
web: rathdowneygolfclub.com

An 18-hole parkland course, with undulating terrain. The 17th hole is a tricky par 3, 12th and 15th are particularly tough par 4s and the 6th is a challenging par 5 (503 metres) into the prevailing wind. A good test for golfers of all abilities.

18 Holes, 5894metres, Par 71, SSS 70, Course record 67. Club membership 500.

Visitors Mon-Sun except BHs. Booking required Sun. Dress code. **Societies** booking required. **Green Fees** €25 per 18 holes (€30 weekends) **Course Designer** Eddie Hackett **Facilities** ⑪ ⑩ ⌸ ᵮ⌶ ⚲ 🖳 ⚷ **Conf** Corporate Hospitality Days **Location** 0.8km SE, follow Johnstown signs from town square
Hotel ★★★★ 78% HL Newpark, KILKENNY, Co Kilkenny
☎ 056 7760500 ▤ 056 7760500 129 en suite

BALLINAMORE Map 1 C4

Ballinamore
☎ 071 9644346

A very dry and very testing nine-hole parkland course along the Ballinamore-Ballyconnell Canal. Not busy on weekdays which makes it ideal for high handicap golfers, while at the same time it tests the ability of even a scratch golfer.

9 Holes, 5194mtrs, Par 70, SSS 68, Course record 66. Club membership 300.

Visitors Mon-Sun & BHs. Booking required weekends & BHs. **Societies** booking required. **Green Fees** €20 per day **Course Designer** A Spring **Facilities** ᗷ ⌸ ᵮ⌶ ⚲ ⚷ **Leisure** fishing **Location** 3km W of town along Shannon-Erne canal

CARRICK-ON-SHANNON Map 1 C4

Carrick-on-Shannon Woodbrook
☎ 071 9667015
e-mail: ckgc3@eircom.net
web: www.carrickgolfclub.ie

An 18 hole course with a delightful diversity of scenery. Extended from 9 holes on preserved marshland that sweeps down to a lake and the Boyle river. The original 9 holes are set in mature parkland and under the new layout constitute the first 5 and last 4 holes of the course. Two spectacular holes are the 8th where the tee is surrounded by water which requires a carry over the river and the 13th, a frightening par 3.

18 Holes, 5728mtrs, Par 70, SSS 68. Club membership 505.

Visitors contact club for details. **Societies** booking required.
Green Fees €40 Mon. Wed, Thu, €25 Tue (€45 Fri-Sun) **Course Designer** Eddie Hackett/ Marc Westenborg (new 9) **Facilities** ⑪ ⑩ ᗷ ⌸ ᵮ⌶ ⚲ 🖅 🖳 ⚷ 🗺 **Location** 6.5km W of town on N4

ADARE Map 1 B3

Adare Manor
☎ 061 396204 ▤ 061 396800
e-mail: info@adaremanorgolfclub.com
web: www.adaremanorgolfclub.com

An 18-hole parkland course surrounding the ruins of a 13th-century castle and a 15th-century abbey.

18 Holes, 5304mtrs, Par 69, SSS 69, Course record 63. Club membership 750.

Visitors contact club for details. **Societies** booking required **Green Fees** €40 per round **Course Designer** Ben Sayers/Eddie Hackett **Facilities** ⑪ ⑩ ᗷ ⌸ ᵮ⌶ ⚲ 🖅 🗺 ⚷ **Location** NE of town off N21
Hotel ★★★★ 80% HL Dunraven Arms, ADARE, Co Limerick
☎ 061 396633 ▤ 061 396633 86 en suite

LIMERICK   Map 1 B3

Castletroy Castletroy
☎ 061 335753   📠 061 335373
e-mail: golf@castletroygolfclub.ie
web: www.castletroygolfclub.ie

Mature, parkland course extensively redeveloped in recent years. Out of bounds left of the first two holes and well maintained fairways demand accuracy off the tee. The long par 5 6th hole is set into water. The par 3 14th hole features a panoramic view from the tee with the green surrounded by water while the picturesque 18th is a stern test to finish with the green guarded by bunkers on both sides.

18 Holes, 6284mtrs, Par 72, SSS 73.
Club membership 1062.

Visitors Mon, Wed, Fri, Sat & BHs. Booking required. Handicap certificate. Dress code. **Societies** booking required. **Green Fees** €50 per 18 holes (€60 Fri-Sat & BHs) **Course Designer** Eddie Connaughton **Facilities** ⓣ 🍴 ⓛ 💻 🍷 ⚐ 🏠 ⚑ ⚘ 🚜 ⚘ **Conf** Corporate Hospitality Days **Location** 5km E of city centre

Limerick Ballyclough
☎ 061 415146   📠 061 319219
e-mail: pat.murray@limerickgolfclub.ie
web: www.limerickgc.com

Tree-lined parkland course. The club is the only Irish winner of the European Cup Winners Team Championship.

18 Holes, 6601mtrs, Par 72, SSS 72, Course record 63.
Club membership 1500.

Visitors Mon, Wed-Sat & BHs. Booking required. Dress code. **Societies** booking required. **Green Fees** €50 per round (€70 Fri-Sat & BHs) **Course Designer** A McKenzie **Prof** Lee Harrington **Facilities** ⓣ 🍴 ⓛ 💻 🍷 ⚐ 🏠 ⚑ ⚘ 🚜 ⚘ **Conf** facs Corporate Hospitality Days **Location** 5km S on R511
Hotel ★★★ 79% HL Maldron Hotel Limerick, Southern Ringroad, Roxboro, LIMERICK, Co Limerick ☎ 061 436100 📠 061 436100 199 en suite

Limerick County Golf & Country Club Ballyneety
☎ 061 351881   📠 061 351384
web: www.limerickcounty.com

Limerick County Golf & Country Club: 18 Holes, 5686mtrs, Par 71, SSS 70, Course record 70.

Course Designer Des Smyth **Location** 8km SE of city on R512
Telephone for further details
Hotel ★★★ 79% HL Maldron Hotel Limerick, Southern Ringroad, Roxboro, LIMERICK, Co Limerick ☎ 061 436100 📠 061 436100 199 en suite

NEWCASTLE WEST   Map 1 B3

Newcastle West, Ardagh
☎ 069 76500   📠 069 76511
e-mail: info@newcastlewestgolf.com
web: www.newcastlewestgolf.com

Course set in 160 acres of countryside, built to the highest standards on sandy free draining soil. A practice ground and driving range are included. Hazards on the course include lakes, bunkers, streams and trees. A signature hole is the par 3 6th playing 185yds over a lake.

18 Holes, 5615mtrs, Par 71, SSS 72, Course record 67.
Club membership 1019.

Visitors Mon-Sat & BHs. Dress code. **Societies** booking required.

Green Fees Mon €35, Tue-Thu €45, Fri-Sat €55 **Course Designer** Dr Arthur Spring **Prof** Conor McCormick **Facilities** ⓣ 🍴 ⓛ 💻 🍷 ⚐ 🏠 ⚑ 🚜 ⚘ 🏌 **Conf** facs Corporate Hospitality Days **Location** 3.5km off N21
Hotel ★★★★ 80% HL Dunraven Arms, ADARE, Co Limerick ☎ 061 396633 📠 061 396633 86 en suite

CO LONGFORD

LONGFORD   Map 1 C4

County Longford, Glack, Dublin Rd
☎ 043 46310   📠 043 47082
e-mail: colonggolf@eircom.net
web: www.countylongfordgolfclub.com

A lovely 18-hole parkland course with lots of trees founded in 1894. A stream comes into play at a number of holes including the last. Additional water features have also been introduced, especially at the signature 13th hole. Fine views of Longford and the surrounding countryside from almost every hole.

18 Holes, 5766metres, Par 72, Course record 71.
Club membership 819.

Visitors Mon-Sun & BHs. Booking required. Dress code. **Societies** booking required. **Green Fees** €25 per round (€30 weekends & BHs) **Course Designer** Irish Golf Design **Prof** David Byrne **Facilities** ⓣ ⓛ 💻 🍷 ⚐ 🏠 ⚑ ⚘ 🚜 ⚘ **Conf** facs Corporate Hospitality Days **Location** E of town
Hotel ★★★★ 73% HL Abbey, Galway Road, ROSCOMMON, Co Roscommon ☎ 090 6626240 📠 090 6626240 50 en suite

CO LOUTH

ARDEE   Map 1 D4

Ardee Townparks
☎ 041 6853227   📠 041 6856137
web: www.ardeegolfclub.com

18 Holes, 5934mtrs, Par 71, SSS 72, Course record 64.

Course Designer Eddie Hackett & Declan Branigan **Location** N33 to Ardee, 400 metres from Fair Green
Telephone for further details
Hotel ★★★★ 77% HL Ballymascanlon House, DUNDALK, Co Louth ☎ 042 9358200 📠 042 9358200 90 en suite

BALTRAY   Map 1 D4

County Louth
☎ 041 9881530   📠 041 9881531
e-mail: reservations@countylouthgolfclub.com
web: www.countylouthgolfclub.com

Generally held to have the best greens in Ireland, this links course was designed by Tom Simpson to have well-guarded and attractive greens without being overly dependant on bunkers. It provides a good test for modern championship play.

18 Holes, 6141mtrs, Par 72, SSS 72, Course record 64.
Club membership 1342.

Visitors contact club for details. **Societies** welcome. **Green Fees** €125 per round (€150 Sat) **Course Designer** Tom Simpson **Prof** Paddy McGuirk **Facilities** ⓣ 🍴 ⓛ 💻 🍷 ⚐ 🏠 ⚑

continued

IRELAND

◇ ✔ 🛏 ✔ ✔ **Leisure** hard tennis courts **Location** 8km NE of Drogheda
Hotel ★★★ 70% HL Boyne Valley Hotel & Country Club, Stameen, Dublin Road, DROGHEDA, Co Louth ☎ 041 9837737 📠 041 9837737 73 en suite

DUNDALK
Map 1 D4

Ballymascanlon House Hotel Carlingford Rd (R170)
☎ 042 9358200 📠 042 9371598
e-mail: info@ballymascanlon.com
web: www.ballymascanlon.com

A testing 18-hole parkland course with numerous water hazards and two difficult holes through woodland, this very scenic course is set at the edge of the Cooley Mountains.

Ballymascanlon House Hotel Golf Course: 18 Holes, 5073mtrs, Par 68, SSS 66.

Visitors Mon-Sun & BHs. Booking required Fri-Sun & BHs. Dress code. **Societies** welcome. **Green Fees** phone **Course Designer** Craddock/Ruddy **Facilities** ⑪ ℟ ⓛ ☐ 🍴 ⚷ 🏠 ✔ 💎 ✔ 🛏 ✔ **Leisure** hard tennis courts, heated indoor swimming pool, sauna, gymnasium **Conf** facs Corporate Hospitality Days **Location** 5km NE of town on R173
Hotel ★★★★ 77% HL Ballymascanlon House, DUNDALK, Co Louth
☎ 042 9358200 📠 042 9358200 90 en suite

Dundalk Blackrock
☎ 042 9321731 📠 042 9322022
web: www.dundalkgolfclub.ie
18 Holes, 6028mtrs, Par 72, SSS 71.

Prof Leslie Walker **Facilities** ⑪ ℟ ⓛ ☐ 🍴 ⚷ 🏠 🛏 ✔ **Leisure** sauna **Location** 4km S of town on R172 coast road
Telephone for further details
Hotel ★★★★ 77% HL Ballymascanlon House, DUNDALK, Co Louth
☎ 042 9358200 📠 042 9358200 90 en suite

Killin Park Killin Park
☎ 042 9339303 📠 042 9320848
18 Holes, 4840metres, Par 69, SSS 65, Course record 65.

Course Designer Eddie Hackett **Location** 4.5km NW of village off N53
Telephone for further details
Hotel ★★★★ 77% HL Ballymascanlon House, DUNDALK, Co Louth
☎ 042 9358200 📠 042 9358200 90 en suite

GREENORE
Map 1 D4

Greenore
☎ 042 9373212 & 9373678 📠 042 9383898
e-mail: greenoregolfclub@eircom.net
web: www.greenoregolfclub.com

Situated amid beautiful scenery on the shores of Carlingford Lough, with views of the Mourne Mountains. The pine trees here are an unusual feature on a part-links course. There are quite a number of water facilities, tight fairways and very good greens.

18 Holes, 6078mtrs, Par 71, SSS 73, Course record 69. Club membership 1074.

Visitors Mon-Sun & BHs. Booking required. Dress code. **Societies** booking required. **Green Fees** €40 per round (€50 weekends & BHs) **Course Designer** Eddie Hackett **Prof** Mr Robert Giles **Facilities** ⑪ ℟ ⓛ ☐ 🍴 ⚷ 🏠 ✔ 🛏 ✔ ✔ **Conf** Corporate Hospitality Days **Location** near village off R175
Hotel ★★★★ 77% HL Ballymascanlon House, DUNDALK, Co Louth
☎ 042 9358200 📠 042 9358200 90 en suite

TERMONFECKIN
Map 1 D4

Seapoint
☎ 041 9822333 📠 041 9822331
e-mail: golflinks@seapoint.ie
web: seapointgolfclub.com

A premier championship links course with a particularly interesting 17th hole. A testing course where all the clubs in the bag will be needed.

18 Holes, 6470mtrs, Par 72, SSS 74. Club membership 580.

Visitors Mon-Sun & BHs. Booking required. Dress code. **Societies** booking required. **Green Fees** €65 (€75 Sat, €100 Sun). Half price for 9 holes **Course Designer** Des Smyth **Prof** David Carroll **Facilities** ⑪ ℟ ⓛ ☐ 🍴 ⚷ 🏠 ✔ ✔ 🛏 ✔ ✔ **Conf** facs Corporate Hospitality Days **Location** 6.5km NE of Drogheda
Hotel ★★★ 70% HL Boyne Valley Hotel & Country Club, Stameen, Dublin Road, DROGHEDA, Co Louth ☎ 041 9837737 📠 041 9837737 73 en suite

CO MAYO

BALLINA
Map 1 B4

Ballina Mossgrove
☎ 096 21050 📠 096 21718
web: ballinagolfclub.com
18 Holes, 5581metres, Par 71, SSS 69, Course record 69.

Course Designer E Hackett **Location** 1.5km W of town on R294
Telephone for further details
Hotel ★★★★ 81% HL Mount Falcon Country House, Mount Falcon Estate, BALLINA, Co Mayo ☎ 096 74472 📠 096 74472 32 en suite

IRELAND

461

BALLINROBE   Map 1 B4

Ballinrobe Cloonacastle
☎ 094 9541118   📄 094 9541889
e-mail: info@ballinrobegolfclub.com
web: ballinrobegolfclub.com

A championship parkland 18-hole course, set in the mature woodlands of a historic estate at Cloonacastle. The layout of the course incorporates seven man-made lakes with the River Robe flowing at the back of the 3rd and 5th greens. Ballinrobe is full of character, typified by the 19th-century residence now used as the clubhouse.

18 Holes, 6334metres, Par 73, SSS 72, Course record 67.
Club membership 750.

Visitors Mon-Sat & BHs. Booking required. Dress code.
Societies booking required. **Green Fees** not confirmed **Course Designer** Eddie Hackett **Prof** Courtney Cougar **Facilities** ⓣ 🍽 🏌
🛒 🍴 🚶 🏠 ⛳ ⛳ 🏌 **Conf** facs Corporate Hospitality Days **Location** NE of town on R331
Hotel ★★★ 70% HL Cill Aodain Court Hotel, Main Street, KILTIMAGH, Co Mayo ☎ 094 9381761 📄 094 9381761   17 en suite

See advert on opposite page

BELMULLET (BÉAL AN MHUIRTHEAD)   Map 1 A5

Carne Carne
☎ 097 82292   📄 097 81477
web: www.carnegolflinks.com

Carne Golf Links: 18 Holes, 6119mtrs, Par 72, SSS 72,
Course record 66.
Course Designer Eddie Hackett **Location** 3km W of town off R313
Telephone for further details
Hotel ★★★★ 81% HL Mount Falcon Country House, Mount Falcon Estate, BALLINA, Co Mayo ☎ 096 74472 📄 096 74472   32 en suite

CASTLEBAR   Map 1 B4

Castlebar Hawthorn Av, Rocklands
☎ 094 9021649   📄 094 9026088
e-mail: info@castlebargolfclub.ie
web: www.castlebargolfclub.ie

Course opened September 2000. Fast greens with severe borrows. Accuracy is essential from the tee on most holes. Long difficult course from blue (championship) tees.

18 Holes, 5698metres, Par 71, SSS 70.
Club membership 650.

Visitors Mon-Sat & BHs. Booking required. Dress code.
Societies booking required. **Green Fees** not confirmed **Course Designer** Peter McEvoy **Facilities** ⓣ 🍽 🏌 🛒 🍴 🚶 🏠 ⛳ ⛳ 🏌 **Location** 1.6km SE of town off N84

CLAREMORRIS   Map 1 B4

Claremorris Castlemacgarrett
☎ 094 9371527   📄 094 9372919
e-mail: info@claremorrisgolfclub.com
web: www.claremorrisgolfclub.com

A 18-hole parkland course designed by Tom Craddock, designer of Druids Glen. It consists of many eye-catching water features, bunkers, trees and wooded backgrounds. The feature hole is the short par 4 14th with its island green.

18 Holes, 6600mtrs, Par 73, SSS 70, Course record 68.
Club membership 675.

Visitors Mon-Sun & BHs. Booking required Thu-Sun & BHs. Handicap certificate. Dress code. **Societies** booking required. **Green Fees** Oct-Mar €26/€32 per round, Apr-Sep €32/€40 **Course Designer** Tom Craddock **Prof** Jimmy Heggarty **Facilities** ⓣ 🍽 🏌 🛒 🍴 🚶
🚶 🚜 🏌 **Location** 2km S of town on N17
Hotel ★★★ 66% HL Belmont, KNOCK, Co Mayo ☎ 094 9388122 📄 094 9388122   62 en suite

KEEL   Map 1 A4

Achill Achill Island, Westport
☎ 098 43456   📄 098 43456
e-mail: achillgolfclub@eircom.net
web: www.achillgolfclub.com

Seaside links in a scenic location by the Atlantic Ocean overlooking Keel Strand with panoramic views of the Minaun Cliffs.

9 Holes, 5416mtrs, Par 70, SSS 66, Course record 69.
Club membership 240.

Visitors handicap certificate. **Societies** booking required. **Green Fees** €15 per round (€20 weekends) **Course Designer** Paddy Skirrit **Facilities** 🚶 🚶 🏌 **Location** E of Keel on R319
Hotel ★★★★ 77% HL Hotel Westport Leisure, Spa & Conference, Newport Road, WESTPORT, Co Mayo ☎ 098 25122 & 0870 876 5432 📄 098 25122   129 en suite

SWINFORD   Map 1 B4

Swinford Brabazon Park
☎ 094 9251378   📄 094 9251378
web: www.swinfordgolf.com

9 Holes, 5542metres, Par 70, SSS 68.
Facilities 🍴 🚶 🏌 **Location** S of town on R320
Telephone for further details

WESTPORT
Map 1 B4

Westport Carrowholly
☎ 098 28262 & 27070 📠 098 27217
e-mail: info@westportgolfclub.com
web: www.westportgolfclub.com

This is a beautiful course with wonderful views of Clew Bay, with its 365 islands, and the holy mountain called Croagh Patrick, famous for the annual pilgrimage to its summit. Golfers indulge in a different kind of penance on this challenging course with many memorable holes. Perhaps the most exciting is the par 5 15th, 580yds long and featuring a long carry from the tee over an inlet of Clew Bay.

18 Holes, 6148mtrs, Par 73, SSS 71, Course record 61. Club membership 600.

Visitors contact club for details. **Societies** booking required. **Green Fees** not confirmed **Course Designer** Fred Hawtree **Prof** Alex Mealia **Facilities** ⑪ ⑩ ⅃ ⌨ ⌷ ᚜ ㅅ ☖ ⚐ ⚔ 🛵 ⚑
Conf Corporate Hospitality Days **Location** 4km from town off N59 **Hotel** ★★★★ 77% HL Hotel Westport Leisure, Spa & Conference, Newport Road, WESTPORT, Co Mayo ☎ 098 25122 & 0870 876 5432 📠 098 25122 129 en suite

CO MEATH

BETTYSTOWN
Map 1 D4

Laytown & Bettystown
☎ 041 9827170 📠 041 9828506
e-mail: links@landb.ie
web: www.landb.ie

A very competitive and trying links course.

18 Holes, 5652mtrs, Par 71, SSS 70, Course record 65. Club membership 950.

Visitors Mon-Sun & BHs. Booking required. Dress code.
Societies booking required. **Green Fees** not confirmed **Prof** Robert J Browne **Facilities** ⑪ ⑩ ⅃ ⌨ ⌷ ᚜ ㅅ ☖ ⚐ ⚔ 🛵 ⚑
Leisure hard tennis courts **Location** N of village on R150
Hotel ★★★ 70% HL Boyne Valley Hotel & Country Club, Stameen, Dublin Road, DROGHEDA, Co Louth ☎ 041 9837737 📠 041 9837737 73 en suite

DUNSHAUGHLIN
Map 1 D4

Black Bush Thomastown
☎ 01 8250021 📠 01 8250400
e-mail: info@blackbushgolfclub.ie
web: www.blackbushgolfclub.ie

Three 9-hole courses, giving three possible 18-hole combinations, set in lovely parkland, with a lake providing a hazard at the 1st. Creeks, trees and bunkers make for challenging and accurate shot-making.

Black Bush: 18 Holes, 6337metres, Par 73, SSS 72.
Agore: 18 Holes, 6033metres, Par 71, SSS 69.
Thomastown: 18 Holes, 5882metres, Par 70, SSS 68.
Club membership 1100.

Visitors Mon, Thu & Sat. Booking required. Handicap certificate. Dress code. **Societies** booking required. **Green Fees** €35 per 18 holes (€40 weekends and BHs) **Course Designer** Bobby Browne **Prof** Shane O'Grady **Facilities** ⑪ ⑩ ⅃ ⌨ ⌷ ᚜ ㅅ ☖ ⚐ ⚔ 🛵 ⚑
Conf Corporate Hospitality Days **Location** 2.5km E of village on R125 **Hotel** ★★★ 77% HL Finnstown Country House Hotel, Newcastle Road, LUCAN, Co Dublin ☎ 01 6010700 📠 01 6010700 81 en suite

IRELAND

KELLS
Map 1 C4

Headfort
☎ 046 9240146 📠 046 9249282
e-mail: info@headfortgolfclub.ie
web: www.headfortgolfclub.ie

Headfort Old Course is a delightful parkland course which is regarded as one of the best of its kind in Ireland. There are ample opportunities for birdies, but even if these are not achieved, provides a challenging test. The New Course is a modern course which criss-crosses the Blackwater river, making use of two islands.

Old Course: 18 Holes, 5973mtrs, Par 72, SSS 71.
New Course: 18 Holes, 6164metres, Par 72, SSS 74.
Club membership 1700.

Visitors dress code. **Societies** welcome. **Green Fees** not confirmed **Course Designer** Christy O'Connor jnr **Prof** Brendan McGovern **Facilities** ⑪ ⑩ 🍴 🛒 🍷 🤸 🏌 🧺 ⚑ 🏌 🛺 ⚑
Location 0.8km E of village on N3
Hotel ★★★ 71% HL The Park Hotel, Virginia Park, VIRGINIA, Co Cavan ☎ 049 8546100 📠 049 8546100 26 en suite

See advert on page 461

KILCOCK
Map 1 C4

Kilcock, Gallow
☎ 01 6287592 📠 01 6287283
e-mail: kilcockgolfclub@eircom.net
web: www.kilcockgolfclub.ie

A parkland course with generous fairways, manicured greens and light rough only. The course has recently undergone a major redevelopment with the installation of USGA sand based tees and greens and a comprehensive drainage programme.

18 Holes, 6046mtrs, Par 72, SSS 70, Course record 69.
Club membership 700.

Visitors Mon-Sun & BHs. Booking required. Dress code.
Societies booking required. **Green Fees** Mon-Thu €25, Fri €32, weekends & BHs €35 **Course Designer** Eddie Hackett **Facilities** ⑪ ⑩ 🍴 🛒 🍷 🤸 ⚑ **Location** M4 exit Kilcock, course 3km
Hotel ★★★ 67% HL Lucan Spa, LUCAN, Co Dublin ☎ 01 6280494 📠 01 6280494 71 en suite

NAVAN
Map 1 C4

Royal Tara Bellinter
☎ 046 25508 & 25244 📠 046 25508
web: royaltaragolfclub.com

New Course: 18 Holes, 5757mtrs, Par 71, SSS 70.
Bellinter Nine: 9 Holes, 2911mtrs, Par 35, SSS 35.

Course Designer Des Smyth **Location** 20km from Navan on N3
Telephone for further details
Guesthouse ★★★★ GA Killyon, Dublin Road, NAVAN, Co Meath, Republic of Ireland ☎ 046 907 1224 📠 046 907 1224 6 en suite

TRIM
Map 1 C4

County Meath Newtownmoynagh
☎ 046 9431463 📠 046 9437554
e-mail: info@countymeathgolfclubtrim.ie
web: trimgolf.net

Originally a 9-hole course, it was extended to 18-holes in 1990. It is maturing into a very challenging and formidable parkland course with four testing par 5s. Luxurious clubhouse with panoramic views across the course.

18 Holes, 6088mtrs, Par 73, SSS 72, Course record 68.
Club membership 900.

Visitors Mon-Sun & BHs. Booking required. Dress code.
Societies booking required. **Green Fees** €35 per round Mon-Thu (€40 Fri-Sun) **Course Designer** Eddie Hackett/Tom Craddock **Prof** Robin Machin **Facilities** ⑪ ⑩ 🍴 🛒 🍷 🤸 🏌 ⚑ **Leisure** snooker **Location** 5km SW of town on R160
Hotel ★★★★ 77% HL Knightsbrook Hotel Spa & Golf Resort, Dublin Road, TRIM, Co Meath ☎ 046 9482100 📠 046 9482100 131 en suite

CO MONAGHAN

CARRICKMACROSS
Map 1 C4

Mannan Castle Donaghmoyne
☎ 042 9663308 📠 042 9663308

18 Holes, 5944metres, Par 70, SSS 69.

Course Designer F Ainsworth **Location** 6.5km N of town
Telephone for further details
Hotel ★★★★ 77% HL Ballymascanlon House, DUNDALK, Co Louth ☎ 042 9358200 📠 042 9358200 90 en suite

Nuremore
☎ 042 9671368 📠 042 9661853
e-mail: nuremore@eircom.net
web: www.nuremore.com

Picturesque parkland course of championship length incorporating the drumlins and lakes that are a natural feature of the Monaghan countryside. Precision is required on the 10th to drive over a large lake and between a narrow avenue of trees. Signature hole 18th.

Nuremore Hotel & Country Club: 18 Holes, 6400yds,
Par 71, SSS 69, Course record 64. Club membership 250.

Visitors Mon-Sun & BHs. Dress code. **Societies** welcome. **Green Fees** €35 (€42 weeekends and BHs) **Course Designer** Eddie Hackett **Prof** Maurice Cassidy **Facilities** ⑪ ⑩ 🍴 🛒 🍷 🤸 🏌 ⚑ 💎 ⚑ 🛺 ⚑ **Leisure** hard tennis courts, heated indoor swimming

continued

pool, squash, fishing, sauna, gymnasium **Conf** facs Corporate Hospitality Days **Location** 1.6km SE of town on N2
Hotel ★★★★ 79% HL Nuremore, CARRICKMACROSS, Co Monaghan ☎ 042 9661438 🖹 042 9661438 72 en suite

CASTLEBLAYNEY
Map 1 C4

Castleblayney Onomy
☎ 042 9740451 🖹 042 9740451
9 Holes, 4918metres, Par 68, SSS 66, Course record 65.
Course Designer Bobby Browne **Location** in town on Hope Castle Estate
Telephone for further details
Hotel ★★★★ 77% HL Ballymascanlon House, DUNDALK, Co Louth ☎ 042 9358200 🖹 042 9358200 90 en suite

CLONES
Map 1 C5

Clones Hilton Park
☎ 047 56017 & 56913 🖹 047 56913
e-mail: clonesgolfclub@eircom.net
web: www.clonesgolfclub.com
A parkland course set in drumlin country and renowned for the quality of the greens and the wildlife. Due to a limestone belt, the course is very dry and playable all year.
18 Holes, 5980mtrs, Par 71, SSS 71, Course record 68.
Club membership 450.
Visitors booking required weekends & BHs. Dress code
Societies booking required. **Green Fees** €30 per day (€35 per round weekends) **Course Designer** Dr Arthur Spring **Facilities** ⓣ ⑩ 🖺 ⬚ 🕪 ⚍ ⚑ ✆ **Conf** Corporate Hospitality Days **Location** 5km S of town on R212
Hotel ★★★★ 74% HL Hillgrove Hotel, Leisure & Spa, Old Armagh Road, MONAGHAN, Co Monaghan ☎ 047 81288 🖹 047 81288 87 en suite

MONAGHAN
Map 1 C5

Rossmore Rossmore Park, Cootehill Rd
☎ 047 71222
e-mail: info@rossmoregc.com
web: www.rossmoregc.com
An undulating, 18-hole parkland course in beautiful countryside with views over Ulster and the surrounding area.
18 Holes, 5590mtrs, Par 70, SSS 69, Course record 68.
Club membership 650.
Visitors Mon-Sun & BHs. Booking required Thu, weekends & BHs. **Societies** booking required. **Green Fees** €35 per round (€45 weekends & BHs) **Course Designer** Des Smyth **Facilities** ⓣ ⑩ 🖺 ⬚ 🕪 ⚍ 🖻 ⚑ ✆ 🛒 ✆ **Leisure** snooker **Location** 3km S of town on R188
Hotel ★★★★ 74% HL Hillgrove Hotel, Leisure & Spa, Old Armagh Road, MONAGHAN, Co Monaghan ☎ 047 81288 🖹 047 81288 87 en suite

CO OFFALY

BIRR
Map 1 C3

Birr The Glenns
☎ 0509 20082 🖹 0509 22155
web: www.globalgolf.com
18 Holes, 5700mtrs, Par 70, SSS 70, Course record 62.
Course Designer Eddie Connaughton **Location** 3km N of town on R439
Telephone for further details

DAINGEAN
Map 1 C4

Castle Barna Tullamore
☎ 057 9353384 🖹 057 9353077
e-mail: info@castlebarna.ie
web: www.castlebarna.ie
Parkland beside the Grand Canal noted for its excellent greens and lush fairways. Many mature trees, natural streams and the naturally undulating landscape provide a great challenge for golfers of all abilities.
18 Holes, 5798mtrs, Par 72, SSS 71, Course record 68.
Club membership 600.
Visitors Mon-Sun & BHs. Booking required weekends & BHs. Dress code. **Societies** booking required. **Green Fees** €25 per round (€35 weekends & BHs) **Course Designer** Alan Duggan/Kieran Monahan **Facilities** ⓣ by prior arrangement ⑩ by prior arrangement 🖺 ⬚ 🕪 ⚍ ⚑ ✆ 🛒 ✆ **Leisure** fishing **Conf** Corporate Hospitality Days **Location** 11km off N6 Dublin-Galway road at Tyrells pass

EDENDERRY
Map 1 C4

Edenderry
☎ 046 9731072 🖹 046 9733911
e-mail: enquiries@edenderrygolfclub.com
web: www.edenderrygolfclub.com
A most friendly club which offers a relaxing game in pleasant surroundings.
18 Holes, 5815metres, Par 72, SSS 72, Course record 66.
Club membership 900.
Visitors dress code. **Societies** booking required. **Green Fees** not confirmed **Course Designer** Havers/Hackett **Facilities** ⓣ ⑩ 🖺 ⬚ 🕪 ⚍ ✆ 🛒 ✆ **Conf** facs Corporate Hospitality Days **Location** 1.2km outside Edenderry on Dublin route

TULLAMORE
Map 1 C4

Esker Hills
☎ 057 9355999 🖹 057 9355021
web: www.eskerhillsgolf.com
18 Holes, 6051mtrs, Par 71, SSS 71, Course record 65.
Course Designer Christy O'Connor jnr **Location** 3m from Tullamore off N80 Tullamore to Clara road
Telephone for further details

IRELAND

Tullamore Brookfield
☎ 057 9321439 📠 057 9341806
e-mail: tullamoregolfclub@eircom.net
web: www.tullamoregolfclub.ie

Course set in mature parkland of oak, beech and chestnut. The original design was by James Braid and this has been radically altered to meet the highest standards of the modern game, with sand-based undulating greens, lakes, bunkering, mounding and more trees.

18 Holes, 5666mtrs, Par 70, SSS 71, Course record 68. Club membership 1200.

Visitors Mon-Sat. Booking required. Dress code **Societies** booking required **Green Fees** not confirmed **Course Designer** James Braid/ Paddy Merrigam **Prof** Donagh McArdle **Facilities** ⑪ 🍴 🏌 🛋 ☕ 🍺 ⚑ 📧 🎽 🚗 ⚙ **Location** 4km SW of town on R421
Hotel ★★★★ 78% HL Hodson Bay, Hodson Bay, ATHLONE, Co Westmeath ☎ 090 6442000 📠 090 6442000 182 en suite

CO ROSCOMMON

ATHLONE   Map 1 C4

Athlone Hodson Bay
☎ 090 6492073 📠 090 6494080
e-mail: athlonegolfclub@eircom.net
web: www.athlonegolfclub.ie

A picturesque course with a panoramic view of Lough Ree. Overall, it is a tight, difficult course with some outstanding holes and is noted for its magnificent greens. All greens and tees have been rebuilt to be sand based. Three water features.

18 Holes, 5983mtrs, Par 71, SSS 71, Course record 66. Club membership 1250.

Visitors Mon-Sun & BHs. Booking required. Dress code.
Societies booking required. **Green Fees** €35 per round (€40 Sat) **Course Designer** J McAllister **Prof** Kevin Grealy **Facilities** ⑪ 🍴 🏌 ☕ 🍺 🛋 📧 🎽 ⚙ 🚗 ⚙ **Conf** Corporate Hospitality Days **Location** 6.5km from town beside Lough Ree off N61
Hotel ★★★★ 78% HL Hodson Bay, Hodson Bay, ATHLONE, Co Westmeath ☎ 090 6442000 📠 090 6442000 182 en suite

BALLAGHADERREEN   Map 1 B4

Ballaghaderreen
☎ 094 9860295

9 Holes, 5237metres, Par 70, SSS 67, Course record 68.
Course Designer Paddy Skerritt **Location** 3.5km S of town
Telephone for further details

BOYLE   Map 1 B4

Boyle Roscommon Rd
☎ 071 9662594

9 Holes, 5324mtrs, Par 68, SSS 66, Course record 65.
Course Designer E Hackett **Location** 3km S off N61
Telephone for further details
Hotel ★★★★ 72% HL The Landmark, CARRICK-ON-SHANNON, Co Leitrim ☎ 071 9622222 📠 071 9622222 50 en suite

CASTLEREA   Map 1 B4

Castlerea Clonalis
☎ 094 9620068

The clubhouse is virtually at the centre of Castlerea course with seven tees visible. A pleasant parkland course incorporating part of the River Francis.

Castlerea Golf Course: 9 Holes, 4974mtrs, Par 68, SSS 66, Course record 62. Club membership 815.

Visitors Mon-Sat & BHs. **Societies** booking required. **Green Fees** €20 per day **Facilities** 🏌 ☕ 🍺 🛋 ⚙ **Location** near town centre on N60
Hotel ★★★★ 73% HL Abbey, Galway Road, ROSCOMMON, Co Roscommon ☎ 090 6626240 📠 090 6626240 50 en suite

ROSCOMMON   Map 1 B4

Roscommon Mote Park
☎ 090 6626382 📠 090 6626043
e-mail: rosegolfclub@eircom.net
web: www.golfclubireland.com/roscommon

Located on the rolling pastures of the Mote Park estate. Numerous water hazards, notably on the tricky 13th, multi-tiered greens and an excellent irrigation to give an all-weather surface.

Roscommon Golf Course: 18 Holes, 6290mtrs, Par 72, SSS 70, Course record 61. Club membership 700.

Visitors Mon-Sun & BHs. Booking required Tue, Thu, weekends & BHs. Handicap certificate. Dress code. **Societies** booking required. **Green Fees** not confirmed **Course Designer** E Connaughton **Facilities** ⑪ 🍴 🏌 ☕ 🍺 🛋 🚗 ⚙ **Location** 0.8km S of town
Hotel ★★★★ 73% HL Abbey, Galway Road, ROSCOMMON, Co Roscommon ☎ 090 6626240 📠 090 6626240 50 en suite

STROKESTOWN   Map 1 C4

Strokestown Bumlin
☎ 071 9633528 & 9633660
e-mail: strokesdowngolfclub@gmail.com
web: www.strokesdowngolfclub.com

Picturesque nine-hole course set in parkland with fine views.

Strokestown Golf Course: 9 Holes, 2615mtrs, Par 70, SSS 67. Club membership 250.

Visitors handicap certificate. Dress code. **Societies** booking required. **Green Fees** not confirmed **Course Designer** Mel Flanagan **Facilities** 🍺 🛋 **Location** 2.5km SW of village off R368
Hotel ★★★★ 73% HL Abbey, Galway Road, ROSCOMMON, Co Roscommon ☎ 090 6626240 📠 090 6626240 50 en suite

CO SLIGO

BALLYMOTE   Map 1 B4

Ballymote Ballinascarrow
☎ 071 9183089
e-mail: kenneth.drury@gmail.com
web: www.ballymotegolfclub.ie

Although Ballymote was founded in 1940, the course dates from 1993 and has matured well into a parkland with ample fairways and large greens. The feature par 4 7th hole has been redesigned with the green

continued

surrounded by water and Ballinascarrow Lake in the background. A challenging course set in breathtaking scenery.

9 Holes, 5302mtrs, Par 70, SSS 68, Course record 63. Club membership 250.

Visitors Mon-Sun & BHs. **Societies** booking required. **Green Fees** €20 per day **Course Designer** Eddie Hacket/Mel Flanagan **Facilities** ⛳ ♨ 🚩 🏌 🚌 ⛳ **Leisure** fishing **Location** 1.5km from Ballymote centre
Hotel ★★★ 79% HL Sligo Park, Pearse Road, SLIGO, Co Sligo ☎ 071 9190400 📠 071 9190400 137 en suite

INISHCRONE   Map 1 B5

Enniscrone
☎ 096 36297   📠 096 36657
web: www.enniscronegolf.com
27 Holes, 6125metres, Par 73, SSS 72, Course record 70.
Course Designer E Hackett/Donald Steel **Location** 0.8km S of village
Telephone for further details

SLIGO   Map 1 B5

County Sligo Rosses Point
☎ 071 9177134 & 9177186   📠 071 9177460
e-mail: teresa@countysligogolfclub.ie
web: countysligogolfclub.ie
Now considered to be one of the top links courses in Ireland, County Sligo is host to a number of competitions, including the West of Ireland championships and internationals. Set in an elevated position on cliffs above three large beaches, the prevailing winds provide an additional challenge. Tom Watson described it as 'a magnificent links, particularly the stretch of holes from the 14th to the 17th'.

18 Holes, 6136mtrs, Par 71, SSS 72, Course record 67. Bomore: 9 Holes, 2785mtrs, Par 35, SSS 69. Club membership 1250.

Visitors handicap certificate. Dress code. **Societies** booking required. **Green Fees** not confirmed **Course Designer** Harry Colt **Prof** Jim Robinson **Facilities** ⛳ 🍴 🏌 ⛳ 🍷 🏌 🏠 🚩 ⛳ 🚌 ⛳ **Conf** facs Corporate Hospitality Days **Location** N of town off N15

Strandhill Strandhill
☎ 071 9168188   📠 071 9168811
18 Holes, 5516mtrs, Par 69, SSS 68.
Prof Anthony Gray **Facilities** ⛳ 🍴 🏌 ⛳ 🍷 🏌 🏠 🚩 ⛳ 🚌 ⛳ **Location** 8km W of town off R292
Telephone for further details
Hotel ★★★ 79% HL Sligo Park, Pearse Road, SLIGO, Co Sligo ☎ 071 9190400 📠 071 9190400 137 en suite

TOBERCURRY   Map 1 B4

Tubbercurry
☎ 071 85849   📠 071 9185888
e-mail: contact@tubbercurrygolfclub.com
web: www.tubbercurrygolfclub.com
A nine-hole parkland course designed by Edward Hackett. The 8th hole, a par 3, is regarded as being one of the most testing in the west of Ireland. An exceptionally dry course, playable all year round.

Tobercurry Golf Club: 9 Holes, 5490mtrs, Par 70, SSS 69, Course record 65. Club membership 350.

Visitors contact club for details. **Societies** welcome. **Green Fees** €20 per day/round **Course Designer** Eddie Hackett **Facilities** ⛳ 🍴 🏌 ⛳ 🍷 🏌 ⛳ **Conf** Corporate Hospitality Days **Location** 0.4km from town centre
Guesthouse ★★★ BB Cruckawn House, Ballymote/Boyle Road, TOBERCURRY, Co Sligo ☎ 071 918 5188 📠 071 918 5188

CO TIPPERARY

CAHIR   Map 1 C3

Cahir Park Kilcommon
☎ 052 41474   📠 052 42717
web: www.cahirparkgolfclub.com
18 Holes, 5806metres, Par 71, SSS 71, Course record 66.
Course Designer Eddie Hackett **Location** 1.6km SW of town centre on R668
Telephone for further details
Guesthouse ★★★★★ GH Hanoras Cottage, Nire Valley, BALLYMACARBRY, Co Waterford ☎ 052 6136134 & 6136442 📠 052 6136134 10 en suite

CLONMEL   Map 1 C2

Clonmel Lyreanearla
☎ 052 24050   📠 052 83349
web: clonmelgolfclub.com
18 Holes, 5804metres, Par 72, SSS 71.
Course Designer Eddie Hackett **Location** 5km from Clonmel off N24
Telephone for further details
Hotel ★★★★ 73% HL Hotel Minella, CLONMEL, Co Tipperary ☎ 052 22388 📠 052 22388 70 en suite

MONARD   Map 1 B3

Ramada Hotel Ballykisteen
☎ 062 33333   📠 062 31555
web: www.ramadaireland.com
Ramada Hotel & Suites: 18 Holes, 6186metres, Par 72, SSS 72.
Course Designer Des Smith **Location** 1.6km SE of village on N24 towards Tipperary
Telephone for further details
Guesthouse ★★★ GH Ach-na-Sheen House, Clonmel Road, TIPPERARY, Co Tipperary ☎ 062 51298 📠 062 51298 8 en suite

IRELAND

NENAGH
Map 1 B3

Nenagh Beechwood
☎ 067 31476 📄 067 34808
e-mail: nenaghgolfclub@eircom.net
web: www.nenaghgolfclub.com

The sand-based greens guarded by intimidating bunkers are a challenge for even the most fastidious putters. Excellent drainage and firm surfaces allow play all year round.

18 Holes, 6029mtrs, Par 72, SSS 72, Course record 68. Club membership 1100.

Visitors Mon-Sat. Booking required. Handicap certificate. Dress code. **Societies** booking required. **Green Fees** not confirmed **Course Designer** Patrick Merrigan **Prof** Ryan McCann **Facilities** 🕯 by prior arrangement 🍴 by prior arrangement 🍺 🖥 🏌 🛪 🛒 ⛳ 🚗 🛍 ⛳ **Location** 5km NE of town on R491
Guesthouse ★★★★ BB Ashley Park House, NENAGH, Co Tipperary ☎ 067 38223 & 38013 📄 067 38223 5 en suite

ROSCREA
Map 1 C3

Roscrea Golf Club Derryvale
☎ 0505 21130 📄 0505 23410
e-mail: info@roscreagolfclub.ie

Course situated on the eastern side of Roscrea in the shadows of the Slieve Bloom Mountains. A special feature of the course is the variety of the par 3 holes, most noteworthy of which is the 150-metre 4th, which is played almost entirely over a lake. It is widely recognised that the finishing six holes will prove a worthy challenge to even the best players. The most famous hole on the course is the 5th, referred to locally as the Burma Road, a par 5 of over 511 metres with the fairway lined with trees and out of bounds on the left side.

Roscrea Golf Club: 18 Holes, 5862mtrs, Par 71, SSS 70, Course record 66. Club membership 600.

Visitors Mon-Sun & BHs. Booking required Tue, Wed, weekends & BHs. Dress code. Handicap certificate. **Societies** booking required. **Green Fees** €30 (€35 weekends) **Course Designer** A Spring **Facilities** 🕯 🍴 🍺 🖥 🏌 🛪 ⛳ 🛒 ⛳ **Conf** facs Corporate Hospitality Days **Location** E of town on N7
Hotel ★★★ 70% HL Racket Hall Country Golf & Conference Hotel, Dublin Road, ROSCREA, Co Tipperary ☎ 050 521748 📄 050 521748 40 en suite

TEMPLEMORE
Map 1 C3

Templemore Manna South
☎ 0504 31400

Flat parkland course with many spinneys masking out the fairways. Drains cross the fairway on the 1st and 8th holes and require golfers to manage shot making to avoid ending up in the hazard. The 4th, a par 4 dog leg and 5th, a par 3, while not very long, demand accuracy to avoid the influence of water hazards and the course boundary.

9 Holes, 5780mtrs, Par 71, SSS 71, Course record 68. Club membership 330.

Visitors contact club for details. **Societies** booking required. **Green Fees** not confirmed **Facilities** 🛪 **Leisure** hard tennis courts **Location** 0.8km S of town on N62
Hotel 🅻 Horse & Jockey Hotel, Horse & Jockey, THURLES, Co Tipperary ☎ 0504 44192 📄 0504 44192 67 en suite

THURLES
Map 1 C3

Thurles Turtulla
☎ 0504 21983 & 24599 📄 0504 24647
18 Holes, 5904mtrs, Par 72, SSS 71, Course record 67.
Course Designer Mr J McMlister **Location** 1.6km S of town on N62
Telephone for further details
Guesthouse ★★★ GH Ach-na-Sheen House, Clonmel Road, TIPPERARY, Co Tipperary ☎ 062 51298 📄 062 51298 8 en suite

TIPPERARY
Map 1 C3

County Tipperary Golf & Country Club Dundrum House Hotel, Dundrum
☎ 062 71717 📄 062 71718
e-mail: golf shop@dundrumhousehotel.com
web: www.dundrumhousehotel.com

The course had been built into a mature Georgian estate using the features of woodland and parkland adorned by the Multeen River. Designed by Philip Walton. The 13th hole is one of the most testing par 5s in Ireland.

County Tipperary Golf & Country Club: 18 Holes, 6447metres, Par 72, SSS 72. Club membership 460.

Visitors contact club for details **Societies** booking required. **Green Fees** €60 per round (€70 weekends) **Course Designer** Philip Walton **Facilities** 🕯 🍴 🍺 🖥 🏌 🛪 🛒 ⛳ 🚗 🛍 ⛳ **Leisure** heated indoor swimming pool, fishing, gymnasium **Conf** facs Corporate Hospitality Days **Location** 12km NE of town on R505
Guesthouse ★★★ GH Ach-na-Sheen House, Clonmel Road, TIPPERARY, Co Tipperary ☎ 062 51298 📄 062 51298 8 en suite

Tipperary Rathanny
☎ 062 51119 📄 062 51119
Tipperary Golf Course: 18 Holes, 5761mtrs, Par 71, SSS 71, Course record 66.
Facilities 🕯 🍴 by prior arrangement 🍺 🖥 🏌 🛪 🛒 🛍 ⛳ **Location** 1.6km S of town on R664
Telephone for further details
Guesthouse ★★★ GH Ach-na-Sheen House, Clonmel Road, TIPPERARY, Co Tipperary ☎ 062 51298 📄 062 51298 8 en suite

CO WATERFORD

DUNGARVAN
Map 1 C2

Dungarvan Knocknagranagh
☎ 058 41605 & 43310 📄 058 44113
e-mail: dungarvangc@eircom.net
web: www.dungarvangolfclub.com

A championship-standard course beside Dungarvan Bay, with lakes and hazards placed to challenge all levels of golfer. The greens are considered to be among the best in Ireland.

18 Holes, 5998metres, Par 72, SSS 71, Course record 66. Club membership 900.

Visitors Mon-Sun & BHs. Booking required. Dress code. **Societies** booking required. **Green Fees** €35 (€45 weekends & BHs). Reductions for on-line booking **Course Designer** Moss Fives **Prof** David Hayes **Facilities** 🕯 🍴 🍺 🖥 🏌 🛪 🛍 ⛳ 🚗 ⛳ **Leisure** snooker **Location** off N25
Hotel ★★★ 68% HL Lawlors, DUNGARVAN, Co Waterford ☎ 058 41122 & 41056 📄 058 41122 89 en suite

IRELAND

Gold Coast Golf & Leisure Ballinacourty
☎ 058 44055 🖷 058 44055
e-mail: goldcoastgolf@cablesurf.com
web: www.goldcoastclub.com

Parkland beside the Atlantic Ocean with unrivalled views of Dungarvan Bay. The mature tree-lined fairways of the old course are tastefully integrated with the long and challenging newer holes to create a superb course.

Gold Coast Golf Club: 18 Holes, 6171mtrs, Par 72, SSS 72, Course record 70. Club membership 600.

Visitors contact club for details. **Societies** welcome. **Green Fees** €37 per 18 holes (€47 weekends & BHs) **Course Designer** Maurice Fives **Facilities** **Leisure** hard tennis courts, heated indoor swimming pool, sauna, gymnasium **Conf** facs **Location** 3km N of town off N25
Hotel ★★★ 68% HL Lawlors, DUNGARVAN, Co Waterford
☎ 058 41122 & 41056 🖷 058 41122 89 en suite

West Waterford Golf 7 Country Club
☎ 058 43216 & 41475 🖷 058 44343
e-mail: info@westwaterfordgolf.com
web: www.westwaterfordgolf.com

Designed by Eddie Hackett, the course is on 150 acres of rolling parkland by the Brickey River with a backdrop of the Comeragh Mountains, Knockmealdowns and Drum Hills. The first nine holes are laid out on a large plateau featuring a stream which comes into play at the 3rd and 4th holes. The river at the southern boundary affects several later holes.

West Waterford Golf & Country Club: 18 Holes, 6137mtrs, Par 72, SSS 72. Club membership 603.

Visitors Mon-Sun & BHs. Booking required weekends & BHs. Dress code. **Societies** welcome. **Green Fees** €35 per 18 holes (€45 weekends and BHs) **Course Designer** Eddie Hackett **Facilities** **Leisure** hard tennis courts **Conf** Corporate Hospitality Days **Location** 5km W of town off N25
Hotel ★★★ 68% HL Lawlors, DUNGARVAN, Co Waterford
☎ 058 41122 & 41056 🖷 058 41122 89 en suite

DUNMORE EAST — Map 1 C2

Dunmore East
☎ 051 383151 🖷 051 383151
e-mail: info@dunmoreeastgolfclub.ie
web: www.dunmoreeastgolfclub.ie

Overlooking the village, bay and the Hook peninsula, this course features a number of holes with cliff top trees and greens, promising challenging golf for the high or low handicap golfer.

18 Holes, 6070mtrs, Par 72, SSS 69, Course record 65. Club membership 500.

Visitors Mon-Sun & BHs. Booking required BHs. Dress code. **Societies** booking required. **Green Fees** Apr-Oct €30 per 18 holes, Nov-Mar €25 per 18 holes (€35/€30 weekends) **Course Designer** W H Jones **Prof** Susan O'Brien **Facilities** **Location** into Dunmore East, first left, left at Strand Inn, right
Hotel ★★★ 74% HL Majestic, TRAMORE, Co Waterford
☎ 051 381761 🖷 051 381761 60 en suite

LISMORE — Map 1 C2

Lismore Ballyin
☎ 058 54026 🖷 058 53338
e-mail: lismoregolf@eircom.net
web: www.lismoregolf.org

Picturesque, tree-dotted, sloping, nine-hole parkland course on the banks of the Blackwater River.

9 Holes, 2748mtrs, Par 69, SSS 68. Club membership 400.

Visitors Mon-Sun & BHs. Booking required weekends & BHs. Handicap certificate. Dress code. **Societies** welcome. **Green Fees** €20 per 18 holes **Course Designer** Eddie Hackett **Prof** T. W. Murphy **Facilities** **Location** 1.6km W of town on R666
Hotel ★★★ 68% HL Lawlors, DUNGARVAN, Co Waterford
☎ 058 41122 & 41056 🖷 058 41122 89 en suite

TRAMORE — Map 1 C2

Tramore Newtown Hill
☎ 051 386170 🖷 051 390961
e-mail: info@tramoregolfclub.com
web: www.tramoregolfclub.com

This course has matured nicely over the years to become a true championship test and has been chosen as the venue for the Irish Professional Matchplay Championship and the Irish Amateur Championship. Most of the fairways are lined by evergreen trees, calling for accurate placing of shots, and the course is continuing to develop. There are water features and all tees and greens are to USGA specification.

18 Holes, 6060mtrs, Par 72, SSS 72, Course record 66. Club membership 1200.

Visitors Mon-Sat & BHs. Booking required. Handicap certificate. Dress code. **Societies** booking required. **Green Fees** May-Sep €45, Apr & Oct €35, Nov-Mar €30 (€60/€45/€35 Fri-Sat) **Course Designer** Capt H C Tippet **Prof** Deirdre Brennan **Facilities** **Location** 0.8km W of town on R675 coast road
Hotel ★★★ 74% HL Majestic, TRAMORE, Co Waterford
☎ 051 381761 🖷 051 381761 60 en suite

WATERFORD — Map 1 C2

Faithlegg, Faithlegg
☎ 051 380000 & 086 3840215 🖷 051 382010
e-mail: golf@faithlegg.com
web: www.faithlegg.com

Set on the banks of the River Suir, the course has been integrated into a landscape textured with mature trees, flowing parkland and five lakes. Length is not the main defence, rather the greens provide a test for all levels making a good score a true reflection of good golf. Long par 3's and tricky to mange par 4's provide a challenge while reachable par 5's may allow you to reclaim a shot or two.

18 Holes, 6629yds, Par 72, SSS 72, Course record 69. Club membership 620.

Visitors Mon-Sun & BHs. Booking required. Dress code. **Societies** booking required. **Green Fees** not confirmed **Course Designer** Patrick Merrigan **Prof** Ryan Hunt & Derry Kiely **Facilities** **Leisure** hard tennis courts, heated indoor swimming pool, fishing, sauna, gymnasium,

continued

IRELAND

full P.G.A. club repair & custom fitting service available, coaching specialists **Conf** facs **Location** 9km E of town off R684 towards Cheekpoint
Hotel ★★★ 75% HL Tower, The Mall, WATERFORD, Co Waterford ☎ 051 875801 & 862300 ▤ 051 875801 139 en suite

Waterford Newrath
☎ 051 876748 ▤ 051 853405
e-mail: info@waterfordgolfclub.com
web: www.waterfordgolfclub.com

One of the finest inland courses in Ireland. This is exemplified by the spectacular closing stretch, in particular the downhill 18th with its elevated tee, a wonderful viewpoint and a narrow gorse lined fairway demanding a very accurate tee shot.

18 Holes, 5722mtrs, Par 71, SSS 70, Course record 64.
Club membership 1102.

Visitors Mon, Wed-Sat & BHs. Booking required. Dress code.
Societies booking required **Green Fees** €40 per round (€50 Sat & BHs) **Course Designer** W Park/J Braid **Facilities** ⑪ ⑩ ㄴ ▯ ⑪ ㅿ ☎ ✔ ㅁ ✔ ☛ **Conf** Corporate Hospitality Days **Location** 1.6km N of town on N77
Hotel ★★★ 75% HL Tower, The Mall, WATERFORD, Co Waterford ☎ 051 875801 & 862300 ▤ 051 875801 139 en suite

Waterford Castle The Island
☎ 051 871633 ▤ 051 871634
web: www.waterfordcastle.com/golf
18 Holes, 6231mtrs, Par 72, SSS 71, Course record 65.
Course Designer Des Smyth **Location** 3km E of town via private ferry
Telephone for further details
Hotel ★★★★ HL Waterford Castle, The Island, WATERFORD, Co Waterford ☎ 051 878203 ▤ 051 878203 19 en suite

CO WESTMEATH

ATHLONE Map 1 C4

Glasson Golf Hotel Glasson
☎ 090 6485120 ▤ 090 6485444
web: www.glassongolf.ie
Glasson Golf Hotel: 18 Holes, 6251mtrs, Par 74, SSS 74, Course record 65.
Course Designer Christy O'Connor Jnr **Location** 10km N of town on N55
Telephone for further details
Hotel ★★★★ 78% HL Hodson Bay, Hodson Bay, ATHLONE, Co Westmeath ☎ 090 6442000 ▤ 090 6442000 182 en suite

DELVIN Map 1 C4

Delvin Castle Clonyn
☎ 044 64315 & 64671 ▤ 044 64315
Delvin Castle Golf Course: 18 Holes, 5800mtrs, Par 70, SSS 68.
Course Designer John Day **Location** on N52
Telephone for further details

MOATE Map 1 C4

Moate
☎ 090 6481271 ▤ 090 6482645
web: www.moategolfclub.ie
Moate Golf Course: 18 Holes, 5742mtrs, Par 72, SSS 70, Course record 67.
Course Designer B Browne **Location** 1.6km N of town
Telephone for further details
Hotel ★★★★ 78% HL Hodson Bay, Hodson Bay, ATHLONE, Co Westmeath ☎ 090 6442000 ▤ 090 6442000 182 en suite

Mount Temple, Mount Temple Village
☎ 090 6481841
e-mail: mttemple@iol.ie
web: www.mounttemplegolfclub.com

A traditionally built, championship course with unique links-type greens and natural undulating fairways. A challenge for all levels of golfers and all year golfing available.

Mount Temple Golf Course: 18 Holes, 6020metres, Par 72, SSS 72, Course record 67. Club membership 250.

Visitors Mon-Sun & BHs. Booking required Fri-Sun & BHs. Handicap certificate. **Societies** booking required. **Green Fees** €35 per round, €15 per 9 holes (€45/€20 weekends & BHs) **Course Designer** Michael Dolan **Prof** Mel Flanagan **Facilities** ⑪ ⑩ ㄴ ▯ ⑪ ㅿ ☎ ⑪ ✔ ☛ ✔ ☛ **Conf** facs Corporate Hospitality Days **Location** M6 junct 6, 5km NW of town to Temple Mount
Hotel ★★★★ 78% HL Hodson Bay, Hodson Bay, ATHLONE, Co Westmeath ☎ 090 6442000 ▤ 090 6442000 182 en suite

MULLINGAR Map 1 C4

Mullingar
☎ 044 48366 ▤ 044 41499
18 Holes, 5858metres, Par 72, SSS 71, Course record 63.
Course Designer James Braid **Location** 5km S of town on N52
Telephone for further details
Hotel ★★★★ 79% HL Mullingar Park, Dublin Road, MULLINGAR, Co Westmeath ☎ 044 9344446 & 9337500 ▤ 044 9344446 95 en suite

CO WEXFORD

ENNISCORTHY Map 1 D3

Enniscorthy Knockmarshall
☎ 053 9233191 ▤ 053 9237367
e-mail: info@enniscorthygc.ie
web: www.enniscorthygc.ie

A pleasant course suitable for all levels of ability.

18 Holes, 6115mtrs, Par 72, SSS 72. Club membership 900.

Visitors dress code. **Societies** booking required **Green Fees** €30 per round (€40 Fri-Sun & BHs) **Course Designer** Eddie Hackett **Prof** Martin Sludds **Facilities** ⑪ ⑩ ㄴ ▯ ⑪ ㅿ ☎ ⑪ ☎ ✔ ☛ **Leisure** sauna **Conf** Corporate Hospitality Days **Location** 1.6km W of town on N30
Hotel ★★★ 72% HL Riverside Park Hotel & Leisure Club, The Promenade, ENNISCORTHY, Co Wexford ☎ 053 9237800 ▤ 053 9237800 62 en suite

GOREY · Map 1 D3

Courtown Kiltennel
☎ 055 25166 📄 055 25553
web: www.courtowngolfclub.com

18 Holes, 5898mtrs, Par 71, SSS 71, Course record 65.
Course Designer Harris & Associates **Location** 5km SE of town off R742
Telephone for further details
Hotel ★★★★ 75% HL Ashdown Park Hotel, The Coach Road, GOREY TOWN, Co Wexford ☎ 053 9480500 📄 053 9480500 79 en suite

NEW ROSS · Map 1 C3

New Ross
☎ 051 421433 📄 051 420098

New Ross Golf Course: 18 Holes, 5259metres, Par 70, SSS 70.
Course Designer Des Smith **Location** 5km from town
Telephone for further details

ROSSLARE · Map 1 D2

Rosslare Rosslare Strand
☎ 053 9132203 📄 053 9132263
e-mail: office@rosslaregolf.com
web: www.rosslaregolf.com

This traditional links course is within minutes of the ferry terminal at Rosslare. Many of the greens are sunken and are always in beautiful condition, but the semi-blind approaches are among features of this course which provide a healthy challenge. Celebrated 100 years of golf in 2005.

Old Course: 18 Holes, 6042mtrs, Par 72, SSS 72, Course record 66.
Burrow: 12 Holes, 3917metres, Par 46.
Club membership 1500.

Visitors Mon-Sun & BHs. Booking required. Dress code.
Societies booking required. **Green Fees** Old Course €50 per day, Burrow Course €20 (€70/€25 weekends & BHs) **Course Designer** Hawtree/Taylor **Prof** Johnny Young **Facilities** 🔟 🍴 🔨 🛒 🍺 ⛳ 🏌 🚕 🏌 🏌 **Leisure** sauna
Conf Corporate Hospitality Days **Location** N of Rosslare village
Hotel ★★★★ HL Kelly's Resort Hotel & Spa, ROSSLARE, Co Wexford ☎ 053 9132114 📄 053 9132114 118 en suite

St Helen's Bay Golf & Country Club St Helens
☎ 053 9133234 📄 053 9133803
web: www.sthelensbay.com

St Helen's Bay Golf Resort: 27 Holes, 5894mtrs, Par 72, SSS 72, Course record 69.
Course Designer Philip Walton **Location** SE of Rosslare Harbour off N25
Telephone for further details

WEXFORD · Map 1 D3

Wexford Mulgannon
☎ 053 42238 📄 053 42243
e-mail: info@wexfordgolfclub.ie
web: www.wexfordgolfclub.ie

Parkland with panoramic view of the Wexford coastline and mountains. Extensive redevelopment in recent years..

18 Holes, 5950mtrs, Par 71, SSS 70. Club membership 800.

Visitors dress code. **Societies** booking required. **Green Fees** €40 per 18 holes, winter €35 (€45/€40 weekends & BHs) **Prof** Llam Bowler **Facilities** 🔟 🍴 🔨 🛒 🍺 ⛳ 🏌 🏌 🚕 🏌 🏌 **Conf** facs
Hotel ★★★★ 74% HL Talbot Hotel Conference & Leisure Centre, The Quay, WEXFORD, Co Wexford ☎ 053 9122566 & 9155559 📄 053 9122566 109 en suite

CO WICKLOW

ARKLOW · Map 1 D3

Arklow Abbeylands
☎ 0402 32492 📄 0402 91604

18 Holes, 5802mtrs, Par 69, SSS 68, Course record 64.
Course Designer Hawtree & Taylor **Location** 0.8km E of town centre
Telephone for further details
Hotel ★★★ CHH Marlfield House Hotel, GOREY, Co Wexford ☎ 053 9421124 📄 053 9421124 19 en suite

BALTINGLASS · Map 1 D3

Baltinglass Dublin Rd
☎ 059 6481350 📄 059 6481842
web: baltinglassgc.com

18 Holes, 5912mtrs, Par 71, SSS 71, Course record 68.
Course Designer Eddie Connaughton **Location** 500 metres N of village
Telephone for further details
Hotel ★★★ 78% HL Seven Oaks, Athy Road, CARLOW, Co Carlow ☎ 059 9131308 📄 059 9131308 89 en suite

BLAINROE · Map 1 D3

Blainroe
☎ 0404 68168 📄 0404 69369
web: www.blainroe.com

Parkland course overlooking the east coast, a challenge to golfers of all abilities. Some holes are situated right on the coast and two notable holes are the 14th, played over the sea from a cliff promontory, and the par 3 15th over a lake.

18 Holes, 6140mtrs, Par 72, SSS 73, Course record 71.
Club membership 1300.

Visitors Mon-Sun & BHs. Booking required Mon, Wed & weekends. Dress code **Societies** booking required. **Green Fees** €30 (€45 weekends) **Course Designer** Fred Hawtree **Prof** John McDonald
Facilities 🔟 🍴 🔨 🛒 🍺 ⛳ 🏌 🚕 🏌 🏌
Conf Corporate Hospitality Days **Location** 5km SE of Wicklow on R750 coast road
Guesthouse ★★★★ FH Kilpatrick House, Redcross, WICKLOW, Co Wicklow ☎ 0404 47137 & 087 6358325 📄 0404 47137 4 rms (3 en suite)

BLESSINGTON   Map 1 D3

Tulfarris Hotel & Golf Resort
☎ 045 867644 & 867600   📄 045 867000
e-mail: info@tulfarris.com
web: www.tulfarris.com

Designed by Paddy Merrigan, this course is on the Blessington
lakeshore with the Wicklow Mountains as a backdrop. The use of the
natural landscape is evident throughout the whole course, the variety
of trees guarding fairways and green approaches.

Tulfarris Hotel & Golf Resort: 18 Holes, 6507metres,
Par 72, SSS 74, Course record 68. Club membership 255.

Visitors dress code. Handicap certificate. **Societies** booking required.
Green Fees not confirmed **Course Designer** Patrick Merrigan
Facilities ⑪ 🅿️ 🍴 🛒 💷 🍳 🔥 🛒 ◇ 🚗 🎣 🏌️
Leisure hard tennis courts, fishing, gymnasium **Conf** facs Corporate
Hospitality Days **Location** 3.5km from village off N81

BRAY   Map 1 D4

Bray Greystones Rd
☎ 01 2763200   📄 01 2763262
e-mail: info@braygolfclub.com
web: www.braygolfclub.com

A USGA standard parkland course of nearly 81 hectares, combining
stunning scenery with a classic layout. The 11th par 4 signature hole
provides a fine view of the coastline.

18 Holes, 5990mtrs, Par 71, SSS 72, Course record 66.
Club membership 790.

Visitors Mon, Thu-Sat. Booking required. Dress code. Handicap
certificate. **Societies** booking required. **Green Fees** €25
before 9:30am, €40 before noon, €50 after noon (€60 Sat) **Course
Designer** Smyth/Brannigan **Prof** Ciaran Carroll **Facilities** ⑪ 🍴
🅱️ 🅿️ 🍳 💷 🛒 🍳 ◇ 🔥 🏌️ **Conf** facs Corporate
Hospitality Days **Location** near town off R761
Hotel ★★★ 73% HL Royal Hotel & Leisure Centre, Main Street,
BRAY, Co Wicklow ☎ 01 2862935 & 2724900 📄 01 2862935
130 en suite

Old Conna Ferndale Rd
☎ 01 2826055 & 2826766   📄 01 2825611

18 Holes, 5989metres, Par 72, SSS 72, Course record 68.
Course Designer Eddie Hackett **Location** 3.5km from town centre
Telephone for further details
Hotel ★★★ 73% HL Royal Hotel & Leisure Centre, Main Street,
BRAY, Co Wicklow ☎ 01 2862935 & 2724900 📄 01 2862935
130 en suite

Woodbrook Dublin Rd
☎ 01 2824799   📄 01 2821950
web: www.woodbrook.ie

18 Holes, 6017metres, Par 72, SSS 71, Course record 65.
Course Designer Peter McEvoy **Location** on N11
Telephone for further details
Hotel ★★★ 73% HL Royal Hotel & Leisure Centre, Main Street,
BRAY, Co Wicklow ☎ 01 2862935 & 2724900 📄 01 2862935
130 en suite

BRITTAS BAY   Map 1 D3

The European Club
☎ 0404 47415   📄 0404 47449
e-mail: info@europeanclub.com
web: www.theeuropeanclub.com

A links course that runs through a large dunes system. Since it was
opened in 1992 it is rapidly gaining recognition as one of Irelands
best courses. Notable holes include the 7th, 13th and 14th.

The European Club: 20 Holes, 6737metres, Par 71,
SSS 73, Course record 67. Club membership 100.

Visitors Mon-Sun & BHs. Booking required. Dress code. Handicap
certificate. **Societies** booking required. **Green Fees** €100 per round
Nov-Mar; €180 Apr-Oct **Course Designer** Pat Ruddy **Facilities** ⑪
🍴 🅱️ 🅿️ 🍳 💷 🛒 🍳 **Conf** Corporate Hospitality Days
Location 1.6km from Brittas Bay
Guesthouse ★★★★ FH Kilpatrick House, Redcross, WICKLOW,
Co Wicklow ☎ 0404 47137 & 087 6358325 📄 0404 47137 4 rms
(3 en suite)

DELGANY   Map 1 D3

Delgany
☎ 01 2874536   📄 01 2873977
e-mail: delganygolf@eircom.net
web: www.delganygolfclub.com

Undulating parkland amid beautiful scenery. Recently remodelled with
sand-based greens and tees to USGA specifications.

18 Holes, 5473mtrs, Par 69, SSS 68, Course record 62.
Club membership 1200.

Visitors Mon, Thu & Fri. Handicap certificate. Dress code.
Societies booking required. **Green Fees** €45 per 18 holes (€55
weekends) **Course Designer** H Vardon **Prof** Gavin Kavanagh
Facilities ⑪ 🍴 🅱️ 🅿️ 🍳 💷 🛒 🍳 🔥 🏌️ 🛒 🍳
Conf Corporate Hospitality Days **Location** 1.2km from village off N11
Hotel ★★★★ 75% HL Glenview, Glen O' the Downs, DELGANY, Co
Wicklow ☎ 01 2873399 📄 01 2873399 70 en suite

Glen of the Downs Coolnaskeagh
☎ 01 2876240   📄 01 2870063
e-mail: info@glenofthedowns.com
web: www.glenofthedowns.com

A parkland course that plays much like a links course with sand-
based greens and tees. Among its features is a five-tier double green,
which is shared by the 8th and 10th holes. Sandwiched in between
is a fine par 5, the 9th, which measures 457 metres off the back.
Panoramic views of the Sugarloaf mountains and rolling hills beyond.

18 Holes, 5980yds, Par 71, SSS 70, Course record 68.
Club membership 650.

Visitors dress code. **Societies** booking required. **Green Fees** from
€35-€80 **Course Designer** Peter McEvoy **Facilities** ⑪ 🍴 🅱️ 🅿️
🍳 💷 🛒 🍳 🔥 🏌️ 🛒 🍳 **Conf** facs Corporate Hospitality Days
Location off N11 southbound at Glenview exit, 4m from Bray
Hotel ★★★★ 75% HL Glenview, Glen O' the Downs, DELGANY, Co
Wicklow ☎ 01 2873399 📄 01 2873399 70 en suite

IRELAND

DRUIDS GLEN GOLF CLUB

CO WICKLOW - NEWTOWN MOUNT KENNEDY - MAP 1 D3

Druids Glen Golf Resort is home to two championship courses, Druids Glen and Druids Heath. Druids Glen held the Irish Open an unprecedented four occasions from 1996-1999, the quality of the tournament reflected in its winners with Colin Montgomerie being a two time champion and the tournament was also the scene for Sergio Garcia's maiden tour victory in 1999. Druids Glen also played host to the inaugural 'Seve Trophy' in 2002. The stunning parkland layout which is known as 'the Augusta of Europe' features tree lined holes which demand driving accuracy while the back nine sees numerous approach shots over water testing the nerve of the most experienced player. In contrast Druids heath is a heathland course with strong links influences. It is set on rolling countryside overlooking the Irish Sea with the Wicklow Mountains as its backdrop and provides stunning panoramic views as well as being a stern test of golf.

☎ 01 2873600 📄 01 2873699
e-mail: info@druidsglen.ie **web:** www.druidsglen.ie
Druids Glen: 18 Holes, 5998metres, Par 71, SSS 73, Course record 62.
Druids Heath: 18 Holes, 6062mtrs, Par 71, SSS 74, Course record 71. Club membership 219.
Visitors Mon-Sun & BHs. Booking required. Dress code. **Societies** booking required. **Green Fees** Druids Glen from €90, Druids Heath from €60 **Course Designer** Tom Craddock/Pat Ruddy **Prof** George Henry **Facilities** ⊕ 🍽 🏃 💻 🎯 🏌 🛒 ♦ 🍺 🚗 ♦ 🏌 **Leisure** heated indoor swimming pool, sauna, gymnasium **Conf** facs Corporate Hospitality Days **Location** S of village on R761

DUNLAVIN Map 1 D3

Rathsallagh
☎ 045 403316 📠 045 403295
e-mail: info@rathsallagh.com
web: www.rathsallagh.com

Designed by Peter McEvoy and Christy O'Connor Jnr, this is a spectacular course which will test the professionals without intimidating the club golfer. Set in 525 acres of lush parkland with thousands of mature trees, natural water hazards and gently rolling landscape. The greens are of high quality, in design, construction and condition.

Rathsallagh House Golf & Country Club: 18 Holes, 6324mtrs, Par 72, SSS 74, Course record 68. Club membership 460.

Visitors Mon-Sun & BHs. Booking required. Dress code. Handicap certificate. **Societies** booking required. **Green Fees** €65 per round (€85 Fri-Sat & BHs). **Course Designer** McEvoy/O'Connor **Prof** Brendan McDaid **Facilities** ⑪ ⑩ 🍴 🛍 ⛳ 🖊️ 🏊 🏠 ⚓ ◇ 🏌️ 🚌 🏌️ 🎣 **Leisure** hard tennis courts, private jacuzzi/steam room, croquet lawn, walled garden **Conf** facs Corporate Hospitality Days **Location** SW of village off N9
Guesthouse ★★★★★ GH Rathsallagh House, DUNLAVIN, CO WICKLOW ☎ 045 403112 📠 045 403112 29 en suite

GREYSTONES Map 1 D3

Charlesland Golf & Country Club Hotel
☎ 01 2874350 & 2878200 📠 01 2874360
e-mail: teetimes@charlesland.com
web: www.charlesland.com

Championship length course with a double dog-leg at the 9th and 18th. Water hazards on seven holes. Signature hole is the par 3 13th which at 229 metres from the championship tee makes it one of the longest par 3's in Ireland.

Charlesland Golf & Country Club Hotel: 18 Holes, 5963mtrs, Par 72, SSS 72, Course record 68. Club membership 680.

Visitors Mon-Sun & BHs. Booking required. Dress code. Handicap certificate. **Societies** booking required. **Green Fees** €35 per 18 holes Mon-Thu (€40 Fri & Sun, €50 Sat) **Course Designer** Eddie Hackett **Prof** Peter Duignan **Facilities** ⑪ ⑩ 🍴 🛍 ⛳ 🖊️ 🏊 🏠 ◇ 🚌 🏌️ **Conf** facs Corporate Hospitality Days **Location** 1.6km S of town on R762
Hotel ★★★★ 75% HL Glenview, Glen O' the Downs, DELGANY, Co Wicklow ☎ 01 2873399 📠 01 2873399 70 en suite

Greystones
☎ 01 2874136 📠 01 2873749
web: www.greystonesgc.com
18 Holes, 5322mtrs, Par 69, SSS 68.
Course Designer P Merrigan
Telephone for further details
Hotel ★★★★ 75% HL Glenview, Glen O' the Downs, DELGANY, Co Wicklow ☎ 01 2873399 📠 01 2873399 70 en suite

NEWTOWN MOUNT KENNEDY Map 1 D3

Druids Glen Golf Club see page 473
☎ 01 2873600 📠 01 2873699
e-mail: info@druidsglen.ie
web: www.druidsglen.ie

Kilcoole
☎ 01 2872066 📠 01 2010497
web: www.kilcoolegolfclub.com
9 Holes, 5506mtrs, Par 70, SSS 69, Course record 66.
Facilities ⑪ ⑩ 🛍 ⛳ 🖊️ 🏊 🏠 🏌️ **Conf** facs Corporate Hospitality Days **Location** S of village on R761
Telephone for further details
Hotel ★★★★ 75% HL Glenview, Glen O' the Downs, DELGANY, Co Wicklow ☎ 01 2873399 📠 01 2873399 70 en suite

RATHDRUM Map 1 D3

Glenmalure Greenane
☎ 0404 46679 📠 0404 46783
e-mail: golf@glenmalure-golf.ie
web: www.glenmalure-golf.ie

A moorland course with elevated tees and greens where accuracy is required. The 3rd, known as the Helicopter Pad, is difficult.

Glenmalure Golf Course: 18 Holes, 4846metres, Par 71, SSS 67, Course record 71. Club membership 250.

Visitors Mon-Sat & BHs. Sun after 11am. Boooking required. **Societies** booking required. **Green Fees** not confirmed **Course Designer** P Suttle **Facilities** ⑪ ⑩ 🛍 ⛳ 🖊️ 🏊 🏌️ 🚌 🏌️ **Conf** Corporate Hospitality Days **Location** 3km W of town
Hotel ★★★ 70% HL Woodenbridge, WOODEN BRIDGE, Co Wicklow ☎ 0402 35146 📠 0402 35146 23 en suite

ROUNDWOOD Map 1 D3

Roundwood Newtown
☎ 01 2818488 & 2802555 📠 01 2843642
web: www.roundwoodgolf.com
18 Holes, 6113mtrs, Par 72, SSS 72, Course record 70.
Prof Seamus Clinton **Facilities** ⑪ ⑩ 🛍 ⛳ 🖊️ 🏊 🏌️ 🚌 **Conf** Corporate Hospitality Days **Location** 4km NE of village on R765
Telephone for further details
Hotel ★★★ 69% HL The Glendalough, GLENDALOUGH, Co Wicklow ☎ 0404 45135 📠 0404 45135 44 en suite

SHILLELAGH Map 1 D3

Coollattin Coollattin
☎ 053 9429125 📠 053 9429930
web: www.coollattingolfclub.com
Coollattin Golf Course: 18 Holes, 5622mtrs, Par 70, SSS 68, Course record 70.
Course Designer Peter McEvoy **Location** off R749
Telephone for further details
Hotel ★★★ CHH Marlfield House Hotel, GOREY, Co Wexford ☎ 053 9421124 📠 053 9421124 19 en suite

WICKLOW Map 1 D3

Wicklow Dunbur Rd
☎ 0404 67379 📠 0404 64756
web: www.wicklowgolfclub.ie

Wicklow Golf Course: 18 Holes, 5437mtrs, Par 71, SSS 70.
Course Designer Craddock & Ruddy **Location** SE of town centre
Telephone for further details
Guesthouse ★★★★ FH Kilpatrick House, Redcross, WICKLOW, Co Wicklow ☎ 0404 47137 & 087 6358325 📠 0404 47137 4 rms (3 en suite)

WOODENBRIDGE Map 1 D3

Woodenbridge Woodenbridge, Arklow
☎ 0402 35202 📠 0402 35754
e-mail: reception@woodenbridge.ie
web: www.woodenbridge.ie

A level parkland course with undulating fairways and greens, traversed by two lovely meandering rivers.

18 Holes, 5852metres, Par 71, SSS 70, Course record 71. Club membership 1200.

Visitors dress code. **Societies** welcome **Green Fees** €55 per 18 holes (€65 Sun & BHs) **Course Designer** Patrick Merrigan **Facilities** **Location** N of village
Hotel ★★★ **70%** HL Woodenbridge, WOODEN BRIDGE, Co Wicklow ☎ 0402 35146 📠 0402 35146 23 en suite

IRELAND

Maps

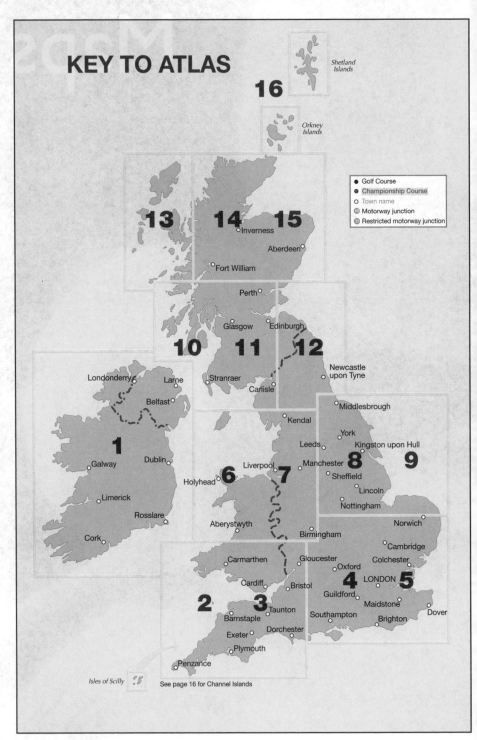

KEY TO ATLAS

Shetland Islands

16

Orkney Islands

Legend:
- ● Golf Course
- ● Championship Course
- ○ Town name
- Ⓜ Motorway junction
- ⓜ Restricted motorway junction

13　**14**　**15**

Inverness

Aberdeen

Fort William

Perth

10　**11**　**12**

Glasgow　Edinburgh

Stranraer　　Newcastle upon Tyne

Carlisle

Londonderry　Larne

Belfast

Kendal　Middlesbrough

York

Leeds　Kingston upon Hull

1

Galway　Dublin

Liverpool　Manchester　**8**　**9**

Holyhead　**6**　**7**　Sheffield

Limerick

Lincoln

Rosslare

Nottingham

Cork

Aberystwyth　Norwich

Birmingham　Cambridge

Carmarthen　Gloucester　Colchester

Oxford

Cardiff　Bristol　**4**　LONDON　**5**

2　**3**　Taunton　Guildford

Barnstaple　Maidstone

Southampton　Brighton　Dover

Exeter　Dorchester

Plymouth

Penzance

Isles of Scilly

See page 16 for Channel Islands

© AA Media Limited 2009

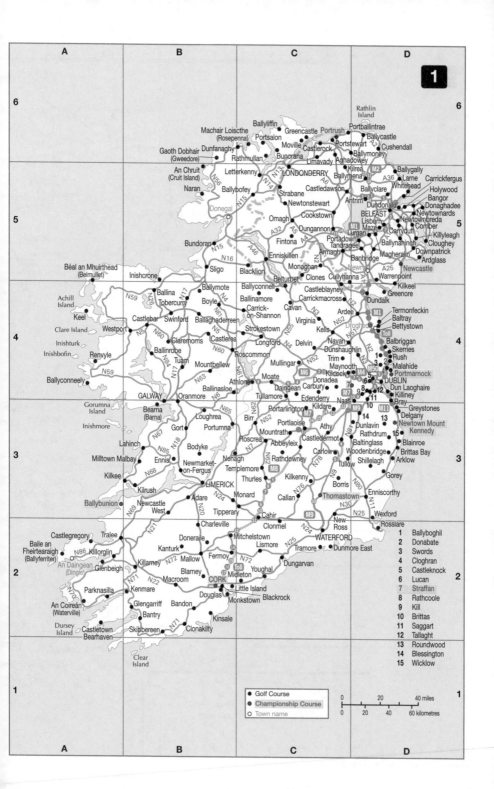

1

A	B	C	D

6 — Rathlin Island — **6**

Ballyliffin
Machair Loiscthe (Rosepenna)
Portsalon
Greencastle Portrush Portballintrae
Moville Castlerock Ballycastle
Gaoth Dobhair (Gweedore) Dunfanaghy
Rathmullan Buncrana Portstewart Cushendall
Ballymoney Aghadowey
An Chruit (Cruit Island)
Letterkenny N13 LONDONDERRY A6 Kilrea Ballymena M2 Ballygally
A36 Larne Carrickfergus
Whitehead
Naran Ballybofey N14 Strabane Castledawson Ballyclare Holywood
Bangor
Newtonstewart Antrim Dundonald Donaghadee
Newtownards
N15 Omagh Cookstown BELFAST Newtownbreda Comber
Lisburn Maze Killyleagh
Dungannon M1 Lurgan Carryduff Cloughey
Donegal A32 A5 Fintona Portadown Ballynahinch Ardglass
Enniskillen Monaghan Armagh Tandragee Magheralin Downpatrick
A46 Banbridge
Béal an Mhuirhead (Belmullet)
Inishcrone Sligo Blacklion Belturbet Clones Cullyhanna Newry A25 Newcastle
Warrenpoint
Achill Island N16 Ballyconnell Castleblayney Kilkeel
Keel Ballina N17 Ballymote Cavan Carrickmacross N2 Greenore
Dundalk
Clare Island Castlebar Tobercurry Ballinamore Virginia Ardee Termonfeckin M1
Westport N5 Swinford N60 Boyle Carrick- N55 Kells N52 Baltray
Inishturk on-Shannon Navan Drogheda Bettystown
Inishbofin Renvyle Claremorris Ballaghaderreen N5 Strokestown Delvin Dunshaughlin N51 Balbriggan Toll
Ballinrobe Longford N4 Trim Maynooth N3 Skerries
Ballyconneely N59 Tuam N63 Roscommon Mullingar N52 Kilcock M4 1 Rush
N84 Moate M6 Donadea 5 6 M50 Malahide
GALWAY Mountbellew Athlone Daingean Carbury 7 Portmarnock
Oranmore N61 Ballinasloe Tullamore Edenderry Kildare DUBLIN
Gorumna Island N6 Moate Naas 8 Dun Laoghaire
Bearna (Barna) Loughrea N65 Birr Portarlington M7 Killiney
Inishmore Gort Portumna N52 Portlaoise Athy 10 Bray
Lahinch N67 Bodyke Roscrea Mountrath Castledermot Dunlavin 14 Greystones
N85 N18 Nenagh Abbeyleix Carlow Rathdrum Delgany
Milltown Malbay Ennis Newmarket- Templemore Rathdowney N78 Woodenbridge Blainroe
Kilkee N68 on-Fergus M8 Thurles Tullow Shillelagh Brittas Bay
Ballybunion LIMERICK Monard Kilkenny N76 Borris N80 Arklow
Newcastle Adare N24 Callan Gorey
West N20 Tipperary M9 Thomastown New Enniscorthy N11
Castlegregory Tralee Charleville Cahir Ross Wexford
Baile an Fheirtearaigh (Ballyferriter) N86 Killorglin Doneraile Clonmel N25 Rosslare
An Daingean (Dingle) Kanturk Mitchelstown WATERFORD
Glenbeigh N71 Killarney N72 Mallow Fermoy Lismore Tramore Dunmore East
Parknasilla N22 Macroom Blarney N72 Dungarvan
An Coireán (Waterville) Kenmare CORK Midleton Youghal
Glengarriff Bandon Douglas Little Island
Dursey Island Bantry Kinsale Monkstown Blackrock
Castletown Bearhaven Skibbereen N71 Clonakilty

Clear Island

1	Ballyboghil
2	Donabate
3	Swords
4	Cloghran
5	Castleknock
6	Lucan
7	Straffan
8	Rathcoole
9	Kill
10	Brittas
11	Saggart
12	Tallaght
13	Roundwood
14	Blessington
15	Wicklow

● Golf Course
● Championship Course
○ Town name

0 — 20 — 40 miles
0 — 20 — 40 — 60 kilometres

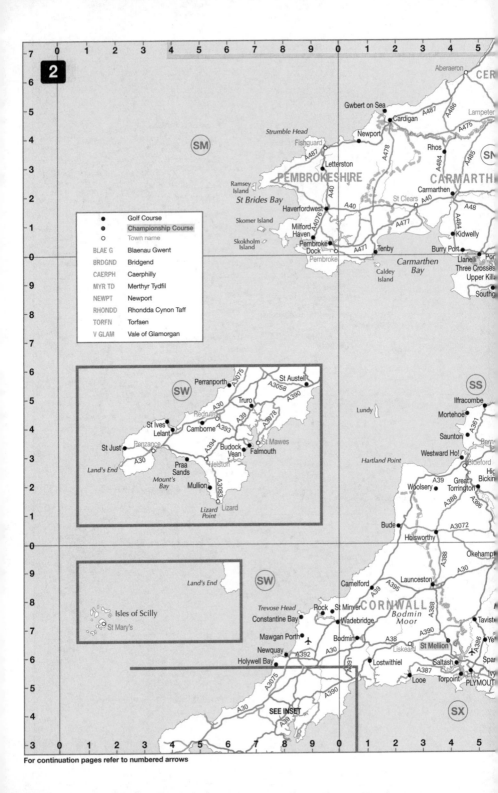

2

Legend

●	Golf Course
●	Championship Course
○	Town name
BLAE G	Blaenau Gwent
BRDGND	Bridgend
CAERPH	Caerphilly
MYR TD	Merthyr Tydfil
NEWPT	Newport
RHONDD	Rhondda Cynon Taff
TORFN	Torfaen
V GLAM	Vale of Glamorgan

SM

PEMBROKESHIRE

CARMARTH

Aberaeron
CER
Gwbert on Sea
Cardigan
Lampeter
Newport
Rhos
SM
Strumble Head
Fishguard
Letterston
Ramsey Island
St Brides Bay
Carmarthen
St Clears
Skomer Island
Haverfordwest
A40
A48
Milford Haven
A477
A484
Kidwelly
Skokholm Island
Pembroke Dock
Tenby
Burry Port
Llanelli
Por
Pembroke
Caldey Island
Carmarthen Bay
Three Crosses
Upper Killa
Southg

SW

Perranporth
St Austell
A3075
A3058
Truro
A390
St Ives
Lelant
Camborne
A393
A39
A3078
St Mawes
St Just
Penzance
A394
Budock Vean
Falmouth
Land's End
A30
Praa Sands
Helston
Mount's Bay
Mullion
A3083
Lizard Point
Lizard

SS
Lundy
Ilfracombe
Mortehoe
Saunton
Berr
Westward Ho!
Bideford
Hartland Point
Hig
Bickin
Woolsery
Great Torrington
A39
A388
A386
Bude
A3072
Holsworthy
Okehamp
A388
A30

SW
Land's End
Camelford
Launceston
A39
A395
Isles of Scilly
St Mary's
Trevose Head
Rock
St Minver
CORNWALL
Bodmin Moor
Constantine Bay
Wadebridge
A388
Tavist
Mawgan Porth
Bodmin
A390
Ye
Newquay
A392
A38
Liskeard
St Mellion
A386
Holywell Bay
Lostwithiel
Saltash
Spar
A3075
A387
Torpoint
Ivy
Looe
PLYMOUT
A30
SEE INSET
A390
SX
A39

For continuation pages refer to numbered arrows

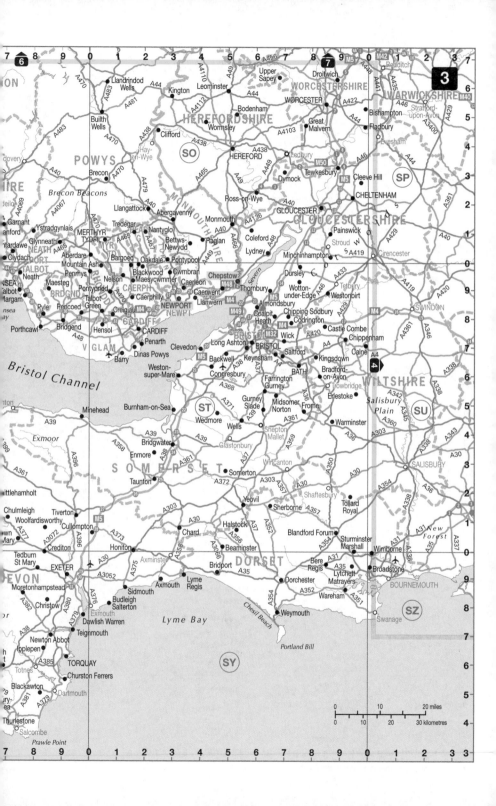

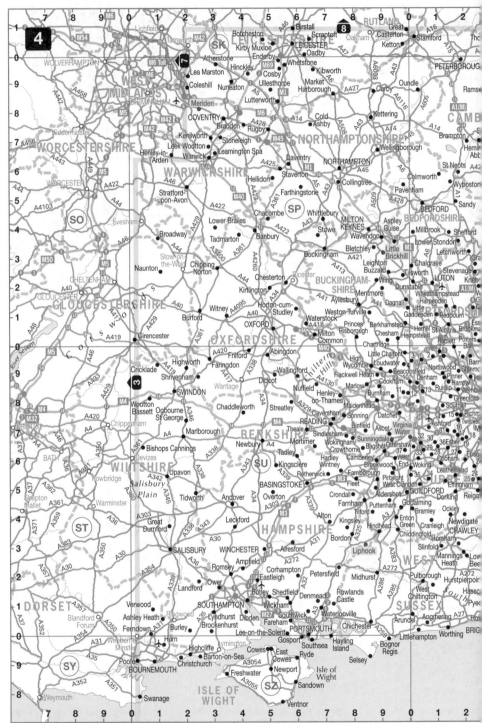

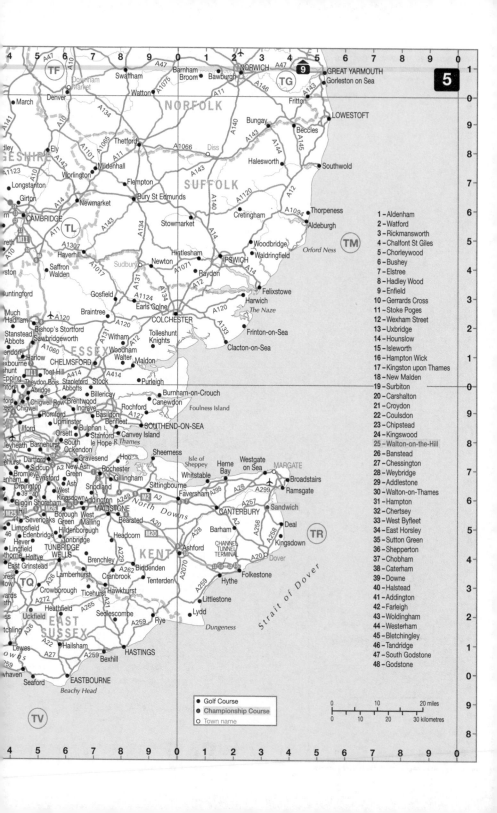

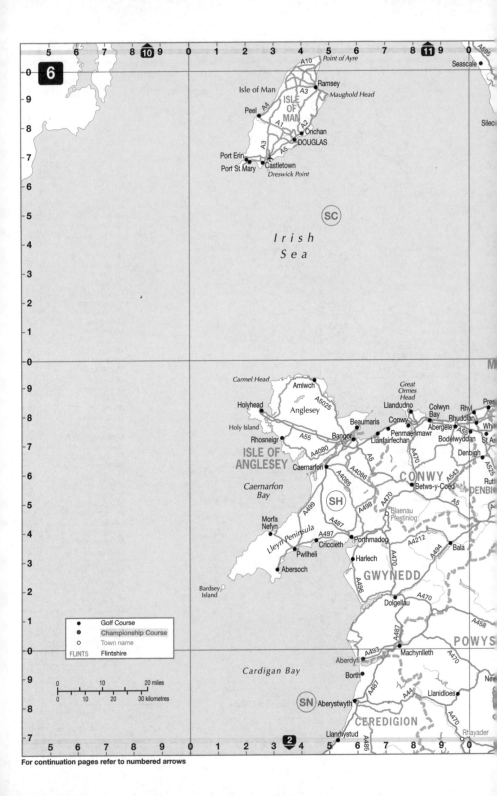

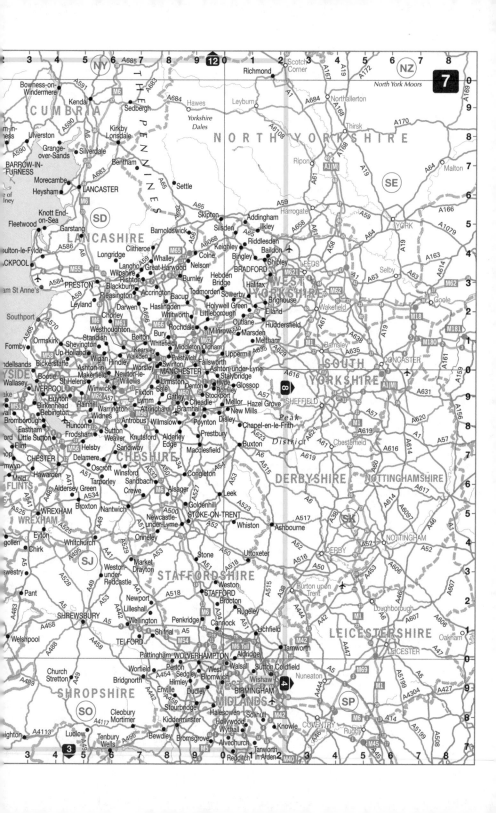

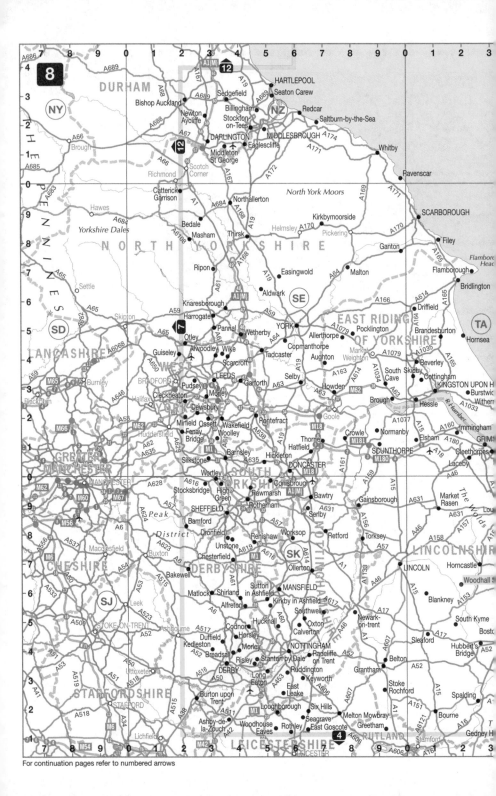

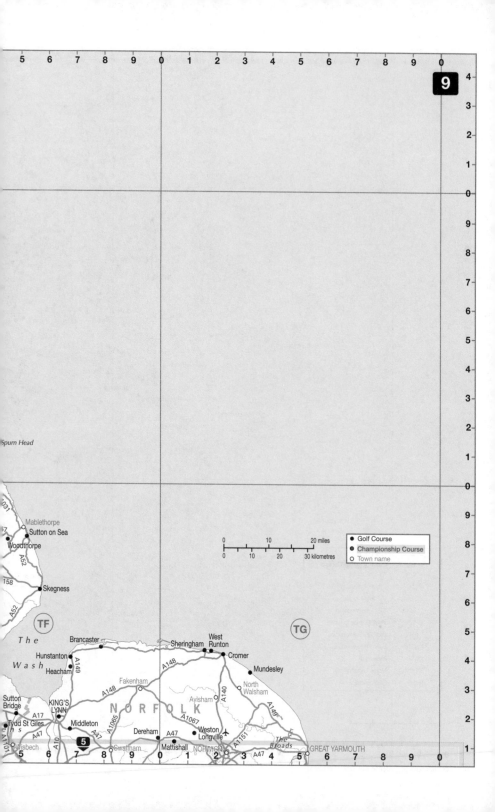

9

5 6 7 8 9 0 1 2 3 4 5 6 7 8 9 0

4
3
2
1
0

9
8
7
6
5
4
3
2
1
0

9
8

Spurn Head

7
6
5
4
3
2
1
0

9

Mablethorpe
Sutton on Sea
Woodthorpe

A52

158

Skegness

A52

| ● Golf Course |
| ● Championship Course |
| ○ Town name |

TF

TG

5
4

The

Brancaster

Sheringham   West
              Runton

Wash

Hunstanton
Heacham

A149

A148

Cromer

Mundesley

4
3

Fakenham

A148

North
Walsham

A140

3
2

Sutton
Bridge

A17

KING'S
LYNN

A1065

Aylsham

A1067

A149

N O R F O L K

Tydd St Giles

A47

A10

Middleton

A47

Dereham

A47

Weston
Longville

A151

*The
Broads*

2
1

Wisbech

5

Swaffham

Mattishall

NORWICH

A47

GREAT YARMOUTH

5 6 7 8 9 0 1 2 3 4 5 6 7 8 9 0

0   10   20 miles
0 10 20 30 kilometres

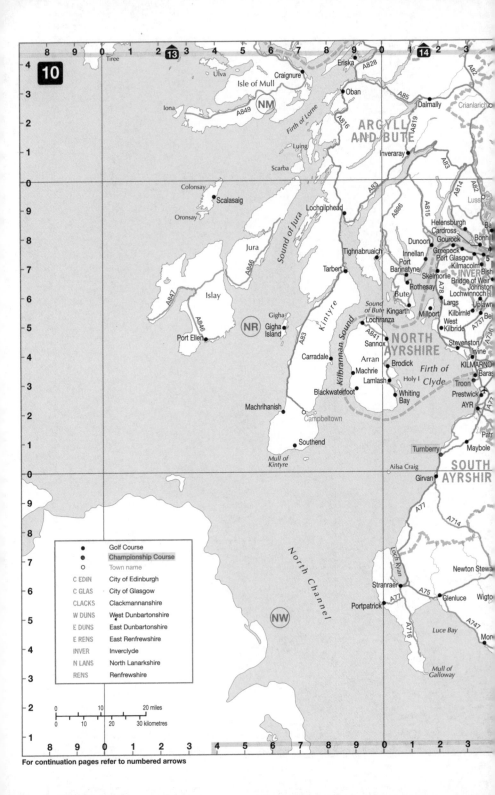

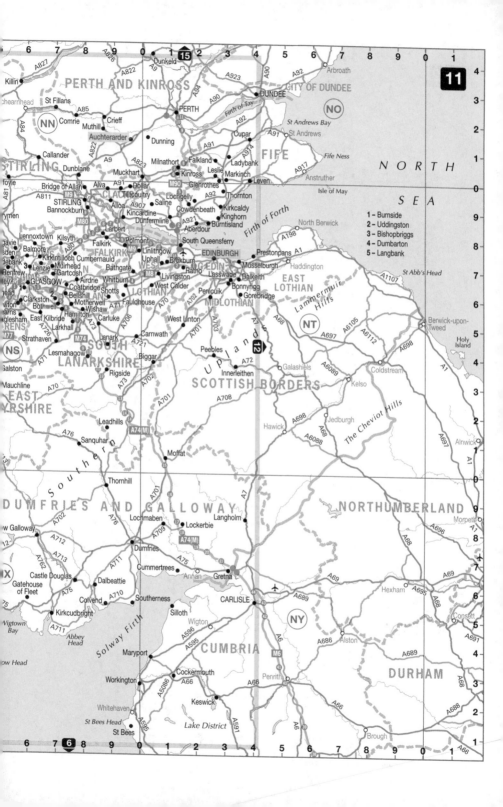

For continuation pages refer to numbered arrows

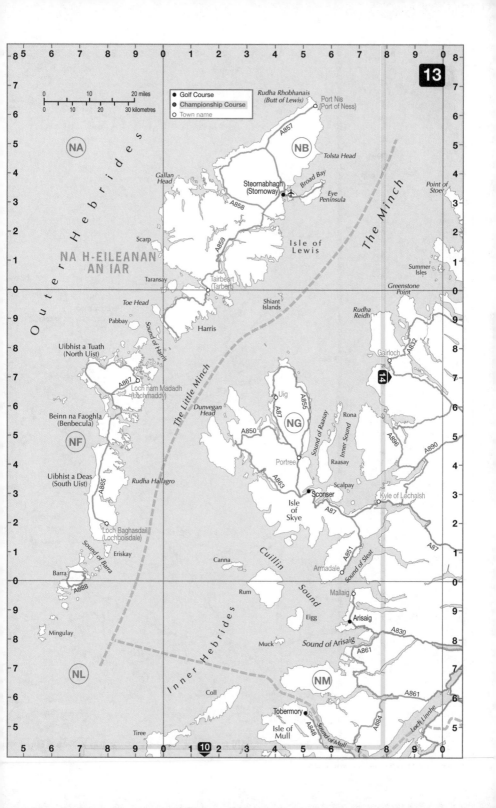

13

Golf Course
Championship Course
Town name

0   10   20 miles
0   10   20   30 kilometres

Rudha Rhobhanais
(Butt of Lewis)
Port Nis
(Port of Ness)

A857

NB

Tolsta Head

Gallan
Head

Steornabhagh
(Stornoway)

Broad Bay

A858

Eye
Peninsula

Isle of
Lewis

Point of
Stoer

NA

O   u   t   e   r   H   e   b   r   i   d   e   s

NA H-EILEANAN
AN IAR

Scarp

A859

Summer
Isles

Taransay

Tairbeart
(Tarbert)

Greenstone
Point

The   Minch

Toe Head

Shiant
Islands

Pabbay

Harris

Rudha
Reidh

Gairloch

A852

Uibhist a Tuath
(North Uist)

A867

Loch nam Madadh
(Lochmaddy)

The   Little   Minch

Dunvegan
Head

Uig

A855

Rona

A896

14

Beinn na Faoghla
(Benbecula)

A850

A87

NG

Sound of Raasay

Inner Sound

A890

NF

Portree

Raasay

Uibhist a Deas
(South Uist)

A865

Rudha Hallagro

A863

Sconser

Scalpay

Kyle of Lochalsh

A87

Isle
of
Skye

A87

Loch Baghasdail
(Lochboisdale)

Eriskay

Canna

Cuillin

A851

Armadale

Sound of Sleat

A87

Barra

A888

Sound of Barra

Rum

Sound

Mallaig

A830

Mingulay

Eigg

Arisaig

Sound of Arisaig

A861

NL

Muck

Inner   Hebrides

NM

A861

Coll

A864

Loch Linnhe

Tobermory

A848

Sound of Mull

Tiree

Isle of
Mull

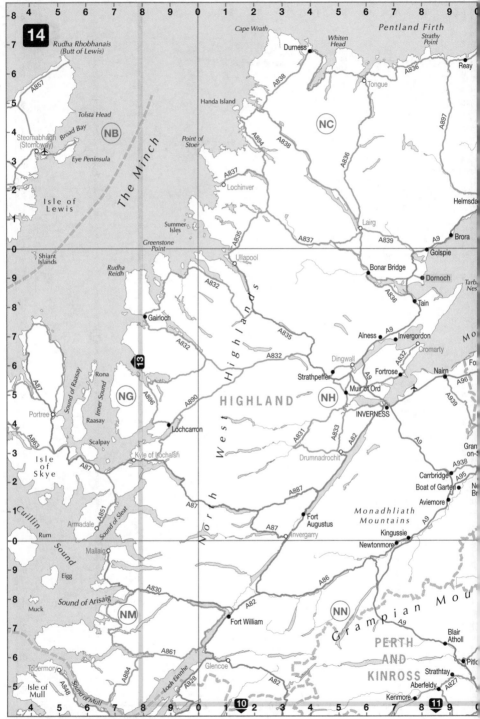

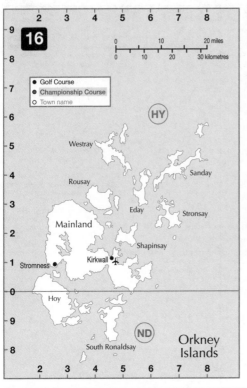

- ● Golf Course
- ● Championship Course
- ○ Town name

Orkney Islands

Westray

Sanday

Rousay

Eday

Stronsay

Mainland

Shapinsay

Stromness ●   Kirkwall ●

Hoy

ND

HY

South Ronaldsay

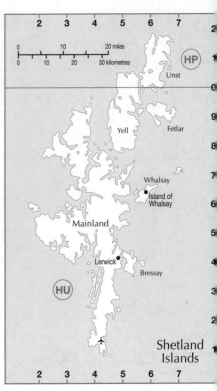

HP

Unst

Yell

Fetlar

Whalsay
Island of
Whalsay

Mainland

Lerwick ●

Bressay

HU

Shetland Islands

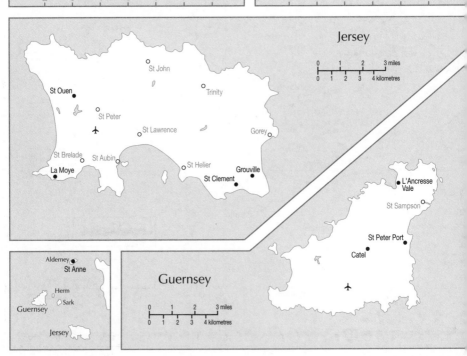

Jersey

St John

St Ouen ●

Trinity

St Peter

St Lawrence

Gorey

St Brelade

St Aubin

St Helier

Grouville ●

La Moye ●

St Clement ●

L'Ancresse
Vale ●

St Sampson

St Peter Port ●

Catel ●

Alderney ●
St Anne

Herm

Sark

Guernsey

Jersey

Guernsey

Driving Ranges

ENGLAND

BEDFORDSHIRE

BEDFORD
Bedford 16
Bedfordshire 16
Mowsbury 16
COLMWORTH
Colmworth & North Bedfordshire 17
DUNSTABLE
Caddington 17
LUTON
Stockwood Park 18
SHEFFORD
Beadlow Manor Hotel & Golf &
  Country Club 18
TILSWORTH
Tilsworth 19
WYBOSTON
Wyboston Lakes 19

BERKSHIRE

ASCOT
Berkshire 19
Lavender Park 19
BINFIELD
Blue Mountain Golf Centre 20
CAVERSHAM
Caversham Heath 20
CHADDLEWORTH
West Berkshire 20
DATCHET
Datchet 21
MAIDENHEAD
Bird Hills 21
READING
Hennerton 22
SINDLESHAM
Bearwood 22
SUNNINGDALE
Sunningdale 23
THEALE
Theale 24
WOKINGHAM
Downshire 24
Sand Martins 24

BRISTOL

BRISTOL
Bristol and Clifton 25

BUCKINGHAMSHIRE

AYLESBURY
Aylesbury Golf Centre 26

BEACONSFIELD
Beaconsfield 27
BLETCHLEY
Windmill Hill 27
BURNHAM
Burnham Beeches 27
Lambourne 27
CHALFONT ST GILES
Oakland Park 28
DAGNALL
Whipsnade Park 28
DENHAM
Buckinghamshire 28
IVER
Iver 29
Richings Park Golf & Country
  Club 29
LITTLE BRICKHILL
Woburn 30
LOUDWATER
Wycombe Heights Golf Centre 30
MARLOW
Harleyford 30
MENTMORE
Mentmore Golf & Country Club 30
MILTON KEYNES
Abbey Hill 30
STOKE POGES
Stoke Park 32
STOWE
Silverstone 32
WAVENDON
Wavendon Golf Centre 32
WEXHAM STREET
Wexham Park 33
WING
Aylesbury Vale 33

CAMBRIDGESHIRE

BRAMPTON
Brampton Park 34
CAMBRIDGE
Gog Magog 34
LONGSTANTON
Cambridge 34
MELDRETH
Malton 35
PETERBOROUGH
Elton Furze 35
Peterborough Milton 35
PIDLEY
Lakeside Lodge 35
ST NEOTS
Abbotsley Golf & Squash Club 36
THORNEY
Thorney 36

TYDD ST GILES
Tydd St Giles Golf & Country Club ... 37

CHESHIRE

ANTROBUS
Antrobus 37
BROXTON
De Vere Carden Park Hotel 38
CHESTER
Eaton 38
Vicars Cross 38
CREWE
Wychwood Park 39
DELAMERE
Delamere Forest 39
HELSBY
Helsby 40
KNUTSFORD
Heyrose 40
Mere Golf & Country Club 40
MACCLESFIELD
Tytherington 42
PRESTBURY
Prestbury 42
TARPORLEY
Macdonald Portal Hotel Golf &
  Spa 43
WILMSLOW
De Vere Mottram Hall 45
Styal 45
WINWICK
Alder Root 45

CORNWALL & ISLES OF SCILLY

BODMIN
Lanhydrock Hotel 45
CAMELFORD
Bowood Park Hotel 46
CONSTANTINE BAY
Trevose 47
FALMOUTH
Falmouth 47
LAUNCESTON
Trethorne 48
LOSTWITHIEL
Lostwithiel Hotel, Golf & Country
  Club 48
MAWGAN PORTH
Merlin 48
ROCK
St Enodoc 50
ST AUSTELL
Porthpean 50
St Austell 50
ST MELLION
St Mellion 51

ST MINVER
Roserrow Golf & Country Club 52
SALTASH
China Fleet Country Club 52
TRURO
Killiow Park 52
WADEBRIDGE
St Kew 52

CUMBRIA

BRAMPTON
Brampton 54
CARLISLE
Carlisle 54
Stony Holme Municipal 54
CROSBY-ON-EDEN
Eden 55
KENDAL
Carus Green 55
PENRITH
Penrith 56
SEASCALE
Seascale 56

DERBYSHIRE

BREADSALL
Marriot Breadsall Priory Hotel &
 Country Club 58
BUXTON
Cavendish 59
CHESTERFIELD
Grassmoor Golf Centre 59
HORSLEY
Horsley Lodge 61
KEDLESTON
Kedleston Park 61
LONG EATON
Trent Lock Golf Centre 61
MORLEY
Morley Hayes 61
STANTON BY DALE
Erewash Valley 62

DEVON

BLACKAWTON
Dartmouth Golf & Country Club 63
CULLOMPTON
Padbrook Park 65
HIGH BICKINGTON
Libbaton 66
HOLSWORTHY
Holsworthy 66
ILFRACOMBE
Ilfracombe 67
IPPLEPEN
Dainton Park 67
MORETONHAMPSTEAD
Bovey Castle 67

NEWTON ABBOT
Hele Park Golf Centre 68
OKEHAMPTON
Ashbury Golf Hotel 68
SAUNTON
Saunton 69

DORSET

BERE REGIS
Dorset Golf & Country Club 71
BOURNEMOUTH
Iford Golf Centre 72
Solent Meads 73
BRIDPORT
Bridport & West Dorset 73
FERNDOWN
Dudsbury 74
Ferndown Forest 74
HALSTOCK
Halstock 74
HURN
Parley 74
LYME REGIS
Lyme Regis 74
POOLE
Parkstone 75
STURMINSTER MARSHALL
Sturminster Marshall 75
VERWOOD
Crane Valley 75
WEYMOUTH
Weymouth 76
WIMBORNE
Canford Magna 76

CO DURHAM

CHESTER-LE-STREET
Roseberry Grange 77
DARLINGTON
Stressholme 78
DURHAM
Ramside Hall 79
MIDDLETON ST GEORGE
Dinsdale Spa 79
NEWTON AYCLIFFE
Oakleaf Golf Complex 80
SEDGEFIELD
Knotty Hill Golf Centre 80

ESSEX

ABRIDGE
Abridge Golf and Country Club 81
BRENTWOOD
Warley Park 82
CANVEY ISLAND
Castle Point 83
CHELMSFORD
Channels 83
Regiment Way 83

CHIGWELL ROW
Hainault Forest Golf Complex 84
COLCHESTER
Colchester 84
Lexden Wood 84
EPPING
Epping 85
Nazeing 85
HARLOW
North Weald 86
MALDON
Forrester Park 86
SAFFRON WALDEN
Saffron Walden 87
STOCK
Crondon Park 88
TOLLESHUNT KNIGHTS
Five Lakes Hotel, Golf, Country
 Club & Spa 88
TOOT HILL
Toot Hill 89
WOODHAM WALTER
Warren 89

GLOUCESTERSHIRE

ALMONDSBURY
Bristol 89
CHELTENHAM
Lilley Brook 91
CIRENCESTER
Cirencester 91
COALPIT HEATH
The Kendleshire 92
CODRINGTON
Players Club 92
COLEFORD
Forest Hills 92
GLOUCESTER
Brickhampton Court Golf
 Complex 93
Ramada Gloucester 93
Rodway Hill 93
MINCHINHAMPTON
Minchinhampton (New Course) 94
TEWKESBURY
Tewkesbury Park Hotel Golf &
 Country Club 95
THORNBURY
Thornbury Golf Centre 95
WESTONBIRT
Westonbirt 96
WICK
Park Resort 96

GREATER LONDON

BARNET
The Shire London 97
BIGGIN HILL
Cherry Lodge 98

YORKSHIRE, EAST RIDING OF

AUGHTON
Oaks Golf Club & Spa ... 281
BRIDLINGTON
Bridlington Links ... 282
BURSTWICK
Burstwick Country Golf ... 282
COTTINGHAM
Cottingham Parks Golf & Country
  Club ... 282
DRIFFIELD (GREAT)
Driffield ... 283
HOWDEN
Boothferry ... 283
SKIDBY
Skidby Lakes ... 284

YORKSHIRE, NORTH

COPMANTHORPE
Pike Hills ... 287
EASINGWOLD
Easingwold ... 287
HARROGATE
Rudding Park ... 288
MALTON
Malton & Norton ... 288
MIDDLESBROUGH
Middlesbrough Municipal ... 289
NORTHALLERTON
Romanby ... 290
PANNAL
Pannal ... 290
REDCAR
Cleveland ... 290
RIPON
Ripon City ... 291
SELBY
Selby ... 292
YORK
Forest of Galtres ... 293
Forest Park ... 293

YORKSHIRE, SOUTH

BARNSLEY
Sandhill ... 294
BAWTRY
Bawtry ... 294
HATFIELD
Kings Wood ... 295
RAWMARSH
Wath ... 295
ROTHERHAM
Grange Park ... 295
Phoenix ... 296
SHEFFIELD
Concord Park ... 296
Hillsborough ... 297
Rother Valley Golf Centre ... 297

YORKSHIRE, WEST

BINGLEY
Bingley St Ives ... 299
BRIGHOUSE
Willow Valley Golf ... 300
GUISELEY
Bradford (Hawksworth) ... 301
HUDDERSFIELD
Bradley Park ... 302
Huddersfield ... 302
LEEDS
Cookridge Hall Golf & Country
  Club ... 303
De Vere Oulton Hall ... 303
Leeds Golf Centre, Wike Ridge ... 304
Moor Allerton ... 304
Moortown ... 304
OTLEY
Otley ... 306
PONTEFRACT
Mid Yorkshire ... 306
SCARCROFT
Scarcroft ... 307
SHIPLEY
Marriott Hollins Hall Hotel &
  Country Club ... 307
WETHERBY
Wetherby ... 309
WOOLLEY
Woolley Park ... 309

CHANNEL ISLANDS

GUERNSEY

CASTEL
La Grande Mare Golf & Country
  Club ... 309
ST PETER PORT
St Pierre Park Golf Club ... 310

JERSEY

LA MOYE
La Moye ... 310
ST CLEMENT
St Clement ... 310
ST OUEN
Les Mielles Golf & Country Club ... 310

ISLE OF MAN

DOUGLAS
Mount Murray Hotel & Country
  Club ... 311

SCOTLAND

ABERDEEN, CITY OF

ABERDEEN
Deeside ... 314
Murcar Links ... 314

ABERDEENSHIRE

BALMEDIE
East Aberdeenshire Golf Centre ... 316
BANCHORY
Inchmarlo Resort & Golf Club ... 316
CRUDEN BAY
Cruden Bay ... 316
HUNTLY
Huntly ... 317
NEWBURGH
Newburgh on Ythan ... 318
NEWMACHAR
Newmachar ... 318
OLDMELDRUM
Old Meldrum ... 318

ANGUS

CARNOUSTIE
Carnoustie Golf Links ... 321
EDZELL
Edzell ... 320

ARGYLL & BUTE

ERISKA
Isle of Eriska ... 323

DUMFRIES & GALLOWAY

CUMMERTREES
Powfoot ... 326
DUMFRIES
Dumfriesshire Golf Centre ... 326
KIRKCUDBRIGHT
Brighouse Bay ... 327

DUNDEE, CITY OF

DUNDEE
Ballumbie Castle ... 329

EAST DUNBARTONSHIRE

BISHOPBRIGGS
Bishopbriggs ... 331

EAST LOTHIAN

GIFFORD
Castle Park ... 333

CO DONEGAL

BALLYLIFFIN
Ballyliffin 439
NARIN (NARAN)
Narin & Portnoo 440
ROSEPENNA
Rosapenna 441
GWEEDORE
Gweedore 441

CO DUBLIN

CASTLEKNOCK
Elm Green 442
Luttrellstown Castle 442
DONABATE
Turvey Golf Club & Hotel 443
DUBLIN
Elm Park Golf & Sports Club 444
Howth 444
Royal Dublin 444
St Margaret's Golf & Country
   Club 445

CO GALWAY

BALLYCONNEELY
Connemara 449
MOUNTBELLEW
Mountbellew 450
ORANMORE
Athenry 450

CO KERRY

BALLYBUNION
Ballybunion 451
KENMARE
Ring of Kerry Golf & Country Club 451
KILLARNEY
Killarney Golf & Fishing Club 452
WATERVILLE (AN COIREÁN)
Waterville House & Golf Links 454

CO KILDARE

KILDARE
The Curragh 456
STRAFFAN
The K Club 458

CO KILKENNY

KILKENNY
Kilkenny 458
THOMASTOWN
Mount Juliet Hotel 458

CO LAOIS

PORTLAOISE
The Heath 459

CO LEITRIM

CARRICK-ON-SHANNON
Carrick-on-Shannon 459

CO LIMERICK

NEWCASTLE WEST
Newcastle West 460

CO LONGFORD

LONGFORD

CO LOUTH

BALTRAY
County Louth 460
DUNDALK
Ballymascanlon House Hotel 461
Dundalk 461
GREENORE
Greenore 461
TERMONFECKIN
Seapoint 461

CO MAYO

BALLINROBE
Ballinrobe 462
WESTPORT
Westport 463

CO MEATH

DUNSHAUGHLIN
Black Bush 463
TRIM
County Meath 464

CO MONAGHAN

CLONES
Clones 465
MONAGHAN
Rossmore 465

CO TIPPERARY

TIPPERARY
Tipperary 468

CO WATERFORD

DUNGARVAN
Gold Coast Golf & Leisure 469
LISMORE
Lismore 469
WATERFORD
Waterford 470

CO WESTMEATH

MOATE
Mount Temple 470
MULLINGAR

CO WEXFORD

ENNISCORTHY
Enniscorthy 470
ROSSLARE
Rosslare 471
WEXFORD
Wexford 471

CO WICKLOW

BLESSINGTON
Tulfarris Hotel & Golf Resort 472
BRAY
Bray 472
DUNLAVIN
Rathsallagh 474
GREYSTONES
Charlesland Golf & Country Club
   Hotel 474
NEWTOWN MOUNT KENNEDY
Druids Glen Golf Club 474

Location Index

C

Golf Course Index

C

T